LOCATOR MAPS

12e

Anthropology
The Human Challenge

WILLIAM A. HAVILAND
University of Vermont

HARALD E. L. PRINS
Kansas State University

DANA WALRATH
University of Vermont

BUNNY MCBRIDE
Kansas State University

WADSWORTH

™

THOMSON LEARNING

Australia • Brazil • Canada • Mexico • Singapore • Spain • United Kingdom • United States

WADSWORTH

THOMSON LEARNING™

Anthropology: The Human Challenge, Twelfth Edition

William A. Haviland, Harald E. L. Prins, Dana Walrath, Bunny McBride

Senior Acquisitions Editor: Lin Marshall

Editorial Assistant: Jessica Jang

Technology Project Manager: Dave Lionetti

Marketing Manager: Caroline Concilla

Marketing Assistant: Mary Anne Payumo

Marketing Communications Manager: Shemika Britt

Project Manager, Editorial Production: Jerilyn Emori

Creative Director: Rob Hugel

Art Director: Maria Epes

Print Buyer: Judy Inouye

Permissions Editor: Bob Kauser

Production Service: Robin Hood

Text Designer: Lisa Buckley

Photo Researcher: Billie L. Porter

Copy Editor: Jennifer Gordon

Cover Designer: Larry Didona

Cover Images: Background image © Yann Arthus-Bertrand/Altitude; remaining images, clockwise from top left: © NASA; © David J. Simchock/vagabondvistas.com; Yoav Lemmer/AFP/Getty Images; © Art Wolfe/Photo Researchers, Inc.; © Franz Aberham/Getty Images; © Peter Adams Photography/Alamy; © David J. Simchock/vagabondvistas.com

Text and Cover Printer: Courier Corporation/Kendallville

Compositor: Newgen–Austin

Thomson Higher Education
10 Davis Drive
Belmont, CA 94002-3098
USA

For more information about our products, contact us at:
Thomson Learning Academic Resource Center
1-800-423-0563

For permission to use material from this text or product, submit a request online at **http://www.thomsonrights.com.**
Any additional questions about permissions can be submitted by e-mail to **thomsonrights@thomson.com.**

Library of Congress Control Number: 2006909141

Student Edition:
ISBN-13: 978-0-495-09559-0
ISBN-10: 0-495-09559-1

Dedicated to
the World's Indigenous Peoples
in Their Quest for Human Rights

Putting the World in Perspective

Although all humans that we know about are capable of producing accurate sketches of localities and regions with which they are familiar, CARTOGRAPHY (the craft of mapmaking as we know it today) had its beginnings in 13th century Europe, and its subsequent development is related to the expansion of Europeans to all parts of the globe. From the beginning, there have been two problems with maps: the technical one of how to depict on a two-dimensional, flat surface a three-dimensional spherical object, and the cultural one of whose world-view they reflect. In fact, the two issues are inseparable, for the particular projection one uses inevitably makes a statement about how one views one's own people and their place in the world. Indeed, maps often shape our perception of reality as much as they reflect it.

In cartography, a PROJECTION refers to the system of intersecting lines (of longitude and latitude) by which part or all of the globe is represented on a flat surface. There are more than 100 different projections in use today, ranging from polar perspectives to interrupted "butterflies" to rectangles to heart shapes. Each projection causes distortion in size, shape, or distance in some way or another. A map that shows the shape of land masses correctly will of necessity misrepresent the size. A map that is accurate along the equator will be deceptive at the poles.

Perhaps no projection has had more influence on the way we see the world than that of Gerhardus Mercator, who devised his map in 1569 as a navigational aid for mariners. So well suited was Mercator's map for this purpose that it continues to be used for navigational charts today. At the same time, the Mercator projection became a standard for depicting land masses, something for which it was never intended. Although an accurate navigational tool, the Mercator projection greatly exaggerates the size of land masses in higher latitudes, giving about two-thirds of the map's surface to the northern hemisphere. Thus, the lands occupied by Europeans and European descendants appear far larger than those of other people. For example, North America (19 million square kilometers) appears almost twice the size of Africa (30 million square kilometers), while Europe is shown as equal in size to South America, which actually has nearly twice the land mass of Europe.

A map developed in 1805 by Karl B. Mollweide was one of the earlier equal-area projections of the world. Equal-area projections portray land masses in correct relative size, but, as a result, distort the shape of continents more than other projections. They most often compress

MERCATOR

MOLLWEIDE

VAN DER GRINTEN

ROBINSON

and warp lands in the higher latitudes and vertically stretch land masses close to the equator. Other equal-area projections include the Lambert Cylindrical Equal-Area Projection (1772), the Hammer Equal-Area Projection (1892), and the Eckert Equal-Area Projection (1906).

The Van der Grinten Projection (1904) was a compromise aimed at minimizing both the distortions of size in the Mercator and the distortion of shape in equal-area maps such as the Mollweide. Allthough an improvement, the lands of the northern hemisphere are still emphasized at the expense of the southern. For example, in the Van der Grinten, the Commonwealth of Independent States (the former Soviet Union) and Canada are shown at more than twice their relative size.

The Robinson Projection, which was adopted by the National Geographic Society in 1988 to replace the Van der Grinten, is one of the best compromises to date between the distortion of size and shape. Although an improvement over the Van der Grinten, the Robinson projection still depicts lands in the northern latitudes as proportionally larger at the same time that it depicts lands in the lower latitudes (representing most third-world nations) as proportionally smaller. Like European maps before it, the Robinson projection places Europe at the center of the map with the Atlantic Ocean and the Americas to the left, emphasizing the cultural connection between Europe and North America, while neglecting the geographical closeness of northwestern North America to northeast Asia.

The following pages show four maps that each convey quite different "cultural messages." Included among them is the Peters Projection, an equal-area map that has been adopted as the official map of UNESCO (the United Nations Educational, Scientific, and Cultural Organization), and a map made in Japan, showing us how the world looks from the other side.

The Robinson Projection

The map above is based on the Robinson Projection, which is used today by the National Geographic Society and Rand McNally. Although the Robinson Projection distorts the relative size of land masses, it does so to a much lesser degree than most other projections. Still, it places Europe at the center of the map. This particular view of the world has been used to identify the location of many of the cultures discussed in this text.

The Peters Projection

The map above is based on the Peters Projection, which has been adopted as the official map of UNESCO. While it distorts the shape of continents (countries near the equator are vertically elongated by a ratio of two to one), the Peters Projection does show all continents according to their correct relative size. Though Europe is still at the center, it is not shown as larger and more extensive than the third world.

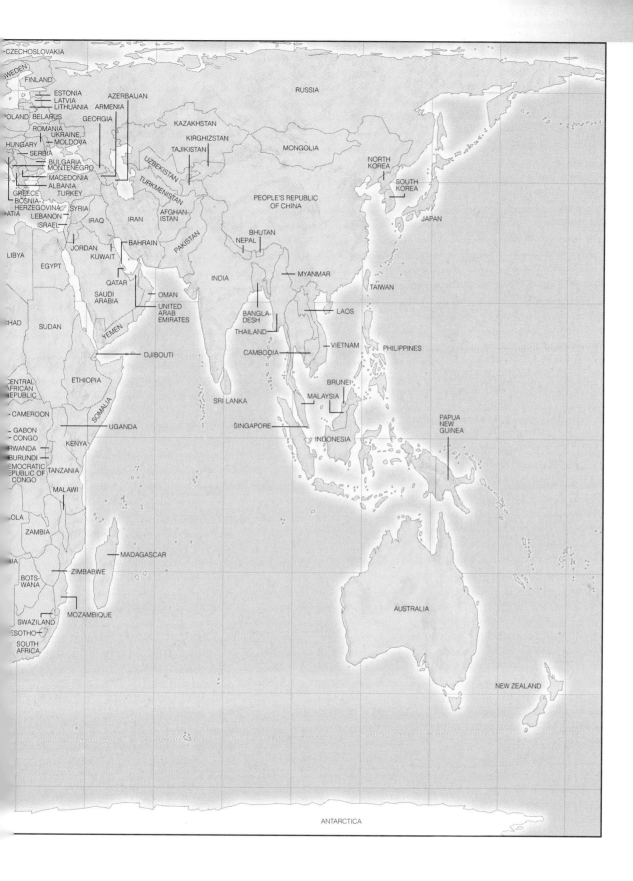

Japanese Map

Not all maps place Europe at the center of the world, as this
Japanese map illustrates. Besides reflecting the importance the
Japanese attach to themselves in the world, this map has the virtue
of showing the geographic proximity of North America to Asia, a
fact easily overlooked when maps place Europe at their center.

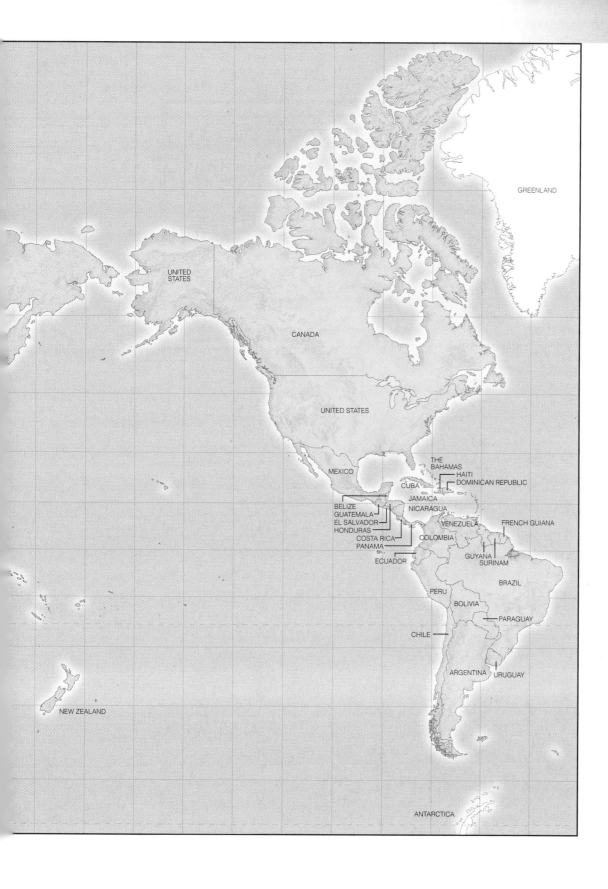

GREENLAND

UNITED
STATES

CANADA

UNITED STATES

MEXICO

THE
BAHAMAS

HAITI

CUBA

DOMINICAN REPUBLIC

JAMAICA

BELIZE

NICARAGUA

GUATEMALA

EL SALVADOR

VENEZUELA

FRENCH GUIANA

HONDURAS

COSTA RICA

COLOMBIA

PANAMA

GUYANA

ECUADOR

SURINAM

BRAZIL

PERU

BOLIVIA

PARAGUAY

CHILE

ARGENTINA

URUGUAY

NEW ZEALAND

ANTARCTICA

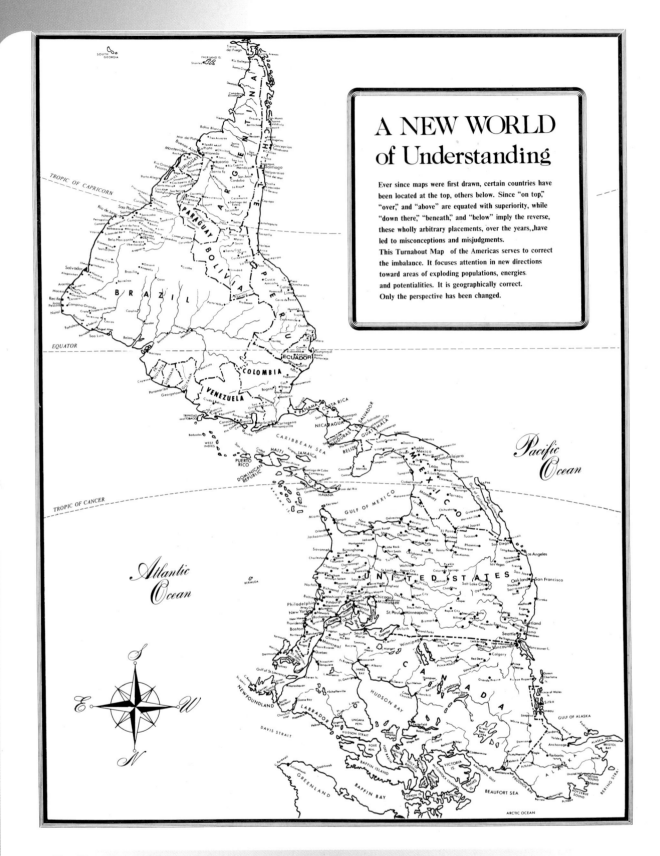

The Turnabout Map

The way maps may reflect (and influence) our thinking is exemplified by the "Turnabout Map," which places the South
Pole at the top and the North Pole at the bottom. Words and phrases such as "on top," "over," and "above" tend to be
equated by some people with superiority. Turning things upside down may cause us to rethink the way North Americans regard themselves in relation to the people of Central America. © 1982 by Jesse Levine Turnabout Map™—Dist. by
Laguna Sales, Inc., 7040 Via Valverde, San Jose, CA 95135

Brief Contents

Contents

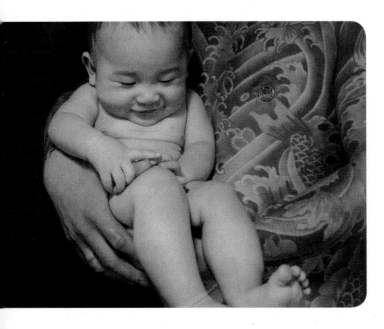

Features Contents

Preface

It is common for students to enter an introductory anthropology class intrigued by the general subject but with little more than a vague sense of what it is all about. Thus, the first and most obvious task of our text is to provide a thorough introduction to the discipline—its foundations as a domain of knowledge and its major insights into the rich diversity of humans as a culture-making species. In doing this, we draw from the research and ideas of a number of traditions of anthropological thought, exposing students to a mix of theoretical perspectives and methodologies. Such inclusiveness reflects our conviction that different approaches offer distinctly important insights about human biology, behavior, and beliefs.

If most students start out with only a vague sense of what anthropology is, they often have less clear—and potentially more problematic—views of the superiority of their own culture and its place in the world. A secondary task for this text, then, is to prod students to appreciate the rich complexity and breadth of human behavior. Along with this is the task of helping them understand why there are so many differences and similarities in the human condition, past and present. Debates regarding globalization and notions of progress, the "naturalness" of the mother/father/child(ren) nuclear family, new genetic technologies, and how gender roles relate to biological variation all benefit greatly from the fresh and often fascinating insights gained through anthropology. This probing aspect of our discipline is perhaps the most valuable gift we can pass on to those who take our classes. If we, as teachers (and textbook authors), do our jobs well, students will gain a wider and more open-minded outlook on the world and a critical but constructive perspective on their own cultures. To paraphrase the famous poet T. S. Eliot: After all our explorations, they will come home and know the place for the first time.

More than ever before, students need anthropological tools to step out of culture-bound ways of thinking and acting so that they can gain tolerance and respect for other ways of life. Thus, we have written this text, in large part, as a tool to help students make sense of our increasingly complex world and to navigate through its interrelated biological and cultural networks with knowledge and skill, whatever professional path they take. We see it as a guide for people entering the often bewildering maze of global crossroads in the 21st century.

A DISTINCTIVE APPROACH

Two key factors distinguish *Anthropology: The Human Challenge* from other introductory anthropology texts: our integrative presentation of the discipline's four fields and a trio of unifying themes that tie the book together to prevent students from feeling lost.

Integration of the Four Fields

Unlike traditional texts that present anthropology's four "fields"—archaeology, linguistics, cultural anthropology, and physical anthropology—as if they were relatively separate or independent, our book takes an integrative approach. This reflects the comprehensive character of our discipline, a domain of knowledge where members of our species are studied in their totality—as social creatures biologically evolved with the inherent capacity of learning and sharing culture by means of symbolic communication. This approach also reflects our collective experience as practicing anthropologists who recognize that we cannot fully understand humanity in all its fascinating complexity unless we appreciate the systemic interplay among environmental, physiological, material, social, ideological, psychological, and symbolic factors, both past and present.

For analytical purposes, of course, we have no choice but to discuss physical anthropology as distinct from archaeology, linguistics, and sociocultural anthropology. Accordingly, there are separate chapters that focus primarily on each field, but the links between them are shown repeatedly. Among many examples of this integrative approach, Chapter 12, "Modern Human Diversity: Race and Racism," discusses the social context of "race" and recent cultural practices that have impacted the human genome. Similarly, material concerning linguistics appears not only in Chapter 16, "Language and Communication" but also in the chapters on living primates (Chapter 3), on early *Homo* and the origins of culture (Chapter 7), on pre-modern humans and the elaboration of culture (Chapter 8), and on the emergence of cities and states (Chapter 11). These chapters include material on the linguistic capabilities of apes, the emergence of human language, and the origin of writing. In addition, every chapter includes a Biocultural Connection feature to further illustrate the interplay of biological and cultural processes in shaping the human experience.

Unifying Themes

In our own teaching, we have come to recognize the value of marking out unifying themes that help students see the big picture as they grapple with the great array of concepts and information encountered in the study of human beings. In *Anthropology* we employ three such themes.

1. We present anthropology as a study of humankind's responses through time to the fundamental **challenges of survival.** Each chapter is framed by this theme, opening with a Challenge Issue paragraph and photograph and ending with Questions for Reflection tied to that particular challenge.

2. We emphasize the integration of human culture and biology in the steps humans take to meet these challenges. This **Biocultural Connection** theme appears throughout the text—as a thread in the main narrative and in a boxed feature that highlights this connection with a topical example for each chapter.

3. We track the emergence of **globalization and its disparate impact on various peoples and cultures around the world.** While European colonization was a global force for centuries, leaving a significant, often devastating, footprint on the affected peoples in Asia, Africa, and the Americas, decolonization began about 200 years ago and became a worldwide wave in the mid-1900s. Since the 1960s, however, political-economic hegemony has taken a new and fast-paced form, namely globalization (in many ways a concept that expands or builds on imperialism). Attention to both forms of global domination—colonialism and globalization—runs through *Anthropology,* culminating in the final chapter where we apply the concept of structural power to globalization, discussing it in terms of hard and soft power and linking it to structural violence.

PEDAGOGY

Anthropology: The Human Challenge features a range of learning aids, in addition to the three unifying themes described above. Each pedagogical piece plays an important role in the learning process—from clarifying and enlivening the material to revealing relevancy and aiding recall.

Accessible Language and a Cross-Cultural Voice

What could be more basic to pedagogy than clear communication? In addition to our standing as professional anthropologists, all four co-authors have made a specialty of speaking to audiences outside of our profession. Using that experience in the writing of this text, we consciously cut through a lot of unnecessary jargon to speak directly to students. Manuscript reviewers recognized this, noting that even the most difficult concepts are presented in prose that is straightforward and easy for today's first- and second-year college students to understand, without feeling they are being "spoken down to." Where technical terms are necessary, they appear in bold-faced type, are carefully defined in the narrative, and are defined again in the running glossary in simple, clear language, as well as appearing in the glossary at the end of the book.

Accessibility involves not only clear writing but also an engaging voice or style. The voice of *Anthropology* is distinct among introductory texts in the discipline, for it has been written from a cross-cultural perspective. This means we strove to avoid the typical Western "we–they" voice in favor of a more inclusive one that will resonate with both Western and non-Western students and professors. Moreover, the book highlights the theories and work of anthropologists from all over the world. Finally, its cultural examples come from industrial and postindustrial societies as well as nonindustral ones.

Challenge Issues and Questions for Reflection

Each chapter opens with a Challenge Issue and accompanying photograph, which together carry forward the book's theme of humankind's responses through time to the fundamental challenges of survival within the context of the particular chapter. And each chapter closes with Questions for Reflection relating back to the Challenge Issue presented on the chapter's opening page. These questions are designed to stimulate and deepen thought, trigger class discussion, and link the material to the students' own lives.

Chapter Preview

In every chapter the page facing the opening Challenge Issue and photo presents three or four preview questions that mark out the key issues covered in the chapter. Beyond orienting students to the chapter contents, these questions provide study points useful when preparing for exams.

Barrel Model of Culture

Every culture, past and present, is an integrated and dynamic system of adaptation that responds to a combination of internal and external factors. This is illustrated by a pedagogical device we refer to as the "barrel model" of culture. Depicted in a simple but telling drawing (Figure 14.2), the barrel model shows the interrelatedness of social, ideological, and economic factors within a cultural system along with outside influences of environment, climate, and other societies. Throughout the book examples are linked back to this point.

Visuals

Maintaining a key pedagogical tradition of the Haviland et al. textbooks, *Anthropology is* richly illustrated with a notable array of maps, photographs, and figures. This is important because humans—like all primates—are visually oriented, and a well-chosen image may serve to "fix" key information in a student's mind. Unlike some competing texts, all of our visuals are in color, enhancing their appeal and impact.

Photographs

This edition features a hard-sought collection of new and truly compelling photographs—with a greater number of them sized larger to increase their effectiveness. With some of the images, we provide longer-than-usual captions, tying concepts directly to visuals in a way that helps students to see the rich photographic content and then hang on to the information. We have retained our popular "Visual Counterpoint" feature—side-by-side photos to compare and contrast cultures from around the world.

Maps

In addition to our various map features—"Putting the World in Perspective" map series, locator maps, and distribution maps providing overviews of key issues such as pollution and energy consumption—this edition introduces a new and highly engaging map feature: Globalscape. Appearing in nine chapters, Globalscape feature charts the global flow of people, goods, and services, as well as pollutants and pathogens. Showing how the world is interconnected through human activity, this feature contributes to the text's globalization theme with topics geared toward student interests. Each one ends with a Global Twister—a question that prods students to think critically about globalization.

The Globalscape features in *Anthropology* are: "A Global Body Shop?," which investigates human organ trafficking around the world; "Gorilla-Hand Ashtrays?," which shows how mining for the cell phone component coltan is linked to gorilla habitat destruction; "Iraqi Artifacts in New York City?," which explores the effects of the war in Iraq on the precious Mesopotamian artifacts that were housed in the National Museum in Baghdad; "Healthy Border Crossings?," which reports on the transfer of Brazil's highly regarded HIV/AIDS programs to Portuguese-speaking countries in Africa; "Operator, Where Are You?," which offers a short story on how outsourcing impacts travelers; "How Much for a Red Delicious?," which follows Jamaican migrant laborers working in Maine and Florida; "Soccer Diplomacy?" which traces the life of an Ivory Coast soccer star and the numerous countries in which he has trained and played; "Do Coffins Fly?," which highlights the work of a Ghanaian custom coffin maker gaining global recognition as art; and "*Probo Koala's* Dirty Secrets," which investigates the dumping of First World toxic waste in Third World countries.

In addition to this innovative new feature, all the maps have been redrawn with a color-blind sensitive palette and with attention to accurate representation in two dimensions of the geographic areas that together make up our world.

Integrated Gender Coverage

In contrast to many introductory texts, *Anthropology* integrates rather than separates gender coverage. Thus, material on gender-related issues is included in *every* chapter. The result of this approach is a measure of gender-related material that far exceeds the single chapter that most books contain.

Why is the gender-related material integrated? Because concepts and issues surrounding gender are almost always too complicated to remove from their context. Moreover, spreading this material through all of the chapters has a pedagogical purpose, for it emphasizes how considerations of gender enter into virtually everything people do. Further, integration of gender into the book's "biological" chapters allows students to grasp the analytic distinction between sex and gender, illustrating the subtle influence of gender norms on biological theories about sex difference. Gender-related material ranges from discussions of gender roles in evolutionary discourse and studies of nonhuman primates, to intersexuality, homosexual identity, same-sex marriage, and female genital mutilation. Through a steady drumbeat of such coverage, this edition avoids ghettoizing gender to a single chapter that is preceded and followed by resounding silence.

Glossary

The running glossary is designed to catch the student's eye, reinforcing the meaning of each newly introduced term. It is also useful for chapter review, as the student may readily isolate the new terms from those introduced in earlier chapters. A complete alphabetical glossary is also included at the back of the book. In the glossaries, each term is defined in clear, understandable language. As a result, less class time is required for going over terms, leaving instructors free to pursue other matters of interest.

Special Boxed Features

Our text includes four types of special boxed features: Biocultural Connections, Original Studies, Anthropology Applied, and Anthropologists of Note. Every chapter contains three of the features: a Biocultural Connection, along with two of the others. These are carefully placed and introduced within the main narrative to alert students to their importance and relevance—and to ensure that they will be read.

Biocultural Connections

Now appearing in every chapter, this signature feature of the Haviland et al. textbooks illustrates how cultural and biological processes interact to shape human biology, beliefs, and behavior. It reflects the integrated biocultural approach central to the field of anthropology today. The twenty-seven Biocultural Connection titles hint at the intriguing array of topics covered by this feature: "The Anthropology of Organ Transplantation"; "The Social Impact of Genetics on Reproduction"; "Ethics of Great Ape Habituation and Conservation: The Costs and Benefits of Ecotourism" by Michele Goldsmith; "Kennewick Man"; "Nonhuman Primates and Human Disease"; "Evolution and Human Birth"; "Sex, Gender, and Female Paleoanthropologists"; "Paleolithic Prescriptions for the Diseases of Civilization"; "Altered States, Art, and Archaeology"; "Breastfeeding, Fertility, and Beliefs"; "Social Stratification and Diseases of Civilization: Tuberculosis"; "Beans, Enzymes, and Adaptation to Malaria"; "Picturing Pesticides"; "Adult Human Stature and the Effects of Culture: An Archaeological Example"; "Pig Lovers and Pig Haters" by Marvin Harris; "The Biology of Human Speech"; "A Cross-Cultural Perspective on Psychosomatic Symptoms and Mental Health"; "Surviving in the Andes: Aymara Adaptation

to High Altitude"; "Cacao: The Love Bean in the Money Tree"; "Marriage Prohibitions in the United States" by Martin Ottenheimer; "Maori Origins: Ancestral Genes and Mythical Canoes"; "African Burial Ground Project" by Michael Blakey; "Sex, Gender, and Human Violence"; "Change Your Karma and Change Your Sex?" by Hillary Crane; "Peyote Art: Divine Visions among the Huichol"; "Studying the Emergence of New Diseases"; and "Toxic Breast Milk Threatens Arctic Culture."

Original Studies

Written expressly for this text, or selected from ethnographies and other original works by anthropologists, these studies present concrete examples that bring specific concepts to life and convey the passion of the authors. Each study sheds additional light on an important anthropological concept or subject area found in the chapter where it appears. Notably, these boxes are carefully integrated within the flow of the chapter narrative, signaling students that their content is not extraneous or supplemental. Appearing in twenty-two chapters, Original Studies cover a wide range of topics, evident from their titles: "Fighting HIV/AIDS in Africa: Traditional Healers on the Front Line" by Suzanne Leclerc-Madlala; "Ninety-Eight Percent Alike: What Our Similarity to Apes Tells Us about Our Understanding of Genetics" by Jonathan Marks; "Reconciliation and Its Cultural Modification in Primates" by Frans B. M. de Waal; "Whispers from the Ice" by Sherry Simpson; "The Unsettling Nature of Variational Change" by Stephen Jay Gould; "Is It Time to Revise the System of Scientific Naming?" by Lee R. Berger; "Humans as Prey" by Donna Hart; "Paleolithic Paint Job" by Roger Lewin; "History of Mortality and Physiological Stress" by Anna Roosevelt; "Action Archaeology and the Community at El Pilar" by Anabel Ford; "A Feckless Quest for the Basketball Gene" by Jonathan Marks; "Dancing Skeletons: Life and Death in West Africa" by Katherine Dettwyler; "The Importance of Trobriand Women" by Annette B. Weiner; "Language and the Intellectual Abilities of Orangutans" by H. Lyn White Miles; "The Blessed Curse" by R. K. Williamson; "Gardens of the Mekranoti Kayapo" by Dennis Werner; "Arranging Marriage in India" by Serena Nanda; "Honor Killings in the Netherlands" by Clementine van Eck; "The Jewish *Eruv*: Symbolic Place in Public Space" by Susan Lees; "Healing among the Ju/'hoansi of the Kalahari" by Marjorie Shostak; "The Modern Tattoo Community" by Margo DeMello; and "Standardizing the Body: The Question of Choice" by Laura Nader.

Anthropology Applied

These succinct and compelling profiles illustrate anthropology's wide-ranging relevance in today's world and give students a glimpse into a variety of the careers anthropologists enjoy. Featured in sixteen chapters, they include: "Forensic Anthropology: Voices for the Dead"; "In the Belly of the Beast: Reflections on a Decade of Service to U.S. Genetics Policy Commissions" by Barbara Koenig and Nancy Press; "Cultural Resource Management" by John Crock; "Paleotourism and the World Heritage List"; "Stone Tools for Modern Surgeons"; "The Real Dirt on Rainforest Fertility" by Charles Mann; "Tell It to the Marines: Teaching Troops about Cultural Heritage" by Jane C. Waldbaum; "New Houses for Apache Indians" by George S. Esber; "Language Renewal among the Northern Ute" by William Leap; "Agricultural Development and the Anthropologist"; "Anthropology in the Corporate Jungle" by Karen Stephenson; "Resolving a Native American Tribal Membership Dispute"; "Anthropologists and Social Impact Assessment"; "Dispute Resolution and the Anthropologist"; "Reconciling Modern Medicine with Traditional Beliefs in Swaziland" by Edward C. Green; and "Development Anthropology and Dams."

Anthropologists of Note

Profiling pioneering and contemporary anthropologists from many corners of the world, this feature puts the work of noted anthropologists in historical perspective and draws attention to the international nature of the discipline in terms of both subject matter and practitioners. This edition highlights twenty-two distinct anthropologists from all four fields of the discipline: Arjun Appadurai, Berhane Asfaw, Gregory Bateson, Ruth Fulton Benedict, Franz Boas, Margaret Conkey, Peter Ellison, Jane Goodall, Kinji Imanishi, Fatimah Jackson, Jomo Kenyatta, Frederica de Laguna, Louis S. B. Leakey, Mary Leakey, Claude Lévi-Strauss, Bronislaw Malinowski, Margaret Mead, Laura Nader, Matilda Coxe Stevenson, Allan Wilson, Eric R. Wolf, and Xinzhi Wu.

TWELFTH EDITION CHANGES AND CHAPTER HIGHLIGHTS

The pedagogical features described above strengthen each of the twenty-seven chapters in *Anthropology,* serving as threads that tie the text together and help students feel the holistic nature of the discipline. In addition, the engagingly presented concepts themselves provide students with a solid foundation in the principles and practices of anthropology today.

The text in hand has a significantly different feel to it than previous editions. Although still rich and varied in content, it is less "busy," for the narrative has been streamlined, the boxed features are more fluidly incorporated, and the photographs are fewer in number but greater in size and quality.

All chapters have been revised extensively—with the word count streamlined by about 15 percent, the data and examples updated, and the chapter openers refreshed with new, up-to-date Challenge Issues and related photographs. In addition to these overall changes, each chapter has undergone specific modifications and additions. The inventory presented below provides brief previews of the chapter contents and changes in this edition.

Chapter 1: The Essence of Anthropology

The book's opening chapter introduces students to the holistic discipline of anthropology, the unique focus of each of its four fields, and the common philosophical and methodological approaches they share. Touching briefly on fieldwork and the comparative method, along with ethical issues and examples of applied anthropology in all four fields, this chapter provides a foundation for our two field methods chapters—a revised one concerning archaeology and paleoanthropology and an entirely new one concerning cultural anthropology. An Anthropology Applied box on forensic anthropology and archaeology illustrates the importance of forensics in the investigations of international human rights abuses. Two boxed features help illustrate the interconnection of biology and culture in the human experience: Suzanne Leclerc-Madlala's compelling Original Study, "Fighting HIV/AIDS in Africa: Traditional Healers on the Front Line," and a Biocultural Connection highlighting Margaret Lock's cross-cultural research on human organ transplantation. The impact of the Biocultural Connection is strengthened by a new Globalscape, which profiles a particular organ donor. The chapter closes with a section titled "Anthropology and Globalization," in which we show the relevance of anthropology to several of today's most significant social and political issues.

Chapter 2: Biology and Evolution

This reorganized and streamlined chapter covers the same topics as in the eleventh edition but does so with more efficiency allowing for the elaboration of some topics. The comparison of religious accounts of creation to the science of evolution, for example, has been expanded to cover creation stories from diverse cultures. Biological mechanisms at the cellular level are explored early in the chapter, leaving the ways that evolutionary forces work on populations to the end of the chapter, thus setting the stage for the discussion of mammalian, primate, and human evolution that follows in later chapters. Updated photos illustrate the concept of homology more clearly. In the history of human classification section, we present this history including alternate taxonomies being used today by practicing anthropologists. The text does not favor one classificatory system so that the text can work for professors using either *hominid* or *hominin* to refer to humans and ancestral bipeds. The work of Rosalind Franklin is included in the history of the discovery of DNA. Clear new figures on protein synthesis and mitosis/meiosis will help students grasp these elegant biological processes. This chapter's boxed features emphasize the importance of culture in interpreting and implementing new genetic knowledge. They include a Biocultural Connection titled "The Social Impact of Genetics on Reproduction" and an Original Study by Jonathan Marks titled "Ninety-Eight Percent Alike: What Our Similarity to Apes Tells Us about Our Understanding of Genetics." A new Anthropology Applied feature titled "In the Belly of the Beast: Reflections on a Decade of Service to U.S. Genetics Policy Commissions" by Barbara Koenig and Nancy Press discusses their contributions as cultural anthropologists to U.S. national genetics policy.

Chapter 3: Living Primates

This beautifully illustrated chapter on the diversity of living primates has also been streamlined and reorganized to make room for some new material. The chapter opens with a new section on methods and ethics in primatology and a new Biocultural Connection by gorilla expert Michele Goldsmith on the ethics of great ape habituation and conservation in the context of ecotourism. Basic characteristics of the primate order and classificatory schemes are explored including new material on baboon behavior. A new Globalscape feature connects mining for the cell phone component coltan to gorilla habitat destruction so that students will connect their actions to protecting our endangered primate cousins. The chapter's Challenge Issue and closing section also focus on the critical issue of primate conservation today. The chapter includes an Anthropologists of Note box on Jane Goodall and Kinji Imanishi along with an excellent Original Study by Frans de Waal titled "Reconciliation and Its Cultural Modification in Primates."

Chapter 4: Field Methods in Archaeology and Paleoanthropology

This chapter clearly conveys the key methodological techniques. It also explores the philosophical approach necessary for successful collaboration between scientists and local peoples and for the successful resolution of the complex questions about who owns the past. Cultural resource management (CRM) is featured in the text narrative and also in a new Anthropology Applied feature by archaeologist John Crock about CRM work that uncovered the first St. Lawrence Iroquoian village in the state of Vermont. The ratio of time between lab work and excavation is illustrated with the new "Lucy's baby" fossils discovered in 2000 and then studied extensively before the release of the first report on this amazing find

in September 2006. The Biocultural Connection on Kennewick Man is updated to include new developments on scientific and legislative fronts. The Kennewick controversy is compared to the cooperation between local people and archaeologists specializing in Native Americans presented in the chapter's excellent Original Study titled "Whispers from the Ice" by Sherry Simpson. A new figure on paleomagnetic reversals makes this dating technique more accessible for the introductory student.

Chapter 5: Macroevolution and the Early Primates

Building on the evolutionary principles laid out in Chapter 2, this chapter provides an excellent overview of macroevolutionary mechanisms and also provides a concise, clear discussion of mammalian primate evolution. New diagrams illustrating cladogenesis and anagenesis help students with these concepts. A more thorough discussion of heterochrony and homeobox genes shows students how very contemporary molecular investigations can shed light on the distant past. A revised timeline helps students grasp geological time and the major events that occurred in the evolutionary history of the earth and its inhabitants. Also, the writing has been tightened throughout the chapter so that the same information is conveyed in fewer pages. Interesting features for this chapter include an Anthropologists of Note box on the pioneering work of New Zealander Allan Wilson on molecular clocks; an Original Study by Stephen Jay Gould titled "The Unsettling Nature of Variational Change," and a Biocultural Connection titled "Nonhuman Primates and Human Disease" that explores the ethical implications of using our closest living relatives for medical research.

Chapter 6: The First Bipeds

The anatomy of bipedalism, the derived trait characteristic of the human line, opens this chapter, which then proceeds to trace the various species of biped that lived in Africa during the Pliocene. Revised diagrams illustrate the differences in the pelvic and lower limb structures of contemporary humans, the other apes, and *Australopithecus*. The chapter explores both the history of discovery of various australopithecenes and provides a clear discussion of gracile versus robust forms. The text develops critical thinking skills through its discussion of *hominid* versus *hominin* classificatory schemes and a presentation of alternate phylogenies. The chapter's Original Study by Lee Berger titled "Is it Time to Revise the System of Scientific Naming?" also expands on this debate. An excellent discussion of gendered interpretation of the fossil record returns to a theme emphasized in the text: Paleoanthropology is a science of discovery that incorporates developments in a variety of disciplines. The chapter's box features emphasize the vitality of paleoanthropology. They include an Anthropologists of Note box on the extraordinary contributions of Louis and Mary Leakey to paleoanthropology and a Biocultural Connection titled "Evolution and Human Birth."

Chapter 7: Early *Homo* and the Origins of Culture

This chapter synthesizes and combines the content of Chapters 7 and 8 on *Homo habilis* and *Homo erectus* from the eleventh edition. While these two species figure prominently in the chapter, grouping them together allows us to provide a nuanced discussion of lumping versus splitting approaches to the fossil record and to provide alternate taxonomies. It also allows for a continuous and streamlined discussion of the trend of increasing cranial capacity and a reliance on culture that is true for *Homo*'s first 2 million or so years. The chapter has an expanded section on gendered interpretations of the fossil record and a new Biocultural Connection, "Sex, Gender, and Female Paleoanthropologists," that documents the important work done since the 1970s to bring a focus on women in human evolutionary history. The Anthropology Applied box, "Paleotourism and the World Heritage List," discusses the importance of paleoanthropological research to people today. A new Original Study by Donna Hart provides a brief version of her thesis (from her book *Man the Hunted,* co-authored with Robert Sussman) that selective pressure from carnivores played a role in increasing brain size over the course of human evolution. The chapter also features recent research on the effects of the myosin gene mutation on anatomical changes in the genus *Homo*. The chapter's figures and locator maps clearly explain the anatomical changes and geographic distribution of the genus *Homo* during its first 2 million years on the planet.

Chapter 8: Pre-Modern Humans and the Elaboration of Culture

This chapter provides a discussion of the fossil evidence of the genus *Homo* leading into and during the Middle Paleolithic, effectively tying together the debates around the relationship between biological change and cultural change. The fate and history of the Neandertals is explored in detail with an examination of the evidence for alternative taxonomies for this infamous fossil group. The chapter also presents the two major theories to account for the appearance of anatomically modern *Homo sapiens*. New features include an improved diagram that presents the Levalloisian tool-making technique and an expanded discussion on the evolution of language that links recent genetic work on the FOXP2 gene with the primate language studies of Sue Savage-Rumbaugh. The

recent genetic work on the Y chromosome and African origins by Spencer Wells is also included. The chapter's global focus is apparent in the Anthropologists of Note box, which features Ethiopian paleoanthropologist Berhane Asfaw and Chinese paleoanthropologist Xinzhi Wu. The Biocultural Connection "Paleolithic Prescriptions for the Diseases of Civilization" has a new home in this chapter as does the Anthropology Applied feature "Stone Tools for Modern Surgeons."

Chapter 9: The Global Expansion of *Homo sapiens* and Their Technology

This chapter includes new diagrams featuring the blade technique and the use of the spear-thrower along with examples of ancient human creativity, which convey the range and complexity of human cultural capabilities in the Upper Paleolithic. A new Biocultural Connection, "Altered States, Art, and Archaeology," links some of the images of cave art from the distant and more recent past to trancing states that are part of the healing traditions of many cultures. The Original Study "Paleolithic Paint Job" examines techniques used to create ancient cave art. The important work on gender in the archaeological record is featured through an Anthropologists of Note box on Margaret Conkey. The chapter also examines the biological evidence for the appearance of "modern" humans. A new figure and text about mitochondrial DNA make this material more accessible for students. The material on the spread of humans to Australia and the Americas has been expanded as well.

Chapter 10: The Neolithic Transition: The Domestication of Plants and Animals

Chapter 10 concentrates on the drastic cultural changes that occurred at the Neolithic transition with the domestication of plants and animals along with the development of permanent settlements in villages. The chapter's theme beginning with the Challenge Issue is the unexpected deleterious consequences of this culture change in terms of overall human health. The chapter features a new Anthropology Applied box, "The Real Dirt on Rainforest Fertility." It focuses on the work by a team of international archaeologists on ancient farming techniques in the Amazon forest that may make this region more productive in the future. The Biocultural Connection "Breastfeeding, Fertility, and Beliefs" and the Original Study by Anna Roosevelt, "History of Mortality and Physiological Stress," both illustrate the ways that cultures shape human biology. The discussion of the Mesolithic that preceded the Neolithic is streamlined and better organized. As well, there is a clear examination of the complex relationship between food production and population growth.

Chapter 11: The Emergence of Cities and States

This chapter on cities and states draws parallels between ancient and modern cities while exploring the origins of this very human way of life. A new Globalscape feature explores the effects of the war in Iraq on the precious Mesopotamian artifacts that were housed in the National Museum in Baghdad and a recent sting operation used to reclaim some of these Mesopotamian wonders in New York City. New discoveries of Olmec writing are included in the chapter along with a classic case study of archaeological work at Tikal. The chapter's Original Study, "Action Archaeology and the Community at El Pilar," illustrates another means through which archaeological projects can contribute to the lives of humans today. A new Anthropology Applied feature by Jane C. Waldbaum, president of the American Archaeological Institute, describes their program in which military personnel are given basic training in archaeology in order to preserve our shared global heritage.

Chapter 12: Modern Human Diversity: Race and Racism

Chapter 12 has been streamlined considerably by moving all sections about the biological effects of pollution and other human-made threats to the new Chapter 13. In addition, the chapter has been restructured so that the sections on biological diversity are all grouped together at the end of the chapter rather than sprinkled throughout. The chapter now opens with a history of human classification that emphasizes how culture shapes human interpretation of biology. It goes on to explore the effects of racism setting the stage for an examination of biological diversity that takes culture into account at all levels. The boxed features for this chapter are all new as well. Material on Ashley Montagu and Franz Boas has been moved into the body of the text, making room for a new Anthropologists of Note on the diverse work of Fatimah Jackson. A new Original Study by Jonathan Marks, "A Feckless Quest for the Basketball Gene," explores the dangers of stereotyping the abilities of any so-called race. Finally a new Biocultural Connection, "Beans, Enzymes, and Adaptation to Malaria," explores the complex interplay between fava beans and G-6-PD deficiency as adaptations to malaria and the folklore surrounding fava beans.

Chapter 13: Human Adaptation to a Changing World

This new chapter weaves together the anthropological study of human adaptation by biological and medical anthropologists with cutting-edge work in evolutionary medicine and the political ecology of health and disease. It examines the way that human alteration of the environment is leading to disease in our species and how political and social forces impact the distribution of health and disease among human populations. The biocultural theme characteristic of the entire textbook is explored in depth here through drawing out the connections between human health and political and economic forces, both globally and locally.

While some of this material appeared in the Epilogue of the seventh edition of *Evolution and Prehistory,* it is all entirely new to this twelfth edition of *Anthropology.* The chapter begins with classic anthropological work on genetic, developmental, and physiological adaptation to natural stressors such as high altitude and extreme cold and heat. It then explores the challenges of the rapidly changing human-made environment characteristic of the world today. The chapter provides students with an introduction to the biological and cultural approaches of medical anthropology that gives them a framework to think about health challenges in an era of globalization. New figures include one on the human pattern of growth and development and one on human population size through time. Work of reproductive ecologist Peter Ellison is featured in the Anthropologists of Note box. The Chapter's Original Study "Dancing Skeletons" is an excerpt from Katherine Dettwyler's monograph of the same name and focuses on childhood growth, nutrition, and disease categories in Mali. The Biocultural Connection "Picturing Pesticides" features Elizabeth Guillette's work on the neurological effects of pesticide exposure in Yaqui children. This chapter also features a new Globalscape concerning the transfer of Brazil's highly regarded HIV/AIDS programs to Portuguese-speaking countries in Africa.

Chapter 14: Characteristics of Culture

Here we address anthropology's core concept of culture, exploring the term and its significance for human individuals and societies. Elaborating on culture as the medium through which humans handle the problems of existence, we mark out its characteristics as something that is learned, shared, based on symbols, integrated, and dynamic. This chapter includes a new and more elaborate treatment of ethnocentrism and cultural relativism, as well as discussions on culture and adaptation; the functions of culture; culture, society and the individual; and culture and change. Our ethnographic narrative on the Amish has been significantly revised and brought forward to the present. The "Functions of Culture" section has also undergone a thorough reworking and now includes a new ethnographic sketch of cremation rituals in Bali. Special boxes include a new Biocultural Connection on "Adult Human Stature and the Effects of Culture," George Esber's revised Anthropology Applied box, "New Houses for Apache Indians," and an Anthropologists of Note box on Bronislaw Malinowski. Also in this chapter is an original illustration we call the "barrel model," which conveys the integrative and dynamic nature of culture and introduces the concepts of infrastructure/ social structure/superstructure.

Theory material that appeared in the last edition has been moved to the new chapter on theory and ethnographic fieldwork (Chapter 15).

Chapter 15: Ethnographic Fieldwork: Its History, Methods, and Theories

This entirely new chapter takes a unique approach to discussing ethnographic research. It begins with a historical overview on the subject—from the colonial era and salvage ethnography to acculturation studies, advocacy anthropology, and multi-sited ethnography in the era of globalization. The work of numerous anthropologists, past and present, are used to illustrate this historical journey. The chapter continues with an overview of research methods—marking out what is involved in choosing a research site and question and how one goes about doing preparatory research and participant observation. This section also covers ethnographic tools and aids, data gathering methods, fieldwork challenges, issues of subjectivity, and the creation of an ethnography in written, film, or digital formats. The third section of this chapter offers an overview of anthropology's theoretical perspectives, contrasts doctrine and theory, discusses the comparative method and the Human Relations Area Files, and explores the moral dilemmas and ethical responsibilities encountered in anthropological research. Special features include a new Biocultural Connection, "Pig Lovers and Pig Haters," adapted from Marvin Harris' work, Annette Weiner's Original Study, "The Importance of Trobriand Women," and an Anthropologists of Note box that profiles the pioneering visual anthropology work of Gregory Bateson and Margaret Mead.

Chapter 16: Language and Communication

This chapter, trimmed and rearranged to flow more smoothly, investigates the nature of language and the three branches of linguistic anthropology—descriptive linguistics, historical linguistics, and the study of language in its social and cultural settings (ethnolinguistics and sociolinguistics). The latter features new discussions of linguistic relativity and linguistic determinism. Also found here are sections on paralanguage and tonal languages, as well as language and gender and body language (proxemics and kinesics)—including new material on the impact of electronic media on language and communication worldwide. The historical sketch about writing takes readers from traditional speech performatives and memory devices to Egyptian hieroglyphics to the conception and spread of the alphabet to the 2003 to 2012 Literacy Decade established by the United Nations. An overhauled section on language loss and revival includes the latest data on the digital divide and its impact on ethnic minority languages—plus a new chart showing Internet language populations. Special features include a revised Biocultural Connection box, "The Biology of Human Speech," a lively new abridged version of H. Lyn White Miles' Original Study, "Language and the Intellectual Abilities of Orangutans," and William Leap's updated telling of his applied anthropology project, "Language Renewal among the Northern Ute." Finally, the chapter includes a new Globalscape on outsourcing.

Chapter 17: Social Identity, Personality, and Gender

Looking at individual identity within a sociocultural context, this chapter surveys a range of issues: the concept of "self," enculturation and the behavioral environment, social identity through personal naming, the development of personality, the concepts of group and modal personality, and the idea of national character. New ethnographic examples include a Navajo naming and First Laugh Ceremony in the section on naming, and a description of *sadhus* (ascetic Hindu monks) in the section "Normal and Abnormal Personality in Social Context." A substantial section titled "Alternative Gender Models from a Cross-Cultural Perspective" provides a thought-provoking historical overview of intersexuality, transsexuality, and transgendering, including current statistics on the incidence of intersexuality worldwide. Boxed features include the Biocultural Connection "A Cross-Cultural Perspective on Psychosomatic Symptoms and Mental Health," a shortened version of R. K. Williamson's stirring Original Study on intersexuality, "The Blessed Curse," and an Anthropologists of Note on Margaret Mead and Ruth Fulton Benedict.

Chapter 18: Patterns of Subsistence

Here we investigate the various ways humans meet their basic needs and how societies adapt through culture to the environment. We begin with a discussion of adaptation, followed by profiles on modes of subsistence in which we look at food-foraging and food-producing societies—pastoralism, crop cultivation, and industrialization. The chapter's boxed features include a new Biocultural Connection on "Surviving in the Andes: Aymara Adaptation to High Altitude," along with a trimmed version of Dennis Werner's Original Study "Gardens of the Mekranoti Kayapo" (which analyzes the productivity of a slash-and-burn gardening community in the central Amazon basin in Brazil), and an Anthropology Applied piece "Agricultural Development and the Anthropologist" (about a rural development organization that revives ancient farming practices). Also in this chapter is a new Globalscape, "How Much for a Red Delicious?," profiling migrant laborers from Jamaica.

Chapter 19: Economic Systems

In this chapter covering the production, distribution, and consumption of goods, we delve into such matters as the control of resources (natural, technological, labor) and types of labor division (gender, age, cooperative labor, craft specialization). A section on distribution and exchange defines various forms of reciprocity (with a detailed and illustrated description of the Kula ring and a new discussion of silent trade), along with redistribution and market exchange. The discussion on leveling mechanisms has been revised and expanded, with new narratives on cargos and the potlatch (including a rare and remarkable contemporary potlatch photograph). The section on market exchange includes a new narrative on the invention and spread of money, including a new Biocultural Connection titled "Cacao: The Love Bean in the Money Tree." Other boxed features are Karen Stephenson's "Anthropology in the Corporate Jungle" and an Anthropologists of Note about independent Kenya's first president, Jomo Kenyatta, who was academically trained in anthropology and took the concept of cooperation from the local level to the state.

Chapter 20: Sex, Marriage, Family

Exploring the close interconnection among sexual reproductive practices, marriage, family, and household, we discuss the household as the basic building block in a culture's social structure, the center where child rearing, as well as shelter, economic production, consumption, and inheritance are commonly organized. Particulars addressed in this chapter include the incest taboo, endogamy and exogamy, dowry and bride-price, cousin marriage, same-sex marriage, divorce, residence patterns, and non-family households. Updated definitions of marriage, family, nuclear family, and extended family encompass current real-life situations around the world, as does a discussion of how new reproductive technologies (NRTs) are impacting the ways humans think about and form families. Boxed features include a shortened version of Serena Nanda's engaging Original Study, "Arranging Marriage in India"; Martin Ottenheimer's Biocultural Connection, "Marriage Prohibitions in the United States"; and an Anthropologists of Note box on Claude Lévi-Strauss.

Chapter 21: Kinship and Descent

This chapter marks out the various forms of descent groups and the roles descent plays as an integrated feature in a cultural system. Details and examples are presented concerning lineages, clans, phratries, and moieties (highlighting Hopi Indian matriclans and Scottish highland patriclans, among others), followed by illustrated examples of a representative range of kinship systems and their kinship terminologies.

There is a new discussion on diasporic communities in today's globalized world. New ethnographic examples include the Han Chinese, Maori of New Zealand, and Canela Indians of Brazil. In addition to the revised Anthropology Applied box that relays the role descent played in "Resolving a Native American Tribal Membership Dispute," this chapter includes two new boxed features: Clementine van Eck's compelling Original Study about Turkish immigrants, "Honor Killings in the Netherlands," and a Biocultural Connection, "Maori Origins: Ancestral Genes and Mythical Canoes," which shows how Maori oral traditions about their origins fit quite well with recent genetic research.

Chapter 22: Grouping by Gender, Age, Common Interest, Class

This much refined chapter includes discussions of grouping by gender, age, common interest, and class or social rank. The section on age grouping features revised and new ethnographic material from the Mundurucu of Brazil and the Tiriki and Maasai of East Africa. Common-interest group examples range from the Shriners to the Crips to the Jewish diaspora. A revised narrative on caste explores its historical context and role in India's Hindu culture and also presents examples of castelike situations from other parts of the world. A new "wealth inequality" chart provides a clear visual of wealth distribution in the United States. Boxed features include a Biocultural Connection box, "African Burial Ground Project" (the archaeological dig in New York City that revealed the physical stress of an entire community brought on by the social institution of slavery); a fully reworked Applied Anthropology piece "Anthropologists and Social Impact Assessment"; and Susan Lees' new Original Study, "The Jewish *Eruv*: Symbolic Place in Public Space." Also new to this chapter is a Globalscape tracing the life of an Ivory Coast soccer star and the numerous countries in which he has trained and played.

Chapter 23: Politics, Power, and Violence

Looking at a range of uncentralized and centralized political systems—from kin-ordered bands and tribes, to chiefdoms and states—this chapter explores the question of power, the intersection of politics and religion, and issues of political leadership and gender. Discussing the maintenance of order, we look at internalized and externalized controls (including a new discussion on gossip's role in curbing socially unacceptable behavior), along with social control through witchcraft and through law. We mark the functions of law and the ways different societies deal with crime, including new sentencing laws in Canada based on traditional Native American restorative justice techniques such as the Talking Circle. Then, shifting our focus from maintaining order *within* a society to political organization and *external* affairs, we discuss warfare and present a 5,000-year overview of armed conflicts among humans right up to today. Special features in this chapter include a Biocultural Connection box, "Sex, Gender, and Human Violence," an Anthropology Applied box, "Dispute Resolution and the Anthropologist," and an Anthropologists of Note box profiling Laura Nader.

Chapter 24: Spirituality, Religion, and the Supernatural

Opening with a description of the anthropological approach to religion and noting current distinctions between religion and spirituality, this chapter goes on to discuss beliefs concerning supernatural beings and forces (gods and goddesses, ancestral spirits, animism, and animatism), religious specialists (priests and priestesses, as well as shamans), and rituals and ceremonies (rites of passage and rites of intensification). A section on shamanism explores the origins of the term and presents our "shamanic complex" model of how shamanic healings take place. A section on religion, magic, and witchcraft highlights Ibibio witchcraft, while another section marks out religion's psychological and social functions, including efforts to heal physical, emotional, and social ills. Touching on religion and cultural change, this chapter looks at revitalization movements and new material on indigenous Christian churches in Africa. Also new to the chapter are discussions on sacred places and women's roles in religious leadership. Of special note are the many new and evocative photographs. Boxed features include Hillary Crane's new and arresting Biocultural Connection about Taiwanese Buddhist nuns, "Change Your Karma and Change Your Sex?," along with Marjorie Shostak's Original Study, "Healing among the Ju/'hoansi," and an Anthropology Applied piece on "Reconciling Modern Medicine with Traditional Beliefs in Swaziland."

Chapter 25: The Arts

This chapter explores in detail three key categories of art—visual, verbal, and musical—illustrating what they reveal about and what functions they play in societies. A long and detailed discussion about aesthetic and interpretive approaches to analyzing art, as applied to rock art in southern Africa has been shortened and reworked to make it more lively and engaging. Among numerous high points in the section "Functions of Art" is a new and remarkable photograph of a sand painting healing ceremony. Of particular note in this chapter is the section on "Art, Globalization, and Cultural Survival," which investigates how threatened indigenous groups use aesthetic traditions as part of a cultural survival strategy. Boxed features include a new Biocultural Connection, "Peyote Art: Divine Visions among the Huichol," a newly illus-

trated Original Study on "The Modern Tattoo Community" by Margo DeMello, and an Anthropologists of Note profile about Frederica de Laguna's work among the Tlingit of Yakutat, Alaska.

Also new in this chapter is the Globalscape highlighting the work of a Ghanaian custom coffin maker that is gaining worldwide recognition as art.

Chapter 26: Processes of Change

The themes and terminology of globalization are woven through this chapter, which includes definitions that distinguish *progress* from *modernization, rebellion* from *revolution,* and *acculturation* from *enculturation.* Here, we discuss mechanisms of change—innovation, diffusion, and cultural loss, as well as repressive change. Our exploration of the latter covers acculturation, ethnocide, and genocide, citing a range of the all-too-many repressive-change examples from around the world—including a new discussion of ethnocide in Tibet. This chapter also looks at reactions to such change, including revitalization movements, rebellions, and revolutions. A discussion on modernization touches on the issue of self-determination among indigenous peoples and highlights two contrasting cases: Skolt Lapp reindeer herders in Finland, and Shuar Indians of Ecuador. Also featured is the historical profile of applied or practical anthropology and the emergence of action or advocacy anthropology in collaboration with indigenous societies, ethnic minorities, and other besieged or repressed groups. The chapter's last pages discuss globalization as a worldwide process of accelerated modernization in which all parts of the earth are becoming interconnected in one vast, interrelated, and all-encompassing system. Boxed features include a Biocultural Connection on the Emergence of new diseases, an Anthropology Applied piece titled "Development Anthropology and Dams," and an Anthropologists of Note box on Eric R. Wolf.

Chapter 27: Global Challenges, Local Responses, and the Role of Anthropology

Our final chapter zeroes in on numerous global challenges confronting the human species today—and prods students to use the anthropological tools they have learned to think critically about these issues and take informed steps to help bring about a future in which humans live in harmony with each other and the nature that sustains us all. Sections on global culture and ethnic resurgence look at Westernization and its counterforce of growing nationalism and the breakup of multi-ethnic states. We present examples of resistance to globalization, and discuss pluralism and multiculturalism. A substantial section about the rise of global corporations places this phenomenon in historical context and highlights the largest corporations (making particular note of media corporations and the emergence of the "global mediascape").

Under the heading "Structural Power in the Age of Globalization," we recount the ever-widening gap between those who have wealth and power and those who do not. We define and illustrate the term *structural power* and its two branches—hard power (military and economic might) and soft power (media might that gains control through ideological influence). We then address "Problems of Structural Violence"—from pollution to epidemics of hunger and obesity. We also touch on "the culture of discontent," including the psychological problems born of powerful marketing messages that shape cultural standards concerning the ideal human body. Tied to this is Laura Nader's Original Study "Standardizing the Body: The Question of Choice." Also featured is a new Biocultural Connection, "Toxic Breast Milk Threatens Arctic Culture," an Anthropologists of Note box on Arjun Appadurai, and a new Globalscape on the deadly results of toxins being shipped to the Third World. The chapter closes with a stirring photo and commentary on indigenous peoples, noting anthropology's potential for helping to solve problems of inequity on local and global levels.

SUPPLEMENTS

Anthropology comes with a strong supplements program to help instructors create an effective learning environment both inside and outside the classroom and to aid students in mastering the material.

Supplements for Instructors

Online Instructor's Manual and Print Test Bank

The Instructor's Manual offers detailed chapter outlines, lecture suggestions, key terms, and student activities such as *InfoTrac College Edition* exercises and Internet exercises. In addition, there are over seventy-five chapter test questions including multiple choice, true/false, fill-in-the-blank, short answer, and essay.

ExamView Computerized and Online Testing

Create, deliver, and customize tests and study guides (both print and online) in minutes with this easy to use assessment and tutorial system. ExamView offers both a Quick Test Wizard and an Online Test Wizard that guide you step-by-step throughout the process of creating tests, while its unique "WYSWYG" capability allows you to see the test you are creating on screen exactly as it will print or display online. You can build tests of up to 250 questions using up to twelve question types. Using ExamView's complete word processing capabilities, you can enter an unlimited number of new questions or edit existing questions.

Multimedia Manager for Anthropology: A Microsoft PowerPoint Link Tool

This new CD-ROM contains digital media and Microsoft PowerPoint presentations for all of Wadsworth's © 2008 introductory anthropology texts, placing images, lectures, and video clips at your fingertips. This CD-ROM includes preassembled Microsoft PowerPoint presentations, and charts, graphs, maps, line art, and images with a NEW zoom feature from all Wadsworth © 2008 anthropology texts. You can add your own lecture notes and images to create a customized lecture presentation. Also, an Earthwatch Institute Research Expedition feature offers even more images.

JoinIn on TurningPoint

The anthropology discipline at Thomson Wadsworth is pleased to offer **JoinIn**™ (clicker) content for Audience Response Systems tailored to this text. Use the program by posing your own questions and display students' answers instantly within the Microsoft® PowerPoint® slides of your existing lecture. Or, utilize any or all of the following content that will be included with your Anthropology JoinIn product:

- **Opinion polls** on issues important to each anthropology chapter (five questions per chapter). Students may feel uncomfortable talking about sensitive subjects such as sexuality or religion. JoinIn gives students complete anonymity and helps students feel connected to the issues.
- **Conceptual quiz questions** for each chapter. Give students a quick quiz during or after the chapter lecture and determine if they have understood the material.
- **Plus, pre-assembled PowerPoint lecture slides** for each chapter of your book are included with the material above integrated into the slides. All of the work integrating clicker questions into the chapter lecture slides has been done for you!

The program can be used to simply take roll, or it can assess your students' progress and opinions with in-class questions. Enhance how your students interact with you, your lecture, and each other. For college and university adopters only. *Contact your local Thomson representative to learn more.*

Wadsworth Anthropology Video Library

Qualified adopters may select full-length videos from an extensive library of offerings drawn from such excellent educational video sources as *Films for the Humanities and Sciences.*

ABC Anthropology Video Series

This exclusive video series was created jointly by Wadsworth and ABC for the anthropology course. Each video contains approximately 60 minutes of footage originally broadcast on ABC within the past several years. The videos are broken into short 2- to 7-minute segments, perfect for classroom use as lecture launchers or to illustrate key anthropological concepts. An annotated table of contents accompanies each video, providing descriptions of the segments and suggestions for their possible use within the course.

A Guide to Visual Anthropology

Prepared by Jayasinhji Jhala of Temple University, this guide provides a compendium of fifty of the most outstanding classic and contemporary anthropological films. The guide describes the films, tells why they are important, and gives suggestions for their use in the classroom.

AIDS in Africa DVD

Southern Africa has been overcome by a pandemic of unparalleled proportions. This documentary series focuses on the new democracy of Namibia and the many actions that are being taken to control HIV/AIDS. Included in this series are four documentary films created by the Periclean Scholars at Elon University: (1) *Young Struggles, Eternal Faith,* which focuses on caregivers in the faith community; (2) *The Shining Lights of Opuwo,* which shows how young people share their messages of hope through song and dance; (3) *A Measure of Our Humanity,* which describes HIV/AIDS as an issue related to gender, poverty, stigma, education, and justice; and (4) *You Wake Me Up,* a story of two HIV-positive women and their acts of courage helping other women learn to survive. Thomson/Wadsworth is excited to offer these award-winning films to instructors for use in class. When presenting topics such as gender, faith, culture, poverty, and so on, the films will be enlightening for students and will expand their global perspective of HIV/AIDS.

Online Resources for Instructors and Students

Anthropology Resource Center

This online center offers a wealth of information and useful tools for both instructors and students in all four fields of anthropology. It includes interactive maps, learning modules, video exercises, and breaking news in anthropology. For instructors, the Resource Center includes a gateway to time-saving teaching tools, such as image banks, sample syllabi, and more. Access to the website is available free when bundled with the text or for purchase at a nominal fee. To purchase online, students are directed to www.thomsonedu.com, where they can create an account through 1Pass.

Book Premium Companion Website

Access to this text-specific website is available free when bundled with the text or for purchase at a nominal fee. This site includes: learning modules on key anthropological concepts, animations, interactive exercises, map exercises, video exercises with questions, tutorial quizzes with feedback, and essay questions, all of which can be e-mailed to professors.

Thomson InSite for Writing and Research—with Turnitin Originality Checker

InSite features a full suite of writing, peer review, online grading, and e-portfolio applications. It is an all-in-one tool that helps instructors manage the flow of papers electronically and allows students to submit papers and peer reviews online. Also included in the suite is Turnitin, an originality check that offers a simple solution for instructors who want a strong deterrent against plagiarism, as well as encouragement for students to employ proper research techniques. Access is available for packaging with each copy of this book. For more information, visit http://insite.thomson.com.

InfoTrac College Edition

InfoTrac College Edition is an online library that offers full-length articles from thousands of scholarly and popular publications. Among the journals available are *American Anthropologist, Current Anthropology,* and *Canadian Review of Sociology and Anthropology.* Contact your local Thomson sales representative for details.

Supplements for Students

Thomson Audio Study Products

Thomson Audio Study Products provide audio reinforcement of key concepts students can listen to from their personal computer or MP3 player. Created specifically for Haviland et al.'s *Anthropology,* 12th edition, *Thomson Audio Study Products* provide approximately 10 minutes of up-beat audio content, giving students a quick and convenient way to master key concepts, test their knowledge with quiz questions, and listen to a brief overview on the major themes of each chapter. Students may purchase access to *Thomson Audio Study Products* for this text online at www.thomsonedu.com.

Study Guide and Workbook

The Study Guide includes learning objectives, detailed chapter outlines and key terms to aid in student study; activities such as InfoTrac College Edition exercises and

Internet exercises to help students apply their knowledge, and over fifty practice test questions per chapter including multiple choice, true/false, fill-in-the-blank, short answer, and essay questions.

Telecourse Study Guide

A new telecourse, **Anthropology: The Four Fields,** available in the fall of 2007 provides online and print companion study guide options that include study aids, interactive exercises, videos, and more.

Additional Student Resources

Basic Genetics for Anthropology CD-ROM: Principles and Applications (Stand–Alone Version), by Robert Jurmain and Lynn Kilgore

This student CD-ROM expands on such biological concepts as biological inheritance (genes, DNA sequencing, and so on) and applications of that to modern human populations at the molecular level (human variation and adaptation, that is, to disease, diet, growth, and development). Interactive animations and simulations bring these important concepts to life for students so they can fully understand the essential biological principles required for physical anthropology. Also available are quizzes and interactive flashcards for further study.

Hominid Fossils CD-ROM: An Interactive Atlas, by James Ahern

The interactive atlas CD-ROM includes over seventy-five key fossils important for a clear understanding of human evolution. The QuickTime Virtual Reality (QTVR) "object" movie format for each fossil enables students to have a near-authentic experience of working with these important finds, by allowing them to rotate the fossil 360 degrees. Unlike some VR media, QTVR objects are made using actual photographs of the real objects and thus better preserve details of color and texture. The fossils used are high-quality research casts and real fossils. The organization of the atlas is nonlinear, with three levels and multiple paths, enabling students to see how the fossil fits into the map of human evolution in terms of geography, time, and evolution. The CD-ROM offers students an inviting, authentic learning environment, one that also contains a dynamic quizzing feature that will allow students to test their knowledge of fossil and species identification, as well as provide more detailed information about the fossil record.

Virtual Laboratories for Physical Anthropology, 4th edition, by John Kappelman

The new edition of this full color, interactive online product provides students with a hands-on computer component for completing lab assignments at school or at home. Through the use of video clips, 3-D animations, sound, and digital images, students can actively participate in twelve labs as part of their physical anthropology and archaeology course. The labs and assignments teach students how to formulate and test hypotheses with exercises that include how to measure, plot, interpret, and evaluate a variety of data drawn from osteological, behavioral, and fossil materials.

Modules in Physical and Cultural Anthropology

Each free-standing module is actually a complete text chapter, featuring the same quality of pedagogy and illustration that are contained in Thomson Wadsworth's anthropology texts.

Coming Fall of 2007, Medical Anthropology!

Coming Fall of 2007, Evolution of the Brain: Neuroanatomy, Development, and Paleontology!

Human Environment Interactions by Cathy Galvin

Cathy Galvin provides students with an introduction to the basic concepts in human ecology, before discussing cultural ecology, human adaptation studies, human behavioral ecology—including material on systems approaches and cognitive and critical approaches—and political ecology. She concludes the module with a discussion of resilience and global change as a result of human–environment interactions today and the tools used.

Readings and Case Studies

Globalization and Change in Fifteen Cultures: Born in One World, Living in Another, edited by George Spindler and Janice E. Stockard

In this volume, fifteen case study authors write about culture change in today's diverse settings around the world. Each original article provides insight into the dynamics and meanings of change, as well as the effects of globalization at the local level.

Case Studies in Cultural Anthropology, edited by George Spindler and Janice E. Stockard

Select from more than sixty classic and contemporary ethnographies representing geographic and topical diversity. Newer case studies focus on culture change and culture continuity, reflecting the globalization of the world.

Case Studies in Contemporary Social Issues, edited by John A. Young

Framed around social issues, these new contemporary case studies are globally comparative and represent the cutting-edge work of anthropologists today.

Case Studies in Archaeology, edited by Jeffrey Quilter

These engaging accounts of cutting-edge archaeological techniques, issues and solutions—as well as studies discussing the collection of material remains—range from site-specific excavations to types of archaeology practiced.

Primate Evolution Module by Robert Jurmain

Robert Jurmain examines primate evolution as it has developed over the last 60 million years, helping students understand the ecological adaptations and evolutionary relationships of fossil forms to each other and to contemporary primates. Using what they know about primate anatomy and social behavior, students will learn to "flesh out" the bones and teeth that make up the evolutionary record of primate origins.

Forensics Anthropology Module: A Brief Review by Diane France

Diane France explores the myths and realities of the search for human remains in crime scenes, what should be expected from a forensic anthropology expert in the courtroom, some of the special challenges in mass fatality incident responses (such as plane crashes and terrorist acts), and what students should consider if they want to purse a career in forensic anthropology.

Molecular Anthropology Module by Leslie Knapp

Leslie Knapp explores how molecular genetic methods are used to understand the organization and expression of genetic information in humans and nonhuman primates. Students will learn about the common laboratory methods used to study genetic variation and evolution in molecular anthropology. Examples are drawn from up-to-date research on human evolutionary origins and comparative primate genomics to demonstrate that scientific research is an ongoing process with theories frequently being questioned and re-evaluated.

Acknowledgments

In this day and age, no textbook comes to fruition without extensive collaboration. Beyond the shared endeavors of our author team, this book owes its completion to a wide range of individuals, from colleagues in the discipline to those involved in the production process. We are particularly grateful for the remarkable group of manuscript reviewers listed below. They provided unusually detailed and thoughtful feedback that helped us to hone and re-hone our narrative.

Tara Devi S. Ashok, University of Massachusetts, Boston

René Bobe, State University of New York University at Buffalo

Barbara Bonnekessen, University of Missouri at Kansas City

Joanna Casey, University of South Carolina

Terri Castaneda, California State University, Sacramento

Rebecca Cramer, Johnson County Community College

Matthea Cremers, University of California at Santa Barbara

Barbra E. Erickson, California State University, Fullerton

Lynn Gamble, San Diego State University

Mikel Hogan, California State University, Fullerton

Frank Hutchins, Spalding University

Stevan R. Jackson, Radford University

Susan Kirkpatrick Smith, Kennesaw State University

Susan Krook, Normandale Community College

Alison Rautman, Michigan State University

Melissa Remis, Purdue University

Monica Rothschild-Boros, Orange Coast College

Suzanne Spencer-Wood, Oakland University

Orit Tamir, New Mexico Highlands University

Melody Yeager, Butte College

Ellen Zimmerman, Framingham State College

We carefully considered and made use of the wide range of comments provided by these individuals. Our decisions on how to utilize their suggestions were influenced by our own perspectives on anthropology and teaching, combined with the priorities and page limits of this text. Thus, neither our reviewers, nor any of the other anthropologists mentioned here should be held responsible for any shortcomings in this book. They should, however, be credited as contributors to many of the book's strengths.

Thanks, too, go to colleagues who provided material for some of the Original Study, Biocultural Connection, and Anthropology Applied boxes in this text: Mary Jo Arnoldi, Michael Blakey, Hillary Crane, John Crock, Margo DeMello, Katherine A. Dettwyler, Clementine van Eck, George Esber, Anabel Ford, Edward C. Green, Michele Goldsmith, Marvin Harris, Michael M. Horowitz, Barbara Koenig, William Leap, Suzanne LeClerc-Madlala, Susan Lees, Charles C. Mann, Jonathan Marks, H. Lyn White Miles, Laura Nader, Serena Nanda, Martin Ottenheimer, Nancy Press, Marjorie Shostak, Sherry Simpson, Clyde C. Snow, Karen Stephenson, William Ury, Frans B. M. de Waal, Dennis Werner, Annette B. Wiener, R. K. Williamson, and Jane C. Waldbaum. Among these individuals we particularly want to acknowledge our admiration, affection, and appreciation for our mutual friend and colleague Jim Petersen, whose life came to an abrupt and tragic end while returning from fieldwork in the Brazilian Amazon. Jim's work is featured in the piece by Charles C. Mann.

We have debts of gratitude to office workers in our departments for their cheerful help in clerical matters: Debbie Hedrick, Karen Rundquist, Emira Smailagic, Gretchen Gross, and Sheri Youngberg. And to research librarian extraordinaire Nancy Bianchi and colleagues Yvette Pigeon, John Fogarty, Lewis First, Martin Ottenheimer, Harriet Ottenheimer, and Michael Wesch for engaging in lively discussions of anthropological and pedagogical approaches. Also worthy of note here are the introductory anthropology teaching assistants who, through the years, have shed light for us on effective ways to reach new generations of students.

Our thanksgiving inventory would be incomplete without mentioning individuals at Wadsworth Publishing who helped conceive this text and bring it to fruition. Special gratitude goes to Senior Acquisitions Editor Lin Marshall for her vision, vigor, and anthropological knowledge and to Developmental Editor Julie Cheng for her calming influence and attention to detail. Our thanks also go out to Wadsworth's skilled and enthusiastic editorial, marketing, design, and production team: Eve Howard (Vice President and Editor-in-Chief), Dave Lionetti (Technology Project Manager), Jessica Jang (Editorial Assistant), Caroline Concilla (Executive Marketing Manager), as well as Jerilyn Emori (Content Project Manager) and Maria Epes (Executive Art Director).

In addition to all of the above, we have had the invaluable aid of several most able freelancers, including Christine Davis of Two Chicks Advertising & Marketing, and our expert and enthusiastic photo researcher Billie Porter, who was always willing to go the extra mile to find the most telling and compelling photographs, and our skilled graphic designer Carol Zuber-Mallison of ZM Graphics who can always be relied upon to deliver fine work and great humor. We are especially thankful to have had the opportunity to work once again with copyeditor Jennifer Gordon and production coordinator Robin Hood, who bring calm efficiency and grace to the demands of meeting difficult deadlines.

And finally, all of us are indebted to family members who have not only put up with our textbook preoccupation but cheered us on in the endeavor. Dana had the tireless support and keen eye of husband Peter Bingham—along with the varied contributions of their three sons Nishan, Tavid, and Aram Bingham. As co-author spouses under the same roof, Harald and Bunny have picked up slack for each other on every front to help this project move along smoothly. But the biggest debt of gratitude may be in Bill's corner: For more than three decades he has had invaluable input and support in his text-book tasks from his spouse Anita de Laguna Haviland.

About the Authors

While distinct from one another, all four members of this author team share overlapping research interests and a similar vision of what anthropology is (and should be) about. For example, all are "true believers" in the four-field approach to anthropology and all have some involvement in applied work.

WILLIAM A. HAVILAND is Professor Emeritus at the University of Vermont, where he founded the Department of Anthropology and taught for thirty-two years. He holds a Ph.D. in Anthropology from the University of Pennsylvania.

He has carried out original research in archaeology in Guatemala and Vermont; ethnography in Maine and Vermont; and physical anthropology in Guatemala. This work has been the basis of numerous publications in various national and international books and journals, as well as in media intended for the general public. His books include The Original Vermonters, coauthored with Marjorie Power, and a technical monograph on ancient Maya settlement. He also served as technical consultant for the award-winning telecourse, *Faces of Culture,* and is coeditor of the series *Tikal Reports,* published by the University of Pennsylvania Museum of Archaeology and Anthropology.

Besides his teaching and writing, Dr. Haviland has lectured to numerous professional, as well as, non-professional audiences in Canada, Mexico, Lesotho, South Africa, and Spain, as well as in the United States. A staunch supporter of indigenous rights, he served as expert witness for the Missisquoi Abenakis of Vermont in an important court case over aboriginal fishing rights.

Awards received by Dr. Haviland include being named University Scholar by the Graduate School of the University of Vermont in 1990, a Certificate of Appreciation from the Sovereign Republic of the Abenaki Nation of Missisquoi, St. Francis/Sokoki Band in 1996, and a Lifetime Achievement Award from the Center for Research on Vermont in 2006. Now retired from teaching, he continues his research, writing, and lecturing from the coast of Maine.

HARALD E. L. PRINS (Ph.D., New School 1988) is a University Distinguished Professor of Anthropology at Kansas State University and guest curator at the National Museum of Natural History, Smithsonian Institution. Born in The Netherlands, he studied at universities in Europe and the United States. He has done extensive fieldwork among indigenous peoples in South and North America, published dozens of articles in five languages,

Authors Bunny McBride, Dana Walrath, Harald Prins, and William Haviland

co-edited some books, and authored "The Mi'kmaq: Resistance, Accommodation, and Cultural Survival" (1996). He also made award-winning documentaries and served as president of the Society for Visual Anthropology and visual anthropology editor of the "American Anthropologist." Dr. Prins has won his university's most prestigious undergraduate teaching awards and held the Coffman Chair for University Distinguished Teaching Scholars (2004–05). Most recently, Dr. Prins was selected as Professor of the Year for the State of Kansas by the Carnegie Foundation for the Advancement of Teaching. Active in human rights, he served as expert witness in Native rights cases in the U.S. Senate and various Canadian courts, and was instrumental in the successful federal recognition and land claims of the Aroostook Band of Micmacs (1991).

DANA WALRATH is Assistant Professor of Family Medicine at the University of Vermont and a Women's Studies affiliated faculty member. She earned her Ph.D. in Anthropology from the University of Pennsylvania and is a medical and biological anthropologist with principal interests in biocultural aspects of reproduction, the cultural context of biomedicine, genetics, and evolutionary medicine. She directs an innovative educational program at the University of Vermont's College of Medicine that brings anthropological theory and practice to first-year medical students. Before joining the faculty at the University of Vermont in 2000, she taught at the University of Pennsylvania and Temple University. Her research has been supported by the National Science Foundation, Health Resources and Services Administration, the Centers for Disease Control and the Templeton Foundation. Dr. Walrath's publications have appeared in *Current Anthropology, American Anthropologist,* and *American*

Journal of Physical Anthropology. An active member of the Council on the Anthropology of Reproduction, she has also served on a national committee to develop women's health-care learning objectives for medical education and works locally to improve health care for refugees and immigrants.

BUNNY MCBRIDE (M.A. Columbia University, 1980) is an award-winning author specializing in cultural anthropology, indigenous peoples, international tourism, and nature conservation issues. Published in dozens of national and international print media, she has reported from Africa, Europe, China, and the Indian Ocean. Highly rated as a teacher, she served as visiting anthropology faculty at Principia College, the Salt Institute for Documentary Field Studies, and since 1996 as adjunct lecturer of anthropology at Kansas State University. McBride's many publications include *Women of the Dawn* (1999) and *Molly Spotted Elk: A Penobscot in Paris* (1995). Collaborating with Native communities in Maine, she curated various museum exhibits based on her books. The Maine state legislature awarded her a special commendation for significant contributions to Native women's history (1999). A community activist and researcher for the Aroostook Band of Micmacs (1981–91), she assisted this Maine Indian community in its successful efforts to reclaim lands, gain tribal status, and revitalize cultural traditions. Currently, McBride serves as co-principal investigator for a National Park Service ethnography project, guest curator for an exhibition on the Rockefeller Southwest Indian Art Collection, oral history advisor for the Kansas Humanities Council, and board member of the Women's World Summit Foundation, based in Geneva, Switzerland.

1 The Essence of Anthropology

CHALLENGE ISSUE

It is a challenge to make sense of who we are. Where did we come from? Why are we so radically different from other animals and so surprisingly similar to others? Why do our bodies look the way they do? How do we explain so many different beliefs, languages, and customs? What makes us tick? As just one of 10 million species, including 4,000 fellow mammals, we humans are the only creatures on earth with the mental capacity to ask such questions about ourselves and the world around us. We do this not only because we are curious but also because knowledge has enabled us to adapt to radically contrasting environments all across the earth and helps us create and improve our material and social living conditions. Adaptations based on knowledge are essential in every culture, and culture is our species' ticket to survival. Understanding humanity in all its biological and cultural variety, past and present, is the fundamental contribution of anthropology. This contribution has become all the more important in the era of globalization, when appreciating our common humanity and respecting cultural differences are essential to human survival.

What Is Anthropology?

Anthropology, the study of human-kind everywhere, throughout time, produces knowledge about what makes people different from one another and what they all share in common. Anthropologists work within four fields of the discipline. While physical anthropologists focus on humans as biological organisms (tracing evolutionary development and looking at biological variations), cultural anthropologists investigate the contrasting ways groups of humans think, feel, and behave. Archaeologists try to recover information about human cultures—usually from the past—by studying material objects, skeletal remains, and settlements. Meanwhile, linguists study languages—communication systems by which cultures are maintained and passed on to succeeding generations. Practitioners in all four fields are informed by one another's findings and united by a common anthropological perspective on the human condition.

How Do Anthropologists Do What They Do?

Anthropologists, like other scholars, are concerned with the description and explanation of reality. They formulate and test hypotheses—tentative explanations of observed phenomena—concerning humankind. Their aim is to develop reliable theories— interpretations or explanations supported by bodies of data—about our species. These data are usually collected through fieldwork—a particular kind of hands-on research that makes anthropologists so familiar with a situation that they can begin to recognize patterns, regularities, and exceptions. It is also through careful observation (combined with comparison) that anthropologists test their theories.

How Does Anthropology Compare to Other Disciplines?

In studying humankind, early anthropologists came to the conclusion that to fully understand the complexities of human thought, feelings, behavior, and biology, it was necessary to study and compare all humans, wherever and whenever. More than any other feature, this unique cross-cultural, long-term perspective distinguishes anthropology from other social sciences. Anthropologists are not the only scholars who study people, but they are uniquely holistic in their approach, focusing on the interconnections and interdependence of all aspects of the human experience, past and present. It is this holistic and integrative perspective that equips anthropologists to grapple with an issue of overriding importance for all of us today: globalization.

or as long as they have been on earth, people have sought answers to questions about who they are, where they come from, and why they act as they do. Throughout most of human history, though, people relied on myth and folklore for answers, rather than on the systematic testing of data obtained through careful observation. Anthropology, over the last 150 years, has emerged as a tradition of scientific inquiry with its own approaches to answering these questions. Simply stated, **anthropology** is the study of humankind in all times and places. While focusing primarily on *Homo sapiens*—the human species—anthropologists also study our ancestors and close animal relatives for clues about what it means to be human.

THE DEVELOPMENT OF ANTHROPOLOGY

Although works of anthropological significance have a considerable antiquity—two examples being cross-cultural accounts of people written by the Greek historian Herodotus about 2,500 years ago and the North African Arab scholar Ibn Khaldun nearly 700 years ago—anthropology as a distinct field of inquiry is a relatively recent product of Western civilization. In the United States, for example, the first course in general anthropology to carry credit in a college or university (at the University of Rochester in New York) was not offered until 1879. If people have always been concerned about themselves and their origins, and those of other people, then why did it take such a long time for a systematic discipline of anthropology to appear?

The answer to this is as complex as human history. In part, it relates to the limits of human technology. Throughout most of history, people have been restricted in their geographic horizons. Without the means of traveling to distant parts of the world, observation of cultures and peoples far from one's own was a difficult—if not impossible—undertaking. Extensive travel was usually the exclusive privilege of a few; the study of foreign peoples and cultures was not likely to flourish until improved modes of transportation and communication could be developed.

> **THOMSON** AUDIO **STUDY PRODUCTS**
> Take advantage of the MP3-ready Audio Lecture Overviews and comprehensive audio glossary of key terms for each chapter. See the preface for information on how to access this on-the-go study and review tool.

anthropology The study of humankind in all times and places.

This is not to say that people have been unaware of the existence of others in the world who look and act differently from themselves. The Bible's Old and New Testaments, for example, are full of references to diverse ancient peoples, among them Babylonians, Egyptians, Greeks, Jews, and Syrians. However, the differences among these people pale by comparison to those among any of the more recent European nations and (for example) traditional indigenous peoples of the Pacific islands, the Amazon rainforest, or Siberia.

© Documentary Educational Resources

Anthropologists come from many corners of the world and carry out research in a huge variety of cultures all around the globe. Dr. Jaya-sinhji Jhala, pictured here, hails from the old city of Dhrangadhra in Gujarat, northwest India. A member of the Jhala clan of Rajputs, an aristocratic caste of warriors, he grew up in the royal palace of his father, the maharaja. After earning a bachelor of arts degree in India, he came to the United States and earned a master's in visual studies from MIT, followed by a doctorate in anthropology from Harvard. Currently a professor and director of the programs of Visual Anthropology and the Visual Anthropology Media Laboratory at Temple University, he returns regularly to India with students to film cultural traditions in his own caste-stratified society.

With the invention of the magnetic compass for use aboard better-equipped sailing ships, it became easier to determine geographic direction and travel to truly faraway places and meet for the first time such radically different groups. It was the massive encounter with hitherto unknown peoples—which began 500 years ago as Europeans sought to extend their trade and political domination to all parts of the world—that focused attention on human differences in all their amazing variety.

Another significant element that contributed to the emergence of anthropology was that Europeans gradually came to recognize that despite all the differences, they might share a basic humanity with people everywhere. Initially, Europeans labeled societies that did not share their fundamental cultural values as "savage" or "barbarian." Over time, however, Europeans came to recognize such highly diverse groups as fellow members of one species and therefore relevant to an understanding of what it is to be human. This growing interest in human diversity, coming at a time when there were increasing efforts to explain things in scientific terms, cast doubts on the traditional explanations based on religious texts such as the Torah, Bible, or Koran and helped set the stage for the birth of anthropology.

Although anthropology originated within the historical context of European culture, it has long since gone global. Today, it is an exciting, transnational discipline whose practitioners come from a wide array of societies all around the world. Societies that have long been studied by European and North American anthropologists—several African and Native American societies, for example—have produced anthropologists who have made and continue to make a mark on the discipline. Their distinct perspectives shed new light not only on their own cultures but also on those of others. It is noteworthy that in one regard diversity has long been a hallmark of the discipline: From its earliest days both women and men have entered the field. Throughout this text, we will be spotlighting individual anthropologists, illustrating the diversity of these practitioners and their work.

THE ANTHROPOLOGICAL PERSPECTIVE

Many academic disciplines are concerned in one way or another with our species. For example, biology focuses on the genetic, anatomical, and physiological aspects of organisms. Psychology is concerned primarily with cognitive, mental, and emotional issues, while economics examines the production, distribution, and management of material resources. And various disciplines in the humanities look into the artistic and philosophical achievements of human cultures. But anthropology is distinct because of its focus on the interconnections and interdependence of all aspects of the human experience in all places and times—both biological and cultural, past and present. It is this **holistic perspective** that best equips anthropologists to broadly address that elusive phenomenon we call human nature.

Anthropologists welcome the contributions of researchers from other disciplines and in return offer their own findings for the benefit of these other disciplines. Anthropologists do not expect, for example, to know as much about the structure of the human eye as anatomists or as much about the perception of color as psychologists. As synthesizers, however, anthropologists are prepared to understand how these bodies of knowledge relate to color-naming practices in different human societies. Because they look for the broad basis of human ideas and practices without limiting themselves to any single social or biological aspect, anthropologists can acquire an especially expansive and inclusive overview of the complex biological and cultural organism that is the human being.

The holistic perspective also helps anthropologists stay keenly aware of ways that their own culture's perspective and social values may influence their research. As the old saying goes, people often see what they believe, rather than what appears before their eyes. By maintaining a critical awareness of their own assumptions about human nature—checking and rechecking the ways their beliefs and actions might be shaping their research—anthropologists strive to gain objective knowledge about people. Equipped with this awareness, anthropologists have contributed uniquely to our understanding of diversity in human thought, biology, and behavior, as well as our understanding of the many things humans have in common.

While other social sciences have concentrated predominantly on contemporary peoples living in North American and European (Western) societies, anthropologists have traditionally focused on non-Western peoples and cultures. Anthropologists believe that to fully understand the complexities of human ideas, behavior, and biology, all humans, wherever and whenever, must be studied. A cross-cultural and long-term evolutionary perspective not only distinguishes anthropology from other social sciences, but also guards against the danger that theories of human behavior will be **culture-bound:**

holistic perspective A fundamental principle of anthropology: that the various parts of human culture and biology must be viewed in the broadest possible context in order to understand their interconnections and interdependence.
culture-bound Theories about the world and reality based on the assumptions and values of one's own culture.

VISUAL COUNTERPOINT

Although infants in the United States typically sleep apart from their parents, cross-cultural research shows that co-sleeping, of mother and baby in particular, is the rule. The photo on the right shows a Nenet family sleeping together in their *chum* (reindeer-skin tent). Nenet people are arctic reindeer pastoralists living in Siberia.

that is, based on assumptions about the world and reality that come from the researcher's own particular culture.

As a case in point, consider the fact that infants in the United States typically sleep apart from their parents. To most North Americans, this may seem normal, but cross-cultural research shows that co-sleeping, of mother and baby in particular, is the rule. Only in the past 200 years, generally in Western industrial societies, has it been considered proper for parents to sleep apart from their infants. In a way, this practice amounts to a cultural experiment in child rearing.

Recent studies have shown that separation of mother and infant in Western societies has important biological and cultural consequences. For one thing, it increases the length of the child's crying bouts. Some mothers incorrectly interpret the cause as a deficiency in breast milk and switch to less healthy bottle formulas; and in extreme cases the crying may provoke physical abuse. But the benefits of co-sleeping go beyond significant reductions in crying: Infants also nurse more often and three times as long per feeding; they receive more stimulation (important for brain development); and they are apparently less susceptible to sudden infant death syndrome (SIDS or "crib death"). There are benefits to the mother as well: Frequent nursing prevents early ovulation after childbirth, and she gets at least as much sleep as mothers who sleep without their infants.[1]

These benefits may lead us to ask, Why do so many mothers continue to sleep apart from their infants? In North America the cultural values of independence and consumerism come into play. To begin building individual identities, babies are provided with rooms (or at least space) of their own. This room of one's own also provides parents with a place for the toys, furniture, and other paraphernalia associated with good parenting in North America.

Anthropology's early emphasis on studying traditional, non-Western peoples has often led to findings that run counter to generally accepted opinions derived from Western studies. Thus, anthropologists were the first to demonstrate

> that the world does not divide into the pious and the superstitious; that there are sculptures in jungles and paintings in deserts; that political order is possible without centralized power and principled justice without codified rules; that the norms of reason were not fixed in Greece, the evolution of morality not consummated in England. . . . We have, with no little success, sought to keep the world off balance; pulling out rugs, upsetting tea tables, setting off firecrackers. It has been the office of others to reassure; ours to unsettle.[2]

Although the findings of anthropologists have often challenged the conclusions of sociologists, psychologists, and economists, anthropology is absolutely indispensable to them, as it is the only consistent check against

[1]Barr, R. G. (1997, October). The crying game. *Natural History, 47.* Also, McKenna, J. J. (2002, September-October). Breastfeeding and bedsharing. *Mothering,* 28–37; and McKenna, J. J., & McDade, T. (2005, June). Why babies should never sleep alone: A review of the co-sleeping controversy in relation to SIDS, bedsharing, and breast feeding. *Pediatric Respiratory Reviews 6(2),* 134–152.

[2]Geertz, C. (1984). Distinguished lecture: Anti anti-relativism. *American Anthropologist 86,* 275.

culture-bound assertions. In a sense, anthropology is to these disciplines what the laboratory is to physics and chemistry: an essential testing ground for their theories.

ANTHROPOLOGY AND ITS FIELDS

Individual anthropologists tend to specialize in one of four fields or subdisciplines: physical anthropology, archaeology, linguistic anthropology, or cultural anthropology (Figure 1.1). Some anthropologists consider archaeology and linguistics as part of the broader study of human cultures, but, archaeology and linguistics also have close ties to biological anthropology. For example, while linguistic anthropology focuses on the cultural aspects of language, it has deep connections to the evolution of human language and the biological basis of speech and language studied within physical anthropology. Each of anthropology's fields may take a distinct approach to the study of humans, but all gather and analyze data that are essential to explaining similarities and differences among humans, across time and space. Moreover, all of them generate knowledge that has numerous practical applications.

Within the four fields are individuals who practice **applied anthropology,** which entails using anthropological knowledge and methods to solve practical problems, often for a specific client. Applied anthropologists do not offer their perspectives from the sidelines. Instead, they actively collaborate with the communities in which they work—setting goals, solving problems, and

Figure 1.1

The four fields of anthropology. Note that the divisions among them are not sharp, indicating that their boundaries overlap. Moreover, each operates on the basis of a common body of knowledge. All four are involved in theory building, developing their own research methodologies, and solving practical problems through applied anthropology.

conducting research together. In this book, examples of how anthropology contributes to solving a wide range of the challenges humans face appear in Anthropology Applied features.

One of the earliest contexts in which anthropological knowledge was applied to a practical problem was

applied anthropology The use of anthropological knowledge and methods to solve practical problems, often for a specific client.

Biocultural
Connection   The Anthropology of Organ Transplantation

In 1954, the first organ transplant occurred in Boston when surgeons removed a kidney from one identical twin to place it inside his sick brother. Though some transplants rely upon living donors, routine organ transplantation depends largely upon the availability of organs obtained from individuals who have died.

From an anthropological perspective, the meanings of death and the body vary cross-culturally. While death could be said to represent a particular biological state, social agreement about this state's significance is of paramount importance. Anthropologist Margaret Lock has explored differences between Japanese and North American acceptance of the biological state of "brain death" and how it affects the practice of organ transplants.

Brain death relies upon the absence of measurable electrical currents in the brain and the inability to breathe without technological assistance. The brain-dead individual, though attached to machines, still seems alive with a beating heart and pink cheeks. North Americans find brain death acceptable, in part, because personhood and individuality are culturally located in the brain. North American comfort with brain death has allowed for the "gift of life" through organ donation and subsequent transplantation.

By contrast, in Japan, the concept of brain death is hotly contested and organ transplants are rarely performed. The Japanese do not incorporate a mind–body split into their models of themselves and locate personhood throughout the

body rather than in the brain. They resist accepting a warm pink body as a corpse from which organs can be harvested. Further, organs cannot be transformed into "gifts" because anonymous donation is not compatible with Japanese social patterns of reciprocal exchange.

Organ transplantation carries far greater social meaning than the purely biological movement of an organ from one individual to another. Cultural and biological processes are tightly woven into every aspect of this new social practice.

(Based on M. Lock (2001). Twice dead: Organ transplants and the reinvention of death. Berkeley: University of California Press.)

the international public health movement that began in the 1920s, marking the beginning of *medical anthropology*—a specialization that brings theoretical and applied approaches from the fields of cultural and biological anthropology to the study of human health and disease. The work of medical anthropologists sheds light on the connections between human health and political and economic forces, both globally and locally. Examples from this specialization appear in some of the Biocultural Connections featured in this text, including the one presented in this chapter, "The Anthropology of Organ Transplantation."

Physical Anthropology

Physical anthropology, also called *biological anthropology,* is the systematic study of humans as biological organisms. Traditionally, biological anthropologists concentrated on human evolution, primatology, growth and development, human adaptation, and forensics. Today, **molecular anthropology,** or the anthropological study of genes and genetic relationships, is another vital component of biological anthropology. Comparisons among groups separated by time, geography, or the frequency of a particular gene can reveal how humans have adapted and where they have migrated. As experts in the anatomy of human bones and tissues, physical anthropologists lend their knowledge about the body to applied areas such as gross anatomy laboratories, public health, and criminal investigations.

Paleoanthropology

Human evolutionary studies (known as **paleoanthropology**) investigate the origins and predecessors of the present human species, focusing on biological changes through time to understand how, when, and why we became the kind of organisms we are today. In biological terms, we humans are primates, one of the many kinds of mammal. Because we share a common ancestry with other primates, most specifically apes, paleoanthropologists look back to the earliest primates (65 or so million years ago) or even the earliest mammals (225 million years ago) to reconstruct the complex path of human evolution. Paleoanthropology unlike other evolutionary studies, takes a **biocultural** approach, focusing on the interaction of biology and culture.

physical anthropology Also known as biological anthropology. The systematic study of humans as biological organisms.
molecular anthropology A branch of biological anthropology that uses genetic and biochemical techniques to test hypotheses about human evolution, adaptation, and variation.
paleoanthropology The study of the origins and predecessors of the present human species.
biocultural Focusing on the interaction of biology and culture.

The fossilized skeletons of our ancestors allow paleoanthropologists to reconstruct the course of human evolutionary history. They compare the size and shape of these fossils to one another and to the bones of living species. With each new fossil discovery, paleoanthropologists have another piece to add to human evolutionary history. Biochemical and genetic studies add considerably to the fossil evidence. As we will see in later chapters, genetic evidence establishes the close relationship between humans and ape species—chimpanzees, bonobos, and gorillas. Genetic analyses indicate that the human line originated 5 to 8 million years ago. Physical anthropology therefore deals with much greater time spans than archaeology or other fields of anthropology.

Human Growth, Adaptation, and Variation

Another specialty of physical anthropologists is the study of human growth and development. Anthropologists examine biological mechanisms of growth as well as the impact of the environment on the growth process. Franz Boas (see Anthropologists of Note box, page 15), a pioneer of anthropology of the early 20th century, compared the heights of European immigrants who spent their childhood in "the old country" to the increased heights obtained by their children who grew up in the United States. Today, physical anthropologists study the impacts of disease, pollution, and poverty on growth. Comparisons between human and nonhuman primate growth patterns can provide clues to the evolutionary history of humans. Detailed anthropological studies of the hormonal, genetic, and physiological basis of healthy growth in living humans also contribute significantly to the health of children today.

Studies of human adaptation focus on the capacity of humans to adapt or adjust to their material environment—biologically and culturally. This branch of physical anthropology takes a comparative approach to humans living today in a variety of environments. Humans are remarkable among the primates in that they now inhabit the entire earth. Though cultural adaptations make it possible for our species to live in some environmental extremes, biological adaptations also contribute to survival in extreme cold, heat, and high altitude.

Some of these biological adaptations are built into the genetic makeup of populations. The long period of human growth and development provides ample opportunity for the environment to shape the human body. These *developmental adaptations* are responsible for some features of human variation such as the enlargement of the right ventricle of the heart to help push blood to the lungs among the Quechua Indians of highland Peru. *Physiological adaptations* are short-term changes in response to a particular environmental stimulus. For example, a person who normally lives at sea level will undergo a series of physiological responses if she suddenly moves to a high altitude. All of these kinds of biological adaptation contribute to present-day human variation.

Variation in visible traits such as height, body build, and skin color, as well as biochemical factors such as blood type and susceptibility to certain diseases, contribute to human biological diversity. Still, we remain members of a single species. Physical anthropology applies all the techniques of modern biology to achieve fuller understanding of human variation and its relationship to the different environments in which people have lived. Research in physical anthropology on human variation has debunked false notions of biologically defined races—a notion based on widespread misinterpretation of human variation.

Forensic Anthropology

One of the many practical applications of physical anthropology is **forensic anthropology:** the identification of human skeletal remains for legal purposes. Although they are called upon by law enforcement authorities to identify murder victims, forensic anthropologists also investigate human rights abuses such as systematic genocides, terrorism, and war crimes. These specialists use details of skeletal anatomy to establish the age, sex, and stature of the deceased; forensic anthropologists can also determine whether the person was right- or left-handed, exhibited any physical abnormalities, or experienced trauma. While forensics relies upon differing frequencies of certain skeletal characteristics to establish population affiliation, it is nevertheless false to say that all people from a given population have a particular type of skeleton. (See the Anthropology Applied feature to read about the work of several forensic anthropologists and forensic archaeologists.)

Primatology

Studying the anatomy and behavior of the other primates helps us understand what we share with our closest living relatives and what makes humans unique. Therefore, **primatology,** or the study of living and fossil primates, is a vital part of physical anthropology. Primates include the Asian and African apes, as well as monkeys, lemurs, lorises, and tarsiers. Biologically, humans are apes—large-bodied, broad-shouldered primates with no tail. Detailed studies of ape behavior in the wild indicate that the sharing of learned behavior is a significant part of their social life. Increasingly, primatologists designate the shared, learned behavior of nonhuman apes as culture. For example, tool use and communication systems indicate the elementary basis of language in some ape societies.

Primate studies offer scientifically grounded perspectives on the behavior of our ancestors, as well as greater appreciation and respect for the abilities of our closest living relatives. As human activity encroaches on

all parts of the world, many primate species are endangered. Primatologists often advocate for the preservation of primate habitats so that these remarkable animals will continue to inhabit the earth with us.

Cultural Anthropology

Cultural anthropology (also called *social* or *sociocultural anthropology*) is the study of customary patterns in human behavior, thought, and feelings. It focuses on humans as culture-producing and culture-reproducing creatures. Thus, in order to understand the work of the cultural anthropologist, we must clarify what we mean by **culture**—a society's shared and socially transmitted ideas, values, and perceptions, which are used to make sense of experience and which generate behavior and are reflected in that behavior. These standards are socially learned, rather than acquired through biological inheritance. Because they determine, or at least guide, normal day-to-day behavior, thought, and emotional patterns of the members of a society, human activities, ideas, and feelings are above all culturally acquired and influenced. The manifestations of culture may vary considerably from place to place, but no person is "more cultured" in the anthropological sense than any other.

Cultural anthropology has two main components: ethnography and ethnology. An **ethnography** is a detailed description of a particular culture primarily based on **fieldwork,** which is the term anthropologists use for on-location research. Because the hallmark of ethnographic fieldwork is a combination of social participation and personal observation within the community being studied, as well as interviews and discussions with individual members of a group, the ethnographic method is commonly referred to as **participant observation.**

forensic anthropology Applied subfield of physical anthropology that specializes in the identification of human skeletal remains for legal purposes.
primatology The study of living and fossil primates.
cultural anthropology Also known as social or sociocultural anthropology. The study of customary patterns in human behavior, thought, and feelings. It focuses on humans as culture-producing and culture-reproducing creatures.
culture A society's shared and socially transmitted ideas, values, and perceptions, which are used to make sense of experience and which generate behavior and are reflected in that behavior.
ethnography A detailed description of a particular culture primarily based on fieldwork.
fieldwork The term anthropologists use for on-location research.
participant observation In ethnography, the technique of learning a people's culture through social participation and personal observation within the community being studied, as well as interviews and discussion with individual members of the group over an extended period of time.

Anthropology Applied

Forensic Anthropology: Voices for the Dead ▪ Clyde C. Snow, Karen Burns, Amy Zelson Mundorff, and Michael Blakey

Forensic anthropology is the analysis of skeletal remains for legal purposes. Law enforcement authorities call upon forensic anthropologists to use skeletal remains to identify murder victims, missing persons, or people who have died in disasters, such as plane crashes. Forensic anthropologists have also contributed substantially to the investigation of human rights abuses in all parts of the world by identifying victims and documenting the cause of their death.

Among the best-known forensic anthropologists is Clyde C. Snow. He has been practicing in this field forty years, first for the Federal Aviation Administration and more recently as a freelance consultant. In addition to the usual police work, Snow has studied the remains of General George Armstrong Custer and his men from the 1876 battlefield at Little Big Horn, and in 1985 he went to Brazil, where he identified the remains of the notorious Nazi war criminal Josef Mengele.

He was also instrumental in establishing the first forensic team devoted to documenting cases of human rights abuses around the world. This began in 1984 when he went to Argentina at the request of a newly elected civilian gov-

ernment to help with the identification of remains of the *desaparecidos*, or "disappeared ones," the 9,000 or more people who were eliminated by government death squads during seven years of military rule. A year later, he returned to give expert testimony at the trial of nine junta members and to teach Argentineans how to recover, clean, repair, preserve, photograph, x-ray, and analyze bones. Besides providing factual accounts of the fate of victims to their surviving kin and refuting the assertions of revisionists that the massacres never happened, the work of Snow and his Argentinean associates was crucial in convicting several military officers of kidnapping, torture, and murder.

Since Snow's pioneering work, forensic anthropologists have become increasingly involved in the investigation of human rights abuses in all parts of the world, from Chile to Guatemala, Haiti, the Philippines, Rwanda, Iraq, Bosnia, and Kosovo. Meanwhile, they continue to do important work for more typical clients. In the United States these clients include the Federal Bureau of Investigation and city, state, and county medical examiners' offices.

Forensic anthropologists specializing in skeletal remains commonly work closely with forensic archaeologists.

Physical anthropologists do not just study fossil skulls. Here Clyde Snow holds the skull of a Kurd who was executed by Iraqi security forces. Snow specializes in forensic anthropology and is best known for his work identifying victims of state-sponsored terrorism.

Ethnographies provide the information used to make systematic comparisons among cultures all across the world. Known as **ethnology,** such cross-cultural research allows anthropologists to develop anthropological theories that help explain why certain important differences or similarities occur among groups.

Ethnography

Through participant observation—eating a people's food, sleeping under their roof, learning how to speak and behave acceptably, and personally experiencing their habits

ethnology The study and analysis of different cultures from a comparative or historical point of view, utilizing ethnographic accounts and developing anthropological theories that help explain why certain important differences or similarities occur among groups.

Sociologists conduct structured interviews and administer questionnaires to *respondents,* while psychologists experiment with *subjects.* Anthropologists, by contrast, learn from and often collaborate with *informants.* The researcher here is Dutch anthropologist Harald Prins, a coauthor of this book. Doing fieldwork among the Plains Apache Indians in Oklahoma, he is using a camera to document part of the community's oral history project with tribal chief Alfred Chalepah.

The relation between them is rather like that between a forensic pathologist, who examines a corpse to establish time and manner of death, and a crime scene investigator, who searches the site for clues. While the forensic anthropologist deals with the human remains—often only bones and teeth—the forensic archaeologist controls the site, recording the position of all relevant finds and recovering any clues associated with the remains. In Rwanda, for example, a team assembled in 1995 to investigate a mass atrocity for the United Nations included archaeologists from the U.S. National Park Service's Midwest Archaeological Center. They performed the standard archaeological procedures of mapping the site, determining its boundaries, photographing and recording all surface finds, and excavating, photographing, and recording buried skeletons and associated materials in mass graves.[a]

In another example, Karen Burns of the University of Georgia was part of a team sent to northern Iraq after the 1991 Gulf War to investigate alleged atrocities. On a military base where there had

been many executions, she excavated the remains of a man's body found lying on its side facing Mecca, conforming to Islamic practice. Although there was no intact clothing, two threads of polyester used to sew clothing were found along the sides of both legs. Although the threads survived, the clothing, because it was made of natural fiber, had decayed. "Those two threads at each side of the leg just shouted that his family didn't bury him," says Burns.[b] Proper though his position was, no Islamic family would bury their own in a garment sewn with polyester thread; proper ritual would require a simple shroud.

In recent years two major anthropological analyses of skeletal remains have occurred in New York City dealing with both past and present atrocities. Amy Zelson Mundorff, a forensic anthropologist for New York City's Office of the Chief Medical Examiner, was injured in the September 11, 2001, terrorist attack on the World Trade Center. Two days later she returned to work to supervise and coordinate the management, treatment, and cataloguing of people who lost their lives in the attack.

Just a short walk away, construction workers in lower Manhattan discovered a 17th- and 18th-century African burial ground in 1991. Archaeological investigation of the burial ground revealed the horror of slavery in North America, showing that even young children were worked so far beyond their ability to endure that their spines were fractured. Biological archaeologist Michael Blakey, who led the research team, notes:

> Although bioarchaeology and forensics are often confused, when skeletal biologists use the population as the unit of analysis (rather than the individual), and incorporate cultural and historical context (rather than simply ascribing biological characteristics), and report on the lifeways of a past community (rather than on a crime for the police and courts), it is bioarchaeology rather than forensics.[c]

Thus, several kinds of anthropologists analyze human remains for a variety of purposes, contributing to the documentation and correction of atrocities committed by humans of the past and present.

[a]Conner, M. (1996). The archaeology of contemporary mass graves. *SAA Bulletin 14*(4), 6, 31.

[b]Cornwell, T. (1995, November 10). Skeleton staff. *Times Higher Education,* 20.

[c]Blakey, M. Personal communication, October 29, 2003.

and customs—the ethnographer seeks to understand a particular way of life to a far greater extent than any nonparticipant researcher ever could. Being a participant observer does not mean that the anthropologist must join in a people's battles in order to study a culture in which warfare is prominent; but by living among a warlike people, the ethnographer should be able to understand how warfare fits into the overall cultural framework. She or he must observe carefully to gain an overview without placing too much emphasis on one part at the expense of another. Only by discovering how *all* aspects of a culture—its social, political, economic, and religious practices and institutions—relate to one another can the ethnographer begin to understand the cultural system. This is the holistic perspective so basic to the discipline.

The popular image of ethnographic fieldwork is that it occurs among people who live in far-off, isolated places. To be sure, much ethnographic work has been done in the remote villages of Africa or South America,

the islands of the Pacific Ocean, the Indian reservations of North America, the deserts of Australia, and so on. However, as the discipline of anthropology developed in response to the end of colonialism since the mid-20th century, peoples and cultures in industrialized nations, including Europe and the United States, also became a legitimate focus of anthropological study. Some of this shift occurred as scholars from non-Western nations became anthropologists. An even more significant factor is *globalization,* a worldwide process that rapidly transforms cultures—shifting, blurring, and even breaking long-established boundaries between different peoples.

Ethnographic fieldwork has changed from anthropological experts observing, documenting, and analyzing people from distant "other places" to collaborative efforts among anthropologists and the communities in which they work, producing knowledge that is valuable not only in the academic realm but also to the people being studied. Today, anthropologists from all parts of the globe employ research techniques similar to those developed in the study of traditional non-Western peoples to investigate a wide range of cultural niches, including those in industrial and postindustrial societies—from religious movements to conflict resolution, street gangs, schools, corporate bureaucracies, and health-care systems.

Ethnology

Although ethnographic fieldwork is basic to cultural anthropology, it is not the sole occupation of the cultural anthropologist. Largely descriptive in nature, ethnography provides the raw data needed for ethnology—the branch of cultural anthropology that involves cross-cultural comparisons and theories that explain differences or similarities among groups.

Intriguing insights into one's own beliefs and practices may come from cross-cultural comparisons. Consider, for example, the amount of time spent on domestic chores by industrialized peoples and traditional food foragers (people who rely on wild plant and animal resources for subsistence). Anthropological research among food foragers has shown that they work far less at domestic tasks, and indeed less at all subsistence pursuits, than do people in industrialized societies. Urban women in the United States who were not working for wages outside their homes put 55 hours a week into their housework—this despite all the "labor-saving" dishwashers, washing machines, clothes dryers, vacuum cleaners, food processors, and microwave ovens; in contrast, aboriginal women in Australia devoted 20 hours a week to their chores.[3]

Considering such cross-cultural comparisons, one may think of ethnology as the study of alternative ways of doing things. But more than that, by making systematic comparisons, ethnologists seek to arrive at scientific conclusions concerning the function and operation of cultural practices in all times and places. Today many cultural anthropologists apply such insights in a variety of contexts ranging from business to education to governmental interventions to humanitarian aid.

Archaeology

Archaeology is the field of anthropology that studies human cultures through the recovery and analysis of material remains and environmental data. Material products scrutinized by archaeologists include tools, pottery, hearths, and enclosures that remain as traces of cultural

[3]Bodley, J. H. (1985). *Anthropology and contemporary human problems* (2nd ed., p. 69). Palo Alto, CA: Mayfield.

archaeology The study of human cultures through the recovery and analysis of material remains and environmental data.

practices in the past, as well as human, plant, and animal remains, some of which date back 2.5 million years. The details of exactly how these traces were arranged when they were found reflect specific human ideas and behavior. For example, shallow, restricted concentrations of charcoal that include oxidized earth, bone fragments, and charred plant remains, located near pieces of fire-cracked rock, pottery, and tools suitable for food preparation, indicate cooking and food processing. Such remains can reveal much about a people's diet and subsistence practices. Together with skeletal remains, these material remains help archaeologists reconstruct the biocultural context of human life in the past.

Archaeologists can reach back for clues to human behavior far beyond the mere 5,000 years to which historians are confined by their reliance on written records. Calling this time period "prehistoric" does not mean that these societies were less interested in their history or that they did not have ways of recording and transmitting history. It simply means that written records do not now exist. That said, archaeologists are not limited to the study of societies without written records; they may also study those for which historic documents are available to supplement the material remains. In most literate societies, written records are associated with governing elites rather than with farmers, fishers, laborers, or slaves. Although written records can tell archaeologists much that might not be known from archaeological evidence alone, it is equally true that material remains can tell historians much about a society that is not apparent from its written documents.

Although most archaeologists concentrate on the human past, some of them study material objects in contemporary settings. One example is the Garbage Project, founded by William Rathje at the University of Arizona in 1973. This carefully controlled study of household waste continues to produce thought-provoking information about contemporary social issues. Among its accomplishments, the project has tested the validity of survey techniques, upon which sociologists, economists, and other social scientists and policymakers rely heavily.

For example, in 1973 conventional techniques were used to construct and administer a questionnaire to find out about the rate of alcohol consumption in Tucson. In one part of town, 15 percent of respondent households affirmed consumption of beer, but no household reported consumption of more than eight cans a week. Analysis of garbage from the same area, however, demonstrated that some beer was consumed in over 80 percent of households, and 50 percent discarded more than eight empty cans a week. Another interesting finding of the Garbage Project is that when beef prices reached an all-time high in 1973, so did the amount of beef wasted by households (not just in Tucson but in other parts of the country as well). Although common sense would lead us to suppose

Few places have caused as much speculation as Rapa Nui, a tiny volcanic island in the middle of the southern Pacific Ocean. Better known as Easter Island, it is one of the most remote and remarkable places on earth. The landscape is punctuated by nearly 900 colossal stone "heads," some towering to 65 feet. The islanders call them *moai,* and they have puzzled visitors ever since Dutch seafarers first discovered the island on Easter Day, 1722. By then, it was a barren land with a few thousand people for whom the *moai* were already ancient relics. Since the 1930s, anthropologists have used evidence from many subfields, especially oral traditions and archaeological excavations, to reconstruct a fascinating but troubling island history of environmental destruction and internal warfare.[4]

just the opposite, high prices and scarcity correlate with more, rather than less, waste. Such findings are important for they demonstrate that ideas about human behavior based on conventional interview-survey techniques alone can be seriously in error. Likewise, they show that what people actually do does not always match what they think they do.

In 1987, the Garbage Project began a program of excavating landfills in different parts of the United States and Canada. From this work came the first reliable data on what materials actually go into landfills and what happens to them there. And once again, common beliefs turned out to be at odds with the actual situation. For example, biodegradable materials such as newspapers take far longer to decay when buried in deep compost landfills than anyone had previously expected. This kind of information is a vital step toward solving waste disposal problems.[5]

Cultural Resource Management

While archaeology may conjure up images of ancient pyramids and the like, much archaeological research is carried out as **cultural resource management.** This branch of archaeology is tied to government policies for the protection of cultural resources and involves surveying and/or excavating archaeological and historical remains threatened by construction or development. For example, in the United States, if the transportation department of a state government plans to replace an inadequate highway bridge, steps have to be taken to identify and protect any significant prehistoric or historic resources that might be affected by this new construction. Federal legislation passed since the mid-1960s now requires cultural resource management for any building project that is partially funded or licensed by the U.S. government. As a result, the practice of cultural resource management has flourished. Many archaeologists are employed by such agencies as the U.S. Army Corps of Engineers, the National Park Service, the U.S. Forest Service, and the U.S. Soil and Conservation Service to assist in the preservation, restoration, and salvage of archaeological resources.

Archaeologists are also employed by state historic preservation agencies. Moreover, they consult for engineering firms to help them prepare environmental impact statements. Some of these archaeologists operate out of universities and colleges, while others are on the staffs of independent consulting firms. Finally, some archaeologists now also work for American Indian nations involved in cultural resource management on reservation lands.

---

[4]For more information, see the following: Anderson, A. (2002). Faunal collapse, landscape change, and settlement history in Remote Oceania. *World Archaeology 33*(3),375–390; Van Tilburg, J. A. (1994). *Easter Island: Archaeology, ecology, and culture.* London: British Museum Press.

[5]Details about the Garbage Project's past and present work can be seen on its website:http://info-center.ccit.arizona.edu/~bara/report.htm.

cultural resource management A branch of archaeology tied to government policies for the protection of cultural resources and involving surveying and/or excavating archaeological and historical remains threatened by construction or development.

Linguistic Anthropology

Perhaps the most distinctive feature of the human species is language. Although the sounds and gestures made by some other animals—especially by apes—may serve functions comparable to those of human language, no other animal has developed a system of symbolic communication as complex as that of humans. Language allows people to preserve and transmit countless details of their culture from generation to generation.

The field of anthropology that studies human languages is called **linguistic anthropology.** Linguists may deal with the description of a language (such as the way a sentence is formed or a verb conjugated), the history of languages (the way languages develop and change with the passage of time), or with language in relation to social and cultural contexts. All three approaches yield valuable information about how people communicate and how they understand the world around them. The everyday language of English-speaking North Americans, for example, includes a number of slang words, such as *dough, greenback, dust, loot, bucks, change,* and *bread,* to identify what an indigenous inhabitant of Papua New Guinea would recognize only as "money." The profusion of names helps to identify a thing of special importance to a culture.

Anthropological linguists also make a significant contribution to our understanding of the human past. By working out relationships among languages and examining their spatial distributions, they may estimate how long the speakers of those languages have lived where they do. By identifying those words in related languages that have survived from an ancient ancestral tongue, they can also suggest not only where, but how, the speakers of the ancestral language lived. Such work shows linguistic ties between geographically distant groups such as the people of Finland and Turkey.

Linguistic anthropology is practiced in a number of applied settings. For example, linguistic anthropologists have collaborated with indigenous communities and ethnic minorities in the preservation or revival of languages lost during periods of oppression by dominant societies. Anthropologists have helped to create written forms of some languages that previously existed only by word of mouth. These examples of applied linguistic anthropology represent the kind of true collaboration that is characteristic of much anthropological fieldwork today.

linguistic anthropology The study of human languages, looking at their structure, history, and/or relation to social and cultural contexts.
empirical Based on observations of the world rather than on intuition or faith.
hypothesis A tentative explanation of the relation between certain phenomena.

ANTHROPOLOGY, SCIENCE, AND THE HUMANITIES

Anthropology has been called the most humane of the sciences and the most scientific of the humanities—a designation that most anthropologists accept with pride. Given their intense involvement with people of all times and places, it should come as no surprise that anthropologists have amassed considerable information about human failure and success, weakness and greatness—the real stuff of the humanities. While anthropologists steer clear of an impersonal scientific approach that reduces people and the things they do and think to mere numbers, their quantitative studies have contributed substantially to the scientific study of the human condition. But even the most scientific anthropologists always keep in mind that human societies are made up of individuals with rich assortments of emotions and aspirations that demand respect.

Beyond this, anthropologists remain committed to the proposition that one cannot fully understand another culture by simply observing it; as the term *participant observation* implies, one must *experience* it as well. This same commitment to fieldwork and to the systematic collection of data, whether it is qualitative or quantitative, is also evidence of the scientific side of anthropology. Anthropology is an **empirical** social science based in observations about humans. But what distinguishes anthropology from other sciences are the diverse ways in which scientific research is conducted within anthropology.

Science, a carefully honed way of producing knowledge, aims to reveal and explain the underlying logic, the structural processes that make the world "tick." It is a creative endeavor that seeks testable explanations for observed phenomena, ideally in terms of the workings of hidden but unchanging principles, or laws. Two basic ingredients are essential for this: imagination and skepticism. Imagination, though capable of leading us astray, is required to help us recognize unexpected ways phenomena might be ordered and to think of old things in new ways. Without it, there can be no science. Skepticism is what allows us to distinguish fact (an observation verified by others) from fancy, to test our speculations, and to prevent our imaginations from running away with us.

In their search for explanations, scientists do not assume that things are always as they appear on the surface. After all, what could be more obvious than that the earth is a stable entity, around which the sun travels every day? And yet, it isn't so.

Like other scientists, anthropologists often begin their research with a **hypothesis** (a tentative explanation or hunch) about the possible relationships between certain observed facts or events. By gathering various kinds of data that seem to ground such suggested explanations on evidence, anthropologists come up with a

Anthropologists of Note
Franz Boas (1858–1942) ▪ Matilda Coxe Stevenson (1849–1915)

Franz Boas was not the first to teach anthropology in the United States, but it was he and his students, with their insistence on scientific rigor, who made anthropology courses a common part of college and university curricula. Born and raised in Germany, where he studied physics, mathematics, and geography, Boas did his first ethnographic research among the Inuit (Eskimos) in Arctic Canada in 1883–1884. After a brief academic career in Berlin, he came to the United States. There, after work in museums interspersed with ethnographic research among Kwakiutl Indians in the Canadian Pacific, he became a professor at Columbia University in New York City in 1896. He authored an incredible number of publications, founded professional organizations and journals, and taught

© Bettmann/Corbis

two generations of great anthropologists, including numerous women and ethnic minorities.

As a Jewish immigrant, Boas recognized the dangers of ethnocentrism and especially racism. Through ethnographic fieldwork and comparative analysis, he demonstrated that white supremacy theories and other schemes ranking non-European peoples and cultures as inferior were biased, ill-informed, and unscientific. Throughout his long and illustrious academic career, he not only promoted anthropology as a human science but also as an instrument to combat racism and prejudice in the world.

Among the founders of North American anthropology were a number of women who were highly influential among women's rights advocates in the late 1800s. One such pioneering anthropologist was **Matilda Coxe Stevenson,** who did fieldwork among the Zuni Indians of Arizona. In 1885, she founded the Women's Anthropological Society in Washington, D.C., the first professional association for women scientists. Three years later, hired by the Smithsonian's Bureau of American Ethnology, she became one of the first women in the world to receive a full-time official position in science.

The tradition of women being active in anthropology continues. In fact,

© Smithsonian Institution Photo # 56196

since World War II more than half the presidents of the now 12,000-member American Anthropological Association have been women.

Recording observations on film as well as in notebooks, Stevenson and Boas were also pioneers in visual anthropology. Stevenson used an early box camera to document Pueblo Indian religious ceremonies and material culture, while Boas photographed Inuit (Eskimos) in northern Canada in 1883 and Kwakiutl Indians from the early 1890s for cultural as well as physical anthropological documentation. Today, these old photographs are greatly valued not only by anthropologists and historians, but also by indigenous peoples themselves.

---

theory—an explanation supported by a reliable body of data. In their effort to demonstrate linkages between known facts or events, anthropologists may discover unexpected facts, events, or relationships. An important function of theory is that it guides us in our explorations and may result in new knowledge. Equally important, the newly discovered facts may provide evidence that certain explanations, however popular or firmly believed to be true, are unfounded. When the evidence is lacking or fails to support the suggested explanations, anthropologists are forced to drop promising hypotheses or attractive hunches. In other words, anthropology relies on empirical evidence. Moreover, no scientific theory, no matter how widely accepted by the international community of scholars, is beyond challenge.

Straightforward though the scientific approach may seem, its application is not always easy. For instance, once a hypothesis has been proposed, the person who

suggested it is strongly motivated to verify it, and this can cause one to unwittingly overlook negative evidence and unanticipated findings. This is a familiar problem in all science as noted by paleontologist Stephen Jay Gould: "The greatest impediment to scientific innovation is usually a conceptual lock, not a factual lock."[6] Because culture provides humans with their concepts and shapes our very thoughts, it can be challenging to frame hypotheses or develop interpretations that are not culture-bound. By encompassing both humanism and science, the discipline of anthropology can draw on its internal diversity to overcome conceptual locks.

---

[6]Gould, S. J. (1989). *Wonderful life* (p. 226). New York: Norton.

theory In science, an explanation of natural phenomena, supported by a reliable body of data.

Fieldwork

All anthropologists are aware that personal and cultural background may shape their research questions and, more importantly, modify or even distort their actual observations. Engaging in such critical self-reflection, they rely on a technique that also has proved successful in other disciplines: They immerse themselves in the data to the fullest extent possible. In the process, anthropologists become so thoroughly familiar with even the smallest details that they may begin to identify possible relationships and underlying patterns in the data. Recognition of such suspected relationships and patterns enables anthropologists to frame meaningful hypotheses, which then may be subjected to further testing on location or "in the field." Within anthropology, such fieldwork brings additional rigor to the concept of total immersion in the data.

Touched upon above in our discussion of cultural anthropology, fieldwork is also characteristic of the other anthropological subdisciplines. Archaeologists and paleoanthropologists excavate sites in the field. A biological anthropologist interested in the effects of globalization on nutrition and human growth will reside in the particular community of people selected for study. A primatologist might live among a group of chimpanzees or baboons just as a linguist will study the language of a people by living among them and sharing their daily life. Fieldwork, being on location and fully immersed in another way of life, challenges the anthropologist to be constantly aware of the possible ways that otherwise unsuspected cultural factors may influence the research questions, observations, and explanations.

Fieldwork requires researchers to step out of their cultural comfort zone into a world that is unfamiliar and sometimes unsettling. Anthropologists in the field are likely to face a host of challenges—physical, social, mental, political, and ethical. They may have to deal with the physical challenge of adjusting to unfamiliar food, climate, and hygiene conditions. Typically, anthropologists in the field struggle with such mental challenges as loneliness, feeling like a perpetual outsider, being socially clumsy and clueless in their new cultural setting, and having to be alert around the clock because anything that is happening or being said may be significant to their research. Political challenges include the possibility of unwittingly letting oneself be used by factions within the community or being viewed with hostility by government authorities who may suspect the anthropologist is a spy. And there are ethical dilemmas: what to do if faced with a cultural practice one finds troubling, such as female circumcision; how to deal with demands for food supplies and/or medicine; how to handle the temptation to use deception to gain vital information; and so on.

At the same time, fieldwork often leads to tangible and meaningful personal, professional, and social rewards, ranging from lasting friendships to vital knowledge and insights concerning the human condition that make positive contributions to people's lives. Something of the meaning of anthropological fieldwork—its usefulness and its impact on researcher and subject—is conveyed in the following Original Study by Suzanne Leclerc-Madlala, an anthropologist who left her familiar New England surroundings two decades ago to do AIDS research among Zulu-speaking people in South Africa. Her research interest has changed the course of her own life, not to mention the lives of individuals who have HIV/AIDS and the type of treatment they receive.

Original Study ▪ By Suzanne Leclerc-Madlala

Fighting HIV/AIDS in Africa: Traditional Healers on the Front Line

In the 1980s, as a North American anthropology graduate student at George Washington University, I met and married a Zulu-speaking student from South Africa. It was the height of apartheid, and upon moving to that country I was classified as "honorary black" and forced to live in a segregated township with my husband. The AIDS epidemic was in its infancy, but it was clear from the start that an anthropological understanding of how people perceive and engage with this disease would be crucial for developing interventions. I wanted to learn all

that I could to make a difference, and this culminated in earning a Ph.D. from the University of Natal on the cultural construction of AIDS among the Zulu. The HIV/AIDS pandemic in Africa became my professional passion.

Faced with overwhelming global health-care needs, the World Health Organization passed a series of resolutions in the 1970s promoting collaboration between traditional and modern medicine. Such moves held a special relevance for Africa where traditional healers typically outnumber practitioners

of modern medicine by a ratio of 100 to 1 or more. Given Africa's disproportionate burden of disease, supporting partnership efforts with traditional healers makes sense. But what sounds sensible today was once considered absurd, even heretical. For centuries Westerners generally viewed traditional healing as a whole lot of primitive mumbo jumbo practiced by witchdoctors with demonic powers who perpetuated superstition. Yet, its practice survived. Today, as the African continent grapples with an HIV/AIDS epidemic of crisis proportion, millions of sick people who are either too poor or too distant to access modern health care are proving that traditional healers are an invaluable resource in the fight against AIDS.

Of the world's estimated 40 million people currently infected by HIV, 70 percent live in sub-Saharan Africa, and the vast majority of children left orphaned by AIDS are African. From the 1980s onward, as Africa became synonymous with the rapid spread of HIV/AIDS, a number of prevention programs involved traditional healers. My initial research in South Africa's KwaZulu-Natal province—where it is estimated that 36 percent of the population is HIV infected—revealed that traditional Zulu healers were regularly consulted for the treatment of sexually transmitted disease (STD). I found that such diseases, along with HIV/AIDS, were usually attributed to transgressions of taboos related to birth, pregnancy, marriage, and death. Moreover, these diseases were often understood within a framework of pollution and contagion, and like most serious illnesses, ultimately believed to have their causal roots in witchcraft.

In the course of my research, I investigated a pioneer program in STD and HIV education for traditional healers in the province. The program aimed to provide basic biomedical knowledge about the various modes of disease transmission, the means available for prevention, the diagnosing of symptoms, the keeping of records, and the making of patient referrals to local clinics and hospitals.

Interviews with the healers showed that many maintained a deep suspicion of modern medicine. They perceived AIDS education as a one-way street intended to press them into formal health struc-

tures and convince them of the superiority of modern medicine. Yet, today, few of the 6,000-plus KwaZulu-Natal healers who have been trained in AIDS education say they would opt for less collaboration; most want to have more.

Treatments by Zulu healers for HIV/AIDS often take the form of infusions of bitter herbs to "cleanse" the body, strengthen the blood, and remove misfortune and "pollution." Some treatments provide effective relief from common ailments associated with AIDS such as itchy skin rashes, oral thrush, persistent diarrhea, and general debility. Indigenous plants such as *unwele (Sutherlandia*

Medical anthropologist Suzanne Leclerc-Madlala visits with "Doctor" Koloko in KwaZulu-Natal, South Africa. This Zulu traditional healer proudly displays her official AIDS training certificate.

frutescens) and African potato *(Hypoxis hemerocallidea)* are well-known traditional medicines that have proven immuno-boosting properties.

Both have recently become available in modern pharmacies packaged in tablet form. With modern anti-retroviral treatments still well beyond the reach of most South Africans, indigenous medicines that can delay or alleviate some of the suffering caused by AIDS are proving to be valuable and popular treatments.

Knowledge about potentially infectious bodily fluids has led healers to change some of their practices. Where porcupine quills were once used to give a type of indigenous injection, patients are now advised to bring their own sewing needles to consultations. Patients provide their own individual razor blades for making incisions on their skin, where

previously healers reused the same razor on many clients. Some healers claim they have given up the practice of biting clients' skin to remove foreign objects from the body. It is not uncommon today, especially in urban centers like Durban, to find healers proudly displaying AIDS training certificates in their inner-city "surgeries" where they don white jackets and wear protective latex gloves.

Politics and controversy have dogged South Africa's official response to HIV/AIDS. But back home in the waddle-and-daub, animal-skin-draped herbariums and divining huts of traditional healers, the politics of AIDS holds little relevance. Here the sick and dying are coming in droves to be treated by healers who have been part and parcel of community life (and death) since time immemorial. In many cases traditional healers have transformed their homes into hospices for AIDS patients. Because of the strong stigma that still plagues the disease, those with AIDS symptoms are often abandoned or sometimes chased away from their homes by family members. They seek refuge with healers who provide them with comfort in their final days. Healers' homes are also becoming orphanages as healers respond to what has been called the "third wave" of AIDS destruction: the growing legions of orphaned children.

The practice of traditional healing in Africa is adapting to the changing face of health and illness in the context of HIV/AIDS. But those who are suffering go to traditional healers not only in search of relief for physical symptoms. They go to learn about the ultimate cause of their disease—something other than the immediate cause of a sexually transmitted "germ" or "virus." They go to find answers to the "why me and not him" questions, the "why now" and "why this." As with most traditional healing systems worldwide, healing among the Zulu and most all African ethnic groups cannot be separated from the spiritual concerns of the individual and the cosmological beliefs of the community at large. Traditional heal-

CONTINUED

ers help to restore a sense of balance between the individual and the community, on one hand, and between the individual and the cosmos, or ancestors, on the other hand. They provide health care that is personalized, culturally appropriate, holistic, and tailored to meet the needs and expectations of the patient. In many ways it is a far more satisfactory form

of healing than that offered by modern medicine.

Traditional healing in Africa is flourishing in the era of AIDS, and understanding why this is so requires a shift in the conceptual framework by which we understand, explain, and interpret health. Anthropological methods and its comparative and holistic perspective

can facilitate, like no other discipline, the type of understanding that is urgently needed to address the AIDS crisis.
(By Suzanne Leclerc-Madlala. Adapted in part from S. Leclerc-Madlala (2002). Bodies and politics: Healing rituals in the democratic South Africa. In V. Faure (Ed.), Les cahiers de 'l'IFAS, No. 2. Johannesburg: The French Institute.) ∎

ANTHROPOLOGY'S COMPARATIVE METHOD

The end product of anthropological research, if properly carried out, is a coherent statement about a people that provides an explanatory framework for understanding the beliefs, behavior, or biology of those who have been studied. And this, in turn, is what permits the anthropologist to frame broader hypotheses about human beliefs, behavior, and biology. A single instance of any phenomenon is generally insufficient for supporting a plausible hypothesis. Without some basis for comparison, the hypothesis grounded in a single case may be no more than a particular historical coincidence. On the other hand, a single case may be enough to cast doubt on, if not refute, a theory that had previously been held to be valid. For example, the discovery in 1948 that aborigines living in Australia's northern Arnhem Land put in an average workday of less than 6 hours, while living well above a level of bare sufficiency, was enough to call into question the widely accepted notion that food-foraging peoples are so preoccupied with finding scarce food that they lack time for any of life's more pleasurable activities. The observations made in the Arnhem Land study have since been confirmed many times over in various parts of the world.

Hypothetical explanations of cultural and biological phenomena may be tested through comparison of archaeological, biological, linguistic, historical, and/or ethnographic data for several societies found in a particular region. Carefully controlled comparison provides a broader basis for drawing general conclusions about humans than does the study of a single culture or population. The anthropologist who undertakes such a comparison may be more confident that events or features believed to be related really are related, at least within the area under investigation; however, an explanation that is valid in one area is not necessarily so in another.

Ideally, theories in anthropology are generated from worldwide comparisons or comparisons across species or

through time. Anthropologists examine a global sample of societies in order to discover whether or not hypotheses proposed to explain cultural phenomena or biological variation are universally applicable. However, cross-cultural researchers depend upon data gathered by other scholars as well as their own. Similarly, archaeologists and biological anthropologists rely on artifacts and skeletal collections housed in museums, as well as published descriptions of these collections.

QUESTIONS OF ETHICS

The kinds of research carried out by anthropologists, and the settings within which they work, raise a number of important moral questions about the potential uses and abuses of our knowledge. Who will utilize our findings and for what purposes? Who decides what research questions are asked? Who, if anyone, will profit from the research? For example, in the case of research on an ethnic or religious minority whose values may be at odds with dominant mainstream society, will governmental or corporate interests use anthropological data to suppress that group? And what of traditional communities around the world? Who is to decide what changes should, or should not, be introduced for community "betterment"? And who defines what constitutes betterment—the community, a national government, or an international agency like the World Health Organization? What are the limits of cultural relativism when a traditional practice is considered a human rights abuse globally?

Then there is the problem of privacy. Anthropologists deal with matters that are private and sensitive, including things that individuals would prefer not to have generally known about them. How does one write about such important but delicate issues and at the same time protect the privacy of the individuals who have shared their stories? The American Anthropological Association (AAA) maintains a Statement of Ethics, which is regularly examined and modified to reflect the practice of anthropology in a changing world. This educational document lays out the rules and ideals applicable to anthropologists in all the subdisciplines. While the AAA has no legal authority, it does issue policy statements on research ethics questions as they come up. For example, recently the AAA recommended that field notes from medical settings should be protected and not subject to subpoena in malpractice lawsuits. This honors the ethical imperative to protect the privacy of individuals who have shared their stories with anthropologists.

Anthropologists recognize that they have special obligations to three sets of people: those whom they study, those who fund the research, and those in the profession who expect us to publish our findings so that they may be used to further our collective knowledge. Because fieldwork requires a relationship of trust between fieldworkers and the community in which they work, the anthropologist's first responsibility clearly is to the individuals who have shared their stories and the greater community. Everything possible must be done to protect their physical, social, and psychological welfare and to honor their dignity and privacy. This task is frequently complex. For example, telling the story of a group of people gives information both to relief agencies who might help them and to others who might take advantage of them.

While anthropologists regard as basic a people's right to maintain their own culture, any connections with outsiders can endanger the cultural identity of the community being studied. To overcome these obstacles, anthropologists frequently collaborate with and contribute to the communities in which they are working, allowing the people being studied to have some say about how their stories are told.

ANTHROPOLOGY AND GLOBALIZATION

A holistic perspective and a long-term commitment to understanding the human species in all its variety is the essence of anthropology. Thus, anthropology is well equipped to grapple with an issue that has overriding importance for all of us at the beginning of the 21st century: **globalization.** This term refers to worldwide interconnectedness, evidenced in global movements of natural resources, human labor, finance capital, information, infectious diseases, and trade goods (including human organs as described in this chapter's Globalscape). Although worldwide travel, trade relations, and information flow have existed for several centuries, the pace and magnitude of these long-distance exchanges has picked up enormously in recent decades; the Internet, in particular, has greatly expanded information exchange capacities.

The powerful forces driving globalization are technological innovations, lower transportation and commu-

nication costs, faster knowledge transfers, and increased trade and financial integration among countries. Touching almost everybody's life on the planet, globalization is about economics as much as politics, and it changes human relations and ideas as well as our natural environments. Even geographically remote communities are quickly becoming more interdependent through globalization.

Doing research in all corners of the world, anthropologists are confronted with the impact of globalization on human communities wherever they are located. As participant observers, they describe and try to explain how individuals and organizations respond to the massive changes confronting them. Anthropologists may also find out how local responses sometimes change the global flows directed at them.

Dramatically increasing every year, globalization can be a two-edged sword. It may generate economic growth and prosperity, but it also undermines long-established institutions. Generally, globalization has brought significant gains to higher-educated groups in wealthier countries, while doing little to boost developing countries and actually contributing to the erosion of traditional cultures. Upheavals born of globalization are key causes for rising levels of ethnic and religious conflict throughout the world.

Since all of us now live in a global village, we can no longer afford the luxury of ignoring our neighbors, no matter how distant they may seem. In this age of globalization, anthropology may not only provide humanity with useful insights concerning diversity, but it may also assist us in avoiding or overcoming significant problems born of that diversity. In countless social arenas, from schools to businesses to hospitals to emergency centers, anthropologists have done cross-cultural research that makes it possible for educators, businesspeople, doctors, and humanitarians to do their work more effectively.

The wide-ranging relevance of anthropological knowledge in today's world may be illustrated by three quite different examples. In the United States today, discrimination based on notions of race continues to be a serious issue affecting economic, political, and social relations. Far from being a biological reality, anthropologists have shown that the concept of race emerged in the 18th century as a device for justifying European dominance over Africans and American Indians. In fact, differences of skin color are simply surface adaptations to different climatic zones and have nothing to do with physical or mental capabilities. Indeed, geneticists find

globalization Worldwide interconnectedness, evidenced in global movements of natural resources, trade goods, human labor, finance capital, information, and infectious diseases.

GLOBALSCAPE

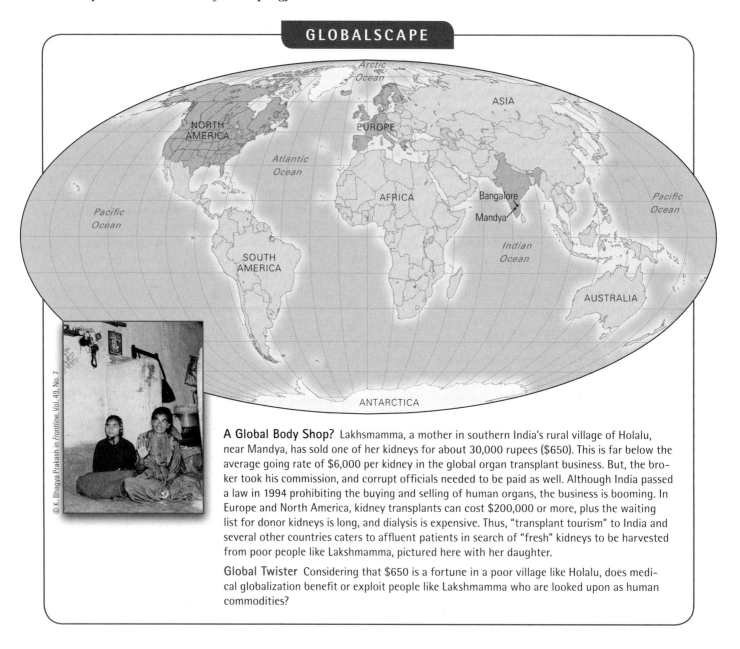

A Global Body Shop? Lakhsmamma, a mother in southern India's rural village of Holalu, near Mandya, has sold one of her kidneys for about 30,000 rupees ($650). This is far below the average going rate of $6,000 per kidney in the global organ transplant business. But, the broker took his commission, and corrupt officials needed to be paid as well. Although India passed a law in 1994 prohibiting the buying and selling of human organs, the business is booming. In Europe and North America, kidney transplants can cost $200,000 or more, plus the waiting list for donor kidneys is long, and dialysis is expensive. Thus, "transplant tourism" to India and several other countries caters to affluent patients in search of "fresh" kidneys to be harvested from poor people like Lakshmamma, pictured here with her daughter.

Global Twister Considering that $650 is a fortune in a poor village like Holalu, does medical globalization benefit or exploit people like Lakshmamma who are looked upon as human commodities?

far more biological variation *within* any given human population than *among* them. In short, human "races" are divisive categories based on prejudice, false ideas of differences, and erroneous notions of the superiority of one's own group. Given the importance of this issue, race and other aspects of biological variation will be discussed further in upcoming sections of the text.

A second example involves the issue of same-sex marriage. In 1989, Denmark became the first country to enact a comprehensive set of legal protections for same-sex couples, known as the Registered Partnership Act. At this writing, more than a half-dozen other countries and some individual states within the United States have passed similar laws, variously named, and numerous countries around the world are considering or have passed legislation providing people in homo-

sexual unions the benefits and protections afforded by marriage.[7] In some societies—including Spain, Canada, Belgium, and the Netherlands—same-sex marriages are considered socially acceptable and allowed by law, even though opposite-sex marriages are far more common.

As individuals, countries, and states struggle to define the boundaries of legal protections they will grant to same-sex couples, the anthropological perspective on

---

[7]Merin, Y. (2002). *Equality for same-sex couples: The legal recognition of gay partnerships in Europe and the United States.* Chicago: University of Chicago Press; "Court says same-sex marriage is a right" (2004, February 5), *San Francisco Chronicle;* current overviews and updates on the global status of same-sex marriage are posted on the Internet by the Partners Task Force for Gay & Lesbian Couples at www .buddybuddy.com.

marriage is useful. Anthropologists have documented same-sex marriages in many human societies in various parts of the world, where they are regarded as acceptable under appropriate circumstances. Homosexual behavior occurs in the animal world just as it does among humans.[8] The key difference between people and other animals is that human societies entertain beliefs regarding homosexual behavior, just as they do for heterosexual behavior—beliefs that specify when, where, how, and with whom sexual relations are appropriate or "normal." An understanding of global variation in marriage patterns and sexual behavior does not dictate that one pattern is more right than another. It simply illustrates that all human societies define the boundaries for social relationships.

A final example relates to the common confusion of *nation* with *state*. Anthropology makes an important distinction between these two: States are politically organized territories that are internationally recognized, whereas nations are socially organized bodies of people, who putatively share ethnicity—a common origin, language, and cultural heritage. For example, the Kurds constitute a nation, but their homeland (Kurdistan) is divided among several states, primarily Turkey, Iraq, and Iran. The modern boundaries of these states were drawn up after World War I, with little regard for the region's ethnic groups or nations. Similar processes have taken place throughout the world, especially in Asia and Africa, often making political conditions in these countries inherently unstable.

As we will see in later chapters, states and nations rarely coincide, nations being split among different states, and states typically being controlled by members of one nation who commonly use their control to gain access to the land, resources, and labor of other nationalities within the state. Most of the armed conflicts in the world today, such as the many-layered conflicts among the peoples of the former Yugoslavia, are of this sort and are not mere acts of tribalism or terrorism, as commonly asserted.

As these examples show, ignorance about other peoples and their ways causes serious problems throughout the world, especially now that we have developed a global system of fast information exchange and mass transportation that greatly increase our interaction and interdependence. Anthropology offers a way of looking at and understanding the world's peoples—insights that are nothing less than basic skills for survival in this age of globalization.

---

[8]Kirkpatrick, R. C. (2000). The evolution of human homosexual behavior. *Current Anthropology 41,* 384.

Questions for Reflection

1. Anthropology uses a holistic approach to explain all aspects of human beliefs, behavior, and biology. How might anthropology challenge your personal perspective on the following questions: Where did we come from? Why do we act in certain ways? What makes us tick?

2. From the holistic anthropological perspective, humans have one leg in culture and the other in nature. Are there examples from your life that illustrate the interconnectedness of human biology and culture?

3. Globalization can be described as a two-edged sword. How does it foster growth and destruction simultaneously?

4. The textbook definitions of *state* and *nation* are based on scientific distinctions between both organizational types. However, this distinction is commonly lost in everyday language. Consider, for instance, the names *United States of America* and the *United Nations*. How does confusing the terms contribute to political conflict?

5. The Biocultural Connection in this chapter contrasts different cultural perspectives on brain death, while the Original Study features a discussion about traditional Zulu healers and their role in dealing with AIDS victims. What do these two accounts suggest about the role of applied anthropology in dealing with cross-cultural health issues around the world?

Suggested Readings

Bonvillain, N. (2000). *Language, culture, and communication: The meaning of messages* (3rd ed.). Upper Saddle River, NJ: Prentice-Hall.

An up-to-date text on language and communication in a cultural context.

Fagan, B. M. (1999). *Archeology: A brief introduction* (7th ed.). New York: Longman.

This primer offers an overview of archaeological theory and methodology, from field survey techniques to excavation to analysis of materials.

Jones, S., Martin R., & Pilbeam, D. (Eds.). (1992). *Cambridge encyclopedia of human evolution.* New York: Cambridge University Press.

This comprehensive introduction to the human species covers the gamut of biological anthropology, from genetics, primatology, and the fossil evidence to a detailed exploration of contemporary human ecology, demography, and disease. Contributions by over seventy scholars.

Kedia, S., & Van Willigen, J. (2005). *Applied anthropology: Domains of application.* New York: Praeger.

Compelling essays by prominent scholars on the potential, accomplishments, and methods of applied anthropology in domains including development, agriculture, environment, health and medicine, nutrition, population displacement and resettlement, business and industry, education, and aging. The contributors show how anthropology can be used to address today's social, economic, health, and technical challenges.

Peacock, J. L. (2002). *The anthropological lens: Harsh light, soft focus* (2nd ed.). New York: Cambridge University Press.

This lively and innovative book gives the reader a good understanding of the diversity of activities undertaken by cultural anthropologists, while at the same time identifying the unifying themes that hold the discipline together. Additions to the second edition include such topics as globalization, gender, and postmodernism.

Thomson Audio Study Products

 Enjoy the MP3-ready Audio Lecture Overviews for each chapter and a comprehensive audio glossary of key terms for quick study and review. Whether walk-ing to class, doing laundry, or studying at your desk, you now have the freedom to choose when, where, and how you interact with your audio-based educational media. See the preface for information on how to access this on-the-go study and review tool.

The Anthropology Resource Center

www.thomsonedu.com/anthropology

The Anthropology Resource Center provides extended learning materials to reinforce your understanding of key concepts in the four subfields of anthropology. For each of the four subdisciplines, the Resource Center includes dynamic exercises including video exercises, map exercises, simulations, and "Meet the Scientists" interviews, as well as critical thinking questions that can be assigned and e-mailed to instructors. The Resource Center also provides breaking news in anthropology and interesting material on applied anthropology to help you link what you are learning to the world around you.

2 Biology and Evolution

© Charles C. Benton

CHALLENGE ISSUE

Monumental sculptures of DNA, the molecule that contains the human genetic code, grace a variety of public spaces today. They illustrate the molecular structure of DNA as well as its profound social meaning. Through sculptures like this one, from the Lawrence Hall of Science (a public science museum and research center for education at the University of California, Berkeley), the structure of DNA becomes internalized as a normal part of daily life. Will the scientific understanding of the human genetic code fundamentally reshape our understanding of what it means to be human? How much of our lives are dictated by the structure of DNA? And what will be the social consequences of depicting humans as entities programmed by their DNA? Individuals and societies can answer these challenging questions using an anthropological perspective that emphasizes the connections between human biology and culture.

What Is Evolution?

Although all living creatures ultimately share a common ancestry, they have come to differ from one another through the process of evolution. Biological evolution refers to genetic change over successive generations. The process of change is characterized by descent with modification, as descendant populations come to differ from ancestral ones. As a population's genetic variation changes from one generation to another, genetic change is reflected in visible differences between organisms.

What Is the Molecular Basis of Evolution?

Scientists began to understand the mechanics of heredity and how evolution works in populations long before molecular biologists identified the genetic basis of evolutionary change. With the discovery of DNA (deoxyribonucleic acid) molecules in 1953, scientists came to understand how genetic information is stored in the chromosomes of a cell. Genes, specific portions of DNA molecules, direct the synthesis of the protein molecules upon which all living organisms depend.

What Are the Forces Responsible for Evolution?

Four evolutionary forces—mutation, genetic drift, gene flow, and natural selection—account for change in the genetic composition of populations. Random mutations introduce new genetic variation into individual organisms. Gene flow (the introduction of new gene variants from other populations), genetic drift (random changes in frequencies of gene variants in a population), and natural selection shape genetic variation at the population level. Natural selection is the mechanism of evolution that results in adaptive change, favoring individuals with genetic variants relatively better adapted to local environment conditions.

A common part of the mythology of most peoples is a story explaining the appearance of humans on earth. The accounts of creation recorded in the Bible's Book of Genesis, for example, explain human origins. A vastly different example, serving the same function, is the traditional belief of the Nez Perce, a people native to eastern Oregon and Idaho. For the Nez Perce, humanity is the creation of Coyote, a trickster-transformer inhabiting the earth before humans. Coyote chased Wishpoosh, the giant beaver monster, over the earth, leaving a trail to form the Columbia River. When Coyote caught Wishpoosh, he killed him, dragged his body to the riverbank, and cut it into pieces; each body part transformed into one of the various peoples of this region. The Nez Perce were made from Wishpoosh's head, thus conferring on them great intelligence and horsemanship.[1]

Creation stories depict the relationship between humans and the rest of the natural world, sometimes reflecting a deep connection among people, other animals, and the earth. In the traditional Nez Perce creation story, groups of people derive from specific body parts—each possessing a special talent and relationship with a particular animal. By contrast, the story of creation depicted in the Book of Genesis emphasizes human uniqueness and the concept of time. Creation is depicted as a series of actions occurring over the course of six days. God's final act of creation is to fashion the first human from the earth in his own image before the seventh day of rest.

This linear creation story from the Book of Genesis—shared by Jews, Christians, and Muslims—differs from the cyclical creation stories characteristic of the Hindu religion, which emphasize reincarnation and the cycle of life, including creation and destruction. The diversity of life on earth comes from three gods—Lord Brahma, the creator; Lord Vishnu, the preserver; and Lord Shiva, the destroyer and re-creator—all of whom are part of the Supreme One. When Lord Brahma sleeps the world is destroyed, then re-created again when he awakes. Similarly, some sort of supreme being is integral to creation according to the intelligent design movement centered at the Discovery Institute, a conservative think tank based in Seattle, Washington.

Evolution, the major organizing principle of the biological sciences, also accounts for the diversity of life on earth. However, evolution differs from creation stories in that it explains the diversity of life in a consistent scientific language, using testable ideas (hypotheses) that are grounded in verifiable evidence. Contemporary scientists make comparisons among living organisms to test

---

[1]Clark, E. E. (1966). *Indian legends of the Pacific Northwest* (p. 174). Berkeley: University of California Press.

hypotheses drawn from evolutionary theories. Through their research, scientists have deciphered the molecular basis of evolution and the mechanisms through which evolutionary forces work on populations of organisms. Scientific accounts of evolution also differ from the traditional Judeo-Christian-Islamic creation story in that it situates humans firmly within the natural world. Though scientific theories of evolution treat humans as natural biological organisms, at the same time historical and cultural processes also shape evolutionary theory and our understanding of it.

THE CLASSIFICATION OF LIVING THINGS

The development of biology and its central concept, evolution, provide an excellent example of the ways that historical and cultural processes can shape scientific thought. As the exploitation of foreign lands by European explorers, including Columbus, changed the prevailing European approach to the natural world, the discovery of new life forms challenged the previously held notion of fixed, unchanging life on earth. The invention of instruments such as the microscope to study the previously invisible interior of cells led to new levels of appreciation of the diversity of life on earth.

Before this time, Europeans organized living things and inanimate objects alike into a ladder or hierarchy known as the Great Chain of Being—an approach to nature first developed by Aristotle in ancient Greece over 2,000 years ago. The categories were based upon visible similarities, and one member of each category was considered its "primate" (from the Latin *primus*), meaning the first or best of the group. For example, the primate of rocks was the diamond, and the primate of birds was the eagle, and so forth. Humans were at the very top of the ladder, just below the angels.

This classificatory system was in place until Carl von Linné, writing with a Latin pen name Carolus Linnaeus, developed the *Systema Naturae* or system of nature in the 18th century, classifying all living things. A professor of medicine and botany in Sweden, Linnaeus prepared and prescribed medicinal plants as did other physicians of the time. He arranged for his students to join the major European voyages such as Captain James Cook's circumnavigation of the globe so they could bring back new medicinal plants and other life forms. Von Linné's compendium reflected a new understanding of life on earth and of the place of humanity among the animals.

Linnaeus noted the similarity among humans, monkeys, and apes, classifying them together as primates.

COLUMBUS AT THE COURT OF BARCELONA

© Art Resource, NY

An unforeseen consequence of the exploitation of foreign lands by European explorers beginning with Columbus (here at the court of Spain) was a change in the approach to the natural world. New life forms challenged the previously held notion of fixed, unchanging life on earth. Another unforeseen consequence was the widespread death of American Indians from exposure to Old World infectious diseases the explorers brought with them to the New World.

But instead of being the first or the best of the animals on earth, primates are just one of several kinds of **mammal,** animals who suckle or nurse their young and possess body hair or fur (though this body hair is very fine in humans). Besides humans, **primates** include the other mammals to which humans are most closely related: lemurs, lorises, tarsiers, monkeys, and apes. In other words, Linnaeus classified living things into a series of categories that are progressively more inclusive on the basis of internal and external visual similarities.

Species are the smallest working units in biological classificatory systems. Species are defined as reproductively isolated populations or groups of populations capable of interbreeding to produce fertile offspring. Species are subdivisions of larger, more inclusive groups, called **genera** (singular, **genus**). Humans, for example, are classified in the genus *Homo* and species *sapiens*. This binomial nomenclature, or two-part naming system, mirrors the naming patterns in many European societies where individuals possess two names—one personal and the other reflecting their membership in a larger group of related individuals.

Linnaeus based his classificatory system on the following criteria:

1. *Body structure:* A Guernsey cow and a Holstein cow are the same species because unlike a cow and a horse, they have identical body structure.
2. *Body function:* Cows and horses give birth to live young. Although they are different species, they are closer than either cows or horses are to chickens, which lay eggs and have no mammary glands.
3. *Sequence of bodily growth:* At the time of birth—or hatching out of the egg—young cows and chickens resemble their parents in their body plan. They are therefore more closely related to each other than either one is to the frog, whose tadpoles

mammal The class of vertebrate animals distinguished by bodies covered with fur, self-regulating temperature, and in females milk-producing mammary glands.

primate The group of mammals that includes lemurs, lorises, tarsiers, monkeys, apes, and humans.

species The smallest working unit in the system of classification. Among living organisms, species are populations or groups of populations capable of interbreeding and producing fertile viable offspring.

genus, genera (pl.) In the system of plant and animal classification, a group of like species.

VISUAL COUNTERPOINT

The wings of birds and butterflies exemplify analogy. Both are used for flight and share similar appearance due to their common function. However, the course of their development and their structure differs.

undergo a series of changes before attaining the basic adult form.

Modern **taxonomy,** or the science of classification (from the Greek for naming divisions), while retaining the structure of the Linnaean system, is based on more than body structure, function, and growth. Today, scientists also compare protein structure and genetic material to construct the relationship among living things. Such molecular comparisons can even be made between species of parasites, bacteria, or viruses, allowing scientists to classify or trace the origins of particular diseases, such as SARS (sudden acute respiratory syndrome) or HIV (human immunodeficiency virus).

In addition, cross-species comparisons identify anatomical features of similar function as **analogies,** while anatomical features that have evolved from a common ancestral feature are called **homologies.** For example, the hand of a human and the wing of a bat evolved from the forelimb of a common ancestor, though they have

taxonomy The science of classification.
analogies In biology, structures possessed by different organisms that are superficially similar due to similar function; without sharing a common developmental pathway or structure.
homologies In biology, structures possessed by two different organisms that arise in similar fashion and pass through similar stages during embryonic development though they may possess different functions.
hominoid The taxonomic division superfamily within the old world primates that includes gibbons, siamangs, orangutans, gorillas, chimpanzees, bonobos, and humans.

acquired different functions: The human hand and bat wing are homologous structures.

During their early embryonic development, homologous structures arise in a similar fashion and pass through similar stages before differentiating. The wings of birds and butterflies look similar and have a similar function (flying): These are analogous, but not homologous, structures because the butterfly wing does not develop from a forelimb.

Through careful comparison and analysis of organisms, Linnaeus and his successors have grouped species into genera and also into even larger groups such as families, orders, classes, phyla, and kingdoms. Each taxonomic level is distinguished by characteristics shared by all the organisms in the group. Table 2.1 presents the main categories of contemporary taxonomy applied to the classification of the human species, with a few of the more important distinguishing features noted for each category.

Taxonomies are human ways of organizing the natural world. Because taxonomies reflect scientists' understanding of the evolutionary relationships among living things, these classificatory systems are continually under construction. With new scientific discoveries, taxonomic categories have to be redrawn, and scientists often differ in their acceptance of a particular category. The classification of humans contains a prime example of a taxonomy under construction.

Humans are placed in the **hominoid** or ape superfamily with chimpanzees, gorillas, orangutans, and gibbons, due to physical similarities such as broad shoulder, absent tail, and long arms. Human characteristics such as bipedalism (walking on two legs) and culture

VISUAL COUNTERPOINT

An example of homology: The same bones of the mammalian forelimb differentiate into the human arm and hand and the bat wing. These structures have the same embryonic origin but come to take on different functions.

led scientists to think that all the other apes were more closely related to one another than any of them were to humans. Thus, humans and their ancestors were classified in the **hominid** family to distinguish them from the other apes. As will be discussed in more detail in later chapters, genetic and fossil studies have shown that humans are more closely related to African apes (chimps, bonobos, and gorillas) than they are to orangutans and gibbons. Some scientists then proposed that African apes should be included in the hominid family, with humans and their ancestors distinguished from the other African hominoids at the taxonomic level of subfamily, as **hominins.**

Although all scientists today agree about the close relationship among humans, chimpanzees, bonobos, and gorillas, they differ as to whether they use the term *hominid* or *hominin* to describe the taxonomic grouping of humans and their ancestors. Museum displays and much of the popular press tend to retain the old term *hominid,* emphasizing the visible differences between humans and the other African apes. Scientists and publications using *hominin* (such as *National Geographic)* are emphasizing the importance of genetics in establishing relationships among species. These word choices are more than name games: They reflect theoretical relationships among closely related species.

THE DISCOVERY OF EVOLUTION

Just as European seafaring and exploitation brought about an awareness of the diversity of life across the earth, the digging involved in construction and mining, which came with the onset of industrialization in Europe, brought about an awareness of change in life forms through time. Through cutting a railway line or some other work involving moving the earth, all sorts of fossils, or preserved remains, of past life forms were brought into the light.

At first, the fossilized remains of elephants and giant saber-toothed tigers in Europe were interpreted according to religious doctrine. For example, the early 19th-century theory of "catastrophism" invoked natural

hominid African hominoid family that includes humans and their ancestors. Some scientists, recognizing the close relationship of humans, chimps, bonobos, and gorillas, use the term *hominid* to refer to all African hominoids. They then divide the hominid family into two subfamilies: the Paninae (chimps, bonobos, and gorillas) and the Homininae (humans and their ancestors).

hominin The taxonomic subfamily or tribe within the primates that includes humans and our ancestors.

TABLE 2.1   **CLASSIFICATION OF HUMANS**

Taxonomic Category	Category to Which Humans Belong	Biological Features Used to Define and Place Humans in this Category
Kingdom	Animalia	Humans are animals. We do not make our own food (as plants do) but depend upon intake of living food.
Phylum	Chordata	Humans are chordates. We have a **notochord** (a rodlike structure of cartilage) and nerve chord running along the back of the body as well as gill slits in the embryonic stage of our life cycle.
Subphylum*	Vertebrata	Humans are vertebrates possessing an internal backbone, with a segmented spinal column.
Class	Mammalia	Humans are mammals, warm-blooded animals covered with fur, possessing mammary glands for nourishing their young after birth.
Order	Primates	Humans are primates, a kind of mammal with a generalized anatomy, relatively large brains, and grasping hands and feet.
Suborder	Anthropoidea	Humans are anthropoids, social, daylight-active primates.
Superfamily	Hominoidea	Humans are hominoids with broad flexible shoulders and no tail. Chimps, bonobos, gorillas, orangutans, gibbons, and siamangs are also hominoids.
Family Subfamily	Hominidae Homininae	Humans are hominids. We are hominoids from Africa, genetically more closely related to chimps, bonobos, and gorillas than to hominoids from Asia. Some scientists use hominid to refer only to humans and their ancestors. Others include chimps and gorillas in this category, using the subfamily hominin to distinguish humans and their ancestors from chimps and gorillas and their ancestors.
Genus Species	*Homo* *sapiens*	Humans have large brains and rely on cultural adaptations to survive. Ancestral fossils are placed in this genus and species depending upon details of the skull shape and interpretations of their cultural capabilities. Genus and species names are always italicized.

*Most categories can be expanded or narrowed by adding the prefix "sub" or "super." A family could thus be part of a superfamily and in turn contain two or more subfamilies.

The large-scale movement of earth in 19th-century Europe, due to mining and construction of railroad lines, unearthed fossils such as mastodons. Such discoveries indicated that life forms of the past were not the same as the present and that change had occurred.

notochord A rodlike structure of cartilage that, in vertebrates, is replaced by the vertebral column.

events like the Great Flood of the Bible to account for the disappearance of these species in European lands. With industrialization, however, Europeans became more comfortable with the ideas of change and progress. In hindsight, it seems inevitable that someone would hit upon the idea of evolution. So it was that, by the start of the 19th century, many naturalists had come to accept the idea that life had evolved, even though they were not clear about how it happened. It remained for Charles Darwin (1809–1882) to formulate a theory that has withstood the test of time.

Grandson of Erasmus Darwin (a physician, scientist, poet, and originator of a theory of evolution himself), Charles Darwin tried several careers on for size before undertaking the work for which he is so well known. He began the study of medicine at the University of Edinburgh, Scotland but dropped out after two years. Next, he went to Christ's College, Cambridge, to study theology. He then left Cambridge to take the position of naturalist and companion to Captain Fitzroy on the *H.M.S. Beagle,* on an expedition to various poorly mapped parts of the world.

The voyage lasted for almost five years, taking Darwin along the coasts of South America, to the Galapagos Islands, across the Pacific to Australia, and then across the Indian and Atlantic oceans to South America before returning to England in 1836. Observing the tremendous diversity of living creatures as well as the astounding fossils of extinct animals, Darwin began to note that species varied according to the environments they inhabited. The observations he made on this voyage, his readings of Sir Charles Lyell's *Principles of Geology* (1830), and the arguments he had with the orthodox and opinionated Fitzroy all contributed to the ideas culminating in Darwin's most famous book, *On the Origin of Species*. This book, published in 1859, over twenty years after he returned from his voyage, described a theory of evolution accounting for change within species and for the emergence of new species in purely naturalistic terms.

Darwin added observations from English farm life and intellectual thought to the ideas he began to develop on the *Beagle*. He paid particular attention to domesticated animals and farmers' practice of breeding their stock to select for specific traits. Darwin's theoretical breakthrough derived partly from an essay by economist Thomas Malthus (1766–1834), which warned of the potential consequences of increased human population. Malthus observed that animal populations, unlike human populations, remained stable, due to a large proportion of animal offspring not surviving to maturity.

Darwin combined his observations into the theory of **natural selection** as follows: All species display a range of variation, and all have the ability to expand beyond their means of subsistence. It follows that, in their "struggle for existence," organisms with variations that help them to survive in a particular environment will reproduce with greater success than those without them. Thus, as generation succeeds generation, nature selects the most advantageous variations, and species evolve. So obvious did the idea seem in hindsight that Thomas Henry Huxley, one of the era's most prominent scientists, remarked, "How extremely stupid of me not to have thought of that."[2]

As often happens in the history of science, Darwin was not alone in authoring the theory of natural selection. A Welshman, Alfred Russel Wallace, independently came up with the same idea at the same time while on a voyage to the Malay archipelago in Southeast Asia to collect specimens for European zoos and museums. According to his autobiography, a theory of evolution came to Wallace while he was in a feverish delirium from malaria. He shared excitedly his idea with other scientists in England, including Darwin, whose own theory was yet unpublished. The two scientists jointly presented their findings.

However straightforward the idea of evolution by natural selection may appear, the theory was (and has continued to be) a source of considerable controversy. The most contentious question of human origins was avoided by Darwin, who limited his commentary in the original work to a single sentence near the end: "much light will be thrown on the origin of man and his history." The feisty Thomas Henry Huxley, however, took up the subject of human origins explicitly through comparative anatomy of apes and humans and an examination of the fossils in his book, *On Man's Place in Nature,* published in 1863.

Two problems plagued Darwin's theory throughout his career. First, how did variation arise in the first place? Second, what was the mechanism of heredity by which variable traits could be passed from one generation to the next? Ironically, some of the information Darwin needed, the basic laws of heredity, were available by 1866, through the experimental work of Gregor Mendel (1822–1884), an obscure monk, working in the monastery gardens in Brno, a city in the southeast of today's Czech Republic.

Mendel, who was raised on a farm, possessed two particular talents: a flair for mathematics and a passion for gardening. As with all farmers, Mendel had an intuitive understanding of biological inheritance. He went a step farther, though, in that he recognized the need for a more systematic understanding. Thus, at age 34, he began careful breeding experiments in the monastery garden, starting with pea plants.

Over eight years, Mendel planted over 30,000 plants—controlling their pollination, observing the results, and figuring out the mathematics behind it all. This allowed him to predict the outcome of hybridization, or breeding that combined distinct varieties of the same species, over successive generations, in terms of basic laws of heredity. Though his findings were published in 1866 in a respected scientific journal, no one seemed to recognize the importance of Mendel's work during his lifetime.

Interestingly, a copy of this journal was found in Darwin's own library with the pages still uncut (journals were printed on long continuous sheets of paper and then folded into pages to be cut by the reader), an indication that the journal had never been read. In 1900, cell biology had advanced to the point where rediscovery of Mendel's laws was inevitable, and in that year three European botanists, working independently of one another,

---

[2]Quoted in Durant, J. C. (2000, April 23). Everybody into the gene pool. *New York Times Book Review*, p. 11.

natural selection The evolutionary process through which factors in the environment exert pressure, favoring some individuals over others to produce the next generation.

rediscovered not only the laws but also Mendel's original paper. With this rediscovery, the science of genetics began. Still, it would be another fifty-three years before the molecular mechanisms of heredity, and the discrete units of inheritance, would be discovered. Today, a comprehensive understanding of heredity, molecular genetics, and population genetics support evolutionary theory.

HEREDITY

In order to understand how evolution works, one has to have some understanding of the mechanics of heredity, because heritable variation constitutes the raw material for evolution. Our knowledge of the mechanisms of heredity is fairly recent; most of the fruitful research into the molecular level of inheritance has taken place in the past five decades. Although some aspects remain puzzling, the outlines by now are reasonably clear.

The Transmission of Genes

Today we define a **gene** as a portion of the DNA molecule containing a sequence of base pairs that is the fundamental physical and functional unit of heredity. Interestingly, the molecular basis of the gene was not known at the turn of the 20th century when biologists coined the term from the Greek word for "birth."

Mendel had deduced the presence and activity of genes by experimenting with garden peas to determine how various traits are passed from one generation to the next. Specifically, he discovered that inheritance was *particulate,* rather than *blending,* as Darwin and many others thought. That is, the units controlling the expression of visible traits come in pairs, one from each parent, and retain their separate identities over the generations rather than blending into a combination of parental traits in offspring. This was the basis of Mendel's first **law of seg-**

© Vittorio Luzzati/National Portrait Gallery, London

British scientist Rosalind Franklin's pioneering work in x-ray crystal photography played a vital role in unlocking the secret of the genetic code in 1953. Without her permission, Franklin's colleague Maurice Wilkins showed one of her images to James Watson. In his book *The Double Helix,* Watson wrote, "The instant I saw the picture my mouth fell open and my pulse began to race." While her research was published simultaneously in the prestigious journal *Nature* in 1953 alongside that of James Watson, Francis Crick, and Maurice Wilkins, only the gentlemen received the Nobel Prize for the double-helix model of DNA in 1962.

regation, which states that pairs of genes separate and keep their individuality and are passed on to the next generation, unaltered. Another of his laws—that of **independent assortment**—states that different traits (under the control of distinct genes) are inherited independently of one another.

Mendel's laws were abstract formulations based on statistical frequencies of observed characteristics such as color and texture in generations of plants. His inferences about the mechanisms of inheritance were confirmed through the discovery of the cellular and molecular basis of inheritance in the first half of the 20th century. When **chromosomes,** the cellular structures containing the genetic information, were discovered at the start of the 20th century, they provided a visible vehicle for separate transmission of traits proposed in Mendel's law of independent assortment.

It was not until 1953 that James Watson and Francis Crick found that genes are actually portions of molecules of deoxyribonucleic acid (**DNA**)—long strands of which form the chromosomes. DNA is a complex molecule with an unusual shape, rather like two strands of a rope twisted around each other with ladderlike steps between the two strands. X-ray crystallographic photographs of the DNA molecule created by British scientist Rosalind Franklin contributed significantly to deciphering the molecule's structure.

Alternating sugar and phosphate molecules form the backbone of these strands, connected to each other by

---

gene A portion of the DNA molecule containing a sequence of base pairs that is the fundamental physical and functional unit of heredity.

law of segregation The Mendelian principle that variants of genes for a particular trait retain their separate identities through the generations.

law of independent assortment The Mendelian principle that genes controlling different traits are inherited independently of one another.

chromosome In the cell nucleus, the structure visible during cellular division containing long strands of DNA combined with a protein.

DNA Deoxyribonucleic acid. The genetic material consisting of a complex molecule whose base structure directs the synthesis of proteins.

four base pairs: adenine, thymine, guanine, and cytosine (usually written as A, T, G, and C). Connections between the strands occur between so-called complementary pairs of bases (A to T, G to C; see Figure 2.1). Sequences of three complementary bases specify the sequence of amino acids in protein synthesis. This arrangement also confers upon genes the unique property of being able to replicate or make exact copies of themselves. As long as no errors are made in this replication process, cells within organisms can divide to form daughter cells that are exact genetic copies of the parent cell.

How is the DNA recipe converted into a protein? Through a series of intervening steps, each three-base sequence of a gene, called a **codon,** specifies production of a particular amino acid, strings of which build proteins. Because DNA cannot leave the cell's nucleus (Figures 2.2 and 2.3), the directions for a specific protein are first converted into ribonucleic acid or **RNA** in a process called **transcription.** RNA differs from DNA in the structure of its sugar phosphate backbone and in the presence of the base uracil rather than thymine. Next the RNA travels to the **ribosomes,** the cellular structure (see Figure 2.2)

codon Three-base sequence of a gene that specifies a particular amino acid for inclusion in a protein.
RNA Ribonucleic acid; similar to DNA but with uracil substituted for the base thymine. Transcribes and carries instructions from DNA from the nucleus to the ribosomes where it directs protein synthesis. Some simple life forms contain RNA only.
transcription Process of conversion of instructions from DNA into RNA.
ribosomes Structures in the cell where translation occurs.

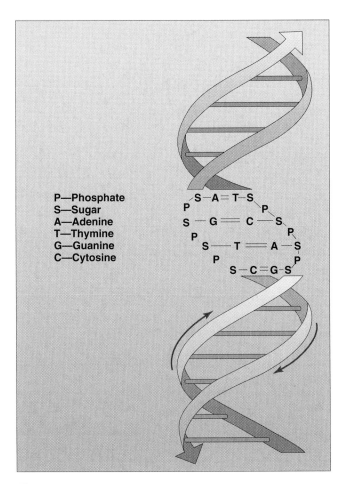

P—Phosphate
S—Sugar
A—Adenine
T—Thymine
G—Guanine
C—Cytosine

Figure 2.1

This diagrammatic representation of a portion of deoxyribonucleic acid (DNA) illustrates its twisted ladderlike structure. Alternating sugar and phosphate groups form the structural sides of the ladder. The connecting "rungs" are formed by pairings between complementary bases—adenine with thymine and cytosine with guanine.

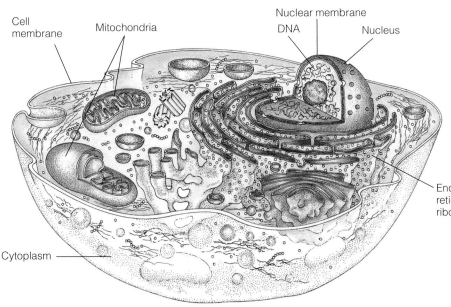

Cell membrane
Mitochondria
Nuclear membrane
DNA
Nucleus
Endoplasmic reticulum with ribosomes
Cytoplasm

Figure 2.2

Structure of a generalized eukaryotic, or nucleated, cell, illustrating the cell's three-dimensional nature. DNA is located in the nucleus. Because DNA cannot leave the nucleus, genes must first be transcribed into RNA, which carries genetic information to the ribosomes, where protein synthesis occurs. Note also the mitochondria, which contain their own circular chromosomes and mitochondrial DNA.

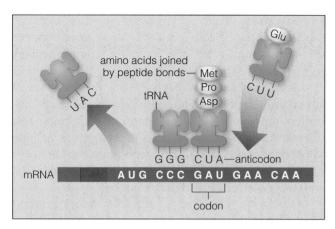

Figure 2.3

Codons (a sequence of three bases) are transcribed into the complementary codons of RNA. In the ribosomes, these codons specify particular amino acids that are strung together to form chains that create the primary structures of proteins.

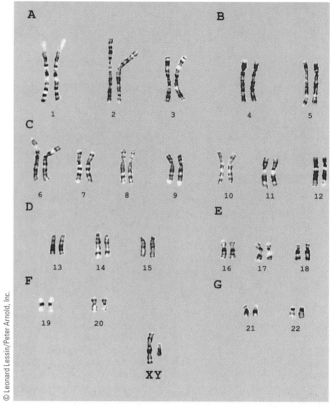

© Leonard Lessin/Peter Arnold, Inc.

In addition to the twenty-two pairs of somatic or body chromosomes, humans possess one pair of sex chromosomes for a total of forty-six chromosomes. In the lower right corner is the pair of sex chromosomes found in the normal male phenotype: a larger X chromosome (left) and smaller Y. The female phenotype is determined by the presence of two X chromosomes. Offspring inherit an X chromosome from their mothers but either an X or a Y from their fathers, resulting in approximately equal numbers of male and female offspring in subsequent generations. Though the Y chromosome is critical for differentiation into a male phenotype, compared to other chromosomes the Y is tiny and carries little genetic information.

where **translation** of the directions found in the codons into proteins occurs. For example, the sequence of CGA specifies the amino acid arginine, GCG alanine, CAG glutamine, and so on.

There are twenty amino acids, which are strung together in different amounts and sequences to produce an almost infinite number of different proteins. This is the so-called **genetic code,** and it is the same for every living thing, whether it be a worm or a human being. In addition to the genetic information stored in the chromosomes of the nucleus, complex organisms also possess cellular structures called *mitochondria,* each of which has a single circular chromosome. The genetic material known as *mitchondiral DNA* or *mtDNA* has figured prominently in human evolutionary studies. On the other end of the spectrum, simple living things without nucleated cells, such as the retrovirus that causes AIDS, contain their genetic information only as RNA.

Genes and Alleles

A sequence of chemical bases on a molecule of DNA (a gene) constitutes a recipe for the production of RNA, which in turn can direct the production of specific proteins. As science writer Matt Ridley puts it, "Proteins . . . do almost every chemical, structural, and regulatory thing that is done in the body: they generate energy, fight infection, digest food, form hair, carry oxy-

gen, and so on and on."[3] Almost everything in the body is made *of* or *by* proteins.

Thus, when we speak of the gene for a human blood type in the A-B-O system, we are referring to the portion of a DNA molecule that is 1,062 "letters" long—a medium-sized gene—that specifies production of an **enzyme,** a particular kind of protein that initiates and directs a chemical reaction. This particular enzyme causes molecules involved in immune responses to attach to the surface of red blood cells. Alternate forms of genes, known as **alleles** exist, in this case corresponding to the specific blood type (the A allele and B allele). Genes, then, are not really separate structures, as had once been imagined, but locations, like dots on a map. These genes provide the recipe for the many proteins that keep us alive and healthy.

---

translation   Process of conversion of RNA instructions into proteins.
genetic code   The sequence of three bases (a codon) that specifies the sequence of amino acids in protein synthesis.
enzyme   Protein that initiates and directs chemical reactions.
allele   Alternate form of a single gene.

---

[3]Ridley, M. (1999). *Genome: The autobiography of a species in 23 chapters* (p. 40). New York: HarperCollins.

Connection

The Social Impact of Genetics on Reproduction

While pregnancy and childbirth have been traditional subjects for cultural anthropological study, the genetics revolution has raised new questions for the biocultural study of reproduction. At first glance, the genetics revolution has simply expanded biological knowledge. Individuals today, compared to a hundred years ago, can now see their own genetic makeup even to the level of base pair sequence. A deeper look illustrates that this new biological knowledge has the capacity to profoundly transform cultures.

In many cultures, the social experience of pregnancy and childbirth has changed dramatically as a result of the genetic revolution. New reproductive technologies (NRTs) allow for the genetic assessment of fertilized eggs and embryos (the earliest stage of animal development), with far-reaching social consequences. These NRTs have also become the object of anthropological study as cultural anthropologists study the social impact of biological knowledge.

For more than twenty years, anthropologist Rayna Rapp has studied the social impact of prenatal (before birth) genetic testing in North America. Her work illustrates how biological knowledge is generated and interpreted by humans every step of the way.

Prenatal genetic testing is conducted most frequently through amniocentesis, a technique developed in the 1960s

Courtesy of Rayna Rapp

through which fluid, containing cells from the developing embryo, is drawn from the womb of a pregnant woman. The chromosomes and specific genes are then analyzed for abnormalities. Rapp traces the development of amniocentesis from an experimental procedure to one routinely used in pregnancy in the United States. For example, today pregnant women over the age of 35 routinely undergo this test because certain genetic conditions are associated with older maternal age. Trisomy 21 or Down syndrome, in which individuals have an extra 21st chromosome, can be easily identified through amniocentesis.

Through ethnographic study Rapp shows that a biological fact (such as an extra 21st chromosome) present "potential parents" with new reproductive choices. She also illustrates how genetic testing may lead to the labeling of disabled people as undesirable. Rapp's anthropological investigation of the social impact of amniocentesis illustrates the complex interplay between biological knowledge and cultural practices.

The human **genome**—the complete sequence of human DNA—contains 3 billion chemical bases, with about 20,000 to 25,000 functioning genes, a number similar to that found in most mammals. Of the 3 billion bases, humans and mice are about 90 percent identical. Both species have a mere three times as many genes as in the fruit fly, but half the number of genes found in the rice plant. In other words the number of genes or base pairs does not explain every difference among organisms.

At the same time, those 20,000 to 25,000 human genes account for only 1 to 1.5 percent of the entire genome, indicating that scientists still have far more to learn about how genes work. Frequently, genes themselves are split by long stretches of DNA that are not part of the known protein code. The 1,062 bases of the A-B-O blood group gene, for example, are interrupted by five such stretches. In the course of producing proteins, these stretches of DNA are metaphorically snipped out and left on the cutting-room floor.

Some of this seemingly useless, noncoding DNA (often called *junk DNA*) has been inserted by retroviruses. *Retroviruses* are some of the most diverse and widespread infectious entities of vertebrates—responsible for AIDS,

hepatitis, anemias, and some neurological disorders.[4] Other junk DNA consists of decaying hulks of once-useful but now functionless genes: damaged genes that have been "turned off." As cells divide and reproduce, junk DNA, like known genes, also replicates. In the replication process mistakes are made fairly frequently, adding or subtracting repeats of the four bases: A, C, G, and T. This happens with some frequency and differently in every individual. As these "mistakes" accumulate over time, each person develops his or her unique DNA fingerprint.

Cell Division

In order to grow and maintain good health, the body cells of an organism must divide and produce new cells. Cell division is initiated when the chromosomes repli-

---

[4]Amábile-Cuevas, C. F., & Chicurel, M. E. (1993). Horizontal gene transfer. *American Scientist 81*, 338.

genome The complete structure sequence of DNA for a species.

cate, forming a second pair that duplicates the original pair of chromosomes in the nucleus. To do this, the DNA metaphorically "unzips" between the base pairs—adenine from thymine and guanine from cytosine—following which each base on each now-single strand attracts its complementary base, reconstituting the second half of the double helix. Each new pair is surrounded by a membrane and becomes the nucleus that directs the activities of a new cell. This kind of cell division is called **mitosis,** and it produces new cells that have exactly the same number of chromosome pairs, and hence genes, as did the parent cell.

Like most animals, humans reproduce sexually. One reason sex is so popular, from an evolutionary perspective, is that it provides opportunity for increased genetic variation. All animals contain two copies of each chromosome, having inherited one from each parent. In humans this involves twenty-three pairs of chromosomes. Sexual reproduction can bring beneficial alleles together, purge the genome of harmful ones, and allow beneficial alleles to spread without being held back by the baggage of disadvantageous variants of other genes. Without sexual reproduction, we would lack genetic diversity, without which we would be more open to attack by various microbes. Nor would we be able to adapt to changing environments.

Because of its importance to survival, human societies have always regulated sexual reproduction in some ways. Recently, the science of genetics has had a tremendous impact on social aspects of reproduction, as seen in this chapter's Biocultural Connection.

When new individuals are produced through sexual reproduction, the process involves the merging of two cells, one from each parent. If two regular body cells, each containing twenty-three pairs of chromosomes, were to merge, the result would be a new individual with forty-six pairs of chromosomes; such an individual surely could not survive. But this increase in chromosome number does not occur, because the sex cells that join to form a new individual are the product of a different kind of cell division, called **meiosis.**

Although meiosis begins like mitosis, with the replication and doubling of the original genes in chromosomes, it proceeds to divide that number into four new cells rather than two (Figure 2.4). Thus each new cell has only half the number of chromosomes with their genes

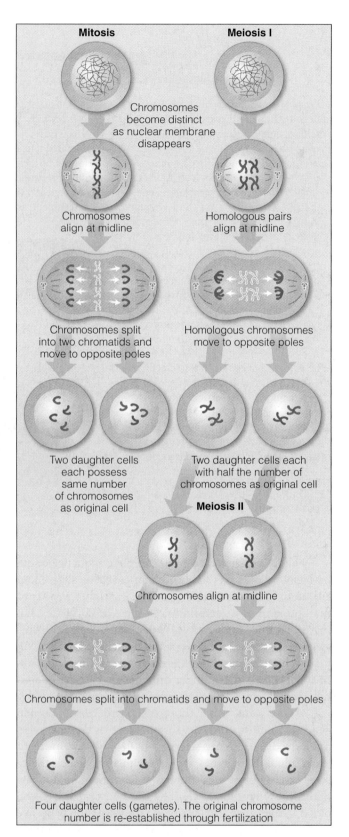

Figure 2.4

Because a chromatid can replicate itself, mitosis (a) results in daughter cells that are exact copies of the parent cell. In meiosis (b) the first division halves the chromosome number. The second meiotic division is essentially like mitosis and involves the separation of chromatids. Chromosomes in red originally came from one parent, those in blue from the other.

mitosis A kind of cell division that produces new cells having exactly the same number of chromosome pairs, and hence copies of genes, as the parent cell.

meiosis A kind of cell division that produces the sex cells, each of which has half the number of chromosomes found in other cells of the organisms.

found in the parent cell. Human eggs and sperm, for example, have only twenty-three single chromosomes (half of a pair), whereas body cells have twenty-three pairs, or forty-six chromosomes.

The process of meiotic division has important implications for genetics. Because paired chromosomes are separated, two different types of new cells will be formed; two of the four new cells will have one-half of a pair of chromosomes, and the other two will have the second half of the original chromosome pair. At the same time, corresponding portions of one chromosome may "cross over" to the other one, somewhat scrambling the genetic material compared to the original chromosomes.

Sometimes, the original pair is **homozygous,** possessing identical alleles for a specific gene. For example, if in both chromosomes of the original pair the gene for A-B-O blood type is represented by the allele for type A blood, then all new cells will have the "A" allele. But if the original pair is **heterozygous,** with the "A" allele on one chromosome and the allele for type B blood on the other, then half of the new cells will contain only the "B" allele; the offspring have a 50-50 chance of getting either one. It is impossible to predict any single individual's **genotype,** or genetic composition, but (as Mendel originally discovered) statistical probabilities can be established.

What happens when a child inherits the allele for type O blood from one parent and that for type A from the other? Will the child have blood of type A, O, or some mixture of the two? While Mendel's original experiments did not include traits with multiple alleles (as in the A-B-O blood system) his work answered many of these questions.

Mendel discovered that certain alleles are able to mask the presence of others; one allele is dominant, whereas the other is recessive. Actually, it is the traits that are dominant or recessive, rather than the alleles themselves; geneticists merely speak of dominant and recessive alleles for the sake of convenience. Among your biological relatives you can trace classic examples of visible traits governed by simple dominance such as a widow's peak (dominant), attached earlobes (recessive), or the presence of hair on the back of the middle section of each finger (dominant). A person with a widow's peak may be either homozygous or heterozygous because the presence of one allele will mask the allele for an unpeaked hairline. Similarly, one might speak of the allele for type A blood as being dominant to the one for type O. An individual whose blood-type genes are heterozygous, with one "A" and one "O" allele, will have type A blood. In other words, the heterozygous condition (AO) will show exactly the same physical characteristic, or **phenotype,** as the homozygous (AA), even though the two have a somewhat different genetic composition, or genotype. Only the homozygous recessive genotype (OO) will show the phenotype of type O blood.

The **dominance** of one allele does not mean that the **recessive** one is lost or in some way blended. A type A heterozygous parent (AO) will produce sex cells containing both "A" and "O" alleles. (This is an example of Mendel's law of segregation, that alleles retain their separate identities.) Recessive alleles can be handed down for generations before they are matched with another recessive in the process of sexual reproduction and show up in the phenotype. The presence of the dominant allele simply masks the expression of the recessive allele.

All of the traits Mendel studied in garden peas showed this dominant-recessive relationship, and so for some years it was believed that this was the only relationship possible. Later studies, however, have indicated that patterns of inheritance are not always so simple. In some cases, neither allele is dominant; they are both co-dominant. An example of co-dominance in human heredity can be seen also in the inheritance of blood types. Type A is produced by one allele; type B by another. A heterozygous individual will have a phenotype of AB, because neither allele can dominate the other.

The inheritance of blood types points out another complexity of heredity. Although each of us has at most two alleles for any given gene, the number of *possible* alleles is by no means limited to two. Certain traits have three or more allelic forms. For example, over a hundred alleles exist for **hemoglobin,** the blood protein that carries oxygen. Only one allele can appear on each of the two homologous chromosomes, so each individual is limited to two genetic alleles.

Polygenetic Inheritance

So far, we have spoken as if the traits of organisms are determined by just one gene. However, multiple genes control most physical traits—such as height, skin color, or liability to disease. In such cases, we speak of **polygenetic inheritance,** where the respective alleles of two or more

homozygous Refers to a chromosome pair that bears identical alleles for a single gene.
heterozygous Refers to a chromosome pair that bears different alleles for a single gene.
genotype The alleles possessed for a particular trait.
phenotype The observable or testable appearance of an organism that may or may not reflect a particular genotype due to the variable expression of dominant and recessive alleles.
dominance The ability of one allele for a trait to mask the presence of another allele.
recessive An allele for a trait whose expression is masked by the presence of a dominant allele.
hemoglobin The protein that carries oxygen in the red blood cells.
polygenetic inheritance When two or more genes contribute to the phenotypic expression of a single characteristic.

genes influence phenotype. Because so many genes are involved, each of which may have alternative alleles, it is difficult to unravel the genetic underpinnings of any continuous trait. For this reason, characteristics subject to polygenetic inheritance exhibit a continuous range of variation in their phenotypic expression and illustrate

difficulties inherent with reconciling visible traits with their underlying genetic bases.

As biological anthropologist Jonathan Marks demonstrates in the following Original Study, tracing the relationship between genetics and continuous traits is a mystery still to be unraveled.

Original Study ▪ By Jonathan Marks

Ninety–Eight Percent Alike: What Our Similarity to Apes Tells Us about Our Understanding of Genetics

It's not too hard to tell Jane Goodall from a chimpanzee. Goodall is the one with long legs and short arms, a prominent forehead, and whites in her eyes. She's the one with a significant amount of hair only on her head, not all over her body. She's the one who walks, talks, and wears clothing.

A few decades ago, however, the nascent field of molecular genetics recognized an apparent paradox: However easy it may be to tell Jane Goodall from a chimpanzee on the basis of physical characteristics, it is considerably harder to tell them apart according to their genes.

More recently, geneticists have been able to determine with precision that humans and chimpanzees are over 98 percent identical genetically, and that figure has become one of the most well-known factoids in the popular scientific literature. It has been invoked to argue that we are simply a third kind of chimpanzee, together with the common chimp and the rarer bonobo; to claim human rights for nonhuman apes; and to explain the roots of male aggression.

Using the figure in those ways, however, ignores the context necessary to make sense of it. Actually, our amazing genetic similarity to chimpanzees is a scientific fact constructed from two rather more mundane facts: our familiarity with the apes and our unfamiliarity with genetic comparisons.

To begin with, it is unfair to juxtapose the differences between the bodies of people and apes with the similarities in their genes. After all, we have been comparing the bodies of humans and chimpanzees for 300 years, and we have been comparing DNA sequences for less than 20 years.

Now that we are familiar with chimpanzees, we quickly see how dif-

ferent they look from us. But when the chimpanzee was a novelty, in the 18th century, scholars were struck by the overwhelming similarity of human and ape bodies. And why not? Bone for bone, muscle for muscle, organ for organ, the bodies of humans and apes differ only in subtle ways. And yet, it is impossible to say just how physically similar they are. Forty percent? Sixty percent? Ninety-eight percent? Three-dimensional beings that develop over their lifetimes don't lend themselves to a simple scale of similarity.

Genetics brings something different to the comparison. A DNA sequence is a one-dimensional entity, a long series of A, G, C, and T subunits. Align two sequences from different species and you can simply tabulate their similarities; if they match 98 out of 100 times, then the species are 98 percent genetically identical.

But is that more or less than their bodies match? We have no easy way to tell, for making sense of the question "How similar are a human and a chimp?"

By Jonathan Marks (2000)

requires a frame of reference. In other words, we should be asking: "How similar are a human and a chimp, compared to what?" Let's try and answer the question. How similar are a human and a chimp, compared to, say, a sea urchin? The human and chimpanzee have limbs, skeletons, bilateral symmetry, a central nervous system; each bone, muscle, and organ matches. For all intents and purposes, the human and chimpanzee aren't 98 percent identical, they're 100 percent identical.

On the other hand, when we compare the DNA of humans and chimps, what does the percentage of similarity mean? We conceptualize it on a linear scale, on which 100 percent is perfectly identical, and 0 percent is totally different. But the structure of DNA gives the scale a statistical idiosyncrasy.

Because DNA is a linear array of those four bases—A, G, C, and T—only four possibilities exist at any specific point in a DNA sequence. The laws of chance tell us that two random sequences from species that have no ancestry in common will match at about one in every four sites.

Thus, even two unrelated DNA sequences will be 25 percent identical, not 0 percent identical. (You can, of course, generate sequences more different than that, but greater differences would not occur randomly.) The most different two DNA sequences can be, then, is 75 percent different.

Now consider that all multicellular life on earth is related. A human, a chimpanzee, and the banana the chimpanzee is eating share a remote common ancestry, but a common ancestry nevertheless. Therefore, if we compare any particular DNA sequence in a human and a banana, the sequence would have to be more than 25 percent identical. For the sake of argument, let's say 35 percent. In other words, your DNA is over one-third the same as a banana's. Yet, of course, there are few ways other than genetically in which a human could be shown to be one-third identical to a banana.

That context may help us to assess the 98 percent DNA similarity of humans and chimpanzees. The fact that our DNA is 98 percent identical to that of a chimp is not a transcendent statement about our natures, but merely a decontextualized and culturally interpreted datum.

Moreover, the genetic comparison is misleading because it ignores qualitative differences among genomes. Genetic evolution involves much more than simply replacing one base with another. Thus, even among such close relatives as human and chimpanzee, we find that the chimp's genome is estimated to be about 10 percent larger than the human's; that one human chromosome contains a fusion of two small chimpanzee chromosomes; and that the tips of each chimpanzee chromosome contain a DNA sequence that is not present in humans.

In other words, the pattern we encounter genetically is actually quite close to the pattern we encounter anatomically. In spite of the shock the figure of 98 percent may give us, humans are obviously identifiably different from, as well as very similar to, chimpanzees. The apparent paradox is simply a result of how mundane the apes have become, and how exotic DNA still is.
(By Jonathan Marks (2000, May 12). 98% alike (what our similarity to apes tells us about our understanding of genetics). Chronicle of Higher Education, *B7.)* ■

EVOLUTION, INDIVIDUALS, AND POPULATIONS

At the level of the individual, the study of genetics shows how traits are transmitted from parent to offspring, enabling a prediction about the chances that any given individual will display some phenotypic characteristic. At the level of the group, the study of genetics takes on additional significance, revealing how evolutionary processes account for the diversity of life on earth.

A key concept in genetics is that of the **population,** or a group of individuals within which breeding takes place. It is within populations that natural selection occurs, as some members contribute a disproportionate share of the next generation. Over generations, the relative proportions of alleles in a population changes (biological evolution) according to the varying reproductive success of individuals within that population. In other words, at the level of population genetics, **evolution** can be defined as changes in allele frequencies in populations. This is also known as *microevolution.*

Four evolutionary forces—mutation, gene flow, genetic drift, and natural selection—are responsible for the genetic changes that underlie the biological variation present in species today. As we shall see, variation is at the heart of evolution. These evolutionary forces create and pattern diversity.

The Stability of the Population

In theory, the characteristics of any given population should remain stable. For example, generation after generation, the bullfrogs in a farm pond look much alike, have the same calls, and exhibit the same behavior when breeding. The **gene pool** of the population—the genetic variants available to that population—appears to remain stable over time.

Although some alleles may be dominant to others, recessive alleles are not just lost or destroyed. Statistically, an individual who is heterozygous for a particular gene with one dominant (A) and one recessive allele (a) has a 50 percent chance of passing on the dominant allele, and a 50 percent chance of passing on the recessive allele. Even if another dominant allele masks the presence of the recessive allele in the next generation, the recessive allele nonetheless will continue to be a part of the gene pool.

Because alleles are not "lost" in the process of reproduction, the frequency of the different alleles within a population should remain exactly the same from one generation to the next in the absence of evolution. In 1908, the English mathematician G. H. Hardy (1877–1947) and the German obstetrician W. Weinberg (1862–1937) worked this idea into a mathematical formula called the **Hardy-Weinberg principle.** The principle algebraically demonstrates that the percentage of individuals homozygous for the dominant allele, homozygous for the recessive allele, and heterozygous will remain the same from

population In biology, a group of similar individuals that can and do interbreed.
evolution Changes in allele frequencies in populations; also known as microevolution.
gene pool All the genetic variants possessed by members of a population.
Hardy-Weinberg principle Demonstrates algebraically that the percentage of individuals that are homozygous for the dominant allele, homozygous for the recessive allele, and heterozygous should remain constant from one generation to the next, provided that certain specified conditions are met.

one generation to the next provided that certain specified conditions are met. These conditions include that mating is entirely random; that the population is sufficiently large for statistical averages to express themselves; that no new variants will be introduced into the population's gene pool; and that all individuals are equally successful at surviving and reproducing. The last four conditions are equivalent to the absence of evolution. Geographical, physiological, or social factors may favor mating between certain individuals over others.

Thus, changes in the gene pools of populations, without which there could be no evolution, can and do take place. The mechanisms by which these changes might lead to the formation of new species will be discussed in detail in Chapter 5.

EVOLUTIONARY FORCES
Mutation

The ultimate source of evolutionary change is **mutation** of genes because mutation constantly introduces new variation. Although some mutations may be harmful or beneficial to individuals, most mutations are neutral. But in an evolutionary sense, random mutation is inherently positive, as it provides the ultimate source of new genetic variation. New body plans—such as walking on two legs compared to knuckle-walking like our closest relatives, chimpanzees and gorillas—ultimately depended on genetic mutation. A random mutation might create a new allele that creates a modified protein making a new biological task possible. Without the variation brought in through random mutations, populations cannot change over time in response to changing environments.

For sexually reproducing species like humans, the only mutations of any *evolutionary* consequence are those occurring in sex cells, since these cells form future generations. Mutations may arise whenever copying mistakes are made during cell division. This may involve a change in a single base of a DNA sequence, or at the other extreme, relocation of large segments of DNA, including entire chromosomes. As you read this page, the DNA in each cell of your body is being damaged.[5] Fortunately, DNA repair enzymes constantly scan DNA for mistakes, slicing out damaged segments and patching up gaps. These repair mechanisms prevent diseases like cancer and ensure that we get a faithful copy of our parental in-

---

[5]Culotta, E., & Koshland, D. E., Jr. (1994). DNA repair works its way to the top. *Science 266,* 1,926.

mutation Chance alteration of genetic material that produces new variation.

Mutagens—such as pollutants, preservatives, cigarette smoke, radiation, and even some medicines—threaten people in industrial societies. While the mutations from these environmental hazards are generally negative, mutation is overall a positive force in evolutionary terms, as the ultimate source of all new genetic variation. The positive side of mutation is fictionalized in the special talents of the X-Men.

heritance. Genes controlling DNA repair therefore form a critical part of any species' genetic makeup.

Because no species has perfect DNA repair, new mutations arise continuously, so that all species continue to evolve. Geneticists have calculated the rate at which various types of mutant genes appear. In human populations, they run from a low of about five mutations per million sex cells formed, in the case of a gene abnormality that leads to the absence of an iris in the eye, to a high of about a hundred per million, in the case of a gene involved in a form of muscular dystrophy. The average is about thirty mutants per million. Environmental factors may increase the rate at which mutations occur. These include certain dyes, antibiotics, and chemicals used in the preservation of food. Radiation, whether of industrial or solar origin, represents another important cause of mutations. There is even evidence that stress can raise mutation rates, increasing the diversity necessary for selection if successful adaptation is to occur.[6]

In humans, as in all multicellular animals, the very nature of genetic material ensures that mutations will occur. For instance, the fact that genes are split by stretches of DNA that are not a part of that gene increases the chances that a simple editing mistake in the process of copying DNA will cause mutations. To cite one example, no fewer than fifty such segments of DNA fragment the gene for collagen—the main structural protein of the skin, bones, and teeth. One result of this seemingly inefficient situation is that it becomes possible to shuffle the gene segments themselves like a deck of cards, putting together new proteins with new functions. Although individuals may suffer as a result, mutations also confer versatility at the population level, making it possible for an evolving species to adapt more quickly to environmental changes. It is important to realize that mutations occur randomly and thus do not arise out of need for some new adaptation.

Genetic Drift

Genetic drift refers to chance fluctuations of allele frequencies in the gene pool of a population. These changes at the population level come about due to random events at the individual level. Over the course of their lifetime, each individual is subject to a number of random events affecting its survival. For example, an individual squirrel in good health and possessed of a number of advantageous traits may be killed in a forest fire; a genetically well-adapted baby cougar may not live longer than a day if its mother gets caught in an avalanche, whereas the weaker offspring of a mother that does not die may survive.

In a large population, such accidents of nature are unimportant; the accidents that preserve individuals with certain alleles will be balanced out by the accidents that destroy them. However, in small populations, such averaging out may not be possible. Because human populations today are so large, we might suppose that human beings are unaffected by chance events. Although it is true that a rock slide that kills five campers whose home community has a total population of 100,000 is not statistically significant, a rock slide that kills five hunters from a small group of food foragers could significantly alter frequencies of alleles in the local gene pool. The group size of typical food foragers (people who hunt, fish, and gather other wild foods for subsistence) tends to vary between about twenty-five and fifty.

These random events ultimately result in changes in frequencies of gene variants in a population, defined as the evolutionary force of genetic drift. The effects of genetic drift are most powerful in small populations. A particular kind of genetic drift, known as the **founder effect,** may occur when an existing population splits up into two or more new ones, especially if one of these new populations is founded by a particularly small number of individuals. In such cases, it is unlikely that the gene frequencies of the smaller population will be representative of those of the larger one.

Isolated island populations may possess limited variability due to the founder effect. For example, in 1790, nine British sailors from the *H.M.S. Bounty,* six Tahitian men, and eight or nine Tahitian women settled on Pitcairn Island in the South Pacific. These individuals possessed only a small fraction of the total genetic variation in either Great Britain or Tahiti. After a conflict between the Tahitians and the British, the population was further reduced to one British man, Alexander Smith, the women, and some children. Thus today's island population descended from a small number of individuals with a very narrow gene pool, which results in high frequency of some genetic traits.

Genetic drift is likely to have been an important factor in human evolution, because until 10,000 years ago all humans were food foragers who probably lived in relatively small, self-contained populations. Whenever biological variation is observed, whether it is the distant past or the present, it is always possible that chance events of genetic drift can account for the presence of this variation.

Gene Flow

Another factor that brings change to the gene pool of a population is **gene flow,** or the introduction of new alleles from nearby populations. Interbreeding allows "road-tested" genes to flow in and out of populations, thus increasing the total amount of variation present within the population. Migration of individuals or groups into the territory occupied by others may lead to gene flow. Geographical factors also affect gene flow. For example, if a river separates two populations of small mammals preventing interbreeding, these populations

genetic drift Chance fluctuations of allele frequencies in the gene pool of a population.
founder effect A particular form of genetic drift deriving from a small founding population not possessing all the alleles present in the original population.
gene flow The introduction of alleles from the gene pool of one population into that of another.

[6]Chicurel, M. (2001). Can organisms speed their own evolution? *Science 292,* 1,824–1,827.

Anthropology Applied

In the Belly of the Beast: Reflections on a Decade of Service to U.S. Genetics Policy Commissions
By Barbara A. Koenig and Nancy Press

Medicine is in the midst of a foundational transformation based on the science of genomics. In an odd bit of chance, we as anthropologists have been involved in a process to consider and institute regulation regarding the introduction of new genetic tests into the marketplace and into clinical practice. Each of us has served on a variety of federal policy bodies in the field of genetics, charged with the oversight of new genetic tests. Barbara Koenig served on the Secretary's Advisory Committee on Genetic Testing (SACGT); Nancy Press served on the precursor group to the SACGT, the National Institutes of Health, Department of Energy Task Force on Genetic Testing, and more recently has worked on efforts related to specific genetic technologies, such as population-based testing for cystic fibrosis carrier status.

There is a commonly held assumption that anthropologists should be engaged in policy because we offer a unique voice that otherwise would remain silent. But the difficulties and uneasy relationships that a policy orientation in anthropology can entail have also been well described. For example, it has been pointed out that

the field of applied anthropology has a history of complicity with colonial authorities as well as a contemporary political economy that rewards collaboration with institutions that promote social inequality. In addition, many anthropology practitioners are funded by federal "soft money," which may inadvertently sap anthropology's independent voice of its vigor by affecting the choice of research agendas, methods, and conclusions.

We cannot claim to be exempt from any of these charges. Both of us "serve" government authorities; both are funded through grant money from the National Institutes of Health (NIH). In fact, we are always consciously poised between two disturbing possibilities: First, that we may be collaborating and providing "cover" for the institutions and practices we seek to critique and influence; and second, that we may be making no difference at all, either on the level of policy or the level of anthropological theory.

We are aware of the potentially pernicious effects of the genetics revolution, but we also believe that the magnitude of the potential improvement that genetics can bring to the broad arena of medicine

should not be minimized. It seems likely, in fact, that all aspects of health-care practice—research into disease etiology, public health screening, clinic-based prevention and treatment, modes of reproduction, and development of personalized therapeutics—are in the process of being transformed.

"High throughput technologies" for genetic analysis will allow for the testing of hundreds if not thousands of genes simultaneously. And what is tested for will not be confined to a narrow range of "genetic diseases"—such as Huntington disease or cystic fibrosis. As the genetic component to more and more conditions is located, differential levels of individual susceptibility to common diseases—and common environmental elements—will be the target of testing. In addition, the pathways to testing will also expand beyond the physician–patient encounter. They will include the hospital pathologist's lab, where a cancerous tumor may be examined for indications of a familial cancer predisposition, or to DNA samples, perhaps easily obtained at home by a consumer rubbing the inside of her cheek with a little swab and mailing it directly to a biotechnology company.

---

will begin to accrue random genetic differences from their isolation. If the river changes course and the two populations can interbreed freely again, new alleles that may have been present in only one population will now be present in both populations due to gene flow.

Among humans, social factors such as mating rules, intergroup conflict, and our ability to travel great distances affect gene flow. For example, the last 500 years have seen the introduction of alleles into Central and South American populations from both the Spanish colonists and the Africans whom Europeans imported as slaves. More recent migrations of people from East Asia have added to this mix. When gene flow is present, variation within populations increases. Throughout the history of human life on earth, gene flow has been im-

portant because it keeps populations from developing into separate species.

Natural Selection

Although the factors discussed above may produce change in a population, that change would not necessarily make the population better adapted to its biological and social environment. Genetic drift, for example, often produces strange characteristics that have no survival value; mutant genes may be either helpful or harmful to survival, or simply neutral. Natural selection, the evolutionary force described by Darwin, accounts for *adaptive* change. **Adaptation** is a series of beneficial adjustments to the environment. As we will explore throughout this textbook, humans adapt to their environment through culture as well as biology. When biological adaptation occurs at a genetic level, natural selection is at work.

Natural selection refers to the evolutionary process through which genetic variation at the population level

adaptation A series of beneficial adjustments to the environment.

There is also the danger that genetics will increase the medicalization of daily life: as increasing ability to communicate disease risk numbers to perfectly healthy people; or as more and more tests become available for testing prenatally to detect, but not treat, traits and conditions; or as advances in testing increase the likelihood of various sorts of insurance discrimination.

Genetics is particularly dangerous because of the way it captures the public imagination, linking the glamour of high technology with the allure of the fortune teller. But, unusually, genetics presents a case in which there has been public awareness, from the very beginning of the Human Genome Project, that its power might, in fact, be hazardous. This led to the immediate establishment of the Ethical, Legal and Social Implications (ELSI) branch of what became the National Human Genome Research Institute (NHGRI).

As anthropologists on national genetics policy committees, we both felt accepted. And such social acceptance should not be discounted, because social acceptance seems to be a *sine qua non* for functioning in such a policy forum.

Our training and techniques, developed from thirty-five years between us of studying doctors and the biomedical industrial complex, remind us of the need to understand *why* people act the way they act and believe what they believe; to examine what social role they are occupying and what the forces are that shape and drive that social role; to remember that no individual is to blame and no one is assigned to a pre-existing villain category. These techniques—that is, creating an ethnography of the policy group—can also suggest where a lever can be applied to change the process.

As anthropologists we have helped these policy groups frame questions such as, *Why* are we doing this testing? What health outcome will accrue to a person tested? What are the psychological and social benefits (or risks) to the person and his/her family in doing the test? How do people value, and how does society value, and *why* might society value the provision of genetic information absent a clear health outcome benefit? That is, the concept of clinical utility provides a research agenda, and it is a research agenda that is as key and

accessible to the social scientist as to the epidemiologist.

We have also used the insights of medical anthropology about the concept of "risk" in biomedicine to try to bring to the fore more hidden perils of genetics. While psychologists on these boards, or involved in other ELSI conversations, may express concern about the possibility of psychological damage to living with uncertainty, it is only an anthropological voice that raises the issue of why the idea of parsing one's "risk" for various things has become such a central focus in medicine.

So, are these real accomplishments? Is this a worthwhile tradeoff? Perhaps only the reader can answer that question. As participant observers in the national genetics policy debate, sometimes we refer to our work as digging away in the genetics policy trenches. A better metaphor might come from the title, *In the Belly of the Beast,* a book by Jack Henry Abbott containing letters to Norman Mailer about life in prison. To us, it seems a useful and appropriate place for a medical anthropologist to be.

---

is shaped to fit local environmental conditions. In other words, instead of a completely random selection of individuals whose traits will be passed on to the next generation, there is selection by the forces of nature. In the process, the frequency of genetic variants for harmful or nonadaptive traits within the population is reduced while the frequency of genetic variants for adaptive traits is increased. Over time, changes in the genetic structure of the population are visible in the biology or behavior of a population, and such genetic changes can result in the formation of new species.

In popular writing, natural selection is often thought of as "survival of the fittest," a phrase coined by British philosopher Herbert Spencer (1820–1903). The phrase implies that the physically weak, being unfit, are eliminated from the population by disease, predation, or starvation. Obviously, the survival of the fittest has some bearing on natural selection. But there are many cases in which individuals survive, and even do quite well, but do not reproduce. They may be incapable of attracting mates, or they

may be sterile, or they may produce offspring that do not survive after birth. For example, among the Uganda kob, a kind of antelope native to East Africa, males that are unable to attract females form bachelor herds in which they live out their lives. As members of a herd, they are reasonably well protected against predators, and so they may survive to relatively old ages. They do not, however, pass on their genes to succeeding generations.

Change in the frequency with which certain genetic variants occur in human populations can be a very slow process. For example, if an environment changed such that a recessive allele that had been present in humans at a modest frequency suddenly became lethal, this allele's frequency would still decrease only gradually. Even with complete selection against those homozygous for this allele, the allele would persist in the offspring of heterozygotes. In the first several generations, the frequency of the allele would decrease at a relatively rapid rate. However, with time, as the frequency of the recessive allele drops, the probability of forming a recessive ho-

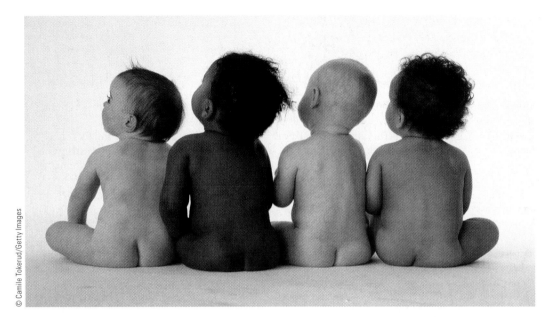

© Camile Tokerud/Getty Images

Across the globe, newborn babies weigh on average between 5 and 8 pounds. Stabilizing selection seems to be operating here to keep infant size well matched to the size of the human birth canal for successful childbirth. Natural selection can promote stability as well as change.

mozygote also drops, so that it would take many generations to realize even a small decrease in allele frequency. This is compounded by the fact that a human generation takes about twenty-five years (forty generations would span over a thousand years). Nevertheless, even such small and slow changes can have a significant cumulative impact on both the genotypes and phenotypes of any population.

By contrast the social impact of genetics is sometimes quite rapid, as people face the challenges posed by the scientific study of the human genome, described in this chapter's Anthropology Applied feature.

As a consequence of the process of natural selection, populations generally become well adapted to their environments. Anyone who has ever looked carefully at the plants and animals that survive in the deserts of the western United States can cite many instances of adaptation. For example, members of the cactus family have extensive root networks close to the surface of the soil, enabling them to soak up the slightest bit of moisture; they are able to store large quantities of water whenever it is available; they are shaped so as to expose the smallest possible surface to the dry air and are generally leafless as adults, thereby preventing water loss through evaporation; and a covering of spines discourages animals from chewing into the juicy flesh of the plant.

Desert animals are also adapted to their environment. The kangaroo rat can survive without drinking water; many reptiles live in burrows where the temperature is lower; most animals are nocturnal or active only in the cool of the night.

By extrapolation, biologists assume that the same mechanisms work on behavioral traits as well. It seems reasonable that individuals in a group of vervet monkeys capable of warning one another of the presence of predators would have a significant survival advantage over those without this capability. However, such situations have constituted an enigma for evolutionary biologists who typically see individuals as "survival machines," acting always in their own self-interest. By giving an alarm call, an individual calls attention to itself, thereby becoming an obvious target for the predator. How, then, could **altruism,** or concern for the welfare of others, evolve in which individuals place themselves at risk for the good of the group? One biologist's simple solution substitutes money for reproductive fitness to illustrate one way in which such cooperative behavior may come about:

> You are given a choice. Either you can receive $10 and keep it all or you can receive $10 million if you give $6 million to your next door neighbor. Which would you do? Guessing that most selfish people would be happy with a net gain of $4 million, I consider the second option to be a form of selfish behavior in which a neighbor gains an incidental benefit. I have termed such selfish behavior benevolent.[7]

Natural selection of beneficial social traits was probably an important influence on human evolution, since in the primates some degree of cooperative social behavior became important for food-getting, defense, and mate attraction. Indeed, anthropologist Christopher Boehm

altruism Acts of selflessness or self-sacrificing behavior.

[7]Nunney, L. (1998). Are we selfish, are we nice, or are we nice because we are selfish? *Science 281,* 1,619.

argues, "If human nature were merely selfish, vigilant punishment of deviants would be expected, whereas the elaborate prosocial prescriptions that favor altruism would come as a surprise."[8]

Natural selection may also promote stability, rather than change. **Stabilizing selection** occurs in populations that are already well adapted or where change would be disadvantageous. In cases where change is disadvantageous, natural selection will favor the retention of allele frequencies more or less as they are. However, the evolutionary history of most forms of life is not one of constant change, proceeding as a steady, stately progression over vast periods of time; rather, it is one of prolonged periods of relative stability or gradual change punctuated by shorter periods of more rapid change (or extinction) when altered conditions require new adaptations or when a new mutation produces an opportunity to adapt to some other available environment. According to the fossil record, most species survive somewhere between 3 and 5 million years.[9]

Many of the creation stories traditionally offered to explain observable cases of adaptation rely heavily on the purposeful acts of a supreme being as described earlier. The "Just So" stories of Rudyard Kipling such as "How the Leopard Got His Spots," or the elephant his trunk, are literary caricatures of this approach. Ironically, because specific examples of adaptation can be difficult to prove at times, scientists will sometimes suggest that their colleagues' scenarios about adaptation are "Just So" stories.

The adaptability of organic structures and functions, no matter how much a source of wonder and fascination, nevertheless falls short of perfection. This is so because natural selection can only work with what the existing store of genetic variation provides; it cannot create something entirely new. In the words of one evolutionary biologist, evolution is a process of tinkering, rather than design. Often tinkering involves balancing beneficial and harmful effects of a specific allele, as the case of sickle-cell anemia illustrates.

The Case of Sickle-Cell Anemia

Among human beings, a particularly well-studied case of an adaptation paid for by the misery of many individuals brings us to the case of **sickle-cell anemia,** a painful disease in which the oxygen-carrying red blood cells change shape (sickle) and clog the finest parts of the circulatory system. This disorder first came to the atten-

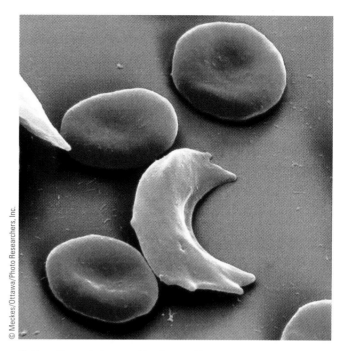

© Meckes/Ottawa/Photo Researchers, Inc.

Sickle-cell anemia is caused by abnormal hemoglobin, called hemoglobin S. Those afflicted by the disease are homozygous for the "S" allele, causing their red blood cells to "sickle." Co-dominance is observable with the sickle and normal alleles. Heterozygotes make some percentage of normal hemoglobin and some percentage of sickle hemoglobin. Shown here is a sickle hemoglobin red blood cell among normal red blood cells.

tion of geneticists in Chicago when it was observed that most North Americans who suffer from it are of African ancestry. Investigation traced the abnormality to populations that live in a clearly defined belt across central Africa where the sickle-cell allele is found at surprisingly high frequencies.

Geneticists were curious to know why such a harmful hereditary disability persisted in these populations. According to the theory of natural selection, any alleles that are harmful will tend to disappear from the group, because the individuals who are homozygous for the abnormality generally die—are "selected out"—before they are able to reproduce. Why, then, had this seemingly harmful condition remained in populations from central Africa?

The answer to this mystery began to emerge when it was noticed that the areas with high rates of sickle-cell anemia are also areas in which falciparum malaria is common (Figure 2.5). This particularly deadly form

[8]Boehm, C. (2000). The evolution of moral communities. *School of American Research, 2000 Annual Report, 7.*

[9]Thomson, K. S. (1997). Natural selection and evolution's smoking gun. *American Scientist 85,* 516.

stabilizing selection Natural selection acting to promote stability, rather than change, in a population's gene pool.
sickle-cell anemia An inherited form of anemia caused by a mutation in the hemoglobin protein that causes the red blood cells to assume a sickle shape.

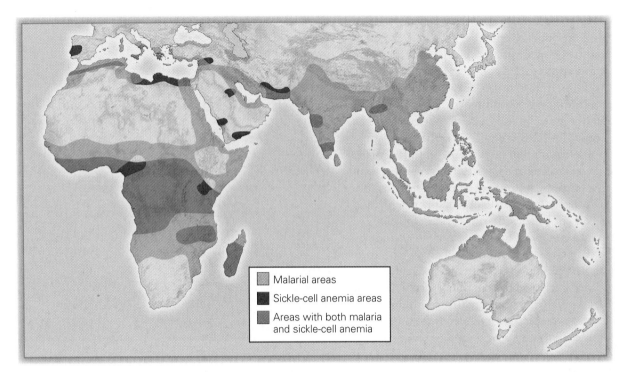

Figure 2.5
The allele that, in homozygotes, causes sickle-cell anemia makes heterozygotes resistant to falciparum malaria. Thus, the allele is most common in populations native to regions where this strain of malaria is common.

of malaria causes high fevers that significantly interfere with the reproductive abilities of those who do not actually die from the disease. Moreover, it was discovered that the same hemoglobin abnormalities are found in people living in parts of the Arabian Peninsula, Greece, Algeria, Syria, and India—all regions where falciparum malaria is (or was) common.

Further research established that the abnormal hemoglobin was associated with an increased ability to survive the effects of the malarial parasite; it seems that the effects of the abnormal hemoglobin in limited amounts were less injurious than the effects of the malarial parasite. Thus, selection favored heterozygous individuals (HbᴬHbˢ). The loss of alleles for abnormal hemoglobin caused by the death of those homozygous for it (from sickle-cell anemia) was balanced out by the loss of alleles for normal hemoglobin, as those homozygous for it experienced reproductive failure.

Expression of normal versus sickle hemoglobin in a heterozygous individual represents an example of incomplete dominance. The sickle abnormality is caused by a change in a single base pair in the DNA of the hemoglobin gene. The resulting mutant allele codes for an amino acid substitution in the hemoglobin protein that leads red blood cells to take on a characteristic sickle shape. In homozygous individuals with two sickle-hemoglobin alleles, collapse and clumping of the abnormal red cells blocks the capillaries and creates tissue damage—causing the symptoms of sickle-cell disease. Afflicted individuals commonly die before reaching adulthood.

The homozygous dominant condition (HbᴬHbᴬ; normal hemoglobin is known as hemoglobin A, not to be confused with blood type A) produces only normal molecules of hemoglobin whereas the heterozygous condition (HbᴬHbˢ) produces some percentage of normal and some percentage of abnormal hemoglobin. Except under low oxygen or other stressful conditions, such individuals suffer no ill effects. The heterozygous condition can actually improve individuals' resilience to malaria relative to the "normal" homozygous condition.

This example points out how adaptations tend to be specific; the abnormal hemoglobin was an adaptation to the particular parts of the world in which the malarial parasite flourished. When Africans adapted to that region were brought to North America, where in recent times falciparum malaria is almost never seen, what had been an adaptive characteristic became an injurious one. Where there was no malaria to attack those with normal hemoglobin, the abnormal hemoglobin became comparatively disadvantageous.

Although the rates of sickle-cell trait are still relatively high among African Americans—about 9 percent show the sickling trait—this represents a significant decline from the approximately 22 percent who are estimated to have shown the trait when the first slaves were brought from Africa. A further decline over the next several generations is to be expected, as selection pressure continues to work against the frequency of the sickle-cell allele.

This example also illustrates the important role culture may play even with respect to biological adaptation. In Africa, falciparum malaria was not a significant problem until humans abandoned food foraging for farming a few thousand years ago. In order to farm, people had to clear areas of the natural forest cover. In the forest, decaying vegetation on the forest floor had imparted an absorbent quality to the ground so that the heavy rainfall of the region rapidly soaked into the soil. But once stripped of its natural vegetation, the soil lost this quality. Furthermore, the forest canopy was no longer there to break the force of the rainfall, and so the impact of the heavy rains tended to compact the soil further.

The result was that stagnant puddles commonly formed after rains, providing the perfect breeding environment for the type of mosquito that is the host to the malarial parasite. These mosquitoes then began to flourish and transmit the malarial parasite to humans. Thus, humans unwittingly created the kind of environment that made a hitherto disadvantageous trait, the abnormal hemoglobin associated with sickle-cell anemia, advantageous.

Natural Selection, Time, and Nonadaptive Traits

Although it is true that all living organisms have many adaptive characteristics, it is not true that all characteristics are adaptive. All male mammals, for example, possess nipples, even though they serve no useful purpose. To female mammals, however, nipples are essential to reproductive success, which is why males have them. The two sexes are not separate entities, shaped independently by natural selection, but are variants upon a single body plan, elaborated in later embryology. Precursors of mammary glands are built in all mammalian fetuses, enlarging later in the development of females, but remaining small and without function in males.

Nor is it true that current utility is a reliable guide to historical origin or future use. For one thing, nonadaptive characters may be co-opted for later utility following origins as developmental consequences of changing patterns in embryonic and postnatal growth. The unusually large size of a kiwi's egg, for example, enhances the survivability of kiwi chicks, in that they are particularly large and capable when hatched.

Otorohanga Zoological Society

This x-ray showing the unusually large size of a kiwi egg illustrates that evolution does not proceed by preplanned design but rather by a process of tinkering with preexisting body forms.

Nevertheless, kiwi eggs probably did not evolve such large size because it is adaptive. Kiwis evolved from large, moa-sized ancestors, and in birds, egg size reduces at a slower rate than does body size. Therefore, the outsized eggs of kiwi birds seem to be no more than a developmental by-product of a reduction in body size.[10] Similarly, an existing adaptation may come under strong selective pressure for some new purpose, as did insect wings. These did not arise so that insects might fly, but rather as structures that were used to "row," and later skim, across the surface of the water.[11] Later, the larger ones by chance proved useful for purposes of flight. In both these cases, what we see is natural selection operating as "a creative scavenger, taking what is available and putting it to new use."[12]

As primatologist Frans de Waal notes, "Evolution is a magnificent idea that has won over essentially everyone in the world willing to listen to scientific arguments."[13] We will return to the topic in Chapter 5, as we look at how the primates evolved to produce the many species in the world today. First, however, we will survey the living primates (in Chapter 3) in order to understand the kinds of animals they are, what they have in common, and what distinguishes the various forms.

[10]Gould, S. J. (1991). *Bully for brontosaurus* (pp. 109–123). New York: Norton.

[11]Kaiser, J. (1994). A new theory of insect wing origins takes off. *Science 266,* 363.

[12]Doist, R. (1997). Molecular evolution and scientific inquiry, misperceived. *American Scientist 85,* 475.

[13]de Waal, F. (2001). Sing the song of evolution. *Natural History 110*(8), 77.

Questions for Reflection

1. Has a scientific understanding of the human genetic code challenged you to rethink your conception of what it means to be human? How much of your life, or of the lives of the people around you, is dictated by the structure of DNA?

2. Creation myths and evolutionary theories for human origins share a number of features but differ in critical ways. Is it possible for spiritual and scientific models of human origins to co-exist? How?

3. What do you think about genetic testing for diseases? Would you like to know if you carry the recessive allele for a harmful condition?

4. The four evolutionary forces—mutation, genetic drift, gene flow, and natural selection—all exert effects on biological variation. Some are at work in individuals while others function at the population level. Compare and contrast these evolutionary forces, outlining their contributions to biological variation.

5. The frequency of the sickle-cell allele in populations provides a classic example of adaptation on a genetic level. Describe the adaptive benefits of this deadly allele. Are mutations good or bad?

Suggested Readings

Berra, T. M. (1990). *Evolution and the myth of creationism.* Stanford, CA: Stanford University Press.

Written by a zoologist, this book is a basic guide to the facts in the debate over evolution. It is not an attack on religion but a successful effort to assist in understanding the scientific basis for evolution.

Eugenides, J. (2002). *Middlesex: A novel.* New York: Farrar, Straus and Giroux.

This fascinating novel explores the lives of a family carrying a recessive allele that results in hermaphroditic phenotype in the third generation. It demonstrates the intersection of genetics and culture, deals with age-old questions of nature versus nurture, and explores the importance of the cultural meaning given any phenotypic state.

Gould, S. J. (1996). *Full house: The spread of excellence from Plato to Darwin.* New York: Harmony.

In this highly readable book, Gould explodes the misconception that evolution is inherently progressive. In the process, he shows how trends should be read as changes in variation within systems.

Rapp, R. (1999). *Testing the woman, testing the fetus: The social impact of amniocentesis in America.* New York: Routledge.

This beautifully written, meticulously researched book provides an in-depth historical and sophisticated cultural analysis, as well as a deeply felt personal account of the geneticization of reproduction in America. It demonstrates the importance of cultural analyses of science without ever resorting to an antiscientific stance.

Ridley, M. (1999). *Genome: The autobiography of a species in 23 chapters.* New York: HarperCollins.

Written just as the mapping of the human genome was about to be announced, this book made the *New York Times* bestseller list. The twenty-three chapters discuss DNA on each of the twenty-three human chromosomes. A word of warning, however: The author uncritically accepts some ideas (one example relates to IQ). Still, there's much food for thought here.

Zimmer, C. (2001). *Evolution: The triumph of an idea.* New York: HarperCollins.

This is the companion volume to the seven-part television series broadcast by PBS in fall 2001 covering a broad range of topics in modern evolutionary biology in a readable manner. Though it may pay too much attention to the tension between contemporary biblical literalism and the life sciences, it provides a good basic reference.

Thomson Audio Study Products

 Enjoy the MP3-ready Audio Lecture Overviews for each chapter and a comprehensive audio glossary of key terms for quick study and review. Whether walking to class, doing laundry, or studying at your desk, you now have the freedom to choose when, where, and how you interact with your audio-based educational media. See the preface for information on how to access this on-the-go study and review tool.

The Anthropology Resource Center

www.thomsonedu.com/anthropology
The Anthropology Resource Center provides extended learning materials to reinforce your understanding of key concepts in the four subfields of anthropology. For each of the four subdisciplines, the Resource Center includes dynamic exercises including video exercises, map exercises, simulations, and "Meet the Scientists" interviews, as well as critical thinking questions that can be assigned and e-mailed to instructors. The Resource Center also provides breaking news in anthropology and interesting material on applied anthropology to help you link what you are learning to the world around you.

3 Living Primates

Fotostock/SuperStock

CHALLENGE ISSUE

Other primates have long fascinated humans owing to our many shared anatomical and behavioral characteristics. Our similarities are evident in the way these Japanese macaques, a species of Old World monkey, enjoy a hot tub on a cold day, much in the same way that a human would. Our differences, however, have had devastating consequences for our closest living relatives in the animal world. As a result of human destruction of primate habitats and hunting of primates for bush-meat or souvenirs, seventy-six primate species are now in danger of extinction. In the 21st century, humans face the challenge of making sure that other primates do not go extinct due to human actions.

What Is the Place of Humanity among the Other Animals?

Biologists classify humans as belonging to the primate order, a mammalian group that also includes lemurs, lorises, tarsiers, monkeys, and apes. Among the primates, humans are most closely related to the apes, particularly to chimpanzees, bonobos, and gorillas. A common evolutionary history is responsible for the characteristics shared by humans and other primates. By studying the anatomy, physiology, and molecular structure of the other primates, we can gain a better understanding of what human characteristics we owe to our general primate ancestry and what traits are uniquely human.

What Are the Characteristics of the Primates Inhabiting the World Today?

Compared to other mammals, primates possess a relatively unspecialized anatomy, while their behavioral patterns are diverse and flexible. Although the earliest primates were active at night and tree dwelling, relatively few of today's primates still behave in this way. Most primate groups today live in social groups and are quite active in the day. Brain expansion and development of visual acuity in place of a reliance on sense of smell accompanied this behavioral shift. While some primates still live in the trees, many species today are ground dwelling; some move into the trees only to forage or to sleep at night. A relatively long period of growth and development allows young primates to learn the behaviors of their social group.

Why Do Anthropologists Study the Social Behavior of Primates?

The study of the social behavior of primates has contributed significantly to ecology and evolutionary theory. In addition, analysis of the behavior of monkeys and apes living today—especially those most closely related to us—provides important clues from which to reconstruct the adaptations and behavior patterns involved in the emergence of our earliest ancestors. The more we know about our nearest living relatives, the more it becomes clear that many of the differences between apes and humans reflect differences in degree of expression of shared characteristics.

The diversity of life on earth attests to the fact that the challenge of survival can be solved in many ways. In evolutionary terms, survival means continued existence of the species beyond one individual's lifespan. It includes reproducing subsequent generations and avoiding extinction. Over the course of countless generations, each species has followed its own unique journey, an evolutionary history including random turns as well as patterned adaptation to the environment. Because new species are formed as populations diverge from one another, closely related species resemble one another due to their more recent common ancestry. In other words, closely related species have shared a longer part of their evolutionary journey together. With each step, living creatures can only build on what already exists, making today's diversity a product of tinkering with ancestral body plans, behaviors, and physiology.

In this chapter we will look at the biology and behavior of the primates, the group of animals to which humans belong. By doing so, we will gain a firm understanding of those characteristics we share with other primates, as well as those that distinguish us from them and make us human. By studying social behavior, communication, and tool use among our primate cousins today, we draw closer to an understanding of how and why humans developed as they did.

METHODS AND ETHICS IN PRIMATOLOGY

Just as anthropologists employ diverse methods to study humans, primatologists today use a variety of methods to study the biology, behavior, and evolutionary history of our closest living relatives. Some primatologists concentrate on the comparative anatomy of ancient skeletons, while others trace evolutionary relationships by studying the comparative physiology and genetics of living species. Primatologists study the biology and behavior of living primates both in their natural habitats and in captivity in zoos, primate research colonies, or learning laboratories.

The classic image of a primatologist is someone like Jane Goodall, a world-renowned British researcher who has devoted her career to in-depth observation of chimpanzees in their natural habitat. While documenting the range and nuance of chimpanzee behavior, she has also championed primate habitat conservation and humane treatment of primates in captivity. This philosophy of conservation and preservation has led to further innovations in primate research methods. For example, primatologists have developed a number of noninvasive methods that allow them to link primate biology and behavior

in the field, while minimizing physical disruption. Primatologists gather hair, feces, or other body secretions left by the primates in the environment for later analysis in the laboratory. These analyses provide invaluable information about characteristics such as dietary habits, or genetic relatedness among a group of individuals.

Work with captive animals provides more than knowledge about the basic biology of primates. It has also allowed primatologists to document the "humanity" of our closest living relatives. Many of the amazing linguistic and conceptual abilities of primates became known through captive animal studies. Individual primatologists have devoted their careers to working with primates in captivity, teaching the primate to communicate through pictures on a computer screen or with American Sign Language. Of course, even compassionate captivity imposes stress on primates. Still, the knowledge gained through these studies will contribute ultimately to primate conservation and survival.

At first glance it might seem that work with captive animals is inherently less humane when compared to field studies. But as noted in this chapter's Biocultural Connection, even field studies raise important ethical issues for primatologists to consider. Primatologists must maintain an awareness of how their presence affects the behavior of the group. For example, does becoming tolerant of human observers make the primates more vulnerable? Primates habituated to humans commonly range beyond established preserves and come in close contact with other humans who may be more interested in hunting than observation. Contact between primates and humans can also expose endangered primates to infectious diseases carried by humans. Whether working with primates in captivity or in the field, primatologists seriously consider the well-being of the primates they study.

OUR MAMMALIAN (PRIMATE) HERITAGE

Biologists classify humans within the primate order, a subgroup of the class Mammalia. The other primates include lemurs, lorises, tarsiers, monkeys, and apes. Humans—together with chimpanzees, bonobos, gorillas, orangutans, gibbons, and siamangs—form the hominoids, colloquially known as apes, a superfamily within the primate order. As hominoids, humans are a kind of ape!

The primates are only one of several kinds of mammals, such as rodents, carnivores, ungulates (hoofed mammals), and so on. Primates, like other mammals, are intelligent animals, having more in the way of brains than reptiles or other kinds of vertebrates. This increased brain power, along with the mammalian pattern

Ethics of Great Ape Habituation and Conservation: The Costs and Benefits of Ecotourism ▪

By Michele Goldsmith

For the past ten years I have been studying the impact of habituation for the purpose of ecotourism on mountain gorillas living in Bwindi Impenetrable National Park, Uganda. "Habituation" refers to the acceptance by wild animals of a human observer as a neutral element in their environment. Habituation allows the natural behavior of a species to be observed and documented. Although information from habituated primates has been instrumental in providing a wealth of information for research and conservation, little attention has been given to the costs these animals bear when their fear of humans is removed. As a behavioral ecologist, great ape researcher, and conservationist, I am interested in how their lack of fear of humans influences both their behavior and their well-being.

All great apes are listed as "endangered species," and some subspecies (such as *Gorilla gorilla beringei*) are "critically endangered."[a] Therefore, attempts at research and conservation, such as ecotourism, should improve local population numbers and conditions.

Although I study how habituation influences primate behavior, it is important to note that even the habituation process itself impacts primate behavior. For example, during the habituation process, a group of western lowland gorillas exhibited fear in their vocalizations, increased their aggressive behavior, and changed their daily ranging pattern.[b] Such stress can lead to loss of reproductive function and a weakened immune system. The process can also be dangerous to the people performing the habituation process as many of them have been charged, bitten, and hit.

Unfortunately, gorillas are still hunted for a number of reasons. Gorillas who have lost their fear of humans are especially vulnerable. Five Bwindi gorillas habituated for research were found dead, having been killed by poachers for a young infant. In addition, humans have also brought great instability and warfare to areas where gorilla populations live. Sudden evacuation of research and tourist sites leaves behind habituated gorillas who become easy targets for the poacher's gun.

Courtesy Michele L. Goldsmith/Photograph ©Katherine Hope

With regard to long-term changes in ecology and behavior, my research has shown that the diet, nesting, and ranging patterns of habituated gorilla groups are different from other "wild" gorillas in the same study area. The Nkuringo group, habituated in 1998 for tourism that started in 2004, lives near the edge of the protected preserve. These gorillas spend close to 90 percent of their time outside the national park, in and around human-inhabited areas and farms. These behavioral changes have many costs to the gorillas, such as increased contact with humans and human waste, conflict with farmers that could result in injury, increased exposure to hunting as these areas are mostly open fields, and increased risk of disease transmission.

Another effect on behavior may be an artificial increase in group size. For example, a group of some forty-four animals now exist in the Virungas where the average group size is usually ten individuals. Furthermore, it is thought that, due to their fear of humans, nonhabituated adult male gorillas that would normally challenge other dominant males are either deterred from presenting a challenge or are less successful in their challenge against habituated groups.

Perhaps the biggest threat to habituated great apes is disease. There are over nineteen viruses and eighteen parasites that are known to infect both great apes and humans. These diseases have been responsible for between sixty-three and eighty-seven ape deaths in habituated groups (both research and tourist groups) in the Virungas, Bwindi, Mahale, Tai, and Gombe.[c] As for the gorillas in Bwindi, it has been shown that the prevalence of parasites such as *Crytopsporidium* and *Giardia* are most prevalent in habituated groups living near humans along the border of the park.

In highlighting the costs of habituation in field primatology, as a great ape primatologist, I know full well the benefits that have come out of this process. Weighing these costs and benefits as a biological anthropologist, I wonder if primatological field studies on endangered great apes for the sake of understanding humans is still a viable option. Perhaps primatologists should study apes only when it directly benefits the welfare and conservation of the study animals, rather than our interest or curiosity in learning more ourselves. Ethical considerations are crucial as the numbers of great apes in the wild continue to dwindle. Habituation may not be an ape's salvation.

[a] International Union for Conservation of Nature and Natural Resources (IUCN). (2000).
[b] Blom, A., et al. (2001). A survey of the apes in the Dzanga-Ndoki National Park, Central African Republic. *African Journal of Ecology* 39, 98–105.

[c] Butynski, T. M. (2001). Africa's great apes. In B. Beck et al. (Eds.), *Great apes and humans: The ethics of co-existence* (pp. 3–56). Washington, D.C.: Smithsonian Institution Press.

© Peter Arnold, Inc.

Nursing their young is an important part of the general mammalian tendency to invest high amounts of energy into rearing relatively few young at a time. The reptile pattern is to lay many eggs, with the young fending for themselves. Interestingly, ape mothers, such as this one, tend to nurse their young for up to four or five years. The practice of bottle-feeding infants in the United States and Europe is a massive departure from the ape pattern. Although the health benefits of breastfeeding for mothers (such as lowered breast cancer rates) and children (strengthened immune systems) are clearly documented, cultural norms have presented obstacles to breastfeeding. Across the globe, however, women nurse their children on average for about three years.

of growth and development, forms the biological basis of the flexible behavior patterns typical of mammals. In most species, the young are born live, the egg being retained within the womb of the mother until the embryo achieves an advanced state of growth. Once born, the young receive milk from their mothers' mammary glands, the structures from which the class Mammalia gets its name. During this period of infant dependency, young mammals are able to learn some of the things they will need for survival as adults.

Relative to other members of the animal kingdom, mammals are highly active. This activity is made possible by a relatively constant body temperature, an effi-

cient respiratory system featuring a separation between the nasal (nose) and mouth cavities (allowing them to breathe while they eat), a diaphragm to assist in drawing in and letting out breath, and an efficient four-chambered heart that prevents mixing of oxygenated and deoxygenated blood.

Mammals possess a skeleton in which the limbs are positioned beneath the body, rather than out at the sides. This arrangement allows for direct support of the body and easy flexible movement. The bones of the limbs have joints constructed to permit growth in the young while simultaneously providing strong, hard joint surfaces that will stand up to the stresses of sustained activity. Mammals stop growing when they reach adulthood, while reptiles continue to grow throughout their lives.

The teeth of mammals and reptiles also differ. Reptiles possess identical, pointed, peglike teeth while mammals have teeth specialized for particular purposes: incisors for nipping, gnawing, and cutting; canines for ripping, tearing, killing, and fighting; premolars that may either slice and tear or crush and grind (depending on the kind of animal); and molars for crushing and grinding (Figure 3.1). This enables mammals to eat a wide variety of food—an advantage to them, since they require more food than reptiles to sustain their high activity level. But they pay a price: reptiles have unlimited tooth replacement throughout their lives, whereas mammals are limited to two sets. The first set serves the immature animal and is replaced by the "permanent" or adult teeth. The specializations of mammalian teeth al-

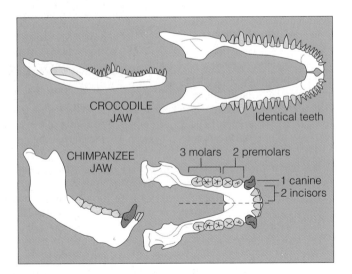

Figure 3.1

The crocodile jaw, like jaws of all reptiles, contains a series of identical teeth. If a tooth breaks or falls out, a new tooth will emerge in its place. Mammals, by contrast, possess precise numbers of specialized teeth, each with a particular shape characteristic of the group, as indicated on the chimpanzee jaw: Incisors in front are shown in blue, canines behind in red, followed by two premolars and three molars in yellow (the last being the wisdom teeth in humans).

low species and evolutionary relationships to be identified through dental comparisons.

Evidence from ancient skeletons indicates that the first mammals appeared over 200 million years ago as small **nocturnal** (active at night) creatures. The earliest primatelike creatures came into being about 65 million years ago when a new mild climate favored the spread of dense tropical and subtropical forests over much of the earth. The change in climate and habitat, combined with the sudden extinction of dinosaurs, favored mammal diversification, including the evolutionary development of **arboreal** (tree-living) mammals from which primates evolved.

The ancestral primates possessed biological characteristics that allowed them to adapt to life in the forests. Their relatively small size enabled them to use tree branches not accessible to larger competitors and predators. Arboreal life opened up an abundant new food supply. The primates were able to gather leaves, flowers, fruits, insects, bird eggs, and even nesting birds, rather than having to wait for them to fall to the ground. Natural selection favored those who judged depth correctly and gripped the branches tightly. Those individuals who survived life in the trees passed on their genes to the succeeding generations. Although the earliest primates were nocturnal, today most primate species are **diurnal** (active in the day). The transition to diurnal life in the trees involved important biological adjustments that helped shape the biology and behavior of humans today.

 THOMSON AUDIO STUDY PRODUCTS Take advantage of the MP3-ready Audio Lecture Overviews and comprehensive audio glossary of key terms for each chapter. See the preface for information on how to access this on-the-go study and review tool.

PRIMATE TAXONOMY

Anthropologists use two classificatory systems to categorize primate species. The older system, dating back to the time of Linnaeus, is based on visible physical characteristics, while a more recent system depends upon genetic analyses. The Linnaean system divides primates into two sub-orders: the **Prosimii** (from the Latin for "before monkeys"), which includes lemurs, lorises, and tarsiers, and the **Anthropoidea** (from the Greek for "humanlike"), which includes monkeys, apes, and humans. This division was based on the overall similarity of the body plans within each group, a phenomenon biologists refer to as a **grade.**

The prosimians have also been called the lower primates because they resemble the earliest fossil primates. On the whole, prosimians are cat-sized or smaller, although some larger forms existed in the past. The prosimians also retain certain features common among nonprimate mammals, such as claws and moist, naked skin on their noses, not retained by the anthropoids.

In Asia and Africa, all prosimians are nocturnal and arboreal creatures—again, like the fossil primates. The isolated but large island of Madagascar, off the coast of Africa, however, is home to a variety of diurnal ground-dwelling prosimians. In the rest of the world, the diurnal (active in daytime) primates are all anthropoids. This group is sometimes called the higher primates, because they appeared later in evolutionary history and because of a lingering belief that the group including humans was more "evolved." From a contemporary biological perspective, no species is more evolved than any other.

The anthropoid suborder is further divided into two infraorders; the **Platyrrhini,** or New World monkeys; and the **Catarrhini,** consisting of the superfamilies Cercopithecoidea (Old World monkeys) and Hominoidea (apes). Although the terms *New World* and *Old World* reflect a Eurocentric vision of history (whereby the Americas were considered new only to European explorers and not to the indigenous people already living there), these terms have evolutionary and geological relevance with respect to primates, as we will see in Chapter 5. Old World monkeys and apes, including humans, have a 40 million-year shared evolutionary history in Africa distinct from the course taken by anthropoid primates in the tropical Americas. "Old World" in this context represents the evolutionary origins of anthropoid primates rather than a political or historical focus on Europe.

Establishing Relationships among the Primates Through Genetics

Molecular evidence has confirmed the close relationship between humans and other primates. Genetic comparisons have also challenged evolutionary relationships that

nocturnal Active at night and at rest during the day.
arboreal Living in the trees.
diurnal Active during the day and at rest at night.
Prosimii A suborder of the primates that includes lemurs, lorises, and tarsiers.
Anthropoidea A suborder of the primates that includes New World monkeys, Old World monkeys, and apes (including humans).
grade A general level of biological organization seen among a group of species, useful for constructing evolutionary relationships.
Platyrrhini An anthropoid infraorder that includes New World monkeys.
Catarrhini An anthropoid infraorder that includes Old World monkeys, apes, and humans.

TABLE 3.1	TWO ALTERNATIVE TAXONOMIES FOR THE PRIMATE ORDER: DIFFERING IN PLACEMENT OF TARSIERS

Suborder	Infraorder	Superfamily (family)	Location
I. Prosimii (lower primates)	Lemuriformes	Lemuroidea (lemurs, indriids, and aye-ayes)	Madagascar
	Lorisiformes	Lorisoidea (lorises)	Asia and Africa
		Tarsioidea (tarsiers)	Asia
Anthropoidea (higher primates)	Platyrrhini (New World monkeys)	Ceboidea	Tropical Americas
	Catarrhini	Cercopithecoidea (Old World monkeys)	Africa and Asia
		Hominoidea (Apes and humans)	Africa and Asia (humans worldwide)
II. Strepsirhini	Lemuriformes	Lemuroidea (lemurs, indriids, and aye-ayes)	Madagascar
	Lorisiformes	Lorisoidea (lorises)	Asia and Africa
Haplorhini	Tarsiiformes	Tarsioidea (tarsiers)	Asia
	Platyrrhini (New World monkeys)	Ceboidea	Tropical Americas
	Catarrhini	Cercopithecoidea (Old World monkeys)	Africa and Asia
		Hominoidea (Apes and humans)	Africa and Asia (humans worldwide)

had been inferred from physical characteristics. Laboratory methods involving genetic comparisons range from scanning species' entire genomes, to comparisons of the precise sequences of base pairs in DNA or amino acids in proteins.

Such research led to the proposal of a new primate taxonomy (Table 3.1). A close genetic relationship was discovered between the tarsiers—nocturnal tree dwellers who resemble lemurs and lorises—and monkeys and apes.[1] The taxonomic scheme reflecting this genetic relationship places lemurs and lorises in the suborder **Strepsirhini** (from the Greek for "turned nose"). Tarsiers are placed with monkeys and apes in the suborder **Haplorhini** (Greek for "simple nose"). Although this classificatory scheme accurately reflects genetic relationships, it is still useful to make comparisons between "grades," or general levels of organization in the older prosimian and anthropoid classification.

[1]Goodman, M., et al. (1994). Molecular evidence on primate phylogeny from DNA sequences. *American Journal of Physical Anthropology 94,* 7.

Strepsirhini In the alternate primate taxonomy, the suborder that includes the lemurs and lorises without the tarsiers.
Haplorhini In the alternate primate taxonomy, the suborder that includes tarsiers, monkeys, apes, and humans.

Most relevant to human evolution, however, are the evolutionary relationships established from the molecular evidence among the hominoids. On the basis of tests with blood proteins and DNA, it has been shown that among the apes, the bonobo, chimpanzee, and gorilla are closest to humans; next comes the orangutan, then the smaller apes (gibbons and siamangs), Old World monkeys, New World monkeys, tarsiers, and then finally the lemurs and lorises (Figure 3.2).

Though the DNA sequence of humans and African apes is 98 percent identical, the organization of DNA into chromosomes differs between humans and the other great apes. Bonobos and chimps, like gorillas and orangutans, have an extra pair of chromosomes compared to humans, in which two medium-sized chromosomes have fused together to form chromosome 2. (The chromosomes are numbered according to their size as they are viewed microscopically, so that chromosome 2 is the second largest of the human chromosomes.) Of the other pairs, eighteen are virtually identical between humans and the genus *Pan,* whereas the remaining ones have been reshuffled.

Overall, the differences are fewer than those between gibbons (with twenty-two pairs of chromosomes) and siamangs (twenty-five pairs of chromosomes)—closely related species that, in captivity, have produced live hybrid offspring. Although some studies of molecular similarities have suggested a closer relationship between *Pan*

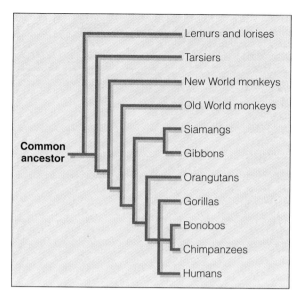

Figure 3.2

Based on molecular similarities and differences, a relationship can be established among various primate groups. Based on molecular evidence, tarsiers are more closely related to monkeys and apes than to the lemurs and lorises that they resemble physically. Present thinking is that the split between the human and African ape lines took place between 5 and 8 million years ago.

and humans than either has to gorillas, others disagree, and the safest course at the moment is to regard all three genera as having an equal degree of relationship (the two species of genus *Pan* are, of course, more closely related to each other than either is to gorillas or humans).[2]

PRIMATE CHARACTERISTICS

While the living primates are a varied group of animals, they do share a number of features. We humans, for example, can grasp, throw, and see in three dimensions because of shared primate characteristics. Compared to other mammals, primates possess a relatively unspecialized anatomy while their behavioral patterns are diverse and flexible.

Many primate characteristics are useful to arboreal animals, although (as any squirrel knows) they are not essential to life in the trees. For animals preying upon the many insects living on the fruit and flowers of trees and shrubs, however, primate characteristics such as dexterous hands and keen vision would have been enormously adaptive. Life in the trees, along with the visual predation of insects, played a role in the evolution of primate biology.

[2]Rogers, J. (1994). Levels of the genealogical hierarchy and the problem of hominid phylogeny. *American Journal of Physical Anthropology 94*, 81.

Primate Dentition

The varied diet available to arboreal primates—shoots, leaves, insects, and fruits—did not require specializations of the teeth seen in other mammals. In most primates (humans included), on each side of each jaw, in front, are two straight-edged, chisel-like broad teeth called incisors (see Figure 3.3). Behind the two incisors is a canine tooth, which in many mammals is large, flaring, and fanglike. The canines are used for defense as well as for tearing and shredding food.

In humans, canine tooth size is relatively small, although it has an oversized root, suggestive of larger canines some time back in our ancestry. Behind the canines are the premolars and molars (the "cheek teeth") for grinding and chewing food. Molars erupt through the gums while a young primate is maturing (6-year molars, 12-year molars, and wisdom teeth in humans). Thus the functions of grasping, cutting, and grinding were served by different kinds of teeth. The exact number of premolars and molars and the shape of individual teeth differ among primate groups (see Table 3.2).

The evolutionary trend for primate dentition has been toward a reduction in the number and size of the teeth. The ancestral **dental formula** or pattern of tooth type and number in mammals consisted of three incisors, one canine, five premolars, and three molars (expressed as 3-1-5-3) on each side of the jaw, top and bottom, for a total of forty-eight teeth. In the early stages of primate evolution, one incisor and one premolar were lost on each side of each jaw, resulting in a dental pattern of 2-1-4-3 in the early fossil primates. This change differentiated the primates from other mammals.

Over the millennia, as the first and second premolars became smaller and eventually disappeared altogether, the third and fourth premolars grew larger and added a second pointed projection, or cusp, thus becoming "bicuspid." In humans, all eight premolars are bicuspid, but in other Old World anthropoids, the lower first premolar is not bicuspid. Instead, it is a specialized, single-cusped tooth with a sharp edge to act with the upper canine as a shearing mechanism. The molars, meanwhile, evolved from a three-cusp pattern to one with four and even five cusps. The five-cusp pattern is characteristic of the lower molars of living and extinct hominoids (Figure 3.3). Because the grooves separating the five cusps of a hominoid lower molar looks like the letter Y, hominoid lower molars are said to have a Y5 pattern. In humans there has

dental formula The number of each tooth type (incisors, canines, premolars, and molars) on one half of each jaw. Unlike other mammals, primates possess equal numbers on their upper and lower jaws so the dental formula for the species is a single series of numbers.

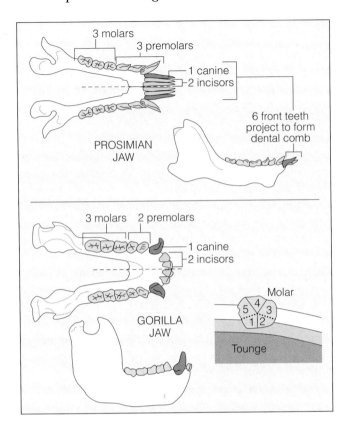

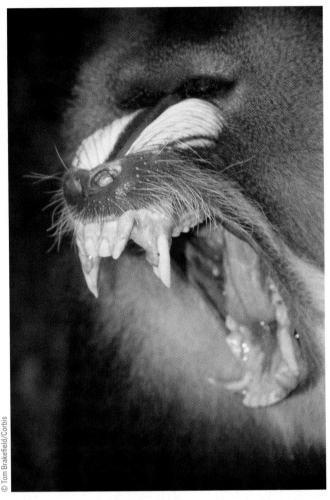

© Tom Brakefield/Corbis

Figure 3.3

Because the exact number and shape of the teeth differs among primate groups, teeth are frequently used to identify evolutionary relationships and group membership. Prosimians (top), with a dental formula of 2-1-3-3, possess two incisors, one canine, three premolars, and three molars on each side of their upper and lower jaws. Also, lower canines and incisors project forward, forming a "dental comb," which they use for grooming. A dental formula of 2-1-2-3, typical of Old World monkeys and apes, can be seen in the gorilla jaw (bottom). Note the large projecting canines. On one of the molars, the cusps are numbered to illustrate the Y5 pattern found in hominoids.

Though the massive canine teeth of some male anthropoids such as this mandrill are serious weapons, they are used more often to communicate rather than to draw blood. Raising his lip to flash his canines to young members of the group will get them in line right away. Over the course of human evolution, overall canine size and sexual dimorphism of the canines reduced. Nevertheless, we associate projecting canines with drawing blood.

been some departure from the Y5 pattern associated with the reduction in tooth and jaw size such that the second and third molars generally have only four cusps. Four- and five-cusp molars economically combined the functions of grasping, cutting, and grinding in one tooth.

The evolutionary trend for human dentition has generally been toward economy, with fewer, smaller, more efficient teeth doing more work. Thus our own thirty-two teeth (a 2-1-2-3 dental formula shared with the Old World monkeys and apes) are fewer in number than those of some, and more generalized than those of most, primates. However, this trend does not indicate that species with more teeth are less evolved, only that their evolutionary history followed different trends.

sexual dimorphism Within a single species, differences in the shape or size of a feature for males and females in body features not directly related to reproduction such as body size or canine tooth shape and size.

The canines of most primates develop into long, daggerlike teeth that enable them to rip open tough husks of fruit and other foods. In many species, males possess larger canine teeth compared to females. This sex difference is an example of **sexual dimorphism**— differences between the sexes in the shape or size of a feature. These large canines are used frequently for social communication. All an adult male gorilla or baboon needs to do to get a youngster to be submissive is to raise his upper lip to display his large, sharp canines.

Sensory Organs

The primates' adaptation to arboreal life involved changes in the form and function of their sensory organs. The sense of smell was vital for the earliest ground-dwelling, night-active mammals. It enabled them to operate in the dark, to sniff out their food, and to detect hidden predators. However, for active tree life during daylight, good vision is a better guide than smell in judging the location of the next branch or tasty morsel. Accordingly, the sense of smell declined in primates, while vision became highly developed.

Travel through the trees demands judgments concerning depth, direction, distance, and the relationships of objects hanging in space, such as vines or branches. Monkeys, apes, and humans achieved this through binocular stereoscopic color vision (Figure 3.4), the ability to see the world in the three dimensions of height, width, and depth. **Binocular vision** (in which two eyes sit next to each other on the same plane so that their visual fields overlap), together with nerve connections that run from each eye to both sides of the brain, confers complete depth perception characteristic of three-dimensional or **stereoscopic vision.** This arrangement allows nerve cells to integrate the images derived from each eye. Increased brain size in the visual area in primates, and a greater complexity at nerve connections, also contribute to stereoscopic color vision.

Visual acuity, however, varies throughout the primate order both in terms of color and spatial perception. Prosimians, most of whom are nocturnal, lack color vision. The eyes of lemurs and lorises (but not tarsiers) are capable of reflecting light off the back of the retina, the surface where nerve fibers gather images in the back of the eye to intensify the limited light available in the forest at night. In addition, prosimian vision is binocular without the benefits of stereoscopy. Their eyes look out from either side of their muzzle or snout. Though there is some overlap of visual fields, their nerve fibers do not cross from each eye to both halves of the brain.

By contrast, monkeys, apes, and humans possess both color and stereoscopic vision. Color vision markedly improves the diet of these primates compared to most other mammals. The ability to distinguish colors promotes the identification of food by allowing anthropoid primates to choose ripe fruits or tender immature leaves due to their red rather than green coloration. In addition, anthropoid primates possess a unique structure called the **fovea centralis,** or central pit, in the retina of each eye. Like a camera lens, this feature enables the animal to focus on a particular object for acutely clear perception without sacrificing visual contact with the object's surrounding.

The primates' emphasis on visual acuity came at the expense of their sense of smell. Smells are processed in the forebrain, a part of the brain that projects into the snout of animals depending upon smells. A large protruding snout, however, may interfere with stereoscopic vision. But smell is an expendable sense to tree-dwelling animals in search of insects; they no longer needed to live a "nose to the ground" existence, sniffing the ground in

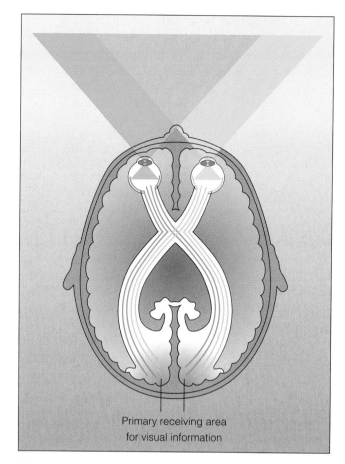

Figure 3.4

Anthropoid primates possess binocular stereoscopic vision. Binocular vision refers to overlapping visual fields associated with forward-facing eyes. Three-dimensional or stereoscopic vision comes from binocular vision and the transmission of information from each eye to both sides of the brain.

Primary receiving area for visual information

search of food. The anthropoids especially have the least-developed sense of smell of all land animals. Though humans can smell fear, distinguish perfumes, and even distinguish family members from strangers, our brains have come to emphasize vision rather than smell. Prosimians, by contrast, still rely more on smell than on vision, possessing numerous scent glands for marking objects in their territories.

Arboreal primates also possess an acute sense of touch. An effective feeling and grasping mechanism

binocular vision Vision with increased depth perception from two eyes set next to each other allowing their visual fields to overlap.

stereoscopic vision Complete three-dimensional vision (or depth perception) from binocular vision and nerve connections that run from each eye to both sides of the brain allowing nerve cells to integrate the images derived from each eye.

fovea centralis A shallow pit in the retina of the eye that enables an animal to focus on an object while maintaining visual contact with its surroundings.

helps prevent them from falling and tumbling while speeding through the trees. The early mammals from which primates evolved possessed tiny touch-sensitive hairs at the tips of their hands and feet. In primates, sensitive pads backed up by nails on the tips of the animals' fingers and toes replaced these hairs.

The Primate Brain

These changes in sensory organs have corresponding changes to the primate brain. In addition, an increase in brain size, particularly in the cerebral hemispheres—the areas supporting conscious thought—occurred in the course of primate evolution. In monkeys, apes, and humans, the cerebral hemispheres completely cover the cerebellum, the part of the brain that coordinates the muscles and maintains body balance.

One of the most significant outcomes of this development is the flexibility seen in primate behavior. Rather than relying on reflexes controlled by the cerebellum, primates constantly react to a variety of features in the environment. Messages from the hands and feet, eyes and ears, as well as from the sensors of balance, movement, heat, touch, and pain, are simultaneously relayed to the cerebral cortex. Obviously the cortex had to evolve considerably in order to receive, analyze, and coordinate these impressions and transmit the appropriate response back down to the motor nerves. The enlarged, responsive, cerebral cortex provides the biological basis for flexible behavior patterns found in all primates, including humans.

The reasons for the increased capacity of the brain for learning are many, but they likely began as the earliest primates, along with many other mammals, began to carry out their activities in the daylight hours. Prior to 65 million years ago, mammals seem to have been nocturnal in their habits. The extinction of the dinosaurs and climate change at that time opened new **ecological niches**—a species' way of life considered in the full context of its environment, including other species, geology, climate, and so on. With the change to a diurnal life, the sense of vision took on greater importance, and so visual acuity was favored by natural selection. Unlike reptile vision, where the information-processing neurons are in the retina, mammalian vision is processed in the brain, permitting integration with information received through sound, touch, taste, and smell.

If the evolution of visual acuity led to larger brains, it is likely that the primates' insect predation in an arboreal setting also played a role in enlargement of the brain. This would have required great agility and muscular coordination, favoring development of the brain centers. Thus it is of interest that much of the higher mental faculties are apparently developed in an area alongside the motor centers of the brain.[3]

Another related hypothesis that may help account for primate brain enlargement involves the use of the hand as a tactile organ to replace the teeth and jaws or snout. The hands assumed some of the grasping, tearing, and dividing functions of the jaws, again requiring development of the brain centers for more complete coordination.

The Primate Skeleton

The skeleton gives animals with internal backbones, or **vertebrates,** their basic shape or silhouette, supports the soft tissues, and helps protect vital internal organs (Figure 3.5). In primates, for example, the skull protects the brain and the eyes. A number of factors are responsible for the shape of the primate skull as compared with those of most other mammals: changes in dentition, changes in the sensory organs of sight and smell, and increased brain size. The primate braincase, or **cranium,** tends to be high and vaulted. A solid partition exists in anthropoid primates between the eye and the temple, affording maximum protection to the eyes from the contraction of the chewing muscles positioned directly next to the eyes.

The **foramen magnum** (the large opening at the base of the skull through which the spinal cord passes and connects to the brain) is an important clue to evolutionary relationships. In most mammals, as in dogs and horses, this opening faces directly backward, with the skull projecting forward from the vertebral column. In humans, by contrast, the vertebral column joins the skull toward the center of its base, thereby placing the skull in a balanced position as required for habitual upright posture. Other primates, though they frequently cling, sit, or hang with their bodies upright, are not as fully committed to such posture as humans and so their foramen magnum is not as far forward.

In anthropoid primates, the snout or muzzle portion of the skull reduced as the acuity of the sense of smell

---

ecological niche A species' way of life considered in the full context of its environment, including factors such as diet, activity, terrain, vegetation, predators, prey, and climate.
vertebrate An animal with a backbone including fish, amphibians, reptiles, birds, and mammals.
cranium The braincase of the skull.
foramen magnum A large opening in the skull through which the spinal cord passes and connects to the brain.

---

[3]Romer, A. S. (1945). *Vertebrate paleontology* (p. 103). Chicago: University of Chicago Press.

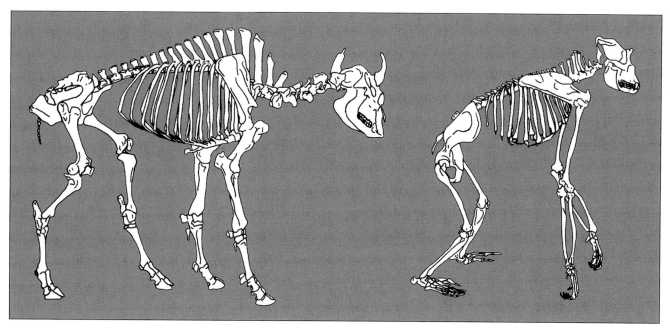

Figure 3.5

All primates possess the same ancestral vertebrate limb pattern as seen in reptiles and amphibians, consisting of a single upper long bone, two lower long bones, and five radiating digits, as seen in this gorilla (right) skeleton. Most other mammals such as bison (left) have modified this pattern in some way. Bison have lost all but two of their digits, and the second long bone in the lower portion of the limb is reduced. Note also that in bison (as in most mammals) the skull projects forward from the vertebral column, but in the semi-erect gorilla, the vertebral column is further beneath the skull.

declined. The smaller snout offers less interference with stereoscopic vision; it also enables the eyes to take a frontal position. As a result, primates have flatter faces than some other mammals.

Below the primate skull and the neck is the **clavicle,** or collarbone, a bone found in ancestral mammals though lost in mammals such as cats. The size of the clavicle is reduced in quadrupedal primates like monkeys that possess a narrow sturdy body plan. In the apes, by contrast, it is broad, orienting the arms at the side rather than at the front of the body and forming part of the **suspensory hanging apparatus** of this group (Table 3.2). The clavicle also supports the **scapula** (shoulder blade) and allows for the muscle development that is required for flexible, yet powerful, arm movement—permitting large-bodied apes to hang suspended below the tree branches and to **brachiate,** or swing from tree to tree.

The limbs of the primate skeleton follow the same basic ancestral plan seen in the earliest vertebrates. Other animals possess limbs specialized to optimize a particular behavior such as speed. In each primate arm or leg, the upper portion of the limb has a single long bone, the lower portion two long bones, and then hands or feet with five radiating digits. Their grasping feet and hands have sensitive pads at the tips of their digits, backed up (except in some prosimians) by flattened nails. This unique combination of pad and nail provides the

animal with an excellent **prehensile** (grasping) device for use when moving from branch to branch. The structural characteristics of the primate foot and hand make grasping possible; the digits are extremely flexible, the big toe is fully **opposable** to the other digits in all but humans and their immediate ancestors, and the thumb is opposable to the other digits to varying degrees.

The retention of the flexible vertebrate limb pattern in primates was a valuable asset to evolving humans. It was, in part, having hands capable of grasping that enabled our own ancestors to manufacture and use tools and to embark on the evolutionary pathway that led to the revolutionary ability to adapt through culture.

clavicle The collarbone connecting the sternum (breastbone) with the scapula (shoulder blade).
suspensory hanging apparatus The broad powerful shoulder joints and muscles found in all the hominoids, allowing these large-bodied primates to hang suspended below the tree branches.
scapula The shoulder blade.
brachiation Using the arms to move from branch to branch, with the body hanging suspended beneath the arms.
prehensile Having the ability to grasp.
opposable Able to bring the thumb or big toe in contact with the tips of the other digits on the same hand or foot in order to grasp objects.

| TABLE 3.2 | PRIMATE ANATOMICAL VARIATION AND SPECIALIZATION | | | |

Primate Group	Skull and Face	Dental Formula and Specializations	Locomotor Pattern and Morphology	Tail and Other Skeletal Specializations
Earliest fossil primates	Eye not fully surrounded by bone	2-1-4-3		
Prosimians	Complete ring of bone surrounding eye Upper lip bound down to the gum Long snout	2-1-3-3 Dental comb for grooming	Hind leg dominance for vertical clinging and leaping	Tail present
Anthropoids	Forward facing eyes fully enclosed in bone Free upper lip Shorter snout			
New World monkeys		2-1-3-3	Quadrupedal	Prehensile (grasping) tail
Old World monkeys		2-1-2-3 Four-cusped molars	Quadrupedal	Tail present
Apes		2-1-2-3 Y5 molars on lower jaw	Suspensory hanging apparatus	No tail

Humans are able to grasp and throw things as they do because of characteristics of their hands and shoulders inherited from ape ancestors. The suspensory hanging apparatus also allows humans to hang from "monkey bars," which should really be called "ape bars."

To sum up, what becomes apparent when humans are compared to other primates is how many of the characteristics we consider distinctly human are not in fact uniquely ours; rather, they are variants of typical primate traits. The fact is, we humans look the way we do *because* we are primates, and the differences between us and others of this order—especially the apes—are more differences of degree than kind.

THE LIVING PRIMATES

Except for a few species of Old World monkeys who live in temperate climates and humans who inhabit the entire globe, the living primates inhabit warm areas of the world. We will briefly explore the diversity of the five natural groupings of living primates: (1) lemurs and lorises, (2) tarsiers, (3) New World monkeys, (4) Old World monkeys, and (5) apes. Each group's distinctive habitat, biological features, and behavior will be examined.

Lemurs, lorises, and tarsiers are the living primates whose anatomy and behavior most closely resembles the ancestral primate condition. Monkeys, apes, and humans resemble one another more than any of these groups resemble lemurs, lorises, and tarsiers. New World and Old World species are separated from one another at the classificatory level of infraorder: the Platyrrhini (New World monkeys) and Catarrhini (Old World monkeys, apes, and humans). Humans are remarkably like monkeys, but we are even more like the other apes, in appearance.

VISUAL **COUNTER**POINT

Wherever there is competition from anthropoid primates, prosimian species, such as this loris on the right, retain the arboreal nocturnal pattern of the earliest fossil primates. Notice its large eyes, long snout, and moist split nose—all useful in its relatively solitary search for food in the trees at night. Only on the large Island of Madagascar off the eastern coast of Africa, where no anthropoids existed until humans arrived there, have prosimians come to occupy the diurnal ground-dwelling niche. Prosimians still rely on smell, marking their territory and communicating through "smelly" messages left for others with a squirt from glands located on their wrists. Though a dependence on smell is a characteristic typical of the earliest fossil primates and the insectivores from which primates evolved, it would be incorrect to think of prosimians as "less evolved."

Lemurs and Lorises

Although lemurs are restricted to the island of Madagascar (off the east coast of Africa), lorises range from Africa to southern and eastern Asia. Only on Madagascar, where there was no competition from anthropoid primates until humans arrived, are lemurs diurnal, or active during the day; lorises, by contrast, are all nocturnal and arboreal.

All these animals are small, with none larger than a good-sized dog. In general body outline, they resemble rodents and insectivores, with short pointed snouts, large pointed ears, and big eyes. In the anatomy of the upper lip and snout, lemurs and lorises resemble nonprimate mammals, in that the upper lip is bound down to the gum, and the naked skin on the nose around the nostrils is moist and split. They also have long tails, with that of a ring-tail lemur somewhat like the tail of a raccoon.

Lemurs and lorises have typical primate "hands," although they use them in pairs, rather than one at a time. Sensitive pads and flattened nails are located at the tips of the fingers and toes, although they retain a claw on their second toe, sometimes called a grooming claw, which they use for scratching and cleaning. Lemurs and lorises possess another unique structure for grooming: a dental comb made up of the lower incisors and canines, which projects forward from the jaw and which can be run through their fur. Behind the incisors and canines,

lemurs and lorises have three premolars and molars, resulting in a dental formula of 2-1-3-3.

The hind legs of lemurs and lorises are longer than their front legs, and when they move on all fours, the forelimbs are in a palms-down position. Some species can also move from tree to tree by vertical clinging and leaping. First they hang onto the trunk of one tree in an upright position, with their long legs curled up tightly like springs and their heads twisted to look in the direction they are moving. They propel themselves into the air, do a "180," and land facing the trunk on their tree of choice.

With their distinctive mix of characteristics, lemurs and lorises appear to occupy a place between the anthropoid primates and insectivores, the mammalian order that includes moles and shrews.

Tarsiers

Outwardly, tarsiers resemble the lemurs and lorises. Molecular evidence, however, indicates a closer relationship to the monkeys, apes, and humans. The head, eyes, and ears of these kitten-sized arboreal creatures are huge in proportion to the body. They have the remarkable ability to turn their heads 180 degrees, so they can see where they have been as well as where they are going. The digits end in platelike adhesive discs. Tarsiers are named for the elongated tarsal, or foot bone, that provides leverage

With their large eyes, tarsiers are well adapted for nocturnal life. If humans possessed eyes proportionally the same size as tarsiers relative to the size of our faces, our eyes would be approximately the size of oranges. In their nocturnal habit and outward appearance, tarsiers resemble the lemurs and lorises. Genetically, however, they are more closely related to monkeys and apes, causing scientists to rework the suborder divisions in primate taxonomy to reflect this evolutionary relationship.

for jumps of 6 feet or more. Tarsiers are mainly nocturnal insect eaters and so occupy a niche that is similar to that of the earliest ancestral primates. In the structure of the nose and lips, and the part of the brain governing vision, tarsiers resemble monkeys.

New World Monkeys

New World monkeys live in tropical forests of South and Central America. They are characterized by flat noses with widely separated, outward-flaring nostrils, from which comes their name of platyrrhine (from the Greek for "flat nosed") monkeys. All are arboreal and possess long tails, which in some groups are prehensile or grasping and used as a fifth limb. The naked skin on the undersides of their tails resembles the sensitive skin found at the tips of our fingers and is even covered with whorls like fingerprints. These features and a 2-1-3-3 dental formula (three, rather than two, premolars on each side of each jaw) distinguish them from the Old World monkeys, apes, and humans.

Platyrrhines walk on all fours with their palms down and scamper along tree branches in search of fruit, which they eat sitting upright. Although New World monkeys spend much of their time in the trees, they rarely hang suspended below the branches or swing from limb to limb by their arms and have not developed the extremely long forelimbs and broad shoulders characteristic of the apes.

Old World Monkeys

Old World or catarrhine (from the Greek for "sharp nosed") primates are characterized by noses with closely spaced, downward-pointing nostrils. The Old World monkeys, divided from the apes at the taxonomic level of superfamily, possess a 2-1-2-3 dental formula (two, rather than three, premolars on each side of each jaw) and nonprehensile tails. They may be either arboreal or terrestrial, using a quadrupedal pattern of locomotion on the ground or in the trees in a palms-down position. Their body plan is narrow with hind limbs and forelimbs of equal length, a reduced clavicle (collarbone), and relatively fixed and sturdy shoulder, elbow, and wrist joints. The arboreal species include the guereza monkey, the Asiatic langur, and the strange-looking proboscis monkey. Some are equally at home on the ground and in the trees, such as the macaques, of which some nineteen species range from tropical Africa

Grasping hands and three-dimensional vision enable primates like these South American monkeys to effectively lead active lives in the trees. In some New World monkey species, a grasping or prehensile tail makes life in the trees even easier. The naked skin on the undersides of their tails resembles the sensitive skin found at the tips of our fingers and is even covered with whorls like fingerprints. This sensory skin allows New World monkeys to use their tails as a fifth limb.

The behavior of baboons, a kind of Old World monkey, has been particularly well studied. There are several distinct species of baboon, each with their own social rules. In the troops of hamadryas baboons (pictured), the sacred baboons of ancient Egypt, each male has a harem of females over which he dominates. Female hamadryas baboons, if transferred to a troop of olive baboons, where females are less submissive, maintain the passive behaviors learned in their original troop. But a female olive baboon placed in the hamadryas troop quickly learns submissive behaviors in order to survive.

and Asia to Gibraltar on the southern coast of Spain to Japan.

Some species of baboon, a kind of Old World monkey, have been of particular interest to paleoanthropologists because they live in environments similar to those in which humans may have originated. These baboons have abandoned trees (except for sleeping and refuge) and are largely terrestrial, living in the savannahs, deserts, and highlands of Africa. They have long, fierce faces and eat a diet of leaves, seeds, insects, and lizards. They live in large, well-organized troops comprised of related females and adult males that have transferred out of other troops. Other species of baboons live in different environments.

Small and Great Apes

The apes of the hominoid superfamily are the closest living relatives we humans have in the animal world. Like us, apes are large wide-bodied primates with no tails. As described earlier in this chapter, apes possess a shoulder anatomy specialized for hanging suspended below tree branches. All apes possess this suspensory hanging apparatus, though among apes only small lithe gibbons and talented gymnasts swing from branch to branch in the pattern known as brachiation. At the opposite extreme are gorillas, which generally climb trees, using their prehensile hands and feet to grip the trunk and branches. While smaller gorillas may swing between branches, in large individuals swinging is limited to leaning outward while reaching for fruit and clasping a limb for support. Still, most of their time is spent on the ground. All apes

While all apes or hominoids possess a suspensory hanging apparatus that allows them to hang from the branches of the forest canopy, only the gibbon is a master of brachiation—swinging from branch to branch. The nonhuman hominoids can also walk bipedally for brief periods of time when they need their arms free for carrying something, but they cannot sustain bipedal locomotion for more than 50 to 100 yards. Hominoid anatomy is better adapted to knuckle-walking and hanging in the trees.

except humans and their immediate ancestors possess arms that are longer than their legs.

In moving on the ground, the African apes "knuckle-walk" on the backs of their hands, resting their weight on the middle joints of the fingers. They stand erect when reaching for fruit, looking over tall grass, or in any activity where they find an erect position advantageous. The semi-erect position is natural in apes when on the ground because the curvature of their vertebral column places their center of gravity, which is high in their bodies, in front of their hip joint. Thus, they are both "top heavy" and "front heavy." Though apes can walk on two legs, or bipedally, for short distances, the structure of the ape pelvis is not well suited to support the weight of the torso and limbs for more than several minutes.

Gibbons and siamangs, the small apes that are native to Southeast Asia and Malaya, have compact, slim bodies with extraordinarily long arms compared to their short legs and stand about 3 feet high. Although their usual form of locomotion is brachiation, they can run erect, holding their arms out for balance. Gibbon and siamang males and females are similar in size, living in family groups of two parents and offspring.

Orangutans are found in Borneo and Sumatra. They are considerably taller than gibbons and siamangs and are much heavier, with the bulk characteristic of the great apes. In the closeness of the eyes and facial prominence, an orangutan looks very humanlike. The people of Sumatra gave orangutans their name, "person of the forest," using the Malay term *oran,* which means "person." On the ground, orangutans walk with their forelimbs in a fists-sideways or a palms-down position. They are, however, more arboreal than the African apes. Although sociable by nature, the orangutans of upland

The least well known of the great apes, orangutans also possess incredible intellectual capacities. This adult male holds a stick from which he has stripped off all side twigs so that he can use it as a probe to extract termites, ants, or honey.

Borneo spend most of their time alone (except in the case of females with young), as they have to forage over a wide area to obtain sufficient food. By contrast, fruits and insects are sufficiently abundant in the swamps of Sumatra to sustain groups of adults and permit coordinated group travel. Thus, gregariousness is a function of habitat productivity.[4]

Gorillas, found in equatorial Africa, are the largest of the apes; an adult male can weigh over 450 pounds, with females about half that size. The body is covered with a thick coat of glossy black hair, and mature males have a silvery gray upper back. There is a strikingly human look about the face, and like humans, gorillas focus on things in their field of vision by directing the eyes rather than moving the head.

Gorillas are mostly ground dwellers, but the lighter females and young may sleep in trees in carefully constructed nests. Because of their weight, adult males spend less time in the trees but raise and lower themselves among the tree branches when searching for fruit. Gorillas knuckle-walk, using all four limbs with the fingers of the hand flexed, placing the knuckles instead of the palm of the hand on the ground. They stand erect to reach for fruit, to see something more easily, or to threaten perceived sources of danger with their famous chest-beating displays. Though known for these displays to protect the members of their troop, adult male silverback gorillas are the gentle giants of the forest. As vegetarians, gorillas devote a major portion of each day to eating volumes of plant matter to sustain their massive bodies. Although gorillas are gentle and tolerant, bluffing is an important part of their behavioral repertoire.

Chimpanzees and bonobos are two closely related species of the same genus (*Pan*), pictured frequently throughout this chapter. Bonobos are restricted in their distribution to the rainforests of the Democratic Republic of Congo. The common chimpanzee, by contrast, is widely distributed in the forested portions of sub-Saharan Africa. Chimpanzees and bonobos are probably the best known of the apes and have long been favorites in zoos and circuses. In the past, bonobos were known as pygmy chimpanzees—not because they are smaller than the common chimps but due to prejudices linking African pygmy people to the apes.

Although thought of as particularly quick and clever, all four great apes are of equal intelligence, despite some differences in cognitive styles. More arboreal than gorillas, but less so than orangutans, chimpanzees and bonobos forage on the ground much of the day, knuckle-walking like gorillas. At sunset, they return to the trees, where they build their nests.

[4]Normile, D. (1998). Habitat seen as playing larger role in shaping behavior. *Science 279,* 1,454.

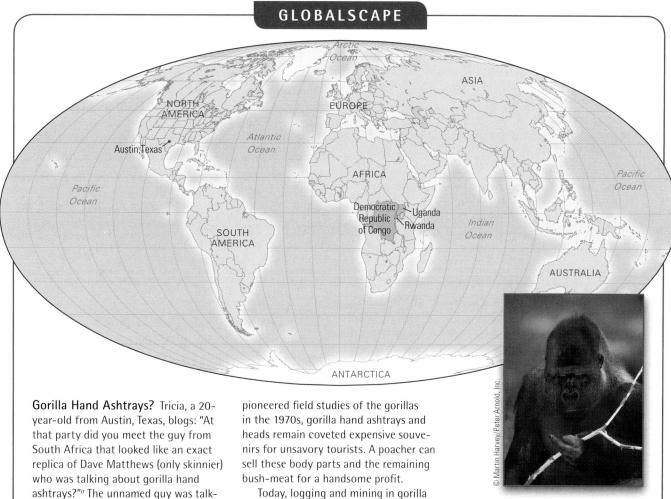

GLOBALSCAPE

Gorilla Hand Ashtrays? Tricia, a 20-year-old from Austin, Texas, blogs: "At that party did you meet the guy from South Africa that looked like an exact replica of Dave Matthews (only skinnier) who was talking about gorilla hand ashtrays?"[a] The unnamed guy was talking about one of the many real threats to gorillas in the wild. With no natural enemies, human actions alone are responsible for the shrinking population size of gorillas in their natural habitats in Rwanda, Uganda, and the Congo. Despite conservation work, begun by the late primatologist Dian Fossey who

[a]http://profile.myspace.com/index.cfm ?fuseaction=user.viewprofile&friendid =40312227. Accessed July 3, 2006.

pioneered field studies of the gorillas in the 1970s, gorilla hand ashtrays and heads remain coveted expensive souvenirs for unsavory tourists. A poacher can sell these body parts and the remaining bush-meat for a handsome profit.

Today, logging and mining in gorilla habitats not only destroy these forests, but roads make it easier for poachers to access the gorillas. Local governments of Rwanda and Uganda in partnership with the Fossey Fund and the Bush Meat Project have set up poaching patrols and community partnerships to protect the endangered gorillas. Thousands of miles away, Tricia and her friends can also help by recycling their cell phones. The mineral coltan that is found in cell phones is mined primarily from gorilla habitats

in the Democratic Republic of Congo. Recycling will reduce the amount of new coltan needed.

Global Twister Encouraging recycling of cell phones and discouraging poaching both will impact gorilla survival. How would you go about convincing the average cell phone user or the poacher to change their habits and/or livelihood to protect endangered gorillas?

© Martin Harvey/Peter Arnold, Inc.

PRIMATE SOCIAL BEHAVIOR

In addition to the physical resemblance between human beings and other catarrhine primates, striking similarities in social behavior also exist. These primates spend more time reaching adulthood compared to many other mammals. During their lengthy growth and development, young primates learn the behaviors of their social group.

Observations of primates in their natural habitats over the past decades have shown that social organization, learning, reproduction and care of the young, and communication among our primate relatives have many similarities to humans, differing in degree, rather than in kind. Because the full range of primate behavior is beyond the scope of this book, we shall focus upon the behavior of those species most closely related to humans: bonobos, chimpanzees, and gorillas.

The Group

Primates are social animals, living and traveling in groups that vary in size from species to species. Among chimps and bonobos, the largest social organizational unit is the **community,** composed of fifty or more individuals who collectively inhabit a large geographic area. Rarely, however, are all these animals together at one time. Instead, they are usually found ranging singly or in small subgroups consisting of adult males together, females with their young, or males and females together with young. In the course of their travels, subgroups may join forces and forage together, but sooner or later these subgroups break up again into smaller units. When they do, some individuals split off and others join, so that the new subunits may be different in their composition from the ones that initially came together.

The gorilla group is a "family" of five to twenty individuals led by a mature, silver-backed male and including younger (black-backed) males, females, the young, and occasionally other silverbacks. Subordinate males, however, are usually prevented by the dominant male from mating with the group's females. Thus, young silverbacks often leave their **natal group**—the community they have known since birth—to start their own social group by winning outside females. If the dominant male is weakening with age, however, one of his sons may remain with the group to succeed to his father's position. Alternatively, an outside male may take over the group. Unlike chimpanzees, gorillas rarely fight over food, territory, or sex but will fight fiercely to maintain the integrity of the group.

In many primate species, including humans, adolescence is a time during which individuals change the relationships they have had with their natal group. Among primates this change takes the form of migration to new social groups. In many species, females constitute the core of the social system. For example, offspring tend to remain with the group to which their mother, rather than their father, belongs. Among gorillas, male adolescents leave their natal groups more frequently than females. However, adolescent female chimpanzees and bonobos are frequently the ones to migrate.

In two Tanzanian chimpanzee communities studied, about half of females may leave the community they have known since birth to join another group.[5] Other females may also temporarily leave their group to mate with males of another group. Among bonobos, adolescent females appear to always transfer to another group, where they promptly establish bonds with females of their new group. While biological factors such as the hormonal influences on sexual maturity play a role in adolescent migration, the variation across species, and within the chimpanzees in dispersal patterns, indicates that differences may also derive from the learned social traditions of the group.

Relationships among individuals within the ape community are relatively harmonious. In the past, primatologists believed that male **dominance hierarchies,** in which some animals outrank and could dominate others, formed the basis of primate social structures. They noted that physical strength and size play a role in determining an animal's rank. By this measure males generally outrank females.

However, the gender-biased cultures of the human primatologist contributed disproportionately to this theory, with its emphasis on domination through superior size and strength. Male dominance hierarchies seemed "natural" to the early primatologists who often came from human social systems organized according to similar principles. With the benefit of detailed field studies over the last forty years, many of which were pioneered by female primatologists like Jane Goodall (see Anthropologists of Note), the nuances of primate social behavior and the importance of female primates has been documented. High-ranking (alpha) females may dominate low-ranking males. In groups such as bonobos, females dominate overall. While strength and size contribute to an animal's rank, other important factors include the rank of its mother and effectiveness at creating alliances with other individuals. For males, drive or motivation to achieve high status also influences rank. For example, in the community studied by Goodall, one male chimp hit upon the idea of incorporating noisy kerosene cans into his charging displays, thereby intimidating all the other males.[6] As a result, he rose from relatively low status to the number one (alpha) position.

Among bonobos, female–female bonds play an important role in determining rank. Further, the strength of the bond between mother and son may interfere with the ranking among males. Not only do bonobo males defer to females in feeding, but alpha females have been observed chasing high-ranking males. Alpha males even yield to low-ranking females, and groups of females form alliances in which they may cooperatively attack males,

community A unit of primate social organization composed of fifty or more individuals who inhabit a large geographic area together.

natal group The group or the community an animal has inhabited since birth.

dominance hierarchies An observed ranking system in primate societies ordering individuals from high (alpha) to low standing corresponding to predictable behavioral interactions including domination.

[5]Moore, J. (1998). Comment. *Current Anthropology 39,* 412.

[6]Goodall, J. (1986). *The chimpanzees of Gombe: Patterns of behavior* (p. 424). Cambridge, MA: Belknap Press.

Jane Goodall (b. 1934) ▪ Kinji Imanishi (1902–1992)

In July 1960, **Jane Goodall** arrived with her mother at the Gombe Chimpanzee Reserve on the shores of Lake Tanganyika in Tanzania. Goodall was the first of three women Kenyan anthropologist Louis Leakey sent out to study great apes in the wild (the others were Dian Fossey and Birute Galdikas, who were to study gorillas and orangutans, respectively); her task was to begin a long-term study of chimpanzees. Little did she realize that, more than forty years later, she would still be at it.

Born in London, Jane grew up and was schooled in Bournemouth, England. As a child, she dreamed of going to live in Africa, so when an invitation arrived to visit a friend in Kenya, she jumped at the opportunity. While in Kenya, she met Leakey, who gave her a job as an assistant secretary. Before long, she was on her way to Gombe. Within a year, the outside world began to hear the most extraordinary things about this pioneering woman: tales of tool-making apes, cooperative hunts by chimpanzees, and what seemed like exotic chimpanzee rain dances. By the mid-1960s, her work had earned her a doctorate from Cambridge University, and Gombe was on its way to

becoming one of the most dynamic field stations for the study of animal behavior anywhere in the world.

Although Goodall is still very much involved with her chimpanzees, she spends a good deal of time these days lecturing, writing, and overseeing the work of others. She also is heavily committed to primate conservation, and no one is more dedicated to efforts to halt the illegal trafficking in chimps nor a more eloquent champion of humane treatment of captive chimpanzees.

Kinji Imanishi, a naturalist, explorer, and mountain climber, profoundly influenced primatology in Japan and throughout the world. Like all Japanese scholars, he was fully aware of Western methods and theories but developed a radically different approach to the scientific study of the natural world.

He dates his transformation to a youthful encounter with a grasshopper: "I was walking along a path in a valley, and there was a grasshopper on a leaf in a shrubbery. Until that moment I had happily caught insects, killed them with chloroform, impaled them on pins, and looked up their names, but I realized I knew nothing at all about how this grasshopper lived in the wild."[a] In his most important work, *The World of Living Things,* first published in 1941, Imanishi developed a comprehensive theory about the natural world rooted in Japanese cultural beliefs and practices.

Imanishi's work challenged Western evolutionary theory in several ways. First, Imanishi's theory, like Japanese culture, does not emphasize differences between

humans and other animals. Second, rather than focusing on the biology of individual organisms, Imanishi suggested that naturalists examine "specia" (a species society) to which individuals belong as the unit of analysis. Rather than focusing on time, Imanishi emphasized space in his approach to the natural world. He highlighted the harmony of all living things rather than conflict and competition among individual organisms.

Imanishi's research techniques, now standard worldwide, developed directly from his theories: long-term field study of primates in their natural societies using methods from ethnography.

Imanishi and his students conducted pioneering field studies of African apes, and Japanese and Tibetan macaques, long before Louis Leakey sent the first Western primatologists into the field. Japanese primatologists were the first to document the importance of kinship, the complexity of primate societies, patterns of social learning, and the unique character of each primate social group. Because of the work by Imanishi and his students, we now think about the distinct cultures of primate societies.

© Bunataro Imanishi

© Michael Nichols/National Geographic Image Collection

---

[a]Heita, K. (1999). Imanishi's world view. *Journal of Japanese Trade and Industry 18*(2), 15.

---

to the point of inflicting blood-drawing injuries.[7] Thus, instead of the male dominance characteristic of chimps, one sees female dominance.

Western primatologists' focus on social rank and attack behavior may be a legacy of the militaristic, competitive nature of the societies in which evolutionary theory originated. To a certain degree, natural selection

relies upon a struggle between living creatures rather than peaceful coexistence. By contrast, noted Japanese primatologist Kinji Imanishi (see Anthropologists of Note) developed a harmonious theory of evolution and initiated field studies of bonobos that have demonstrated the importance of social cooperation rather than competition. As the work of Dutch primatologist Frans de Waal illustrates in the following Original Study, reconciliation after an attack may be even more important from an evolutionary perspective than the actual attack.

---

[7]de Waal, F., Kano, T., & Parish, A. R. (1998). Comments. *Current Anthropology 39*, 408, 410, 413.

Reconciliation and Its Cultural Modification in Primates

Despite the continuing popularity of the struggle-for-life metaphor, it is increasingly recognized that there are drawbacks to open competition, hence that there are sound evolutionary reasons for curbing it. The dependency of social animals on group life and cooperation makes aggression a socially costly strategy. The basic dilemma facing many animals, including humans, is that they sometimes cannot win a fight without losing a friend.

This photo shows what may happen after a conflict—in this case between two female bonobos. About 10 minutes after their fight, the two females approach each other, with one clinging to the other and both rubbing their clitorises and genital swellings together in a pattern known as genito-genital rubbing, or GG-rubbing. This sexual contact, typical of bonobos, constitutes a so-called reconciliation. Chimpanzees, which are closely related to bonobos (and to us: bonobos and chimpanzees are our closest animal relatives), usually reconcile in a less sexual fashion, with an embrace and mouth-to-mouth kiss.

There is now evidence for reconciliation in more than twenty-five different primate species, not just in apes but also in many monkeys. The same sorts of studies have been conducted on human children in the schoolyard, and of course children show reconciliation as well. Researchers have even found reconciliation in dolphins, spotted hyenas, and some other nonprimates. Reconciliation seems widespread: a common mechanism found whenever relationships need to be maintained despite occasional conflict.[a,b]

The definition of reconciliation used in animal research is a friendly reunion between former opponents not long after a conflict. This is somewhat different from definitions in the dictionary, primarily because we look for an empirical definition that is useful in observational studies—in our case, the stipulation that the reunion happen not long after the conflict. There is no intrinsic reason that a reconciliation could not occur after hours or days, or, in the case of humans, generations.

Let me describe two interesting elaborations on the mechanism of reconciliation. One is *mediation*. Chimpanzees are the only animals to use mediators in conflict resolution. In order to be able to mediate conflict, one needs to understand relationships outside of oneself, which may be the reason why other animals fail to show this aspect of conflict resolution.

Two adult female bonobos engage in so-called GG-rubbing, a sexual form of reconciliation typical of this species.

For example, if two male chimpanzees have been involved in a fight, even on a very large island as where I did my studies, they can easily avoid each other, but instead they will sit opposite from each other, not too far apart, and avoid eye contact. They can sit like this for a long time. In this situation, a third party, such as an older female, may move in and try to solve the issue. The female will approach one of the males and groom him for a brief while. She then gets up and walks slowly to the other male, and the first male walks right behind her.

We have seen situations in which, if the first male failed to follow, the female turned around to grab his arm and make him follow. So the process of getting the two males in proximity seems intentional on the part of the female. She then begins grooming the other male, and the first male grooms her. Before long, the female disappears from the scene, and the males continue grooming: She has in effect brought the two parties together.

There exists a limited anthropological literature on the role of conflict resolution, a process absolutely crucial for the maintenance of the human social fabric in the same way that it is crucial for our primate relatives. In human society, mediation is often done by high-ranking or senior members of the community, sometimes culminating in feasts in which the restoration of harmony is celebrated.[c]

The second elaboration on the reconciliation concept is that it is not purely instinctive, not even in our animal relatives. It is a learned social skill subject to what primatologists now increasingly call "culture" (meaning that the behavior is subject to learning from others as opposed to genetic transmission.[d] To test the learnability of reconciliation, I conducted an experiment with young rhesus and stumptail monkeys. Not nearly as conciliatory as stumptail monkeys, rhesus monkeys have the reputation of being rather aggressive and despotic. Stumptails are considered more laid-back and tolerant. We housed members of the two species together for 5 months. By the end of this period, they were a fully integrated group: They slept, played and groomed together.

After 5 months, we separated them again, and measured the effect of their time together on conciliatory behavior.

The research controls—rhesus monkeys who had lived with one an-

[a]de Waal, F. B. M. (2000). Primates—A natural heritage of conflict resolution. *Science 28*, 586–590.

[b]Aureli, F., & de Waal, F. B. M. (2000). *Natural conflict resolution*. Berkeley: University of California Press.

[c]Reviewed by Frye, D. P. (2000). Conflict management in cross-cultural perspective. In F. Aureli & F. B. M. de Waal, *Natural conflict resolution* (pp. 334–351). Berkeley: University of California Press.

[d]See de Waal, F. B. M. (2001). *The ape and the sushi master*. New York: Basic Books, for a discussion of the animal culture concept.

other, without any stumptails—showed absolutely no change in the tendency to reconcile. Stumptails showed a high rate of reconciliation, which was also expected, because they also do so if living together. The most interesting group was the experimental rhesus monkeys, those who had lived with stumptails. These monkeys started out at the same low level of reconciliation as the rhesus controls, but after they had lived with the stumptails, and after we have segregated them again so that they were now housed only with

other rhesus monkeys who had gone through the same experience, these rhesus monkeys reconciled as much as stumptails do. This means that we created a "new and improved" rhesus monkey, one that made up with its opponents far more easily than a regular rhesus monkey.[c]

---

[c]de Waal, F. B. M., & Johanowicz, D. L. (1993). Modification of reconciliation behavior through social experience: An experiment with two macaque species. *Child Development 64*, 897–908.

This was in effect an experiment on social culture: We changed the culture of a group of rhesus monkeys and made it more similar to that of stumptail monkeys by exposing them to the practices of this other species. This experiment also shows that there exists a great deal of flexibility in primate behavior. We humans come from a long lineage of primates with great social sophistication and a well-developed potential for behavioral modification and learning from others.

■

Individual Interaction and Bonding

One of the most notable primate activities is **grooming,** the ritual cleaning of another animal's coat to remove parasites, shreds of grass, or other matter. The grooming animal deftly parts the hair of the one being groomed and removes any foreign object, often eating it. Interestingly, different chimp communities have different styles of grooming. In one East African group, for example, the two chimps groom each other face to face, with one hand, while clasping their partner's free hand. In another group 90 miles distant, the hand clasp is unknown. In East Africa, all communities incorporate leaves in their

grooming, but in West Africa they do not. However hygienic it may be, grooming is also an important gesture of friendliness, submission, appeasement, or closeness. Embracing, touching, and jumping up and down are forms of greeting behavior among chimpanzees. Touching is also a form of reassurance.

Gorillas, though gentle and tolerant, are also aloof and independent, and individual interaction among adults tends to be quite restrained. Friendship or closeness between adults and infants is more evident. Among bonobos, chimpanzees, and gorillas, as among most other primates, the mother–infant bond is the strongest and most long-lasting in the group. It may endure for many years—commonly for the lifetime of the mother. Gorilla infants share their mothers' nests but have also been seen sharing nests with mature, childless females. Bonobo, chimpanzee, and gorilla males are attentive to juveniles and play a role in their socialization. Bonobo males even carry infants on occasion. Their interest in a youngster does not elicit the nervous reaction from the mother that it does among chimps. The latter may relate to the occasional infanticide on the part of chimpanzee males, a behavior never observed among bonobos.

Sexual Behavior

Most mammals mate only during specified breeding seasons occurring once or twice a year, but many primate species are able to breed at any time during the course of the year. Among the African apes, as with humans, no fixed breeding season exists. In chimps, sexual activity—initiated by either the male or the female—occurs

© Anita de Laguna Haviland

Grooming is an important activity among all catarrhine primates, as shown here. Such activity is important for strengthening bonds among individual members of the group.

grooming The ritual cleaning of another animal's coat to remove parasites and other matter.

frequently during **estrus,** the period when the female is receptive to impregnation. In chimpanzees, estrus is signaled by vivid swelling of the skin around the genitals. Bonobo females, by contrast, appear as if they are fertile at all times due to their constantly swollen genitals and interest in sex. Gorillas appear to show less interest in sex compared to either the chimp or bonobos.

By most human standards, chimps' sexual behavior is promiscuous. A dozen or so males have been observed to have as many as fifty copulations in one day with a single female in estrus. For the most part, females mate with males of their own group. Dominant males try to monopolize females in full estrus, although cooperation from the female is usually required for this to succeed. In addition, an individual female and a lower ranking male sometimes form a temporary bond, leaving the group together for a few "private" days during the female's fertile period. Interestingly, the relationship between reproductive success and social rank differs for males and females. In the chimpanzee community studied by Goodall, about half the infants were sired by low- or mid-level males. Although for females high rank is linked with successful reproduction, social success—achieving alpha male status—does not translate neatly into the evolutionary currency of reproductive success.

In contrast to chimpanzees, bonobos (like humans) do not limit their sexual behavior to times of female fertility. Whereas the genitals of chimpanzee females are swollen only at times of fertility, female bonobo genitals are perpetually swollen. The constant swelling, in effect, conceals the females' **ovulation,** or moment when an egg released into the womb is receptive for fertilization. Ovulation is also concealed in humans, by the absence of genital swelling at all times.

Concealed ovulation in humans and bonobos may play a role in the separation of sexual activity for social reasons and pleasure from the purely biological task of reproduction. In fact, among bonobos (as among humans) sexuality goes far beyond male–female mating for purposes of biological reproduction. Primatologists have observed virtually every possible combination of ages and sexes engaging in a remarkable array of sexual activities, including oral sex, tongue-kissing, and massaging each other's genitals.[8] Male bonobos may mount each other, or one may rub his scrotum against that of the other. They have also been observed "penis fencing"—hanging face to face from a branch and rubbing their erect penises together as if crossing swords. Among females, genital rubbing is particularly common. As described in this chapter's Original Study, the primary function of most of this sex, both hetero- and homosexual, is to reduce tensions and resolve social conflicts. Since the documentation of a variety of sexual activities among bonobos, field studies by primatologists working with other species are now recording a variety of sexual behaviors among these species as well.

In gorilla families, the dominant silverback has exclusive breeding rights with the females, although he may allow a young silverback occasional access to a low-ranking female. In one group studied in Rwanda, in which there was more than one adult male, a single male fathered all but one of ten juveniles.[9] So it is that a young silverback must leave "home," luring partners away from other established groups, in order to have reproductive success.

Although the vast majority of primate species are not **monogamous**—bonded exclusively to a single sexual partner—in their mating habits, many smaller species of New World monkeys, a few island-dwelling populations of leaf-eating Old World monkeys, and all of the smaller apes (gibbons and siamangs) appear to mate for life with a single individual of the opposite sex. None of these species is closely related to human beings, nor do monogamous species ever display the degree of sexual dimorphism—anatomical differences between males and females—that is characteristic of our closest primate relatives, or that was characteristic of our own ancient ancestors. Evolutionary biologists propose that sexual dimorphism (for example, larger male size in the apes, beautiful feathers as in peacocks) relates to competition among males for access to females. The variation in ape reproductive behavior suggests that social processes contribute to reproductive success as much as variation in a biological feature such as body size.

Reproduction and Care of Young

The average adult female monkey or ape spends most of her adult life either pregnant or nursing her young, times at which she is not sexually receptive. Apes generally nurse each of their young for about four years. After her infant is weaned, she will come into estrus periodically, until she becomes pregnant again. Many human societies modify the succession of pregnancy and lactation by a variety of cultural means.

---

[8] de Waal, F. (2001). *The ape and the sushi master* (pp. 131–132). New York: Basic Books.

estrus In some primate females, the time of sexual receptivity during which ovulation is visibly displayed.
ovulation Moment when an egg released from the ovaries into the womb is receptive for fertilization.
monogamous Mating for life with a single individual of the opposite sex.

---

[9] Gibbons, A. (2001). Studying humans—and their cousins and parasites. *Science 292,* 627.

Among primates, as among some other mammals, females generally give birth to one infant at a time. Natural selection may have favored single births among primate tree dwellers because the primate infant, which has a highly developed grasping ability (the grasping reflex can also be seen in human infants), must be transported about by its mother, and more than one clinging infant would interfere with movement in the tree tops. Only among the smaller nocturnal prosimians, the primates closest to the ancestral condition, are multiple births common. Among the anthropoids, only the true marmoset has a pattern of habitual twinning. Other species like humans will twin occasionally. In marmosets, both parents share infant care, with fathers doing most of the carrying.

Primates follow a pattern of bearing few young, but devoting more time and effort to the care of each individual offspring. Compared to other mammals such as mice, which pass from birth to adulthood in a matter of weeks, primates spend a great deal of time growing up. As a general rule, the more closely related to humans the species is, the longer the period of infant and childhood dependency (Figure 3.6). For example, a lemur is dependent upon its mother for only a few months after birth, while an ape is dependent for four or five years. A chimpanzee infant cannot survive if its mother dies before it reaches the age of 4 at the very least. During the juvenile period, young primates are still dependent upon the larger social group rather than on their mothers alone, using this period for learning and refining a variety of behaviors. If a juvenile primate's mother dies, he or she will be "adopted" by an older male or female member of the social group.

The long interval between births, particularly among the apes, results in small population sizes in our closest relatives. A female chimpanzee, for example, does not reach sexual maturity until about the age of 10, and once she produces her first live offspring, there is a period of five or six years before she will bear another. Thus, assuming that none of her offspring die before adulthood, a female chimpanzee must survive for at least twenty or twenty-one years just to maintain the size of chimpanzee populations at existing levels. In fact, chimpanzee infants and juveniles do die from time to time, and not all females live full reproductive lives. This is one reason why apes are far less abundant in the world today than are monkeys.

A long slow period of growth and development, particularly among the hominoids, also provides opportunities. Born without built-in responses dictating specific behavior in complex situations, the young monkey or ape, like the young human, learns how to strategically interact with others, and even manipulate them for his or her own benefit—by trial and error, observation, imitation, and practice. Young primates make mis-

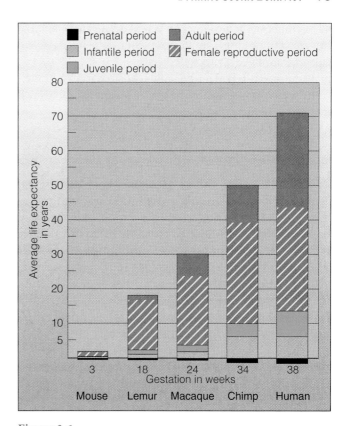

Figure 3.6

A long life cycle, including a long period of childhood dependency, is characteristic of the primates. In biological terms, infancy ends when young mammals are weaned, and adulthood is defined as sexual maturation. In many species, such as mice, animals become sexually mature as soon as they are weaned. Among primates, a juvenile period for social learning occurs between infancy and adulthood. For humans, the biological definitions of infancy and adulthood are modified according to cultural norms.

takes along the way, learning to modify their behavior based on the reactions of other members of the group. Each member of the community has a unique physical appearance and personality. Youngsters learn to match their interactive behaviors according to each individual's social position and temperament. Anatomical features common to all monkeys and apes—such as a free upper lip (unlike lemurs and cats, for example)—allow for varied facial expression, contributing to communication between individuals.

Play

Frequent play activity among primate infants and juveniles is a means of learning about the environment, learning about social skills, and testing a variety of behaviors. Chimpanzee infants mimic the food-getting activities of adults, "attack" dozing adults, and "harass" adolescents.

Observers have watched young gorillas do somersaults, wrestle, and play various organized games such as jostling for the position on top of a hillside or following and mimicking a single youngster. One juvenile, becoming annoyed at repeated harassment by an infant, picked it up, climbed a tree, and deposited it on a branch from which it was unable to get down on its own, until its mother came to retrieve it.

Communication

Primates, like many animals, vocalize. They have a great range of calls that are often used together with movements of the face or body to convey a message. Observers have not yet established the meaning of all the sounds, but a good number have been distinguished, such as warning calls, threat calls, defense calls, and gathering calls. The behavioral reactions of other animals hearing the call have also been studied. Among bonobos, chimpanzees, and gorillas, vocalizations are emotional rather than propositional. Much of these species' communication takes place by the use of specific gestures and postures. Indeed, a number of these, such as kissing and embracing, are in virtually universal use today among humans, as well as apes.

Primatologists have classified numerous kinds of chimpanzee vocalization and visual communication signals. Facial expressions convey emotional states such as distress, fear, or excitement. Numerous distinct vocalizations or calls have been associated with a variety of sensations. For example, chimps will smack their lips or clack their teeth to express pleasure with sociable body contact. Calls called "pant-hoots" can be differentiated into specific types used for arrival of individuals or inquiring. Together, these facilitate group protection, coordination of group efforts, and social interaction in general.

One form of communication appears to be unique to bonobos: the use of trail markers. When foraging, the community breaks up into smaller groups, rejoining again in the evening to nest together. To keep track of each party's whereabouts, those in the lead will, at the intersections of trails or where downed trees obscure trails, deliberately stomp down the vegetation so as to indicate their direction, or rip off large leaves and place them carefully for the same purpose. Thus, they all know where to come together at the end of the day.[10]

Experiments with captive apes, carried out over several decades, reveal that their communicative abilities exceed what they make use of in the wild. In some of

© Tim Davis/Corbis

Many ape nonverbal communications are easily recognized by humans as we share these same gestures.

these experiments, bonobos and chimpanzees have been taught to communicate using symbols, as in the case of Kanzi, a bonobo who uses a keyboard. Other chimpanzees, gorillas, and orangutans have been taught American Sign Language. Although this research provoked controversy, it has become evident that apes are capable of understanding language quite well, even using rudimentary grammar. They are able to generate original utterances, ask questions, distinguish naming something from asking for it, develop original ways to tell lies, coordinate their actions, and even spontaneously teach language to others. Even though they cannot literally *speak*, it is now clear that all of the great ape species can develop *language skills* to the level of a 2- to 3-year-old human child.[11] From such studies, we may learn something about the origin of human language.

Home Range

Primates usually move about within a circumscribed area, or **home range,** which is of varying size, depending on the size of the group and on ecological factors such as availability of food. Ranges often change seasonally. The number of miles traveled by a group in a day varies. Some areas of a range, known as *core areas,* are used more often than others. Core areas typically contain water, food

---

[10]Recer, P. (1998, February 16). Apes shown to communicate in the wild. *Burlington Free Press,* 12A.

home range The geographical area within which a group of primates usually moves.

---

[11]Lestel, D. (1998). How chimpanzees have domesticated humans. *Anthropology Today 12* (3); Miles, H. L. W. (1993). Language and the orangutan: The "old person" of the forest. In P. Cavalieri & P. Singer (Eds.), *The great ape project* (pp. 45–50). New York: St. Martin's Press.

sources, resting places, and sleeping trees. The ranges of different groups may overlap, as among bonobos, where 65 percent of one community's range may overlap with that of another.[12] By contrast, chimpanzee territories, at least in some regions, are exclusively occupied.

Gorillas do not defend their home range against incursions of others of their kind, although they certainly will defend their group if it is in any way threatened. In the lowlands of Central Africa, it is not uncommon to find several families feeding in close proximity to one another.[13] In encounters with other communities, bonobos will defend their immediate space through vocalizations and displays, but rarely through fighting. Usually, they settle down and feed side by side, not infrequently grooming, playing, and engaging in sexual activity between groups as well.

Chimpanzees, by contrast, have been observed patrolling their territories to ward off potential trespassers. Moreover, Goodall has recorded the destruction of one chimpanzee community by another invading group. This sort of deadly intercommunity interaction has never been observed among bonobos. Some have interpreted this apparent territorial behavior as an expression of the supposedly violent nature of chimpanzees. However, another interpretation is that the violence that Goodall witnessed was a response to crowding as a consequence of human activity.[14]

Learning

Observations of monkeys and apes have shown learning abilities remarkably similar to those of humans. Numerous examples of inventive behavior have been observed among Japanese macaques, as well as among apes. One newly discovered example is a technique of food manipulation on the part of captive chimpanzees in the Madrid zoo. It began when a 5-year-old female rubbed apples against a sharp corner of a concrete wall in order to lick the mashed pieces and juice left on the wall. From this youngster, the practice of "smearing" spread to her peers, and within five years, most group members were performing the operation frequently and consistently. The innovation has become standardized and durable, having transcended two generations in the group.[15]

Another dramatic example of learning is afforded by the way chimpanzees in West Africa crack open oil-palm

© Martin Harvey/Peter Arnold, Inc.

Chimps use a variety of tools in the wild. Here a chimp is using a long stick stripped of its side branches to fish for termites. Chimps will select a stick when still quite far from a termite mound and modify its shape on their way to the snacking spot.

nuts. For this they use tools: an anvil stone with a level surface on which to place the nut and a good-sized hammer stone to crack it. Not any stone will do; it must be of the right shape and weight, and the anvil may require leveling by placing smaller stones beneath one or more edges. Nor does random banging away do the job; the nut has to be hit at the right speed and the right trajectory, or else the nut simply flies off into the forest. Last but not least, the apes must avoid mashing their fingers, rather than the nut. According to fieldworkers, the expertise of the chimps far exceeds that of any human who tries cracking these hardest nuts in the world.

Youngsters learn this process by staying near to adults who are cracking nuts, where their mothers share some of the food. This teaches them about the edibility of the nuts, but not how to get at what's edible. This they learn by observing and by "aping" (copying) the adults. At first they play with a nut or stone alone; later they be-

---

[12]Parish, A. R. (1998). Comment. *Current Anthropology 39,* 414.

[13]Parnell, R. (1999). Gorilla exposé. *Natural History 108* (8), 43.

[14]Power, M. G. (1995). Gombe revisited: Are chimpanzees violent and hierarchical in the "free" state? *General Anthropology 2*(1), 5–9.

[15]Fernandez-Carriba, S., & Loeches, A. (2001). Fruit smearing by captive chimpanzees: A newly observed food-processing behavior. *Current Anthropology 42,* 143–147.

gin to randomly combine objects. They soon learn, however, that placing nuts on anvils and hitting them with a hand or foot gets them nowhere.

Only after three years of futile efforts do they begin to coordinate all of the multiple actions and objects, but even then it is only after a great deal of practice, by the age of 6 or 7 years, that they become proficient in this task. They do this for over a thousand days. Evidently, it is *social* motivation that accounts for their perseverance after at least three years of failure, with no reward to reinforce their effort. At first, they are motivated by a desire to act like the mother; only later does the desire to feed on the tasty nut-meat take over.[16]

Use of Objects as Tools

A **tool** may be defined as an object used to facilitate some task or activity. The nut cracking just discussed is the most complex tool-use task known from the field, involving both hands, two tools, and exact coordination. It is not, however, the only case of tool use among apes in the wild. Chimpanzees, bonobos, and orangutans make and use tools.

Here, a distinction must be made between simple *tool use,* as when one pounds something with a convenient stone when a hammer is not available, and *tool making,* which involves deliberate modification of some material for its intended use. Thus, otters that use unmodified stones to crack open clams may be tool users, but they are not toolmakers. Not only do chimpanzees modify objects to make them suitable for particular purposes, but chimps to some extent modify them to regular and set patterns. They also pick up, and even prepare, objects for future use at some other location, and they can use objects as tools to solve new and novel problems. Thus, chimps have been observed using stalks of grass, twigs that they have stripped of leaves, and even sticks up to 3 feet long that they have smoothed down to "fish" for termites. They insert the modified stick into a termite nest, wait a few minutes, pull the stick out, and eat the insects clinging to it, all of which requires considerable dexterity. Chimpanzees are equally deliberate in their nest building. They test the vines and branches to make sure they are usable. If they are not, the animal moves to another site.

---

[16]de Waal, F. (2001). *The ape and the sushi master* (pp. 227–229). New York: Basic Books.

tool An object used to facilitate some task or activity. Although tool making involves intentional modification of the material of which it is made, tool use may involve objects either modified for some particular purpose or completely unmodified.

Other examples of chimpanzee use of tools involve leaves, used as wipes or as sponges, to get water out of a hollow to drink. Large sticks may serve as clubs or as missiles (as may stones) in aggressive or defensive displays. Twigs are used as toothpicks to clean teeth as well as to extract loose baby teeth. They use these dental tools not just on themselves but on other individuals as well.[17]

In the wild, bonobos have not been observed making and using tools to the extent seen in chimpanzees. However, the use of large leaves as trail markers may be considered a form of tool use. That these animals do have further capabilities is exemplified by a captive bonobo who has figured out how to make tools of stone that are remarkably like the earliest such tools made by our own ancestors.

Medicinal use of plants by chimpanzees illustrates their selective use of raw materials, a quality related to tool manufacture. Chimps that are ill by outward appearance have been observed to seek out specific plants of the genus *Aspilia*. They will eat the leaves singly without chewing them, letting the leaves soften in their mouths for a long time before swallowing. Primatologists have discovered that the leaves pass through their digestive system whole and relatively intact having scraped parasites off the intestine walls in the process.

Although gorillas (like bonobos and chimps) build nests, they are the only one of the four great apes that have not been observed to make and use other tools in the wild. The reason for this is probably not that gorillas lack the intelligence or skill to do so; rather, their easy diet of leaves and nettles makes tools of no particular use.

Hunting

Although fruits, other plant foods, and invertebrate animals constitute the bulk of their diet, both chimps and bonobos will kill and eat other animals such as small monkeys, something unusual among primates. Chimpanzee females sometimes hunt, but males do so far more frequently. When on the hunt, they may spend up to 2 hours watching, following, and chasing intended prey. Moreover, in contrast to the usual primate practice of each animal finding its own food, hunting frequently involves teamwork to trap and kill prey particularly when hunting for baboons. Once a potential victim has been partially isolated from its troop, three or more adult chimps will carefully position themselves so as to block off escape routes while another climbs toward the prey for the kill. Following the kill, most of those present get a share of the meat, either by grabbing a piece as chance affords, or by sitting and begging for a piece.

---

[17]McGrew, W. C. (2000). Dental care in chimps. *Science 288,* 1,747.

Whatever the nutritional value of meat, hunting is not done purely for protein but for social and sexual reasons as well. The giving of meat helps forge alliances between males, and its sharing may be used also to entice a receptive female to have sex. In fact, males are more apt to hunt if a fertile female is present, and fertile females are more successful at begging for meat.

In bonobos, females are more likely to hunt than males. The female hunters regularly share carcasses with other females, but less often with males. Even when the most dominant male throws a tantrum nearby, he may still be denied a share.[18] Not only do females share the spoils of the hunt with one another, they are also unusual in their willingness to share other foods such as fruits.

PRIMATE CONSERVATION AND THE QUESTION OF CULTURE

The more we learn of the behavior of our nearest primate relatives, the more we become aware of the importance to chimps of learned, socially shared practices and knowledge. This raises two important questions: Do chimpanzees, bonobos, and the other apes have culture? Do we have responsibilities towards preserving the lifeways of our closest living relatives?

The answer to both questions appears to be yes. The detailed study of ape behavior has revealed variation among groups in use of tools and patterns of social engagement that seem to derive from the traditions of the group rather than a biologically determined script. Humans share with the other apes an ability to learn the complex but flexible patterns of behavior particular to a social group during a long period of childhood dependency. While documenting the presence of cultural capacities among primate groups is an important scholarly pursuit, the matter of primate conservation is an urgent concern for all of us.

At present, no fewer than seventy-six species of primates are recognized as being in danger of extinction. Included among them are all of the great apes, as well as such formerly widespread and adaptable species as rhesus macaques. In the wild, these animals are threatened by habitat destruction in the name of economic development.

As humans encroach on primate habitats, translocation of the primates to a protected area is an excellent strategy for primate conservation. The field studies by primatologists for such relocations are invaluable. For example, when the troop of free-ranging baboons Shirley Strum studied for fifteen years in Kenya began raiding people's crops and garbage on newly established farms, she was instrumental in successfully moving this troop and two other local troops—130 animals in all—to more sparsely inhabited country 150 miles away. Knowing their habits, Strum was able to trap, tranquilize, and transport the animals to their new home while preserving the baboons' vital social relationships.

Strum's careful work allowed for a smooth transition. With social relations intact, the baboons did not abandon their new homes nor did they block the transfer of new males, with their all-important knowledge of local resources, into the troop. The success of her effort, which had never been tried with baboons, proves that translocation is a realistic technique for saving endangered primate species. As this method is dependent upon available land, preserves must be established to provide habitats for endangered primates.

Primates are also vulnerable to being hunted for food or recreation, and by trapping for use as pets and for research. Because monkeys and apes are so closely related to humans, they are regarded as essential for biomedical research in which humans cannot be used. Ironically, using live primates to supply laboratories can be a major factor in their local extinction.

A second strategy to preventing primate extinction is to maintain breeding colonies in captivity. Such colonies must carefully provide the kind of physical and social environment that will encourage psychological and physical well-being, as well as reproductive success. Primates in zoos and laboratories do not successfully reproduce when deprived of such amenities as opportunities for climbing, materials to use for nest building, others with which to socialize, and places for privacy.

While the sensitivity and knowledge primatologists contribute to primate conservation is invaluable, they cannot prevent primate extinction alone. Whole societies and coordinated global efforts are required. Many of the states that contain the natural primate habitats are beset by a variety of political and economic problems that threaten the well-being of their human populations as well. Western societies, without primate habitats, have much to contribute to solving these larger issues that affect humans and their primate cousins alike.

When it comes to the nonhumans, powerful social barriers exist that work against the well-being of our animal relatives. In Western societies there has been an unfortunate tendency to erect what paleontologist Stephen Jay Gould refers to as "golden barriers" that set us apart from the rest of the animal kingdom.[19] It is unfortunate, for it blinds us to the fact that a continuum exists between "us" and "them" (animals). We have already seen that the physical differences between humans and apes are largely differences of degree, rather than kind. It now

---

[18]Ingmanson, E. J. (1998). Comment. *Current Anthropology 39*, 409.

[19]Quoted in de Waal, F. (2001). *The ape and the sushi master* (p. 235). New York: Basic Books.

appears that the same is true with respect to behavior. As primatologist Richard Wrangham once put it,

> Like humans, [chimpanzees] laugh, make up after a quarrel, support each other in times of trouble, medicate themselves with chemical and physical remedies, stop each other from eating poisonous foods, collaborate in the hunt, help each other over physical obstacles, raid neighboring groups, lose their tempers, get excited by dramatic weather, invent ways to show off, have family traditions and group traditions, make tools, devise plans, deceive, play tricks, grieve, and are cruel and are kind.[20]

[20]Quoted in Mydens, S. (2001, August 12). He's not hairy, he's my brother. *New York Times*, sec. 4, 5.

This is not to say that we are "just" another ape; obviously, "degree" does make a difference. Nevertheless, the continuities between us and our primate kin reflect a common evolutionary heritage and a responsibility to help our cousins today. Because of our common evolutionary heritage, the biology and behavior of the other living primates, like the contemporary study of genetics, provide valuable insight into understanding human origins. The methods scientists use to recover data directly from fossilized bones and preserved cultural remains in order to study the human past are the subject of the next chapter.

Questions for Reflection

1. Does knowing more about the numerous similarities among the primates including humans motivate you personally to want to meet the challenge of preventing the extinction of our closest living relatives?

2. Considering some of the trends seen among the primates, such as increased brain size or reduced tooth number, why can't we say that some primates are more evolved than others? What is wrong with the statement that humans are more evolved than chimpanzees?

3. Two systems exist for dividing the primate order into suborders because of difficulties with classifying tarsiers. Should classification systems be based on genetic relationships or based on the biological concept of grade? Is the continued use of the older terminology an instance of inertia or a difference in philosophy? How do the issues brought up by the "tarsier problem" translate to the hominoids?

4. Given the variation seen in the specific behaviors of chimp, bonobo, and gorilla groups, is it fair to say that our close relatives possess culture?

5. Many primate species, particularly apes, are endangered today. Though some features of ape biology may be responsible for apes' limited population size, humans, with an ever-expanding population, share these same biological features. Besides life cycle biology, what factors are causing endangerment of primates, and how can humans work to prevent the extinction of our closest living relatives?

Suggested Readings

de Waal, F. (2001). *The ape and the sushi master*. New York: Basic Books.

This masterful discussion of the presence of culture among apes moves this concept from an anthropocentric realm and ties it instead to communication and social organization. In an accessible style, Frans de Waal, one of the world's foremost experts on bonobos, demonstrates ape culture while challenging human intellectual theories designed to exclude animals from the "culture club."

Fossey, D. (1983). *Gorillas in the mist*. Burlington, MA: Houghton Mifflin.

The late Dian Fossey is to gorillas what Jane Goodall is to chimpanzees. Fossey devoted years to the study of gorilla behavior in the field. This book is about the first thirteen years of her study; as well as being readable and informative, it is well illustrated.

Galdikas, B. (1995). *Reflections on Eden: My years with the orangutans of Borneo*. New York: Little Brown.

Birute Galdikas is the least known of the trio of young women sent by Louis Leakey in 1971 to study apes in the wild. Her work with the orangutans of Borneo, however, is magnificent. In this book she presents rich scientific information as well as her personal reflections on a life spent fully integrated with orangutans and the culture of Borneo.

Goodall, J. (1990). *Through a window: My thirty years with the chimpanzees of Gombe*. Boston: Houghton Mifflin.

This fascinating book is a personal account of Jane Goodall's first thirty years experiences studying wild chimpanzees in Tanzania. A pleasure to read and a fount of information on the behavior of these apes, the book is profusely illustrated as well.

Goodall, J. (2000). *Reason for hope: A spiritual journey*. New York: Warner Books.

Jane Goodall's most recent book is a memoir linking her monumental life's work with the chimpanzees of Gombe to her inner spiritual convictions. She makes clear her commitment to conferring chimpanzees with the same rights and respect experienced by humans through the exploration of difficult topics such as environmental destruction, animal abuse, and genocide. She expands the concept of humanity while providing us with powerful reasons to maintain hope.

Rowe, N., & Mittermeier, R. A. (1996). *The pictorial guide to the living primates*. East Hampton, NY: Pogonias Press.

Filled with dynamic photographs of primates in nature, this book also provides concise descriptions (including anatomy, taxonomy, diet, social structure, maps, and so on) for 234 species of primates. The book is useful for students and primatologists alike.

Thomson Audio Study Products

 Enjoy the MP3-ready Audio Lecture Overviews for each chapter and a comprehensive audio glossary of key terms for quick study and review. Whether walking to class, doing laundry, or studying at your desk, you now have the freedom to choose when, where, and how you interact with your audio-based educational media. See the preface for information on how to access this on-the-go study and review tool.

The Anthropology Resource Center

www.thomsonedu.com/anthropology
The Anthropology Resource Center provides extended learning materials to reinforce your understanding of key concepts in the four subfields of anthropology. For each of the four subdisciplines, the Resource Center includes dynamic exercises including video exercises, map exercises, simulations, and "Meet the Scientists" interviews, as well as critical thinking questions that can be assigned and e-mailed to instructors. The Resource Center also provides breaking news in anthropology and interesting material on applied anthropology to help you link what you are learning to the world around you.

4 Field Methods in Archaeology and Paleoanthropology

CHALLENGE ISSUE

Given the radical changes taking place in the world today, a scientific understanding of the past has never been more important. But scientific investigation of ancient remains challenges us to solve the complex question of who owns the past. In a particularly chilling example, the Khmer Rouge—the totalitarian regime responsible for the genocide that killed millions during the 1970s in Cambodia—also threatened to destroy the 12th-century Buddhist temple of Angkor Wat. Destroying both the people and the temple were part of the Khmer Rouge's campaign to eliminate evidence of the past. When this murderous government was finally ousted, its troops fled to the temple complex, knowing that international opinion regarding these spectacular archaeological remains would afford them some safety. In the chaos that followed, even small temple artifacts became very expensive collectibles. To whom do such ancient remains belong—to the local government, to the global community, to scientists, to people living in the region, to those who happen to have possession of them at the moment? At peaceful Angkor Wat today, collaboration among local people, scientists, local governments, and the international community not only shields ancient remains from this type of trade and destruction, but it honors the connections of indigenous people to the places and remains under study.

How Are the Physical and Cultural Remains of Past Humans Investigated?

Archaeologists and paleoanthropologists investigate our past by excavating sites where biological and cultural remains are found. Unfortunately, excavation results in the site's destruction. Thus, every attempt is made to excavate in such a way that the location and context of everything recovered, no matter how small, is precisely recorded. Through careful analysis of the physical and cultural remains recovered through excavation, scientists make sense of the data and enhance our knowledge of the biology, behavior, and beliefs of our ancestors. The success of an excavation also depends upon cooperation and respect between anthropologists who are investigating the past and the living people connected to the sites and remains being studied.

Are Human Physical and Cultural Remains Always Found Together?

Archaeological sites are places containing the cultural remains of past human activity. Sites are revealed by the presence of artifacts as well as soil marks, changes in vegetation, and irregularities of the earth's surface. While skeletons of recent peoples are frequently associated with their cultural remains, as we go back in time, the association of physical and cultural remains becomes less likely. Fossils are defined as any surviving trace or impression of an organism from the past. Fossils sometimes accompany archaeological sites, but many of them predate the first stone tools or other cultural artifacts. The human cultural practice of burying the dead, starting about 100,000 years ago, changed the nature of the fossil record, providing relatively complete skeletons as well as information about this cultural practice.

How Are Archaeological or Fossil Remains Dated?

Calculating the age of physical and cultural remains is an essential aspect of interpreting the past. Remains can be dated by noting their stratigraphic position, by measuring the amount of chemicals contained in fossil bones, or through association with other plant, animal, or cultural remains. More precise dating methods rely upon advances in the disciplines of chemistry and physics that use properties such as rates of decay of radioactive elements. These elements may be present in the remains themselves or in the surrounding soil. By comparing dates and remains across a variety of sites, anthropologists can make inferences about human origins, migrations, and technological developments. Sometimes the development of a new dating technique leads to an entirely new interpretation of physical and cultural remains.

While the focus of anthropology is on peoples of all places and times, paleoanthropology and archaeology are the specialties most concerned with our past. Paleoanthropology and archaeology share a focus on **prehistory,** a conventional term used to refer to the period of time before written records. For some people, the term *prehistoric* might conjure up images of "primitive" cavemen and women, but it does not imply a lack of history or any inferiority—merely a lack of written history. Since the next seven chapters of this book focus upon the past, this chapter will look at the methods archaeologists and paleoanthropologists use to study the past.

Most of us are familiar with some kind of archaeological material: the coin dug out of the earth, the fragment of an ancient pot, the spear point used by some ancient hunter. Finding and cataloguing such objects is often thought to be the chief goal of archaeology. While this was true in the 19th and early 20th century, when professional and amateur archaeologists alike collected cultural treasures, the situation changed by the mid-20th century. Today, the aim is to use archaeological remains to reconstruct the culture and worldview of past human societies. Archaeologists examine every recoverable detail from past societies, including all kinds of structures (not just palaces and temples), hearths, garbage dumps, bones, and plant remains. Although it may appear that archaeologists are digging up things, they are really digging up human biology, behavior, and beliefs.

Similarly, paleoanthropologists who study the physical remains of our ancestors and other ancient primates do more than find and catalogue old bones. Paleoanthropologists recover, describe, and organize these remains to see what they can tell us about human biological evolution. It is not so much a case of finding the ancient bones but finding out what the bones mean.

prehistory A conventional term used to refer to the period of time before the appearance of written records. Does not deny the existence of history, merely of *written* history.
artifact Any object fashioned or altered by humans.
material culture The durable aspects of culture such as tools, structures, and art.

RECOVERING CULTURAL AND BIOLOGICAL REMAINS

Archaeologists and paleoanthropologists face a dilemma. The only way to thoroughly investigate our past is to excavate sites where biological and cultural remains are found. Unfortunately, excavation results in the site's destruction. Thus, every attempt is made to excavate in such a way that the location and context of everything recovered, no matter how small, is precisely recorded. These records help scientists make sense of the data and enhance our knowledge of the past. Knowledge that can be derived from physical and cultural remains diminishes dramatically if accurate and detailed records of the excavation are not kept. As the U.S. anthropologist Brian Fagan has put it:

> The fundamental premise of excavation is that all digging is destructive, even that done by experts. The archaeologist's primary responsibility, therefore, is to record a site for posterity as it is dug because there are no second chances.[1]

Archaeologists work with **artifacts,** any object fashioned or altered by humans—a flint scraper, a basket, an axe, or such things as house ruins or walls. An artifact expresses a facet of human culture. Because it is something that someone made, archaeologists like to say that an artifact is a product or representation of human behavior and beliefs or, in more technical terms, artifacts are **material culture.**

Artifacts are not considered in isolation; rather, they are integrated with biological and ecological remains. And just as important as the artifacts or physical remains themselves is the way they were left in the ground. For example, what people do with the things they have made, how they dispose of them, and how they lose them reflect important aspects of human culture. In other words, context allows archaeologists to understand the cultures of the past.

Similarly, context provides important information about biological remains. It provides information about which fossils are earlier or later in time than other fossils. Also, by noting the association of ancient human fossils with the remains of other species, the paleoanthropologist may make significant progress in reconstructing environmental settings of the past.

While cultural and physical remains represent distinct kinds of data, the fullest interpretations of the human past require the integration of ancient human

[1]Fagan, B. M. (1995). *People of the earth* (8th ed., p. 19). New York: HarperCollins.

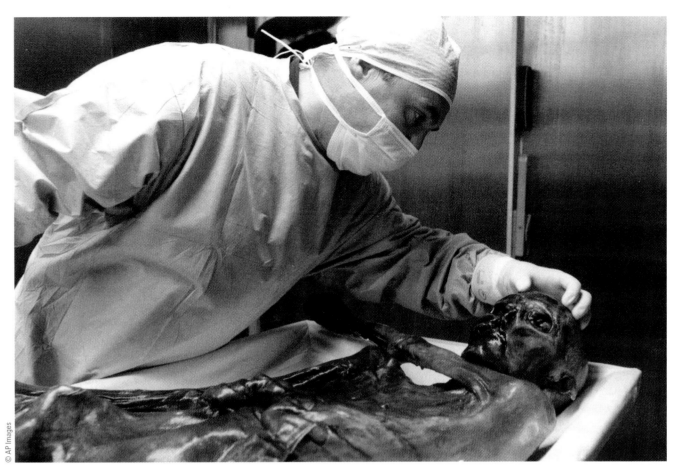

© AP Images

In rare circumstances, human bodies are so well preserved that they could be mistaken for recent corpses. Such is the case of "Ötzi," the 5,200-year-old "Ice Man," exposed by the melting of an alpine glacier in the Tyrolean Alps in 1991. Both the Italian and the Austrian governments felt they had legitimate claims on this rare find, and they mounted legal, geographic, and taphonomic arguments for housing the body in their country. These arguments continued as the specimen, just released from the ice, began to thaw.

biology and culture. Often paleoanthropologists and archaeologists work together to systematically excavate and analyze fragmentary remains, placing scraps of bone, shattered pottery, and scattered campsites into broad interpretive contexts.

The Nature of Fossils

Broadly defined, a **fossil** is any mineralized trace or impression of an organism that has been preserved in the earth's crust from past geologic time. Fossilization typically involves the hard parts of an organism. Bones, teeth, shells, horns, and the woody tissues of plants are the most successfully fossilized materials. Although the soft parts of an organism are rarely fossilized, the casts or impressions of footprints, brains, and even whole bodies have sometimes been found. Because dead animals quickly attract meat-eating scavengers and bacteria that cause decomposition, they rarely survive long enough to

become fossilized. For an organism to become a fossil, it must be covered by some protective substance soon after death.

An organism or part of an organism may be preserved in a number of ways. The whole animal may be frozen in ice, like the famous mammoths found in Siberia, safe from the actions of predators, weathering, and bacteria. Or it may be enclosed in a natural resin exuding from evergreen trees, later becoming hardened and fossilized as amber. Specimens of spiders and insects dating back millions of years have been preserved in the Baltic Sea area, which is rich in resin-producing evergreens such as pine, spruce, or fir trees.

An organism may be preserved in the bottoms of lakes and sea basins, where the body or body part may

fossil Any mineralized trace or impression of an organism that has been preserved in earth's crust from past geological time.

be quickly covered with sediment. An entire organism may also be mummified or preserved in tar pits, peat, oil, or asphalt bogs, in which the chemical environment prevents the growth of decay-producing bacteria.

Cases in which an entire organism of any sort, let alone a human, is preserved are especially rare. Fossils generally consist of such things as scattered teeth and fragments of bones found embedded in rock deposits. Most have been altered in some way in the process of becoming fossilized. **Taphonomy** (from the Greek for "tomb"), the study of the biological and geological processes by which dead organisms become fossils, provides systematic understanding of the fossilization process vital for the scientific interpretations of the fossils themselves.

Fossilization is most apt to occur among marine animals and other creatures living near water. Concentrations of shells and other parts of organisms are covered and completely enclosed by the soft waterborne sediments that eventually harden into shale and limestone in the following fashion: As the remains of organisms accumulate on shallow sea, river, or lake bottoms, they become covered by sediments and silt, or sand. These materials gradually harden, forming a protective shell around the skeleton of the organism. The internal cavities of bones or teeth and other parts of the skeleton fill in with mineral deposits from the sediment immediately surrounding the specimen. Then the external walls of the bone decay and are replaced by calcium carbonate or silica.

Unless protected in some way, the bones of a land dweller are generally scattered and exposed to the deteriorating influence of the elements, predators, and scavengers. Occasionally, terrestrial animals living near lakes or rivers become fossilized if they happen to die next to or in the water. A land dweller may also become fossilized if it happens to die in a cave, or if some other meat-eating animal drags its remains to a site protected from erosion and decay. In caves, conditions are often excellent for fossilization, as minerals contained in water dripping from the ceiling may harden over bones left on the cave floor. In northern China, for example, many fossils of *Homo erectus* (discussed in Chapter 7) and other animals were found in a cave at a place called Zhoukoudian, in deposits consisting of consolidated clays and rock that had fallen from the cave's limestone ceiling. The cave had been frequented by both humans and predatory animals, which left remains of many a meal there.

Burial of the Dead

Entirely preserved fossil skeletons dating before the cultural practice of burial about 100,000 years ago are quite rare. The human fossil record from before this period consists primarily of fragmentary remains. The fossil record for many other primates is even poorer, because organic materials decay rapidly in the tropical forests where they lived. The records are much more complete for primates (such as evolving humans) that lived on the grassy plains or in savannah environments, where conditions were far more favorable to the formation of fossils. This was particularly true in places where ash deposited from volcanic eruptions or waterborne sediments along lakes and streams could quickly cover organisms that died there. At several localities in Ethiopia, Kenya, and Tanzania in East Africa, numerous fossils important for our understanding of human evolution have been found near ancient lakes and streams, often sandwiched between layers of volcanic ash.

In more recent times, such complete remains, although not common, are often quite spectacular and may be particularly informative. As an example, consider the recovery in 1994 of an Eskimo girl's remains in Barrow, Alaska, described in the Original Study. As seen in this case study, successful exploration of the past depends upon cooperation and respect between anthropologists and the living people with ancestral connections to the physical and cultural remains being studied.

taphonomy The study of how bones and other materials come to be preserved in the earth as fossils.

Original Study ▪ By Sherry Simpson

Whispers from the Ice

People grew excited when a summer rainstorm softened the bluff known as Ukkuqsi, sloughing off huge chunks of earth containing remains of historic and prehistoric houses, part of the old village that predates the modern community of Barrow. Left protruding from the slope was a human head. Archaeologist Anne Jensen happened to be in Barrow buying strapping tape when the body appeared. Her firm, SJS Archaeological Services, Inc., was closing a field season at nearby Point Franklin, and Jensen offered the team's help in a kind of archaeological triage to remove the body before it eroded completely from the earth.

The North Slope Borough hired her and Glenn Sheehan, both associated with Pennsylvania's Bryn Mawr College, to conduct the work. The National Science Foundation, which supported the 3-year Point Franklin project, agreed to fund the autopsy and subsequent analysis of the body and artifacts. The Ukkuqsi excavation quickly became a community event. In remarkably sunny and calm weather, volunteers troweled and picked through the thawing soil, finding trade beads, animal bones, and other items. Teenage boys worked alongside grandmothers. The smell of sea mammal oil, sweet at first then corrupt, mingled with ancient organic odors of decomposed vegetation. One man searched the beach for artifacts that had eroded from the bluff, discovering such treasures as two feather parkas. Elder Silas Negovanna, originally of Wainwright, visited several times, "more or less out of curiosity to see what they have in mind," he said. George Leavitt, who lives in a house on the bluff, stopped by one day while carrying home groceries and suggested a way to spray water to thaw the soil without washing away valuable artifacts. Tour groups added the excavation to their rounds.

"This community has a great interest in archaeology up here just because it's so recent to their experience," says oral historian Karen Brewster, a tall young woman who interviews elders as part of her work with the North Slope Borough's division of Inupiat History, Language, and Culture. "The site's right in town, and everybody was really fascinated by it."

Slowly, as the workers scraped and shoveled, the earth surrendered its historical hoard: carved wooden bowls, ladles, and such clothing as a mitten made from polar bear hide, bird-skin parkas, and mukluks. The items spanned prehistoric times, dated in Barrow to before explorers first arrived in 1826.

The work prompted visiting elders to recall when they or their parents lived in traditional sod houses and relied wholly on the land and sea for sustenance. Some remembered sliding down the hill as children, before the sea gnawed away the slope. Others described the site's use as a lookout for whales or ships. For the

archaeologists, having elders stand beside them and identify items and historical context is like hearing the past whispering in their ears. Elders often know from experience, or from stories, the answers to the scientists' questions about how items were used or made. "In this instance, usually the only puzzled people are the archaeologists," jokes archaeologist Sheehan.

A modern town of 4,000, Barrow exists in a cultural continuum, where history is not detached or remote but still pulses through contemporary life. People live, hunt, and fish where their ancestors did, but they can also buy fresh vegetables at the store and jet to other places. Elementary school classes include computer and Inupiaq language studies. Caribou skins, still ruddy with blood, and black brant carcasses hang near late-model cars outside homes equipped with television antennas. A man uses power tools to work on his whaling boat. And those who appear from the earth are not just bodies, but relatives. "We're not a people frozen in time," says Jana Harcharek, an Inupiat Eskimo who teaches Inupiaq and nurtures her culture among young people. "There will always be that connection between us [and our ancestors]. They're not a separate entity."

The past drew still closer as the archaeologists neared the body. After several days of digging through thawed soil, they used water supplied by the local fire station's tanker truck to melt through permafrost until they reached

the remains, about 3 feet below the surface. A shell of clear ice encased the body, which rested in what appeared to be a former meat cellar. With the low-pressure play of water from the tanker, the archaeologists teased the icy casket from the frozen earth, exposing a tiny foot. Only then did they realize they had uncovered a child. "That was kind of sad, because she was about my daughter's size," says archaeologist Jensen.

The girl was curled up beneath a baleen toboggan and part of a covering that Inupiat elder Bertha Leavitt identified as a kayak skin by its stitching. The child, who appeared to be 5 or 6, remained remarkably intact after her dark passage through time. Her face was cloaked by a covering that puzzled some onlookers. It didn't look like human hair, or even fur, but something with a feathery residue. Finally they concluded it was a hood from a feather parka made of bird skins. The rest of her body was delineated muscle that had freeze-dried into a dark brick-red color. Her hands rested on her knees, which were drawn up to her chin. Frost particles coated the bends of her arms and legs.

"We decided we needed to go talk to the elders and see what they wanted, to get some kind of feeling as to whether they wanted to bury her right away, or whether they were willing to allow some studies in a respectful manner—studies that would be of some use to residents of the North Slope," Jensen says. Working with community elders is not a radical idea to Jensen or Sheehan, whose previous work in the Arctic has earned them high regard from local officials who appreciate their sensitivity. The researchers feel obligated not only to follow community wishes, but to invite villagers to sites and to share all information through public presentations. In fact, Jensen is reluctant to discuss findings with the press before the townspeople themselves hear it.

"It seems like it's a matter of simple common courtesy," she says. Such consideration can only help researchers, she points out. "If people don't get along with you, they're not going to talk to you, and they're liable to throw you out on your ear." In the past, scientists were

CONTINUED

not terribly sensitive about such matters, generally regarding human remains—and sometimes living natives—as artifacts themselves. Once, the girl's body would have been hauled off to the catacombs of some university or museum, and relics would have disappeared into exhibit drawers in what Sheehan describes as "hit-and-run archaeology."

"Grave robbers" is how Inupiat Jana Harcharek refers to early Arctic researchers. "They took human remains and their burial goods. It's pretty gruesome. But, of course, at the time they thought they were doing science a big favor. Thank goodness attitudes have changed."

Today, not only scientists but municipal officials confer with the Barrow Elders Council when local people find skeletons from traditional platform burials out on the tundra, or when bodies appear in the house mounds. The elders appreciate such consultations, says Samuel Simmonds, a tall, dignified man known for his carving. A retired Presbyterian minister, he presided at burial ceremonies of the famous "frozen family," ancient Inupiats discovered in Barrow thirteen years ago. "They were part of us, we know that," he says simply, as if the connection between old bones and bodies and living relatives is self-evident. In the case of the newly discovered body, he says, "We were concerned that it was re-buried in a respectful manner. They were nice enough to come over and ask us."

The elders also wanted to restrict media attention and prevent photographs of the body except for a few showing her position at the site. They approved a limited autopsy to help answer questions about the body's sex, age, and state of health. She was placed in an orange plastic body bag in a stainless steel morgue with the temperature turned down to below freezing.

With the help of staff at the Indian Health Service Hospital, Jensen sent the girl's still-frozen body to Anchorage's Providence Hospital. There she assisted with an autopsy performed by Dr. Michael Zimmerman of New York City's Mount Sinai Hospital. Zimmerman, an expert on prehistoric frozen bodies, had autopsied Barrow's frozen family in 1982, and was on his way to work on the prehistoric man recently discovered in the Alps.

The findings suggest the girl's life was very hard. She ultimately died of starvation, but also had emphysema caused by a rare congenital disease—the lack of an enzyme that protects the lungs. She probably was sickly and needed

In the long cool days of the Alaska summer, archaeologist Anne Jensen and her team excavate artifacts that will be exhibited at the newly built Inupiat Heritage Center in Barrow, Alaska. In addition to traditional museum displays honoring the past, the center actively promotes the continuation of Inupiat Eskimo cultural traditions through innovations such as the elder-in-residence program.

Courtesy of Anne Jensen and Glenn Sheehan

extra care all her brief life. The autopsy also found soot in her lungs from the family's sea mammal oil lamps, and she had osteoporosis, which was caused by a diet exclusively of meat from marine mammals. The girl's stomach was empty, but her intestinal tract contained dirt and animal fur. That remains a mystery and raises questions about the condition of the rest of the family. "It's not likely that she would be hungry and everyone else well fed," Jensen says.

That the girl appears to have been placed deliberately in the cellar provokes further questions about precontact burial practices, which the researchers hope Barrow elders can help answer. Historic accounts indicate the dead often were wrapped in skins and laid out on the tundra on wooden platforms, rather than buried in the frozen earth. But perhaps the entire family was starving and too weak to remove the dead girl from the house, Jensen speculates. "We probably won't ever be able to say, 'This is the way it was,'" she adds. "For that you need a time machine."

The scientific team reported to the elders that radiocarbon dating places the girl's death in about AD 1200. If correct—for dating is technically tricky in the Arctic—the date would set the girl's life about 100 years before her people formed settled whaling villages, Sheehan says.

Following the autopsy and the body's return to Barrow in August, one last request by the elders was honored. The little girl, wrapped in her feather parka, was placed in a casket and buried in a small Christian ceremony next to the grave of the other prehistoric bodies. Hundreds of years after her death, an Inupiat daughter was welcomed back into the midst of her community.

The "rescue" of the little girl's body from the raw forces of time and nature means researchers and the Inupiat people will continue to learn still more about the region's culture. Sheehan and Jensen returned to Barrow in winter 1994 to explain their findings to townspeople. "We expect to learn just as much from them," Sheehan said before the trip. A North Slope Cultural Center scheduled for completion in 1996 will store and display artifacts from the dig sites.

Laboratory tests and analysis also will contribute information. The archaeologists hope measurements of heavy metals in the girl's body will allow comparisons with modern-day pollution contaminating the sea mammals that Inupiats eat today. The soot damage in her lungs might offer health implications for Third World people who rely on oil lamps, dung fires, and charcoal for heat and light. Genetic tests could illuminate

early population movements of Inupiats. The project also serves as a model for good relations between archaeologists and Native people. "The larger overall message from this work is that scientists and communities don't have to be at odds," Sheehan says. "In fact, there are mutual interests that we all have. Scientists have obligations to communities. And when more scientists realize that, and when more communities hold scientists to those standards, then everybody will be happier."
(Adapted from Sherry Simpson (1995, April). Whispers from the ice. Alaska, 23–28.) ■

SEARCHING FOR ARTIFACTS AND FOSSILS

Where are artifacts and fossils found? Places containing archaeological remains of previous human activity are known as *sites*. There are many kinds of sites, and sometimes it is difficult to define their boundaries, for remains may be strewn over large areas. Sites are even found underwater. Some examples of sites identified by archaeologists and paleoanthropologists are hunting campsites, from which hunters went out to hunt game; kill sites, in which game was killed and butchered; village sites, in which domestic activities took place; and cemeteries, in which the dead, and sometimes their belongings, were buried.

While skeletons of recent peoples are frequently associated with their cultural remains, archaeological sites may or may not contain any physical remains. As we go back in time, the association of physical and cultural remains becomes less likely. Physical remains dating from before 2.5 million years ago are found in isolation. This is not proof of the absence of material culture but rather that the earliest forms of material culture were not preserved in the archaeological record. It is likely that the earliest tools were made of organic materials (such as the termiting sticks used by chimpanzees) that were much less likely to be preserved in the archaeological record. Similarly, fossils are found only in geological contexts where conditions are known to have been right for fossilization. By contrast, archaeological sites may be found just about anywhere, perhaps because many date from more recent periods.

Site Identification

The first task for the archaeologist is actually finding sites to investigate. Archaeological sites, particularly very old ones, frequently lie buried underground covered by layers of sediment deposited since the site was in use. Most sites are revealed by the presence of artifacts. Chance may play a crucial role in the site's discovery, as in the previously discussed case of the site at Barrow, Alaska. Usually, however, the archaeologist will have to survey a region in order to plot the sites available for excavation. A survey can be made from the ground, but more and more use is made of remote sensing techniques, many of them by-products of space-age technology. Aerial photographs have been used by archaeologists since the 1920s and are widely used today. Among other things, such photographs were used for the discovery and interpretation of the huge geometric and zoomorphic (from

Courtesy Dana Walrath

Sometimes archaeological sites are marked by dramatic ruins, such as this temple from the ancient Maya city of Tikal. Built by piling up rubble and facing it with stone blocks held together with mortar, it towers above the trees. While the scaffolding provides the opportunity for tourists to appreciate the grandeur of its full height, the benefits of learning about the ancient Maya through the experience of such a climb must be balanced with preserving these archaeological remains.

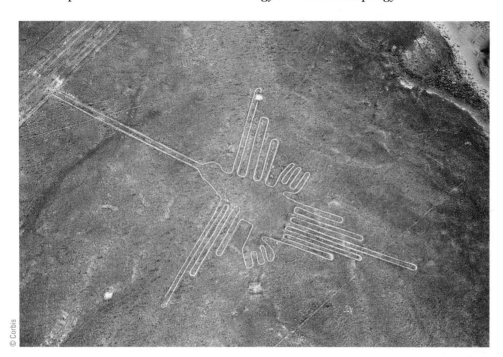

© Corbis

Some archaeological features are best seen from the air, such as this figure of a hummingbird made in prehistoric times on the Nazca Desert of Peru.

Latin for "animal-shaped") markings on the coastal desert of Peru.

More recently, use of high-resolution aerial photographs, including satellite imagery, resulted in the astonishing discovery of over 500 miles of prehistoric roadways connecting sites in the four-corners region of the United States (where Arizona, New Mexico, Colorado, and Utah meet) with other sites in ways that archaeologists had never suspected. This discovery led to a new understanding of prehistoric Pueblo Indian economic, social, and political organization. Evidently, large centers in this region governed a number of smaller satellite communities, mobilized labor for large public works, and saw to the distribution of goods over substantial distances.

More obvious sites, such as the human-made mounds or *tells* of the Middle East, are easier to spot from the ground, for the country is open. But it is more difficult to locate ruins, even those that are well above ground, where there is a heavy forest cover. Thus, the discovery of archaeological sites is strongly affected by local geography and climate.

Some sites may be spotted by changes in vegetation. For example, the topsoil of ancient storage and refuse pits is often richer in organic matter than that of the surrounding areas, and so it grows distinctive vegetation. At Tikal, an ancient Maya site in Guatemala, breadnut trees usually grow near the remains of ancient houses,

so that archaeologists looking for the remains of houses at this site can use these trees as guideposts.

On the ground, sites can be spotted by **soil marks,** or stains, showing up on the surface of recently plowed fields. Soil marks led archaeologists to many of the Bronze Age burial mounds in northern Hertfordshire and southwestern Cambridgeshire, England. The mounds hardly rose out of the ground, yet each was circled at its core by chalky soil marks. Sometimes the very presence of certain chalky rock is significant.

Documents, maps, and folklore are also useful to the archaeologist. Heinrich Schliemann, the famous and controversial 19th-century German archaeologist, was led to the discovery of Troy after a reading of Homer's *Iliad.* He assumed that the city described by Homer as Ilium was really Troy. Place names and local lore often are an indication that an archaeological site is to be found in the area. Archaeological surveys therefore often depend upon amateur collectors and local people who are usually familiar with the history of the land.

Sometimes natural processes, such as soil erosion or droughts, expose sites or fossils. For example, in eastern North America erosion along the coastlines and river banks has exposed prehistoric refuse mounds known as **middens,** which are filled with shells indicating that shellfish consumption was common. Similarly, a whole village of stone huts was exposed at Skara Brae in Scotland's Orkney Islands by the action of wind as it blew away sand.

Though natural forces sometimes expose fossils and sites, human physical and cultural remains are more often accidentally discovered in the course of some other human activity. In Chapter 2 we saw how the discovery

soil mark A stain that shows up on the surface of recently plowed fields that reveals an archaeological site.

middens A refuse or garbage disposal area in an archaeological site.

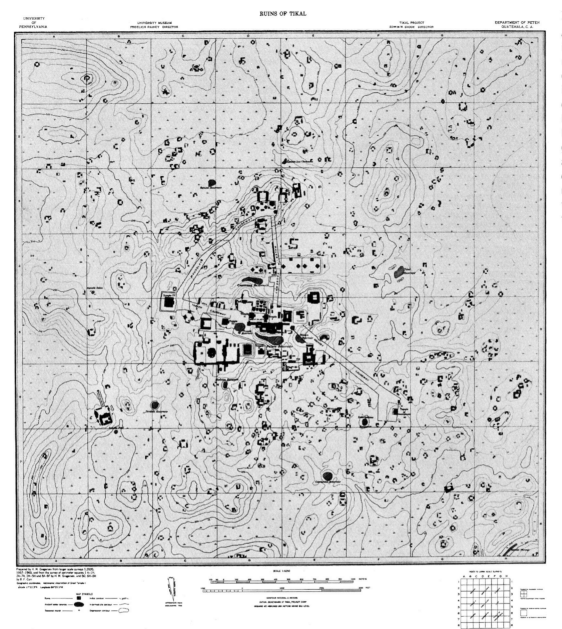

Figure 4.1

At large sites covering several square miles, a giant grid is constructed, as shown in this map of the center of the ancient Maya city of Tikal. Each square of the grid is one-quarter of a square kilometer; individual structures are numbered according to the square in which they are found.

of fossils of extinct animals in Europe from construction and quarrying played a role in the development of evolutionary theory. Similarly, limestone quarrying at a variety of sites in South Africa early in the 20th century led to the discovery of the earliest humanlike fossils from millions of years ago (see Chapter 6). Smaller scale disturbances of earth such as plowing sometimes turn up bones, fragments of pots, and other archaeological objects.

So frequently do construction projects uncover archaeological remains that in many countries, including the United States, construction projects require government approval in order to ensure the identification and protection of archaeological remains. Archaeological work known as cultural resource management (see the

Anthropology Applied feature) is now routinely carried out as part of the environmental review process for federally funded or licensed construction projects in the United States as it is in Europe.

Archaeological Excavation

Once a researcher identifies a site likely to contribute to his or her research agenda, the next step is to plan and carry out excavation. To begin, the land is cleared, and the places to be excavated are plotted as a **grid system** (Figure 4.1). The surface of the site is divided into squares

grid system A system for recording data in three dimensions from an archaeological excavation.

Anthropology Applied

Cultural Resource Management ■ By John Crock

In the United States and Europe, cultural resource management or "regulatory" archaeology employs more archaeologists than universities and museums combined. This work is mandated by laws like Section 106 of the National Historic Preservation Act, which requires a cultural resources review for federally funded or regulated development projects, like the construction of new highways. These federal requirements have provided the funds for me and many other archaeologists to do what we love the best: to reconstruct the lives of people in the past through excavation of the material traces they have left behind.

For example, the Vermont Agency of Transportation's Missisquoi Bay Bridge project at the northern end of Lake Champlain resulted in the discovery of one of the most significant archaeological sites ever found in Vermont. The initial Phase I survey sampling for the project included the excavation of small shovel test pits across the level field that would one day become the new bridge approach. Seven of the initial fifty-seven pits contained evidence of an archaeological site, including a total of just eight artifacts. Fortunately, this limited evidence was enough to document the presence of a pre-contact Native American habitation, later named the Bohannon site after the landowner.

To determine its size and significance, we conducted a Phase II evaluation of the site. Native American deposits were recovered from thirty-nine of the additional sixty-seven Phase II test pits excavated. The majority of the artifacts recovered are small fragments of clay pottery, including a portion of a turtle head effigy from a pipe or vessel. It was this artifact, the likes of which had never before been excavated in Vermont, which helped indicate the site was significant

and eligible for the National Register of Historic Places. The effigy, and the style and thickness of pottery shards, indicated the site dated to the late pre-contact or contact period, between about 1400 and 1700. Since the site could not be avoided during construction, Phase III data recovery excavations were necessary to salvage a sample of the endangered site.

It was only during this final phase of work that the true size and significance of the Bohannon site was revealed. Excavation of large areas uncovered a substantial sample of decorated clay pipes and jars. Paleobotanist Nancy Sidell identified corn kernels and parts of corn plants in hearth and trash pit features at the site, indicating that the residents of the site grew corn close by. Zooarchaeologist Nanny Carder identified twenty-four different species in bone refuse from the same features, revealing a broad diet of animals ranging from flying squirrel to black bear. Living floors, trash pits, and the former location of house posts also were identified.

© John Crock

To salvage as much information as possible from the site before construction, an acre of the project area was stripped of topsoil to try to determine more about the layout of the site. Hundreds of post "mold" stains were revealed, from which portions of several longhouses have been reconstructed. A sample of corn kernels found were radiocarbon dated using accelerator mass spectrometry (AMS) to around AD 1600. Other dates and their error ranges place the site occupation between 1450 and 1650.

We believe the site was occupied just prior to 1609, when the first Europeans entered the region, based on the style of the pottery, the radiocarbon dates, and the fact that no European artifacts were recovered. The decorated clay pipes and pottery jars from the site are identical to material that has been found at late pre-contact village sites along the St. Lawrence River in Quebec. The inventory of artifacts, food resources, and house patterns from the site all suggest that the people at the Bohannon site were closely related to the St. Lawrence Iroquoians, a First Nations people who lived in what is now Quebec and Ontario.

From its humble identification in the early stages of archaeological survey for the new bridge, the Bohannon site has yielded an incredible amount of information; it represents the first St. Lawrence Iroquoian village discovered in Vermont.

To recover very small objects easily missed in excavation, archaeologists routinely screen the earth they remove. Here archaeologists are using the flotation technique for the recovery of charred plant remains.

© Tony Arruza/Corbis

of equal size, and each square is numbered and marked with stakes. Each object found may then be located precisely in the square from which it came. (Remember, context is everything!) The starting point of a grid system, which is located precisely in three dimensions, may be a large rock, the edge of a stone wall, or an iron rod sunk into the ground; this point is also known as the reference or **datum point.**

At a large site covering several square miles, the plotting may be done in terms of individual structures, numbered according to the square of a "giant grid" in which they are found. In a gridded site, each square is dug separately with great care. Trowels are used to scrape the soil, and screens are used to sift all the loose soils so that even the smallest artifacts, such as flint chips or beads, are recovered.

A technique employed when looking for very fine objects, such as fish scales or very small bones, is called

datum point The starting, or reference, point for a grid system.

This photo shows a section excavated through a building at the ancient Maya site of Tikal and illustrates stratigraphy. Inside the building's base are the remains of walls and floors for earlier buildings. Oldest are the innermost and deepest walls and floors. As time wore on, the Maya periodically demolished upper portions of older buildings, the remains of which were buried beneath new construction.

© William A. Haviland

flotation. Flotation consists of immersing soil in water, causing the particles to separate. Some will float, others will sink to the bottom, and the remains can be easily retrieved.

If the site is **stratified**—that is, if the remains lie in layers one upon the other—each layer, or stratum, will be dug separately. Each layer, having been laid down during a particular span of time, will contain artifacts deposited at the same time and belonging to the same culture. Culture change can be traced through the order in which artifacts were deposited—deeper layers reveal older artifacts. But, archaeologists Frank Hole and Robert F. Heizer suggest,

> because of difficulties in analyzing stratigraphy, archaeologists must use the greatest caution in drawing conclusions. Almost all interpretations of time, space, and culture contexts depend on stratigraphy. The refinements of laboratory techniques for analysis are wasted if archaeologists cannot specify the stratigraphic position of their artifacts.[2]

If no stratification is present, then the archaeologist digs by arbitrary levels. Each square must be dug so that its edges and profiles are straight; walls between squares are often left standing to serve as visual correlates of the grid system.

Excavation of Fossils

Although fossil excavating is similar to archaeological excavation, some key differences exist. The paleoanthropologist must be particularly skilled in the techniques of geology, or have ready access to geological expertise, because a fossil is of little value unless its place in the sequence of rocks that contain it can be determined.

In order to provide all the necessary expertise, paleoanthropological expeditions these days generally are made up of teams of experts in various fields in addition to physical anthropology. Surgical skill and caution are required to remove a fossil from its burial place without damage. An unusual combination of tools and materials is usually contained in the kit of the paleoanthropologist—pickaxes, dental tools, enamel coating, burlap for bandages, and sculpting plaster.

---

[2]Hole, F., & Heizer, R. F. (1969). *An introduction to prehistoric archeology* (p. 113). New York: Holt, Rinehart & Winston.

flotation An archaeological technique employed to recover very tiny objects by immersion of soil samples in water to separate heavy from light particles.
stratified Layered; said of archaeological sites where the remains lie in layers, one upon another.

To remove newly discovered bones, the paleoanthropologist begins uncovering the specimen, using pick and shovel for initial excavation, then small camel-hair brushes and dental picks to remove loose and easily detachable debris surrounding the bones. Once the entire specimen has been uncovered (a process that may take days of back-breaking, patient labor), the bones are covered with shellac and tissue paper to prevent cracking and damage during further excavation and handling.

Both the fossil and the earth immediately surrounding it, or the matrix, are prepared for removal as a single block. The bones and matrix are cut out of the earth (but not removed), and more shellac is applied to the entire block to harden it. The bones are covered with burlap bandages dipped in plaster. Then the entire block is enclosed in more plaster and burlap bandages, perhaps splinted with tree branches and allowed to dry overnight. After it has hardened, the entire block is carefully removed from the earth, ready for packing and transport to a laboratory. Before leaving the discovery area, the investigator makes a thorough sketch map of the terrain and pinpoints the find on geological maps to aid future investigators.

State of Preservation of Archaeological and Fossil Evidence

The results of excavation depend upon the nature of the remains as much as upon the excavator's digging skills. Inorganic materials such as stone and metal are more resistant to decay than organic ones such as wood and bone. Sometimes the anthropologist discovers an assemblage—a collection of artifacts—made of durable inorganic materials, such as stone tools, and traces of organic ones long since decomposed, such as woodwork (Figure 4.2), textiles, or food.

Climate, local geological conditions, and cultural practices also play a role in the state of preservation. For example, our knowledge of ancient Egyptian culture stems not only from their burial practices but from the effects of climate and soil on the state of preservation. The ancient Egyptians believed that eternal life could be achieved only if the dead person were buried with his or her worldly possessions. Hence, their tombs are usually filled with a wealth of artifacts even including the skeletons of other humans owned by dynastic rulers.

Under favorable climatic conditions, even the most perishable objects may survive over vast periods of time. Even the earliest Egyptian burials consisting of shallow pits in the sand often yield well-preserved corpses. Because these bodies were buried long before mummification was ever practiced, their preservation can only be the result of rapid desiccation, or complete drying out, in the warm desert climate. The elaborate tombs of the rul-

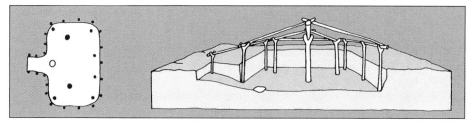

Figure 4.2
Although the wooden posts of a house may have long since decayed, their positions may still be marked by discoloration of the soil. The plan shown on the left—of an ancient posthole pattern and depression at Snaketown, Arizona—permits the hypothetical house reconstruction on the right.

ers of dynastic Egypt often contain wooden furniture, textiles, flowers, and written scrolls on paper made from papyrus reeds, barely touched by time, seemingly as fresh looking as they were when deposited in the tomb as long as 5,000 years ago—a consequence of the region's arid climatic conditions. Of course, the ancient Egyptian burial practices selectively preserved more information about the elite members of society than the average individual.

The dryness of certain caves is also a factor in the preservation of **coprolites,** the scientific term for fossilized human or animal feces. Coprolites provide information on prehistoric diet and health. From the analysis of elements preserved in coprolites such as seeds, insect skeletons, and tiny bones from fish or amphibians, archaeologists and paleoanthropologists can directly determine diets from the past. This information, in turn, can shed light on overall health. Because many sources of food are available only in certain seasons, it is even

possible to tell the time of year in which the food was eaten.

Certain climates can obliterate all evidence of organic remains. Maya ruins found in the tropical rainforests of Mesoamerica (the geographical area including southern Mexico and northern Central America) are often in a state of collapse—notwithstanding that many are massive structures of stone—as a result of the pressure exerted upon them by the heavy forest vegetation. The rain and humidity soon destroy almost all traces of woodwork, textiles, or basketry. Fortunately, impressions of these artifacts can sometimes be preserved in plaster, and some objects made of wood or plant fibers are depicted in stone carvings and pottery figurines. Thus, even in the face of substantial decay of organic substances, something may still be learned about them.

Sorting Out the Evidence

Excavation records include a scale map of all the features, the stratification of each excavated square, a description of the exact location and depth of every artifact or bone unearthed, and photographs and scale drawings of the objects. This is the only way archaeological evidence can later be pieced together so as to arrive at a plausible reconstruction of a culture. Although the archaeologist or paleoanthropologist may be interested only in certain kinds of remains, every aspect of the site must be recorded, whether it is relevant to the particular investigation or not, because such evidence may be useful to others and would otherwise be permanently lost. In sum, archaeological sites are nonrenewable resources. The disturbance of the arrangement of artifacts, even by proper excavation, is permanent.

Looting of sites for personal profit can also cause permanent loss not only of artifacts but of the sites that held them. Looting has long been a threat to the archaeological record. But today, looting has become a high-

At the Maya site of Tikal, these manikin scepter figures, originally made of wood, were recovered from a king's tomb by pouring plaster into a cavity in the soil, left when the original organic material decayed.

coprolites Preserved fecal material providing evidence of the diet and health of past organisms.

© AFP/Getty images

In September 2006, research-ers announced the discovery of a spectacular new fossil—the skeleton of a young child dated to 3.3 million years ago. The fossil was actually discovered in the Dikika area of northern Ethiopia in 2000. Since then, researchers worked on careful recovery and analysis of the fos-silized remains so that when the announcement was made, a great deal was already known about the specimen. Their analyses have determined that this child, a little girl about 3 years old who likely died in a flash flood, was a member of the *Australopithecus afarensis*, the same species as the famous "Lucy" specimen (see Chapter 6). Due to the importance of this find, some sci-entists have referred to this child as "Lucy's baby" though the child lived about 150,000 years before "Lucy."

tech endeavor. Avid collectors and fans of archaeological sites unwittingly aid looting activity through sharing detailed knowledge about site and artifact location over the Internet. The Internet has also provided a market for artifacts.

Once the artifact or fossil has been freed from the surrounding matrix, a variety of other laboratory meth-ods come into play. For example, dental specimens are frequently analyzed under the microscope to examine markings on teeth that might provide clues about diet in the past. Specimens are now regularly scanned using computed tomography (CT scans) to analyze structural details of the bone. Imprints or **endocasts** of the insides of skulls are taken to determine the size and shape of an-cient brains.

The genetics revolution has carried over even to an-cient human remains. Anthropologists extract genetic material from skeletal remains in order to perform DNA comparisons between the specimen, other fossils, and living people. Small fragments of DNA are amplified or copied repeatedly using **polymerase chain reaction (PCR)** technology to provide a sufficient amount of ma-

endocast A cast of the inside of a skull; helps determine the size and shape of the brain.
polymerase chain reaction (PCR) A technique for amplifying or creating multiple copies of fragments of DNA so that it can be studied in the laboratory.
bioarchaeology The archaeological study of human remains emphasizing the preservation of cultural and social processes in the skeleton.

terial to perform these analyses. However, unless DNA is preserved in a stable material such as amber, it will decay over time. Therefore, analyses of DNA extracted from specimens older than about 50,000 years ago become in-creasingly unreliable due to the decay of DNA.

Archaeologists and paleoanthropologists, as a rule of thumb, plan on at least three hours of laboratory work for each hour of fieldwork. In the lab, artifacts that have been recovered must first be cleaned and catalogued—often a tedious and time-consuming job—before they are ready for analysis. From the shapes of the artifacts as well as from the traces of manufacture and wear, ar-chaeologists can usually determine their function. For example, the Russian archaeologist S. A. Semenov de-voted many years to the study of prehistoric technology. In the case of a flint tool used as a scraper, he was able to determine, by examining the wear patterns of the tool under a microscope, that the prehistoric individuals who used it began to scrape from right to left and then scraped from left to right, and in so doing avoided strain-ing the muscles of the hand.[3] From the work of Semenov and others, we now know that right-handed individuals made most stone tools preserved in the archaeological record, a fact that has implications for brain structure. The relationships among populations can also be traced through material remains (Figure 4.3).

Bioarchaeology, which seeks to understand past cultures through analysis of skeletal remains, is a grow-

---

[3]Semenov, S. A. (1964). *Prehistoric technology*. New York: Barnes & Noble.

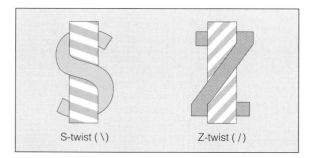

Figure 4.3

In northern New England, prehistoric pottery was often decorated by impressing the damp clay with a cord-wrapped stick. Examination of cord impressions reveals that coastal people twisted fibers used to make cordage to the left (Z-twist), while those living inland did the opposite (S-twist). The nonfunctional differences reflect motor habits so deeply ingrained as to seem completely natural to the cordage makers. From this, we may infer two distinctively different populations.

ing area within anthropology. It combines the biological anthropologists' expertise in skeletal biology with the archaeological reconstruction of human cultures. Analysis of human skeletal material provides important insights into ancient peoples' diets, gender roles, social status, and patterns of activity. For example, analysis of human skeletons showed that elite members of society had access to better diets than lower-ranking members of society, allowing them to reach their full growth potential.[4]

Gender roles in a given society can be assessed through skeletons as well. In fully preserved adult skel-

---

[4]Haviland W. (1967). Stature at Tikal, Guatemala: Implications for ancient Maya, demography, and social organization. *American Antiquity 32*, 316–325.

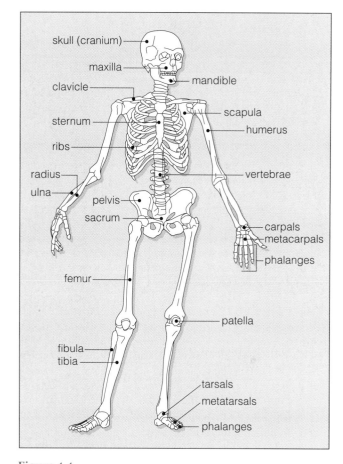

Figure 4.4

The complete male and female skeletons differ on average in some consistent ways that allow skeletal biologists to identify the sex of the deceased individual. In addition to noting some of these features labeled above, learning the basic skeleton will be useful in the chapters ahead as we trace the history of human evolution.

Skulls from peoples of the Tiwanaku empire, who tightly bound the skulls of their children. The shape of the skull distinguished people from various parts of the empire.

Biocultural

Connection

Kennewick Man

The "Ancient One," or "Kennewick Man," both refer to the 9,300-year-old skeletal remains that were found in 1996 below the surface of Lake Wallula, part of the Columbia River, in Kennewick, Washington State. This discovery has been the center of continuing controversy since it was made. Who owns these human remains? Who can determine what shall be done with them? Do the biological characteristics preserved in these remains play a role in determining their fate?

This particular conflict involves three major parties. Because the skeleton was found on a location for which the United States Army Corps of Engineers is responsible, this federal agency first took possession of the remains. Appealing to a new federal law, the Native American Graves Protection and Repatriation Act of 1990, a nearby American Indian group named the Confederated Tribes of the Umatilla Indian Reservation (representing the region's Umatilla, Cayuse, and Walla Walla nations) claimed the remains. Because Kennewick Man was found within their ancestral homeland, they argue that they are "culturally affiliated" with the individual they refer to as the

Ancient One. Viewing these human bones as belonging to an ancestor, they wish to return them to the earth in a respectful ceremony.

This claim was challenged in federal court by a group of scientists, including some archaeologists and biological anthropologists. They view these human remains, among the oldest ever discovered in the western hemisphere, as scientifically precious, with potential to shed light on the earliest population movements in the Americas. The scientists do not want to "own" the remains but want the opportunity to study them. By means of DNA analysis, for instance, these scientists expect to determine possible prehistoric linkages between this individual and ancient human remains found elsewhere, including Asia. Moreover, scientific analysis may determine whether there actually exists any biological connection between these remains and currently living Native peoples, including individuals residing on the Umatilla Indian Reservation.

Fearing the loss of a unique scientific specimen, they have filed a lawsuit in federal court to prevent reburial before

these bones are researched and analyzed. Their legal challenge is not based on "cultural affiliation," which is a very difficult concept when it concerns such ancient human remains, but focuses on the fact that the region's Native peoples cannot prove they are direct lineal descendants. Unless such ties have been objectively established, they argue, Kennewick Man should be released for scientific study.

In 2004 federal court rulings permitted initial scientific investigations. Just as these investigations were wrapping up in July 2005, the Senate Indian Affairs Committee heard testimony on a proposal by Arizona Senator John McCain to expand the Native American Graves Protection and Repatriation Act so that remains such as these would be once again prohibited from study. Doug Owsley, the forensic anthropologist from the Smithsonian Institution leading the research team, has said that scientific investigation is yielding even more information than expected. Because conflicting worldviews are at the center of this controversy, it is unlikely that it will be easily resolved.

etons, the sex of the deceased individual can be assessed with a high accuracy, allowing for comparisons of male and female life expectancy, mortality, and health status. These analyses can help establish the social roles of men and women in past societies.

Recently, skeletal analyses have become more difficult to carry out, especially in the United States, where Native American communities now often request the return of skeletons from archaeological excavations for reburial as required by federal law. Anthropologists find themselves in a quandary over this requirement. As scientists, anthropologists know the importance of the information that can be gleaned from studies of human skeletons, but as scholars subject to ethical principles, they are bound to respect the feelings of those who vest the skeletons with cultural and spiritual significance.

New techniques, such as 3D digital images of Native American skeletons, help to resolve this conflict as they allow for both rapid repatriation and continued study of skeletal remains. This chapter's Original Study provides an excellent example of archaeologists consulting with

representatives of Native American communities to work out procedures agreeable to both parties. By contrast, scientists and American Indians sometimes have been unable to move beyond their conflicting views as seen with "Kennewick Man," the 9,300-year-old skeleton that was dislodged by the Columbia River in Washington State in 1996. This chapter's Biocultural Connection focuses on how this controversy has been playing out in the federal courts.

Dating the Past

With accurate and detailed records of their excavations in hand, archaeologists and paleoanthropologists are able to deal with a crucial research issue: the question of age. As we have seen, analysis of physical and cultural remains is dependent on knowledge about the age of the artifacts or specimens. How, then, are the materials retrieved from excavations reliably dated? Calculating the age of physical and cultural remains is an essential aspect of interpreting the past. Because archaeologists and paleoanthropologists deal so often with peoples and events in times far removed from our own, the calendar of historic times is of little use to them.

Remains can be dated by noting their position in the earth, by measuring the amount of chemicals contained in fossil bones, or through association with other plant, animal, or cultural remains. These are known as **relative dating** techniques because they do not establish precise dates for remains but rather the relationship among a series of remains. **Absolute dating** or **chronometric dating** (from the Latin for "measuring time") methods provide actual dates calculated in years "before the present" (BP). These methods rely upon advances in the disciplines of chemistry and physics that use properties such as rates of decay of radioactive elements. These elements may be present in the remains themselves or in the surrounding soil. Absolute dating methods scientifically establish actual dates for the major events of geological and evolutionary history. By comparing dates and remains across a variety of sites, anthropologists can reconstruct human origins, migrations, and technological developments.

Many relative and chronometric techniques are available. However, most of these techniques are applicable only for certain time spans and in certain environmental contexts. Bear in mind that each of the chronometric dating techniques also has a margin of error. Ideally, archaeologists and paleoanthropologists try to utilize as many methods as are appropriate, given the materials available and the funds at their disposal. By doing so, they significantly reduce the risk of error. Several of the most frequently employed dating techniques are presented in Table 4.1.

Methods of Relative Dating

Of the many relative dating techniques available, **stratigraphy** is probably the most reliable. Stratigraphy is based on the simple principle that the oldest layer, or stratum, was deposited first (it is the deepest) whereas the newest layer was deposited last (in undisturbed situations, it lies at the top). Similarly, archaeological evidence is usually deposited in chronological order. The lowest stratum contains the oldest artifacts and/or fossils, whereas the uppermost stratum contains the most recent ones. Thus, even in the absence of precise dates, one knows the *relative* age of objects in one stratum compared with the ages of those in other strata. Defining the stratigraphy of a given site can be complicated by geological activities such as earthquakes that shift the position of stratigraphic layers.

Another method of relative dating is the **fluorine** method. It is based on the fact that the amount of fluorine deposited in bones is proportional to the amount of time they have been in the earth. The oldest bones contain the greatest amount of fluorine and vice versa. The fluo-

Some ancient societies devised precise ways of recording dates that archaeologists have been able to correlate with our own calendar. Here is the tomb of an important ruler, Siyaj Chan K'awil II, at the ancient Maya city of Tikal. The glyphs painted on the wall give the date of the burial in the Maya calendar, which is the same as March 18, AD 457, in the Gregorian calendar.

© University of Pennsylvania Museum

rine test is useful in dating bones that cannot be ascribed with certainty to any particular stratum. A shortcoming of this method is that the amount of naturally occurring fluorine is not constant, but varies from region to region making cross-site comparisons of fluorine values invalid. This method was vital for uncovering the infamous Pilt-

relative dating In archaeology and paleoanthropology, designating an event, object, or fossil as being older or younger than another.
absolute or **chronometric dating** In archaeology and paleoanthropology, dates for recovered material based on solar years, centuries, or other units of absolute time.
stratigraphy In archaeology and paleoanthropology, the most reliable method of relative dating by means of strata.
fluorine dating In archaeology or paleoanthropology, a technique for relative dating based on the fact that the amount of fluorine in bones is proportional to their age.

TABLE 4.1	ABSOLUTE AND RELATIVE DATING METHODS USED BY ARCHAEOLOGISTS AND PALEOANTHROPOLOGISTS		
Dating Method	**Time Period**	**Method's Process**	**Drawbacks**
Stratigraphy	Relative only	Based on the law of superposition, which states that lower layers or strata are older than higher layers.	Site specific; natural forces, such as earthquakes, and human activity, such as burials, disturb stratigraphic relationships.
Fluorine analysis	Relative only	Compares the amount of fluorine from surrounding soil absorbed by specimens after deposition.	Site specific.
Faunal and floral series	Relative only	Sequencing remains into relative chronological order based on an evolutionary sequence established in another region with reliable absolute dates. Called palynology when done with pollen grains.	Dependent upon known relationships established elsewhere.
Seriation	Relative only	Sequencing cultural remains into relative chronological order based on stylistic features.	Dependent upon known relationships established elsewhere.
Dendrochronology	About 3,000 years BP maximum	Compares tree growth rings preserved in a site with a tree of known age.	Requires ancient trees of known age.
Radiocarbon	Accurate < 50,000 BP	Compares the ratio of radioactive ^{14}C (with a half-life of 5,730 years) to stable ^{12}C in organic material.	Increasingly inaccurate when assessing remains from greater than 50,000 years ago.
Potassium argon (K-Ar)	> 200,000 BP	Compares the amount of radioactive potassium (^{40}K with a half-life of 1.3 billion years) to stable argon (^{40}Ar).	Requires volcanic ash; requires cross-checking due to contamination from atmospheric argon.
Amino acid racemization	40,000– 180,000 BP	Compares the change in the number of proteins in a right- vs. left-sided three-dimensional structure.	Amino acids leached out from soil variably cause error.
Thermoluminescence	Possibly up to 200,000 BP	Measures the amount of light given off due to radioactivity when sample heated to high temperatures.	Technique developed for recent materials such as Greek pottery; not clear how accurate the dates will be for older remains.
Electron spin resonance	Possibly up to 200,000 BP	Measures the resonance of trapped electrons in a magnetic field.	Works with tooth enamel—not yet developed for bone; problems with accuracy.
Fission track	Wide range of times	Measures the tracks left in crystals by uranium as it decays; good cross-check for K-Ar technique.	Useful for dating crystals only.
Paleomagnetic reversals	Wide range of times	Measures orientation of magnetic particles in stones and links them to whether magnetic field of earth pulled toward the north or south during their formation.	Large periods of normal or reversed magnetic orientation require dating by some other method; some smaller events known to interrupt the sequence.
Uranium series	40,000–180,000	Measures the amount of uranium decaying in cave sites.	Large error range.

down hoax in which a human skull and orangutan jaw were placed together in the earth as false evidence for an early human ancestor in England (see Chapter 6).

seriation A technique for relative dating by putting groups of objects into a sequence in relation to one another.

Relative dating can also be done by establishing sequences of plant, animal, or even cultural remains. For these methods, the order of appearance of a succession (or series) of plants, animals, or artifacts provides relative dates for a site based on a series established in another area. An example of **seriation** based on cultural artifacts is the Stone–Bronze–Iron Age series established by prehistorians (see Chapter 11). Within a given region, sites containing artifacts made of iron are generally more recent than sites containing only stone tools. In well-investigated culture areas, series have even been developed for particular styles of pottery.

Similar inferences are made with animal or faunal series. For example, very early North American Indian sites have yielded the remains of mastodons and mammoths—animals now extinct—and on this basis the sites can be dated to a time before these animals died out, roughly 10,000 years ago. For dating some of the earliest African fossils in human evolution, faunal series have been developed in regions where accurate chronometric dates can be established. These series can then be used to establish relative sequences in other regions. Similar series have been established for plants, particularly using grains of pollen. This approach has become known as **palynology.** The kind of pollen found in any geologic stratum depends on the kind of vegetation that existed at the time that stratum was deposited. A site or locality can therefore be dated by determining what kind of pollen was found associated with it. In addition, palynology also helps to reconstruct environments in which prehistoric people lived.

Methods of Chronometric Dating

Chronometric dating methods rely upon advances in the disciplines of chemistry and physics, allowing scientists to calculate the ages of physical and cultural remains. Several methods use naturally occurring radioactive elements that are present either in the remains themselves or in the surrounding soil.

One of the most widely used methods of absolute dating is **radiocarbon dating.** This method uses the fact that while they are alive, all organisms absorb radioactive carbon (known as carbon 14 or ^{14}C) as well as ordinary carbon 12 (^{12}C) in proportions identical to those found in the atmosphere. Absorption of ^{14}C ceases at the time of death, and the ratio between the two forms of carbon begins to change as the unstable radioactive element ^{14}C begins to "decay." Each radioactive element decays, or transforms into a stable nonradioactive form, at a specific rate. The amount of time it takes for one-half of the material originally present to decay is expressed as the "half-life." In the case of ^{14}C, it takes 5,730 years for half of the amount of ^{14}C present to decay to stable nitrogen 14. In another 5,730 years (11,460 years total), half of the remaining amount will also decay to nitrogen 14 so that only one-quarter of the original amount of ^{14}C will be present. Thus the age of an organic substance such as charcoal, wood, shell, or bone can be measured through determining the changing proportion of ^{14}C relative to the amount of stable ^{12}C.

Though scientists can measure the amount of radioactive carbon left in even a few milligrams of a given organic substance of a recent specimen, as we get into the more distant past, the amounts of carbon 14 present become so small that it becomes difficult to detect it accurately. The radiocarbon method can adequately date organic materials up to about 50,000 years old, but dates for older material are far less reliable. Of course, one has to be sure that the organic remains were truly contemporaneous with the archaeological materials. For example, charcoal found on a site may have gotten there from a recent forest fire rather than more ancient activity; or wood used to make something by the people who lived at a site may have been retrieved from some older context.

Because there is always a certain amount of error involved, radiocarbon dates (like all chronometric dating methods) are not as absolute as is sometimes thought. This is why any stated date always has a plus-or-minus ($\pm$) factor attached to it corresponding to one standard deviation above and below the mean value. For example, a date of 5,200 $\pm$ 120 years ago means that there is about a 2 out of 3 chance (or a 67 percent chance) that the true date falls somewhere between 5,080 and 5,320 radiocarbon years ago. The qualification "radiocarbon years" is used because radiocarbon years are not precisely equivalent to calendar years.

The discovery that radiocarbon years are not precisely equivalent to calendar years was made possible by another method of absolute dating: **dendrochronology.** Originally devised for dating Pueblo Indian sites in the North American Southwest, this method is based on the fact that in the right kind of climate, trees add one (and only one) new growth ring to their trunks every year. The rings vary in thickness, depending upon the amount of rainfall received in a year, so that climatic fluctuation is registered in the growth ring. By taking a sample of wood, such as a beam from a Pueblo Indian house, and by comparing its pattern of rings with those in the trunk of a tree of known age, archaeologists can date the archaeological material.

Dendrochronology is applicable only to wooden objects. Furthermore, it can be used only in regions in which trees of great age, such as the giant sequoias and the bristlecone pine, are known to grow. Radiocarbon

palynology In archaeology and paleoanthropology, a method of relative dating based on changes in fossil pollen over time.
radiocarbon dating In archaeology and paleoanthropology, a technique for chronometric dating based on measuring the amount of radioactive carbon (^{14}C) left in organic materials found in archaeological sites.
dendrochronology In archaeology, a method of chronometric dating based on the number of rings of growth found in a tree trunk.

dating of wood from bristlecone pines dated by dendro-chronology allows scientists to correct carbon 14 dates so as to bring them into agreement with calendar dates.

Potassium-argon dating, another commonly used method of absolute dating, is based on a technique similar to that of radiocarbon analysis. Following intense heating, as from a volcanic eruption, radioactive potassium decays at a known rate to form argon—any previously existing argon having been released by the heating of the molten lava. The half-life of radioactive potassium is 1.3 billion years. Deposits that are millions of years old can now be dated by measuring the ratio of potassium to argon in a given rock.

Volcanic debris at various localities in East Africa is routinely dated by potassium-argon analysis, indicating when the volcanic eruption occurred. If fossils or artifacts are found sandwiched between layers of volcanic ash, as they are at Olduvai and other sites in East Africa, they can be dated with some precision. As with radiocarbon dates, there are limits to that precision, and potassium-argon dates are always stated with a plus-or-minus margin of error attached. The precision of this method is limited to time periods older than about 200,000 years ago.

Though these radiocarbon and potassium-argon methods are extremely valuable, neither technique works well during the time period dating from about 50,000 years ago to about 200,000 years ago. Because this same time period happens to be very important in human evolutionary history, scientists have developed a number of other important methods to obtain accurate dates during this critical period.

One such method, amino acid racemization, is based on the fact that amino acids trapped in organic materials gradually change, or racemize, after death, from left-handed forms to right-handed forms. Thus, the ratio of left- to right-handed forms should indicate the specimen's age. Unfortunately, in substances like bone, moisture and acids in the soil can leach out the amino acids, thereby introducing a serious source of error. However, ostrich eggshells have proved immune to this problem, the amino acids being so effectively locked up in a tight mineral matrix that they are preserved for thousands of years. Because ostrich eggs were widely used as food, and the shells as containers in Africa and the Middle East, they provide a powerful means of dating sites of the later parts of the Old Stone Age (Paleolithic), between 40,000 and 180,000 years ago.

Electron spin resonance, which measures the number of trapped electrons in bone, and thermoluminescence, which measures the amount of light emitted from a specimen when heated to high temperatures, are two additional methods that have been developed to fill in prehistorical time gaps. Dates derived from these two methods changed the interpretation of key sites in present-day Israel vital for reconstructing human origins (see Chapter 8).

A few other chronometric techniques rely on the element uranium. Fission track dating, for example, counts radiation damage tracks on mineral crystals. Like amino acid racemization, all these methods have problems: They are complicated and tend to be expensive; many can be carried out only on specific kinds of materials, and some are so new that their reliability is not yet unequivocally established. It is for these reasons that

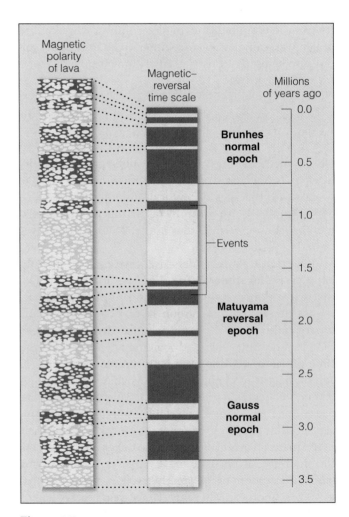

Figure 4.5

Scientists have documented a geomagnetic polarity time scale in which the changes in the earth's magnetic force—to north or south—have been calibrated. This geomagnetic time scale provides opportunities to cross-check other dating methods.

potassium-argon dating In archaeology and paleoanthropology, a technique for chronometric dating that measures the ratio of radioactive potassium to argon in volcanic debris associated with human remains.

they have not been as widely used as radiocarbon and potassium-argon dating techniques.

Paleomagnetic reversals contribute another interesting dimension to absolute dating methodologies by providing a method to cross-check dates. This method is based on the shifting magnetic pole of the earth—the same force that controls the orientation of a compass needle. Today, a compass points to the north because we are in a period defined as the geomagnetic "normal." Over the past several million years, there have been extended periods of time during which the magnetic field of the earth pulled toward the South Pole. Geologists call these periods "geomagnetic reversals." Iron particles in stones will be oriented into positions determined by the dominant magnetic pole at the time of their formation, allowing scientists to derive broad ranges of dates for them. Human evolutionary history contains a geomagnetic reversal starting 5.2 million years ago that ended 3.4 million years ago, followed by a normal period until 2.6 million years ago; then a second reversal began, lasting until about 700,000 years ago when the present normal period began. This paleomagnetic sequence can be used to date sites to either normal or reversed periods and can be correlated with a variety of other dating methods to cross-check their accuracy.

Establishment of dates for human physical and cultural remains is a vital part of understanding our past. For example, as paleoanthropologists reconstruct human evolutionary history and the movement of the genus *Homo* out of Africa, dates determine the story told by the bones. In the next chapters we will see that many of the theories about human origins are dependent upon dates. Similarly, as archaeologists dig up material culture, interpretations of the movement and interactions of past peoples depend on dating methods to provide a sequence to the cultural remains.

CHANCE AND THE STUDY OF THE PAST

The archaeological and fossil records are imperfect. Chance circumstances of preservation have determined what has and what has not survived the ravages of time. Thus, the biology and culture of our ancestors are reconstructed on the basis of incomplete and, possibly, unrepresentative samples of physical and cultural remains. The problems are further compounded by the role that chance continues to play in the discovery of prehistoric remains. Remains may come to light due to factors ranging from changing sea level, vegetation, or even a local government's decision to build a highway.

In addition, past cultural processes have also shaped the archaeological and fossil record. We know more about the past due to the cultural practice of deliberate burial. We know more about the elite segments of past societies because they have left more material culture behind. However, as archaeologists have shifted their focus from gathering treasures to the reconstruction of human behavior, they have gained a more complete picture of past societies. Similarly, paleoanthropologists no longer simply catalog fossils; they interpret data about our ancestors in order to reconstruct the biological processes responsible for who we are today. The challenge of reconstructing our past will be met by a continual process of re-examination and modification as anthropologists discover new evidence in the earth, among living people, and in the laboratory leading to new understanding of human origins.

Questions for Reflection

1. How would you answer the challenge of deciding who owns the past? Have there been any examples of contested ownership in your community?

2. The cultural practice of burial of the dead altered the fossil record and provided valuable insight into the beliefs and practices of past cultures. The same is true today. What beliefs are reflected in the traditions for treatment of the dead in your culture?

3. Controversy has surrounded Kennewick Man since this skeleton eroded from the banks of the Columbia River in Washington in 1996. Scientists and Native American people both feel they have a right to these remains. What kinds of evidence support these differing perspectives? How should this controversy be resolved?

4. Why is dating so important for paleoanthropologists and archaeologists? Would an interpretation of physical or cultural remains change depending upon the date assigned to the remains?

5. How have random events as well as deliberate cultural practices shaped both the fossil and archaeological records? Why do we know more about some places and peoples than others?

Suggested Readings

Fagan, B. M., Beck, C., & Silberman, N. A. (1998). *The Oxford companion to archaeology*. New York: Oxford University Press.

This encyclopedia of archaeology and prehistory contains 700 entries written in an engaging style by over 300 experts in the field. Topics range from fossils to historical sites conveying the field's critical transition from an amateur to a scientific discipline.

Feder, K. L. (1999). *Frauds, myths, and mysteries* (3rd ed.). Mountain View, CA: Mayfield.

This very readable book enlightens readers about the many pseudo-scientific and even crackpot theories about past cultures that all too often have been presented to the public as "solid" archaeology.

Joukowsky, M. (1980). *A complete field manual of archaeology: Tools and techniques of fieldwork for archaeologists.* Englewood Cliffs, NJ: Prentice-Hall.

This book, encyclopedic in its coverage, explains for the novice and professional alike all of the methods and techniques used by archaeologists in the field.

Sharer, R. J., & Ashmore, W. (2002). *Archaeology: Discovering our past* (3rd ed.). New York: McGraw-Hill.

One of the best presentations of the body of method, technique, and theory that most archaeologists accept as fundamental to their discipline. The authors confine themselves to the operational modes, guiding strategies, and theoretical orientations of anthropological archaeology in a manner well designed to lead the beginner into the discipline.

Shipman, P. (1981). *Life history of a fossil: An introduction to taphonomy and paleoecology.* Cambridge, MA: Harvard University Press.

In order to understand what a fossil has to tell us, one must know how it came to be where the paleoanthropologist found it (taphonomy). In this book, anthropologist-turned-science writer Pat Shipman explains how animal remains are acted upon and altered from death to fossilization.

Thomas, D. H. (1998). *Archaeology* (3rd ed.). Fort Worth, TX: Harcourt Brace.

Some books tell us how to do archaeology, some tell us what archaeologists have found out, but this one tells us why we do archaeology. It does so in a coherent and thorough way, and Thomas' blend of ideas, quotations, biographies, and case studies makes for interesting reading.

Thomson Audio Study Products

 Enjoy the MP3-ready Audio Lecture Overviews for each chapter and a comprehensive audio glossary of key terms for quick study and review. Whether walking to class, doing laundry, or studying at your desk, you now have the freedom to choose when, where, and how you interact with your audio-based educational media. See the preface for information on how to access this on-the-go study and review tool.

The Anthropology Resource Center

www.thomsonedu.com/anthropology

The Anthropology Resource Center provides extended learning materials to reinforce your understanding of key concepts in the four subfields of anthropology. For each of the four subdisciplines, the Resource Center includes dynamic exercises including video exercises, map exercises, simulations, and "Meet the Scientists" interviews, as well as critical thinking questions that can be assigned and e-mailed to instructors. The Resource Center also provides breaking news in anthropology and interesting material on applied anthropology to help you link what you are learning to the world around you.

5 Macroevolution and the Early Primates

© Russell L. Ciochon

CHALLENGE ISSUE

In the centuries to come, humans will face increasing challenges in maintaining an ecosystem on earth that can sustain diverse species. The principles of macroevolution and the evolutionary history of the primate order provide a foundation for understanding future changes such as the impact of the formation of new species and the extinction of others. Paleoanthropologists use fossil, molecular, and geologic data to reconstruct the biology and behavior of extinct groups. This model of a member of the extinct ape genus *Gigantopithecus*, for example, is based on evidence from jaw bones and teeth found in China combined with the anatomy of living species such as the gorilla. The teeth indicate that a vegetarian ape larger than the gorilla lived in East Asia at about the same time that members of the genus *Homo* began to inhabit the region. The model was created by Hollywood monster maker Bill Munn and anthropologist Russell Ciochon (pictured).

What Is Macroevolution?

While microevolution refers to changes in the allele frequencies of populations, macroevolution focuses upon the formation of new species (speciation) and on the evolutionary relationships among groups of species. Speciation may proceed in a branching manner, as when reproductive isolation of populations prevents gene flow between them, leading to the formation of separate species. Alternatively, in the absence of isolation, a species may evolve without branching in response to environmental changes. The accumulation of small changes from generation to generation may transform an ancestral species into a new one.

When and Where Did the First Primates Appear, and What Were They Like?

Fossil evidence indicates that the earliest primates began to develop around 65 million years ago, when the mass extinction of the dinosaurs opened new ecological opportunities for mammals. By 55 million years ago, primates inhabited North America and Eurasia, which at that time were joined together as the supercontinent Laurasia and separated from Africa. The earliest primates were small nocturnal insect eaters adapted to life in the trees.

When Did the First Monkeys and Apes Appear, and What Were They Like?

By the late Eocene epoch, about 40 million years ago, diurnal anthropoid primates appeared. Many of the Old World anthropoid species became ground dwellers. By the Miocene epoch (beginning 23.5 million years ago), apes were widespread in Asia, Africa, and Europe. While some of these hominoids were relatively small, others were even larger than present-day gorillas. Sometime between 5 and 8 million years ago, a branch of the African hominoid line became bipedal, beginning the evolutionary line that later produced humans.

Today, humans are the only primate to have a global distribution. We inhabit every continent, including areas as inhospitable as the icy Antarctic or the scorching Sahara Desert. This extended geographic range reflects the adaptability of *Homo sapiens*. By comparison, our relatives in the hominoid superfamily live in very circumscribed areas of the Old World tropical rainforest. Chimpanzees, bonobos, and gorillas can be found only in portions of Central and West Africa. Orangutans are limited to the treetops on the Southeast Asian islands of Sumatra and Borneo. Gibbons and siamangs swing through the branches of a variety of Southeast Asian forests.

Such comparisons between humans and the other primates feel natural to biologists and anthropologists today, because they accept that modern humans, apes, and monkeys are descended from the same prehistoric ancestors. However, almost a century and a half ago, when Charles Darwin published *Origin of Species* (1859), this notion was so controversial that Darwin limited himself to a single sentence on the subject. Today, anthropologists, as well as the global scientific community in general, accept that human origins are revealed in the evolutionary history of the primates. We now know that much of who we are, as culture-bearing biological organisms, derives from our mammalian primate heritage.

 THOMSON AUDIO STUDY PRODUCTS Take advantage of the MP3-ready Audio Lecture Overviews and comprehensive audio glossary of key terms for each chapter. See the preface for information on how to access this on-the-go study and review tool.

Although many of the primates discussed in this chapter no longer exist, their descendants (discussed in Chapter 3), now live in South and Central America, Africa, Asia, and Gibraltar at the southern tip of Spain. The successful adaptation of the primates largely reflects their intelligence, a characteristic that provides for behavioral flexibility. Other physical traits, such as stereoscopic vision and a grasping hand, have also been instrumental in the success of the primates.

Why do paleoanthropologists attempt to recreate primate evolutionary history from ancient evidence?

macroevolution Evolution above the species level.
speciation The process of forming new species.
isolating mechanism A factor that separates breeding populations, thereby preventing gene flow, creating divergent subspecies, and ultimately (if maintained) divergent species.
cladogenesis Speciation through a branching mechanism whereby an ancestral population gives rise to two or more descendant populations.

The study of these ancestral primates gives us a better understanding of the physical forces that caused these early creatures to evolve into today's primates. It gives us a fuller knowledge of the processes through which an insect-eating, small-brained mammal evolved into a toolmaker, a thinker, a human being.

MACROEVOLUTION AND THE PROCESS OF SPECIATION

While microevolution refers to changes in the allele frequencies of populations, **macroevolution** focuses upon the formation of new species (**speciation**) and on the evolutionary relationships among groups of species. To understand how the primates evolved, we must first look at how the evolutionary forces discussed in Chapter 2 led to macroevolutionary change. As noted in that chapter, the term *species* is usually defined as a population or group of populations that is capable of interbreeding and producing fertile, viable offspring. In other words, species are reproductively isolated. This definition, however, is not altogether satisfactory, because in nature isolated populations may be in the process of evolving into different species, and it is hard to tell exactly when they become biologically distinct without conducting breeding experiments. Furthermore, this definition can only be tested among living groups.

Certain factors, known as **isolating mechanisms,** can separate breeding populations and lead to the appearance of new species. Because isolation prevents gene flow, changes that affect the gene pool of one population cannot be introduced into the gene pool of the other. Random mutation may introduce new alleles in one of the isolated populations but not in the other. Genetic drift and natural selection may affect the two populations in different ways. Over time, as the two populations come to differ from each other, speciation occurs in a branching fashion known as **cladogenesis** (Figure 5.1) (from the Greek *klados* meaning "branch" or "shoot").

Some isolating mechanisms are geographical—preventing contact, hence gene flow, between members of separated populations. Biological aspects of organisms can also serve as isolating mechanisms. For example, early miscarriage of the hybrid offspring or sterility of the hybrid offspring, as in the case of closely related species such as horses and donkeys (producing sterile mules), serve as mechanisms to keep populations reproductively isolated from one another.

Isolating mechanisms may also be social rather than physical. Speciation due to this mechanism is particularly common among birds. For example, cuckoos (birds that do not build nests of their own but lay their eggs in other birds' nests) attract mates by mimicking the song

VISUAL **COUNTER**POINT

Regulatory genes turn other genes on and off, and a mere change in their timing can cause significant evolutionary change. This may have a played a role in differentiating chimps and humans; for example, adult humans retain the flat facial profile of juvenile chimps.

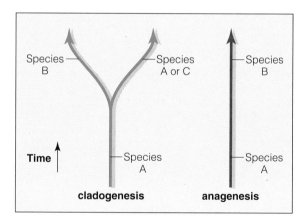

Figure 5.1

Cladogenesis occurs as different populations of an ancestral species become reproductively isolated. Through drift and differential selection, the number of descendant species increases. By contrast, anagenesis can occur through a process of variational change that takes place as small differences in traits that (by chance) are advantageous in a particular environment accumulate in a species' gene pool. Over time, this may produce sufficient change to transform an old species into a new one. Genetic drift may also account for anagenesis.

Sometimes mutations in a single gene can cause reorganization of an organism's body plan. Here the "bithorax" homeobox gene has caused this fruit fly to have two thoraxes and two sets of wings. Another homeobox gene "antennepedia" caused legs to develop in the place of antennae on the heads of fruit flies.

of the bird species in whose nests they place their eggs. Thus, cuckoos that are physically capable of mating may be isolated due to differences in courtship song behavior, which effectively isolates them from other cuckoos singing different tunes. Though social rules about marriage might be said to impose reproductive isolation among humans, these social barriers have no biological counterpart. For humans, no sufficiently absolute or long-lasting barriers to gene flow exist.

Because speciation is a process, it can occur at various rates. Speciation through the process of adaptive change to the environment as proposed in Darwin's *Origin of Species* is generally considered to occur at a slow rate. In this model, speciation may occur as organisms become more adapted to their environments. Sometimes, however, speciation can occur quite rapidly. For example, a genetic mutation, such as one involving a key regulatory gene, can lead to the formation of a new body plan. Such genetic accidents may involve material that is broken off, transposed, or transferred from one chromosome to another.

heterochrony Change in the timing of developmental events that is often responsible for changes in the shape or size of a body part.
homeobox gene A gene responsible for large-scale effects on growth and development that are frequently responsible for major reorganization of body plans in organisms.
punctuated equilibria A model of macroevolutionary change that suggests evolution occurs via long periods of stability or stasis punctuated by periods of rapid change.

Genes that regulate the growth and development of an organism may have a major effect on its adult form. Developmental change in the timing of events, a phenomenon known as **heterochrony** (from Latin for "different time"), is often responsible for changes in the shape or size of a body part. A kind of heterochrony called *neotony,* in which juvenile traits are retained in the adult state, may be responsible for some of the visible differences between humans and chimps. Scientists have discovered certain key genes called **homeobox genes** that are responsible for large-scale effects on the growth and development of the organism. If a new body plan happens to be adaptive, natural selection will maintain this new form during long periods of time rather than promoting change.

Paleontologists Stephen Jay Gould and Niles Eldred proposed that speciation occurs in a pattern of **punctuated equilibria**—the alternation between periods of rapid speciation and times of stability. Often, this conception of evolutionary change is contrasted with speciation through adaptation, sometimes known as *Darwinian gradualism.* A close look at the genetics and the fossil record indicate that both models of evolutionary change are important. Gould, the champion of the punctuated equilibrium model, describes the importance of the Darwinian approach to change in the following Original Study.

Original Study ▪ By Stephen Jay Gould

The Unsettling Nature of Variational Change

The Darwinian principle of natural selection yields temporal change—evolution in the biological definition—by the two-fold process of producing copious and undirected variation within a population and then passing along only a biased (selected) portion of this variation to the next generation. In this manner, the variation within a population at any moment can be converted into differences in mean values (average size, average braininess) among successive populations through time. For this fundamental reason, we call such theories of change *variational* as opposed to the more conventional, and more direct, models of *transformational* change imposed by natural laws that mandate a particular trajectory based on inherent (and therefore predictable) properties of substances and environments. (A ball rolling down

an inclined plane does not reach the bottom because selection has favored the differential propagation of moving versus stable elements of its totality but because gravity dictates this result when round balls roll down smooth planes.)

To illustrate the peculiar properties of variational theories like Darwin's in an obviously caricatured, but not inaccurate, description: Suppose that a population of elephants inhabits Siberia during a warm interval before the advance of an ice sheet. The elephants vary, at random, and in all directions, in their amount of body hair. As the ice advances and local conditions become colder, elephants with more hair will tend to cope better, by the sheer good fortune of their superior adaptation to changing climates—and they will leave more offspring on average. (This differential reproductive success

must be conceived as broadly statistical and not guaranteed in every case: In any generation, the hairiest elephant of all may fall into a crevasse and die.) Because offspring inherit their parents' degree of hairiness, the next generation will contain a higher proportion of more densely clad elephants (who will continue to be favored by natural selection as the climate becomes still colder). This process of increasing hairiness may continue for many generations, leading to the evolution of woolly mammoths.

This little fable can help us understand how peculiar and how contrary to all traditions of Western thought and explanation the Darwinian theory of evolution, and variational theories of historical change in general, must sound to the common ear. All the odd and fascinating properties of Darwinian

CONTINUED

evolution—the sensible and explainable but quite unpredictable nature of the outcome (dependent upon complex and contingent changes in local environments), the nonprogressive character of the alteration (adaptive only to these unpredictable local circumstances and not inevitably building a "better" elephant in any cosmic or general sense)—flow from the variational basis of natural selection.

Transformational theories work in a much simpler and more direct manner. If I want to go from A to B, I will have so much less conceptual (and actual) trouble if I can postulate a mechanism that will push me there directly than if I must rely upon the selection of "a few good men" from a random cloud of variation about

point A, then constitute a new generation around an average point one step closer to B, then generate a new cloud of random variation about this new point, then select "a few good men" once again from this new array—and then repeat this process over and over until I finally reach B.

When one adds the oddity of variational theories in general to our strong cultural and psychological resistance against their application to our own evolutionary origin (as an unpredictable and not necessary progressive little twig on life's luxuriant tree), then we can better understand why Darwin's revolution surpassed all other scientific discoveries in reformatory power and why so many

people still fail to understand, and may even resist, its truly liberal content. (I must leave the issue of liberation for another time, but once we recognize that the specification of morals and the search for a meaning to our lives cannot be accomplished by scientific study in any case, then Darwin's variational mechanism will no longer seem threatening and may even become liberating in teaching us to look within ourselves for answers to these questions and to abandon a chimerical search for the purpose of our lives, and for the source of our ethical values, in the external workings of nature.) *(By Stephen Jay Gould (2000). What does the dreaded "E" word mean anyway?* Natural History 109 *(1), 34–36.)* ■

Gould also described a fundamental puzzle in the fossil record in his Original Study: The precise moment when variational change led to the formation of a new species—in this case, the woolly mammoth—remained elusive. More recent populations may appear sufficiently changed from ancestral populations to be called different species. The difficulty arises because, given a reasonably good fossil record, one species will appear to grade into the other without any clear break. This gradual directional change over time can occur within a single line, without any evident branching, and is called **anagenesis** (see Figure 5.1). Speciation is inferred as organisms take on a different appearance over time.

It may be difficult to determine whether variation preserved in the fossil record presents evidence of separate species. How can we tell whether two sets of fossilized bones represent organisms capable of interbreeding and producing viable fertile offspring? Paleoanthropologists use as many sources of data as possible, checking the proposed evolutionary relationships, in order to approximate an answer to this question. Today, paleoanthropologists use genetic data as well as observations about the biology and behavior of living groups to support theories about speciation in the past. Thus, reconstructing evolutionary relationships draws on much more than bones alone. Fossil finds are always interpreted against the backdrop of scientific discoveries as well as prevailing beliefs and biases. Fortunately the self-correcting nature of scientific investigation allows evolutionary lines to be redrawn in light of all new discoveries and more compelling explanations.

Constructing Evolutionary Relationships

In addition to designating species in the fossil record, paleoanthropologists and paleontologists construct evolutionary relationships among fossil groups. Scientists pay particular attention to features appearing more recently in evolutionary history that are unique to a line, calling these features **derived.** The counterpart to derived traits are **ancestral** characteristics, which are present not only in the particular species at hand but in ancestral forms as well. For example, bilateral symmetry, a body plan in which the right and left sides of the body are mirror images of each other, is an ancestral trait in humans. Because it is a characteristic of all vertebrates including fish, reptiles, birds, and mammals, bilateral symmetry does not contribute to the reconstruction of evolutionary relationships among fossil primates. Instead, paleoanthropologists pay particular attention to recently evolved derived features in order to construct evolutionary relationships among fossil groups. For example, because changes in bones associated with bipedalism are present only in the human line, these derived features can be used to separate humans and their ancestors from other hominoids.

anagenesis A sustained directional shift in a population's average characteristics.
derived Characteristics that define a group of organisms that did not exist in ancestral populations.
ancestral Characteristics possessed by an organism or group of organisms due to shared ancestry.

VISUAL COUNTERPOINT

The characteristic long legs of prosimians and humans are not the result of a close evolutionary relationship. This is instead the result of convergence of homologous structures.

Sorting out evolutionary relationships among fossil species may be complicated by a phenomenon called **convergent evolution,** in which two more distant forms develop greater similarities. The classic examples of convergence involve analogies discussed in Chapter 2 such as the wings of birds and butterflies, which resemble each other because these structures serve similar functions. Convergent evolution occurs when an environment exerts similar pressures on distantly related organisms causing these species to resemble each other. Distinguishing the physical similarities produced by convergent evolution from those resulting from shared ancestry may be difficult, complicating the reconstruction of the evolutionary history of any given species.

Among more closely related groups, convergence of homologous structures can occur as when an identical structure present within several distinct species takes on a similar form in distantly related groups. Among the primates, an example is hind-leg dominance in both lemurs and humans. In most primates, the hind limbs are either shorter or of the same length as the forelimbs. Lemurs and humans are not as closely related to each other as are humans and chimps for example, but both have longer hind limbs related to their patterns of locomo-

tion. Humans are bipedal while lemurs use their long legs to push off and propel them from tree to tree. Hind-leg dominance appeared separately in these two groups and is not indicative of a close evolutionary relationship. Only shared derived features can be used to establish relationships among groups of species.

The Nondirectedness of Macroevolution

Among the lay public, evolution is often seen as leading in a predictable and determined way from one-celled organisms, through various multicelled forms, to humans, who occupy the top rung of a ladder of progress. However, even though one-celled organisms appeared long before multicellular forms, single-celled organisms were not replaced by multicellular descendants. Single-celled organisms exist in greater numbers and diversity than all forms of multicellular life and live in a greater variety of habitats.[1]

As for humans, we are indeed recent arrivals in the world (though not as recent as some new strains of bacteria). Our appearance—like that of any kind of organism—was made possible only as a consequence of a whole string of accidental happenings in the past. To cite but one example, about 65 million years ago the earth's

convergent evolution In biological evolution a process by which unrelated populations develop similarities to one another due to similar function rather than shared ancestry.

[1]Gould, S. J. (1996). *Full house: The spread of excellence from Plato to Darwin* (pp. 176–195). New York: Harmony Books.

climate changed drastically. Evidence suggests that a meteor or some other sort of extraterrestrial body slammed into earth where the Yucatan Peninsula of Mexico now exists, cooling global temperatures to such an extent as to cause the extinction of the dinosaurs (and numerous other species as well). For 100 million years, dinosaurs dominated most terrestrial environments available for vertebrate animals and would probably have continued to do so were it not for this event. Although mammals appeared at about the same time as reptiles, they existed as small, inconspicuous creatures that an observer from outer space would probably have dismissed as insignificant.

But with the demise of the dinosaurs, all sorts of opportunities became available allowing mammals to begin their great expansion into a variety of species including our own ancestors, the earliest primates. Therefore, an essentially random event—the collision with a comet or asteroid—made our own existence possible. Had it not happened, or had it happened at some other time (before the existence of mammals), we would not be here.[2]

The history of any species is an outcome of many such occurrences. At any point in the chain of events, had any one element been different, the final result would be markedly different. As Gould puts it, "All evolutionary sequences include . . . a fortuitous series of accidents with respect to future evolutionary success. Human brains and bodies did not evolve along a direct and inevitable ladder, but by a circuitous and tortuous route carved by adaptations evolved for different reasons, and fortunately suited to later needs."[3]

CONTINENTAL DRIFT AND GEOLOGICAL TIME

As described in Chapter 4, context and dating are vital for the interpretation of fossils. Because primate evolution extends so far back in time, paleoanthropologists reconstruct primate evolution in conjunction with information about the geological history of the earth. The scale of geological time is not similar to other conceptions of time that most humans use in their daily lives. Few of us deal with hundreds of millions of anything, let alone time, on a regular basis.

To understand geological time, astronomer Carl Sagan correlated the geological time scale for the history of the earth to a single calendar year. In this "cosmic calendar," the earth itself originates on January 1, the first

organisms appear approximately 9 months later around September 25, followed by the earliest vertebrates around December 20, mammals on December 25, primates on December 29, hominoids at 12:30 PM on New Year's Eve, bipeds at 9:30 PM, with our species appearing in the last minutes before midnight. In this chapter, we will consider human evolutionary history beginning with the appearance of the mammals in the Mesozoic era, roughly 245 million years ago.

Over such vast amounts of time, the earth itself has changed considerably. During the past 200 million years, the position of the continents has changed through a process called **continental drift** that accounts for the rearrangement of adjacent land masses through the theory of plate tectonics. According to this theory, the continents, embedded in platelike segments of the earth, move their positions as the edges of the underlying plates are created or destroyed (Figure 5.2). Plate movements are also responsible for geological phenomena such as earthquakes, volcanic activity, and mountain formation. Continental drift is important for understanding the distribution of fossil primate groups whose history we will now explore. The shifting orientation of the earth's continents is also responsible for climatic changes in the environment that affected the course of primate evolutionary history.

EARLY MAMMALS

By 190 million years ago—the end of what geologists call the Triassic period—true mammals were on the scene. Mammals from the Triassic, Jurassic (135–190 million years ago), and Cretaceous (65–135 million years ago) periods are largely known from hundreds of fossils, especially teeth and jaw parts. Because teeth are the hardest, most durable structures, they often outlast other parts of an animal's skeleton. Fortunately, investigators often are able to infer a good deal about the total animal on the basis of only a few teeth found lying in the earth.

For example, as described in Chapter 3, unlike the relatively homogeneous teeth of reptiles, mammals possess distinct tooth types, the structure of which varies by species. Knowledge of the way the teeth fit together indicates the arrangement of muscles needed to operate the jaws. Reconstruction of the jaw muscles, in turn, indicates how the skull must have been shaped to provide

[2]Gould, S. J. (1985). *The flamingo's smile: Reflections in natural history* (p. 409). New York: Norton.
[3]Ibid., p. 4100.

continental drift According to the theory of plate tectonics, the movement of continents embedded in underlying plates on the earth's surface in relation to one another over the history of life on earth.

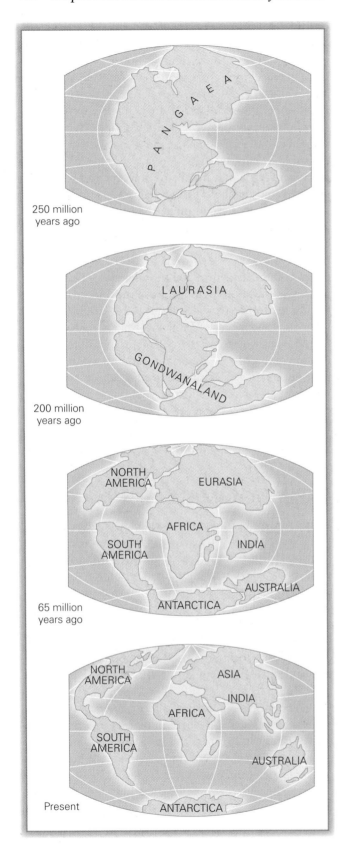

Figure 5.2
Continental drift is illustrated by the position of continents during several geological periods. At the end of the Cretaceous period some 65 million years ago, the time of the dinosaurs' extinction, the seas, opened up by continental drift, created isolating barriers between major land masses. During the Miocene epoch, African and Eurasian land masses reconnected.

a place for these muscles to attach. The shape of the jaws and details of the teeth also suggest the type of food that these animals consumed. Thus, a mere jawbone fragment with a few teeth contains a great deal of information about the animal from which it came.

An interesting observation about the evolution of the mammals is that the diverse forms with which we are familiar today, including the primates, are the products of an **adaptive radiation,** the rapid increase in number of related species following a change in their environment. This did not begin until after mammals had been present on the earth for over 100 million years. With the mass extinction of many reptiles at the end of the Cretaceous, however, a number of existing *ecological niches,* or functional positions in their habitats, became available to mammals. A species' niche incorporates factors such as diet, activity, terrain, vegetation, predators, prey, and climate.

The story of mammalian evolution starts as early as 230 to 280 million years ago (Figure 5.3). From deposits of this period, which geologists call the Permian, we have the remains of reptiles with features pointing in a distinctly mammalian direction. These mammal-like reptiles were slimmer than most other reptiles and were flesh eaters. A series of graded fossils demonstrate trends toward a mammalian pattern such as a reduction in the number of bones, the shifting of limbs underneath the body, the development of a separation between the mouth and nasal cavity, differentiation of the teeth, and so forth.

Eventually these creatures became extinct, but not before some of them developed into true mammals by the Triassic period. During the Jurassic period that followed, dinosaurs and other large reptiles dominated the earth, and mammals remained tiny, inconspicuous creatures occupying a nocturnal niche.

By chance, mammals were **preadapted**—possessing the biological equipment to take advantage of the new opportunities available to them through the mass extinction of the dinosaurs and other reptiles 65 million years ago. As **homeotherms,** mammals possess the ability to maintain a constant body temperature, a trait that appears to have promoted the adaptive radiation of the mammals. Mammals can be active at a wide range of environmental temperatures, whereas reptiles, as **isotherms** who take their body temperature from the

adaptive radiation Rapid diversification of an evolving population as it adapts to a variety of available niches.
preadapted Possessing characteristics that, by chance, are advantageous in future environmental conditions.
homeotherm An animal that maintains a relatively constant body temperature despite environmental fluctuations.
isotherm An animal whose body temperature rises or falls according to the temperature of the surrounding environment.

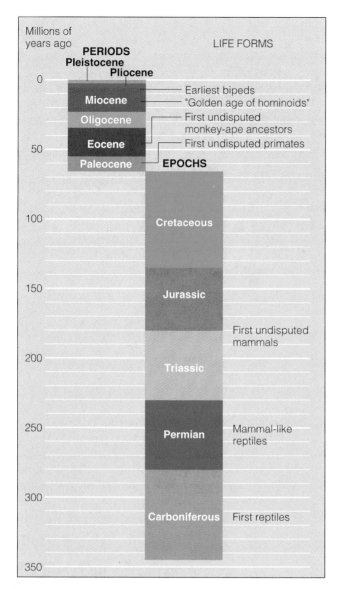

Figure 5.3

This timeline highlights some major milestones in the evolution of those mammals from which humans are descended.

Though popular media depict the co-existence of humans and dinosaurs, in reality the extinction of the dinosaurs occurred 65 million years ago while the first bipeds ancestral to humans appeared between 5 and 8 million years ago.

surrounding environment, become progressively sluggish as the surrounding temperature drops. Cold global temperatures 65 million years ago appear to be responsible for the mass extinction of the reptiles, while mammals, as homeotherms, were preadapted for this climate change.

The mammalian trait of maintaining constant body temperature however, requires a diet high in calories. Based on evidence from their teeth, scientists know that early mammals ate such foods as insects, worms, and eggs. As animals with nocturnal habits, mammals have well-developed senses of smell and hearing relative to reptiles. Although things cannot be seen as well in the dark as they can in the light, they can be heard and smelled just as well.

The mammalian pattern also differs from reptiles in terms of how they care for their young. Mammals are considered **k-selected** species. This means that they produce relatively few offspring at a time, providing them with considerable parental care. A universal feature of how mammals care for their young is the production of food (milk) via the mammary glands. Reptiles are relatively **r-selected,** which means that they produce many young at a time and invest little effort caring for their young after they are born. Though among mammals some species are relatively more k- or r-selected, the relatively high energy requirements of mammals, entailed by parental investment and the maintenance of a constant body temperature, demand more nutrition than required by reptiles. During their adaptive radiation, the fruits, nuts, and seeds of flowering plants that became more common in the late Cretaceous period provided mammals with high-quality nutrition.

THE RISE OF THE PRIMATES

Early primates began to emerge during this time of great global change at the start of the Paleocene epoch. The distribution of fossil primates on the earth makes sense only when one understands that the positions of the continents today differ tremendously from what was found in the past (see Figure 5.3). During this period, as noted

k-selected Reproduction involving the production of relatively few offspring with high parental investment in each.
r-selected Reproduction involving the production of large numbers of offspring with relatively low parental investment in each.

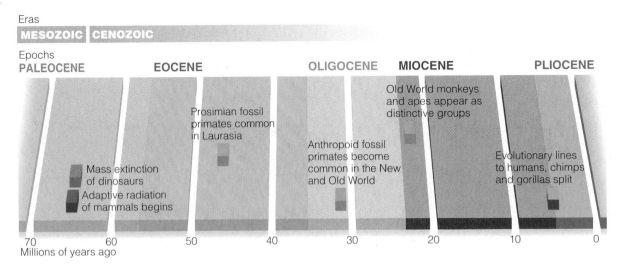

Eras
MESOZOIC   CENOZOIC

Epochs
PALEOCENE   EOCENE   OLIGOCENE   MIOCENE   PLIOCENE

Old World monkeys
and apes appear as
distinctive groups

Prosimian fossil
primates common
in Laurasia

Anthropoid fossil
primates become
common in the New
and Old World

Evolutionary lines
to humans, chimps
and gorillas split

Mass extinction
of dinosaurs
Adaptive radiation
of mammals begins

70   60   50   40   30   20   10   0
Millions of years ago

Figure 5.4
This timeline depicts some of the major events of primate evolution.

earlier, North America and Eurasia were connected in the supercontinent called Laurasia. South America, Africa, Antarctica, Australia, and the Indian subcontinent—previously joined together as the supercontinent Gondwanaland—were beginning to separate from one another through continental drift. Africa was separated from Eurasia by a narrow body of water.

On land, the dinosaurs had become extinct, and the mammals were undergoing the great adaptive radiation that ultimately led to the development of the diverse forms with which we are familiar today. At the same time, the newly evolved grasses, shrubs, and other flowering plants were undergoing an enormous proliferation. This diversification, along with a milder climate, favored the spread of dense, lush tropical and subtropical forests over much of the earth, including North and South America and much of Eurasia and Africa. With the spread of these huge belts of forest, the stage was set for the movement of some mammals into the trees. Forests would provide our early ancestors with the ecological niches in which they would flourish. Fossil evidence of primatelike mammals from the Paleocene forests has been found in North America and Eurasia. See Figure 5.4 for a full timeline of primate evolution.

One theory for primate evolution, the **arboreal hypothesis,** proposes that life in the trees was responsible for enhanced visual acuity and manual dexterity in primates. Misjudgments and errors of coordination, lead-

ing to falls that injured or killed the individuals poorly adapted to arboreal life may have been a part of the initial forays into the trees. Natural selection would favor those that judged depth correctly and gripped the branches strongly. Early primates that took to the trees were probably in some measure preadapted by virtue of behavioral flexibility, better vision, and more dexterous fingers than their contemporaries.

Primatologist Matt Cartmill further suggests that primate visual and grasping abilities were also promoted through the activity of hunting for insects by sight. His **visual predation** hypothesis accounts for the observa-

The appearance of angiosperm plants provided not only highly nutritious fruits, seeds, and flowers but also a host of habitats for numerous edible insects and worms—just the sorts of foods required by mammals with their high metabolism.

arboreal hypothesis A theory for primate evolution that proposes that life in the trees was responsible for enhanced visual acuity and manual dexterity in primates.
visual predation A hypothesis for primate evolution that proposes that hunting behavior in tree-dwelling primates was responsible for their enhanced visual acuity and manual dexterity.

© Anita de Laguna Haviland

tion that other tree-dwelling species and hunting species do not necessarily possess the same combination of visual and manual abilities possessed by the primates. The relatively small size of the early primates allowed them to make use of the smaller branches of trees; larger, heavier competitors, and most predators, could not follow. The move to the smaller branches also gave them access to an abundant food supply; the primates were able to gather insects, leaves, flowers, and fruits directly rather than waiting for them to fall to the ground.

The strong selection in a new environment led to an acceleration in the rate of change of primate characteristics. Paradoxically, these changes eventually made possible a return to the ground by some primates, including the ancestors of the genus *Homo*.

True Primates

The first well-preserved "true" primates appeared by about 55 million years ago at the start of the Eocene epoch. During this time period, an abrupt warming trend began on earth, causing many older forms of mammals to become extinct, to be replaced by recognizable forerunners of some of today's forms. Among the latter was an adaptive radiation of prosimian primates, of which over fifty fossil genera are known. Fossils of these creatures have been found in Africa, North America, Europe, and Asia, where the warm, wet conditions of the Eocene sustained extensive rainforests. Relative to ancestral primatelike mammals, these early primate families had enlarged braincases, slightly reduced snouts, and a somewhat forward position of the eye orbits, which, though not completely walled in, are surrounded by a complete bony ring called a postorbital bar (Figure 5.5).

During the Eocene, the first signs of anthropoid primates also begin to appear in the fossil record. The earliest evidence is of a tiny species *Eosimias* (pronounced ee-o-sim-ee-us, Latin for "dawn of the monkeys") represented by fossils from China, dated to about 45 million years ago. The Chinese fossils represent several species of tiny, insect-eating animals and are the smallest primates ever documented.[4] Some scientists have challenged whether these tiny fossils are truly anthropoids as they are reconstructed largely from foot bones rather than skulls or teeth.

Numerous fossils from Fayum, Egypt, show a unique mix of prosimian and anthropoid characteristics. The front teeth resemble those of the Eocene prosimian primates, with the derived dental formula shared by Old World monkeys and apes of two incisors, a canine, two

Figure 5.5

Ancestral features seen in the Eocene genus *Adapis* are found in prosimians today. Like modern lemurs, it has a postorbital bar, a bony ring around the eye orbit. Note that the orbit is open behind the ring.

Illustration by Nancy J Perkins, Carnegie Museum of Natural History

The scientists who discovered tiny leg bones, placed in the genus *Eosimias*, suggest these fossils are the earliest anthropoids. Other experts do not think such claims can be made from leg bones alone. Although its bones suggest overall body form, this reconstruction is otherwise speculative.

premolars, and three molars on each side of the jaw. The eye orbits have a complete wall, the latter being a feature of anthropoid primates.[5]

Although there is still much to be learned about the Eocene primates, it is clear that they were abundant, diverse, and widespread. Among them were ancestors of

[4]Gebo, D. L., et al. (2001). Middle Eocene primate tarsals from China: Implications for haplorhine evolution. *American Journal of Physical Anthropology 116,* 83–107.

[5]Simons, E. (1995). Skulls and anterior teeth of *Catopithecus* (Primates: Anthropoidea) from the Eocene and anthropoid origins. *Science 268,* 1,885–1,888.

today's prosimians and anthropoids.[6] With the end of the Eocene, substantial changes took place among the primates, as among other mammals. In North America, now well isolated from Eurasia, primates became extinct, and elsewhere their range seems to have been reduced considerably.

Climate change affected primate and mammalian evolution. Through the late Eocene, climates were becoming somewhat cooler and drier, but then temperatures took a sudden dive, triggering the formation of an ice cap over previously forested Antarctica. The result was a marked reduction in the range of suitable environments for primates. At the same time, cold climate led to lower sea levels through the formation of ice caps, perhaps changing opportunities for migration of primates.

Oligocene Anthropoids

During the Oligocene epoch, from about 23 to 34 million years ago, the anthropoid primates diversified and expanded their range. Fossil evidence from Egypt's Fayum region has yielded sufficient fossils (more than 1,000) to reveal that by 33 million years ago, Old World anthropoid primates existed in considerable diversity. Moreover, the cast of characters is growing, as new fossils continue to be found in the Fayum, as well as in newly discovered localities in Algeria (North Africa) and Oman (Arabian Peninsula). At present, we have evidence of at least sixty genera included in two families. During the Oligocene, prosimian fossil forms became far less prominent than anthropoids. Only on the large island of Madagascar (off the coast of East Africa), which was devoid of anthropoids until humans arrived, is prosimian diversity still evident. In their isolation, they underwent a further adaptive radiation.

Fossil evidence indicates that these Old World anthropoids were quadrupeds who were diurnal, as evidenced through their smaller orbits (eyes). Many of these Oligocene species possess a mixture of monkey and ape features. Of particular interest is the genus *Aegyptopithecus* (pronounced "Egypt"-o-pith-ee-kus, Greek for "Egyptian ape"), an Oligocene anthropoid that has sometimes been called a monkey with an ape's teeth. *Aegyptopithecus* possessed a mosaic of monkey and ape features as well as features shared by both groups. Its lower molars have the five cusps of an ape, and the upper canine and lower first premolar exhibit the sort of shearing surfaces found in monkeys and apes. Its skull possesses eye sockets that are in a forward position and completely protected by a bony wall, as is typical of modern monkeys and apes. The endocast of its skull indicates that it pos-

sessed a larger visual cortex than that found in prosimians. Relative to its body size, the brain of *Aegyptopithecus* was smaller than that of more recent anthropoids. Still, this primate seems to have had a larger brain than any prosimian, past or present. Possessed of a monkeylike skull and body, and fingers and toes capable of powerful grasping, it evidently moved about in a quadrupedal, monkeylike manner.[7]

The teeth of *Aegyptopithecus* suggest that this species may be closely related to an ancestor of humans and modern apes. Although no bigger than a modern house cat, *Aegyptopithecus* was nonetheless one of the larger Oligocene primates. Differences between males and females include larger body size, more formidable canine teeth, and deeper mandibles (lower jaws) in the males. In modern anthropoids, such sexual dimorphism correlates with social systems in which male competition is high.

New World Monkeys

The earliest evidence of primates in South America dates from this time. These fossil primates are certainly anthropoid monkeys, with the eyes fully encased in bone and limb bones for quadrupedal locomotion. Scientists hypothesize that these primates came to South America from Africa, because the earliest fossil evidence of anthropoids is from the Old World.

Some of the African anthropoids arrived in South America, which at the time was not attached to any other land mass, probably by means of floating masses of vegetation of the sort that originate even today in the great rivers of West and Central Africa. In the Oligocene, the distance between the two continents was far less than it is today; favorable winds and currents could easily have carried "floating islands" of vegetation across within a period that New World monkey ancestors could have survived.[8] Nearly all living and fossil New World primates possess the ancestral dental formula (2-1-3-3) of prosimians compared to the derived pattern (2-1-2-3) found in Old World anthropoids.

Miocene Apes

True apes first appeared in the fossil record during the Miocene epoch, 5 to 23 million years ago. It was also during this time period that the African and Eurasian land masses made direct contact. For most of the preceding 100 million years, the Tethys Sea, a continuous body

[6]Kay, R. F., Ross, C., & Williams, B. A. (1997). Anthropoid origins. *Science 275*, 803–804.

[7]Ankel-Simons, F., Fleagle, J. G., & Chatrath, P. S. (1998). Femoral anatomy of *Aegyptopithecus zeuxis*, an early Oligocene anthropoid. *American Journal of Physical Anthropology 106*, 421–422.

[8]Houle, A. (1999). The origin of platyrrhines: An evaluation of the Antarctic scenario and the floating island model. *American Journal of Physical Anthropology 109*, 554–556.

of water that more or less joined what are now the Mediterranean and Black seas to the Indian Ocean, created a barrier to migration between Africa and Eurasia. Once joined through what is now the Middle East and Gibraltar, Old World primate groups such as the apes that got their start in Africa could expand their ranges into Eurasia. Miocene ape fossil remains have been found everywhere from the caves of China, to the forests of France, to eastern Africa where the earliest fossil remains of bipeds have been found.

So varied and ubiquitous were the fossil apes of this period that the Miocene has even been labeled by some as the "golden age of the hominoids." The word *hominoid* comes from the Latin roots *Homo* and *Homin* (meaning "human being") and the suffix *oïdes* ("resembling"). As a group, the hominoids get their name from their resemblance to humans.

In addition to the Old World anthropoid dental formula of 2-1-2-3 and Y5 molars, hominoids can be characterized by the derived characteristics of having no tail and having broad flexible shoulder joints. The likeness between humans and the other apes bespeaks an important evolutionary relationship that, as explained in the Biocultural Connection feature, makes other living hominoids vulnerable to human needs in today's world. In the distant past, one of the Miocene apes is the direct ancestor of the human line. Exactly which one is a question still to be resolved.

An examination of the history of the "contenders" for direct human ancestor among the Miocene apes demonstrates how reconstruction of evolutionary relationships draws on much more than bones alone. Scientists interpret fossil finds by drawing on existing beliefs and knowledge. With new discoveries, interpretations change.

The first Miocene ape fossil remains were found in Africa in the 1930s and 1940s by A. T. Hopwood and the renowned paleoanthropologist Louis Leakey. These fossils turned up on one of the many islands in Lake Victoria, the 27,000-square-mile lake where Kenya, Tanzania, and Uganda meet. Impressed with the chimplike appearance of these fossil remains, Hopwood suggested that the new species be named *Proconsul,* combining the Latin root for "before" *(pro)* with the stage name of a chimpanzee who was performing in London at the time.

Dated to the early Miocene 17 to 21 million years ago, *Proconsul* has some of the classic hominoid features, lacking a tail and having the characteristic pattern of Y5 grooves in the lower molar teeth. However, the adaptations of the upper body seen in later apes (including humans) were absent. These included a skeletal structure adapted for hanging suspended below tree branches. In

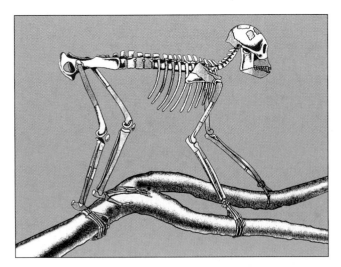

Figure 5.6
Reconstructed skeleton of *Proconsul*. Note the apelike absence of tail but monkeylike limb and body proportions. *Proconsul*, however, was capable of greater rotation of forelimbs than monkeys.

other words, *Proconsul* had some apelike features as well as some features of four-footed Old World monkeys (Figure 5.6). This mixture of ape and monkey features makes *Proconsul* a contender for a missing link between monkeys and apes but not as a connection between Miocene apes and later-appearing bipeds.

At least seven fossil hominoid groups besides *Proconsul* have been found in East Africa from the early to middle Miocene. But between 5 and 14 million years ago this fossil record thins out. It is not that all the apes suddenly moved from Africa to Eurasia, but rather that the environmental conditions made it less likely that any of the African remains would fossilize. Tropical forests inhabited by chimps and gorillas today make poor conditions for the preservation of bones. As mentioned in Chapter 4, in order to become a fossil, bones must be quickly incorporated into the earth before any rotting or decomposition occurs. In tropical forests, the heat, humidity, and general abundance of life make this unlikely. The bones' organic matrix is consumed by other creatures before it can be fossilized.

Nevertheless, the scarcity of African fossil evidence from this time period fit well with prevailing notions about human origins. Two factors conspired to take the focus away from Africa. First, investigators initially did not consider that humans were any more closely related to the African apes than they were to the other intelligent great ape—the Asian orangutan. Chimps, bonobos, gorillas, and orangutans were thought to be more closely related to one another than any of them were to humans. The construction of evolutionary relationships still relied upon visual similarities among species, much as it did in the mid-1700s when Linnaeus developed the taxonomic scheme that grouped humans with other primates. Chimps, bonobos, gorillas, and orangutans all possess the same basic body plan, adapted to hanging by their arms from branches or knuckle-walking on the ground. Humans and their ancestors had an altogether different form of locomotion: walking upright on two legs. On an anatomical basis, the first Miocene ape to become bipedal could have come from any part of the vast Old World range of the Miocene apes.

The second factor at work to pull attention away from African origins was more subtle and embedded not in the bones from the earth but in the subconscious of the scientists of the past. It was hard for these scientists to imagine that humans originated entirely in Africa. European scientists in the early 20th century therefore concentrated on the various species of European ape—all members of the genus *Dryopithecus* (pronounced dry-o-pith-ee-kus). They believed that humans evolved where "civilization" developed and that these apes could be the missing link to humans.

As we will see in the next chapter, it took many years for the first bipedal fossils discovered in South Africa in the 1920s to be accepted by the scientific community as a key part of the human line. Instead, human origins were imagined to involve a close link between those who invented the first tools and the people responsible for Western civilization.

During the 1960s, it appeared as though this Miocene human ancestor lived in the Siwaliks, the foothills of the majestic Himalayan mountain range along the northern borders of India and Pakistan, near the ruins of the later Indus Valley civilization. The Himalayas are some of the youngest mountains of the world. They began forming during the Miocene when the Indian subcontinent collided with the rest of Eurasia, and they have been becoming taller ever since.

In honor of the Hindu religion practiced in the region where the fossils were found, the contender was given the name *Ramapithecus,* after the Indian deity Rama and the Greek word for "ape," *pithekos.* Rama is the physical embodiment, or incarnation, of the major Hindu god Vishnu, the preserver. He is meant to portray what a perfect human can be. He is benevolent, protects the weak, and embodies all noble human characteristics. Features like the relative delicacy and curvature of the jaw and palate as well as thick tooth enamel led paleoanthropologists David Pilbeam and Elwyn Simons to suggest that this was the first hominoid to become part of the direct human line. They suggested that *Ramapithecus* was a bipedal tool user—the earliest human ancestor. With these qualities, *Ramapithecus* was perfectly named.

Other Miocene apes were also present in the foothills of the Himalayas. *Sivapithecus* was named after the Hindu deity Siva, the god of destruction and regeneration. In the Hindu religion Siva is depicted as an asocial hermit who, when provoked, reduces his enemies to smoldering ashes in fits of rage. Though never consid-

© Art Resource, NY

Miocene ape fossils proposed as direct ancestors to humans in the 1960s from the foothills of the Himalayan mountains were named after the Indian deity Rama (shown here in a marriage ceremony with his
brother) as a reference to humanlike qualities observed in the teeth and jaws. Subtle cultural biases in the
earlier 20th century led scientists to expect to find the missing link between the other apes and humans in
one of the cradles of ancient civilization rather than Africa.

ered a human ancestor, *Sivapithecus* also had the humanlike characteristic of thick molar tooth enamel (unlike
the African apes but like the orangutans). *Sivapithecus*
also had large projecting canine teeth more suitable to
a destroyer than to a human ancestor. The *Sivapithecus*
and *Ramapithecus* fossils were dated to between 7 and
12 million years ago.

The interpretation of these fossils changed with discoveries in the laboratory. By the 1970s, the use of biochemical and genetic evidence to establish evolutionary
relationships among species had begun. A University
of California, Berkeley, biochemist named Vince Sarich
working in the laboratory of Allan Wilson (see Anthropologist of Note) brought molecular techniques to evolutionary studies and developed the revolutionary concept
of a **molecular clock.** Such clocks help detect when the
branching of related species from a common ancestor
took place in the distant past.

Sarich used a molecular technique that had been
around since the beginning of the 20th century: comparison of the blood proteins of living groups. He worked
on serum albumin, a protein from the fluid portion of
the blood (like the albumin that forms egg whites) that
can be precipitated out of solution. *Precipitation* refers
to when a dissolved substance is removed from a liquid
form through chemical transformation into a solid. One
of the forces that will cause such precipitation is contact
of this protein with antibodies directed against it. Antibodies are proteins produced by organisms as part of an
immune response to an infection. The technique relies
on the notion that the stronger the biochemical reaction
between the protein and the antibody (the more precipi-
tate), the closer the evolutionary relationship. The antibodies and proteins of closely related species resemble

molecular clock The hypothesis that dates of divergences
among related species can be calculated through an examination
of the genetic mutations that have accrued since the divergence.

Anthropologists of Note

Allan Wilson (1934–1991)

Though a biochemist by training, New Zealander Allan Wilson has made key contributions to anthropology through his pioneering work in applying the principles of biochemistry to human evolutionary questions. Wilson forged a new "hybrid science," combining fossil and molecular evidence with ground-breaking results. Because the molecular evidence required rethinking long-held theories about the relationships among fossil groups, Wilson's work has been surrounded by controversy. According to those close to Wilson, he enjoyed his role as an outsider—being on the edges of anthropology and shaking things up.

Wilson was born in Ngaruwahia, New Zealand, and grew up on a farm in Pukekohe. After attending school in New Zealand and Australia, he was invited to study biochemistry at the University of California, Berkeley, in 1955. His father was reluctant to have his son travel so far from home, but his mother saw this as an opportunity for him and encouraged him to head to California.

Wilson stayed at Berkeley for the next thirty-five years, running one of the

© Roger Ressmeyer/Corbis

Allan Wilson (right) observes as a laboratory rabbit is injected.

world's most creative biochemistry labs. In the 1960s, Berkeley was a center of academic liberalism and social protest. Wilson's highly original work was conducted with a similar revolutionary spirit, garnering him a MacArthur "genius" award, two Guggenheim fellowships,

and a place on the short list for the Nobel Prize.

He developed the notion of a "molecular clock" with his graduate student Vince Sarich and published the ground-breaking paper "Immunological Time-Scale for Human Evolution" in the journal *Science* in 1967. The molecular clock proposes that evolutionary events such as the split between humans and apes can be dated through an examination of the number of genetic mutations that accumulated since two species diverged from a common ancestor. In the 1980s, his laboratory (including Rebecca Cann and Mark Stoneking) was also responsible for seminal work with the mitochondrial Eve hypothesis that continues to be widely debated today (see Chapter 8).

Sadly, Wilson died from leukemia at the age of 56. Joseph Felsenstein, one of his biographers, stated in his obituary in the journal *Nature*, "while others concentrated on what evolution could tell them about molecules, Wilson always looked for ways that molecules could say something about evolution."

---

one another more than the antibodies and proteins of distant species.

Sarich made immunological comparisons between a variety of species and suggested that he could establish dates for evolutionary events by calculating a molecular rate of change over time. By assuming a constant rate of change in the protein structure of each species over time, Sarich used these results to predict times of divergence between related groups. Each molecular clock needs to be set, or calibrated, by the dates associated with a known event such as the divergence between prosimian and anthropoid primates or Old World monkeys and apes as established by absolute dating methods.

Using this technique, Sarich proposed a sequence of divergence for the living hominoids showing that human, chimp, and gorilla lines split roughly 5 million years ago. He boldly stated that it was impossible to have a separate human line before 7 million years ago "no matter what it looked like." In other words, anything that old would also have to be ancestral to chimps and gorillas as well as humans. Because *Ramapithecus,* even with its humanlike jaws, was dated to between 7 and 12 million years ago, it could no longer be considered a human ancestor.

In the meantime, Pilbeam continued fossil hunting in the Himalayan foothills. Further specimens began to show that *Ramapithecus* was actually a smaller, perhaps female version of *Sivapithecus.*[9] Eventually all the specimens referred to as *Ramapithecus* were "sunk" or absorbed into the *Sivapithecus* group, so that today *Ramapithecus* no longer exists as a valid name for a Miocene ape. Instead of two distinct groups, one of which went on to evolve into humans, they are considered males and females of the sexually dimorphic genus *Sivapithecus.* A spectacular complete specimen found in the Potwar Plateau of Pakistan by Pilbeam showed that *Sivapithecus* was undoubtedly the ancestor of orangutans. This conclusion matched well with the molecular evidence that the separate line to orangutans originated 10 to 12 million years ago.

All of these changes reflect the fact that paleoanthropologists participate in an unusual kind of science. Paleoanthropology, like all paleontology, is a science of

---

[9]Pilbeam, D. R. (1987). Rethinking human origins. In R. L. Ciochon & J. G. Fleagle (Eds.), *Primate evolution and human origins* (p. 217). Hawthorne, NY: Aldine de Gruyter.

discovery. As new fossil discoveries come to light, interpretations inevitably change, making for better understanding of our evolutionary history. Today, discoveries can occur in the laboratory as easily as on the site of an excavation. Molecular studies since the 1970s provide a new line of evidence much the same way that fossils provide new data as they are unearthed. A discovery in the laboratory, like Sarich's molecular clocks, can drastically change the interpretation of the fossil evidence.

MIOCENE APES AND HUMAN ORIGINS

As described above, determining which Miocene apes were directly ancestral to humans is one of the key questions in primate evolution. Molecular evidence directs our attention to Africa between 5 and 8 million years ago (Figure 5.7). Though any fossil discoveries in Africa from this critical time period have the potential to be the

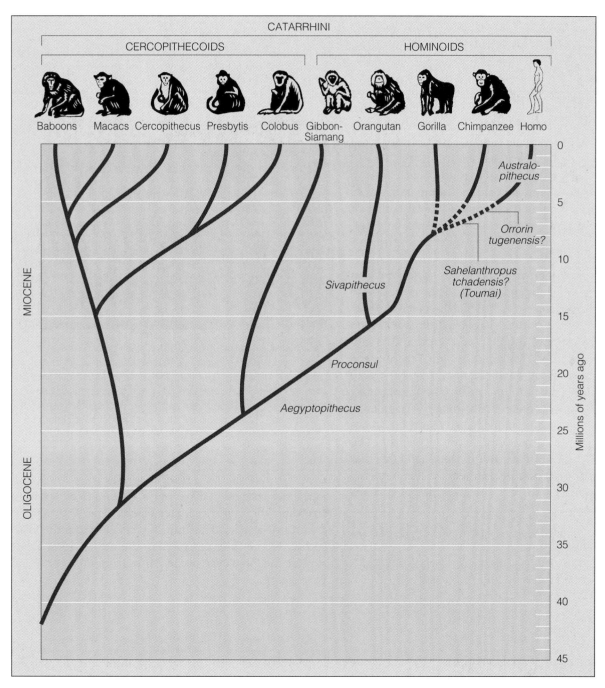

Figure 5.7
Although debate continues over details, this chart represents a reasonable reconstruction of evolutionary relationships among the Old World anthropoid primates. (Extinct evolutionary lines are not shown.)

missing link between humans and the other African ape species, the evidence from this period has until recently been particularly scrappy. Controversy surrounds the interpretation of many of these new fossil finds.

For example, in Chad in the summer of 2002 a team of international researchers led by Michel Brunet of France unearthed a well-preserved skull dated to between 6 and 7 million years ago.[10] Calling their find *Sahelanthropus tchadensis* ("Sahel man of Chad," referring to the Sahel region south of the Sahara Desert), the researchers suggested that this specimen represented the earliest known ancestor of humans, or earliest biped. Nicknamed "Toumai," from the region's Goran-language word meaning "hope for life" (a name typically given to babies born just before the dry season), this specimen is the only skull from this time period.

Considering that bipedalism is the derived characteristic that indicates inclusion in the human subfamily, some paleoanthropologists argue that the relationship of this specimen to humans cannot be established from skull bones alone. The research team argues that derived features such as a reduced canine tooth can be seen in the face of the Toumai specimen, indicating its status as a member of the human evolutionary line. Whether or not this specimen proves to be a direct human ancestor, as the only skull from this time period, it is nevertheless a very important find.

In 2001, 6-million-year-old fossils discovered in Kenya by Brigitte Senut and Martin Pickford were also reported as human ancestors.[11] Officially given the species name *Orrorin tugenensis* (*Tugensis* from the Tugen hills, *Orrorin* meaning "original man" in the local language) but nicknamed "Millennium Man," these specimens have also been surrounded by controversy.

The evidence for *Orrorin* consists of fragmentary arm and thigh bones, a finger bone, some jaw fragments, and teeth of at least five individuals. The thigh bones demonstrate possible, but not definite, bipedalism. Unfortunately, the distal or far ends of the thigh bone that would prove this are not fully preserved. The humerus (upper arm) appears to be more like that of humans

© Michael Brunet

The spectacular recently discovered skull from Chad nicknamed "Toumai" (hope for life) has been proposed as the earliest direct human ancestor. While the 6- to 7-million-year-old specimen is a beautifully preserved skull and has some derived features, some paleoanthropologists feel that alone, it does not establish bipedalism, the derived trait characteristic of the human line.

© Orban, Thierry/Corbis Sygma.

These 6 million-year-old fossils, discovered in Kenya in 2001, represent a new species, *Orrorin tugenensis,* that has also been proposed as the earliest human ancestor. Like Toumai these bones are surrounded by controversy. The thigh bones (femora) strongly suggest bipedalism, and the upper arm bone (humerus) may be more like that of humans than it is like some of the later bipeds. More discoveries and scientific comparisons will solve controversies surrounding both *Orrorin* and Toumai.

than it is like the later bipedal species we will explore in the next chapter. Also *Orrorin* appears to be larger in size than some of these later bipeds. The way that paleoanthropologists determine bipedalism from the fossil record will be fully described in the next chapter as we explore the fossil evidence in Africa from 2.5 to 5 million years ago.

---

[10]Brunet, M., et al. (2002). A new hominid from the Upper Miocene of Chad, Central Africa. *Nature 418,* 145–151.

[11]Senut, B., et al. (2001). First hominid from the Miocene (Lukeino formation, Kenya). *C. R. Acad. Sci. Paris 332,* 137–144.

Questions for Reflection

1. How can humans face the challenge of maintaining our ecosystem so that it can sustain diverse species? What role does understanding the impact of the formation of new species and the extinction of others play in facing this challenge? Will humans be just another primate to go extinct?

2. Why are shared derived characteristics more important than shared ancestral characteristics in evolutionary reconstructions? Using the Miocene apes and humans, think about

the ways that conclusions about evolution would change if ancestral rather than derived characteristics were used to figure out evolutionary relationships among species.

3. The biological definition of a species is a population or a group of populations that is capable of interbreeding and producing fertile, viable offspring. Why is this definition of species difficult to apply to the fossil record?

4. The interpretation of fossil material changes with the discovery of new specimens and with discoveries in the laboratory. How has that happened? Can you imagine a different conception of human evolutionary history in the future?

5. An understanding of the changing position of the earth's continents through the past several hundred million years is important for the reconstruction of primate evolutionary history. Do you think the evolutionary history of the primates can be understood without knowledge of continental drift?

Suggested Readings

Fleagle, J. (1998). *Primate adaptation and evolution.* New York: Academic Press.

This beautifully illustrated book is an excellent introduction to the field of primate evolution, synthesizing the fossil record with primate anatomical and behavioral variation.

Hartwig, W. C. (2002). *The primate fossil record.* New York: Cambridge University Press.

This book contains an up-to-date and comprehensive treatment of the discovery and interpretation of primate fossils.

Jones, S., Martin, R., & Pilbeam, D. (1992). *Cambridge encyclopedia of human evolution.* New York: Cambridge University Press.

This comprehensive introduction to the human species covers the gamut from genetics, primatology, and the fossil evidence to a detailed exploration of contemporary human ecology, demography, and disease. Over seventy scholars from throughout the world contributed to this encyclopedia.

Mayr, E., & Diamond, J. (2002). *What evolution is.* New York: Basic Books.

Written for a general educated audience, this engaging book provides a comprehensive treatment of evolutionary theory.

Thomson Audio Study Products

 Enjoy the MP3-ready Audio Lecture Overviews for each chapter and a comprehensive audio glossary of key terms for quick study and review. Whether walking to class, doing laundry, or studying at your desk, you now have the freedom to choose when, where, and how you interact with your audio-based educational media. See the preface for information on how to access this on-the-go study and review tool.

The Anthropology Resource Center

www.thomsonedu.com/anthropology
The Anthropology Resource Center provides extended learning materials to reinforce your understanding of key concepts in the four subfields of anthropology. For each of the four subdisciplines, the Resource Center includes dynamic exercises including video exercises, map exercises, simulations, and "Meet the Scientists" interviews, as well as critical thinking questions that can be assigned and e-mailed to instructors. The Resource Center also provides breaking news in anthropology and interesting material on applied anthropology to help you link what you are learning to the world around you.

6 The First Bipeds

© Gregory Manchess, 2004

CHALLENGE ISSUE

The fossilized remains of the earliest bipeds from eastern, southern, and central Africa challenge us to rethink what separates us from the other animals. While it is our intelligence and large brains that most humans think of first, the characteristic that sets us apart is the simple fact that we walk on two legs. Clear evidence of bipedalism is preserved in various aspects of the skeleton and in footprints that have been sealed in volcanic ash. From evidence in fossil skeletons and from the specimens' surrounding environment, we now know that there were many species of ancient biped—one of whom eventually became human. Here an artist has depicted one of the most ancient bipeds, from the species *Ardipithecus ramidus,* a small-brained bipedal forest ape that is a side branch of the human evolutionary tree. Many species of bipedal apes inhabited the earth for several million years before the larger-brained genus *Homo* appeared.

What Is the Anatomy of Bipedalism, and How Is It Preserved in the Fossil Record?

Bipedalism is the shared derived characteristic used to establish whether a fossilized hominoid is a part of the evolutionary line that produced humans. Evidence for bipedalism is preserved literally from head to toe. Bipedalism can be inferred from the forward position of the large opening in the base of the skull, a series of curves in the spinal column, the basin-shaped structure of the pelvis, the angle of the lower limbs from the hip joint to the knees, and the shape of the foot bones. Thus even fragmentary evidence can prove bipedalism, providing the "right" fragment is preserved. Several groups from between 4 and 7 million years ago have been proposed as the earliest bipedal human ancestor.

Who Were the Australopithecines, and What Were They Like?

The fossil record indicates that some time during the early Pliocene, beginning 5 million years ago, the genus *Australopithecus* appeared in Africa. Australopithecines include a diverse group of fully bipedal species still possessing relatively small-sized brains in proportion to their body size. Some of the later australopithecines, known as "robust" forms, possessed particularly large teeth, jaws, and chewing muscles and represent an evolutionary dead end, disappearing from the fossil record completely by 1 million years ago. One of the other australopithecine species, though it is not clear which one, appears to be a direct ancestor of the genus *Homo*.

What Role Did Bipedalism Play in Human Evolutionary History?

Numerous theories stressing adaptation have been proposed to account for the appearance of bipedalism in human evolutionary history. These theories range from the adaptive advantage of having hands free to carry young or wield weapons to adaptation to damaging buildup of heat in the brain from direct exposure to the sun in a hot, treeless environment. Bipedalism appeared in human evolutionary history several million years before brain size expanded.

Though genetic evidence established that the human line diverged from those leading to chimpanzees and gorillas between 5 and 8 million years ago, for a long time the fossil evidence of the early stages of human evolution was both sparse and tenuous. Today, however, several interesting specimens from Africa fill in this important period. Inclusion of any fossil specimen in the human evolutionary line depends upon evidence for **bipedalism** (also called *bipedality*), the defining characteristic of the human line. The possible human ancestors from the Miocene recently found in Chad (*Sahelanthropus tchadensis*) and Kenya (*Orrorin tugenensis*), dated 6 to 7 million years ago, were described in the last chapter. In this chapter, we will pick up our story with a diverse array of fossil bipeds from the Pliocene—the geological epoch that began 5 million years ago.

Most of the early bipeds are members of the genus *Australopithecus,* a genus that includes species from eastern, southern, and central Africa. The name for this group of fossils was coined back in 1924 when the first important fossil from Africa proposed to be a human ancestor came to light. This unusual fossil, consisting of a partial skull and natural brain cast of a young individual, was brought to the attention of Professor Raymond Dart of the University of Witwatersrand in Johannesburg, South Africa. The "Taung child," named for the limestone quarry in which it was found, was unlike any creature Dart had ever seen before. Recognizing an intriguing mixture of ape and human characteristics in this unusual fossil, anatomist Dart proposed a new taxonomic category for his discovery—*Australopithecus africanus,* or southern ape of Africa—suggesting that this specimen represented an extinct form that was ancestral to humans.

Although the anatomy of the base of the skull indicated that the Taung child was probably a biped, the scientific community was not ready to accept the notion of a small-brained African ancestor to humans. Dart's original paper describing the Taung child was published in the February 1925 edition of the prestigious journal

THOMSON AUDIO STUDY PRODUCTS Take advantage of the MP3-ready Audio Lecture Overviews and comprehensive audio glossary of key terms for each chapter. See the preface for information on how to access this on-the-go study and review tool.

bipedalism The mode of locomotion in which an organism walks upright on its two hind legs characteristic of humans and their ancestors.
Australopithecus The genus including several species of early bipeds from eastern, southern, and central Africa living between about 1.1 and 4.3 million years ago, one of whom was directly ancestral to humans.

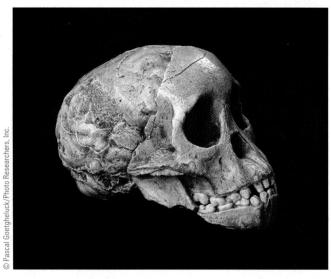

The Taung child, discovered in South Africa in 1924, was the first fossil specimen placed in the genus *Australopithecus*. Though Raymond Dart correctly diagnosed the Taung child's bipedal mode of locomotion as well as its importance in human evolution, other scientists rejected Dart's claims that this small-brained biped with a humanlike face was a direct ancestor to humans. In the early 20th century scientists were expecting the ancestors to humans to possess large brains and an apelike face and to originate from Europe or Asia rather than Africa.

Nature. The next month's issue was filled with venomous critiques rejecting Dart's proposal that this specimen represented an ancestor to humans. Critiques ranged from biased to fussy to sound. Fussy critiques included chastising Dart for incorrectly combining Latin and Greek in the genus and species name he coined. Valid criticisms included questions concerning inferences made about the appearance of an adult of the species based only on the fossilized remains of a young individual.

The biggest stumbling block, however, to the acceptance of Dart's proposal lay in the realm of bias. Paleoanthropologists of the early 20th century expected that the ancestor to humans already had a large brain. Moreover, most European scientists expected to find evidence of this large-brained ancestor in Europe or, barring that, Asia.

In fact, many scientists of the 1920s even believed that the ancestor to humans had already been found in the Piltdown gravels of Sussex, England, in 1910. The Piltdown specimens consisted of a humanlike skull and an apelike jaw that seemed to fit together though the crucial joints connecting the two were missing. They were discovered along with the bones of some other animal species known to be extinct. Charles Dawson—the amateur archaeologist, paleontologist, and practicing lawyer who found these remains—immodestly named them *Eoanthropus dawsoni* or "Dawson's dawn man." Until the 1950s the Piltdown remains were widely accepted as representing the missing link between apes and humans rather than as one of the biggest hoaxes in the history of science that we know them to be today.

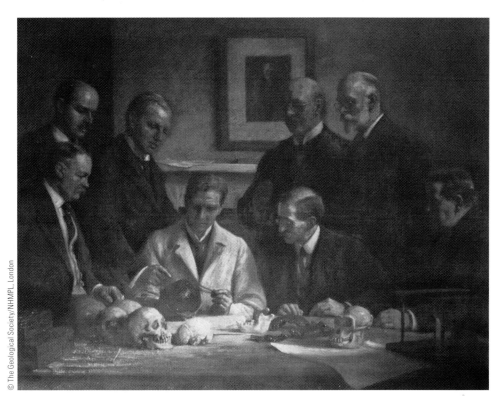

The Piltdown forgery was widely accepted as ancestral to humans, in large part because it fit with public expectations that the missing link would have a large brain and an apelike face. No one knows with certainty how many of the "Piltdown Gang," scientists supporting this specimen as the missing link, were actually involved in the forgery. It is likely that Charles Dawson had help from at least one scientist. Sir Arthur Conan Doyle, the author of the Sherlock Holmes detective stories, has also been implicated.

© The Geological Society/NHMPL, London

The reasons for widespread acceptance of Dawson's dawn man were as follows. As Darwin's theory of evolution by natural selection began to gain acceptance in the early 20th century, intense interest developed in finding traces of prehistoric human ancestors. Accordingly, predictions were made as to what those ancestors looked like. Darwin himself, on the basis of his knowledge of embryology and the comparative anatomy of living apes and humans, suggested in his 1871 book, *The Descent of Man,* that early humans had, among other things, a large brain and an apelike face and jaw.

Although the tools made by prehistoric peoples were commonly found in Europe, their bones were not. A few fossilized skeletons had come to light in France and Germany, but they were not at all like the predicted missing link, nor had any human fossils been discovered in England. Given this state of affairs, the Piltdown finds could not have come at a better time. Here at last was the long-awaited missing link, and it was almost exactly as predicted. Even better, so far as English-speaking scientists were concerned, it was found in English soil.

In the context of the evidence available in the early 1900s, the idea of an ancient human with a large brain and an apelike face became widely accepted as valid. Fortunately, the self-correcting nature of science has prevailed, exposing the Piltdown specimens as a forgery. The discovery (primarily in South Africa, China, and Java) of more and more fossils, of smaller-brained bipeds from the distant past, caused scientists to question Piltdown's authenticity. Ultimately, the application of the newly developed fluorine dating method (described in Chapter 4) by Kenneth Oakley and colleagues in 1953 proved conclusively that Piltdown was a forgery. The skull, which was indeed human, was approximately 600 years old, while the jaw, which proved to be from an orangutan, was even more recent. Finally, Dart and the Taung child were fully vindicated.

Today, genetic and fossil evidence both indicate that the human evolutionary line begins with a small-brained bipedal ape from Africa. Numerous international expeditions—including researchers from Kenya, Ethiopia, Japan, Belgium, Great Britain, Canada, France, Israel, the Netherlands, South Africa, and the United States—scoured East, South, and central Africa recovering unprecedented amounts of fossil material. This wealth of fossil evidence has allowed scientists to constantly refine our understanding of early human evolution. Today there is widespread agreement over its broad outline, even though debate continues over details.

What is clear is that the course of human evolution began with a shift toward bipedalism—the shared derived characteristic distinguishing humans and their ancestors from the other African apes. As described in Chapter 2, many scientists continue to restrict the term "hominid" for humans and the other fossil bipeds while others now call these specimens "hominins." The following Original Study by Lee Berger, the director of the paleoanthropology unit at the University of Witwatersrand in South Africa, weighs the issue.

Original Study ▪ By Lee R. Berger

Is It Time to Revise the System of Scientific Naming?

A team of researchers led by paleo-anthropologist Meave Leakey sparked a controversy among evolutionary scientists and the press alike earlier this year when they announced the discovery of a new genus and species of ape-man. They named their find *Kenyanthropus platyops,* the "flat-faced man of Kenya."

Ordinarily, the find itself would be enough to spark a flame of controversy in the heart of any follower of human origins research. But this find also highlighted an ongoing debate within the scientific community over the adoption of a new system for naming, ranking, and classifying organisms. The debate is not confined to ivory tower scientists. The fossil discovery was widely reported. The *New York Times* referred to the new genus as a "hominid"; *National Geographic* reported on the find as a "hominin." *National Geographic* subsequently received several hundred e-mails complaining about the poor editorial work of the staff that had clearly erred by replacing a "d" with an "n." But were they really wrong, and more important, does it really matter?

Linnaean Classification

The taxonomic classification system devised by Linnaeus in 1758 is still used in modified form today. Animals are identified, in descending order, as belonging to a kingdom, phylum, class, order, family, genus, and finally a species. This classification system is based largely on the animal's physical characteristics; things that looked alike were placed together. In the Linnaean system, humans would be categorized first as Animalia; then Chordata because we have a backbone; Mammalia because we have hair and suckle our young; primates because we share with apes, monkeys, and lemurs certain morphological characteristics; Hominidae because, among a

few other criteria, we are separated from the other apes by being bipedal; *Homo* being our generic classification as human; and finally *sapiens,* a species name meaning, rightly or wrongly, "wise."

The Linnaean system also recognizes such groupings as superfamilies and subfamilies. In the case of the human lineage, the most often recognized superfamily is the Hominoidea (hominoids), which includes all of the living apes. It is from this point onward that most of the present human origins classification debate begins.

The traditional view has been to recognize three families of hominoid: the Hylobatidae, the Hominidae, and the Pongidae. The Hylobatidae include the so-called lesser apes of Asia, the gibbons, and siamangs. The Hominidae include living humans and typically fossil apes

© Kenneth Garrett/National Geographic Society Images

Lee Berger excavating at the South African site Sterkfontein.

that possess a suite of characteristics such as bipedalism, reduced canine size, and increasing brain size such as the australopithecines. The Pongidae include the remaining African great apes including gorillas, chimpanzees, and the Asian orangutan.

New Molecular Evidence

Modern-day genetic research is providing evidence that morphological distinctions are not necessarily proof of evolutionary relatedness. Recent evidence suggests that humans are in fact more closely related to the chimpanzee and bonobo than either species is to the gorilla. Chimps and humans share something like 98 percent of genes, indicating that we share a common ape ancestor.

Divergence times between the two groups based on a molecular clock suggest that the chimpanzee/human split occurred between 5 and 7 million years ago. In turn, the African apes, including humans, are more closely related to each other than any are to the orangutan.

In recognition of these and other genetic relationships, some argue that we must overhaul the present morphologically based classification system for one that is more representative of our true evolutionary relationships as evinced by our genes.

Reworking the Family Tree

This is where the term *hominin* comes into play. Under the new classification model, hominoids would remain a primate superfamily, as has always been the case. Under this hominoid umbrella would fall orangutans, gorillas, chimps, and humans, all in the family Hominidae.

In recognition of their genetic divergence some 11 to 13 million years ago, the orangutans would be placed in the subfamily Ponginae, and the African apes, including humans, would all be lumped together in the subfamily Homininae. The bipedal apes—all of the fossil species as well as living humans—would fall into the tribe Hominini (thus hominin). All of the fossil genera, such as *Australopithecus, Ardipithecus, Kenyanthropus*, and *Homo*, would fall into this tribe.

A few evolutionary biologists want a more extreme classification, which would include humans and chimpanzees within the same genus, the genus *Homo*.

Old Versus New

So hominid or hominin? Is it just a matter of semantics that only purists should be worried about? The *New York Times'* use of "hominid" and *National Geographic*'s use of "hominin" were both right in the broadest sense. In either the "old" or "new" classification system, hominid works; it just means different things.

In the old system, hominid refers solely to the bipedal ape line. In the new classification system it refers to the broader grouping of all the great apes,

© Dr. Fred Spoor/National Museums of Kenya

This 3- to 4-million-year-old skull could be another australopithecine or, as its discoverers suggest, a separate genus *Kenyanthropus platyops*.

which would by definition certainly include the new *Kenyanthropus* fossils.

The use of hominin by *National Geographic* is technically more correct in that it recognizes the relationship of *Kenyanthropus* to the other bipedal apes and distinguishes it from other living and fossil African apes, which are not so closely related to us based on the molecular evidence we have to date.

In the long run, "hominin" is likely to win out against the term "hominid." It is more precise and recognizes the biological reality that moves beyond physical morphology.

Do I like it? Well, I would never try to stand in the way of the advancement of science, but just try saying Hominidae, Homininae, Hominini three times fast in front of a first-year Introduction to Anthropology class, and you will have some sympathy for the scientist who clings to the term "hominid" for a few more years.

So what's in a name? The classification debate is not just a debate for the purist; it cuts to the very core of our understanding of human's place in nature and our evolutionary relationships with our closest living relatives. All hominins are hominids, but not all hominids are hominins.

(By Lee R. Berger for National Geographic News, *December 4, 2001.)* ■

THE ANATOMY OF BIPEDALISM

For a hominoid fossil to be definitively classified as part of the human evolutionary line, certain evidence of bipedalism—the shared derived characteristic distinguishing humans and their ancestors from the other African apes—is required. Bipedalism is associated with anatomical changes literally from head to toe (Figures 6.1 and 6.2).

As noted in the Taung child, evidence of bipedalism can even be preserved in the skull. Evidence of walking on two feet is preserved in the skull because balancing the skull above the spinal column in an upright posture requires a skull position relatively centered above the spinal column. The spinal cord leaves the skull at its base through an opening called the *foramen magnum* (Latin for "big opening"). In a knuckle-walker like a chimp, the foramen magnum is placed more toward the back of the skull while in a biped it is in a more forward position.

Extending down from the skull of a biped, the spinal column makes a series of convex and concave curves that together maintain the body in an upright posture by positioning the body's center of gravity above the legs rather than forward. The curves correspond to the neck (cervical), chest (thoracic), lower back (lumbar), and pelvic (sacral) regions of the spine, respectively. In a chimp, the shape of the spine follows a single arching curve. Interestingly, at birth the spines of human babies have a single arching curve as seen in adult apes. As they mature the curves characteristic of bipedalism appear, the cervical curve at about three months on average and the lumbar curve at around twelve months—a time when many babies begin to walk.

The shape of the pelvis also differs considerably between bipeds and other apes. Rather than an elongated shape following the arch of the spine as seen in chimps, the biped pelvis is wider and foreshortened so that it can provide structural support for the upright body. With a wide bipedal pelvis, the lower limbs would be oriented away from the body's center of gravity if the thigh bones (femora) didn't angle in toward each other from the hip to the knee, a phenomenon described as "kneeing-in."

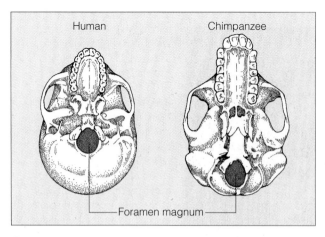

Figure 6.1

Bipedalism can be inferred from the position of the foramen magnum, the large opening at the base of the skull. Note its relatively forward position on the human skull (left) compared to the chimp skull.

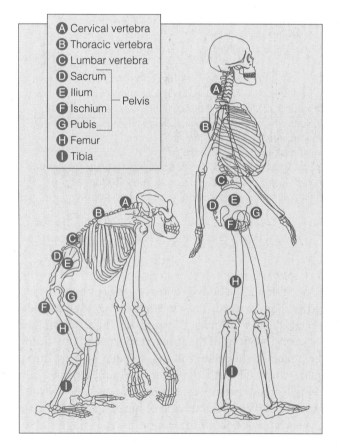

Ⓐ Cervical vertebra
Ⓑ Thoracic vertebra
Ⓒ Lumbar vertebra
Ⓓ Sacrum
Ⓔ Ilium
Ⓕ Ischium — Pelvis
Ⓖ Pubis
Ⓗ Femur
Ⓘ Tibia

Figure 6.2

Differences between skeletons of chimps and humans reflect their mode of locomotion.

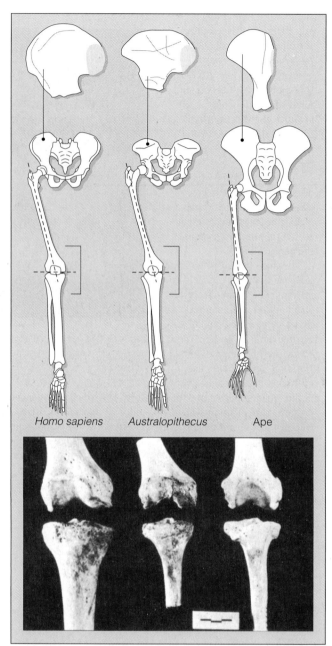

Homo sapiens   *Australopithecus*   Ape

Figure 6.3

Examination of the upper hip bones and lower limbs of (from left) *Homo sapiens, Australopithecus,* and an ape can be used to determine means of locomotion. The similarities of the human and australopith-ecine bones are striking and are indicative of bipedal locomotion.

(Notice how your own knees and feet can touch when standing while your hip joints remain widely spaced.)

This angling does not continue past the knee to the shin bones (tibia), which are oriented vertically. The resulting knee joint is not symmetrical, allowing the thigh and shin bones to meet despite their different orientations (Figure 6.3). Another characteristic of bipeds is their stable arched feet and the absent opposable big toe. In general, humans and their ancestors possess shorter toes than the other apes.

These anatomical features allow paleoanthropologists to "diagnose" bipedal locomotion even in fragmentary remains such as the top of the shin bone or the base of a skull. In addition, bipedal locomotion can also be established through fossilized footprints, preserving not so much the shape of foot bones but the characteristic stride used by humans and their ancestors. In fact, bipedal locomotion is a process of shifting the body's

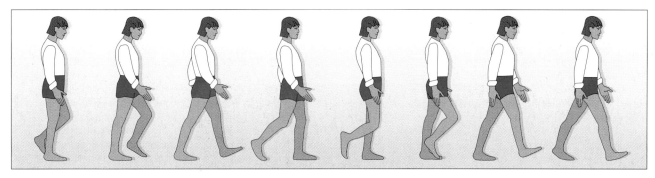

Figure 6.4

The bipedal gait in some regards is really "serial monopedalism" or locomotion one foot at a time through a series of controlled falls. Note how the body's weight shifts from one foot to the other as an individual moves through the swing phase to heel strike and toe off.

weight from one foot to the other as the nonsupporting foot swings forward. While the body is supported in a one-legged stance, a biped takes a stride by swinging the other leg forward. The heel of the foot is the first part of the swinging leg to hit the ground. Then as the biped continues to move forward, he or she rolls from the heel toward the toe, pushing or "toeing off" into the next swing phase of the stride. While one leg is moving from heel strike to toe off of the stance phase, the other leg is moving forward through the swing phase of walking (Figure 6.4).

The most dramatic confirmation of australopithecines' walking ability comes from Laetoli, Tanzania, where, 3.6 million years ago, three individuals walked across newly fallen volcanic ash. Because it was damp, the ash took the impressions of their feet, and these were sealed beneath subsequent ash falls until discovered by chemist Paul Abell in 1978. Abell was part of a team led by paleoanthropologist Mary Leakey in search of human origins at Laetoli (see Anthropologists of Note). The shape of the footprints, the linear distance between the heel strikes and toe off, are all quite human.

Once bipedalism is established in a fossil specimen, paleoanthropologists turn to other features such as the skull or teeth to establish relationships among the various fossil groups.

THE PLIOCENE FOSSIL EVIDENCE: *AUSTRALOPITHECUS* AND OTHER BIPEDS

As described in the previous chapter, the Miocene epoch was a time of tremendous geological change. The effects of these changes continued into the Pliocene. The steady

© Anthro-Photo

Fossilized footprints were preserved in volcanic ash at the 3.6-million-year-old Tanzanian site of Laetoli. As shown here, the foot of a living human fits right inside this ancient footprint, which shows the characteristic pattern of bipedal walking.

Anthropologists of Note

Louis S. B. Leakey (1903–1972) ▪ Mary Leakey (1913–1996)

Few figures in the history of paleoanthropology discovered so many key fossils, received so much public acclaim, or stirred up as much controversy as Louis Leakey and his second wife, Mary Leakey. Born in Kenya of missionary parents, Louis received his early education from an English governess and subsequently was sent to England for a university education. He returned to Kenya in the 1920s to begin his career there.

It was in 1931 that Louis and his research assistant from England, Mary Nicol (whom he married in 1936), began working in their spare time at Olduvai Gorge in Tanzania, searching patiently and persistently for remains of early human ancestors. It seemed a good place to look, for there were numerous animal fossils, as well as crude stone tools lying scattered on the ground and eroding out of the walls of the gorge.

Their patience and persistence were not rewarded until 1959, when Mary found the first fossil. A year later, another skull was found, and Olduvai was on its way to being recognized as one of the most important sources of fossils important to human evolution in all of Africa. While Louis reconstructed, described,

© Melville Bell Grosvenor/National Geographic Society Images

and interpreted the fossil material, Mary made the definitive study of the Oldowan tools.

The Leakeys' important discoveries were not limited to those at Olduvai. In the early 1930s, they found the first fossils of Miocene apes in Africa at Rusinga Island in Lake Victoria. Also in the 1930s, Louis found a number of skulls at Kanjera, Kenya, that show a mixture of derived and more ancestral features. In 1948, at Fort Ternan, Kenya, the Leakeys found the remains of a late Miocene ape with features that seemed appropriate for an ancestor of the bipeds. After Louis' death, a member of an expedition led by Mary Leakey

found the first footprints of *Australopithecus* at Laetoli, Tanzania.

In addition to their own work, Louis Leakey promoted a good deal of important work on the part of others. He made it possible for Jane Goodall to begin her landmark field studies of chimpanzees; later on, he was instrumental in setting up similar studies among gorillas (by Dian Fossey) and orangutans (by Birute Galdikas). He set into motion the fellowship program responsible for the training of numerous paleoanthropologists from Africa. Last but not least, the Leakey tradition has been continued by son Richard, his wife, Meave, and their daughter Louise.

Louis Leakey had a flamboyant personality and a way of making interpretations of fossil materials that frequently did not stand up well to careful scrutiny, but this did not stop him from publicly presenting his views as if they were the gospel truth. It was this aspect of the Leakeys' work that generated controversy. Nonetheless, the Leakeys accomplished and promoted more work that resulted in the accumulation of knowledge about human origins than anyone before them. Anthropology clearly owes them a great deal.

---

movement of geological plates supporting the African and Eurasian continents resulted in a collision of the two landmasses at either end of what now is the Mediterranean Sea (Figure 6.5). This contact allowed for the spread of species between these continents.

Associated with this collision is a suite of geological changes that produced the Great Rift Valley system. This system consists of a separation between geological plates, extending from the Middle East through the Red Sea and eastern Africa into southern Africa. Part of rifting involves the steady increase in the elevation of the

eastern third of the African continent, which experienced a cooler and drier climate and a transformation of vegetation from forest to dry grassy **savannah.**

The system also contributed to the volcanic activity in the region, which provides opportunities for accurate dating of fossil specimens. Also in the Miocene, the Indian subcontinent, which had been a solitary landmass for many millions of years, came into its present position through a collision with Eurasia, contributing further to cooler, drier conditions globally. In addition to causing global climate change, these geological events also provided excellent opportunities for the discovery of fossil specimens as layers of the earth become exposed through the rifting process.

savannah Semi-arid plains environment as in eastern Africa.

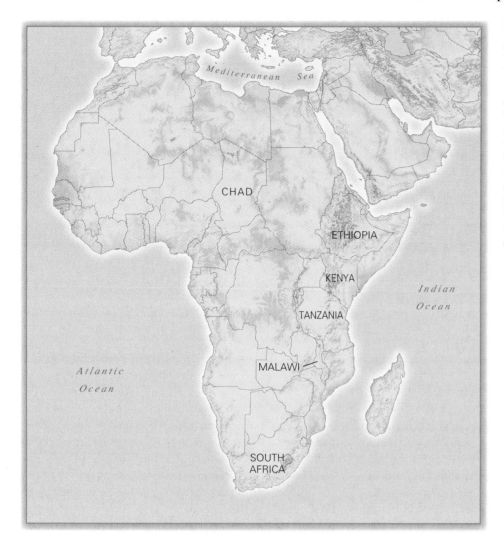

Figure 6.5

Australopithecine fossils have been found in South Africa, Malawi, Tanzania, Kenya, Ethiopia, and Chad. In the Miocene the Eurasian and African continents made contact at the eastern and western ends of what now is the Mediterranean Sea. As these land masses met, "rifting" also occurred, gradually raising the elevation of the eastern third of Africa. The dryer climates that resulted may have played a role in human evolution in the distant past. In the present this rifting also created excellent geological conditions for finding fossils.

Since Dart's original find, hundreds of other fossil bipeds have been discovered, first in South Africa and later in Tanzania, Malawi, Kenya, Ethiopia, and Chad. As they were discovered, many were placed in a variety of different genera and species, but now usually all are considered to belong to the single genus *Australopithecus*. Anthropologists recognize up to eight species of the genus (Table 6.1). In addition, some other groups of fossil bipeds from the Pliocene epoch (1.6 to 5 million years ago) have been discovered.

First we will describe those species and the australopithecines in the order in which they inhabited the earth up to the middle Pliocene (2.5 million years ago) when the genus *Homo* first appeared. The East African and South African evidence will be presented separately because the dating for East African sites is more reliable. Next we will examine late-appearing australopithecines, including a grade of australopithecine found in both eastern and southern Africa that co-existed with the genus *Homo*.

East Africa

Geological and climatic changes in human evolutionary history have been frequently incorporated in theories about the evolution of bipedalism with an emphasis on adaptation to the dry savannah environment. As more fossil evidence is discovered from the early Pliocene, we increasingly see that some of the early bipeds may have inhabited a forested environment. For example, in 1994 pieces of several individuals were discovered in 4.4-million-year-old deposits along Ethiopia's Awash River accompanied by fossils of forest animals. Subsequent finds in the same region date between 5.2 and 5.8 million years ago. They are thought to represent early and later varieties of a single species, **Ardipithecus ramidus.** The name is fitting for an ultimate human ancestor as

Ardipithecus ramidus One of the earliest bipeds that lived in eastern Africa about 4.4 to 5.8 million years ago.

TABLE 6.1	SPECIES OF *AUSTRALOPITHECUS**		
Species	**Location**	**Dates**	**Notable Features/Fossil Specimens**
A. anamensis	Kenya	3.9–4.2 mya[†]	Oldest australopithecine
A. afarensis	Ethiopia and Tanzania	2.9–3.9 mya	Well represented in fossil record (Lucy, First Family, Laetoli footprints, "Lucy's baby")
A. africanus	South Africa	2.3–3 mya	First discovered, gracile, well represented in fossil record (Taung)
A. aethiopicus	Kenya	2.5 mya	Oldest robust australopithecine ("Black Skull")
A. bahrelghazali	Chad	3–3.5 mya	Only australopithecine from central Africa
A. boisei	Kenya	1.2–2.3 mya	Later robust form co-existed with early *Homo* ("Zinj")
A. garhi	Ethiopia	2.5 mya	Later East African australopithecine with humanlike dentition
A. robustus	South Africa	1–2 mya	Robust co-existed with early *Homo*

*Paleoanthropologists differ in the number of species they recognize, some suggesting separate genera.
[†]Million years ago.

Ardi means "floor" and *ramid* means "root" in the local Afar language.

Careful examination of the *Ardipithecus* specimens proved that all early bipeds are not necessarily direct ancestors to later humans. *Ardipithecus* was much smaller than a modern chimpanzee, but it was chimpanzeelike in other features, such as the shape and enamel thickness of its teeth. On the other hand, a partially complete skeleton of one *Ardipithecus* individual suggests that unlike chimpanzees, and like all other species in the human line, this creature was bipedal. Given the combination of bipedalism and chimpanzeelike characteristics, many paleoanthropologists consider it a side branch of the human evolutionary tree. Fossil evidence shows that over the next several million years, many bipedal species inhabited Africa—making it more accurate to refer to an evolutionary bush rather than a tree.

The *Ardipithecus* finds along with the *Orrorin* and Toumai specimens described in the previous chapter have begun to provide evidence for the time period before australopithecines appeared. So what are we to make of these fossils? Until we have better samples, we will not know for sure. What seems likely on present genetic and fossil evidence is that bipeds evolved from late Miocene apes, becoming distinct by at least 5 million years ago. It seems that more than one line of biped appeared at this time, but just how many is not known. Australopithecines emerged from this early branching. In turn, one of these species from the middle Pliocene evolved into the genus *Homo*.

The oldest australopithecine species known so far consists of some jaw and limb bones from Kenya that date to between 3.9 and 4.2 million years ago (see *Australopithecus anamensis* in Table 6.1). Meave and Louise Leakey, daughter-in-law and granddaughter of Louis

and Mary Leakey, discovered these fossils in 1995 and decided to place them in a separate species from other known australopithecines. Its name means "ape-man of the lake," and it shows particularities in the teeth such as a true "sectorial" premolar tooth shaped to hone the upper canine as seen in apes. As in other australopithecines and humans, the enamel in the molar teeth is thick. The limb bone fragments indicate bipedalism.

Moving closer to the present, the next species defined in the fossil record is *Australopithecus afarensis*. No longer the earliest australopithecine species, it still remains one of the best known due to the Laetoli footprints from Tanzania, the famous "Lucy" specimen and the recent discovery of the 3.3-million-year-old remains of a young child called "Lucy's baby," both from Ethiopia. Lucy consists of bones from almost all parts of a single skeleton discovered in 1974 in the Afar triangle of Ethiopia (hence the name *afarensis*). The Afar region is also famous for the "First Family," a collection of bones from at least thirteen individuals, ranging in age from infancy to adulthood, who died together as a result of some single calamity.

At least sixty individuals have been removed from fossil localities in Ethiopia and Tanzania. Specimens from Ethiopia's Afar region are securely dated by potassium argon to between 2.9 and 3.9 million years ago. Material from Laetoli, in Tanzania, is securely dated to 3.6 million years ago. Altogether, *A. afarensis* appears to be a sexually dimorphic bipedal species with estimates of body size and weight ranging between 1.1 and 1.6 meters (3½–5 feet) and 29 and 45 kilograms (64–100 pounds), respectively.[1]

---

[1]McHenry, H. M. (1992). Body size and proportions in early hominids. *American Journal of Physical Anthropology* 87, 407.

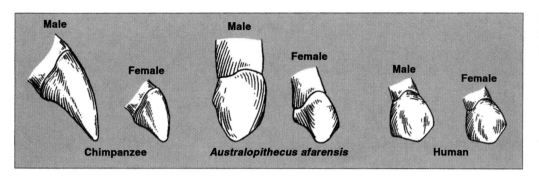

Figure 6.6
Sexual dimorphism in canine teeth.

If paleoanthropologists are correct in assuming that larger fossil specimens were males and smaller specimens females, males were about 1½ times the size of females. In this respect, they were somewhat like the Miocene African apes, with sexual dimorphism greater than one sees in a modern chimpanzee but less than one sees in gorillas and orangutans. Male canine teeth, too, are significantly larger than canine teeth of females,

though canine size is reduced compared to that of chimps (Figure 6.6).

Nearly 40 percent complete, the Lucy specimen has provided invaluable information about the shape of the pelvis and torso of early human ancestors. *A. afarensis'* physical appearance was unusual by human standards: They may be described as looking like an ape from the waist up and like a human from the waist down (Figure 6.7). In addition, a forearm bone from Lucy, which is relatively shorter than that of an ape, suggests that the upper limb was lighter and the center of gravity lower in the body than in apes. Still, the arms of Lucy and other early australopithecines are long in proportion to their legs when compared to the proportions seen in humans. Though fully competent as bipeds, the curvature of the fingers and toes and the somewhat elevated position of the shoulder joint indicate *A. afarensis* was more adapted to tree climbing compared to more recent human ancestors.

Though she lived about 150,000 years before her namesake, "Lucy's baby," the discovery from Ethiopia announced in 2006, will add considerably to our knowledge about *A. afarensis*.[2] These fossilized remains of a young child dated to 3.3 million years ago were discovered in the Dikika area of northern Ethiopia in 2000. Because the remains of this child, thought to have died in a flash flood, are particularly well preserved, scientists can investigate new aspects of this species' biology and behavior. For example, a preserved hyoid bone (located in the throat region) allows scientists to reconstruct australopithecine patterns of vocalization. While the lower limbs clearly indicate bipedalism, the specimen's scapula and long curved finger bones are more apelike.

The skull of *A. afarensis* is relatively low, the forehead slopes backward, and the brow ridge that helps give apes such massive-looking foreheads is also present. The lower half of the face is chinless and accented by jaws that are quite large, relative to the size of the skull. The brain is small and apelike, and the general conformation of the skull seems nonhuman. Even the semicircular canal, a part of the ear crucial to maintenance of balance, is

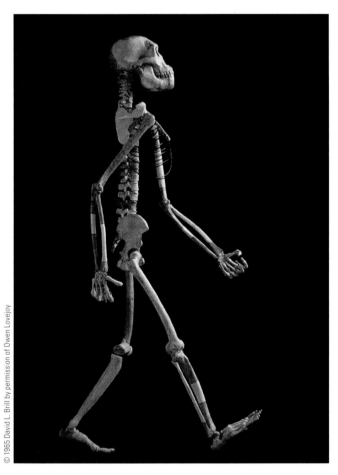

© 1985 David L. Brill by permission of Owen Lovejoy

A 40 percent complete australopithecine skeleton "Lucy," named after the Beatles' song "Lucy in the Sky with Diamonds," popular at the time of discovery, indicates that these australopithecine ancestors were bipedal. This adult female was only 3½ feet tall, typical of the small size of female australopithecines. By understanding the shapes of bones, paleoanthropologists have reconstructed the entire skeleton from the remains that were discovered. (Note the darker color of the actual fossil remains, as opposed to the lighter reconstructed portions).

---

[2] Zeresenay, A., et al. (2006). A juvenile early hominin skeleton from Dikika, Ethiopia. *Nature 443*, 296–301.

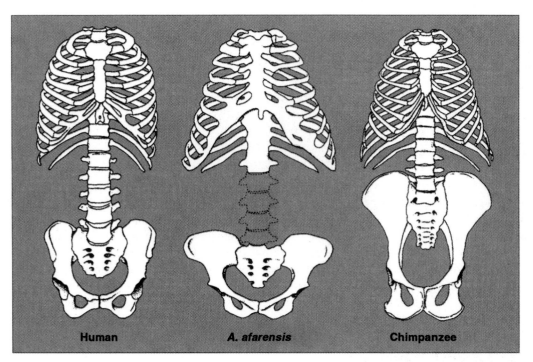

Figure 6.7
Trunk skeletons of modern human, *A. afarensis,* and chimpanzee, compared. In its pelvis, the australopithecine resembles the modern human, but its rib cage shows the pyramidal configuration of the ape.

Human   **A. afarensis**   **Chimpanzee**

apelike. Cranial capacity, commonly used as an index of brain size for *A. afarensis,* averages about 420 cubic centimeters (cc), roughly equivalent to the size of a chimpanzee and about one-third the size of living humans.[3] Intelligence, however, is indicated not only by absolute brain size alone but also by the ratio of brain to body size. Unfortunately, with such a wide range of adult weights, it is

not clear whether australopithecine brain size was larger than a modern ape's, relative to body size.

Much has been written about australopithecine teeth because they are one of the primary means for distinguishing between closely related groups. In *A. afarensis,* unlike humans, the teeth are all quite large, particularly the molars. The premolar is no longer fully sectorial as in *A. anamensis,* but most other features of the teeth represent a more ancestral rather than derived condition. For example, the rows of the teeth are more parallel (the ancestral ape condition) compared to the arch seen in the human tooth rows. The canines project slightly, and a slight space or gap known as a **diastema** remains between the upper incisors and canines as found in the apes (Figure 6.8).

[3]Grine, F. E. (1993). Australopithecine taxonomy and phylogeny: Historical background and recent interpretation. In R. L. Ciochon & J. G. Fleagle (Eds.), *The human evolution source book* (pp. 201–202). Englewood Cliffs, NJ: Prentice-Hall.

diastema A space between the canines and other teeth allowing large projecting canines space within the jaw.

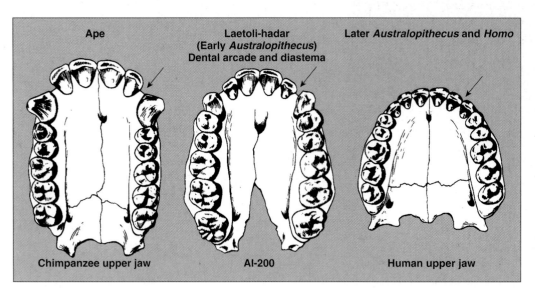

Ape   Laetoli-hadar (Early *Australopithecus*) Dental arcade and diastema   Later *Australopithecus* and *Homo*

Chimpanzee upper jaw   AI-200   Human upper jaw

Figure 6.8
The upper jaws of an ape, *Australopithecus,* and modern human show important differences in the shape of the dental arch and the spacing between the canines and adjoining teeth. Only in the earliest australopithecines can a diastema (a large gap between the upper canine and incisor) be seen.

To further complicate the diversity seen in *A. afarensis,* in 2001 Meave and Louise Leakey announced the discovery of an almost complete cranium, parts of two upper jaws, and assorted teeth from a site in northern Kenya, dated to between 3.2 and 3.5 million years ago.[4] Contemporary with early East African *Australopithecus,* the Leakeys see this as a different genus named **Kenyanthropus platyops** ("flat-faced man of Kenya"). Unlike early australopithecines, *Kenyanthropus* is said to have a small braincase and small molars set in a large, humanlike, flat face. But again, there is controversy; the Leakeys see the fossils as ancestral to the genus *Homo.* Other paleoanthropologists are not convinced, suggesting that the Leakeys' interpretation rests on a questionable reconstruction of badly broken fossil specimens.[5]

Central Africa

Dated to the same time period as *Kenyanthropus platyops* is another recent discovery of an australopithecine from Chad in central Africa. The new species, *Australopithecus bahrelghazali,* is named after the Arabic name for a nearby riverbed and consists of a jaw and several teeth dated to between 3 and 3.5 million years ago.[6] This is the first australopithecine discovered in central Africa. With time, perhaps more discoveries from this region will give a fuller understanding of the role of *A. bahrelghazali* in human evolution and their relationship to the possible bipeds from the Miocene.

South Africa

Throughout the 20th century and into the present, paleoanthropologists have continued to recover australopithecine fossils from a variety of sites in South Africa. Included in this group are numerous fossils found beginning in the 1930s at Sterkfontein and Makapansgat, in addition to Dart's original find from Taung.

It is important to note, however, that South African sites, lacking the clear stratigraphy and volcanic ash of East African sites, are much more difficult to date and interpret (Figure 6.9). One unusually complete skull and skeleton has been dated by paleomagnetism to about 3.5 million years ago,[7] as was a partial foot skeleton (Fig-

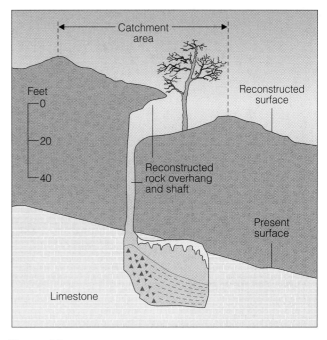

Figure 6.9

Many of the fossil sites in South Africa were limestone caverns connected to the surface by a shaft. Over time, dirt, bones, and other matter that fell down the shaft accumulated inside the cavern, becoming fossilized. In the Pliocene, the earth next to the shaft's opening provided a sheltered location for trees that, in turn, may have been used by predators for eating without being bothered by scavengers.

ure 6.10) described in 1995.[8] The other South African remains are difficult to date. A faunal series established in East Africa places these specimens between 2.3 and 3 million years ago. These specimens are all classified in the australopithecine species named by Dart—*A. africanus,* also known as **gracile australopithecines.**

The reconstruction of australopithecine biology is controversial. Some researchers think they see evidence for some expansion of the brain in *A. africanus,* while others vigorously disagree. Paleoanthropologists also compare the outside appearance of the brain, as revealed by casts of the insides of skulls. Some researchers suggest that cerebral reorganization toward a human condition is present,[9] while others state the organization of

[4]Leakey, M. G., et al. (2001). New hominin genus from eastern Africa shows diverse middle Pliocene lineages. *Nature 410,* 433–440.

[5]White, T. D. (2003). Early hominids—diversity or distortion? *Science 299,* 1,994–1,997.

[6]Brunet, M., et al. (1995).The first australopithecine 2,500 kilometers west of the Rift Valley (Chad). *Nature 16,* 378(6554), 273–275.

[7]Clarke, R. J. (1998). First ever discovery of a well preserved skull and associated skeleton of Australopithecus. *South African Journal of Science 94,* 460–464.

[8]Clarke, R. J., & Tobias, P. V. (1995). Sterkfontein member 2 foot bones of the oldest South African hominid. *Science 269,* 521–524.

[9]Holloway, R. L., & de LaCoste-Lareymondie, M. C. (1982). Brain endocast asymmetry in pongids and hominids: Some preliminary

Kenyanthropus platyops A new proposed genus and species of bipeds contemporary with early australopithecines; may not be separate genus.

gracile australopithecines Members of the genus *Australopithecus* possessing a more lightly built chewing apparatus; likely had a diet that included more meat than that of the robust australopithecines.

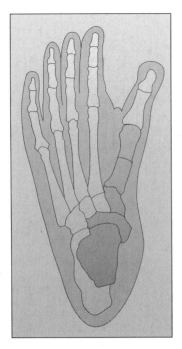

Figure 6.10

Drawing of the foot bones of a 3- to 3.5-million-year-old *Australopithecus* from Sterkfontein, South Africa, as they would have been in the complete foot. Note how long and flexible the first toe (at right) is.

the brain is more apelike than human.[10] At the moment, the weight of the evidence favors mental capabilities for all gracile australopithecines as being comparable to those of modern great apes (chimps, bonobos, gorillas, orangutans).

Using patterns of tooth eruption in young australopithecines such as Taung, North American paleoanthropologist Alan Mann and colleagues suggested that the developmental pattern of australopithecines was more humanlike than apelike,[11] though some other paleoanthropologists do not agree. Evidence from the recent

findings on the paleontology of cerebral dominance. *American Journal of Physical Anthropology 58*, 101–110.

[10]Falk, D. (1989). Apelike endocast of "ape-man" Taung. *American Journal of Physical Anthropology 80*, 335–339.

[11]Mann A., Lampl, M., & Monge, J. (1990). Patterns of ontogeny in human evolution: Evidence from dental development. *Yearbook of Physical Anthropology, 33*, 111–150.

robust australopithecines Several species within the genus *Australopithecus*, who lived from 2.5 and 1.1 million years ago in eastern and southern Africa; known for the rugged nature of their chewing apparatus (large back teeth, large chewing muscles, and a bony ridge on their skull tops for the insertion of these large muscles).

sagittal crest A crest running from front to back on the top of the skull along the midline to provide a surface of bone for the attachment of the large temporal muscles for chewing.

discovery of the young *A. afarensis* specimen will help scientists to resolve this debate. A current understanding of genetics and the macroevolutionary process indicates that a developmental shift is likely to have accompanied a change in body plan such as the emergence of bipedalism among the African hominoids.

Other South African sites have yielded fossils whose skulls and teeth looked quite different from the gracile australopithecines described above. These South African fossils are known as *Australopithecus robustus*. They are notable for having teeth, jaws, and chewing muscles that are massive (robust) relative to the size of the braincase. The gracile forms are slightly smaller on average and lack such robust chewing structures. Over the course of evolution, several distinct groups of **robust australopithecines** have appeared not only in South Africa, but throughout East Africa as well.

Robust Australopithecines

The remains of robust australopithecines were first found at Kromdraai and Swartkrans in South Africa by paleoanthropologists Robert Broom and John Robinson in the 1930s in deposits that, unfortunately, cannot be securely dated. Current thinking puts them anywhere from 1 and 1.8 million years ago. Usually referred to as *A. robustus* (see Table 6.1), this species possessed a characteristic robust chewing apparatus including a **sagittal crest** running from front to back along the top of the skull. This feature provides sufficient area on a relatively small braincase for attachment of the huge temporal muscles required to operate powerful jaws. Because it is present in robust australopithecines and gorillas today, this feature provides an example of convergent evolution.

The first robust australopithecine to be found in East Africa was discovered by Mary Leakey in the summer of 1959, the centennial year of the publication of Darwin's *On the Origin of Species*. She found it in Olduvai Gorge, a fossil-rich area near Ngorongoro Crater, on the Serengeti Plain of Tanzania, East Africa. Olduvai is a huge gash in the earth, about 25 miles long and 300 feet deep, which cuts through Plio-Pleistocene and recent geological strata revealing close to 2 million years of the earth's history.

Mary Leakey's discovery was reconstructed by her husband Louis, who gave it the name *Zinjanthropus boisei* (Zinj, an Arabic word for "East Africa," boisei after the benefactor who funded their expedition). At first, he thought this ancient fossil seemed more humanlike than *Australopithecus* and extremely close to modern humans in evolutionary development, in part due to the stone tools found in association with this specimen. Further study, however, revealed that *Zinjanthropus*, the remains of which consisted of a skull and a few limb bones, was

VISUAL COUNTERPOINT

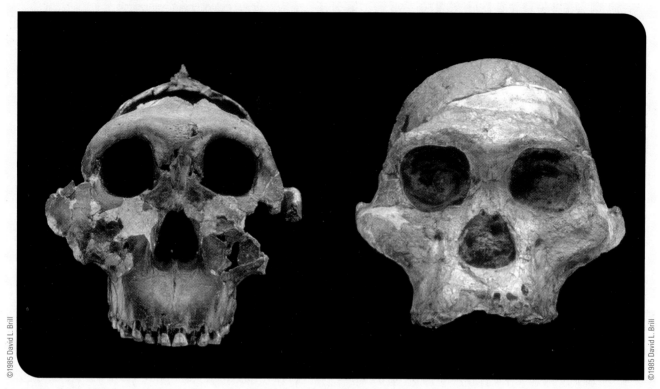

The differences between gracile and robust australopithecines are related primarily to their chewing apparatus. Robust species have extremely large cheek teeth, large chewing muscles, and a bony ridge on the top of their skulls for the attachment of large temporal muscles for chewing. The front and back teeth of gracile species are balanced in size, and their chewing muscles (reflected in a less massive skull) are more like those seen in the later genus *Homo*. If you place your own hands on the sides of your skull above your ears while opening and closing your jaw, you can feel where your temporal muscles attach to your skull. By moving your hands toward the top of your skull you can feel where these muscles end in humans.

an East African species of robust australopithecine. Although similar in many ways to *A. robustus*, "Zinj" is now most commonly referred to as *Australopithecus boisei* (see Table 6.1). Potassium-argon dating places this early species at about 1.75 million years old.

Since the time of Mary Leakey's original find, numerous other fossils of this robust species have been found at Olduvai, as well as north and east of Lake Turkana in Kenya. Although one fossil specimen often referred to as the "Black Skull" (see *A. aethiopicus* in Table 6.1) is known to be as much as 2.5 million years old, some date to as recently as 1.1 million years ago.

Like robust australopithecines from South Africa, East African robust forms possessed enormous molars and premolars. Despite a large mandible and palate, the anterior teeth (canines and incisors) were often crowded, owing to the room needed for the massive molars.

The heavy skull, more massive even than seen in the robust forms from South Africa, has a sagittal crest and prominent brow ridges. Cranial capacity ranges from about 500 to 530 cubic centimeters. Body size, too,

is somewhat larger; whereas the South African robust forms are estimated to have weighed between 32 and 40 kilograms, the East African robusts probably weighed from 34 to 49 kilograms.

Because the earliest robust skull from East Africa (2.5 million years), the so-called Black Skull from Kenya, retains a number of ancestral features shared with earlier East African australopithecines, it is possible that it evolved from *A. afarensis*, giving rise to the later robust East African forms. Whether the South African robust australopithecines represent a southern offshoot of the East African line or convergent evolution from a South African ancestor is so far not settled; arguments can be presented for both interpretations. In either case, what happened was that the later robust australopithecines developed molars and premolars that are both absolutely and relatively larger than those of earlier australopithecines who possessed front and back teeth more in proportion to those seen in the genus *Homo*.

Larger teeth require more bone to support them, hence the prominent jaws of the robust australopith-

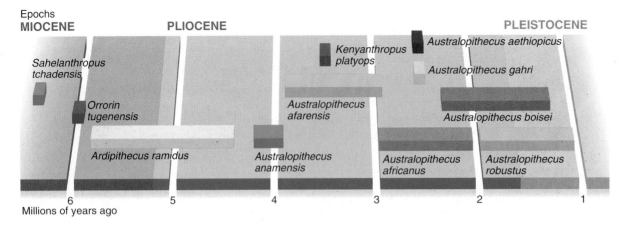

Figure 6.11

The Pliocene fossil bipeds and the scientific names by which they have been known, arranged according to when they lived. *A. aethiopicus*, *A. boisei*, and *A. robustus* are all robust australopithecines. Whether all the different species names are warranted is debated.

ecines. Larger jaws and heavy chewing activity require more jaw musculature that attaches to the skull. The marked crests seen on skulls of the late australopithecines provide for the attachment of chewing muscles on a skull that has increased very little in size. In effect, robust australopithecines had evolved into highly efficient chewing machines. Clearly, their immense cheek teeth and powerful chewing muscles bespeak the kind of heavy chewing a diet of uncooked plant foods requires. This kind of general level of biological organization shared by separate fossil groups as seen in the robust australopithecines is referred to as a *grade*.

Many anthropologists believe that, by becoming a specialized consumer of plant foods, the late australopithecines avoided competing for the same niche with early *Homo*, with which they were contemporaries. In the course of evolution, the **law of competitive exclusion** dictates that when two closely related species compete for the same niche, one will out-compete the other, bringing about the loser's extinction. That early *Homo* and late *Australopithecus* did not compete for the same niche is suggested by their co-existence for something like 1.5 million years from about 1 million to 2.5 million years ago (Figure 6.11).

Australopithecines and the Genus *Homo*

A variety of bipeds inhabited Africa about 2.5 million years ago, around the time the first evidence for the genus *Homo* begins to appear. In 1999, discoveries in

law of competitive exclusion When two closely related species compete for the same niche, one will out-compete the other, bringing about the latter's extinction.

East Africa added another australopithecine to the mix. Found in the Afar region of Ethiopia, these fossils were named *Australopithecus garhi* after the word for "surprise" in the local Afar language. Though the teeth were large, this australopithecine possessed an arched dental arcade and a ratio between front and back teeth more like humans and South African gracile australopithecines rather than like robust groups. For this reason, some have proposed that *A. garhi* is ancestral to the genus *Homo*. More evidence will be needed to prove whether or not this is true.

The precise relationship among all the australopithecine species (and other bipeds) that have been defined during the Pliocene is still not settled. In this mix, the question of which australopithecine was ancestral to humans remains particularly controversial. A variety of scenarios have been proposed, each one giving a different australopithecine group the "starring role" as the immediate human ancestor (Figure 6.12). Though paleoanthropologists debate which species is ancestral to humans, they agree that the robust australopithecines, though successful in their time, ultimately represent an evolutionary side branch.

ENVIRONMENT, DIET, AND AUSTRALOPITHECINE ORIGINS

Having described the fossil material, we may now consider *how* evolution transformed an early ape into *Australopithecus*. Generally, such paleoanthropological reconstructions rely heavily on the evolutionary role of natural selection in their hypotheses. The question at hand is not so much *why* did bipedalism appear as *how* did bipedalism allow these ancestors to adapt to their environment?

In 1999, Ethiopian paleoanthropologist Y. Haile Selassie discovered fossil material placed into the new species *Australopithecus garhi.*

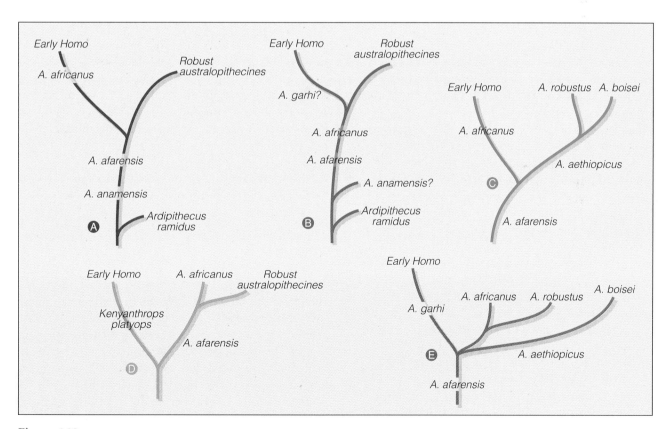

Figure 6.12

The relationship among the various australopithecine (and other) Pliocene groups, and the question of which group is ancestral to the genus *Homo,* is debated by anthropologists. Several alternative hypotheses are presented in these diagrams. Most agree, however, that the robust australopithecines represent an evolutionary side branch.

Hypotheses about adaptation begin with features evident in the fossil evidence. For example, the fossil record indicates that once bipedalism appeared, over the next several million years the shape of the face and teeth shifted from a more apelike to a humanlike condition. To refine their hypotheses, paleoanthropologists add scientifically reconstructed environmental conditions and inferences made from data gathered on living nonhuman primates and humans to the fossil evidence. In this regard, evolutionary reconstructions involve piecing together a coherent story or narrative about the past. Sometimes these narratives are tenuous. But as paleoanthropologists consider their own biases and incorporate new evidence as it is discovered, the quality of the narrative improves.

For many years, the human evolutionary narrative has been tied to the emergence of the savannah environment in eastern Africa as the global climate changes of the Miocene led to increasingly cooler and drier conditions. The size of tropical forests decreased or, more commonly, broke up into mosaics where patches of forest were interspersed with savannah or other types of open country. The forebears of the human line are thought to have lived in places with access to both trees and open country. With the breaking up of forests, these early ancestors found themselves spending more and more time on the ground and had to adapt to this new, more open environment.

The most obvious problem facing these ancestors in their new situation, other than getting from one patch of trees to another, was getting food. As the forest thinned or shrank, the traditional ape-type foods found in trees became less available to them, especially in seasons of reduced rainfall. Therefore, it became more and more necessary to forage on the ground for foods such as seeds, grasses, and roots. With reduced canine teeth, early bipeds were relatively defenseless when down on the ground and were easy targets for numerous carnivorous predators. That predators were a problem is revealed by the South African fossils, most of which are from individuals that were dropped into rock fissures by leopards or, in the case of Dart's original find, by an eagle.

Many investigators have argued that the hands of early bipeds took over the weapon functions of the reduced canine teeth, by enabling them to threaten predators by using wooden objects as clubs and throwing stones. This quality is shared with many of the other hominoids. Recall the male chimpanzee (Chapter 3) who wielded objects as part of his display to obtain alpha status. In australopithecines the use of clubs and throwing stones may have set the stage for the much later manufacture of more efficient weapons from bone, wood, and stone.

Although the hands of the later australopithecines were suitable for tool making, no evidence exists that any of them actually *made* stone tools. Similarly, experiments with captive bonobos have shown that they are capable of making crude chipped stone tools, but they have never been known to do so outside of captivity. Thus, to be able to do something is not necessarily equivalent to doing it. In fact, the earliest known stone tools, dating to about 2.5 million years ago, are about 2 million years more recent than the oldest fossils of *Australopithecus*. However, *Australopithecus* certainly had no less intelligence and dexterity than do modern great apes, all of whom make use of tools when it is to their advantage to do so. Orangutans, bonobos, chimpanzees, and even gorillas have all been observed in the wild making and using simple tools such as those described in Chapter 3. Most likely, the ability to make and use simple tools is something that goes back to the last common ancestor of the Asian and African apes, before the appearance of the first bipeds.

It is reasonable to suppose, then, that australopithecine tool use was similar to that of the other great apes. Unfortunately, few tools that they used are likely to have survived for a million and more years, and any that did would be hard to recognize as such. Although we cannot be certain about this, in addition to clubs and objects thrown for defense, sturdy sticks may have been used to dig edible roots, and convenient stones may have been used (as some chimpanzees do) to crack open nuts. In fact, some animal bones from australopithecine sites in South Africa show microscopic wear patterns suggesting their use to dig edible roots from the ground. We may also allow the possibility that, like chimpanzees, females may have used tools more often to get and process food than males, but the latter may have used tools more often as "weapons."[12]

Humans Stand on Their Own Two Feet

From the broad-shouldered, long-armed, tailless ape body plan, the human line became fully bipedal. Their late Miocene forebears seem to have been primates that combined quadrupedal tree climbing with at least some swinging below the branches. On the ground, they were capable of assuming an upright stance, at least on occasion (optional, versus obligatory, bipedalism).

Paleoanthropologists generally take the negative aspects of bipedal locomotion into account when considering the advantages of this pattern of locomotion. For example, paleoanthropologists have suggested that bipedalism makes an animal more visible to predators, exposes its soft underbelly or gut, and interferes with the ability to change direction as instantly while running.

---

[12]Goodall, J. (1986). *The chimpanzees of Gombe: Patterns of behavior* (pp. 552, 564). Cambridge, MA: Belknap Press.

Biocultural Connection

Evolution and Human Birth

Because biology and culture have always shaped human experience, it can be a challenge to separate the influences of each of these factors on human practices. For example, in the 1950s, paleoanthropologists developed the theory that human childbirth is particularly difficult compared to birth in other mammals. This theory was based in part on the observation of a "tight fit" between the human mother's birth canal and the baby's head, though several other primates also possess similarly tight fits between the newborn's head or shoulders and the birth canal. Nevertheless, changes in the birth canal associated with bipedalism coupled with the evolution of large brains were held responsible for difficult birth in humans.

At the same historical moment, American childbirth practices were changing. In one generation from the 1920s to the 1950s birth shifted from the home to the hospital. In the process childbirth transformed from something a woman normally accomplished at home, perhaps with the help of a midwife or relatives, into the high-tech delivery of a neonate (the medical term for a newborn) with the assistance of medically trained personnel. During the 1950s women were generally fully anesthetized during the birth process.

Paleoanthropological theories mirrored the cultural norms, providing a scientific explanation for the change in American childbirth practices.

As a scientific theory, the idea of difficult human birth stands on shaky ground. No fossil neonates have ever been recovered, and only a handful of complete pelves (the bones forming the birth canal) exist. Instead, scientists must examine the birth process in living humans and nonhuman primates to reconstruct the evolution of the human birth pattern.

Cultural beliefs and practices, however, shape every aspect of birth. Cultural factors determine where a birth occurs, the actions of the individuals present, and beliefs about the nature of the experience. When paleoanthropologists of the 1950s and 1960s asserted that human childbirth is more difficult than birth in other mammals, they may have been drawing upon their own North American cultural beliefs that childbirth is dangerous and belongs in a hospital.

A quick look at global neonatal mortality statistics indicates that in countries such as The Netherlands and Sweden, healthy well-nourished women give birth successfully outside of hospitals as they did throughout human evolutionary history. In other countries, deaths related to childbirth reflect malnutrition, infectious disease, and the low social status of women, rather than an inherently faulty biology.

They also emphasize that bipedalism does not result in particularly fast running; quadrupedal chimpanzees and baboons, for example, are 30 to 34 percent faster than we bipeds. For 100-meter distances, our best athletes today may attain speeds of 34 to 37 kilometers per hour, while the larger African carnivores that bipeds might run from can attain speeds up to 60 to 70 kilometers per hour. The consequences of a serious leg or foot injury are more serious for a biped while a quadruped can do amazingly well on three legs. A biped with only one functional leg is seriously hindered—an easy meal for some carnivore.

Because each of these drawbacks would have placed our early ancestors at risk from predators, paleoanthropologists have tended to ask, what made bipedal locomotion worth paying such a high price? Paleoanthropologists have found it hard to imagine bipedalism becoming a viable adaptation in the absence of strong selective pressure in its favor; therefore, a number of theories have been proposed to account for the adaptive advantages of bipedalism.

One once-popular suggestion is that bipedal locomotion allowed males to gather food on the savannah and transport it back to females, who were restricted from doing so by the dependence of their offspring.[13] This explanation is unlikely, however, because female apes, not to mention women among food-foraging peoples, routinely combine infant care with foraging for food. Indeed, among most food foragers, it is the women who commonly supply the bulk of the food eaten by both sexes.

Moreover, the pair bonding (one male attached to one female) presumed by this model is not characteristic of terrestrial primates, nor of those displaying the degree of sexual dimorphism that was characteristic of *Australopithecus*. Nor is it really characteristic of *Homo sapiens*. In a substantial majority of recent human societies, including those in which people forage for their food, some form of polygamy—marriage to two or more individuals at the same time—is not only permitted, but preferred. And even in the supposedly monogamous United States, it is relatively common for an individual to marry (and hence mate with) two or more others (the only requirement is that he or she not be married to them at the same time).

Although we may reject as culture-bound the idea of male "breadwinners" provisioning "stay-at-home moms," it is true that bipedal locomotion does make transport of bulky foods possible. (See the Biocultural Connection for another example of the influence of socially defined roles and theories about evolution of human childbirth.)

---

[13]Lovejoy, C. O. (1981). The origin of man. *Science 211*, 341–350.

Nevertheless, a fully erect biped on the ground—whether male or female—has the ability to gather such foods for transport back to a tree or other place of safety for consumption. The biped does not have to remain out in the open, exposed and vulnerable, to do all of its eating.

Besides making food transport possible, bipedalism could have facilitated the food quest in other ways. With their hands free and body upright, the animals could reach otherwise unobtainable food on thorn trees too flimsy and too spiny to climb. Furthermore, with both hands free, they could gather other small foods more quickly using both hands. And in times of scarcity, their ability to travel far without tiring would help get them between widely distributed sources of food. Distant sources of food and water can be located more easily with the head positioned higher than in a quadrupedal stance.

Food may not have been the only thing transported by early bipeds. As we saw in Chapter 3, infants must be able to cling to their mothers in order to be transported; because the mother is using her forelimbs in locomotion, to either walk or swing, she can't hold her infant as well. Chimpanzee infants, for example, must cling by themselves to their mother, and even at the age of 4, they make long journeys on their mothers' backs. Injuries caused by falling from the mother are a significant cause of infant mortality among apes. Thus, the ability to carry infants would have made a significant contribution to the survivorship of offspring, and the ancestors of *Australopithecus* would have been capable of doing just this.

Another suggestion—that bipedal locomotion arose as an adaptation for nonterritorial scavenging of meat[14]—is unlikely. Although it is true that a biped is able to travel long distances without tiring, and that a daily supply of dead animal carcasses would have been available to early bipeds only if they were capable of ranging over vast areas, no evidence exists to indicate that they did much in the way of scavenging prior to about 2.5 million years ago. Furthermore, the heavy wear seen on australopithecine teeth is indicative of a diet high in tough, fibrous plant foods. Thus, scavenging was likely an unforeseen by-product of bipedal locomotion, rather than a cause of it.

Yet more recent is the suggestion that our ancestors stood up as a way to cope with heat stress out in the open. In addition to bipedalism, one of the most obvious differences between humans and other living hominoids is our relative nakedness. Body hair in humans is generally limited to a fine sparse layer over most of the body with a very dense cover of hair limited primarily to the head. Peter Wheeler, a British physiologist, has suggested that bipedalism and the human pattern of body

hair growth are both adaptations to the heat stress of the savannah environment.[15] Building upon the earlier "radiator" theory of North American paleoanthropologist Dean Falk, Wheeler developed this hypothesis through comparative anatomy, experimental studies, and the observation that humans are the only apes to inhabit the savannah environment.

Many other animals, however, inhabit the savannah, and each of them possesses some mechanism for coping with heat stress. Some animals, like many of the carnivores, are active only when the sun is low in the sky, early or late in the day, or when it is absent altogether at night. Some, like antelope, are evolved to tolerate high body temperatures that would kill humans due to overheating of the brain tissue. They accomplish this through cooling their blood in their muzzles through evaporation before it enters the vessels leading to the delicate tissues of the brain.

According to Wheeler, the interesting thing about humans and other primates is that

> We can't uncouple brain temperature from the rest of the body, the way an antelope does, so we've got to prevent any damaging elevations in body temperature. And of course the problem is even more acute for an ape, because in general, the larger and more complex the brain, the more easily it is damaged. So, there were incredible selective pressures on early hominids favoring adaptations that would reduce thermal stress-pressures that may have favored bipedalism.[16]

Though the idea that bipedal posture reduces the amount of heat from solar radiation to which humans are exposed is not completely new, Wheeler has scientifically studied this phenomenon. He took a systematic series of measurements on the exposure of an early biped like Lucy to solar radiation in upright and quadrupedal stances. He found that the bipedal stance reduced exposure to solar radiation by 60 percent, indicating that a biped would require less water to stay cool in a savannah environment compared to a quadruped.

Wheeler further suggests that bipedalism made the human body hair pattern possible. Fur can keep out solar radiation as well as retaining heat. A biped, with reduced exposure to the sun everywhere except the head, would benefit from hair loss on the body surface to increase the efficiency of sweating to cool down. On the head, hair serves as a shield, blocking the solar radiation.

An objection to the above scenario might be that when bipedalism developed, savannah was not as extensive in Africa as it is today (Figure 6.13). In both East

[14]Lewin, R. (1987). Four legs good, two legs bad. *Science 235*, 969–971.

[15]Quoted in Folger, T. (1993). The naked and bipedal. *Discover 14*(11), 34–35. Reprinted with permission.
[16]Ibid.

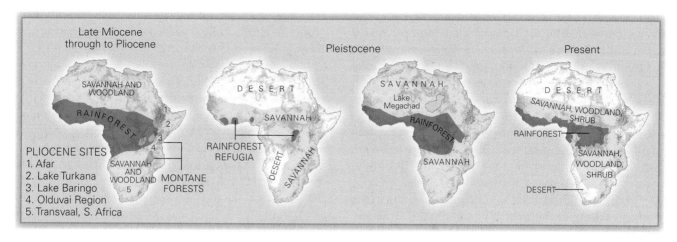

Figure 6.13

Since the late Miocene, the vegetation zones of Africa have changed considerably.

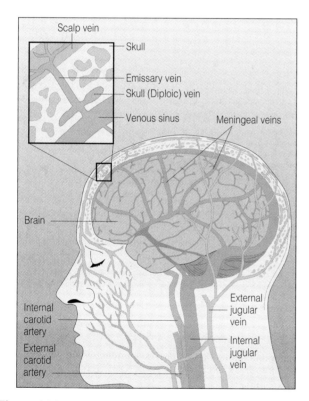

Figure 6.14

In humans, blood from the face and scalp, instead of returning directly to the heart, may be directed instead into the braincase, and then to the heart. Already cooled at the surface of the skin, it is able to carry away heat from the brain.

and South Africa, environments included both closed and open bush and woodlands. Moreover, fossil flora and fauna found with *Ardipithecus* and the possible human ancestors from the Miocene are typical of a moist, closed, wooded habitat.

However, the presence of bipedalism in the fossil record without a savannah environment does not indicate that bipedalism was not adaptive to these conditions. It merely indicates that bipedalism appeared without any particular adaptive benefits at first, likely through a random macromutation. Bipedalism provided a body plan preadapted to the heat stress of the savannah environment.

In an earlier era of human evolutionary studies, larger brains were thought to have permitted the evolution of bipedalism. Around the mid-20th century, theories for the adaptability of bipedalism involved a feedback loop between tool use, brain expansion, and free hands brought about by bipedalism. We now know not only that bipedality preceded the evolution of larger brains by several million years, but we can also now consider the possibility that bipedalism may have preadapted human ancestors for brain expansion. According to Wheeler,

> The brain is one of the most metabolically active tissues in the body. . . . In the case of humans it accounts for something like 20 percent of total energy consumption. So you've got an organ producing a lot of heat that you've got to dump. Once we'd become bipedal and naked and achieved this ability to dump heat, that may have allowed the expansion of the brain that took place later in human evolution. It didn't cause it, but you can't have a large brain unless you can cool it.[17]

Consistent with Wheeler's hypothesis is the fact that the system for drainage of the blood from the cranium of the earlier australopithecines is significantly different from that of the genus *Homo* (Figure 6.14).

Though paleoanthropologists cannot resolve every detail of the exact course of human evolution from the available data, over time the narrative they have constructed has improved. Human evolution evidently took

[17]Ibid.

place in fits and starts, rather than at a steady pace. To-day we know that bipedalism preceded brain expansion by several million years. Bipedalism likely occurred as a sudden shift in body plan while the tempo for the evolution of brain size differed considerably. For example, fragments of an *Australopithecus* skull 3.9 million years old are virtually identical to the corresponding parts of one 3 million years old. Evidently, once a viable bipedal adaptation was achieved, stabilizing selection took over, and there was little change for at least a few million years.

Then, 2.5 million years ago, change was again in the works, resulting in the branching out of new forms, including several robust species as well as the first appearance of the genus *Homo*. But again, from about 2.3 mil-lion years ago until robust australopithecines became extinct around 1 million years ago, the robust forms underwent relatively little change.[18]

Evidently, the pattern in early human evolution has been relatively short periods of marked change with diversification, separated by prolonged periods of relative stasis or stability in the surviving species. In the following chapters, we will trace the next period of change as seen in the steady course of brain expansion beginning with the first appearance of the genus *Homo* 2.5 million years ago until brain size reached its current state.

---

[18]Wood, B., Wood, C., & Konigsberg, L. (1994). Paranthropus boisei: An example of evolutionary stasis? *American Journal of Physical Anthropology 95*, 134.

Questions for Reflection

1. Has the Pliocene fossil evidence showing that bipedalism preceded brain expansion by several million years challenged you to rethink the differences between humans and the other animals? How have beliefs and biases affected the interpretation of this fossil material?

2. Describe the anatomy of bipedalism, providing examples from head to toe of how bipedalism can be "diagnosed" from a single bone. Do you think evidence from a single bone is enough to determine whether an organism from the past was bipedal?

3. Who were the robust australopithecines? What evidence is used to demonstrate that they are an evolutionary dead end?

4. How do paleoanthropologists decide whether a fossil specimen from the distant past is male or female? Do our cultural ideas about males and females in the present affect the interpretation of behavior in human evolutionary history?

5. Do you think that australopithecines were tool users? What evidence would you use to support a case for tool use in these early bipeds?

Suggested Readings

Ciochon, R. L., & Fleagle, J. G. (Eds.). (1993). *The human evolution source book*. Englewood Cliffs, NJ: Prentice-Hall.

In the first four parts of this book, the editors have assembled articles to present data and survey different theories on the evolution and diversification of the earliest human ancestors. A short editors' introduction to each section places the various articles in context.

Falk, D. (1992). *Braindance*. New York: Henry Holt & Company.

In this book Falk presents her "radiator theory" to account for the lag between the appearance of bipedalism and the increase in the size of the brain over the course of human evolutionary history.

Johanson, D. C., & Edey, M. (1981). *Lucy: The beginnings of humankind*. New York: Simon & Schuster.

This book tells the story of the discovery of Lucy and the other fossils of *Australopithecus afarensis* and how they have enhanced our understanding of the early stages of human evolution. It reads like a first-rate detective story, while giving an excellent description of australopithecines and an accurate account of how paleoanthropologists analyze their fossils.

Johanson, D. C., Edgar, B., & Brill, D. (1996). *From Lucy to language*. New York: Simon & Schuster.

This coffee table-sized book includes more than 200 color pictures of major fossil discoveries along with a readable, intelligent discussion of many of the key issues in paleoanthropology.

Larsen, C. S., Matter, R. M., & Gebo, D. L. (1998). *Human origins: The fossil record*. Long Grove, IL: Waveland Press.

This volume covers all the major fossils discoveries relevant to the study of human origins beginning with the Miocene apes. It has detailed drawings and clear brief descriptions of each specimen, introducing the reader to the nature of the fossil evidence.

Zimmer, C. (2005) *Smithsonian intimate guide to human origins*. New York: HarperCollins.

This book by science writer Carl Zimmer is an intelligent and engaging presentation of the evidence of human evolution that includes discoveries up to 2005. It is also beautifully illustrated.

Thomson Audio Study Products

Enjoy the MP3-ready Audio Lecture Overviews for each chapter and a comprehensive audio glossary of key terms for quick study and review. Whether walking to class, doing laundry, or studying at your desk, you now have the freedom to choose when, where, and how you interact with your audio-based educational media. See the preface for information on how to access this on-the-go study and review tool.

The Anthropology Resource Center

www.thomsonedu.com/anthropology
The Anthropology Resource Center provides extended learning materials to reinforce your understanding of key concepts in the four subfields of anthropology. For each of the four subdisciplines, the Resource Center includes dynamic exercises including video exercises, map exercises, simulations, and "Meet the Scientists" interviews, as well as critical thinking questions that can be assigned and e-mailed to instructors. The Resource Center also provides breaking news in anthropology and interesting material on applied anthropology to help you link what you are learning to the world around you.

7 Early *Homo* and the Origins of Culture

CHALLENGE ISSUE

With the appearance of the genus *Homo* 2.5 million years ago, integrated biological and cultural capabilities allowed our ancestors to meet the challenges of survival. The series of skulls pictured here illustrates the evolutionary trend of increasing brain size that occurred over the course of the next 2 million years. Without this brain expansion, reliance on culture could not have occurred. In turn, the archaeological record, starting with the oldest known artifacts—stone tools dated to between 2.5 and 2.6 million years ago from Gona, Ethiopia—provides tangible evidence of culture in the distant past.

When, Where, and How Did the Genus *Homo* Develop?

Since the late 1960s, a number of sites in South and East Africa have produced the fossil remains of lightly built bipeds all but indistinguishable from the earlier gracile australopithecines, except that the teeth are smaller and the brain is significantly larger relative to body size. The earliest fossils to exhibit these trends appeared around 2.5 million years ago, along with the earliest evidence of stone tool making. *Homo habilis* or "handy man" was the name given to the first members of the genus as a reflection of their tool-making capacities. While paleoanthropologists debate the number of species of early *Homo* existing during this time period, most concur that the genus *Homo* developed from one of the smaller-brained bipedal australopithecines in Africa by 2.5 million years ago.

What Is the Relationship Between Biological Change and Cultural Change in the Genus *Homo*?

Paleoanthropologists make species designations in the fossil record according to their interpretation of physical traits such as skull shape and size combined with archaeological evidence. Because the earliest stone tools appear in the archaeological record along with fossil evidence of increased brain size, paleoanthropologists attribute the cultural change—the making of stone tools—to the associated increase in brain size. The fabrication and use of stone tools needed to crack open the bones of animals for marrow or to butcher dead animals required improved eye–hand coordination and a precision grip. These behavioral abilities depended on the capacity to learn and communicate. This exquisite ability to learn to coordinate vision and movement depended upon larger, more complex brains.

Who Was *Homo erectus*?

By 1.8 million years ago, brain size along with cultural capabilities increased considerably, marking the appearance of the species *Homo erectus*. Because the earliest fossils identified as *Homo erectus* come from Africa, this fossil group appears to have descended directly from *Homo habilis*. Variation within this taxon has led some scientists to split *H. erectus* into separate species.

What Were the Cultural Capabilities of *Homo erectus*?

Having a larger brain than its ancestors, *Homo erectus* became increasingly able to adapt to different challenges through the medium of culture. Evidence of *H. erectus'* cultural capabilities is preserved in the archaeological record through better-made tools, a greater variety of tool types, regional diversification of tool kits, and the controlled use of fire. Through these cultural adaptations, life for the genus *Homo* appears to have become more secure, allowing population size to expand. Evidence of increased reproductive success can be inferred by the spread of *Homo* from Africa into previously uninhabited regions of Eurasia.

By 2.5 million years ago, long after the appearance of bipedalism separated the human evolutionary line from that of chimpanzees, bonobos, and gorillas, a new kind of evolutionary change was set in motion. The fossil record reveals an increase in brain size, proceeding for the next 2 million years or so. Simultaneously, the archaeological record begins to provide evidence of increased cultural manipulation of the physical world by these early ancestors through their use of stone tools. These new bipeds were the first members of the genus *Homo*. With the passage of time, they came to intensify their reliance on cultural adaptation as a rapid and effective way of adjusting to their environments.

While the evolution of culture became critical for human survival, it was intricately tied to underlying biological capacities, specifically the evolution of the human brain. Increasing brain size and specialization of function (evidence preserved in fossilized skulls), eventually permitted the development of language, planning, new technologies, and artistic expression. With the evolution of a brain that made versatile behavior possible, members of the genus *Homo* became biocultural beings.

U.S. anthropologist Misia Landau has noted that human evolutionary history follows the narrative form of a heroic epic because of the role culture plays in human evolution. The hero, or evolving human, is faced with a series of natural challenges that cannot be overcome from a strictly biological standpoint. Endowed with the gift of intelligence, the hero can meet these challenges and become fully human. In this narrative, culture increasingly separates humans from other evolving animals.

THOMSON AUDIO **STUDY PRODUCTS** Take advantage of the MP3-ready Audio Lecture Overviews and comprehensive audio glossary of key terms for each chapter. See the preface for information on how to access this on-the-go study and review tool.

Differences in the rates of biological and cultural change account for some of the complications and debates relating to human evolutionary history. Cultural equipment and techniques can change rapidly with innovations occurring during the lifetime of individuals. By contrast, because it depends upon heritable traits, biological change requires many generations.

Paleoanthropologists try to decipher whether an evident cultural change in the past corresponds to a major biological change, such as the appearance of a new species. In the fossil record, the evidence for new species often consists of small changes in the shape or size of the skull. When we take into account the variation present today within the species *Homo sapiens,* we can see why reconciling the relation between differences in skulls and culture change is often a source of debate within paleoanthropology.

EARLY REPRESENTATIVES OF THE GENUS *HOMO*

The renowned paleoanthropologists Louis and Mary Leakey began their search for human origins at Olduvai Gorge, Tanzania, because of the presence of crude stone tools found there. The tools were found in deposits dating back to very early in the Pleistocene epoch, which began almost 2 million years ago. In 1959, when the Leakeys found the bones of the first specimen of robust *Australopithecus boisei* in association with some of these tools and the bones of birds, reptiles, antelopes, and pigs, they thought they had found the remains of one of the toolmakers. Fossils unearthed a few months later and a few feet below this first discovery led them to change their minds. These fossil remains consisted of more than one individual, including a few cranial bones, a lower jaw, a clavicle, some finger bones (Figure 7.1), and the nearly complete left foot of an adult (Figure 7.2). Skull and jaw fragments indicated that these specimens represented a larger-brained biped without the specialized chewing apparatus of the robust australopithecines.

The Leakeys and colleagues named that contemporary ***Homo habilis*** (Latin for "handy man") and suggested that tool-wielding *H. habilis* may have eaten the animals and possibly had the *A. boisei* for dessert. Of course, we don't really know whether *A. boisei* from Olduvai Gorge met its end in this way, but we do know that cut marks from a stone tool are present on a 2.4-million-year-old australopithecine mandible from South Africa.[1] This was done, presumably, to remove the mandible, but for what purpose we do not know. In any event, it does lend credibility to the idea of *A. boisei* on occasion being dismembered by *H. habilis*.

Subsequent work at Olduvai has unearthed not only more skull fragments but other parts of the skeleton of *H. habilis* as well. Since the late 1960s, fossils of the genus *Homo* that are essentially contemporaneous with those from Olduvai have been found elsewhere in Africa

Homo habilis *"Handy man." The first fossil members of the genus* Homo *appearing 2.5 million years ago, with larger brains and smaller faces than australopithecines.*

---

[1]White, T. D., & Toth, N. (2000). Cutmarks on a Plio-Pleistocene hominid from Sterkfontein, South Africa. *American Journal of Physical Anthropology 111,* 579–584.

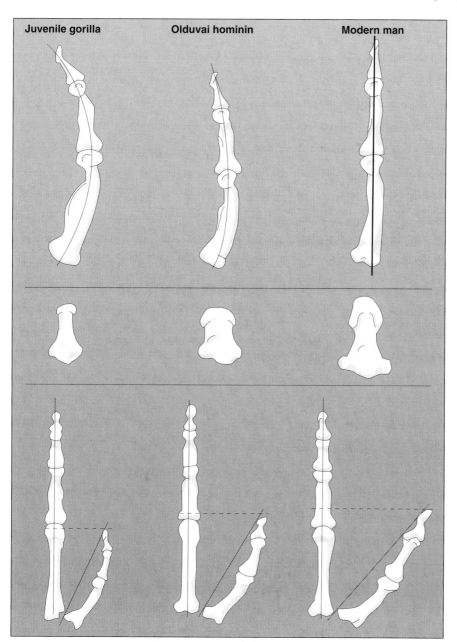

Juvenile gorilla   Olduvai hominin   Modern man

Figure 7.1

A comparison of hand bones of a juvenile gorilla, *Homo habilis* from Olduvai, and a modern human, highlights important differences in the structure of fingers and thumbs. In the top row are fingers, and in the second row are terminal (end) thumb bones. Although terminal finger bones are more human, lower finger bones are more curved and powerful. The bottom row compares thumb length and angle relative to the index finger.

such as South Africa, Ethiopia, and several sites in Kenya (Figure 7.3).

The eastern shores of Lake Turkana, on the border between Kenya and Ethiopia, have been particularly rich with fossils from earliest *Homo*. One of the best of these fossils, known as KNM ER 1470, was discovered by the Leakeys' son Richard. (The letters KNM stand for Kenya National Museum; the ER, for East Rudolf, the name for Lake Turkana during the colonial era in Kenya.) The deposits in which it was found are about 1.9 million years old; these deposits, like those at Olduvai, also contain crude stone tools. The KNM ER 1470 skull is more modern in appearance than any *Australopithecus* skull and has a cranial capacity of 752 cubic centimeters. However, the

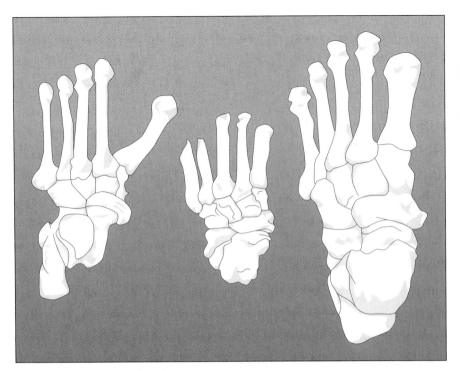

Figure 7.2

A partial foot skeleton of *Homo habilis* (center) is compared with the same bones of a chimpanzee (left) and modern human (right). Note how *H. habilis'* bone at the base of the great toe is in line with the others, as in modern humans, making for effective walking but poor grasping.

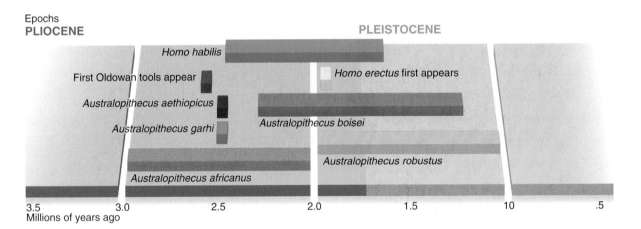

Figure 7.3

Homo habilis and other early bipeds. When found with fossil specimens, Oldowan tools are always associated with genus *Homo*.

large teeth and face of this specimen resemble the earlier australopithecines.

From this same site another well-preserved skull from the same time period (KNM ER 1813) possesses a cranial capacity of less than 600 cubic centimeters but has the derived characteristics of a smaller, less projecting face and teeth. Generally, specimens attributed to *H. habilis* have cranial capacities greater than 600 cubic centimeters. However, cranial capacity of any individual is also in proportion to its body size. Therefore, many paleoanthropologists interpret KNM ER 1813 and ER 1470 as a female and male of a very sexually dimorphic spe-

cies, and the small cranial capacity of KNM ER 1813 as a reflection of her small body size.

Lumpers or Splitters

Other paleoanthropologists do not agree with placing specimens as diverse as KNM ER 1813 and KNM ER 1470 in the single taxonomic group of *H. habilis*. Instead they feel that the diversity represented in these specimens warrants separating the fossils like the larger-brained KNM ER 1470 into a distinct co-existing group called *Homo rudolphensis*. Whether one chooses to call these

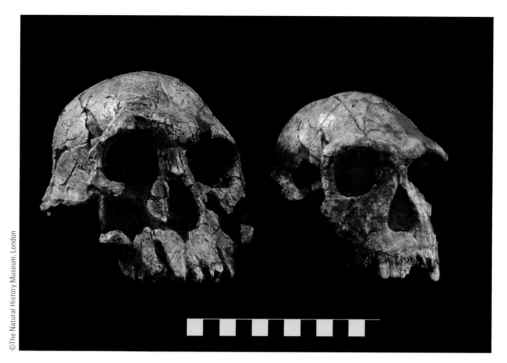

The KNM ER 1470 skull—one of the most complete skulls of *Homo habilis*—is close to 2 million years old and is probably a male; it contrasts with the considerably smaller KNM ER 1813 skull, probably a female. Some paleoanthropologists feel this variation is too great to place these specimens in the same species.

or any other contemporary fossils *Homo rudolphensis* or *Homo habilis* is more than a name game. Fossil names indicate researchers' perspectives about evolutionary relationships among groups. When specimens are given separate species names, it signifies that they form part of a reproductively isolated group.

Some paleoanthropologists approach the fossil record with the perspective that making such detailed biological determinations is arbitrary and that variability exists within any group.[2] Arguing that it is impossible to prove whether or not a collection of ancient bones and teeth represents a distinctive species, they tend to be "lumpers," placing more or less similar-looking fossil specimens together in more inclusive groups. For example, gorillas show a degree of sexual dimorphism that lumpers attribute to *H. habilis*. "Splitters," by contrast, focus on the variation in the fossil record, interpreting minor differences in the shape of skeletons or skulls as evidence of distinctive biological species with corresponding cultural capacities. Referring to the variable shape of the bony ridge above ancient eyes, South African paleoanthropologist Philip Tobias has quipped, "Splitters will create a new species at the drop of a brow ridge."[3] Splitting has the advantage of specificity while lumping has the advantage of simplicity. We will use a lumping approach in our discussion of early *Homo* below.

Differences between Early *Homo* and *Australopithecus*

By 2.4 million years ago, the evolution of the genus *Homo* was proceeding in a direction different from that of *Australopithecus*. In terms of body size, early *Homo* differs little from *Australopithecus*. Early *Homo* had undergone enlargement of the brain far in excess of values predicted on the basis of body size alone. Therefore, early *Homo*'s mental abilities probably exceeded those of *Australopithecus*. This means that early *Homo* likely possessed a marked increase in ability to learn and to process information compared with australopithecines.

Because larger brains generate more heat, it is not surprising to find that *H. habilis*' brain was provided with a heat exchanger of a sort not seen in the earliest bipeds or in the apes.[4] This heat-exchange system consists of small openings in the braincase through which veins pass, allowing cooled blood from the face and scalp to be directed back to the braincase before returning to the heart to carry off excess heat as described in Chapter 6 (see Figure 6.14). This physiologic mechanism prevents damage to the brain from excessive heat.

Although early *Homo* had teeth that are large by modern standards—or even by those of a half-million years ago—they are smaller in relation to the size of the skull than those of any australopithecine. Because major brain-size increase and tooth-size reduction are impor-

---

[2]Miller, J. M. A. (2000). Craniofacial variation in *Homo habilis*: An analysis of the evidence for multiple species. *American Journal of Physical Anthropology 112*, 122.

[3]Personal communication.

[4]Falk, D. (1993). A good brain is hard to cool. *Natural History 102*(8), 65.

tant trends in the evolution of the genus *Homo,* but not of *Australopithecus,* it looks as if early *Homo* was becoming somewhat more human. Consistent with this are the indications that the brain of *H. habilis* was less apelike and more humanlike in structure. It is probably no accident that the earliest fossils to exhibit these features appear close to the same time as the earliest evidence (to be discussed shortly) for stone tool making and the use of these tools to process meat.

The later robust australopithecines from East and South Africa that co-existed with early *Homo* evolved into more specialized "grinding machines" as their jaws and back teeth became markedly larger for processing plant foods. Robust australopithecine brain size did not change, nor is there firm evidence that they made stone tools. Thus, in the period between 1 and 2.5 million years ago, two kinds of bipeds were headed in very different evolutionary directions: the robust australopithecines, specializing in plant foods and ultimately becoming extinct, and the genus *Homo,* with expanding cranial capacity and a varied diet that included meat.

LOWER PALEOLITHIC TOOLS

The earliest stone tools have been found in the vicinity of Lake Turkana in northwestern Kenya, in southern Ethiopia, in Olduvai Gorge in Tanzania, and in Hadar in Ethiopia— often in the same geological strata as *Homo habilis* fossils. These earliest *identifiable* tools consist of a number of implements made using a system of manufacture called the **percussion method** (Figure 7.4). Sharp-edged flakes were obtained from a stone (often a large, water-worn pebble) either by using another stone as a hammer (a hammerstone) or by striking the pebble against a large rock (anvil) to remove the flakes. The finished flakes had two sharp edges, effective for cutting and scraping. Microscopic wear patterns show that these flakes were used for cutting meat, reeds, sedges, and grasses and for cutting and scraping wood. Small indentations on their surfaces suggest that the leftover cores were transformed into choppers, for breaking open bones, and they may also have been employed to defend the user. The appearance of these tools marks the beginning of the **Lower Paleolithic,** the first part of the Old Stone Age.

percussion method A technique of stone tool manufacture performed by striking the raw material with a hammerstone or by striking raw material against a stone anvil to remove flakes.
Lower Paleolithic The first part of the Old Stone Age beginning with the earliest Oldowan tools spanning from about 200,000 or 250,000 to 2.6 million years ago.

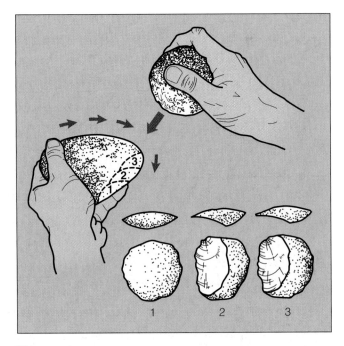

Figure 7.4

By 2.5 million years ago, early *Homo* in Africa had invented the percussion method of stone tool manufacture. This technological breakthrough, which is associated with a significant increase in brain size, made possible the butchering of meat from scavenged carcasses.

The makers of these early tools were highly skilled, consistently and efficiently producing many well-formed flakes.[5] The apparent objective of the task was to obtain large, sharp-edged flakes from available raw materials with the least effort. Thus, the toolmaker had to have in mind an abstract idea of the tool to be made, as well as a specific set of steps that would accomplish the transfor-

[5]Ambrose, S. H. (2001). Paleolithic technology and human evolution. *Science 291,* 1,749.

The oldest stone tools, dated to between 2.5 and 2.6 million years ago, were discovered in Gona, Ethiopia, in 1996, by Ethiopian paleoanthropologist Silesi Semaw.

© Michael Rogers, Southern Connecticut State University

Anthropology Applied

Paleotourism and the World Heritage List

Travel to early fossil sites and to museums where original fossil specimens are housed is an important part of the paleoanthropologist's life. Increasingly, these same destinations are becoming popular with tourists traveling across the globe. Making sites accessible for tourists while protecting the sites for further excavation requires considerable skill and knowledge.

The paleoanthropologist's expertise is indispensable for responsible paleotourism. Features such as footpaths for tourists, access roads, and even the numbers of tourists allowed to visit on a given day must be planned carefully so that paleotourism does not damage the sites permanently.

Since 1972, UNESCO's World Heritage List has been an important part of maintaining paleoanthropological sites for responsible tourism while preserving these sites for the global community. The goal of the World Heritage List is "protecting natural and cultural properties of outstanding value against the threat of damage in a rapidly developing world." Individual states apply to UNESCO for

site designation, receiving financial and political support for maintaining the sites if approved.

The tasks of documenting the value of a fossil site and working to effectively maintain the site for research and tourism fall to the paleoanthropological experts. When designated sites are threatened by natural disaster, war, pollution, or poorly managed tourism, they are placed on a danger list, forcing the local governments to institute measures to protect the sites in order to continue receiving UNESCO support.

Each year approximately thirty new World Heritage sites are designated. In 2003 the list had grown to 754 sites: 149 natural preserves, 582 cultural sites,

© Tom Brown

and 23 mixed sites. Fossil and archaeological sites are well represented on the World Heritage List. Sites important for human evolution are generally designated as cultural sites because the knowledge gained from these sites is considered to be of cultural importance to the world community.

Occasionally, important fossil remains have been recovered within an area that is designated as a larger natural reserve. For example, Olduvai Gorge—known for *Homo habilis* and robust australopithecine remains as well as Oldowan tools—is within the Ngorongoro Conservation Area of Tanzania, as are the Laetoli footprints mentioned in Chapter 6.

The Maasai people have inhabited this region for hundreds of years. Today, the Maasai near Olduvai Gorge remind us that paleotourism affects both the present and the past. Responsible tourism at these sites promotes public education on the subject of human evolution while preserving our common heritage for future generations. Paleotourism may also benefit local inhabitants, helping them preserve their culture.

mation from raw material to finished product. Furthermore, only certain kinds of stone have the flaking properties that will allow the transformation to take place. The toolmaker must know about these, as well as where such stone can be found. The archaeological record also provides evidence of thinking and planning, since tool fabrication required the transport of raw materials over great distances. Such planning for the future undoubtedly was associated with natural selection favoring changes in brain structure.

At Olduvai and Lake Turkana, these tools are close to 2 million years old. The Ethiopian tools are older at 2.5 to 2.6 million years. Before this time, early bipeds probably used tools such as heavy sticks to dig up roots or ward off animals, unshaped stones to use as thrown objects for defense or to crack open nuts, and perhaps simple carrying devices made of knotted plant fibers. Perishable tools, like unmodified stones, are not preserved in the archaeological record.

Olduvai Gorge and Oldowan Tools

Part of what is now Olduvai Gorge was once a lake. Almost 2 million years ago, its shores were inhabited not only by numerous wild animals but also by a variety of bipeds, including robust australopithecines and *H. habilis* as well as (later) *Homo erectus*. The gorge, therefore, is a rich source of Paleolithic remains as well as a key site providing evidence of human evolutionary change. Among the finds are assemblages of stone tools that are about 2 million years old. As described in this chapter's Anthropology Applied, today the Olduvai Gorge is still a vital part of the daily lives of many people.

The oldest tools found at Olduvai Gorge belong to the **Oldowan tool tradition** and were made by the per-

Oldowan tool tradition   The first stone tool industry, beginning between 2.5 and 2.6 million years ago.

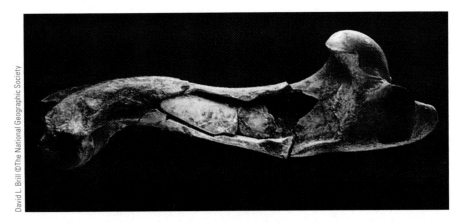

The stone tools used by *Homo habilis* included lava cobbles, choppers, and flakes. Most choppers were probably the result of flakes being struck from one cobble by another. These flakes were used to remove meat from bones, leaving cut marks. The cobbles and choppers were used to break open bones to get at the marrow, as pictured here.

David L. Brill ©The National Geographic Society

cussion method described above. Crude as they were, Oldowan tools mark an important technological advance for early *Homo;* previously, they depended on found objects requiring little or no modification, such as bones, sticks, or conveniently shaped stones. Oldowan tools made new additions to the diet possible because, without such tools, early *Homo* could eat few animals (only those that could be skinned by tooth or nail); therefore, their diet was limited in terms of animal proteins.

The advent of Oldowan tools meant more than merely saving labor and time: They made the addition of meat to the diet on a frequent rather than occasional basis possible. Much popular literature has been written about this penchant for meat in early human evolution, often with numerous colorful references to "killer apes." Such references are misleading because no one knows whether these ancestors were very aggressive, as "killer" suggests. Meat can be obtained, after all, by scavenging or by stealing it from other predators. What is significant is that a dentition such as that possessed by *Australopithecus* and early *Homo* is poorly suited for meat eating. Without teeth like those possessed by carnivorous animals (or even chimpanzees), early *Homo* needed sharp tools for butchering to eat substantial amounts of meat.

Increased consumption of animal flesh on the part of evolving humans was important for human evolution. On the arid savannah, it is hard for a primate with a humanlike digestive system to satisfy its protein requirements from available plant resources. Moreover, failure to do so has serious consequences: growth stunting, malnutrition, starvation, and death. Leaves and legumes (nitrogen-fixing plants, familiar modern examples being beans and peas) provide most readily accessible plant sources of protein. The problem is that these plants are difficult for primates to digest unless they are cooked. The leaves and legumes available contain substances causing the proteins to pass right through the gut without being absorbed.[6]

Chimpanzees have a similar problem when out on the savannah. In such a setting, they spend about a third of their time foraging for insects (ants and termites), eggs, and small vertebrate animals. Such animal foods not only are easily digestible, but they provide high-quality proteins that contain all the essential amino acids, the building blocks of protein. No single plant food can provide this nutritional balance. Only a combination of plants can supply the range of amino acids provided by meat alone.

Lacking long, sharp teeth for shearing meat, our earliest ancestors likely solved their protein problem in much the same way that chimps on the savannah do today. Even chimpanzees, whose canine teeth are far larger and sharper than ours or those of early *Homo,* frequently have trouble tearing through the skin of other animals.[7] For efficient utilization of meat, our ancestors needed sharp tools for butchering. The initial use of tools by early *Homo* may be related to adaptation to an environment that we know was changing since the Miocene from forests to grasslands (see Figure 6.13).[8] The physical changes that adapted bipeds for spending increasing amounts of time on the new grassy terrain may have encouraged tool making.

SEX, GENDER, AND THE BEHAVIOR OF EARLY *HOMO*

Paleoanthropological depictions of early *Homo* from the 1960s and 1970s focused on "man the hunter," wielding tools in a savannah teeming with meat, while females stayed at home tending their young. Because these behavioral speculations relate to proposed differences between males and females in the distant past, they were generally attributed to biologically determined sex dif-

---

[6]Stahl, A. B. (1984). Hominid dietary selection before fire. *Current Anthropology 25*, 151–168.

[7]Goodall, J. (1986). *The chimpanzees of Gombe: Patterns of behavior* (p. 372). Cambridge, MA: Belknap Press.

[8]Behrensmeyer, A. K., et al. (1997). Late Pliocene faunal turnover in the Turkana basin, Kenya, and Ethiopia. *Science 278*, 1,589–1,594.

Biocultural Connection

Sex, Gender, and Female Paleoanthropologists

Up until the 1970s, the study of human evolution, from its very beginnings, was permeated by a deep-seated bias reflecting the privileged status enjoyed by men in Western society. Beyond the obvious labeling of fossils as particular types of "men," irrespective of the sex of the individual represented, it took the form of portraying males as the active players in human evolution. Thus, it was males who were seen as providers and innovators, using their wits to become ever-more effective providers of food and protection for passive females. The latter were seen as spending their time preparing food and caring for offspring, while the men were getting ahead by becoming ever smarter. Central to such thinking was the idea of "man the hunter," constantly honing his wits through the pursuit and killing of animals. Thus, hunting by men was seen as the pivotal humanizing activity in evolution.

We now know that such ideas are culture-bound, reflecting the hopes and expectations of Euramerican culture in the late 19th and early 20th centuries. This recognition came in the 1970s and was a direct consequence of the entry of a number of highly capable women into the profession of paleoanthropology.

Up until the 1960s, there were few women in any field of physical anthropology, but with the expansion of graduate programs and changing attitudes toward the role of women in society, increasing numbers of women went on to earn doctorates. One of these was Adrienne Zihlman, who earned her doctorate at the University of California at Berkeley in 1967. Subsequently, she authored a number of important papers critical of "man the hunter" scenarios. She was not the first to do so; as early as 1971, Sally Linton had published a preliminary paper on "woman the gatherer," but it was Zihlman who from 1976 on especially

elaborated on the importance of female activities for human evolution. Others have joined in the effort, including Zihlman's companion in graduate school and later colleague, Nancy Tanner, who collaborated with Zihlman on some of her papers and has produced important works of her own.

The work of Zihlman and her coworkers was crucial in forcing a reexamination of existing "man the hunter" scenarios, out of which came recognition of the importance of scavenging in early human evolution as well as the value of female gathering and other activities.

Although there is still plenty to learn about human evolution, thanks to these women we now know that it was not a case of females being "uplifted" as a consequence of their association with progressively evolving males. Rather, the two sexes evolved together, with each making its own important contribution to the process.

---

ferences rather than the socially defined category of **gender.** However, the gender roles internalized by the working paleoanthropologist from his or her own culture may be inadvertently applied to the fossil specimens. Similarly, until the 1960s, most anthropologists doing fieldwork among foragers stressed the role of male hunters and underreported the significance of female gatherers in providing food for the community. As anthropologists became aware of their own biases, they began to set the record straight, documenting the vital role of "woman the gatherer" in provisioning the social group in foraging cultures, past and present.

Paleoanthropologists' behavioral reconstructions from fragments of bone and stone have relied heavily on observations of living primates, including both human and nonhuman living primates. For example, the observation that food sharing and a division of labor by gender characterize many modern food foragers has been used to support depictions of our male and female ancestors as "hunter" and "gatherer," respectively. However, the division of labor among contemporary food foragers, like all gender relations, reflects both cultural and biological factors. Division of labor by food-foraging societies does not conform to fixed boundaries defined through biologically based sex differences. Instead, it is influenced by

cultural and environmental factors. It appears likely that the same principle applied to our human ancestors.

Evidence from chimpanzees and bonobos casts further doubt on the notion of a strict, sex-based division of labor in human evolutionary history. As described in Chapter 3, among chimpanzees, females have been observed participating in male hunting expeditions. Meat gained from the successful hunt of a smaller mammal is shared within the group whether provided by a male or a female chimpanzee. Among bonobos, females hunt regularly and share meat as well as plant foods with one another. In other words patterns of food sharing and hunting behaviors in these apes are variable, lending credit to the notion that culture plays a role in establishing these behaviors. Similarly, in our evolutionary history it is likely that culture—the shared learned behaviors of each early *Homo* group—played a role in food-sharing behaviors rather than strict biological differences between the sexes.

Though increased consumption of scavenged meat on the part of early *Homo* may have promoted more food

gender The cultural elaborations and meanings assigned to the biological differentiation between the sexes.

In this artist's reconstruction separate roles are portrayed for males and females from early *Homo.* Do the roles depicted here derive from biological differences between the sexes or culturally established gender differences?

sharing among adults, this remains a hypothesis, as does the notion that a division of labor characterized early *Homo.* The fossil and archaeological records provide evidence only of cut marks on bones, the stone tools that made these marks, along with information about our ancestors' bodies and brains. No evidence exists to establish definitively how procured foods may have been shared.

When the evidence is fragmentary, as it is in all paleoanthropological reconstructions of behavior, gaps are all too easily filled in with behaviors that seem "natural" and familiar such as contemporary gender roles. In reconstructing the behavior of our ancestors from the distant past, current paleoanthropologists today pay careful attention to the ways in which contemporary gender norms and other cultural factors inform their models. A return to the evidence with an awareness of its limits will define which inferences can be legitimately made about behaviors in human evolutionary history.

Hunters or Scavengers?

What do these assemblages of Oldowan tools and broken animal bones have to tell us about the life of early *Homo*? First, they tell us that both *H. habilis* and large carnivorous animals were active at these locations, for in addi-

tion to marks on the bones made by slicing, scraping, and chopping with stone tools, there are tooth marks from gnawing. Some of the gnawing marks overlie the butcher marks, indicating that enough flesh remained on the bones after *Homo* was done with them to attract other carnivores. In other cases, though, the butcher marks overlie the tooth marks of carnivores, indicating that the animals got there first. This is what we would expect if *H. habilis* were scavenging the kills of other animals, rather than doing its own killing.

Consistent with this picture is that whole carcasses are not represented in the fossil record; apparently, only parts were transported away from the original location where they were obtained, again what we would expect if they were "stolen" from the kill of some other animal. The stone tools, too, were made of raw material procured at distances of up to 60 kilometers from where they were used to process the parts of carcasses. Finally, the incredible density of bones at some of the sites and patterns of weathering indicate that the sites were used repeatedly over periods guessed to be on the order of five to fifteen years.

All of this is quite unlike the behavior of historically known and contemporary food-foraging peoples or hunters, who typically bring whole carcasses back to camp or form camp around a large animal in order to fully process it. After processing, neither meat nor **marrow** (the tissue inside of long bones where blood cells are produced) is left as they were at Oldowan sites. The bones themselves are broken up not just to get at the marrow (as at Oldowan sites) but to fabricate tools and other objects of bone (unlike at Oldowan sites).

The picture that emerges of our Oldowan forebears, then, is of scavengers, getting their meat from the Lower Paleolithic equivalent of modern-day road kills, taking the spoils of their scavenging to particular places where tools, and the raw materials for making them (often procured from faraway sources), had been stockpiled in advance for the purpose of butchering. At the least, this may have required fabrication of carrying devices such as net bags and trail signs of the sort (described in Chapter 3) used by modern bonobos. Thus, the Oldowan sites were not campsites or "home bases" at all. Quite likely, *H. habilis* continued to sleep in trees or rocky cliffs, as do modern small-bodied terrestrial or semi-terrestrial primates, in order to be safe from predators. However, the advanced preparation for meat processing implied by the storing of stone tools, and the raw materials for making tools, attests to considerable foresight and ability to plan ahead.

In addition, microscopic analysis of cut marks on bones has revealed that the earliest members of the genus *Homo* were actually **tertiary scavengers**—that is, third in line to get something from a carcass after a lion or leopard managed to kill some prey. Leopards, for example, generally chew a limb from a zebra it has felled and haul it into the treetops for a relaxed feast. *Homo habilis* might have climbed into the trees to scavenge meat hauled there by a leopard. If the carcass remains on the ground, hyenas grab what they can, followed by vultures who swarm the rotting carcass. By the time a lightly built *H. habilis* could get near the carcass of a dead zebra, only bones remained.

Fortunately, these tool-wielding ancestors could break open the shafts of long bones to get at the rich marrow inside. A small amount of marrow is a concentrated source of both protein and fat. Muscle alone, particularly from lean game animals, contains very little fat. Furthermore, as shown in the following Original Study, evolving humans may even have been prey themselves; the selective pressure imposed by predators played a role in brain expansion.

marrow The tissue inside of long bones where blood cells are produced.
tertiary scavenger In a food chain, the third animal group (second to scavenge) to obtain meat from a kill made by a predator.

Original Study ▪ By Donna Hart

Humans as Prey

There's little doubt that humans, particularly those in Western cultures, think of themselves as the dominant form of life on earth. And we seldom question whether that view holds true for our species' distant past—or even for the present, outside of urban areas. We swagger like the toughest kids on the block as we spread our technology over the landscape and irrevocably change it for other species.

Current reality does appear to perch humans atop a planetary food chain. The vision of our utter superiority may even hold true for the last 500 years, but that's just the proverbial blink of an eye when compared to the seven million years that our hominid ancestors wandered the planet.

"Where did we come from?" and "What were the first humans like?" are questions that have been asked since Darwin first proposed his theory of evolution. One commonly accepted answer is that our early ancestors were killers of other species and of their own kind, prone to violence and even cannibalism. In fact a club-swinging "Man the Hunter" is the stereotype of early humans that permeates literature, film, and even much scientific writing.

Man the Hunter purports to be based on science. Even the great paleontologist Louis S. B. Leakey endorsed it when he emphatically declared that we were not "cat food." Another legendary figure in the annals of paleontology, Raymond A. Dart, launched the killer-ape-man scenario in the mid-20th century with the help of the best public-relations juggernaut any scientist ever had: the writer Robert Ardrey and his best-selling book, *African Genesis.*

Dart had interpreted the finds in South African caves of fossilized bones from savannah herbivores together with damaged hominid skulls as evidence that our ancestors had been hunters. The fact that the skulls were battered in a peculiar fashion led to Dart's firm conviction that violence and cannibalism on the part of killer ape-men formed the stem from which our own species eventually flowered. In his 1953 article "The Predatory Transition from Ape to Man," Dart wrote that early hominids were "carnivorous creatures, that seized living quarries by violence, battered them to death, tore apart their broken bodies, [and] dismembered them limb from limb, ... greedily devouring livid writhing flesh."

But what is the evidence for Man the Hunter? Could smallish, upright creatures with relatively tiny canine teeth and flat nails instead of claws, and with no tools or weapons in the earliest millennia, really have been deadly predators? Is it possible that our ancestors lacked the

CONTINUED

CONTINUED

spirit of cooperation and desire for social harmony? We have only two reliable sources to consult for clues: the fossilized remains of the human family tree, and the behaviors and ecological relationships of our living primate relatives.

When we investigate those two sources, a different view of humankind emerges. First, consider the hominid fossils that have been discovered. Dart's first and most famous find, the cranium of an *Australopithecus* child who died over 2 million years ago (called the "Taung child" after the quarry in which the fossil was unearthed), has been reassessed by Lee Berger and Ron Clarke of the University of the Witwatersrand, in light of recent research on eagle predation. The same marks that occur on the Taung cranium are found on the remains of similarly sized African monkeys eaten today by crowned hawk eagles, known to clutch the monkeys' heads with their sharp talons.

C. K. Brain, a South African paleontologist like Dart, started the process of relabeling Man the Hunter as Man the Hunted when he slid the lower fangs of a fossil leopard into perfectly matched punctures in the skull of another australopithecine, who lived between 1 million and 2 million years ago. The paradigm change initiated by Brain continues to stimulate reassessment of hominid fossils.

The idea that our direct ancestor *Homo erectus* practiced cannibalism was based on the gruesome disfigurement of faces and brain-stem areas in a cache of skulls a half-million years old, found in the Zhoukoudian cave, in China. How else to explain these strange manipulations except as relics of Man the Hunter? But studies over the past few years by Noel T. Boaz and Russell L. Ciochon—of the Ross University School of Medicine and the University of Iowa, respectively—show that extinct giant hyenas could have left the marks as they crunched their way into the brains of their hominid prey.

The list of our ancestors' fossils showing evidence of predation continues to grow. A 1.75-million-year-old hominid skull unearthed in the Republic of Georgia

shows punctures from the fangs of a saber-toothed cat. Another skull, about 900,000 years old, found in Kenya, exhibits carnivore bite marks on the brow ridge. A 6-million-year-old hominid, also found in Kenya, may well have been killed by a leopard. A fragment of a 1.6-million-year-old hominid skull was found in the den of an extinct hyena, in Spain. A cranium from 250,000 years ago, discovered in South Africa in 1935, has a depression on the forehead caused by a hyena's tooth. Those and other fossils provide rock-hard proof that a host of large, fierce animals preyed on human ancestors.

It is equally clear that, outside the West, no small amount of predation occurs today on modern humans. Although we are not likely to see these facts in American newspaper headlines, each year 3,000 people in sub-Saharan Africa are eaten by crocodiles, and 1,500 Tibetans are killed by bears about the size of grizzlies. In one Indian state between 1988 and 1998, over 200 people were attacked by leopards; 612 people were killed by tigers in the Sundarbans delta of India and Bangladesh between 1975 and 1985. The carnivore zoologist Hans Kruuk, of the University of Aberdeen, studied death records in Eastern Europe and concluded that wolf predation on humans is still a fact of life in the region, as it was until the 19th century in Western European countries like France and Holland.

The fact that humans and their ancestors are and were tasty meals for a wide range of predators is further supported by research on nonhuman primate species still in existence. My study of predation found that 178 species of predatory animals included primates in their diets. The predators ranged from tiny but fierce birds to 500-pound crocodiles, with a little of almost everything in between: tigers, lions, leopards, jaguars, jackals, hyenas, genets, civets, mongooses, Komodo dragons, pythons, eagles, hawks, owls, and even toucans.

Our closest genetic relatives, chimpanzees and gorillas, are prey to humans and other species. Who would have thought that gorillas, weighing as much as 400 pounds, would end up as cat food? Yet Michael Fay, a researcher with the Wildlife Conservation Society and the National Geographic Society, has found the remnants of a gorilla in leopard feces in the Central African Republic. Despite their obvious intelligence and strength, chimpanzees often fall victim to leopards and lions. In the Tai Forest in the Ivory Coast, Christophe Boesch, of the Max Planck Institute, found that over 5 percent of the chimp population in his study was consumed by leopards annually. Takahiro Tsukahara reported, in a 1993 article, that 6 percent of the chimpanzees in the Mahale Mountains National Park of Tanzania may fall victim to lions.

The theory of Man the Hunter as our archetypal ancestor isn't supported by archaeological evidence, either. Lewis R. Binford, one of the most influential figures in archaeology during the last half of the 20th century, dissented from the hunting theory on the ground that reconstructions of early humans as hunters were based on a priori positions and not on the archaeological record. Artifacts that would verify controlled fire and weapons, in particular, are lacking until relatively recent dates. Because no hominids possess the dental equipment or digestive tract to eat raw flesh, we need to be able to cook our meat, but the first evidence of controlled fire is from only 790,000 years ago.

And, of course, there's also the problem of how a small hominid could subdue a large herbivore. The first true weapon we know of is a wooden spear about 400,000 years old, although the archaeologist John Shea, of the State University of

© J & B Photos/Animals, Animals

Whether hunters or hunted, early *Homo* was in competition with formidable adversaries like hyenas. Communication and cooperation helped early *Homo* avoid carnivores who saw them as prey.

New York at Stony Brook, likened it to a glorified toothpick. Large-scale, systematic hunting of big herbivores for meat may not have occurred any earlier than 60,000 years ago—over 6 million years after the first hominids evolved.

What I am suggesting, then, is a less powerful, more ignominious beginning for our species. Consider this alternate image: smallish beings (adult females maybe weighing 60 pounds, with males a bit heavier), not overly analytical because their brain-to-body ratio was rather small, possessing the ability to stand and move upright, who basically spent millions of years as meat walking around on two legs. Rather than Man the Hunter, we may need to visualize ourselves as more like Giant Hyena Chow, or Protein on the Go.

Our species began as just one of many that had to be careful, to depend on other group members, and to communicate danger. We were quite simply small beasts within a large and complex ecosystem.

Is Man the Hunter a cultural construction of the West? Belief in a sinful, violent ancestor does fit nicely with Christian views of original sin and the necessity to be saved from our own awful, yet natural, desires. Other religions don't necessarily emphasize the ancient savage in the human past; indeed, modern-day hunter–gatherers, who have to live as part of nature, hold animistic beliefs in which humans are a part of the web of life, not superior creatures who dominate or ravage nature and each other.

Think of Man the Hunted, and you put a different face on our past. The shift forces us to see that for most of our evolutionary existence, instead of being the toughest kids on the block, we were merely the 90-pound (make that 60-pound) weaklings. We needed to live in groups (like most other primates) and work together to avoid predators. Thus an urge to cooperate can clearly be seen as a functional tool rather than a Pollyannaish nicety, and deadly competition among individuals or nations may be highly aberrant behavior, not hard-wired survival techniques. The same is true of our destructive domination of the earth by technological toys gone mad.

Raymond Dart declared that "the loathsome cruelty of mankind to man . . . is explicable only in terms of his carnivorous, and cannibalistic origin." But if our origin was not carnivorous and cannibalistic, we have no excuse for loathsome behavior. Our earliest evolutionary history is not pushing us to be awful bullies. Instead, our millions of years as prey suggest that we should be able to take our heritage of cooperation and interdependency to make a brighter future for ourselves and our planet.

(By D. Hart (2006, April 21). Humans as prey. Chronicle of Higher Education.) ■

Whether as hunters or as the hunted, brain expansion and tool use played a significant role in the evolution of the genus *Homo*. Just after 2 million years ago, bipeds with brains significantly larger than earlier *Homo* began to appear in Africa and mark the beginning of the species *Homo erectus*.

HOMO ERECTUS

In 1887, long before the discovery of *Australopithecus* and early *Homo* in Africa, the Dutch physician Eugene Dubois set out to find the "missing link" between humans and apes. The presence of humanlike orangutans in the Dutch East Indies (now Indonesia), along with cultural biases against African origins, led him to start his search there. He joined the colonial service as an army surgeon and set sail.

After several years of searching in vain, Dubois found fossilized remains consisting of a skull cap, a few teeth, and a thighbone at Trinil, on the island of Java. Its features seemed to Dubois part ape, part human. The flat skull, for example, with its low forehead and enormous brow ridges, appeared to be like that of an ape; but at about 775 cubic centimeters it possessed a cranial capacity much larger than an ape's, even though small by modern human standards. The femur, or thighbone, was clearly human in shape, and its proportions indicated the creature was a biped.

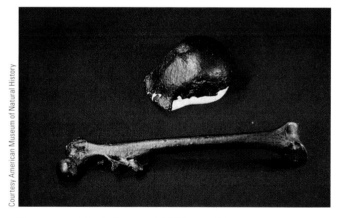

Courtesy American Museum of Natural History

These casts of the skull cap and thighbone of *Homo erectus* were made from the original bones found by Eugene Dubois at Trinil, Java.

Several years earlier, the German zoologist Ernst Haeckel, who strongly supported Darwin's theory of evolution, had proposed that if the missing link were ever found that it should be placed in the genus *Pithecanthropus* (from the Greek *pithekos* meaning "ape," *anthropus* meaning "man"). Believing that his specimens represented the missing link and that the thighbone indicated this creature was bipedal, Dubois named his find *Pithecanthropus erectus*, or "erect ape man."

As with the Taung child, the first australopithecine discovered in the 1920s, many in the scientific community ridiculed and criticized Dubois' claim, suggesting instead that the apelike skull and humanlike femur came from different individuals. Controversy surrounded these specimens throughout Dubois' lifetime. He eventually retreated from the controversy, keeping the fossil specimens stored safely under the floorboards of his dining room. Ultimately, the discovery of more fossils provided evidence to support Dubois' claim fully. In the 1950s, the Trinil skull cap and similar specimens from Indonesia and China were assigned to the species *Homo erectus* because they were more human than apelike.

HOMO ERECTUS FOSSILS

Until about 1.8 million years ago, Africa was the only home to the bipedal primates. It was on this continent that the first bipeds, and the genus *Homo*, originated. It was also in Africa that the first stone tools were invented. But by the time of *Homo erectus,* members of the genus *Homo* had begun to spread far beyond their original homeland. Fossils of this species are now known from a number of localities not just in Africa, but in China,

western Europe, Georgia (in the Caucasus Mountains), and India, as well as Java (Figure 7.5).

Although remains of *H. erectus* have been found in many different places in three continents, "lumpers" emphasize that they are unified by a number of shared characteristics. However, because the fossil evidence also suggests some differences within and among populations of *H. erectus* inhabiting discrete regions of Africa, Asia, and Europe, other paleoanthropologists prefer to split *H. erectus* into several distinct groups, limiting the species *H. erectus* only to the specimens from Asia. In this taxonomic scheme *Homo ergaster* is used for African specimens from the early Pleistocene period that others describe as early *H. erectus* (Table 7.1).

Regardless of species designation, it is clear that beginning 1.8 million years ago these larger-brained members of the genus *Homo* lived not only in Africa but also had spread to Eurasia. Fossil specimens dating to 1.8 million years old have been recovered from Dmanisi, Georgia, as well as from Mojokerto, Indonesia. Many additional specimens have been found at a variety of sites in Europe and Asia.

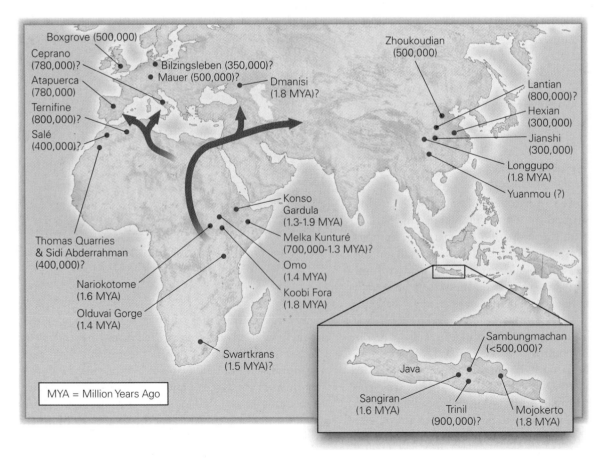

Figure 7.5

Sites, with dates, at which *Homo erectus* remains have been found. The arrows indicate the proposed routes by which *Homo* spread from Africa to Eurasia.

TABLE 7.1	ALTERNATE SPECIES DESIGNATIONS FOR *HOMO ERECTUS* FOSSILS FROM EURASIA AND AFRICA
Name	**Explanation**
Homo ergaster	Some paleoanthropologists feel that the large-brained successors to *H. habilis* from Africa and Asia are too different to be placed in the same species. Therefore, they use *H. ergaster* for the African specimens, saving *H. erectus* for the Asian fossils. Some paleoanthropologists place the recent discoveries from Dmanisi into this taxon.
Homo antecessor	This name was coined by splitters for the earliest *Homo* fossils from western Europe discovered in Spain; *antecessor* is Latin for "explorer" or "pioneer."
Homo heidelbergensis	Originally coined for the Mauer jaw (Mauer is not far from Heidelberg, Germany), this name is now used by some as a designation for all European fossils from about 500,000 years ago until the appearance of the Neandertals (Chapter 8).

Physical Characteristics of *Homo erectus*

The specific features characteristic of *H. erectus* are best known from the skull. Interestingly many of the *H. erectus* fossils consist of isolated skull caps as in Dubois' original discovery. Cranial capacity in *H. erectus* ranges from 600 to 1,225 cubic centimeters (average about 1,000 cc). Thus cranial capacity overlaps with the nearly 2-million-year-old KNM ER 1470 skull from East Africa (752 cc) and the 1,000 to 2,000 cc range (average 1,300 cc) for modern human skulls (Figure 7.6).

The cranium itself has a low vault (height of the dome of the skull top), and the head is long and narrow. When viewed from behind, its width is greater than its height, with its greatest width at the base. The skulls of modern humans when similarly viewed are higher than they are wide, with the widest dimension in the region above the ears. The shape of the inside of *H. erectus*' braincase shows near-modern development of the brain, especially in the speech area. Although some anthropologists argue that the vocal apparatus was not adequate for speech, others argue that asymmetries of the brain suggest the same pattern of right-handedness with left cerebral dominance that, in modern peoples, is correlated with the capacity for language.[9]

H. erectus possessed massive brow ridges (Figure 7.7). When viewed from above, a marked constriction or "pinching in" of the skull can be seen just behind the massive brow ridges. *H. erectus* also possessed a sloping forehead and a receding chin. Powerful jaws with large teeth, a protruding mouth, and huge neck muscles added to *H. erectus*' generally rugged appearance. Nevertheless, the face, teeth, and jaws of this species are smaller than those of *Homo habilis*.

Apart from its skull, the skeleton of *H. erectus* differs only subtly from that of modern humans. Although

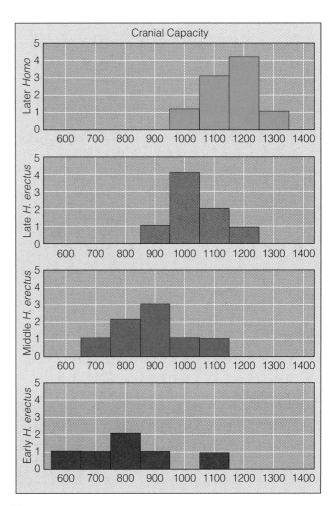

Figure 7.6

Cranial capacity in *Homo erectus* increased over time, as illustrated by these bar graphs, shown in cubic centimeters. The cranial capacity of late *Homo erectus* overlaps with the range seen in living humans.

its bodily proportions are like ours, it was more heavily muscled. Stature seems to have increased from the smaller size typical of the australopithecines and the earliest members of the genus *Homo*. The best evidence for this comes from a remarkably well-preserved skeleton of an adolescent male from Lake Turkana in Kenya. Sexual

---

[9]Holloway, R. L. (1981). The Indonesian *Homo erectus* brain endocasts revisited. *American Journal of Physical Anthropology 55*, 521.

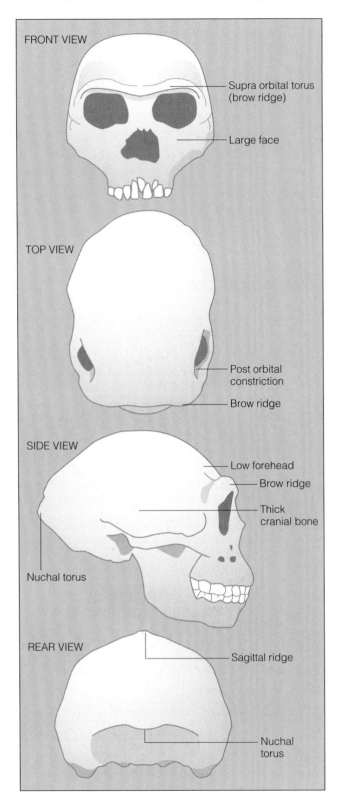

FRONT VIEW

Supra orbital torus (brow ridge)

Large face

TOP VIEW

Post orbital constriction

Brow ridge

SIDE VIEW

Low forehead

Brow ridge

Thick cranial bone

Nuchal torus

REAR VIEW

Sagittal ridge

Nuchal torus

Figure 7.7

dimorphism in body size also appears to have decreased in *H. erectus* compared to earlier bipeds. A reduction in sexual dimorphism may be due to the increase in female size as an adaptation to childbirth.[10]

Relationship among *Homo erectus, Homo habilis,* and Other Proposed Fossil Groups

The smaller teeth and larger brains of *H. erectus* seem to mark continuation of a trend first seen in *Homo habilis*. Increased body size, reduced sexual dimorphism, and more "human" body form of *H. erectus* are newly derived characteristics. Nonetheless, some skeletal resemblance to *H. habilis* exists, for example, in the long neck and low neck angle of the thighbone, the long low vault and marked constriction of the skull behind the eyes, and smaller brain size in the earliest *H. erectus* fossils. Indeed, as already noted, it is very difficult to distinguish between the earliest *H. erectus* and the latest *H. habilis* fossils. Presumably the one form evolved from the other, fairly abruptly, around 1.8 to 1.9 million years ago (Figure 7.8).

Generally speaking, African *H. erectus* skulls are similar to those from Asia; one difference is that their bones aren't quite as thick; another is that some Africans had smaller brow ridges. It may be, too, that individuals living in Asia were shorter and stockier, on the whole, than those living in Africa. However, the detailed anatomical comparisons indicate levels of variation approximating those seen in *H. sapiens*.[11]

Consistent with the notion of a single species is the observation that 1.8-million-year-old specimens from Dmanisi, in the Caucasus—a region that lies more or less halfway between Africa and Indonesia—show a mix of characteristics seen in African and Asian *H. erectus* populations.[12]

Overall, it seems that comparisons between African and Asian populations of *Homo erectus* possess levels of variations similar to those seen if modern human populations from the east and the west are compared. As in Asia, the most recent African fossils are more derived in appearance, and the oldest fossils (up to 1.8 million years old) display features reminiscent of the earlier *Homo habilis*. Indeed, distinguishing early *H. erectus* from late

[10]Hager, L. (1989). The evolution of sex differences in the hominid bony pelvis. Ph. D. dissertation, University of California, Berkeley.

[11]Rightmire, G. P. (1998). Evidence from facial morphology for similarity of Asian and African representatives of *Homo erectus*. *American Journal of Physical Anthropology 106,* 61.

[12]Rosas, A., & Bermudez de Castro, J. M. (1998). On the taxonomic affinities of the Dmanisi mandible (Georgia). *American Journal of Physical Anthropology 107,* 159.

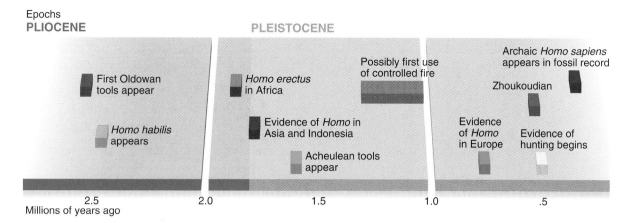

Figure 7.8

Timeline of early *Homo* and the cultural changes from this time period.

H. habilis is problematic—precisely what one would expect if the one evolved from the other. We will explore the *H. erectus* finds by region, beginning with the fossil evidence from Africa.

Homo erectus from Africa

Although our samples of *H. erectus* fossils from Asia remain among the best, several important specimens are also known from Africa. Fossils now assigned to this species were discovered there as long ago as 1933, but the better-known finds have been made since 1960, at Olduvai Gorge and at Lake Turkana, Kenya. Among them is the most complete *H. erectus* skeleton ever found, that of an adolescent boy who died 1.6 million years ago. Paleoanthropologists infer the age of this specimen from his teeth (the 12-year molars are fully erupted) and the state of maturity of the bones. With a height of about 5 feet 3 inches at adolescence, this specimen was expected to attain a stature of about 6 feet by adulthood.

Another partial skeleton, this time of an adult, had diseased bones, possibly the result of a massive overdose of vitamin A. This excess could have come from eating the livers of carnivorous animals, for they accumulate vitamin A in their livers at levels that are poisonous to human beings. More probable might have been heavy consumption of bee brood (larvae) and other immature insects, producing the same result.

Homo erectus from Eurasia

Evidence of the spread of *H. erectus* from Africa into Eurasia is well preserved at the interesting site of Dmanisi in the Caucasus Mountains of Georgia. Dmanisi was first excavated as an archaeological site because of its importance as a crossroads for the caravan routes of Armenia, Persia, and Byzantium in medieval times. When Oldo-

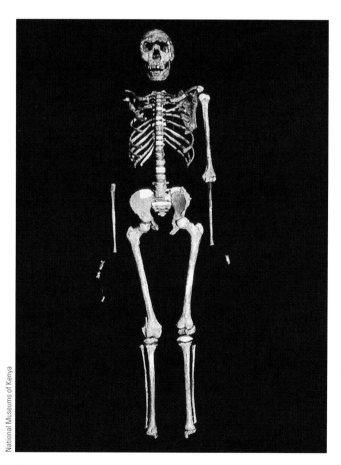

One of the oldest and certainly one of the most complete *Homo erectus* fossils is the "Nariokotome Boy" from Lake Turkana, Kenya. The remains are those of a tall adolescent boy.

wan stone tools were found at this site in 1984, the hunt for fossil specimens began here as well.

Since then, paleoanthropologists have recovered some remarkable remains that can be accurately dated to 1.8 million years ago through past volcanic activity in the region. In 1999, two well-preserved skulls, one with a partial face, were discovered. Thus the early habi-

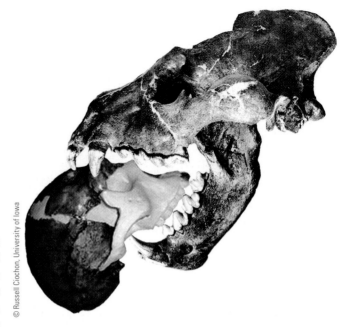

Many of the *Homo erectus* fossils consist of isolated skull caps. This reconstruction suggests that the faces may be missing because they are the isolated remains of individuals who were consumed by the now-extinct giant hyena. This composite shows how the giant hyena could have attacked the face.

tation of this region by members of the genus *Homo* is supported at Dmanisi by archaeological, anatomical, and geological evidence. Because rising sea levels since the Pleistocene make it impossible for paleoanthropologists to document coastal routes for the spread of *Homo* from Africa to Eurasia, the evidence from Georgia constitutes the only direct evidence of the spread of evolving humans from Africa to Europe, and Asia.

Homo erectus from Indonesia

While it took many years for the skull cap and thighbone discovered by Dubois to be accepted as part of the human line, these specimens are now considered typical Asian *Homo erectus*. In the 1930s, a number of *H. erectus* fossils were discovered by German paleoanthropologist G. H. R. von Königswald at Sangiran, Java. Von Königswald found a small skull that fluorine analysis and (later) potassium-argon dating assigned to the Early Pleistocene. This indicated that these fossils were older than the Trinil skull cap found by Dubois, dating to approximately 500,000 to 700,000 years ago.

Since 1960, additional fossils have been found in Java, and we now have remains of around forty individuals. A long continuity of *H. erectus* populations in Southeast Asia is indicated, from perhaps as many as 500,000 to 1.8 million years ago. Interestingly, the teeth and jaws of some of the earliest Javanese fossils are in many ways quite similar to those of *Homo habilis*.[13] When considering the spread of *H. erectus* to Java, it is important to note that in the past, lower sea levels resulted in a continuous landmass between Indonesia and the Asian continent.

Homo erectus from China

In the mid-1920s another group of fossils from Asia, now known as *H. erectus*, was found by Davidson Black, a Canadian anatomist teaching at Peking Union Medi-

cal College. Black was led to this site after purchasing a few ancient humanlike teeth offered for their medicinal properties from a Beijing drugstore. He set out for the nearby countryside to discover the "owner" of the teeth and perhaps a species of early human ancestor. At a place called Dragon Bone Hill in Zhoukoudian, 30 miles from Beijing, on the day before closing camp at the end of his first year of excavation, he found one molar tooth. Subsequently, Chinese paleoanthropologist W. C. Pei, who worked closely with Black, found a skull encased in limestone.

Between 1929 and 1934, the year of his death from silicosis—a lung disease caused by exposure to silica particles in the cave—Black labored along with Pei and French paleontologist Pierre Teilhard de Chardin in the fossil-rich deposits of Zhoukoudian, uncovering fragment after fragment of ancient remains. On the basis of the anatomy of that first molar tooth, Black named these fossils *Sinanthropus pekinensis*, or "Chinese human of Peking" (Beijing), called "Peking Man" for short at the time. They are now recognized as an East Asian representative of *H. erectus*.

After Black's death, Franz Weidenreich, a German anatomist and paleoanthropologist, was sent to China by the Rockefeller Foundation to continue this work. As a Jew in Nazi Germany in the early 1930s, Weidenreich had sought refuge in the United States. By 1938, Wiedenreich and his colleagues recovered the remains of more than forty individuals, more than half of them women and

---

[13]Tobias, P. V., & von Königswald, G. H. R. (1964). A comparison between the Olduvai hominines and those of Java and some implications for hominid phylogeny. *Nature 204*, 515–518.

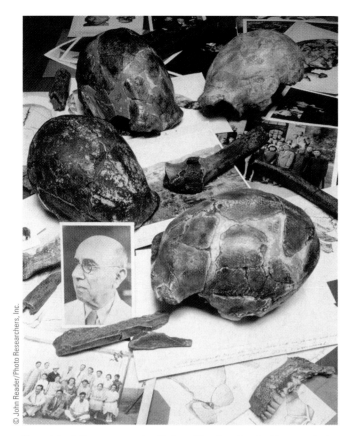

© John Reader/Photo Researchers, Inc.

The original *Homo erectus* fossils from Zhoukoudian had been packed for shipment to the United States for safekeeping during World War II, but they mysteriously disappeared. Fortunately, excellent casts of the specimens and detailed anatomical descriptions (by Weidenreich) were made before the fossils were lost during the war.

children, from the limestone deposits of Zhoukoudian. Most fossils were fragmentary, represented by teeth, jawbones, and incomplete skulls. A spectacular composite specimen has been reconstructed from the most complete remains. World War II (1939–1945) brought a halt to the digging, and the original Zhoukoudian specimens were lost during the Japanese occupation of China. The fossils had been carefully packed by Weidenreich and his team and placed with the U.S. Marines, but in the chaos of war, these precious fossils disappeared.

Fortunately, Weidenreich had made superb casts of most of the Zhoukoudian fossil specimens and sent them to the United States before the war. After the war, other specimens of *H. erectus* were discovered in China, at Zhoukoudian and a number of other localities (see Figure 7.5). The oldest skull is about 700,000 to 800,000 years old and comes from Lantian in central China. Even older is a fragment of a lower jaw from a cave in south-central China (Lunggupo) that is as old as the oldest Indonesian fossils. Like some of their Indonesian contemporaries, this Chinese fossil is reminiscent of African *H. habilis*. In contrast to these ancient remains, the original Zhoukoudian fossils appear to date between 300,000 and 600,000 years ago.

Although the two populations overlap in time, the majority of the Chinese fossils are, on the whole, not quite as old as those from Indonesia. Not surprisingly, Chinese *H. erectus* is less ancestral in appearance. Its average cranial capacity is about 1,000 cubic centimeters, compared to 900 cc for Indonesian *H. erectus*. The smaller teeth and short jaw of the Chinese fossil specimens are further evidence of their more derived status.

Homo erectus from Western Europe

Although the fossil evidence indicates the presence of the genus *Homo* on the Eurasian landmass 1.8 million years ago (at Dmanisi, Georgia), the fossil evidence from western Europe dates to about 800,000 years ago. The evidence from the Grand Dolina site in north-central Spain (see Table 7.1) consists of fragments of four individuals dating to 780,000 years ago. A skull from Ceprano in Italy is thought to be approximately the same age if not older. Again, whether one lumps these specimens into the inclusive but varied species *H. erectus* or into several separate species differs according to the approach taken by paleoanthropologists with regard to the fossil record.

Some other fossils attributable to *H. erectus*—such as a robust shinbone from Boxgrove, England, and a large lower jaw from Mauer, Germany—are close to half a million years old. The jaw certainly came from a skull wide at the base, typical of *H. erectus*. As might be expected, these remains are similar to *H. erectus* material from North Africa from the same time period. This observation, and the fact that the earliest evidence of the genus *Homo* in western Europe comes from Spain and Italy, suggests that they arrived there by crossing from northern Africa.[14] At the time, a mere 6 or 7 kilometers separated Gibraltar from Morocco (compared to 13 kilometers today), and islands dotted the straits from Tunisia to Sicily. The only direct land connection between Africa and Eurasia is through the Middle East and into Turkey and the Caucasus. Otherwise *H. erectus* may have come to western Europe by crossing open water. Though evidence (discussed later in this chapter) demonstrates that *H. erectus* was capable of crossing open water by 800,000 years ago, no definite proof of such a crossing exists in Europe.

THE CULTURE OF *HOMO ERECTUS*

As one might expect given its larger brain, *H. erectus* outstripped its predecessors in cultural ability. In Africa, Europe, and Asia, a refinement of the stone tool-

[14]Balter, M. (2001). In search of the first Europeans. *Science 291*, 1,724.

making technology begun by the makers of earlier flake and chopper tools is evident. At some point, fire began to be used for protection, warmth, and cooking, though precisely when is still a matter for debate. Finally, there is indirect evidence that the organizational and planning abilities of *H. erectus,* or at least the later ones, were improved over those of their predecessors. Many sites preserve a rich array of archaeological remains without any fossil specimens. Therefore the following discussion will draw on larger geographic areas rather than limiting the discussion only to the specific sites where actual *H. erectus* fossils have been found.

Paleoanthropological reconstructions of the culture and behavior of our ancestors differ considerably from simple interpretations of biological change based on comparative anatomy. Behavioral reconstructions combine evidence about the environment, archaeological evidence of tools, hearths, and shelters, with biological data about brain size and structure. Because the cultural capacity of our ancestors is rooted in biology, paleoanthropologists are faced with the challenge of integrating biology and culture in the interpretation of the fragmentary evidence from the past. However, it is in these reconstructions that paleoanthropologists shift into a narrative mode, telling the "heroic story" of human evolution in which our ancestors increasingly use their cultural capabilities rather than biology to survive.

In the following paleoanthropological reconstructions of the culture of *H. erectus,* a curious blend of scientific method and storytelling co-exist. In this regard, as with our earlier discussion of gender, paleoanthropologists must work to keep their own cultural beliefs and values out of the paleoanthropological reconstructions.

The Acheulean Tool Tradition

Associated with the remains of *Homo erectus* in Africa, Europe, and Southwest Asia are tools of the **Acheulean tradition.** The signature piece of this tradition first identified in stone tools discovered at Saint Acheul, France, is the hand-axe: a teardrop-shaped tool pointed at one end with a sharp cutting edge all around.

The earliest hand-axes, from East Africa are about 1.6 million years old. Those found in Europe are no older than about 500,000 years. At the same time that hand-axes appeared, archaeological sites in Europe became dramatically more common than earlier ones. This suggests an influx of individuals bringing Acheulean technology with them, implying continued gene flow into

Acheulean tradition The tool-making tradition of *Homo erectus* in Africa, Europe, and Southwest Asia in which hand-axes were developed from the earlier Oldowan chopper.

© R. Potts/Smithsonian Institution

To fabricate this Acheulean hand-axe from flint, the toolmaker imposed a standardized arbitrary form on the naturally occurring raw material.

Europe. Because the spread of the genus *Homo* from Africa into Asia took place before the invention of the hand-axe, it is not surprising to find that different forms of tools were developed in East Asia.

That the Acheulean grew out of the Oldowan tradition is indicated by an examination of the evidence discovered at Olduvai Gorge. In Bed I, the lowest level, chopper tools were found along with remains of *Homo habilis.* Above, in lower Bed II, the first crude hand-axes were found intermingled with chopper tools. The more finished-looking Acheulean hand-axes appear in middle Bed II together with *H. erectus* remains.

Early Acheulean tools represent a significant step beyond the generalized cutting, chopping, and scraping tools of the Oldowan tradition. The shapes of Oldowan tools were largely controlled by the original form, size, and mechanical properties of raw materials. The shapes of hand-axes and some other Acheulean tools, by contrast, are more standardized, apparently reflecting arbitrary preconceived designs imposed upon a diverse range of raw materials.[15] Overall, sharper points, more regular cutting edges, and more cutting edge were produced from the same amount of stone.

---

[15]Ambrose, S. H. (2001). Paleolithic technology and human evolution. *Science 291,* 1,750.

In regions where bamboo was readily available for the fabrication of effective tools, the same stone tool industries might not have developed. This contemporary scaffolding demonstrates bamboo's strength and versatility.

During this part of the Lower Paleolithic, or Old Stone Age, tool kits began to diversify. Besides hand-axes, *H. erectus* used tools that functioned as cleavers (hand-axes with a straight, sharp edge where the point would otherwise be), picks and knives (variants of the hand-axe form), and flake tools (generally smaller tools made by hitting a flint core with a hammerstone, thus knocking off flakes with sharp edges). Many flake tools were by-products of hand-axe and cleaver manufacture. Their sharp edges made them useful "as is," but many were retouched (modified again by ancient flint knappers) to make points, scrapers, borers, and other sorts of tools. Diversification of tool kits is also indicated by the smaller numbers of hand-axes in northern and eastern Europe where people relied more on simple flaked choppers; a wide variety of unstandardized flakes; and supplementary tools of bone, antler, and wood.

In eastern Asia, by contrast, people developed a variety of choppers, scrapers, points, and burins (chisel-like tools) different from those in western Asia, Europe, and Africa. Besides direct percussion, anvil (striking the raw material against a stationary stone) and bipolar percussion (holding the raw material against an anvil, but striking it at the same time with a hammerstone) methods were used in tool manufacture. Although tens of thousands of stone tools have been found with *H. erectus* remains at Zhoukoudian, stone implements are not at all common in Southeast Asia. Here, favored materials likely were ones that do not preserve well such as bamboo and other local woods, from which excellent knives, scrapers, and so on can be made.

Use of Fire

The use of fire provides another sign of *H. erectus'* developing culture and technology. The 700,000-year-old Kao Poh Nam rock shelter in Thailand provides compelling evidence for deliberate controlled use of fire. Here, a roughly circular arrangement of fire-cracked basalt cobbles was discovered in association with artifacts and animal bones. Because basalt rocks are not native to the rock shelter and are quite heavy, they probably had to have been carried in by *H. erectus.* Limestone rocks, more readily available in the shelter, cannot be used for hearths because, when burned, limestone produces quicklime, a caustic substance that causes itching and burning skin rashes.[16] The hearth, located near the rock shelter entrance, away from the deeper recesses favored by animals making dens, is associated with bones, showing clear evidence of cut marks from butchering, as well as burning.

Homo erectus may have been using fire even earlier, based on evidence from Swartkrans in South Africa. Here, in deposits estimated to date between 1 and 1.3 million years ago, bones have been found that had been heated to temperatures far in excess of what one would expect as the result of natural fires. Natural grass fires in the region will not heat bones above 212 degrees Fahrenheit, whereas coals in campfires reach temperatures from 900° to 1200° F. Consequently, bones thrown into controlled fires reach higher temperatures. Furthermore, the burned bones at Swartkrans do not occur in older, deeper deposits. If these fires were natural they would be distributed among all archaeological layers. Because the bones indicate heating to such high temperatures that any meat on them would have been inedible, South African paleoanthropologists Andrew Sillen and C. K. Brain suggest that the Swartkrans fires functioned as protection from predators.[17] Thus, fire may not have

---

[16]Pope, G. C. (1989). Bamboo and human evolution. *Natural History 10,* 56.

[17]Sillen, A., & Brain, C. K. (1990). Old flame. *Natural History 4,* 10.

Archaeologists excavate a hearth at a rock shelter in Kao Poh Nam, Thailand. This hearth testifies to human use of controlled fire 700,000 years ago.

been "tamed" initially for cooking or to keep people warm; such uses may have come later.

Whatever the reason for *H. erectus'* original use of fire, it proved invaluable to populations that spread from the tropics into regions with cooler climates. Not only did fire provide warmth, but it may have assisted in the quest for food. In places like central Europe and China, food would have been hard to come by in the long, cold winters when edible plants were unavailable and the large herds of animals dispersed and migrated. One solution could have been to search out the frozen carcasses of animals that had died naturally in the late fall and winter, using long wooden probes to locate them beneath the snow, wooden scoops to dig them out, and fire to thaw them so that they could be butchered and eaten.[18] Furthermore, such fire-assisted scavenging would have made available meat and hides of woolly mammoths, woolly rhinoceroses, and bison, which were probably beyond the ability of *H. erectus* to kill, at least until late in the species' career.

Perhaps it was the use of fire to thaw carcasses that led to the idea of cooking food. Some paleoanthropologists suggest that this behavioral change altered the forces of natural selection, which previously favored individuals with heavy jaws and large, sharp teeth (food is tougher and needs more chewing when it is uncooked), favoring instead further reduction in tooth size along with supportive facial structure.

Alternatively, the reduction of tooth size and supporting structure may have occurred outside the context of adaptation. For example, the genetic changes responsible for increasing brain size may also have caused a reduction in tooth size as a secondary effect. Recently, researchers at the University of Pennsylvania announced discovery of a genetic mutation, shared by all humans but absent in apes, that acts to prevent growth of powerful jaw muscles. They calculated that the mutation arose between 2.1 and 2.7 million years ago, the period when early *Homo* first appeared. They argue that, without heavy jaw muscles attaching to the outside of the brain case, a significant constraint to brain growth was removed. In other words, humans may have developed large brains as an accidental by-product of jaw-size reduction.[19] Natural selection added to the effects of the sudden change of the jaw through the gradual brain expansion that continued in the genus *Homo* until some 200,000 years ago. By then, brain size had approximately tripled and reached the levels of today's humans. Sometimes it is not possible to infer the reasons for an anatomical change visible in the fossil record. Instead, paleoanthropologists must remain content with making observations such as that, between early and late *H. erectus,* chewing-related structures undergo reduction at a rate markedly above the fossil vertebrate average.[20]

---

[18]Gamble, C. (1986). *The Paleolithic settlement of Europe* (p. 387). Cambridge, England: Cambridge University Press.

[19]Stedman, H. H., et al. (2004). Myosin gene mutation correlates with anatomical changes in the human lineage. *Nature 428,* 415–418.

[20]Wolpoff, M. H. (1993). Evolution in *Homo erectus:* The question of stasis. In R. L. Ciochon & J. G. Fleagle (Eds.), *The human evolution*

Hypotheses regarding the benefits of certain cultural innovations such as cooking are another matter altogether. Cooking does more than soften food. It detoxifies a number of otherwise poisonous plants; alters digestion-inhibiting substances so that important vitamins, minerals, and proteins can be absorbed while in the gut, rather than just passing through it unused; and makes high-energy complex carbohydrates like starch digestible. With cooking, the nutritional resources available to humans were substantially increased and made more secure.

In the story of human evolution, the biological consequences of cultural change can sometimes be inferred. For example, the partial predigestion of food by cooking also may have allowed a reduction in the size of the digestive tract. To establish this biological change, paleoanthropologists do not have the benefit of fossilized digestive tracts. Instead they turn to comparative anatomy of the living hominoids. Despite its overall similarity of form to those of apes, the digestive tract of modern humans is substantially smaller. The advantage of this gut reduction is that it draws less energy to operate, thereby competing less with the high energy requirements of a larger brain. Although a mere 2 percent of body weight, the brain accounts for about 20 to 25 percent of energy consumed at resting metabolic rate in modern human adults.[21]

Like tools, then, fire gave people more control over their environment. Possibly, *H. erectus* in Southeast Asia used fire, as have more recent populations living there, to keep areas in the forest clear for foot traffic. Certainly, the resistance to burning, which is characteristic of many hardwood trees in this forest today, indicates that fire has long been important in their evolution. Fire may also have been used by *H. erectus,* as it was by subsequent members of the genus *Homo,* not just for protection from animals out in the open but to frighten away cave-dwelling predators so that the fire-users might live in the caves themselves. In addition, fire could be used to provide warmth and light in these otherwise cold and dark habitations.

Even more, fire modified the natural succession of day and night, perhaps encouraging *H. erectus* to stay up after dark to review the day's events and plan the next day's activities. Though we cannot know whether *H. erectus* enjoyed socializing and planning around campfires at night, we do have evidence at least of some planning behavior. Planning is implied by the existence of populations in temperate climates, where the ability to anticipate the needs of the winter season by preparing in advance to protect against the cold would have been crucial to survival.[22]

With *H. erectus* came the first evidence of ancestral populations living outside the Old World tropics. Without controlled use of fire, it is unlikely that early humans could have moved successfully into regions where winter temperatures regularly dropped to temperate climate levels—as they must have in northern China, the mountain highlands of central Asia, or most of Europe. Members of the genus *Homo* spread to these colder regions some 780,000 years ago.

Although considerable variation exists, studies of modern humans indicate that most people can remain reasonably comfortable down to 50 degrees Fahrenheit (10 degrees Celsius) with minimal clothing so long as they keep active. Below that temperature, hands and feet cool to the point of pain.[23] Clothing, like many other aspects of material culture, does not fossilize, so we have no direct evidence of the kind of clothing worn by *H. erectus.* We only know that it must have been more sophisticated than was required in warmer climates. In short, when our human ancestors learned to employ fire to warm and protect themselves and to cook their food, they dramatically increased their geographic range and nutritional options.

This sort of missing evidence creates controversy around many of the behavioral constructions suggested for *H. erectus.* The Chinese *H. erectus* site, Zhoukoudian, provides an excellent case in point. Many paleoanthropologists interpret evidence of fires, hackberries, and animal bones as demonstrating hunting, gathering, and occupation of this cave site by *Homo erectus.* Archaeologist Lewis Binford suggests instead that the fires were natural—that due to the presence of bat guano (feces), a reliable fuel, high temperature and fires occurred naturally. He suggests too that the hackberries were brought into the cave in animal feces and that all the animal remains including those of humans were brought into this cave by carnivores. However, the well-documented use of controlled fire by *H. erectus* 700,000 years ago in Thailand, described above, suggests that fire could have been in use at Zhoukoudian as well.

Hunting

Evidence that *H. erectus* developed the ability to organize in order to hunt large animals is suggested by remains such as those from the 400,000-year-old sites of Ambrona

source book (p. 396). Englewood Cliffs, NJ: Prentice-Hall.

[21]Leigh, S. R., & Park, P. B. (1998). Evolution of human growth prolongation. *American Journal of Physical Anthropology 107,* 347.

[22]Goodenough, W. H. (1990). Evolution of the human capacity for beliefs. *American Anthropologist, 92,* 601.

[23]Whiting, J. W. M., Sodergem, J. A., & Stigler, S. M. (1982). Winter temperature as a constraint to the migration of preindustrial peoples. *American Anthropologist 84,* 289.

and Torralba, in Spain. At the latter site, in what was an ancient swamp, the remains of several elephants, horses, red deer, wild oxen, and rhinoceroses were found. Their skeletons were dismembered and scattered, a finding that cannot be explained as a result of any natural geological process. Therefore, it is clear that these animals did not accidentally get mired in a swamp where they simply died and decayed.[24] In fact, the bones are closely associated with a variety of stone tools—a few thousand of them. Furthermore, there is very little evidence of carnivorous animal activity and none at all for the really big carnivores. Clearly, the genus *Homo* was involved—not just in butchering the animals but evidently in killing them as well.

It appears that the animals were actually driven into the swamp so that they could be easily dispatched. The remains of charcoal and carbon, widely but thinly scattered in the vicinity, raise the possibility that grass fires were used to drive the animals into the swamp. In any event, this evidence indicates more than opportunistic scavenging. Not only was *H. erectus* able to hunt, but considerable organizational and communicative skills are implied as well.

Additional evidence for hunting 400,000 years ago was discovered accidentally in 1995 in the course of strip-mining at Schöningen in northern Germany. Here five well-constructed and finely balanced spears made entirely of wood, the longest one measuring more than 7 feet in length, were found. These are sophisticated weapons made by hunters who clearly knew what they were doing. The nearby bones of more than a dozen horses attest to the effectiveness of their weapons.

There is no reason to suppose that *H. erectus* became an accomplished hunter all at once. As described in Chapter 3, coordinated hunting behavior is seen in chimpanzees and bonobos. Presumably, the most ancient members of this species, like *Homo habilis* and australopithecines before them, got the bulk of their meat through scavenging with occasional hunting of smaller prey. As their cultural capabilities increased, however, they could have devised ways of doing their own killing, rather than waiting for larger animals to die or be killed by other predators. As they became more proficient predators over time, they would have been able to count on a more reliable supply of meat.

Other Evidence of Complex Thought

Yet other evidence of *H. erectus'* capabilities comes from the island of Flores in Indonesia. This island lies east of a deepwater strait that has acted throughout the Pleisto-

cene as a barrier to the passage of animals to and from Southeast Asia. To get to Flores, even at times of lowered sea levels, required crossing open water: at minimum 25 kilometers from Bali to Sumbawa, with an additional 19 kilometers to Flores. That early humans did just this is indicated by the presence of 800,000-year-old stone tools.[25] Precisely how they navigated across the deep, fast-moving water is not known, but at the least it required some sort of substantial raft.

Evidence for a developing symbolic life is suggested by the increased standardization and refinement of Acheulean hand-axes over time. Moreover, at several sites in Europe, deliberately marked objects of stone, bone, and ivory have been found in Acheulean contexts. These include several objects from Bilzingsleben, Germany—among them a mastodon bone with a series of regular lines that appear to have been deliberately engraved. Though a far cry from the later Upper Paleolithic cave art of France and Spain, these are among the earliest Paleolithic artifacts that have no obvious utility or model in the natural world.

Such apparently symbolic artifacts became more common in later phases of the Paleolithic, as more derived forms of the genus *Homo* appeared on the scene. Similarly, the world's oldest known rock carvings are associated with Acheulean tools in a cave in India.[26] Archaeologist Alexander Marshack argues that the use of such symbolic images requires some sort of spoken language, not only to assign meaning to the images but to maintain the tradition they seem to represent.[27] That such a symbolic tradition did exist is suggested by similar motifs on later Paleolithic artifacts. It is also in late Acheulean contexts on three continents that we have our

[24]Freeman, L. G. (1992). *Ambrona and Torralba: New evidence and interpretation.* Paper presented at the 91st Annual Meeting, American Anthropological Association, San Francisco.

[25]Gibbons, A. (1998). Ancient island tools suggest *Homo erectus* was a seafarer. *Science 279*, 1,635.

[26]Bednarik, R. G. (1995). Concept-mediated marking in the Lower Paleolithic. *Current Anthropology 36*, 610–611.

[27]Marshack, A. (1976). Some implications of the Paleolithic symbolic evidence for the origin of language. *Current Anthropology 17*, 280.

earliest evidence for the use of red ochre. More modern forms of *Homo* employed this pigment to color symbolic as well as utilitarian artifacts, to stain the bodies of the dead, to paint the bodies of the living, and (ultimately) to make notations and paint pictures.

THE QUESTION OF LANGUAGE

We do not, of course, know anything definitive about *H. erectus'* linguistic abilities. Still, the evidence for a developing symbolic life, as well as the need to plan for seasonal changes and to coordinate hunting activities (and cross stretches of open water), implies improving linguistic competence.

Stone tools provide another interesting source for evidence of evolving humans' linguistic capabilities. The vast majority of the stone tools preserved in the fossil record were made by right-handed individuals, providing evidence of the specialization and lateralization of the brain. In other primates and most mammals, the right and left sides of the brain duplicate each other's function; therefore these animals use the right and left sides of their bodies equally and interchangeably. In humans, the emergence of handedness seems closely linked both ontogenetically (at about the age of 1 year) and evolutionarily with the appearance of language (Figure 7.9). Thus evidence of handedness in Lower Paleolithic tools

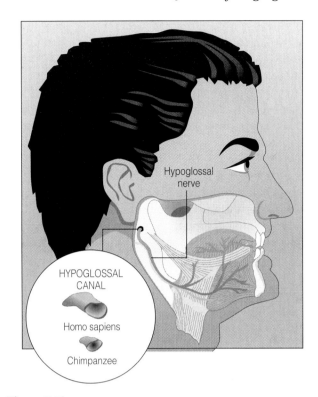

Figure 7.10

The size of the hypoglossal canal is much larger in humans than in chimpanzees. The nerve that passes through this canal controls tongue movement, and complex tongue movements are involved in spoken language. All members of the genus *Homo* after about 500,000 years ago have an enlarged hypoglossal canal.

indicates that the kind of brain specialization required for language was well underway.

The vocal tract and brain of *H. erectus* are intermediate between those of *H. sapiens* on the one hand and earlier *Australopithecus* on the other. Another clue is the increasing size of the **hypoglossal canal.** This passageway through the skull accommodates the nerve that controls tongue movements, so important for spoken language (Figure 7.10). In contemporary people this is twice the size that it is in any ape. This characteristic first appears in fossilized skulls of late *H. erectus* about 500,000 years ago.[28]

Possibly, a changeover from reliance on gestural to spoken language was a driving force in these evolutionary changes. The reduction of tooth and jaw size, facilitating the ability to articulate speech sounds may have

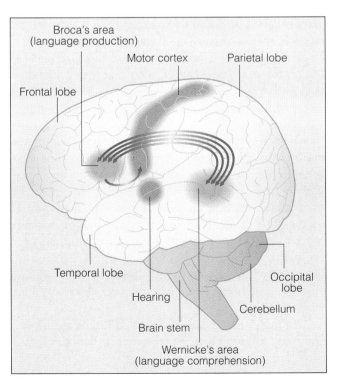

Figure 7.9

Language areas in the left side of the brain.

---

[28]Cartmill, M. (1998). The gift of gab. *Discover 19*(11), 64.

hypoglossal canal The opening in the skull that accommodates the tongue-controlling hypoglossal nerve.

also played a role. From an evolutionary standpoint, spoken language could be said to provide some advantages over a gestural one. Individuals do not have to stop whatever they are doing with their hands to "talk" (useful to a species increasingly dependent on tool use), and it is possible to talk in the dark, past opaque objects, or among people whose gaze is concentrated on something else (potential prey, for example).

With *H. erectus,* then, we find a clearer manifestation of the interplay among cultural, physical, and environmental factors than ever before. However slowly, social organization, technology, and communication developed in tandem with an increase in brain size and complexity. In fact, the cranial capacity of late *H. erectus* is 31 percent greater than the mean for early *H. erectus,* a rate of increase more rapid than the average fossil vertebrate rate.[29]

As a consequence of these changes, *H. erectus'* resource base was enlarged significantly; the supply of meat could be increased by hunting as well as by scavenging, and the supply of plant foods was increased as cooking allowed the consumption of vegetables that otherwise are toxic or indigestible. This, along with an increased ability to modify the environment in advantageous ways—for example, by using fire to provide warmth—undoubtedly contributed to a population increase and territorial expansion. In all living creatures, any kind of adaptation that enhances reproductive success causes population growth. This growth causes fringe populations to spill over into neighboring regions previously uninhabited by the species. Thus, *Homo erectus* was able to move into areas that had never been inhabited by bipedal primates before—first into the warm, southern regions of Eurasia and ultimately into the cooler regions of China and Europe.

TOOLS, FOOD, AND BRAIN EXPANSION

With the appearance of the genus *Homo* and the tools of the Old Stone Age, human evolution began a course of brain expansion through variational change (see Chapter 5) that continued until about 200,000 years ago. By this point, brain size had approximately tripled and reached the levels of contemporary people.

During this time period, the increasing cultural capabilities accompanying larger brains required parallel improvements in diet. The energy demands of nerve tissue, of which the brain is made, are high—higher, in fact, than the demands of other types of tissue in the hu-

man body. One can meet these demands on a vegetarian diet, but the overall energy content of a given amount of plant food is generally less than that of the same amount of meat. Thus, the use of meat, marrow in particular, in addition to plant foods, ensured the availability of a reliable source of high-quality protein to support a more highly developed brain.

In addition, animals that live on plant foods must spend their time eating large quantities of vegetation. Gorillas, for example, spend all day munching on plants to maintain their large bodies. Meat eaters, by contrast, have no need to eat so much, or so often. Consequently, meat-eating bipeds may have had more leisure time available to explore and manipulate their environment. Like lions and leopards, they would have time for activities other than eating.

The archaeological record provides us with a tangible record of our ancestors' cultural abilities that corresponds with the simultaneous biological expansion of the brain. Tool making itself puts a premium on manual dexterity, precision, and fine manipulation. Stone tools provide evidence of handedness that bespeaks specialization and lateralization of the brain associated with language. Beginning with the appearance of the genus *Homo* in Africa 2.5 million years ago, human evolution began a sure course of increasing brain size and increasing cultural development, each presumably acting to promote the other.

The importance of increased consumption of meat for brain development in early *Homo* is suggested by the size of their brains: The cranial capacity of the largely plant-eating *Australopithecus* ranged from 310 to 530 cubic centimeters (cc); that of the earliest known meat eater, *Homo habilis* from East Africa, ranged from 580 to 752 cc; whereas *Homo erectus,* who eventually hunted as well as scavenged for meat, possessed a cranial capacity of 775 to 1,225 cc.

Many scenarios about behavioral adaptation in early *Homo,* such as the relationship among tools, food, and brain expansion, propose a kind of feedback loop between brain size and behavior. The behaviors made possible by larger brains confer advantages to large-brained individuals, contributing to their increased reproductive success. Over time, large-brained individuals contribute more to successive generations, so that the population evolves to a larger-brained form. Natural selection for increases in learning ability has thus led to the evolution of larger and more complex brains over about 2 million years.

Though it preceded increases in brain size by several more million years, bipedalism set the stage for the evolution of large brains and human culture. It freed the hands for activities such as tool making and carrying of resources or infants. This new body plan, bipedalism, opened new opportunities for change.

[29]Wolpoff, M. H. (1993). Evolution in *Homo erectus:* The question of stasis. In R. L. Ciochon & J. G. Fleagle (Eds.), *The human evolution source book* (pp. 392, 396). Englewood Cliffs, NJ: Prentice-Hall.

VISUAL COUNTERPOINT

A power grip (left) utilizes more of the hand while the precision grip (right) relies on the fingers for control, requiring corresponding organizational changes in the brain.

Questions for Reflection

1. The earliest members of the genus *Homo* drew upon integrated biological and cultural capabilities to face the challenges of existence. Provide examples of how early *Homo* increasingly relied on cultural abilities and how these abilities are tied to biological evidence preserved in the fossil record.

2. Paleoanthropologists can be characterized as either "lumpers" or "splitters" depending upon their approach to the identification of species in the fossil record. Using *Homo habilis* and *Homo erectus*, which of these approaches do you prefer and why?

3. In his 1871 book *Descent of Man and Selection in Relation to Sex*, Charles Darwin stated, "Thus man has ultimately become superior to woman. It is indeed fortunate that the law of equal transmission of characters prevails with mammals. Otherwise it is probable that man would have become as superior in mental endowment to woman as the peacock is in ornamental plumage to the peahen." How were the cultural norms of Darwin's time reflected in his statement? Can 21st-century paleoanthropologists speak about differences between the sexes in evolutionary contexts without introducing their own cultural biases?

4. Animals ranging from rabbits to plants have come to occupy new niches without the benefits of culture. How does the spread of *Homo* out of the African continent tell paleoanthropologists anything about this species' cultural capabilities?

5. Though language itself does not "fossilize," the archaeological and fossil records provide some evidence of the linguistic capabilities of our ancestors. Using the evidence available for *Homo habilis* and *Homo erectus*, what sort of linguistic abilities do you think early *Homo* possessed?

Suggested Readings

Corballis, M. C. (2003). *From hand to mouth: The origins of human language.* Princeton, NJ: Princeton University Press.

This book, written by a psychologist, takes the position that facial and manual gestures rather than vocalization are key to the development of language. It brings data from linguistics, molecular genetics, animal behavior, psychology, and neurology to the anthropological question of when human language arose.

Delson, E., Tattersal, I., Brooks, A., & Van Couvering, J. (1999). *Encyclopedia of human evolution and prehistory*. New York: Garland.

Using an A to Z format, this user-friendly encyclopedia includes over 800 entries relating to human evolution and prehistory. It includes excellent diagrams, illustrations, and descriptions of key archaeological sites.

Potts, R. (1997). *Humanity's descent: The consequences of ecological instability*. New York: Avon.

Written by the director of the Smithsonian Institution's Human Origins Program, this book suggests that environmental instability was the unifying factor contributing to the acquisition of human language and culture.

Stanford, C. B. (2001). *The hunting apes: Meat eating and the origins of human behavior*. Princeton, NJ: Princeton University Press.

Though updated and less gender biased, this work revisits the old "Man the Hunter" hypothesis, suggesting that human intelligence is linked to the acquisition of meat and food sharing.

Walker, A., & Shipman, P. (1997). *The wisdom of the bones: In search of human origins*. New York: Vintage Books.

This book provides an engaging description of the discovery of the most complete *Homo erectus* specimen—the Nariokotome Boy from Lake Turkana, Kenya—as well as placing it within the context of the larger story of human evolution.

Zihlman, A. (2001). *The human evolution coloring book*. New York: Harper Resources.

Do not be deceived by the title or the book's visual hands-on format. This book provides an authoritative scientific approach to all aspects of the study of human evolution.

Thomson Audio Study Products

 Enjoy the MP3-ready Audio Lecture Overviews for each chapter and a comprehensive audio glossary of key terms for quick study and review. Whether walking to class, doing laundry, or studying at your desk, you now have the freedom to choose when, where, and how you interact with your audio-based educational media. See the preface for information on how to access this on-the-go study and review tool.

The Anthropology Resource Center

www.thomsonedu.com/anthropology
The Anthropology Resource Center provides extended learning materials to reinforce your understanding of key concepts in the four subfields of anthropology. For each of the four subdisciplines, the Resource Center includes dynamic exercises including video exercises, map exercises, simulations, and "Meet the Scientists" interviews, as well as critical thinking questions that can be assigned and e-mailed to instructors. The Resource Center also provides breaking news in anthropology and interesting material on applied anthropology to help you link what you are learning to the world around you.

8 Pre-Modern Humans and the Elaboration of Culture

© Mary Evans Picture Library/Alamy

CHALLENGE ISSUE

When we imagine the appearance and behavior of members of the genus *Homo*, having brains the size of modern humans and living closer to the present, we are challenged to avoid imposing contemporary beliefs upon the mysteries of the past. For example, this early 20th-century portrayal of a Neandertal, based on the research of paleoanthropologist Marcellin Boule, makes a powerfully negative statement about the capabilities of this group as well as their distance from living humans. In looking at this sorry specimen, it is easy to forget that this portrayal is not derived directly from the fossil remains, but from the collective imagination of early 20th-century Europeans. While paleoanthropologists uniformly recognize the inaccuracies and biases present in this engraving, present-day reconstructions of Neandertals still vary tremendously and reflect the conflicting scientific theories and beliefs about their place in our evolutionary history.

What Is the Relationship Between Brain Size and Culture Change?

Between 200,000 and 400,000 years ago, the brain size of genus *Homo* throughout the Old World began to reach modern proportions. Still, fossil skulls retain a number of ancestral features, as well as some specialized features typically not seen in modern *Homo sapiens*. Archaeological evidence shows that as the human brain reached its modern size, cultures throughout the globe had become rich and varied compared to cultures of earlier members of the genus *Homo*. A wide variety of tools for special purposes, objects for purely symbolic purposes, ceremonial activities, and care for the old and disabled existed. The appearance of more sophisticated stone tool industries marks the beginning of the Middle Paleolithic. Some of these large-brained fossils are called archaic *Homo sapiens,* while the place of others in human evolutionary history is hotly debated. Paleoanthropologists disagree about whether alterations in the shape of the skull indicate differences in brain structure sufficient to affect the cultural capabilities of these fossil groups.

Who Were the Neandertals, and What Became of Them?

The Neandertals were large-brained, robust, muscular members of the genus *Homo* from Southwest Asia and Europe whose remains date from about 30,000 to 125,000 years ago. The first Neandertals were discovered in the mid-19th century, before scientific theories to account for human evolution had gained acceptance. Much debate has surrounded the fate of the Neandertals. Some paleoanthropologists consider the Neandertals as early members of our species, *Homo sapiens*. Others suggest that distinctive features in Neandertal skulls place them outside of the evolutionary line leading to contemporary people.

What Is the Relationship Between Middle Paleolithic *Homo* and Modern *Homo sapiens?*

Some paleoanthropologists propose that Neandertals, like other archaic forms, evolved into anatomically modern versions of *Homo sapiens* as different features of modern anatomy arising in other regional populations were carried to them through gene flow. In this framework, human populations throughout Africa, Europe, and Asia contributed to the making of modern humans. Other paleoanthropologists propose that anatomically modern humans with superior cultural capabilities appeared first in Africa about 200,000 years ago, replacing existing archaic forms as they spread from Africa to the rest of the world.

As well as being a scholar, the anthropologist attempting to piece together the innumerable parts of the puzzle of human evolution must be a detective, and creative thinker, for the available evidence is often scant, enigmatic, or full of misleading and even contradictory clues. The quest for the origin of modern humans from more ancient representatives of the genus *Homo* has elements of a detective story, for it contains mysteries concerning the emergence of humanity, none of which has been completely resolved to this day. The mysteries involve the appearance of the first fossils with human-sized brains, the identity of the Neandertals, and the relationship of changes in the shape of the skull to cultural abilities.

THE APPEARANCE OF MODERN-SIZED BRAINS

At various sites in Africa, Asia, and Europe, a number of fossils from the genus *Homo*—primarily skulls, jaws, and jaw fragments—have been found that seem to date roughly to between 200,000 and 400,000 years ago. Most fossil finds consist of parts of one or a very few individuals, the one exception being a large number of bones and teeth from the Sierra de Atapuerca in northern Spain. Here, at some time between 205,000 and 325,000 years ago,[1] the remains of at least twenty-eight individuals of both sexes, juveniles as well as adults, were deliberately

dumped (after defleshing their skulls) by their contemporaries into a deep cave shaft known today as Sima de los Huesos ("Pit of the Bones"). This makes it the best population sample from this time period anywhere in the world (Figure 8.1). The presence of other animal bones in the same pit with humans raises the possibility that early humans simply used the site as a dump. Alternatively, the treatment of the dead at Atapuerca may have involved ritual activity that presaged burial of the dead, a practice that became common after 100,000 years ago.

As expected of any population, this one displays a significant degree of variation. Cranial capacity, for example, ranges from 1,125 to 1,390 cubic centimeters, overlapping the upper end of the range for *H. erectus* and the average size of *H. sapiens'* range (1,300 cc). Overall, the bones display a mix of features, some typical of *H. erectus,* others of *H. sapiens,* including some incipient Neandertal characteristics. Despite this variation, the sample appears to show no more sexual dimorphism than displayed by modern humans.[2]

Other remains from Africa and Europe dating between 200,000 and 400,000 years ago have shown a combination of *H. erectus* and *H. sapiens* features. Some—such as skulls from Ndutu in Tanzania, Swanscombe (England), and Steinheim (Germany)—have been classified as *H. sapiens,* while others—from Arago (France), Bilzingsleben (Germany), and Petralona (Greece), and several African sites—have been classified as *H. erectus.* Yet all have cranial capacities that fit within the range exhibited by the Sima de los Huesos skulls.

[1]Parés, J. M., et al. (2000). On the age of hominid fossils at the Sima de los Huesos, Sierra de Atapuerca, Spain: Paleomagnetic evidence. *American Journal of Physical Anthropology* 111, 451–461.

[2]Lorenzo, C., et al. (1998). Intrapopulational body size variation and cranial capacity variation in middle Pleistocene humans: The Sima de los Huesos sample (Sierra de Atapuerca, Spain). *American Journal of Physical Anthropology* 106, 30.

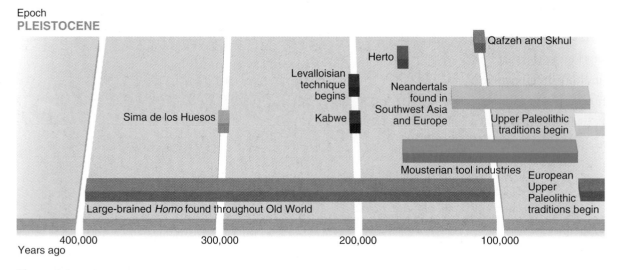

Figure 8.1

Around 400,000 years ago, large-brained members of the genus *Homo* began to be found throughout Africa and Eurasia; corresponding culture changes are evident as well.

Javier Trueba/Madrid Scientific Films

The fossils from Sima de los Huesos, Sierra de Atapuerca, Spain, represent the best collection of *Homo* fossils from this period. With the well-preserved remains of at least twenty-eight individuals, paleo-anthropologists can interpret these fossils in the context of the range of variation seen within this population.

Comparisons of these skulls to those of living people or of *H. erectus* reflect their transitional nature. The Swanscombe and Steinheim skulls are large and robust, with their maximum breadth lower on the skull, more prominent brow ridges, larger faces, and bigger teeth. Similarly, the face of the Petralona skull from Greece resembles European Neandertals, while the back of the skull looks like *H. erectus*. Conversely, a skull from Salé in Morocco, which had a rather small brain for *H. sapiens* (930–960 cc), looks surprisingly modern from the back. Finally, various jaws from France and Morocco (in northern Africa) seem to combine features of *H. erectus* with those of the later European Neandertals.

A similar situation exists in East Asia, where skulls from several sites in China exhibit the same mix of *H. erectus* and *H. sapiens* characteristics. "Lumpers" suggest that calling some of these early humans "late *H. erectus*" or "early *H. sapiens*" (or any of the other proposed species names within the genus *Homo*) serves no useful purpose and merely obscures their apparently transitional status.

They tend to lump these fossils into the archaic *Homo sapiens,* a category that reflects both their large brain size and the ancestral features in the skull. "Splitters" use a series of discrete names for specimens from this period that take into account some of the geographic and morphological variation present in these fossils. Both approaches correspond to statements about evolutionary relationships among fossil groups.

Levalloisian Technique

With the appearance of large-brained members of the genus *Homo,* the pace of culture change began to accelerate. Although hand-axes and other Acheulean tools were still made, a new method of flake manufacture was invented: the **Levalloisian technique,** so named after the French site where such tools were first excavated. Flake tools produced by this technique have been found widely in Africa, Europe, Southwest Asia, and even China. In China, the technique could represent a case of independent invention, or it could indicate the spread of ideas from one part of the inhabited world to another.

The Levalloisian technique initially involves preparing a core by removing small flakes over the stone's surface. Following this, a striking platform is set up by a crosswise blow at one end of the core of stone (Figure 8.2). Striking the platform removes three or four long flakes, whose size and shape have been predetermined by the preceding preparation. What is left, besides small waste flakes, is a nodule that looks like a tortoise shell. This method produces a longer edge for the same amount of flint than the previous ones used by evolving humans. The edges are sharper and can be produced in less time.

THOMSON AUDIO STUDY PRODUCTS
Take advantage of the MP3-ready Audio Lecture Overviews and comprehensive audio glossary of key terms for each chapter. See the preface for information on how to access this on-the-go study and review tool.

At about the same time the Levalloisian technique was developed, hafting—the fastening of small stone bifaces and flakes to handles of wood—was invented. Hafting led to the development of knives and spears. Unlike the older handheld tools made simply by reduction (flaking of stone or working of wood), these new composite tools involved three components: a handle or shaft, a stone insert, and the materials to bind them. The ac-

Levalloisian technique Tool-making technique by which three or four long triangular flakes were detached from a specially prepared core. Developed by members of the genus *Homo* transitional from *H. erectus* to *H. sapiens.*

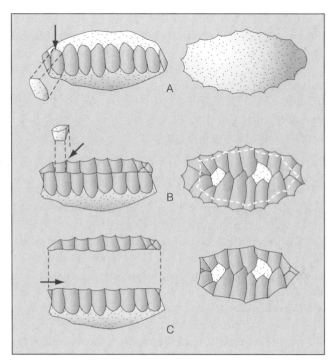

Figure 8.2
These drawings show side (left) and top (right) views of the steps in the Levalloisian technique. Drawing A shows the preparatory flaking of the stone core; B, the same on the top surface; and C, the final step of detaching a flake; and D, the final step of detaching a flake of a size and shape predetermined by the preceding steps.

quisition and modification of each component involved planned sequences of actions that could be performed at different times and places.

With this new technology, regional stylistic and technological variants appear in the archaeological record, suggesting the emergence of distinct cultural traditions and culture areas. At the same time, the proportions of raw materials procured from faraway sources increase; whereas sources of stone for Acheulean tools were rarely more than 12 miles away, Levalloisian tools are found up to 200 miles from the sources of their stone.[3]

Another development, first identified in Africa, was the use of yellow and red pigments of iron oxide, called ochre, becoming especially common by 130,000 years ago.[4] The use of ochre may signal a rise in ritual activity, similar to the deliberate placement of the human

---

[3]Ambrose, S. H. (2001). Paleolithic technology and human evolution. *Science 291*, 1,752.

[4]Barham, L. S. (1998). Possible early pigment use in South-Central Africa. *Current Anthropology 39*, 703–710.

Neandertals A distinct group within the genus *Homo* inhabiting Europe and Southwest Asia from approximately 30,000 to 125,000 years ago.

© PhotoDisc/Getty Images

The practice of hafting, the fastening of small stone bifaces and flakes to handles of wood, was a major technological advance appearing in the archaeological record at about the same time as the invention of the Levalloisian technique.

remains in the Sima de los Huesos, Atapuerca, already noted. The use of red ochre in ancient burials may relate to its similarity to the color of blood as a powerful symbol of life.

THE NEANDERTALS

Of all the remains of *Homo* from the Late Pleistocene, the **Neandertals** are perhaps the most notorious. Neandertals are typically represented as the classic cave men, frequently depicted as brutes in popular media such as cartoons, films, and even natural history museum displays. One of the most contentious issues in paleoanthropology today concerns whether the Neandertals represent an inferior side branch of human evolution, that went extinct following the appearance of modern humans. Alternatively, descendents of the Neandertals may walk the earth today.

Neandertals were an extremely muscular people living from approximately 30,000 to 125,000 years ago in Europe and southwestern Asia. While having brains of modern size, Neandertals possessed faces distinctively different from those of modern humans. Their large noses and teeth projected forward. They had prominent bony brow ridges over their eyes. On the back of their skull, there was a bunlike bony mass for attachment of powerful neck muscles. These features, not in line with classic forms of Western beauty, may have contributed to the depiction of Neandertals as brutes. Their rude reputation may also derive from the timing of their discovery.

One of the first Neandertals was found in a cave in the Neander Valley (*thal* pronounced "tal" means "valley" in German) near Düsseldorf, Germany, in 1856—well before scientific theories to account for human evolution had gained acceptance. (Darwin published his book, *On the Origins of Species by Means of Natural Selection* three years later in 1859.)

Initially, experts were at a loss as to what to make of this discovery. Examination of the fossil skull, a few ribs, and some limb bones revealed that the individual was a human being, but it did not look "normal." Some people believed the bones were those of a sickly and deformed contemporary. Others thought the skeleton belonged to a soldier who had succumbed to "water on the brain" during the Napoleonic Wars. One prominent anatomist thought the remains were those of an idiot suffering from malnutrition, whose violent temper had gotten him into many fights, flattening his forehead and making his brow ridges bumpy.

The idea that Neandertals were somehow deformed or abnormal was given impetus by an analysis of a skeleton found in 1908 near La Chapelle-aux-Saints in France. The analysis mistakenly concluded that the specimen's brain was apelike and that he walked like an ape. Although a team of North American investigators subsequently proved that this French Neandertal specimen was that of an elderly male who had suffered from malnutrition, severe arthritis, and other deformities, the brutish image has persisted.

To many nonanthropologists, the Neandertal has become the quintessential cave man, portrayed by imaginative cartoonists as a slant-headed, stooped, dim-witted individual clad in animal skins and carrying a big club as he plods across the prehistoric landscape, perhaps dragging an unwilling female or a dead saber-toothed tiger. The stereotype has been perpetuated in novels and film. The popular image of Neandertals as brutish and incapable of spoken language, abstract or innovative thinking, or even planning ahead may, in turn, have influenced the interpretation of the fossil and archaeological evidence.

The evidence indicates that Neandertals were nowhere near as brutish and apelike as originally portrayed,

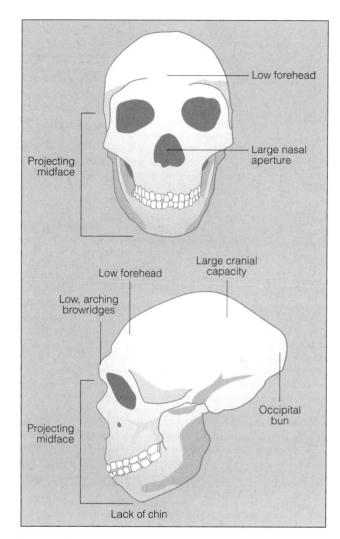

Figure 8.3

This figure depicts features of the skull seen in "classic" Neandertals.

and some scholars now see them as the archaic *H. sapiens* of Europe and Southwest Asia, ancestral to the more derived, anatomically modern populations of Europe and Southwest Asia of the last 30,000 years. For example, paleoanthropologist C. Loring Brace of the University of Michigan observes that "classic" Neandertal features (Figure 8.3) are commonly present in 100,000-year-old skulls from Denmark and Norway.[5]

Nevertheless, Neandertals are somewhat distinctive when compared to more recent populations. Although they held modern-sized brains (average cranial capacity 1,400 cc versus 1,300 cc for modern *H. sapiens*), Neandertal skulls are notable for the protruding appearance of the mid-facial region. The wear patterns on their large front teeth indicate that they may have been heavily used for tasks other than chewing. In many individuals, front teeth were worn down to the stubs of their roots

[5]Ferrie, H. (1997). An interview with C. Loring Brace. *Current Anthropology 38*, 861.

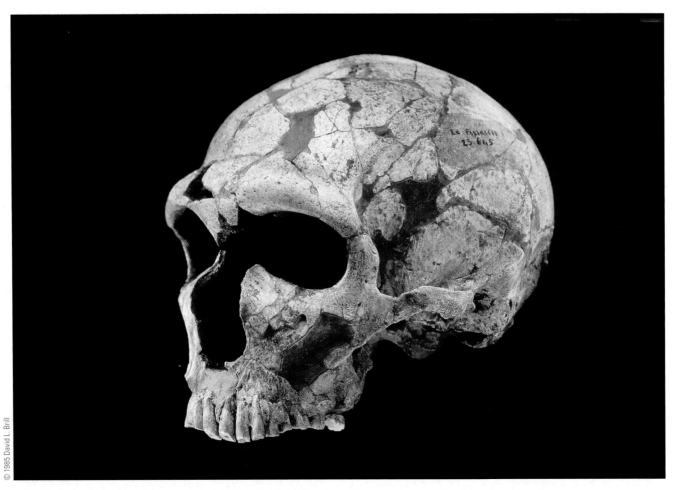

© 1985 David L. Brill

This Neandertal from La Ferrassie in France shows the marked bony ridge above the eyes, the receding forehead, and heavy wear on the front teeth typical of this fossil group.

by 35 to 40 years of age. The large noses of Neandertals probably were necessary to warm, moisten, and clean the dry, dusty frigid air of the glacial climate, preventing damage to the lungs and brain as seen in cold-adapted people of recent times. At the back of the skull, the bun-like bony mass providing attachment for the powerful neck muscles counteracted the weight of a heavy face.

All Neandertal fossils indicate that both sexes were muscular, with extremely robust and dense limb bones. Relative to body mass, the limbs were short (as they are in modern humans native to especially cold climates). Details of the shoulder blades indicate the importance of over-arm and downward thrusting movements. Their arms were exceptionally powerful, and pronounced attachments on their hand bones attest to a remarkably strong grip. Science writer James Shreeve suggests that a healthy Neandertal could lift an average North American football player over his head and throw him through the goalposts.[6] Their massive dense foot and leg bones suggest high levels of strength and endurance, compa-

rable to robust individuals who live today. Because brain size is related to overall body mass, heavy robust Neandertal bodies account for the large average size of the Neandertal brain.

Throughout the previous chapters increasing brain size was linked to increasing cultural capabilities of the genus *Homo*. Neandertal brain size, like that of other members of the genus *Homo* from this time period, falls at the high end of the range for contemporary humans. With these and later fossil groups, the challenge for paleoanthropologists is to decide whether changes in the shape of the skull indicate changes in cultural capabilities.

Though the interpretation of Neandertal fossils has changed dramatically compared to when Neandertals were first discovered, they are still surrounded by controversy. Academic debates relating to their fate rely upon the shape of the Neandertal skeleton and the relationship between the skeleton and human cultural capacities. Those who propose that the Neandertal line went extinct emphasize a notion of Neandertal biological difference and cultural inferiority. Those who include Neandertals in our direct ancestry emphasize the sophis-

[6]Shreeve, J. (1995). *The Neandertal enigma: Solving the mystery of modern human origins* (p. 5). New York: William Morrow.

As this face-off between paleoanthropologist Milford Wolpoff and his reconstruction of a Neandertal shows, the latter did not differ all that much from modern humans of European descent.

tication of Neandertal culture, attributing differences in skull shape and body form to regional adaptation to an extremely cold climate and the retention of ancestral traits in an isolated population.

JAVANESE, AFRICAN, AND CHINESE ARCHAIC *HOMO SAPIENS*

Other parts of the world were inhabited by variants of archaic *H. sapiens* lacking the extreme mid-facial projection and massive muscle attachments on the back of the skull characteristic of the Neandertals. Skulls found in Java, Africa, and China date from roughly the same time period.

The eleven skulls found near the Solo River in Ngandong, Java, are a prime example. Though their dating was not precisely known at the time of their discovery in the 1930s, they were generally considered to be Southeast Asian equivalents of the Neandertals. These skulls indicated modern-sized brains ranging from 1,013 to

1,252 ccs, while retaining features of earlier Javanese *H. erectus.*

With time, opinion on the dating of these fossils changed, with most scholars coming to regard them as considerably earlier than the Neandertals. This opinion focused attention on their resemblance to *H. erectus,* so that when their dating was recently revised (to some time between 27,000 and 53,000 years ago) some concluded that this proved a late survival of *H. erectus* in Asia, contemporary with *H. sapiens* elsewhere. But the Ngandong skulls remain what they always were: representatives of archaic *H. sapiens,* with modern-sized brains in otherwise ancient-looking skulls. Fossils from various parts of Africa, the most famous being a 200,000-year-old skull from Kabwe (Zambia), show a similar combination of ancient and modern traits. Equivalent remains have been found at several localities in China.

African and eastern Asian contemporaries of the Neandertals differ from the Neandertals primarily in their lack of mid-facial projection and massive muscle attachments on the back of the skull. Thus, the Neandertals could be said to represent an extreme form of archaic *H. sapiens.* Elsewhere, the archaics look like robust versions of the early modern populations that lived in the same regions or like somewhat more derived versions of the *H. erectus* populations that preceded them. All appear to have contained fully modern-sized brains, with their skulls retaining some ancestral features.

MIDDLE PALEOLITHIC CULTURE

Adaptations to the environment by *Homo* from the **Middle Paleolithic,** or middle part of the Old Stone Age, were both biological and cultural, but the capacity for cultural adaptation was predictably superior to what it had been in earlier members of the genus *Homo*. Possessing brains of modern size, these members of the genus *Homo* had, as we would expect, greater cultural capabilities than their ancestors. Such a brain played a role in technological innovations, conceptual thought of considerable sophistication, and, almost surely, communication through spoken language. In addition to the Levalloisian traditions already described, the Middle Paleolithic also included the development of the Mousterian tradition.

The Mousterian Tradition

The improved tool-making capabilities of evolving humans are represented by various traditions. The **Mousterian** and Mousterian-like tool traditions of Europe, western Asia, and North Africa, dating between about 40,000 and 166,000 years ago, are the best known of these. Comparable traditions are found in China and Japan, where they likely arose independently from local tool-making traditions.

All these traditions represent a technological advance over preceding industries. For example, the 16 inches of working edge that an Acheulean flint worker could get from a 2-pound core compares with the 6 feet the Mousterian could get from the same core. Mousterian tools were used by *all* people—Neandertals as well as other members of the genus *Homo* said to possess more anatomically modern skulls, in Europe, North Africa, and Southwest Asia during this time period.

At around 35,000 years ago, the Mousterian traditions were replaced by the Upper Paleolithic traditions that will be the subject of the next chapter. As seen in this chapter's Anthropology Applied feature, stone tools continue to be important for humans today.

Middle Paleolithic The middle part of the Old Stone Age characterized by the development of the Mousterian tradition of tool making and the earlier Levalloisian traditions.
Mousterian tradition The tool industry of the Neandertals and their contemporaries of Europe, Southwest Asia, and northern Africa from 40,000 to 125,000 years ago.

This assemblage of Mousterian tools from southwestern France show the range of Mousterian tool types and their workmanship.

The Mousterian tradition is named after the Neandertal cave site of Le Moustier, in southern France. The presence of Acheulean hand-axes at Mousterian sites is one indication that this culture was ultimately rooted in the older Acheulean tradition. Mousterian tools are generally lighter and smaller than those of earlier traditions. Whereas previously only two or three flakes could be obtained from the entire core, Mousterian toolmakers obtained many smaller flakes, which they skillfully retouched and sharpened. Their tool kits also contained a greater variety of types than the earlier ones: hand-axes, flakes, scrapers, borers, notched flakes for shaving wood, and many types of points that could be attached to wooden shafts to make spears. This variety of tools facilitated more effective use of food resources and enhanced the quality of clothing and shelter.

With the Mousterian cultural traditions, for the first time members of the genus *Homo* could cope with the nearly Arctic conditions that supervened in Eurasia as the glaciers expanded about 70,000 years ago. People likely came to live in cold climates as a result of a slow but steady population increase during the Pleistocene.

Population expansion into previously uninhabited colder regions was made possible through a series of

Anthropology Applied

Stone Tools for Modern Surgeons

When anthropologist Irven DeVore of Harvard University was to have some minor melanomas removed from his face, he did not leave it up to the surgeon to supply his own scalpels. Instead, he had graduate student John Shea make a scalpel. Making a blade of obsidian (a naturally occurring volcanic "glass") by the same techniques used by Upper Paleolithic people to make blades, he hafted this in a wooden handle, using melted pine resin as glue and then lashing it with sinew. After the procedure, the surgeon reported that the obsidian scalpel was superior to metal ones.[a]

DeVore was not the first to undergo surgery in which stone scalpels were used. In 1975, Don Crabtree, then at Idaho State University, prepared the scalpels that his surgeon would use in Crabtree's heart surgery. In 1980, Payson Sheets at the University of Colorado prepared obsidian scalpels that were used successfully in eye surgery. And in 1986, David Pokotylo of the Museum of Anthropology at the University of British Columbia underwent reconstructive surgery on his hand with blades he himself had made (the hafting was done by his museum colleague, Len McFarlane).

The reason for these uses of scalpels modeled on ancient stone tools is that the anthropologists realized that obsidian is superior in almost every way to materials normally used to make scalpels: It is 210 to 1,050 times sharper than surgical steel, 100 to 500 times sharper than a razor blade, and three times sharper than a diamond blade (which not only costs much more but cannot be made with more than 3 mm of cutting edge).

Obsidian blades are easier to cut with and do less damage in the process (under a microscope, incisions made with the sharpest steel blades show torn ragged edges and are littered with bits of displaced flesh).[b] As a consequence, the surgeon has better control over what she or he is doing, and the incisions heal faster with less scarring and pain. Because of the superiority of obsidian scalpels, Sheets went so far as to form a corporation in partnership with Boulder, Colorado, eye surgeon Dr. Firmon Hardenbergh. Together, they developed a means of producing cores of uniform size from molten glass, as well as a machine to detach blades from the cores.

[a]Shreeve, J. (1995). *The Neandertal enigma: Solving the mystery of modern human origins* (p. 134). New York: William Morrow.

[b]Sheets, P. D. (1987). Dawn of a New Stone Age in eye surgery. In R. J. Sharer & W. Ashmore (Eds.), *Archaeology: Discovering our past* (p. 231). Palo Alto, CA: Mayfield.

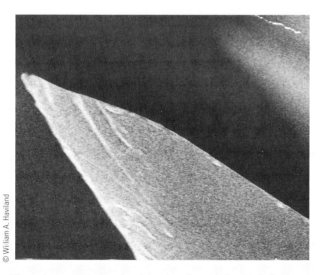
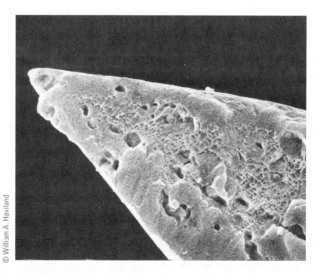

These electron micrographs of the tips of an obsidian blade (left) and a modern steel scalpel illustrate the superiority of the obsidian.

cultural adaptations to cold climate. Under such cold conditions, vegetable foods are only rarely or seasonally available, and meat becomes a critical staple. In particular, animal fats, rather than carbohydrates, become the chief source of energy. Energy-rich animal fat in the diets of cold-climate meat eaters provides them with the extra energy needed for hunting, as well as for keeping the body warm.

The importance of meat to Mousterian tool makers is indicated by an abundance of associated animal bones, often clearly showing cut marks. Frequently, the remains consist almost entirely of very large game—wild cattle (including the European bison known as the aurochs), wild horses, and even mammoths and woolly rhinoceroses. At several sites evidence indicates that particular species were singled out for the hunt. For example, at one

Biocultural

Connection

Paleolithic Prescriptions for the Diseases of Civilization

Though increased life expectancy is often hailed as one of modern civilization's greatest accomplishments, in some ways we in the developed world lead far less healthy lifestyles than our ancestors. Throughout most of our evolutionary history, humans led more physically active lives and ate a more varied low-fat diet than we do now. They did not drink or smoke. They spent their days scavenging or hunting for animal protein while gathering vegetable foods with some insects thrown in for good measure. They stayed fit through traveling great distances each day over the savannah and beyond.

Today we may survive longer but in old age are beset by chronic disease. Heart disease, diabetes, high blood pressure, and cancer shape the experience of old age in wealthy industrialized nations. The prevalence of these "diseases of civilization" has increased rapidly over the past sixty years. Anthropologists Melvin Konner and Marjorie Shostak and physician Boyd Eaton have suggested that our Paleolithic ancestors have provided a prescription for a cure. They propose that as "stone-agers in a fast lane," people's health will improve by returning to the lifestyle to which their bodies are adapted. Such Paleolithic prescriptions are an example of evolutionary medicine—a branch of medical anthropology that uses evolutionary principles to contribute to human health.

Evolutionary medicine bases its prescriptions on the idea that rates of cultural change exceed the rates of biological change. Our food-forager physiology was shaped over millions of years, while the cultural changes leading to contemporary lifestyles have occurred rapidly.

Anthropologist George Armelagos suggests that the downward trajectory for human health began with the earliest human village settlements some 10,000 years ago. When humans began farming rather than gathering, they often switched to single-crop diets. In addition, settlement into villages led directly to the increase in infectious disease. While the cultural invention of antibiotics has cured many infectious diseases, it also led to the increase in chronic diseases.

In many cases, alternative treatments for these conditions stem from evolutionary medicine.

---

site in the French Pyrenees, well over 90 percent of the faunal assemblage (representing at least 108 animals) consists of large members of the cattle family. These bones accumulated at the foot of a steep riverside escarpment, over which the animals were evidently stampeded.

Remains found at other Mousterian sites indicate similar mass-hunting techniques. At La Quina in western France, a dense accumulation of wild cattle, horse, and reindeer bones (many with cut marks from butchering) occurred at the base of a steep cliff. At another site in the Channel Islands just off the northwest coast of France, dense deposits of mammoth and woolly rhinoceros bones indicate use of a deep coastal ravine for cliff-fall hunting.

Clearly, the Neandertals were not merely casual or opportunistic hunters but engaged in carefully planned and organized hunting of very large and potentially dangerous game.[7] This required careful planning, forethought, and logistical organization. The active lifestyle and healthy diet characteristic of ancient hominoids, australopithecines, and early *Homo* continued into the Middle and Upper Paleolithic. These ancient lifeways may provide keys to improving the health of people today, as discussed in the Biocultural Connection.

Mousterian hunting implements, which are more standardized with respect to size and shape than are household tools, also reflect the importance of hunting for these ancient peoples. At the same time, the complexity of the tool kit needed for survival in a cold climate may have decreased the mobility of the users of these possessions. Decreased mobility is suggested by the greater depth of deposits and thus longer habitation at Mousterian sites compared with those from the earlier Lower Paleolithic. Such sites contain evidence of long production sequences, resharpening and discarding of tools, and large-scale butchering and cooking of game. Pebble paving, construction of simple walls, and the digging of postholes and artificial pits shows how the inhabitants worked to improve living conditions in some caves and rock shelters. This evidence suggests that Mousterian sites were not simply stopovers in peoples' constant quest for food.

In addition, evidence suggests that Neandertal social organization had developed to the point of providing care for physically disabled members of the group. For the first time, the remains of old people are well represented in the fossil record. Furthermore, many elderly Neandertal skeletons show evidence of trauma having been treated, with extensive healing of wounds and little or no infection.[8]

One particularly dramatic example is Shanidar Cave in Iraq, which includes the remains of a partially blind

---

[7]Mellars, P. (1989). Major issues in the emergence of modern humans. *Current Anthropology 30*, 356–357.

[8]Conroy, G. C. (1997). *Reconstructing human origins: A modern synthesis* (p. 427). New York: Norton.

man (the eye socket indicates serious injury) with a withered upper arm indicating loss of the arm from the elbow on down. Remains of another individual found at Krapina in Croatia suggests the possibility of surgical amputation of a hand. In La Chapelle, France, fossil remains indicate prolonged survival of a man badly crippled by arthritis. The earliest example comes from a 200,000-year-old site in France, where a toothless man was able to survive probably because others in his group processed or pre-chewed his food so he could swallow it. Whether this evidence indicates true compassion on the part of these early people is not clear; but it is certain that cultural factors helped ensure survival, allowing individuals to provide care for others.

The Symbolic Life of Neandertals

Indications of a rich symbolic life of Neandertals exist. For example, at several sites, there is clear evidence for deliberate burial of the dead. This is one reason for the relative abundance of reasonably complete Neandertal skeletons. The difficulty of digging an adult-sized grave without access to metal shovels suggests how important a social activity this was. Moreover, intentional positioning of dead bodies, whatever the specific reason may have been, constitutes evidence of symbolism.[9]

To date, at least seventeen sites in Europe, South Africa, and Southwest Asia include Middle Paleolithic burials. For example, at Kebara Cave in Israel, around 60,000 years ago, a Neandertal male aged between 25 and 35 years was placed in a pit on his back, with his arms folded over his chest and abdomen. Some time later, after complete decay of attaching ligaments, the grave was reopened and the skull removed (a practice that, interestingly, is sometimes seen in burials in the same region roughly 50,000 years later).

Another example is from Shanidar Cave in Iraq, where evidence was found of a burial accompanied by what may have been funeral ceremonies. In the back of the cave a Neandertal was buried in a pit. Pollen analysis of the soil around the skeleton indicated that flowers had been placed below the body and in a wreath about the head. Because the key pollen types came from insect-pollinated flowers, few if any of the pollen grains could have found their way into the pit via air currents. The flowers in question consist solely of varieties valued in historic times for their medicinal properties.

Other evidence for symbolic behavior in Mousterian culture comes from the naturally occurring pigments: manganese dioxide and the red and yellow forms of ochre as described above. Recovered chunks of these pigments reveal clear evidence of scraping to produce pow-

© Kenneth Garrett/National Geographic Images

The position of the body and the careful removal of the skull indicate that the fossil from Kebara Cave in Israel was deliberately buried there about 60,000 years ago.

der, as well as facets, like those that appear on a crayon, from use. A Mousterian "artist" also applied color to the carved and shaped section of a mammoth tooth about 50,000 years ago. This mammoth tooth may have been made for cultural symbolic purposes. In addition, it is similar to objects made of bone and ivory dated to the later Upper Paleolithic and to the *churingas* made of wood by Australian aborigines.

The mammoth tooth, which was once smeared with red ochre, has a highly polished face suggesting it was handled a lot. Microscopic examination reveals that it was never provided with a working edge for any utilitarian purpose. Such objects imply, as archaeologist Alexander Marshack observed, "that the Neandertals did in fact have conceptual models and maps as well as problem-solving capacities comparable to, if not equal to, those found among anatomically modern humans."[10]

Evidence for symbolic activity on the part of Neandertals raises the possibility of the presence and use

[9]Schepartz, L. A. (1993). Language and modern human origins. *Yearbook of Physical Anthropology 36,* 113.

[10]Marshack, A. (1989). Evolution of the human capacity: The symbolic evidence. *Yearbook of Physical Anthropology 32,* 22.

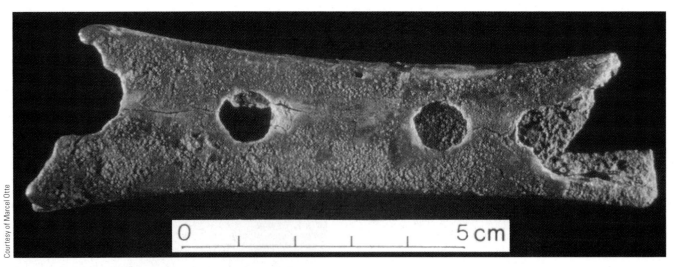

The first musical instrument? There is a strong possibility that this object, found in trash left by Neandertals, is the remains of a flute made of bone.

of musical instruments, such as a proposed bone flute from a Mousterian site in Slovenia in southern Europe. This object, consisting of a hollow bone with perforations, has sparked controversy. Some see it as nothing more than a cave bear bone that was chewed on by carnivores—hence the perforations. Its discoverer, French archaeologist Marcel Otte, on the other hand, sees it as a flute.

Unfortunately, the object is fragmentary; surviving are five holes, four on one side and one on the opposite side. The regular spacing of the four holes, fitting perfectly to the fingers of a human hand, and the location of the fifth hole at the base of the opposite side, at the natural location of the thumb, all lend credence to the flute hypothesis. While signs of gnawing by animals are present on this bone, they are superimposed on traces of human activity.[11] Were it found in an Upper Paleolithic context, it would probably be accepted as a flute without argument. However, because its early date indicates it was made by a Neandertal, the interpretation of this object is tied to the larger controversy about Neandertals' cultural abilities and their place in human evolutionary history.

Speech and Language in the Middle Paleolithic

Among modern humans, the sharing of thoughts and ideas, as well as the transmission of culture from one generation to the next, is dependent upon language. Because the Neandertals and other Middle Paleolithic *Homo*

had modern-sized brains and a sophisticated Mousterian tool kit, it might be supposed that they had some form of language.

As pointed out by paleoanthropologist Stanley Ambrose, the Mousterian tool kit included composite tools involving the assembly of parts in different configurations to produce functionally different tools. He likens this ordered assembly of parts into tools to grammatical language, "because hierarchical assemblies of sounds produce meaningful phrases and sentences, and changing word order changes meaning."[12] Furthermore, "a composite tool may be analogous to a sentence, but explaining how to make one is the equivalent of a recipe or a short story."[13] In addition, the evidence for the manufacture of objects of symbolic significance supports the presence of language in Middle Paleolithic *Homo*. Objects such as the colored section of mammoth tooth already described would seem to have required some form of explanation through language.

While the archaeological evidence supports the symbolic thinking characteristic of language, specific anatomical features can be examined to determine whether this language was spoken or gestural. Some have argued that the Neandertals lacked the physical features necessary for speech. For example, an early 20th-century reconstruction of the angle at the base of the Neandertal skull was said to indicate that the larynx was higher in the throat than it is in modern humans, precluding humanlike speech. This reconstruction is now known to be faulty. Further, the hyoid bone associated with the muscles of speech in the larynx is preserved from a skeleton

[11]Otte, M. (2000). On the suggested bone flute from Slovenia. *Current Anthropology 41*, 271.

[12]Ambrose, S. H. (2001). Paleolithic technology and human evolution. *Science 291*, 1,751.

[13]Ibid.

from the Kebara Cave burial in Israel. Its shape is identical to that of contemporary humans, indicating that the vocal tract was adequate for speech.

With respect to the brain, paleoneurologists, working from endocranial casts, are agreed that Neandertals had the neural development necessary for spoken language. Indeed, they argue that the changes associated with language began even before the appearance of archaic *Homo sapiens*,[14] as described in previous chapters. Consistent is the size of the hypoglossal canal, which in Neandertals is like that of modern humans and unlike that of apes.[15] As discussed in the previous chapter, this feature is apparent in *Homo* fossils that are at least 400,000 years old and indicates an ability to make the tongue movements necessary for articulate speech.

Consistent, too, is an expanded thoracic vertebral canal (the thorax is the upper part of the body), a feature Neandertals share with modern humans but not early *Homo erectus* (or any other primate). This feature suggests the increased breath control required for speech.[16] This control enables production of long phrases or single expirations of breath, punctuated with quick inhalations at meaningful linguistic breaks.

Another argument—that a relatively flat base in Neandertal skulls would have prevented speech—has no merit, as some modern adults show as much flattening, yet have no trouble talking. Clearly, when the anatomical evidence is considered in its totality, there seems no compelling reason to deny Neandertals the ability to speak.

The recent discovery of a "language gene" by Svante Pääbo and colleagues at the Max Planck Institute for Evolutionary Anthropology in Leipzig, Germany, adds an interesting new dimension to the study of the evolution of language.[17] The gene, called FOXP2 found on chromosome 7, was identified through the analysis of a family in which members spanning several generations have severe language problems. Changes in the gene are hypothesized to control the ability to make fine movements of the mouth and larynx necessary for spoken language. The identification of this gene in humans allowed scientists to compare its structure to that found in other mammalian species.

The human FOXP2 gene differs from versions of the gene found in chimpanzee, gorilla, orangutan, rhesus macaque, and mouse. While these differences among living species can be known, applying this knowledge to the earlier members of the genus *Homo* is far more difficult. We do not know precisely when in human evolution the human form of the FOXP2 gene appeared or whether this gene was associated with the formation of a new species of *Homo*.

In light of these genetic discoveries it is also interesting to consider the work done on language capacity in the great apes. For example, in her work with the bonobo named Kanzi, Sue Savage-Rumbaugh documented his ability to understand hundreds of spoken words and associate them with lexigrams (pictures of words) on a computer display while unable to create the sounds himself.[18]

CULTURE, SKULLS, AND MODERN HUMAN ORIGINS

For Middle Paleolithic *Homo*, cultural adaptive abilities relate to the fact that brain size was comparable to that of people living today. Archaeological evidence indicates sophisticated technology, as well as conceptual thought of considerable complexity, matching the increased cranial capacity. During this same time period, large-brained individuals with skulls with an anatomically modern shape began to appear. The earliest specimens with this skull shape—a more vertical forehead, diminished brow ridge, and a chin—appear first in Africa and later in Asia and Europe. Whether the derived features in the skull indicate the appearance of a new species with improved cultural capabilities remains a hotly debated question.

The transition from the Middle Paleolithic to the tools of the Upper Paleolithic occurred around 40,000 years ago, some 100,000 years or so after the appearance of the first anatomically modern specimens. The Upper Paleolithic is known not only for a veritable explosion of tool industries, but also for clear artistic expression preserved in representative sculptures, paintings, and engravings (see Chapter 9). But the earliest anatomically modern humans used tools of the Middle Paleolithic traditions like the Neandertals and other archaic forms.

The relationship between cultural developments of the Upper Paleolithic and underlying biological differences between anatomically modern humans and archaic forms remains one of the most contentious debates in paleoanthropology. Discussions concerning the fate of

[14]Schepartz, L. A. (1993). Language and modern human origins. *Yearbook of Physical Anthropology 36*, 98.

[15]Cartmill, M. (1998). The gift of gab. *Discover 19* (11), 62.

[16]MacLarnon, A. M., & Hewitt, G. P. (1999). The evolution of human speech: The role of enhanced breathing control. *American Journal of Physical Anthropology 109*, 341–363.

[17]Lai, C. S. L., et al. (2001). A forkhead-domain gene is mutated in severe speech and language disorder. *Nature, 413*, 519–523; Enard, W., et al. (2002). Molecular evolution of FOXP2, a gene involved in speech and language. *Nature 418*, 869–872.

[18]Savage-Rumbaugh, S., & Lewin, R. (1994). *Kanzi: The ape at the brink of the human mind*. New York: Wiley.

the Neandertals and their cultural abilities are integral to this debate. Whether or not a new kind of human—anatomically modern with correspondingly superior intellectual and creative abilities—is responsible for the cultural explosion of the Upper Paleolithic is a difficult question to resolve. The biological and cultural evidence preserved in fossil and archaeological records, respectively, do not tell a simple story.

On a biological level, the great debate can be distilled to a question of whether one, some, or all populations of the archaic groups played a role in the evolution of modern *H. sapiens*. Those supporting the multiregional hypothesis argue for a simultaneous local transition from *Homo erectus* to modern *Homo sapiens* throughout the parts of the world inhabited by members of the genus *Homo*. By contrast, those supporting a theory of recent African origins argue that all contemporary people are derived from one single population of archaic *H. sapiens* from Africa. This model proposes that the improved cultural capabilities of anatomically modern humans allowed this group to replace other archaic forms as they began to migrate out of Africa some time after 100,000 years ago. Both theories are explored in detail below.

The Multiregional Hypothesis

As several anthropologists have noted, African, Chinese, and Southeast Asian fossils of archaic *Homo sapiens* imply continuity within these respective populations, from *Homo erectus* through to modern *Homo sapiens*,[19] and lend strong support to the interpretation that there was genetic continuity in these regions. For example, in China Pleistocene fossils from the genus *Homo* consistently have small forward-facing cheeks and flatter faces

---

[19]Wolpoff, M. H., Wu, X. Z. & Thorne, A. G. (1984). Modern *Homo sapiens* origins: A general theory of hominid evolution involving fossil evidence from East Asia (pp. 411–483). In F. H. Smith & F. Spencer (Eds.), *The origins of modern humans*. New York: Alan R. Liss; Wolpoff, M. H., & Caspari, R. (1997). *Race and human evolution*. New York: Simon & Schuster; Pope, G. C. (1992). Craniofacial evidence for the origin of modern humans in China. *Yearbook of Physical Anthropology 35*, 291.

multiregional hypothesis The hypothesis that modern humans originated through a process of simultaneous local transition from *Homo erectus* to *Homo sapiens* throughout the inhabited world.

recent African origins or "Eve" hypothesis The hypothesis that all modern people are derived from one single population of archaic *H. sapiens* from Africa who migrated out of Africa after 100,000 years ago, replacing all other archaic forms due to their superior cultural capabilities. Also called the *out of Africa hypothesis*.

than their contemporaries elsewhere, as is still true today. In Southeast Asia and Australia, by contrast, skulls are consistently robust, with huge cheeks and forward projection of the jaws.

In this model, gene flow among populations keeps the human species unified throughout the Pleistocene. No speciation events remove ancestral populations such as *Homo erectus* or Neandertals from the line leading to *Homo sapiens*. Although proponents of the **multiregional hypothesis** accept the idea of continuity from the earliest European fossils through the Neandertals to living people, many other paleoanthropologists reject the idea that Neandertals were involved in the ancestry of modern Europeans.

The Recent African Origins or "Eve" Hypothesis

The **recent African origins or "Eve" hypothesis** (also called the *out of Africa hypothesis*) states that anatomically modern humans are descended from one specific population of *H. sapiens*, replacing not just the Neandertals but other populations of archaic *H. sapiens* as our ancestors spread out of their original homeland. This idea did not originate from fossils, but from a relatively new technique that uses mitochondrial DNA (mtDNA) to reconstruct family trees.

Unlike nuclear DNA (in the cell nucleus), mtDNA is located in the mitochondria, the cellular structures that produce the energy needed to keep cells alive. Because sperm contribute virtually no mtDNA to the fertilized egg, all of mtDNA is inherited only from one's mother and is not subject to recombination through meiosis and fertilization with each succeeding generation as is nuclear DNA. Therefore, changes in mtDNA over time occur only through mutation. By comparing the mtDNA of living individuals from diverse geographic populations, anthropologists and molecular biologists seek to determine when and where modern *H. sapiens* originated (Figure 8.4).

As widely reported in the popular press (including cover stories in *Newsweek* and *Time*), preliminary results suggest that the mitochondrial DNA of all living humans could be traced back to a "mitochondrial Eve" who lived in Africa some 200,000 years ago. If so, all other populations of archaic *H. sapiens*, as well as non-African *H. erectus*, would have to be ruled out of the ancestry of modern humans.

For many years, the absence of good fossil evidence from Africa to support the recent African origins hypothesis has been a weakness of this theory. In 2003, however, skulls of two adults and one child described as anatomically modern discovered in 1997 in Ethiopia in East Africa were reconstructed and dated to 160,000 years ago

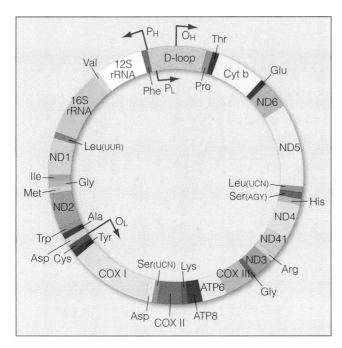

Figure 8.4
The 16,569 bases in mitochondrial DNA (mtDNA) are organized into circular chromosomes present in large numbers in every cell. The human mtDNA sequence has been entirely sequenced with functional genes identified. Because mtDNA is maternally inherited and not subject to recombination it can be used to establish evolutionary relationships. However, the effects of population size on the amount of mtDNA variation preserved, complicates using contemporary mtDNA variation to calibrate a molecular clock.

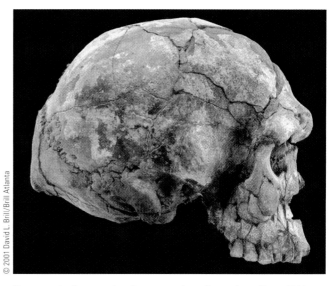

The recently discovered well-preserved specimens from Herto, Ethiopia, provide the best fossil evidence in support of the recent African origins hypothesis. Though these fossils unquestionably possess an anatomically modern appearance, they are still relatively robust. In addition, the question of whether the higher skull and forehead indicate superior cultural abilities still remains open.

(see Anthropologists of Note).[20] The discoverers of these fossils called them *Homo sapiens idaltu* (meaning "elder" in the local Afar language). While conceding that these skulls are robust, they believe that these skulls have conclusively proved the recent African origins hypothesis, relegating Neandertals to a side branch of human evolution with these finds.

RECONCILING THE EVIDENCE

Though the recent African origins hypothesis is the majority position among Western paleoanthropologists, the theory does not prevail throughout the globe. Chinese paleoanthropologists, for example, favor the multiregional hypothesis because it fits well with the fossil discoveries from Asia and Australia. By contrast, the recent African origins hypothesis depends more upon the interpretation of fossils and cultural remains from Europe, Africa, and Southwest Asia

The recent African origins hypothesis can be critiqued on several additional grounds. For example, the

molecular evidence upon which it is based has come under considerable criticism. Genetic studies indicate that Africa was not the sole source of DNA in modern humans.[21] In addition, because both theories proposed African origins for the human line, molecular data could be interpreted as evidence supporting the African origins of the genus *Homo,* rather than the more recent species *Homo sapiens.* Both models place ultimate human origins firmly in Africa.

Other assumptions made by DNA analysts are problematic. For example, it is assumed that rates of mutation are steady, when in fact they can be notoriously uneven. Another assumption is that mtDNA is not subject to selection, when in fact variants have been implicated in epilepsy and a disease of the eye.[22] A third is that DNA is seen as traveling exclusively *from* Africa, when it is known that, over the past 10,000 years, there has been plenty of movement of humans into Africa as well. In fact, one study of DNA carried on the Y chromosome (the sex chromosome inherited exclusively in the male line) suggests that some DNA seen on the Y chromosome of some Africans was introduced from Asia, where it originated some 200,000 years ago.[23] Nevertheless, recent work on the Y chromosome by anthropologist and

[20]White, T., et al. (2003). Pleistocene *Homo sapiens* from the Middle Awash, Ethiopia. *Nature 423,* 742–747.

[21]Templeton, A. R. (1995). The "Eve" Hypothesis: A genetic critique and reanalysis. *American Anthropologist 95* (1), 51–72.

[22]Shreeve, J. (1995). *The Neandertal enigma: Solving the mystery of modern human origins* (p. 121). New York: William Morrow.

[23]Gibbons, A. (1997). Ideas on human origins evolve at anthropology gathering. *Science 276,* 535–536.

Anthropologists of Note

Berhane Asfaw (b. 1953–) ▪ Xinzhi Wu (b. 1930)

Born in Addis Ababa, Ethiopia, in 1953, **Berhane Asfaw** is a world-renowned paleoanthropologist leading major expeditions in Ethiopia. He is co-leader of the international Middle Awash Research Project, the research team responsible for the discovery of ancestral fossils dating from the entire 6-million-year course of human evolutionary history, including *Ardipithecus ramidus, Australopithecus afarensis, Australopithecus garhi, Homo erectus,* and, most recently, the *Homo sapiens idaltu* fossils from Herto, Ethiopia.

At the June 2003 press conference, organized by Teshome Toga, Ethiopia's minister of culture, Asfaw described the Herto specimens as the oldest "anatomically modern" humans, likening Ethiopia to the "Garden of Eden." This conference marked a shift in the Ethiopian government's stance toward the paleoanthropological research spanning Asfaw's career. Previous discoveries in the Middle Awash were also very important, but the government did not participate or support this research.

Asfaw entered the discipline of paleoanthropology through a program administered by the Leakey Foundation providing fellowships for Africans to pursue graduate studies in Europe and the United States. Since this program's inception in the late 1970s, the Leakey Foundation has awarded sixty-eight fellowships totaling $1.2 million to Kenyans, Ethiopians, and Tanzanians to pursue graduate education in paleoanthropology.

Asfaw, mentored by American paleoanthropologist Desmond Clark at the University of California, Berkeley, was among the earliest fellows in this program. They first met in 1979 when Asfaw was a senior studying geology in Addis Ababa. Asfaw obtained his doctorate in 1988 and returned to Ethiopia, where he had few Ethiopian anthropological colleagues and the government had halted fossil exploration. Since that time, Asfaw has recruited and mentored many Ethiopian scholars, including Sileshi Semaw (see Chapter 7), and now has about a dozen on his team. Local scientists can protect the antiquities, keep fossils from disappearing, and marshal government support.

Asfaw's leadership in paleoanthropology has played a key role in helping the Ethiopian government to recognize how important prehistory is for the country of Ethiopia.

Xinzhi Wu is one of China's foremost paleoanthropological scholars, contributing to the development of the discipline for the past fifty years. As with many other paleoanthropologists, the study of human anatomy has been of vital importance to him. He began his academic career with a degree from Shanghai Medical College followed by teaching in the Department of Human Anatomy at the Medical College in Dalian before beginning graduate studies in paleoanthropology. He is presently a professor at the Chinese Academy of Sciences Institute of Vertebrate Paleontology and Paleoanthroplogy in Beijing and the honorary president of the Chinese Society of Anatomical Sciences.

In addition to managing excavations in China and other parts of Asia, Wu has played a major role in the development of theories about modern human origins in cooperation with scholars internationally. He collaborated with Milford Wolpoff of the United States and Alan Thorne of Australia in the development of the theory of multiregional continuity for modern human origins. This theory fits well with the Asian fossil evidence proposing an important place for *Homo erectus* in

modern human origins. Interestingly it builds upon the model for human origins developed by Franz Weidenreich.

According to Wu, early humans from China are as old if not older than humans anyplace else. He suggests that the reason more fossils have been found in Africa recently is that more excavations are occurring there than elsewhere.

Zhoukoudian remains a site of particular importance for Wu, as it documents continuous habitation of early humans and one of the earliest controlled use of fire. Wu has predicted that more important discoveries will still be made at Zhoukoudian as one-third of this site has still not been fully excavated. The Chinese government has responded to Wu's suggestions and is presently constructing a 2.4-square kilometer "Peking Man" exhibition and paleoanthropology research area at Zhoukoudian.

Wu has welcomed many international scholars to China to study the Asian evidence. He also has led efforts to make descriptions of fossil material available in English. Collaborating with U.S. anthropologist Frank Poirier, he published the comprehensive volume *Human Evolution in China,* describing all of the fossil evidence and archaeological sites with great accuracy and detail.

© 1988 David L. Brill

The notion of a single African "Eve," mother of all humans, living a mere 200,000 years ago, captured the public's imagination and the media's attention. Both the recent African origins hypothesis and multiregional continuity hypothesis place the roots of the human line firmly in Africa.

geneticist Spencer Wells traces the human lineage to a single population living in Africa about 60,000 years ago.[24]

Since 1997, studies of mitochondrial DNA have not been limited to living people. In that year, mtDNA was extracted from the original German Neandertal remains, and two other Neandertals have since been studied. Because the mtDNA of each of these differs substantially from modern Europeans, many have concluded that there can be no Neandertal ancestry in living humans and that Neandertals must constitute a separate species that went extinct.

But biological anthropologist John Relethford (a specialist in anthropological genetics) points out that these conclusions are premature.[25] For one thing, the average differences are not as great as those seen among living subspecies of the single species of chimpanzee. For another, the differences between populations separated in time by tens of thousands of years tell us nothing about differences between populations contemporaneous with each other. More meaningful would be comparison of the DNA from a late Neandertal with an early anatomically modern European.

Finally, if we are to reject Neandertals in the ancestry of modern Europeans because their DNA cannot be

detected in their supposed ancestors, then we must also reject any connection between a 40,000- to 62,000-year-old skeleton from Australia (that everyone agrees is anatomically modern) and more recent native Australians. In this case, a mtDNA sequence present in an ancient human seems to have become extinct, in which case we must allow the same possibility for the Neandertals.[26] In short, it is definitely premature to remove from modern human ancestry all populations of archaic *H. sapiens* save those of Africa. Not even the Neandertals can be excluded.

Though the recent fossil discoveries certainly provide evidence of the earliest anatomically modern specimens in Africa, they do not resolve the relationship between biological change in the shape of the skull and culture change as preserved in the archaeological record. The changes in the archaeological record and the appearance of anatomically modern skulls are separated by some 100,000 years. The evidence from Southwest Asia is particularly interesting in this regard. Here, at a variety of sites dated to between 50,000 and 100,000 years ago, fossils described as both anatomically modern and Neandertal are present and associated with Mousterian technology.

Nevertheless, recent African origins proponents argue that anatomically modern people co-existed for a time with other archaic populations until the superior cultural capacities of the "moderns" resulted in extinction of the archaic peoples. Especially clear evidence of this is said to exist in Europe, where Neandertals and "moderns" are said to co-exist in close proximity between 30,000 and 40,000 years ago. However, defining fossils as either Neandertals or "moderns" illustrates the difficulty with defining a distinct biological species, given the presence of variation found in humans.

If we think in terms of varied populations, as seen in living humans today,[27] we find that features reminiscent of modern humans can be discerned in some of the latest Neandertals. A specimen from Saint Césaire in France, for example, has a higher forehead and chin. A number of other Neandertals, too, show incipient chin development as well as reduced facial protrusion and smaller brow ridges. Conversely, the earliest anatomically modern human skulls from Europe often exhibit features reminiscent of Neandertals (see Chapter 9). In addition, some typical Neandertal features such as the occipital bun are found in diverse living populations today such as Bushmen from Southern Africa, Finns and Lapps from Scandanavia, and Australian aborigines. Accordingly, we might view the population of this region between 30,000 and 40,000 years ago as a varied one, with some individu-

[24]Wells, S. (2002). *The journey of man: A genetic odyssey.* Princeton, NJ: Princeton University Press.

[25]Relethford, J. H. (2001). Absence of regional affinities of Neandertal DNA with living humans does not reject multiregional evolution. *American Journal of Physical Anthropology 115,* 95–98.

[26]Gibbons, A. (2001). The riddle of coexistence. *Science 291,* 1,726.

[27]Gould, S. J. (1996). *Full house: The spread of excellence from Plato to Darwin* (pp. 72–73). New York: Harmony Books.

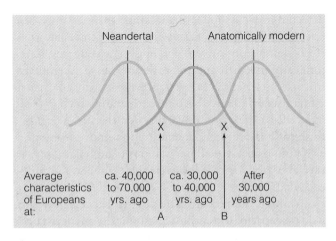

Figure 8.5

Graphically portrayed here is a shift in average characteristics of an otherwise varied population over time from Neandertal to more modern features. Between 30,000 and 40,000 years ago, we would expect to find individuals with characteristics such as those of the Saint Césaire Neandertal (A) and the almost (but not quite) modern Cro-Magnon (B; this fossil is discussed in Chapter 9).

als retaining a stronger Neandertal heritage than others, in whom modern characteristics are more prominent (Figure 8.5).

A mix of "modern" and Neandertal features is so strong in a child's skeleton recently found in Portugal as to lead several specialists to regard it as clear evidence of hybridization, or successful reproduction between the two groups.[28] This would mean that the two forms are

---

[28]Holden, C. (1999). Ancient child burial uncovered in Portugal. *Science 283*, 169.

Aurignacian tradition   Tool-making tradition in Europe and western Asia at the beginning of the Upper Paleolithic.

of a single rather than separate species. Others, of course, argue that features interpreted as Neandertal-like might instead be related to this child's "chunky" build.[29]

Scientists supporting the hypothesis that Neandertals are members of the species *Homo sapiens* suggest that the simplest explanation that accounts for all the evidence is that all of these fossils belong to a single varied population, with some individuals showing more of typical Neandertal features than others. This accords with archaeological evidence that the intellectual abilities of "late Neandertals" were no different from those of "early moderns."[30]

It is difficult to find evidence for something in the physical or mental makeup of Neandertals that would have prevented them from leading a typical Upper Paleolithic way of life. In fact, the latest Neandertals of Europe developed their own Upper Paleolithic technology (the Châtelperronian) comparable to the industries used by anatomically modern *H. sapiens*. No earlier than 36,500 years ago,[31] a new Upper Paleolithic technology, known as the **Aurignacian tradition**—named after Aurignac, France, where tools of this sort were first discovered—appeared in Europe (Figure 8.6).

Though commonly considered to have spread from Southwest Asia, a recent re-analysis failed to sustain this idea, suggesting instead that the Aurignacian is a distinctively European development.[32] Skeletal remains are rarely associated with Aurignacian tools, although ana-

---

[29]Tattersall, I., & Schwartz, J. H. (1999). Hominids and hybrids: The place of Neanderthals in human evolution. *PNAS 96* (13), 7,117–7,119.

[30]d'Errico, F., et al. (1998). Neandertal acculturation in Western Europe? *Current Anthropology 39*, 521.

[31]Zilhão, J. (2000). Fate of the Neandertals. *Archaeology 53* (4), 30.

[32]Clark, G. A. (2002). Neandertal archaeology: Implications for our origins. *American Anthropologist 104* (1), 50–67.

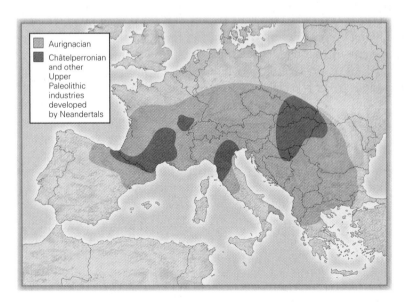

Figure 8.6

Between 30,000 and 36,500 years ago, Upper Paleolithic industries developed from the Mousterian tradition by European Neandertals co-existed with the Aurignacian industry, usually associated with anatomically modern humans.

Living people today such as this native Australian do not all meet the definition of anatomical modernity proposed in the recent African origins model. Some paleoanthropologists suggest that this proves that the definition is problematic because all living people are clearly full-fledged members of the species *Homo sapiens*.

tomically modern humans are generally considered the makers of these tools. A notable exception to this notion is the central European site of Vindija, Croatia, where Neandertals are associated with an Aurignacian split-bone point.[33]

However, some argue that the Upper Paleolithic technology of the Neandertals was a crude imitation of the truc technological advancements practiced by anatomically modern humans. In some respects, Neandertals outdid their anatomically modern contemporaries, as in the use of red ochre, a substance less frequently used by Aurignacian peoples than by their late Neandertal neighbors.[34] This cannot be a case of borrowing ideas and techniques from Aurignacians, as these developments clearly predate the Aurignacian.[35]

Neandertals and anatomically modern humans also co-existed in Southwest Asia long before the cultural innovations of the Upper Paleolithic. Here neither the skeletal nor the archaeological evidence supports cultural difference between the fossil groups or absolute biological difference. Although Neandertal skeletons are clearly present at sites such as Kebara and Shanidar caves, skeletons from some older sites have been described as anatomically modern. At the Mount Carmel site of Qafzeh in Israel, for example, 90,000-year-old skeletons are said to show none of the Neandertal hallmarks; although their faces and bodies are large and heavily built by today's standards, they are nonetheless claimed to be within the range of living peoples. Yet, a statistical study comparing a number of measurements among Qafzeh, Upper Paleolithic, and Neandertal skulls found those from Qafzeh to fall in between the anatomically modern and Neandertal norms, though slightly closer to the Neandertals.[36] Nor is the dentition functionally distinguishable when Qafzeh and Neandertal are compared.[37]

[33]Karavani, I., & Smith, F. H. (2000). More on the Neanderthal problem: The Vindija case. *Current Anthropology 41,* 839.

[34]Bednarik, R. G. (1995). Concept-mediated marking in the lower Paleolithic. *Current Anthropology 36,* 606.

[35]Zilhão, J. (2000). Fate of the Neandertals. *Archaeology 53* (4), 40.

[36]Corruccini, R. S. (1992). Metrical reconsideration of the Skhul IV and IX and Border Cave I crania in the context of modern human origins. *American Journal of Physical Anthropology 87,* 433–445.

[37]Brace, C. L. (2000). *Evolution in an anthropological view* (p. 206). Walnut Creek, CA: Altamira.

While skeletons from another Mount Carmel site of the same period called Skhul are similar to those from Qafzeh, they were also part of a population whose continuous range of variation included individuals with markedly Neandertal characteristics. Furthermore, the idea of two distinctly different but co-existing populations receives no support from the archaeological evidence. Individuals living at Skhul and Qafzeh were making and using the same Mousterian tools as those at Kebara and Shanidar, arguing against biologically distinct groups with different cultural abilities.

The examination of sites continuously inhabited throughout the Upper Pleistocene provides no significant evidence for behavioral differences between Middle Paleolithic and early Upper Paleolithic at these sites. For example, the Upper Paleolithic people who used Kebara Cave continued to live in exactly the same way as their Neandertal predecessors: They procured the same foods, processed them in the same way, used similar hearths, and disposed of their trash in the same way. The only evident difference is that the Neandertals did not bank their fires for warmth with small stones or cobbles as did their Upper Paleolithic successors.[38]

Nevertheless, by 28,000 years ago, many of the extreme anatomical features seen in archaic groups like Neandertals seem to disappear from the fossil record in Europe and Southwest Asia. Instead, people with higher foreheads, smoother brow ridges, and distinct chins seemed to have Europe more or less to themselves. However, an examination of the full range of individual human variation across the globe and into the present reveals contemporary humans with skulls not meeting the anatomical definition of modernity proposed in the standard evolutionary arguments.[39] Similarly, many Neandertal features can be seen in living people today such as the occipital buns mentioned earlier. As is usual in human populations, contemporary people and Upper Paleolithic people exhibit considerable physical variability.

---

[38]Corruccini, R. S. (1992). Metrical reconsideration of the Skhul IV and IX and Border Cave I crania in the context of modern human origins. *American Journal of Physical Anthropology 87*, 436.

[39]Wolpoff, M. H., & Caspari, R. (1997). *Race and human evolution.* New York: Simon & Schuster.

RACE AND HUMAN EVOLUTION

The Neandertal question can be viewed as more than simply a fascinating discussion about interpreting the fossil evidence. It raises fundamental issues about the relationship between biological and cultural variation. Can a series of biological features indicate particular cultural abilities?

As we examined the fossil record throughout this chapter and others, we made inferences about the cultural capabilities of our ancestors based on biological features in combination with archaeological features. The increased brain size of *Homo habilis* noted around 2.5 million years ago supported the notion that these ancestors were capable of more complex cultural activities than australopithecines, including the manufacture of stone tools. When we get closer to the present, can we make the same kinds of assumptions? Can we say that only the anatomically modern humans with high foreheads and reduced brow ridges and not archaic *Homo sapiens,* even with their modern-sized brains, were capable of making sophisticated tools and representational art?

Supporters of the multiregional hypothesis argue that we cannot.[40] They suggest that using a series of biological features to represent a type of human being (Neandertals) with certain cultural capacities (inferior) is like making assumptions about cultural capabilities of living humans based on their appearance. In living people, such an assumption represents a stereotype at best or racist prejudice at worst. Supporters of the recent African origins hypothesis counter that because their theory embraces African human origins, it could hardly be considered prejudicial.

While paleoanthropologists all acknowledge African origins for the first bipeds and the genus *Homo,* considerable disagreement exists with regard to the interpretation of the relationship between biological change and culture change as we approach the present. The fossil and archaeological evidence from the Middle Paleolithic does not indicate a simple one-to-one correspondence between cultural innovations and a biological change preserved in the shape of the skull.

---

[40]Ibid.

Questions for Reflection

1. When we imagine the appearance and behavior of the members of the genus *Homo* that lived closer to the present and possessed brains the size of modern humans, we are challenged to avoid imposing contemporary beliefs upon the mysteries of the past. What aspects of the reconstruction of Middle Paleolithic *Homo* are the most free from present-day beliefs?

2. What does it mean to be "modern," biologically or culturally? How should we define "human"?

3. Compare and contrast the recent African origins and multiregional hypotheses for the origins of humans. Describe

the kinds of data each of these theories use to support their arguments.

4. How do you feel personally about the possibility of having Neandertals as part of your ancestry? How might you relate the Neandertal debates to stereotyping or racism in contemporary society?

5. What is the difference between speech and language? Describe the evidence for each in Neandertals.

Suggested Readings

Shreeve, J. (1995). *The Neandertal enigma: Solving the mystery of modern human origins.* New York: William Morrow.

Shreeve is a science writer who has written extensively about human evolution. This book is engagingly written and covers most of the major issues in the Neandertal–modern debate.

Stringer, C. B., & McKie, R. (1996). *African exodus: The origins of modern humanity.* London: Jonathan Cape.

Chris Stringer of the British Museum is a leading champion of the recent African origins hypothesis; this book is a vigorous presentation of his arguments.

Trinkaus, E., & Shipman, P. (1992). *The Neandertals: Changing the image of mankind.* New York: Knopf.

The senior author of this book is a long-time specialist on the Neandertals. Eminently readable, the book chronicles the changing interpretations of these fossils since the first recognized find in 1856. For a good look at what is known about the Neandertals, there is no better place to go than this.

Wells, S. (2002). *The journey of man: A genetic odyssey.* Princeton, NJ: Princeton University Press.

Anthropologist and geneticist Spencer Wells presents recent genetic evidence from the Y chromosome from all over the world to support the recent African origins theory. He suggests that all contemporary humans evolved from a small population in Africa about 60,000 years ago.

Wolpoff, M., & Caspari, R. (1997). *Race and human evolution.* New York: Simon & Schuster.

One of the problems in evaluating the multiregional and recent African origins hypotheses is that many writers misrepresent the former. That is no problem in this book, written by the leading champions of multiregionalism. The hypothesis is presented and defended in a straightforward and thorough way so that anyone can understand it.

Thomson Audio Study Products

 Enjoy the MP3-ready Audio Lecture Overviews for each chapter and a comprehensive audio glossary of key terms for quick study and review. Whether walking to class, doing laundry, or studying at your desk, you now have the freedom to choose when, where, and how you interact with your audio-based educational media. See the preface for information on how to access this on-the-go study and review tool.

The Anthropology Resource Center

www.thomsonedu.com/anthropology

The Anthropology Resource Center provides extended learning materials to reinforce your understanding of key concepts in the four subfields of anthropology. For each of the four subdisciplines, the Resource Center includes dynamic exercises including video exercises, map exercises, simulations, and "Meet the Scientists" interviews, as well as critical thinking questions that can be assigned and e-mailed to instructors. The Resource Center also provides breaking news in anthropology and interesting material on applied anthropology to help you link what you are learning to the world around you.

9 The Global Expansion of *Homo sapiens* and Their Technology

Réunion de Musées Nationaux/Art Resource, NY

CHALLENGE ISSUE

Around 40,000 years ago the archaeological record becomes richer, not only with varied and sophisticated tool industries but also with evidence of increased human creativity, ingenuity, and problem solving. Spectacular evidence of early artistic creativity among our ancestors appears in exquisite works of ancient art on cave walls and in sculptures such as this 23,000-year-old Venus figurine carved from ivory discovered in Brassempouy, France. Such creations suggest that humans, as a thoughtful and self-reflecting species, have always faced the challenge of understanding where and how we fit in the larger natural system of all life forms, past and present. This figurine also embodies one of the classic paleoanthropological debates: Were the biological features evident in both fossils and in this ancient artistic expression—features such as a chin and a high forehead—at the root of this creative expression?

When Did Anatomically Modern Forms of *Homo sapiens* Appear?

Although 160,000-year-old fossils from Ethiopia have been described as anatomically modern, the answer to this question is quite complex. Anatomical modernity refers to particular characteristics in the shape of the skull. While all humans today are members of a single species, and as such are equally "modern," some contemporary populations do not meet the definition of anatomical modernity used by some paleoanthropologists. To exclude contemporary humans from the species based on the shape of their skulls is an obvious impossibility. By extension, the application of this definition of anatomical modernity to the fossil record is a source of debate. Still, it is generally agreed that by 30,000 years ago, Upper Paleolithic populations in all parts of the inhabited world showed greater resemblance to more recent human populations than earlier large-brained *Homo*.

What Was the Culture of Upper Paleolithic Peoples Like?

Upper Paleolithic cultures generally include a greater diversity of tools than before as well as a greater frequency of blade tools. Pressure flaking techniques and the use of burins to fashion implements of bone and antler became widespread. In Europe, success of large game hunting increased with the invention of the spear-thrower, or atlatl, and nets aided in hunting of small game. In Africa the earliest small points appropriate for arrowheads appear during this time period. There was as well an explosion of creativity, represented by impressive works of art discovered in a variety of sites from Africa, Australia, and Eurasia.

When and How Did Humans Spread to Australia and the Americas?

Around the time of the Upper Paleolithic, humans expanded into new regions, most dramatically Australia and the Americas. Expansion into Australia and New Guinea required crossing a deep, wide ocean channel and was thus dependent upon some sort of watercraft. Spread to the Americas involved successful adaptation to Arctic conditions and movement over land through northeastern Asia to the Americas and/or the use of watercraft over even more extended distances. Anthropologists use archaeological, linguistic, and biological evidence to reconstruct the spread of humans into these new regions.

The remains of ancient people who looked more like contemporary Europeans than Neandertals were first discovered in 1868 at Les Eyzies in France, in a rock shelter together with tools of the **Upper** (late) **Paleolithic.** Consisting of eight skeletons, they are commonly referred to as **Cro-Magnons,** after the rock shelter in which they were found. The name was extended to thirteen other specimens recovered between 1872 and 1902 in the caves of southern coastal France and, since then, to other Upper Paleolithic skeletons discovered in other parts of Europe.

Because Cro-Magnons were found with Upper Paleolithic tools and seemed responsible for the production of impressive works of art, they were seen as particularly clever when compared with the Neandertals. The idea that Neandertals were basically dim-witted fit comfortably with the prevailing stereotype of their supposedly brutish appearance. Their Mousterian tools were interpreted as evidence of cultural inferiority. Hence the idea was born of an anatomically modern people with a superior culture sweeping into Europe and replacing a primitive local population. This idea was not unlike the image Europeans had of themselves regarding their colonial expansion.

With the invention of reliable dating techniques in the 20th century, we now know that many Neandertal specimens of Europe and the later Cro-Magnon specimens date from different time periods. The Middle Paleolithic Mousterian technology is associated with earlier fossil specimens and Upper Paleolithic technology and art with later fossil specimens. Perhaps the most Eurocentric aspect of all is that historically this discussion focused on the European fossil evidence. Recent fossil evidence for early anatomical modernity in Africa, evidence of regional continuity from Asia, and associated genetic studies allow paleoanthropologists to develop theories for the origins of modern humans that are more complete and more complex.

Upper Paleolithic The last part (10,000 to 40,000 years ago) of the Old Stone Age, featuring tool industries characterized by long slim blades and an explosion of creative symbolic forms.
Cro-Magnon A European of the Upper Paleolithic after about 36,000 years ago.

UPPER PALEOLITHIC PEOPLES: THE FIRST MODERN HUMANS

As noted in Chapter 8, scholars debate whether the transition from archaic large-brained *Homo* to anatomically modern *H. sapiens* took place in one specific population or whether it involved populations living in Africa, Asia, and even Europe between 40,000 and 100,000 years ago evolving together. Further, when we refer to modernity with regard to these ancient humans, are we considering the shape of their skulls, their cultural practices, or both?

As Upper Paleolithic remains (from various parts of Africa and Asia as well as Europe) have become better

In the novel and movie *Clan of the Cave Bear*, the anatomically modern heroine is depicted as a tall blonde beauty while Neandertals are depicted as dark and sloppy. These images conform both to the stereotypes about Neandertals and aesthetic standards in the Western dominant culture.

Jonesfilm/Warner Bros./The Kobal Collection

VISUAL COUNTERPOINT

With a high forehead, the Cro-Magnon skull (left) is more like contemporary Europeans than the prominent brow ridge and sloping forehead seen in the Neandertal skull (right). Whether these differences in
skull shape account for their cultural differences rather than their relative age is hotly debated. The more
recent Cro-Magnon skull even preserves evidence of cultural continuity in diet with local contemporary
French people. This skull has evidence of a fungal infection, perhaps from eating tainted mushrooms.
Mushrooms are a tremendous delicacy in this region of France to this day.

understood, it has become clear that the differences from
earlier populations have been exaggerated. In the case of
Europeans, for example, there is some resemblance between Cro-Magnons and later populations: in braincase
shape, high broad forehead, narrow nasal openings, and
common presence of chins. But Cro-Magnon faces were
on average shorter and broader than those of modern
Europeans, their brow ridges were a bit more prominent, and their teeth and jaws were as large as those
of Neandertals. Some (a skull from the original Cro-
Magnon site, for instance) even display the distinctive occipital bun of the Neandertals on the back of the skull.[1]
Nor were they particularly tall, as their height of 5 feet
7 or 8 inches (170–175 centimeters) does not fall outside
the Neandertal range. Similarly, early Upper Paleolithic
skulls from Brno, Mladec, and Predmosti, in the Czech
Republic, retain heavy brow ridges and Neandertal-like
muscle attachments on their backs.[2]

Conversely, a late Neandertal from Vindija, northern Croatia, shows a thinning of brow ridges toward
their outer margins. Of course, these features could all
be the result of interbreeding between two populations
that overlapped in time, rather than simple evolution
from one into the other. Or, they could represent a single
varied population whose average characters were shifting in a more modern direction. In either case, they do
not fit with the idea of the complete extinction of the
older population.

Although the Cro-Magnons and Upper Paleolithic
peoples from Africa and Asia are now routinely referred
to as "anatomically modern," it is surprisingly difficult
to be precise about what we mean by this. We think of
people with brains the size of modern people, but this
had already been achieved by archaic *H. sapiens*. Average
brain size actually peaked in Neandertals at 10 percent
larger than the contemporary human average. The reduction to today's average size correlates with a reduction in brawn, as bodies have become less massive overall. Modern faces and jaws are, by and large, less massive
as well, but there are exceptions. For example, anthropologists Milford Wolpoff and Rachel Caspari have pointed
out that any definition of modernity that excludes Neandertals also excludes substantial numbers of recent and
living aboriginal Australians, although they are, quite
obviously, a contemporary people. The fact is, no multi-
dimensional diagnosis of anatomical modernity can be

[1]Brace, C. L. (1997). Cro-Magnons "R" us? *Anthropology Newsletter*
38(8), 1.

[2]Bednarik, R. G. (1995). Concept-mediated marking in the Lower
Paleolithic. *Current Anthropology 36,* 627; Minugh-Purvis, N. (1992).
The inhabitants of Ice Age Europe. *Expedition 34* (3), 33–34.

both exclusive of archaic populations and inclusive of all contemporary humans.[3]

It is impossible to know just how much gene flow took place among ancient human populations, but that some took place is consistent with the sudden appearance of novel traits in one region later than their appearance elsewhere. For example, some Upper Paleolithic remains from North Africa exhibit the kind of mid-facial flatness previously seen only in East Asian fossils; similarly, various Cro-Magnon fossils from Europe show the short upper jaws, horizontally oriented cheek bones, and rectangular eye orbits previously seen in East Asians. Conversely, the round orbits, large frontal sinuses, and thin cranial bones seen in some archaic *H. sapiens* skulls from China represent the first appearance there of traits that have greater antiquity in Europe.[4]

What appears to be happening, then, is that genetic variants from the East are being introduced into Western gene pools and vice versa. Some studies of the Y chromosome in humans (found only in males) indicate that some DNA carried by this chromosome originated in Asia at least 200,000 years ago and spread from there to Africa.[5] Other Y chromosome studies indicate African origins for our species.[6] Despite the seeming conflict, all of these data indicate that gene flow has been an important aspect of human evolutionary history. The multiregional hypothesis and recent African origins hypothesis differ in terms of whether this gene flow occurred over the course of 200,000 or 2 million years.

Not only is such gene flow consistent with the remarkable tendency humans have to "swap genes" between populations, even in the face of cultural barriers to gene flow, but it is also consistent with the tendency of other primates to produce hybrids when two subspecies (and sometimes even species) come into contact.[7] Moreover, without such gene flow, evolution inevitably would have resulted in the appearance of multiple species of modern humans, something that clearly has not

happened. In fact, the low level of genetic differentiation among modern human populations can be explained easily as a consequence of high levels of gene flow.[8]

Whatever the underlying genetic mechanism, the appearance of modern-sized brains in archaic *Homo* was related to increased reliance on cultural adaptation. Ultimately, this emphasis on cultural adaptation led to the development of more complex tool kits. Technological improvements may also have reduced the intensity of selective pressures that had previously favored especially massive robust bodies, jaws, and teeth. With new emphasis on elongate tools having greater mechanical advantages, more effective techniques of hafting, a switch from thrusting to throwing spears, and development of net hunting, there was a marked reduction in overall muscularity. In addition, as the environment changed to milder conditions from the extreme cold that prevailed in Eurasia during the last Ice Age, selective pressure for short stature as an adaptation to conserve body heat may have also diminished.

UPPER PALEOLITHIC TECHNOLOGY

The Upper Paleolithic was a time of great technological innovation. Upper Paleolithic tool kits are known for a preponderance of blade tools, with flint flakes at least twice as long as they are wide. The earliest blade tools come from sites in Africa, but these tools do not make up the majority of the tool types until well into the Upper Paleolithic. New techniques of core preparation allowing more intensive production of highly standardized blades permitted the proliferation of this tool type. The toolmaker formed a cylindrical core, struck the blade off near the edge of the core, and repeated this procedure, going around the core in one direction until finishing near its center (Figure 9.1). The procedure is analogous to peeling long leaves off an artichoke. With this **blade technique,** an Upper Paleolithic flint knapper could get 75 feet of working edge from a 2-pound core; a Mousterian knapper could get only 6 feet from the same-sized core.

Other efficient techniques of tool manufacture also came into common use at this time. One such method was **pressure flaking,** in which a bone, antler, or wooden tool was used to press rather than strike off small flakes as the final step in stone tool manufacture (Figure 9.2). The advantage of this technique was that the toolmaker had greater control over the final shape of the tool than is possible with percussion flaking alone. The so-called Solutrean laurel leaf bifaces found in Spain and France

[3]Wolpoff, M., & Caspari, R. (1997). *Race and human evolution* (pp. 344–345, 393). New York: Simon & Schuster.

[4]Pope, G. C. (1992). Craniofacial evidence for the origin of modern humans in China. *Yearbook of Physical Anthropology 35,* 287–288.

[5]Gibbons, A. (1997). Ideas on human origins evolve at anthropology gathering. *Science 276,* 535–536.

[6]Wells, S. (2002). *The journey of man: A genetic odyssey.* Princeton, NJ: Princeton University Press.

[7]Simons, E. L. (1989). Human origins. *Science 245,* 1,349.

blade technique A technique of stone tool manufacture by which long, parallel-sided flakes are struck off the edges of a specially prepared core.
pressure flaking A technique of stone tool manufacture in which a bone, antler, or wooden tool is used to press, rather than strike off, small flakes from a piece of flint or similar stone.

[8]Relethford, J. H., & Harpending, H. C. (1994). Craniometric variation, genetic theory, and modern human origins. *American Journal of Physical Anthropology 95,* 265.

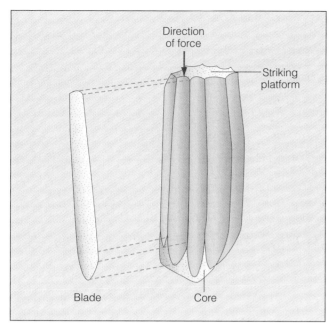

Figure 9.1
During the Upper Paleolithic, a new technique was used to manufacture blades. The stone is worked to create a striking platform; long almost parallel-sided flakes then are struck around the sides, providing sharp-edged blades.

Figure 9.2
Two methods used for pressure flaking in which a bone, antler, or wooden tool is used to press rather than strike off small flakes.

are examples of this technique. The longest of these tools is 13 inches in length but only about a quarter of an inch thick. Through pressure flaking, tools could be worked with great precision into a variety of final forms, and worn tools could be effectively resharpened over and over until they were too small for further use.

Although invented in the Middle Paleolithic, the **burin,** a tool with a chisel-like edge like blade tools, became more common in the Upper Paleolithic. Burins facilitated the working of bone, horn, antler, and ivory into such useful things as fishhooks, harpoons, and eyed needles, all of which made life easier for *H. sapiens,* especially in colder northern regions where the ability to stitch together animal hides was particularly important for warmth.

The spear-thrower, also known by its Aztec name atlatl, appeared at this time as well. Atlatls are wooden

burin A stone tool with chisel-like edges used for working bone and antler.

The techniques of the Upper Paleolithic allowed for the manufacture of a wide variety of tool types. The finely wrought Solutrean bifaces of Europe (shaped like the leaf of a plant) were made using the pressure technique. Tools such as eyed needles and harpoons began to be manufactured out of bone as well.

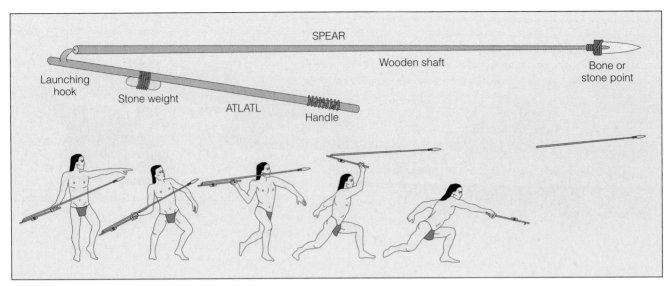

Figure 9.3

Spear-throwers (atlatls) allowed individual Upper Paleolithic people to throw spears at animals from a safe distance while still maintaining reasonable speed and accuracy. Upper Paleolithic artists frequently combined artistic expression with practical function, ornamenting their spear-throwers with animal figures.

devices, one end of which is gripped in the hunter's hand, while the other end has a hole or hook, in or against which the end of the spear is placed. It is held so as to effectively extend the length of the hunter's arm, thereby increasing the velocity of the spear when thrown. Using a spear-thrower greatly added to the efficiency of the spear as a hunting tool (Figure 9.3).

With handheld spears, hunters had to get close to their quarry to make the kill. Because many of the animals they hunted were large and fierce, this was a dangerous business. The need to approach closely, and the improbability of an instant kill, exposed the spear hunter to considerable risk. But with the spear-thrower, the effective killing distance was increased; experiments demonstrate that the effective killing distance of a spear when used with a spear-thrower is between 18 and 27 meters as opposed to less than a meter without.[9] Killing distance can be safely shortened when the kill is assured. The use of poison on spear tips, as employed by contemporary hunters such as the Hadza of Tanzania will decrease the risk to a hunter at shorter range. It is not clear from the archaeological record when this innovation began though the invention of tiny sharp stone blades for dart tips to provide a vehicle for poison delivery is clear. The earliest examples of these "microliths" began during the Upper Paleolithic in Africa, but did not become widespread till the Mesolithic or Middle Stone Age, as will be described in detail in Chapter 10.

Another important innovation, net hunting, appeared some time between 22,000 and 29,000 years ago.[10] Knotted nets, made from the fibers of wild plants such as hemp or nettle, left their impression on the clay floors of huts when people walked on them. When the huts later burned, these impressions, baked into the earth, provide evidence that nets existed. Their use accounts for the high number of hare, fox, and other small mammal and bird bones at archaeological sites. Like historically known and contemporary net hunters, such as the Mbuti of the Congo, everyone—men, women, and children—probably participated, frightening animals with loud noises to drive them to where hunters were stationed with their nets. In this way, large amounts of meat could be amassed without requiring great speed or strength on the part of the hunters.

A further improvement of hunting techniques came with the invention of the bow and arrow, which appeared first in Africa, but not until the end of the Upper Paleolithic in Europe. The greatest advantage of the bow is that it increases the distance between hunter and prey. Beyond 24 meters, the accuracy and penetration of a spear thrown with a spear-thrower is not very good, whereas even a poor bow will shoot an arrow further, with greater accuracy and penetrating power. A good bow is effective even at nearly 91 meters. Thus, hunters were able to maintain more distance between themselves and dangerous prey, dramatically decreasing their chances of being seriously injured by an animal fighting

---

[9]Frayer, D. W. (1981). Body size, weapon use, and natural selection in the European Upper Paleolithic and Mesolithic. *American Anthropologist 83,* 58.

[10]Pringle, H. (1997). Ice Age communities may be earliest known net hunters. *Science 277,* 1,203.

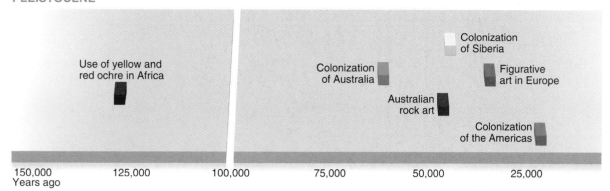

Figure 9.4

This timeline indicates the dates for some of the cultural innovations associated with the Upper Paleolithic.

for its life as well as decreasing the chance of startling an animal and triggering its flight.

Upper Paleolithic peoples not only had better tools but also a greater diversity of types than earlier peoples. The highly developed Upper Paleolithic kit included tools for use during different seasons, and regional variation in tool kits was greater than ever before. Thus, it is really impossible to speak of a single Upper Paleolithic culture even in Europe, a relatively small and isolated region compared to Asia and Africa. For foot nomads, the size of Europe and the rest of the inhabited world was formidable. Geological features such as mountain ranges, oceans, and glaciers isolated groups of people from each other.

To understand the Upper Paleolithic, one must make note of the many different traditions that made it possible for people to adapt ever more specifically to the various environments in which they were living. Just how proficient people had become at securing a livelihood is indicated by bone yards containing thousands of animal skeletons. At Solutré in France, for example, Upper Paleolithic hunters killed 10,000 horses; at Predmostí in the Czech Republic, they were responsible for the deaths of 1,000 mammoths. The favored big game of European hunters, however, was reindeer, which they killed in even greater numbers.

UPPER PALEOLITHIC ART

Although tools and weapons demonstrate the ingenuity of Upper Paleolithic peoples, artistic expression provides the best evidence of their creativity. Some have argued that artistic expression was made possible by a newly evolved biological ability to manipulate symbols and make images. However, the modern-sized brains of

archaic *H. sapiens* and increasingly compelling evidence of the presence of language or behaviors involving symbolism—such as burials—undercut this notion. Like agriculture, which came later (see Chapter 10), the artistic explosion may have been no more than a consequence of innovations made by a people who had the capacity to make them for tens of thousands of years already.

In fact, just as many of the distinctive tools that were commonly used in Upper Paleolithic times first appear in the Middle Paleolithic, so too do objects of art. In Southwest Asia, a crude figurine of volcanic tuff is some 250,000 years old.[11] While some scholars contest whether this was carved, those who believe it is state that it indicates that people had the ability to carve all sorts of things from wood, a substance easier to work than volcanic tuff but rarely preserved for long periods of time. Furthermore, ochre "crayons" from Middle Paleolithic contexts in various parts of the world must have been used to decorate or mark. In southern Africa, for example, regular use of yellow and red ochre goes back 130,000 years, with some evidence as old as 200,000 years.[12] Perhaps pigments were used on people's bodies, as well as objects, as the 50,000-year-old mammoth-tooth *churinga* discussed in Chapter 8 might suggest. The timeline in Figure 9.4 shows some of the cultural events of the Upper Paleolithic.

The presence of bone flutes and whistles in sites, some up to 30,000 years old, documents music played a role in the lives of Upper Paleolithic peoples. But again, such instruments may have their origin in Middle Paleolithic prototypes, such as the probable Neandertal flute

---

[11]Appenzeller, T. (1998). Art: Evolution or revolution? *Science 282*, 1,452.

[12]Barham, L. S. (1998). Possible early pigment use in South-Central Africa. *Current Anthropology 39*, 709.

These 17,000-year-old images, painted on a wall in the multi-chambered Lascaux Cave in the Dordogne region of southwest France, were discovered in 1940 by 4 teenage boys. In addition to the Ice Age animals depicted here—horses, wild ox, rhino, and bison—the chambers of Lascaux feature renderings of many other recognizable species. The carved and painted interiors of such caves were often deep underground and difficult to reach. Upper Paleolithic artists burned animal fat in sandstone lamps to light their way. In 1963 Lascaux Cave was closed to the public because carbon dioxide from the breath of thousands of visitors was damaging the ancient paintings. The French government built an exact replica of the cave so that visitors can still experience the wonder of these ancient works.

discussed in Chapter 8. Although we cannot be sure just where and when it happened, some genius discovered that bows could be used not just for killing, but to make music as well. Because the bow and arrow is an Upper Paleolithic invention, the musical bow likely is as well. We do know that the musical bow is the oldest of all stringed instruments, and its invention ultimately made possible the development of all of the stringed instruments with which we are familiar today.

The earliest evidence of figurative pictures goes back 32,000 years in Europe although they do not become common until much later. Pictorial art is probably equally old in Africa. Both engravings and paintings are known from many rock shelters and outcrops in southern Africa, where they continued to be made by Bushmen peoples until recently. Scenes feature both humans and animals, depicted with extraordinary skill, often in association with geometric and other abstract motifs. Some people still have the seemingly irresistible urge to add to existing rock paintings, while others create new sites for what we today call graffiti.

Because this rock art tradition continues unbroken into the present, it has been possible to discover what this art means. There is a close connection between the art and shamanism, and many scenes depict visions seen in states of trance. Distortions in the art, usually of human figures, represent sensations felt by individuals in a state of trance, whereas the geometric designs depict illusions that originate in the central nervous system in altered states of consciousness. These **entoptic phenomena** are luminous grids, dots, zigzags, and other designs that seem to shimmer, pulsate, rotate, and expand and are seen as one enters a state of trance (sufferers of migraines experience similar hallucinations).

In many recent cultures, geometric designs are used as symbolic expressions of genealogical patterns, records of origins, and the afterlife.[13] The animals depicted in this art, often with startling realism, are not the ones most often eaten. Rather, they are powerful beasts like the eland (a large African antelope), and this power is important to shamans—individuals skilled at manipulating supernatural powers and spirits for human benefit—who try to harness it for their rain-making and other rituals. See the Biocultural Connection for more on this fascinating topic.

Rock art in Australia goes back at least 45,000 years; the earliest examples consist entirely of entoptic motifs. Later art, as seen in the chapter opening photograph, is largely figurative. But the most famous Upper Paleolithic art is that of Europe, largely because most researchers of prehistoric art are themselves of European background. The earliest of this art took the form of sculpture and engravings often portraying such animals as reindeer, horses, bears, and ibexes.

There are also numerous portrayals of voluptuous women with exaggerated sexual and reproductive characteristics. Many appear to be pregnant, and some are shown in birthing postures. These so-called Venus figures have been found at sites from southwestern France

---

entoptic phenomena Bright pulsating forms that are generated by the central nervous system and seen in states of trance.

[13]Schuster, C., & Carpenter, E. (1996). *Patterns that connect: Social symbolism in ancient and tribal art.* New York: Abrams.

Biocultural Connection

Altered States, Art, and Archaeology

Many human societies today not only accept the practice of inducing altered states of consciousness, but actively encourage it as an accepted means of contacting and interacting with supernatural beings and powers. These induced states do not necessarily depend on consuming a drug, but they do reflect an individual's powers of concentration and imagination.

Because all human beings have essentially the same nervous system—be they urban dwellers in the United States, horticulturalists in the Amazon forests, or the Upper Paleolithic people who painted cave walls—the visual sensations of the trance experience will be similar. Initially, the nervous system often generates a variety of luminous, pulsating, revolving, and constantly shifting geometric patterns known as *entoptic phenomena.* Many individuals who have suffered from migraine will be familiar with such visual sensations. Typical imagery includes grids, parallel lines, zigzags, dots, nested curves, and filigrees, often in a spiral pattern.

Often, the brain tries to "make sense" of these abstract forms, just as it does of sensations received in more usual states of consciousness. In this process, known as *construal,* differences in culture and experience come into

play. Commonly, a South African Bushman in trance will construe a grid pattern as markings on the skin on a giraffe and nested curves as a honeycomb (honey is a local delicacy, and the auditory sensation of buzzing that often accompanies trance promotes the illusion). Obviously, we would expect different visual associations from an Inuit living in the arctic or from someone living in Los Angeles.

In deeper states of trance, people cease to be observers of their visions and report that they feel as though they have become, physically or spiritually, part of them. Though some observers might describe this as an out-of-body experience, it is not clear that the individual loses bodily sensation. The individual might report a feeling of passing into a rotating

tunnel or vortex with latticelike sides on which appear images of animals, humans, and monsters of various sorts.

Entoptic forms of the earlier stages may become integrated into these *iconic images.* These are also culture specific: Individuals see what their culture disposes them to see, and often the images have high emotional content. Bushmen often see the eland, an animal thought to be imbued with especially strong potency, particularly for rain-making. Given this, one of the things shamans try to do in trance is to "capture" elands ("rain animals") for purposes of making rain.

In many societies, individuals have recorded the visions they saw when in trance. The Bushmen are a prime example; as early as 27,000 years ago, they began to paint or engrave their visions on rock faces. Such depictions inevitably include the geometric elements and visual distortions that are common components of the trance experience. These records have led archaeologists to identify such diverse prehistoric art as the famous cave paintings of Europe, or graffiti etched into the plaster walls of ancient Maya palaces as related to the altered state of consciousness known as trance. The dots and other geometric patterns preserved in the art of the Upper Paleolithic may well be the product of trancing in the distant past.

© John Van Hasselt/Corbis Sygma

Rock art, like these paintings from Australia, may depict things seen by dancers while in states of trance. Simple geometric designs such as zigzags, notches, dots, and spirals (as on the cave ceiling) as well as human and animal figures are common in these paintings.

---

to as far east as Siberia. Made of stone, ivory, antler, or baked clay, they differ little in style from place to place, testifying to the sharing of ideas over vast distances. Although some have interpreted the Venuses as objects associated with a fertility cult, others suggest that they may have been exchanged to cement alliances among groups. Art historian LeRoy McDermott has suggested that the Venus figurines are "ordinary women's views of their own bodies" and the earliest examples of self-representation.[14] Paleolithic archaeologist Margaret Con-

key (see Anthropologist of Note) opened the door to such interpretations through her work combining gender theory and feminist theory with the science of archaeology.

Figurative art abounds in the spectacular paintings on the walls of 200 or so caves in southern France and northern Spain, the oldest of which date from about 32,000 years ago. Visually accurate portrayals of Ice Age mammals, including bison, bulls, horses, mammoths, and stags, were often painted one on top of another. Although well represented in other media, humans are not commonly portrayed in cave paintings, nor are scenes or depictions of events at all common. Instead, the animals are often abstracted from nature and rendered two-

[14]McDermott, L. (1996). Self-representation in Upper Paleolithic female figurines. *Current Anthropology* 37 ,227–276.

Anthropologists of Note

Margaret Conkey (b. 1943)

Courtesy of Theresa Babineau

Throughout her career, Margaret Conkey has blended the science of archaeology with theoretical perspectives from feminist scholarship and gender studies. Her goal has not been to create a separate "feminist archaeology" but rather to practice archaeology as a feminist. This consists of asking different kinds of research questions as well as challenging the ways that gender affects the practice of archaeology.

Conkey attended Mount Holyoke College, graduating in 1965. She is currently professor in the anthropology department at the University of California, Berkeley. She is co-author (with Joan Gero) of the major 1991 work that brought feminist perspectives into archaeology: *Engendering Archaeology*. Recently her work in this field brought her recognition as one of the "Fifty Most Important Women in Science," named by *Discover* magazine.

With a particular interest in the Upper Paleolithic art of Europe, Conkey has spent decades challenging the traditional notion that Paleolithic art was made by male artists as an expression of spiritual beliefs related to hunting activities. She emphasizes that many reconstructions of behavior in the past rely upon contemporary gender norms to fill in blanks left in the archaeological record. In other words, she is interested in the role of gender today in shaping the reconstruction of gender in the past. In the archaeological research she conducts, she is looking for clues about gender in the deep past, evidence that is not shaped by gender stereotypes from the present.

For example, she is currently directing a field project called "between the caves" in the French Midi-Pyrenees. The goal of this large-scale project is to provide a context for the art and material culture of this region's Cro-Magnons through surveying the regions between the caves. With a multidisciplinary international team, she aims to reconstruct daily life and the environments in which Upper Paleolithic people expressed themselves through art.

---

dimensionally—no small achievement for these early artists. Sometimes the artists made use of bulges and other features of the rock to impart a more three-dimensional feeling. Frequently, the paintings are in hard-to-get-at places while suitable surfaces in more accessible places remain untouched. In some caves, the lamps by which the artists worked have been found; these are spoon-shaped objects of sandstone in which animal fat was burned. Experimentation has shown that such lamps would have provided adequate illumination over several hours.

The techniques used by Upper Paleolithic peoples to create their cave paintings were unraveled a decade ago through the experimental work of Michel Lorblanchet. Interestingly, they turn out to be the same ones used by aboriginal rock painters in Australia. Lorblanchet's experiments are described in the following Original Study by science writer Roger Lewin.

VISUAL COUNTERPOINT

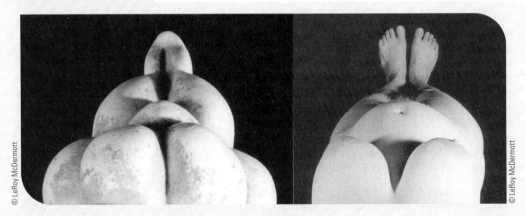

© LeRoy McDermott

According to art historian LeRoy McDermott, the distortions and exaggerations of the female form visible in the Venus figurines are a result of the perspective taken by female artists representing their own bodies.

Original Study • By Roger Lewin

Paleolithic Paint Job

Lorblanchet's recent bid to re-create one of the most important Ice Age images in Europe was an affair of the heart as much as the head. "I tried to abandon my skin of a modern citizen, tried to experience the feeling of the artist, to enter the dialogue between the rock and the man," he explains. Every day for a week in the fall of 1990 he drove the 20 miles from his home in the medieval village of Cajarc into the hills above the river Lot. There, in a small, practically inaccessible cave, he transformed himself into an Upper Paleolithic painter.

And not just any Upper Paleolithic painter, but the one who 18,400 years ago crafted the dotted horses inside the famous cave of Pech Merle.

You can still see the original horses in Pech Merle's vast underground geologic splendor. You enter through a narrow passageway and soon find yourself gazing across a grand cavern to where the painting seems to hang in the gloom. "Outside, the landscape is very different from the one the Upper Paleolithic people saw," says Lorblanchet. "But in here, the landscape is the same as it was more than 18,000 years ago. You see what the Upper Paleolithic people experienced." No matter where you look in this cavern, the eye is drawn back to the panel of horses.

The two horses face away from each other, rumps slightly overlapping, their outlines sketched in black. The animal on the right seems to come alive as it merges with a crook in the edge of the panel, the perfect natural shape for a horse's head. But the impression of naturalism quickly fades as the eye falls on the painting's dark dots. There are more than 200 of them, deliberately distributed within and below the bodies and arcing around the right-hand horse's head and mane. More cryptic still are a smattering of red dots and half-circles and the floating outline of a fish. The surrealism is completed by six disembodied human hands stenciled above and below the animals.

Lorblanchet began thinking about re-creating the horses after a research trip to Australia over a decade ago. Not only is Australia a treasure trove of rock art, but its aboriginal people are still creating it. "In Queensland I learned how people painted by spitting pigment onto the rock," he recalls. "They spat paint and used their hand, a piece of cloth, or a feather as a screen to create different lines and other effects. Elsewhere in Australia people used chewed twigs as paintbrushes, but in Queensland the spitting technique worked best." The rock surfaces there were too uneven for extensive brushwork, he adds—just as they are in Quercy.

When Lorblanchet returned home he looked at the Quercy paintings with a

This spotted horse in the French cave of Pech Merle was painted by an Upper Paleolithic artist.

new eye. Sure enough, he began seeing the telltale signs of spit-painting—lines with edges that were sharply demarcated on one side and fuzzy on the other, as if they had been airbrushed—instead of the brushstrokes he and others had assumed were there. Could you produce lines that were crisp on both edges with the same technique, he wondered, and perhaps dots too? Archeologists had long recognized that hand stencils, which

are common in prehistoric art, were produced by spitting paint around a hand held to the wall. But no one had thought that entire animal images could be created this way. Before he could test his ideas, however, Lorblanchet had to find a suitable rock face—the original horses were painted on a roughly vertical panel 13 feet across and 6 feet high. With the help of a speleologist, he eventually found a rock face in a remote cave high in the hills and set to work.

Following the aboriginal practices he had witnessed, Lorblanchet first made a light outline sketch of the horses with a charred stick. Then he prepared black pigment for the painting. "My intention had been to use manganese dioxide, as the Pech Merle painter did," says Lorblanchet, referring to one of the minerals ground up for paint by the early artists. "But I was advised that manganese is somewhat toxic, so I used wood charcoal instead." (Charcoal was used as pigment by Paleolithic painters in other caves, so Lorblanchet felt he could justify his concession to safety.) To turn the charcoal into paint, Lorblanchet ground it with a limestone block, put the powder in his mouth, and diluted it to the right consistency with saliva and water. For red pigment he used ochre from the local iron-rich clay.

CONTINUED

CONTINUED

He started with the dark mane of the right-hand horse. "I spat a series of dots and fused them together to represent tufts of hair," he says, unself-consciously reproducing the spitting action as he talks. "Then I painted the horse's back by blowing the pigment below my hand held so"—he holds his hand flat against the rock with his thumb tucked in to form a straight line—"and used it like a stencil to produce a sharp upper edge and a diffused lower edge. You get an illusion of the animal's rounded flank this way."

He experimented as he went. "You see the angular rump?" he says, pointing to the original painting. "I reproduced that by holding my hand perpendicular to the rock, with my palm slightly bent, and I spat along the edge formed by my hand and the rock." He found he could produce sharp lines, such as those in the tail and in the upper hind leg, by spitting into the gap between parallel hands.

The belly demanded more ingenuity; he spat paint into a V-shape formed by his two splayed hands, rubbed it into a curved swath to shape the belly's outline, then finger-painted short protruding lines to suggest the animals' shaggy hair. Neatly outlined dots, he found, could not be made by blowing a thin jet of charcoal onto the wall. He had to spit pigment through a hole made in an animal skin. "I spent seven hours a day for a week," he says. "Puff . . . puff . . . puff. . . . It was exhausting, particularly because there was carbon monoxide in the cave. But you experience something special, painting like that. You feel you are breathing the image onto the rock—projecting your spirit from the deepest part of your body onto the rock surface."

Was that what the Paleolithic painter felt when creating this image? "Yes, I know it doesn't sound very scientific," Lorblanchet says of his highly personal style of investigation, "but the intellectual games of the structuralists haven't got us very far, have they? Studying rock art shouldn't be an intellectual game. It is about understanding humanity. That's why I believe the experimental approach is valid in this case."
(By Roger Lewin (1993). Paleolithic paint job. Discover *14 (7), 67-69. Copyright ©1993 The Walt Disney Co. Reprinted with permission of Discover Magazine.)* ∎

Theories to account for the early European cave art are difficult because they so often depend on conjectural and subjective interpretations. Some have argued that it is art for art's sake; but if that is so, why were animals so often painted over one another, and why were they so often placed in inaccessible places? The latter might suggest that they were for ceremonial purposes and that the caves served as religious sanctuaries.

One suggestion is that the animals were drawn to ensure success in the hunt, another that their depiction was seen as a way to promote fertility and increase the size of the herds on which humans depended. In Altamira Cave in northern Spain, for example, the art shows a pervasive concern for the sexual reproduction of the bison.[15] In cave art generally, though, the animals painted show little relationship to those most frequently hunted. Furthermore, there are few depictions of animals being hunted or killed, nor are there depictions of animals copulating or with exaggerated sexual parts as there are in the Venus figures.

Another suggestion is that rites by which youngsters were initiated into adulthood took place in the painted galleries. In support of this idea, footprints, most of which are small, have been found in the clay floors of several caves, and in one, they even circle a modeled clay bison. The animals painted, so this argument goes, may have had to do with knowledge being transmitted from the elders to the youths. Furthermore, the transmission of information might be implied by countless so-called signs, apparently abstract designs that accompany much Upper Paleolithic art. Some have interpreted these as tallies of animals killed, a reckoning of time according to a lunar calendar, or both.

These abstract designs, including such ones as the spots on the Pech Merle horses, suggest yet another possibility. For the most part, these are just like the entoptic designs seen by subjects in experiments dealing with altered states of consciousness and that are so consistently present in the rock art of southern Africa. Furthermore, the rock art of southern Africa shows the same painting of new images over older ones, as well as the same sort of fixation on large, powerful animals instead of the ones most often eaten. Thus, the cave art of Europe may well represent the same depictions of trance experiences, painted after the fact. Consistent with this interpretation, the isolation of the cave and the shimmering light on the cave walls themselves are conducive to the sort of sensory distortion that can induce trance.

Artistic expression, whatever its purpose may have been, was not confined to rock surfaces and portable objects. Upper Paleolithic peoples also ornamented their bodies with necklaces of perforated animal teeth, shells, beads of bone, stone, and ivory; rings; bracelets; and anklets. Clothing, too, was adorned with beads. Quite a lot of art was probably also executed in perishable materials such as wood carving, paintings on bark, or animal skins, which have not been preserved. Thus, the rarity or

---

[15]Halverson, J. (1989). Review of the book *Altimira revisited and other essays on early art. American Antiquity* 54, 883.

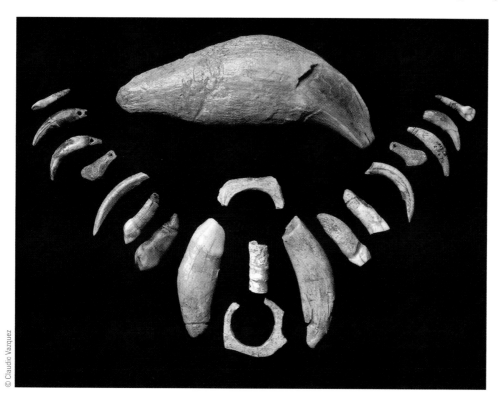

© Claudio Vazquez

Pendants and beads for personal adornment became common in the Upper Paleolithic. In Europe, most were made by Cro-Magnons, but some—like these shown here—were made by Neandertals. The earliest undisputed items of personal adornment are some 40,000-year-old beads from Africa made from ostrich egg shell.

absence of Upper Paleolithic art in some parts of the inhabited world may be more apparent than real, as people elsewhere worked with materials unlikely to survive so long in the archaeological record.

OTHER ASPECTS OF UPPER PALEOLITHIC CULTURE

Upper Paleolithic peoples lived not only in caves and rock shelters, but also in structures built out in the open. In Ukraine, for example, the remains have been found of sizable settlements, in which huts were built on frameworks of intricately stacked mammoth bones. Where the ground was frozen, cobblestones were heated and placed in the earth to sink in, thereby providing sturdy, dry floors. Their hearths, no longer shallow depressions or flat surfaces that radiated back little heat, were instead stone-lined pits that conserved heat for extended periods and made for more efficient cooking.

For the outdoors, they had the same sort of tailored clothing worn in historic times by Arctic and sub-Arctic peoples. And they engaged in long-distance trade, as indicated, for example, by the presence of seashells and Baltic amber at sites several hundred kilometers from the sources of these materials. Although Middle Paleolithic peoples also made use of rare and distant ma-

terials, they did not do so with the regularity seen in the Upper Paleolithic.

THE SPREAD OF UPPER PALEOLITHIC PEOPLES

Upper Paleolithic peoples expanded into regions previously uninhabited by their archaic forebears. Colonization of Siberia began about 42,000 years ago, although it took something like 10,000 years before humans reached the northeastern part of that region.

Much earlier, possibly by at least 60,000 years ago, people managed to get to Australia, Tasmania, and New Guinea, then connected to one another in a single landmass called the **Sahul** (Figure 9.5).[16] To do this, they had to use some kind of watercraft because the Sahul was separated from the islands (which are geologically a part

[16]Rice, P. (2000). Paleoanthropology 2000—part 1. *General Anthropology* 7 (1), 11; Zimmer, C. (1999). New date for the dawn of dream time. *Science 284*, 1,243.

Sahul The greater Australian landmass including Australia, New Guinea, and Tasmania. At times of maximum glaciation and low sea levels, these areas were continuous.

Reconstruction of an Upper Paleolithic hut with walls of interlocked mammoth mandibles.

of the Asian landmass) of Java, Sumatra, Borneo, and Bali. At times of maximum glaciation and low sea levels, these islands were joined to one another in a single landmass called **Sunda,** but a deep ocean trench (called the Wallace trench, after Alfred Russel Wallace who, as described in Chapter 2, discovered natural selection at the same time as Charles Darwin) always separated Sunda and Sahul.

Anthropologist Joseph Birdsell suggested several routes of island hopping and seafaring to make the crossing between these landmasses.[17] Each of these routes still involves crossing open water without land visible on the horizon. The earliest known site in New Guinea dates to 40,000 years ago. Sites in Australia are dated to even earlier, but these dates are especially contentious because they relate back to the critical question about the relationship between anatomical modernity and the presence of humanlike culture. Early dates for the habi-

---

[17]Birdsell, J. H. (1977). The recalibration of a paradigm for the first peopling of Greater Australia. In J. Allen, J. Golson, & R. Jones (Eds.), *Sunda and Sahul: Prehistoric studies in Southeast Asia, Melanesia, and Australia* (pp. 113–167). New York: Academic Press.

Sunda The combined landmass of the contemporary islands of Java, Sumatra, Borneo, and Bali that was continuous with mainland Southeast Asia at times of low sea levels corresponding to maximum glaciation.

Figure 9.5

Habitation of Australia and New Guinea (joined together with Tasmania as a single landmass called Sahul) was dependent upon travel across the open ocean even at times of maximum glaciation when sea levels were low. This figure represents the coastlines of Sahul and Sunda (Southeast Asia plus the island of Java, Sumatra, Borneo, and Bali) now and in the past. As sea levels rose with melting glaciers, sites of early human habitation were submerged under water.

tation of the Sahul indicate that archaic *Homo* rather than anatomically modern forms possessed the cultural capacity for navigation to the Sahul. Once in Australia, these people created some of the world's earliest sophisticated rock art, perhaps some 10,000 to 15,000 years earlier than the more famous European cave paintings.

Interestingly, considerable physical variation is seen in Australian fossil specimens from this period. Some specimens have the high forehead characteristic of anatomical modernity while others possess traits providing excellent evidence of continuity between living aboriginal people and the earlier *Homo erectus* and archaic *Homo sapiens* fossils from Indonesia. Willandra Lakes, the fossil lake region of southeastern Australia far from where the earliest archaeological evidence of human habitation of the continent was found, is particularly rich with fossils. The variation present in these fossils illustrates the problems inherent with making a one-to-one correspondence between the skull of a certain shape and cultural capabilities.

Other evidence for sophisticated ritual activity in early Australia is provided by the burial of a man at least 40,000 and possibly 60,000 years ago from the Willandra Lakes region. His body was positioned with his fingers intertwined around one another in the region of his penis, and red ochre had been scattered over the body. It may be that this pigment had more than symbolic value; for example, its iron salts have antiseptic and deodorizing properties, and there are recorded instances in which red ochre is associated with prolonging life and is used medicinally to treat particular conditions or infections. One historically known aboriginal Australian society is reported to have used ochre to heal wounds, scars, and burns. A person with internal pain was covered with the substance and placed in the sun to promote sweating.

As in many parts of the world, paleoanthropologists conducting research on human evolution in Australia are essentially constructing a view of the history of people and the world that conflicts with the beliefs of Australian aborigines. The story of human evolution is utterly dependent on Western conceptions of time, relationships established through genetics, and a definition of what it means to be human. While aboriginal creation stories account for human origins very differently, paleoanthropologists in Australia have worked closely with and advocated for Australian aboriginal peoples while conducting their research on evolution.

THE AMERICAS

While scientists concur that American Indian ancestry can be traced ultimately back to Asian origins, just when people arrived in the Americas has been a matter

Figure 9.6

The Arctic conditions and glaciers in northeastern Asia and northwestern North America provided opportunity and challenges for ancient people spreading to the Americas. On the one hand, the Arctic conditions provided a land bridge (Beringia) between the continents, but on the other hand, these harsh environmental conditions pose considerable challenges to humans. Ancient people may have also come to the Americas by sea. Once in North America, glaciers spanning a good portion of the continent determined the areas open to habitation.

of lively debate. This debate draws upon geographic, cultural, and biological evidence.

The conventional wisdom has long been that the first people spread into North America over dry land that connected Siberia to Alaska. This so-called land bridge was a consequence of the buildup of great continental glaciers. As these ice masses grew, there was a worldwide lowering of sea levels, causing an emergence of land in places like the Bering Strait where seas today are shallow. Thus, Alaska became, in effect, an eastward extension of Siberia (Figure 9.6). Climatic patterns of the Ice Age kept this land bridge, known as Beringia or the Bering Land Bridge, relatively ice free and covered instead with lichens and mosses that could support herds of grazing animals. It is possible that Upper Paleolithic peoples could have come to the Americas simply by following herd animals.

According to geologists, conditions were right for ancient humans and herd animals to traverse Beringia between 11,000 and 25,000 years ago. Though this land bridge was also open between 40,000 and 75,000 years ago, there is no evidence that conclusively confirms human migration at these earlier dates. As with the Sahul, early dates open the possibility of spread to the Americas by archaic *Homo.*

Although ancient Siberians did indeed spread eastward, it is now clear that their way south was blocked by massive glaciers until 13,000 years ago at the earliest.[18] By then, people were already living further south in the Americas. Thus the question of how people first came to this hemisphere has been reopened. One possibility is that, like the first Australians, the first Americans may have come by boat or rafts, perhaps traveling between islands or ice-free pockets of coastline, from as far away as the Japanese islands and down North America's northwest coast. Hints of such voyages are provided by a handful of North American skeletons (such as Kennewick Man) that bear a closer resemblance to the aboriginal Ainu people of northern Japan and their forebears than they do to other Asians or contemporary Native Americans. Unfortunately, because sea levels were lower than they are today, coastal sites used by early voyagers would now be under water.

Securely dated objects from Monte Verde, a site in south-central Chile, place people in southern South America by 12,500 years ago, if not earlier. Assuming the first populations spread from Siberia to Alaska, linguist Johanna Nichols suggests that the first people to arrive in North America did so by 20,000 years ago. She bases

this estimate on the time it took various other languages to spread from their homelands—including Eskimo languages in the Arctic and Athabaskan languages from interior western Canada to New Mexico and Arizona (Navajo). Her conclusion is that it would have taken at least 7,000 years for people to reach south-central Chile.[19] Others suggest people arrived in the Americas closer to 30,000 years ago or even earlier.

The picture currently emerging, then, is of people, who may not have looked like modern Native Americans, arriving by boats or rafts and spreading southward and eastward over time. In fact, contact back and forth between North America and Siberia never stopped. In all probability, it became more common as the glaciers melted away. As a consequence, through gene flow as well as later arrivals of people from Asia, people living in the Americas came to have the broad faces, prominent cheekbones, and round cranial vaults that tend to characterize the skulls of many Native Americans today. Still, Native Americans, like all human populations, are physically variable. The Kennewick Man controversy described in Chapter 4 illustrates the complexities of establishing ethnic identity based on the shape of the skull. In order to trace the history of the peopling of the Americas, anthropologists must combine archaeological, linguistic, and cultural evidence with evidence of biological variation.

Although the earliest technologies in the Americas remain poorly known, they gave rise in North America, about 12,000 years ago, to the distinctive fluted spear points of **Paleoindian** hunters of big game, such as mammoths, mastodons, caribou, and now extinct forms of bison. Fluted points are finely made, with large channel flakes removed from one or both surfaces. This thinned section was inserted into the notched end of a spear shaft for a sturdy haft. Fluted points are found from the Atlantic seaboard to the Pacific coast, and from Alaska down into Panama. The efficiency of the hunters who made and used these points may have hastened the extinction of the mammoth and other large Pleistocene mammals. By driving large numbers of animals over cliffs, they killed many more than they could possibly use, thus wasting huge amounts of meat.

Upper Paleolithic people in Australia and the Americas, like their counterparts in Africa and Eurasia, possessed sophisticated technology that was efficient and appropriate for the environments they inhabited. As in other parts of the world, when a technological innovation such as the fluted points begins, this technology is rapidly disseminated among the people inhabiting the region.

---

[18]Marshall, E. (2001). Preclovis sites fight for acceptance. *Science* *291,* 1,732.

Paleoindian The earliest inhabitants of North America.

---

[19]The first Americans, ca. 20,000 (1998). *Discover 19* (6), 24.

Paleoindians, like their Upper Paleolithic contemporaries in Eurasia, were such accomplished hunters that they, too, could kill more animals than could possibly be used at one time. These bones are the remains of some 200 bison that Paleoindian hunters stampeded over a cliff 8,500 years ago.

MAJOR PALEOLITHIC TRENDS

Looking at the larger picture, since the time the genus *Homo* appeared, evolving humans came to rely increasingly on cultural, as opposed to biological, adaptation. To handle environmental challenges, evolving humans developed appropriate tools, clothes, shelter, use of fire, and so forth rather than relying upon biological adaptation of the human organism. This was true whether human populations lived in hot or cold, wet or dry, forest or grassland areas. Though culture is ultimately based on what might loosely be called "brain power" or, more formally, **cognitive capacity,** it is learned and not carried by genes. Therefore, cultural innovations may occur rapidly and can easily be transferred among individuals and groups.

Certain trends stand out from the information anthropologists have gathered about the Old Stone Age in most parts of the world. One was toward increasingly more sophisticated, varied, and specialized tool kits. Tools became progressively lighter and smaller, resulting in the conservation of raw materials and a better ratio between length of cutting edge and weight of stone. Tools became specialized according to region and function. Instead of crude all-purpose tools, more effective particularized devices were made to deal with the differing conditions of savannah, forest, and shore.

As humans came to rely increasingly on culture as a means to meet the challenges of existence, they were able to inhabit new environments. With more efficient tool technology, human population size could increase allowing humans to spill over into more diverse environments. Improved cultural abilities may also have played a role in the reduction of heavy physical features, favoring instead decreased size and weight of face and teeth, the development of larger and more complex brains, and ultimately a reduction in body size and robustness. This dependence on intelligence rather than bulk provided the key for humans' increased reliance on cultural rather than physical adaptation. The development of conceptual thought can be seen in symbolic artifacts and signs of ritual activity throughout the world.

Through Paleolithic times, at least in the colder parts of the world, hunting became more important, and people became more proficient at it. Humans' intelligence enabled them to develop composite tools as well as the social organization and cooperation so important for survival and population growth. As discussed in the next chapter, this trend was reversed during the Mesolithic, when hunting lost its preeminence, and the gathering of wild plants and seafood became increasingly important.

As human populations grew and spread, cultural differences between regions also became more marked. While some indications of cultural contact and intercommunication are evident in the development of long-distance trade networks, tool assemblages developed in response to the specific challenges and resources of specific environments.

As Paleolithic peoples eventually spread over all the continents of the world, including Australia and the Americas, changes in climate and environment called for new kinds of adaptations. In forest environments, people needed tools for working wood; on the open savannah and plains, they came to use the bow and arrow to hunt the game they could not stalk closely; the people in settlements that grew up around lakes and along rivers and coasts developed harpoons and hooks; in the sub-Arctic regions they needed tools to work the heavy skins of seals and caribou. The fact that culture is first and foremost a mechanism by which humans adapt means that as humans faced new challenges in the Paleolithic throughout the globe, their cultures differentiated regionally.

cognitive capacity A broad concept including intelligence, educability, concept formation, self-awareness, self-evaluation, attention span, sensitivity in discrimination, and creativity.

Joe Ben Wheat Photo/University of Colorado Museum, Boulder.

Questions for Reflection

1. Upper Paleolithic art suggests that humans have always been challenged to understand where we fit in the larger system of life forms, past and present. What are your thoughts about how the impulse to create art relates to human efforts to make sense of our place in nature?

2. What evidence from the Upper Paleolithic supports a one-to-one relationship between biological change and culture change? What evidence from the Upper Paleolithic indicates that culture change in that era is not connected to an underlying biological change? Which approach do you think is correct?

3. Why do you think that most of the studies of prehistoric art have tended to focus on Europe? Is it ethnocentrism or biases about the definition of art in Western cultures?

4. Many animals without culture have spread to new environments. What is it about the spread of humans to Australia and the Americas that tells us about the cultural capabilities of past people?

5. Do you think that gender has played a role in anthropological interpretations of the behavior of our ancestors and the way that paleoanthropologists and archaeologists conduct their research? Do you believe that feminism has a role to play in the interpretation of the past?

Suggested Readings

Clottes, J., & Bennett, G. (2002). *World rock art* (conservation and cultural heritage series). San Francisco: Getty Trust Publication.

Written by Jean Clottes, a leading authority on rock art (and discoverer of the Upper Paleolithic cave art site Grotte de Cahuvet), this book provides excellent descriptions and beautiful images of rock art from throughout the world, beginning with the earliest rock art from Australia to rock art from the 20th century.

Dillehay, T. D. (2001). *The settlement of the Americas.* New York: Basic Books.

In an engaging, clear style, this book provides a detailed account of the evidence from South America that has recently challenged theories about the peopling of the Americas with particular emphasis on the author's work in Chile.

Klein, R. (2002). *The dawn of human culture.* New York: Wiley.

While this book covers the entire history of human evolution, it provides a particular focus on the theory of recent African origins of the species *Homo sapiens* and associated cultural abilities.

White, R. (2003). *Prehistoric art: The symbolic journey of humankind.* New York: Abrams.

This sumptuously illustrated volume demonstrates the power of prehistoric imagery as well as providing a comprehensive overview of the theoretical approaches to studying prehistoric art. White presents a global survey of prehistoric art and demonstrates that Western notions of art have interfered with interpretations of art made in the past.

Wolpoff, M., & Caspari, R. (1997). *Race and human evolution.* New York: Simon & Schuster.

This book is a detailed but readable presentation of the multiregional hypothesis of modern human origins. Among its strengths is a discussion of the problem of defining what "anatomically modern" means.

Thomson Audio Study Products

 Enjoy the MP3-ready Audio Lecture Overviews for each chapter and a comprehensive audio glossary of key terms for quick study and review. Whether walking to class, doing laundry, or studying at your desk, you now have the freedom to choose when, where, and how you interact with your audio-based educational media. See the preface for information on how to access this on-the-go study and review tool.

The Anthropology Resource Center

www.thomsonedu.com/anthropology
The Anthropology Resource Center provides extended learning materials to reinforce your understanding of key concepts in the four subfields of anthropology. For each of the four subdisciplines, the Resource Center includes dynamic exercises including video exercises, map exercises, simulations, and "Meet the Scientists" interviews, as well as critical thinking questions that can be assigned and e-mailed to instructors. The Resource Center also provides breaking news in anthropology and interesting material on applied anthropology to help you link what you are learning to the world around you.

10 The Neolithic Transition: The Domestication of Plants and Animals

© The Art Archive/Dagli Orti

CHALLENGE ISSUE

Beginning some time around 10,000 years ago, some of the world's people embarked on a new way of life, presenting them with a host of new challenges. By chance rather than design, they developed sedentary communities in which people relied upon domesticated animals and plants for their livelihood. The shift from food foraging to food production so drastically transformed human existence that this cultural period, the Neolithic, has been described as revolutionary. While farming and village life solved some of the challenges of existence, these cultural innovations have also posed risks to human health, both in the past and the present. Crowded living conditions and close contact with animals in Neolithic villages promoted the spread of infectious disease. Diets limited by reliance on single crops sometimes led to malnutrition and even famine when these crops failed. In addition to health issues, the development of village life and the domestication of animals and plants introduced new beliefs, daily routines, social relationships, and political structures that together continue to challenge humans globally.

When and Where Did the Change from Food Foraging to Food Production Begin?

Independent centers of early plant and animal domestication exist in Africa, China, Mesoamerica, North and South America, as well as Southwest and Southeast Asia. From these places, food production spread to most other parts of the world. Food production began independently at more or less the same time around 10,000 years ago in these different places—perhaps a bit earlier in Southwest Asia than elsewhere. Though farming has changed dramatically over the millennia, crops people rely on today, such as rice, wheat, and maize, originated with those earliest farmers.

Why Did the Change Take Place?

Though the Neolithic transition can appear to be a cultural advancement because later cities and states developed from Neolithic villages, food production is not necessarily a more secure means of subsistence than food foraging. In the Neolithic, farming often limited the diversity of the human diet and required more work than hunting, gathering, and fishing. In addition, being sedentary created new vulnerability to disease. It may be that people did not become food producers due to clear-cut advantages of this way of life. Of various theories that have been proposed, the most likely is that food production came about as a consequence of a chance convergence of separate natural events and cultural developments.

What Were the Consequences of the Neolithic Transition?

Although food production generally leaves less leisure time than food foraging, it does permit some reallocation of the workload. Some people can produce enough food to support those who undertake other tasks, and so a number of technological developments, such as weaving and pottery making, generally accompany food production. In addition, a sedentary lifestyle in villages allows for the construction of more substantial housing. Finally, the new modes of work and resource allocation require new ways of organizing people, generally into lineages, clans, and common-interest associations.

Throughout the Paleolithic, people depended exclusively on wild sources of food for their survival. They followed wild herds and gathered wild plant foods, relying on their wits and muscles to acquire what nature provided. Whenever favored sources of food became scarce, people adjusted by increasing the variety of foods eaten and incorporating less desirable foods into their diets.

Over time, the subsistence practices of some people began to change in ways that radically transformed their way of life as they became food producers rather than food foragers.[1] Food production had important implications for humans, for it meant that people could lead a more sedentary existence. Moreover, by reorganizing the workload, some individuals could be freed from the food quest to devote their energies to other tasks. Over the course of thousands of years, food production and permanent settlement in villages brought about an unforeseen way of life. With good reason, the **Neolithic,** when this change took place, has been called a revolutionary one in human history.

THOMSON AUDIO STUDY PRODUCTS Take advantage of the MP3-ready Audio Lecture Overviews and comprehensive audio glossary of key terms for each chapter. See the preface for information on how to access this on-the-go study and review tool.

THE MESOLITHIC ROOTS OF FARMING AND PASTORALISM

By 12,000 years ago, recession of the glaciers that had covered much of the northern hemisphere caused changes in human habitats globally. As climates warmed and sea levels rose, many areas flooded that had been above sea level during periods of glaciation. This occurred in areas such as the Bering Strait, parts of the North Sea, and an extensive land area that had joined the eastern is-

lands of Indonesia to mainland Asia. In some northern regions, higher temperatures brought about particularly marked changes, allowing the replacement of tundra with forests.

In the process, the herd animals—which northern Paleolithic peoples had depended upon for much of their food, clothing, and shelter—disappeared from many areas. Some, like the reindeer and musk ox, moved to colder climates; others, like the mammoths, died out completely. In the new forests, animals were often more solitary in their habits. As a result, large cooperative hunts were less productive than before. Diets shifted to abundant plant foods as well as fish and other foods around lakeshores, bays, and rivers. In Europe, Asia, and Africa this transitional period between the Paleolithic and the Neolithic is called the **Mesolithic,** or Middle Stone Age. In the Americas, comparable cultures are referred to as **Archaic cultures.**

New technologies accompanied the changed postglacial environment. People began to manufacture ground stone tools, shaped and sharpened by grinding the tool against sandstone, often using sand as an additional abrasive. These shaped, sharpened stones were set into wooden or sometimes antler handles to make effective axes and adzes (a cutting tool for squaring off logs) with a sharp blade set at right angles to a handle. Though such implements take longer to make, they are less prone to breakage under heavy-duty usage than those made of chipped stone. Thus, they were helpful in clearing forest areas and in the woodwork needed for the creation of dugout canoes and skin-covered boats. Evidence for the presence of seaworthy watercraft at Mesolithic sites indicates that human foraging for food likely took place on the water as well as the land. Thus, it was possible to make use of deepwater resources as well as those of coastal areas, rivers, and lakes.

The **microlith,** a small but hard, sharp, blade, was the characteristic tool of the Mesolithic. Although a microlithic tradition existed in Central Africa by about 40,000 years ago,[2] such tools did not become common elsewhere until the Mesolithic. Microliths could be mass produced because they were small, easy to make, and could be fashioned from sections of blades. These small tools could be attached to arrow or other tool shafts by using melted resin (from pine trees) as a binder.

Microliths provided Mesolithic people with an important advantage over their Upper Paleolithic forebears: The small size of the microlith enabled them to devise a wider array of composite tools made out of stone and wood or bone. Thus, they could make sickles, harpoons, arrows, knives, and daggers by fitting microliths into slots in wood, bone, or antler handles. Later experimen-

---

[1]Rindos, D. (1984). *The origins of agriculture: An evolutionary perspective* (p. 99). Orlando: Academic Press.

Neolithic The New Stone Age; prehistoric period beginning about 10,000 years ago in which peoples possessed stone-based technologies and depended on domesticated crops and/or animals.
Mesolithic The Middle Stone Age period between the end of the Paleolithic and the start of the Neolithic; referred to as Archaic cultures in the Americas.
Archaic cultures Term used to refer to Mesolithic cultures in the Americas.
microlith A small blade of flint or similar stone, several of which were hafted together in wooden handles to make tools; widespread in the Mesolithic.

---

[2]Bednarik, R. G. (1995). Concept-mediated marking in the Lower Paleolithic. *Current Anthropology 36,* 606.

The Natufians from Southwest Asia were the earliest Mesolithic people known to have stored plant foods. Basin-shaped depressions are preserved in the rocks outside of their homes.

tation with these forms led to more sophisticated tools and weapons such as bows to propel arrows.

Dwellings from the Mesolithic provide some evidence of a more sedentary lifestyle during this period. By contrast, most hunting peoples, and especially those depending on herd animals, are highly mobile. To be successful, hunters must follow migratory game. People subsisting on diets of seafood and plants in the milder northern forested environments of this time period did not need to move regularly over large geographic areas.

In the warmer parts of the world, the collection of wild plant foods complemented hunting in the Upper Paleolithic more than had been the case in the colder northern regions. Hence, in areas like Southwest Asia, the Mesolithic represents less of a changed way of life than was true in Europe. Here, the important **Natufian culture** flourished.

The Natufians lived between 10,200 and 12,500 years ago at the eastern end of the Mediterranean Sea in caves, rock shelters, and small villages with stone- and mud-walled houses. They are named after the Wadi en-Natuf, a ravine near Jerusalem, Israel, where the remains of this culture were first found. They buried their dead in communal cemeteries, usually in shallow pits without any other burial objects or decorations. A small collective shrine is known from one of their villages, a 10,500-year-old settlement at Jericho in the Jordan River Valley. Basin-shaped depressions in the rocks found outside homes and plastered storage pits beneath the floors of the houses indicate that the Natufians were the earliest Mesolithic people known to have stored plant foods. Certain tools found among Natufian remains bear evidence of their use to cut grain. These Mesolithic sickles consisted of small stone blades set in straight handles of wood or bone.

The new lifeways of the various Mesolithic and Archaic cultures generally provided supplies of food sufficiently abundant to permit people in some parts of the world to live in larger and more sedentary groups. They became village dwellers, and some of these settlements went on to expand into the first farming villages, towns, and ultimately cities.

THE NEOLITHIC REVOLUTION

The Neolithic, or New Stone Age derives its name from the polished stone tools that are characteristic of this period. But more important than the presence of these tools is the transition from a foraging economy based on hunting, gathering, and fishing to one based on food production, representing a major change in the subsistence practices of early peoples. It was by no means a smooth or instantaneous transition; in fact, the switch to food production spread over many centuries—even millennia—and was a direct outgrowth of the preceding Mesolithic. Where to draw the line between the two periods is not always clear.

One of the first regions to undergo this transition, and certainly the most intensively studied, was Southwest Asia. The remains of domesticated plants and animals are known from parts of Israel, Jordan, Syria, Turkey, Egypt, Iraq, and Iran, from well before 10,000 years ago.

The transition to relatively complete reliance on domesticates took several thousand years. Archaeological evidence for food production also exists from other parts of the world such as China and the Americas at similar or somewhat earlier dates. The critical point is not which region invented farming first, but rather the independent but more or less simultaneous invention of food production throughout the globe.

Domestication: What Is It?

Domestication is an evolutionary process whereby humans modify, either intentionally or unintentionally, the genetic makeup of a population of plants or animals, sometimes to the extent that members of the population are unable to survive and/or reproduce without human assistance. Domestication is essentially a special case of interdependence between different species frequently

---

Natufian culture A Mesolithic culture living in the lands that are now Israel, Lebanon, and western Syria, between about 10,200 and 12,500 years ago.
domestication An evolutionary process whereby humans modify, either intentionally or unintentionally, the genetic makeup of a population of plants or animals, sometimes to the extent that members of the population are unable to survive and/or reproduce without human assistance.

seen in the natural world, where one species depends on another (that feeds upon it) for its protection and reproductive success. For example, certain ants native to the American tropics grow fungi in their nests, and these fungi provide the ants with most of their nutrition. Like human farmers, the ants add manure, which provides nutrients to stimulate fungal growth. They also eliminate competing weeds both mechanically and through use of antibiotic herbicides.[3] The fungi are protected and ensured reproductive success while providing the ants with a steady food supply.

Numerous other examples of such cooperation between species exist, all characterized by mutual benefit. In plant–human interactions, for instance, domestication ensures the plants' reproductive success while providing humans with food. From a human point of view, domestication involves selection to eliminate thorns, toxins, and bad-tasting chemical compounds that in the wild had served to ensure a plant species' survival and selecting for larger, tastier edible parts attractive to humans. U.S. journalist Michael Pollan has turned this idea around by looking at domestication from a plant's perspective. He suggests that domesticated plant species successfully exploit human desires and considers "agriculture as something grasses did to people to conquer trees."[4]

Evidence of Early Plant Domestication

Domesticated plants generally differ from their wild ancestors in ways favored by humans, including increased size, at least of edible parts; reduction or loss of natural means of seed dispersal; reduction or loss of protective devices such as husks or distasteful chemical compounds that keep animals from eating them; loss of delayed seed germination (important to wild plants for survival in times of drought or other adverse conditions of temporary duration); and development of simultaneous ripening of the seed or fruit. Many of these characteristics can be seen in plant remains from archaeological sites. Paleobotanists can often tell the fossil of a wild plant species from a domesticated one, for example, by studying the shape and size of various plant structures.

Wild cereals have a very fragile stem, whereas domesticated ones have a tough stem. Under natural conditions, plants with fragile stems scatter their seed for themselves, whereas those with tough stems do not. When humans began to harvest wild grain stalks with a sickle, the soft stems would shatter and many seeds would be lost. Inevitably, though unintentionally, most

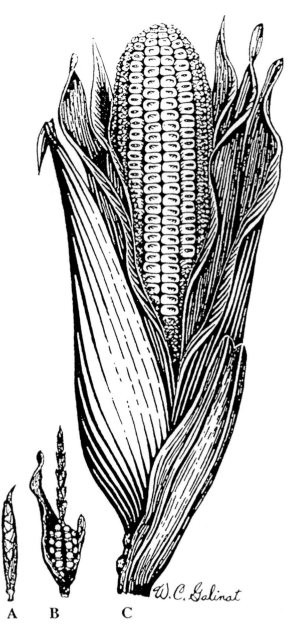

Teosinte (A), compared to 5,500-year-old maize (B) and modern maize (C). Teosinte, the wild grass from highland Mexico from which maize originated, is far less productive and doesn't taste very good. Like most plants that were domesticated, it was not a favored food for foraging people. Domestication transformed it into something highly desirable.

of the seeds that people harvested would have been taken from the tough plants. Early domesticators probably also tended to select seed from plants having few husks or none at all—eventually breeding them out—because husking prior to pounding the grains into meal or flour required extra labor.

Size of plants is another good indicator of the presence of domestication. For example, the large ear of corn (maize) we know today is a far cry from the tiny ears (about an inch long) characteristic of earliest maize. In fact, the ear of maize may have arisen when a simple

---

[3]Diamond, J. (1998). Ants, crops, and history. *Science 281*, 1,974–1,975.

[4]Pollan, M. (2001). *The botany of desire: A plant's-eye view of the world.* New York: Random House.

gene mutation transformed male tassel spikes of the wild grass called teosinte into small earliest versions of the female maize ear.[5] Small as these were (an entire ear contained less nourishment than a single kernel of modern maize), they were radically different in structure from the ears of teosinte.

Evidence of Early Animal Domestication

Domestication also produced changes in the skeletal structure of some animals. For example, the horns of wild goats and sheep differ from those of their domesticated counterparts. Most domesticated female sheep have no horns at all. Similarly, the size of an animal or its parts can vary with domestication as seen in the smaller size of certain teeth of domesticated pigs compared to those of wild ones.

A study of age and sex ratios of butchered animals at an archaeological site may indicate whether animal domestication was practiced. Investigators have determined that if the age and/or sex ratios at the site differ from those in wild herds, the imbalances are due to domestication. Archaeologists documented a sharp rise in the number of young male goats killed at 10,000-year-old sites in the Zagros Mountains of Iran. Evidently people were slaughtering the young males for food and saving the females for breeding. Although such herd management does not prove that the goats were fully domesticated, it does indicate at least a step in that direction.[6]

In the Andean highlands, the high frequency of bones of newborn llamas at archaeological sites, dating to around 6,300 years ago, is probably indicative of the beginning of domestication. Such high mortality rates for newborn animals are uncommon in wild herds but are common where animals are penned up. Under confined conditions, the inevitable buildup of mud and filth harbors bacteria and viruses that can be deadly to newborn animals.

Beginnings of Domestication

Over the past forty years, a good deal of information has accumulated about the beginnings of domestication, primarily in Southwest Asia, Central America, and the Andes. We still do not have all the answers about how and why it took place. Nonetheless, some generally valid observations can be made that help us to understand how the switch to food production may have occurred.

The first of these observations is that the switch to food production was not the result of people making certain discoveries, such as that seeds, if planted, grow into plants. Contemporary food foragers are far from ignorant about the forces of nature and are perfectly aware of the role of seeds in plant growth, that plants grow better under certain conditions than others, and so forth. Physiologist Jared Diamond aptly describes contemporary food foragers as "walking encyclopedias of natural history with individual names for as many as a thousand or more plant and animal species, and with detailed knowledge of those species' biological characteristics, distribution, and potential uses."[7] What's more, they frequently apply their knowledge so as to actively manage the resources on which they depend. For example, indigenous people living in northern Australia deliberately alter the runoff channels of creeks so as to flood extensive tracts of land, converting them into fields of wild grain. Indigenous Australians choose to continue to forage while also managing the land.

A second observation is that a switch from food foraging to food production does not free people from hard work. In fact, available ethnographic data indicate just the opposite—that farmers, by and large, work far longer hours compared to most food foragers.

A final observation is that food production is not necessarily a more secure means of subsistence than food foraging. Seed crops in particular—of the sort originally domesticated in Southwest Asia, Central America, and the Andean highlands—are highly productive but not stable from an ecological perspective because of low species diversity. Without constant human attention, their productivity suffers.

For these reasons, it is little wonder that food foragers do not necessarily regard farming and animal husbandry as superior to hunting, gathering, or fishing. Thus, there are some people in the world who have remained food foragers into the present. However, it has become increasingly difficult for them, because food-producing peoples (including postindustrial societies) have deprived them of more and more of the land base necessary for their way of life. For food foragers, as long as existing practices work well, there is no need to abandon them especially if their practices are in balance with other aspects of their society's culture. Noting that hunter–gatherers have more leisure time than farmers, U.S. anthropologist Marshall Sahlins has called them "the original affluent society."[8] Farming brings with it a whole new system of relationships that disturbs an age-old balance between humans and nature.

[5]Gould, S. J. (1991). *The flamingo's smile: Reflections in natural history* (p. 368). New York: Norton.

[6]Zeder, M. A., & Hesse, B. (2000). The initial domestication of goats (*Capra hircus*) in the Zagros Mountains 10,000 years ago. *Science 287,* 2,254–2,257.

[7]Diamond, J. (1997). *Guns, germs, and steel* (p. 143). New York: Norton.

[8]Sahlins, M. (1972). *Stone age economics.* Chicago: Aldine.

WHY HUMANS BECAME FOOD PRODUCERS

In view of what has been said so far, we may well ask: Why did any human group abandon food foraging in favor of food production?

Several theories have been proposed to account for this change in human subsistence practices. One older theory, championed by Australian archaeologist V. Gordon Childe, is the desiccation (from the Latin "to dry completely"), or oasis, theory, which is based on climatic determinism. Its proponents advanced the idea that the glacial cover over Europe and Asia caused a shift in rain patterns from Europe to northern Africa and Southwest Asia. When the glaciers retreated northward, so did the rain patterns. As a result, formerly lush regions of northern Africa and Southwest Asia became dryer, and people were forced to congregate at oases for water. Because of the relative food scarcity in such an environment, necessity drove people to collect the wild grasses and seeds growing around the oases, congregating in a part of Southwest Asia known as the Fertile Crescent (Figure 10.1). Eventually they began to cultivate various plants to provide enough food for the community. According to this theory, animal domestication began because the oases attracted hungry animals, such as wild goats, sheep, and also cattle, which came to graze on the stubble of the grain fields and to drink. Finding that these animals were often too thin to kill for food, people began to fatten them up.

Although Childe's oasis theory can be critiqued on a number of grounds and many other theories have been proposed to account for the shift to domestication, it remains historically significant as the first scientifically testable explanation for the origins of food production. Childe's theory set the stage for the development of archaeology as a science. Later theories build on Childe's ideas and take into account the role of historical as well as environmental circumstances.

The Fertile Crescent

Present evidence indicates that the earliest plant domestication took place gradually in the Fertile Crescent, the lands just east of the Mediterranean Sea. Archaeological data suggest the domestication of rye as early as

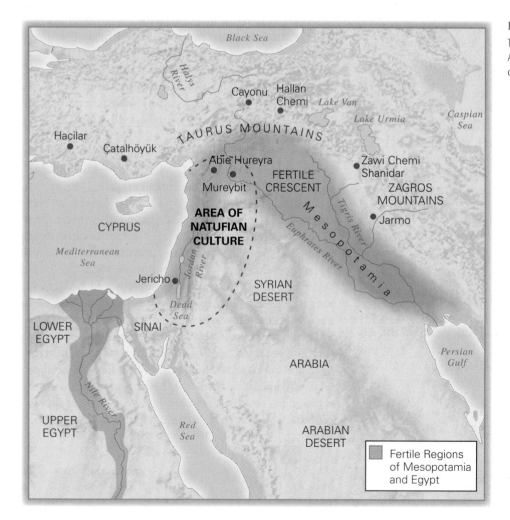

Figure 10.1

The Fertile Crescent of Southwest Asia and the area of Natufian culture.

13,000 years ago by people living at a site (Abu Hureyra) east of Aleppo, Syria, although wild plants and animals continued to be their major food sources. Over the next several millennia they became full-fledged farmers, cultivating rye and wheat.[9] By 10,300 years ago, others in the region were also growing crops.

The domestication process was a consequence of a chance convergence of independent natural events and other cultural developments.[10] The Natufians, whose culture we looked at earlier in this chapter, illustrate this process. These people lived at a time of dramatically changing climates in Southwest Asia. With the end of the last glaciation, temperatures not only became significantly warmer but markedly seasonal as well. Between 6,000 and 12,000 years ago, the region experienced the most extreme seasonality in its history, with dry summers significantly longer and hotter than today. As a consequence of increased evaporation, many shallow lakes dried up, leaving just three in the Jordan River Valley.

At the same time, the region's plant cover changed dramatically. Environmental instability and seasonal dryness favored annual plants, including wild cereal grains and legumes (such as peas, lentils, and chickpeas). Because they complete their life cycle in a single year, annuals can evolve very quickly under unstable conditions. Moreover, they store their reproductive abilities for the next wet season in abundant seeds, which can remain dormant for prolonged periods.

The Natufians, who lived where these conditions were especially severe, adapted by modifying their subsistence practices in two ways: First, they probably burned the landscape regularly to encourage browsing by red deer and grazing by gazelles, the main focus of their hunting activities. Burning the landscape removed saplings and weeds and promoted the growth of fresh green grass to lure grazing animals. Second, they placed greater emphasis on the collection of wild seeds from the annual plants that could be effectively stored to see people through the dry season. The importance of stored foods, coupled with the scarcity of reliable water sources, promoted more sedentary living patterns, reflected in the substantial villages of late Natufian times. The reliance upon seeds in Natufian subsistence was made possible by the fact that they already possessed sickles (originally used to cut reeds and sedges for baskets) for harvesting grain and grinding stones for processing a variety of wild foods.[11]

The use of sickles to harvest grain turned out to have important consequences, again unexpected, for the Natufians. In the course of harvesting, it was inevitable that many easily dispersed seeds would be lost at the harvest site, whereas those from plants that did not readily scatter their seeds would mostly be carried back to where people processed and stored them.[12] The periodic burning of vegetation carried out to encourage the deer and gazelle herds to feed nearby may have also affected the development of new genetic variation. Among plants, heat is known to affect mutation rates. Also, fire removes individuals from a population, which change the genetic structure of a group drastically and quickly. With seeds for nondispersing variants being carried back to settlements, it was inevitable that some lost seeds would germinate and grow there on dump heaps and other disturbed sites (latrines, areas cleared of trees, or burned-over terrain).

As it turns out, many of the plants that became domesticated were "colonizers," variants that do particularly well in disturbed habitats. Moreover, with people becoming increasingly sedentary, disturbed habitats became more extensive as resources closer to settlements were depleted over time. Thus, variants of plants particularly susceptible to human manipulation had more opportunities to flourish where people were living. Under such circumstances, it was inevitable that eventually people would begin to actively promote their growth, even by deliberately sowing them. Ultimately, people realized that they could play a more active role in the process by deliberately trying to breed the strains they preferred. With this, domestication may be said to have shifted from a process that was unintentional to one that was intentional.

The development of animal domestication in Southwest Asia seems to have proceeded along somewhat similar lines in the hilly country of southeastern Turkey, northern Iraq, and the Zagros Mountains of Iran. Large herds of wild sheep and goats, as well as much environmental diversity, characterized these regions. From the flood plains of the valley of the Tigris and Euphrates rivers, for example, travel to the north or east takes one into high country through three other zones: first steppe; then oak and pistachio woodlands; and, finally, high plateau country with grass, scrub, or desert vegetation. Valleys that run at right angles to the mountain ranges afford relatively easy access across these zones. Today, a number of peoples in the region still graze their herds of sheep and goats on the low steppe in the winter and move to high pastures on the plateaus in the summer.

[9]Pringle, H. (1998). The slow birth of agriculture. *Science 282*, 1,449.

[10]McCorriston, J., & Hole, F. (1991). The ecology of seasonal stress and the origins of agriculture in the Near East. *American Anthropologist 93*, 46–69.

[11]Olszewski, D. I. (1991). Comment. *Current Anthropology 32*, 43.

[12]Blumer, M. A., & Byrne, R. (1991). The ecological genetics and domestication and the origins of agriculture. *Current Anthropology 32*, 30.

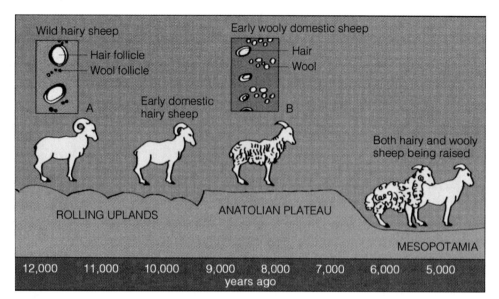

Figure 10.2

Domestication of sheep resulted in evolutionary changes that created more wool. Inset A shows a section, as seen through a microscope, of skin of wild sheep, showing the arrangement of primary (hair) and secondary (wool) follicles. Inset B shows a section of similarly enlarged skin of domestic sheep, showing the changed relationship and the change in size of follicles that accompanied the development of wool.

Prior to the domestication of plants and animals, people who inhabited this region, like the Natufians, practiced a subsistence pattern of food foraging. Different plants were found in different ecological zones, and because of the difference in altitude, plant foods matured at different times in different zones. Many animal species were hunted for meat and hides by these people, most notably, the hoofed animals: deer, gazelles, wild goats, and wild sheep. Their bones are far more common in human refuse piles than those of other animals. This is significant, for most of these animals naturally move back and forth from low winter pastures to high summer pastures.

People followed these animals in their seasonal migrations, making use along the way of other wild foods in the zones through which they passed: palm dates in the lowlands; acorns, almonds, and pistachios higher up; apples and pears higher still; wild grains maturing at different times in different zones; woodland animals in the forested zone between summer and winter grazing lands. All in all, it was a rich, varied fare.

The archaeological record indicates that, at first, animals of all ages and sexes were hunted by the people of the Southwest Asian highlands. But, beginning about 11,000 years ago, the percentage of immature sheep eaten increased to about 50 percent of the total. At the same time, the percentage of female animals eaten decreased. Apparently, people were learning that they could increase yields by sparing the females for breeding, while feasting on male lambs. This marks the beginning of human management of sheep.

As this management of flocks became more efficient, sheep were increasingly shielded from the effects of natural selection, allowing variants preferred by humans to have increased reproductive success. Variants attractive to humans did not arise out of need but at random, as mutations do. But then humans selectively bred the varieties they favored. In such a way, those features characteristic of domestic sheep—such as greater fat and meat production, excess wool, and so on—began to develop. By 9,000 years ago, the shape and size of the bones of domestic sheep had become distinguishable from those of wild sheep (Figure 10.2). At about the same time, similar developments were taking place in southeastern Turkey and the lower Jordan River Valley, where pigs were the focus of attention.[13]

Some researchers have recently linked animal domestication to the development of fixed territories and settlements. Without a notion of resource ownership, they suggest that hunters would not be likely to postpone the short-term gain of killing prey for the long-term gain of continued access to animals in the future.[14] Eventually, animal species domesticated in one area were introduced into areas outside their natural habitat.

To sum up, the domesticators of plants and animals sought only to maximize the food sources available to them. They were not aware of the long-term and revolutionary cultural consequences of their actions. But as the process continued, the productivity of the domestic species increased relative to wild species. Thus they became increasingly more important to subsistence, resulting in

[13]Pringle, H. (1998). The slow birth of agriculture. *Science 282*, 1,448.

[14]Alvard, M. S., & Kuznar, L. (2001). Deferred harvest: The transition from hunting to animal husbandry. *American Anthropologist 103* (2), 295–311.

The Dani people of New Guinea specialize in growing sweet potatoes, a crop introduced in the 16th century into a region with a long history of vegeculture. Today villagers grow more than seventy species of sweet potato and have incorporated this root crop into many important rituals.

by about 11,000 years ago.[15] It was not until 4,000 years later, however, that domestic rice dominated wild rice to become the dietary staple.

In Southeast Asia, decorations on pottery depicting rice dated to between 5,000 and 8,800 years ago document it as the earliest species to be domesticated in this region. Nevertheless, this region is primarily known for the domestication of root crops, most notably yams and taro. Root crop farming, or **vegeculture,** typically involves the growing of many different species together in a single field. Because this approximates the complexity of the natural vegetation, vegeculture tends to be more stable than seed crop cultivation. Propagation or breeding of new plants typically occurs through vegetative means—the planting of cuttings—rather than the planting of seeds.

In the Americas, the domestication of plants began about as early as it did in these other regions. One species of domestic squash may have been grown as early as 10,000 years ago in the coastal forests of Ecuador; at the same time another species was being grown in an arid region of highland Mexico.[16] Evidently, these developments were independent of each other. The ecological diversity of the highland valleys of Mexico, like the

Today, deliberate attempts to create new varieties of plants take place in many a greenhouse, experiment station, or lab. But when first begun, the creation of domestic plants was not deliberate; rather, it was the unforeseen outcome of traditional food-foraging activities. Today genetically engineered crops are being created to survive massive applications of herbicides and pesticides and not to produce viable seeds (the latter solidifies corporate control on the food industry). One may wonder what the long-term consequences will be.

further intensification of, interest in, and management of, the domesticates.

OTHER CENTERS OF DOMESTICATION

In addition to Southwest Asia, the domestication of plants and, in some cases, animals took place independently in Southeast Asia, parts of the Americas (Central America, the Andean highlands, the tropical forests of South America, and eastern North America), northern China, and Africa (Figure 10.3). In China, domestication of rice was underway along the middle Yangtze River

---

[15]Pringle, H. (1998). The slow birth of agriculture. *Science 282,* 1,449.

[16]Ibid., 1,447.

vegeculture The cultivation of domesticated root crops, such as yams and taro.

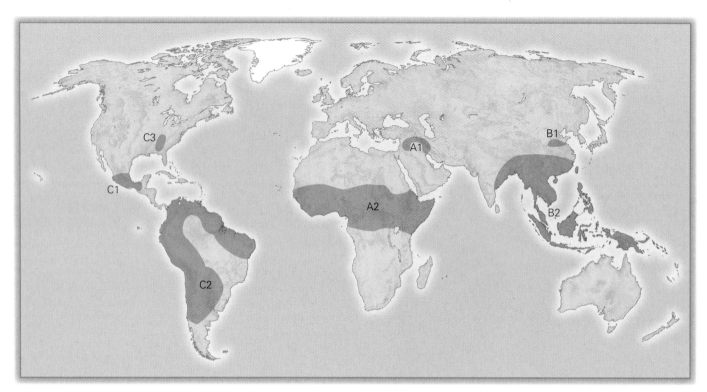

Figure 10.3
Early plant and animal domestication took place in such widely scattered areas as Southwest Asia (A1), Central Africa (A2), China (B1), Southeast Asia (B2), Mesoamerica (C1), South America (C2), and North America (C3).

In coastal Peru, the earliest domesticates were the non-edible bottle gourd (like the one shown here) and cotton. They were used to make nets and floats to catch fish, which was an important source of food.

hill country of Southwest Asia, provided an excellent environment for domestication (Figure 10.4). Movement of people through a variety of ecological zones as they changed altitude brought plant and animal species into new habitats, providing opportunities for "colonizing" species and humans alike.

Farmers in the Andean highlands of Peru, another environmentally diverse region, domesticated a variety of root crops, of which the potato is the best known. Andean farmers grew about 3,000 varieties of potato compared to the mere 250 grown in North America today. South Americans also domesticated guinea pigs, llamas, alpacas, and ducks, whereas people in the Mexican highlands never did much with domestic livestock. They limited themselves to dogs, turkeys, and bees. American Indians living north of Mexico developed some of their own indigenous domesticates. These included local varieties of squash and sunflower.

Ultimately, American Indians domesticated over 300 food crops, including two of the four most important ones in the world today: potatoes and maize (the other two are wheat and rice). In fact, America's indigenous peoples first cultivated over 60 percent of the crops grown in the world today. They remain not only the de-

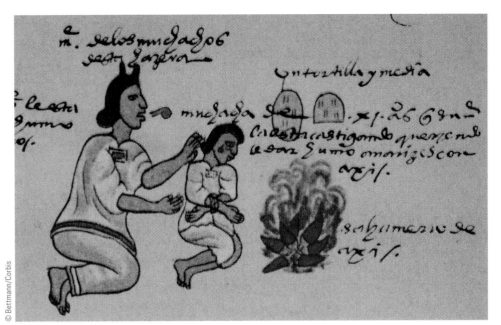

In Mexico, chili peppers have been a part of the diet for millennia. Chili peppers enhance the flavor of foods and aid digestion by helping with the breakdown of cellulose in diets heavy in plant foods. They had other uses as well: This illustration from a 16th-century Aztec manuscript shows a woman threatening her child with punishment by being exposed to smoke from chili peppers. Chili smoke was also used as a kind of chemical weapon in warfare.

© Bettmann/Corbis

CULTIGENS		PERCENTAGE		Years ago
		Hunting	Horti-culture	Wild plant use	
Squash Chili Amaranth Avocado	Cotton Maize Beans Gourd Sapote	29%		31%	3,000 — 3,500 — 4,000
Squash Chili Amaranth Avocado	Maize Beans Gourd Sapote	25%		50%	4,500 — 5,000
Squash Chili Amaranth Avocado	Maize Beans Gourd Sapote	34%		52%	5,500 — 6,000 — 6,500 — 7,000
Squash Chili Amaranth Avocado		54%		40%	7,500 — 8,000 — 8,500

Figure 10.4
Subsistence trends in Mexico's Tehuacan Valley show that here, as elsewhere, dependence of horticulture came about gradually, over a prolonged period of time.

velopers of the world's largest array of nutritious foods but are also the primary contributors to the world's varied cuisines.[17] After all, where would Italian cuisine be without tomatoes? Thai cooking without peanuts? Northern European cooking without potatoes? Small wonder American Indians have been called the world's greatest farmers.[18]

An international team of archaeologists and other scientists is beginning to decipher the farming methods used by Indians in the Amazon rainforest. These ancient methods, which left behind rich dark soils, may have important applications for humans today, as explained in this chapter's Anthropology Applied. Reviving these ancient soil-enrichment techniques could contribute to better global management of rainforests and climate today.

Considering the separate innovations of plant domestication, it is interesting to note that in all cases people developed the same categories of foods. Everywhere, starchy grains (or root crops) combine with one or more legumes: wheat and barley with peas, chickpeas, and lentils in Southwest Asia; maize with various kinds of beans in Mexico, for example. Together the amino acids (building blocks of proteins) in these starch and legume combinations provide humans with sufficient protein. The

[17]Weatherford, J. (1988). *Indian givers: How the Indians of the Americas transformed the world* (pp. 71, 115). New York: Fawcett Columbine.

[18]Weatherford, J. (1988). *Indian givers: How the Indians of the Americas transformed the world* (p. 95). New York: Fawcett Columbine.

Anthropology Applied

The Real Dirt on Rainforest Fertility ■ By Charles Mann

IRANDUBA, AMAZÔNAS STATE, BRAZIL—Above a pit dug by a team of archaeologists here is a papaya orchard filled with unusually vigorous trees bearing great clusters of plump green fruit. Below the surface lies a different sort of bounty: hundreds, perhaps thousands, of burial urns and millions of pieces of broken ceramics, all from an almost unknown people who flourished here before the conquistadors. But surprisingly, what might be most important about this central Amazonian site is not the vibrant orchard or the extraordinary outpouring of ceramics but the dirt under the trees and around the ceramics. A rich, black soil known locally as *terra preta do Indio* (Indian dark earth), it sustained large settlements on these lands for 2 millennia, according to the Brazilian-American archaeological team working here.

Throughout Amazonia, farmers prize terra preta for its great productivity—some farmers have worked it for years with minimal fertilization. Such long-lasting fertility is an anomaly in the tropics. Despite the exuberant growth of rainforests, their red and yellow soils are notoriously poor: weathered, highly acidic, and low in organic matter and essential nutrients. In these oxisols, as they are known, most carbon and nutrients are stored not in the soil, as in temperate

regions, but in the vegetation that covers it. When loggers, ranchers, or farmers clear the vegetation, the intense sun and rain quickly decompose the remaining organic matter in the soil, making the land almost incapable of sustaining life—one reason ecologists frequently refer to the tropical forest as a "wet desert."

Because terra preta is subject to the same punishing conditions as the surrounding oxisols, "its existence is very surprising," says Bruno Glaser, a chemist at the Institute of Soil Science and Soil Geography at the University of Bayreuth, Germany. "If you read the textbooks, it shouldn't be there." Yet according to William I. Woods, a geographer at Southern Illinois University, Edwardsville, terra preta might cover as much as 10 percent of Amazonia, an area the size of France. More remarkable still, terra preta appears to be the product of intensive habitation by precontact Amerindian populations. "They practiced agriculture here for centuries," Glaser says. "But instead of destroying the soil, they improved it—and that is something we don't know how to do today."

In the past few years, a small but growing group of researchers—geographers, archaeologists, soil scientists, ecologists, and anthropologists—has been investigating this "gift from the past," as

terra preta is called by one member of the Iranduba team, James B. Petersen of the University of Vermont, Burlington.[a] By understanding how indigenous groups created Amazonian dark earths, these researchers hope, today's scientists might be able to transform some of the region's oxisols into new terra preta. Indeed, experimental programs to produce "terra preta nova" have already begun. Population pressure and government policies are causing rapid deforestation in the tropics, and poor tropical soils make

---

[a]James B. Petersen died in 2005 while working in the Amazon.

---

starchy grains form the core of the diet and are eaten at every meal in the form of bread, some sort of food wrapper (like a tortilla) or a gruel or thickening agent in a stew along with one or more legumes. Being rather bland, these sources of carbohydrates and proteins are invariably combined with flavor-giving substances that help the food go down.

In Mexico, for example, the flavor enhancer par excellence is the chili pepper; in other cuisines it may be a bit of meat, a dairy product, or mushrooms. Anthropologist Sidney Mintz refers to this as the core-fringe-legume pattern (CFLP), noting that only recently has it been upset by the worldwide spread of processed sugars and high-fat foods.[19]

FOOD PRODUCTION AND POPULATION SIZE

Since the Neolithic, human population size has grown steadily. The exact relationship between population growth and food production resembles the old chicken and egg question. Some assert that population growth creates pressures that result in innovations such as food production while others suggest that population growth is a consequence of food production. As already noted, domestication inevitably leads to higher yields, and higher yields make it possible to feed more people, albeit at the cost of more work.

While increased dependence on farming is associated with increased fertility across human populations,[20]

---

[19]Mintz, S. (1996). A taste of history. In W. A. Haviland & R. J. Gordon (Eds.), *Talking about people* (2nd ed., pp. 81–82). Mountain View, CA: Mayfield.

[20]Sellen, D. W., & Mace, R. (1997). Fertility and mode of subsistence: A phylogenetic analysis. *Current Anthropology 38*, 886.

much of the clearing as economically nonviable in the long run as it is ecologically damaging.

The Good Earth

Terra preta is scattered throughout Amazonia, but it is most frequently found on low hills overlooking rivers—the kind of terrain on which indigenous groups preferred to live. According to Eduardo Neves, an archaeologist at the University of São Paulo who is part of the Iranduba team, the oldest deposits date back more than 2,000 years and occur in the lower and central Amazon; terra preta then appeared to spread to cultures upriver. By AD 500 to 1000, he says, "it appeared in almost every part of the Amazon Basin."

Typically, black-soil regions cover 1 to 5 hectares, but some encompass 300 hectares or more. The black soils are generally 40 to 60 centimeters deep but can reach more than 2 meters. Almost always they are full of broken ceramics. Although they were created centuries ago—probably for agriculture, researchers such as Woods believe—patches of terra preta are still among the most desirable land in the Amazon. Indeed, terra preta is valuable enough that locals sell it as potting soil. To the consternation of archaeologists, long planters full of terra preta, complete with pieces of pre-Columbian pottery, greet visitors to the airport in the lower Amazon town of Santarém.

As a rule, terra preta has more "plant-available" phosphorus, calcium, sulfur, and nitrogen than surrounding oxisols; it also has much more organic matter, retains moisture and nutrients better, and is not rapidly exhausted by agricultural use when managed well.

The key to terra preta's long-term fertility, Glaser says, is charcoal: Terra preta contains up to 70 times as much as adjacent oxisols. "The charcoal prevents organic matter from being rapidly mineralized," Glaser says. "Over time, it partly oxidizes, which keeps providing sites for nutrients to bind to." But simply mixing charcoal into the ground is not enough to create terra preta. Because charcoal contains few nutrients, Glaser says, "high nutrient inputs via excrement and waste such as turtle, fish, and animal bones were necessary." Special soil microorganisms are also likely to play a role in its persistent fertility, in the view of Janice Thies, a soil ecologist who is part of a Cornell University team studying terra preta. "There are indications that microbial biomass is higher in terra preta," she says, which raises the possibility that scientists might be able to create a "package" of charcoal, nutrients, and microfauna that could be used to transform oxisols into terra preta.

Slash-and-Char

Surprisingly, terra preta seems not to have been created by the "slash-and-burn" agriculture famously practiced in the tropics. In slash-and-burn, farmers clear and then burn their fields, using the ash to flush enough nutrients into the soil to support crops for a few years; when productivity declines, they move on to the next patch of forest. Glaser, Woods, and other researchers believe that the long-ago Amazonians created terra preta by a process that Christoph Steiner, a University of Bayreuth soil scientist, has dubbed "slash-and-char." Instead of completely burning organic matter to ash, in this view, ancient farmers burned it only incompletely, creating charcoal, then stirred the charcoal directly into the soil. Later they added nutrients and, in a process analogous to adding sourdough starter to bread, possibly soil previously enriched with microorganisms. In addition to its potential benefits to the soil, slash-and-char releases less carbon into the air than slash-and-burn, which has potential implications for climate change. *(By Charles C. Mann (2002). The real dirt on rainforest fertility.* Science *297, 920–923. Reprinted by permission of the AAAS.)*

the reasons behind this illustrate the complex interplay between human biology and culture in all human activity. Some researchers have suggested that the availability of soft foods for infants brought about by farming promoted population growth. In humans, frequent breastfeeding has a dampening effect on mothers' ovulation, inhibiting pregnancy in nursing mothers who breastfeed exclusively. Because breastfeeding frequency declines when soft foods are introduced, fertility tends to increase.

However, it would be overly simplistic to limit the explanation for changes in fertility to the introduction of soft foods. Many other pathways can also lead to fertility changes. For example, among farmers, numerous children are frequently seen as assets to help out with the many household chores. Further, it is now known that sedentary lifestyles and diets emphasizing a narrow range of resources characteristic of the Neolithic led to growing rates of infectious disease and higher mortality. High infant mortality may well have led to a cultural value placed on increased fertility. In other words, the relationship between farming and fertility is far from simple, as explored in this chapter's Biocultural Connection.

THE SPREAD OF FOOD PRODUCTION

Paradoxically, although domestication increases productivity, it also increases instability. This occurs because those varieties with the highest yields become the focus of human attention, while other varieties are less valued and ultimately ignored. As a result, farmers become dependent on a rather narrow range of resources, compared to the wide range utilized by food foragers. Today,

Biocultural Connection

Breastfeeding, Fertility, and Beliefs

Cross-cultural studies indicate that farming populations tend to have higher rates of fertility than hunter–gatherers. These differences in fertility were calculated in terms of the average number of children born per woman and through the average number of years between pregnancies or birth spacing. Hunter–gatherer mothers have their children about four to five years apart while some contemporary farming populations not practicing any form of birth control have another baby every year and a half.

For many years this difference was interpreted as a consequence of nutritional stress among the hunter–gatherers. This theory was based in part on the observation that humans and many other mammals require a certain percentage of body fat in order to reproduce successfully. The theory was also grounded in the mistaken cultural belief that the hunter–gatherer lifestyle,

supposedly inferior to that of "civilized" people, could not provide adequate nutrition for closer birth spacing.

Detailed studies by anthropologists Melvin Konner and Carol Worthman, among the !Kung or Ju'hoansi people of the Kalahari Desert in southern Africa, disproved this theory, revealing instead a remarkable interplay between cultural and biological processes in human infant feeding.

Konner and Worthman combined detailed observations of Ju'hoansi infant feeding practices with studies of hormonal levels in nursing Ju'hoansi mothers. Ju'hoansi mothers do not believe that babies should be fed on a schedule, as recommended by some North American child-care experts, nor do they believe that crying is "good" for babies. Instead, they respond rapidly to their infants and breastfeed them whenever the infant shows any signs of fussing both during

the day and night. The resulting pattern is breastfeeding in short very frequent bouts.

As Konner and Worthman document,[a] this pattern of breastfeeding stimulates the body to suppress ovulation, or the release of a new egg into the womb for fertilization. They documented that hormonal signals from nipple stimulation through breastfeeding controls the process of ovulation. Thus, the average number of years between children among the Ju'hoansi is not a consequence of nutritional stress. Instead, Ju'hoansi infant feeding practices and beliefs directly affect the biology of fertility.

[a]Konner, M., & Worthman, C. (1980). Nursing frequency, gonadal function, and birth spacing among !Kung hunter-gatherers. *Science 207*, 788–791.

---

this range has narrowed further. Modern agriculturists rely on a mere dozen species for about 80 percent of the world's annual tonnage of all crops.[21]

This dependence upon fewer varieties means that when a crop fails, for whatever reason, farmers have less to fall back on than do food foragers. Furthermore, the likelihood of failure is increased by the common farming practice of planting crops together in one locality, so that a disease contracted by one plant easily spreads to others. Moreover, by relying on seeds from the most productive plants of a species to establish next year's crop, farmers favor genetic uniformity over diversity. As a result, if some virus, bacterium, or fungus is able to destroy one plant, it will likely destroy them all. The famous Irish potato famine of 1845–1850 provides an example of this from a more recent time period. The massive potato crop failure caused the deaths of about 1 million people due to hunger and disease and forced another 1.5 million to abandon their homes and emigrate. The population of Ireland dropped from 8 million people before the famine to only 5 million after the famine was over.

The Irish potato famine illustrates how the combination of increased productivity and vulnerability may

contribute to the geographic spread of farming. Time and time again in the past, population growth, followed by crop failure, has triggered movements of people from one place to another, where they have re-established their familiar subsistence practices. Thus, once farming came into existence, its spread to neighboring regions through such migrations was more or less guaranteed. From Southwest Asia, for instance, farming spread northwestward eventually to all of Europe, westward to North Africa, and eastward to India. Domesticated variants also spread from China and Southeast Asia westward. Those who brought crops to new locations brought other things as well, including languages, beliefs, and new alleles for human gene pools.

A similar spread occurred from West Africa, to the southeast, creating the modern far-reaching distribution of speakers of Bantu languages. Crops including sorghum (so valuable today it is grown in hot, dry areas on all continents), pearl millet, watermelon, black-eyed peas, African yams, oil palms, and kola nuts (source of modern cola drinks) were first domesticated in West Africa but began spreading eastward by 5,000 years ago. Between 2,000 and 3,000 years ago, Bantu speakers with their crops reached the continent's east coast and a few centuries later reached deep into what is now the country of South Africa. Being well adapted to summer rains,

---

[21]Diamond, J. (1997). *Guns, germs, and steel* (p. 132). New York: Norton.

VISUAL **COUNTER**POINT

The higher fertility of the Hutterites, a religious farming culture in North America, compared to that of the !Kung hunter–gatherers from the Kalahari Desert, was originally attributed to differences in nutrition. It is now known to be related to differences in child-rearing beliefs and practices.

African crops spread no further, for the Cape of South Africa has a Mediterranean climate with winter rains.

CULTURE OF NEOLITHIC SETTLEMENTS

A number of Neolithic settlements have been excavated, particularly in Southwest Asia. The structures, artifacts, and food debris found at these sites have revealed much about the daily activities of their former inhabitants as they pursued the business of making a living. Perhaps the best known of these sites is Jericho, an early farming community in the Jordan River Valley of Palestine.

Jericho: An Early Farming Community

Excavations at the Neolithic settlement that later grew to become the biblical city of Jericho revealed the remains of a sizable farming community inhabited as early as 10,350 years ago. Here, in the Jordan River Valley, crops could be grown almost continuously, due to the presence of a bounteous spring and the rich soils of an Ice Age lake that had dried up some 3,000 years earlier. In addition, flood-borne deposits originating in the Judean highlands to the west regularly renewed the fertility of the soil.

To protect their settlement against these floods and associated mudflows, as well as invaders, the people of Jericho built massive walls of stone around it.[22] Within

these walls (6½ feet wide and 12 feet high), as well as a large rock-cut ditch (27 feet wide and 9 feet deep), an estimated 400 to 900 people lived in houses of mud brick with plastered floors arranged around courtyards. In addition to these houses, a stone tower that would have taken 100 people 104 days to build was located inside one corner of the wall, near the spring. A staircase inside it probably led to a mud-brick building on top. This massive wall—near mud-brick storage facilities as well as peculiar structures of possible ceremonial significance—provide evidence of social changes in these early farming communities. A village cemetery also reflects the sedentary life of these early people; nomadic groups, with few exceptions, rarely buried their dead in a single central location.

Close contact between the farmers of Jericho and other villages is indicated by common features in art, ritual, use of prestige goods, and burial practices. Other evidence of trade consists of obsidian and turquoise from Sinai as well as marine shells from the coast, all discovered inside the walls of Jericho.

Neolithic Material Culture

Various innovations in the realms of tool making, pottery, housing, and clothing characterized life in Neolithic villages. All of these are examples of material culture.

Tool Making

Early harvesting tools were made of wood or bone into which razor sharp flint blades were inserted. Later tools continued to be made by chipping and flaking stone, but

[22]Bar-Yosef, O. (1986), The walls of Jericho: An alternative interpretation. *Current Anthropology 27,* 160.

during the Neolithic period, stone that was too hard to be chipped was ground and polished for tools. People developed scythes, forks, hoes, and simple plows to replace their digging sticks. Mortars and pestles were used to grind and crush grain. Later, when domesticated animals became available for use as draft animals, plows were redesigned. Along with the development of diverse technologies, individuals acquired specialized skills for creating a variety of implements including leatherworks, weavings, and pottery.

Pottery

Hard work on the part of those producing the food would also support other members of the society who could then apply their skills and energy to various craft specialties such as pottery. In the Neolithic, different forms of pottery were created for transporting and storing food, water, and various material possessions.

Because pottery vessels are impervious to damage by insects, rodents, and dampness, they could be used for storing small grain, seeds, and other materials. Moreover, food can be boiled in pottery vessels directly over the fire rather than by such ancient techniques as dropping stones heated directly in the fire into the food being cooked. Pottery was also used for pipes, ladles, lamps, and other objects, and some cultures used large vessels for disposal of the dead. Significantly, pottery containers remain important for much of humanity today.

Widespread use of pottery, which is made of clay and fired in very hot ovens, is a good, though not foolproof, indication of a sedentary community. It is found in abundance in all but a few of the earliest Neolithic settlements. Its fragility and weight make it less practical for use by nomads and hunters, who more commonly use woven bags, baskets, and animal hide containers. Nevertheless, there are some modern nomads who make and use pottery, just as there are farmers who lack it. In fact, food

This pottery vessel from Turkey was made around 7,600 years ago. Pigs were under domestication as early as 10,500 to 11,000 years ago in southeastern Turkey.

foragers in Japan were making pottery by 13,000 years ago, long before it was being made in Southwest Asia.

The manufacture of pottery requires artful skill and considerable technological sophistication. To make a useful vessel requires knowledge of clay: how to remove impurities from it, how to shape it into desired forms, and how to dry it in a way that does not cause cracking. Proper firing is tricky as well; it must be heated to over 600 degrees Fahrenheit so that the clay will harden and resist future disintegration from moisture, but care must be taken to prevent the object from cracking or even exploding as it heats and later cools down.

Pottery is decorated in various ways. For example, designs can be engraved on the vessel before firing, or special rims, legs, bases, and other details may be made separately and fastened to the finished pot. Painting is the most common form of pottery decoration, and there are literally thousands of painted designs found among the pottery remains of ancient cultures.

Housing

Food production and the new sedentary lifestyle brought about another technological development—house building. Because they move frequently, most food foragers show little interest in permanent housing. Cave shelters, pits dug in the earth, and simple lean-tos made of hides and tree limbs serve the purpose of keeping the weather out. In the Neolithic, however, dwellings became more complex in design and more diverse in type. Some Neolithic peoples constructed houses of wood, while others built more elaborate shelters made of stone, sun-dried brick, or poles plastered together with mud or clay.

Although permanent housing frequently goes along with food production, there is evidence that substantial housing could exist without food production. For example, on the northwestern coast of North America, people lived in substantial houses made of heavy planks hewn from cedar logs, yet their food consisted entirely of wild plants and animals, especially salmon and sea mammals.

Clothing

During the Neolithic, for the first time in human history, clothing was made of woven textiles. The raw materials and technology necessary for the production of clothing came from several sources: flax and cotton from farming; wool from domesticated sheep, llamas, or goats; silk from silk worms. Human invention contributed the spindle for spinning and the loom for weaving.

Social Structure

Evidence of all the economic and technological developments listed thus far have enabled archaeologists to draw certain inferences concerning the organization of

Sometimes Neolithic villages got together to carry out impressive communal works. Shown here is Stonehenge, the famous ceremonial and astronomical center in England, which dates back to about 4,500 years ago. Its construction relates to the new attitudes toward the earth and forces of nature associated with food production.

© John Kegan

Neolithic societies. Although indication of ceremonial activity exists, little evidence of a centrally organized and directed religious life has been found. Burials, for example, show a marked absence of social differentiation. Early Neolithic graves were rarely constructed of or covered by stone slabs and rarely included elaborate objects. Evidently, no person had attained the kind of exalted status that would have required an elaborate funeral. The small size of most villages and the absence of elaborate buildings suggest that the inhabitants knew one another very well and were even related, so that most of their relationships were probably highly personal ones, with equal emotional significance.

A general picture emerges that Neolithic societies were relatively egalitarian with minimal division of labor but did have some development of new and more specialized social roles. Villages seem to have been made up of several households, each providing for most of its own needs. The organizational needs of society beyond the household level were probably met by kinship groups.

Neolithic Culture in the Americas

In the Americas the shape and timing of the Neolithic transition differed compared to other parts of the world. For example, Neolithic agricultural villages were common in Southwest Asia between 8,000 and 9,000 years ago, but similar villages did not appear in the Americas until about 4,500 years ago, in **Mesoamerica** (southern Mexico and northern Central America) and the central Andes. Moreover, pottery, which developed in Southwest Asia shortly after plant and animal domestication, did not emerge in the Americas until about 4,500 years

ago. The potter's wheel was not used by early Neolithic people in the Americas. Instead, elaborate pottery was manufactured by hand. Looms and the hand spindle appeared in the Americas about 3,000 years ago.

None of these absences indicate any backwardness on the part of Native American peoples, many of whom, as we have already seen, were highly sophisticated farmers and plant breeders. Rather, the effectiveness of existing practices was such that they continued to be satisfactory. When food production developed in Mesoamerica and the Andean highlands, it did so wholly independently of Europe and Asia, with different crops, animals, and technologies.

Outside Mesoamerica and the Andean highlands, hunting, fishing, and the gathering of wild plant foods remained important elements in the economy of Neolithic peoples in the Americas. Apparently, most American Indians chose not to make as complete a change from a food-foraging to a food-producing mode of life, even though maize and other domestic crops came to be cultivated just about everywhere that climate permitted.

THE NEOLITHIC AND HUMAN BIOLOGY

Although we tend to think of the invention of food production in terms of its cultural impact, it obviously had a biological impact as well. From studies of human skel-

Mesoamerica The region encompassing southern Mexico and northern Central America.

etons from Neolithic burials, physical anthropologists have found evidence for a somewhat lessened mechanical stress on peoples' bodies and teeth. Although there are exceptions, the teeth of Neolithic peoples show less wear, their bones are less robust, and osteoarthritis (the result of stressed joint surfaces) is not as marked as in the skeletons of Paleolithic and Mesolithic peoples. Though Neolithic teeth show less wear, recent discoveries from Pakistan provide the earliest evidence of human dentistry: tiny holes made in the molar teeth of ancient live humans, with fine flint drills.[23] Whether dentistry accompanied an increase in dental decay brought about by the dietary shift of this period remains to be seen. This would parallel the clear evidence for a marked overall deterioration in health and mortality during the Neolithic. Anthropologist Anna Roosevelt sums up our knowledge of this in the following Original Study.

---

[23]Coppa, A., et al. (2006). Early Neolithic tradition of dentistry. *Nature 440*, 755–756.

Original Study ▪ By Anna Roosevelt

History of Mortality and Physiological Stress

Although there is a relative lack of evidence for the Paleolithic stage, enough skeletons have been studied that it seems clear that seasonal and periodic physiological stress regularly affected most prehistoric hunting-gathering populations, as evidenced by the presence of enamel hypoplasias [horizontal linear defects in tooth enamel] and Harris lines [horizontal lines near the ends of long bones].

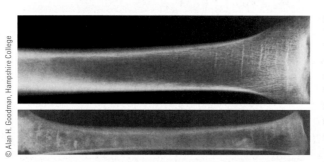

© Alan H. Goodman, Hampshire College

Harris lines near the ends of these youthful thigh bones, found in a prehistoric farming community in Arizona, are indicative of recovery after growth arrest, caused by famine or disease.

What also seems clear is that severe and chronic stress, with high frequency of hypoplasias, infectious disease lesions, pathologies related to iron-deficiency anemia, and high mortality rates, is not characteristic of these early populations. There is no evidence of frequent, severe malnutrition, and so the diet must have been adequate in calories and other nutrients most of the time.

During the Mesolithic, the proportion of starch in the diet rose, to judge from the increased occurrence of certain dental diseases, but not enough to create an impoverished diet. At this time, diets seem to have been made up of a rather large number of foods, so that the failure of one food source would not be catastrophic. There is a possible slight tendency for Paleolithic people to be healthier and taller than Mesolithic people, but there is no apparent trend toward increasing

physiological stress during the Mesolithic. Thus, it seems that both hunter–gatherers and incipient agriculturalists regularly underwent population pressure, but only to a moderate degree.

During the periods when effective agriculture first comes into use, there seems to be a temporary upturn in health and

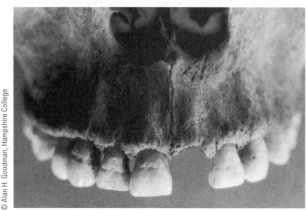

© Alan H. Goodman, Hampshire College

Enamel hypoplasias, such as those shown on these teeth, are indicative of arrested growth caused by famine or disease. These teeth are from an adult who lived in an ancient farming community in Arizona.

survival rates in a few regions: Europe, North America, and the eastern Mediterranean. At this stage, wild foods are still consumed periodically, and a variety of plants are cultivated, suggesting the availability of adequate amounts of different nutrients. Based on the increasing frequency of tooth disease related to high carbohydrate consumption, it seems that cultivated plants probably increased the storable calorie supply, removing for a time any seasonal or periodic problems in food supply. In most regions, however, the development of agriculture seems not to have had this effect, and there seems to have been a slight increase in physiological stress.

Stress, however, does not seem to have become common and widespread until after the development of high degrees of sedentism, population density, and reliance on intensive agriculture. At this stage in all regions the incidence of physiological stress increases greatly, and average mortality rates increase appreciably.

Most of these agricultural populations have high frequencies of porotic hyperostosis and cribra orbitalia [bone deformities indicative of chronic iron-deficiency anemia], and there is a substantial increase in the number and severity of enamel hypoplasias and pathologies associated with infectious disease. Stature in many populations appears to have been considerably lower than would be expected if genetically determined height maxima had been reached, which suggests that the growth arrests documented by pathologies were causing stunting.

Accompanying these indicators of poor health and nourishment, there is a universal drop in the occurrence of Harris lines, suggesting a poor rate of full recovery from the stress. Incidence of carbohydrate-related tooth disease increases, apparently because subsistence by this time is characterized by a heavy emphasis on a few starchy food

crops. Populations seem to have grown beyond the point at which wild food resources could be a meaningful dietary supplement, and even domestic animal resources were commonly reserved for farm labor and transport rather than for diet supplementation.

It seems that a large proportion of most sedentary prehistoric populations under intensive agriculture underwent chronic and life-threatening malnutrition and disease, especially during infancy and childhood. The causes of the nutritional stress are likely to have been the poverty of the staple crops in most nutrients except calories, periodic famines caused

by the instability of the agricultural system, and chronic lack of food due to both population growth and economic expropriation by elites. The increases in infectious disease probably reflect both a poorer diet and increased interpersonal contact in crowded settlements, and it is, in turn, likely to have aggravated nutritional problems.

(By Anna C. Roosevelt (1984). Population, health, and the evolution of subsistence: Conclusions from the conference. In M. N. Cohen & G. J. Armelagos (Eds.), Paleopathology at the origins of agriculture (pp. 572–574). Orlando: Academic Press.) ∎

Like many infectious diseases, mad cow disease is a result of domestication and human manipulation of animal diets. In this case the infectious particle is not a virus or bacteria, but rather a prion—a newly discovered infectious protein particle. Prions were introduced to cows through their feed, which included ground remains of other animals with the infected prions. By eating infected beef, the disease may be transmitted to humans.

For the most part, the crops on which Neolithic peoples came to depend were selected for their higher productivity and storability rather than their nutritional value. Moreover, as already noted, their nutritional shortcomings would have been exacerbated by their susceptibility to periodic failure, particularly as populations grew in size. Thus, the worsened health and mortality of Neolithic peoples is not surprising. Some have gone so far as to assert that the switch from food foraging to food production was the worst mistake that humans ever made!

Another key contributor to the increased incidence of disease and mortality was probably the new mode of life in Neolithic communities. Sedentary life in fixed villages brings with it sanitation problems as garbage and

human waste accumulate. These are not a problem for small groups of people who move about from one campsite to another. Moreover, airborne diseases are more easily transmitted where people are gathered into villages. Another factor, too, was the close association between humans and their domestic animals, a situation conducive to the transmission of some animal diseases to humans. A host of life-threatening diseases—including smallpox, chicken pox, and in fact all of the infectious diseases of childhood that were not overcome by medical science until the latter half of the 20th century—were transmitted to humans through their close association with domestic animals (Table 10.1).

TABLE 10.1	**DISEASES ACQUIRED FROM DOMESTICATED ANIMALS**
Human Disease	**Animal with Most Closely Related Pathogen**
Measles	Cattle (rinderpest)
Tuberculosis	Cattle
Smallpox	Cattle (cowpox) or other livestock with related pox viruses
Influenza	Pigs, ducks
Pertussis ("whooping cough")	Pigs, dogs

Some of the diseases that humans have acquired from domestic animals. Close contact with animals provides a situation in which variants of animal pathogens may establish themselves in humans.

Source: Diamond, J. (1997). *Guns, germs, and steel* (p. 207). New York: Norton.

The abnormal hemoglobin responsible for sickle-cell anemia, discussed in Chapter 2, provides another example of the impact of food production on human biology. Other abnormal hemoglobins are associated with the spread of farming from Southwest Asia westward around the Mediterranean as well as eastward to India, and also with the spread of farming in Southeast Asia. In all these regions, changes in human gene pools took place as a biological response to malaria, which had become a problem as a result of farming practices.

Higher mortality rates in Neolithic villages were offset by increased fertility, for population growth accelerated dramatically at precisely the moment that health and mortality worsened. The factors responsible for higher birthrates have already been discussed in this chapter.

THE NEOLITHIC AND THE IDEA OF PROGRESS

Despite the fact that the overall health of Neolithic peoples often worsened as a consequence of this cultural shift, many view the transition from food foraging to food production as a great step upward on a ladder of progress. In part this interpretation is due to one of the more widely held beliefs of Western culture: that human history is basically a record of steady progress over time. To be sure, farming allowed people to increase the size of their populations, to live together in substantial sedentary communities, and to reorganize the workload in ways that permitted craft specialization. This is not progress in a universal sense but, rather, a set of cultural beliefs about the nature of progress. Each culture, after all, defines progress (if it does so at all) in its own terms.

Whatever the benefits of food production, however, a substantial price was paid.[24] As anthropologists Mark Cohen and George Armelagos put it, "Taken as a whole, indicators fairly clearly suggest an overall decline in the quality—and probably in the length—of human life associated with the adoption of agriculture."[25]

Rather than imposing ethnocentric notions of progress on the archaeological record, it is best to view the advent of food production as but one more factor contributing to the diversification of cultures, something that had begun in the Paleolithic. Although some societies continued to practice various forms of hunting, gathering, and fishing, others became **horticultural**—small communities of gardeners working with simple hand tools and using neither irrigation nor the plow. Horticulturists typically cultivate a variety of crops in small gardens they have cleared by hand. Some horticultural societies, however, developed **agriculture.** Technologically more complex than horticultural societies, agriculturalists practice intensive crop cultivation, employing plows, fertilizers, and possibly irrigation. They may use a wooden or metal plow pulled by one or more harnessed draft animals, such as the horse, oxen, or water buffalo, to produce food on larger plots of land. The distinction between horticulturalist and intensive agriculturalist is not always an easy one to make. For example, the Hopi Indians of the North American Southwest traditionally employed irrigation in their farming while at the same time using basic hand tools.

Pastoralism arose in environments that were too dry, too grassy, too steep, too cold, or too hot for effective horticulture or intensive agriculture. Pastoralists breed and manage migratory herds of domesticated grazing animals, such as goats, sheep, cattle, llamas, or camels. For example, the Russian steppes, with their heavy grass cover, were not suitable to farming without a plow, but they were ideal for herding. Thus, a number of peoples living in the arid grasslands and deserts that stretch from northwestern Africa into Central Asia kept large herds of domestic animals, relying on their neighbors for plant foods. Finally, some societies went on to develop civilizations—the subject of the next chapter.

---

[24]Cohen, M. N., & Armelagos, G. J. (1984). *Paleopathology at the origins of agriculture.* Orlando: Academic Press; Goodman, A., &

horticulture Cultivation of crops carried out with simple hand tools such as digging sticks or hoes.
agriculture Intensive crop cultivation, employing plows, fertilizers, and/or irrigation.
pastoralism Breeding and managing migratory herds of domesticated grazing animals, such as goats, sheep, cattle, llamas, or camels.

Armelagos, G. J. (1985). Death and disease at Dr. Dickson's mounds. *Natural History Magazine* 94(9), 12–18.

[25]Cohen, M. N., & Armelagos, G. J. (1984). Paleopathology at the origins of agriculture: Editors' summation. In *Paleopathology at the origins of agriculture* (p. 594). Orlando: Academic Press.

Questions for Reflection

1. The changed lifeways of the Neolithic included the domestication of plants and animals as well as settlement into villages. How did these cultural transformations both solve the challenges of existence while creating new challenges for humans of the past and today?

2. Why do you think some people of the past chose not to make the change from food foragers to food producers? What problems existing in today's world have their origins in the lifeways of the Neolithic?

3. Though human biology and culture are always interacting, the rates of biological change and culture change uncoupled at some point in the history of our development. Think of examples of how the differences in these rates had consequences for humans in the Neolithic and in the present.

4. Why are the changes of the Neolithic sometimes mistakenly associated with progress? Why have the social forms that originated in the Neolithic come to dominate the earth?

5. Although the archaeological record indicates some differences in the timing of domestication of plants and animals in different parts of the world, why is it incorrect to say that one region was more advanced than another?

Suggested Readings

Childe, V. G. (1951). *Man makes himself.* New York: New American Library.

In this classic, originally published in 1936, Childe presented his concept of the Neolithic revolution. He places special emphasis on the technological inventions that helped transform humans from food gatherers to food producers.

Coe, S. D. (1994). *America's first cuisines.* Austin: University of Texas Press.

Writing in an accessible style, Coe discusses some of the more important crops grown by Native Americans and explores their early history and domestication. Following this she describes how these foods were prepared, served, and preserved by the Aztec, Maya, and Incas.

Diamond, J. (1997). *Guns, germs, and steel.* New York: Norton.

This Pulitzer Prize-winning best-seller tries to answer the question, Why are wealth and power distributed as they are in the world today? For Diamond, the answer requires an understanding of events associated with the origin and spread of food production. Although Diamond falls into various ethnocentric traps, he provides a great deal of solid information on the domestication and spread of crops and the biological consequences for humans.

MacNeish, R. S. (1992). *The origins of agriculture and settled life.* Norman: University of Oklahoma Press.

MacNeish was a pioneer in the study of the start of food production in the New World. In this book, he reviews the evidence from around the world in order to develop general laws about the development of agriculture and evolution of settled life.

Rindos, D. (1984). *The origins of agriculture: An evolutionary perspective.* Orlando: Academic Press.

This is one of the most important books on agricultural origins. After identifying the weaknesses of existing theories, Rindos presents his own evolutionary theory of agricultural origins.

Zohary, D., & Hopf, M. (1993). *Domestication of plants in the Old World* (2nd ed.). Oxford: Clarenden Press.

This book deals with the origin and spread of domestic plants in western Asia, Europe, and the Nile Valley. Included is a species-by-species discussion of the various crops, an inventory of remains from archaeological sites, and a conclusion summarizing present knowledge.

Thomson Audio Study Products

 Enjoy the MP3-ready Audio Lecture Overviews for each chapter and a comprehensive audio glossary of key terms for quick study and review. Whether walking to class, doing laundry, or studying at your desk, you now have the freedom to choose when, where, and how you interact with your audio-based educational media. See the preface for information on how to access this on-the-go study and review tool.

The Anthropology Resource Center

www.thomsonedu.com/anthropology
The Anthropology Resource Center provides extended learning materials to reinforce your understanding of key concepts in the four fields of anthropology. For each of the four fields, the Resource Center includes dynamic exercises including video exercises, map exercises, simulations, and "Meet the Scientists" interviews, as well as critical thinking questions that can be assigned and e-mailed to instructors. The Resource Center also provides breaking news in anthropology and interesting material on applied anthropology to help you link what you are learning to the world around you.

11 The Emergence of Cities and States

© Tavid Rankin Bingham

CHALLENGE ISSUE

With the emergence of cities and states, people began to face the challenge of social stratification in which a ruling elite controls the means of subsistence and many other aspects of daily life, often resulting in the oppression of others. While the people of such societies are interdependent, the elite classes have disproportionate access to and control of all resources including human labor. The centralized governments that emerged with cities and states have commonly used their power to mobilize and supervise labor for the construction of large-scale dwellings, monuments, and military works, all of which served to strengthen or extend their rule. One such monumental undertaking was the Great Wall of China, a 4,163-mile wall built over 2,000 years ago, for protection from plundering nomadic peoples to the north.

When and Where Did the World's First Cities Develop?

Cities are urban settlements with well-defined centers and populations that are large, dense, and diversified both economically and socially. They are characteristic of civilizations that developed independently in Eurasia, Africa, and the Americas. Between 4,500 and 6,000 years ago, cities began to develop in China, the Indus and Nile valleys, Mesopotamia, Mesoamerica, and the central Andes. The world's oldest cities were those of Mesopotamia, but one of the largest was located in Mesoamerica.

What Changes in Culture Accompanied the Rise of Cities?

Four basic cultural changes mark the transition from Neolithic village existence to life in urban centers: agricultural innovation, as new farming methods were developed; diversification of labor, as more people were freed from food production to pursue a variety of full-time craft specialties; the emergence of centralized governments to deal with the new problems of urban life; and the emergence of social classes, as people were ranked according to the work they did or the position of the families into which they were born.

Why Did Cities Develop into States?

Ancient cities developed into what anthropologists call civilizations: societies in which large numbers of people live in cities, are socially stratified, and are governed by centrally organized political systems called states. A number of theories have been proposed to explain why civilizations develop. For example, population growth led to competition for space and scarce resources. This competition favored the development of centralized authority to control resources and, incidentally, organized warfare. Some civilizations, though, appear to have developed as a result of unifying beliefs and values. In some cases, the self-promoting actions of powerful individuals may have played a role. Thus, it may be that civilizations arose in different places for different reasons.

A walk down a busy street of a city such as New York or San Francisco brings us in contact with numerous activities essential to life in North American society. Sidewalks are crowded with people going to and from offices and stores. Heavy traffic of cars, taxis, and trucks periodically comes to a standstill. A brief two-block stretch may contain a grocery store; sidewalk vendors; shops selling clothing, appliances, or books; a restaurant; a newsstand; a gasoline station; and a movie theater. Other features such as a museum, a police station, a school, a hospital, or a church distinguish some neighborhoods.

Each of these services or places of business is dependent on others from outside this two-block radius. A butcher shop, for instance, depends on slaughterhouses and beef ranches. A clothing store could not exist without designers, farmers who produce cotton and wool, and workers who manufacture synthetic fibers. Restaurants rely on refrigerated trucking and vegetable and dairy farmers. Hospitals need insurance companies, pharmaceutical companies, and medical equipment industries to function. All institutions, finally, depend on the public utilities—the telephone, gas, water, and electric companies. Although interdependence is not immediately apparent to the passerby, it is an important aspect of modern cities.

The interdependence of goods and services in a big city makes a variety of products readily available to people. But interdependence also creates vulnerability. If strikes, bad weather, or acts of violence cause one service to stop functioning, other services can deteriorate. At the same time, cities are resilient in their response to stresses. When one service breaks down, others take over its functions. During a long newspaper strike in New York City in the 1960s, for example, several new magazines were launched, and television networks expanded their coverage of news and events. In many parts of the world the violence of war has caused extensive damage to basic infrastructure, leading to the development of alternative systems to cope with everything from the most basic tasks such as procuring food to communication within global political systems.

On the surface, city life seems so orderly that we take it for granted; but a moment's reflection reminds us that the intricate fabric of city life did not always exist, and the concentrated availability of diverse goods is a very recent development in human history.

DEFINING CIVILIZATION

The word *civilization* comes from the Latin *civis,* which refers to one who is an inhabitant of a city, and *civitas,* which refers to the urban community in which one dwells. The concept of civilization therefore contains the idea of "citification" or "the coming-to-be of cities."

In everyday North American and European usage, the word *civilization* carries the notion of refinement

The violence of war destroys the basic facilities of cities, as seen in Kabul, Afghanistan, the site of years of constant war.

© AP Images

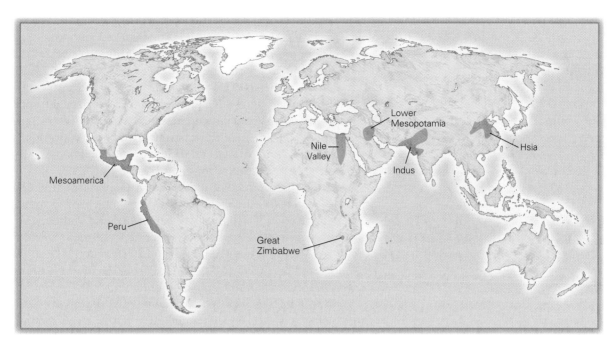

Figure 11.1

The major early civilizations sprang from Neolithic villages in various parts of the world. Those of the Americas developed wholly independently of those in Africa and Eurasia; Chinese civilization seems to have developed independently of Southwest Asia (including the Nile and Indus) civilizations.

and progress, and the term may imply judgments about cultures according to an ethnocentric standard. In anthropology, by contrast, the term has a more precise meaning that avoids culture-bound notions. As used by anthropologists, **civilization** refers to societies in which large numbers of people live in cities, are socially stratified, and are governed by a ruling elite working through centrally organized political systems called states. We shall elaborate on all of these points in the course of this chapter.

As Neolithic villages grew into towns, the world's first cities developed. This happened between 4,500 and 6,000 years ago, first in Mesopotamia (modern-day Iraq), then in Egypt's Nile Valley and the Indus Valley (today's India and Pakistan). In China, civilization was underway by 5,000 years ago. Independent of these developments in Eurasia and Africa, the first American Indian cities appeared in Peru around 4,000 years ago and in Mesoamerica about 2,000 years ago (Figure 11.1).

THOMSON AUDIO STUDY PRODUCTS
Take advantage of the MP3-ready Audio Lecture Overviews and comprehensive audio glossary of key terms for each chapter. See the preface for information on how to access this on-the-go study and review tool.

What characterized these first cities? Why are they called the birthplaces of civilization? The first feature of cities—and of civilization—is their large size and population.

But cities are more than overgrown towns. Consider the case of Çatalhöyük, a compact 9,500-year-old village settlement in south-central Turkey.[1] The tightly packed houses for its more than 5,000 inhabitants left no room for streets. People traversed the roofs of neighboring houses and dropped through a hole in the roof to get into their own homes. While house walls were covered with all sorts of paintings and bas-reliefs, the houses were structurally similar to one another, and no known public

---

[1]Material on Çatalhöyük is drawn from Balter, M. (1998). Why settle down? The mystery of communities. *Science 282,* 1,442–1,444; Balter, M. (1999). A long season puts Çatalhöyük in context. *Science 286,* 890–891; Balter, M. (2001). Did plaster hold Neolithic society together? *Science 294,* 2,278–2,281; Kunzig, R. (1999). A tale of two obsessed archaeologists, one ancient city and nagging doubts about whether science can ever hope to reveal the past. *Discover 20* (5), 84–92.

civilization In anthropology, a type of society marked by the presence of cities, social classes, and the state.

tral authority, technological intensification, and social stratification. For example, flood control and protection were vital components of the great ancient cities of the Indus River Valley, located in today's India and Pakistan. Mohenjo-Daro—an urban center at its peak some 4,500 years ago with a population of at least 20,000—was built on an artificial mound, safe from flood waters. Further, the streets of this densely populated city were laid out in a grid pattern and included individual homes with sophisticated drainage systems.

Ancient peoples incorporated their spiritual beliefs and social order into the cities they built. For example, the layout of the great Mesoamerican city Teotihuacan, founded 2,200 years ago, translated the solar calendar into a unified spatial pattern. The Street of the Dead—a grand north-south axis running from the Pyramid of the Moon at the north end and bordered by the Pyramid of the Sun, the royal palace compound, and other major structures—was deliberately oriented to an astronomical marker, east of true north. Ancient city planners even channeled the San Juan River to conform to the grid where it runs through the city (Figure 11.2). Surrounding this core were thousands of apartment compounds, separated from one another by a grid of narrow streets, maintaining the east-of-north orientation throughout the city. It is estimated that over 100,000 people inhabited this great city until its sudden collapse possibly in the 7th century.

architecture existed. People grew some crops and tended livestock but also collected significant amounts of food from wild plants and animals, never intensifying their agricultural practices. Evidence of a division of labor or of a centralized authority is minimal or nonexistent. It was as if several Neolithic villages were crammed together in one place at Çatalhöyük.

Archaeological evidence from early urban centers, by contrast, demonstrates organized planning by a cen-

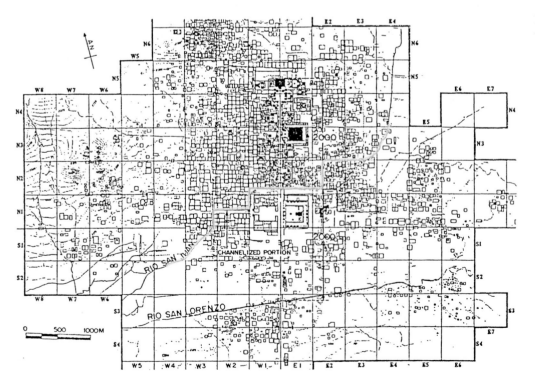

Figure 11.2

The founders of Teotihuacan imposed an audacious plan on several square kilometers of landscape in central Mexico. At the center is the Street of the Dead, running from the Pyramid of the Moon (near top), past the Pyramid of the Sun, and, south of the San Juan River (Rio), the palace compound. Note the gridded layout of surrounding apartment compounds and the channeled San Juan River.

VISUAL **COUNTER**POINT

Looking south down Teotihuacan's principal avenue, the Street of the Dead, an urban axis unequaled in its scale until the construction of such modern-day avenues as the Champs Elysées in Paris.

Finally, clear evidence for both social and economic diversity exists in Teotihuacan. Some six levels of society can be recognized by variation in size and quality of apartment rooms. Those at and near the top of the social scale lived on or near the Street of the Dead. The Pyramid of the Sun along this avenue was built above a cave, which was seen as a portal to the underworld and as the home of deities associated with death. Teotihuacan artisans worked on exotic goods and raw materials imported from afar, and at least two neighborhoods housed people with foreign affiliations—one with Oaxaca, the other (the "merchant's barrio") with the Gulf and Maya lowlands. Farmers, whose labor in fields (some of them irrigated) supplied the food to fellow city dwellers, also resided in the city.[2]

Mohenjo-Daro and Teotihuacan, like other early cities throughout the globe, were far more than expanded Neolithic villages. Such great changes took place in the transition from village to city that the emergence of urban living is considered by some to be one of the great transformations in human culture. The following case study gives us a glimpse of another of the world's ancient cities, how archaeologists studied it, and how it may have grown from a smaller farming community.

---

[2]Cowgill, G. L. (1997). State and society at Teotihuacan, Mexico. *Annual Review of Anthropology 26*, 129–161.

TIKAL: A CASE STUDY

The ancient city of Tikal, one of the largest lowland Maya centers in existence, is situated in Central America about 300 kilometers north of Guatemala City. Tikal was built on a broad limestone terrace in a rainforest. Here the Maya settled 3,000 years ago. Because the Maya calendar can be precisely correlated with our own, it is known that their civilization flourished until 1,100 years ago.

At its height, Tikal covered about 120 square kilometers (km^2), and its center or nucleus was the Great Plaza, a large, paved area surrounded by about 300 major structures and thousands of houses. Starting from a small, dispersed population, Tikal swelled to at least 45,000 people. By 1,550 years ago, its population density had reached 600 to 700 persons per square kilometer, which was three times that of the surrounding region.

Tikal and the surrounding region were intensively explored under the joint auspices of the University of Pennsylvania Museum and the Guatemalan government from 1956 through the 1960s. At the time, it was the most ambitious archaeological project undertaken in the western hemisphere.

In the first few years of the Tikal Project, archaeologists investigated only major temple and palace structures found in the vicinity of the Great Plaza, at the site's epicenter. But in 1959, aiming to gain a balanced view of Tikal's development and composition, they turned their attention to hundreds of small mounds that surrounded

© William A. Haviland

At Tikal only the tallest temples are visible above the forest canopy. The two farthest temples are at either end of the Great Plaza, the civic and ceremonial heart of the city. (Those familiar with the original *Star Wars* movie will recognize this view.)

larger buildings and were thought to be the remains of dwellings. In some senses, this represented a shift in the practice of archaeology toward studying the complexities of everyday life. Imagine how difficult it would be to get a realistic view of life in a major city such as Washington, D.C., or Beijing by looking only at their monumental public buildings. Similarly, a realistic view of Tikal cannot be reconstructed without examining the full range of ruins in the area.

The excavation of small structures, most of which were probably houses, permitted the estimation of Tikal's population size and density. This information was critical for testing hypotheses regarding the city's Maya inhabitants. These data allowed archaeologists to test the conventional assumption that the Maya's subsistence practices were inadequate to sustain large population concentrations.

Extensive excavation also provided a sound basis for a reconstruction of the everyday life and social organization of the Maya, a people who had been known almost entirely through the study of ceremonial remains. For example, differences in architecture, house construction, and associated artifacts and burials suggest social class differences. Features of house distribution seem to reflect the existence of extended families or other types of kin groups. The excavation of both large and small structures revealed the social structure of the total population of Tikal.[3]

Surveying and Excavating the Site

Mapping crews extensively surveyed 6 km² of forested land surrounding the Great Plaza, providing a preliminary map to guide the small structure excavation process.[4] Aerial photography could not be used for this mapping, because the tree canopy in this area is often 30 meters (about 100 feet) above the ground, obscuring all but the tallest temples. Many of the small ruins are practically invisible even to observers on the ground. Four years of mapping revealed that ancient Tikal was far larger than the 6 km² originally surveyed. More time and money were required to continue surveying the area in order to fully define the city's boundaries and calculate its overall size.[5]

The initial excavation of six structures, two plazas, and a platform revealed new structures not visible before excavation, the architectural complexity of the structures, and an enormous quantity of artifacts that had to be washed and catalogued. Consequently, not every structure was completely excavated, and some remained uninvestigated. Following this initial work, the archaeological team excavated over 100 additional small structures in different parts of the site in order to ensure investigation of a representative sample. The team also sunk numerous test pits in various other small structure

---

[3]Haviland, W. A. (2002). Settlement, society and demography at Tikal. In J. Sabloff (Ed.), *Tikal.* Santa Fe: School of American Research.

---

[4]Haviland, W. A., et al. (1985). *Excavations in small residential groups of Tikal: Groups 4F-1 and 4F-2.* Philadelphia: University Museum.

[5]Puleston, D. E. (1983). *The settlement survey of Tikal.* Philadelphia: University Museum.

groups to supplement the information gained from more extensive excavations.

Evidence from the Excavation

Excavation at Tikal produced considerable evidence about the social organization, technology, and diversity in this ancient city, as well as the relationship between people in Tikal and other regions. For example, the site provides evidence of trade in nonperishable items. Granite, quartzite, hematite, pyrite, jade, slate, and obsidian all were imported, either as raw materials or finished products. Marine materials came from Caribbean and Pacific coastal areas.

Tikal is located on top of an abundant source of chert (a flintlike stone used to manufacture tools), which may have been exported in the form of raw material and finished objects. The site is located between two river systems to the east and west, and so may have been on a major overland trade route between the two. Also, evidence exists for trade in perishable goods such as textiles, feathers, salt, and cacao. We can safely

This painting from Cacaxtla in southern Mexico shows a deity with the typical backpack of a Maya merchant. Imported raw materials and finished objects made from exotic materials provide abundant evidence of the presence of merchants and trade at Tikal.

© Enrico Ferorelli

conclude that there were full-time traders among the Tikal Maya.

In the realm of technology, specialized woodworking, pottery, obsidian, and shell workshops have been found. The skillful stone carving displayed on stone monuments suggests that occupational specialists did this work. The same is true of the fine artwork exhibited on ceramic vessels. Ancient artists had to envision what their work would look like after their pale, relatively colorless ceramics had been fired. Although we do not have direct evidence, there are clues to the existence of textile workers, dental workers, makers of bark-cloth "paper," scribes, masons, astronomers, and other occupational specialists.

To control the large population, some form of bureaucratic organization must have existed in Tikal. From Maya written records (glyphs), we know that the government was headed by a hereditary ruling dynasty with sufficient power to organize massive construction and maintenance. This included a system of defensive ditches and embankments on the northern and southern edges of the city. The longest of these ran for a distance of perhaps 19 to 28 km.

The religion of the Tikal Maya may have developed initially as a means to cope with the uncertainties of agriculture. Soils at Tikal are thin, and the only available water comes from rain that has been collected in ponds. Rain is abundant in season, but its onset tends to be unreliable. Conversely, the elevation of Tikal, high relative to surrounding terrain, may have caused it to be perceived as a "power place," especially suited for making contact with supernatural forces and beings.

The Maya priests tried not only to win over and please the deities in times of drought but also to honor them in times of plenty. Priests, the experts on the Maya calendar, determined the most auspicious time to plant crops and were concerned with other agricultural matters. This tended to keep people in or near the city. The population in and around Tikal depended upon their priesthood to influence supernatural beings and forces on their behalf, so that their crops would not fail.

As the population increased, land for agriculture became scarce, forcing the Maya to find new methods of food production that could sustain the dense population concentrated at Tikal. They added the planting and tending of fruit trees and other crops that could be grown around their houses in soils enriched by human waste (unlike houses at Teotihuacan, those at Tikal were not built close to one another).

Along with increased reliance on household gardening, the Maya constructed artificially raised fields in areas that were flooded each rainy season. In these fields, crops could be intensively cultivated year after year, as

© Anita de Laguna Haviland

Carved monuments like this were commissioned by Tikal's rulers to commemorate important events in their reigns. Portrayed on this one is a king who ruled about 1,220 years ago. Such skilled stone carving could only have been accomplished by a specialist. (For a translation of the inscription on the monument's left side, see Figure 11.4.)

long as they were carefully maintained. Measures were taken to maximize collection of water for the dry season, by converting low areas into reservoirs and constructing channels to carry runoff from plazas and other architecture into these reservoirs.

As these changes were taking place, a class of artisans, craftspeople, and other occupational specialists emerged to serve the needs of an elite consisting of the priesthood and a ruling dynasty. The Maya built numerous temples, public buildings, and various kinds of houses appropriate to the distinct social classes of their society.

For several hundred years, Tikal was able to sustain its ever-growing population. When the pressure for food and land reached a critical point, population growth stopped. At the same time, warfare with other cities was becoming increasingly destructive. All of this is marked archaeologically by abandonment of houses on prime land in rural areas, by the advent of nutritional problems visible in skeletons recovered from burials, and by the construction of the previously mentioned defensive ditches and embankments. In other words, a period of readjustment set in, which must have been directed by an already strong central authority. Activities then continued as before, but without further population growth for another 250 years or so.

As this case study shows, excavations at Tikal demonstrated the splendor, the social organization, the belief systems, and the agricultural practices of the ancient Maya civilization, among other things. This chapter's Original Study illustrates a very different approach to another Maya site, just a day's walk from Tikal.

Original Study ▪ By Anabel Ford

Action Archaeology and the Community at El Pilar

Resource management and conservation are palpable themes of the day. Nowhere is this more keenly felt than the Maya forest, one of the world's most biodiverse areas and among the last terrestrial frontiers. Over the next two decades this area's population will double, threatening the integrity of the tropical ecosystems with contemporary development strategies. Curiously, in the past the Maya forest was home to a major civilization with at least three to nine times the current population of the region.

I began my work as an archaeologist in the Maya forest in 1972. I was interested in the everyday life of the Maya through the study of their cultural

ecology—the multifaceted relationships of humans and their environment—rather than monumental buildings. Despite my interest in daily life in the forest, monumental buildings became a part of my work. While conducting a settlement survey in the forest, I discovered El Pilar, a Maya urban center with temples and plazas covering more than 50 hectares. The observation that the ancient Maya evolved a sustainable economy in the tropics of Mesoamerica led my approach to developing El Pilar.

Astride the contemporary border separating Belize from Guatemala, El Pilar has been the focus of a bold conservation design for an international friendship park on a troubled border. My vision for

El Pilar is founded on the preservation of cultural heritage in the context of the natural environment. With a collaborative and interdisciplinary team of local villagers, government administrators, and

scientists, we have established the El Pilar Archaeological Reserve for Maya Flora and Fauna.

Since 1993, the innovations of the El Pilar program have forged new ground in testing novel strategies for community participation in the conservation development of the El Pilar Reserve. This program touches major administrative themes of global importance: tourism, natural resources, foreign affairs, and rural development and education. Yet the program's impacts go further. Working with traditional forest gardeners impacts agriculture, rural enterprise, and capacity building. There are few areas untouched by the program's inclusive sweep, and more arenas can contribute to its evolution.

At El Pilar, I practice what I call "action archaeology," a pioneering conservation model that draws on lessons learned from the recent and distant past to benefit contemporary populations. For example, the co-evolution of Maya society and the environment provide clues

about sustainability in this region today. At El Pilar we have advanced programs that will simulate "Maya forest gardens" as an alternative to resource-diminishing, plow and pasture farming methods. The forest survives and demonstrates resil-

ience to impacts brought on by human expansion. The ancient Maya lived with this forest for millennia, and the El Pilar program argues there are lessons to be learned from that past.

The El Pilar program recognizes the privilege it has enjoyed in forging an innovative community participatory process, in creating a unique management planning design, and in developing a new tourism destination. The success of local outreach at El Pilar can best be seen in the growth of the community organization Amigos de El Pilar (Friends of El Pilar). With groups based in both Belize and Guatemala, the Amigos de El Pilar have worked together with the El Pilar program to build an inclusive relationship between the community and the reserve that is mutually beneficial. The development of this dynamic relationship lies at the heart of the El Pilar philosophy—resilient and with the potential to educate communities, reform local-level resource management, and inform conservation designs for the Maya Forest. ∎

CITIES AND CULTURE CHANGE

If someone who grew up in a rural North American village today moved to Chicago, Montreal, or Los Angeles, that person would experience a number of marked changes in his or her way of life. Similarly, changes in daily life would have been felt 5,500 years ago by a Neolithic village dweller upon moving into one of the world's first cities in Mesopotamia. Four basic changes mark the transition from Neolithic village life to life in the first urban centers: agricultural innovation, diversification of labor, central government, and social stratification.

Agricultural Innovation

The first culture change characteristic of early civilizations occurred in farming methods. The ancient Sumerians, for example, built an extensive system of dikes, canals, and reservoirs to irrigate their farmlands. With such a system, they could control water resources at will; water could be held and then run off into the fields as necessary. Irrigation was an important factor affecting an increase of crop yields. Freedom from seasonal rain cycles allowed farmers to harvest more crops in one year. Increased crop yields, resulting from agricultural innovations, were undoubtedly a factor contributing to the high population densities of ancient civilizations.

This clay tablet map of farmland outside of the Mesopotamian city of Nippur dates to 3,300 years ago. Shown are irrigation canals separating the various fields, each of which is identified with the name of the owner.

Diversification of Labor

The second culture change characteristic of early civilizations was the diversification of labor. In a Neolithic village without irrigation or plow farming, every family member participated in the raising of crops. The high crop yields made possible by new farming methods and the increased population permitted a sizable number of people to pursue nonagricultural activities on a full-time basis.

Ancient public records document a variety of specialized workers. For example, an early Mesopotamian document from the old Babylonian city of Lagash lists the artisans, craftspeople, and others paid from crop surpluses stored in the temple granaries. These lists included coppersmiths, silversmiths, sculptors, merchants, potters, tanners, engravers, butchers, carpenters, spinners, barbers, cabinetmakers, bakers, clerks, and brewers.

With specialization came the expertise that led to the invention of new ways of making and doing things. In Eurasia and Africa, civilization ushered in what archaeologists often refer to as the **Bronze Age,** a period marked by the production of tools and ornaments made of this metal. Metals were in great demand for the manufacture of farmers' and artisans' tools, as well as for weapons. Copper and tin (the raw materials from which bronze is made) were smelted, or separated from their ores, then purified, and cast to make plows, swords, axes, and shields. Later, such tools were made from smelted iron. In wars over border disputes or to extend a state's territory, stone knives, spears, and slings could not stand up against metal spears, arrowheads, swords, helmets, or armor.

The indigenous civilizations of the Americas also used metals. In South America, copper, silver, and gold were used for tools as well as ceremonial and ornamental objects. The Aztecs and to a lesser extent the Maya used the same soft metals for ceremonial and ornamental objects while continuing to rely on stone for their everyday tools. To those who assume that metal is inherently superior, this seems puzzling. However, the ready availability of obsidian (a glass formed by volcanic activity), its extreme sharpness (many times sharper than the finest steel), and the ease with which it could be worked made it perfectly suited to their needs. Moreover, unlike bronze and especially iron, copper, silver, and gold are soft metals and have limited practical use. Obsidian tools provide some of the sharpest cutting edges ever made.

Bronze Age In the Old World, the period marked by the production of tools and ornaments of bronze; began about 5,000 years ago in China and Southwest Asia and about 500 years earlier in Southeast Asia.

This 2,900-year-old Etruscan vase is a fine example of the artistry that became possible with the introduction of bronze.

Early civilizations developed extensive trade systems to procure the raw materials needed for their technologies. In many parts of the world, boats gave greater access to trade centers for transporting large loads of imports and exports between cities at less cost than if they had been carried overland. A one-way trip from the ancient Egyptian cities along the Nile River to the Mediterranean port city of Byblos in Phoenicia (not far from the present city of Beirut, Lebanon) took far less time by rowboat compared to the overland route. With a sailboat, it took even less time.

Egyptian kings, or pharaohs, sent expeditions south to Nubia (northern Sudan) for gold; east to the Sinai Peninsula for copper; to Arabia for spices and perfumes; to Asia for lapis lazuli (a blue semiprecious stone) and other jewels; north to Lebanon for cedar, wine, and funerary oils; and southwest to central Africa for ivory, ebony, ostrich feathers, leopard skins, cattle, and the captives they enslaved. Evidence of trading from Great Zimbabwe in southern Africa indicates that these trading networks extended throughout the Old World. Increased contact with foreign peoples through trade brought new knowledge into trading economies, furthering the spread of innovations and even bodies of knowledge such as geometry and astronomy.

Central Government

The third culture change characteristic of early civilizations was the emergence of a governing elite, a strong central authority required to deal with the challenges new cities faced because of their size and complexity. The

The construction of elliptical granite walls held together without any mortar at Great Zimbabwe in southern Zimbabwe, Africa, attest to the skill of the people who built these structures. When European explorers unwilling to accept the notion of civilization in sub-Saharan Africa discovered these magnificent ruins, they wrongly attributed them to white non-Africans. This false notion persisted until archaeologists demonstrated that these structures were part of a city with 12,000 to 20,000 inhabitants that served as the center of a medieval Bantu state.

governing elite saw to it that different interest groups, such as farmers or craft specialists, provided their respective services and did not infringe on one another's rights (to the extent that they had rights).

The government ensured that the city was safe from its enemies by constructing fortifications and raising an army. It levied taxes and appointed tax collectors so that construction workers, the army, and other public expenses could be paid. It saw to it that merchants, carpenters, or farmers who made legal claims received justice according to standards of the legal system. It guaranteed safety for the lives and property of ordinary people and assured them that any harm done to one person by another would be justly handled. In addition, surplus food had to be stored for times of scarcity, and public works such as extensive irrigation systems or fortifications had to be supervised by competent, fair individuals. The mechanisms of government served all these functions.

Evidence of Centralized Authority

Evidence of centralized authority in ancient civilizations comes from such sources as law codes, temple records, and royal chronicles. Excavation of the city structures themselves provides further evidence because they can show definite signs of city planning. The precise astronomical layout of the Mesoamerican city Teotihuacan, described earlier, attests to strong, centralized control.

Monumental buildings and temples, palaces, and large sculptures are usually found in ancient civilizations. For example, the Great Pyramid, which is the tomb of Khufu, an Egyptian pharaoh, is 755 feet long and

481 feet high. It contains about 2,300,000 stone blocks, each with an average weight of 2.5 tons. The Greek historian Herodotus reports that it took 100,000 men twenty years to build this tomb. Such gigantic structures could be built only because a powerful central authority could harness the considerable labor force, engineering skills, and raw materials necessary for their construction.

Another indicator of the existence of centralized authority is writing, or some form of recorded information (Figure 11.3). With writing, central authorities could disseminate information and store, systematize, and deploy memory for political, religious, and economic purposes.

Scholars attribute the initial motive for the development of writing in Mesopotamia to record keeping of state affairs. Writing allowed early governments to track accounts of their food surplus, tribute records, and other business receipts. Some of the earliest documents appear to be just such records—lists of vegetables and animals bought and sold, tax lists, and storehouse inventories.

Before 5,500 years ago, records consisted initially of "tokens," ceramic pieces with different shapes indicative of different commercial objects. Thus, a cone shape could represent a measure of grain, or a cylinder could be an animal. As the system developed, tokens represented different animals; processed foods such as oil, trussed ducks, or bread; and manufactured or imported goods such as textiles and metal.[6] Ultimately, clay tablets with impressed marks representing objects replaced these tokens.

[6] Lawler, A. (2001). Writing gets a rewrite. *Science 292*, 2,419.

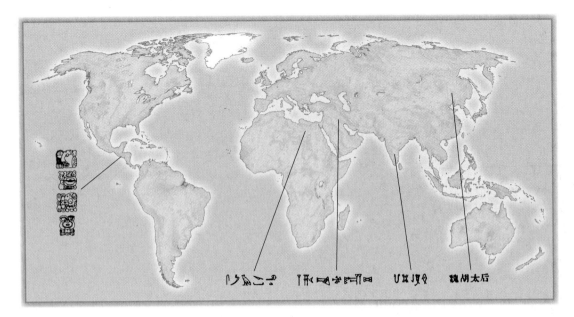

Figure 11.3
The impermanence of spoken words contrasts with the relative permanence of written records. In all of human history, writing has been independently invented at least five times.

In the Mesopotamian city of Uruk, by 5,100 years ago, a new writing technique emerged in which writers used a reed stylus to make wedge-shaped markings on a tablet of damp clay. Originally, each marking stood for a word. Because most words in this language were monosyllabic, the markings came, in time, to stand for syllables.

Controversy surrounds the question of the earliest evidence of writing. Traditionally, the earliest writing was linked to Mesopotamia. However, in 2003 archaeologists working in the Henan Province of western China discovered signs carved into 8,600-year-old tortoise shells; these markings resemble later-written characters and predate the Mesopotamian evidence by about 2,000 years.[7]

In the Americas, writing systems came into use among various Mesoamerican peoples, but the Maya system was particularly sophisticated. The Maya writing system, like other aspects of Maya culture, appears to have roots in the earlier writing system of the Olmec civilization,[8] though discoveries announced in 2006 of a stone tablet with a distinctive writing system indicate that the Olmec had another form of writing distinct from Maya glyphs.[9] The Maya hieroglyphic system had less to do with keeping track of state properties than with extravagant celebrations of the accomplishments of their rulers. Maya lords glorified themselves by recording their dynastic genealogies, important conquests, and royal marriages; by using grandiose titles to refer to themselves; and by associating their actions with important astronomical events (Figure 11.4). Different though this may be from the record keeping of ancient Mesopotamia, all writing systems share a concern with political power and its maintenance.

The Earliest Governments

A king and his advisors typically headed the earliest city governments. Of the many ancient kings known, one stands out as truly remarkable for the efficient government organization and highly developed legal system characterizing his reign. This is Hammurabi, the Babylonian king who lived in Mesopotamia some time between 3,700 and 3,950 years ago. He issued a set of laws for his kingdom, now known as the Code of Hammurabi, notable for its thorough detail and standardization. It prescribed the correct form for legal procedures and determined penalties for perjury and false accusation.

[7]Li, X., et al. (2003). The earliest writing? Sign use in the seventh millennium BC at Jiahu, Henan Province, China. *Antiquity 77,* 31–44.

[8]Pohl, M. E. D., Pope, K. O., & von Nagy, C. (2002). Olmec origins of Mesoamerican writing, *Science 298,* 1,984–1,987.

[9]del Carmen Rodríguez Martínez, M. (2006). Oldest writing in the New World. *Science 313,* 1,610–1,614.

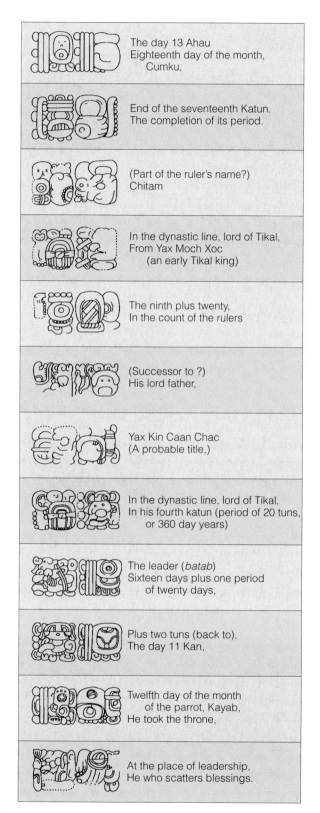

	The day 13 Ahau Eighteenth day of the month, Cumku,
	End of the seventeenth Katun. The completion of its period.
	(Part of the ruler's name?) Chitam
	In the dynastic line, lord of Tikal, From Yax Moch Xoc (an early Tikal king)
	The ninth plus twenty, In the count of the rulers
	(Successor to ?) His lord father,
	Yax Kin Caan Chac (A probable title,)
	In the dynastic line, lord of Tikal, In his fourth katun (period of 20 tuns, or 360 day years)
	The leader (*batab*) Sixteen days plus one period of twenty days,
	Plus two tuns (back to), The day 11 Kan,
	Twelfth day of the month of the parrot, Kayab, He took the throne,
	At the place of leadership, He who scatters blessings.

Figure 11.4

The translation of the text on the monument shown on page 250 gives some indication of the importance of dynastic genealogy to Maya rulers. The "scattering" mentioned may refer to bloodletting as part of the ceremonies associated with the end of one twenty-year period, or Katun, and the beginning of the next.

It contained laws applying to property rights, loans and debts, family rights, and even damages paid for malpractice by a physician. It defined fixed rates to be charged in various trades and branches of commerce and mechanisms to protect the poor, women, children, and slaves against injustice.

Officials had the code publicly displayed on huge stone slabs so that no one accused could plead ignorance. Even the poorest citizen was supposed to know his or her rights and responsibilities. Distinct social classes were clearly reflected in the law ("rule of law" does not necessarily mean "equality before the law"). For example, if an aristocrat put out the eye of a fellow aristocrat, the law required that his own eye be put out in turn; hence, the saying "an eye for an eye." However, if the aristocrat put out the eye of a commoner, the punishment was simply a payment of silver.[10]

While some civilizations flourished under a single ruler with extraordinary governing abilities, other civilizations possessed a widespread governing bureaucracy that was very efficient at every level. The government of the Inca empire is one such example.

The Inca civilization of Peru and its surrounding territories reached its peak 500 years ago, just before the arrival of the Spanish invaders. By 1525, it stretched 2,500 miles from north to south and 500 miles from east to west, making it at the time one of the largest empires on the face of the earth. Its population, which numbered in the millions, was composed of people of many different ethnic groups. In the achievements of its governmental and political system, Inca civilization surpassed every other civilization of the Americas and most of those of Eurasia. An emperor, regarded as the divine son of the Sun God, headed the government. Under him came the royal family, the aristocracy, imperial administrators, and lower nobility, and below them the masses of artisans, craftspeople, and farmers.

The empire was divided into four administrative regions, further subdivided into provinces, and so on down to villages and families. Government agricultural and tax officials closely supervised farming activities such as planting, irrigation, and harvesting. Teams of professional relay runners could carry messages up to 250 miles in a single day over a network of roads and bridges that remains impressive even today.

Considering the complexity of the Inca civilization, it is surprising that they had no known form of conventional writing. Instead, public records and historical chronicles were kept in the form of an ingenious coding system of colored strings with knots.

---

[10]Moscati, S. (1962). *The face of the ancient orient* (p. 90). New York: Doubleday.

GLOBALSCAPE

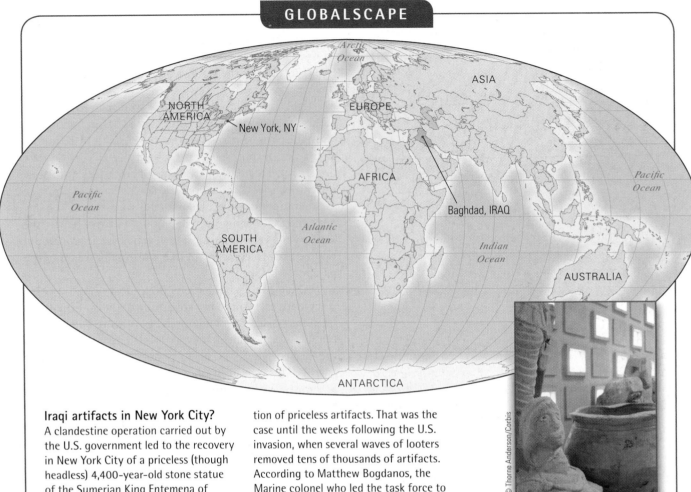

Iraqi artifacts in New York City?

A clandestine operation carried out by the U.S. government led to the recovery in New York City of a priceless (though headless) 4,400-year-old stone statue of the Sumerian King Entemena of Lagash. The statue will be returned to its rightful place in the center of the Sumerian Hall of the Iraqi National Museum in Baghdad. The modern-day state of Iraq, located in an area known as the cradle of civilization, is home to 10,000 archaeological sites preserving evidence of the earliest cities, laws, and civilizations. Though many Mesopotamian artifacts were brought to museums in Europe and the United states in the 19th and early 20th centuries, the Iraqi National Museum in Baghdad still housed an extraordinary collec-tion of priceless artifacts. That was the case until the weeks following the U.S. invasion, when several waves of looters removed tens of thousands of artifacts. According to Matthew Bogdanos, the Marine colonel who led the task force to track down and recover these artifacts, "The list of missing objects read like a 'who's who' of Near Eastern archaeol-ogy." Ironically, looting during the first Gulf War had led local archaeologists to move artifacts from regional museums to the National Museum of Baghdad for their safety. This statue, like many other stolen artifacts, was first taken across the border into Syria and then made its way into the international black market in antiquities. Many artifacts have been returned to the museum through a no-questions-asked amnesty program.

© Thorne Anderson/Corbis

Others have required a combination of international cooperation and investiga-tion, along with raids and seizures once artifacts have been tracked down.

Global Twister If artifacts from ancient civilizations from throughout the world represent our shared global heritage, how can such treasures be kept safe from the chaos and desperation that results from war?

Social Stratification

The rise of large, economically diversified populations presided over by centralized governing authorities brought with it the fourth culture change characteristic of civilization: social stratification, or the emergence of social classes. For example, symbols of special status and privilege appeared in the ancient cities of Mesopotamia, and people were ranked according to the kind of work they did or the family into which they were born.

People who stood at or near the head of government were the earliest holders of high status. Although spe-cialists of one sort or another—metal workers, tanners, traders, or the like—generally outranked farmers, such specialization did not necessarily bring with it high sta-tus. Rather, people engaged in these kinds of economic

Grave goods frequently indicate the status of deceased individuals in stratified societies. For example, China's first emperor was buried with 7,000 life-size terra cotta figures of warriors.

© Courtesy of Tavid Rankin Bingham

activities were either members of the lower classes or outcasts.[11] Merchants of the past could sometimes buy their way into a higher class. With time, the possession of wealth and the influence it could buy became in itself a requisite for high status, as it is in some cultures today.

Evidence of Social Stratification

How do archaeologists know that different social classes existed in ancient civilizations? As described earlier, laws and other written documents as well as archaeological features including dwelling size and location can reflect social stratification.

It is also revealed by burial customs. Graves excavated at early Neolithic sites are mostly simple pits dug in the ground, containing few, if any, grave goods. **Grave goods** consist of things such as utensils, figurines, and personal possessions, symbolically placed in the grave for the deceased person's use in the afterlife. Early Neolithic grave sites reveal little variation, indicating essentially classless societies. Graves excavated in civilizations, by contrast, vary widely in size, mode of burial, and the number and variety of grave goods. This reflects a stratified society, divided into social classes. The graves of important persons contain not only various artifacts made from precious materials, but sometimes, as in some early Egyptian burials, the remains of servants evidently killed to serve their master in the afterlife.

Skeletons from the burials may also provide evidence of stratification. Age at death as well as presence of certain diseases can be determined from skeletal re-

mains. In stratified societies of the past, the dominant groups usually lived longer, ate better, and enjoyed an easier life than lower-ranking members of society, just as they do today.

THE MAKING OF STATES

From northeastern Africa to China to the South American Andes, ancient civilizations are almost always associated with magnificent palaces built high above ground; sculptures so perfect as to be unrivaled by those of today's artists; and engineering projects so vast and daring as to awaken in us a sense of wonder. These impressive accomplishments could indicate that civilization is superior to other cultural forms, particularly when civilizations have come to dominate peoples with other social systems.

It is important to bear in mind that domination relates more to an aggressive attitude, size, and power than to cultural superiority. In other words, the emergence of centralized governments, characteristic of civilizations, has allowed some cultures to dominate others and for civilizations to flourish. Anthropologists have proposed several theories to account for the transition from small, egalitarian farming villages to large urban centers in which population density, social inequality, and diversity of labor required a centralized government.

grave goods Items such as utensils, figurines, and personal possessions, symbolically placed in the grave for the deceased person's use in the afterlife.

---

[11]Sjoberg, G. (1960). *The preindustrial city* (p. 325). New York: Free Press.

Anthropology Applied

Tell It to the Marines: Teaching Troops about Cultural Heritage ▪ By Jane C. Waldbaum

The need to protect ancient sites, museums, and antiquities in war-torn Iraq and Afghanistan has led the Archaeological Institute of America (AIA) to begin an innovative program to help educate troops soon to be sent to those countries. Conceived by AIA vice president C. Brian Rose, the program sends experienced lecturers to military bases to teach the basics of Middle Eastern archaeology and the importance of protecting the evidence of past cultures. The class, taken by both officers and enlisted men and women, is mandatory.

The effort is a supplement to the AIA's long-standing, nationwide lecture program in which scholars in archaeology and related fields present the latest research and developments to more than 102 local societies in the United States and Canada. The lectures for the troops focus specifically on the areas where military personnel will be deployed and on the specific sites, monuments, museums, and artifacts

that they might be called upon to protect.

The current lectures, funded in part by the Packard Humanities Institute, emphasize Mesopotamia's role in the development of writing, schools, libraries, law codes, calendars, and astronomy, as well as connections with familiar biblical figures such as Abraham and Daniel and ancient sites such as Ur and Babylon. Afghanistan's position as a crossroads of ancient civilizations and the route of Alexander the Great through the region are discussed. Troops also learn about basic archaeological techniques, the importance of preserving context, the necessity of working with archaeologists and conservators, and the most effective ways to protect sites against looters.

The first series of lectures was given at the Marine Corps base at Camp Lejeune, North Carolina, and there are plans to expand the program to other bases and services in the near future. "Many

of the officers have M.A. degrees; some are reservists and high-school history teachers," says Rose, who delivered the inaugural lectures last spring. "They care a great deal about the history of the areas in which they serve; some of them have actually lived in or near Babylon on earlier tours of duty. All of us have been struck by their thirst for knowledge during and after our lectures."

Many have helped get this program up and running, including U.S. Marine Colonel Matthew Bogdanos, who was instrumental in securing the return of many antiquities stolen from the Iraq Museum. "When it comes to clearing a building, neutralizing a land mine, or making a neighborhood safe for children, we know what to do," says Bogdanos. "When it comes to protecting a country's cultural heritage, we are just as eager to do the right thing—we just don't always know the best way to do it. This is where Brian Rose's groundbreaking program will pay dividends for generations."

Ecological Approaches

Ecological approaches emphasize the role of the environment in the development of states. Among these, the irrigation or **hydraulic theory** holds that civilizations developed when Neolithic peoples realized that the best farming occurred in the fertile soils of river valleys, provided periodic flooding was controlled.[12] The centralized effort to control the irrigation process blossomed into the first governing body, elite social class, and civilization.

Another theory suggests that in regions of ecological diversity, trade is necessary to procure scarce resources. In Mexico, for example, trade networks distributed chilies grown in the highlands, cotton and beans from intermediate elevations, and salt from the coasts to people

throughout the region. Some form of centralized authority developed to organize trade for the procurement of these commodities and to redistribute them.

A third theory suggests that states develop where populations are hemmed in by such environmental barriers as mountains, deserts, seas, or other human populations.[13] As these populations grow, they have no space in which to expand, and so they begin to compete for increasingly scarce resources. Internally, this may result in the development of social stratification, in which an elite controls important resources to which lower classes have limited access. Externally, this leads to warfare and even conquest, which, to be successful, require elaborate organization under a centralized authority. As this chapter's Anthropology Applied feature shows, in times of war centralized authorities such as the U.S. military are drawing upon archaeological expertise to protect cultural resources.

Problems exist with each of these ecological theories. Across the globe and through time, cultures can be found that do not fit these models. For example, some

---

[12]Wittfogel, K. A. (1957). *Oriental despotism, a comparative study of total power.* New Haven, CT: Yale University Press.

hydraulic theory The theory that explains civilization's emergence as the result of the construction of elaborate irrigation systems, the functioning of which required full-time managers whose control blossomed into the first governing body and elite social class.

[13]Carneiro, R. L. (1970). A theory of the origin of the state. *Science 169,* 733–738.

of the earliest large-scale irrigation systems developed in highland New Guinea, where strong centralized governments never emerged. North American Indians possessed trade networks that extended from Labrador in northeastern Canada to the Gulf of Mexico and the Yellowstone region of the Rocky Mountains and even to the Pacific without centralized control.[14] In many of the cultures that do not fit the theories of environmental determinism, neighboring cultures learned to co-exist rather than pursuing warfare to the point of complete conquest.

Although few anthropologists would deny the importance of the human–environment relationship, many are dissatisfied with theories that do not take into account the beliefs and values that regulate the interaction between people and their environment.[15] For example, as described in the case study of Tikal, while religion was tied to the earth in that the priests determined the most promising time for planting crops, the beliefs and power relations that developed within Maya culture were not environmentally determined. Human societies past and present bring their beliefs and values into their interactions with the environment.

Action Theory

One criticism of the above theories is that they fail to recognize the capacity of aggressive, charismatic leaders to shape the course of human history. Accordingly, anthropologists Joyce Marcus and Kent Flannery have developed what they call **action theory.**[16] This theory acknowledges the relationship of society to the environment in shaping social and cultural behavior, but it also recognizes that forceful leaders strive to advance their positions through self-serving actions. In so doing, they may create change.

In the case of Maya history, for example, local leaders, who once relied on personal charisma for the economic and political support needed to sustain them in their positions, may have seized upon religion to solidify their power. Through religion they developed an ideology that endowed them and their descendants with supernatural ancestry and privileged access to the gods on which their followers depended. In this case, certain individuals could monopolize power and emerge as divine kings, using their power to subjugate any rivals.

As the above example makes clear, the context in which a forceful leader operates is critical. In the case of the Maya, the combination of existing cultural and ecological factors combined to open the way to the emergence of political dynasties. Thus, explanations of civilization's emergence are likely to involve multiple causes, rather than just one. Furthermore, we may also have the cultural equivalent of what biologists call *convergence,* where similar societies come about in different ways. Consequently, a theory that accounts for the rise of civilization in one place may not account for its rise in another.

CIVILIZATION AND ITS DISCONTENTS

Living in the context of civilization ourselves, we are inclined to view its development as a great step upward on a so-called ladder of progress. Whatever benefits civilization has brought, the cultural changes it represents have produced new problems. Among them is the problem of waste disposal. In fact, waste disposal probably began to be a problem in settled, farming communities even before civilizations emerged. But as villages grew into towns and towns grew into cities, the problem became far more serious, as crowded conditions and the buildup of garbage and sewage created optimum environments for infectious diseases such as bubonic plague, typhoid, and cholera. Early cities therefore tended to be disease-ridden places, with relatively high death rates.

Genetically based adaptation to diseases may also have influenced the course of civilization. In northern Europeans, for example, the mutation of a gene on chromosome 7 makes carriers resistant to cholera, typhoid, and other bacterial diarrheas.[17] Because of the mortality caused by these diseases, selection favored spread of this allele among northern Europeans. But, as with sickle-cell anemia, protection comes at a price. That price is cystic fibrosis, a usually fatal disease present in people who are homozygous for the altered gene.

The rise of towns and cities brought with it other acute, infectious diseases. In a small population, diseases such as chicken pox, influenza, measles, mumps, pertussis, polio, rubella, and smallpox will kill or immunize so high a proportion of the population that the virus cannot

[14]Haviland, W. A., & Power, M. W. (1994). *The original Vermonters* (2nd ed., chs. 3 & 4). Hanover, NH: University Press of New England.

[15]Adams, R. M. (2001). Scale and complexity in archaic states. *Latin American Antiquity, 11,* 188.

[16]Marcus, J., & Flannery, K. V. (1996). *Zapotec civilization: How urban society evolved in Mexico's Oaxaca Valley.* New York: Thames & Hudson.

[17]Ridley, M. (1999). *Genome, the autobiography of a species in 23 chapters* (p. 142). New York: HarperCollins.

action theory The theory that self-serving actions by forceful leaders play a role in civilization's emergence.

Biocultural Connection

Social Stratification and Diseases of Civilization: Tuberculosis

Before the discovery of antibiotics in the early 20th century, individuals infected with the bacteria causing the disease tuberculosis (TB) would invariably waste away and die. But before the development of cities, the disease TB in humans was rare. The bacteria that cause TB cannot survive in the presence of sunlight and fresh air. Therefore, TB, like many other sicknesses, can be called a disease of civilization.

Before humans lived in dark, crowded urban centers, if an infected individual coughed and released the TB bacteria into the air, sunlight would prevent the spread of infection. But civilization affects disease in another powerful way. The social distribution of TB indicates that social stratification is as much a determinant of disease as any bacterium, past and present.

For example, Ashkenazi Jews of eastern Europe were forced into urban ghettos over several centuries, becoming especially vulnerable to the TB thriving in crowded, dark, confined neighborhoods. As we have seen with the genetic response to malaria (sickle cell and other abnormal hemoglobins) and bacterial diarrheas (the cystic fibrosis gene), TB triggered a genetic response in the form

© Paul Almasy/Corbis

The difficult living conditions in urban slums promote the spread of infectious disease. For example, the rates of tuberculosis, AIDS, hepatitis, and other infectious diseases are very high in this *favella*, or bustling slum neighborhood in postindustrial cities of Brazil, as in many other parts of the world.

of the Tay-Sachs allele. Individuals heterozygous for the Tay-Sachs allele were protected from this disease.[a]

Unfortunately, homozygotes for the Tay-Sachs allele develop a lethal, degenerative condition that remains common in Ashkenazi Jews. Without the selective

[a]Ridley, M. (1999). *Genome, the autobiography of a species in 23 chapters* (p. 191). New York: HarperCollins.

pressure of TB, the frequency of the Tay-Sachs allele would never have increased. Similarly, without the strict social rules confining poor Jews to the ghettos (compounded by rules about marriage), the frequency of the Tay-Sachs allele would never have increased. In recent times, cultural mechanisms such as prenatal and premarital genetic testing have resulted in a decrease in the frequency of the Tay-Sachs allele.

While antibiotics have reduced deaths from TB, resistant forms of the bacteria require an expensive regime of multiple drugs. Not only are poor individuals more likely to become infected with TB, they are also less likely to be able to afford expensive medicines required to treat this disease. For people in poor countries and for disadvantaged people in wealthier countries, TB—like AIDS—can be an incurable, fatal, infectious disease. As Holger Sawert from the World Health Organization has said, "Both TB and HIV thrive on poverty." The difficult living conditions in urban slums promote the spread of infectious disease. Poverty also makes medical treatment inaccessible.

Before the social stratification accompanying the emergence of cities and states, as far as infectious microbes were concerned, all humans were the same.

---

continue to propagate. Measles, for example, is likely to die out in any human population with fewer than half a million people.[18] Hence, such diseases, when introduced into small communities, spread immediately to the whole population and then die out. Their continued existence depends upon the presence of large population aggregates as found in cities. Survivors possessed immunity to these deadly diseases.

Infectious disease played a major role in European colonization of the Americas. When Europeans with immunity to Old World diseases came to the Americas for the first time, they brought these devastating diseases with them. Millions of Native Americans who had never been in contact with the microbes that cause diseases such as smallpox, typhus, measles, and bubonic plague died as a result.

Not until relatively recent times did public health measures reduce the risk of living in cities, and had it not been for a constant influx of rural peoples, areas of high

[18]Diamond, J. (1997). *Guns, germs, and steel* (p. 203). New York: Norton.

population density might not have persisted. Europe's urban population, for example, did not become self-sustaining until early in the 20th century.[19]

What led people to live in such unhealthy places? Most likely, people were attracted by the same things that lure people to cities today: They are vibrant, exciting places that provide people with new opportunities and protection in times of warfare. Of course, people's experience in the cities did not always live up to advance expectations, particularly for the poor, as described in this chapter's Biocultural Connection.

In addition to health problems, many early cities faced social problems strikingly similar to those found in many cities all over the world today. Dense population and the inequalities of class systems and oppressive centralized governments created internal stress. The poor saw that the wealthy had all the things that they themselves lacked. It was not just a question of luxury items; the poor did not have enough food or space in which to live with comfort, dignity, and health.

Evidence of warfare in early civilizations is common. Cities were fortified. Ancient documents list battles, raids, and wars between groups. Cylinder seals, paintings, and sculptures depict battle scenes, victorious kings, and captured prisoners of war. Increasing population and the accompanying scarcity of good farming land often led to boundary disputes and quarrels over land between civilized states or between so-called tribal peoples and a state. When war broke out, people crowded into walled cities for protection and to be near irrigation systems.

What we would call "development" today also posed problems in the past. At the Maya city of Copan, in the present-day country of Honduras, much of the fertile bottom lands along the Copan River were paved over as the city grew, making the people more and more dependent on food grown in the fragile soils of the valley slopes. This ultimately led to catastrophic soil loss through erosion and a breakdown of food production. Similarly, in ancient Mesopotamia, evaporation of water from extensive irrigation works resulted in a buildup of salt in the soil, ruining it for agricultural use.

It is discouraging to note that many of the problems associated with the first civilizations are still with us. Waste disposal, pollution-related health problems, crowding, social inequities, and warfare continue to be serious problems. Through the study of past civilizations, and through comparison of contemporary societies, we now stand a chance of understanding such problems. Such understanding represents a central part of the anthropologist's mission. In this sense, then, anthropology represents an effort to adapt, so that the next cultural revolution may see our species transcend these problems.

---

[19]Ibid.

Questions for Reflection

1. In large-scale societies of the past and present, people face the challenge of social stratification. Elite classes have disproportionate access to and control of all resources. Is social stratification an inevitable consequence of the emergence of cities and states? How can the study of social stratification in the past contribute to the resolution of contemporary issues of social justice?

2. In previous chapters it was emphasized that human evolutionary history should not be thought of as progress. Why is it similarly incorrect to think of the shift from village to city to state as progress?

3. What are some of the ways that differences in social stratification are expressed in your community? Does your community have any traditions surrounding death that serve to restate the social differentiation of individuals?

4. With today's global communication and economic networks, will it be possible to shift away from social systems involving centralized governments or will a centralized authority have to control and protect resources for the entire world?

5. With many archaeological discoveries there is a value placed on "firsts," such as the earliest writing, the first city, or the earliest government. Given the history of the independent emergence of cities and states throughout the world, do you think that scientists should place more value on some of these events just because they are older?

Suggested Readings

Diamond, J. (1997). *Guns, germs, and steel*. New York: Norton.

Also recommended in the last chapter, this book has an excellent discussion of the relation among diseases, social complexity, and social change.

Fagan, B. (2001). *The seventy great mysteries of the ancient world*. New York: Thames & Hudson.

Archaeologist Brian Fagan edited contributions from twenty-eight other archaeologists and historians about some of the great controversies in the field in this readable book.

Marcus, J., & Flannery, K. V. (1996). *Zapotec civilization: How urban society evolved in Mexico's Oaxaca Valley.* New York: Thames & Hudson.

With its lavish illustrations, this looks like a book for coffee table adornment, but it is a thoughtful and serious work on the rise of a pristine civilization. In it, the authors present their action theory.

McNeill W. (1992). *Plagues and people.* New York: Anchor Books.

This book offers an interpretation of world history through the impact of infectious disease. It documents the role disease played in the colonization of the Americas as well as continuing the investigation into the present with a social history of AIDS.

Sabloff, J. A. (1997). *The cities of ancient Mexico* (Rev. ed.). New York: Thames & Hudson.

This well-written and lavishly illustrated book describes the major cities of the Olmecs, Zapotecs, Maya, Teotihuacans, Toltecs, and Aztecs. Following the descriptions, Sabloff discusses the question of origins, the problems of archaeological reconstruction, and the basis on which he provides vignettes of life in the ancient cities. The book concludes with a gazetteer of fifty sites in Mesoamerica.

Thomson Audio Study Products

 Enjoy the MP3-ready Audio Lecture Overviews for each chapter and a comprehensive audio glossary of key terms for quick study and review. Whether walking to class, doing laundry, or studying at your desk, you now have the freedom to choose when, where, and how you interact with your audio-based educational media. See the preface for information on how to access this on-the-go study and review tool.

The Anthropology Resource Center

www.thomsonedu.com/anthropology
The Anthropology Resource Center provides extended learning materials to reinforce your understanding of key concepts in the four fields of anthropology. For each of the four fields, the Resource Center includes dynamic exercises including video exercises, map exercises, simulations, and "Meet the Scientists" interviews, as well as critical thinking questions that can be assigned and e-mailed to instructors. The Resource Center also provides breaking news in anthropology and interesting material on applied anthropology to help you link what you are learning to the world around you.

12 Modern Human Diversity: Race and Racism

© White Packert/Iconica/Getty Images

CHALLENGE ISSUE

Biological diversity contributes to our ability to adapt to a variety of environments. It is also a challenge, calling upon us to recognize our common origins and to avoid oversimplification, discrimination, bigotry, and even bloodshed fueled by superficial differences. While some people view so-called racial groups as natural and separate divisions within our species based on visible physical differences, biological evidence demonstrates that separate races do not exist. Broadly defined geographic "racial" groupings differ from one another in only 7 percent of their genes. Having exchanged genes throughout history, human populations continue to do so today. Instead of leading to the development of distinctive subspecies (biologically defined races), this genetic exchange has maintained all of humankind as a single species. While race is an important social and political category in some societies, it is a cultural construct without objective scientific merit.

What Is the History of Human Classification?

European scholars of the 18th through early 20th centuries classified humans into a series of subspecies based on geographic location and phenotypic features such as skin color, body size, head shape, and hair texture. Some scholars went a step further and placed these types into a hierarchical framework in which the "white" race was considered to be superior to other races. With time, these efforts to classify humans into higher and lower forms were discredited for being racist and unscientific.

Is the Biological Concept of Race Useful for Studying Physical Variation in the Human Species?

No. Biologically defined, "race" refers to subspecies, and no subspecies exist within modern *Homo sapiens*. The vast majority of biological variation within our species occurs *within* populations rather than among them. Furthermore, the differences that do exist among populations occur in gradations from one neighboring population to another without sharp breaks. For these and other reasons, anthropologists have actively worked to expose the fallacy of race as a biological concept while recognizing the existence of race as a social construct.

Is Studying Differences in Intelligence among Populations Valid?

These studies are flawed in many ways. First, studies attempting to document biological differences generally involve comparisons among races—a category that for humans is biologically false. Second, intelligence is a multifaceted phenomenon, and cultures vary in terms of which aspects of intelligence they value. Third, most instruments (tests) used to measure intelligence are biased toward the dominant culture of the people who created the test. Finally, as a complex set of traits, intelligence cannot be linked to discrete evolutionary forces acting in a particular environment.

What Are the Causes of Physical Variability?

Physical variability is a product of underlying genetic variation as it is expressed in a particular environment. Some physical traits are controlled by single genes, with variation present in alternate forms of the gene (alleles). Many physical characteristics like height, weight, or skin color are controlled by multiple genes and are thus expressed continuously, meaning this variation cannot be divided into discrete categories. Because evolutionary forces such as natural selection and random drift act on each physical trait independently, human biological variation can be studied only "one trait at a time."

From male to female, short to tall, light to dark, biological variation can be categorized in a number of ways, but in the end we are all members of the same species. Minute variations of our DNA give each of us a unique genetic "fingerprint," yet this variation remains within the bounds of being genetically human. Visible differences among modern humans are expressed within the framework of biological features shared throughout the species, and as a species, humans are highly variable.

Human genetic variation generally is distributed across the globe in a continuous fashion. From a biological perspective, this variation sometimes follows a pattern imposed by interaction with the environment through the evolutionary process of natural selection. At other times, the variation results from random genetic drift. The significance we give our biological variation, however, is always patterned, because the way we perceive variation—in fact, whether we perceive it at all—is determined by culture. For example, in many Polynesian cultures, where skin color is not a determinant of social status, people pay little attention to this physical characteristic. By contrast, in countries such as the United States, Brazil, and South Africa, where skin color is a significant social and political category, it is one of the first things people notice.

Biological diversity, therefore, cannot be studied without an awareness of the cultural dimensions that shape the questions asked about diversity as well as the history of how this knowledge has been used. When European scholars first began their systematic study of human variation in the 18th and 19th centuries, some were concerned with documenting differences among human groups in order to divide them hierarchically into progressively superior "types" of humans. Today, this hierarchical approach has been appropriately abandoned. Before exploring how contemporary biological variation is studied today, we will examine the effects of social ideas about race and racial hierarchy on the interpretation of biological variation, past and present.

THE HISTORY OF HUMAN CLASSIFICATION

Early European scholars tried to systematically classify *Homo sapiens* into subspecies, based on geographic location and phenotypic features such as skin color, body size, head shape, and hair texture. The 18th-century Swedish naturalist Carolus Linnaeus originally divided humans into subspecies based on geographic location and classified all Europeans as "white," Africans as "black," American Indians as "red," and Asians as "yellow."

The German physician Johann Blumenbach (1752–1840) introduced some significant changes to this four-race scheme in the 1795 edition of his book *On the Natural Variety of Mankind.* Most notably this book formally put forth the notion of a hierarchy of human types. Based on a comparative examination of his human skull collection, Blumenbach judged as most beautiful the skull of a woman from the Caucasus Mountain range (located between the Black Sea and the Caspian Sea of southeastern Europe and southwestern Asia). It was more symmetrical than the others, and he saw it as a reflection of nature's ideal form: the circle. Surely, Blumenbach reasoned, this "perfect" specimen resembled God's original creation. Moreover, he thought that the living inhabitants of the Caucasus region were the most beautiful in the world. Based on these criteria, he concluded that this high mountain range, not far from the lands mentioned in the Bible, was the place of human origins.

Blumenbach concluded that all light-skinned peoples in Europe and adjacent parts of western Asia and northern Africa belonged to the same race. On this basis, he dropped the "European" race label and replaced it with "Caucasian." Although he continued to distinguish American Indians as a separate race, he regrouped dark-skinned Africans as "Ethiopian" and split those Asians not considered Caucasian into two separate races: "Mongolian" (referring to most inhabitants of Asia, including China and Japan) and "Malay" (indigenous Australians, Pacific Islanders, and others).

Convinced that Caucasians were closest to the original ideal humans supposedly created in God's image, Blumenbach ranked them as superior. The other races, he argued, were the result of "degeneration"; moving away from their place of origin and adapting to different environments and climates, they had degenerated physically and morally into what many Europeans came to think of as inferior races.[1]

Critically reviewing this and other historical efforts at classifying humanity into higher and lower forms, we now clearly recognize their factual errors and ethnocentric prejudices with respect to the concept of race. Especially disastrous is the notion of superior and inferior races, as this has been used to justify brutalities ranging from repression to slavery to mass murder or genocide. It has also been employed to rationalize cruel mockery, as painfully illustrated in the tragic story of Ota Benga, an African pygmy man who in the early 1900s was caged in a New York zoo with an orangutan.

Captured in a raid in Congo, Ota Benga somehow came into the possession of a North American missionary-explorer looking for exotic "savages" for exhibition in the United States. In 1904, Ota and a group of fellow Pyg-

---

[1]Gould, S. J. (1994). The geometer of race. *Discover 15* (11), 65–69.

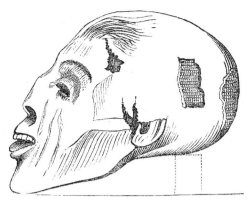

Head of an embalmed idiot, from Thebes.

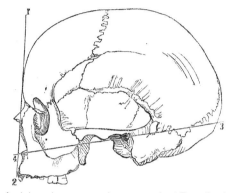

The facial angle measured on an ancient Egyptian head.

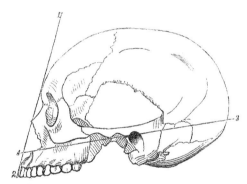

The facial angle measured on a Shoshonee Indian.

The work of 19th-century Philadelphia physician Samuel Morton is an example of ideologically biased research conducted to justify popular prejudices about so-called racial hierarchies. He measured a series of skulls in an attempt to demonstrate the supposed biological superiority of groups of people through features of skull shape and size.

mies were shipped across the Atlantic and exhibited at the World's Fair in Saint Louis, Missouri. About 23 years old at the time, Ota was 4 feet 11 inches in height and weighed 103 pounds. Throngs of visitors came to see displays of dozens of indigenous peoples from around the globe, shown in their traditional dress and living in replica villages doing their customary activities. The fair was a success for the organizers, and all the Pygmies survived to be shipped back to their homeland. The en-

terprising missionary also returned to Congo and with Ota's help collected artifacts to be sold to the American Museum of Natural History in New York City.

In the summer of 1906 Ota came back to the United States with the missionary, who soon went bankrupt and lost his entire collection to the bank. Left stranded in the big city, Ota was placed in the care of the museum and then taken to the Bronx Zoo and exhibited in the monkey house, with an orangutan as company. Ota's sharpened teeth (a cultural practice among his own people) were seen as evidence of his supposedly cannibal nature. After intensive protest, zoo officials released Ota from his cage and during the day let him roam free in the park, where he was often harassed by teasing visitors. Ota (usually referred to as a "boy") was then turned over to an orphanage for African American children. In 1916, upon hearing that he would never return to his homeland, he took a revolver and shot himself through the heart.[2]

The racist display at the Bronx Zoo a century ago was by no means unique. Just a tip of the ethnocentric iceberg, it was the manifestation of a powerful ideology in which one small part of humanity sought to demonstrate and justify its claims of biological and cultural superiority. This had particular resonance in North America, where people of European descent were thrown together in a society with Native Americans, African slaves, and (later) Asians who had been imported as a source of cheap labor. Indeed, such claims, based on false notions of race, have resulted in the oppression and genocide of millions of humans because of the color of their skin or the shape of their skulls.

Fortunately, by the early 20th century, some scholars began to challenge the concept of racial hierarchies. Among the strongest critics was Franz Boas (1858–1942), a Jewish scientist who immigrated to the United States because of rising anti-Semitism in his German homeland and went on to become a founder of North America's academic anthropology. As president of the American Association for the Advancement of Science, Boas criticized false claims of racial superiority in an important speech titled "Race and Progress," published in the prestigious journal *Science* in 1909.

Ashley Montagu (1905–1999), a student of Boas and one of the best-known anthropologists of his time, devoted much of his career to combating scientific racism. Born Israel Ehrenberg to a working-class Jewish family in England, he also felt the sting of anti-Semitism. After changing his name in the 1920s, he immigrated to the United States, where he went on to fight racism in his writing and in academic and public lectures. Of all his works, none is more important than his book *Man's*

---

[2]Bradford, P. V., & Blume, H. (1992). *Ota Benga: The pygmy in the zoo.* New York: St. Martin's Press.

While at first glance Fatimah Jackson's research areas seem quite diverse, they are unified by consistent representation of African American perspectives in biological anthropological research.

With a keen awareness of how culture determines the content of scientific questions, Jackson chooses hers carefully. One of her earliest areas of research concerned the use of common African plants as foods and medicines. She has examined the co-evolution of plants and humans and the ways plant compounds serve to attract and repel humans at various stages of ripeness. Through laboratory and field research, she has documented that cassava, a New World root crop providing the major source of dietary energy for over 500 million people, also guards against malaria. This crop has become a major food

Courtesy of Robert T. Jackson

throughout Africa in areas where malaria is common.

Jackson is also the genetics group leader for the African Burial Ground Project (mentioned in Chapter 1). In a

small area uncovered during a New York City construction project, the remains of thousands of Africans and people of African descent were uncovered. Jackson is recovering DNA from skeletal remains and attempting to match the dead with specific regions of Africa through the analysis of genetic markers in living African people.

Jackson, one of the early advocates for appropriate ethical treatment of minorities in the human genome project, is very concerned with making sure that the genetic work for the African Burial Ground Project is conducted with sensitivity to African people. She is therefore working to establish genetic laboratories and repositories in Africa. For Jackson, these laboratories are symbolic of the fact of human commonality and that all humans today have roots in Africa.

Most Dangerous Myth: The Fallacy of Race. Published in 1942, it took the lead in debunking the concept of clearly bounded races as a "social myth." The book has since gone through six editions, the last in 1999. Montagu's once controversial ideas have now become mainstream, and his text remains one of the most comprehensive treatments of its subject. For a contemporary example of a culturally informed approach to human biological variation, see this chapter's Anthropologists of Note.

The fact is, generalized references to human types such as "Asiatic" or "Mongoloid," "European" or "Caucasoid," and "African" or "Negroid" were at best mere statistical abstractions about populations in which certain physical features appeared in higher frequencies than in other populations; no example of "pure" racial types could be found. These categories turned out to be

THOMSON AUDIO STUDY PRODUCTS Take advantage of the MP3-ready Audio Lecture Overviews and comprehensive audio glossary of key terms for each chapter. See the preface for information on how to access this on-the-go study and review tool.

neither definitive nor particularly helpful. The visible traits were generally found to occur not in abrupt shifts from population to population but in a continuum that changed gradually, with few sharp breaks. To compound the problem, one trait might change gradually over a north-south gradient, whereas another might show a similar change from east to west. Human skin color, for instance, becomes progressively darker as one moves from northern Europe to central Africa, whereas blood type B becomes progressively more common as one moves from western to eastern Europe.

Finally, there are many variations within each group, and those within groups are often greater than those between groups. In Africa, the light-brown skin color of someone from the Kalahari Desert might more closely resemble that of a person from Southeast Asia than the darkly pigmented person from southern Sudan who is supposed to be of the same race.

RACE AS A BIOLOGICAL CONCEPT

To understand why the racial approach to human variation has been so unproductive and even damaging, we must first understand the race concept in strictly biological terms. In biology, a **race** is defined as a subspecies, or a population of a species differing geographically, morphologically, or genetically from other populations of the same species.

race In biology, the taxonomic category of subspecies that is not applicable to humans because the division of humans into discrete types does not represent the true nature of human biological variation. In some societies race is an important social category.

© Laurence Dutton/ Getty Images

Fingerprint patterns of loops, whorls, and arches are genetically determined. Grouping people on this basis would place most Europeans, sub-Saharan Africans, and East Asians together as "loops," Australian aborigines and the people of Mongolia together as "whorls," and central Europeans and the Bushmen of southern Africa together as "arches."

© AP Photo/Eugene Hoshiko

Yao Ming, center for the Houston Rockets, receives his Special Olympics Global Ambassador jersey from athlete Xu Chuang (left) and Special Olympics East Asia President Dicken Yung. Standing side-by-side, these three individuals illustrate the wide range of variation seen within a single so-called racial category.

Simple and straightforward as such a definition may seem, there are three very important things to note about it. First, it is arbitrary; there is no agreement on how many differences it takes to make a race. For example, if one researcher emphasizes skin color while another emphasizes blood group differences, they will not classify people in the same way. Ultimately, it proved impossible to reach agreement on the number of genes and precisely which ones are the most important for defining races.

After arbitrariness, the second thing to note about the biological definition of race is that it does not mean that any one race has exclusive possession of any particular variant of any gene or genes. In human terms, the frequency of a trait like the type O blood group, for example, may be high in one population and low in another, but it is present in both. In other words, populations are genetically "open," meaning that genes flow between them. Because populations are genetically open, no fixed racial groups can exist. The primary reproductive barriers that exist for humans are cultural.

Another important consideration about the biological definition of race with respect to humans is that the differences among individuals and *within* a population are generally greater than the differences *among* populations. Evolutionary biologist Richard Lewontin demonstrated this through genetic analyses in the 1970s. He compared the amount of genetic variation within populations and among so-called racial types, finding a mere 7 percent of human variation existing among groups.[3] Instead, the vast majority of genetic variation exists within groups. As the science writer James Shreeve puts it, "most of what separates me genetically from a typical African or Eskimo also separates me from another average American of European ancestry."[4] This follows from the genetic openness of races; no one race has an exclusive claim to any particular form of a gene or trait.

---

[3]Lewontin, R. C. (1972). The apportionment of human diversity. In T. Dobzhansky, et al. (Eds.), *Evolutionary biology* (pp. 381–398). New York: Plenum Press.

[4]Shreeve, J. (1994). Terms of estrangement. *Discover 15* (11), 60.

THE CONCEPT OF HUMAN RACES

While the biological race concept is not applicable to human variation, nevertheless, race exists as a significant cultural category. Human groups frequently insert a false notion of biological difference into the social category of race to make it appear more factual and objective. In various ways, cultures define religious, linguistic, and ethnic groups as races, thereby confusing linguistic and cultural traits with physical traits.

For example, in many Central and South American countries, people are commonly classified as Indian, Mestizo (mixed), or Ladino (of Spanish descent). Despite the biological connotations of these terms, the criteria used for assigning individuals to these categories consist of things such as whether they wear shoes, sandals, or go barefoot; speak Spanish or an Indian language; live in a thatched hut or a European-style house; and so forth. Thus, an Indian—by speaking Spanish, wearing Western-style clothes, and living in a house in a non-

Indian neighborhood—ceases to be an Indian, no matter how many "Indian genes" he or she may possess.

This sort of confusion of nonbiological characteristics with the biological notion of heredity is by no means limited to Central and South American societies. To various extents, such confusion is found in most societies of Europe and North America. Take, for example, the fact that the racial categories used by the U.S. Census Bureau change with every census. The current large catch-all categories (white, black, American Indian or Alaskan Native, Asian, and Pacific Islander or native Hawaiian) include diverse peoples. Asian, for example, includes such different people as Chinese and East Indians, whereas native Hawaiian and Alaskan are far more restrictive. The Census Bureau also asks people to identify Hispanic ethnicity, a category that includes people who, in their countries of origin, might be classified as Indian, Mestizo, or Ladino. The addition of categories for native Hawaiians, Middle Easterners, and people who consider themselves multiracial does nothing to improve the situation. To compound the confusion, inclusion in one or another of these categories is usually based on self-identification, which means that these are not biological categories at all but rather cultural constructs.

In the United States, the Census Bureau statistics are applied in a variety of ways that add to the confusion between biological and social categories. For example, health statistics are gathered using the same Census Bureau categories for the purposes of correcting health disparities among social groups. Unfortunately, the false biological concept of race is frequently inferred in these analyses. As a result, the increased risk of dying from a heart attack for African Americans compared to whites is attributed to biological difference rather than healthcare disparities or other social factors contributing to the development of heart attacks.

Similarly, medical genetics research is regularly oversimplified into the comparisons among the racial types defined in the 18th and 19th centuries. Whether this genetic research will avoid the trap of recreating false genetic types that do not reflect the true nature of human variation remains to be seen. The recent claims made for race-specific drugs and vaccines based on limited scientific data indicate that the social category of race may again be limiting our ability to grasp the true nature of human genetic diversity.

To make matters worse, the confusion of social with biological factors is frequently combined with prejudices that then serve to exclude whole categories of people from certain roles or positions in society. Take for example, the racial hierarchy among European settlers, American Indians, and Africans imported as slaves that characterized colonial North America. A racial worldview that had antecedents in the unequal power relations between the supposed English or Saxon and the Irish or Celtic

© Scott Nelson/Getty Images

Persecution and killing based on race or ethnic identity is far from being a thing of the past. Conflict in the Darfur region of western Sudan between the Janjaweed, a militia group recruited from local Arab tribes, and the non-Arab peoples of the region is a major humanitarian crisis today. Recently the number of internally displaced persons in Darfur was estimated to be 1.65 million people, with more than an additional 200,000 refugees from Darfur fleeing to neighboring Chad. In this photo, refugees stop to take water from a muddy well dug in an intermittent stream on the border between Sudan and Chad.

races in Europe assigned some groups to perpetual low status on the basis of their supposed biological inferiority, whereas access to privilege, power, and wealth was reserved for favored groups of European descent.[5]

Because of the colonial association of lighter skin with greater power and higher social status, people whose history includes domination by lighter-skinned Europeans have sometimes valued this phenotype. In Haiti, for example, the "color question" has been the dominant force in social and political life. Skin texture, facial features, hair color, and socioeconomic class collectively play a role in the ranking. According to Haitian anthropologist Michel-Rolph Trouillot, "a rich black becomes a mulatto, a poor mulatto becomes black."[6]

The Nazis in Germany elevated a racialized worldview to state policy, with particularly evil consequences. The Nuremberg race laws of 1935 declared the superior-

---

[5]American Anthropological Association. (1998). Statement on "race." Available: www.ameranthassn.org.

[6]Trouillot, M. R. (1996). Culture, color, and politics in Haiti. In S. Gregory & R. Sanjek (Eds.), *Race*. New Brunswick, NJ: Rutgers University Press.

ity of the Aryan race and the inferiority of the Gypsy and Jewish races. The Nazi doctrine justified, on supposed biological grounds, political repression and extermination. In all, 11 million people (Jews, Gypsies, homosexuals, and other so-called inferior people, as well as political opponents of the Nazi regime) were deliberately put to death.

Tragically, the Nazi Holocaust (from the Greek word for "wholly burnt" or "sacrificed by fire") is not unique in human history. Such genocides, programs of extermination of one group by another, have a long history that predates World War II and continues today. Recent and ongoing genocide in parts of South America, Africa, Europe, and Asia, like previous genocides, are accompanied by a rhetoric of dehumanization and a depiction of the people being exterminated as a lesser type of human.

Considering the problems, confusion, and horrendous consequences, it is small wonder that most anthropologists have abandoned the race concept as being of no particular utility in understanding human biological variation. Instead, they have found it more productive to study the distribution and significance of single, specific, genetically based characteristics and continuous traits related to adaptation without grouping a series of unlinked traits together. They examine human variation within small breeding populations, the smallest units in which evolutionary change occurs.

THE SOCIAL SIGNIFICANCE OF RACE: RACISM

Scientific facts, unfortunately, have been slow to change what people think about race. **Racism,** a doctrine of superiority by which one group justifies the dehumanization of others based on their distinctive physical characteristics, is not just about discriminatory ideas, values, or attitudes but is also a political problem. Indeed, politicians have often exploited this concept as a means to mobilize support, demonize opponents, and eliminate rivals. Racial conflicts result from social stereotypes, not known scientific facts.

Race and Behavior

The assumption that behavioral differences exist among human "races" remains an issue to which many people today cling tenaciously. Throughout history, certain characteristics have been attributed to groups of people under a variety of names—national character, spirit, temperament—all of them vague and standing for a number of concepts totally unrelated to any biological phenomena. Common myths involve the coldness of Scandinavians or the warlike character of Germans or the lazy na-

ture of Africans. Such unjust characterizations rely upon a false notion of biological difference.

To date, no innate behavioral characteristic can be attributed to any group of people (which the nonscientist might term a "race") that cannot be explained in terms of cultural practices. If the Chinese happen to exhibit exceptional visual-spatial skills, it is probably because the business of learning to read Chinese characters requires a visual-spatial kind of learning that is not needed to master Western alphabets.[7] Similarly, the exclusion of African Americans from honors in the sport of golf (until Tiger Woods) had more to do with the social rules of country clubs and the sport's expense. All such differences or characteristics can be explained in terms of culture.

Similarly, high crime rates, alcoholism, and drug use among certain groups can be explained with reference to culture rather than biology. Individuals alienated and demoralized by poverty, injustice, and unequal opportunity tend to display antisocial behaviors more frequently than those who are integrated into the dominant culture. In a racialized society, poverty and all its ill consequences disproportionately affect some groups of people more than others.

Race and Intelligence

A question frequently asked by those unfamiliar with the fallacy of biological race in humans is whether some races are inherently more intelligent than others. First we must ask, what do we mean by the term *intelligence?* Unfortunately, there is no general agreement as to what abilities or talents actually make up what we call intelligence, even though some psychologists insist that it is a single quantifiable thing measured by IQ tests. Many more psychologists consider intelligence to be the product of the interaction of different sorts of cognitive abilities: verbal, mathematical-logical, spatial, linguistic, musical, bodily kinesthetic, social, and personal.[8] Each may be thought of as a particular kind of intelligence, unrelated to the others. This being so, they must be independently inherited (to the degree they are inherited), just as height, blood type, skin color, and

---

[7]Chan, J. W. C., & Vernon, P. E. (1988). Individual differences among the peoples of China. In J. W. Berry (Ed.), *Human abilities in cultural context* (pp. 340–357). Cambridge, England: Cambridge University Press.

[8]Jacoby, R., & Glauberman, N. (Eds.). (1995). *The Bell Curve debate* (pp. 7, 55–56, 59). New York: Random House.

racism A doctrine of superiority by which one group justifies the dehumanization of others based on their distinctive physical characteristics.

so forth are independently inherited. Thus, the various abilities that constitute intelligence are independently distributed like phenotypic traits such as skin color and blood type.

The next question is, are IQ tests a valid measure of inborn intelligence? Unfortunately, an IQ test measures performance (something that one does) rather than genetic disposition (something with which the individual was born). Performance reflects past experiences and present motivational state, as well as innate ability. In sum, it is fair to say that an IQ test is not a reliable measure of inborn intelligence.

Attempts to prove the existence of significant differences in intelligence among human populations have been going on for at least a century. In the United States, systematic comparisons of intelligence between people categorized as whites and blacks began in the early 20th century and were frequently combined with data gathered by physical anthropologists about skull shape and size. During World War I, for example, a series of IQ tests known as Alpha and Beta were regularly given to draftees. The results showed that the average score attained by European Americans was higher than that obtained by African Americans. Even though African Americans from the urban northern states scored higher than European Americans from the rural South, and some African Americans scored higher than most European Americans, many people took this as proof of the intellectual superiority of white people. But all the tests really showed was that, on the average, whites outperformed blacks in the social situation of IQ testing. The tests did not measure intelligence per se, but the ability, conditioned by culture, of certain individuals to respond appropriately to certain questions conceived by Americans of European descent for comparable middle-class whites. These tests frequently require knowledge of white middle-class values and linguistic behavior.

For such reasons, intelligence tests continue to be the subject of controversy. Many psychologists as well as anthropologists are convinced that they are of limited use, because they are applicable only to particular cultural settings. When researchers controlled for cultural and environmental factors, African and European Americans tended to score equally well.[9]

Nevertheless, some researchers still insist upon significant differences in intelligence among human populations. Recent proponents of this view are the psychologist Richard Herrnstein and the social scientist Charles Murray, who at the time was a fellow of the American Enterprise Institute, a conservative think tank in the United States. Their argument, in a lengthy (and highly publicized) book entitled *The Bell Curve,* is that the difference in IQ scores between Americans of African, Asian, and European descent is primarily determined by genetic factors and therefore immutable.

Herrnstein and Murray's book has been justly criticized on many grounds, including violation of statistical principles and the citation of flawed studies, that support their thesis, while ignoring or barely mentioning those that contradict it. In addition, they are also wrong on purely theoretical grounds. Because genes are inherited independently of one another, whatever alleles that may be associated with intelligence bear no relationship with the ones for skin pigmentation or with any other aspect of human variation such as blood type.

Further, the expression of genes always occurs in an environment. Among humans, culture shapes all aspects of the environment. In the following Original Study, U.S. physical anthropologist Jonathan Marks extends the discussion of race and intelligence to stereotypes about athletic abilities of different so-called races.

[9]Sanday, P. R. (1975). On the causes of IQ differences between groups and implications for social policy. In M. F. A. Montagu (Ed.), *Race and IQ* (pp. 232–238). New York: Oxford.

Original Study ▪ By Jonathan Marks

A Feckless Quest for the Basketball Gene

You know what they say about a little knowledge. Here's some: The greatest sprinters and basketball players are predominantly black. Here's some more: Nobel laureates in science are predominantly white.

What do we conclude? That blacks have natural running ability, and whites have natural science ability? Or perhaps

that blacks have natural running ability, but whites don't have natural science ability, because that would be politically incorrect?

Or perhaps that we can draw no valid conclusions about the racial distribution of abilities on the basis of data like these.

That is what modern anthropology would say.

But it's not what a new book, *Taboo: Why Black Athletes Dominate Sports and Why We're Afraid to Talk About It,* says. It says that blacks dominate sports because of their genes and that we're afraid to talk about it on account of a cabal of high-ranking politically correct postmodern professors—myself, I am flattered to observe, among them.

The book is a piece of good old-fashioned American anti-intellectualism (those dang perfessers!) that plays to vulgar beliefs about group differences of the sort we recall from *The Bell Curve* six years ago. These are not, however, issues that anthropologists are "afraid to talk about"; we talk about them a lot. The author, journalist, and former television producer Jon Entine, simply doesn't like what we're saying. But to approach the subject with any degree of rigor, as anthropologists have been trying to do for nearly a century, requires recognizing that it consists of several related questions.

First, how can we infer a genetic basis for differences among people? The answer: Collect genetic data. There's no substitute. We could document consistent differences in physical features, acts, and accomplishments until the Second Coming and be entirely wrong in thinking they're genetically based. A thousand Nigerian Ibos and a thousand Danes will consistently be found to differ in complexion, language, and head shape. The first is genetic, the second isn't, and the third we simply don't understand.

What's clear is that, developmentally, the body is sufficiently plastic that subtle differences in the conditions of growth and life can affect it profoundly. Simple observation of difference is thus not a genetic argument.

Which brings us to the second question: How can we accept a genetic basis for athletic ability and reject it for intelligence? The answer: We can't. Both conclusions are based on the same standard of evidence. If we accept that blacks are genetically endowed jumpers because "they" jump so well, we are obliged to accept that they are genetically unendowed at schoolwork because "they" do so poorly.

In either case, we are faced with the scientifically impossible task of drawing conclusions from a mass of poorly controlled data. Controls are crucial in science: If every black schoolboy in America knows he's supposed to be good at basketball and bad at algebra, and we have no way to measure schoolboys outside the boundaries of such an expectation, how can we gauge their "natural" endowments? Lots of things go into the observation of excellence or failure, only one of which is genetic endowment.

But obviously humans differ. Thus, the last question: What's the relationship between patterns of human genetic variation and groups of people? The answer: It's complex.

All populations are heterogeneous and are built in some sense in opposition to other groups. Jew or Muslim, Hutu or Tutsi, Serb or Bosnian, Irish or English, Harvard or Yale—one thing we're certain of is that the groups of most significance to us don't correspond to much in nature.

Consider, then, the category "black athlete"—and let's limit ourselves to men here. It's broad enough to encompass Arthur Ashe, Mike Tyson, and Kobe Bryant.

When you read about the body of the black male athlete, whose body do you imagine? Whatever physical gift these men share is not immediately apparent from looking at them.

Black men of highly diverse builds enter athletics and excel.

Far more don't excel. In other words, there is a lot more to being black and to being a prominent athlete than mere biology. If professional excellence or overrepresentation could be regarded as evidence for genetic superiority, there would be strong implications for Jewish comedy genes and Irish policeman genes.

Inferring a group's excellence from the achievements of some members hangs on a crucial asymmetry: To accomplish something means that you had the ability to do it, but the failure to do it doesn't mean you didn't have the ability. And the existing genetic data testify that known DNA variations do not respect the boundaries of human groups.

To be an elite athlete, or elite anybody, presumably does require some kind of genetic gift. But those gifts must be immensely diverse, distributed broadly across the people of the world—at least to judge from the way that the erosion of social barriers consistently permits talent to manifest itself in different groups of people.

In an interview with *The Philadelphia Daily News* in February, Mr. Entine observed that Jews are overrepresented among critics of the views he espouses. But is that a significantly Jewish thing? Or is it simply a consequence of the fact that among any group of American intellectuals you'll find Jews overrepresented because they are a well-educated minority? There's certainly no shortage of non-Jews who find the ideas in "Taboo" to be demagogic quackery.

Of course, Jewish academics may sometimes be speaking as academics, not as Jews. Likewise black athletes may perform as athletes, not just as embodied blackness.

How easy it is to subvert Michael Jordan, the exceptional and extraordinary man, into merely the representative of the black athlete.

The problem with talking about the innate superiority of the black athlete is that it is make-believe genetics applied to naïvely conceptualized groups of people. It places a spotlight on imaginary natural differences that properly belongs on real social differences.

More important, it undermines the achievements of individuals as individuals. Whatever gifts we each have are far more likely, from what we know of genetics, to be unique individual constellations of genes than to be expressions of group endowments.

(By Jonathan Marks, professor of biological anthropology at the University of North Carolina, Charlotte.) ∎

There are enormous problems in attempting to separate genetic components of intelligence from environmental contributors.[10] Most studies of intelligence rely on comparisons between identical twins, genetically identical individuals raised in the same or different environments. As biologists Richard Lewontin and Steven Rose with psychologist Leon Kamin observe, twin studies are plagued by a host of problems: inadequate sample sizes, biased subjective judgments, failure to make sure that "separated twins" really were raised separately, unrepresentative samples of adoptees to serve as controls, and

[10]Andrews, L. B., & Nelkin, D. (1996). The Bell Curve: A statement. *Science 271,* 13.

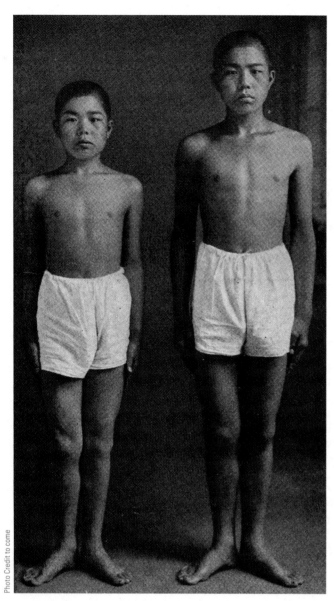

Photo Credit to come

While genetically identical, differences in the growth process can lead to very different outcomes in terms of size as seen in these twins. Even starting from inside their mother's womb, twins may experience environmental differences in terms of blood and nutrient supply. This can impact not only size but cognitive development.

untested assumptions about similarity of environments. In fact, children reared by the same mother resemble her in IQ to the same degree, whether or not they share her genes.[11] Clearly, the degree to which intelligence is inherited through genes is far from understood.[12]

Undoubtedly, the effects of social environment are important for intelligence. This should not surprise us, as other genetically determined traits are influenced by environmental factors. Height in humans, for example,

has a genetic basis while also being dependent both upon nutrition and health status (severe illness in childhood arrests growth, and renewed growth never makes up for this loss).

While it is possible to see the effects of the environment on growth, the exact relative contributions of genetic and environmental factors on either the height or the intelligence of an individual is unknown. Nevertheless, documentation of the importance of the environment in the expression of intelligence exposes further the problems with generalizations about IQ and race. For example, IQ scores of all groups in the United States, as in most industrial and postindustrial countries, have risen some 15 points since World War II. In addition, the gap between Americans of African and European descent, for example, is narrower today than in the past. Other studies show impressive IQ scores for African American children from socially deprived and economically disadvantaged backgrounds who have been adopted into highly educated and prosperous families. It is now known that underprivileged children adopted into such privileged families can boost their IQs by 20 points. It is also well known that IQ scores rise in proportion to the test-takers' amount of schooling.

More such cases could be cited, but these suffice to make the point: The assertion that IQ is biologically fixed and immutable is clearly false. Ranking human beings with respect to their intelligence scores in terms of racial difference is doubly false.

But despite all the efforts to confirm it, the hypothesis that differences in intelligence exist among races remains unproved. Nor is it ever likely to be proved, in view of the major thrust in the evolution of the genus *Homo*. Over the past 2.5 million years, all populations of this genus have adapted primarily through culture—actively inventing solutions to the problems of survival, rather than relying only on biological adaptation. Thus, we would expect a comparable degree of intelligence in all present-day human populations.

One final criticism of the race–intelligence difference hypothesis is purely practical. The only way to be sure that individual human beings develop their innate abilities and skills to the fullest is to make sure they have access to the necessary resources and the opportunity to do so. This certainly cannot be accomplished if whole populations are assumed at the outset to be inferior.

STUDYING HUMAN BIOLOGICAL DIVERSITY

Although the biological concept of race is not applicable to humans, this is not to say that differences in various biological traits such as skin color do not exist. In fact,

---

[11]Lewontin, R. C., Rose, S., & Kamin, L. J. (1984). *Not in our genes* (pp. 100, 113, 116). New York: Pantheon.

[12]Ibid., pp. 9, 121.

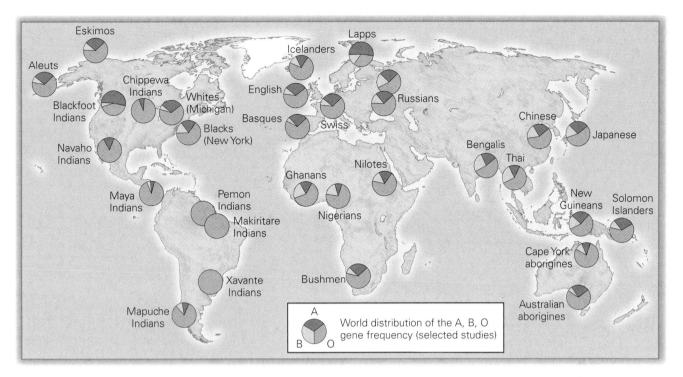

Figure 12.1

Frequencies of the three alleles for the A, B, and O blood groups for selected populations around the world illustrate the polytypic nature of *Homo sapiens*. The frequency of the alleles differs among populations.

skin color provides an excellent example of the role of natural selection in shaping human variation.

The physical characteristics of both populations and individuals are a product of the interaction between genes and environments. For example, genes predispose people to a particular skin color, but an individual's skin color is also influenced by cultural and environmental factors. The skin of sailors, for example, is darkened or burned after many hours of exposure to the sun, depending not only on genetic predisposition but cultural practices regarding exposure to the sun. In other cases, such as A-B-O blood type, phenotypic expression closely reflects genotype.

For characteristics controlled by a single gene, different versions of that gene, known as alleles, also mediate variation. Such traits are called **polymorphic** (meaning "many shapes"). Our blood types, determined by the alleles for types A, B, and O blood, are an example of a polymorphism, may appear in any of four distinct phenotypic forms (A, B, O, and AB).

A species can also be considered polymorphic, meaning that there is wide variation among individuals (beyond differences between males and females). Here "polymorphic" refers to continuous phenotypic variation that may be genetically controlled by interactions among multiple different genes, in addition to the allelic variation described above. When a polymorphic species faces changing environmental conditions, the variation it has within its gene pool fosters survival of the species,

since some of those individuals may possess traits that prove adaptive in the altered environment. Individuals whose physical characteristics enable them to do well in the new environment will usually reproduce more successfully, so that their genes will become more common in subsequent generations. Similarly, the polymorphism of the human species has allowed us to thrive in a wide variety of environments.

When polymorphisms of a species are distributed into geographically dispersed populations, biologists describe this species as **polytypic** ("many types"); that is, genetic variability is unevenly distributed among groups. For example, in the distribution of the polymorphism for blood type (four distinct phenotypic groups: A, B, O, or AB), the human species is polytypic. The frequency of the "O" allele is highest in American Indians, especially among some populations native to South America; the highest frequencies of the allele for type A blood tend to be found among certain European populations (although the highest frequency of all is found among the Blackfoot Indians of North America); the highest frequencies of the "B" allele are found in some Asian populations (Figure 12.1). Even though single traits may be grouped

polymorphic A term to describe species with alternative forms (alleles) of particular genes.

polytypic The expression of genetic variants in different frequencies in different populations of a species.

VISUAL COUNTERPOINT

A thick, stocky body and relatively short limbs tend to be characteristic of populations adapted to the cold of the Arctic or high altitude, as in this person from the Andean highlands of Peru, because this body type is excellent at conserving heat. A tall, thin body on the other hand, as seen in the Maasai of Kenya, is well adapted to the heat as it provides additional surface area from which body heat can be radiated into the environment.

within specific geographic regions, when a greater number of traits are considered, specific human "types" cannot be identified. Instead each of these traits is independently subject to evolutionary forces.

Today anthropologists study biological diversity in terms of **clines,** or the continuous gradation over space in the form or frequency of a trait. As mentioned in Chapter 2, the spatial distribution or cline for the sickle-cell allele allowed anthropologists to identify the adaptive function of this gene in a malarial environment. Clinal analysis of a continuous trait such as body shape, which

cline A gradual change in the frequency of an allele or trait over space.

is controlled by a series of genes, allows anthropologists to interpret human global variation in body build as an adaptation to climate.

Generally, people long native to regions with cold climates tend to have greater body bulk (not to be equated with fat) relative to their extremities (arms and legs) than do people native to regions with hot climates, who tend to be relatively long and slender. Interestingly, these differences show up as early as the time of *Homo erectus,* as described in Chapter 7. A person with larger body bulk and relatively shorter extremities may suffer more from summer heat than someone whose extremities are relatively long and whose body is slender. But they will conserve needed body heat under cold conditions. A bulky body tends to conserve more heat than a less bulky one, because it has less surface area relative to volume. In hot, open country, by contrast, people benefit from a long slender body that can get rid of excess heat quickly. A small slender body can also promote heat loss due to a high surface area to volume ratio.

In addition to these sorts of very long-term effects that climate may have imposed on human variation, climate can also contribute to human variation through its impact on the process of growth and development (developmental adaptation). For example, some of the physiological mechanisms for withstanding cold or dissipating heat have been shown to vary depending upon the climate that an individual experiences as a child. Individuals spending their youths in very cold climates develop circulatory system modifications that allow them to remain comfortable at temperatures that people from warmer climates cannot tolerate. Similarly, hot climate promotes the development of a higher density of sweat glands, creating a more efficient system for sweating to keep the body cool.

Cultural processes complicate studies of body build and climatic adaptation. For example, dietary differences

The epicanthic eye fold is common among people native to East Asia. While some anthropologists have suggested that this feature might be an adaptation to cold, genetic drift could also be responsible for the frequency of this trait among people of East Asia.

© Steve Elmore

particularly during childhood will cause variation in body shape through their effect on the growth process. Another complicating factor is clothing. Much of the way people adapt to cold is cultural, rather than biological. For example, Inuit peoples of northern Canada live in a region where much of the year is very cold. To cope with this, they long ago developed efficient clothing to keep the body warm. Because of this, the Inuit are provided with what amount to artificial tropical environments inside their clothing. Such cultural adaptations allow humans to inhabit the entire globe.

Some anthropologists have also suggested that variation in such features as face and eye shape relate to climate. For example, biological anthropologist Carleton Coon and colleagues once proposed that the "Mongoloid face," common in populations native to East and Central Asia, as well as Arctic North America, exhibits features adapted to life in very cold environments. The **epicanthic eye fold,** which minimizes eye exposure to the cold, a flat facial profile, and extensive fatty deposits may help to protect the face against frostbite.

Although experimental studies have failed to sustain the frostbite hypothesis, it is true that a flat facial profile generally goes with a round head. A significant percentage of body heat may be lost from the head. A round head, having less surface area relative to volume, loses less heat than a longer, more elliptical head. As one would predict from this, long-headed populations are generally found in hotter climates; round-headed ones are more common in cold climates. However, these same features could be also present in populations due to genetic drift.

Culture and Biological Diversity

While cultural adaptation has reduced the importance of biological adaptation and physical variation, at the same time, cultural forces impose their own selective pressures. For example, take the reproductive fitness of individuals with diabetes—a disease with a known genetic predisposition. In North America and Europe today, where medication is relatively available, people with diabetes are as biologically fit as anyone else. However, if diabetics are denied access to the needed medication, as they are in many parts of the world, their biological fitness is lost and they die out. In fact, one's financial status affects one's access to medication, and so, however unintentional it may be, one's biological fitness may be decided by one's financial status.

epicanthic eye fold A fold of skin at the inner corner of the eye that covers the true corner of the eye; common in Asiatic populations.

Cultural factors can also contribute directly to the development of disease. For example, one type of diabetes is very common among overweight individuals who get little exercise—a combination that describes 61 percent of people from the United States today who are increasingly beset by this condition. As people from traditional cultures throughout the world adopt a Western high sugar diet and activity pattern, the frequency of diabetes and obesity increases.

Another example of culture acting as an agent of biological selection has to do with lactose tolerance: the ability to digest **lactose,** the primary constituent of fresh milk. This ability depends on the capacity to make a particular enzyme, **lactase.**

Most mammals as well as most human populations—especially Asian, Native Australian, Native American, and many (but not all) African populations—do not continue to produce lactase into adulthood. Failure to retain lactase production into adulthood causes gas pains and diarrhea for individuals who consume milk. Only 10 to 30 percent of Americans of African descent and 0 to 30 percent of adult Asians are lactose tolerant.[13] By contrast, lactase retention and lactose tolerance are normal for over 80 percent of adults of northern European descent. Eastern Europeans, Arabs, and some East Africans are closer to northern Europeans in lactase retention than they are to Asians and other Africans. Generally speaking, a high retention of lactase is found in populations with a long tradition of dairying. For them, fresh milk is an important dietary item. In such populations, selection in the past favored those individuals with the allele that confers the ability to assimilate lactose, selecting out those without this allele.

Because milk is associated with health in North American and European countries, powdered milk has long been a staple of economic aid to other countries. In fact, such practices work against the members of populations in which lactase is not commonly retained into adulthood. Those individuals who are not lactose tolerant will be unable to utilize the many nutrients in milk. Frequently they will also suffer diarrhea, abdominal cramping, and even bone degeneration, with serious results. In fact, the shipping of powdered milk to victims of

---

[13]Harrison, G. G. (1975). Primary adult lactase deficiency: A problem in anthropological genetics. *American Anthropologist 77,* 815–819.

lactose A sugar that is the primary constituent of fresh milk.
lactase An enzyme in the small intestine that enables humans to assimilate lactose.
thrifty genotype Human genotype that permits efficient storage of fat to draw on in times of food shortage and conservation of glucose and nitrogen.

The "got milk?" ad campaign emphasizes that milk is good for all people's health, yet the vast majority of adults globally are unable to digest milk. Only populations with long traditions of dairying have high frequencies of the alleles for this biological capacity.

South American earthquakes in the 1960s caused many deaths among them.

Among Europeans, lactose tolerance is linked with the evolution of a non-thrifty genotype as opposed to the **thrifty genotype** that characterized humans until about 6,000 years ago.[14] The thrifty genotype permits efficient storage of fat to draw on in times of food shortage. In times of scarcity individuals with the thrifty genotype conserve glucose (a simple sugar) for use in brain and red blood cells (as opposed to other tissues such as muscle), as well as nitrogen (vital for growth and health).

Regular access to glucose through the lactose in milk led to selection for the non-thrifty genotype as protection against adult-onset diabetes, or at least its onset relatively late in life (at a nonreproductive age). Populations that are lactose intolerant retain the thrifty genotype. As a consequence, when they are introduced to Western-style diets (characterized by abundance, particularly of foods high in sugar content), the incidence of obesity and diabetes skyrockets. This chapter's Biocultural Connection describes another example of genetic and cultural adaptations working at cross purposes.

Skin Color: A Case Study in Adaptation

Generally, the notion of race is most commonly equated with skin color. Skin color is subject to great variation and is attributed to several key factors: the transparency or thickness of the skin; a copper-colored pigment called carotene; reflected color from the blood vessels (responsible for the rosy color of lightly pigmented people); and,

---

[14]Allen, J. S., & Cheer, S. M. (1996). The non-thrifty genotype. *Current Anthropology 37,* 831–842.

Biocultural Connection

Beans, Enzymes, and Adaptation to Malaria

Some human adaptations to the deadly malarial parasite are biological while other adaptations are strictly tied to cultural practices such as local cuisine. The phenotype of the genetic sickle-cell allele, for example, manifests in red blood cells. With the interaction between one form of the glucose-6-phosphate-dehydrogenase (G-6-PD) enzyme and fava bean consumption, we see biological and dietary adaptations to malaria converge. The fava bean is a broad flat bean (*Vivia faba*) that is a dietary staple in malaria-endemic areas along the Mediterranean coast.

G-6-PD is an enzyme that serves to reduce one sugar, glucose-6-phosphate, to another sugar—in the process releasing an energy-rich molecule. The malaria parasite lives in red blood cells off of energy produced via G-6-PD. Individuals with a mutation in the G-6-PD gene, so-called G-6-PD deficiency, produce energy by an alternate pathway not involving this enzyme that the parasite cannot use. Furthermore, G-6-PD deficient red blood cells seem to turn over more quickly, thus allowing less time for the parasite to grow and multiply. While a different form of G-6-PD deficiency is also found in some sub-Saharan African populations, the form found in Mediterranean populations is at odds with an adaptation embedded in the cuisine of the region.

Enzymes naturally occurring in fava beans also contain substances that interfere with the development of the malarial parasite. In cultures around the Mediter-

© Charles O. Cecil/Alamy

Fava beans, a dietary staple in the countries around the Mediterranean Sea, also provide some protection against malaria. However, in individuals with G-6-PD deficiency, the protective aspects of fava beans turn deadly. This dual role has led to a rich folklore surrounding fava beans.

ranean Sea, where malaria is common, fava beans are incorporated into the diet through foods eaten at the height of the malaria season. However, if an individual with G-6-PD deficiency eats fava beans, the result is that the substances toxic to the parasite become toxic to humans. With G-6-PD deficiency, fava bean consumption leads to *hemolytic crisis* (Latin

for "breaking of red blood cells") and a series of chemical reactions that release free radicals and hydrogen peroxide into the blood stream. This condition is known as *favism*.

The toxic effect of fava bean consumption in G-6-PD individuals has led to a rich folklore around this simple food, including the ancient Greek belief that fava beans contain the souls of the dead. The link between favism and G-6-PD deficiency has led parents of children with this condition to limit consumption of this favorite dietary staple.

Unfortunately, this has sometimes led to the generalized elimination of many excellent sources of protein such as peanuts, lentils, chick peas, soy beans, and nuts. Another biocultural connection is again at the root of this unnecessary deprivation. The Arabic name for fava beans is *foul* (pronounced "fool"), while the soy beans are called *foul-al-Soya*, and peanuts are *foul-al-Soudani*, linguistically linking plants that are unrelated biologically.[a]

An environmental stressor as potent as malaria has led to a number of human adaptations. In the case of fava beans and G-6-PD deficiency, these adaptations can work at cross-purposes. Cultural knowledge of the biochemistry of these interactions will allow humans to adapt, regardless of their genotype.

[a]Babiker, M. A., et al. (1996). Unnecessary deprivation of common food items in glucose-6-phosphate dehydrogenase deficiency. *Annals of Saudi Arabia 16* (4), 462–463.

---

most significantly, the amount of **melanin** (from *melas*, a Greek word meaning "black")—a dark pigment in the skin's outer layer. People with dark skin have more melanin-producing cells than those with light skin, but everyone (except albinos) has a measure of melanin. Exposure to sunlight increases melanin production, causing skin color to deepen.

Melanin is known to protect skin against damaging ultraviolet solar radiation;[15] consequently, dark-skinned

peoples are less susceptible to skin cancers and sunburn than are those with less melanin. They also seem to be less susceptible to destruction of certain vitamins under intense exposure to sunlight. Because the highest concentrations of dark-skinned people tend to be found in the tropical regions of the world, it appears that natural selection has favored heavily pigmented skin as a protection against exposure where ultraviolet radiation is most constant.

---

[15]Neer, R. M. (1975). The evolutionary significance of vitamin D, skin pigment, and ultraviolet light. *American Journal of Physical Anthropology 43*, 409–416.

melanin The chemical responsible for dark skin pigmentation that helps protect against damage from ultraviolet radiation.

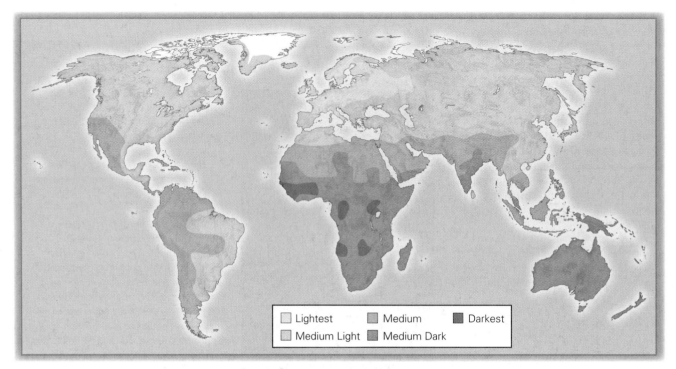

Figure 12.2

This map illustrates the distribution of dark and light human skin pigmentation before 1492. Medium-light skin color in Southeast Asia reflects the spread into that region of people from southern China, whereas the medium darkness of people native to southern Australia is a consequence of their tropical Southeast Asian ancestry. Lack of dark skin pigmentation among tropical populations of Native Americans reflects their ancestry in Northeast Asia a mere 20,000 years ago.

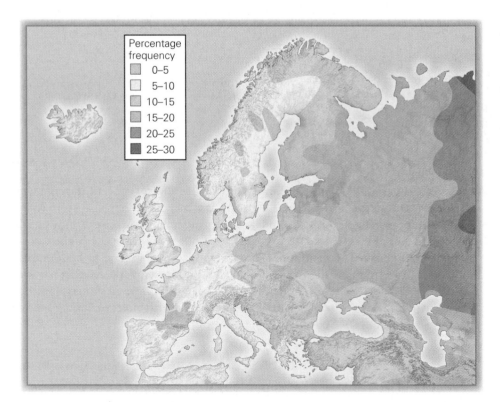

Figure 12.3

The east-west gradient in the frequency of the type B blood in Europe contrasts with the north-south gradient in skin color shown in Figure 12.2. Whatever genes are involved in the various abilities lumped together as "intelligence" must be independently assorted as well.

The inheritance of skin color involves several genes (rather than variants of a single gene), each with several alleles, thus creating a continuous range of phenotypic expression for this trait. In addition, the geographic distribution or cline of skin color, with few exceptions, tends to be continuous (Figures 12.2 and 12.3). The exceptions have to do with the historic movement of certain populations from their original homelands to other regions, or the practice of selective mating, or both.

Because skin cancers generally do not develop until later in life, they are less likely to have interfered with the reproductive success of lightly pigmented individuals in the tropics, and so are unlikely to have been the agent of selection. On the other hand, severe sunburn, which is especially dangerous to infants, causes the body to overheat and interferes with its ability to sweat and rid itself of excess heat. Furthermore, it makes one susceptible to other kinds of infection. In addition to all this, decomposition of folate, an essential vitamin sensitive to heavy doses of ultraviolet radiation, can cause anemia, spontaneous abortion, and infertility.[16]

In northern latitudes light skin has an adaptive advantage related to the skin's important biological function as the manufacturer of vitamin D through a chemical reaction dependent upon sunlight. Vitamin D is vital for maintaining the balance of calcium in the body. In northern climates with little sunshine, light skin allows enough sunlight to penetrate the skin and stimulate the

---

[16]Branda, R. F., & Eatoil, J. W. (1978). Skin color and photolysis: An evolutionary hypothesis. *Science 201*, 625–626.

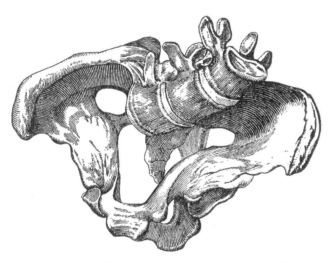

Bone diseases caused by vitamin D deficiency can deform the birth canal of the pelvis to the degree that it can interfere with successful childbirth. Because sunshine is the source of the body's vitamin D, this disease was very common in the past among the poor in northern industrial cities whose exposure to sunlight was limited. Though food supplements have reduced the impact of rickets today, it continues to be a problem where social conventions such as complete veiling limit access to sunlight by women and girls.

formation of vitamin D, essential for healthy bones. Dark pigmentation interferes with this process.

The severe consequences of vitamin D deficiency can be avoided through cultural practices. Until recently, children in northern Europe and northern North America were regularly fed a spoonful of cod liver oil during the dark winter months. Today, pasteurized milk is often fortified with vitamin D.

RACE AND HUMAN EVOLUTION REVISITED

Given what we know about the adaptive significance of human skin color and the fact that, until 800,000 years ago, the genus *Homo* exclusively inhabited the tropics, it is likely that lightly pigmented skins are a recent development in human history. Darkly pigmented skins likely are quite ancient. Consistent with humanity's African origins, the enzyme tyrosinase, which converts the amino acid tyrosine into the compound that forms melanin, is present in lightly pigmented peoples in sufficient quantity to make them very "black." The reason it does not is that they have genes that inactivate or inhibit it.[17]

Human skin, more liberally endowed with sweat glands and lacking heavy body hair compared to other primates, effectively eliminates excess body heat in a hot climate as described in Chapter 6. This would have been especially advantageous to our ancestors on the savannah, who could have avoided confrontations with carnivorous animals by carrying out most of their activities in the heat of the day. For the most part, large carnivores such as lions rest during this period, being active from dusk until early morning. Without much hair to cover their bodies, selection would have favored dark skins in our ancestors. All humans appear to have had a "black" ancestry, no matter how "white" some of them may appear to be today.

An interesting question is how long it took for light pigmentation to develop in populations living outside the tropics. Whether or not one subscribes to the multi-regional continuity model or the recent African origins hypothesis (Chapters 8 and 9), the settling of Greater Australia can be used to examine this question, as we know that the first people to reach Australia did so about 60,000 or so years ago. These people came there from tropical Southeast Asia, spreading throughout Australia eventually to what is now the island of Tasmania, with a latitude and levels of ultraviolet radiation similar to New York City, Rome, or Beijing.

As aboriginal Australians originally came from the tropics, we would expect them to have had darkly pig-

---

[17]Wills, C. (1994). The skin we're in. *Discover 15* (11), 79.

Photo Credit to come

These boys from the Jarawa tribe, one of the five indigenous tribes from the Andaman and Nicobar archipelago in the Bay of Bengal, are direct descendants of the original inhabitants of Southeast Asia. Southeast Asia also includes people whose ancestors spread into the region from China after the invention of agriculture. In the process there was a mixing of gene pools. The Andaman and Nicobar archipelago located close to the epicenter earthquake of December 2004 was devastated by the tsunami that followed. The Jarawa emerged safely in January 2005, and seem to have been saved by their ability to understand patterns of movement of the wind, ocean, and wildlife.

mented skin. In Australia, those populations that spread south of the tropics (where, as in northern latitudes, ultraviolet radiation is less intense) underwent some reduction of pigmentation. But for all that, their skin color is still far darker than that of Europeans or East Asians. Most of today's Southeast Asian population spread there from southern China following the invention of farming. This expansion of lighter skinned populations effectively "swamped" the original populations of this region, except in a few out-of-the-way places like the Andaman Islands, in the Bay of Bengal between India and Thailand.[18] The obvious conclusion is that 60,000 years is not enough to produce significant depigmentation.[19] These observations also suggest that Europeans and East Asians may have lived outside the tropics for far longer than the people of Tasmania or that settlement in latitudes even more distant from the equator were required for depigmentation to occur.

One should not conclude that, because it is newer, lightly pigmented skin is better, or more highly evolved, than heavily pigmented skin. The latter is clearly better adapted to the conditions of life in the tropics, although with cultural adaptations like protective clothing, hats, and sunscreen lotions, very lightly pigmented peoples can survive there. Conversely, the availability of supplementary sources of vitamin D allows heavily pigmented peoples to do quite well away from the tropics. In both cases, culture has rendered skin color differences largely irrelevant from a biological perspective. With time, skin color may lose its social significance as well.

---

[18]Diamond, J. (1996). Empire of uniformity. *Discover 17* (3), 83–84.

[19]Ferrie, H. (1997). An interview with C. Loring Brace. *Current Anthropology 38*, 864.

Questions for Reflection

1. Humans are challenged to find ways to embrace and comprehend the range of biological diversity without succumbing to oversimplification, discrimination, and even bloodshed fueled by superficial differences. How do anthropological approaches to race contribute to meeting this challenge?

2. From an evolutionary perspective, why is human biological diversity a key component of our collective identity as a species?

3. Why do biological anthropologists and evolutionary biologists use clines to study human variation rather than the biological concept of subspecies? Can you imagine another species of animal, plant, or microorganism for which the subspecies concept makes sense?

4. How do you define the concept of intelligence? Do you think scientists will ever be able to discover the genetic basis of intelligence?

5. Globally, health statistics are gathered by country. In addition, some countries such as the United States gather health statistics by race. How are these two endeavors different and similar? Should health statistics be gathered by group?

Suggested Readings

Cohen, M. N. (1998). *Culture of intolerance: Chauvinism, class, and racism in the United States.* New Haven, CT: Yale University Press.

This very readable book summarizes what scientific data really say about biological differences among humans and exposes questionable assumptions in U.S. culture that promote intolerance and generate problems where none need exist.

Gould, S. J. (1996). *The mismeasure of man* (2nd ed.). New York: Norton.

This is an update of a classic critique of supposedly scientific studies that attempt to rank all people on a linear scale of intrinsic and unalterable mental worth. The revision was prompted by what Gould refers to as the "latest cyclic episode of biodeterminism" represented by the publication of the widely discussed book, *The Bell Curve*.

Graves, J. L. (2001). *The emperor's new clothes: Biological theories of race at the millennium*. New Brunswick, NJ: Rutgers University Press.

Graves, a laboratory geneticist, aims to show that there is no biological basis for separation of human beings into races and that the idea of race is a relatively recent social and political construction. His grasp of science is solid and up-to-date.

Jacoby, R., & Glauberman, N. (Eds.). (1995). *The Bell Curve debate*. New York: Random House.

This collection of articles by a wide variety of authors (biologists, anthropologists, psychologists, mathematicians, essayists) critically examines the claims raised in *The Bell Curve*. For anyone who hopes to understand the race and intelligence debate, this book is a must.

Marks, J. (1995). *Human biodiversity: Genes, race, and history*. Hawthorne, NY: Aldine de Gruyter.

In this book, Marks shows how genetics has undermined the fundamental assumptions of racial taxonomy. In addition to its presentation of the nature of human biodiversity, the book also deals with the history of cultural attitudes toward race and diversity.

Smedley, A. (1998). *Race in North America: Origin and evolution of a worldview*. Boulder, CO: Westview Press.

Audrey Smedley traces the cultural invention of the idea of race and how this false biological category has been used to rationalize inequality in North America.

Thomson Audio Study Products

 Enjoy the MP3-ready Audio Lecture Overviews for each chapter and a comprehensive audio glossary of key terms for quick study and review. Whether walking to class, doing laundry, or studying at your desk, you now have the freedom to choose when, where, and how you interact with your audio-based educational media. See the preface for information on how to access this on-the-go study and review tool.

The Anthropology Resource Center

www.thomsonedu.com/anthropology
The Anthropology Resource Center provides extended learning materials to reinforce your understanding of key concepts in the four fields of anthropology. For each of the four fields, the Resource Center includes dynamic exercises including video exercises, map exercises, simulations, and "Meet the Scientists" interviews, as well as critical thinking questions that can be assigned and e-mailed to instructors. The Resource Center also provides breaking news in anthropology and interesting material on applied anthropology to help you link what you are learning to the world around you.

13 Human Adaptation to a Changing World

© Roberto Escobar/epa/Corbis

CHALLENGE ISSUE

Among the primate species, humans are the only ones capable of inhabiting the entire globe. Over the course of human evolutionary history, both our cultural and biological capabilities have contributed to our adaptability as a species. Today, however, the actions of human societies are changing the world on such a massive scale and at such a rapid pace that we, as a species, are facing novel challenges often manifest in sickness and suffering. Consider this Maya woman, displaced from her home by war and civil unrest, inhabiting the dump in Guatemala City. Her well-being and that of her children is utterly tied to the local political situations that led her family to leave their home. But global forces, both positive and negative, also impact their well-being. For example, Safe Passage, an American-based organization, works to support families so these children can stay in school and ultimately leave the dump behind. At the same time, other global processes keep these people poor and dependent while increasing the toxicity and danger of the dump they inhabit.

How Have Humans Adapted Biologically to Naturally Occurring Environmental Stressors?

When faced with an environmental stressor, the human species can adapt biologically at three distinct levels: genetically, developmentally, and physiologically. Some genetic adaptations are expressed in terms of phenotypic variation of continuous traits. Even when the genetic bases to these adaptations are not precisely known, scientists can study them through comparative measurement of the associated phenotypic variation. In addition, the long period of human growth and development allows the environment to interact with genes and shape the human body. Short-term changes or physiological adaptations occur in response to a particular environmental stimulus. Today, the rapid rates at which cultural processes change human environments pose new biological challenges with important consequences for our species.

What Is Evolutionary Medicine?

Evolutionary medicine, a branch of medical anthropology, uses the principles of evolutionary theory to contribute to human health. Basic to this approach is framing health issues in terms of the relationship between biological change and cultural change. Biological evolution shaped humans slowly over millions of years while cultural change occurs relatively quickly. The resulting disconnect between human biology and current cultural practices may lead to disease. Also, because culture shapes even scientific interpretations of the human body, evolutionary medicine acknowledges that some physiological phenomena regarded as symptoms of disease can also be understood as naturally evolving defense mechanisms.

How Are Humans Adapting in the Face of Globalization?

The interconnectedness of humans to one another and to the environment is critical for understanding human adaptation and disease. Because local human environments are shaped by culture—including global political and economic systems—these cultural features directly impact the global distribution of health and disease. Simply describing disease in terms of biological processes, such as those associated with infection or malnutrition, leaves out the ultimate reasons that some individuals are more likely to become sick than others. By examining the political ecology of disease, we can reveal its social causes, bringing us closer to finding long-lasting cures.

Throughout millions of years of human evolutionary history, biology and culture interacted to make humans the species we are today. A look at the archaeological record and contemporary human variation reveal that biology and culture continue to shape all areas of human experience, including health and disease. Indeed, an inside joke among anthropologists is that if you do not know the answer to an exam question about biology and culture, the answer is always "both" or "malaria." Our current understanding of malaria, as explained in previous chapters, illustrates how answering "malaria" is just like answering "both." Farming practices (culture) of the past created the perfect environment for the malarial parasite. The genetic response to this environmental change (biology) was increased frequencies of the sickle-cell allele.

To add a few more layers closer to the present, think about how contemporary global inequalities (culture) contribute to the continued devastating effects of malaria (biology) in poorer countries today. For example, if malaria were a problem plaguing North America or Europe today, would most citizens of the countries with rampant malaria still be without adequate treatment or cure? Similarly, public health initiatives for genetic counseling (culture) to reduce frequencies of sickle-cell anemia (biology) in the United States have been met with distrust by African Americans who have experienced racism rooted in a false message of biological difference (culture).[1] Would white citizens of the United States feel as comfortable with genetic testing to eliminate a disease gene if they had experienced some of the wrongs underprivileged ethnic minorities had experienced in the name of science?

Consider for example, the Tuskegee Syphilis Study, carried out by the U.S. Public Health Service in Macon County, Alabama, from 1932 to 1972. This study involved withholding adequate treatment for syphilis to a group of poor African American men without their knowledge, to learn more about the biology of syphilis in the "Negro." These methods are now widely recognized as a moral breach that caused unnecessary pain and suffering to the men and their families. The unethical practices of the study caused the U.S. government to change its research policies involving the biological study of human subjects. In short, when examining a seemingly biological phenomenon such as disease, cultural factors must be considered at every level—from how that phenomenon is represented in each social group (reflected in this case in the false notion that the biology of syphilis would differ between people of different skin colors) to how biological research is conducted.

An integrated biocultural approach is one of the hallmarks of anthropology. In examples ranging from infant feeding and sleeping practices to the relationship between poverty and tuberculosis, biocultural connections have been emphasized throughout this book. In this chapter, we take a deeper look at this connection and examine some of the theoretical approaches biological and medical anthropologists use to examine the interaction of biology and culture.

While humans possess a number of exquisite biological mechanisms through which they have adapted to

---

[1]Tapper, M. (1999). *In the blood: Sickle-cell anemia and the politics of race*. Philadelphia: University of Pennsylvania Press.

The Tuskegee Syphilis Study wrongly justified the denial of appropriate medical therapy to African American men in order to study the supposed differences in the biology of the disease in the "Negro." This human experimentation was not only false from a biological perspective but represents a moral breach in research conduct. Public outcry about this experiment led to regulations that protect all human subjects in biomedical research.

© Corbis/Sygma

the natural environment, as human cultures change the environment in today's globalizing world, these biological mechanisms can fall terribly short. Before turning to the challenges we face in today's human-made environments, we will explore the biological mechanisms humans have used over millennia to adapt to three naturally occurring environmental extremes: high altitude, cold, and heat.

HUMAN ADAPTATION TO NATURAL ENVIRONMENTAL STRESSORS

Studies of human adaptation traditionally focus on the capacity of humans to adapt or adjust to their environ-

THOMSON AUDIO STUDY PRODUCTS
Take advantage of the MP3-ready Audio Lecture Overviews and comprehensive audio glossary of key terms for each chapter. See the preface for information on how to access this on-the-go study and review tool.

ment through biological and/or cultural mechanisms. Darwin's theory of natural selection accounts for discrete genetic changes built into the allele frequencies of populations, such as the various adaptations to malaria that we have examined. It also provides the mechanism for understanding that adaptations, evident in population variation of continuous phenotypic traits, depend upon multiple interacting genes. Even when the genetic bases to these adaptations (such

as skin color or body build) are not precisely known, scientists can study them through comparative measurement of the associated phenotypic variation. Humans possess two additional biological mechanisms through which they can adapt.

The first of these, **developmental adaptation,** also produces permanent phenotypic variation as the environment shapes the expression of the genes each individual possesses. The extended period of growth and development characteristic of humans allows for a prolonged time period during which the environment can exert its effects on the developing organism.

The anthropological focus on growth and development has a long history dating back to the work of Franz Boas, one of the founders of four-field anthropology. Boas is credited with discovering the features of the human growth curve (Figure 13.1). He demonstrated that the rate of human growth varies in typical patterns until adulthood, when physical growth ceases. Humans experience a period of very rapid growth after birth through infancy, followed by a gradually slower rate of growth during childhood. At adolescence, the rate of growth increases again during the adolescent growth spurt.

In addition to describing the long-term pattern of human growth, anthropologists have also demonstrated that within periods of growth, the actual growth process proceeds as a series of alternating bursts and rela-

developmental adaptation A permanent phenotypic variation derived from interaction between genes and the environment during the period of growth and development.

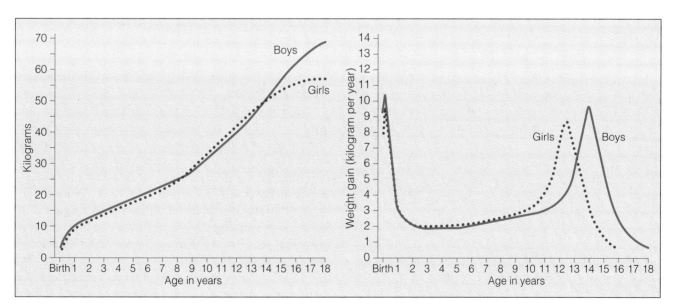

Figure 13.1
Franz Boas defined the features of the human growth curve. The graph on the left depicts distance, or the amount of growth attained over time, while the graph on the right shows the velocity, or rate of growth over time. These charts are widely used throughout the globe to determine the health status of children.

Anthropologist of Note

Peter Ellison (b. 1950)

Reproductive biology and human health across cultures have been the focus of the work of biological anthropologist Peter Ellison. In the 1970s, Ellison first read Darwin's *Origin of Species* as a college student at St. John's College in Annapolis, Maryland. He found Darwin's text transformative and went to the University of Vermont to study biology; later he earned a doctorate in biological anthropology from Harvard, where he now runs a comprehensive program in reproductive ecology.

Ellison has pioneered techniques for hormonal analysis from saliva, and he uses this technique to monitor individuals' hormonal response to a variety of environmental stressors. This non-invasive technique has allowed Ellison to conduct hormonal studies throughout

Courtesy Martha Stewart

the world and to correlate hormonal levels with social events. People from long-term field sites in the Congo, Poland, Japan, Nepal, and Paraguay have participated in this research, allowing

Ellison to document the hormonal variation around biological events, such as egg implantation and breastfeeding, as well as cultural factors such as farm work or foraging.

He is especially interested in how behavior and social stimuli affect reproductive physiology. In Western societies, he has explored hormonal levels of males and females in response to stimuli, such as winning a championship or taking a stressful exam. He has also studied the relationship cancer development has to exercise and stress. In his recent book *On Fertile Ground*, Ellison illustrates how evolutionary forces have shaped human reproductive physiology into a system capable of precise responses to environmental stimuli.

---

tive quiet.[2] When challenged by malnutrition, physical growth slows to permit immediate survival at the expense of height in adulthood. This adaptive mechanism may have negative consequences for subsequent generations as individuals who were malnourished as children have been shown to experience reduced reproductive success as adults.[3]

Boas also demonstrated differences in the growth of immigrant children in the United States compared to their parents. This work was the earliest documentation of the variable effects of different environments on the growth process. Presumably, immigrant children resemble their parents genetically; therefore, size differences between immigrant children and their parents could be attributed to the environment alone. These kinds of

differences, known as **secular trends,** allow anthropologists to make inferences about environmental effects on growth and development.

For example, across the globe tremendous variation is seen in the age at menarche or first menstruation. Some of this variation can be attributed to genetically based population differences, while the remainder is due to environmental effects. The Bundi of New Guinea have the oldest average age at menarche (18). An important theory accounting for the timing of sexual maturation ties age at menarche to the percentage of body fat possessed by growing individuals as a regulator of hormonal production.

Over the past fifty years a secular trend has become evident in North America with a trend to lower age at menarche. Whether the secular trend to lower age at menarche is attributable to healthy or problematic environmental stimuli (such as childhood obesity or hormones in the environment) has yet to be determined. Biological anthropologist Peter Ellison works extensively on the connections between hormones and the environment—a subspecialty defined as reproductive ecology (see Anthropologist of Note).

While genetic and developmental adaptations are permanent parts of an adult's phenotype, **physiological adaptations,** short-term changes in response to a specific environmental stimulus, come and go. Along with cultural adaptations, these various biological mechanisms allow humans to be the only primate species to inhabit

---

[2]Lampl, M., Velhuis, J. D., & Johnson, M. L. (1992). Saltation and stasis: A model of human growth. *Science 258* (5083), 801–803.

[3]Martorell, R. (1988). Body size, adaptation, and function. *GDP,* 335–347.

---

secular trend   A physical difference among related people from distinct generations that allows anthropologists to make inferences about environmental effects on growth and development.
physiological adaptation   A short-term physiological change in response to a specific environmental stimulus. An immediate short-term response is not very efficient and is gradually replaced by a longer term response (see acclimatization).

the entire globe. Over the course of our evolutionary history, most environmental stressors were climatic and geographic. Today, humans face a series of new environmental stressors of their own making.

Adaptation to High Altitude

High altitude differs from other natural environmental stressors because it is the least amenable to cultural adaptation. The major challenge of high altitude is the reduced availability of oxygen. Before the invention of oxygen masks and pressurized cabins in airplanes, there was no way to modify this environmental stressor.

When people speak of the air being "thinner" at high altitude, they are referring to the concentration ("partial pressure") of oxygen available to the lungs (and so the circulatory system). At high altitudes, the partial pressure of oxygen is sufficiently reduced so that most lowlanders experience severe oxygen deprivation.

Populations that have lived at high altitudes for generations, such as the Quechua Indians of Highland Peru and the Sherpa native to the Himalaya Mountains, possess a remarkable ability to tolerate oxygen deprivation, living and working at altitudes as high as 17,000 to 20,000 feet above sea level. Physiological adaptation to the lower partial pressure of oxygen in the environment has rendered their body tissues resistant to oxygen deprivation.

Typical lowlanders can make both short- and long-term physiological adjustments to high altitude. In general, short-term changes help an individual avoid an immediate crisis, but their poor efficiency makes them difficult to sustain. Instead, long-term responses take over as the individual's physiological responses attain an equilibrium with the environment. This process is known as **acclimatization.** Most lowlanders stepping off an airplane in Lima, Peru, will increase their respiratory rate, cardiac output, and pulse rate. Their arteries will expand as blood pressure increases in order to get oxygen to the tissues. This kind of response cannot be maintained indefinitely. Instead, lowlanders acclimatize as their bodies begin to produce more red blood cells and hemoglobin in order to carry more oxygen. Individuals vary at the altitude at which these physiological responses begin due to their genetic makeup.

Developmental adaptations are seen in individuals who spend their childhood period of growth and development at high altitude. Among the highland Quechua, for example, both the chest cavity and the right ventricle of the heart (which pushes blood to the lungs) are enlarged compared to lowland Quechua. This may have genetic underpinnings in that all Quechua experience a long period of growth and development compared to the average person in the United States.

Observing that Kenyan runners have won most of the major marathon competitions over the past several decades, coaches have emulated the Kenyan approach. Adaptation to the hot, dry yet mountainous region leads to a long lean build (a product of the heat adaptation) and increased oxygen-carrying capacity. Although runners worldwide tend to be tall and lean, many athletes now train at high altitude so that when race day comes, their red blood cell count and hemoglobin levels allow them to carry more oxygen.

The process of growth and development of course begins with reproduction, and high altitude exerts considerable effects on this process. For populations who have not adapted to high altitude, successful reproduction is not possible without some cultural interventions. For example, when Spanish colonists founded the city of Potosi high in the Andes to mine the "mountain of silver" that towers above the community, for the first fifty-four years of this city's existence no Spanish child was born who survived childhood. Indigenous populations did not have these problems. To ensure reproductive success, Spanish women began the cultural practice of retreating to lower altitude for their pregnancies and the first year of their children's lives.[4]

---

[4]Wiley, A. S. (2004). An ecology of high-altitude infancy: A biocultural perspective series. *Cambridge Studies in Medical Anthropology* (12). Cambridge.

acclimatization Long-term physiological adjustments made in order to attain an equilibrium with a specific environmental stimulus.

At high altitudes cold stress is also a problem. As described in the previous chapter, a stocky body and short limbs help individuals conserve heat while the opposite facilitates heat loss. These phenomena have been formalized into two rules named after the naturalist who made such observations in mammals. **Bergman's rule** refers to the tendency for the bodies of mammals living in cold climates to be shorter and rounder than members of the same species living in warm climates. **Allen's rule** refers to the tendency of mammals living in cold climates to have shorter appendages (arms and legs) than members of the same species living in warm climates.

Adaptation to Cold

Cold stress can exist without high altitude, as it does in the Arctic. While the same pattern of body and limb shape and size is evident in Arctic populations, additional cold responses are seen.

In extreme cold, the limbs need enough heat to prevent frostbite, but giving up heat to the periphery takes it away from the body core. Humans balance this through a cyclic expansion and contraction of the blood vessels of their limbs called the **hunting response.** Blood vessels oscillate between closing down to prevent heat loss and opening up to warm the hands and feet. When first exposed to cold by taking off gloves, blood vessels immediately constrict. Initial alternations between the open (warm) and shut (cold) and the corresponding temperature of the skin range dramatically. But the oscillations become smaller and more rapid, allowing a hunter to maintain the warmth-derived manual dexterity required for tying knots or sewing.

Eskimos also deal with cold through a high metabolic rate: the rate at which their bodies burn energy. This may result from a diet high in protein and fat (whale blubber is the common food). In addition, genetic factors likely also contribute to Eskimos' high metabolic rate.

Short-term physiological responses to cold include shivering. Shivering generates heat for the body quickly but cannot be maintained for long periods of time. Instead, as an individual acclimatizes to the cold, adjust-

ments to diet, activity pattern, metabolic rate, and the circulatory system must occur.

Adaptation to Heat

The human body's primary physiological mechanism for coping with extreme heat is sweating or perspiring. Sweating is a process through which water released from sweat glands gives up body heat as the sweat evaporates. Therefore, water availability is a crucial aspect of adaptation to heat. Without replacing sweat through drinking water, exposure to heat can be fatal.

Though some individual and population variation exists, each human has roughly 2 million sweat glands. These glands are spread out over a greater surface area on tall, thin bodies, facilitating water evaporation and heat loss. Thus Bergman's and Allen's rules also apply to heat adaptation. The more surface area a body has, the more surface for the sweat glands. In addition, because heat is produced by unit of volume, having a high surface area to volume ratio is beneficial for heat loss. A long, slender body is best for dissipating heat. In a hot and humid environment such as a rainforest, water evaporation is a major challenge. In this environment, human populations minimize heat production through a reduction in overall size while keeping a slender, lean build.

Of course, culture can play an important role in modifying both heat and cold stress. Housing, diet, and clothing traditions modify these stressors considerably. But in today's globalizing world, the effects of culture are much more complex. Rather than alleviating physical stressors through simple cultural adaptations such as housing, diet, and clothing, cultural processes are adding stressors of their own. The dramatic and rapid human alteration of the environment has rendered simple biological adaptation to these unnatural stressors very difficult. Instead, human-made pollution, global warming, and unhealthy diets and lifestyle lead directly to human sickness and suffering.

THE DEVELOPMENT OF MEDICAL ANTHROPOLOGY IN A GLOBALIZING WORLD

Medical anthropology, a specialization that cuts across all four fields of anthropology, contributes significantly to the understanding of sickness and suffering in the 21st century. Some of the earliest medical anthropologists were individuals trained as physicians and ethnographers who investigated the health beliefs and practices of people in exotic places while also providing them with

---

Bergman's rule　The tendency for the bodies of mammals living in cold climates to be shorter and rounder than members of the same species living in warm climates.

Allen's rule　The tendency of mammals living in cold climates to have shorter appendages (arms and legs) than members of the same species living in warm climates.

hunting response　A cyclic expansion and contraction of the blood vessels of the limbs that balances releasing enough heat to the limbs to prevent frostbite, maintaining heat in the body core.

Western medicine. Medical anthropologists during this early period translated local experiences of sickness into the scientific language of Western biomedicine. Following a re-evaluation of this ethnocentric approach in the 1970s, **medical anthropology** emerged as a specialization that brings theoretical and applied approaches from cultural and biological anthropology to the study of human health and sickness.

Medical anthropologists study **medical systems,** or patterned sets of ideas and practices relating to illness, as cultural systems similar to any other social institution. They examine healing traditions and practices cross-culturally and use scientific models drawn from biological anthropology to understand and improve human health. Medical anthropologists have also turned their attention toward biomedicine, focusing on the social and cultural aspects of health care in their own societies. Their work sheds light on the connections between human health and political and economic forces, both globally and locally. Because global flows of people, germs, cures, guns, and pollution underlie the distribution of sickness and health in the world today, a broad anthropological understanding of the origins of sickness is vital for alleviating human suffering.

The theoretical relationship between biological and cultural knowledge transformed during the course of medical anthropology's development as a distinct specialty within anthropology. The earliest research on medical systems was carried out by physician anthropologists—individuals trained as medical doctors and as anthropologists who participated in the international public health movement emerging early in the 20th century. While delivering the medical care developed in Europe and North America, they simultaneously studied the health beliefs and practices of the cultures they were sent to help. Local cultural categories about sickness were translated into Western biomedical terms. Initially, these Western approaches were thought to be culture-free depictions of human biology and were therefore used as an interpretive framework for examining the medical beliefs and practices of other cultures. Implicit in this work was a notion that the Western approach, with its supposed objectivity, was superior.

Science, Illness, and Disease

Gradually the superiority of biomedicine eroded as a consequence of fieldwork conducted by cultural anthropologists who began to examine health beliefs outside of traditional public health interventions. For example, French cultural anthropologist Claude Lévi-Strauss described the healing powers of *shamans* (the name for indigenous healers, originally from Siberia, and now applied to many traditional healers) in terms that could also apply

to medical practices in Europe and North America.[5] In both cases, the healer has access to a world of restricted knowledge (spiritual or scientific) from which the average community member is excluded.

Similarly, other studies revealed how medical categories, like other aspects of a people's unique worldview, reflect the value system of their particular culture. For example, the Subinam people of Mindinao, one of the large islands of the Philippines, give different names to fungal infections of the skin depending on whether the infection is openly visible or hidden under clothes.[6] The biomedical and scientific categorization of fungal infections refer only to genus and species.

In the 1970s the place of biological and cultural knowledge in medical anthropology was dramatically reorganized. The admission of mainland China to the United Nations in 1971, and the subsequent improvement of diplomatic and other relationships between that communist country and Western powers, played a role in this theoretical shift.[7] Cultural exchanges revealed a professional medical system in the East rivaling that of Western biomedicine in its scientific basis and technical feats. For example, the practice of open heart surgery in China, using only acupuncture needles as an anesthetic, challenged the assumption of biomedical superiority within anthropological thought. At this time scholars proposed that biomedicine was a cultural system, just like the medical systems in other cultures, and that it, too, was worthy of anthropological study.[8]

To effectively compare medical systems and health cross-culturally, medical anthropologists have made a theoretical distinction between the terms *disease* and *illness*. **Disease** refers to a specific pathology: a physical or biological abnormality. **Illness** refers to the meanings

[5]Lévi-Strauss, C. (1963). The sorcerer and his magic. In *Structural anthropology.* New York: Basic Books.

[6]Frake, C. (1961). The diagnosis of disease among the Subinam of Mindinao. *American Anthropologist 63,*113–132.

[7]Young, A. (1981). The creation of medical knowledge: Some problems in interpretation. *Social Science and Medicine 17,* 1,205–1,211.

[8]Kleinman, A. (1976). Concepts and a model for the comparison of medical systems as cultural systems. *Social Science and Medicine 12* (2B), 85–95.

medical anthropology A specialization that brings theoretical and applied approaches from cultural and biological anthropology to the study of human health and disease.
medical system A patterned set of ideas and practices relating to illness.
disease Refers to a specific pathology; a physical or biological abnormality.
illness Refers to the meanings and elaborations given to a particular physical state.

VISUAL COUNTERPOINT

Shamans and biomedical doctors both rely upon manipulation of symbols to heal their patients. The physician's white coat is a powerful symbol of medical knowledge and authority that communicates to patients just as clearly as does the shaman's drum. Interestingly, medical schools in the United States are increasingly incorporating a "white coat" ceremony into medical education, conferring the power of the white coat onto new doctors.

and elaborations given to particular physical states. Disease and illness do not necessarily overlap. An individual may experience illness without having a disease, or a disease may occur in the absence of illness.

In cultures with scientific medical systems, a key component of the social process of illness involves delineating human suffering in terms of biology. At times this even extends to labeling an illness as a disease even though the biology is poorly understood. Think about alcoholism in the United States, for example. A person who is thought of as a drunk, partier, barfly, or boozer tends not to get sympathy from the rest of society. By contrast, a person struggling with the disease alcoholism receives cultural help from physicians, support from groups such as Alcoholics Anonymous, and financial aid from health insurance covering medical treatment. It matters little that the biology of this disease is still poorly understood and that alcoholism is treated through social support rather than expert manipulation of biology. By calling al-

coholism a disease, it becomes a socially sanctioned and recognized illness within the dominant medical system of the United States.

Disease can also exist without illness. Schistosomiasis, infection with a kind of parasitic flatworm called a blood fluke, is an excellent example. Scientists have fully documented the life cycle of this parasite that alternates between water snail and human hosts. The adult worms live for many years inside the human intestines or urinary tract. Human waste then spreads the mobile phase of the parasite to freshwater snails. Inside the snails, the parasite develops further to a second mobile phase of the flatworm life cycle, releasing thousands of tiny creatures into freshwater. If humans swim, wade, or do household chores such as laundry in this infested water, the parasite can bore its way through the skin, traveling to the intestine or bladder where the life cycle continues.

The idea of parasites boring through the skin and living permanently inside the bladder or intestine may well be revolting. Ingesting poisons to rid the body of these parasites may be acceptable for people at certain social and economic levels. But to people living in parts of the world where schistosomiasis is **endemic** (the public health term for a disease that is widespread in the

endemic   The public health term for a disease that is widespread in a population.

Building the Aswan Dam in Egypt was a vital part of modernization for that country. Unfortunately, the dam has also caused problems. It increased the rates of schistosomiasis in the Nile River by creating a massive artificial lake upstream from the dam that provides the ideal environment for water snails. Downstream, the reduced flow of Nile waters into the Mediterranean Sea has meant that the sea has encroached upon people's homes.

© Reza, Webistan/Corbis

population), this disease state is regarded as normal, and no treatment is sought. In other words schistosomiasis is not an illness. Individuals may know about expensive effective biomedical treatments but given the likelihood of re-infection and the inaccessibility of the drugs, treatment with pharmaceutical agents is not the social norm. Over time, the forces of evolution have led to a tolerance between parasite and host so that infected individuals can live normal lives. So normal is the parasitic infection in some societies that the appearance of bloody urine at the time of adolescence (due to a high enough parasite load to cause this symptom) is regarded as a male version of menstruation.[9]

Cultural perspectives can thus be at odds with international public health goals that are based on a strictly Western biomedical understanding of disease. In the following Original Study, biological anthropologist Katherine Dettwyler shows that each perspective brings with it particular challenges and benefits.

_____

[9]Desowitz, R. S. (1987). *New Guinea tapeworms and Jewish grandmothers.* New York: Norton.

Original Study ▪ Katherine Dettwyler

Dancing Skeletons: Life and Death in West Africa

I stood in the doorway, gasping for air, propping my arms against the door frame on either side to hold me up. I sucked in great breaths of cool, clean air and rested my gaze on the distant hills, trying to compose myself. Ominous black thunderclouds were massed on the horizon and moved rapidly toward the schoolhouse. . . .

The morning had begun pleasantly enough, with villagers waiting patiently under the huge mango tree in the center of the village. But before long, the approaching storm made it clear that we would have to move inside. The only building large enough to hold the crowd was the one-room schoolhouse, located on the outskirts of the village. . . .

Inside the schoolhouse, chaos reigned. It was 20 degrees hotter, ten times as noisy, and as dark as gloom. What little light there was from outside entered through the open doorway and two small windows. The entire population of the village crowded onto the rows of benches, or stood three deep around the periph-

CONTINUED

ery of the room. Babies cried until their mothers pulled them around front where they could nurse, children chattered, and adults seized the opportunity to converse with friends and neighbors. It was one big party, a day off from working in the fields, with a cooling rain thrown in for good measure. I had to shout the measurements out to Heather, to make myself heard over the cacophony of noise. . . .

A middle-aged man dressed in a threadbare pair of Levis shoved a crying child forward. I knelt down to encourage the little boy to step up onto the scales and saw that his leg was wrapped in dirty bandages. He hesitated before lifting his foot and whimpered as he put his weight onto it. . . .

"What's the matter with his leg?" I asked his father.

"He hurt it in a bicycle accident," he said.

I rolled my eyes at Heather. "Let me guess. He was riding on the back fender, without wearing long pants, or shoes, and he got his leg tangled in the spokes." Moussa translated this aside into Bambara, and the man acknowledged that that was exactly what had happened. . . .

The festering wound encompassed the boy's ankle and part of his foot, deep enough to see bone at the bottom. His entire lower leg and foot were swollen and putrid; it was obvious that gangrene had a firm hold. . . .

"You have to take him to the hospital in Sikasso immediately," I explained.

"But we can't afford to," he balked.

"You can't afford not to," I cried in exasperation, turning to Moussa. "He doesn't understand," I said to Moussa. "Please explain to him that the boy is certain to die of gangrene poisoning if he doesn't get to a doctor right away. It may be too late already, but I don't think so. He may just lose his leg." Moussa's eyes widened with alarm. Even he hadn't realized how serious the boy's wounds were. As the father took in what Moussa was saying, his face crumpled. . . . Father and son were last seen leaving Merediela, the boy perched precariously on the back of a worn-out donkey hastily borrowed from a neighbor, while the father trotted alongside, shoulders drooping, urging the donkey to greater speed. . . .

Lunch back at the animatrice's compound provided another opportunity for learning about infant feeding beliefs in rural Mali, through criticism of my own child feeding practices. This time it was a chicken that had given its life for our culinary benefit. As we ate, without even thinking, I reached into the center pile of chicken meat and pulled pieces of meat off the bone. Then I placed them over in Miranda's section of the communal food bowl and encouraged her to eat.

"Why are you giving her chicken?" Bakary asked.

"I want to make sure she gets enough to eat," I replied. "She didn't eat very much porridge for breakfast, because she doesn't like millet."

"But she's just a child. She doesn't need good food. You've been working hard all morning, and she's just been lying around. Besides, if she wanted to eat, she would," he argued.

"It's true that I've been working hard," I admitted, "but she's still growing. Growing children need much more food, proportionately, than adults. And if I didn't encourage her to eat, she might not eat until we get back to Bamako."

Bakary shook his head. "In Dogo," he explained, "people believe that good food is wasted on children. They don't appreciate its good taste or the way it makes you feel. Also, they haven't worked hard to produce the food. They have their whole lives to work for good food for themselves, when they get older. Old people deserve the best food, because they're going to die soon." . . .

. . . In rural southern Mali, "good food" (which included all the high protein/high calorie foods) was reserved for elders and other adults. Children subsisted almost entirely on the carbohydrate staples, flavored with a little sauce. My actions in giving Miranda my share of the chicken were viewed as bizarre and misguided—I was wasting good food on a mere child, and depriving myself. . . .

In N'tenkoni the next morning, we were given use of the men's sacred meeting hut for our measuring session. A round hut about 20 feet in diameter, it had a huge center pole made from the trunk of a tree that held up the thatched roof. Because it had two large doorways,

it was light and airy and would provide protection in the event of another thunderstorm. . . .

There was some initial confusion caused by the fact that people outside couldn't really see what we were doing, and everyone tried to crowd in at once. That was straightened out by the chief, however, and measuring proceeded apace, men, women, children, men, women, children. One family at a time filed into the hut through one door, had their measurements taken, and departed through the other door. It was cool and pleasant inside the hut, in contrast to the hot sun and glare outside. Miranda sat off to one side, reading a book, glancing up from time to time, but generally bored by the whole thing.

"Mommy, look!" she exclaimed in mid-morning. "Isn't that an *angel*?" she asked, using our family's code word for a child with Down syndrome. Down syndrome children are often (though not always!) sweet, happy, and affectionate kids, and many families of children with Down syndrome consider them to be special gifts from God, and refer to them as angels. I turned and followed the direction of Miranda's gaze. A little girl had just entered the hut, part of a large family with many children. She had a small round head, and all the facial characteristics of a child with Down syndrome—Oriental-shaped eyes with epicanthic folds, a small flat nose, and small ears. There was no mistaking the diagnosis. Her name was Abi, and she was about 4 years old, the same age as Peter.

I knelt in front of the little girl. "Hi there, sweetie," I said in English. "Can I have a hug?" I held out my arms, and she willingly stepped forward and gave me a big hug.

I looked up at her mother. "Do you know that there's something 'different' about this child?" I asked, choosing my words carefully.

"Well, she doesn't talk," said her mother, hesitantly, looking at her husband for confirmation. "That's right," he said. "She's never said a word."

"But she's been healthy?" I asked.

"Yes," the father replied. "She's like the other kids, except she doesn't talk. She's always happy. She never cries. We know she can hear, because she does what we tell her to. Why are you so interested in her?"

"Because I know what's the matter with her. I have a son like this." Excitedly, I pulled a picture of Peter out of my bag and showed it to them. They couldn't see any resemblance, though. The difference in skin color swamped the similarities in facial features. But then, Malians think all white people look alike. And it's not true that all kids with Down syndrome look the same. They're "different in the same way," but they look most like their parents and siblings.

"Have you ever met any other children like this?" I inquired, bursting with curiosity about how rural Malian culture dealt with a condition as infrequent as Down syndrome. Children with Down syndrome are rare to begin with, occurring about once in every 700 births. In a community where thirty or forty children are born each year at the most, a child with Down syndrome might be born only once in twenty years. And many of them would not survive long enough for anyone to be able to tell that they were different. Physical defects along the midline of the body (heart, trachea, intestines) are common among kids with Down syndrome; without immediate surgery and neonatal intensive care, many would not survive. Such surgery is routine in American children's hospitals, but nonexistent in rural Mali. For the child without any major physical defects, there are still the perils of rural Malian life to survive: malaria, measles, diarrhea, diphtheria,

and polio. Some, like Peter, have poor immune systems, making them even more susceptible to childhood diseases. The odds against finding a child with Down syndrome, surviving and healthy in a rural Malian village, are overwhelming.

Not surprisingly, the parents knew of no other children like Abi. They asked if I knew of any medicine that could cure her. "No," I explained, "this condition can't be cured. But she will learn to talk, just give her time. Talk to her a lot. Try to get her to repeat things you say. And give her lots of love and attention. It may take her longer to learn some things, but keep trying. In my country, some people say these children are special gifts from God." There was no way I could explain cells and chromosomes and non-disjunction to them, even with Moussa's help. And how, I thought to myself, would that have helped them anyway? They just accepted her as she was.

We chatted for a few more minutes, and I measured the whole family, including Abi, who was, of course, short for her age. I gave her one last hug and a balloon and sent her out the door after her siblings. . . .

I walked out of the hut, . . . trying to get my emotions under control. Finally I gave in, hugged my knees close to my chest, and sobbed. I cried for Abi—what a courageous heart she must have; just think what she might have achieved given all the modern infant stimulation programs available in the West. I cried for Peter—another courageous heart; just

think of what he might achieve given the chance to live in a culture that simply accepted him, rather than stereotyping and pigeonholing him, constraining him because people didn't think he was capable of more. I cried for myself—not very courageous at all; my heart felt as though it would burst with longing for Peter, my own sweet angel.

There was clearly some truth to the old adage that ignorance is bliss. Maybe pregnant women in Mali had to worry about evil spirits lurking in the latrine at night, but they didn't spend their pregnancies worrying about chromosomal abnormalities, the moral implications of amniocentesis, or the heart-wrenching exercise of trying to evaluate handicaps, deciding which ones made life not worth living. Women in the United States might have the freedom to choose not to give birth to children with handicaps, but women in Mali had freedom from worrying about it. Children in the United States had the freedom to attend special programs to help them overcome their handicaps, but children in Mali had freedom from the biggest handicap of all—other people's prejudice.

I had cried myself dry. I splashed my face with cool water from the bucket inside the kitchen and returned to the task at hand.
(Adapted from Katherine A. Dettwyler (1994). Dancing skeletons: Life and death in West Africa (ch. 8). Prospect Heights, IL: Waveland Press.)

While diseases are generally described in biological terms as understood through scientific investigation, the medical anthropological framework admits that notions of disease are not universal. Whether these are based in the scientific study of biological processes, each culture's medical system provides individuals with a "map" of how to think about themselves in sickness and health. All cultures define specific terms and mechanisms for thinking about, preventing, and managing illness. In this way, Western medical systems define whether a particular biological state such as malnutrition, Down syndrome, or schistosomiasis is recognized as an illness. Each cultural system delineates the choices and constraints available to individuals afflicted by particular disease states.

EVOLUTIONARY MEDICINE

The new field of **evolutionary medicine**—an approach to human sickness and health combining principles of evolutionary theory and human evolutionary history—constitutes one of the interesting recent developments within scientific medicine with roots in anthropology. While it may seem at first to concentrate on human biological mechanisms, evolutionary medicine's emphasis is

evolutionary medicine An approach to human sickness and health combining principles of evolutionary theory and human evolutionary history.

true to the biocultural integration that figures so prominently in anthropological approaches. Biological processes are given cultural meanings, and cultural practices affect human biology. These two insights provide alternative approaches to promoting human health.

As with evolutionary theory in general, it is difficult to prove conclusively that some of the specific ideas and theories from evolutionary medicine are indeed beneficial to human health. Instead, scientists work to amass a sufficient body of knowledge that supports their theories. Where appropriate, the theories can lead to hypotheses that can be tested experimentally. Frequently treatments derived from evolutionary medicine lead to altering cultural practices and to a return to a more natural state in terms of human biology. As described in the Biocultural Connection of Chapter 8, evolutionary medicine contributes a variety of Paleolithic prescriptions for the diseases of civilization.

The work of biological anthropologist James McKenna is an excellent example of evolutionary medicine. McKenna has suggested that the human infant, immature compared to some other mammals, has evolved to co-sleep with adults who provide breathing cues to the sleeping infant, protecting the child from sudden infant death syndrome (SIDS).[10] He uses cross-cultural data of sleeping patterns and rates of SIDS to support his claim.

McKenna conducted a series of experiments documenting differences between the brainwave patterns of mother–infant pairs who co-sleep compared to mother–infant pairs who sleep in separate rooms. These data fit McKenna's theory, challenging North America's predominant cultural practice of solitary sleeping. Further, McKenna shows how the cultural pattern of sleeping directly impacts infant feeding practices demonstrating that co-sleeping and breastfeeding are mutually reinforcing behaviors.

Evolutionary medicine suggests that cultural practices in industrial and postindustrial societies are responsible for a variety of other biomedically defined diseases, ranging from psychological disorders to hepatitis (inflammation of the liver).

Symptoms as a Defense Mechanism

Scientists have documented that when faced with infection from a bacterium or virus, the human body mounts a series of physiological responses. For example, as a young individual learns his or her culture's medical sys-

tem, the person might learn to recognize an illness as a "cold" or "flu" by responses of the body, such as fever, aches, runny nose, sore throat, vomiting, or diarrhea.

Think of how you may have learned about sickness as a young child. A caregiver or parent might have touched your forehead or neck with the back of the hand or lips to gauge your temperature. They may have placed a thermometer under your arm, in your mouth, or some other place to see if you had an elevated temperature or fever. (In the past, children's temperatures were usually taken rectally in North America.) If any of these methods revealed a temperature above the value defined as normal, the result might be giving a medicine to lower the fever.

Evolutionary medicine proposes that many of the symptoms that biomedicine treats are themselves nature's treatments developed over millennia. Some of these symptoms, such as fever, perhaps should be tolerated rather than suppressed, so the body can heal itself. An elevated temperature is part of the human body's response to infectious particles, whereas eliminating the fever provides favorable temperatures for bacteria or viruses. Similarly within some physiological limits, vomiting, coughing, and diarrhea may be adaptive as they remove harmful substances or organisms from the body. In other words, the cultural prescription to lower a fever or suppress a cough might actually prolong the disease.

Evolutionary biologist Margie Profet proposed a particular benefit for the symptoms of nausea and vomiting during early pregnancy.[11] She suggests that many plants, particularly those in the broccoli and cabbage family, naturally contain toxins developed through the plants' evolutionary process to prevent them from being eaten by animals. Profet suggests that eating these plants during the first weeks of pregnancy, when the developing embryo is rapidly creating new cells through mitosis and differentiation into specific body parts, makes the embryo vulnerable to mutation. Therefore, a heightened sense of smell and lowered nausea threshold serves as the body's natural defense. It causes women to avoid these foods, thus protecting the developing embryo.

Evolution and Infectious Disease

Understanding infectious disease is all the more important in a globalizing world where people, viruses, and bacteria cross national boundaries freely. Evolutionary medicine provides two key insights with regard to in-

[10]McKenna, J. (1999). Co-sleeping and SIDS. In W. Trevathan, E. O. Smith, & J. J. McKenna (Eds.), *Evolutionary medicine.* London: Oxford University Press.

[11]Profet, M. (1991). The function of allergy: Immunological defense against toxins. *Quarterly Review of Biology* 66 (1), 23–62; Profet, M. (1995). *Protecting your baby to be.* New York: Addison Wesley.

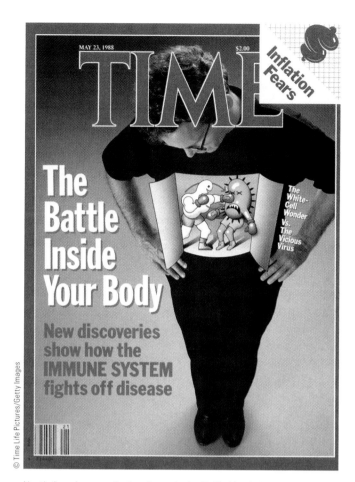

North American medical anthropologist Emily Martin has shown that scientific depictions of infectious disease draw upon military imagery common to the culture of the United States. Biomedical treatments involve taking antibiotics to kill "invading" organisms. An evolutionary perspective suggests that the quick life cycle of microorganisms makes this "battle" a losing proposition for humans.

fectious disease. First, if infectious disease is viewed as competition between microorganisms and humans—as it is in biomedicine where patients and doctors "fight" infectious disease—microorganisms possess one very clear advantage. Viruses, bacteria, fungi, and parasites all have very short life cycles compared to humans. Therefore, when competing on an evolutionary level, they will continue to pose new threats to health, because any new genetic variants appearing through a random mutation will become incorporated in the population's genome more quickly. This notion is of particular importance with regard to the use of antibiotics to fight infectious disease.

While antibiotics will kill many bacteria, increasingly resistant strains of bacteria are becoming more common. "Resistant strains" refers to genetic variants of a specific bacterium that are not killed by antibiotics. If a resistant strain appears in an infected individual who is being treated with antibiotics, the removal of all the nonresistant strains essentially opens up an entire ecological niche for that resistant strain inside the infected human. Here, without competition from the original form of the bacterium wiped out by the antibiotic, this mutant can proliferate easily and then spread to other individuals. The practice of taking antibiotics artificially alters the environment inside the human body.

In order to avoid the development of resistant strains, complex lengthy treatment regimes, often of multiple drugs, must be followed exactly. These expensive treatments are cost-prohibitive in many parts of the world. The unfortunate result is not only increased human suffering but also the possibility of creating environments for the development of resistant strains as individuals receive partial treatments.

Although treatments are provided to individuals within their own country's health care system, infectious microbes do not observe these same national boundaries. To eradicate or control any infectious process, the world has to be considered in its entirety. On a positive note, treatments can also be allowed to flow freely across national boundaries. As seen in this chapter's Globalscape, successful treatment of many infectious diseases involves far more than simply taking antibiotics or antiviral agents.

Thus, antibiotic resistance illustrates a key perspective evolutionary medicine contributes to the understanding of infectious disease: Infectious disease and the human efforts to stop infectious disease always occur in the context of the human-made environment. Humans have been altering their external environments with increasing impact since the Neolithic transition, resulting in an increase in a variety of infectious diseases. In this regard, evolutionary medicine shares much with political ecology—a discipline closely related to medical anthropology and described below.

THE POLITICAL ECOLOGY OF DISEASE

An ecological perspective considers organisms in the context of their environment. Because local human environments are shaped not only by local culture but by global political and economic systems, these features must all be included in a comprehensive examination of human disease from an ecological perspective. Simply describing disease in terms of biological processes leaves out the deeper, ultimate reasons that some individuals are more likely to become sick than others. A strictly biological approach also leaves out differences in the resources available to individuals, communities, and states to cope with disease and illness.

GLOBALSCAPE

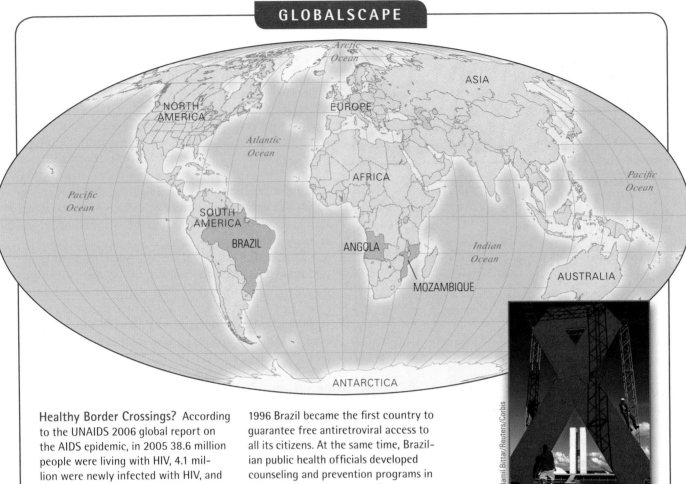

© Jamil Bittar/Reuters/Corbis

Healthy Border Crossings? According to the UNAIDS 2006 global report on the AIDS epidemic, in 2005 38.6 million people were living with HIV, 4.1 million were newly infected with HIV, and 2.8 million people lost their lives to AIDS. International public health officials often point out the fact that the HIV retrovirus does not observe national boundaries, whereas the transfer of treatments and preventive approaches is far more complex. Each culture possesses its own health beliefs and practices, along with systems and infrastructure for distribution and financing of HIV prevention and treatments.

The Brazil HIV/AIDS program is internationally recognized as a model for prevention, education, and treatment for several reasons. Through a national policy of developing generic alternative antiretroviral agents and negotiating for reduced prices on patented agents, in 1996 Brazil became the first country to guarantee free antiretroviral access to all its citizens. At the same time, Brazilian public health officials developed counseling and prevention programs in collaboration with community groups and religious organizations. Their AIDS program's success is in part due to the candid public education on disease transmission targeted at heterosexual women and young people, who are now the fastest-growing groups affected by HIV.

In 2004, Brazil continued its innovations with the "South to South Initiative" providing assistance to the HIV and AIDS programs in the Portuguese-speaking African countries of Mozambique and Angola. The Brazilian approach of providing free antiretroviral agents can be modeled directly in these African countries. The Brazilian philosophy of collaboration with civil and religious groups to develop appropriate counseling, education, and prevention will lead to strategies specific for the people of Mozambique and Angola.

Global Twister Brazil's AIDS program provides antiretroviral agents at a cost of $2,000 per person per year and puts medicines within reach for people from poor countries like Angola and Mozambique. In developed nations, including the United States, these same medicines cost $10,000 to $15,000 per person per year. What aspects of the Brazilian HIV/AIDS program should developed nations emulate?

Mad Cow, Kuru, and Other Prion Diseases

In 1997 the North American physician scientist Stanley Prusiner won the Nobel Prize in medicine for his discovery of an entirely new disease agent called a **prion**—a protein lacking any genetic material that behaves as an infectious particle. Prions are a kind of protein that can cause the reorganization and destruction of other proteins and result in neurodegenerative disease as brain tissue and the nervous system are destroyed.

This discovery provided a mechanism for understanding mad cow disease, a serious problem in postindustrial societies. But knowing the biological mechanism alone is not enough to truly grasp how this disease spreads. The beef supply of several countries in Europe and North America became tainted by prions introduced through the cultural practice of grinding up sheep carcasses and adding them to the commercial feed of beef cattle. This practice began before prions were discovered, but postindustrial farmers were aware that these sheep had a condition known as *scrapie;* they just did not know that this condition was infectious. Thus, through the wide distribution of tainted feed, prion disease spread from sheep to cows and then to humans who consumed tainted beef. Today countries without confirmed mad cow disease ban the importation of beef from neighboring countries with documented prion disease. Such bans have tremendous effects on the local economies.

While mad cow disease besets postindustrialized countries today, prion disease was a major concern for the Fore (pronounced "foray") people of Papua New Guinea during the middle of the 20th century. Kuru is the name given in the local language to the prion disease that was claiming the lives of great numbers of women and children in Fore communities. With such devastation in their midst, the Fore welcomed assistance provided by an international team of health workers led by a physician from the United States, Carleton Gajdusek. As with mad cow disease, local and global cultural processes affected both the transmission of kuru and the measures taken to prevent transmission of this deadly condition long before prion biology was understood.

Kuru did not fit neatly into any known biomedical categories. Because the disease seemed to be limited to families of related individuals, cultural anthropologists Shirley Lindenbaum from Australia and Robert Glasse from the United States, who were doing fieldwork in the region, were recruited to contribute documentation of Fore kinship relationships. It was hoped this knowledge would reveal an underlying genetic mechanism for this disease.[12]

When documentation of the kin relationships did not reveal a pattern of genetic transmission, the medical team turned instead to the notion of infectious disease, even though the slow progression of kuru seemed to weigh against an infectious cause. Material derived from infected individuals was injected into chimpanzees (see Chapter 5's Biocultural Connection for a discussion of the ethics of this practice) to see whether they developed the disease. After 18 months, injected chimpanzees succumbed to the classic symptoms of kuru, and their autopsied brains indicated the same pathologies as seen in humans with kuru. At this point, the disease was defined as infectious (garnering Gajdusek a Nobel Prize). Because prions had not yet been discovered, scientists defined this infectious agent as an unidentified "slow virus."

Though scientists knew that kuru is infectious, the story of kuru is not complete without an examination of why some individuals were infected and not others. For this, one has to return to the local cultural and larger global perspectives of anthropology, as Lindenbaum explains in her book *Kuru Sorcery*. Lindenbaum demonstrates that kuru is related to cultural practices regarding the bodies of individuals who had died from kuru and the way global factors impacted local practices.

Culturally, Fore women are responsible for preparing the bodies of their loved ones for the afterlife. This practice alone put women at a greater risk for exposure to kuru. Lindenbaum also discovered that women and children were at risk due to a combination of these local practices with more global forces. In Fore society, men were responsible for raising pigs and slaughtering and distributing meat. The middle of the 20th century was a time of hardship and transition for the Fore people. Colonial rule by Australia had changed the fabric of society, threatening traditional subsistence patterns and

---

[12]Lindenbaum, S. (1978). *Kuru sorcery: Disease and danger in the New Guinea highlands.* New York: McGraw-Hill.

prion An infectious protein lacking any genetic material but capable of causing the reorganization and destruction of other proteins.

resulting in a shortage of protein in the form of pigs. The limited amount of pig meat available was distributed by men preferentially to other men.

Fore women told Lindenbaum that, as a practical solution to their hunger they consumed their own dead. Fore women preferred eating their loved ones who had died in a relatively "meaty" state from kuru compared to eating individuals wasted from malnutrition. This temporary practice was abandoned as the Fore subsistence pattern recovered, and the biological mechanisms of transmission were communicated to the Fore.

The Fore medical system had its own explanations for the causes of kuru, primarily involving sorcery, that were compatible with biomedical explanations for the mechanisms of disease. Such blending of medical systems is common throughout the globe today.

Medical pluralism refers to the presence of multiple medical systems, each with its own practices and beliefs in a society. As illustrated with the Fore, individuals generally can reconcile conflicting medical systems and incorporate diverse elements from a variety of systems to ease their suffering. While Western biomedicine has contributed some spectacular treatments and cures for a variety of diseases, many of its practices and values are singularly associated with the Euramerican societies in which it developed. The international public health movement attempts to bring many of the successes of biomedicine based on the scientific understanding of human biology to the rest of the world. But to do so successfully, cultural practices and beliefs must be taken into account.

Both mad cow disease and kuru illustrate that no sickness in the 21st century can be considered in isolation; an understanding of these diseases must take into account political and economic forces as well as how these forces affect the ability to treat or cure.

GLOBALIZATION, HEALTH, AND STRUCTURAL VIOLENCE

One generalization that can be made across the globe is that with regard to most diseases, wealth means health. The World Health Organization defines health as "a complete state of physical, psychological, and social well-

being, not the mere absence of disease or infirmity."[13] While the international public health community works to improve human health throughout the globe, heavily armed states, megacorporations, and very wealthy elites are using their powers to structure or rearrange the emerging world system and direct global processes to their own competitive advantage. When such power relationships undermine the well-being of others, we may speak of **structural violence**—physical and/or psychological harm (including repression, environmental destruction, poverty, hunger, illness, and premature death) caused by exploitative and unjust social, political, and economic systems.

As we saw in Chapter 11, **health disparities,** or differences in the health status between the wealthy elite and the poor in stratified societies, are nothing new. Globalization has expanded and intensified structural violence, leading to enormous health disparities among individuals, communities, and even states. Medical anthropologists have examined how structural violence leads not only to unequal access to treatments but also to the likelihood of contracting disease through exposure to malnutrition, crowded conditions, and toxins.

Population Size, Poverty, and Health

At the time of the speciation events of early human evolutionary history, population size was relatively small compared to what it is today. With human population size at over 6 billion and still climbing, we are reaching the carrying capacity of the earth. India and China alone have over 1 billion inhabitants each. And population growth is still rapid in South Asia, which is expected to become even more densely populated in the early 21st century (Figure 13.2). Population growth threatens to increase the scale of hunger and pollution—and the many problems associated with these two issues.

Desirable though it may be to halt population growth, programs to do so, and their consequences, pose many new health (and ethical) problems. These are well illustrated by China's much publicized "one child" policy, introduced in 1979 to control its soaring population growth. This policy led to a sharp upward trend in sex-selective abortions, as well as female infanticide and high female infant mortality due to abandonment and neglect. This trend has created an imbalance in China's male and female populations, referred to as the "missing girl gap" of some 50 million. One study reported that China's male to female sex ratio had become so distorted that 111 million men would not be able to find a wife. Government regulations softened slightly in the 1990s, when it became legal for rural couples to have a second

medical pluralism The presence of multiple medical systems, each with its own practices and beliefs in a society.
structural violence Physical and/or psychological harm (including repression, environmental destruction, poverty, hunger, illness, and premature death) caused by exploitative and unjust social, political, and economic systems.
health disparity A difference in the health status between the wealthy elite and the poor in stratified societies.

[13]World Health Organization. http://www.who.int/about/definition/en.

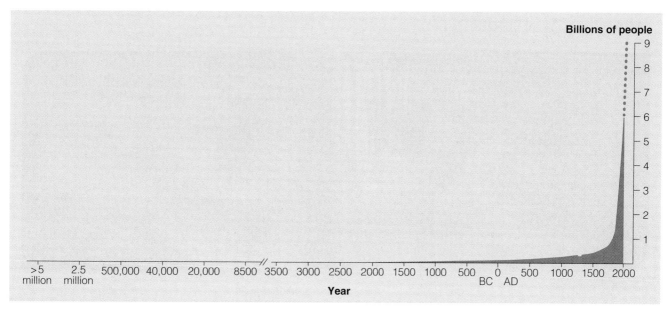

Figure 13.2

Human population growth grew at a relatively steady pace until the industrial revolution when a geometric pattern of growth began. Since that time, human population size has been doubling at an alarming rate. The earth's natural resources will not be able to accommodate ever-increasing human population if the rates of consumption seen in Western industrialized nations, particularly the United States, persist.

child if their first was a girl—and if they paid a fee. Millions of rural couples have circumvented regulations by not registering births—resulting in millions of young people who do not "officially" exist.[14]

With an ever-expanding population, a shocking number of people worldwide face hunger on a regular basis leading to a variety of health problems including premature death. It is no accident that poor countries and poorer citizens of wealthier countries are disproportionately malnourished. All told, about 1 billion people in the world are undernourished. Some 6 million children age 5 and under die every year due to hunger, and those who survive often suffer from physical and mental impairment.[15]

In wealthy industrialized countries a particular version of malnourishment—obesity—is becoming increasingly common. Obesity also affects poor working-class people who are no longer physically active at their work (because of increasing automation) and who cannot afford more expensive, healthy foods to stay fit. High sugar and fat content of mass-marketed foods and "super size" portions underlie this dramatic change. The risk of diabetes, heart disease, and stroke is also greatly in-

creased in the presence of obesity. High rates of obesity among U.S. youth has led public health officials to project that the current generation of adults may be the first generation to outlive their children due to a cause other than war.

Much of the famine and associated death experienced disproportionately by the disenfranchised over the past hundred years can be attributed to human-made causes. Similarly, the generation and disposition of pollutants represent another aspect of how population health may

After a natural disaster such as Hurricane Katrina, the ability to recover is determined by the relative wealth and resources available to the community. In the hard-hit Lower 9th Ward of New Orleans, for example, a year after water levels rose to above the rooflines of houses, much of the neighborhood is still in disarray. Here a car sits exactly where it was pushed after the levees broke—underneath a house.

---

[14]Bongaarts, J. (1998). Demographic consequences of declining fertility. *Science 282*, 419; Wattenberg, B. J. (1997, November 23). The population explosion is over. *New York Times Magazine,* 60.

[15]Hunger Project 2003; Swaminathan, M. S. (2000). Science in response to basic human needs. *Science, 287,* 425. *Historical atlas of the twentieth century.* http://users.erols.com/mwhite28/20centry.htm.

VISUAL COUNTERPOINT

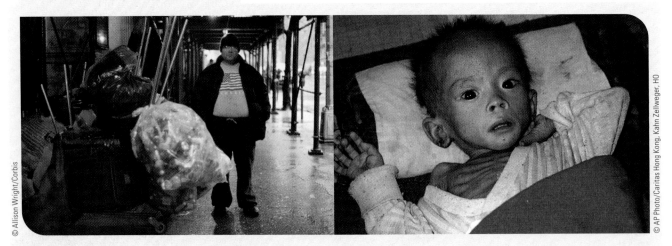

The scientific definition of malnutrition includes undernutrition as well as excess consumption of unhealthy foods. Malnutrition leading to obesity is increasingly common among poor working-class people
in industrialized countries. Starvation is more common in poor countries or in those that have been beset
by years of political turmoil, as evident in this emaciated North Korean child.

be impacted by disparities in the distribution of wealth. The industries of wealthier communities and states create the majority of the pollutants that are changing the earth today. For example, in recent years, the use of chlorofluorocarbons in aerosol sprays, refrigeration, and air conditioning and the manufacture of Styrofoam have contributed substantially to the ozone layer's deterioration. Because the ozone layer screens out some of the sun's ultraviolet rays, its continued deterioration will expose humans to increased ultraviolet radiation. As we saw in the previous chapter, some ultraviolet radiation is necessary for the production of vitamin D, but excessive amounts lead, among other things, to an increased incidence of skin cancers. Hence, a rising incidence of skin cancers—particularly melanoma, a fatal cancer if not caught quickly—represents a predictable consequence of ozone layer depletion. Unfortunately, ozone continues to deteriorate despite international treaties limiting the use of chlorofluorocarbons. In many places such as Australia and the United States, melanoma is becoming a leading cause of death.

Global warming represents another challenge humans face as a consequence of their industrial activity. Rates of deadly infectious diseases such as malaria may increase as the carbon emissions from the combustion of petroleum warm the climate globally. Annually it is estimated that 1.5 million to 2.7 million deaths worldwide are caused by malaria, making it the fifth largest infectious killer in the world. Children account for about 1 million of these deaths, and more than 80 percent of these cases are in tropical Africa. It is possible that over the next century, an average temperature increase of 3 degrees Celsius could result in 50 million to 80 million new malaria cases per year.[16]

Experts predict that global warming will lead to an expansion of the geographic ranges of tropical diseases and increase the incidence of respiratory diseases due to additional smog caused by warmer temperatures. Also, they expect an increase in deaths due to heat waves, as witnessed in the 15,000 deaths attributed to the 2003 heat wave in France.[17] Added to this is the flow of industrial and agricultural chemicals via air and water currents to Arctic regions where their long life (due to icy temperatures) allows these toxins to enter the food chain. As a result toxins generated in temperate climates end up in the bodies (and breast milk) of Arctic peoples who do not produce the toxins but merely eat primarily foods that they hunt and fish.

Unfortunately, public concern about global warming is minimal. To solve this global challenge our species needs to evolve new cultural tools in order to anticipate environmental consequences that eventuate over decades. Public relations campaigns from energy interests implying that global warming is not real, hearkening back to tobacco companies' former campaigns claiming that smoking was not hazardous, have not helped.

Ozone depletion and global warming are merely two of a host of problems confronting humans today that

---

[16]Stone, R. (1995). If the mercury soars, so may health hazards. *Science 267,* 958.

[17]World Meteorological Organization, quoted in "Increasing heat waves and other health hazards." greenpeaceusa.org/climate/index.fpl/7096/article/907.html.

will ultimately have an impact on human gene pools. In view of the consequences for human biology of such seemingly benign innovations as dairying or farming (as discussed in Chapter 10), we may wonder about many recent practices—for example, the effects of increased exposure to radiation from increased use of x-rays, nuclear accidents, increased production of radioactive wastes, and the like.

In addition to exposure to radiation, humans also face increased exposure to other known mutagenic agents, including a wide variety of chemicals, such as pesticides. Despite repeated assurances about their safety, there have been tens of thousands of cases of poisonings in the United States alone and thousands of cases of cancer related to the manufacture and use of pesticides. The impact may be greater in so-called underdeveloped countries, where substances banned in the United States are routinely used.

All this on top of the several million birds killed each year (many of which would otherwise have been happily gobbling down bugs and other pests), serious fish kills, and decimation of honey bees (bees are needed for the efficient pollination of many crops). In all, pesticides alone (never mind other agricultural chemicals) are responsible for billions of dollars of environmental and public health damage in the United States each year.[18] Anthropologists are documenting the effects on individuals as described in the Biocultural Connection feature.

The shipping of pollutant waste between countries represents an example of structural violence. Individuals in the government or business sector of either nation may profit from these arrangements, creating another obstacle to addressing this problem. Similar issues may arise within countries, when authorities attempt to coerce ethnic minorities to accept disposal of toxic waste on their lands.

In addition to pesticides, hormone-disrupting chemicals pose health threats. For example, in 1938 a synthetic estrogen known as DES (diethylstilbestrol) was developed and subsequently prescribed for a variety of ailments ranging from acne to prostate cancer. Moreover, DES is routinely added to animal feeds. It was not until 1971, however, that the first indication that DES causes vaginal cancer in young women came to light. Subsequent research has shown that DES causes problems with the male reproductive system and causes deformities of the female reproductive tract. DES, like many other synthetic organic compounds, mimics the natural sex hormones, binding with receptors in and on cells.[19]

DES is not alone in its effects: At least fifty-one chemicals—many of them in common use—are now

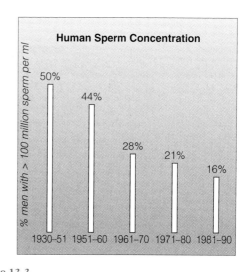

Figure 13.3

A documented decline in human male sperm counts worldwide may be related to widespread exposure to hormone-disrupting chemicals.

known to disrupt hormones, and this could be just the tip of the iceberg. Some of these chemicals mimic hormones in the manner of DES, whereas others interfere with other parts of the endocrine system, such as thyroid and testosterone metabolism. Included are such seemingly inert substances as plastics widely used in laboratories and chemicals added to polystyrene and polyvinyl chloride (PVCs) to make them more stable and less breakable. These plastics are widely used in plumbing, food processing, and food packaging. Hormone-disrupting chemicals are also found in many detergents and personal care products, contraceptive creams, the giant jugs used to bottle drinking water, and plastic linings in cans (about 85 percent of food cans in the United States are so lined).

The implications of all these developments are sobering. We know that pathologies result from extremely low levels of exposure to harmful chemicals. Yet, besides those used domestically, the United States exports millions of pounds of these chemicals to the rest of the world.[20] It is possible that hormone disruptions are at least partially responsible for certain trends that have recently become causes for concern among scientists. These range from increasingly early onset of puberty in human females to dramatic declines in human sperm counts. With respect to the latter, some sixty-one separate studies confirm that sperm counts have dropped almost 50 percent from 1938 to 1990 (Figure 13.3). Most of these studies were carried out in the United States and Europe, but some from Africa, Asia, and South America show that this is essentially a worldwide phenomenon. If this trend continues, it will have profound results.

[18]Pimentel, D. (1991). Response. *Science 252*, 358.

[19]Colburn, T., Dumanoski, D., & Myers, J. P. (1996). Hormonal sabotage. *Natural History 3*, 45–46.

[20]Ibid., 45–46.

Biocultural Connection

Picturing Pesticides

The toxic effects of pesticides have long been known. After all, these compounds are designed to kill bugs. However, documenting the toxic effects of pesticides on humans has been more difficult, as they are subtle—sometimes taking years to become apparent.

Anthropologist Elizabeth Guillette, working in a Yaqui Indian community in Mexico, combined ethnographic observation, biological monitoring of pesticide levels in the blood, and neurobehavioral testing to document the impairment of child development by pesticides.[a] Working with colleagues from the Technological Institute of Sonora in Obregón, Mexico, Guillette compared children and families from two Yaqui communities: one living in farm valleys who were exposed to large doses of pesticides and one living in ranching villages in the foothills nearby.

Guillette documented the frequency of pesticide use among the farming Yaqui to be forty-five times per crop cycle with two crop cycles per year. In the farming valleys she also noted that families tended to use household bug sprays on a daily basis, thus increasing their exposure to toxic pesticides. In the foothill ranches, she found that the only pesticides that the Yaqui were exposed to consisted of DDT sprayed by the government to control malaria. In these communities, indoor bugs were swatted or tolerated.

Pesticide exposure was linked to child health and development through two sets of measures. First, levels of pesticides in the blood of valley children at birth and throughout their childhood were examined and found to be far higher than in the children from the foothills. Further, the presence of pesticides in breast milk of nursing mothers from the valley farms was also documented. Second, children from the two communities were asked to perform a variety of normal childhood activities, such as jumping, memory games, playing catch, and drawing pictures.

The children exposed to high doses of pesticides had significantly less stamina, eye–hand coordination, large motor coordination, and drawing ability compared to the Yaqui children from the foothills. These children exhibited no overt symptoms of pesticide poisoning—instead exhibiting delays and impairment in their neurobehavioral abilities that may be irreversible.

Though Guillette's study was thoroughly embedded in one ethnographic community, she emphasizes that the exposure to pesticides among the Yaqui farmers is typical of agricultural communities globally and has significance for changing human practices regarding the use of pesticides everywhere.

[a]Guillette, E. A., et al. (1998, June). An anthropological approach to the evaluation of preschool children exposed to pesticides in Mexico. *Environmental Health Perspectives 106*, 347.

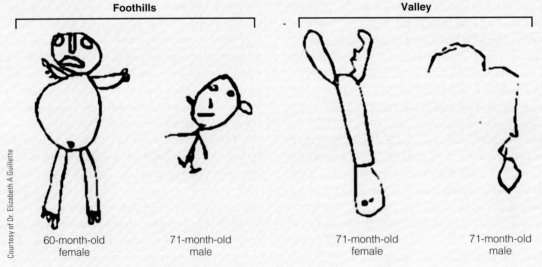

Courtesy of Dr. Elizabeth A Guillette

Foothills

60-month-old female

71-month-old male

Valley

71-month-old female

71-month-old male

Compare the drawings typically done by Yaqui children heavily exposed to pesticides (valley) to those made by Yaqui children living in nearby areas who were relatively unexposed (foothills).

THE FUTURE OF *HOMO SAPIENS*

One of the difficulties with managing environmental and toxic health risks is that serious consequences of new cultural practices are often not apparent until years or even decades later. By then, of course, these practices are fully embedded in the cultural system. Genetic toxicity, with associated risk of cancer and birth defects, represents just one example of the prices paid for many of the material benefits of civilization we enjoy today. Cultural practices thus exert deleterious effects on the human gene pools as never before.

The long-term effects on the human species remain to be seen. If the promise of genetic engineering offers hope of alleviating some of the misery and death that result from our own practices, it also raises the possibility of rendering us susceptible to infection or other biological stressors.

In addition to the problems human cultures are creating through changing the environment, new challenges arise from expectations set in motion through cultural means. The values of wealthy consumers living in industrialized countries spread to the inhabitants of poorer and developing countries, influencing their expectations and dreams. Of course, the resources necessary to maintain a luxurious standard of living are limited. Instead of globalizing a standard of living that the world's natural resources cannot meet, it is time for all of humanity to use today's global connections to learn how to live within the carrying capacity of the earth.

We are a social species with origins on the African continent over 5 million years ago. Over the course of our evolutionary history, we came to inhabit the entire globe. In each corner of this round earth, human cultures became distinct from one another, each devising its own specific beliefs and practices to meet the challenges of survival. In the future, dramatic changes in cultural values will be required if our species is to thrive. "New, improved" values might, for example, include a worldview that sees humanity as *part of* the world, rather than as *master over* it as it is in many of the worlds' cultures today. Included, too, might be a sense of social responsibility that recognizes and affirms respect among ethnic groups as well as our collective stewardship for the earth we inhabit.

Our continued survival will depend on our ability to cultivate positive social connections among all kinds of people and to recognize the ways we impact one another in a world interconnected by the forces of globalization. Together, we can use the adaptive faculty of culture, the hallmark of our species, to ensure our continued survival.

These Gambian children are spending their Saturday in the school library to make up skits and songs about health issues that they will take out into their local community. They are a part of a peer health educator group, a tradition that stretches throughout The Gambia and beyond. Both in school lessons and in extracurricular activities these students are reminded of their connections to the rest of the world. The survival of the human species depends on the knowledge of our common humanity and our collective responsibility for the world we share.

Questions for Reflection

1. Considering that sickness has challenged humans throughout our evolutionary history, why is an understanding of global process so critical for human health today?

2. The anthropological distinction between illness and disease provides a way to separate biological states from cultural elaborations given to those biological states. Can you think of some examples of illness without disease and disease without illness?

3. What do you think of the notion of letting a fever run its course instead of taking a medicine to lower it? Do these "Paleolithic prescriptions" suggested by evolutionary medicine run counter to your own medical beliefs and practices?

4. Are there any examples in your experience of how the growth process or human reproductive physiology served to help you adapt to environmental stressors? Does this ability help humans from an evolutionary perspective?

5. Do you see examples of structural violence in your community that make some individuals more vulnerable to disease than others?

Suggested Readings

Farmer, P. (2001). *Infections and inequalities: The modern plagues* (updated edition with a new preface). Berkeley: University of California Press.

Paul Farmer, continuing the tradition of the physician anthropologist, traces the relationship between structural violence and infectious disease, demonstrating that the world's poor bear a disproportionate burden of disease.

Helman, C. B. (2003). *Culture, health, and illness: An introduction for health professionals*. New York: Butterworth Heinemann Medical.

This well-referenced book provides a good overview and introduction to medical anthropology. Though written with health professionals in mind, it is very accessible for North American students who have firsthand experience with biomedicine, the dominant medical system of North America.

McElroy, A., & Townsend, P. K. (2003). *Medical anthropology in ecological perspective*. Boulder, CO: Westview Press.

Now in its fourth edition, this text lays out ecological approaches in medical anthropology, including biocultural, environmental, and evolutionary perspectives. In addition to providing a clear theoretical perspective, it offers excellent examples of applied work by medical anthropologists to improve health globally.

Nesse, R. M., & Williams, G. C. (1996). *Why we get sick*. New York: Vintage.

The authors expanded on a scholarly article to bring health-promoting ideas from evolutionary medicine to the public.

Trevathan, W., Smith, E. O., &.McKenna, J. J. (Eds.). (1999). *Evolutionary medicine*. London: Oxford University Press.

This comprehensive edited volume collects primary research conducted by leaders in the field of evolutionary medicine. Examples from throughout the human life cycle range from sexually transmitted diseases to cancer.

Thomson Audio Study Products

Enjoy the MP3-ready Audio Lecture Overviews for each chapter and a comprehensive audio glossary of key terms for quick study and review. Whether walking to class, doing laundry, or studying at your desk, you now have the freedom to choose when, where, and how you interact with your audio-based educational media. See the preface for information on how to access this on-the-go study and review tool.

The Anthropology Resource Center

www.thomsonedu.com/anthropology
The Anthropology Resource Center provides extended learning materials to reinforce your understanding of key concepts in the four fields of anthropology. For each of the four fields, the Resource Center includes dynamic exercises including video exercises, map exercises, simulations, and "Meet the Scientists" interviews, as well as critical thinking questions that can be assigned and e-mailed to instructors. The Resource Center also provides breaking news in anthropology and interesting material on applied anthropology to help you link what you are learning to the world around you.

14 Characteristics of Culture

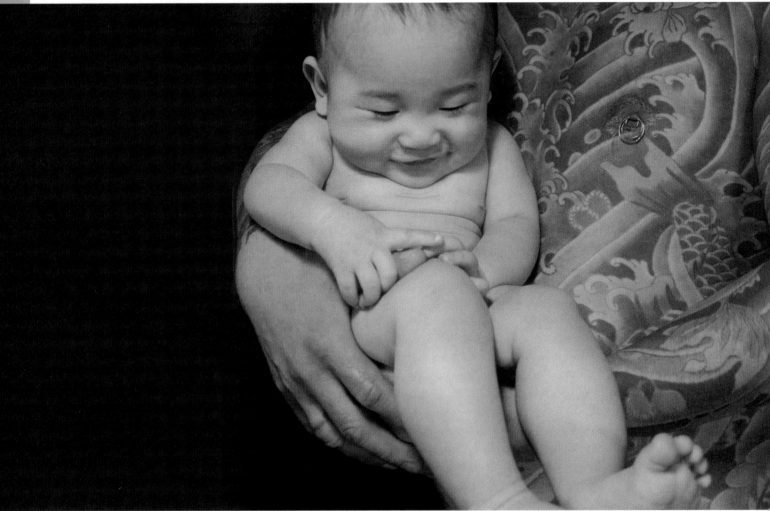

© Sandi Fellman, 1984

CHALLENGE ISSUE

Born naked and speechless, we are naturally incapable of surviving alone. As humans, we rely on culture, a shared way of living, to meet the physical, social, economic, and ideological challenges of human survival. In fact, it is through culture that we become fully human. Culture is manifested in countless ways, but one of its most visible expressions is self-adornment—the distinctive ways groups of people dress, style their hair, and otherwise decorate their bodies. We may enter the world in a natural state with a biological profile, but over time we acquire a cultural identity, etched into our minds and sometimes into our very skin—as shown in this photograph of Japanese tattoo artist Horiyoshi II, holding his unmarked newborn son.

What Is Culture?

Culture consists of the abstract ideas, values, and perceptions of the world that inform and are reflected in people's behavior. Culture is shared by members of a society and produces behavior that is intelligible to other members of that society. Cultures are learned rather than inherited biologically, and all the different parts of a culture function as an integrated whole.

Why Do Cultures Exist?

Every culture provides a design for thought and action that helps people survive and deal with all the challenges of existence. To endure, a culture must satisfy the basic needs of those who live by its rules, and it must provide an orderly existence for the members of a society. In doing so, a culture must strike a balance between the self-interests of individuals and the needs of society as a whole. Moreover, it must have the capacity to change in order to adapt to new circumstances or to altered perceptions of existing circumstances.

Ethnocentrism: Are Some Cultures Better than Others?

Humans are born into families forming part of wider communities. Raised by relatives and other members of these groups, we learn to behave, speak, and think like others in our society. Because each of us is reared to regard the world from the vantage point of our own social group, the human perspective is typically "ethnocentric"—believing that the ways of one's own culture are the only proper ones. Crossing cultural boundaries, we discover that people in our own society are not unique in being ethnocentric. Anthropologists challenge ethnocentrism by striving to understand each culture in its own right.

Students of anthropology are bound to find themselves studying a seemingly endless variety of human societies, each with its own distinctive environment and system of economics, politics, and religion. Yet for all this variety, these societies have one thing in common: Each is a group of people cooperating to ensure their collective survival and well-being. Group living and cooperation are impossible unless individuals know how others are likely to behave in any given situation. Thus, some degree of predictable behavior is required of each person within the society. In humans, it is culture that sets the limits of behavior and guides it along predictable paths that are generally acceptable to those who fall within the culture.

THE CONCEPT OF CULTURE

Anthropologists conceived the modern concept of culture toward the end of the 19th century. The first really clear and comprehensive definition came from the British anthropologist Sir Edward Tylor. Writing in 1871, he defined culture as "that complex whole which includes knowledge, belief, art, law, morals, custom, and any other capabilities and habits acquired by man as a member of society."

Since Tylor's time, definitions of culture have proliferated, so that by the early 1950s, North American anthropologists A. L. Kroeber and Clyde Kluckhohn were able to collect over a hundred of them from the academic literature. Recent definitions tend to distinguish more clearly between actual behavior and the abstract ideas, values, and perceptions of the world that inform that behavior. To put it another way, **culture** goes deeper than observable behavior; it is a society's shared and socially transmitted ideas, values, and perceptions, which are used to make sense of experience and generate behavior and are reflected in behavior.

THOMSON AUDIO STUDY PRODUCTS Take advantage of the MP3-ready Audio Lecture Overviews and comprehensive audio glossary of key terms for each chapter. See the preface for information on how to access this on-the-go study and review tool.

culture A society's shared and socially transmitted ideas, values, and perceptions, which are used to make sense of experience and which generate behavior and are reflected in that behavior.

enculturation The process by which a society's culture is transmitted from one generation to the next and individuals become members of their society.

CHARACTERISTICS OF CULTURE

Through the comparative study of many human cultures, past and present, anthropologists have gained an understanding of the basic characteristics evident in all of them: Every culture is learned, shared, based on symbols, integrated, and dynamic. A careful study of these characteristics helps us to see the importance and the function of culture itself.

Culture Is Learned

All culture is learned rather than biologically inherited, prompting U.S. anthropologist Ralph Linton to refer to it as humanity's "social heredity." One learns one's culture by growing up with it, and the process whereby culture is transmitted from one generation to the next is called **enculturation.**

Most animals eat and drink whenever the urge arises. Humans, however, are enculturated to do most of their eating and drinking at certain culturally prescribed times and feel hungry as those times approach. These eating times vary from culture to culture, as does what is eaten, how it is prepared, how it is eaten, and where. To add complexity, food is used to do more than merely satisfy nutritional requirements. When used to celebrate rituals and religious activities, as it often is, food "establishes relationships of give and take, of cooperation, of sharing, of an emotional bond that is universal."[1]

Through enculturation every person learns socially appropriate ways of satisfying the basic biologically determined needs of all humans: food, sleep, shelter, companionship, self-defense, and sexual gratification. It is important to distinguish between the needs themselves, which are not learned, and the learned ways in which they are satisfied—for each culture determines in its own way how these needs will be met. For instance, a North American's idea of a comfortable way to sleep may vary greatly from that of a Japanese person.

Learned behavior is exhibited in some degree by most, if not all, mammals. Several species may even be said to have elementary culture, in that local populations share patterns of behavior that, just like humans, each generation learns from the one before and that differ from one population to another. Elizabeth Marshall Thomas, for example, has described a distinctive pattern of behavior among lions of southern Africa's Kalahari Desert—behavior that fostered nonaggressive interaction with the region's indigenous hunters and gatherers and that each generation of lions passed on

[1]Caroulis, J. (1996). Food for thought. *Pennsylvania Gazette 95* (3), 16.

VISUAL COUNTERPOINT

In all human societies adults teach social roles and pass on cultural skills to the next generation. Here a North American mother introduces her child to the computer, and a Maya Indian mother in Guatemala shows her daughter how to handle a machete—useful for a multitude of tasks, from gardening to chopping food to cutting wood for fire and buildings.

to the next.[2] She has shown as well how Kalahari lion culture changed over a thirty-year period in response to new circumstances. That said, it is important to note that not all learned behavior is cultural. For instance, a pigeon may learn tricks, but this behavior is reflexive, the result of conditioning by repeated training, not the product of enculturation.

Beyond our species, examples of cultural behavior are particularly evident among other primates. A chimpanzee, for example, will take a twig, strip it of all leaves, and smooth it down to fashion a tool for extracting termites from their nest. Such tool making, which juveniles learn from their elders, is unquestionably a form of cultural behavior once thought to be exclusively human. In Japan, macaques that learned the advantages of washing sweet potatoes before eating them passed the practice on to the next generation. Within any given primate species, the culture of one population often differs from that of others, just as it does among humans. We have discovered both in captivity and in the wild that primates in general and apes in particular "possess a near-human intelligence generally, including the use of sounds in representational ways, a rich awareness of the aims and objec-

tives of others, the ability to engage in tactical deception, and the ability to use symbols in communication with humans and each other."[3]

Given the remarkable degree of biological similarity between apes and humans, it should come as no surprise that they are like us in other ways as well. In fact, in many respects the differences between apes and humans are differences of degree rather than kind (although the degree *does* make a major difference). Growing knowledge of ape/human similarities contradicts a belief that is deeply embedded in Western cultures: the idea that there is a vast and unbridgeable gap between people and animals. It has not been easy to overcome this bias, and indeed we still have not come to grips fully with the moral implications with respect to the way humans treat fellow primates in research laboratories.

Culture Is Shared

As a shared set of ideas, values, perceptions, and standards of behavior, culture is the common denominator that makes the actions of individuals intelligible to other members of their society. It enables them to predict how

[2]Thomas, E. M. (1994). *The tribe of the tiger: Cats and their culture* (pp. 109–186). New York: Simon & Schuster.

[3]Reynolds, V. (1994). Primates in the field, primates in the lab. *Anthropology Today 10* (2), 4.

others are most likely to behave in a given circumstance, and it tells them how to react accordingly. A group of people from different cultures, stranded for a time on a desert island, may become a society of sorts. They would have a common interest—survival—and would develop techniques for living and working together. However, each person would retain his or her own cultural identity and the group would disintegrate once everyone was rescued from the island and returned home. It would have been merely an aggregate in time and not a cultural entity. **Society** may be defined as an organized group or groups of interdependent people who generally share a common territory, language, and culture and who act together for collective survival and well-being. The ways in which these people depend upon one another can be seen in such features as their economic, communication, and defense systems. They are also bound together by a general sense of common identity.

Because culture and society are such closely related concepts, anthropologists study both. Obviously, there can be no culture without a society. Conversely, there are no known human societies that do not exhibit culture. This cannot be said for all other animal species. Ants and bees, for example, instinctively cooperate in a manner that clearly indicates a remarkable degree of social organization, yet this instinctual behavior is not a culture. Whether or not animals other than humans exhibit cultural behavior is a question that we will deal with shortly.

Although a culture is shared by members of a society, it is important to realize that all is not uniform. For one thing, no two people share the exact same version of their culture. And there are bound to be other variations. At the very least, there is some difference between the roles of men and women. This stems from the fact that women give birth but men do not and that there are obvious differences between male and female reproductive anatomy and physiology. Every society gives cultural meaning to biological sexual differences by explaining them in a particular way and specifying what their significance is in terms of social roles and expected patterns of behavior.

Because each culture does this in its own way, there can be tremendous variation from one society to another. Anthropologists use the term **gender** to refer to the cultural elaborations and meanings assigned to the biological differentiation between the sexes. So, although one's sex is biologically determined, one's gender is so-

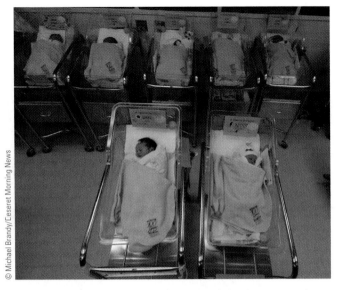

Newborn girls (under pink blankets) and boys (under blue blankets) in hospital nursery. Euramerican culture requires that newborn infants be assigned a gender identity of either male or female. Yet, significant numbers of infants are born each year whose genitalia do not conform to cultural expectations. Because only two genders are recognized, the usual reaction is to make the young bodies conform to cultural requirements through gender assignment surgery that involves constructing male or female genitalia. This is in contrast to many Native American cultures in which more than two genders are recognized.[4]

cially constructed within the context of one's particular culture.

The distinction between sex, which is biological, and gender, which is cultural, is an important one. Presumably, gender differences are at least as old as human culture—about 2.5 million years—and arose from the biological differences between early human males and females. As in chimps and gorillas today, the species most closely related to humans, early human males were on average substantially larger than females (although size contrasts were not as great as among gorillas). Average male–female size difference in modern humans appears to be significantly less than among our remote ancestors. Moreover, technological advancements in the home and workplace over the last century or two have greatly diminished the cultural significance of many remaining male–female biological differences in many societies all across the world.

Thus, apart from sexual differences directly related to reproduction, any biological basis for contrasting gender roles has largely disappeared in modern industrialized and postindustrial societies. (For example, hydraulic lifts used to move heavy automobile engines in an assembly line eliminate the need for muscular strength in

society An organized group or groups of interdependent people who generally share a common territory, language, and culture and who act together for collective survival and well-being.
gender The cultural elaborations and meanings assigned to the biological differentiation between the sexes.

---

[4]For statistics on this, see Blackless, M., et al. (2000). How sexually dimorphic are we? Review and synthesis. *American Journal of Human Biology 12*, 151–166.

that task.) Nevertheless, all cultures exhibit at least some role differentiation related to biology—some far more so than others.

In addition to cultural variation associated with gender, there is also variation related to age. In any society, children are not expected to behave as adults, and the reverse is equally true. But then, who is a child and who is an adult? Again, although age differences are "natural," cultures give their own meaning and timetable to the human life cycle. In North America, for example, individuals are generally not regarded as adults until the age of 18; in many others, adulthood begins earlier—often around age 12. That said, the status of adulthood often has less to do with age than with passage through certain prescribed rituals.

Subcultures: Groups Within a Larger Society

Besides age and gender variation, there may be cultural variation between subgroups in societies that share an overarching culture. These may be occupational groups in societies where there is a complex division of labor, or social classes in a stratified society, or ethnic groups in some other societies. When such groups exist within a society, each functioning by its own distinctive standards of behavior while still sharing some common standards, we speak of **subcultures.** The word *subculture* carries no suggestion of lesser status relative to the word *culture*.

Amish communities comprise one example of a subculture in North America. Specifically, they are an **ethnic group**—people who collectively and publicly identify themselves as a distinct group based on various cultural

features such as shared ancestry and common origin, language, customs, and traditional beliefs. The Amish originated in western Europe during the Protestant revolutions that swept through Europe in the 16th century. Today members of this group number about 100,000 and live mainly in Pennsylvania, Ohio, Illinois, and Indiana in the United States, and in Ontario, Canada.

These pacifist, rural people base their lives on their traditional Anabaptist beliefs, which hold that only adult baptism is valid and that "true Christians" as they define them should not hold government office, bear arms, or use force. They prohibit marriage outside their faith, which calls for obedience to radical Christian teachings, including social separation from what they see as the wider "evil world" and rejection of material wealth as "vainglorious." Among themselves they usually speak a German dialect known as Pennsylvania Dutch (from *Deutsch,* meaning "German"). They use High German for religious purposes, and children learn English in school. Valuing simplicity, hard work, and a high degree of neighborly cooperation, they dress in a distinctive plain garb and even today rely on the horse for transpor-

subculture A distinctive set of standards and behavior patterns by which a group within a larger society operates, while still sharing common standards with that larger society.
ethnic group People who collectively and publicly identify themselves as a distinct group based on various cultural features such as shared ancestry and common origin, language, customs, and traditional beliefs.

The Amish people have held on to their traditional agrarian way of life in the midst of industrialized North American society. By maintaining their own schools to instill Amish values in their children, prohibiting mechanized vehicles and equipment, and dressing in their distinctive plain clothing, the Amish proclaim their own special identity.

tation as well as agricultural work.[5] In short, they share the same **ethnicity.** This term, rooted in the Greek word *ethnikos* ("nation") and related to *ethnos* ("custom") is the expression of the set of cultural ideas held by an ethnic group.

The goal of Amish education is to teach youngsters reading, writing, and arithmetic, as well as Amish values. Adults in the community reject what they regard as "worldly" knowledge and the idea of schools producing good citizens for the state. Resisting all attempts to force their children to attend regular public schools, they insist that education take place near home and that teachers be committed to Amish ideals.

Their nonconformity to many standards of mainstream culture has caused frequent conflict with state authorities, as well as legal and personal harassment. Pressed to compromise, they have introduced "vocational training" beyond junior high to fulfill state requirements, but they have managed to retain control of their schools, and maintain their way of life.

Confronted with economic challenges that make it impossible for most Amish groups to subsist solely on farming, some work outside their communities. Many more have established cottage industries and actively market homemade goods to tourists and other outsiders. Yet, while their economic separation from mainstream society has declined over the past four decades, their cultural separation has not.[6] They remain a reclusive community, more distrustful than ever of the dominant North American culture surrounding them and mingling as little as possible with non-Amish people.

The Amish are but one example of the way a subculture may develop and be dealt with by the larger culture within which it functions. Different as they are, the Amish actually put into practice many values that other North Americans primarily respect in the abstract: thrift, hard work, independence, a close family life. The degree of tolerance accorded to them, in contrast to some other ethnic groups, is also due in part to the fact that the Amish are "white" Europeans; they are defined as being of the same "race" as those who comprise dominant mainstream society. Although the concept of race has been shown to have no biological validity when applied

to humans, it still persists as a powerful social classification. This can be seen in the general lack of tolerance shown toward American Indians, typically viewed as racially different by members of the dominant society.

Implicit in the discussion thus far is that subcultures may develop in different ways. On the one hand, Amish subculture in the United States emerged as the product of the way these European immigrants have communicated and interacted in pursuit of their common goals within the wider society. On the other hand, North American Indian subcultures are formerly independent cultural groups that underwent colonization by European settlers and were forcibly brought under the control of federal governments in the United States and Canada.

Although all American Indian groups have experienced enormous changes due to colonization, many have held on to traditions significantly different from those of the dominant Euramerican culture surrounding them, so that it is sometimes difficult to decide whether they remain as distinct cultures as opposed to subcultures. In this sense, *culture* and *subculture* represent opposite ends of a continuum, with no clear dividing line in the gray area between. The Anthropology Applied feature examines the intersection of culture and subculture with an example concerning Apache Indian housing.

This raises the issue of the multi-ethnic or **pluralistic society** in which two or more ethnic groups or nationalities are politically organized into one territorial state but maintain their cultural differences. Pluralistic societies could not have existed before the first politically centralized states arose a mere 5,000 years ago. With the rise of the state, it became possible to bring about the political unification of two or more formerly independent societies, each with its own culture, thereby creating what amounts to a more complex order that transcends the theoretical one culture–one society linkage.

Pluralistic societies, which are common in the world today (Figure 14.1), all face the same challenge: They are comprised of groups that, by virtue of their high degree of cultural variation, are all essentially operating by different sets of rules. Since social living requires predictable behavior, it may be difficult for the members of any one subgroup to accurately interpret and follow the different standards by which the others operate. This can lead to significant misunderstandings, such as the following case reported in the *Wall Street Journal* of May 13, 1983:

> Salt Lake City—Police called it a cross-cultural misunderstanding. When the man showed up to buy the Shetland pony advertised for sale, the owner asked what he intended to do with the animal. "For my son's birthday," he replied, and the deal was closed.

---

[5]Hostetler, J., & Huntington, G. (1971). *Children in Amish society.* New York: Holt, Rinehart & Winston.

[6]Kraybill, D. B. (2001). *The riddle of Amish culture* (pp. 1–6, 244, 268–269). Baltimore: Johns Hopkins University Press.

ethnicity This term, rooted in the Greek word *ethnikos* ("nation") and related to *ethnos* ("custom"), is the expression of the set of cultural ideas held by an ethnic group.
pluralistic society A society in which two or more ethnic groups or nationalities are politically organized into one territorial state but maintain their cultural differences.

Anthropology Applied

New Houses for Apache Indians ▪ George S. Esber

The United States, in common with other industrialized countries of the world, contains a number of more or less separate subcultures. Those who live by the standards of one particular subculture have their closest relationships with one another, receiving constant reassurance that their perceptions of the world are the only correct ones and coming to take it for granted that the whole culture is as they see it. As a consequence, members of one subculture frequently have trouble understanding the needs and aspirations of other such groups. For this reason anthropologists, with their special understanding of cultural differences, are frequently employed as go-betweens in situations requiring interaction between peoples of differing cultural traditions.

As an example, while I was still a graduate student in anthropology, one of my professors asked me to work with architects and a community of Tonto Apache Indians to research housing needs for a new Apache community.[a] Although

the architects knew of the cross-cultural differences in the use of space, they had no idea of how to get relevant information from the Indian people. For their part, the Apaches had no explicit awareness of their needs, for these were based on unconscious patterns of behavior. For that matter, few people are consciously aware of the space needs for their own social patterns of behavior.

My task was to persuade the architects to hold back on their planning long enough for me to gather, through participant observation and a review of written records, the data from which Apache housing needs could be abstracted. At the same time, I had to overcome Apache anxieties over an outsider coming into their midst to learn about matters as personal as their daily lives as they are acted out, in and around their homes. With these hurdles overcome, I was able to identify and successfully communicate to the architects those features of Apache life having importance for home and community design. At the same

time, discussions of my findings with the Apaches enhanced their own awareness of their unique needs.

As a result of my work, the Apaches moved into houses that had been designed with *their* participation, for *their* specific needs. Among my findings was the realization that the Apaches preferred to ease into social interactions rather than to shake hands and begin interacting immediately, as is more typical of the Anglo pattern. Apache etiquette requires that people be in full view of one another so each can assess the behavior of others from a distance prior to engaging in social interaction with them. This requires a large, open living space. At the same time, hosts feel compelled to offer food to guests as a prelude to further social interaction. Thus, cooking and dining areas cannot be separated from living space. Nor is standard middle-class Anglo kitchen equipment suitable, since the need for handling large quantities among extended families requires large pots and pans, which in turn calls for extra-large sinks and cupboards. Built with such ideas in mind, the new houses accommodated long-standing native traditions.

[a]Adapted from Esber, G. (1987). Designing Apache houses with Apaches. In R. M. Wulff & S. J. Fiske (Eds.), *Anthropological praxis: Translating knowledge into action.* Boulder, CO: Westview Press.

The buyer thereupon clubbed the pony to death with a two-by-four, dumped the carcass in his pickup truck and drove away. The horrified seller called the police, who tracked down the buyer. At his house they found a birthday party in progress. The pony was trussed and roasting in a *luau pit.* "We don't ride horses, we eat them," explained the buyer, a recent immigrant from Tonga [an island in the Pacific Ocean].

Unfortunately, the difficulty members of one subgroup within a pluralistic society may have making sense of the standards by which members of other groups operate can go far beyond mere misunderstanding. It can intensify to the point of anger and violence. Among many examples of this is the pluralistic society of Guatemala, where a central government distrustful of the country's largely rural Maya Indian majority unleashed a deadly reign of terror against them.

Every culture includes individuals who behave in abnormal ways that earn them such labels as "oddball," "eccentric," or "crazy." Typically, because they differ too much from the acceptable standard, they are looked upon with disapproval by their society. And if their behavior becomes too peculiar, they are sooner or later excluded from participating in the activities of the group. Such exclusion acts to keep what is defined as deviant behavior outside the group.

Interestingly, behavior viewed as deviant in one society may not be in another. In many American Indian societies, for example, a few exceptional individuals were permitted to assume for life the role normally associated with people of the opposite sex. Thus, a man could dress as a woman and engage in what were conventionally defined as female activities; conversely, women could achieve renown in activities normally in the masculine domain. In effect, four different gender identities were available: masculine men, feminine men, feminine women, and masculine women. Furthermore,

Figure 14.1
Shown here are some of the ethnic groups of the Russian Federation, the dominant and by far the largest
part of the former Union of Soviet Socialist Republics.

masculine women and feminine men were not merely
accepted, but were highly respected.

Culture Is Based on Symbols

Much of human behavior involves **symbols**—signs,
sounds, emblems, and other things that are linked to
something else and represent them in a meaningful way.
Because often there is no inherent or necessary relationship between a thing and its representation, symbols are
commonly arbitrary, acquiring specific meanings when
people agree on usage in their communications.

In fact, symbols—ranging from national flags to
wedding rings to money—enter into every aspect of culture, from social life and religion to politics and economics. We're all familiar with the fervor and devotion that
a religious symbol can elicit from a believer. An Islamic
crescent, Christian cross, or a Jewish Star of David, as

symbol A sign, sound, emblem, or other thing that is arbitrarily
linked to something else and represents it in a meaningful way.

well as the sun among the Inca, a cow among the Hindu,
a white buffalo calf among Plains Indians, or any other
object of worship, may bring to mind years of struggle
and persecution or may stand for a whole philosophy or
creed.

The most important symbolic aspect of culture is
language—using words to represent objects and ideas.
Through language humans are able to transmit culture
from one generation to another. In particular, language
makes it possible to learn from cumulative, shared experience. Without it, one could not inform others about
events, emotions, and other experiences to which they
were not a party. Language is so important that an entire
chapter in this book is devoted to the subject.

Culture Is Integrated

For purposes of comparison and analysis, anthropologists customarily imagine a culture as a well-structured
system made up of distinctive parts that function together as an organized whole. While they may sharply
distinguish each part as a clearly defined unit with its

own characteristic features and special place within the larger system, anthropologists recognize that reality is a more complex intertwining, and divisions between cultural units are often blurry. However, because all aspects of a culture must be reasonably well integrated in order to function properly, anthropologists seldom focus on an individual feature in isolation. Instead, they view each in terms of its larger context and carefully examine its connections to related cultural features.

Broadly speaking, a society's cultural features fall within three categories: social structure, infrastructure, and superstructure. **Social structure** concerns rule-governed relationships—with all their rights and obligations—that hold members of a society together. Households, families, associations, and power relations, including politics, are all part of social structure. It establishes group cohesion and enables people to consistently satisfy their basic needs, including food and shelter for themselves and their dependents, by means of work. So, there is a direct relationship between a group's social structure and its economic foundation, which includes subsistence practices and the tools and other material equipment used to make a living.

Because subsistence practices involve tapping into available resources to satisfy a society's basic needs, this aspect of culture is known as **infrastructure.** Supported by this economic foundation, a society is also held together by a shared sense of identity and worldview. This collective body of ideas, beliefs, and values by which a group of people makes sense of the world—its shape, challenges, and opportunities—and their place in it is known as ideology or **superstructure.** Including religion and national ideology, it structures the overarching ideas that people in a society have about themselves and everything else that exists around them—and it gives meaning and direction to their lives. Influencing and reinforcing one another, these three interdependent structures together form part of a cultural system (Figure 14.2).

The integration of economic, social, and ideological aspects of a culture can be illustrated by the Kapauku Papuans, a mountain people of Western New Guinea, studied in 1955 by the North American anthropologist Leopold Pospisil.[7] The Kapauku economy relies on plant cultivation, along with pig breeding, hunting, and fishing. Although plant cultivation provides most of the people's food, it is through pig breeding that men achieve political power and positions of legal authority.

Among the Kapauku, pig breeding is a complex business. Raising a lot of pigs requires a lot of food to feed them. The primary fodder is sweet potatoes, grown in garden plots. According to Kapauku culture, certain garden activities and the caring of pigs are tasks that fall

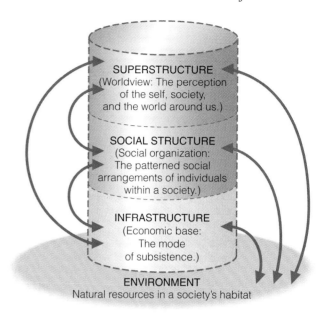

Figure 14.2

The barrel model of culture. Every culture is an integrated and dynamic system of adaptation that responds to a combination of internal factors (economic, social, ideological) and external factors (environmental, climatic). Within a cultural system, there are functional relationships among the economic base (infrastructure), the social organization (social structure), and the ideology (superstructure). A change in one leads to a change in the others.

exclusively in the domain of women's work. So, to raise many pigs, a man needs numerous women in the household. Thus, in Kapauku society, multiple wives (polygyny) are not only permitted, they are highly desired. For each wife, however, a man must pay a bride price, and this can be expensive. Furthermore, wives have to be compensated for their care of the pigs. Put simply, it takes pigs, by which wealth is measured, to get wives, without whom pigs cannot be raised in the first place. Needless to say, this requires considerable entrepreneurship. It is this ability that produces leaders in Kapauku society.

The interrelatedness of the various parts of Kapauku culture is even more complicated. For example, one condition that encourages polygyny is a surplus of adult fe-

---

[7]Pospisil, L. (1963). *The Kapauku Papuans of west New Guinea.* New York: Holt, Rinehart & Winston.

social structure The rule-governed relationships—with all their rights and obligations—that hold members of a society together. This includes households, families, associations, and power relations, including politics.

infrastructure The economic foundation of a society, including its subsistence practices and the tools and other material equipment used to make a living.

superstructure A society's shared sense of identity and worldview. The collective body of ideas, beliefs, and values by which a group of people makes sense of the world—its shape, challenges, and opportunities—and their place in it. This includes religion and national ideology.

Biocultural Connection

Adult Human Stature and the Effects of Culture: An Archaeological Example

Among human beings, each of us is genetically programmed at conception to achieve a certain stature as an adult. Whether or not we actually wind up as tall as our genes would allow, however, is influenced by experiences during our period of growth and development.

For example, if an individual becomes severely ill, this may arrest growth temporarily, a setback that will not be made up when growth resumes. Critically important as well is the quality of diet. Without adequate nutrition, a person will not grow up to be as tall as would otherwise be possible. Thus, in class-structured societies, individuals of upper-class standing have tended to be the tallest individuals, as they generally have access to the best diets and are shielded from many of life's harsher realities. Conversely, individuals of lower class standing have tended to be shorter, owing to poor diets and generally harsher lives.

At the ancient Maya city of Tikal, in the Central American country of Guatemala, analysis of human skeletons from burials reveal stature differences characteristic of stratified societies. On average, males interred in rich "tombs" were taller than those in simple graves associated with relatively small houses. Those buried near intermediate-sized houses are generally taller than those from simple graves, but not as tall as those from "tombs."

Thus, the analysis provides strong support for a reconstruction of Tikal society into three strata: lower class commoners, higher class commoners, and (at the top) the ruling elite.

males, sometimes caused by loss of males through warfare. Among the Kapauku, recurring warfare has long been viewed as a necessary evil. By the rules of Kapauku warfare, men may be killed but women may not. This system works to promote the sort of imbalanced sex ratio that fosters polygyny. Polygyny tends to work best if a man's wives all come to live in his village, and so it is among the Kapauku. With this arrangement, the men of a village are typically "blood" relatives of one another, which enhances their ability to cooperate in warfare. Considering all of this, it makes sense that Kapauku typically trace descent (ancestry) through men.

Descent reckoning through men, coupled with near-constant warfare, tends to promote male dominance. So it is not surprising to find that positions of leadership in Kapauku society are held exclusively by men, who appropriate the products of women's labor in order to play their political "games." Such male dominance is by no means characteristic of all human societies. Rather, as in the Kapauku case, it arises only under particular sets of circumstances that, if changed, will alter the way in which men and women relate to each other.

In sum, for a culture to function properly, its various parts must be consistent with one another. But consistency is not the same as harmony. In fact, there is often friction and potential for conflict within every culture—among individuals, factions, and competing institutions. Even on the most basic level of a society, individuals rarely experience the enculturation process in precisely the same way, nor do they perceive their reality in precisely identical fashion. Moreover, conditions may change, brought on by inside or outside forces.

A society will function reasonably well as long as its culture is capable of handling the daily strains and tensions. However, when a culture no longer provides adequate solutions or when its component parts are no longer consistent, a situation of cultural crisis ensues. Also, as this chapter's Biocultural Connection illustrates, the cultural system in stratified societies generally favors the ruling elite, while the groups scraping by on the bottom benefit the least. The difference may be measured in terms of material wealth as well as physical health.

Culture Is Dynamic

Cultures are dynamic systems that respond to motions and actions within and around them. When one element within the system shifts or changes, the entire system strives to adjust, just as it does when an outside force applies pressure. To function adequately, a culture must be flexible enough to allow such adjustments in the face of unstable or changing circumstances.

All cultures are, of necessity, dynamic, but some are far less so than others. When a culture is too rigid or static and fails to provide its members with the means required for long-term survival under changing conditions, it is not likely to endure. On the other hand, some cultures are so fluid and open to change that they may lose their distinctive character. The Amish mentioned earlier in this chapter typically resist change as much as possible but are constantly making balanced decisions to adjust when absolutely necessary. North Americans in general, however, have created a culture in which change has become a positive ideal.

CULTURE AND ADAPTATION

In the course of their evolution, humans, like all animals, have continually faced the challenge of adapting to their environment. The term *adaptation* refers to a gradual process by which organisms adjust to the conditions of the locality in which they live. Organisms have generally adapted biologically as the frequency of advantageous anatomical and physiological features increase in a population through a process known as natural selection. For example, body hair coupled with certain other physiological traits protects mammals from extremes of temperature; specialized teeth help them to procure the kinds of food they need; and so on.

Humans, however, have increasingly come to depend on cultural adaptation, using a unique combination of brain power and physical skills to alter their circumstances. Biology has not provided them with built-in fur coats to protect them in cold climates, but it has given them the ability to make their own coats, build fires, and construct shelters to shield themselves against the cold. They may not be able to run as fast as a cheetah, but they are able to invent and build vehicles that can carry them faster and further than any other creature. Through culture and its many constructions, the human species has secured not just its survival but its expansion as well. By manipulating environments through cultural means, people have been able to move into a vast range of environments, from the icy Arctic to the Sahara Desert. They have even set foot on the moon.

This is not to say that everything that humans do they do *because* it is adaptive to a particular environment. For one thing, people do not just react to an environment as given; rather, they react to it as they perceive it, and different groups of people may perceive the same environment in radically different ways. They also react to things other than the environment: their own biological natures; their beliefs and attitudes; and the short- and long-term consequences of their behavior for themselves and other life forms that share their habitats. Although people maintain cultures to deal with problems, some cultural practices have proved to be maladaptive and have actually created new problems—such as toxic water and air caused by certain industrial practices, or North America's obesity epidemic brought on by the culture of cars, fast food, television, and personal computers.

A further complication is the relativity of any given adaptation: What is adaptive in one context may be seriously maladaptive in another. For example, the sanitation practices of food-foraging peoples—their toilet habits and methods of garbage disposal—are appropriate to contexts of low population densities and some degree of residential mobility. But these same practices become serious health hazards in the context of large, fully sedentary populations. Similarly, behavior that is adaptive in the short run may be maladaptive over the long run. Thus, the development of irrigation in ancient Mesopotamia (modern-day Iraq) made it possible over the short run to increase food production, but over time it favored the gradual accumulation of salts in the soils. This, in turn, contributed to the collapse of civilization there about 4,000 years ago.

Likewise, today, the development of prime farmland in places like the eastern United States for purposes other than food production makes us increasingly dependent on food raised in marginal environments. High yields on marginal lands are presently possible through the application of expensive technology, but continuing loss of topsoil, increasing salinity of soils through evaporation of irrigation waters, and silting of irrigation works, not to mention impending shortages of water and fossil fuels, make continuing high yields over the long term unlikely. All of this said, it should be clear that for a culture to sur-

What is adaptive at one time may not be at another. In the United States, the principal source of fruits, vegetables, and fiber is the Central Valley of California, where irrigation works have made the desert bloom. As happened in ancient Mesopotamia, evaporation concentrates salts in the water, but here pollution is made even worse by chemical fertilizers. These poisons are now accumulating in the soil and threaten to make the valley a desert again, but this time a true wasteland.

Anthropologists of Note

Bronislaw Malinowski (1884–1942)

Courtesy Phoebe Apperson Hearst Museum of Anthropology

Polish-born Bronislaw Malinowski argued that people everywhere share certain biological and psychological needs and that the ultimate function of all cultural institutions is to fulfill those needs. Everyone, for example, needs to feel secure in relation to the physical universe. Therefore, when science and technology are inadequate to explain certain natural phenomena—such as eclipses or earthquakes—people develop religion and magic to account for those phenomena and to establish a feeling of security. The nature of the institution, according to Malinowski, is determined by its function.

Malinowski outlined three fundamental levels of needs that he claimed had to be resolved by all cultures:

1. A culture must provide for biological needs, such as the need for food and procreation.
2. A culture must provide for instrumental needs, such as the need for law and education.
3. A culture must provide for integrative needs, such as religion and art.

If anthropologists could analyze the ways in which a culture fills these needs for its members, Malinowski believed that they could also deduce the origin of cultural traits.

Although this belief was never justified, the quality of data called for by Malinowski's approach set new standards for anthropological fieldwork. He was the first to insist that it was necessary to settle into the community being studied for an extended period of time in order to really understand it. He himself showed the way with his work in the Trobriand Islands between 1915 and 1918. Never before had such in-depth work been done, nor had such insights been gained into the workings of another culture. Such was the quality of Malinowski's Trobriand research that, with it, ethnography (the detailed description of a particular culture based primarily on fieldwork) can be said to have come of age as a scientific enterprise.

vive, it must produce behavior that is generally adaptive to the natural environment.

Functions of Culture

Polish-born anthropologist Bronislaw Malinowski argued that people everywhere share certain biological and psychological needs and that the ultimate function of all cultural institutions is to fulfill these needs (see Anthropologist of Note). Others have marked out different criteria and categories, but the idea is basically the same: A culture cannot endure if it does not deal effectively with basic challenges. It must include strategies for the production and distribution of goods and services considered necessary for life. To ensure the biological continuity of its members, it must also provide a social structure for reproduction and mutual support. It must offer ways to pass on knowledge and enculturate new members so they can assist one another and contribute to their community as well-functioning adults. It must facilitate social interaction and provide ways to avoid or resolve conflicts within their group as well as with outsiders.

Since a culture must support all aspects of life, as indicated in our barrel model, it must also meet the psychological and emotional needs of its members. This last function is met, in part, simply by the measure of predictability that each culture, as a shared design for thought and action, brings to everyday life. Of course it involves much more than that, including a worldview that helps individuals understand their place in the world and face major changes. For example, every culture provides its members with certain customary ideas and rituals that enable them to think creatively about the meaning of life and death. Many cultures even make it possible for people to imagine an afterworld that no one has actually been to and returned from to tell about. Invited to suspend disbelief and engage in such imaginings, people find the means to deal with the grief of losing a loved one.

In Bali, for instance, Hindu worshipers stage spectacular cremation rituals at special places where they burn the physical remains of their dead. After a colorful procession with musicians, the corpse is carried to the cremation site in a large cremation tower, or *wadah*, representing the three-layered cosmos. It is then transferred into a large and beautifully decorated sarcophagus, made of wood and cloth artfully shaped in the form of an animal—a bull when the deceased belonged to the highest caste of priests (*brahman*), a winged lion for the second highest caste of warriors and administrators (*satria*), and a half-fish/half-elephant for the next caste of merchants (*wesia*). After relatives and friends place their last offerings atop or inside the sarcophagus, a Hindu priest sets the structure on fire. Soon, the body burns, and according to Balinese Hindu belief the animal sarcophagus symbolically guides the soul of the deceased to Bali's "mother" mountain Gunung Angung. This is the sacred dwelling place of the island's gods and ancestors, the place many Balinese believe they return to when they die. Freed from the flesh, the soul may later transmigrate and return in the flesh. This belief in reincarnation of the soul allows the Balinese to cope with death as a celebration of life.

In addition to meeting such emotional needs and all of the other functions noted above, a culture must be able to change if it is to remain adaptive under shifting conditions.

Culture and Change

Cultures have always changed over time, although rarely as rapidly or as massively as many are doing today. Changes take place in response to such events as population growth, technological innovation, environmental crisis, the intrusion of outsiders, or modification of behavior and values within the culture.

Changes are often signified by apparel. For example, in North America, where swift change is driven by capitalism and the need for incessant market growth, clothing fashions change quickly. Over the past half century or so, as advertisers increasingly utilized sexuality to promote sales, it became culturally permissible for men and women alike to wear clothing that revealed more and more of their bodies. Along with this has come greater permissiveness about body exposure in photographs, movies, and television, as well as less restrictive sexual attitudes and practices among many. In our current age of globalization we are witnessing a much accelerated pace of widespread and radical cultural change, discussed in detail in the last two chapters of this book.

Although cultures must have some flexibility to remain adaptive, culture change can also bring unexpected and often disastrous results. For example, consider the relationship between culture and the droughts that periodically afflict so many people living in African countries just south of the Sahara Desert. The lives of some 14 million pastoral nomadic people native to this region are centered on cattle and other livestock, herded from place to place as required for pasturage and water. For thousands of years these people have been able to go about their business, efficiently utilizing vast areas of arid lands in ways that allowed them to survive severe droughts many times in the past. Unfortunately, their way of life is frowned upon by the central governments of modern states in the region because it involves moving back and forth across relatively new international boundaries, making the nomads difficult to track for purposes of taxation and other governmental controls.

Seeing nomads as a challenge to their authority, these governments have gone all out to stop them from ranging through their traditional grazing territories and to convert them into sedentary villagers. Imposed loss of mobility has resulted in overgrazing; moreover, the problem has been compounded by government efforts to press pastoralists into a market economy by giving them

Pastoralists herd their grazing animals, moving slowly across vast territories in search of food. As nomadic peoples who depend on their mobility for survival, they may cross unmarked international borders. Difficult to control by central governments trying to impose taxes on them, these nomads face major obstacles in pursuing their customary way of life. No longer able to range through their traditional grazing territories due to government restrictions on land use, these African herders and their cattle are hit all the harder when droughts occur. So it is in this photo taken in Kenya, where the combination of limited grazing lands and severe drought resulted in the death of many animals and turned others into "bones on hoofs."

© Tony Karumba/AFP/Getty Images

incentives to raise many more animals than required for their own needs in order to have a surplus to sell and thus add to the tax base. The resulting devastation, where there had previously been no significant overgrazing or erosion, now makes droughts far more disastrous than they would otherwise be. In fact, it places the very existence of the nomads' traditional way of life in jeopardy.

CULTURE, SOCIETY, AND THE INDIVIDUAL

Ultimately, a society is no more than a union of individuals, all of whom have their own special needs and interests. To survive, it must succeed in balancing the immediate self-interest of its individual members against the needs and demands of the collective well-being of society as a whole. To accomplish this, a society offers rewards for adherence to its culturally prescribed standards. In most cases, these rewards assume the form of social approval. For example, in contemporary North American society a person who holds a good job, takes care of family, pays taxes, and does volunteer work in the neighborhood may be spoken of as a "model citizen" in the community. To ensure the survival of the group, each person must learn to postpone certain immediate personal satisfactions. Yet the needs of the individual cannot be suppressed too far or the result may be a degree of emotional stress and growing resentment that results in protest, disruption, and sometimes even violence.

Consider, for example, the matter of sexual expression, which, like anything that people do, is shaped by culture. Sexuality is important in any society, for it helps to strengthen cooperative bonds among members of society, ensuring the perpetuation of society itself. Yet sex can be disruptive to social living. If the issue of who has sexual access to whom is not clearly spelled out, competition for sexual privileges can destroy the cooperative bonds on which human survival depends. Uncontrolled sexual activity, too, can result in reproductive rates that cause a society's population to outstrip its resources. Hence, as it shapes sexual behavior, every culture must balance the needs of society against the individual's sexual needs and desires so that frustration does not build up to the point of being disruptive in itself.

Of course, cultures vary widely in the way they go about this. On one end of the spectrum, societies such as the Amish in North America or the Muslim Brotherhood in Egypt have taken an extremely restrictive approach, specifying no sex outside of marriage. On the other end are such societies as the Norwegians in northern Europe who generally accept premarital sex and often choose to have children outside marriage, or even more extreme, the Canela Indians in Brazil, whose social codes guar-

Some people whose needs are not readily met by society direct their frustrations against scapegoats, usually minorities. In Australia, Europe, and North America, such resentment fueled the rise of "skinheads" who express their hatred with Nazi symbols such as swastikas.

antee that, sooner or later, everyone in a given village has had sex with just about everyone of the opposite sex. Yet, even as permissive as the latter situation may sound, there are nonetheless strict rules as to how the system operates.[8]

Not just in sexual matters, but in all life issues, cultures must strike a balance between the needs and desires of individuals and those of society as a whole. When those of society take precedence, people experience excessive stress. Symptomatic of this are increased levels of mental illness and behavior regarded as antisocial: violence, crime, abuse of alcohol and other drugs, depression, suicide, or simply alienation. If not corrected, the situation can result in cultural breakdown. But just as problems develop if the needs of society take precedence

[8]Crocker, W. A., & Crocker, J. (1994). *The Canela, bonding through kinship, ritual and sex* (pp. 143–171). Fort Worth: Harcourt Brace.

over those of the individual, so too do they develop if the balance is upset in the other direction.

EVALUATION OF CULTURE

We have knowledge of numerous highly diverse cultural solutions to the challenges of human existence. The question often arises, Which is best? Anthropologists have been intrigued to find that all cultures tend to see themselves as the best of all possible worlds. This is reflected in the way individual societies refer to themselves: Typically, a society's traditional name for itself translates roughly into "true human beings." In contrast, their names for outsiders commonly translate into

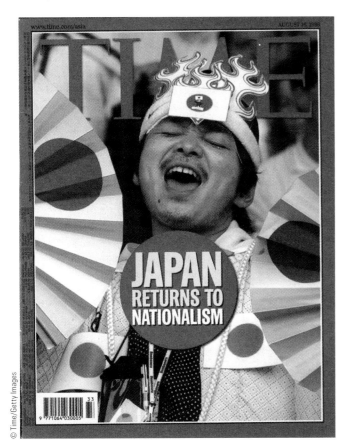

Japanese traditionally referred to their own people as a "divine nation," governed by the *mikado* (emperor) who was revered as a god. Today, a revival of Japanese nationalism is expressed by the restoration of controversial symbols in public places. These include singing (at public events and in some schools) the *kimigayo*, a hymn of praise to the divine emperor that served as Imperial Japan's national anthem. And the *hinomaru* (the rising sun flag), once raised by Japanese soldiers in conquered territories, can increasingly be seen flying in public places and private homes. Historically associated with militant Japanese imperialism, these nationalist symbols reflect a tradition of ethnocentrism not unlike those of other nations claiming a divine association, as in "One Nation under God," "God's Own Country," "God's Chosen People," and "God's Promised Land."

various versions of "subhumans," including "monkeys," "dogs," "weird-looking people," "funny talkers," and so forth. We now know that any adequately functioning culture regards its own ways as the only proper ones, a view known as **ethnocentrism.**

Anthropologists have been actively engaged in the fight against ethnocentrism ever since they started to study and actually live among traditional peoples with radically different cultures—thus learning by personal experience that they were no less human than anyone else. Resisting the common urge to rank cultures, anthropologists have instead aimed to understand individual cultures and the general concept of culture. To do so, they have examined each culture on its own terms, aiming to discern whether or not the culture satisfies the needs and expectations of the people themselves. If a people practiced human sacrifice or capital punishment, for example, anthropologists asked about the circumstances that made the taking of human life acceptable according to that particular group's values.

The idea that one must suspend judgment on other peoples' practices in order to understand them in their own cultural terms is called **cultural relativism.** Only through such an approach can one gain a meaningful view of the values and beliefs that underlie the behaviors and institutions of other peoples and societies as well as clearer insights into the underlying beliefs and practices of one's own society.

Take, for example, the 16th-century Aztec practice of sacrificing humans for religious purposes. Few (if any) North Americans today would condone such practices, but by suspending judgment one can get beneath the surface and discern how it functioned to reassure the populace that the Aztec state was healthy and that the sun would remain in the heavens.

Moreover, an impartial and open-minded exploration of Aztec sacrifice rituals may offer a valuable comparative perspective on the death penalty in countries such as the United States today. Numerous studies by social scientists have clearly shown that the death penalty does not deter violent crime, any more than Aztec sacrifice really provided sustenance for the sun. In fact, cross-cultural studies show that homicide rates mostly decline after its abolition.[9] Similar to Aztec human sacrifice, capital punishment may be seen as an institutionalized

[9]Ember, C. R., & Ember, M. (1996). What have we learned from cross-cultural research? *General Anthropology 2* (2), 5.

ethnocentrism The belief that the ways of one's own culture are the only proper ones.
cultural relativism The idea that one must suspend judgment of other people's practices in order to understand them in their own cultural terms.

magical response to perceived disorder. As U.S. anthropologists Anthony Paredes and Elizabeth D. Purdum point out, it "reassures many that society is not out of control after all, that the majesty of the law reigns, and that God is indeed in his heaven."[10]

Clearly, cultural relativism is essential as a research tool. However, employing it as a tool does not mean suspending judgment forever, nor does it require the anthropologist to defend a people's right to engage in any cultural practice, no matter how destructive. All that is necessary is that we avoid *premature* judgments until we have a full understanding of the culture in which we are interested. Then, and only then, may the anthropologist adopt a critical stance and in an informed way consider the advantages and disadvantages particular beliefs and behaviors have for a society and its members. As British anthropologist David Maybury-Lewis emphasizes, "one does not avoid making judgments, but rather postpones them in order to make informed judgments later."[11]

Forty years ago U.S. anthropologist Walter Goldschmidt devised a still-useful formula to help colleagues avoid the pitfalls of ethnocentrism without ending up in the "anything goes" position of cultural relativism pushed to absurdity.[12] In his view the important question to ask is, How well does a given culture satisfy the physical and psychological needs of those whose behavior it guides?

Specific indicators are to be found in the nutritional status and general physical and mental health of its population; the incidence of violence, crime, and delinquency; the demographic structure, stability, and tranquility of domestic life; and the group's relationship to its resource base. The culture of a people who experience high rates of malnutrition, violence, crime, delinquency, suicide, emotional disorders and despair, and environmental degradation may be said to be operating less well than that of another people who exhibit few such problems. In a well-working culture, people "can be proud, jealous, and pugnacious, and live a very satisfactory life without feeling 'angst,' 'alienation,' 'anomie,' 'depression,' or any of the other pervasive ills of our own inhuman and civilized way of living."[13] When traditional ways of coping no longer seem to work, and people feel helpless to shape

San Quentin Prison cell block. One sign that a culture is not adequately satisfying a people's needs and expectations is a high incidence of crime and delinquency. It is sobering to note that 25 percent of all imprisoned people in the world are incarcerated in the United States. In the past ten years the country's jail and prison population jumped by more than 600,000—from 1.6 to 2.2 million. Ironically, people in the United States think of their country as "the land of the free," yet it has the highest incarceration rate in the world (724 per 100,000 inhabitants).

their own lives in their own societies, symptoms of cultural breakdown become prominent.

In short, a culture is essentially a maintenance system to ensure the continued well-being of a group of people. Therefore, it may be deemed successful as long as it secures the survival of a society in a way that its members find to be reasonably fulfilling. What complicates matters is that any society is made up of groups with different interests, raising the possibility that some people's interests may be served better than those of others. Therefore, a culture that is quite fulfilling for one group within a society may be less so for another.

[10]Paredes, J. A., & Purdum, E. D. (1990). "Bye, bye Ted . . . " *Anthropology Today 6* (2), 9.

[11]Maybury-Lewis, D. H. P. (1993). A special sort of pleading. In W. A. Haviland & R. J. Gordon (Eds.), *Talking about people* (2nd ed., p. 17). Mountain View, CA: Mayfield.

[12]Bodley, J. H. (1990). *Victims of progress* (3rd ed., p. 138). Mountain View, CA: Mayfield.

[13]Fox, R. (1968). *Encounter with anthropology* (p. 290). New York: Dell.

For this reason, the anthropologist must always ask, *Whose* needs and *whose* survival are best served by the culture in question? Only by looking at the overall situation can a reasonably objective judgment be made as to how well a culture is working. But anthropologists today recognize that few peoples still exist in total or near-total isolation and understand that globalization affects the dynamics of culture change in almost every corner of our global village. Accordingly, as will be detailed in many of the following chapters, we must widen our scope and develop a truly worldwide perspective that enables us to appreciate cultures as increasingly open and interactive (and sometimes reactive) systems.

Questions for Reflection

1. Like everyone else in the world, you are meeting daily challenges of survival through your culture. And since you are made "fully human" by your own culture, how do you express your individual identity in your own community? What do your hairstyle, clothes, shoes, jewelry, and perhaps tattoos communicate about who you are? How do you think people from a different cultural background might interpret your choices of self-adornment?

2. Many large modern societies are pluralistic. Are you familiar with any subcultures in your own society? How different are these subcultures from one another? Could you make friends or even marry someone from another subculture? What kind of problems would you be likely to encounter?

3. Although all cultures across the world display some degree of ethnocentrism, some are more ethnocentric than others. In what ways is your own society ethnocentric? Considering the modern fact of globalization (as described in Chapter 1), do you think ethnocentrism poses more of a problem in today's world than in the past?

4. The barrel model offers you a simple framework to imagine what a culture looks like from an analytical point of view. How would you apply that model to your own community?

5. If culture is a maintenance system to continue the well-being of a group of people, how do you think an anthropologist would explain why, in some societies, many members end up in jail or prison? What does a society's incarceration rate tell you about its cultural system?

Suggested Readings

Brown, D. E. (1991). *Human universals*. New York: McGraw-Hill.

Fascination with cultural diversity should not eclipse the study of human universals, which have relevance for our understanding of the nature of all humanity and raise issues transcending boundaries of biological and social science, as well as the humanities.

Gamst, F. C., & Norbeck, E. (1976). *Ideas of culture: Sources and uses*. New York: Holt, Rinehart & Winston.

Selected writings (with editorial comments) on the culture concept, illustrating how the concept has grown and given rise to narrow specializations within the field of anthropology.

Hatch, E. (1983). *Culture and morality: The relativity of values in anthropology*. New York: Columbia University Press.

Traces anthropological grapplings with the concept of cultural relativity—looking at it in relation to relativity of knowledge, historical relativism, and ethical relativism.

Lewellen, T. C. (2002). *The anthropology of globalization: Cultural anthropology enters the 21st century*. Westport, CT: Greenwood Publishing.

A useful and digestible undergraduate textbook on the anthropology of globalization—looking at theory, migration, and local–global relationships.

Urban, G. (2001). *Metaculture: How cultures move through the modern world*. Westport, CT: Greenwood Press.

Examines the dynamics and implications of the rapid circulation of contemporary capitalist culture with its constant striving for "newness."

Thomson Audio Study Products

 Enjoy the MP3-ready Audio Lecture Overviews for each chapter and a comprehensive audio glossary of key terms for quick study and review. Whether walking to class, doing laundry, or studying at your desk, you now have the freedom to choose when, where, and how you interact with your audio-based educational media. See the preface for information on how to access this on-the-go study and review tool.

The Anthropology Resource Center

www.thomsonedu.com/anthropology

The Anthropology Resource Center provides extended learning materials to reinforce your understanding of key concepts in the four fields of anthropology. For each of the four fields, the Resource Center includes dynamic exercises including video exercises, map exercises, simulations, and "Meet the Scientists" interviews, as well as critical thinking questions that can be assigned and e-mailed to instructors. The Resource Center also provides breaking news in anthropology and interesting material on applied anthropology to help you link what you are learning to the world around you.

15 Ethnographic Research: Its History, Methods, and Theories

© Julia Jean

CHALLENGE ISSUE

Anthropologists take on the challenge of studying and describing cultures around the world and finding scientific explanations for their differences and similarities. Why do people think, feel, and act in certain ways—and find it wrong or impossible to do otherwise? Answers must come from fact-based knowledge about cultural diversity—knowledge that is not culture-bound and is widely recognized as significant. Over the years, anthropology has generated such knowledge through various theories and research methods. In particular, anthropologists obtain information through long-term, full-immersion fieldwork based on participant observation—illustrated by this photo of anthropologist Julia Jean (in the orange blouse), who is both observing *and* participating in a Hindu ritual at a temple for the Goddess Kamakhya in northeastern India.

How and Why Did Ethnographic Research Evolve?

In the early years of the discipline, many anthropologists documented traditional cultures they assumed would disappear due to disease, warfare, or acculturation imposed by colonialism, growing state power, or international market expansion. Some worked as government anthropologists, gathering data used to formulate policies concerning indigenous peoples or to help predict the behavior of enemies during wartime. After the colonial era ended in the 1960s, anthropologists established a code of ethics to ensure their research does not harm the groups they study. Today it is common for anthropologists to collaborate with minority groups and communities under siege and to assist in cultural revitalization efforts. Anthropological methods and knowledge are also applied to a range of globalization challenges, including economic development, conflict resolution, business, and politics. Finally, anthropologists do research to better understand what makes us tick and to explain cross-cultural differences and similarities.

What Are Ethnographic Research Methods?

Although anthropology relies on various research methods, its hallmark is extended fieldwork in a particular community or cultural group. This fieldwork features participant observation in which the researcher not only observes and documents the daily life of the community being studied, but also participates in that life. Typically, an anthropologist's initial fieldwork is carried out solo and lasts a full year. However, some anthropologists work in teams, and some field stays may be briefer or longer. It is not uncommon for anthropologists to return to their field sites periodically over the course of several decades.

How Is Research Related to Theory?

Data resulting from research, whether collected through fieldwork or another method, provide anthropologists with material needed to produce a comprehensive written (or filmed) *ethnography,* or description, of a culture. Moreover, it supplies details that are fundamental to *ethnology*—cross-cultural comparisons and theories that explain different cultural beliefs and behaviors. Beyond offering explanations, theories help us frame new questions that deepen our understanding of cultural phenomena. Anthropologists have come up with a wide variety of theories, some of which have been replaced or improved through the discovery of new information or better explanations. Gradually, much of what was puzzling or unknown about our complex species and its fascinating social and cultural diversity is exposed, revealed, or made clearer through theoretically informed research.

As briefly discussed in Chapter 1, cultural anthropology has two main scholarly components: *ethnography* (a detailed description of a particular culture primarily based on fieldwork) and *ethnology* (the study and analysis of different cultures from a comparative or historical point of view, utilizing ethnographic accounts and developing anthropological theories that help explain why certain important differences or similarities occur among groups).

Historically, anthropology focused on non-Western traditional peoples whose languages were not recorded in writing—people whose communication is often direct and face-to-face, and whose knowledge about the past is based primarily on oral tradition. Even in societies where writing exists, most of what is of interest to anthropologists is not documented. Thus, anthropologists have made a point of going to these places in person to see and experience people and their culture firsthand. This is called *fieldwork*.

Today, anthropological fieldwork takes place not only in small-scale communities in distant corners of the world, but also in modern urban neighborhoods in industrial or postindustrial societies. Anthropologists can be found doing fieldwork in a wide range of places and within a host of diverse groups, including transnational corporations, international migrant workers, and peoples scattered and dispersed because of wars, famines, poverty, or persecution.

In our unsettled and globalizing world, where long-standing boundaries between cultures are being erased, new social networks and cultural constructs are emerging, made possible by long-distance mass transportation and communication technology—including electronic media such as radio, television, cell phones, and the Internet. Anthropologists today are adjusting their research methods to better describe, explain, and understand these complex but fascinating dynamics in the rapidly changing human condition of the 21st century.

HISTORY OF ETHNOGRAPHIC RESEARCH AND ITS USES

Cultural anthropology emerged as a formal discipline during the heyday of colonialism (1870s–1950s) when many European anthropologists focused on the study of traditional peoples and their cultures in the colonies overseas. For instance, French anthropologists did most of their research in North and West Africa and Southeast Asia; British anthropologists in southern and East Africa;

urgent anthropology Ethnographic research that documents endangered cultures; also known as salvage ethnography.

Dutch anthropologists in what has become Indonesia, Western New Guinea, and Suriname; and Belgian anthropologists in the Congo of Africa.

Meanwhile, anthropologists in Canada and the United States focused primarily on their own countries' American Indian and Eskimo communities—usually residing on tracts of land known as reservations, or in remote Arctic villages. Because these indigenous groups are surrounded by a more dominant society that has settled on what used to be exclusively native lands, and they are no longer completely independent from that larger and more complex society's national government, their reservations are sometimes described as *internal colonies.*

At one time it was common practice to compare peoples still pursuing traditional lifeways, based on hunting, fishing, gathering, and/or small-scale farming or herding, with the ancient prehistoric ancestors of Europeans and to categorize the cultures of these traditional peoples as "primitive." Although anthropologists have long abandoned such ethnocentric terminology, many others continue to think and speak of these traditional cultures in terms of being "underdeveloped" or even "undeveloped." This misconception helped state societies, commercial enterprises, and other powerful outside groups justify expanding their activities and even invading the lands belonging to these peoples, often exerting overwhelming pressure on them to change their ancestral ways.

THOMSON AUDIO STUDY PRODUCTS Take advantage of the MP3-ready Audio Lecture Overviews and comprehensive audio glossary of key terms for each chapter. See the preface for information on how to access this on-the-go study and review tool.

Salvage Ethnography or Urgent Anthropology

In the disturbing and often violent historical context of expansion and domination by European and other powerful political states and commercial enterprises, the survival of thousands of traditional communities worldwide has been at stake. In fact, many of these threatened peoples have become physically extinct. Others survived but could not hold onto their territories or were forced to give up their way of life. Although anthropologists have seldom been able to prevent such tragic events, they did try to make a record of these cultural groups. This important early anthropological practice of documenting endangered cultures was called *salvage ethnography* and is now also known as **urgent anthropology.**

By the late 1800s, many European and North American museums were sponsoring anthropological expeditions to collect cultural artifacts and other material remains (including skulls, bones, utensils, weapons, clothing, and ceremonial objects), as well as vocabularies, myths, and other relevant cultural data. Some early anthropologists also began taking ethnographic photographs, and by the 1890s some began shooting documentary films or recording speech, songs, and music of these so-called vanishing peoples.

Although the first generation of anthropologists often began their careers working for museums, increasingly those coming later were academically trained in the emerging discipline and became active in newly founded anthropology departments. In North America, most of the latter did their fieldwork on tribal reservations where indigenous communities were falling apart in the face of disease, poverty, and despair brought on by pressures of forced culture change. These anthropologists interviewed American Indian elders still able to recall the ancestral way of life prior to their reservation confinement. They also collected oral histories, traditions, myths, legends, and other information, as well as old artifacts for research, preservation, and public display.

Beyond documenting social practices, beliefs, artifacts, and other disappearing cultural features, anthropologists also sought to reconstruct traditional ways of life that had already been abandoned and that were often only remembered by surviving elders. Although anthropological theories have come and gone during the past

hundred years, the plight of indigenous peoples struggling for cultural survival endures. Anthropologists can and still do contribute to that effort, assisting in cultural preservation efforts. In that work, utilizing a variety of new methods, they can tap into and continue to build on a professional legacy of salvage ethnography.

Acculturation Studies

Since the 1930s, anthropologists have been aware that the number of traditional cultures is quickly diminishing. In response, some began studying asymmetrical (sharply uneven) culture contact, or *acculturation*—the often disruptive process of culture change occurring in traditional societies coming in contact with more powerful state societies, in particular industrialized or capitalist societies.

Typically, as the dominant (often foreign) power establishes its superiority, local indigenous cultures are made to appear inferior, ridiculous, or otherwise not worth preserving—and are often forced to adopt the ways of the dominant society pressing in on them. Government-sponsored programs designed to force indigenous groups to abandon their traditional languages, religious beliefs, and social practices for those of mainstream society have ripped apart the unique cultural fabric of one group after another. These programs left

© Harald E. L. Prins

Until recently, Ayoreo Indian bands lived largely isolated in the Gran Chaco, a vast wilderness in South America's heartland. One by one, these migratory foragers have been forced to "come out" due to outside encroachment on their habitat. Today, most dispossessed Ayoreo Indians find themselves in different stages of acculturation. This photo shows Ayoreo women of Zapocó in Bolivia's forest. Dressed in Western hand-me-downs and surrounded by plastic from the modern society that is pressing in on them, they weave natural plant fibers into traditionally patterned bags to sell for cash, while the men make money by cutting trees for logging companies.

many indigenous families impoverished, demoralized, and desperate.

One of the first U.S. anthropologists to study acculturation was Margaret Mead in her 1932 fieldwork among the Omaha Indians of Nebraska. In that research, she focused on community breakdown and cultural disintegration of this traditional American Indian tribe. In the course of the 20th century, numerous other anthropologists carried out acculturation studies in Asia, Africa, Australia, Oceania, the Americas, and even in parts of Europe itself, thereby greatly contributing to our knowledge of complex and often disturbing processes of culture change.

Applied Anthropology

In identifying the disintegrating effects of asymmetrical culture contact, acculturation studies gave birth to *applied anthropology*—the use of anthropological knowledge and methods to solve practical problems in communities confronting new challenges. For societies in colonized territories or on reservations, government officials began looking at how anthropological research might help these traditional groups struggling with imposed economic, social, and political changes. Voicing the need for an applied anthropology to address the negative effects of colonial policies, British anthropologist Bronislaw Malinowski (born in Poland) commented: "The anthropologist who is unable to . . . register the tragic errors committed at times with the best intentions . . . remains an antiquarian covered with academic dust and in fool's paradise."[1]

In 1937 the British government set up an anthropological research institute in what is now Zambia to study the impact of international markets on Central Africa's traditional societies. In the next decade, anthropologists worked on a number of problem-oriented studies throughout Africa, including the disruptive effects of the mining industry and labor migration on domestic economies and cultures.

Facing similar problems in North America, the U.S. Bureau of Indian Affairs (BIA), which oversees federally recognized tribes on Indian reservations, established an applied anthropology branch in the mid-1930s. Beyond studying the problems of acculturation, the handful of applied anthropologists hired by the BIA were to identify practical culturally appropriate ways for the U.S. government to introduce social and economic development programs to reduce poverty, promote literacy, and solve a host of other problems on the reservations.

In 1941, the now international Society for Applied Anthropology was founded at Harvard University to promote scientific investigation of the principles controlling the relations of human beings to one another and the encouragement of their wide application. Today, a large number of professionally trained anthropologists specialize in applied research, working for a variety of local, regional, national, and international institutions, in particular nongovernmental organizations (NGOs), and are active on numerous fronts in every corner of the world.

Studying Cultures at a Distance

During World War II (1939–1945) and the early years of the Cold War (between capitalist countries led by the United States and communist countries led by Russia), some anthropologists shifted their attention from small-scale traditional communities to modern state societies. Aiming to discover basic personality traits, or psychological profiles, shared by the majority of the people in modern state societies, several U.S. and British anthropologists became involved in a wartime government program of "national character" studies. Such studies were believed to be significant in order to better understand and deal with the newly declared enemy states of Japan and Germany (in World War II) and later Russia and others.

Since on-location ethnographic fieldwork in enemy societies during wartime was impossible, and in most other foreign countries difficult if not prohibitive, Mead, Ruth Benedict, and other anthropologists developed innovative techniques for studying "culture at a distance"—through the analysis of newspapers, literature, photographs, and popular films. They also collected information through structured interviews with immigrants and refugees from the enemy nations, as well as foreigners from other countries.[2]

For instance, by investigating child-rearing practices, cultural beliefs, and attitudes, and by examining any documented material for the appearance of recurrent themes and values, these anthropologists tried to portray the national character of the peoples inhabiting these distant countries. This cultural information and anthropological understanding of foreign societies was also used for propaganda and psychological warfare. After the war, some of the information and insights based on such long-distance anthropological studies were found useful in temporarily governing the occupied territories and dealing with newly liberated populations in other parts of the world.

---

[1]In Mair, L. (1957). *An introduction to social anthropology* (p. 4). London: Oxford University Press. See also Malinowski, B. (1945). *The dynamics of culture change: An inquiry into race relations in Africa* (pp. 1–13). New Haven and London: Yale University Press.

[2]Mead, M., & Métraux, R. (Eds.). (1953). *The study of culture at a distance*. Chicago: University of Chicago Press.

Studying Contemporary State Societies

Although there were theoretical flaws in the national character studies and methodological problems in studying cultures at a distance, anthropological research on contemporary state societies was more than just a war-related endeavor. Even in the early decades of the discipline, when anthropologists devoted themselves primarily to researching non-Western small-scale communities, they recognized that a generalized understanding of human ideas and behavior depends upon knowledge of *all* cultures and peoples, including those in complex, large-scale industrial societies organized in political states, such as modern France or the United States. Thus, already during the years of the Great Depression (1930s), several anthropologists worked in their own countries in settings ranging from factories to farming communities and suburban neighborhoods.

One interesting example of an early anthropologist doing research on the home front is Hortense Powdermaker. After studying anthropology in London, this U.S. anthropologist did her first major ethnographic fieldwork among Melanesians in the southern Pacific. Then, returning to the United States, she researched a racially segregated town in Mississippi in the 1930s.[3] During the next decade, she focused on combating dominant society's racism against African Americans and other ethnic minorities.

While in the South, Powdermaker became keenly aware of the importance of the mass media in shaping people's worldviews.[4] To further explore this ideological force in modern culture, she cast her critical eye on the domestic film industry and did a year of fieldwork in Hollywood (1946–1947).

As Powdermaker was wrapping up her Hollywood research, several other anthropologists were launching other kinds of studies in large-scale societies. For instance, Benedict and Mead, convinced that governments and colonial administrations, as well as new global institutions such as the United Nations (founded in 1945), could and should benefit from anthropological insights, initiated a team project in comparative research on contemporary cultures based at Columbia University in New York (1947–1952).

In 1950, Swiss anthropologist Alfred Métraux put together an international team of U.S., French, and Brazilian researchers to study contemporary race relations in the South American country, Brazil. The project, sponsored by UNESCO (the United Nations Education, Science, and Culture Organization), was part of the UN's global campaign against racial prejudice and discrimination. Headquartered in Paris, Métraux selected Brazil as a research site primarily for comparative purposes. Like the United States, it was a former European colony with a large multi-ethnic population and a long history of black slavery. Brazil had abolished slavery twenty-five years later than the United States but had made much more progress in terms of its race relations. In contrast to the racially segregated United States, Brazil was believed to be an ideal international example of harmonious, tolerant, and overall positive cross-racial relations. The research findings yielded unexpected results, showing that dark-skinned Brazilians of African descent did face systemic social and economic discrimination—albeit not in the political and legal form of racial segregation as was the case in the United States at the time.[5]

In 1956 and 1957, U.S. anthropologist Julian Steward supervised an anthropological research team in developing countries such as Kenya, Nigeria, Peru, Mexico, Japan, Burma, Malaya, and Indonesia—to study the comparative impact of industrialization and urbanization upon these different populations. Other anthropologists launched similar projects in other parts of the world.

Peasant Studies

As anthropologists widened their scope to consider more fully the complex state societies that were impacting traditional small-scale indigenous communities central to early anthropological study, some zeroed in on peasant communities. Peasants represent an important category, standing midway between modern industrial society and traditional subsistence foragers, herders, farmers, and fishers. Forming part of larger, more complex societies, peasant communities exist worldwide, and peasants number in the many hundreds of millions.

Peasantry represents the largest social category of our species so far. Because peasant unrest over economic and social problems fuels political instability in many "developing countries," anthropological studies of these rural populations in Latin America, Africa, Asia, and elsewhere are considered significant and practical.[6] In addition to improving policies aimed at social and economic development in rural communities, anthropological peasant studies may offer insights into how to deal with peasants resisting challenges to their traditional way of life. Such anthropological research may be useful

[3]Powdermaker, H. (1939). *After freedom: A cultural study in the Deep South.* New York: Viking.

[4]Wolf, E. R., & Trager, G. L. (1971). Hortense Powdermaker 1900–1970. *American Anthropologist 73* (3), 784.

[5]Prins, H. E. L., & Krebs, E. (2006). Toward a land without evil: Alfred Métraux as UNESCO anthropologist 1948–1962. In *60 years of UNESCO history. Proceedings of the international symposium in Paris, 16–18 November 2005.* Paris: UNESCO.

[6]Redfield, R. (1953). *The primitive world and its transformations* (pp. 40–41). Ithaca, NY: Cornell University Press; Wolf, E. R. (1966). *Peasants* (p. 1). Englewood Cliffs, NJ: Prentice-Hall.

A peasant leader addresses a crowd in front of the presidential palace in Paraguay's capital city Asuncion at a massive protest rally against land dispossession.

in promoting social justice by helping to solve, manage, or avoid social conflicts and political violence, including rebellions and guerrilla warfare or insurgencies.[7]

Advocacy Anthropology

By the 1960s, European colonial powers had lost almost all of their overseas territorial possessions. Many anthropologists turned their attention to the newly independent countries in Africa and Asia, while others focused on South and Central America. However, as political unrest made fieldwork increasingly difficult in many parts of the world, significant numbers of anthropologists investigated important issues of culture change and conflict inside Europe and North America. Many of these issues, which remain focal points to this day, involve

immigrants and refugees who come from places where anthropologists have conducted research.

Some anthropologists have gone beyond studying such groups to playing a role in helping them adjust to their new circumstances—an example of applied anthropology. Others have become *advocates* for peasant communities, ethnic or religious minorities, or indigenous groups struggling to hold onto their ancestral lands, natural resources, and customary ways of life.

Although anthropologists have privately long championed the rights of indigenous peoples and other culture groups under siege, one of the first anthropological research projects explicitly and publicly addressing the quest for social justice and cultural survival took place among the Meskwaki, or Fox Indians, on their reservation in the state of Iowa (1948–1959). Based on long-term fieldwork with this North American Indian community, U.S. anthropologist Sol Tax challenged government-sponsored applied anthropological research projects and proposed instead that researchers work directly with "disadvantaged, exploited, and oppressed communities [to help *them*] identify and solve their [*own*] problems."[8]

Especially over the past few decades, anthropologists committed to social justice and human rights have become actively involved in efforts to assist indigenous groups, peasant communities, and ethnic minorities. Today, most anthropologists committed to community-based and politically involved research refer to their work as **advocacy anthropology.**

U.S. anthropologist Robert Hitchcock has practiced advocacy anthropology for over three decades. Specializing in development issues, he has focused primarily on land rights, as well as the social, economic, and cultural rights, of indigenous peoples in southern Africa—especially Bushmen (San, Basarwa) groups in Botswana. Hitchcock's work has involved helping Bushmen to ensure their rights to land—for foraging, pasturing, farming, and income-generation purposes—in the face of development projects aimed at setting aside land for the ranching, mining, or conservation interests of others. He helped draw up legislation on subsistence hunting in Botswana, making it the only country in Africa that allows broad-based hunting rights for indigenous peoples who forage for part of their livelihoods.[9]

[7]Firth, R. (1946). *Malay fishermen: Their peasant economy* (pp. ix–x). London: Kegan Paul, Trench, Trubner & Co., Ltd.; see also Wolf, E. R. (1969). *Peasant wars of the twentieth century* (pp. ix–xiii, 276–302). New York: Harper & Row.

advocacy anthropology Research that is community-based and politically involved.

[8]Field, L. W. (2004). Beyond "applied" anthropology. In T. Biolsi (Ed.), *A companion to the anthropology of American Indians* (pp. 472–489). Oxford: Blackwell Publishing. See also Lurie, N. O. (1973). Action anthropology and the American Indian. In *Anthropology and the American Indian: A symposium* (p. 6). San Francisco: Indian Historical Press.

[9]Hitchcock, R. K., & Enghoff, M. (2004). *Capacity-building of first people of the Kalahari, Botswana: An evaluation.* Copenhagen: International Work Group for Indigenous Affairs.

Today's most wide ranging advocacy anthropologist is Rodolfo Stavenhagen, special rapporteur on indigenous rights for the United Nations High Commission on Human Rights. A research professor at the Colegio de Mexico since 1965, he is founder and first president of the Mexican Academy of Human Rights. Dr. Stavenhagen leads investigations on the human rights situation and fundamental freedoms of indigenous peoples, discusses claims of injustice with government officials, and seeks solutions. Here he greets indigenous leader Lourdes Tiban after reporting on the situation of Ecuador's indigenous peoples at a 2006 conference in Quito.

AP Photo/Dolores Ochoa R.

Studying Up

Especially since the 1960s, growing numbers of anthropologists have been doing ethnographic research in their own countries. Largely because of a well-established tradition of participant observation in small-scale communities, most still prefer to do fieldwork in rural villages and urban neighborhoods among culturally distinctive groups such as immigrants or ethnic and religious minorities.

Nevertheless, because of anthropology's mission to gain a more comprehensive understanding of the human condition in its full cross-cultural range and complexity, not just in distant places or at the margins of our own societies, some scholars have urged ethnographic research in the centers of political and economic power in the world's dominant societies. Of particular note is U.S. anthropologist Laura Nader. Coining the term "study up," she has called upon anthropologists to focus on Western elites, government bureaucracies, global corporations, philanthropic foundations, media empires, business clubs, and so on.

Of course, studying up is easier said than done, because it is a formidable challenge to do participant observation in such well-guarded circles. And when these elites are confronted with research projects or findings not of their liking, they have the capacity and political power to stop or seriously obstruct the research or the dissemination of its results.

Globalization and Multi-Sited Ethnography

As noted in Chapter 1, the impact of globalization is everywhere. Of relevance to anthropologists is the fact that distant localities are becoming linked in such a way that local events and situations are shaped by forces and activities occurring thousands of miles away, and vice versa. Connected by modern transportation, world trade, finance capital, transnational labor pools, and information superhighways, even the most geographically remote communities are becoming increasingly interdependent. Indeed, all of humanity now lives in what we refer to in this text as a "globalscape"—a worldwide interconnected landscape with multiple intertwining and overlapping peoples and cultures on the move.

One of the many consequences of globalization is the formation of *diasporic* populations (*diaspora* is a Greek word, originally meaning "scattering"), living and working far from their original homelands. While this has left some people feeling displaced and fragmented, others are transcending vast distances and staying in touch with family and friends from home with the aid of modern transportation and communication technologies. Through e-mail, Internet forums, and World Wide Web access to local news, geographically dispersed individuals spend part of their lives in cyberspace, dubbed "ethnoscapes" by anthropologist Arjun Appadurai from

India.[10] This electronically mediated environment enables people who are far from home to remain informed, to maintain their social networks, and even to hold onto a shared sense of ethnic identity that distinguishes them from the collectivity of individuals with whom they share their daily routines in actual geographic space.

Globalization has given rise to a new trend in anthropological research and analysis known as **multi-sited ethnography**—the investigation and documentation of peoples and cultures embedded in the larger structures of a globalizing world, utilizing a range of methods in various locations of time and space. Engaged in such mobile ethnography, researchers seek to capture the emerging dimension of the global by following individual actors, organizations, objects, images, stories, conflicts, and even pathogens as they move about in various interrelated transnational situations and locations.[11]

An example of multi-sited ethnographic research on a diasporic ethnic group is a recent study on transnational Chinese identities by Chinese American anthropologist Andrea Louie. Louie's fieldwork carried her to an array of locations in San Francisco, Hong Kong, and southern China—including her ancestral home in the Cantonese village Tiegang in Guangdong Province. Her paternal great grandfather left the village in the 1840s, crossing the Pacific Ocean to work on railroad construction during the California Gold Rush. But other family members remained in the area. Investigating Chinese identities from different and changing perspectives, Louie described her research like this:

> My fieldwork on Chinese identities employed a type of mobile [ethnography] aimed at examining various parts of a "relationship" being forged anew across national boundaries that draws on metaphors of shared heritage and place. In my investigation of "Chineseness" I conducted participant observation and interviews in San Francisco with Chinese American participants of the In Search of Roots program,[12] as well as later

Courtesy of Andrea Louie

In her explorations on the construction of Chinese identities in the context of U.S. and Chinese racial and multicultural politics, anthropologist Andrea Louie (center) has done multi-sited research in St. Louis, San Francisco, Hong Kong, and China. Here she sits with a couple and the daughter they adopted from China in 1995, who have been part of her research. (The child on Louie's lap is her own.)

in China when they visited their ancestral villages and participated in government-sponsored Youth Festivals. In China, I researched from a number of bases the shifting attitudes of Chinese living in the Pearl River Delta region of Guangdong, including a village in the emigrant region of Zhongshan County, the Taishan region, and a middle school in the Special Economic Zone of Shenzhen. I interviewed people in their homes, and apartments; in cafes, culture centers, and MacDonald's restaurants; and in rural Chinese villages and on jet planes, focusing on various moments and contexts of interaction within which multiple and often discrepant discourses of Chineseness are brought together. . . .[13]

Also emerging in multi-sited ethnography are greater interdisciplinary approaches to fieldwork, bringing in theoretical ideas and research methods from cul-

---

[10]Appadurai, A. (1996). *Modernity at large: Cultural dimensions of globalization.* Minneapolis: University of Minnesota Press.

[11]Marcus, G. (1995). Ethnography in/of the world system: The emergence of multi-sited ethnography. *Annual review of anthropology 24,* 95–117; Robben, A. C. G. M., & Sluka, J. A. (Eds.). (2007). *Ethnographic fieldwork: An anthropological reader* (Part VII). Malden, MA: Blackwell Publishers.

[12]This program, run by organizations in Guangzhou and San Francisco, provides an opportunity for young adults (ages 17 to 25) of Cantonese descent to visit their ancestral villages in China.

multi-sited ethnography The investigation and documentation of peoples and cultures embedded in the larger structures of a globalizing world, utilizing a range of methods in various locations of time and space.

[13]Louie, A. (2004). *Chineseness across borders: Renegotiating Chinese identities in China and the United States* (pp. 8–9). Durham and London: Duke University Press.

tural studies, media studies, and mass communication, among others. One example is the emergence of ethnographic studies of online "imagined communities" or *cyberethnography.*

Even in the fast-changing, globalizing world of the 21st century, core ethnographic research methods developed about a century ago continue to be relevant and revealing. New technologies have been added to the anthropologist's toolkit, but the hallmarks of our discipline—holistic research through fieldwork with participant observation—is still a valued and productive tradition. Having presented a sweeping historical overview of shifting anthropological research challenges and strategies, we turn now to the topic of research methods.

DOING ETHNOGRAPHY: CULTURAL ANTHROPOLOGY RESEARCH METHODS

Every culture comprises underlying rules or standards that are rarely obvious. A major challenge to the anthropologist is to identify and analyze those rules. Fundamental to the effort is **ethnographic fieldwork**—extended on-location research to gather detailed and in-depth information on a society's customary ideas, values, and practices through participation in its collective social life.

While it is true that early anthropologists worked primarily in small-scale societies and that the scope of social-cultural anthropology has since expanded to include urban life in complex industrial and postindustrial societies, ethnographic fieldwork methods developed in the early stage of the discipline continue to be central to anthropological research in all types of communities. For instance, they still feature personal observation of and participation in the everyday activities of the community, along with interviews, mapping, collection of genealogical data, and recording of sounds and visual images—all toward the gathering and analysis of data. However, it all begins with selecting a research site and a research problem or question.

Site Selection and Research Question

Anthropologists usually work outside their own culture, society, or ethnic group, most often in a foreign country. Although it has much to offer, anthropological study within one's own society may present special problems, as described by noted British anthropologist Sir Edmund Leach:

> Surprising though it may seem, fieldwork in a cultural context of which you already have intimate first hand experience seems to be

much more difficult than fieldwork which is approached from the naïve viewpoint of a total stranger. When anthropologists study facets of their own society their vision seems to become distorted by prejudices which derive from private rather than public experience.[14]

For this reason, most successful anthropological studies of societies to which the researchers themselves belong are done by individuals who first worked in some other culture. The more one learns of other cultures, the more one gains a fresh and more revealing perspective on one's own.

But wherever the site, the research requires advance planning. This includes finding funding and securing permission from the community to be studied (and, where mandated, from government officials as well). If possible, researchers make a preliminary trip to the field site to make these and other arrangements before moving there for more extended research. After spending time exploring the local conditions and circumstances, they have the opportunity to better define their specific research question or problem. For instance, what is the psychological impact of a new highway on members of a traditionally isolated farming community? Or how does the introduction of new electronic media such as cell phones influence long-established gender relations in cultures with religious restrictions on social contact between men and women?

Preparatory Research

Before heading into the field, anthropologists do preparatory research. This includes delving into any existing written, visual, or sound information available about the people and place one has chosen to study. It may involve contacting and interviewing others who have some knowledge about or experience with the community, region, or country.

Because anthropologists must be able to communicate with the people they have chosen to study, they will also have to learn the language used in the community selected for fieldwork. Because many of the more than 6,000 languages currently spoken in the world have already been recorded and written down, especially during the past 100 years or so, it is possible to learn some foreign languages prior to fieldwork. However, as in the

[14]Leach, E. (1982). *Social anthropology* (p. 124). Glasgow: Fontana Paperbacks.

ethnographic fieldwork Extended on-location research to gather detailed and in-depth information on a society's customary ideas, values, and practices through participation in its collective social life.

early days of the discipline, some of today's anthropologists do research among peoples whose native languages have not yet been written down. In such a case, they may find bilingual or multilingual individuals to help them gain some basic linguistic proficiency. Another possibility is to first learn an already recorded and closely related language, which may provide the researcher with some elementary communication skills during the first phase of the actual fieldwork.

Finally, anthropologists prepare for fieldwork by studying theoretical, historical, ethnographic, and other literature relevant to the research problem to be investigated. For instance, anthropologists interested in the problem of human violence, both between and within groups, will read studies describing and theoretically explaining conflicts such as wars, feuds, vengeance killing, and so on. Having delved into the existing literature, they may then formulate a theoretical framework and research question to guide them in their fieldwork. Such was the case when U.S. anthropologist Napoleon Chagnon applied natural selection theory to his study of violence within Yanomami Indian communities in South America's tropical rainforest, suggesting that males with

an aggressive reputation as killers are reproductively more successful than those without such a status.[15]

Christopher Boehm took a different theoretical approach in his research on blood revenge among Slavic mountain people in Montenegro. He framed his research question in terms of the ecological function of this violent tradition, as it regulated relations between groups competing for survival in a harsh environment with scarce natural resources.[16]

Participant Observation

Once in the field, anthropologists are anything but passive onlookers. They rely on *participant observation*—a research method in which one learns about a group's beliefs and behaviors through social participation and personal observation within the community, as well as interviews and discussion with individual members of

---

[15]Chagnon, N. A. (1988). Life histories, blood revenge, and warfare in a tribal population. *Science 239*, 935–992.

[16]Boehm, C. (1984). *Blood revenge*. Lawrence: University of Kansas Press.

During fieldwork, anthropologists use computers not only for recording and processing data, but as a means of communicating with the peoples being studied. Here we see ecologist James Kremer and anthropologist Stephen Lansing (behind Kremer) who have researched the traditional rituals and network of water temples linked to the irrigation management of rice fields on the island of Bali in Indonesia. They are explaining a computer simulation of this system to the high priest of the supreme water temple, as other temple priests look on. Located on the crater rim above the caldera and lake of Mount Batur, this temple is associated with the Goddess of the Crater Lake. Every year people from hundreds of villages bring offerings here, expressing gratitude to this deity for the gift of water.

the group over an extended stay in the community. Although researchers may focus on a particular cultural aspect or issue, they will consider the culture as a whole for the sake of context. This requires being tuned in to nearly countless details of daily life—both the ordinary and the extraordinary. By taking part in community life anthropologists learn why and how events are organized and carried out. Through alert and sustained participation—carefully watching, questioning, listening, and analyzing over a period of time—they can usually identify, explain, and often predict a group's behavior.

Ethnographic Tools and Aids

An anthropologist's most essential ethnographic tools in the field are notebooks, pen/pencil, camera, sound recorder, and, increasingly, a laptop computer sometimes equipped with a variety of specific data processing programs. Beyond such tools of the trade, he or she needs to be able to socially and psychologically adapt to a strange community with a different way of life. Keen personal observation skills are also essential. One must cultivate the ability to perceive collective life in the other culture with *all* the senses—sight, touch, smell, taste, and hearing.

When participating in an unfamiliar culture, anthropologists are often helped by one or more generous individuals in the village or neighborhood. They may also be taken in by a family and through participation in the daily routine of a household, they will soon become familiar with the community's basic shared cultural features.

Anthropologists may also formally enlist the assistance of **key consultants**—members of the society being studied, who provide information that helps researchers understand the meaning of what they observe. (Early anthropologists referred to such individuals as *informants*.) Just as parents guide a child toward proper behavior, so do these insiders help researchers unravel the mysteries of what at first is a strange world full of puzzles. To compensate local individuals for their help in making anthropologists feel welcome in the community and gain access to the treasure troves of inside information, fieldworkers may thank them for their time and expertise with goods, services, or cash.

Data Gathering: The Ethnographer's Approach

Information collected by ethnographers falls in two main categories: quantitative and qualitative data. **Quantitative data** consist of statistical or measurable information, such as: population density, demographic composition of people and animals, and the number and size of houses; the hours worked per day; the types and quantities of crops grown; the amount of carbohydrates or animal protein consumed per individual; the quantity of wood, dung, or other material for fuel used to cook food or heat dwellings; the number of children born out of wedlock; the ratio of spouses born and raised within or outside the community, and so on.

Qualitative data concern nonstatistical information about such features as settlement patterns, natural resources, social networks of kinship relations, customary beliefs and practices, personal life histories, and so on. Often, these nonquantifiable data are the most important part of ethnographic research because they capture the essence of a culture and provide us with deeper insights into the unique lives of different peoples, making us truly understand what, why, and how they feel, think, and act in their own distinctive ways.

Beyond the generalities of participant observation, how exactly do ethnographers gather data? Field methods include formal and informal interviewing, mapping, collection of genealogical data, and recording sounds and images. Cultural anthropologists may also use surveys, but not in the way you might think. Below we touch on several key methods for collecting information.

Taking Surveys

Unlike many other social scientists, anthropologists do not usually go into the field equipped with prefigured surveys or questionnaires; rather, they recognize that there are many things that can be discovered only by keeping an open mind while thoughtfully watching, listening, participating, and asking questions. As fieldwork proceeds, anthropologists sort their complex impressions and observations into a meaningful whole, sometimes by formulating and testing limited or low-level hypotheses, but just as often by making use of imagination or intuition and following up on hunches. What is important is that the results are constantly checked for accuracy and consistency, for if the parts fail to fit together in a way that is internally coherent, it may be that a mistake has been made, and further inquiry is necessary.

This is not to say that anthropologists do not conduct surveys. Some do. But these are just one part of a much larger research strategy that includes a considerable amount of qualitative data as well as quantitative.

key consultant A member of the society being studied, who provides information that helps researchers understand the meaning of what they observe; early anthropologists referred to such individuals as informants.
quantitative data Statistical or measurable information, such as demographic composition, the types and quantities of crops grown, or the ratio of spouses born and raised within or outside the community.
qualitative data Nonstatistical information such as personal life stories and customary beliefs and practices.

Also, in ethnographic fieldwork, surveys are usually carried out after one has spent enough time on location to have gained the community's confidence and to know how to compose a questionnaire with categories that are culturally relevant.

Two studies of a village in Peru illustrate the contrast between anthropological and other social science approaches. One was carried out by a sociologist who, after conducting a survey by questionnaire, concluded that people in the village invariably worked together on one another's privately owned plots of land. By contrast, a cultural anthropologist who lived in the village for over a year (including the brief period when the sociologist did his study) witnessed that particular practice only once. The anthropologist's long-term participant observation revealed that although the idea of labor exchange relations was important to the people's sense of themselves, it was not a common economic practice.[17]

The point here is *not* that all sociological research is flawed, and all anthropological research is solid. It is that relying exclusively or even primarily on questionnaire surveys is a risky business, no matter who does it. That is because questionnaires all too easily embody the concepts and categories of the researcher, who is an outsider, rather than those of the people being studied. Even where this is not a problem, questionnaire surveys alone are not good ways of identifying causal relationships. They tend to concentrate on what is measurable, answerable, and acceptable as a question, rather than probing the less obvious and more complex qualitative aspects of society or culture.

Moreover, for a host of reasons—fear, caution, wishful thinking, ignorance, exhaustion, hostility, hope of benefit—people may give partial, false, or self-serving information.[18] Keeping culture-bound ideas out of research methods, as illustrated through the example of standardized questionnaires, is an important point in all ethnographic research.

Interviewing

Asking questions is fundamental to ethnographic fieldwork and takes place in **informal interviews** (unstructured, open-ended conversations in everyday life) and **formal interviews** (structured question/answer sessions

In addition to using photographs for cultural documentation, anthropologists sometimes use them during fieldwork as eliciting devices, sharing pictures of cultural objects or activities for example, to encourage locals to talk about and explain what they see. Here anthropologists Nadine Peacock and Bob Bailey show photos to Efe people in the Ituri Forest in Congo, Africa.

carefully notated as they occur and based on prepared questions). Informal interviews may be carried out anytime and anywhere—on horseback, in a canoe, by a cooking fire, during ritual events, while walking through the community with a local inhabitant, and the list goes on. Such casual exchanges are essential, for it is often in these conversations that people share most freely. Moreover, questions put forth in formal interviews typically grow out of cultural knowledge and insights gained during informal ones.

Getting people to open up is an art born of a genuine interest in both the information and the person who is sharing it. It requires dropping all assumptions and cultivating the ability to *really* listen. It may even require a willingness to be the village idiot by asking simple questions to which the answers may seem obvious. Also, effective interviewers learn early on that numerous followup questions are vital since first answers may mask truth rather than reveal it. Questions generally fall into

---

[17]Chambers, R. (1983). *Rural development: Putting the last first* (p. 51). New York: Longman.

[18]Sanjek, R. (1990). On ethnographic validity. In R. Sanjek (Ed.), *Field notes* (p. 395). Ithaca, NY: Cornell University Press.

informal interview An unstructured, open-ended conversation in everyday life.
formal interview A structured question/answer session carefully notated as it occurs and based on prepared questions.

one of two categories: broad, *open-ended questions,* such as, Can you tell me about your childhood?, and *closed questions* seeking specific pieces of information, such as, Where and when were you born?

In ethnographic fieldwork, interviews are used to collect a vast range of cultural information, from life histories, genealogies, and myths to craft techniques and midwife procedures, to beliefs concerning everything from illness to food taboos. Genealogical data can be especially useful, as it provides information about a range of social practices (such as cousin marriage), worldview (such as ancestor worship), political relations (such as alliances), and economic arrangements (such as hunting or harvesting on clan-owned lands).

Researchers employ numerous **eliciting devices**—activities and objects used to draw out individuals and encourage them to recall and share information. There are countless examples of this: taking a walk with a local and asking about a legend, inviting the person to comment on it or to offer another; sharing details about one's own family and neighborhood and inviting a telling in return; joining in a community activity and asking a local to explain the practice and why they are doing it; taking and sharing photographs of cultural objects or activities and asking locals to explain what they see in the pictures.

Mapping

Because many anthropologists still do fieldwork among traditional peoples in all corners of the earth, they may find themselves in distant places about which there is little detailed geographic knowledge. Although cartographers may already have mapped the region, standard maps seldom show geographic and spatial features that are culturally significant to the people living there. People inhabiting areas that form part of their ancestral homeland have a particular understanding of the area and their own names for local places. These native names may convey essential geographic information, describing the distinctive features of a locality such as its physical appearance, its specific dangers, or its precious resources.

Some place names may derive from certain political realities such as headquarters, territorial boundaries, and so on. Others may make sense only in the cultural context of a local people's worldview as recounted in their myths, legends, songs, or other narrative traditions. Thus, to truly understand the lay of the land, anthropologists may have to make their own detailed geographic maps documenting culturally relevant geographic features in the landscape inhabited by the people they study.

Especially since the early 1970s, anthropologists have become involved in indigenous land use and occupancy studies for various reasons, including the documenta-

tion of traditional land claims. Information based on a combination of local oral histories, early written descriptions of explorers, traders, missionaries, and other visitors, combined with data obtained from archaeological excavations may be collected as general background for individual map biographies.

One such ethnogeographic research project took place in northwestern Canada, during the planning stage of the building of the Alaska Highway natural gas pipeline. Since the line would cut directly though Native lands, local indigenous community leaders and federal officials insisted that a study be done to determine how the new construction would affect indigenous inhabitants. Canadian anthropologist Hugh Brody, one of the researchers in this ethnogeographic study, explained: "These maps are the key to the studies and their greatest contribution. Hunters, trappers, fishermen, and berry-pickers mapped out all the land they had ever used in their lifetimes, encircling hunting areas species by species, marking gathering location and camping sites—everything their life on the land had entailed that could be marked on a map."[19]

In addition to mapping the local place names and geographic features, anthropologists may also map out information relevant to the local subsistence such as animal migration routes, favorite fishing areas, places where medicinal plants can be harvested or firewood cut, and so on.

Today, by means of the technology known as global positioning system (GPS), researchers can measure precise distances by triangulating the travel time of radio signals from various orbiting satellites. They can create maps that pinpoint human settlement locations and the layout of dwellings, gardens, public spaces, water holes, pastures, surrounding mountains, rivers, lakes, seashores, islands, swamps, forests, deserts, and any other relevant feature in the regional environment.

To store, edit, analyze, integrate, and display this geographically referenced spatial information, some anthropologists use cartographic digital technology, known as geographic information systems (GIS). GIS makes it possible to map the geographic features and natural resources in a certain environment—and to link these data to ethnographic information about population density and distribution, social networks of kinship relations, seasonal patterns of land use, private or collective claims of ownership, travel routes, sources of water, and so on. With GIS researchers can also integrate infor-

---

[19]Brody, H. (1981). *Maps and dreams* (p. 147). New York: Pantheon Books.

eliciting device An activity or object used to draw out individuals and encourage them to recall and share information.

Anthropologists of Note

Gregory Bateson (1904–1980) ▪ Margaret Mead (1901–1978)

From 1936 to 1938 Margaret Mead and Gregory Bateson did collaborative ethnographic fieldwork in Bali. Bateson, Mead's husband at the time, was a British anthropologist trained by Alfred C. Haddon, who led the 1898 Torres Strait expedition and is credited with making the first ethnographic film in the field. During their stay in Bali, Bateson took about 25,000 photographs and shot 22,000 feet of motion picture film. Afterward, the couple co-authored the photographic ethnography *Balinese Character: A Photographic Analysis* (1942).

That same year, Bateson worked as an anthropological film analyst studying German motion pictures. Soon Mead and a few other anthropologists became involved in thematic analysis of foreign fictional films. She later compiled a number of such visual anthropology studies in a co-edited volume titled *The Study of Culture at a Distance* (1953).

Mead became a tireless promoter of the scholarly use of ethnographic

Library of Congress

In 1938, after two years of fieldwork in Bali, Margaret Mead and Gregory Bateson began research in Papua New Guinea, where they staged this photograph of themselves to highlight the importance of cameras as part of the ethnographic toolkit. (Note camera on tripod behind Mead and other cameras atop the desk.)

photography and film. In 1960, the year the portable sync-sound film camera was invented, Mead was serving as president of the American Anthropology Association. In her presidential address at the association's annual gathering, she pointed out what she saw as shortcom-

ings in the discipline and urged anthropologists to use cameras more effectively.[a] Chiding her colleagues for not fully utilizing new technological developments, she complained that anthropology had come "to depend on words, and words, and words."

Mead's legacy is commemorated in numerous venues, including the Margaret Mead Film Festival hosted annually since 1977 by the American Museum of Natural History in New York City. Thus it was fitting that during the Margaret Mead Centennial celebrations in 2001 the American Anthropological Association endorsed a landmark visual media policy statement urging academic committees to consider ethnographic visuals—and not just ethnographic writing—when evaluating scholarly output of academics up for hiring, promotion, and tenure.

---

[a]Mead, M. (1960). Anthropology among the sciences. *American Anthropologist 63,* 475–482.

---

mation about beliefs, myths, legends, songs, and other culturally relevant data associated with distinct locations. Moreover, they can create interactive inquiries for analysis of research data as well as natural and cultural resource management.[20]

Photographing and Filming

Most anthropologists use cameras for fieldwork, as well as notepads, computers, or sound recording devices to record their observations. In fact, photography has been instrumental in anthropological research for more than a century. For instance, German-born U.S. anthropologist Franz Boas already took photographs during his first fieldwork among the Inuit in the Canadian Arctic in the early 1880s. And just a few years after the invention of

the moving picture camera in 1894, anthropologists began filming traditional dances by indigenous Australians and other ethnographic subjects of interest.

Especially following the invention of the portable synchronous-sound camera in 1960, ethnographic filmmaking took off. New technological developments were making it increasingly obvious that visual media could serve a wide range of cross-cultural research purposes. Some anthropologists employed still photography in community surveys and elicitation techniques. Others turned to film to document and research traditional patterns of nonverbal communication such as body language and social space use. Cameras have also been (and continue to be) instrumental in documenting the disappearing world of traditional foragers, herders, and farmers surviving in remote places. The Anthropologists of Note feature details the long history of such equipment in anthropology.

---

[20]Schoepfle, M. (2001). Ethnographic resource inventory and the National Park Service. *Cultural Resource Management 5,* 1–7.

Challenges of Ethnographic Fieldwork

While ethnographic fieldwork offers a range of opportunities to gain better and deeper insight into the community being studied, it comes with a Pandora's box of challenges. Certainly it involves at least a measure of strain and pain, for it usually requires researchers to step out of their cultural comfort zone into an unknown world that is sometimes unsettling. As touched upon in Chapter 1, anthropologists in the field are likely to face a wide array of challenges—physical, social, mental, political, and ethical.

Among the numerous mental challenges anthropologists commonly face are culture shock, loneliness, feeling like an ignorant outsider, and being socially awkward in a new cultural setting. Physical challenges typically include adjusting to unfamiliar food, climate, and hygiene conditions, along with needing to be constantly alert because anything that is happening or being said may be significant to one's research. In addition to engaging fully in work and social activities with the community, ethnographers must spend considerable time doing a host of other things, such as interviewing, making copious notes, and analyzing data.

In the following paragraphs we offer details on some of the most common personal struggles anthropologists face in the field.

Gaining Social Acceptance in the Community

Having decided where to do ethnographic research and what to focus on, anthropologists embark on the journey to their field site. Because few choose to do research in their own home communities, fieldwork almost always involves making new social contacts with strangers who do not know who you are, why you have come, or what you want from them. In short, a visiting anthropologist is as much a mystery to those she or he intends to study as the group is to the researcher.

Although there is no sure way of predicting how one will be received, it is certain that success in ethnographic fieldwork depends on mutual goodwill and the ability to develop friendships and other meaningful social relations. As New Zealand anthropologist Jeffrey Sluka noted, "The classic image of successful rapport and good fieldwork relations in cultural anthropology is that of the ethnographer who has been 'adopted' or named by the tribe or people he or she studies."[21]

Among the numerous ethnographic examples of anthropologists being adopted by a family, lineage, or clan is the case of Canadian anthropologist Richard Lee, adopted by a group of Ju/'hoansi (Bushmen) foragers in the Kalahari Desert. He describes the informal way in which this took place:

> One day in March 1964, I was visiting a !Xabe village, when Hwan//a, a woman about my age who was married to one of the Tswana Headman Isak's three sons, playfully began to call me, "Uncle, uncle, /Tontah, come see me."
>
> Puzzled, I drew closer; until that time the Ju had referred to me simply as the White Man (/Ton) or the bearded one. . . . Hwan//a smiled and said, "You are all alone here and I have no children, so I will name you /Tontah after my *tsu* /Tontah who is dead, and, as I have named you, you shall call me mother."
>
> Pleased, I asked Hwan//a to tell me how she decided on the name /Tontah. She explained that I was a European, a "/ton," and the traditional Ju name /Tontah sounds like it. Since her late *tsu* had no namesake, she decided to name me /Tontah to do honor to him and to my exotic status. [This] was the famous name relationship—the Ju/'hoan custom of naming everyone after an older person according to a repertoire of personal names [and] I was excited to be named in this way. The name stuck. Soon people all over the Dobe area were calling me /Tontah.[22]

Anthropologists adopted into networks of kinship relations not only gain social access and certain rights but also assume a range of social obligations associated with their new kinship status. These relationships can be deep and enduring—as illustrated by Smithsonian anthropologist William Crocker's description of his 1991 return to the Canela community after a twelve-year absence. He had lived among these Amazonian Indians in Brazil for a total of 66 months from the 1950s through the 1970s. When he stepped out of the single-motor missionary plane that had brought him back, he was quickly surrounded by Canela:

> Once on the ground, I groped for names and terms of address while shaking many hands. Soon my Canela mother Tutkhwey (dove-woman), pulled me over to the shade of a plane's wing and pushed me down to a mat on the ground. She put both hands on my shoulders and, kneeling beside me, her head by mine, cried out words of mourning in a loud yodeling manner. Tears and phlegm dripped onto my shoulder and knees. According to a custom now abandoned by the younger women, she was cry-

[21]Sluka, J. A. (2007). Fieldwork relations and rapport: Introduction. In A. C. G. M. Robben & J. A. Sluka (Eds.), *Ethnographic fieldwork: An anthropological reader* (p. 122). Malden, MA: Blackwell Publishers.

[22]Lee, R. B. (1993). *The Dobe Ju/'hoansi* (p. 61). Ft. Worth: Harcourt Brace.

U.S. anthropologist William Crocker did fieldwork among Canela Indians in Brazil over several decades. He still visits the community regularly. In this 1964 photograph, a Canela woman (M~i~i- kw'ej, or Alligator Woman) gives him a traditional haircut while other members of the community look on. She is the wife of his adoptive Canela "brother" and therefore a "wife" to Crocker in Canela kinship terms. Among the Canela, it was improper for a mother, sister, or daughter to cut a man's hair.

ing for the loss of a grown daughter, Tsep-khwey (bat-woman), as well as for my return.[23]

Since that 1991 reunion, Crocker has visited the Canela community every other year—always receiving a warm welcome and staying with locals. Although many anthropologists are successful in gaining social acceptance and even adoption status in communities where they do participant observation, they rarely go completely native and abandon their own homeland. For even after long stays in a community, after learning to behave appropriately and communicate well, few fieldworkers become true insiders.

Political Challenges

Political challenges during fieldwork include the possibility of being caught in rivalries and used unwittingly by factions within the community; the anthropologist may be viewed with suspicion by government authorities who may suspect the anthropologist is a foreign spy.

U.S. anthropologist June Nash, for instance, has faced serious political and personal challenges doing fieldwork in various Latin American communities experiencing violent changes. As an outsider, Nash tried to avoid becoming embroiled in local conflicts but could not maintain her position as an impartial observer while researching a tin mining community in the Bolivian highlands. When the conflict between local miners and bosses controlling the armed forces became violent, Nash found herself in a revolutionary setting in which miners viewed her tape

recorder as an instrument of espionage and suspected her of being a CIA agent.[24]

All anthropologists face the overriding challenge of winning the trust that allows people to be themselves and share an unmasked version of their culture with a newcomer. Some do not succeed in meeting this challenge. So it was with U.S. anthropologist Lincoln Keiser in his difficult fieldwork in the remote town of Thull, situated in the Hindu Kush Mountains of northwestern Pakistan. Keiser ventured there to explore customary blood feuding among a Kohistani tribal community of 6,000 Muslims making their living by a mix of farming and herding in the rugged region. However, many of the people he had traveled so far to study did not appreciate his presence. As Keiser recounted, many of the fiercely independent tribesmen in this area, "where the AK-47 [sub-machine gun] symbolizes the violent quality of male social relations," treated him as a foreign "infidel" and with great disdain and suspicion:

> Throughout my stay in Thull, many people remained convinced I was a creature sent by the devil to harm the community. The stories of my alleged evil doings always amazed me, both in their number and detail. [Doing fieldwork in Thull] was a test I failed, for a *jirga* [political council] of my most vocal opponents ultimately forced me to leave Thull three months before I had planned. . . . Obviously, I have difficulty claiming the people of Thull as "my people"

[23]Crocker, W. H., & Crocker, J. G. (2004). *The Canela: Kinship, ritual, and sex in an Amazonian tribe* (p. 1). Belmont, CA: Wadsworth.

[24]Nash, J. (1976). Ethnology in a revolutionary setting. In M. A. Rynkiewich & J. P. Spradley (Eds.), *Ethics and anthropology: Dilemmas in fieldwork* (pp. 148–166). New York: Wiley.

because so many of them never ceased to despise me. . . . Still, I learned from being hated.[25]

Challenges Linked to Gender, Age, Ideology, Ethnicity, and Skin Color

Keiser's fieldwork challenges stemmed in part from his non-Muslim religious identity, marking him as an outsider in the local community of the faithful. Gender, age, ethnicity, and skin color can also impact a researcher's access to a community. For instance, African American anthropologist Norris Brock-Johnson encountered social obstacles while doing fieldwork in the American Midwest, but his dark skin color helped him gain "admission to the world of black Caribbean shipwrights" on the island of Bequia where he studied traditional boatmaking.[26]

In earlier days, when anthropologist Hortense Powdermaker did fieldwork in a Mississippi town during the early 1930s, she became sharply aware of her own status as a white person in what was then a racially segregated state in the Christian conservative center of the southern Bible Belt. Although she could not change her skin color, she did conceal her Jewish identity to avoid problems.[27]

With respect to gender, male ethnographers may face prohibitions or severe restrictions in interviewing women or observing certain women's activities. Similarly, a female researcher may not find ready reception among males in communities with gender-segregation traditions.

And there are other political, personal, and ethical dilemmas facing anthropologists doing fieldwork: What does the researcher do if faced with a troubling or even reprehensible cultural practice? How does the researcher deal with demands for food supplies and/or Western medicines? What about the temptation to use deception to gain vital information? Finally, all ethnographers must grapple with the very real challenge of subjectivity—his or her own and that of members in the community being studied.

The Problem of Subjectivity: Things Are Not as They Seem

Whether working near home or abroad, when endeavoring to identify the rules that underlie each culture, ethnographers must contend with bias or subjectivity—with the fact that perceptions of reality vary. Consider, for example, the following discussion of exogamy (marriage outside one's own group) among the Trobriand Islanders in Melanesia, as described by Polish anthropologist Bronislaw Malinowski:

> If you were to inquire into the matter among the Trobrianders, you would find that . . . the natives show horror at the idea of violating the rules of exogamy and that they believe that sores, diseases, even death might follow clan incest. [But] from the viewpoint of the native libertine, *suvasova* (the breach of exogamy) is indeed a specially interesting and spicy form of erotic experience.[28]

Malinowski himself determined that although such breaches did occur, they were much less frequent than gossip would have it. Had he relied solely on what the Trobrianders told him, his description of their culture would have been flawed. The same sort of discrepancy between cultural ideals and the way people actually behave can be found in any culture, as illustrated in our Chapter 1 discussion of William Rathje's Garbage Project, which revealed that people consumed notably more alcohol than they said they did. Because of this, an anthropologist must be extremely careful in describing a culture. To do so accurately, he or she needs to seek out and consider three kinds of data:

1. The people's own understanding of their culture and the general rules they share—that is, their ideal sense of the way their own society ought to be.
2. The extent to which people believe they are observing those rules—that is, how they think they really behave.
3. The behavior that can be directly observed—that is, what the anthropologist actually sees happening. (In the example of the Trobrianders, one would watch to see whether or not the rule of exogamy is actually violated.)

Clearly, the way people think they *should* behave, the way in which they think they *do* behave, and the way in which they *actually* behave may be distinctly different. By carefully examining and comparing these elements, anthropologists can draw up a set of rules that may explain the acceptable range of behavior within a culture.

Beyond the possibility of drawing false conclusions based on a group's ideal sense of itself, anthropologists run the risk of misinterpretation due to personal feelings and biases shaped by their own culture, as well as gender and age. It is important to recognize this challenge and make every effort to overcome it, for otherwise one may seriously misconstrue what one sees.

[25]Keiser, L. (1991). *Friend by day, enemy by night: Organized vengeance in a Kohistani community* (p. 103). Fort Worth: Holt, Rinehart & Winston.

[26]Robben, A. C. G. M. (2007). Fieldwork identity: Introduction. In A. C. G. M. Robben & J. A. Sluka (Eds.), *Ethnographic fieldwork: An anthropological reader* (p. 61). Malden, MA: Blackwell Publishers; Johnson, N. B. (1984). Sex, color, and rites of passage in ethnographic research. *Human Organization* 43 (2), 108–120.

[27]Powdermaker, H. (1976). *Stranger and friend: The way of an anthropologist.* London: Secker and Warburg.

[28]Malinowski, B. (1922). *Argonauts of the western Pacific.* London: Routledge & Kegan Paul.

A case in point is the story of how male bias in the Polish culture that Malinowski grew up in caused him to ignore or miss significant factors in his pioneering study of the Trobrianders. Unlike today, when anthropologists receive special training before going into the field, Malinowski set out to do fieldwork early in the 20th century with little formal preparation. The follow-ing Original Study, written by anthropologist Annette Weiner who ventured to the same islands sixty years after Malinowski, illustrates how gender can impact one's research findings—both in terms of the bias that may affect a researcher's outlook and in terms of what key consultants may feel comfortable sharing with a particular researcher.

Original Study ▪ By Annette B. Weiner

The Importance of Trobriand Women

Walking into a village at the beginning of fieldwork is entering a world without cultural guideposts. The task of learning values that others live by is never easy. The rigors of fieldwork involve listening and watching, learning a new language of speech and actions, and most of all, letting go of one's own cultural assumptions in order to understand the meanings others give to work, power, death, family, and friends. During my fieldwork in the Trobriand Islands of Papua New Guinea, I wrestled doggedly with each of these problems—and with the added challenge that I was working in the footsteps of a celebrated anthropological ancestor, Bronislaw Kasper Malinowski. . . .

In 1971, before my first trip to the Trobriands, I thought I understood many things about Trobriand customs and beliefs from having read Malinowski's exhaustive writings. Once there, however, I found that I had much more to discover about what I thought I already knew. For many months I worked with these discordant realities, always conscious of Malinowski's shadow, his words, his explanations. Although I found significant differences in areas of importance, I gradually came to understand how he reached certain conclusions. The answers we both received from informants were not so dissimilar, and I could actually trace how Malinowski had analyzed what his informants told him in a way that made sense and was scientifically signifi-cant—given what anthropologists gener-ally then recognized about such societies. Sixty years separate our fieldwork, and any comparison of our studies illustrates not so much Malinowski's mistaken interpretations but the developments in anthropological knowledge and inquiry from his time to mine. . . .

My most significant point of depar-ture from Malinowski's analyses was the attention I gave to women's produc-tive work. In my original research plans, women were not the central focus of study, but on the first day I took up residence in a village I was taken by them to watch a distribution of their own wealth—bundles of banana leaves and ba-nana fiber skirts—which they exchanged with other women in commemoration of someone who had recently died. Watch-ing that event forced me to take women's economic roles more seriously than I would have from reading Malinowski's studies. Although Malinowski noted the high status of Trobriand women, he attributed their importance to the fact that Trobrianders reckon descent through women, thereby giving them genealogical significance in a matrilineal society. Yet he never considered that this signifi-cance was underwritten by women's own

wealth because he did not systemati-cally investigate the women's productive activities. Although in his field notes he mentions Trobriand women making these seemingly useless banana bundles to be exchanged at a death, his published work only deals with men's wealth.

My taking seriously the importance of women's wealth not only brought women as the neglected half of society clearly into the ethnographic picture but also forced me to revise many of Malinowski's assumptions about Trobriand men. For

In the Trobriand Islands, women's wealth consists of skirts and banana leaves, large quantities of which must be given away on the death of a relative.

example, Trobriand kinship as described by Malinowski has always been a subject of debate among anthropologists. For Malinowski, the basic relationships within a Trobriand family were guided by the matrilineal principle of "mother-right" and "father-love." A father was called "stranger" and had little authority over his own children. A woman's brother was the commanding figure and exercised control over his sister's sons because they were members of his matrilineage rather than their father's matrilineage....

In my study of Trobriand women and men, a different configuration of matrilineal descent emerged. A Trobriand father is not a "stranger" in Malinowski's definition, nor is he a powerless figure as the third party to the relationship between a woman and her brother. The father is one of the most important persons in his child's life, and remains so even after his child grows up and marries. Even his procreative importance is incorporated into his child's growth and development. He gives his child many opportunities to gain things from his matrilineage, thereby adding to the available resources that he or she can draw upon.

At the same time, this giving creates obligations on the part of a man's children toward him that last even beyond his death. Thus, the roles that men and their children play in each other's lives are worked out through extensive cycles of exchanges, which define the strength of their relationships to each other and eventually benefit the other members of both their matrilineages. Central to these exchanges are women and their wealth.

That Malinowski never gave equal time to the women's side of things, given the deep significance of their role in societal and political life, is not surprising. Only recently have anthropologists begun to understand the importance of taking women's work seriously.... In the past, both women and men ethnographers generally analyzed the societies they studied from a male perspective. The "women's point of view" was largely ignored in the study of gender roles, since anthropologists generally perceived women as living in the shadows of men—occupying the private rather than the public sectors of society, rearing children rather than engaging in economic or political pursuits.
(Excerpted from A. B. Weiner (1988). The Trobrianders of Papua New Guinea *(pp. 4–7). New York: Holt, Rinehart & Winston.)* ■

Ethnographic Reflexivity: Acknowledging the Researcher as Subject

As the Original Study makes clear, validation of anthropological research is uniquely challenging. In the natural sciences, replication of observations and/or experiments is a major means of establishing the reliability of a researcher's conclusions. Thus, one can see for oneself if one's colleague has "gotten it right."

Validation in ethnographic research is uniquely challenging because observational access is often limited. Access to sites previously researched may be constrained by a number of factors: insufficient funding, logistical difficulties in reaching the site, problems in obtaining permits, and the fact that cultural and environmental conditions often change. Factors such as these mean that what could be observed in a certain context at one particular time cannot be at others. Thus, one researcher cannot easily confirm the reliability or completeness of another's account. For this reason, anthropologists bear a heavy responsibility for accurate reporting, including disclosing key issues related to their research: Why was a particular location selected as a research site and for which research objectives? What were the local conditions during fieldwork? Who provided the key information and major insights? How were data collected and recorded? Without such background information, it is difficult to judge the validity of the account and the soundness of the researcher's conclusions.

In anthropology, researchers are expected to self-monitor through constantly checking their own personal or cultural biases and assumptions as they work and presenting these self-reflections along with their observations, a practice known as *reflexivity*. Commenting on the development of this reflexive ethnography since the 1970s, Dutch anthropologist Antonius Robben recently noted that this:

> conscious self-examination of the ethnographer's interpretive presuppositions [has] enriched fieldwork by making anthropologists pay much closer attention to the interactional processes through which they acquired, shared, and transmitted knowledge.... Reflexivity also prompted an interest in narrative styles, because if ethnography was all about intercultural and intersubjective translation and construction, then form, style, and rhetoric were of central importance.[29]

Putting It All Together: Completing an Ethnography

After collecting ethnographic information, the next challenge is to piece together all that has been gathered into a coherent whole that accurately describes the culture. Traditionally, ethnographies are detailed written descriptions comprised of chapters on topics such as the circumstances and place of fieldwork itself; historical background; the community or group today; its natural

---

[29]Robben, A. C. G. M. (2007). Reflexive ethnography: Introduction. In A. C. G. M. Robben & J. A. Sluka (Eds.), *Ethnographic fieldwork: An anthropological reader* (pp. 443–446). Malden, MA: Blackwell Publishers.

environment; settlement patterns; subsistence practices; networks of kinship relations and other forms of social organization; marriage and sexuality; economic exchanges; political institutions; myths, sacred beliefs, and ceremonies; and current developments. These may be illustrated with photographs and accompanied by maps, kinship diagrams, and figures showing social and political organizational structures, settlement layout, floor plans of dwellings, seasonal cycles, and so on.

Sometimes ethnographic research is documented not only in writing but also with sound recordings and on film. Visual records may be used for documentation and illustration as well as for analysis or as a means of gathering additional information in interviews. Moreover, footage shot for the sake of documentation and research may also be edited into a documentary film. Not unlike a written ethnography, such a film is a structured whole composed of numerous selected sequences, visual montage, juxtaposition of sound and visual image, and narrative sequencing, all coherently edited into an accurate visual representation of the ethnographic subject.[30]

In recent years some anthropologists have been experimenting with digital media. Today, anthropology's potential in research, interpretation, and presentation appears to be greater than ever with the emergence of digital ethnography. Sometimes called *hypermedia ethnography,* **digital ethnography** is the use of digital technologies (audio and visual) for the collection, analysis, and representation of ethnographic data. Digital recording devices provide ethnographers with a wealth of material to analyze and utilize toward building hypotheses. They also open the door to sharing findings in new, varied, and interactive ways in the far-reaching digitalized realm of the Internet.[31] Digital ethnographers, having amassed a wealth of digital material while researching, are able to share their findings through DVDs, CD-ROMs, photo essays, podcasts, or blogs.

---

[30]See Collier, J., & Collier, M. (1986). *Visual anthropology: Photography as a research method.* Albuquerque: University of New Mexico Press; el Guindi, F. (2004). *Visual anthropology: Essential method and theory.* Walnut Creek, CA: Altamira Press.

[31]Michael Wesch, personal communication.

digital ethnography The use of digital technologies (audio and visual) for the collection, analysis, and representation of ethnographic data.

ethnohistory A study of cultures of the recent past through oral histories, accounts of explorers, missionaries, and traders, and through analysis of records such as land titles, birth and death records, and other archival materials.

theory In science an explanation of natural phenomena, supported by a reliable body of data.

doctrine An assertion of opinion or belief formally handed down by an authority as true and indisputable. Also known as dogma.

Ethnohistory

Ethnohistory is a kind of historical ethnography that studies cultures of the recent past through oral histories, the accounts of explorers, missionaries, and traders, and through analysis of such records as land titles, birth and death records, and other archival materials. The ethnohistorical analysis of cultures is a valuable approach to understanding change and plays an important role in theory building.

ETHNOLOGY: FROM DESCRIPTION TO INTERPRETATION AND THEORY

Largely descriptive in nature, ethnography provides the basic data needed for *ethnology*—the branch of cultural anthropology that makes cross-cultural comparisons and develops theories that explain why certain important differences or similarities occur between groups. As noted in Chapter 1, the end product of anthropological research, if properly carried out, is a theory or coherent statement about culture or human nature that provides an explanatory framework for understanding the ideas and actions of the people who have been studied. In short, a **theory** is an explanation or interpretation supported by a reliable body of data.

Anthropologists do not claim any theory about culture to be the only and final word or absolute truth. Rather they judge or measure a theory's validity and soundness by varying degrees of probability; what is considered to be "true" is what is most probable. But while anthropologists are reluctant about making absolute statements about complex issues such as exactly how cultures function or change, they can and do provide fact-based evidence about whether assumptions have support or are unfounded and thus not true. Thus, a theory, contrary to widespread misuse of the term, is much more than mere speculation; it is a critically examined explanation of observed reality.

In this respect, it is important to distinguish between scientific theories—which are always open to future challenges born of new evidence or insights—and doctrine. A **doctrine,** or dogma, is an assertion of opinion or belief formally handed down by an authority as true and indisputable.

For instance, those who accept a creationist doctrine on the origin of the human species as recounted in sacred texts or myths passed down the generations do so on the basis of religious authority, conceding that such views may be contrary to genetic, geological, biological, or other scientific explanations. Such doctrines cannot be tested or proved one way or another: They are basically accepted as matters of faith.

In contrast to religious doctrine, however, scientific theory depends on demonstrable, fact-based evidence and repeated testing. So it is that, as our cross-cultural knowledge expands, the odds favor some anthropological theories over others; old explanations or interpretations must sometimes be discarded as new theories based on better or more complete evidence are shown to be more effective or probable.

Ethnology and the Comparative Method

A single instance of any phenomenon is generally insufficient for supporting a plausible hypothesis. Without some basis for comparison, the hypothesis grounded in a single case may be no more than a hunch born of a unique happenstance or particular historical coincidence. Theories in anthropology may be generated from worldwide cross-cultural or historical comparisons or even comparisons with other species. For instance, anthropologists may examine a global sample of societies in order to discover whether a hypothesis proposed to explain certain phenomena is supported by fact-based evidence. Of necessity, the cross-cultural researcher depends upon evidence gathered by other scholars as well as his or her own.

A key resource that makes this possible is the **Human Relations Area Files (HRAF),** a vast collection of cross-indexed ethnographic and archaeological data catalogued by cultural characteristics and geographic location. Initiated at Yale University in the mid-1900s, this ever-growing data bank classifies more than 700 cultural characteristics and includes nearly 400 societies, past and present, from all around the world. Archived in about 300 libraries (on microfiche and/or online) and approaching a million pages of information, the HRAF facilitates comparative research on almost any cultural feature imaginable—warfare, subsistence practices, settlement patterns, marriage, rituals, and so on.

Among other things, anthropologists interested in finding explanations for certain social or cultural beliefs and practices can use HRAF to test their hypotheses. For example, Peggy Reeves Sanday examined a sample of 156 societies drawn from HRAF in an attempt to answer such questions as: Why do women play a more dominant role in some societies than others? Why, and under what circumstances, do men dominate women? Her study, published in 1981 (*Female Power and Male Dominance*), disproves the common misperception that women are universally subordinate to men, sheds light on the way men and women relate to each other, and ranks as a major landmark in the study of gender.

Although HRAF is a valuable research tool, it should be used with caution. For instance, the files only allow us to establish correlations between cultural features; they do not permit conclusions about cause and effect. In other words, while HRAF makes it possible to develop functional explanations (how things work), it does not provide us with causal explanations. For that, anthropologists may have to engage in more in-depth historical analysis of particular cultural practices.

Cultural comparisons are not restricted to contemporary ethnographic data. Indeed, anthropologists frequently turn to archaeological or historical data to test

Human Relations Area Files (HRAF) A vast collection of cross-indexed ethnographic and archaeological data catalogued by cultural characteristics and geographic locations. Archived in about 300 libraries (on microfiche and/or online).

Anthropologist David Maybury-Lewis interviews Xavante Indians in the Brazilian savannah where he has made numerous fieldwork visits since the 1950s. Maybury-Lewis is founder of the indigenous advocacy organization Cultural Survival, based in Cambridge, Massachusetts. He, like other anthropologists around the world, reaches beyond the "do no harm" clause of the AAA ethics code to actually work on behalf of indigenous groups.

© Anthro-Photo

hypotheses about culture change. Cultural characteristics thought to be caused by certain specified conditions can be tested archaeologically by investigating similar situations where such conditions actually occurred. Also useful are data provided in ethnohistories.

Anthropology's Theoretical Perspectives: A Brief Overview

Entire books have been written about each of anthropology's numerous theoretical perspectives. Here we offer a general overview to convey the scope of anthropological theory and its role in explaining and interpreting cultures.

In the previous chapter, we presented the barrel model of culture as a dynamic system of adaptation in which infrastructure, social structure, and superstructure are intricately interactive. Helping us to imagine culture as an integrated whole, this model allows us to think about something very complex by reducing it to a simplified scheme or basic design. Anthropologists refer to such a perspective on culture as holistic and integrative.

Although most anthropologists generally agree with a perspective on culture as holistic and integrative, they may have very different takes on the relative significance of different elements comprising the whole and exactly how they relate to one another. When analyzing a culture, some anthropologists argue that humans act primarily on the basis of their ideas, concepts, or symbolic representations. In their research and analysis, these anthropologists usually emphasize that to understand or explain why humans behave as they do, one must first get into other people's heads and try to understand how they imagine, think, feel, and speak about the world in which they live. Because of the primacy of the superstructure (ideas, values), this is known as an **idealistic perspective** (not to be confused with idealism in the sense of fantasy or hopeful imagination).

Examples of idealist perspectives include psychological and cognitive anthropology (culture and personality), ethnoscience, structuralism, and postmodernism, as well as symbolic and interpretive anthropology. The latter approach is most famously associated with U.S. anthropologist Clifford Geertz, who viewed humans primarily as "symbolizing, conceptualizing, and meaning-seeking" creatures. Drawing on words from German historical sociologist Max Weber, he wrote: "Man is an animal suspended in webs of significance he himself has spun. I take culture to be those webs, and the analysis of it to be therefore not an experimental science in search of law but an interpretive one in search of meaning."[32] Geertz developed an artful ethnographic research strategy in which a culturally significant event or social drama (for instance, a Balinese cockfight) is chosen for observation and analysis as a form of "deep play" that may provide essential cultural insights. Peeling back layer upon layer of socially constructed meanings, the anthropologist offers what Geertz called a "thick description" of the event in a detailed ethnographic narrative.

Many other anthropologists hold a theoretical perspective in which they stress explaining culture by first analyzing the material conditions that they see as determining people's lives. They may begin their research with an inventory of available natural resources for food and shelter, the number of mouths to feed and bodies to keep warm, the tools used in making a living, and so on. Anthropologists who highlight such environmental or economic factors as primary in shaping cultures basically share a **materialist perspective.**

Examples of materialist theoretical approaches include Marxism, cultural ecology, neo-evolutionism, and cultural materialism. In cultural ecology, anthropologists focus primarily on the subsistence mechanisms in a culture that enable a group to successfully adapt to its natural environment. Building on cultural ecology, some anthropologists include considerations of political economy such as industrial production, capitalist markets, wage labor, and finance capital. A political economy perspective is closely associated with Marxist theory, which essentially explains major change in society as the result of growing conflicts between opposing social classes, namely those who possess property and those who do not.

One result of widening the scope—combining cultural ecology and political economy to take into account the emerging world systems of international production and trade relations—is known as political ecology. Closely related is cultural materialism, a theoretical research strategy identified with Marvin Harris.[33] Placing primary emphasis on the role of environment, demography, technology, and economy in determining a culture's mental and social conditions, he argued that anthropologists can best explain ideas, values, and beliefs as adaptations to economic and environmental conditions (see Biocultural Connection).

idealist perspective A theoretical approach stressing the primacy of superstructure in cultural research and analysis.
materialist perspective A theoretical approach stressing the primacy of infrastructure (material conditions) in cultural research and analysis.

---

[32]Geertz, C. (1973). *The interpretation of culture.* London: Hutchinson.

[33]Harris, M. (1979). *Cultural materialism: The struggle for a science of culture.* New York: Random House.

Biocultural Connection

Pig Lovers and Pig Haters ▪ By Marvin Harris

In the Old Testament of the Bible, the Israelite's God (Yahweh) denounced the pig as an unclean beast that pollutes if tasted or touched. Later, Allah conveyed the same basic message to his prophet Muhammad. Among millions of Jews and Muslims today, the pig remains an abomination, even though it can convert grains and tubers into high-grade fats and protein more efficiently than any other animal.

What prompted condemnation of an animal whose meat is relished by the greater part of humanity? For centuries, the most popular explanation was that the pig wallows in its own urine and eats excrement. But linking this to religious abhorrence leads to inconsistencies. Cows kept in a confined space also splash about in their own urine and feces.

These inconsistencies were recognized in the 12th century by Maimonides, a widely respected Jewish philosopher and physician in Egypt, who said God condemned swine as a public health measure because pork had "a bad and damaging effect upon the body." The mid-1800s discovery that eating undercooked pork caused trichinosis appeared to verify Maimonides's reasoning. Reform-minded Jews then renounced the taboo, convinced that if well-cooked pork did not endanger public health, eating it would not offend God.

Scholars have suggested this taboo stemmed from the idea that the animal was once considered divine—but this explanation falls short since sheep, goats, and cows were also once worshiped in the Middle East, and their meat is enjoyed by all religious groups in the region.

I think the real explanation for this religious condemnation lies in the fact that pig farming threatened the integrity of the basic cultural and natural ecosystems of the Middle East. Until their conquest of the Jordan Valley in Palestine over 3,000 years ago, the Israelites were nomadic herders, living almost entirely from sheep, goats, and cattle. Like all pastoralists, they maintained close relationships with sedentary farmers who held the oases and the great rivers. With this mixed farming and pastoral complex, the pork prohibition constituted a sound ecological strategy. The pastoralists could not raise pigs in their arid habitats, and among the semi-sedentary farming populations pigs were more of a threat than an asset.

The basic reason for this is that the world zones of pastoral nomadism correspond to unforested plains and hills that are too arid for rainfall agriculture and that cannot easily be irrigated. The domestic animals best adapted to these zones are ruminants (including cattle, sheep, and goats), which can digest grass, leaves, and other cellulose foods more effectively than other mammals.

The pig, however, is primarily a creature of forests and shaded riverbanks. Although it is omnivorous, its best weight gain is from foods low in cellulose (nuts, fruits, tubers, and especially grains), making it a direct competitor of man. It cannot subsist on grass alone and is ill-adapted to the hot, dry climate of the grasslands, mountains, and deserts in the Middle East. To compensate for its lack of protective hair and an inability to sweat, the pig must dampen its skin with external moisture. It prefers to do this by wallowing in fresh clean mud, but will cover its skin with its own urine and feces if nothing else if available. So there is some truth to the theory that the religious uncleanliness of the pig rests upon actual physical dirtiness.

Among the ancient mixed farming and pastoralist communities of the Middle East, domestic animals were valued primarily as sources of milk, cheese, hides, dung, fiber, and traction for plowing. Goats, sheep, and cattle provided all of this, plus an occasional supplement of lean meat. From the beginning, therefore, pork must have been a luxury food, esteemed for its succulent, tender, and fatty qualities.

Between 4,000 and 9,000 years ago, the human population in the Middle East increased sixty-fold. Extensive deforestation accompanied this rise, largely due to damage caused by sheep and goat herds. Shade and water, the natural conditions appropriate for raising pigs, became ever more scarce, and pork became even more of a luxury.

The Middle East is the wrong place to raise pigs, but pork remains a luscious treat. People find it difficult to resist such temptations on their own. Hence Yahweh and Allah were heard to say that swine were unclean—unfit to eat or touch. In short, it was ecologically maladaptive to try to raise pigs in substantial numbers, and small-scale production would only increase the temptation. Better then, to prohibit the consumption of pork entirely.

(Excerpted from M. Harris (1989). Cows, pigs, wars, and witches: The riddles of culture (pp. 35–60). New York: Vintage Books/Random House.)

Not all anthropologists can be easily grouped in idealist or materialist camps. Giving primacy to social structure, many analyze a cultural group by first and foremost focusing on this middle layer in our barrel model. Although it is difficult to neatly pigeonhole various perspectives in this group, theoretical explanations worked out by pioneering French social thinkers like Emile Durkheim and his student Marcel Mauss influenced the development of structural-functionalism. Primarily associated with British anthropologists in the mid-1900s, this approach focuses on the underlying patterns or structures of social relationships, attributing functions to cultural institutions in terms of the contributions they make toward maintaining a group's social order.

Beyond these three general groups, there exist various other anthropological approaches. Some stress the importance of identifying general patterns or even discovering laws. Early anthropologists believed that they could discover such laws by means of the theory of *unilinear cultural evolution* of universal human progress, beginning with what was then called "savagery," followed by "barbarism," and gradually making progress toward a condition of human perfection known as "high civilization."[34]

Although anthropologists have long abandoned such sweeping generalizations as unscientific and ethnocentric, some continued to search for universal laws in the general development of human cultures by focusing on technological development as measured in the growing capacity for energy capture per capita of the population. This theoretical perspective is sometimes called *neoevolutionism*. Others seek to explain recurring patterns in human social behavior in terms of laws of natural selection by focusing on possible relationships with human genetics, a theoretical perspective identified with sociobiology. Yet others stress that broad generalizations are impossible because each culture is distinct and can only be understood as resulting from unique historical processes and circumstances. Some even go a step further and focus on in-depth description and analysis of personal life histories of individual members in a group in order to reveal the work of a culture.

Beyond these cultural historical approaches, there are other theoretical perspectives that do not aim for laws or generalizations to explain culture. Theoretical perspectives that reject measuring and evaluating different cultures by means of some sort of universal standard, and stress that they can only be explained or interpreted

in their own unique terms, are associated with the important anthropological principle known as *cultural relativism*, discussed in the previous chapter.

MORAL DILEMMAS AND ETHICAL RESPONSIBILITIES IN ANTHROPOLOGICAL RESEARCH

Today, universities require that anthropologists, like other researchers, communicate in advance the nature, purpose, and potential impact of the planned study to individuals who provide information—and obtain their **informed consent** or formal recorded agreement to participate in the research. Of course, this requirement is easier to fulfill in some societies or cultures than in others, as most anthropologists recognize. When it is a challenge to obtain informed consent, or even impossible to precisely explain the meaning and purpose of this concept and its actual consequences, anthropologists may protect the identities of individuals, families, or even entire communities by altering their names and locations. For example, when anthropologists study violent secret groups such as the Sicilian mafia, they may find it difficult or even unwise to obtain informed consent and instead opt not to disclose their real identities.

The dilemma facing anthropologists is also recognized in the preamble of the American Anthropological Association's Code of Ethics (discussed in Chapter 1), first formalized in 1971 and modified in its current form in 1998. This document outlines the various ethical responsibilities and moral obligations of anthropologists, including this central maxim: "Anthropological researchers must do everything in their power to ensure that their research does not harm the safety, dignity, or privacy of the people with whom they work, conduct research, or perform other professional activities."

---

[34]Carneiro, R. L. (2003). *Evolutionism in cultural anthropology: A critical history.* Boulder, CO: Westview Press.

informed consent   Formal, recorded agreement to participate in research.

Questions for Reflection

1. In describing and interpreting human cultures, anthropologists have long relied on ethnographic fieldwork, including participant observation. What makes this research method uniquely challenging and effective—and of what use might the findings be for meeting the unique challenges of our globalizing world?

2. Early anthropologists engaged in salvage ethnography to create a reliable record of indigenous cultures once widely expected to vanish. Although many indigenous communities did lose customary practices due to acculturation, descendants of those cultures can now turn to anthropological records to re-

vitalize their ancestral ways of life. Do you think this is a good thing or not?

3. In our globalizing world, a growing number of anthropologists carry out multi-sited ethnography rather than conduct research in a single community. If you would do such a multi-sited research project, what would you focus on, and where would you conduct your actual participant observations and interviews?

4. If you were invited to "study up," on which cultural group would you focus? How would you go about getting access to that group for participant observation, and what are some of the serious obstacles you might expect to run into?

5. Although many people talk about the importance of ethics in research, how can anthropologists get informed consent from nonliterate members of a closed traditional community?

Suggested Readings

Angrosino, M. V. (2004). *Projects in ethnographic research*. Long Grove, IL: Waveland Press.

Presenting a related set of three very doable research projects with clear instructions and guidelines, this compact volume is a useful introduction to some important field techniques. Rich with examples, it lays out relevant concepts and the how-to details of ethnographic research—from methods, principles, and site selection, to observation and interviewing, to analysis and presentation.

Bernard, H. R. (2002). *Research methods in anthropology: Qualitative and quantitative approaches* (3rd ed.). Walnut Creek, CA: Altamira Press.

Written in a conversational style and rich with examples, this extremely useful and accessible book has twenty chapters divided into three sections: preparing for fieldwork, data collection, and data analysis. It touches on all the basics, from literature search and research design to interviewing, field note management, multivariate analysis, ethics, and more.

Dicks, B., et al (2005). *Qualitative research and hypermedia: Ethnography for the digital age (New technologies for social research)*. Thousand Oaks, CA: Sage Publications.

Introducing emerging ethnographic research methods that utilize new technologies, the authors explain how to conduct data collection, analysis, and representation using new technologies and hypermedia—and discuss how digital technologies may transform ethnographic research.

Erickson, P. A., & Murphy, L. D. (2003). *A history of anthropological theory*. (2nd ed.). Peterborough, Ontario: Broadview Press.

A clear and concise survey that spans from antiquity to the modern era, effectively drawing the lines between the old and new. This edition features several new and expanded sections on topics including feminist anthropology, globalization, and medical anthropology.

Pink, S. (2001). *Doing visual ethnography: Images, media and representation in research*. Thousand Oaks, CA: Sage Publications.

Exploring the use and potential of photography, video, and hypermedia in ethnographic and social research, this text offers a reflexive approach to the practical, theoretical, methodological, and ethical issues of using these media. Following each step of research, from planning to fieldwork to analysis and representation, the author suggests how visual images and technologies can be combined to form an integrated process from start to finish.

Robben, A. C. G. M., & Sluka, J. A. (Eds.). (2007). *Ethnographic fieldwork: An anthropology reader*. Malden, MA: Blackwell Publishers.

This up-to-date text provides a comprehensive selection of classic and contemporary reflections, examining the tensions between self and other, the relationships between anthropologists and key consultants, conflicts and ethical challenges, various types of ethnographic research (including multi-sited fieldwork), and different styles of writing about fieldwork.

Thomson Audio Study Products

 Enjoy the MP3-ready Audio Lecture Overviews for each chapter and a comprehensive audio glossary of key terms for quick study and review. Whether walking to class, doing laundry, or studying at your desk, you now have the freedom to choose when, where, and how you interact with your audio-based educational media. See the preface for information on how to access this on-the-go study and review tool.

The Anthropology Resource Center

www.thomsonedu.com/anthropology
The Anthropology Resource Center provides extended learning materials to reinforce your understanding of key concepts in the four fields of anthropology. For each of the four fields, the Resource Center includes dynamic exercises including video exercises, map exercises, simulations, and "Meet the Scientists" interviews, as well as critical thinking questions that can be assigned and e-mailed to instructors. The Resource Center also provides breaking news in anthropology and interesting material on applied anthropology to help you link what you are learning to the world around you.

16 Language and Communication

© Strauss/Curtis/Corbis

CHALLENGE ISSUE

As social creatures dependent upon one another for survival, humans face the challenge of finding effective ways to communicate clearly in a multiplicity of situations about countless things connected to our well-being. We do this in many ways, including touch, gesture, and posture. Our most distinctive and complex form of communication, however, is language—a foundation stone of culture.

What Is Language?

A language is a system of symbolic communication using sounds and/or gestures that are put together according to rules resulting in meanings that are based on agreement by a society and intelligible to all who share that language. Although humans rely heavily on spoken language, or speech, to communicate with one another, it is not their sole means of communication. Human language is embedded in an age-old gesture-call system in which body motions and facial expressions, along with vocal features such as tone and volume, play vital roles in conveying messages.

How Is Language Related to Culture?

Without our capacity for complex language, human culture as we know it could not exist. Languages are shared by people who belong to societies that have their own distinctive cultures. Social variables, such as age, gender, and economic status, may influence how people use language. Moreover, people communicate what is meaningful to them, and that is largely defined by their particular culture. In fact, our use of language has an effect on, and is influenced by, our culture.

How Do Languages Change?

All languages are constantly transforming—new words are adopted or coined, others are dropped, and some shift in meaning. Languages change for various reasons, ranging from selective borrowing by one language from another, or the need for new vocabulary to deal with technological innovations or altered social realities. On one hand, domination of one society by another may result in erosion or loss of a particular language. On the other, cultural revitalization may result in the resurgence or revival of a threatened or even extinct language.

All normal humans are born with the ability to communicate through language and may spend a considerable part of each day doing so. Indeed, language is so much a part of our lives that it involves everything we do, and everything we do involves language.

There is no doubt that our ability to communicate, whether through sounds or gestures (sign languages, such as the American Sign Language (ASL) used by the hearing impaired, are fully developed languages in their own right), rests squarely upon our biological makeup. We are "programmed" for language, although only in a general sort of way. Beyond the cries of babies, which are not learned but which do communicate, humans must learn their language. So it is that any normal child from anywhere in the world readily learns the language of his or her culture.

We define **language** as a system of communication using sounds and/or gestures that are put together according to certain rules, resulting in meanings that are intelligible to all who share that language. These sounds and gestures fall into the category of a *symbol* (defined as a sign, sound, gesture, or other thing that is arbitrarily linked to something else and represents it in a meaningful way). For example, the word *crying* is a symbol, a combination of sounds to which we assign the meaning of a particular action and which we can use to communicate that meaning, whether or not anyone around us is actually crying. **Signals,** unlike culturally learned symbols, are instinctive sounds and gestures that have a natural or self-evident meaning. Screams, signs, or coughs, for example, are signals that convey some kind of emotional or physical state.

THOMSON AUDIO STUDY PRODUCTS Take advantage of the MP3-ready Audio Lecture Overviews and comprehensive audio glossary of key terms for each chapter. See the preface for information on how to access this on-the-go study and review tool.

---

language A system of communication using sounds or gestures that are put together in meaningful ways according to a set of rules.

signal An instinctive sound or gesture that has a natural or self-evident meaning.

Today's language experts are not certain how much credit to give to animals, such as dolphins or chimpanzees, for the ability to use symbols as well as signals. But it has become evident that these animals and many others communicate in remarkable ways. Apes have demonstrated an ability to understand language quite well, even using rudimentary grammar. Several chimpanzees, gorillas, and orangutans have been taught American Sign Language. Researchers have discovered that even vervet monkeys utilize distinct calls for communication. These calls go beyond merely signaling levels of fear or arousal. Among other things, these small African monkeys have specific calls to signify the type of predator threatening the group. According to primatologist Allison Jolly,

> [The calls] include which direction to look in or where to run. There is an audience effect: calls are given when there is someone appropriate to listen . . . monkey calls are far more than involuntary expressions of emotion.[1]

What are the implications of this for our understanding of the nature and evolution of language? No final answer will be evident until we gain more knowledge about the various systems of animal communication. Meanwhile, even as debate continues over how human and animal communication relate to each other, we cannot dismiss communication among nonhuman species as a set of simple instinctive reflexes or fixed action patterns.[2]

A remarkable example of the many scientific efforts underway on this subject is the story of an orangutan named Chantek, featured in the following Original Study. Among other things, it illustrates the creative process of language development and the capacity of a nonhuman primate to recognize symbols.

---

[1]Jolly, A. (1991). Thinking like a vervet. *Science 251,* 574. See also Seyfarth, R. M., et al. (1980). Monkey responses to three different alarm calls: Evidence for predator classification and semantic communication. *Science 210,* 801–803.

[2]Armstrong, D. F., Stokoe, W. C., & Wilcox, S. E. (1993). Signs of the origin of syntax. *Current Anthropology 34,* 349–368; Burling, R. (1993). Primate calls, human language, and nonverbal communication. *Current Anthropology 34,* 25–53.

Language and the Intellectual Abilities of Orangutans

In 1978, after researchers began to use American Sign Language for the deaf to communicate with chimpanzees and gorillas, I began the first long-term study of the language ability of an orangutan named Chantek. There was criticism that symbol-using apes might just be imitating their human caregivers, but there is now growing agreement that orangutans, gorillas, and both chimpanzee species can develop language skills at the level of a 2- to 3-year-old human child.

The goal of Project Chantek was to investigate the mind of an orangutan through a developmental study of his cognitive and linguistic skills. It was a great ethical and emotional responsibility to engage an orangutan in what anthropologists call "enculturation," since I would not only be teaching a form of communication, I would be teaching aspects of the culture upon which that language was based. If my project succeeded, I would create a symbol-using creature that would be somewhere between an ape living under natural conditions and an adult human. This threatened to raise as many questions as I sought to answer.

A small group of caregivers at the University of Tennessee, Chattanooga, began raising Chantek when he was 9 months old. They communicated with him by using gestural signs based on the American Sign Language for the deaf. After a month, Chantek produced his own first sign and eventually learned to use approximately 150 different signs, forming a vocabulary similar to that of a very young child. Chantek learned names for people (LYN, JOHN), places (YARD, BROCK-HALL), things to eat (YOGURT, CHOCOLATE), actions (WORK, HUG), objects (SCREWDRIVER, MONEY), animals (DOG, APE), colors (RED, BLACK), pronouns (YOU, ME), location (UP, POINT), attributes (GOOD, HURT), and emphasis (MORE, TIME-TO-DO).

Though the orangutans diverged from humans, chimps, and gorillas about 12 million years ago, all of these ape species share a number of qualities. Orangutans have an insightful, humanlike thinking style characterized by longer attention spans and quiet deliberate action. Orangutans make shelters, tie knots, recognize themselves in mirrors, use one tool to make another, and are the most skilled of the apes in manipulating objects. In this photo, Chantek begins the sign for "tomato."

We found that Chantek's signing was spontaneous and nonrepetitious. He did not merely imitate his caregivers, but rather he actively used signs to initiate communications and meet his needs. Almost immediately, he began using signs in combinations and modulated their meanings with slight changes in how he articulated and arranged his signs. He commented "COKE DRINK" after drinking his coke, "PULL BEARD" while pulling a caregiver's hair through a fence, and "TIME HUG" while locked in his cage as his caregiver looked at her watch. But, beyond using signs in this way, could he use them as symbols, that is, more abstractly to represent a person, thing, action, or idea, even apart from its context or when it was not present?

One indication of the capacity of both deaf and hearing children to use symbolic language is the ability to point, which some researchers argued that apes could not do spontaneously. Chantek began to point to objects when he was 2 years old, somewhat later than human children. First, he showed and gave us objects, and then he began pointing where he wanted to be tickled and to where he wanted to be carried. Finally, he could answer questions like WHERE HAT? WHICH DIF-FERENT? and WHAT WANT? by pointing to the correct object.

As Chantek's vocabulary increased, the ideas that he was expressing became more complex, such as when he signed BAD BIRD at noisy birds giving alarm calls, and WHITE CHEESE FOODEAT for cottage cheese. He understood that things had characteristics or attributes that could be described. He also created combinations of signs that we had never used before.

In the way that a child learns language, Chantek began to over- or under-extend the meaning of his signs, which gave us insight into his emotions and how he was beginning to classify his world. For example, he used the sign DOG for actual dogs, as well as for a picture of a dog in his Viewmaster, orangutans on television, barking noises on the radio, birds, horses, a tiger at the circus, a herd of cows, a picture of a cheetah, and a noisy helicopter that presumably sounded like it was barking. For Chantek, the sign BUG included crickets, cockroaches, a picture of a cockroach, beetles, slugs, small moths, spiders, worms, flies, a picture of a graph shaped like a butterfly, tiny brown pieces of cat food, and small bits of feces. He signed BREAK before he broke and shared pieces of crackers, and after he broke his toilet. He signed BAD to himself before he grabbed a cat, when he bit into a radish, and for a dead bird.

We also discovered that Chantek could comprehend our spoken English (after the first couple of years we used speech as well as signing). When he was 2 years old, Chantek began to sign for things that were not present. He frequently asked to go to places in his yard to look for animals, such as his pet squirrel and cat, who served as playmates. He also made requests for ICE CREAM, signing CAR RIDE and pulling us toward the parking lot for a trip to a local ice-cream shop.

CONTINUED

We learned that an orangutan can tell lies. Deception is an important indicator of language abilities since it requires a deliberate and intentional misrepresentation of reality. In order to deceive, you must be able to see events from the other person's perspective and negate his or her perception. Chantek began to deceive from a relatively early age, and we caught him in lies about three times a week. He learned that he could sign DIRTY to get into the bathroom to play with the washing machine, dryer, soap, and so on, instead of using the toilet. He also used his signs deceptively to gain social advantage in games, to divert attention in social interactions, and to avoid testing situations and coming home after walks on campus.

On one occasion, Chantek stole food from my pocket while he simultaneously pulled my hand away in the opposite direction. On another occasion, he stole a pencil eraser, pretended to swallow it, and "supported" his case by opening his mouth and signing FOOD-EAT, as if to say that he had swallowed it. However, he really held the eraser in his cheek, and later it was found in his bedroom where he commonly hid objects.

We carried out tests of Chantek's mental ability using measures developed for human children. Chantek reached a mental age equivalent to that of a 2- to 3-year-old child, with some skills of even older children. On some tasks done readily by children, such as using one object

to represent another and pretend play, Chantek performed as well as children, but less frequently. He engaged in chase games in which he would look over his shoulder as he darted about, although no one was chasing him. He also signed to his toys and offered them food and drink.

By 4½ years of age, Chantek showed evidence of planning, creative simulation, and the use of objects in novel relations to one another to invent new meanings. For example, he simulated the context for food preparation by giving his caregiver two objects needed to prepare his milk formula and staring at the location of the remaining ingredient. A further indication that Chantek had mental images is found in his ability to respond to his caregiver's request that he improve the articulation of a sign. When his articulation became careless, we would ask him to SIGN BETTER. Looking closely at us, he would sign slowly and emphatically, taking one hand to put the other into the proper shape.

Chantek was extremely curious and inventive. When he wanted to know the name of something, he offered his hands to be molded into the shape of the proper sign. But language is a creative process, so we were pleased to see that Chantek began to invent his own signs. He invented: NO-TEETH (to show us that he would not use his teeth during rough play); EYE-DRINK (for contact lens solution used by his caregivers); and DAVE-MISSING-FINGER (a name for a favorite university employee who had a

hand injury). Like our ancestors, Chantek had become a creator of language. *(See H. L. W. Miles. (1993). Language and the orangutan: The old "person" of the forest. In P. Cavalieri & P. Singer (Eds.), The great ape project (pp. 45–50). New York: St. Martin's Press.)*

2004 update: My relationship and research with Chantek continues, through the Chantek Foundation in Atlanta, Georgia. Chantek now uses several hundred signs and has invented new signs for CAR WATER (bottled water that I bring in my car), KATSUP, and ANNOYED. He makes stone tools, arts and crafts, necklaces, and other jewelry, and small percussion instruments used in my rock band Animal Nation. He even co-composes songs with the band.

Plans are in the making for Chantek and other enculturated apes to live in culture-based preserves where they have more range of choices and learning opportunities than zoos or research centers. An exciting new project under the auspices of ApeNet will give Chantek an opportunity to communicate with other apes via the Internet. It is of special note that based on great ape language skills, efforts will be underway in the next decade to obtain greater legal rights for these primates, as well as greater recognition of them as another type of "person." (For more information, see www.chantek.org.) ■

While language studies such as the one involving Chantek are fascinating and reveal much about primate cognition, the fact remains that human culture is ultimately dependent on an elaborate system of communication far more complex than that of any other species—including our fellow primates. The reason for this is the sheer amount of what must be learned by each person from other individuals in order to control the knowledge and rules for behavior necessary for full participation in society. Of course, a significant amount of learning can and does take place in the absence of language by way of observation and imitation, guided by a limited number of meaningful signs or symbols. However, all known human cultures are so rich in content that they require communication systems that not only can give precise labels to various classes of phenomena but also permit

people to think and talk about their own and others' experiences and expectations—past, present, and future.

The central and most highly developed human system of communication is language. Knowledge of the workings of language, then, is essential to a full understanding of what culture is about and how it operates.

LINGUISTIC RESEARCH AND THE NATURE OF LANGUAGE

Any human language—Chinese, English, Swahili, or whatever—is obviously a means of transmitting information and sharing with others both collective and individual experiences. Because we tend to take language

For linguists studying language in the field, laptops and recording devices are indispensable tools. Here Tiffany Kershner of Kansas State University works with native Sukwa speakers in northern Malawi, Africa.

for granted, it is perhaps not so obvious that language is also a system that enables us to translate our concerns, beliefs, and perceptions into symbols that can be understood and interpreted by others.

In spoken language, this is done by taking a few sounds—no language uses more than about fifty—and developing rules for putting them together in meaningful ways. Sign languages, such as American Sign Language, do the same thing but with gestures rather than sounds. The vast array of languages in the world—some 6,500 or so different ones—may well astound and mystify us by their great variety and complexity, yet language experts have found that all languages, as far back as we can trace them, are organized in the same basic way.

The roots of **linguistics**—the systematic study of all aspects of language—go back a long way, to the works of ancient language specialists in India more than 2,000 years ago. The European age of exploration from the 16th through the 18th centuries set the stage for a great leap forward in the scientific study of language. Explorers, invaders, and missionaries accumulated information about a huge diversity of languages from all around the world. An estimated 10,000 languages still existed when they began their inquiries.

Linguists in the 19th century, including anthropologists, made a significant contribution in discovering system, regularity, and relationships in the data and tentatively formulating laws and regular principles concerning language. In the 20th century, while still collecting data, they made considerable progress in unraveling the reasoning process behind language construction, testing and working from new and improved theories.

Insofar as theories and facts of language are verifiable by independent researchers looking at the same materials, there may now be said to be a science of linguistics. This science has three main branches: descriptive linguistics, historical linguistics, and a third branch that focuses on language in relation to social and cultural settings.

DESCRIPTIVE LINGUISTICS

How can an anthropologist, a trader, a missionary, a diplomat, or anyone else approach and make sense of a language that has not yet been described and analyzed, or for which there are no readily available written materials? There are hundreds of such undocumented languages in the world; fortunately, effective methods have been developed to help with the task. Descriptive linguistics involves unraveling a language by recording, describing, and analyzing all of its features. It is a painstaking process, but it is ultimately rewarding in that it provides deeper understanding of a language—its structure, its unique linguistic repertoire (figures of speech, word plays, and so on), and its relationship to other languages.

The process of unlocking the underlying rules of a spoken language requires a trained ear and a thorough understanding of the way multiple different speech

linguistics The modern scientific study of all aspects of language.

sounds are produced. Without such know-how, it is extremely difficult to write out or make intelligent use of any data concerning a particular language. To satisfy this preliminary requirement, most people need special training in phonetics, discussed below. As for the biology that makes human speech possible, that is explained in this chapter's Biocultural Connection.

Phonology

Rooted in the Greek word *phone* (meaning "sound"), **phonetics** is defined as the systematic identification and description of the distinctive sounds of a language. Phonetics is basic to **phonology,** the study of language sounds. In order to analyze and describe any language, one needs first an inventory of all its distinctive sounds.

While some of the sounds used in other languages may seem very much like those of the researcher's own speech pattern, others may be unfamiliar. For example, the *th* sound common in English does not exist in the Dutch language and is difficult for most Dutch speakers to pronounce, just as the *r* sound used in numerous languages is tough for Japanese speakers. And the unique "click" sounds used in Bushman languages in southern Africa are difficult for speakers of just about every other language. Sometimes words that feature sounds notoriously difficult for outsiders to pronounce are used as passwords to identify foreigners. For instance, because Germans find it hard to pronounce the sound *sch* the way their Dutch neighbors do, resistance fighters in the Netherlands during World War II chose the place name *Scheveningen* as a test word to identify Dutch-speaking German spies trying to infiltrate their groups. Such a password is known as a *shibboleth.*

While collecting speech sounds or utterances, the linguist works to isolate the **phonemes**—the smallest units of sound that make a difference in meaning. This isolation and analysis may be done by a process called the minimal-pair test. The researcher tries to find two

phonetics The systematic identification and description of distinctive speech sounds in a language.
phonology The study of language sounds.
phoneme The smallest unit of sound that makes a difference in meaning in a language.
morphology The study of the patterns or rules of word formation in a language (including such things as rules concerning verb tense, pluralization, and compound words).
morpheme The smallest unit of sound that carries a meaning in language. It is distinct from a phoneme, which can alter meaning but has no meaning by itself.
syntax The patterns or rules by which morphemes are arranged into phrases and sentences.
grammar The entire formal structure of a language, including morphology and syntax.

short words that appear to be exactly alike except for one sound, such as *bit* and *pit* in English. If the substitution of *b* for *p* in this minimal pair makes a difference in meaning, as it does in English, then those two sounds have been identified as distinct phonemes of the language and will require two different symbols to record. If, however, the linguist finds two different pronunciations (as when "butter" is pronounced "budder") and then finds that there is no difference in their meaning for a native speaker, the sounds represented will be considered variants of the same phoneme. In such cases, for economy of representation only one of the two symbols will be used to record that sound wherever it is found.

Morphology

While making and studying an inventory of distinctive sounds, linguists also look into **morphology,** the study of the patterns or rules of word formation in a language (including such things as rules concerning verb tense, pluralization, and compound words). They do this by marking out specific sounds and sound combinations that seem to have meaning. These are called **morphemes**—the smallest units of sound that carry a meaning in a language.

Morphemes are distinct from phonemes, which can alter meaning but have no meaning by themselves. For example, a linguist studying English in a North American farming community would soon learn that *cow* is a morpheme—a meaningful combination of the phonemes *c, o,* and *w*. Pointing to two of these animals, the linguist would elicit the word *cows* from local speakers. This would reveal yet another morpheme—the *s*—which can be added to the original morpheme to indicate "plural."

Syntax and Grammar

The next step in unraveling a language is to identify its **syntax**—the patterns or rules by which morphemes are arranged into phrases and sentences. The **grammar** of the language will ultimately consist of all observations about its morphemes and syntax. An important component of syntax is the identification of *form classes*—the parts of speech or categories of words that function the same way in a sentence. This can be done by using *substitution frames*. For example, there exists a category we call "nouns," defined as any word that will fit the substitution frame "I see a ___." The linguist simply makes the frame, tries out a number of words in it, and has a native speaker indicate yes or no for whether the words work. In English, the words *house* and *cat* will fit this frame and will be said to belong to the same form class, but the word *think* will not.

Biocultural Connection

The Biology of Human Speech

While other primates have shown some capacity for language (a socially agreed upon code of communication), actual speech is unique to humans. It comes at a price, for the anatomical organization of the human throat and mouth that make speech possible also increase the risk of choking.

Of particular importance are the positions of the human larynx (voice box) and the epiglottis. The larynx, situated in the respiratory tract between the pharynx (throat) and trachea (wind pipe), contains the vocal chords. The epiglottis is the structure that separates the esophagus or food pipe from the wind pipe as food passes from the mouth to the stomach. (See Figure 16.1 for comparative diagrams of the anatomy of this region in chimps and humans.)

The overlapping routes of passage for food and air can be seen as a legacy of our evolutionary history. Fish, the earliest vertebrates (animals with backbones), obtained both food and oxygen from water entering through their mouths. As land vertebrates evolved, separate means for obtaining food and air developed out of the preexisting combined system. As a result, the pathways for air and food overlap. In most mammals, including human infants and apes of all ages, choking on food is not a problem because the larynx is relatively high in the throat so that the epiglottis seals the windpipe from food with every swallow. The position of the larynx and trachea make it easy for babies to coordinate breathing with eating.

However, as humans mature and develop the neurological and muscular coordination for speech, the larynx and epiglottis shift to a downward position. The human tongue bends at the back of the throat and is attached to the pharynx, the region of the throat where the food and airways share a common path. Sound occurs as air exhaled from the lungs passes over the vocal cords and causes them to vibrate.

Through continuous interactive movements of the tongue, pharynx, lips, and teeth, as well as nasal passages, the sounds are alternately modified to produce speech—the uniquely patterned sounds of a particular language. Based on long-standing socially learned patterns of speech, different languages stress certain distinctive types of sounds as significant and ignore others. For instance, languages belonging to the Iroquoian family, such as Mohawk, Seneca, and Cherokee, are among the few in the world that have no bilabial stops (*b* and *p* sounds). They also lack the labio-dental spirants (*f* and *v* sounds), leaving the bilabial nasal *m* sound as the only consonant requiring lip articulation.

It takes many years of practice for people to master the muscular movements needed to produce the precise sounds of any particular language. But no human could produce the finely controlled speech sounds without a lowered position of the larynx and epiglottis.

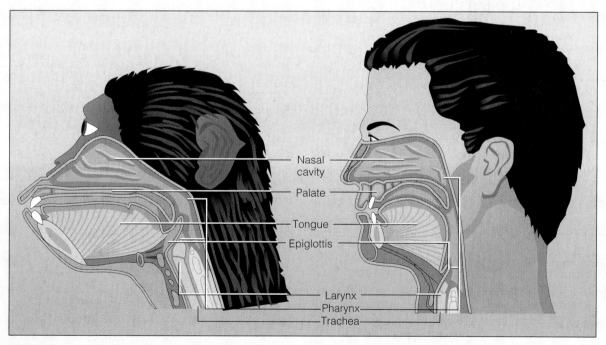

Nasal cavity
Palate
Tongue
Epiglottis
Larynx
Pharynx
Trachea

Figure 16.1

One of the strengths of modern descriptive linguistics is the objectivity of its methods. For example, an English-speaking anthropologist who specializes in this will not approach a language with the idea that it must have nouns, verbs, prepositions, or any other of the form classes identifiable in English. She or he instead sees what turns up in the language and makes an attempt to describe it in terms of its own inner workings. This allows for unanticipated discoveries. For instance, unlike many other languages, English does not distinguish between feminine and masculine nouns. So it is that English speakers use the definite article *the* in front of any noun, while French requires two types of such definite articles: *la* for feminine nouns and *le* for masculine—as in *la lune* (the moon) and *le soleil* (the sun). German speakers go one step further, utilizing three types of articles: *der* in front of masculine nouns, *die* for feminine, and *das* for neutral. It is also interesting to note that in contrast to their French neighbors, Germans consider the moon as masculine, so they say *der Mon,* and the sun as feminine, which makes it *die Sonne.* In another corner of the world, the highlands of Peru and Bolivia in South America, indigenous peoples who speak Quechua are not concerned about such gendered nouns, for there are no definite articles in their language.

HISTORICAL LINGUISTICS

While descriptive linguistics focuses on all features of a particular language as it is at any one moment in time, historical linguistics deals with the fact that languages change. In addition to deciphering "dead" languages that are no longer spoken, specialists in this field investigate relationships between earlier and later forms of the same language, study older languages for developments in modern ones, and examine interrelationships among older languages. For example, they attempt to sort out the development of Latin (spoken almost 1,500 years ago in southern Europe) into Italian, Spanish, Portuguese, French, and Romanian by identifying natural shifts in the original language, as well as modifications brought on by direct contact during the next few centuries with Germanic-speaking invaders from northern Europe.

That said, historical linguists are not limited to the faraway past, for even modern languages are constantly transforming—adding new words, dropping others, or changing meaning. Over the last decade or so, Internet use has widened the meaning of a host of already existing English words—from *hacking* and *surfing* to *spam.* Entirely new words, such as *blogging,* have been coined.

Especially when focusing on long-term processes of change, historical linguists depend on written records of languages. They have achieved considerable success in working out the relationships among different languages, and these are reflected in schemes of classification. For example, English is one of approximately 140 languages classified in the larger Indo-European language family (Figure 16.2). A **language family** is a group of languages descended from a single ancestral language. This family is subdivided into some eleven subgroups, which reflects the fact that there has been a long period (6,000 years or so) of **linguistic divergence** from an ancient unified language (reconstructed as Proto-Indo-European) into separate "daughter" languages. English is one of several languages in the Germanic subgroup (Figure 16.3), all of which are more closely related to one another than they are to the languages of any other subgroup of the Indo-European family.

So it is that, despite the differences between them, the languages of one subgroup share certain features when compared to those of another. As an illustration, the word for "father" in the Germanic languages always starts with an *f* or closely related *v* sound (Dutch *vader,* German *Vater,* Gothic *Fadar*). Among the Romance languages, by contrast, the comparable word always starts with a *p:* French *père,* Spanish and Italian *padre*—all derived from the Latin *pater.* The original Indo-European word for "father" was *p'tēr,* so in this case, the Romance languages have retained the earlier pronunciation, whereas the Germanic languages have diverged. Thus, many words that begin with *p* in the Romance languages, like Latin *piscis* and *pes,* become words like English *fish* and *foot* in the Germanic languages.

language family A group of languages descended from a single ancestral language.
linguistic divergence The development of different languages from a single ancestral language.

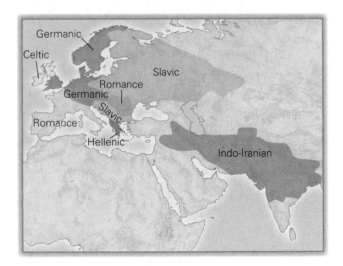

Figure 16.2
The Indo-European languages.

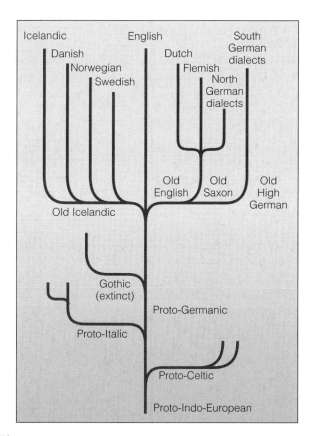

Figure 16.3

English is one of a group of languages in the Germanic subgroup of the Indo-European family. This diagram shows its relationship to other languages in the same subgroup. The root was Proto-Indo-European, an ancestral language originally spoken by early farmers and herders who spread north and west over Europe, bringing with them both their customs and their language.

In addition to describing the changes that have taken place as languages have diverged from ancient parent languages, historical linguists have also developed methods to estimate when such divergences occurred. One such technique is known as **glottochronology,** a term derived from the Greek word *glottis,* which means "tongue" or "language." This method compares the **core vocabularies** of languages—pronouns, lower numerals, and names for body parts and natural objects. It is based on the assumption that these basic vocabularies change more slowly than other words and at a more or less constant rate of 14 to 19 percent per 1,000 years. (Linguists determined this rate by calculating changes documented in thirteen historic written languages.) By applying a mathematical formula to two related core vocabularies, one can roughly determine the approximate number of years since the languages separated. Although not as precise as we might like, glottochronology, in conjunction with other chronological dating methods such as those based on archaeological and genetic data, can help determine the time of linguistic divergence.

Processes of Linguistic Divergence

Studying modern languages in their specific cultural contexts can help us understand the processes of change that may have led to linguistic divergence. Clearly, one force for change is selective borrowing by one language from another. This is evident in the many French words present in the English language—and in the growing number of English words cropping up in languages all around the world due to globalization. Technological breakthroughs resulting in new equipment and products also prompt linguistic shifts. For instance, the electronic revolution that brought us radio, television, and computers has created entirely new vocabularies.

Increasing professional specialization is another driving force. We see one of many examples in the field of biomedicine where today's students must learn the specialized vocabulary and idioms of the profession—over 6,000 new words in the first year of medical school. There is also a tendency for any group within a larger society to create its own unique vocabulary, whether it is a street gang, sorority, religious group, prison inmates, or platoon of soldiers. By changing the meaning of existing words or inventing new ones, members of the "in-group" can communicate with fellow members while effectively excluding outsiders who may be within hearing range. Finally, there seems to be a human tendency to admire the person who comes up with a new and clever idiom, a useful word, or a particularly stylish pronunciation, as long as these do not seriously interfere with communication. All of this means that no language stands still.

Phonological differences among groups may be regarded in the same light as vocabulary differences. In a class-structured society, for example, members of the upper class may try to keep their pronunciation distinct from that of lower classes, or vice versa, as a means of reinforcing social boundaries.

Language Loss and Revival

Perhaps the most powerful force for linguistic change is the domination of one society over another, as demonstrated during 500 years of European colonialism. Such dominations persist in many parts of the world to the present time, such as Taiwan's aboriginal peoples being governed by Mandarin-speaking Chinese, Tarascan Indians by Spanish-speaking Mexicans, or Bushmen by English-speaking Namibians.

glottochronology In linguistics, a method for identifying the approximate time that languages branched off from a common ancestor. It is based on analyzing core vocabularies.
core vocabularies The most basic and long-lasting words in any language—pronouns, lower numerals, and names for body parts and natural objects.

GLOBALSCAPE

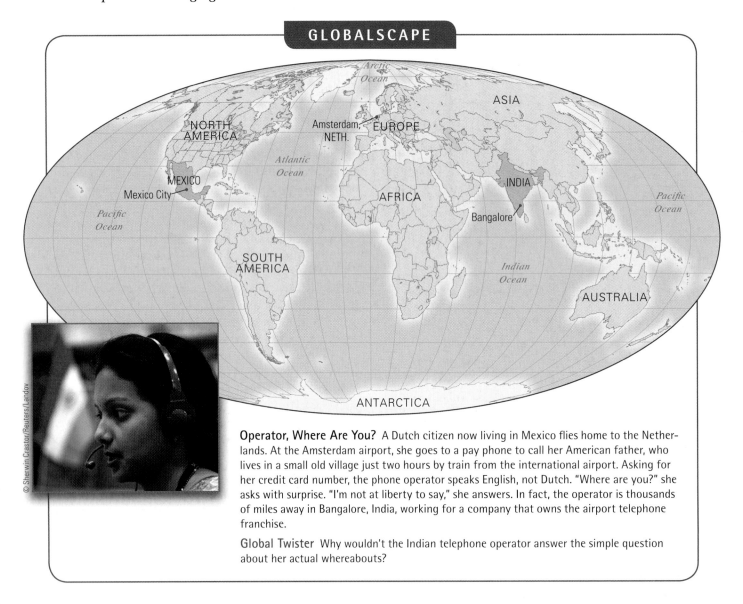

Operator, Where Are You? A Dutch citizen now living in Mexico flies home to the Netherlands. At the Amsterdam airport, she goes to a pay phone to call her American father, who lives in a small old village just two hours by train from the international airport. Asking for her credit card number, the phone operator speaks English, not Dutch. "Where are you?" she asks with surprise. "I'm not at liberty to say," she answers. In fact, the operator is thousands of miles away in Bangalore, India, working for a company that owns the airport telephone franchise.

Global Twister Why wouldn't the Indian telephone operator answer the simple question about her actual whereabouts?

In many cases, foreign political control has resulted in linguistic erosion or even complete disappearance, sometimes leaving only a faint trace in old, indigenous names for geographic features such as hills and rivers. In fact, over the last 500 years about 3,500 of the world's 10,000 or so languages have become extinct as a direct result of warfare, epidemics, and forced assimilation brought on by colonial powers and other aggressive outsiders. Most of the remaining 6,500 languages are spoken by very few people, and many of them are losing speakers rapidly due to globalization. In fact, half have fewer than 10,000 speakers each, and a quarter have fewer than 1,000. In North America, for instance, only 150 of the original 300 indigenous languages still exist, and many of these surviving tongues are seriously endangered and moving toward extinction at an alarming rate.

Anthropologists predict that the number of languages still spoken in the world today will be cut in half by the year 2100, in large part because children born in ethnic minority groups no longer use the ancestral language when they go to school, migrate to cities, join the larger workforce, and are exposed to printed and electronic media. The printing press, radio, satellite television, Internet, and text messaging on cell phones are driving the need for a shared language that many understand, and increasingly that is English. In the past 500 years, this language—originally spoken by about 2.5 million people living only in part of the British Isles in northwestern Europe—has spread around the world. Today some 375 million people (6 percent of the global population) claim English as their native tongue. Close to a billion others (about 15 percent) speak it as a second or foreign language.

While a common language allows people from different ethnic backgrounds to communicate, there is the risk that a global spread of one language may contribute to the disappearance of others. And with the extinction of each language, a measure of humankind's richly varied cultural heritage, including countless insights on life, is lost.

The United Nations Educational, Scientific, and Cultural Organization (UNESCO) recently marked out key factors used to assess the endangerment status of a language.[3] Beyond obvious points—such as declining numbers of speakers, discriminatory governmental policies, non-literacy, and insufficient means for language education—a key issue is the impact electronic media such as the Internet have on language groups. Today, Internet content exists in only a handful of languages, and 80 percent of Internet users are native speakers of just ten of the world's 6,500 languages. On one hand, there is the serious risk that such overwhelming presence of a handful of already dominant languages on the Internet further threatens endangered languages. On the other hand, the Internet offers a powerful tool for maintaining and revitalizing disappearing languages and the cultures they are tied to—as indicated in the ever-growing number of indigenous groups developing computer programs to help teach their native tongues.

Ensuring digital access to local content is a new and important component in language preservation efforts. In 2001, UNESCO established Initiative B@bel, which uses information and communication technologies to support linguistic and cultural diversity. Promoting multilingualism on the Internet, this initiative aims to bridge the digital divide—to make access to Internet content and services more equitable for users worldwide (Figure 16.4).

Sometimes, in reaction to a real or perceived threat of cultural dominance by powerful foreign societies, ethnic groups and even entire countries may seek to maintain or reclaim their unique identity by purging their vocabularies of "foreign" terms. Emerging as a significant force for linguistic change, such **linguistic nationalism** is particularly characteristic of the former colonial countries of Africa and Asia today. It is by no means limited to those countries, however, as one can see by periodic French attempts to purge their language of such Americanisms as *le hamburger*. A recent example of this is France's decision to substitute the word *e-mail* with the newly minted government-approved term *couriel*.

Also in the category of linguistic nationalism are revivals of languages long out of daily use by ethnic minorities and sometimes even whole nations. Examples include efforts among American Indian groups to restore their language and Greece's successful revival of Greek after many centuries of Turkish domination. Perhaps the most remarkable example is the revival of ancient He-

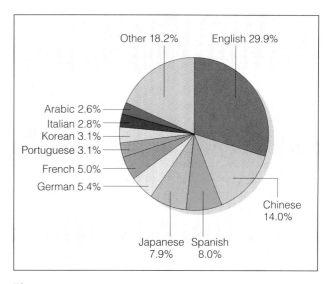

Figure 16.4

Although the world's digital divide is diminishing, it is still dramatic. As illustrated here, 80 percent of today's Internet users are native speakers of just ten of the world's 6,500 languages.
Source: www.internetworldstats.com, 2006.

brew (after it had not been spoken as a daily language for almost 2,000 years) as the basis for the national language of Jews in the modern state of Israel.

For many ethnic minorities, efforts to counter the threat of linguistic extinction or to resurrect already extinct languages form part of their struggle to maintain a sense of cultural identity and dignity. A prime means by which powerful groups try to assert their dominance over minorities living within their borders is to actively suppress their languages.

A dramatic illustration of this is an old government-sanctioned effort to repress Native American cultures in Canada and the United States and fully absorb these cultures into the main body of North American society. Government polices included taking Indian children away from their parents and putting them in boarding schools where only English was allowed, and students were often punished for speaking their traditional languages. Upon returning to their homes, many could no longer communicate with their own close relatives and neighbors.

While now abolished, these institutions and the historical policies that shaped them did lasting damage to American Indian groups striving to maintain their cultural heritage. Especially over the past three decades many of these besieged indigenous communities have

linguistic nationalism The attempt by ethnic minorities and even countries to proclaim independence by purging their language of foreign terms.

---

[3]www.unesco.org/webworld/babel.

Anthropology Applied

Language Renewal among the Northern Ute ▪ By William Leap

On April 10, 1984, the Northern Ute tribe became the first community of American Indians in the United States to affirm the right of its members to regain and maintain fluency in their ancestral language, as well as their right to use it as a means of communication throughout their lives. Like many other Native Americans, they had experienced a decline in fluency in their native tongue, as they were forced to interact more and more intensively with outsiders who spoke only English.

Once the on-reservation boarding school was closed in 1953, Ute children had to attend schools where teachers and most other students were ignorant of the Ute language. Outside the classroom as well, children and adults alike were increasingly bombarded by English as they sought employment off reservation, traded in non-Indian communities, or were exposed to television and other popular media. By the late 1960s, although Ute language fluency was still highly valued, many members of the community could no longer speak it.

Alarmed by this situation, a group of Ute parents decided that action needed to be taken, lest their native language be lost altogether. With the help of other community leaders and educators, they organized meetings to discuss how to remedy the situation. Aware of my work on language education with other tribes, they invited me to participate in the discussions, and subsequently the Utes

asked me to assist with their linguistic renewal efforts.

The first thing I did when I began working with the Utes in 1978 was to conduct a first-ever, reservation-wide language survey. The survey revealed that many individuals had retained a "passive fluency" in the language and could understand it, even though they couldn't speak it.[a] It also showed that children who were still able to speak Ute had fewer problems with English in school than did nonspeakers.

Over the next few years, I helped set up a Ute language renewal program within the tribe's Division of Education, helped secure funding, led staff training workshops in linguistic transcription and grammatical analysis, provided assistance in designing a practical writing system for the language, and supervised data-gathering sessions with already fluent speakers of the language.

In 1980, the local public school established an in-school program to provide instruction in English and Ute for Indian and other interested children. I helped train the language teachers (all of whom were Ute and none of whom had degrees in education) and did research

[a]See Leap, W. L. (1987). Tribally controlled culture change: The Northern Ute language renewal project. In R. M. Wulff & S. J. Fiske (Eds.), *Anthropological praxis: Translating knowledge into action.* Boulder, CO: Westview Press.

that resulted in numerous technical reports, publications, and workshops. I also helped prepare a Ute language handbook for home use so that parents and grandparents might enrich the children's language learning experience, and I put together a preliminary text for the tribe's statement of policy on language. By 1984, this policy was official, and several language development projects were in place on the reservation, all monitored and coordinated by a tribally approved language and culture committee. Although writing in Ute was not a goal, practical needs resulted in development of writing systems, and a number of people in fact became literate in the language.

I feel that these successes were possible only because the Ute themselves were actively involved in all stages of the process, from identifying the need to designing and carrying out the program. Today, Ute language and culture instruction is part of the curriculum in a tribally operated high school, and community programs have been established to build language awareness and literacy. My involvement with this effort has continued, including working with a Ute language staff to develop a dictionary and complete a grammar of sentence and paragraph structures. Most recently, the Ute's Audiovisual Department has partnered in the effort, helping design materials for Ute language instruction in electronic format.

been actively involved in language reclamation efforts, often with the aid of anthropologists specializing in linguistics—as described in this chapter's Anthropology Applied.

LANGUAGE IN ITS SOCIAL AND CULTURAL SETTINGS

As discussed in the section on descriptive linguistics, language is not simply a matter of combining sounds according to certain rules to come up with meaningful utterances. It is important to remember that languages are

spoken by people who are members of distinct societies. In addition to the fact that most societies have their own unique cultures, individuals within each society tend to vary in the ways they use language based on social factors such as gender, age, class, and ethnicity.

We choose words and sentences to communicate meaning, and what is meaningful in one community or culture may not be in another. Our use of language reflects, and is reflected by, the rest of our culture. For that reason, linguistic anthropologists also research language in relation to its various distinctive social and cultural contexts. This third branch of linguistic study falls into two categories: sociolinguistics and ethnolinguistics.

Sociolinguistics

Sociolinguistics, the study of the relationship between language and society, examines how social categories (such as age, gender, ethnicity, religion, occupation, and class) influence the use and significance of distinctive styles of speech.

Language and Gender

As a major factor in personal and social identity, gender is often reflected in language use, so it is not surprising that numerous thought-provoking sociolinguistic topics fall under the category of language and gender. These include research on **gendered speech**—distinct male and female speech patterns, which vary across social and cultural settings.

One of the first in-depth studies in this vein, done in the early 1970s, asserted that neither language nor gender can be studied independently of the socially constructed communities in which we live. Exploring the relationship of gender and power, it addressed specific issues including social factors said to contribute to North American women exhibiting less decisive speech styles than men. This study and a subsequent wave of related scholarly works have produced new insights about language as a social speech "performance" in both private and public settings.[4]

Gendered speech research also includes the study of distinct male and female syntax exhibited in various languages around the world, such as the Lakota language, still spoken at the Pine Ridge and Rosebud Indian reservations in South Dakota. When a Lakota woman asks someone, "How are you?" she says, *"Tonik*thkahe?*"* But when her brother poses the same question, he says, *"Tonik*tukahwo?*"* As explained by Michael Two Horses, "Our language is gender-specific in the area of commands, queries, and a couple of other things."[5]

Learning these nuances of language is not difficult for a child growing up surrounded by Lakota speakers, but it can be hard for newcomers. So it was for U.S. film director/actor Kevin Costner and other actors in the 1990 film *Dances with Wolves,* which tells the fictional story of a white soldier's relationship with a Lakota Indian community in the 1800s. Since Costner (who plays the soldier) and several of the American Indian actors did not speak Lakota, the producers hired a Lakota woman to coach them, aiming to make the feature film as culturally authentic as possible.

Upon release, the film won critical acclaim and drew crowds to cinemas all across the country. When it showed in a theater in Rapid City, South Dakota, Lakota people

Orion Pictures Corporation/Everett Collection

Makers of the 1990 feature film *Dances with Wolves* aimed for cultural authenticity by casting Native American actors and hiring a language coach to teach Lakota to those who did not know how to speak it. However, the lessons did not include the "gendered speech" aspect of Lakota—the fact that females and males follow different rules of syntax. Consequently, when native speakers of the language later saw the finished film, they were amused to hear the actors who portrayed the Lakota warriors speaking like women.

from the nearby reservations arrived on the scene eager to see this movie about their ancestors. But when they heard Costner and his on-screen warrior friends speak, they began to snicker. As the dramatic scenes unfolded, their laughter grew. What was so hilarious? While it was true that Lakota in the audience were generally pleased to hear their own language in a major Hollywood film, they thought it very funny to hear the white hero, along with some non-Lakota Indian actors dressed as warriors, speak Lakota like women. Because the language coach had had to teach both male and female actors, and because they found the language difficult to learn, she had decided not to bother them with the complexities of gendered speech.

Social Dialects

Sociolinguists are also interested in **dialects**—varying forms of a language that reflect particular regions, occupations, or social classes and that are similar enough to be mutually intelligible.

Distinguishing dialects from languages and revealing the relationship between power and language, the

sociolinguistics The study of the relationship between language and society through examining how social categories (such as age, gender, ethnicity, religion, occupation, and class) influence the use and significance of distinctive styles of speech.

gendered speech Distinct male and female speech patterns, which vary across social and cultural settings.

dialects Varying forms of a language that reflect particular regions, occupations, or social classes and that are similar enough to be mutually intelligible.

---

[4]See Lakoff, R.T. (2004). *Language and woman's place.* M. Bucholtz (Ed.). New York: Oxford University Press.

[5]Personal communication, April 2003.

noted linguist/political activist Noam Chomsky often quoted the saying that a dialect is a language without an army.[6] Technically, all dialects are languages—there is nothing partial or sublinguistic about them—and the point at which two different dialects become distinctly different languages is roughly the point at which speakers of one are almost totally unable to communicate with speakers of the other.

Boundaries may be psychological, geographical, social, or economic, and they are not always very sharp. In the case of regional dialects, there is frequently a transitional territory, or perhaps a buffer zone, where features of both are found and understood, as between central and southern China. The fact is that if you learn the Chinese of Beijing, you will find that a Chinese person from Canton or Hong Kong will understand almost nothing of what you say, although both languages—or dialects—are usually lumped together as Chinese.

A classic example of the kind of dialect that may set one group apart from others within a single society is one spoken by many inner-city African Americans. Technically known as African American Vernacular English (AAVE), it has often been referred to as "black English" and "Ebonics." Unfortunately, there is a widespread misperception among non-AAVE speakers that this dialect is somehow substandard or defective. A basic principle of linguistics is that the selection of a so-called prestige dialect—in this case, what we may call "Standard English" as opposed to AAVE—is determined by social historical forces such as wealth and power and is not dependent on virtues or shortcomings of the dialects themselves. In fact, AAVE is a highly structured mode of speech with patterned rules of sounds and sequences like any other language or dialect. Many of its distinctive features stem from the retention of sound patterns, grammatical rules concerning verbs, and even words of the West African languages spoken by the ancestors of present-day African Americans.[7]

---

[6]See biographical entry for Chomsky in Shook, J. R., et al. (Eds.). (2004). *Dictionary of modern American philosophers, 1860–1960.* Bristol, England: Thoemmes Press. The saying is attributed to Yiddish linguist Max Weinreich.

[7]Monaghan, L., Hinton, L., & Kephart, R. (1997). Can't teach a dog to be a cat? The dialogue on ebonics. *Anthropology Newsletter 38* (3), 1, 8, 9.

code switching Changing from one level of language to another as the situation demands, whether from one language to another or from one dialect of a language to another.
ethnolinguistics A branch of linguistics that studies the relationships between language and culture and how they mutually influence and inform each other.
linguistic relativity The idea that distinctions encoded in one language are unique to that language.

Because the AAVE dialect differs so much from Standard English and has been discredited by mainstream society, those who speak it frequently find themselves at a disadvantage outside of their own communities. Schoolteachers, for example, often view African American children as deficient in verbal skills and have even misdiagnosed some of them as "learning impaired." The great challenge for the schools is to find ways of teaching these children how to use Standard English in those situations where it is to their advantage to do so, without detracting from their ability to use the dialect of their own community.

This has been achieved with considerable success in several other countries that have similar challenges. In Scotland, for example, Scots English is now recognized in the schools as a valid and valued way of speaking and is utilized in the teaching of Standard English. As a consequence, individuals become skilled at switching back and forth between the two dialects, depending on the situation in which one is speaking.

Without being conscious of it, we all do the same sort of thing when we switch from formality to informality in our speech, depending upon where we are and to whom we are talking. The process of changing from one language mode to another as the situation demands, whether from one language to another or from one dialect of a language to another, is known as **code switching,** and it has been the subject of a number of sociolinguistic studies.

Ethnolinguistics

The study of the relationships between language and culture, and how they mutually influence and inform each other, is the domain of **ethnolinguistics.**

In this type of research, anthropologists may investigate how a language reflects the culturally significant aspects of a people's traditional natural environment. Among the Inuit in the Canadian Arctic, for instance, we find numerous words for different types of snow, whereas Americans in a city like Detroit most likely possess a rich vocabulary allowing them to precisely distinguish between many different types of cars, categorized by model, year, and manufacturer. This is an example of **linguistic relativity**—the idea that distinctions encoded in one language are unique to that language. Another example concerns cultural categories of color. Languages have different ways of dividing and naming elements of the color spectrum, which is actually a continuum of multiple hues with no clear-cut boundaries between them. In English we speak of red, orange, yellow, green, blue, indigo, and violet, but other languages mark out different groupings. For instance, Indians in Mexico's northwestern mountains speaking Tarahumara have just one word for both "green" and "blue"—*siyoname*.

Linguistic Determinism

Related to linguistic relativity is the principle of **linguistic determinism,** the idea that language to some extent shapes the way in which people view and think about the world around them. An extreme version of this principle holds that language actually determines thought and thereby shapes behavior and culture itself. A more widely accepted view holds that thought is merely influenced by language.

Linguistic determinism is associated with the pioneering ethnolinguistic research of anthropologist Edward Sapir and his student Benjamin Lee Whorf during the 1930s and 1940s. Their research resulted in what is now known as the *Sapir-Whorf hypothesis:* that each language provides particular grooves of linguistic expression that predispose speakers of that language to perceive the world in a certain way. In Whorf's own words, "The structure of the language one habitually uses influences the manner in which one understands his environment. The picture of the universe shifts from tongue to tongue."[8]

Whorf gained many of these insights while translating English into Hopi, a North American Indian language still spoken in Arizona. Doing this work, he discovered that Hopi differs from English not only in vocabulary but also in terms of its grammatical categories such as nouns and verbs. For instance, Hopi use numbers for counting and measuring things that have physical existence, but they do not apply numbers in the same way to abstractions like time. They would have no problem translating an English sentence such as, "I see fifteen sheep grazing on three acres of grassland," but an equally simple sentence such as, "Three weeks ago, I enjoyed my fifteen minutes of fame" would require a much more complex translation into Hopi.

It is also of note that Hopi verbs express tenses differently than English verbs do. Rather than marking past, present, and future, with *-ed, -ing,* or *will,* Hopi requires additional words to indicate if an event is completed, still ongoing, or is expected to take place. So instead of saying, "Three strangers stayed for fifteen days in our village," a Hopi would say something like, "We remember three strangers stay in our village until the sixteenth day." In addition, Hopi verbs do not express tense by their forms. Unlike English verbs that change form to indicate past, present, and future, Hopi verbs distinguish between a statement of fact (if the speaker actually witnesses a certain event), a statement of expectation, and a statement that expresses regularity. For instance, when you ask an English-speaking athlete, "Do you run?" he may answer, "Yes," when in fact he may at that moment be sitting in an armchair watching TV. A Hopi athlete asked the same question in his own language might respond, "No," because in Hopi the statement of fact "he runs" translates as *wari* ("running occurs"), whereas the statement that expresses regularity—"he runs" (on the track team) translates as *warikngwe* (running occurs characteristically).

Considering such linguistic distinctions between Hopi and English, Whorf concluded that the Hopi language structures thinking and behavior with a focus on the present—on getting ready and carrying out what needs to be done right now. He summed it up like this: "A characteristic of Hopi behavior is the emphasis on preparation. This includes announcing and getting ready for events well beforehand, elaborate precautions to insure persistence of desired conditions, and stress on good will as the preparer of good results."[9]

In the 1990s linguistic anthropologists devised new research strategies to actually test Sapir and Whorf's original hypothesis.[10] One study found that speakers of Swedish and Finnish (neighboring peoples who speak radically different languages) working at similar jobs in similar regions under similar laws and regulations show significantly different rates of on-the-job accidents. The rates are substantially lower among the Swedish speakers. What emerges from comparison of the two languages is that Swedish (one of the Indo-European languages) emphasizes information about movement in three-dimensional space. Finnish (a Ural-Altaic language unrelated to Indo-European languages) emphasizes more static relations among coherent temporal entities. As a consequence, it seems that Finns organize the workplace in a way that favors the individual person over the temporal organization in the overall production process. This in turn leads to frequent production disruptions, haste, and (ultimately) accidents. Intriguing as such studies may be, they are not sufficient by themselves for a full understanding of the relation between language and thought. Supplementary approaches are being developed.

A more obvious ethnolinguistic observation is that language mirrors or reflects, rather than determines, cultural reality. Aymara Indians living in the Bolivian highlands, for example, depend on the potato (or *luki*) as their major source of food. Their language has over

---

[8]Quoted in Hoebel, E. A. (1958). *Man in the primitive world: An introduction to anthropology* (p. 571). New York: McGraw-Hill.

[9]Carroll, J. B. (Ed.). (1956). *Language, thought and reality: Selected writings of Benjamin Lee Whorf* (p. 148). Cambridge, MA: MIT Press.

[10]Lucy, J. A. (1997). Linguistic relativity. *Annual Review of Anthropology 26,* 291–312.

linguistic determinism The idea that language to some extent shapes the way in which we view and think about the world around us; sometimes called the Sapir-Whorf hypothesis after its originators Edward Sapir and his student Benjamin Lee Whorf.

Aymara Indians living in the highlands of Bolivia and Peru in South America depend on the potato as their major source of food. Their language has over 200 words for this vegetable, reflecting the many varieties they traditionally grow and the many different ways that they preserve and prepare it.

Kazuyoshi Namachi/Corbis

200 words for potatoes, reflecting the many varieties they traditionally grow and the many different ways that they preserve and prepare this food. Similarly, anthropologists have noted that the language of the Nuer, a nomadic African people of southern Sudan, is rich in words and expressions having to do with cattle; not only are more than 400 words used to describe cattle, but Nuer boys actually take their names from them. Thus, by studying the language we can determine the significance of cattle in Nuer culture and the whole etiquette of human and cattle relationships.

If language does mirror cultural reality, it would follow that changes in a culture will sooner or later be reflected in changes in the language. We see this happening all around the world today, including in the English language.

Consider, for example, the cultural practice of marriage. Historically, English-speaking North Americans have defined marriage as a legally binding union between one man and one woman. However, a growing tolerance toward homosexuals over the past two decades or so, coupled with legislation prohibiting sexual discrimination, resulted in a ruling by Canada's Supreme Court in summer 2003 that it is illegal to exclude same-sex unions from the definition of marriage. Consequently, the meaning of the word *marriage* is now being stretched. It is no longer possible to automatically assume that the term refers to the union of one man and one woman— or that a woman who mentions her spouse is speaking of a man. Such changes in the English language reflect the wider process of change in North America's cultural reality.

Linguists have found that although language is generally flexible and adaptable, established terminologies do tend to perpetuate themselves, reflecting and revealing the social structure and worldview of groups and people. For example, American English has a wide array of words having to do with conflict and warfare. It also features an abundance of militaristic metaphors, such as "conquering" space, "fighting" the "battle" of the bulge, carrying out a "war" against drugs, making a "killing" on the stock market, "shooting down" an argument, "torpedoing" a plan, "spearheading" a movement, "decapitating" a foreign government, or "bombing" on an exam, to mention just a few. An observer from an entirely different and perhaps less aggressive culture, such as the Hopi in Arizona or the Jain in India, could gain considerable insight into the importance of open competition, winning, and military might in the U.S.A. simply by tuning into such commonly used phrases.

Kinship Terms

Ethnolinguists are also interested in the kinship terms people use when referring to their relatives, for these words can reveal much about a culture. By looking at the names people in a particular society use for their relatives, an anthropologist can glean how families are structured, what relationships are considered especially important, and sometimes what the prevailing attitudes are concerning various relationships.

Kinship terminology varies considerably across cultures. For instance, a number of languages use the same word to denote a brother and a cousin, and others have a single word for cousin, niece, and nephew. Some cultures find it useful to distinguish an oldest brother from his younger brothers and have different words for these brothers. And unlike English, many languages distinguish between an aunt who is mother's sister and one who is father's sister. In an upcoming chapter on kinship, we will discuss in detail the meanings behind these and other contrasting kinship terminologies.

LANGUAGE VERSATILITY

In many societies throughout the world, it is not unusual for individuals to be fluent in two, three, or more different languages. They succeed in this in large part because they experience training in multiple languages as children—not as high school or college students, which is the educational norm in the United States.

In some regions where groups speaking different languages co-exist and interact, people often understand one another but may choose not to speak the other's language. Such is the case in the borderlands of northern Bolivia and southern Peru where Quechua-speaking and Aymara-speaking Indians are neighbors. When an Aymara farmer speaks to a Quechua herder in Aymara, the Quechua will reply in Quechua, and vice versa, each knowing that the other understands both languages even if speaking just one. The ability to comprehend two languages but express oneself in only one is known as *receptive* or *passive bilingualism.*

In the United States, perhaps reflecting the country's enormous size and power, many citizens are not interested in learning a second or foreign language. This is especially significant—and troubling—since the United States is not only one of the world's most ethnically diverse countries, but it is also the world's largest economy and heavily dependent on international trade relations. Moreover, in our globalized world, being bilingual or multilingual may open doors of communication not only for trade but for work, diplomacy, art, and friendship.

BEYOND WORDS: THE GESTURE–CALL SYSTEM

Efficient though languages are at naming and talking about ideas, actions, and things, all are insufficient to some degree in communicating certain kinds of information that people need to know in order to fully understand what is being said. For this reason, human speech is always embedded within a gesture-call system of a type that we share with nonhuman primates.

The various sounds and gestures of this system serve to "key" speech, providing listeners with the appropriate frame for interpreting what a speaker is say-

ing. Messages about human emotions and intentions are effectively communicated by this gesture-call system: Is the speaker happy, sad, mad, enthusiastic, tired, or in some other emotional state? Is he or she requesting information, denying something, reporting factually, or lying? Very little of this information is conveyed by spoken language alone. In English, for example, at least 90 percent of emotional information is transmitted not by the words spoken but by body language and tone of voice.

Body Language

The **gesture** component of the gesture-call system consists of facial expressions and bodily postures and motions that convey intended as well as subconscious messages. The method for notating and analyzing this body language is known as **kinesics.**

Humankind's repertoire of body language is enormous. This is evident if you consider just one aspect of it: the fact that a human being has eighty facial muscles and is thereby capable of making more than 7,000 facial expressions! Thus, it should not be surprising to hear that at least 60 percent of our total communication takes place nonverbally. Often, gestural messages complement spoken messages—for instance, nodding the head while af-

gesture Facial expressions and bodily postures and motions that convey intended as well as subconscious messages.
kinesics A system of notating and analyzing postures, facial expressions, and bodily motions that convey messages.

Learned gestures to which different cultures assign different meanings are known as conventional gestures. The "Hook 'em, horns" salute flashed by U.S. President Bush and his family during his 2005 inauguration shocked many Europeans who interpreted it as a salute to Satan. Known as the "devil's hand" in some parts of the world, in Bush's home state of Texas the gesture is a sign of love for the University of Texas Longhorns, whose fans shout out "Hook 'em, horns!" at sporting events. Here, Bush's daughter Jenna gives the sign.

VISUAL COUNTERPOINT

Cultures around the world have noticeably different attitudes concerning proxemics or personal space—how far apart people should position themselves in nonintimate social encounters. How does the gap between the shirt-sleeved U.S. businessmen pictured here compare with that of the robed men of Saudi Arabia?

firming something verbally, raising eyebrows when asking a question, or using hands to illustrate or emphasize what is being talked about. However, nonverbal signals are sometimes at odds with verbal ones, and they have the power to override or undercut them. For example, a person may say the words "I love you" a thousand times to someone, but if it's not true, the nonverbal signals will likely communicate that falseness.

Little scientific notice was taken of body language prior to the 1950s, but since then a great deal of research has been devoted to this intriguing subject. Cross-cultural studies in this field have shown that there are many similarities around the world in such basic facial expressions as smiling, laughing, crying, and displaying shock or anger. The smirks, frowns, and gasps that we have inherited from our primate ancestry require little learning and are harder to "fake" than conventional or socially obtained gestures that are shared by members of a group, albeit not always consciously so.

Routine greetings are also similar around the world. Europeans, Balinese, Papuans, Samoans, Bushmen, and at least some South American Indians all smile and nod, and if the individuals are especially friendly, they will raise their eyebrows with a rapid movement, keeping them raised for a fraction of a second. By doing so, they signal a readiness for contact. The Japanese, however, suppress the eyebrow flash, regarding it as indecent, showing that there are important differences, as well as similarities, cross-culturally. This can be seen in gestural expressions for yes and no. In North America, one nods

the head down then up for yes or shakes it left and right for no. The people of Sri Lanka also nod to answer yes to a factual question, but if asked to do something, a slow sideways movement of the head means yes. In Greece, the nodded head means yes, but no is indicated by jerking the head back so as to lift the face, usually with the eyes closed and the eyebrows raised.

Another aspect of body language has to do with social space: how people position themselves physically in relation to others. **Proxemics,** the cross-cultural study of humankind's perception and use of space, came to the fore through the work of anthropologist Edward Hall, who coined the term. Growing up in the culturally diverse southwestern United States, Hall glimpsed the complexities of intercultural relations early on in life. As a young man in the 1930s, he worked with construction crews of Hopi and Navajo Indians, building roads and dams. In 1942 he earned his doctorate in anthropology under the famous Franz Boas, who stressed the point that "communication constitutes the core of culture."

This idea was driven home for Hall during World War II when he commanded an African American regiment in Europe and the Philippines and again when he worked with the U.S. State Department to develop the new field of intercultural communication at the Foreign Service Institute (FSI). It was during his years at FSI (1950–1955), while training some 2,000 Foreign Service workers, that Hall's ideas about proxemics began to crystallize. He articulated them and other aspects of nonverbal communication in his 1959 book, *The Silent Language,* now recognized as the founding document for the field of intercultural communication.

His work showed that people from different cultures have different frameworks for defining and organizing

proxemics The cross-cultural study of humankind's perception and use of space.

space—the personal space they establish around their bodies, as well as the macrolevel sensibilities that shape cultural expectations about how streets, neighborhoods, and cities should be arranged. Among other things, his investigation of personal space revealed that every culture has distinctive norms for closeness. (You can see this for yourself if you are watching a foreign film, visiting a foreign country, or find yourself in a multicultural group. How close to one another do the people you are observing stand when talking in the street or riding in a subway or elevator? Does the pattern match the one you are accustomed to in your own cultural corner?)

Hall identified four categories of proxemically relevant spaces or body distances: intimate (0–18 inches), personal-casual (1½ – 4 feet), social-consultive (4–12 feet), and public distance (12 feet and beyond). Hall warned that different cultural definitions of socially accepted use of space within these categories can lead to serious miscommunication and misunderstanding in cross-cultural settings. His research has been a foundation stone for the present-day training of international businesspeople, diplomats, and others involved in intercultural work.

Paralanguage

The second component of the gesture-call system is **paralanguage**—specific voice effects that accompany speech and contribute to communication. These include vocalizations such as giggling, groaning, or sighing, as well as voice qualities such as pitch and tempo.

The importance of paralanguage is suggested by the comment, "It's not so much *what* was said as *how* it was said." Recent studies have shown, for example, that subliminal messages communicated below the threshold of conscious perception by seemingly minor differences in phrasing, tempo, length of answers, and the like are far more important in courtroom proceedings than even the most perceptive trial lawyer may have realized. Among other things, how a witness gives testimony alters the reception it gets from jurors and influences the witness' credibility.[11]

Communication took a radical turn in the 1990s when the use of e-mail and Internet chat rooms became widespread. Both resemble the spontaneity and speed of face-to-face communication but lack the body signals and voice qualifiers that nuance what is being said (and hint how it is being received). According to a recent study, the intended tone of e-mail messages is perceived correctly only 56 percent of the time. A misunderstood message can quickly escalate into a "flame war" with hostile and insulting messages. Because the risk of miscommunica-

tion on the Internet abounds, even with the use of interpretation signals such as LOL (laugh out loud) or the smiley face (☺), certain sensitive exchanges are usually better made in person.[12]

TONAL LANGUAGES

There is an enormous diversity in the ways languages are spoken. In addition to hundreds of vowels and consonants, sounds can be divided into tones—rises and falls in pitch that play a key role in distinguishing one word from another. About 70 percent of the world's languages are **tonal languages** in which the various distinctive sound pitches of spoken words are not only an essential part of their pronunciation but are also key to their meaning; worldwide, at least one-third of the population speaks a tonal language.

Many languages in Africa, Central America, and East Asia are tonal. For instance, Mandarin Chinese, the most common language in China, has four contrasting tones: flat, rising, falling, and falling then rising. These tones are used to distinguish among normally stressed syllables that are otherwise identical. Thus, depending on intonation, *ba* can mean "to uproot," "eight," "to hold," or "a harrow" (farm tool).[13] Cantonese, the primary language in southern China and Hong Kong, uses six contrasting tones, and some Chinese dialects have as many as nine. In nontonal languages such as English, tone can be used to convey an attitude or to change a statement into a question, but tone alone does not change the meaning of individual words as it does in Mandarin, where careless use of tones with the syllable *ma* could cause one to call someone's mother a horse!

THE ORIGINS OF LANGUAGE

Cultures all around the world have sacred stories or myths addressing the age-old question of the origin of human languages. Anthropologists collecting these stories have often found that cultural groups tend to locate the place of origin in their own ancestral homelands and believe that the first humans also spoke their language.

[11]O'Barr, W. M., & Conley, J. M. (1993). When a juror watches a lawyer. In W. A. Haviland & R. J. Gordon (Eds.), *Talking about people* (2nd. ed., pp. 42–45). Mountain View, CA: Mayfield.

[12]Kruger, J., et al. (2005, December). Egocentrism over e-mail: Can people communicate as well as they think? *Journal of Personality and Social Psychology* 89 (6), 925–936.

[13]Catford, J. C. (1988). *A practical introduction to phonetics* (p. 183). Oxford, England: Clarendon Press.

paralanguage Voice effects that accompany language and convey meaning. These include vocalizations such as giggling, groaning, or sighing, as well as voice qualities such as pitch and tempo.
tonal language A language in which the sound pitch of a spoken word is an essential part of its pronunciation and meaning.

The unfinished Tower of Babel, described in the first book of the Bible, symbolizes an ancient West Asian myth about the origins of language diversity.

For example, the Incas of Peru tell the story of Pachamacac, the divine creator, who came to the valley of Tiwanaku in the Andean highlands in ancient times. As the story goes, Pachamacac drew people up from the earth, making out of clay a person of each nation, painting each with particular clothing, and giving to each a language to be spoken and songs to be sung. On the other side of the globe, ancient Israelites believed that it was Yahweh, the divine creator and one true god, who had given them Hebrew, the original tongue spoken in paradise. Later, when humans began building the massive Tower of Babel to signify their own power and to link earth and heaven, Yahweh intervened. He created a confusion of tongues so that people could no longer understand one another, and he scattered them all across the face of the earth, leaving the tower unfinished.

The question of the origin of language has also been a fascinating subject among scientists, who have put forth some reasonable and some not so reasonable ideas on the subject: Exclamations became words, sounds in nature were imitated, or people simply got together and assigned sounds to objects and actions.

The main trouble with early efforts to explain the origin of language was that so little data were available. Today, there is more scientific evidence, including genetic data, to work with—better knowledge of primate brains, new studies of primate communication, more information on the development of linguistic competence in children, more human fossils that can be used to tentatively reconstruct what ancient brains and vocal tracts were like, and a better understanding of the lifeways of early human ancestors. We still cannot conclusively prove how, when, and where human language first developed, but we can now theorize reasonably on the basis of more and better information.

The archaeological record shows that archaic humans known as Neandertals (living from 30,000 to 125,000 years ago in Europe and Southwestern Asia) had the neural development and anatomical features necessary for speech. Recently, scientists at the Max Planck Institute for Evolutionary Anthropology in Leipzig, Germany, reported the discovery of a so-called language gene in humans, named the FOXP2 gene. Differing from versions of the gene found in other primates, it may control the ability to make fine movements of the mouth and larynx necessary for spoken language.[14]

Some noted scientists dismiss the idea of a single language gene.[15] Leading evolutionary theorist Philip Lieberman argues that the human language ability is the confluence of a succession of separate evolutionary developments rigged together by natural selection for an evolutionarily unique ability.[16]

---

[14]Enard, W., et al. (2002). Molecular evolution of FOXP2, a gene involved in speech and language. *Nature 418,* 869–872.

[15]For example, Robbins Burling, professor emeritus of anthropology and linguistics at the University of Michigan, commented, "It's more likely a *symphony* of genes" (personal communication). See also Burling, R. (2005). *The talking ape: How language evolved.* Oxford: Oxford University Press.

[16]Lieberman, P. (2006). *Toward an evolutionary biology of language.* Cambridge, MA: Belknap Press.

As human language is embedded within a gesture-call system of a type that we share with nonhuman primates, anthropologists have gained considerable insight on human language by observing the communication systems of fellow primates (especially apes)—comparing their anatomy with that of humans past and present and testing their ability to learn and use forms of human language such as American Sign Language (ASL). Attempts to teach other primates to actually speak like humans have not been successful. In one famous experiment in communication that went on for seven years, for example, the chimpanzee Viki learned to voice only a very few words, such as *up, mama,* and *papa.* This inability to speak is not the result of any obvious sensory or perceptual deficit, and apes can in fact produce many of the sounds used in speech. Evidently, their failure to speak has to do with either a lack of motor control mechanisms to articulate speech or to the virtually complete preoccupation of the throat and mouth for expressing emotional states, such as anger, fear, or joy.

Better results have been achieved through nonvocal methods. Recognizing the importance of gestural communication to apes, psychologists Allen and Beatrice Gardner began teaching ASL to their young chimpanzee Washoe, the first of several who have since learned to sign. With vocabularies of over 400 signs, chimps have shown themselves able to transfer each sign from its original referent to other appropriate objects and even to pictures of objects. Their vocabularies include verbs, adjectives, and such words as *sorry* and *please;* furthermore, they can string signs together properly to produce original sentences, even inflecting their signs to indicate person, place, and instrument. More impressive still, Washoe was observed spontaneously teaching her adopted son Loulis how to sign by deliberately manipulating his hand. For five years, humans had refrained from signing when in sight of Loulis, over which time he learned no fewer than fifty signs.

Chimps have not been the only subjects of ape language experiments. Gorillas and orangutans have also been taught ASL with results that replicate those obtained with chimps. As a consequence, there is now a growing agreement among researchers that all of the great apes can develop language skills at least to the level of a 2- to 3-year-old human. Not only are comprehension skills similar, but so is acquisition order: *What* and *where, what-to-do* and *who,* as well as *how* questions are acquired in that order by both apes and humans. Like humans, apes are capable of referring to events removed in time and space, a phenomenon known as **displacement** and one of the distinctive features of human language.

One of the most difficult problems for students dealing with the origin of language is the origin of syntax, which was necessary to enable our ancestors to articulate and communicate more complex ideas. Another problem involves the relationship between manual gestures and spoken language. Because continuity exists between gestural and spoken language, the latter could have emerged from the former through increasing emphasis on finely controlled movements of the mouth and throat—a scenario consistent with the appearance of neurological structures underlying language in the earliest representatives of the genus *Homo* and steady en-

displacement Referring to things and events removed in time and space.

Several species of apes have been taught to use American Sign Language. Some chimpanzees have acquired signing vocabularies surpassing 400 words, and a lowland gorilla named Koko has a working vocabulary of more than 1,000 words.

© Susan Kuklin/Photo Researchers, Inc.

largement of the human brain *before* the alteration of the vocal tract began that allows us to speak the way we do.

The advantage of spoken over gestural language to a species increasingly dependent on tool use for survival is obvious. To talk with your hands, you must stop whatever else you are doing with them; speech does not interfere with that. Other benefits include being able to talk in the dark, past opaque objects, or among speakers whose attention is diverted. Just when the changeover to spoken language took place is not known, although all would agree that spoken languages are at least as old as the species *Homo sapiens*.

Early anthropologists searched for a truly "primitive" language spoken by a living people that might show the processes of language just beginning or developing. That search has now been abandoned, for anthropologists have come to realize that there is no such thing as a "primitive" language in the world today, or even in the recent past. So far, all human languages that have been described and studied, even among people with something approximating a Stone Age technology, are highly developed, complex, and capable of expressing infinite meanings. Every language or dialect now known has a long history and has developed its own particular subtleties and complexities that reflect its speakers' way of life and what they want or need to communicate with others. Thus, anthropologists recognize that all languages are more or less equally effective as systems of communication within their own particular cultural contexts.

FROM SPEECH TO WRITING

When anthropology developed as an academic discipline over a century ago, it concentrated its attention on small traditional communities that relied primarily on personal interaction and oral communication for survival. Cultures that depend on talking and listening often have rich traditions of storytelling and speechmaking. For them, oration (from the Latin *orare*, "to speak") plays a central role in education, conflict resolution, political decision making, spiritual or supernatural practices, and many other aspects of life. Consequently, people capable of making expressive and informed speeches usually enjoy great prestige in such societies.

Today as in the past, traditional orators are typically trained from childhood in memorizing genealogies, ritual prayers, customary laws, and diplomatic agreements. In ceremonies that can last many hours, even days, they eloquently recite the oral traditions by heart. Their extraordinary memories are often enhanced by oral devices such as rhyme, rhythm, and melody. Orators may also

employ special objects to help them remember proper sequences and points to be made—memory devices such as notched sticks, knotted strings, bands embroidered with shells, and so forth. Traditional Iroquois Indian orators, for example, often performed their formal speeches with wampum belts made of hemp string and purple-blue and white shell beads (quahog and whelk shells) woven into distinctive patterns. More than artful motifs, wampum designs were used to symbolize any of a variety of important messages or agreements, including treaties with other nations.

Such symbolic designs are found all over the world, some dating back more than 30,000 years. When ancient artifacts of bone, antler, stone, or some other material have been etched or painted, anthropologists try to determine if these markings were created to symbolize specific ideas such as seasonal calendars, kinship relations, trade records, and so forth. From basic visual signs such as these emerged a few writing systems, including the alphabet.

Thousands of languages, past and present, have existed only in spoken form, but many others have been documented in graphic symbols of some sort. Over time, visual representations in the form of simplified pictures of things (pictographs) evolved into more stylized symbolic forms.

Although different peoples invented a variety of graphic styles, anthropologists distinguish an actual **writing system** as a set of visible or tactile signs used to represent units of language in a systematic way. Recently discovered symbols carved into 8,600-year-old tortoise shells found in western China may represent the earliest evidence of elementary writing found anywhere.[17]

A fully developed early writing system is Egyptian hieroglyphics, developed some 5,000 years ago and in use for about 3,500 years. One of the other oldest systems in the world is cuneiform, an arrangement of wedge-shaped imprints developed primarily in Mesopotamia (present-day Iraq), which lasted nearly as long. Cuneiform writing stands out among other early forms in that it led to the first and only phonetic writing system (that is, an alphabet), ultimately spawning a wide array of alphabetic writing systems. About two millennia after these systems were established, others began to appear, developing independently in distant locations around the world. These include the oldest known hieroglyphics in the Americas, used as early as 2,900 years ago by Olmec Indians inhabiting what is now Vera Cruz, Mexico.[18]

writing system A set of visible or tactile signs used to represent units of language in a systematic way.

[17]Li, X. et al. (2003). The earliest writing? Sign use in the seventh millennium BC at Jiahu, Henan Province, China. *Antiquity 77*, 31–44.

[18]del Carmen Rodríguez Martínez, M., et al. (2006). Oldest writing in the New World. *Science 313* (5793), 1,610–1,614.

Tac Yec Neen Ho Gar Ton (Red Indian) Emperor of the Six Nations 1710, Verelst, Johannes or Jan (b. 1648-fl 1719)/Private Collection/The Bridgeman Art Library

Tee Yee Neen Ho Ga Row, Mohawk chief of the Iroquois Confederacy, holding a wampum belt made of hemp string and shell beads (quahog and whelk shells). Wampum designs were used to symbolize a variety of important messages or agreements, including treaties with other nations. (By Dutch painter Johannes Verelst in 1710. National Archives of Canada collections.)

Inscriptions recently discovered in Egypt's western desert suggest that our **alphabet** (a series of symbols representing the *sounds* of a language) was invented almost 4,000 years ago by Semitic-speaking peoples in that region. Analysis of the Semitic inscriptions, which were carved into a natural limestone wall alongside hundreds of Egyptian hieroglyphs, reveals that these early Semites adopted a limited number of Egyptian hieroglyphs as symbols for sounds in their own language. For instance, they took the Egyptian glyph for "ox" and determined that it would stand for the sound at the start of the Semitic word for "ox," which is *aleph*. (This symbol looks like the horned head of an ox—and like the letter *A* upside-down). Likewise, they chose the Egyptian glyph for "house" to stand for the opening sound of the Semitic word for "house," which is *beth*. (This symbol looks like a two-room house—and like the letter *B* tipped back.) The result was a writing system with characters based on a selection of Egyptian glyphs but used to represent sounds in an early Semitic language. Over the next

1,000 years, Semitic-speaking peoples inhabiting the eastern Mediterranean (including Canaanites, Hebrews, and Phoenicians) adopted this system and developed the script into a more linear form.[19]

Most of the alphabets used today descended from the Phoenician one. The Greeks adopted it about 2,800 years ago, modifying the characters to suit sounds in their own language. The word *alphabet* comes from the first two letters in the Greek writing system, *alpha* and *beta* (otherwise meaningless words in Greek.). From Greek colonies in southern Italy, the writing system spread north to Rome. Then, when Latin-speaking Romans expanded their empire throughout much of Europe, northern Africa, and western Asia, small groups of formally educated people from dozens of different nations in the realm communicated in the Latin language and used its associated alphabet. The Roman alphabet, slightly modified from Greek, spread even further from the 15th century onward as European nations expanded their trade networks and built colonial empires overseas. The 15th-century invention of the printing press fueled worldwide diffusion of the alphabet, making it possible to mechanically reproduce writings in any human language.

Although other writing systems, such as Chinese, are very widely used by millions of people, North American inventions such as the Internet in the late 20th century help solidify the use of the alphabet as a global writing system.

Literacy in Our Globalizing World

Thousands of years have passed since literacy first emerged, yet today more than 860 million adults worldwide cannot read and write. Illiteracy condemns already disadvantaged people to ongoing poverty—migrant rural workers, refugees, ethnic minorities, and those living in rural backlands and urban slums throughout the world. For example, a third of India's 1 billion inhabitants cannot read and write, and some 113 million children around the world are not enrolled in school.

Declaring literacy a human right, the United Nations established September 8 as International Literacy Day and proclaimed the period 2003 to 2012 as the Literacy Decade with the objective of extending literacy to all humanity. Every September 8 during this decade the UNESCO awards prizes to individuals or groups making particularly effective contributions to the fight against illiteracy.

---

[19]Himmelfarb, E. J. (2000, January/February). First alphabet found in Egypt. Newsbrief. *Archaeology 53* (1).

alphabet   A series of symbols representing the sounds of a language arranged in a traditional order.

Questions for Reflection

1. In what ways do you feel prepared or unprepared to meet the challenge of communicating effectively in our increasingly globalized world?

2. Up to 4,000 languages have disappeared over the last 500 years, most of them vanishing without a trace. Only 6,500 languages remain. If the same rate of extinction continues, and just one or two languages exist in the year 2500, would that be a loss or a gain? How so?

3. Applying the principle of linguistic determinism to your own language, consider how your perceptions of objective reality might have been shaped by your language. How might your sense of reality be different if you grew up speaking Hopi?

4. Think about the gestures commonly used in your own family. Are they more or less powerful than the words expressed?

5. From its earliest days writing was linked to political power. How does that apply to modern media and globalization?

Suggested Readings

Duranti, A. (2001). Linguistic anthropology: History, ideas, and issues. In A. Duranti (Ed.), *Linguistic anthropology: A reader* (pp. 1–38). Oxford, England: Blackwell.

Good summary of the development of the field of linguistic anthropology.

Gladdol, D. (2006). *English next*. London: British Council.

A fascinating overview of the rise of English as a global language—and the socioeconomic problems this spread presents to monolingual English-speaking people. (PDF available online, free)

Lakoff, R. T. (2004). *Language and woman's place*. M. Bucholtz (Ed.). New York: Oxford University Press.

A new edition of Lakoff's 1975 seminal book on gender and language, featuring annotations by Lakoff and twenty-five essays by scholars whose own language and gender research grew out of positive and negative reactions to her original work.

Lieberman, P. (2006) *Toward an evolutionary biology of language*. Cambridge, MA: Belknap Press.

A leading evolutionary theorist of language draws on evidence from evolutionary biology, genetics, physical anthropology, anatomy, and neuroscience.

Morse, D., et al. (1979). *Gestures: Their origins and distribution*. New York: Stein & Day.

This well-illustrated text explores the derivations and distributions of dozens of gestures, as well as the varied meanings they have in different parts of the world.

Yip, M. (2002). *Tone*. New York: Cambridge University Press.

A comprehensive and clearly organized introduction to tone and tonal phonology, covering the main types of tonal systems found in Africa, the Americas, and Asia.

Thomson Audio Study Products

 Enjoy the MP3-ready Audio Lecture Overviews for each chapter and a comprehensive audio glossary of key terms for quick study and review. Whether walking to class, doing laundry, or studying at your desk, you now have the freedom to choose when, where, and how you interact with your audio-based educational media. See the preface for information on how to access this on-the-go study and review tool.

The Anthropology Resource Center

www.thomsonedu.com/anthropology
The Anthropology Resource Center provides extended learning materials to reinforce your understanding of key concepts in the four fields of anthropology. For each of the four fields, the Resource Center includes dynamic exercises including video exercises, map exercises, simulations, and "Meet the Scientists" interviews, as well as critical thinking questions that can be assigned and e-mailed to instructors. The Resource Center also provides breaking news in anthropology and interesting material on applied anthropology to help you link what you are learning to the world around you.

17 Social Identity, Personality, and Gender

© Richard Lord

CHALLENGE ISSUE

Every society faces the challenge of humanizing its children, teaching them the values and social codes that will enable them to be functioning and contributing members in the community. This is essential, for it helps ensure that the society will perpetuate itself culturally as well as biologically. Ethnographic research has revealed a wide range of approaches to raising children in order to meet this goal. These different child-rearing methods and their possible effects on adult personalities have long been of interest to anthropologists. Here, three Afghani mothers hold their daughters, whose growing up years in their traditional gender-segregated society are likely to be quite distinct from those in many other corners of the world.

What Is Enculturation?

As noted in the previous chapter, enculturation is the process by which culture is passed from one generation to the next and through which individuals become members of their society. In this chapter we investigate the details of this process, which begins soon after birth with the development of self-awareness—the ability to perceive oneself as a unique phenomenon in time and space and to judge one's own actions. For self-awareness to function, the individual must be provided with a behavioral environment. The way a person perceives and gets oriented to surrounding objects is specified by the culture in which he or she grows up. Along with object orientation, a behavioral environment includes spatial, temporal, and normative orientations.

How Does Enculturation Influence Personality?

Studies have shown that there is some kind of structural relationship between enculturation and personality development. It is also clear that each individual begins with certain broad potentials and limitations that are genetically inherited. In some cultures, "particular child-rearing practices seem to promote the development of compliant personalities, while in others different practices seem to promote more independent, self-reliant personalities.

Are Different Personalities Characteristic of Different Cultures?

Every culture emphasizes certain personality traits as good and others as bad—and has distinct ways of encouraging or discouraging those traits accordingly. Nonetheless, it is difficult to characterize cultures in terms of particular personalities. Of the several attempts made, the concept of modal personality is the most satisfactory. This recognizes that any human society has a range of individual personalities, but some will be more typical than others. Those that approximate the modal personality of a particular culture are thought of as normal. Since modal personalities may differ from one culture to another and since cultures may differ in the range of variation they will accept, it is clear that abnormal personality is a relative concept.

In 1690 English philosopher John Locke presented his *tabula rasa* theory in his book *An Essay Concerning Human Understanding*. This notion held that a newborn human was like a blank slate used as a tablet or blackboard for writing on with chalk. And what the individual became in life was written on the slate by his or her life experiences. The implication is that at birth all individuals are basically the same in their potential for personality development and that their adult personalities are exclusively the products of their postbirth experiences, which differ from culture to culture.

Locke's idea offered high hopes for the all-embracing impact of intellectual and moral instruction on a child's character formation, but it missed the mark, for it did not take into consideration what we now know: Based on recent breakthroughs in human genetic research, most anthropologists now recognize that a substantial portion of our behavior is influenced by genetic factors.[1] What scientific research has not determined, however, is which genes or gene combinations are linked to human social behavior, and to what degree social, cultural, environmental, or a variety of other factors play a formative role in determining adult personality. Indeed, even though genetic coding is tied to aspects of personality, cultural factors play a vital role as they shape how biological variations are interpreted and valued. In other words, while this genetic inheritance sets certain broad potentials and limitations, an individual's cultural identity and unique life experiences, particularly in the early years, also play a significant role in this formation.

Since different cultures handle the raising and instruction or education of the young in different ways, child-rearing practices and their effects on adult personalities are important subjects of anthropological inquiry. Such cross-cultural studies gave rise to the specialization of psychological anthropology and are the subjects of this chapter.

ENCULTURATION: THE HUMAN SELF AND SOCIAL IDENTITY

From the moment of birth, a person faces multiple survival challenges. Obviously, newborns cannot take care of their own biological needs. Only in myths and romantic fantasies do we encounter stories about children successfully coming of age alone in the wilderness or accomplishing this feat having been raised by animals in the wild. For example, Italians in Rome still celebrate the mythological founders of their city, the twin broth-

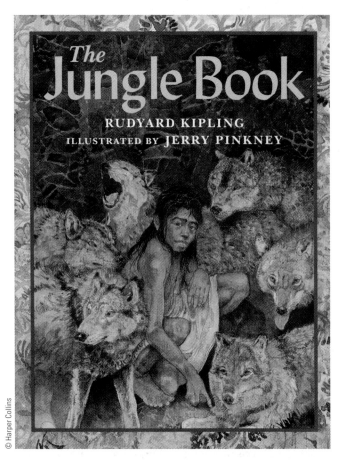

© Harper Collins

In 1916 the international Boy Scout movement expanded to include younger boys in a "cub scout" program inspired by Rudyard Kipling's *The Jungle Book* (1894). Born in former British India (1865), Kipling wrote this story about a young boy in India named Mowgli being raised by a wolf as one of her own cubs. Translated into some forty languages, including Hindi, Swahili, and Chinese, the book has been the subject of many cartoons and movies. Despite happy wild-child legends, human infants are biologically ill-equipped to survive successfully without culture.

ers Romulus and Remus, who according to legend were suckled as infants by a she-wolf. Also, millions of children around the world have been fascinated by stories about Tarzan and the apes or the jungle boy Mowgli and the wolves. Moreover, young and old alike have been captivated by newspaper hoaxes about "wild" children, such as a 10-year-old boy reported to have been found running among gazelles in the Syrian desert in 1946.

Fanciful imaginations aside, human children are biologically ill-equipped to survive without culture. This point has been driven home by several documented cases about feral children (feral comes from *fera*, which is Latin for "wild animal") who grew up deprived of human contact. None of them had a happy ending. For instance, there was nothing romantic about the girl Kamala, supposedly rescued from a wolf den in India in 1920: She moved about on all fours and could not feed herself. And everyone in Paris considered the naked "wild boy" captured in the woods outside Aveyron village in 1800 an

_____

[1]http://www.healthanddna.com/behavioralgenetics.html.

incurable idiot. Clearly, the biological capacity for what we think of as human, which entails culture, must be nurtured to be realized.

Because culture is socially constructed and learned rather than biologically inherited, all societies must somehow ensure that culture is adequately transmitted from one generation to the next—a process we have already defined as *enculturation*. Since each group lives by a particular set of cultural rules, a child will have to learn the rules of his or her society in order to survive. Most of that learning takes place in the first few years when a child learns how to feel, think, speak, and, ultimately, act like an adult who embodies being Japanese, Kikuyu, Lakota, Norwegian, or whatever ethnic or national group into which it is born.

The first agents of enculturation in all societies are the members of the household into which a person is born. Initially, the most important member of this household is the newborn's mother. (In fact, cultural factors are at work even before a child is born, through what a pregnant mother eats, drinks, and inhales, as well as the sound, rhythm, and activity patterns of her daily life.) Soon thereafter, other household members come to play roles in the enculturation process. Just who these others are depends on how households are structured in the particular society.

 THOMSON AUDIO STUDY PRODUCTS Take advantage of the MP3-ready Audio Lecture Overviews and comprehensive audio glossary of key terms for each chapter. See the preface for information on how to access this on-the-go study and review tool.

As the young person matures, individuals outside the household are brought into the enculturation process. These usually include other relatives and certainly the individual's peers. The latter may be included informally in the form of playgroups or formally in age associations, where children actually teach other children. In some societies, and the United States is a good example, professionals are brought into the process to provide formal instruction. In many societies, however, children are pretty much allowed to learn through observation and participation, at their own speed.

Self-Awareness

Enculturation begins with the development of **self-awareness**—the ability to identify oneself as an individual creature, to reflect on oneself, and to evaluate oneself. Humans do not have this ability at birth, even though it is essential for their successful social functioning. It is self-awareness that permits one to assume responsibility for one's conduct, to learn how to react to others, and to assume a variety of roles in society. An important aspect of self-awareness is the attachment of positive value to one's self. Without this, individuals cannot be motivated to act to their advantage rather than disadvantage.

Self-awareness does not come all at once. In modern industrial and postindustrial societies, for example, self and non-self are not clearly distinguished until a child is about 2 years of age. This development of self-awareness in children growing up in such large-scale societies, however, may lag somewhat behind other cultures. Self-awareness develops in concert with neuromotor development, which is known to proceed at a slower rate in infants from industrial societies than in infants in many, perhaps even most, small-scale farming or foraging communities. The reasons for this slower rate are not yet clear, although the amount of human contact and stimulation that infants receive seems to play an important role. In the United States, for example, infants generally do not sleep with their parents, most often being put in rooms of their own. This is seen as an important step in making them into individuals, "owners" of themselves and their capacities, rather than part of some social whole. As a consequence, they do not experience the steady stream of personal stimuli, including smell, movement, and warmth, that they would if co-sleeping. Private sleeping also takes away the opportunity for frequent nursing through the night.

In traditional societies, infants routinely sleep with their parents, or at least their mothers. Also, they are carried or held most other times, usually in an upright position. The mother typically responds to a cry or "fuss" literally within seconds, usually offering the infant her breast. So it is among traditional Ju/'hoansi (pronounced "zhutwasi") people of southern Africa's Kalahari Desert, whose infants breastfeed on demand in short frequent bouts—commonly nursing about four times an hour, for 1 or 2 minutes at a time. Overall, a 15-week-old Ju/'hoansi infant is in close contact with its mother about 70 percent of the time, as compared with 20 percent for home-reared infants in the United States. Moreover, they usually have contact with numerous other adults and children of virtually all ages.

Overall, infants in traditional societies are usually exposed to a steady stream of various stimuli far more than most babies in contemporary North America and most other industrial and postindustrial societies. This is significant, for recent studies show that stimulation plays a key role in the "hard wiring" of the brain—it is necessary for development of the neural circuitry. Looking at breastfeeding in particular, studies show that the longer a child is breastfed, the higher he or she will score on cognitive tests and the lower the risk of attention deficit

self-awareness The ability to identify oneself as an individual, to reflect on oneself, and to evaluate oneself.

VISUAL COUNTERPOINT

Self-awareness is not restricted to humans. This chimpanzee knows that the individual in the mirror is himself and not some other chimp, just as the girl recognizes herself.

hyperactivity disorder. Furthermore, breastfed children have fewer allergies, fewer ear infections, less diarrhea, and are at less risk of sudden infant death syndrome. Nonetheless breastfeeding tends to be relatively short-lived at best in the industrialized world, in part due to workplace conditions that rarely facilitate it.[2]

Social Identity Through Personal Naming

Personal names are important devices for self-definition in all cultures. It is through naming that a social group acknowledges a child's birthright and establishes its social identity. Without a name, an individual has no identity, no self. For this reason, many cultures consider name selection to be an important issue and mark the naming of a child with a special event or ritual known as a **naming ceremony.**

For instance, Aymara Indians in the Bolivian highland village of Laymi do not consider an infant truly human until they have given it a name. And naming does not happen until the child begins to speak the Aymara

language, typically around the age of 2. Once the child shows the ability to speak like a human, he or she is considered fit to be recognized as such with a proper name. The naming ceremony marks their social transition from a state of "nature" to "culture" and consequently to full acceptance into the Laymi community.

There are countless contrasting approaches to naming. Icelanders name babies at birth and still follow an ancient custom in which children use their father's personal given name as their last name. A son adds the suffix *sen* to the name and a daughter adds *dottir.* Thus, a brother and sister whose father is named Sven Olafsen would have the last names Svensen and Svendottir. Among the Netsilik Inuit in Arctic Canada, women experiencing a difficult delivery would call out the names of deceased people of admirable character. The name being called at the moment of birth was thought to enter the infant's body and help the delivery, and the child would bear that name thereafter. Inuit parents may also name their children for deceased relatives in the belief that the spiritual identification will help shape their character.[3]

In many cultures, a person receives a name soon after birth but may acquire new names during subsequent life phases. A Hopi child, for instance, is born into its mother's clan. Cared for by the elder women, the new-

---

[2]Dettwyler, K. A. (1997, October). When to wean. *Natural History,* 49; Stuart-MacAdam, P., & Dettwyler, K. A. (Eds.). (1995). *Breastfeeding: Biocultural perspectives.* New York: Aldine de Gruyter.

naming ceremony   A special event or ritual to mark the naming of a child.

---

[3]Balikci, A. (1970). *The Netsilik Eskimo.* Garden City, NY: Natural History Press.

Navajo babies begin to learn the importance of community at a special First Laugh Ceremony (Chi Dlo Dil). At this event, the person who prompted an infant's first laugh teaches the little child (and reminds the community) about the joy of generosity by helping the baby give symbolic gifts of sweets and rock salt to each guest. Pictured here is the baby daughter of a pediatrician working at a remote clinic on the reservation. She celebrates her first laugh wearing a Navajo dress and jewelry given to her by her mother's Navajo patients.

© Robert H. Rothman/*Focus.* Harvard Medical School

born spends the first nineteen days of its life wrapped in a blanket and secluded indoors. Placed next to the infant are two perfectly shaped ears of corn, referred to as Mother Corn. On the twentieth day, the father's sister gives the baby its name in a sunrise ceremony. At age 6, the child receives another name in a religious ceremony. Reaching adulthood, the person gets yet another name and keeps that one till the end of her or his life. Yet one more name is bestowed upon a Hopi at death, a name that is not to be mentioned after it is given.

Navajo Indians from the southwestern United States name children at birth, but traditionalists often give the baby an additional ancestral clan name soon after the child laughs for the first time. Among the Navajo, the laugh represents an infant's first expression of human language. It signals the beginning of life as a social being and is therefore an occasion for celebration. The person who prompted that very first laugh invites family and close friends to a First Laugh Ceremony (Chi Dlo Dil). At the gathering, the party sponsor holds and helps the child through an important social ritual: Placing rock salt in the baby's hand, he or she helps brush the salt all over the little one's body. Representing tears—of both laughter and crying—the salt is said to provide strength and protection, leading to a long, happy life. Then the ancestral name is given. Next, because a central purpose of the occasion is to ensure that the child will become a generous and selfless adult, the sponsor helps the baby give sweets and a piece of salt to each and every guest as they step forward to greet and welcome the child into the embrace of the community. By accepting these symbolic gifts, guests also receive strength and protection.

And by participating in this laughing ceremony, young and old alike are pleasantly reminded of the importance of generosity and sharing as traditional values in their community. After the ritual, everyone enjoys a great meal together.[4]

Among the many cultural rules that exist in each society, those having to do with naming are unique because they individualize a person while at the same time identify one as part of a group and even connect the person to the spirit world. In short, name-giving customs play an important role in a person's life journey as a socially accepted member of a culture.

The Self and the Behavioral Environment

The development of self-awareness requires basic orientations that structure the psychological field in which the self acts. These include object orientation, spatial orientation, temporal orientation, and normative orientation.

First, each individual must learn about a world of objects other than the self. Through this *object orientation*, each culture singles out for attention certain environmental features, while ignoring others or lumping them together into broad categories. A culture also *explains* the perceived environment. This is important, for a cultural explanation of one's surroundings imposes a measure of

---

[4]Authors' participant observation at traditional Navajo First Laugh ceremony of Wesley Bitsie-Baldwin; personal communication LaVerne Bitsie-Baldwin and Anjanette Bitsie.

order and provides the individual with a sense of direction needed to act meaningfully and effectively.

Behind this lies a powerful psychological drive to reduce uncertainty—part of the common human need for a balanced and integrated perspective on the relevant universe. When confronted with ambiguity and uncertainty, people invariably strive to clarify and give structure to the situation; they do this, of course, in ways that their particular culture deems appropriate. Thus, we should not be surprised to find that observations and explanations of the universe are largely culturally constructed and mediated symbolically through language. In fact, everything in the physical environment varies in the way it is perceived and experienced by humans. In short, we might say that the world around us is perceived through a cultural lens.

The behavioral environment in which the self acts also involves *spatial orientation,* or the ability to get from one object or place to another. In all societies, the names and significant features of places are important references for spatial orientation. Traditionally, geographic place names often contain references to significant features in the landscape. For instance, the name of the Mississippi in North America means literally "big river"; the English coastal city of Plymouth is located at the mouth of the river Plym; and the riverside city of Bamako, Mali, in West Africa translates as "crocodile river." Finding your way to class, remembering where you left your car keys, directing someone to the nearest bus stop, or traveling through deep underground networks in subway tunnels are examples of highly complex cognitive tasks based on spatial orientation and memory. So is a desert nomad's ability to travel long distances from one remote oasis to another—determining the route by means of a mental map of the vast open landscape and gauging his location by the position of the sun in daytime, the stars at night, and even by the winds and smell of the air. Without these spatial orientations, navigating through daily life would be impossible.

Temporal orientation, which gives people a sense of their place in time, is also part of the behavioral environment. Connecting past actions with those of the present and future provides a sense of self-continuity. This is the function of calendars, for example. Derived from the Latin word *kalendae,* which originally referred to a public announcement at the first day of a new month, or moon, such a chart gives people a sense of where they are in the earth's annual cycle. Just as the perceived environment of objects is organized in cultural terms, so too are time and space.

A final aspect of the behavioral environment is the *normative orientation.* Moral values, ideals, and principles, which are purely cultural in origin, are as much a part of the individual's behavioral environment as

Dark and foreboding to outsiders, the Ituri forest in the tropical heart of Africa is viewed with affection by the Mbuti foragers who live there. In their eyes, it is like a benevolent parent, providing them with all they ask for: sustenance, protection, and security.

are trees, rivers, and mountains. Without them people would have nothing by which to gauge their own actions or those of others. In short, the self-evaluation aspect of self-awareness could not be made functional. Normative orientation includes standards that indicate what ranges of behavior are acceptable for males and females in a particular society. Such behavior is embedded in biology but modified by culture, so it should not be surprising that they vary cross-culturally.

PERSONALITY

In the process of enculturation, we have seen that each individual is introduced to the ideas of self and the behavioral environment characteristic of his or her culture. The result is the creation of a kind of mental map of the world in which the individual will think and act. It is his or her particular map of how to run the maze of life. When we speak of someone's personality, we are generalizing about that person's cognitive map over time. Hence, personalities are products of enculturation, as experienced by individuals, each with his or her distinctive genetic makeup.

Personality does not lend itself to a formal definition, but for our purposes we may take it as the distinctive way a person thinks, feels, and behaves. Derived from the Latin word *persōna,* meaning "mask," the term relates to the idea of learning to play one's role on the stage of daily life. Gradually, the "mask," as it is "placed" on the face of a child, begins to shape that person until there is little sense of the mask as a superimposed alien force. Instead it feels natural, as if one were born with it. The individual has successfully internalized the culture.

The Development of Personality

Although *what* one learns is important to personality development, most anthropologists assume that *how* one learns is no less important. Along with psychological theorists, anthropologists view childhood experiences as strongly influencing adult personality. Indeed, many anthropologists have been attracted to Freudian psychoanalytic theory, but with a critical eye.

Psychological literature tends to be long on speculative concepts, clinical data, and studies that are culture-bound. Anthropologists, for their part, are most interested in studies that seek to prove, modify, or at least shed light on the cultural differences in shaping personality. For example, the traditional ideal in Western societies has been for men to be tough, aggressive, assertive, dominant, and self-reliant, whereas women have been expected to be gentle, passive, obedient, and caring. To many, these personality contrasts between the sexes seem so natural that they are thought to be biologically grounded and therefore fundamental, unchangeable, and universal. But are they? Have anthropologists identified any psychological or personality characteristics that universally differentiate men and women?

North American anthropologist Margaret Mead is well known as a pioneer in the cross-cultural study of both personality and gender (see Anthropologists of Note, p. 389). In the early 1930s she studied three ethnic groups in Papua New Guinea—the Arapesh, the Mundugamor, and the Tchambuli. This comparative research suggested that whatever biological differences exist between men and women, they are extremely malleable. In short, she concluded, biology is not destiny. Mead found that among the Arapesh, relations between men and women were expected to be equal, with both genders exhibiting what most North Americans traditionally consider feminine traits (cooperative, nurturing, and gentle).[5] She also discovered gender equality among the Mundugamor (now generally called Biwat); however, in that community both genders displayed supposedly masculine traits (individualistic, assertive, volatile, aggressive). Among the Tchambuli (now called Chambri), however, Mead found that women dominated men.

Recent anthropological research suggests that some of Mead's interpretations of gender roles were incorrect—for instance, Chambri women neither dominate Chambri men, nor vice versa. Yet, overall her research generated new insights into the human condition, showing that male dominance is a cultural construct and, consequently, that alternative gender arrangements can be created. Although biological influence in male–female behavior cannot be ruled out (in fact, debate continues about the genetic and hormonal factors at play), it has nonetheless become clear that each culture provides different opportunities and has different expectations for ideal or acceptable behavior.[6]

To understand the importance of child-rearing practices for the development of gender-related personality characteristics, we may take another brief look at the already mentioned Ju/'hoansi, people native to the Kalahari Desert of Namibia and Botswana in southern Africa. The Ju/'hoansi are one of a number of groups traditionally referred to as Bushmen, who were once widespread through much of southern Africa. Traditionally subsisting as nomadic hunter–gatherers (foragers), in the past three decades many Ju/'hoansi have been forced to settle down—tending small herds of goats, planting gardens for their livelihood, and engaging in occasional wage labor.[7]

Among those who traditionally forage for a living, equality is stressed, and dominance and aggressiveness are not tolerated in either gender. Ju/'hoansi men are as mild-mannered as the women, and women are as energetic and self-reliant as the men. By contrast, among the Ju/'hoansi who have recently settled in permanent villages, men and women exhibit personality characteristics resembling those traditionally thought of as typically masculine and feminine in North America and other industrial societies.

Among the food foragers, each newborn child receives lengthy, intensive care from its mother during the first few years of life, for the space between births is typically four to five years. This is not to say that mothers are constantly with their children. For instance, when

---

[6]Errington, F. K., & Gewertz, D. B. (2001). *Cultural alternatives and a feminist anthropology: An analysis of culturally constructed gender interests in Papua New Guinea.* Cambridge, England, and New York: Cambridge University Press.

[7]Draper, P. (1975). !Kung women: Contrasts in sexual egalitarianism in foraging and sedentary contexts. In R. Reiter (Ed.), *Toward an anthropology of women* (pp. 77–109). New York: Monthly Review Press.

---

[5]Mead, M. (1950). *Sex and temperament in three primitive societies.* New York: New American Library. (orig. 1935).

personality The distinctive way a person thinks, feels, and behaves.

In traditional Ju/'hoansi society, fathers as well as mothers show great indulgence to children, who do not fear or respect men more than women.

women go to collect wild plant foods in the bush, they do not always take their offspring along. At such times, the children are supervised by their fathers or other community adults, one-third to one-half of whom are always found in camp on any given day. Because these include men as well as women, children are as much habituated to the male as to the female presence.

Traditional Ju/'hoansi fathers spend much time with their offspring, interacting with them in nonauthoritarian ways. Although they may correct their children's behavior, so may women who neither defer to male authority nor use the threat of paternal punishment. Thus, among Ju/'hoansi foragers, no one grows up to respect or fear male authority any more than female authority. In fact, instead of being punished, a child who misbehaves will simply be carried away and introduced to some other more agreeable activity.

Neither boys nor girls are assigned chores. Children of both sexes do equally little work. Instead, they spend much of their time in playgroups that include members of both sexes of widely different ages. And when it comes to older children keeping an eye out for the younger ones, this is done spontaneously rather than as an assigned task, and the burden does not fall more heavily on girls than boys. In short, Ju/'hoansi children in traditional foraging groups have few experiences that set one gender apart from the other.

The situation is different among Ju/'hoansi who have been forced to abandon their traditional life as foragers and now reside in permanent settlements: Women spend much of their time in and around the home preparing food, attending to other domestic chores, and tending the children. Men, meanwhile, spend many hours outside the household growing crops, raising animals, or doing wage labor. As a result, children are less habituated to their presence. This remoteness of the men, coupled with their more extensive knowledge of the outside world and their cash, tends to strengthen male influence within the household.

Within village households, gender typecasting begins early. As soon as girls are old enough, they are expected to attend to many of the needs of their younger siblings, thereby allowing their mothers more time to deal with other domestic tasks. This not only shapes but also limits the behavior of girls, who cannot range as widely or explore as freely and independently as they could without little brothers and sisters in tow. Indeed, they must stay close to home and be more careful, more obedient, and more sensitive to the wishes of others than they otherwise might be. Boys, by contrast, have little to do with the handling of infants, and when they are assigned work, it generally takes them away from the household. Thus, the space that village girls occupy becomes restricted, and they are trained in behaviors that promote passivity and nurturance, whereas village boys begin to learn the distant, controlling roles they will later play as adult men.

From this comparison, we may begin to understand how a society's economy helps structure the way a child is brought up, and how this, in turn, influences the adult personality. It also shows that alternatives exist to the way that children are raised—which means that changing the societal conditions in which one's children grow up can alter significantly the way men and women act and interact.

Dependence Training

Some years after Margaret Mead's pioneering comparative research on gender in three Papua communities, psychological anthropologists carried out a significant and more wide-ranging series of cross-cultural studies on the effects of child rearing on personality. Among other things, their work showed that it is possible to distinguish between two general patterns of child rearing. These patterns stem from a number of practices that, regardless of the reason for their existence, have the effect of emphasizing dependence on the one hand and independence on the other. Thus, for convenience, we may speak of "dependence training" and "independence training."[8]

Dependence training socializes people to think of themselves in terms of the larger whole. Its effect is to create community members whose idea of selfhood transcends individualism, promoting compliance in the performance of assigned tasks and keeping individuals within the group. This pattern is typically associated with extended families, which consist of several husband-wife-children units within the same household. It is most likely to be found in societies with an economy based on subsistence farming but also in foraging groups where several family groups may live together for at least part of the year. Big extended families are important, for they provide the labor force necessary to till the soil, tend whatever flocks are kept, and carry out other part-time economic pursuits considered necessary for existence. These large families, however, have built into them certain potentially disruptive tensions. For example, important family decisions must be collectively accepted and followed. In addition, the in-marrying spouses—husbands and/or wives who come from other groups—must conform themselves to the group's will, something that may not be easy for them.

Dependence training helps to keep these potential problems under control and involves both supportive and corrective aspects. On the supportive side, indulgence is shown to young children, particularly in the form of breastfeeding, which is provided on demand and continues for several years. This may be interpreted as rewarding the child for seeking support within the family, the main agent in meeting the child's needs. Also on the supportive side, children at a relatively early age are assigned a number of child-care and domestic tasks, all of which make significant and obvious contributions to the family's welfare. Thus, family members all actively work to help and support one another.

On the corrective side, behavior the adults interpret as aggressive or selfish is likely to be actively discouraged. Moreover, the adults tend to be insistent on overall obedience, which commonly inclines the individual toward being subordinate to the group. This combination of encouragement and discouragement in the socialization process teaches individuals to put the group's needs above their own—to be obedient, supportive, noncompetitive, and generally responsible, to stay within the fold and not do anything potentially disruptive. Indeed, a person's very definition of self comes from the individual being a part of a larger social whole rather than from his or her mere individual existence.

Independence Training

By contrast, **independence training** fosters individual independence, self-reliance, and personal achievement. It is typically associated with societies in which a basic social unit consisting of parent(s) and offspring fends for itself. Independence training is particularly characteristic of mercantile (trading), industrial, and postindustrial societies where self-sufficiency and personal achievement are important traits for success, if not survival—especially for men, and increasingly for women.

Again, this pattern of training involves both encouragement and discouragement. On the negative side, infant feeding is prompted more by schedule than demand. In North America, as noted above, babies are rarely nursed for more than a year, if that. Many parents resort to an artificial nipple or teething ring (pacifier) to satisfy the baby's sucking instincts—typically doing so to calm the child rather than out of an awareness that infants need sucking to strengthen and train coordination in the muscles used for feeding and speech.

In addition, North American parents are comparatively quick to start feeding infants baby food and even try to get them to feed themselves. Many are delighted if they can prop their infants up in the crib or playpen so that they can hold their own bottles. Moreover, as soon after birth as possible, children are commonly given their own private space, away from their parents. As already noted, infants do not receive the amount of attention they so often do in nonindustrial societies. In the United States a mother may be very affectionate with her 15-week-old infant during the 20 percent of the time she is in contact with it, but typically for the other 80 percent of the time the baby is more or less on its own, usually within hearing range of the mother or caretaker(s).

Collective responsibility is not pushed in children; they are not usually given responsible tasks to perform until later in childhood; and these are often carried out for personal benefit (such as to earn an allowance to spend as they wish) rather than as contributions to the family's welfare.

---

[8]Whiting, J. W. M., & Child, I. L. (1953). *Child training and personality: A cross-cultural study.* New Haven, CT: Yale University Press.

dependence training Child-rearing practices that foster compliance in the performance of assigned tasks and dependence on the domestic group, rather than reliance on oneself.
independence training Child-rearing practices that foster independence, self-reliance, and personal achievement.

Displays of individual will, assertiveness, and even aggression are encouraged, or at least tolerated to a greater degree than where dependence training is the rule. In schools, and even in the family, competition and winning are emphasized. Schools in the United States, for example, devote considerable resources to competitive sports. Competition is fostered within the classroom as well: overtly through such devices as spelling bees and awards, covertly through such devices as grading on a curve. In addition, there are various popularity contests, such as crowning a prom queen and king or holding an election to choose the classmate who is "best looking" or "most likely to succeed."

Thus, by the time individuals have grown up in U.S. society, they have received a clear message: Life is about winning or losing, and losing is equal to failure. Often, success is viewed as something that comes at someone else's expense. As anthropologist Colin Turnbull observed, "Even the team spirit, so loudly touted" in U.S. school athletics (or out of school in Little League baseball and the like), "is merely a more efficient way, through limited cooperation, to 'beat' a greater number of people more efficiently."[9]

In sum, independence training generally encourages individuals to seek help and attention rather than to give it and to try to exert individual dominance. Such qualities are useful in societies with hierarchical social structures that emphasize personal achievement and where individuals are expected to look out for their own interests. Its socialization patterns match cultural values and expectations increasingly prevalent in the spread of global capitalism.

Combined Dependence/Independence Training

In actuality, dependence and independence training represent extremes along a continuum, and particular situations may include elements of both. This is the case in child-rearing practices in food-foraging societies, for example. "Share and share alike" is the order of the day, so competitive behavior, which can interfere with the cooperation on which all else depends, is discouraged. Thus, infants receive much in the way of positive, affectionate attention from adults, including extended breastfeeding from the mother. This, as well as low pressure for compliance and a lack of emphasis on competition, encourages individuals to be more supportive of one another than is often the case in modern industrial and postindustrial societies. At the same time, personal achievement and independence are encouraged, for those individuals most capable of self-reliance are apt to be the most successful in the food quest.

---

[9]Turnbull, C. M. (1983). *The human cycle* (p. 74). New York: Simon & Schuster.

In North America the argument is sometimes made that "permissive" child rearing produces irresponsible adults. Yet the practices of food foragers seem to be about as "permissive" as they can get, and socially responsible adults are produced. The fact is that none of these child-rearing systems is inherently better or worse than any other; what matters is whether the system is functional or dysfunctional in the context of a particular society. If compliant adults who are accepting of authority are required, then independence training will not work well in that society. Nor will dependence training serve very well a society whose adults are expected to be self-reliant, questioning of authority, and ready to explore and embrace new ways of doing things.

Group Personality

From studies such as those reviewed here, it is clear that personality, child-rearing practices, and other aspects of culture are systemically interrelated. The existence of a close, if not causal, relationship between child-rearing practices and personality development, coupled with variation in child-rearing practices from one society to another, have led to a number of attempts to characterize whole societies in terms of particular kinds of personalities. Indeed, common sense suggests that personalities appropriate for one culture may be less appropriate for others. For example, an egocentric, aggressive personality would be out of place where cooperation and sharing are the keys to success.

Unfortunately, common sense, like conventional wisdom in general, is not always the truth. A question worth asking is: Can we describe a group personality without falling into stereotyping? The answer appears to be a qualified yes; in an abstract way, we may speak of a generalized "cultural personality" for a society, as long as we do not expect to find a uniformity of personalities within that society. Put another way, each individual develops certain personality characteristics that, from common experience, resemble those of other people. Yet, each human being also acquires distinct personality traits because every individual is exposed to unique sets of experiences and may react to shared experiences in novel ways. Moreover, each person brings to these experiences a one-of-a-kind genetic potential (except in the case of identical twins) that plays a role in determining personality.

This is evident, if not obvious, in every society—including even the most traditional ones. Consider for example the Yanomami Indians, who subsist on foraging and horticulture in the tropical forests of northern Brazil and southern Venezuela. Commonly, Yanomami men strive to achieve a reputation for fierceness and aggressiveness, and they defend that reputation at the risk

Anthropologists of Note

Margaret Mead (1901–1978) ▪ Ruth Fulton Benedict (1887–1947)

© AP Images

Although all of the academic sciences are able to look back and honor certain "founding fathers," anthropologists take pride in the fact that they have a number of "founding mothers" whose pioneering work they celebrate. One is **Margaret Mead,** who was encouraged by her professor Franz Boas to pursue a career in anthropology when few other professions accepted women into their ranks.

As a 24-year-old doctoral candidate, she set out for the Pacific Ocean island of Samoa to test the theory (then widely accepted) that the biological changes of adolescence were always fraught with social, psychological, and emotional stress. Based on her fieldwork there, she later wrote the book *Coming of Age in Samoa: A Psychological Study of Primitive Youth for Western Civilization,* explaining that adolescence does not have to be a time of stress and strain, but cultural conditions may make it so. Published in 1928, this book is generally credited as marking the beginning of psychological anthropology (culture and personality).

Pioneering works, however, are rarely without their faults, and *Coming of Age* is no exception. For one, Mead's time in the field (nine months) was not enough to understand fully the nuances of native speech and body language necessary to comprehend the innermost feelings of her informants. Furthermore, her sample of Samoan adolescents was a mere fifty, half of whom had not yet passed puberty. That she exaggerated her findings is suggested by her dismissal as "deviant" those girls who did not fit her ideal and

by inconsistencies with data collected elsewhere in Polynesia.

Despite its faults, Mead's book stands as a landmark for several reasons: Not only was it a deliberate test of a Euramerican psychological hypothesis, but it also showed psychologists the value of modifying intelligence tests to make them appropriate for the population under study. Furthermore, by emphasizing the lesson to be drawn for Mead's own society, it laid the groundwork for the popularization of anthropology and advanced the cause of applied anthropology.

Ruth Benedict came late to anthropology; after her graduation from Vassar College, she taught high school English, published poetry, and tried her hand at social work. At age 31, she began studying anthropology, first at the New School for Social Research in New York City, and then at Columbia University. Having earned her doctorate under Boas, she joined his department. One of her own first students was Margaret Mead.

As Benedict herself once said, the main purpose of anthropology is "to make the world safe for human differences." In anthropology, she developed the idea that culture was a collective projection of the personality of those who created it. In her most famous book *Patterns of Culture* (1934), she compared the cultures of three peoples—the Kwakiutl Indians of the Pacific Northwest

© The Granger Collection, New York

coast in Canada, the Zuni Indians of the Arizona desert in the United States, and the Melanesians of Dobu Island off the southern shore of Papua New Guinea. She held that each was comparable to a great work of art, with an internal coherence and consistency of its own.

Seeing the Kwakiutl as egocentric, individualistic, and ecstatic in their rituals, she labeled their cultural configuration "Dionysian" (named after the Greek God of wine and noisy feasting). The Zuni, whom she saw as living by the golden mean, wanting no part of excess or disruptive psychological states and distrusting of individualism, she characterized as "Apollonian" (named after the Greek God of poetry who exemplified beauty). The Dobuans, whose culture seemed to her magic-ridden, with everyone fearing and hating everyone else, she characterized as "paranoid."

Another theme of *Patterns of Culture* is that deviance should be understood as a conflict between an individual's personality and the norms of the culture to which the person belongs. Still in print today, *Patterns* has sold close to 2 million copies in a dozen languages. It had great influence on Mead during her cross-cultural gender studies among the Papuans in New Guinea.

Although *Patterns of Culture* still enjoys popularity in some nonanthropological circles, anthropologists have long since abandoned its approach as impressionistic and not susceptible to replication. To compound the problem, Benedict's characterizations of cultures are misleading (the supposedly "Apollonian" Zunis, for example, indulge in such seemingly "Dionysian" practices as sword swallowing and walking over hot coals), and the use of such value-laden terms as "paranoid" prejudices others against the culture so labeled. Nonetheless, the book did have an enormous and valuable influence by focusing attention on the problem of the interrelation between culture and personality and by popularizing the reality of cultural variation.

of serious personal injury and death. Yet, among the Ya-nomami there are men who have quiet and somewhat retiring personalities. It is all too easy for an outsider to overlook these individuals when other, more "typical" Yanomami are in the front row, pushing and demanding attention.

Modal Personality

Obviously, any productive approach to the problem of group personality must recognize that each individual is unique to a degree in both genetic inheritance and life experiences, and it must leave room for a range of different personality types in any society. In addition, personality traits that may be regarded as appropriate in men may not be so regarded in women, and vice versa. Given all this, we may focus our attention on the **modal personality** of a group, defined as the body of character traits that occur with the highest frequency in a culturally bounded population.

Modal personality is a statistical concept rather than the personality of an average person in a particular society. As such, it opens up for investigation the questions of how societies organize diversity and how diversity relates to culture change. Such questions are easily missed if one associates a certain type of personality with one particular culture, as did some earlier anthropologists (see Ruth Benedict in Anthropologists of Note). At the same time, modal personalities of different groups can be compared.

Data on modal personality are best gathered by means of psychological tests administered to a sample of the population in question. Known as projective personality tests, those most often used by anthropologists include the Rorschach "inkblot" test and the Thematic Apperception Test (TAT). Such tests require individuals to look at an indeterminate visual image or meaningless object and tell the researcher what they see. In their description or interpretation of selected standard images or objects, individuals are assumed to project their conscious and unconscious ideas, values, and feelings.

The Rorschach test, named after a Swiss psychiatrist who first published it in the 1920s, contains ten inkblots (five in different colors and five printed in black and white). This test became especially significant for psychological anthropologists interested in modal personality studies in cultures where writing does not exist or is not widely used. The TAT, which was developed in the early 1940s, consists of a series of twenty visual images depicting one or more individuals in nonspecific or

ambiguous everyday scenes or situations. Showing these pictures to different individuals in the study group, the researcher asks them to make up a story about what they are seeing and explain what the people portrayed in each picture are doing, thinking, or feeling.

These and other sorts of projective tests have in common a purposeful ambiguity that forces the individual being tested to structure the situation before responding. The idea is that one's personality is reflected in the sort of structure or definition that he or she projects into the ambiguous situation. Along with such projective tests, recording the frequency of certain behaviors, collecting and analyzing life histories and dreams, and analyzing popular tales, jokes, legends, and traditional myths can yield useful data on modal personality.

While having much to recommend it, the concept of modal personality as a means of dealing with group personality nevertheless presents certain difficulties. One is the complexity of the measurement techniques, which may be difficult to do in the field. For instance, an adequate representative sample of subjects is necessary. The problem here is twofold: making sure the sample is really representative and having the time and personnel necessary to administer the tests, conduct interviews, and so on, all of which can be lengthy proceedings.

In addition to questions about the reliability and validity of the methodology, the projective tests themselves constitute a problem, for those devised in one cultural setting may not be relevant, applicable, or inappropriate in another. (This is more of a problem with the TAT than with some other tests, although different pictures have been devised for other cultures.) To minimize any cultural bias, it is best not to rely on projective tests alone. In addition to all this, language differences or conflicting cultural values between the researcher and the individuals being studied may inhibit communication and/or lead to misinterpretation. Finally, what is being measured must be questioned. Just what, for example, is aggression? Does everyone define it the same way? Is it a legitimate entity, or does it involve other variables?

National Character

In summer 2003, Italy's tourism minister publicly commented on "typical characteristics" of Germans, referring to them as "hyper-nationalistic blondes" and "beer drinking slobs" holding "noisy burping contests" on his country's beaches.[10] Outraged (and proud of his country's excellent beer), Germany's prime minister canceled his planned vacation to Italy and demanded an official apology. Of course, many Germans think of Italians as

---

modal personality The body of character traits that occur with the highest frequency in a culturally bounded population.

[10]Italy-Germany verbal war hots up. (2003, July 9). *Deccan Herald* (Bangalore India).

dark-eyed, hot-blooded spaghetti eaters. To say so in public, however, might cause an uproar.

Unflattering stereotypes about foreigners are deeply rooted in cultural traditions everywhere. Many Japanese believe Koreans are stingy, crude, and aggressive, while many Koreans see the Japanese as cold and arrogant. Similarly, we all have in mind some image, perhaps not well defined, of the typical citizen of Russia or Mexico or England. Essentially, these are simply stereotypes. We might well ask, however, if these stereotypes have any basis in fact. In reality, does such a thing as *national character* exist?

Some anthropologists once thought that the answer might be yes. Accordingly, they embarked upon national character studies in the 1930s and 1940s, aiming to discover basic personality traits shared by the majority of the people of modern state societies. In what came to be known as the *culture and personality* movement, their research emphasized child-rearing practices and education as the factors theoretically responsible for such characteristics.

Objections to National Character Studies

The national character studies, as was recognized early on, were flawed, mainly because they made over-generalized conclusions based on limited data, relatively small samples of informants, and questionable assumptions about developmental psychology. For instance, the concept of modal personality has a certain statistical validity, they argue, but to generalize the qualities of a complex country on the basis of such limited data is to lend insufficient recognition to the countless individuals who vary from the generalization.

Further, such studies tend to be highly subjective; for example, the tendency during the late 1930s and 1940s for anthropologists to characterize the German people as aggressive paranoids was obviously a reflection of wartime hostility rather than scientific objectivity. Finally, it has been pointed out that occupation and social status tend to cut across national boundaries. A French farmer may have less in common with a French lawyer than he does with a German farmer.

These flaws notwithstanding, national character studies were important in that they helped change the anthropological focus from traditional small-scale communities of foragers, herders, and farmers in exotic places to large-scale contemporary state societies. Moreover, they prompted new theoretical and methodological approaches to serious interdisciplinary group research.[11]

---

[11]See Beeman, W. O. (2000). Introduction: Margaret Mead, cultural studies, and international understanding. In M. Mead & R. Métraux (Eds.), *The study of culture at a distance* (pp. xiv–xxxi). New York and Oxford: Berghahn Books.

© Simon Kwong/Corbis

The collectively shared core values of Chinese culture promote the integration of the individual into a larger group, as we see in this large gathering of Hong Kong residents doing Tai Chi together.

Core Values

An alternative approach to national character—one that allows for the fact that not all personalities will conform to cultural ideals—is that of anthropologist Francis Hsu. His approach was to study **core values** (values especially promoted by a particular culture) and related personality traits. The Chinese, he suggested, value kin ties and cooperation above all else. To them, mutual dependence is the very essence of personal relationships and has been for thousands of years. Compliance and subordination of one's will to that of family and kin transcend all else, while self-reliance is neither promoted nor a source of pride.

Perhaps the core value held in highest esteem by North Americans of European descent is rugged individ-

core values Those values especially promoted by a particular culture.

ualism—traditionally for men but in recent decades for women as well. Each individual is supposed to be able to achieve anything he or she likes, given a willingness to work hard enough. From their earliest years, individuals are subjected to relentless pressures to excel, and as we have already noted, competition and winning are seen as crucial to this. Undoubtedly, this contributes to the restlessness and drive seen as characteristic for much of North American society today.

Also, to the degree that it motivates individuals to work hard and to go where the jobs are, it fits well with the demands of a modern economy. Thus, while individuals in Chinese traditional society are firmly bound into a larger group to which they have lifelong obligations, most urban North Americans are isolated from relatives other than their young children and spouse—and even the commitment to marriage has lessened. This is evident in the growing number of North American couples cohabitating without being married or having plans for marriage (Figure 17.1). Increasingly, when couples do marry, prenuptial agreements are made to protect individual assets in case of divorce—and close to 50 percent of marriages do end in divorce. Even parents and children have no legal obligations to one another once the latter have reached the age of majority.[12]

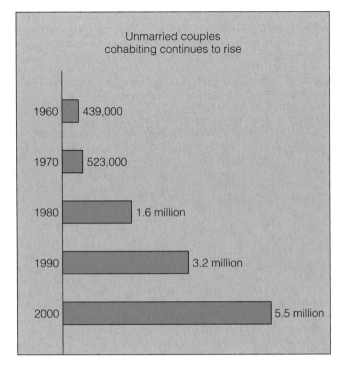

Figure 17.1

Number of unmarried couples cohabiting in the United States, by year. According to the most recent national census, in the year 2000, 8.5 percent of all cohabiting couples in the United States were unmarried. That number continues to rise.

ALTERNATIVE GENDER MODELS FROM A CROSS-CULTURAL PERSPECTIVE

As we have already discussed, the gender roles assigned to each sex vary from culture to culture and have an impact on personality formation. But what if the sex of an individual is not self-evident, as revealed in the following Original Study? Written when its author was an undergraduate student of philosophy at Bryn Mawr College in Pennsylvania, this narrative offers a compelling personal account of the emotional difficulties associated with intersexuality and gender ambiguity, while making the important point that attitudes toward gender vary cross-culturally. However, some of the cultural information is overly generalized and therefore not quite accurate, including the idea that all or most Native American spiritual-religious worldviews were and are nonhierarchical.[13]

---

[12]Observations on North American culture in this section are drawn primarily from Natadecha-Sponsal, P. (1993). The young, the rich and the famous: Individualism as an American cultural value. In P. R. DeVita & J. D. Armstrong (Eds.), *Distant mirrors: America as a foreign culture* (pp. 46–53). Belmont, CA: Wadsworth. See also Whitehead, B. D., & Popenoe, D. (2004). *The state of our unions: The social health of marriage in America 2004.* Rutgers, NJ: Rutgers University National Marriage Project.

---

[13]For scholarly accounts of the issues presented here, readers may turn to several excellent books, including the one mentioned in the Original Study: Roscoe, W. (1991). *Zuni man-woman.* Albuquerque: University of New Mexico Press.

Original Study ▪ R. K. Williamson

The Blessed Curse

One morning not so long ago, a child was born. This birth, however, was no occasion for the customary celebration. Something was wrong: something very

grave, very serious, very sinister. This child was born between sexes, an "intersexed" child. From the day of its birth, this child would be caught in a series of

struggles involving virtually every aspect of its life. Things that required little thought under "ordinary" circumstances were, in this instance, extraordinarily difficult. Simple questions now had an air of complexity: "What is it, a girl or a boy?" "What do we name it?" "How shall we raise it?" "Who (or what) is to blame for this?"

A Foot in Both Worlds

The child referred to in the introductory paragraph is myself. As the great-granddaughter of a Cherokee woman, I was exposed to the Native American view of people who were born intersexed, and those who exhibited transgendered characteristics. This view, unlike the Euramerican one, sees such individuals in a very positive and affirming light. Yet my immediate family (mother, father, and brothers) were firmly fixed in a negative Christian Euramerican point of view. As a result, from a very early age I was presented with two different and conflicting views of myself. This resulted in a lot of confusion within me about what I was, how I came to be born the way I was, and what my intersexuality meant in terms of my spirituality as well as my place in society.

I remember, even as a small child, getting mixed messages about my worth as a human being. My grandmother, in keeping with Native American ways, would tell me stories about my birth. She would tell me how she knew when I was born that I had a special place in life, given to me by God, the Great Spirit, and that I had been given "a great strength that girls never have, yet a gentle tenderness that boys never know" and that I was "too pretty and beautiful to be a boy only and too strong to be a girl only." She rejoiced at this "special gift" and taught me that it meant that the Great Spirit had "something important for me to do in this life." I remember how good I felt inside when she told me these things and how I soberly contemplated, even at the young age of 5, that I must be diligent and try to learn and carry out the purpose designed just for me by the Great Spirit.

My parents, however, were so repulsed by my intersexuality that they would never speak of it directly. They would just refer to it as "the work of Satan." To them, I was not at all blessed with a "special gift" from some "Great Spirit," but was "cursed and given over to the Devil" by God. My father treated me with contempt, and my mother wavered between contempt and distant indifference.

I was taken from one charismatic church to another in order to have the "demon of mixed sex" cast out of me. At some of these "deliverance" services I was even given a napkin to cough out the demon into!

In the end, no demon ever popped out of me. Still I grew up believing that there was something inherent within me that caused God to hate me, that my intersexuality was a punishment for this something, a mark of condemnation.

Whenever I stayed at my grandmother's house, my fears would be allayed, for she would once again remind me that I was fortunate to have been given this special gift. She was distraught that my parents were treating me cruelly and pleaded with them to let me live with her, but they would not let me stay at her home permanently. Nevertheless, they did let me spend a significant portion of my childhood with her. Had it not been for that, I might not have been able to survive the tremendous trials that awaited me in my walk through life.

Blessed Gift:
The Native American View

It is now known that most, if not all, Native American societies had certain individuals that fell between the categories of "man" and "woman." The various nations had different names for such people, but a term broadly used and recognized is *berdache*, a word of French origin that designated a male, passive homosexual. [The preferred term today is *two-spirit*.] Some of these individuals were born physically intersexed. Others appeared to be anatomically normal males, but exhibited the character and the manners of women—or vice versa. The way native people treated such individuals reveals some interesting insights into Native American belief systems.

The Spirit

The extent to which Native Americans see spirituality is reflected in their belief that all things have a spirit: "Every object—plants, rocks, water, air, the moon, animals, humans, the earth itself—has a spirit. The spirit of one thing (including a human) is not superior to the spirit of any other. . . . The function of religion is not to try to condemn or to change what exists, but to accept the realities of the world and to appreciate their contribu-

tions to life. Everything that exists has a purpose."

This paradigm is the core of Native American thought and action. Because everything has a spirit, and no spirit is superior to that of another, there is no "above" or "below," no "superior" or "inferior," no "dominant" and "subordinate." These are only illusions that arise from unclear thinking. Thus, an intersexed child is not derided or viewed as a "freak of nature" in many traditional Native American cultures. Intersexuality (as well as masculinity in a female or effeminacy in a male) is seen as the manifestation of the spirit of the child, so an intersexed child is respected as much as a girl child or a boy child. It is the spirit of the child that determines what the gender of the child will ultimately be. According to a Lakota, Lame Deer, "the Great Spirit made them *winktes* [two-spirit], and we accepted them as such." In this sense, the child has no control over what her or his gender will be. It follows that where there is no choice, there can be no accountability on the part of the child. Indeed, the child who is given the spirit of a *winkte* is unable to resist becoming one.

"When an Omaha boy sees the Moon Being [a feminine Spirit] on his vision quest, the spirit holds in one hand a man's bow and arrow and in the other a woman's pack strap. . . . 'When the youth tried to grasp the bow and arrows, the Moon Being crossed hands very quickly, and if the youth was not very careful he seized the pack strap instead of the bow and arrows, thereby fixing his lot in later life. In such a case he could not help acting [like a] woman, speaking, dressing, and working just as . . . women . . . do.'"

The Curse: The Euramerican View

In contrast to the view of respect and admiration of physical intersexuality and transgendered behavior traditionally held by Native Americans, the Europeans who came to "Turtle Island" (the Cherokee name for North America) brought with them their worldview, shaped by their Judeo-Christian beliefs. According to this religious perspective, there had to be, by mandate of God, a complete dichotomy of the sexes. . .

Will Roscoe, in his book *The Zuni Man-Woman*, reports (pp. 172–73): "Spanish oppression of 'homosexual' practices in the New World took brutal

CONTINUED

forms. In 1513, the explorer Balboa had some forty berdaches thrown to his dogs [to be eaten alive]—'a fine action by an honorable and Catholic Spaniard,' as one Spanish historian commented. In Peru, the Spaniards burned 'sodomites, . . . and in this way they frightened them in such a manner that they left this great sin.'"

It is abundantly clear that Christian Euramericans exerted every effort to destroy Native American culture: "In 1883, the U.S. Office of Indian Affairs issued a set of regulations that came to be known as the Code of Religious Offenses, or Religious Crimes Code. . . . Indians who refused to adopt the habits of industry, or to engage in 'civilized pursuits or employments' were subject to arrest and punishment. . . . By interfering with

native sexuality [and culture], the agents of assimilation effectively undermined the social fabric of entire tribes" (Roscoe, p. 176).

A Personal Resolution

For me, the resolution to the dual message I was receiving was slow in coming, largely due to the fear and self-hatred instilled in me by Christianity. Eventually, though, the spirit wins out. I came to adopt my Grandmother's teaching about my intersexuality. Through therapy, and a new, loving home environment, I was able to shed the constant fear of eternal punishment I felt for something I had no control over. After all, I did not create myself.

Because of my own experience, and drawing on the teaching of my grand-

mother, I am now able to see myself as a wondrous creation of the Great Spirit—but not only me. All creation is wondrous. There is a purpose for everyone in the gender spectrum. Each person's spirit is unique in her or his or her-his own way. It is only by living true to the nature that was bestowed upon us by the Great Spirit, in my view, that we are able to be at peace with ourselves and be in harmony with our neighbor. This, to me, is the Great Meaning and the Great Purpose . . .

(Adapted from R. K. Williamson (1995). The blessed curse: Spirituality and sexual difference as viewed by Euramerican and Native American cultures. The College News, 18(4).) Reprinted with permission of the author.)   ∎

The biological facts of human nature are not always as clear-cut as most people assume. At the level of chromosomes, biological sex is determined according to whether a person's 23rd chromosomal set is XX (female) or XY (male). Some of the genes on these chromosomes control sexual development. This standard biological package does not apply to all humans, for a considerable number are **intersexuals**—people who are born with reproductive organs, genitalia, and/or sex chromosomes that are not exclusively male or female. These individuals do not fit neatly into a binary gender standard.[14]

For example, some people are born with a genetic disorder that gives biological females only one X chromosome instead of the usual two. A person with this chromosomal complex, known as Turner syndrome, develops female external genitalia but has nonfunctional ovaries and is therefore infertile. Other individuals are born with the XY sex chromosomes of a male but have an abnormality on the X chromosome that affects the

body's sensitivity to androgens (male hormones). This is known as androgen insensitivity syndrome (AIS). An adult XY person with complete AIS appears fully female with a normal clitoris, labia, and breasts. Internally, these individuals possess testes (up in the abdomen, rather than in their usual descended position in the scrotal sac), but they are otherwise born without a complete set of either male or female internal genital organs. They generally possess a short, blind-ended vagina.

"Hermaphrodites" comprise a distinct category of intersexuality—although the terms "male pseudohermaphrodite" and "female pseudohermaphrodite" are often used to refer to a range of intersex conditions. The name, objected to by many, comes from a figure in Greek mythology: Hermaphroditus (son of Hermes, messenger of the gods, and Aphrodite, goddess of beauty and love) who became half-male and half-female when he fell in love with a nymph and his body fused with hers.

True hermaphrodites have both testicular and ovarian tissue. They may have a separate ovary and testis, but more commonly they have an ovotestis—a gonad containing both sorts of tissue. About 60 percent of hermaphrodites possess XX (female) sex chromosomes, and the remainder may have XY or a mosaic (a mixture). Their external genitalia may be ambiguous or female, and they may have a uterus or (more commonly) a hemi-uterus (half uterus).

U.S. biologist Anne Fausto-Sterling, a specialist in this area, notes that the concept of intersexuality is "rooted in the very ideas of male and female" in an idealized biological world in which:

---

[14]This section is based on several sources: Chase, C. (1998). Hermaphrodites with attitude. *Gay and Lesbian Quarterly 4* (2), 189–211; Dumurat-Dreger, A. (1998, May/June). "Ambiguous sex" or ambivalent medicine? *The Hastings Center Report 28* (3), 2,435 (posted on the Intersex Society of North America website: www.isna.org); Fausto-Sterling, A. (1993). The five sexes: Why male and female are not enough. *The Sciences 33* (2), 20–24; the Mayo Clinic website.

intersexual A person born with reproductive organs, genitalia, and/or sex chromosomes that are not exclusively male or female.

human beings are divided into two kinds: a perfectly dimorphic species. Males have an X and a Y chromosome, testes, a penis and all of the appropriate internal plumbing for delivering urine and semen to the outside world. They also have well-known secondary sexual characteristics, including a muscular build and facial hair. Women have two X chromosomes, ovaries, all of the internal plumbing to transport urine and ova to the outside world, a system to support pregnancy and fetal development, as well as a variety of recognizable secondary sexual characteristics.

That idealized story papers over many obvious caveats: some women have facial hair, some men have none; some women speak with deep voices, some men veritably squeak. Less well known is the fact that on close inspection, absolute dimorphism disintegrates even at the level of basic biology. Chromosomes, hormones, the internal sex structures, the gonads and external genitalia all vary more than most people realize. Those born outside of the . . . dimorphic mold are called intersexuals.[15]

Intersexuality may be unusual but is not uncommon. In fact, about 1 percent of all humans are intersexed in some (not necessarily visible) way—in other words, over 60 million people worldwide.[16] Until recently, it was rarely discussed publicly in many societies. Since the mid-20th century, individuals with financial means in technologically advanced parts of the world have had the option of reconstructive surgery and hormonal treatments to alter such conditions, and many parents faced with raising a visibly intersexed child in a culture intolerant of such minorities have chosen this option for their baby. However, there is a growing movement to put off such irreversible procedures indefinitely or until the child becomes old enough to be the one to make the choice. Obviously, a society's attitude toward these individuals can impact their personality—their fundamental sense of self and how they express it.

In addition to people who are biologically intersexed, throughout history some individuals have been subjected to a surgical removal of some of their sexual organs. In many cultures, male prisoners or war captives have undergone forced castration, crushing or cutting the testicles. While castration of adult males does not eliminate the sex drive or the possibility of having an

erection, it does put an end to the production of sperm necessary for reproduction.

Archaeological evidence from ancient Egypt, Iraq, Iran, and China suggests that the cultural practice of castrating war captives may have begun several thousand years ago. Young boys captured during war or slave-raiding expeditions were often castrated before being sold and shipped off to serve in foreign households, including royal courts. In the Ottoman Empire of the Turks, where they could occupy a variety of important functions in the sultan's household from the mid-15th century onward, they became known as *eunuchs*. As suggested by the original meaning of the word, which is Greek for "guardian of the bed," castrated men were often put in charge of a ruler's harem, the women's quarters in a household. Eunuchs could also rise to high status as priests and administrators and were even appointed to serve as army commanders. Some powerful lords, kings, and emperors kept hundreds of eunuchs in their castles and palaces.

In addition to forced castration, there were also men who engaged in self-castration or underwent voluntary castration. For example, early Christian monks in Egypt and neighboring regions voluntarily abstained from sexual relationships and sometimes castrated themselves for the sake of the kingdom of heaven. Such genital mutilation was also practiced among Coptic monks in Egypt and Ethiopia, until the early 20th century.[17]

In the late 15th century, Europe saw the emergence of a category of musical eunuchs known as *castrati*. These eunuchs sang female parts in church choirs after Roman Catholic authorities banned women singers on the basis of Saint Paul's instruction, "Let your women keep silence in the churches." Simultaneously, castrati began performing female roles in operas. Castrated before they reached puberty so as to retain their high voices, these selected boys were often orphaned or came from poor families. Without a functioning testis to produce male sex hormones, physical development into manhood is aborted, so deeper voices, as well as body hair, semen production, and other usual male attributes, were not part of a castrati's biology.

During the 1700s, at the height of castrati popularity, an estimated 4,000 boys a year were castrated in Italy alone. Some became celebrated performers, drawing huge fees, adopting fantastic stage names, and gaining notoriety for their eccentricity on and off stage. Not necessarily homosexual, castrati were "gender benders" who could engage in sexual relations with men or women, or both. The phenomenon of castrati continued until about 1900, when Roman Catholic authorities in the Vatican banned their role in church music. By then, the eunuch

[15]Fausto-Sterling, A. (2000, July). The five sexes revisited. *The Sciences*, 20–24.

[16]Fausto-Sterling, A. (2003, August 2). Personal e-mail communication from this recognized expert on the subject. For published statistics, see her article co-authored with Blackless, M., et al. (2000). How sexually dimorphic are we? Review and synthesis. *American Journal of Human Biology 12*,151–166.

[17]Abbot, E. (2001). *A history of celibacy*. Cambridge, MA: Da Capo Press.

systems in the Chinese and Ottoman empires were also about to be abolished.[18]

Although human castration was not practiced among North American Indians, many indigenous communities in the Great Plains and Southwest created alternative social space for intersexed or transgendered individuals. **Transgenders** are people who cross over or occupy a culturally accepted position in the binary male–female gender construction.) For example, the Lakota of the northern Plains had an intermediate category of culturally accepted transgendered males who dressed as women and were thought to possess both male and female spirits. They called (and still call) these third-gender individuals *winkte,* applying the term to a male "who wants to be a woman." Thought to have special curing powers, *winktes* traditionally enjoyed considerable prestige in their communities. Among the neighboring Cheyenne, such a person was called *hemanah,* literally meaning "half-man, half-woman."[19]

French traders who came to the Great Plains in the 1600s eventually encountered cross-dressing Native American men, whom they called *berdache* (also spelled *burdash*). The name derived from the Persian word *bardah,* which referred to eunuchs or slaves. The French term *berdache* had acquired obvious contemptuous applications for effeminacy and celibacy, as well as cowardice, and it was broadly used for eunuchs, castrati, cross-dressers, and homosexuals alike. Although early anthropological literature adopted the word, the preferred term among North American Indians today is "two-spirits," which avoids the negative connotations associated with the term *berdache.*[20]

Mapping the sexual landscape, anthropologists have come to realize that gender bending exists in many cultures all around the world, playing a significant role in shaping behaviors and personalities. For instance, third-gender individuals are well known in Samoa, where males who take on the identity of females are referred to as *fa'afafines* ("the female way"). Becoming a *fa'afafine* is an accepted option for boys who prefer to dance, cook, clean house, and care for children and the elderly. In large families, it is not unusual to find two or three boys

© Photography Hugh Hartshorne/ReAngle Pictures

Transgendering occurs in many cultures, but is not always publicly tolerated. Among Polynesians inhabiting Pacific Ocean islands such as Tonga and Samoa, however, such male transvestites are culturally accepted. Samoans refer to these third genders as *fa'afafines* ("the female way").

being raised as girls to take on domestic roles in their households. As North American anthropologist Lowell Holmes recently reported,

> In fact, they tend to be highly valued because they can do the heavy kinds of labor that most women find difficult. A Samoan nun once told me how fortunate it is to have a fa'afafine in the family to help with the household chores. [There] is also the claim made that fa'afafines never have sexual relations with each other but, rather, consider themselves to be "sisters." [They] are religious and go to church regularly dressed as women and . . . some are even Sunday school teachers. Fa'afafines often belong to women's athletic teams, and some even serve as coaches.[21]

Among many other third genders, the best known may be the *hijra* (or *hijadas*) in India. *Hijra* is an Urdu term that covers transgendered men, castrated males, and her-

---

[18]Taylor, G. (2000). *Castration: Abbreviated history of western manhood* (pp. 38–44, 252–259). New York: Routledge.

[19]Medicine, B. (1994). Gender. In M. B. Davis (Ed.), *Native America in the twentieth century.* New York: Garland.

[20]Jacobs, S. E. (1994). Native American two-spirits. *Anthropology Newsletter 35* (8), 7.

transgender A person who crosses over or occupies a culturally accepted position in the binary male–female gender construction.

---

[21]Holmes, L. D. (2000). Paradise bent (film review). *American Anthropologist 102* (3), 604–605.

maphrodites who dress and behave like women in an exaggerated way. As Hindu devotees of the Mother Goddess Bahuchara Mata, their cultural role is to perform blessings for young married couples and male babies. Beyond small earnings for those rituals, they survive by begging, chanting, running bathhouses, and sometimes prostitution.[22]

None of these transgendered cultural types can be simply lumped together as homosexuals. For example, the Tagalog-speaking people in the Philippines use the word *bakla* to refer to a man who views himself "as a male with a female heart." These individuals cross-dress on a daily basis, often becoming more female than females in their use of heavy makeup, in the clothing they wear, and in the way they walk. Like the Samoan *fa'afafines,* they are generally not sexually attracted to other *bakla* but are drawn to heterosexual men instead.

Since some people are gender variants, permanent or incidental transvestites without being homosexuals, it is obvious that the cross-cultural sex and gender scheme is complex. Indeed, the late 19th-century "homosexuality" label is quite inadequate to cover the full range of sex and gender diversity.

In sum, human cultures in the course of thousands of years have creatively dealt with a wide range of inherited and artificially imposed sexual features. The importance of studying complex categories involving intersexuality and transgendering is that doing so enables us to recognize the existing range of gender alternatives and to debunk false stereotypes. It is one more piece of the human puzzle—an important one that prods us to rethink social codes and the range of forces that shape personality as well as each society's definition of normal.

NORMAL AND ABNORMAL PERSONALITY IN SOCIAL CONTEXT

The cultural standards that define normal behavior for any society are determined by that society itself. So it is that in mainstream European and North American societies, in contrast to those just noted, transgender behavior has traditionally been regarded as culturally abnormal. If a male in those societies dresses as a woman, he is still widely viewed as emotionally troubled, or even mentally ill, and his abnormal behavior may lead to psychiatric intervention. There are countless such examples of the fact that what is considered normal and acceptable (if not always popular) in one society is abnormal and

unacceptable (ridiculous, shameful, and sometimes even criminal) in another.

Not only are the boundaries that distinguish the normal from the abnormal culturally variable (and thus neither absolute nor fixed), but so are the standards of what is socially acceptable. In other words, there are individuals in each society who deviate in appearance or behavior from general social standards or norms but are not considered "abnormal" in the strict sense of the word—and are not socially rejected, ridiculed, censured, condemned, jailed, or otherwise penalized. Quite to the contrary, some cultures tolerate or accept a much wider range of diversity than others and may even accord special status to the deviant or eccentric as unique, extraordinary, even sacred.

A fascinating ethnographic example of a culture in which abnormal individuals are socially accepted and even honored is provided by religious mystics in India and Nepal. This example also illustrates the degree to which one's social identity and sense of personal self are cultural constructs.

Sadhus: Holy Men in Hindu Culture

When a young Hindu man in India or Nepal decides to become an ascetic monk, or *sadhu,* he must transform his personal identity, change his sense of self, and leave his place in the social order. Detaching himself from the pursuit of earthly pleasures (*kama*), power and wealth (*artha*), he makes a radical break with his family and friends and abandons the moral principles and rules of code of conduct prescribed for his caste (*dharma*). Symbolically expressing his "death" as a normal Hindu person, he participates in his own funeral ceremony, followed by a ritual rebirth. As a born-again, he acquires a new identity as a *sadhu* and is initiated into a particular ascetic order or sect.

[22]Nanda, S. (1990). *Neither man nor woman: The hijras of India.* Belmont, CA: Wadsworth.

Shaivite *sadhu* of the Aghori sub-sect drinks from human skull bowl. He is a strict follower of the Hindu god Shiva, whose picture can be seen behind him. The practice of eating and drinking from a human skull is a daily reminder of human mortality. These ascetics remain naked and often wear a rosary made of bones around their neck. To become a *sadhu*, one must transform his personal identity, leave his place in the social order, and surrender all attachments to normal human pleasures.

Having surrendered all social, material, and even sexual attachments to normal human pleasures and delights, the *sadhu* dedicates himself to achieving spiritual union with the divine or universal Soul. This is done through intense meditation (chanting sacred hymns or mystical prayer texts—*mantras*) and yoga (an ascetic and mystic discipline involving prescribed postures and controlled breathing). The goal is to become a fully enlightened soul, liberated from the physical limits of the individual mortal self, including the cycle of life and death.

The *sadhu* path to this divine state of pure consciousness and total inner freedom (*mokshe*) is acutely challenging. It demands extraordinary concentration and near superhuman effort, as can be seen in the most extreme yoga postures. This chosen life of suffering may even include self-torture as a form of extreme penance. For instance, some *sadhus* pierce their tongue or cheeks with a long iron rod, stab a long knife through their arm or leg, or stick their head into a small hole in the ground for

hours on end. Among the more extreme examples, one *sadhu* is known to have kept his right arm continuously stretched up into the air for twenty-five years (transforming his hand into a useless stump).

Most Hindus revere and sometimes even fear *sadhus*. When they encounter one—by a temple or cemetery, or perhaps near a forest, riverbank, or mountain cave, they typically offer him food or other alms. Sightings are not uncommon since an estimated 5 million *sadhus* live in India and Nepal. They belong to different sub-sects of ascetic orders, each with its own characteristics and ritual practices. Some *sadhus* are believed to have succeeded in achieving divine status as *jivan mukta* ("a soul liberated while still alive") and are devoutly honored as great saints or even as gods on earth.

Perhaps the most remarkable *sadhus* belong to a very small sub-sect of the Shaivite Order, devoted to worshiping Shiva, the Hindu god of destruction and reproduction. Known as *aghoris* (meaning "not terrible," one of

Shiva's names), these extremely ascetic monks challenge the cosmic order itself and turn normal rules of Hindu conduct upside-down. Naked or near naked ("sky-clad"), they spend most of their time around cremation grounds. On a regular basis they apply ashes to their body, face, and long matted hair. They also drink and eat from human skull bowls, occasionally challenging themselves in their devotion to Shiva by eating their own excrement and decomposed human flesh torn from a body awaiting cremation.[23]

Of course, if one of these bearded, long-haired, Hindu monks, especially an aghori, decided to practice his extreme yoga exercises and other sacred devotions as a Shiva worshiper in western Europe or North America, such a holy man would be viewed as severely mentally disturbed. And if this *sadhu* was seen walking around naked and drinking from his human skull bowl in a place like Kansas City, he would no doubt face arrest for disorderly and even criminal conduct. In all likelihood, he would be declared insane and forced to spend the rest of his life doing penance of another kind.

A Cross-Cultural Perspective on Mental Disorders

No matter how eccentric or even bizarre certain behaviors might seem in a particular place and time, it is possible for the "abnormal" to become socially accepted in cultures that are changing. In this vein, anthropologist Emily Martin cites recent new attitudes toward manic depression (now more properly called *bipolar disorder*) and attention deficit hyperactivity disorder (ADHD), previously regarded as dreaded liabilities.[24]

She suggests that, in North America, the manic and hyperactivity aspects are gradually becoming viewed as assets in the quest for success. More and more, they are interpreted as indicative of "finely wired, exquisitely alert nervous systems" that make one highly sensitive to signs of change, able to fly from one thing to another while pushing the limits of everything, and doing it all with an intense level of energy focused totally in the future. These are extolled as high virtues in the corporate world, and to be called "hyper" or "manic" is increasingly an expression of approval.

Not only do social attitudes concerning a wide range of both psychological and physical differences

change over time within a society, they also vary across cultures—as evident in this chapter's Biocultural Connection.

Is all of this to suggest that "normalcy" is a meaningless concept when applied to personality? Within the context of a particular culture, the concept of normal personality is quite meaningful. Irving Hallowell, a major figure in the development of psychological anthropology, somewhat ironically observed that it is normal to share the delusions traditionally accepted by one's society. Abnormality involves the development of a delusional system of which the culture does not approve. The individual who is disturbed because he or she cannot adequately measure up to the norms of society and be happy may be termed "neurotic." When a person's delusional system is so different that it in no way reflects his or her society's norms, the individual may be termed "psychotic."

If severe enough, culturally induced conflicts can produce psychosis and also determine the form of the psychosis. In a culture that encourages aggressiveness and suspicion, the insane person may be one who is passive and trusting. In a culture that encourages passivity and trust, the insane person may be the one who is aggressive and suspicious. Just as each society establishes its own norms, each individual is unique in his or her perceptions.

Many anthropologists see the only meaningful criterion for personality evaluation as the correlation between personality and social conformity. From their point of view, insanity is a culturally constructed mental illness, and people are considered insane when they fail to conform to a culturally defined range of normal behavior. This is not to say that psychosis is simply a matter of an especially bad fit between an individual and his or her particular culture.

Although it is true that each particular culture defines what is and is not normal behavior, the situation is complicated by findings suggesting that major categories of mental disorders may be universal types of human affliction. Take, for example, schizophrenia—probably the most common of all psychoses and one that may be found in any culture, no matter how it may manifest itself. Individuals afflicted by schizophrenia experience distortions of reality that impair their ability to function adequately, so they often withdraw from the social world into their own psychological shell. Although environmental factors play a role, evidence suggests that schizophrenia is caused by a biochemical disorder for which there is an inheritable tendency. One of its more severe forms is paranoid schizophrenia. Those suffering from it fear and mistrust nearly everyone. They hear voices that whisper dreadful things to them, and they are convinced that someone is "out to get them." Acting on this con-

---

[23]See Kelly, T. L. (2006). Sadhus, the great renouncers. Photography exhibit, Indigo Gallery, Naxal, Kathmandu, Nepal. Posted online at www.asianart.com/exhibitions/sadhus/index.html. See also Heitzman, J., & R. L. Wordem, R. L. (Eds.). (2006). *India: A country study* (sect. 2, 5th ed.). Washington, D.C.: Federal Research Division, Library of Congress.

[24]Martin, E. (1999). Flexible survivors. *Anthropology News 40* (6), 5–7.

Biocultural Connection

A Cross-Cultural Perspective on Psychosomatic Symptoms and Mental Health

Biomedicine, the dominant medical system of Euramerican cultures, sometimes identifies physical ailments experienced by individuals as "psychosomatic"—a term derived from *psyche* ("mind") and *soma* ("body"). These ailments can be serious and painful, but because a precise physiological cause cannot be identified through scientific methods, the illness is viewed as something rooted in mental or emotional causes—and thus on some level not quite "real."

Each culture possesses its own historically developed ideas about health, illness, and associated healing practices. While biomedicine is based in modern Western traditions of science, it is also steeped in the cultural beliefs and practices of societies within which it operates. Fundamentally informed by a dualistic mind–body model, biomedicine represents the human body as a complex machine with parts that can be manipulated by experts. This approach has resulted in spectacular treatments, such as antibiotics that have eradicated certain infectious diseases.

Today, the remarkable breakthroughs of biomedicine are spreading rapidly throughout the world, and people from cultures with different healing systems are moving into countries where

biomedicine dominates. This makes treating illnesses defined by biomedicine as psychosomatic disorders all the more difficult.

Indicative of our biocultural complexity, psychological factors such as emotional stress, worry, and anxiety may stem from cultural contexts and result in increased physiological agitation like irregular heart pounding or palpitations, heightened blood pressure, headaches, stomach and intestinal problems, muscle pains and tensions, rashes, appetite loss, insomnia, fatigue, and a range of other troubles. Indeed, when individuals are unable to deal successfully with stressful situations in daily life and do not get the opportunity for adequate mental rest and relaxation, even their natural immune systems may weaken, increasing their chances of getting a cold or some other infection. For people forced to adapt to a quickly changing way of life in their own country or immigrants adjusting to a foreign culture, these pressures may result in a range of disorders that are difficult to explain from the perspective of biomedicine.

Medical and psychological approaches developed in European and North American societies are often unsuccessful in dealing with these problems,

for a number of reasons. For one, the various immigrant ethnic groups have different concepts of mind and body than do medical practitioners trained in Western (Euramerican) medicine. Among many Caribbean peoples, for example, a widely held belief is that spiritual forces are active in the world and that they influence human identity and behavior. Thus, for someone with a psychosomatic problem, it is normal to seek help from a local *curandero* or *curandera* (folk healer), *santiguadora* (herbalist), or even a *santéro* (a Santéria priest) rather than a medical doctor or psychiatrist. Not only does the client not understand the symbols of Western psychiatry, but to go to a psychiatrist is often too expensive and may imply that he or she is *loco* (crazy).

During the past few decades, however, anthropologists have become increasingly involved in cross-cultural medical mediation, challenging negative biases and correcting misinformation about non-Western indigenous perceptions of mind–body connections. The inclusion of culturally appropriate healing approaches has gained growing acceptance among the Western medical and psychological establishment in Europe, North America, and many other parts of the world.

---

viction, they engage in bizarre sorts of behaviors, which lead to their removal from society.

Ethnic Psychoses

Ethnic psychoses are mental disorders specific to particular cultural groups (Table 17.1). Among these is Windigo psychosis, limited to northern Algonquian Indian groups such as the Cree and Ojibwa. In their traditional belief systems, these northern Indians recognized the existence of cannibalistic monsters called Windigos. In-

ethnic psychosis A mental disorder specific to a particular ethnic group.

dividuals afflicted by the psychosis developed the delusion that, falling under the control of these monsters, they were transformed into Windigos, with a craving for human flesh. As this happened, the psychotic individuals saw people around them turning into various edible animals—fat, juicy beavers, for instance. Although there are no known instances where sufferers of Windigo psychosis actually ate another human being, they were acutely afraid of doing so, and people around them were genuinely fearful that they might.

Windigo psychosis may seem different from clinical cases of paranoid schizophrenia found in Euramerican cultures, but a closer look suggests otherwise. The disorder was merely being expressed in ways compatible with traditional northern Algonquian cultures. Ideas of perse-

| TABLE 17.1 | ETHNIC PSYCHOSES AND OTHER CULTURE-BOUND SYNDROMES | |

Name of Disorder	Culture	Description
Amok	Malaysia (also observed in Java, Philippines, Africa, and Tierra del Fuego)	A disorder characterized by sudden, wild outbursts of homicidal aggression in which the afflicted person may kill or injure others. The rage disorder is usually found in males who are rather withdrawn, quiet, and inoffensive prior to the onset of the disorder. Stress, sleep deprivation, extreme heat, and alcohol are among the conditions thought to precipitate the disorder. Several stages have been observed: Typically in the first stage the person becomes more withdrawn; then a period of brooding follows in which a loss of reality contact is evident. Ideas of persecution and anger predominate. Finally, a phase of automatism, or *amok*, occurs, in which the person jumps up, yells, grabs a knife, and stabs people or objects within reach. Exhaustion and depression usually follow, with amnesia for the rage.
Anorexia nervosa	Western countries	A disorder occurring most frequently among young women in which a preoccupation with thinness produces a refusal to eat. This condition can result in death.
Latah	Malaysia	A fear reaction often occurring in middle-aged women of low intelligence who are subservient and self-effacing. The disorder is precipitated by the word *snake* or by tickling. It is characterized by echolalia (repetition of the words and sentences of others). The disturbed individual may also react with negativism and the compulsive use of obscene language.
Koro	Southeast Asia (particularly Malaysia)	A fear reaction or anxiety in which the person fears that his penis will withdraw into his abdomen and he will die. This reaction may appear after sexual overindulgence or excessive masturbation. The anxiety is typically very intense and of sudden onset. The condition is "treated" by having the penis held firmly by the patient or by family members or friends. Often the penis is clamped to a wooden box.
Windigo	Algonquian Indians of Canada and northern United States	A fear reaction in which a hunter becomes anxious and agitated, convinced that he is bewitched. Fears center on his being turned into a cannibal by the power of a monster with an insatiable craving for human flesh.
Kitsunetsuki	Japan	A disorder in which victims believe that they are possessed by foxes and are said to change their facial expressions to resemble foxes. Entire families are often possessed and banned by the community.
Pibloktoq and other Arctic hysterias	Circumpolar peoples from Lapland eastward across Siberia, northern Alaska, and Canada to Greenland	A disorder brought on by fright, which is followed by a short period of bizarre behavior; victim may tear clothes off, jump in water or fire, roll in snow, try to walk on the ceiling, throw things, thrash about, and "speak in tongues." Outburst followed by return to normal behavior.

SOURCE: Based on Carson, R. C., Butcher, J. N., & Coleman, J. C. (1990). *Abnormal psychology and modern life* (8th ed., p. 85). Glenview, IL: Scott Foresman.

cution, instead of being directed toward other humans, were directed toward supernatural beings (the Windigo monsters); cannibalistic panic replaced panic expressed in other forms. Northern Algonquian Indians, like Euramericans, expressed their problems in terms compatible with the appropriate view of the self and its behavioral environment. However, the Algonquians protected their families from such seriously deranged individuals by killing them—for in their small-scale communities, there existed nothing resembling what we would recognize as a mental institution.

Windigo behavior has seemed exotic and dramatic to Euramericans, but psychotic individuals draw upon whatever imagery and symbolism their culture has to offer, and in northern Algonquian culture, these include myths featuring cannibal giants. By contrast, the delusions of Irish schizophrenics draw upon the images and symbols of Irish Catholicism and feature virgin and savior motifs. Euramericans, on the other hand, tend toward secular or electromagnetic persecution delusions. The underlying structure of the mental disorder is the same in all cases, but its expression is culturally specific.

Anthropologists view all mental health issues in their cultural context, in recognition of the fact that each individual's social identity, unique personality, and overall sense of mental health is molded by the particular culture within which the person is born and raised to function as a valued member of the community.

Questions for Reflection

1. Every society faces the challenge of humanizing its children, teaching them the values and social codes that will enable them to be functioning and contributing members in the community. What child-rearing practices did you experience that embody the values and social codes of your society?

2. Considering the cultural significance of naming ceremonies in so many societies, what do you think motivated your parents when they named you? Does that have any influence on your sense of self?

3. Margaret Mead's cross-cultural research on gender relations suggests that male dominance is a cultural construct and, consequently, that alternative gender arrangements can be created. Looking at your grandparents, parents, and siblings, do you see any changes in your own family? What about your own community? Do you think such changes are positive?

4. Do you fit within the acceptable range of your society's modal personality? How so?

5. Given that over 60 million people in today's world are intersexed, and in light of the fact that a very small fraction of these people have access to reconstructive sexual surgery, what do you think of societies that have created cultural space for a third-gender option?

Suggested Readings

Barnouw, V. (1985). *Culture and personality* (4th ed.). Homewood, IL: Dorsey Press.

This is a revision of a well-respected text designed to introduce students to psychological anthropology.

Brettell, C. B., & Sargent, C. F. (Eds.). (2000). *Gender in cross-cultural perspective* (3rd. ed.). Upper Saddle River, NJ: Prentice-Hall.

Classic and contemporary gender readings on a range of topics, including the cultural construction of femininity and masculinity and the impact of globalization on gender issues.

LaFont, S. (Ed.). (2003). *Constructing sexualities: Readings in sexuality, gender, and culture.* Upper Saddle River, NJ: Prentice-Hall.

A broad yet detailed look at sexuality and gender behavior. Statistics, ethnographic examples, and theoretical insights on numerous themes—from the biological basics and sex categories to sexual orientation and transsexuality.

Shore, B. (1996). *Culture in mind: Meaning, construction, and cultural cognition.* New York: Oxford University Press.

A readable exploration of developmental and cognitive psychology and the cultural context of individual psychology.

Suárez-Orozoco, M. M., Spindler, G., & Spindler, L. (1994). *The making of psychological anthropology, II.* Fort Worth, TX: Harcourt Brace.

This collection of articles consists of firsthand accounts of the objectives, accomplishments, and failures of well-known specialists in psychological anthropology.

Whiting, J. W. M., & Child, I. (1953). *Child training and personality: A cross-cultural study.* New Haven, CT: Yale University Press.

Exploring the relationship between culture and personality, this classic text is oriented toward testing general hypotheses about human behavior in any and all societies.

Thomson Audio Study Products

Enjoy the MP3-ready Audio Lecture Overviews for each chapter and a comprehensive audio glossary of key terms for quick study and review. Whether walking to class, doing laundry, or studying at your desk, you now have the freedom to choose when, where, and how you interact with your audio-based educational media. See the preface for information on how to access this on-the-go study and review tool.

The Anthropology Resource Center

www.thomsonedu.com/anthropology
The Anthropology Resource Center provides extended learning materials to reinforce your understanding of key concepts in the four fields of anthropology. For each of the four fields, the Resource Center includes dynamic exercises including video exercises, map exercises, simulations, and "Meet the Scientists" interviews, as well as critical thinking questions that can be assigned and e-mailed to instructors. The Resource Center also provides breaking news in anthropology and interesting material on applied anthropology to help you link what you are learning to the world around you.

18 Patterns of Subsistence

© Jeremy Horner/Corbis

CHALLENGE ISSUE

Facing the challenge of getting food, fuel, shelter, and other necessities, humans must gather, produce, or buy the means to satisfy such needs. During the span of human existence, this has been accomplished in a range of highly contrasting natural environments by different biological and cultural adaptations. Inventing and applying various technologies, humans have developed a great variety of distinctive subsistence arrangements to harness energy and process required resources. Thus we may find hunters in Namibia's desert, fishers in Norway, manioc planters in Brazil's rainforest, goat herders in Iran's mountains, automakers in Korea, and Jamaican apple pickers in the United States. While all human activities impact their environments, some are more invasive than others—as we see in this photo of the Andean mountains reshaped with terracing by generations of traditional Indian farmers aiming to capture rainwater and prevent erosion while cultivating the soil.

What Is Adaptation?

Adaptation refers to beneficial adjustments of organisms to their environment, a process that not only leads to changes in the organisms but also impacts their environment. Such dynamic interaction is necessary for the survival of all life forms, including human beings. The human species adapts not only biologically but culturally. In fact, in the course of evolution, humans came to rely increasingly on culture rather than biological change as a means of effectively adapting to different and changing environments.

How Do Humans Adapt Culturally?

Through cultural adaptation, humans develop ways of doing things that are compatible with the resources they have available to them and within the limitations of the various habitats in which they live. In a particular region, people living in similar environments tend to borrow from one another customs that work well in those settings. Once achieved, adaptations may be remarkably stable for long periods of time, even thousands of years. Humankind's unique creative capacity to adapt by means of culture has enabled our species to inhabit an extraordinary variety of environments.

What Sorts of Cultural Adaptations Have Humans Achieved Through the Ages?

Food foraging is the oldest and most universal type of human adaptation and typically involves geographic mobility. Other adaptations, involving domestication of plants and animals, began to develop in some parts of the world about 10,000 years ago. Horticulture (cultivating plants with hand tools) led to more permanent settlements (villages and towns) while pastoralism (herding grazing animals) required mobility to seek out pasture and water. Cities began to develop as early as 5,000 years ago in some world regions, as intensive agriculture and long-distance trading produced sufficient resources to support larger populations and various full-time specialists. These changes led to increasingly complex and large-scale social organizations—but did not necessarily improve the overall conditions of human existence.

All living beings must satisfy certain basic needs to stay alive—including food, water, and shelter. Moreover, because these needs must be met on a regular basis, no creature could long survive if its relations with its environment were random and chaotic. All require regular access to a supply of food and water and a reliable means of obtaining and using it. A lion might die if all its prey disappeared, if its teeth and claws grew soft, or if its digestive system failed.

Although people face similar sorts of problems, they have an overwhelming advantage over other creatures: People have culture. If the rains do not come, and the hot sun turns grassland into desert, we may pump water from deep wells, quenching our thirst, irrigating the pastures, and feeding our grazing animals. Conversely, if the rains do not end, and our pastures turn into marshlands, we may choose to build earth mounds for our villages or dig canals to drain flooded fields. And to keep our food supplies from rotting, we can preserve them by drying or roasting and keep them in safe storage places for protection and future use. When our tools fail or are inadequate, we may choose to replace them or invent better ones. And if our stomachs are incapable of digesting a particular food, we can prepare it by cooking.

We are, nonetheless, subject to similar basic needs and pressures as all other living creatures, and it is important to understand human survival from this point of view. The crucial concept that underlies such a perspective is adaptation or how humans adjust to and act upon the burdens and opportunities presented in daily life.

ADAPTATION

As discussed earlier in this book, adaptation is the process organisms undergo to achieve a beneficial adjustment to a particular environment. What makes human adaptation unique among all other species is our capacity to produce and reproduce culture, enabling us to creatively adapt to an extraordinary range of radically different environments. The biological underpinnings of this capacity include large brains and a long period of growth and

cultural adaptation A complex of ideas, activities, and technologies that enable people to survive and even thrive.

development. How humans adjust to the burdens and opportunities presented in daily life is the basic concern of all cultures. A people's **cultural adaptation** consists of a complex of ideas, activities, and technologies that enable them to survive and even thrive and that, in turn, impact their environment.

The process of adaptation establishes an ever-shifting balance between the needs of a population and the potential of its environment. This process can be illustrated by the Tsembaga people of Papua New Guinea, one of about twenty local groups of Maring speakers who support themselves chiefly through cultivating crops using simple hand tools such as digging sticks or hoes.[1] Although the Tsembaga also raise pigs, they eat them only under conditions of illness, injury, warfare, or celebration. At such times the pigs are sacrificed to ancestral spirits, and their flesh is ritually consumed. (This guarantees a supply of high-quality protein when it is most needed.)

Traditionally, the Tsembaga and their neighbors are bound together in a unique cycle of pig sacrifices that serves to mark the end of hostilities between groups. Hostilities are periodically fueled by ecological pressures in which pigs play a significant role. Pigs are rarely slaughtered because they fulfill important roles: omnivorous eaters, they keep the village free of garbage and even human feces; moreover, they serve as status symbols for their owners who reserve them for significant rituals. But keeping them alive and allowing them to multiply comes at a cost since their numbers grow quickly. Invading the village gardens, the hungry pigs eat the sweet potatoes and other crops, leaving almost nothing for their human owners. In short, they become a problem.

The need to expand food cultivation in order to feed the prestigious but pesky pigs puts a strain on the land

[1]Rappaport, R. A. (1969). Ritual regulation of environmental relations among a New Guinea people. In A. P. Vayda (Ed.), *Environment and cultural behavior* (pp. 181–201). Garden City, NY: Natural History Press.

best suited for farming. Sooner or later, fighting breaks out between the Tsembaga and their neighbors. Hostilities usually end after several weeks, followed by a pig feast ritual. For this event, the Tsembaga butcher and roast almost all of their pigs and feast heartily on them with invited allies. By means of this feast, the Tsembaga not only pay their debts to their allies and gain prestige, but also eliminate a major source of irritation and complaint between neighbors. Moreover, the feast leaves everyone well fed and physically strengthened as a result of the animal protein intake. Even without hostilities over scarce land, such large pig feasts have been held whenever the pig population has become unmanageable—every five to ten years, depending on the groups' success in growing crops and raising animals. Thus, the cycle of fighting and feasting keeps the ecological balance among humans, land, and animals.

Through their distinctive cultures, different human groups have managed to adapt to a very diverse range of natural environments—from Arctic snowfields to Polynesian coral islands, from the Sahara Desert to the Amazon rainforest. In all these different environments, cultural adaptation is fundamental to human survival. Adaptation occurs not only when humans make all kinds of changes in their natural environment, but also when they are biologically changed by their natural environment. The Biocultural Connection provides an example of such a biocultural interaction, found in the central Andean highlands of Bolivia.

The Unit of Adaptation

The unit of adaptation includes both organisms and their environment. Organisms, including human beings, exist as members of a population; populations, in turn, must have the flexibility to cope with variability and change within the natural environment that sustains them. In biological terms, this flexibility means that different organisms within the population have somewhat differing genetic endowments. In cultural terms, it means that variation occurs among individual skills, knowledge, and personalities. Indeed, organisms and environments form dynamic interacting systems. And although environments do not determine culture, they do present certain possibilities and limitations: People might just as easily farm as fish, but we do not expect to find farmers in Siberia's frozen tundra or fishermen in the middle of North Africa's Sahara Desert.

Some anthropologists have adopted the ecologists' concept of **ecosystem,** defined as a system composed of both the natural environment and all the organisms living within it. The system is bound by the activities of the organisms, as well as by such physical processes as erosion and evaporation.

Adaptation in Cultural Evolution

Human groups adapt to their environments by means of their cultures. However, cultures may change over the course of time; they evolve. This is called **cultural evolution.** The process is sometimes confused with the idea of **progress**—the notion that humans are moving forward to a better, more advanced stage in their development toward perfection. Yet, not all changes turn out to be positive in the long run, nor do they improve conditions for every member of a society even in the short run. Complex, urban societies are not more "highly evolved" than those of food foragers. Rather, both are "highly evolved," but in quite different ways.

Cultural adaptation must also be understood from a historical point of view. To fit into an ecosystem, humans (like all organisms) must have the potential to adjust to or become a part of it. A good example of this is the Comanche, whose history begins in the highlands of southern Idaho.[2] Living in that harsh, arid region, these North American Indians traditionally subsisted on wild plants, small animals, and occasionally larger game. Their material equipment was simple and limited to what they (and their dogs) could carry or pull. The size of their groups was restricted, and what little social power could develop was in the hands of the shaman, who was a combination of healer and spiritual guide.

At some point in their nomadic history, the Comanche moved east onto the Great Plains, where bison were abundant and they could hunt. As larger groups could be supported by the new and plentiful food supply, the Comanche needed a more complex political organization.

Eventually the Comanche acquired horses and guns from European settlers, which enhanced their hunting capabilities significantly and led to the emergence of powerful hunting chiefs. The Comanche became raiders in order to get horses (which they did not breed for themselves), and their hunting chiefs evolved into war chiefs. The once materially poor and peaceful hunter–gatherers of the dry highlands became wealthy, and raiding became a way of life.

In the late 18th and early 19th centuries, they dominated the southern plains (now primarily Texas and Oklahoma). In moving from one regional environment

---

[2]Wallace, E., & Hoebel, E. A. (1952). *The Comanches*. Norman: University of Oklahoma Press.

ecosystem A system, or a functioning whole, composed of both the natural environment and all the organisms living within it.
cultural evolution Culture change over time (not to be confused with progress).
progress The notion that humans are moving forward to a better, more advanced stage in their cultural development toward perfection.

Biocultural Connection

Surviving in the Andes: Aymara Adaptation to High Altitude

However adaptable we are as a species through our diverse cultures, some natural environments pose such extreme climatic challenges that the human body must make physical adaptations to successfully survive. The central Andean highlands of Bolivia offer an interesting example of complex biocultural interaction, where a biologically adapted human body type has emerged due to natural selection.

Known as the *altiplano*, this high plateau has an average elevation of 4,000 meters (13,000 feet). Many thousands of years ago, small groups of human foragers in the warm lowlands climbed up the mountain slopes in search of game and other food. The higher they moved, the harder it became to breathe due to decreasing molecular concentration, or partial pressure, of oxygen in the inspired air. However, upon reaching the cold and treeless highlands, they found herds of llamas and hardy food plants, including potatoes—reasons to stay. Eventually (about 4,000 years ago) their descendants domesticated both the llamas and the potatoes and developed a new way of life as high-altitude agropastoralists.

The llamas provided meat and hides, as well as milk and wool. And the potatoes, a rich source of carbohydrates, became their staple food. In the course of many centuries, the Aymara selectively cultivated more than 200 varieties of these tubers on small family-owned tracts of land. They boiled them fresh for immediate consumption and also freeze-dried and preserved them as *chuño*, which is the Aymara's major source of nutrition to this day.

Still surviving as highland subsistence farmers and herders, these Aymara Indians have adapted culturally and biologically to the cold and harsh conditions of Bolivia's altiplano. They live and go about their work at extremely high altitudes (up to 4,800 meters/15,600 feet), where partial pressure of oxygen in the air is far lower than most humans are biologically accustomed to.

Experiencing a marked hypoxeamia (insufficient oxygenation of the blood), a person's normal physiological response to being active at such heights is quick and heavy breathing. Most outsiders visiting the altiplano typically need several days to acclimatize to these conditions. Going too high too quickly can cause *soroche* (mountain sickness), with physiological problems such as pulmonary hypertension, increased heart rates, shortness of breath, headaches, fever, lethargy, and nausea. These symptoms usually disappear when one becomes fully acclimated, but most people will still be quickly exhausted by otherwise normal physical exercise.

For the Aymara Indians whose ancestors have inhabited the altiplano for many thousands of years, the situation is different. Through generations of natural selection, their bodies have become biologically adapted to the low oxygen levels. Short-legged and barrel-chested, their small bodies have an unusually large thoracic volume compared to their tropical lowland neighbors and most other humans. Remarkably, their expanded heart and lungs possess about 30 percent greater pulmonary diffusing capacity to oxygenate blood. In short, the distinctly broad chests of the Aymara Indians are biological evidence of their physiological adaptation to the low-oxygen atmosphere of a natural habitat in which they survive as high-altitude agropastoralists. *(See P. Baker (Ed.). (1978). The biology of high altitude peoples. London: Cambridge University Press; Rupert, J. L., & Hochachka, P. W. (2001). The evidence for hereditary factors contributing to high altitude adaptation in Andean natives: A review.* High Altitude Medicine & Biology 2 *(2), 235–256.)*

© Victor Englebert

---

to another and in adopting a new technology, the Comanche were able to take advantage of existing cultural capabilities to thrive in their new situation.

Sometimes societies that developed independently of one another find similar solutions to similar problems. For example, the Cheyenne Indians moved from the woodlands of the Great Lakes region to the Great Plains and took up a form of plains Indian culture resembling that of the Comanche, even though the cultural historical backgrounds of the two groups differed significantly. (Before they transformed into horse-riding bison hunters, the Cheyenne had cultivated crops and gathered

A Comanche bison hunt as painted by artist George Catlin. Plains Indians such as the Comanche and Lakota developed similar cultures, as they had to adapt to similar environmental conditions. (For a map of Native American culture areas, see Figure 18.1.)

wild rice, which fostered a distinct set of social, political, and religious practices.) This is an example of **convergent evolution**—the development of similar cultural adaptations to similar environmental conditions by different peoples with different ancestral cultures.

Especially interesting is that the Cheyenne gave up crop cultivation completely and focused exclusively on hunting and gathering after their move into the vast grasslands of the northern High Plains. Contrary to the popular notion of evolution as a progressive movement toward increased manipulation of the environment, this ethnographic example shows that cultural historical changes in subsistence practices do not always go from dependence on wild food to farming; they may go the other way as well.

Analogous to the phenomenon of convergent evolution is **parallel evolution,** in which similar cultural adaptations to similar environmental conditions are achieved by peoples whose ancestral cultures were already somewhat alike. For example, the development of farming in Southwest Asia and Mesoamerica took place independently, as people in both regions, whose lifeways were already comparable, became dependent on a narrow range of plant foods that required human intervention for their protection and reproductive success. Both developed intensive forms of agriculture, built large cities, and created complex social and political organizations.

It is important to recognize that stability as well as change is involved in cultural adaptation and evolution; episodes of major adaptive change may be followed by long periods of relative stability in a cultural system. For example, about 5,500 years ago a seasonal migratory way of life had evolved among indigenous peoples in New England and Quebec that was well attuned to the natural environmental conditions of the times.[3] Since those conditions remained fairly stable over the next 5,000 years or so, it is understandable that people's lifeways remained relatively unchanged.

This is not to say that culture change was entirely absent, for it was not. Periodically, people refined and enhanced their way of life: They replaced spears and spear-throwers with far-reaching bows and arrows; they enhanced cooking methods by using pottery vessels instead of containers made from bark, wood, or animal hide; they substituted heavy and cumbersome dugout boats with lightweight birch-bark canoes; and they supplemented foods gained in hunting, gathering, and fishing with cultivated corn, beans, and squash.

Despite these changes, however, the native peoples of the region retained the basic structure of their culture and maintained a balance with their resource base well into the 17th century, when the culture had to adjust to pressures associated with European invasions of North America. Such enduring stability suggests success. Had this culture not effectively satisfied people's physical and psychological needs, it would not have endured as it did for thousands of years.

That said, not every group has implemented the changes needed for long-term survival—and some have made changes that failed to bring expected benefits. Moreover, not everybody benefits from changes, especially if change is forced upon them. As history painfully demonstrates, all too often humans have made changes that have had disastrous results, leading to the deaths of thousands, even millions of people—not to mention other creatures—and to the destruction of the natural environment. In short, we must avoid falling into the ethnocentric trap of equating change with progress or seeing everything as adaptive.

Culture Areas

From early on, anthropologists recognized that ethnic groups living within the same broad habitat often share certain culture traits. This reflects the fact that neighboring peoples may easily borrow from each other and that there exists a basic relationship among their similar natural environment, available resources, and subsistence practices.

---

[3]Haviland, W. A., & Power, M. W. (1994). *The original Vermonters* (2nd ed.). Hanover, NH: University Press of New England.

---

convergent evolution In cultural evolution, the development of similar cultural adaptations to similar environmental conditions by different peoples with different ancestral cultures.
parallel evolution In cultural evolution, the development of similar cultural adaptations to similar environmental conditions by peoples whose ancestral cultures were already somewhat alike.

Classifying groups according to their culture traits, anthropologists have mapped culture clusters known as **culture areas**—geographic regions in which a number of societies have similar ways of life. Such areas often correspond to ecological areas. In sub-Arctic North America, for example, migratory caribou herds graze across the vast tundra. For dozens of different groups that have made this region their home, these animals provide a major source of food as well as material for shelter and clothing. Adapting to more or less the same ecological resources in this sub-Arctic landscape, these groups have developed similar subsistence technologies and practices in the course of generations. They may speak very different languages, but they may all be said to form part of the same culture area.

Because everything in nature is always in a state of flux—daily, seasonal, and annual cycles of abundance and scarcity, as well as permanent changes in the environment due to destruction of habitat and extinction of plant and animal species—culture areas are not always stable. Moreover, new species may be introduced and technologies invented or introduced from more distant cultures. Such was the case with the indigenous culture area of the Great Plains in North America (Figure 18.1). For thousands of years, many indigenous groups with similar ways of life existed in this vast ecological area between the Mississippi River and the Rocky Mountains. Until the mid-1800s, when European immigrants invaded the region and almost completely annihilated the millions of free-ranging bison, these large grazing herds provided an obvious and practical source of food and materials for clothing and shelter.

The efficiency of indigenous groups in the southern plains increased greatly in the 1600s when they gained access to Spanish horses on the northern Mexican frontier and became mounted bison hunters. During the next century, the new horse complex spread northward to almost every indigenous group ranging in the Great Plains culture area. A total of thirty-one politically independent peoples, including the Cheyenne and Comanche, reached a similar adaptation to this particular grassland region.

So it was that by the time of the Euramerican invasion of their vast hunting territories in the 19th century, the Indians of the Great Plains were all bison hunters, dependent upon this animal for food, clothing, shelter, and bone tools. Each native nation was organized into a number of warrior societies, and prestige came from hunting and fighting skills. Their villages were typically arranged in a distinctive circular pattern, and many re-

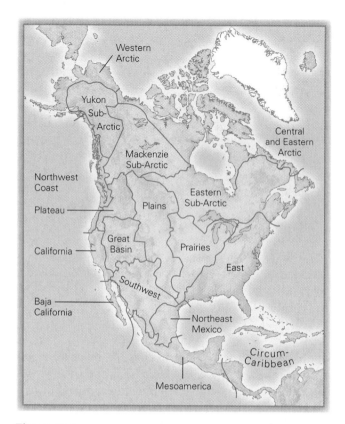

Figure 18.1

The culture area concept was developed by anthropologists in the early part of the 20th century. This map shows the culture areas that have been defined for North and Central America. Within each, there is an overall similarity of native cultures, as opposed to the differences that distinguish the cultures of one area from those of all others.

ligious rituals, such as the Sun Dance, were practiced throughout the region.

During the 1870s and 1880s, railroads were built across the Great Plains, and mass slaughter of bison followed. More than 1 million of these animals were killed every year, mostly by non-Indians interested only in their hides and tongues (tongues were a luxury meat commodity, easily removed and compact to ship). With their herds almost exterminated, Indians of the plains faced starvation, which made it impossible to effectively defend their homelands. This resulted in the near collapse of their traditional cultures from the 1890s onward.

Sometimes geographic regions are not uniform in climate and landscape, so new discoveries do not always spread from one group to another. Moreover, within a culture area, there are variations between local environments, and these favor variations in adaptation. One example of local variations in adaptation is the Great Basin of the western United States—a dry highland area embracing the states of Nevada and Utah, with adjacent portions of California, Oregon, Wyoming, and Idaho.[4]

---

culture area A geographic region in which a number of societies follow similar patterns of life.

---

[4]Steward, J. H. (1972). *Theory of culture change: The methodology of multilinear evolution.* Urbana: University of Illinois Press.

The Shoshone Indians who live there are divided into a northern and a western group. Traditionally, both subsisted as nomadic hunters and gatherers, but there were certain distinctions between them. In the north, a relative abundance of game animals made hunting primary and provided for the maintenance of large human populations, requiring a great deal of cooperation among local groups. In the west, by contrast, game was less plentiful so the western Shoshone depended especially upon rabbit hunting and the gathering of wild plants such as pine nuts for their subsistence. Since plants varied considerably in their seasonal and local availability, the western Shoshone were forced to cover vast distances in search of food. Under such conditions, it was most efficient to travel in groups of but a few families, only occasionally coming together with other groups and not always with the same ones.

The Shoshone were not the only inhabitants of the Great Basin. To the south lived the closely related Paiutes. They, too, were foragers (hunter–gatherers) living under similar environmental conditions as the Shoshone, but some Paiute bands inhabiting areas with swampy lowlands managed their food resources more actively by diverting small streams to irrigate wild crops such as wild hyacinth, nut grass, and spike rush. These bulbs and seeds were the mainstay of their food supply. Because this ecological adaptation provided them with higher yields than their northern neighbors, their populations were larger than those of the Shoshone, and they led a less nomadic existence.

Culture Core

Environment and technology are not the only factors that determine a society's pattern of subsistence; social and political organization also influence how technology is applied to the problem of staying alive. This given, if we wish to understand the rise of irrigation agriculture in the great centers of ancient civilization (such as in what are now Egypt, China, Peru, and Iraq), we need to know not only the technological and environmental factors that made the building of large-scale irrigation works possible but also the social and political organization that made it feasible to mobilize the many workers necessary to build and maintain the systems. For this understanding, we must examine the monarchies and priesthoods that coordinated the work, decided where the water would be used, and determined how the agricultural products of this collective venture would be distributed.

The cultural features that are fundamental in the society's way of making its living are called its **culture core.** This includes the society's food-producing techniques, knowledge of available resources in its environment, and the work arrangements involved in applying those techniques to the local environment. For example,

In Bali, gatherings for rituals at water temples allowed farmers to arrange schedules for flooding their rice paddies.

do people work every day for a fixed number of hours, or is most work concentrated during certain times of the year?

The culture core comprises other aspects of culture that bear on the production and distribution of food. Among these is worldview or ideology, evidenced in the ways religious beliefs sometimes prohibit the use of certain readily available and highly nutritious foods. For example, most Muslims and Jews abstain from eating pork because doing so is prohibited by their religion, and most Hindus do not eat beef because they revere cows as sacred animals. There are countless other food taboos, all varying across cultures: horse meat (regularly part of French fare but generally abhorred in England), dogs (not eaten by Europeans but a typical ingredient in Korean meals), monkeys (appreciated by Amazonian Indians but excluded from North American menus), insects (an important source of nutrition in many tropical cultures but considered creepy in most other parts of the world), and humans (not eaten by most humans).[5]

A number of anthropologists, known as *ethnoscientists,* focus on identifying the principles behind native idea systems, how they inform a people about their environment, and what role they play in survival. For example, on the Indonesian island of Bali, ritual meetings were held regularly at water temples, located at the forks of rivers. Part of the ritual included negotiating seasonal schedules for flooding the farmers' rice fields. When the

---

[5]Pelto, G. H., Goodman, A. H., & Dufour, D. L. (Eds.). (2000). *Nutritional anthropology: Biocultural perspectives on food and nutrition.* Mountain View, CA: Mayfield.

culture core Cultural features that are fundamental in the society's way of making its living—including food-producing techniques, knowledge of available resources, and the work arrangements involved in applying those techniques to the local environment.

Indonesian government forced abandonment of this traditional system in an effort to promote more productive growing techniques, disaster ensued. Without the water temple rituals, irrigation coordination fell apart, and water shortages and pest infestation became the norm. This led to lower and uneven field yields, plus resentment toward those with better harvests.[6] Eventually, the old system was restored because it worked better. The point of this example is that cultural beliefs, no matter how irrelevant they may seem to outsiders, are often anything but irrelevant if one is to understand another society's subsistence or any other long-established collective practice.

MODES OF SUBSISTENCE

Human societies all across the world have developed a cultural infrastructure that is compatible with the natural resources they have available to them and within the limitations of their various habitats. Each mode of subsistence involves not only resources but also the technology required to effectively capture and utilize them, as well as the kinds of work arrangements that are developed to best suit a society's needs. In the next few pages, we will discuss the major types of cultural infrastructure, beginning with the oldest and most universal mode of subsistence: food foraging.

FOOD-FORAGING SOCIETIES

Before the domestication of food plants and animals, all people supported themselves through **food foraging,** a mode of subsistence involving some combination of hunting, fishing, and gathering wild plant foods. When food foragers had the earth to themselves, they had their pick of the best environments. But gradually areas with rich soils and ample supplies of water were appropriated by farming societies and, more recently, by industrial and postindustrial societies. As a result, small foraging communities were edged out of their traditional habitats by these expanding groups.

Today at most a quarter of a million people (less then 0.005 percent of the world population of about 6 billion) still support themselves mainly as foragers. They are found only in the world's most marginal areas—frozen Arctic tundra, deserts, and inaccessible forests—and typically lead a migratory existence that makes it impractical

to accumulate many material possessions. Because foraging cultures have nearly disappeared in areas having a natural abundance of food and fuel resources, anthropologists are necessarily cautious when it comes to making generalizations about the ancient human past based on in-depth studies of still-existing foraging groups that have adapted to more marginal habitats.

Anthropological research shows that forager diets are typically ample and balanced and that foragers are less likely to experience severe famine than farmers. The material possessions of foragers may be limited, but so is their desire to amass things. Notably, they have plenty of leisure time for concentrating on family ties, social life, and spiritual development—apparently far more than people living in farming and industrial societies. Such findings clearly challenge the once widely held view that food foragers live a miserable existence.

All modern food foragers have had some degree of interaction with neighbors whose ways of life often differ radically from their own. For example, the food-foraging Mbuti pygmies of the Republic of Congo's Ituri rainforest have a complex interdependent relationship with their neighbors, Bantu- and Sudanic-speaking peoples who are farmers. They exchange meat and other products of the forest for farm produce and manufactured goods. During part of the year, these pygmies live in their trading partner's village and are incorporated into his kin group, even to the point of allowing him to initiate their sons.

It is important to note that present-day people who subsist by hunting, fishing, and wild plant collection are not following an ancient way of life because they do not know any better. Rather, they have been forced by circumstances into situations where foraging is the best means of survival or they simply prefer to live this way. In fact, foraging constitutes a rational response to particular ecological, economic, and sociopolitical realities. Moreover, for at least 2,000 years, hunters, fishers, and gatherers have met the demands for commodities such as furs, hides, feathers, ivory, pearls, fish, nuts, and honey within larger trading networks. Like everyone else, most food foragers are now part of a larger system with social, economic and political relations extending far beyond regional, national, or even continental boundaries.

Characteristics of Foraging Communities

The hallmarks of food-foraging societies, particularly those still (or until recently) surviving in marginal areas that are not as naturally rich in food and fuel, include mobility, small group size, flexible division of labor by gender, food sharing, egalitarianism, communal property, and rarity of warfare.

---

[6]Fountain, H. (2000, January 30). Now the ancient ways are less mysterious. *New York Times,* News of the Week, 5.

food foraging Hunting, fishing, and gathering wild plant foods.

Human groups (including food foragers) do not exist in isolation except occasionally, and even then not for long. The bicycle this Bushman of southern Africa is riding is indicative of his links with the wider world. For 2,000 years, Bushmen have been interacting regularly with neighboring farmers and pastoralists. Much of the elephant ivory used for the keyboards on pianos so widely sought in 19th-century North America came from the Bushmen.

Although much has been written on the theoretical importance of hunting for shaping the supposedly competitive and aggressive nature of the human species, most anthropologists are unconvinced by these arguments. To be sure, warlike behavior on the part of food-foraging people is known, but such behavior is a relatively recent phenomenon in response to pressure from expansionist states. In the absence of such pressures, food-foraging peoples are remarkably nonaggressive and place more emphasis on peacefulness and cooperation than they do on violent competition. We touch on each of the other characteristics below.

Mobility

Food foragers move as needed within a circumscribed region that is their home range to tap into naturally available food sources. In pursuit of wild game, they are often aided by hunting dogs. Although there are countless varieties of dogs, they all descend from Asian wolves first domesticated more than 15,000 years ago.[7] Some groups, such as the Ju/'hoansi in the Kalahari Desert of southern Africa who depend on the reliable and highly drought-resistant mongongo nut, may keep to fairly fixed annual routes and cover only a restricted territory. Others, such as the traditional Shoshone in the western highlands of North America, had to cover a wider territory, their course determined by the local availability of the erratically productive pine nut.

A crucial factor in this mobility is availability of water. The distance between the food supply and water must not be so great that more energy is required to fetch water than can be obtained from the food.

Small Group Size

Another characteristic of the food-foraging adaptation is the small size of local groups, typically fewer than a hundred people. No completely satisfactory explanation for this has been offered, but both ecological and social factors are involved. Among the ecological factors is the **carrying capacity** of the land—the number of people that the available resources can support at a given level of food-getting techniques. This requires adjusting to seasonal and long-term changes in resource availability. A social factor is the **density of social relations** (the number and intensity of interactions among camp members). Higher social density means more opportunities for conflict.

Both carrying capacity and social density are complex variables. Carrying capacity involves not only the immediate presence of food and water but also the tools and work necessary to secure them, as well as short- and long-term fluctuations in their availability. Social density involves not only the number of people and their interactions but also the circumstances and quality of those interactions, as well as the mechanisms for regulating them. A mob of a hundred angry strangers has a different social density than the same number of neighbors enjoying themselves at a block party.

Among food-foraging populations, social density always seems in a state of flux as people spend more or less time away from camp and as they move to other camps, either on visits or more permanently. Among the Ju/'hoansi of southern Africa, for example, exhaustion

---

[7]Schwartz, M. (1997). *A history of dogs in the early Americas* (pp. 1–28). New Haven: Yale University Press.

carrying capacity The number of people that the available resources can support at a given level of food-getting techniques.
density of social relations The number and intensity of interactions among the members of a camp.

of local food resources, conflict within the group, or the desire to visit friends or relatives living elsewhere cause people to leave one group for another. As Canadian anthropologist Richard Lee notes, "Ju love to go visiting, and the practice acts as a safety valve when tempers get frayed. In fact, the Ju usually move, not when their food is exhausted, but rather when only their patience is exhausted."[8]

If a camp has so many children as to create a burden for the working adults, some young families may be encouraged to join others where fewer children live. Conversely, groups with few children may actively recruit families with young offspring in order to ensure the group's survival. Redistribution of people, then, is an important mechanism for regulating social density, as well as for assuring that the size and composition of local groups is suited to local variations in resources. Thus, cultural adaptations help transcend the limitations of the physical environment.

In addition to seasonal or local adjustments, food foragers must make long-term adjustments to resources. Most food-foraging populations stabilize at numbers well below the carrying capacity of their land. In fact, the home ranges of most food foragers can support from three to five times as many people as they typically do. In the long run, it may be more adaptive for a group to keep its numbers low rather than to expand indefinitely and risk destruction by a sudden and unexpected natural reduction in food resources. The population density of foraging groups surviving in marginal environments today rarely exceeds one person per square mile—a very low density.

How food-foraging peoples regulate population size relates to two things: how much body fat they accumulate and how they care for their children. Ovulation requires a certain minimum of body fat, and in traditional foraging societies, this is not achieved until early adulthood. Hence, female fertility peaks between the early and mid-20s, and teenage pregnancies—at least, successful ones—are virtually unknown.[9] Once a child is born, its mother nurses it several times each hour, even at night, and this continues over a period of four or five years. The constant stimulation of the mother's nipple suppresses the level of hormones that promote ovulation, making conception less likely, especially if work keeps the mother physically active, and she does not have a large store of body fat to draw on for energy.[10]

© Anthony Bannister/ABPL

Frequent nursing of children over four or five years acts to suppress ovulation among food foragers such as Bushmen. As a consequence, women give birth to relatively few offspring at widely spaced intervals.

Continuing to nurse for several years, women give birth only at widely spaced intervals. Thus, the total number of offspring remains low but sufficient to maintain stable population size.

Flexible Division of Labor by Gender

Some form of division of labor has been observed in all human societies and is probably as old as human culture. Among food foragers, the hunting and butchering of large game as well as the processing of hard or tough raw materials are almost universally masculine occupations. By contrast, women's work in foraging societies usually focuses on collecting and processing a variety of plant foods, as well as other domestic chores that can be fit to the demands of breastfeeding and do not endanger pregnancy and childbirth.

Among food foragers today, the work of women is no less arduous than that of men. Ju/'hoansi women,

[8]Lee, R. (1993). *The Dobe Ju/'hoansi* (p. 65). Fort Worth: Harcourt Brace.

[9]Hrdy, S. B. (1999). Body fat and birth control. *Natural History 108* (8), 88. See also Frisch, R. (2002). *Female fertility and the body fat connection.* Chicago: University of Chicago Press.

[10]Small, M. F. (1997). Making connections. *American Scientist 85,* 503. See also Konner, M., & Worthman, C. (1980). Nursing frequency, gonadal function, and birth spacing among !Kung hunter-gatherers. *Science 207,* 788–791.

VISUAL COUNTERPOINT

Food foragers such as the Ju/'hoansi have a division of labor in which women gather and prepare "bush" food (here an ostrich egg omelette) and men usually do the hunting.

for example, may walk as many as 12 miles a day two or three times a week to gather food, carrying not only their children but also, on the return home, anywhere from 15 to 33 pounds of food. Still, they do not have to travel quite as far afield as do men on the hunt, and their work is usually less dangerous than hunting. Also, their tasks require less rapid mobility, do not need complete and undivided attention, and are readily resumed after interruption.

All of this is compatible with those biological differences that remain between the sexes. Certainly women who are pregnant or have infants to nurse cannot travel long distances in pursuit of game as easily as men can. By the same token, of course, women may have preferred and been better at the less risky task of gathering.

To say that differing gender roles among food foragers are compatible with the biological differences between men and women is *not* to say that they are biologically determined. Among the Great Plains Indians of North America, for example, are quite a few reported cases of women who gained fame as hunters and warriors—both historically regarded as men's activities. In fact, the division of labor by gender is often far less rigid among food foragers than it is in most other types of society. Thus, Ju/'hoansi males, willingly and without embarrassment, as the occasion demands, will gather wild plant foods, build huts, and collect water, even though all are regarded as women's work.

The nature of women's work in food-foraging societies is such that it can be done while taking care of chil-

dren. Typically, it is also work that can be in company with other women, which provides adult companionship and opportunities for sharing childrearing tasks and useful ideas, venting frustrations, idle chatter, gossip, and laughter. The food-gathering activities of women play a major role in the survival of their group: Research shows that contemporary food foragers may obtain up to 60 or 70 percent of their diets from plant foods, with perhaps some fish and shellfish provided by women (the exceptions tend to be food foragers living in Arctic regions, where plant foods are not available for much of the year).

Although women in food-foraging societies may spend some time each day gathering plant food, men do not spend all or even the greatest part of their time hunting. The amount of energy expended in hunting, especially in hot climates, is often greater than the energy return from the kill. Too much time spent searching out game might actually be counterproductive. Energy itself is derived primarily from plant carbohydrates, and it is usually the female gatherers who bring in the bulk of the calories. A certain amount of meat in the diet, though, guarantees high-quality protein that is less easily obtained from plant sources, for meat contains exactly the right balance of all of the amino acids (the building blocks of protein) the human body requires. No one plant food does this, and in order to get by without meat, people must hit on exactly the right combination of plants to provide the essential amino acids in the correct proportions.

Food Sharing

Another key feature of human social organization associated with food foraging is the sharing of food among adults. It is easy enough to see why sharing takes place, with women supplying one kind of food and men another. Among the Ju/'hoansi, women have control over the food they collect and can share it with whomever they choose. Men, by contrast, are constrained by rules that specify how much meat is to be distributed and to whom. Thus, a hunter has little effective control over the meat he brings into camp. For the individual hunter, meat sharing is really a way of storing it for the future: His generosity, obligatory though it might be, gives him a claim on the future kills of other hunters. As a cultural trait, food sharing has the obvious survival value of distributing resources needed for subsistence.

Relative to this is the importance of the camp as the center of daily activity and the place where food sharing actually occurs. Among nonhuman primates (and probably among human ancestors until they controlled the use of fire), activities tend to be divided between feeding areas and sleeping areas, and the latter tend to be shifted each evening. Historically known food-foraging people, however, live in camps of some permanence, ranging from the dry season camps of the Ju/'hoansi, which serve for the entire winter, to the wet season camps of the Hadza in Tanzania, which are centered on berry picking and honey collection and serve for a few days or weeks at most. Moreover, human camps are more than sleeping areas; people are in and out all day—eating, working, and socializing in camps to a greater extent than any other primates.

Egalitarian Social Relations

An important characteristic of the food-foraging society is its egalitarianism. Because food foragers are usually highly mobile and lack animal or mechanical transportation, they must be able to travel without many encumbrances, especially on food-getting expeditions. By necessity, the material goods they carry with them are limited to the barest essentials, which include implements for hunting, gathering, fishing, building, and cooking. (For example, the average weight of an individual's personal belongings among the Ju/'hoansi is just under 25 pounds.) In this context, it makes little sense for them to accumulate luxuries or surplus goods, and the fact that no one owns significantly more than another helps to limit status differences. Age and sex are usually the only sources of important status differences.

It is important to realize that status differences by themselves do not constitute inequality, a point that is all too easily misunderstood, especially where relations between men and women are concerned. In most tra-

ditional food-foraging societies, women did not and do not defer to men. To be sure, women may be excluded from some rituals that males participate in, but the reverse is also true. Moreover, the fruits of women's labor are not controlled by men but by the women themselves. Nor do women sacrifice their autonomy even in societies in which male hunting, rather than female gathering, brings in the bulk of the food.

Such was the case, for example, among the Innu (Montagnais) Indians of Labrador. Theirs was a society in which the hunt was of overwhelming importance. For their part, women manufactured clothing and other necessities but provided much less of the food than is common among food foragers. Until recently, women as well as men could be shamans. Nevertheless, women were excluded from ritual feasts having to do with hunting—but then, so were men excluded from ritual feasts held by women. Basically, each gender carried out its own activities, with neither meddling in those of the other. Early missionaries to the Innu hunting bands lamented that men had no inclination to make their wives obey them and worked long and hard to convince the Indians that civilization required men to impose their authority on women. But after 300 years of pressing this point, missionaries achieved only limited success.

Food foragers make no attempt to accumulate surplus foodstuffs, often an important source of status in agrarian societies. This does not mean that they live constantly on the verge of starvation, for their environment is their natural storehouse. Except in the coldest climates (where a surplus must be set aside to see people through the long, lean winter season) or in times of acute ecological disaster, some food can almost always be found in a group's territory. Because food resources are typically distributed equally throughout the group (share and share alike is the order of the day), no one achieves the wealth or status that hoarding might bring. In such a so-

Food-Producing Societies   417

ciety, wealth is a sign of deviance rather than a desirable characteristic.

The food forager's concept of territory contributes as much to social equality as it does to the equal distribution of resources. Most groups have home ranges within which access to resources is open to all members. What is available to one is available to all. If an Mbuti hunter discovers a honey tree, he has first rights; but when he has taken his share, others have a turn. In the unlikely possibility that he does not take advantage of his discovery, others will. No individual within the community privately owns the tree; the system is first come, first served. Therefore, knowledge of the existence of food resources circulates quickly throughout the entire group.

Families move easily from one group to another, settling in any group where they have a previous kinship tie. As noted earlier, the composition of groups among food foragers is always shifting. This loose attitude toward group membership promotes the widest access to resources while maintaining a balance between populations and resources.

Cultural Adaptations and Technology among Foragers

Habitat as well as technology plays an important role in shaping the characteristics of foraging life discussed above. The mobility of food-foraging groups may depend on the availability of water, as among the Ju/'hoansi, or of game animals and other seasonal resources, as among the Mbuti in the Republic of Congo in Central Africa. Different hunting technologies and techniques may also play a part in determining movement, as well as population size, and division of labor by gender.

Consider, for example, the Mbuti pygmies in the Ituri tropical forest. All Mbuti bands hunt elephants with spears. However, for other game, some of the bands use bows and others use large nets. Those equipped with nets have a cooperative division of labor in which men, women, and children collaborate in driving antelope and other game into the net for the kill. Usually, this involves very long hours and movement over great distances as participants surround the animal(s) and beat the woods noisily to chase the game in one direction toward the great nets. Since this sort of "beat-hunt" requires the cooperation of seven to thirty families, those using this method have relatively large camps. Among Mbuti bow hunters, on the other hand, only men go after the game. These archers tend to stay closer to the village for shorter periods of time and live in smaller groups, typically of no more than six families. While there exists no significant difference in overall population densities of net and bow

hunting areas, archers generally harvest a greater diversity of animal species, including monkeys.[11]

FOOD-PRODUCING SOCIETIES

After tool making, which enabled humans to consume significant amounts of meat as well as plant foods, the next truly momentous event in human history was the domestication of plants and animals. Over time, this achievement transformed cultural systems, with humans developing new economic arrangements, social structures, and ideological patterns based either on plant cultivation, breeding and raising animals, or a mixture of both.

The gradual transition from food foraging to food production first took place about 10,000 years ago in Southwest Asia (the Fertile Crescent, including the Jordan River Valley and neighboring regions in the Middle East). This was the beginning of the **Neolithic** or New Stone Age, in which peoples possessed stone-based technologies and depended on domesticated plants and/or animals. Within the next few thousand years, similar early transitions to agricultural economies took place independently in other parts of the world where human groups began to grow and (later) alter wild cereal plants such as wheat, maize (corn), and rice; legumes such as beans; gourds such as squash; and tubers such as potatoes. They did the same with a number of wild animal species ranging in their hunting territories and began to domesticate goats, sheep, pigs, cattle, and llamas (Figure 18.2).

Because these activities brought about a radical transformation in almost every aspect of their cultural systems, Australian-born archaeologist Gordon Childe introduced the term *Neolithic revolution* to refer to the profound culture change associated with the early domestication of plants and animals. Today it is more commonly referred to as the **Neolithic transition.** Marking the beginning of what is traditionally known as the New

---

[11]Bailey, R. C., & Aunger, R. (1989). Net hunters vs. archers: Variation in women's subsistence strategies in the Ituri forest. *Human Ecology 17,* 273–297; Terashima, H. (1983). Mota and other hunting activities of the Mbuti archers: A socio-ecological study of subsistence technology. *African Studies Monograph* (Kyoto), 71–85.

Neolithic The New Stone Age; prehistoric period beginning about 10,000 years ago in which peoples possessed stone-based technologies and depended on domesticated plants and/or animals.
Neolithic transition Sometimes referred to as Neolithic revolution. The profound culture change beginning about 10,000 years ago and associated with the early domestication of plants and animals, and settlement in permanent villages.

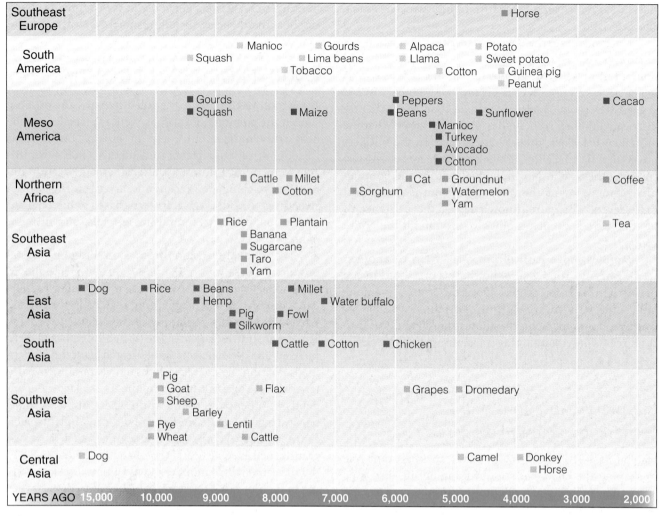

Figure 18.2

Appearance of domesticates in the archaeological record.

Stone Age, this shift changed the very nature of human society. As humans became increasingly dependent on domesticated crops, they mostly gave up their mobile way of life and settled down to till the soil, sow, weed, protect, harvest, and safely store their crops. No longer on the move, they could build more permanent dwellings and began to make pottery for storage of water, food, and so on.

Just why this change came about is one of the important questions in anthropology. Since food production by and large requires more work than food foraging, is more monotonous, is often a less secure means of subsistence, and requires people to eat more of the foods that foragers eat only when they have no other choice, it is unlikely that people voluntarily became food producers.

Initially, it appears that food production arose as a largely unintended by-product of existing food-management practices. Among many examples, we may consider the Paiute Indians, whose desert habitat in the western highlands of North America includes some oasis-like marshlands. These foragers discovered how to irrigate wild crops in their otherwise very dry homeland, thus increasing the quantity of wild seeds and bulbs to be harvested. Although their ecological intervention was very limited, it allowed them to settle down for longer periods in greater numbers than otherwise would have been possible.

Unlike the Paiute, who just stopped short of a Neolithic transition, other groups elsewhere in the world continued to transform their landscapes in ways that favored the appearance of new varieties of particular plants and animals, which came to take on increasing importance for people's subsistence. Although probably at first accidental, it became a matter of necessity as growth outstripped people's ability to sustain themselves through food foraging. For them, food production became a subsistence option of last resort.

Crop Cultivation in Gardens: Horticulture

With the advent of plant domestication, some societies took up **horticulture** (*hortus,* "garden" in Latin) in which small communities of gardeners cultivate crops with simple hand tools, using neither irrigation nor the plow. Typically, horticulturists cultivate several varieties of food plants together in small, hand-cleared gardens. Because they do not usually fertilize the soil, they use a given garden plot for only a few years before abandoning it in favor of a new one. Horticulturists often can (and sometimes do) grow enough food for their subsistence, and many occasionally produce more than they need for purposes such as inter-village feasts and exchange.

Many horticulturists, however, do not depend exclusively on their gardens for their year-round subsistence. As already indicated by the example of Paiute Indian subsistence practices, societies categorized as food foragers by anthropologists may also engage in some wild food plant management. Likewise, horticulturists do not completely give up food foraging. Although their major food supplies may come from their gardens, they will also hunt game, fish, and collect wild plants foods in the forest whenever they need or get a chance.

One of the most widespread forms of horticulture, especially in the tropics, is **slash-and-burn cultivation,** also known as *swidden farming,* in which the natural vegetation is cut, the slash is subsequently burned, and crops then planted among the ashes. Unfortunately, widespread use of fire in connection with the clearing of vast tracts of Amazonian or Indonesian forest for cattle raising and other development schemes has led many people to see this kind of farming in a negative light. In fact, it is an ecologically sophisticated and sustainable way of raising food, especially in the tropics, when carried out under the right conditions: low population densities and adequate amounts of land. It mimics the diversity of the natural ecosystem, growing several different crops in the same field. Mixed together, the crops are less vulnerable to pests and plant diseases than a single crop.

Not only is the system ecologically sound, but it is far more energy efficient than modern farming methods used in developed countries such as the United States where natural resources such as land and fuel are still relatively cheap and abundant, and many farms operate with financial support in the form of government subsidies or tax breaks. While high-tech farming requires more energy input than it yields, swidden farming produces between 10 and 20 units of energy for every unit expended. A good example of how such a system works is provided by the Mekranoti Kayapo Indians of Brazil's Amazon forest, profiled in the following Original Study.

horticulture Cultivation of crops carried out with simple hand tools such as digging sticks or hoes.
slash-and-burn cultivation Also known as swidden farming. An extensive form of horticulture in which the natural vegetation is cut, the slash is subsequently burned, and crops are then planted among the ashes.

Reburning an old, overgrown slash-and-burn plot in the Amazon forest in Venezuela in preparation for new planting. Although it looks destructive, if properly carried out, slash-and-burn cultivation is an ecologically sound way of growing crops in the tropics.

© Jacques Jangoux/Alamy

Original Study ▪ By Dennis Werner

Gardens of the Mekranoti Kayapo

The planting of a Mekranoti garden always follows the same sequence. First, men clear the forest and then burn the debris. In the ashes, both men and women plant sweet potatoes, manioc, bananas, corn, pumpkins, papaya, sugar cane, pineapple, cotton, tobacco, and annatto, whose seeds yield achiote, the red dye used for painting ornaments and people's bodies. Since the Mekranoti don't bother with weeding, the forest gradually invades the garden. After the second year, only manioc, sweet potatoes, and bananas remain. And after three years or so there is usually nothing left but bananas. Except for a few tree species that require hundreds of years to grow, the area will look like the original forest twenty-five to thirty years later.

This gardening technique, known as slash-and-burn, is one of the most common in the world. At one time critics condemned the technique as wasteful and ecologically destructive, but today we know that, especially in the humid tropics, slash-and-burn may be one of the best gardening techniques possible.

Continuous high temperatures encourage the growth of the microorganisms that cause rot, so organic matter quickly breaks down into simple minerals. The heavy rains dissolve these valuable nutrients and carry them deep into the soils, out of the reach of plants. The tropical forest maintains its richness because the heavy foliage shades the earth, cooling it and inhibiting the growth of the decomposers. A good deal of the rain is captured by leaves before ever reaching the ground.

When a tree falls in the forest and begins to rot, other plants quickly absorb the nutrients that are released. In contrast, with open-field agriculture, the sun heats the earth, the decomposers multiply, and the rains quickly leach the soils of their nutrients. In a few years a lush forest, if cleared for open one-crop agriculture, can be transformed into a barren wasteland.

A few months after the Mekranoti plant banana and papaya, these trees shade the soil, just as the larger forest trees do. The mixing of different kinds of plants in the same area means that

minerals can be absorbed as soon as they are released; corn picks up nutrients very fast, while manioc is slow. Also, the small and temporary clearings mean that the forest can quickly reinvade its lost territory.

Because decomposers need moisture as well as warmth, the long Mekranoti dry season could alter this whole picture of soil ecology. But soil samples from recently burned Mekranoti fields and the adjacent forest floor showed that, as in most of the humid tropics, the high fertility of the Indians' garden plots comes from the trees that are burned there, not from the soil, as in temperate climates.

Getting a good burn is a tricky operation. Perhaps for this reason its timing was left to the more experienced and knowledgeable members of the community. If the burn is too early, the rains will leach out the minerals in the ash before planting time. If too late, the debris will be too wet to burn properly. Then, insects and weeds that could plague the plants will not die and few minerals will be released into the soil. If the winds are too weak, the burn will not cover the entire plot. If they are too strong, the fire can get out of hand.

Shortly after burning the plots and clearing away of some of the charred debris, people began the long job of planting, which took up all of September and lasted into October. In the center of the circular garden plot the women dug holes and threw in a few pieces of sweet potatoes. After covering the tubers with dirt they usually asked a male—one of their husbands or anyone else who happened to be nearby—to stomp on the mound and make a ritual noise resembling a Bronx cheer. This magic would ensure a large crop, I was told. Forming a large ring around the sweet potatoes, the Indians rapidly thrust pieces of manioc stems into the ground, one after the other.

When grown, the manioc stems form a dense barrier to the sweet potato patch, and some of the plants must be cut down to gain entrance. Outside of the ring of manioc, the women plant yams, cotton, sugar cane, and annatto. Banana stalks

and papaya trees, planted by simply throwing the seeds on the ground, form the outermost circle. The Indians also plant corn, pumpkins, watermelons, and pineapple throughout the garden. These grow rapidly and are harvested long before the manioc matures. The garden appears to change magically from corn and pumpkins to sweet potatoes and manioc without replanting.

Mekranoti gardens grew well. A few Indians complained now and then about a peccary that had eaten a watermelon they were looking forward to eating, or that had reduced their corn harvest. Capybara, large rodents usually found near the river banks, were known for their love of sugar cane, but in general the animals seemed to leave the crops alone. Even the leaf-cutting ants that are problems in other areas did not bother the Mekranoti. Occasionally a neighbor who had not planted a new garden would make off with a prized first-year crop, such as pumpkin, watermelon, or pineapple. But even these thefts were rare. In general, the Mekranoti could depend on harvesting whatever they planted.

Eventually, I wanted to calculate the productivity of Mekranoti gardens. Western agronomists knew very little about slash-and-burn crop cultivation. They were accustomed to experiments in which a field was given over to one crop only, and in which the harvest happened all at once. Here, the plants were all mixed together, and people harvested piecemeal whenever they needed something. The manioc could stay in the ground, growing for several years before it was dug up.

I began measuring off areas of gardens to count how many manioc plants, ears of corn, or pumpkins were found there. The women thought it strange to see me struggling through the tangle of plants to measure off areas, 10 meters by 10 meters, placing string along the borders, and then counting what was inside. Sometimes I asked a woman to dig up all of the sweet potatoes within the marked-off area. The requests were bizarre, but the women cooperated just the same, holding on to the ends of the measuring tapes, or sending their children to help. For some plants, like bananas, I simply counted the number of clumps of stalks in the garden, and the number of banana bunches I could see growing in various

clumps. By watching how long it took the bananas to grow, from the time I could see them until they were harvested, I could calculate a garden's total banana yield per year.

After returning from the field, I was able to combine the time allocation data with the garden productivities to get an idea of how hard the Mekranoti need to work to survive. The data showed that for every hour of gardening one Mekranoti adult produces almost 18,000 kilocalories of food. (As a basis for comparison, people in the United States consume approximately 3,000 kilocalories of food per day.) As insurance against bad years, and in case they receive visitors from other villages, they grow far more produce than they need. But even so, they don't need to work very hard to survive. A look at

the average amount of time adults spend on different tasks every week shows just how easygoing life in horticultural societies can be:

8.5 hours	Gardening
6.0 hours	Hunting
1.5 hours	Fishing
1.0 hour	Gathering wild foods
33.5 hours	All other jobs

Altogether, the Mekranoti need to work less than 51 hours a week, and this includes getting to and from work, cooking, repairing broken tools, and all of the other things we normally don't count as part of our work week.
(Excerpted from D. Werner (1990). Amazon journey *(pp. 105–112). Englewood Cliffs, NJ: Prentice-Hall.)* ∎

Crop Cultivation: Agriculture

In contrast to horticulture, **agriculture** (*agri*, "field" in Latin) is growing food plants like grains, tubers, fruits, and vegetables in soil prepared and maintained for crop production. This form of more intensive food production involves using technologies other than hand tools, such as irrigation, fertilizers, and the wooden or metal plow pulled by harnessed draft animals. The cultural ecological sophistication of some early agriculturalists is illustrated in this chapter's Anthropology Applied feature. In the so-called developed countries of the world, agriculture relies on fuel-powered tractors to produce food on larger plots of land.

Unlike horticulturists, agriculturists generally grow surplus crops—providing not only for their own needs but food for those of various full-time specialists and nonproducing consumers as well. This surplus may be traded or sold for cash, or it may be coerced out of the farmers through taxes, rent, or tribute (forced gifts acknowledging submission or protection) paid to landowners or other dominant groups. These landowners and specialists—such as traders, carpenters, blacksmiths, sculptors, basket makers, and stonecutters—typically reside in substantial towns or cities, where political power is centralized in the hands of a socially elite class. Dominated by more powerful groups and markets, much of what the farmers do is governed by political and economic forces over which they have little control.

The distinction between horticulture and agriculture is not always an easy one to make. For example, the Hopi Indians of the North American Southwest, in addition to flood plain farming, also irrigate plots near

springs, while using simple hand tools. Moreover, they produce for their own immediate needs and live in small towns without centralized political government.

Early food producers have developed several major crop complexes: two adapted to dry uplands and two to tropical wetlands. In the dry uplands of Southwest Asia, for example, farmers time their agricultural activities with the rhythm of the changing seasons, cultivating wheat, barley, oat, flax, rye, and millet. In the tropical wetlands of Southeast Asia, rice and tubers such as yams and taro are cultivated. In the Americas, people have adapted to natural environments similar to those of Africa and Eurasia, but have cultivated their own indigenous plants. Typically, maize, beans, squash, and the potato are grown in drier areas, whereas manioc is extensively grown in the tropical wetlands.

Characteristics of Agricultural Societies

One of the most significant correlates of plant cultivation was the development of fixed settlements, in which farming families reside together near their cultivated fields. While food foragers stay close to their food by moving around to follow nature's seasonal fluctuations, food producers stay close to theirs by not straying too far from their gardens or farmlands. The task of food production lent itself to a different kind of social organization. Because the hard work of some members of the

agriculture The cultivation of food plants in soil prepared and maintained for crop production. Involves using technologies other than hand tools, such as irrigation, fertilizers, and the wooden or metal plow pulled by harnessed draft animals.

Anthropology Applied

Agricultural Development and the Anthropologist ▪ Ann Kendall

Gaining insight into the traditional practices of indigenous peoples, anthropologists have often been impressed by the ingenuity of their knowledge. This awareness has spread beyond the profession to the Western public at large, giving birth to the popular notion that indigenous groups invariably live in some sort of blissful oneness with the environment. But this was never the message of anthropologists, who know that traditional people are only human, and like all human beings, are capable of making mistakes. Yet, just as we have much to learn from their successes, so can we learn from their failures.

Archaeologist Ann Kendall is doing just this in the Patacancha Valley in the Andes Mountains of southern Peru. Kendall is director and founder of the Cusichaca Trust, near Oxford, England, a rural development organization that revives ancient farming practices. In the late 1980s, after working for ten years on archaeological excavations and rural development projects, she invited botanist Alex Chepstow-Lusty of Cambridge University to investigate climatic change and paleoecological data. His findings, along with Kendall's, provided evidence of in-

tensive farming in the Patacancha Valley, beginning about 4,000 years ago. The research showed that over time widespread clearing to establish and maintain farm plots, coupled with minimal terracing of the hillsides, had resulted in tremendous soil loss through erosion. By 1,900 years ago, soil degradation and a cooling climate had led to a dramatic reduction in farming. Then, about 1,000 years ago, farming was revived, this time with soil-sparing techniques.

Kendall's investigations have documented intensive irrigated terrace construction over two periods of occupation, including Inca development of the area. It was a sophisticated system, devised to counteract erosion and achieve maximum agricultural production. The effort required workers to haul load after load of soil up from the valley floor. In addition, they planted alder trees to stabilize the soil and to provide both firewood and building materials. So successful was this farming system by Inca times that the number of people living in the valley quadrupled to some 4,000, about the same as it is now. However, yet another reversal of fortune occurred when the Spanish took over Peru and the terraces

and trees here and elsewhere were allowed to deteriorate.

Armed with these research findings and information and insights gathered through interviews and meetings with locals, the Cusichaca Trust supported the restoration of the terraces and 5.8 km of canal. The effort relied on local labor working with traditional methods and materials—clay (with a cactus mix to keep it moist), stone, and soil. Local families

group could provide food for all, others became free to devote their time to inventing and manufacturing the equipment needed for a new sedentary way of life. Tools for digging and harvesting, pottery for storage and cooking, clothing made of woven textiles, and housing made of stone, wood, or sun-dried bricks all grew out of the new sedentary living conditions and the altered division of labor.

The Neolithic transition also brought important changes in social structure. At first, social relations were egalitarian and hardly different from those that prevailed among food foragers. As settlements grew, however, and large numbers of people had to share important resources such as land and water, society became more elaborately organized. Most likely, people formed multifamily kinship groups, each culturally elaborated to provide a socially convenient way to handle the distinctive and often thorny problems of individual and group land use and ownership that may arise in food-producing societies.

Mixed Farming: Crop Growing and Animal Breeding

As noted above, indigenous food-producing cultures in the western hemisphere depended primarily on growing domesticated indigenous crops such as manioc, corn, and beans. With some exceptions, including the Aymara and Quechua, who traditionally also keep llamas and alpacas in their high-altitude homeland in the Andes Mountains of South America (see the Biocultural Connection feature), American Indians obtained sufficient meat, fat, leather, and wool from wild game.

On the other side of both oceans, however, Eurasian and African food-producing peoples often do not have an opportunity to obtain enough vitally important animal proteins from wild game, fish, or fowl (although they would not pass up a rare chance to catch some). Instead, many of these farming cultures have developed a mixed subsistence strategy and combine have replanted 160 hectares of the reno-vated pre-conquest terraces with maize, potatoes, and wheat, finding the plots up to ten times more productive than they were. Among other related accomplishments, twenty-one water systems have been installed, which reach more than 800 large families, and a traditional concept of home-based gardens has been adapted to introduce European-style vegetable gardens to improve diet and health and to facilitate market gardening. Since 1997, these projects have been under a new and independent local rural development organization known as ADESA.

The Cusichaca Trust is now continuing its pioneering work in areas of extreme poverty in Peru further to the north, such as Apurimac and Ayacucho, using tried and tested traditional technology in the restoration of ancient canal and terrace systems.

(Adapted from K. Krajick (1998). Green-farming by the Incas? Science 281, *323. The 2003 update and elaboration by textbook authors is based on personal communication with Kendall and Cusichaca Trust reports. For more information see www .cusichaca.org.)*

© Ann Kendall/Cusichaca Trust

crop cultivation with animal husbandry. Thus, in addition to growing crops like cereals, tubers, or vegetables, they may also breed and raise animals for food and other purposes, including selling or trading. The variety of wild animals domesticated by humans in Africa and Eurasia includes chickens, ducks, geese, rabbits, pigs, goats, sheep, cattle, camels, dromedaries, donkeys, and horses.

Depending on cultural traditions, ecological circumstances, and animal habits, some species are kept in barns or fenced-off fields, while others may range quite freely in and around the settlement or designated pastures, albeit under supervision, branded or otherwise marked by their owners as private property. For instance, in some English farming communities (not unlike Papua villages in New Guinea) it was historically not unusual to find ear-marked pigs freely roaming in the surrounding woodlands in search of acorns and any other food appealing to their omnivorous appetite.

Likewise, many ancient agricultural communities adapted to high altitude environments from the Alps to the Himalayas have traditionally herded livestock (cows, sheep, horses, and so on) in high summer pastures, leaving their narrow lowland valleys for alternative use—farming grains, keeping orchards, growing vegetables and hay for animal winter food. After the crop harvest, before the weather turns cold and snow covers the higher pastures, those who left the village to tend the herds bring the animals back to the valley for the winter season. This "vertical" seasonal movement of livestock between high altitude summer pastures and lowland valleys is known as *transhumance*.[12]

---

[12]Cole, J. W., & Wolf, E. R. (1999). *The hidden frontier: Ecology and ethnicity in an alpine valley* (with a new introduction). Berkeley: University of California Press; see also Jones, S. (2005). Transhumance re-examined. *Journal of the Royal Anthropological Institute 11* (4), 841–842.

Pastoralism

One of the more striking examples of human adaptation to the environment is **pastoralism**—breeding and managing large herds of domesticated grazing (and browsing) animals, such as goats, sheep, cattle, horses, llamas, or camels. Unlike the forms of animal husbandry discussed above, pastoralism is a specialized way of life centered on breeding and herding animals.

Completely dependent on livestock for daily survival, families in pastoral cultures may own herds of hundreds of grazing animals whose needs for food and drink determine the pastoralists' everyday routines. When a dozen or more herding families join each other, their collective herds may number in the thousands and sometimes even a few hundred thousand. Unlike crop-cultivators who need to remain close to their fields, pastoral peoples do not usually establish permanent settlements since they must follow or drive their large herds to new pastures on a regular basis. Like their migratory herds, most pastoralists must be mobile and have adjusted their way of life accordingly.

Nomadic Pastoralism:
Bakhtiari Herders in the Zagros Mountains

Nomadic pastoralism is an effective way of living—far more so than sheep or cattle ranching—in environments that are too dry, cold, steep, or rocky for farming, such as the vast, arid grasslands that stretch eastward from northern Africa through the Arabian Desert, across the plateau of Iran and into Turkistan and Mongolia. Today, in Africa and Asia alone, more than 21 million people are pastoralists, still migrating with their herds. These nomadic groups regard movement as a natural part of life. Although some herding groups depend on nearby farmers for certain supplies, and may even earn more from other sources than from their own herds, the nomadic herding lifestyle remains central to their identities.

Counted among the world's pastoral groups are the Bakhtiari, a fiercely independent people who live in the unforgiving Zagros Mountains of western Iran.[13] The Bakhtiari way of life, uniquely adapted to the seasonal fluctuations in their rugged mountainous environment,

[13]Material on the Bakhtiari is drawn mainly from Barth, F. (1960). Nomadism in the mountain and plateau areas of Southwest Asia. *The problems of the arid zone* (pp. 341–355). UNESCO; Coon, C. S. (1958). *Caravan: The story of the Middle East* (2nd ed., ch. 13). New York: Holt, Rinehart & Winston; Salzman, P. C. (1967). Political organization among nomadic peoples. *Proceedings of the American Philosophical Society 111*, 115–131.

pastoralism Breeding and managing large herds of domesticated grazing animals, such as goats, sheep, cattle, horses, llamas, or camels.

involves moving with their grazing animals from winter pastures in low steppe lands to summer pastures on high plateaus. For many thousands of years the Bakhtiari have tended herds of goats and fat-tailed sheep this way. Their lives revolve around these major seasonal migrations needed to provide good grazing lands for their flocks—long hazardous journeys that take them over mountains as high as 12,000 feet and through deep chasms and churning watercourses.

Each fall, before the harsh winter comes to the mountains, these nomads load their tents and other belongings on donkeys and drive their flocks down to the warm plains that border Iraq in the west. Here the grazing land is excellent and well watered during the winter months. In the spring, when the low-lying pastures dry up, the Bakhtiari return to the mountain valleys, where a new crop of grass is sprouting. For this trek, they split into five groups, each containing about 5,000 individuals and 50,000 animals.

The return trip north is especially dangerous because the mountain snows are melting and the gorges are full of turbulent, ice-cold water rushing down from the mountain peaks. This long trek is further burdened by the newborn spring lambs and goat kids. Where the watercourses are not very deep, the nomads ford them. Deeper channels, including one river that is a half-mile wide, are crossed with the help of inflatable goatskin rafts, on which they place infants and elderly or infirm family members, as well as lambs and kids. Men swim alongside the rafts, pushing them through the icy water. If they work from dawn to dusk, the nomads can get all of the people and animals across the river in five days. Not surprisingly, dozens of animals drown each day.

In the mountain passes, where a biting wind numbs the skin and brings tears to the eyes, the Bakhtiari trek a rugged slippery trail. Climbing the steep escarpments is dangerous, and often the stronger men must carry their children and the baby goats on their shoulders as they make their way over the ice and snow to the lush mountain valley that is their destination. During each

In the Zagros Mountains region of Iran, pastoral nomads follow seasonal pastures, migrating with their flocks over rugged terrain that includes perilously steep snowy passes and fast ice-cold rivers.

migration the nomads may cover as many as 200 miles. The journey is familiar but not predictable. It can take weeks, for the flocks travel slowly and require constant attention. Men and older boys walk the route, driving the sheep and goats as they go. Women and children usually ride atop donkeys, along with tents and other equipment.

Reaching their destination, the Bakhtiari set up tents—traditionally black goat-hair shelters woven by the women. The tents are a fine example of adaptation to a changing environment. The goat-hair cloth retains heat and repels water during the winter and keeps out heat during the summer. These portable homes are easy to erect, take down, and transport. Inside, the furnishings are sparse and functional, but also artful. Heavy felt pads or elaborate wool rugs, also woven by the women, cover the ground, and pressed against the inside walls of the tent are stacks of blankets, goatskin containers, copper utensils, clay jugs, and bags of grain.

Central to Bakhtiari subsistence, sheep and goats provide milk, cheese, butter, meat, hides, and wool. Women and girls spend considerable time spinning wool into yarn—sometimes doing so while riding atop donkeys on the less rugged parts of their migration. They use the yarn not only to make rugs and tents, but also clothing, storage bags, and other essentials.

Labor division among the Bakhtiari is according to gender. The chief task of the men is tending the flocks. The women cook, sew, weave, care for the children, and carry fuel and water. With men owning and controlling the animals, which are of primary importance in Bakhtiari life, women have generally lacked both economic and political power. The Bakhtiari live in the political state of Iran but have their own traditional system of justice, including laws and a penal code. They are governed by tribal leaders, or *khans,* men who are elected or inherit their office. Most Bakhtiari *khans* grew wealthy when oil was discovered in their homeland around the start of the 20th century, and many of them are well educated, having attended Iranian or foreign universities.

Despite this, and although some of them own houses in cities, the *khans* spend much of their lives among their people in the mountains. Such prominence of men in both economic and political affairs is common among pastoral nomads; theirs is very much a man's world. That said, elderly Bakhtiari women eventually may gain a good deal of power. And some women of all ages today are gaining a measure of economic control by selling their beautiful handmade rugs to traders, which brings in cash to their households.

Although pastoral nomads like the Bakhtiari depend greatly on their large herds of grazing animals to meet their daily needs, they do trade surplus animals, wool, and woven rugs with farmers or merchants in exchange for crops and valued commodities such as flour, dried fruit, spices, tea, metal knives, pots and kettles, cotton or linen textiles, guns and (more recently) lightweight plastic containers, sheets, and so on. In other words, there are many ties that connect them to surrounding agricultural and industrial societies.

Intensive Agriculture and Nonindustrial Cities

With the intensification of agriculture, some farming villages grew into towns and even cities (Figure 18.3). In these larger population centers, individuals who had

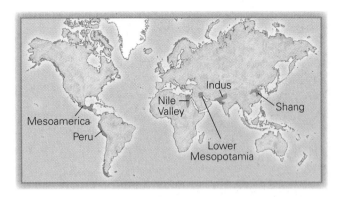

Figure 18.3
Locations of major early civilizations. Those of Central and South America developed wholly independently of those in Africa and Eurasia. Chinese civilization may have developed independently of those that developed earlier in Mesopotamia, the Egyptian Valley, and the Indus Valley.

previously been engaged in farming were freed to specialize in other activities. Thus, craft specialists such as carpenters, blacksmiths, sculptors, basket makers, and stonecutters contribute to the vibrant, diversified life of the city.

Unlike horticulturists and pastoralists, city dwellers are only indirectly concerned with adapting to their natural environment. Far more important is the need to adapt to living and getting along with their fellow urbanites. Urbanization brings with it a new social order: Marked inequality develops as society becomes more complex, and people are ranked according to how much control they hold over resources, the kind of work they do, their gender, or the family they are born into. As social institutions cease to operate in simple, face-to-face groups of relatives, friends, and acquaintances, they become more formal and bureaucratic, with specialized political institutions.

With urbanization came a sharp increase in the tempo of human cultural change. Writing was invented, trade intensified and expanded, the wheel and the sail were invented, and metallurgy and other crafts were developed. In many early cities, monumental buildings, such as royal palaces and temples, were built by thousands of men, often slaves taken in war. These feats of engineering still amaze modern architects and engineers. The inhabitants of these buildings—the ruling class composed of nobles and priests—formed a central government that dictated the social and religious rules

peasant A rural cultivator whose surpluses are transferred to a dominant group of rulers that uses the surpluses both to underwrite its own standard of living and to distribute the remainder to groups in society that do not farm but must be fed for their specific goods and services in turn.

to be followed and carried out by the merchants, craft specialists, warriors, servants, and other city dwellers.

Notably, these urbanized populations mostly depend for much of their daily food (such as bread, tortillas, vegetables, meat, fish, fruit, milk, butter, and cheese) and fuel (especially firewood for cooking and heating their dwellings) on what is produced or foraged in surrounding areas. For this reason, the urban ruling class has sought to widen its territorial power and political control over rural populations. This is how farmers who raised their own crops and livestock as they saw fit, and who determined themselves if and how much surplus they would produce, lost that traditional self-determination.

Once a dominant group managed to impose its rules on the farmers, it also took control over their capacity to produce more food than the farmers actually needed to survive. In other words, these farmers turned into **peasants.** One of the first anthropologists to study peasant communities was Eric Wolf, who defined them as "rural cultivators whose surpluses are transferred to a dominant group of rulers that uses the surpluses both to underwrite its own standard of living and to distribute the remainder to groups in society that do not farm but must be fed for their specific goods and services in turn."[14]

The Aztec State

The Aztec state, which developed in the Mexican highlands in the 15th century, is a good example of a highly developed urban society among America's indigenous peoples and where an urban political elite also gained control over food production in the surrounding countryside.[15] Its capital city Tenochtitlán (modern-day Mexico City) was located in a fertile valley 7,000 feet above sea level. Its population, along with that of its sister city Tlatelolco, reached about 200,000 in the early 16th century.

[14]Wolf, E. R. (1966). *Peasants* (pp. 4–5). Englewood Cliffs: Prentice-Hall.

[15]Most of the following information is taken from Berdan, F. F. (1982). *The Aztecs of Central Mexico.* New York: Holt, Rinehart & Winston.

GLOBALSCAPE

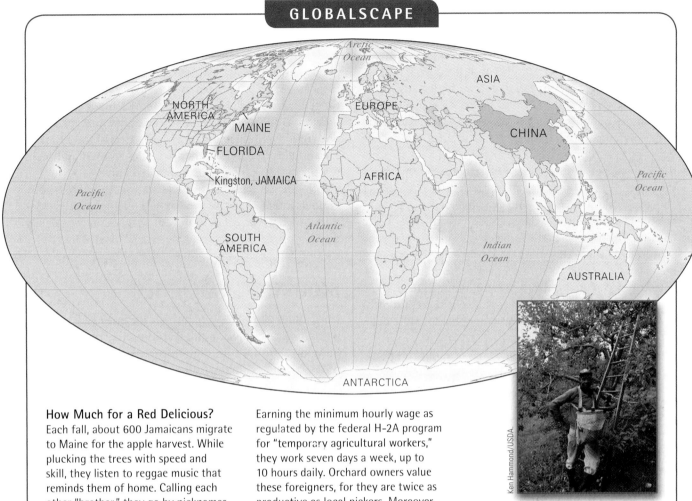

Ken Hammond/USDA.

How Much for a Red Delicious?

Each fall, about 600 Jamaicans migrate to Maine for the apple harvest. While plucking the trees with speed and skill, they listen to reggae music that reminds them of home. Calling each other "brother," they go by nicknames like "Rasta." Most are poor peasants from mountain villages in the Caribbean where they grow yams. But their villages don't produce enough to feed their families, so they go elsewhere to earn cash.

Before leaving Jamaica, they must cut their dreadlocks and shave their beards. Screened and contracted by a labor recruiter in Kingston, they receive a temporary foreign farm workers visa from the U.S. embassy and then fly to Miami. Traveling northward by bus, many work on tobacco farms en route to Maine's orchards (and in Florida's sugar cane fields on the way home).

Earning the minimum hourly wage as regulated by the federal H-2A program for "temporary agricultural workers," they work seven days a week, up to 10 hours daily. Orchard owners value these foreigners, for they are twice as productive as local pickers. Moreover, hand-picked apples graded "extra fancy" earn farmers eight times the price of apples destined for processing.

While in the United States, the Jamaicans remain quite isolated, trying to save as much as they can to send more money home. Just before leaving the country, Rasta and his "brothers" buy things like a television, refrigerator, clothes, and shoes to take home as gifts or as goods to be resold for profit. Lately, their cash-earning opportunities in Maine are disappearing due to a tide of cheaper illegal workers and a diminished demand for U.S.-grown apples due to increasing Chinese competition.

Although rural labor conditions for seasonal migrant workers in the United States have been likened to indentured service (causing some critics to call the federal H-2A program "rent-a-slave"), for Jamaicans like Rasta, it is an opportunity to escape from the dismal poverty on their Caribbean island.

Global Twister When you take a big bite from your next apple, think of a brother like Rasta and ask—what the heck is "fair value" anyway?
See Rathke, L. (1989). To Maine for apples. Salt Magazine 9 *(4), 24–47.*

This makes it five times more populous than the city of London at the same time.

The Aztec social order was stratified into three main classes: nobles, commoners, and serfs. The serfs were bound to the land and the lowest of this class were the slaves. Some had sold themselves into bondage; others were captives taken in war. The state was governed by an absolute monarch, assisted by a large number of government officials who oversaw various functions, such as maintenance of the tax system and the courts of justice, management of government storehouses, and control of military training.

As in early states elsewhere in the world, the foundation of Aztec society was intensive agriculture. Corn was the principal crop. Each family, allotted a plot of land by its kin group, cultivated any of a number of crops, including beans, squash, gourds, peppers, tomatoes, cotton, and tobacco. Only a few animals were domesticated; these included dogs and turkeys (both for eating).

As specialization increased in Aztec society, the market became an extremely important economic and social institution. In addition to the daily markets in each city, larger markets were held in the various cities at different times of year. Buyers and sellers traveled to these from the far reaches of the state. Trade networks between the Aztec capital and other cities brought goods such as chocolate, vanilla beans, and pineapples into Tenochtitlán. The market at Tlatelolco, Tenochtitlán's sister city, was so huge that the Spanish compared it to that of Rome. At the Aztec markets, barter was the primary means of exchange. At times, however, cacao beans and cotton cloaks were used as a form of money. The market also served social functions. People went there not only to buy or to sell but also to meet other people and to hear the latest news.

At Tenochtitlán, with a total area of about 20 square miles, a huge temple and two lavish palaces stood in the central plaza, also called the Sacred Precinct. Surrounding this area were other ceremonial buildings belonging to each kin group. In the city proper stood the houses of the more affluent—graceful, multiroomed, one- and two-story stone and mortar buildings, each surrounding a flower-filled patio and built on a stone platform for protection against floods. It is estimated that there were about 60,000 houses in Tenochtitlán. The focal points of the city were the large pyramidal temples, where religious ceremonies, including human sacrifice, were held.

The Aztec capital sat on an island in the middle of a lake, which has since been drained and filled, and two aqueducts brought in fresh water from springs on the mainland. A 10-mile dike rimmed the eastern end of the city to prevent nearby salty waters from entering the lake around Tenochtitlán. Since the city was surrounded by water, it was unfortified and connected to the mainland by three causeways. Communication among different parts of the city was easy, and people could travel either by land or by water. A series of canals, with footpaths beside them, ran throughout the city. Thousands of canoes plied the canals, carrying passengers and cargo around the city. As in a modern city, housing in Tenochtitlán ranged from squalid to magnificent. Farmers' huts made of wooden posts, thatched straw, and wattle plastered with mud were clustered on the outskirts of the city atop raised fields (*chinampas*) made of piles of mud and plant matter in the shallow lake and marshlands.

While the Spanish invaders were very impressed by Tenochtitlán's magnificence as one of the largest cities in the world, that did not prevent them from completely destroying it soon after their arrival in Mexico in 1519.

INDUSTRIAL SOCIETIES

Until about 200 years ago, human societies all across the world had developed a cultural infrastructure based on foraging, horticulture, agriculture, pastoralism, crafts, trade, or some combination of these. This changed with the invention of the steam engine in England, which brought about an industrial revolution that quickly spread to other parts of the globe. Machines and tools powered by water, wind, and steam (followed by oil, gas, and diesel fuel) replaced human labor and hand tools, increasing factory production and facilitating mass transportation.

Throughout the 1800s and 1900s, this resulted in large-scale industrialization of many societies. Technological inventions utilizing oil, electricity, and (since the 1940s) nuclear energy brought about more dramatic changes in social and economic organization on a worldwide scale. In the late 20th century, the electronic-digital revolution made the production and distribution of information the center of economic activity in some wealthy societies.

Questions for Reflection

1. Since the beginning of human history, our species has met the challenge of survival by adapting to different environments. In capturing essential natural resources, we have also modified these environments. Do you know any examples of landscapes radically transformed for economic reasons? Who benefits from such environmental changes in the long run?

2. What was so radical about the Neolithic transition that prompted some to refer to it as a revolution? Can you think of any equally radical changes in subsistence practices going on in the world today?

3. Consider the ideas of change and progress in light of the agricultural development project described in the Anthropology Applied box. Come up with your own definition of progress that goes beyond the standard idea of technological and material advancement.

4. Technological development in industrial societies often results in highly productive machines effectively replacing animal and human workers. Think of a useful mechanical device and consider its benefits and costs, not only to you but also to others.

5. When shopping for groceries in a supermarket, try to imagine the great chain of human hands that was involved in getting something as simple as a nice red apple from a distant orchard to your own mouth. How many people do you think handled the fruit to get it to you?

Suggested Readings

Bates, D. G. (2001). *Human adaptive strategies: Ecology, culture, and politics* (2nd ed.). Boston: Allyn & Bacon.

Explores different adaptive practices and their correlative political structures. Theoretical issues are made accessible through use of readable ethnographic case studies.

Bogucki, P. (1999). *The origins of human society.* Oxford, England: Blackwell.

Comprehensive global history of the human species, tracing the process of cultural evolution from our prehistoric beginnings as foragers to the creation of agricultural economies leading to complex societies and empires. As a record of human achievements, this book successfully incorporates the explosion in archaeological data accumulated since 1950.

Chatty, D. (1996). *Mobile pastoralists: Development planning and social change in Oman.* New York: Columbia University Press.

This study looks at the forces of modernization in a nomadic community and the resulting shift from herding to wage labor, as well as the changing role of women.

Lee, R. B., & Daly, R. H. (1999). *The Cambridge encyclopedia of hunters and gatherers.* New York: Cambridge University Press.

This is an essential reference text on foragers.

Lustig-Arecco, V. (1975). *Technology: Strategies for survival.* New York: Holt, Rinehart & Winston.

This text focuses especially on the technoeconomic adaptation of hunters, pastoralists, and farmers.

Schrire, C. (Ed.). (1984). *Past and present in hunter-gatherer studies.* Orlando: Academic Press.

This collection of papers demolishes many a myth (including several held by anthropologists) about food-foraging societies. Especially recommended is the editor's introduction, "Wild Surmises on Savage Thoughts."

Thomson Audio Study Products

 Enjoy the MP3-ready Audio Lecture Overviews for each chapter and a comprehensive audio glossary of key terms for quick study and review. Whether walking to class, doing laundry, or studying at your desk, you now have the freedom to choose when, where, and how you interact with your audio-based educational media. See the preface for information on how to access this on-the-go study and review tool.

The Anthropology Resource Center

www.thomsonedu.com/anthropology
The Anthropology Resource Center provides extended learning materials to reinforce your understanding of key concepts in the four fields of anthropology. For each of the four fields, the Resource Center includes dynamic exercises including video exercises, map exercises, simulations, and "Meet the Scientists" interviews, as well as critical thinking questions that can be assigned and e-mailed to instructors. The Resource Center also provides breaking news in anthropology and interesting material on applied anthropology to help you link what you are learning to the world around you.

19 Economic Systems

© Sarah Errington/Eye Ubiquitous/Hutchinson

CHALLENGE ISSUE

All humans face the challenge of gaining and maintaining access to resources needed for immediate and long-term survival. Whatever we lack, we may seek to get by peaceful means through exchange or trade. In today's capitalist societies people can exchange almost anything of value without ever actually meeting in person. But a fundamental characteristic of the market in traditional agricultural and pastoral cultures is that it is a specific location where people meet in person to exchange goods at designated times. In such economic transactions, humans forge and affirm social networks that play a key role in the search for safety and well-being. At this outdoor market by the Niger River in Mali, West Africa, people barter, buy, and sell goods in face-to-face encounters.

How Do Anthropologists Study Economic Systems?

Anthropologists study the means by which goods are produced, distributed, and consumed in the context of the total culture of particular societies. Although they have adopted theories and concepts from economists, most anthropologists recognize that theoretical principles derived from the study of capitalist market economies have limited applicability to economic systems in societies that are not industrialized and where people do not produce and exchange goods for private profit. This is because, in these non-state societies, the economic sphere of behavior is not separate from the social, religious, or political spheres.

How Do Different Societies Organize Their Economic Resources and Labor?

In small-scale nonindustrial societies, land and other valuable resources are usually controlled by groups of relatives, and individual ownership is rare. Division of labor is by age and gender with some craft specialization. Production takes place in the quantity and at the time required, and most goods are consumed by the group that produces them. This is notably different from the economic arrangements in large-scale industrial and postindustrial societies where there is a much more complex division of labor, individuals or business corporations own property, producers and consumers rarely know each other, and transactions take place by means of money.

How and Why Are Goods Exchanged or Redistributed?

People exchange goods through reciprocity, redistribution, and/or market exchange. Reciprocity involves the exchange of goods and services of roughly equivalent value and is often undertaken for ritual or prestige purposes. Redistribution requires a government and/or religious elite to collect and reallocate resources, in the form of either goods or services. Leveling mechanisms ensure that no one accumulates significantly more goods than anyone else. Market exchange in nonindustrial societies takes place in designated locations where people trade goods, meet friends and strangers, and find entertainment. In industrial or capitalist societies, market exchange may be indirect, impersonal, and mediated by money or capital in the form of shares or stock. With the advent of digital technology, trading is also increasingly conducted on the Internet in an entirely impersonal manner.

An **economic system** is an organized arrangement for producing, distributing, and consuming goods. Since a people, in pursuing a particular means of subsistence, necessarily produces, distributes, and consumes things, it is obvious that our discussion of subsistence patterns in the previous chapter involved economic matters. Yet economic systems encompass much more than we have covered so far. Now comes the rest of the story.

ECONOMIC ANTHROPOLOGY

Studying the economies of traditional small-scale societies, researchers from industrial and postindustrial capitalist societies run the risk of interpreting anthropological data in terms of their own technologies, their own values of work and property, and their own determination of what is rational. Take, for example, the following statement from just one respected textbook in economics: "In all societies, the prevailing reality of life has been the inadequacy of output to fill the wants and needs of the people."[1] This ethnocentric assertion fails to take into consideration the fact that in many societies people's wants are maintained at levels that can be fully and continuously satisfied, and without jeopardizing the environment. In such societies, people gather or produce goods in the quantity and at the time required, and to do more than this makes no sense at all.

Thus, no matter how hard they may work when hard work is called for, at other times they will have available hours, days, or even weeks on end to devote to "unproductive" (in the economic sense) activities. To observers from industrial or capitalist societies, such people may seem lazy—and if they happen to be hunters and gatherers, even the skillful or strenuous work they do is likely to be misinterpreted. To those whose livelihoods depend on farming, trading, factory or office work, hunting is typically defined as a sport. Hence, the male hunters in foraging societies are often perceived as spending virtually all of their time in recreational pursuits, while the

 THOMSON AUDIO STUDY PRODUCTS Take advantage of the MP3-ready Audio Lecture Overviews and comprehensive audio glossary of key terms for each chapter. See the preface for information on how to access this on-the-go study and review tool.

female food gatherers are seen as working themselves to the bone.

To understand how the schedule of wants or demands of a given society is balanced against the supply of goods and services available, it is necessary to introduce a noneconomic variable—the anthropological variable of culture. In any given economic system, economic processes cannot be interpreted without culturally defining the demands and understanding the conventions that dictate how and when they are satisfied. The fact is, the economic sphere of behavior is *not* separate from the social, religious, and political spheres and thus is not completely free to follow its own purely economic logic. To be sure, economic behavior and institutions can be analyzed in strictly economic terms, but to do so is to ignore crucial noneconomic cultural considerations, which do, after all, have an impact on the way things are in real life. As a case in point, we may look briefly at yam production among the Trobriand Islanders, who inhabit a group of coral islands that lie in the southern Pacific Ocean off the eastern tip of New Guinea.[2]

The Yam Complex in Trobriand Culture

Trobriand men spend a great deal of their time and energy raising yams—not for themselves or their own households, but to give to others, normally their sisters and married daughters. The purpose of cultivating these starchy edible roots is not to provision the households that receive them, because most of what people eat they grow for themselves in gardens where they plant taro, sweet potatoes, tapioca, greens, beans, and squash, as well as breadfruit and banana trees. The reason a man gives yams to a woman is to show his support for her husband and to enhance his own influence.

Once received by the woman, the gift yams are loaded into her husband's yam house, symbolizing his worth as a man of power and influence in his community. He may use some of these yams to purchase a variety of things, including arm shells, shell necklaces and earrings, betel nuts, pigs, chickens, and locally produced goods such as wooden bowls, combs, floor mats, lime pots, and even magic spells. Some he must use to fulfill social obligations. For instance, a man is expected to present yams to the relatives of his daughter's husband when she marries and again when death befalls a member of the husband's family. Finally, any man who aspires to high status and power is expected to show his worth by organizing a yam competition, during which he gives away huge quantities of yams to invited guests. As anthropologist Annette Weiner explains: "A yam house,

---

[1]Heilbroner, R. L., & Thurow, L. C. (1981). *The economic problem* (6th ed., p. 327). Englewood Cliffs, NJ: Prentice-Hall.

economic system An organized arrangement for producing, distributing, and consuming goods.

---

[2]Weiner, A. B. (1988). *The Trobrianders of Papua New Guinea.* New York: Holt, Rinehart & Winston.

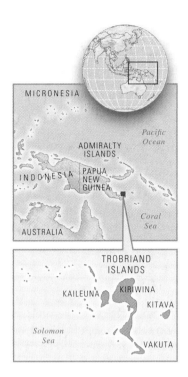

Trobriand Island men devote a great deal of time and energy to raising yams, not for themselves but to give to others. These yams, which have been raised by men related through marriage to a chief, are about to be loaded into the chief's yam house.

then, is like a bank account; when full, a man is wealthy and powerful. Until yams are cooked or they rot, they may circulate as limited currency. That is why, once harvested, the usage of yams for daily food is avoided as much as possible."[3]

By giving yams to his sister or daughter, a man not only expresses his confidence in the woman's husband, but he also makes the latter indebted to him. Although the recipient rewards the gardener and his helpers by throwing a feast, at which they are fed cooked yams, taro, and—what everyone especially looks forward to—ample pieces of pork, this in no way pays off the debt. The debt can only be repaid in women's wealth, which consists of bundles of banana leaves and skirts made of the same material dyed red.

Although the banana leaf bundles are of no utilitarian value, extensive labor is invested in their production, and large quantities of them, along with skirts, are regarded as essential for paying off all the members of other family groups who were close to a recently deceased relative in life and who assisted with the funeral. Also, the wealth and vitality of the dead person's family group is measured by the quality and quantity of the bundles and skirts so distributed. Because a man has received yams from his wife's brother, he is obligated to provide his wife with yams for purchasing the necessary bundles and skirts, beyond those she has produced, to help with payments following the death of a member of her family. Because deaths are unpredictable, and can occur at any time, a man must have yams available for his

wife when she needs them. This, and the fact she may require all of his yams, acts as an effective check on a man's wealth.

Like people the world over, the Trobriand Islanders assign meanings to objects that make those objects worth far more than their cost in labor or materials. Yams, for example, establish long-term relationships that lead to other advantages, such as access to land, protection, assistance, and other kinds of wealth. Thus, yam exchanges are as much social and political transactions as they are economic ones. Banana leaf bundles and skirts, for their part, are symbolic of the political status of families and of their immortality. In their distribution, which is related to rituals associated with death, we see how men in Trobriand society are ultimately dependent on women and their valuables.

So important are these matters to Trobrianders that even with the infiltration of Western culture—money, education, religion, and law—they remain as committed to yam cultivation and to the production of women's

---

[3]Weiner, A. B. (1988). *The Trobrianders of Papua New Guinea* (p. 86). New York: Holt, Rinehart & Winston.

wealth. Looked at in terms of modern capitalist economics, these activities appear meaningless, but viewed in terms of Trobriand values and concerns, they make a great deal of sense.

PRODUCTION AND ITS RESOURCES

In every society, particular customs and rules govern the kinds of work done, who does the work, attitudes toward the work, how it is accomplished, and who controls the resources necessary to produce desired goods, knowledge, and services. The primary resources in any culture are raw materials, technology, and labor. The rules directing the use of these are embedded in a people's culture and determine the way the economy operates within any given natural environment.

Control of Land and Water Resources

All societies regulate allocation of valuable natural resources—especially land and water. Food foragers must determine who will hunt game and gather plants in their home range and where these activities take place. Groups that rely on fishing or growing crops need to make similar decisions concerning who carries out which task on which stretch of water or land. Farmers must have some means of determining title to land and access to water supplies for irrigation. Pastoralists require a system that determines rights to watering places and grazing land, as well as the right of access to land where they move their herds.

In Western capitalist societies, a system of private ownership of land and rights to natural resources generally prevails. Although elaborate laws have been enacted to regulate the buying, owning, and selling of land and water resources, if individuals wish to reallocate valuable farmland to some other purpose, for instance, they generally can.

In traditional nonindustrial societies, land is often controlled by kinship groups such as the family or band rather than by individuals. For example, among the Ju/'hoansi of the Kalahari Desert, each band (a local group of anywhere from ten to thirty people) lives on roughly 250 square miles of land, which they consider to be their territory—their own country. These territories are defined not in terms of boundaries but in terms of water holes that are located within them. The land is said to be "owned" by those who have lived the longest in the band, usually a group of brothers and sisters or cousins. Their concept of ownership, however, is not something easily translated in modern Western terms. Suffice it to say that within their traditional worldview, no part of

their homeland can be sold for money or traded away for goods. Outsiders must ask permission to enter the territory—but denying the request would be unthinkable.

The practice of defining territories on the basis of core features—be they water holes (as among the Ju/'hoansi), watercourses (as among Indians of the northeastern United States), unique sites in the landscape where ancestral spirits are thought to dwell (as among the Aborigines in Australia), or whatever—is typical of food foragers. Typically, territorial boundaries are left rather vaguely defined. To avoid friction, foragers may designate part of their territory as a buffer zone between them and their neighbors. The adaptive value of this is obvious: The size of band territories, as well as the size of the bands, can adjust to keep in balance with availability of resources in any given place. Such adjustment would be more difficult under a system of individual ownership of clearly bounded land.

Among some West African farming groups, a tributary system of land ownership prevails. All land is said to belong to the head chief, who allocates it to various subchiefs, who in turn distribute it to family groups. Then the family group leaders assign individual plots to each farmer. Just as in traditional Europe, these African people owe allegiance to the subchiefs (or nobles) and the head chief (or king). The people who work the land must pay tribute in the form of products or special services such as fighting for the king when necessary.

These people do not really own the land; rather, it is a kind of lease. Yet as long as the land is kept in use, rights to such use will pass to their heirs. No user, however, can give away, sell, or otherwise dispose of a plot of land without approval from the elder of the family group. When an individual no longer uses the allocated land, it reverts to the head of the large family group, who reallocates it to some other group member. The important operative principle here is that the system extends the individual's right to use land for an indefinite pe-

A Ju/'hoansi water hole. The practice of defining territories on the basis of core features such as water holes is typical of food foragers, such as these people of the Kalahari Desert in southern Africa.

© Irven DeVore/Anthro-Photo

riod, but the land is not "owned" outright. This serves to maintain the integrity of valuable farmland as such, preventing its loss through subdivision and conversion to other uses.

Technology Resources

All societies have some means of creating and allocating tools that are used to produce goods, as well as traditions concerning passing them on to succeeding generations. The number and kinds of tools a society uses—which, together with knowledge about how to make and use them constitute its **technology**—are related to the lifestyles of its members. Food foragers and pastoral nomads who are frequently on the move are apt to have fewer and simpler tools than more settled peoples such as sedentary farmers. A great number of complex tools would hinder mobility. Thus, the average weight of an individual's personal belongings among the Ju'hoansi is just under 25 pounds, limited to the barest essentials such as implements for hunting, gathering, fishing, building, and cooking.

Food foragers make and use a variety of tools, many of which are ingenious in their effectiveness. Some of these they make for their individual use, but codes of generosity are such that a person may not refuse to give or loan what is requested. Tools may be given or loaned to others in exchange for the products resulting from their use. For example, a Ju/'hoansi who gives his arrow to another hunter has a right to a share in any animals the hunter kills. Game is considered to "belong" to the man whose arrow killed it, even when he is not present

on the hunt. In this context, it makes little sense for them to accumulate luxuries or surplus goods, and the fact that no one owns significantly more than another helps to limit status differences.

Among horticulturists, the axe, digging stick, and hoe are the primary tools. Since these are relatively easy to produce, almost everyone can make them. Whoever makes a tool has first rights to it, but when he or she is not using it, any family member may ask to use it, and the request is rarely denied. Refusal would cause people to treat the tool owner with scorn for this singular lack of concern for others. If a relative helps raise the crop traded for a particular tool, that relative becomes part owner of the implement, and it may not be traded or given away without his or her permission.

In permanently settled agricultural communities, tools and other productive goods are more complex, heavier, and costlier to make. In such settings, individual ownership tends to be more absolute, as are the conditions under which people may borrow and use such equipment. It is easy to replace a knife lost by a relative during palm cultivation but much more difficult to replace an iron plow or a diesel-fueled harvesting machine. Rights to the ownership of complex tools are more rigidly applied; generally the person who has funded the purchase of a complex piece of machinery is considered the sole owner and may decide how and by whom it will be used.

technology Tools and other material equipment, together with the knowledge of how to make and use them.

Labor Resources and Patterns

In addition to raw materials and technology, labor is a key resource in any economic system. A look around the world reveals many different labor patterns, but two features are almost always present in human cultures: a basic division of labor by gender and by age.

Division of Labor by Gender

Anthropologists have studied extensively the social division of labor by gender in cultures of all sorts. Whether men or women do a particular job varies from group to group, but typically work is divided into the tasks of either one or the other. For example, the practices most commonly regarded as "women's work" tend to be those that can be carried out near home and that are easily resumed after interruption. The tasks historically often regarded as "men's work" tend to be those requiring physical strength, rapid mobilization of high bursts of energy, frequent travel at some distance from home, and assumption of high levels of risk and danger.

Many exceptions occur, however, as in those societies where women regularly carry burdensome loads or put in long hours of hard work cultivating crops in the fields. In some societies, women perform almost three-quarters of all work, and in several societies they have served as warriors. For example, in the 19th-century West African kingdom of Dahomey, in what is now called Benin, thousands of women served in the armed forces of the Dahomean king, and some considered the women to be better fighters than their male counterparts. Also, there are references to female warriors in ancient Ireland, and archaeological evidence indicates their presence among Vikings. During World War II in

the early 1940s, some 58,000 Soviet women engaged in frontline combat defending their homeland against German invaders, and North Vietnamese women fought in mixed-gender army units during the Vietnam War in the 1960s and early 1970s.

Whether or not women should participate in direct combat operations is an ongoing issue in the United States. Clearly, the division of labor by gender cannot be explained simply as a consequence of sex differences, whether they be of male strength and expendability or female reproductive biology.

Instead of looking for key biological factors to explain the social division of labor, a more useful strategy is to examine the kinds of work that men and women do in the context of specific societies to see how it relates to other cultural and historical factors. Researchers find a continuum of patterns, ranging from flexible integration of men and women to rigid segregation by gender.[4]

The *flexible/integrated pattern* is exemplified by the Ju/'hoansi discussed above and is seen most often among food foragers (as well as communities where crops are traditionally cultivated primarily for family consumption). In such societies, men and women perform up to 35 percent of activities with approximately equal participation, and tasks deemed especially appropriate for one gender may be performed by the other, without loss of face, as the situation warrants. Where these practices prevail, boys and girls grow up in much the same way, learn to value cooperation over competition, and become equally habituated to adult men and women, who interact with one another on a relatively equal basis.

Societies following a *segregated pattern* define almost all work as either masculine or feminine, so men and women rarely engage in joint efforts of any kind. In such societies, it is inconceivable that someone would even think of doing something considered the work of the opposite sex. This pattern is frequently seen in pastoral nomadic, intensive agricultural, and industrial societies, where men's work keeps them outside the home for much of the time.

Typically, men in such societies are expected to be tough, aggressive, and competitive—and this often involves assertions of male superiority, and hence authority, over women. Historically, societies segregated by gender often have imposed their control on those featuring integration, upsetting the egalitarian nature of the latter.

In the third pattern of labor division by gender, sometimes called the *dual sex configuration,* men and women carry out their work separately, as in societies segregated

© David Wells/The Image Works

Often, work that is considered inappropriate for women (or men) in one society is performed by them in another. Here we see female stone construction laborers in Bangalore, India, who carry concrete atop their heads.

---

[4]Sanday, P. R. (1981). *Female power and male dominance: On the origins of sexual inequality* (pp. 79–80). Cambridge, England: Cambridge University Press.

by gender, but the relationship between them is one of balanced complementarity rather than inequality. Although competition is a prevailing ethic, each gender manages its own affairs, and the interests of both men and women are represented at all levels. Thus, as in integrated societies, neither gender exerts dominance over the other. The dual sex orientation may be seen among certain American Indian peoples whose economies were based upon subsistence farming, as well as among several West African kingdoms, including that of the aforementioned Dahomeans.

Division of Labor by Age

Division of labor according to age is also typical of human societies. Among the Ju/'hoansi, for example, children are not expected to contribute significantly to subsistence until they reach their late teens. Indeed, until they possess adult levels of strength and endurance, many "bush" foods are tough for them to gather.

The Ju/'hoansi equivalent of retirement comes somewhere around the age of 60. Elderly people, while they will usually do some foraging for themselves, are not expected to contribute much food. However, older men and women alike play an essential role in spiritual matters. Freed from food taboos and other restrictions that apply to younger adults, they may handle ritual substances considered dangerous to those still involved with hunting or having children. By virtue of their old age, they have memories of customary practices and events that happened far in the past. Thus, they are repositories of accumulated wisdom—the libraries of a nonliterate people—and are able to suggest solutions to problems younger adults have never before had to face. Considered useful for their knowledge, they are far from being unproductive members of society.

In some food-foraging societies, women do continue to make a significant contribution to provisioning in their later years. Among the Hadza of East Africa, the input of older women is critical to their daughters, whose foraging abilities are significantly impaired when they have new infants to nurse. This is because lactation is energetically expensive, along with the fact that holding, carrying, and nursing an infant all interfere with the mother's foraging efficiency. Those most immediately affected by this are a woman's weaned children not yet old enough to forage effectively for themselves. The problem is solved by the foraging efforts of grandmothers.[5]

In many traditional farming societies, children as well as older people may make a greater contribution to the economy in terms of work and responsibility than is

This Thai girl exemplifies the use of child labor in many parts of the world, often by large corporations. Even in Western countries, child labor plays a major economic role.

common in industrial or postindustrial societies. For instance, in Maya peasant communities in southern Mexico and Guatemala, children not only look after their younger brothers and sisters but also help with housework. Girls begin to make a substantial contribution to the work of the household by age 7 or 8. By age 11 they are constantly busy with an array of chores—grinding corn, making tortillas, fetching wood and water, sweeping, and so forth. Young boys have less to do but are given small tasks, such as bringing in the chickens or playing with a baby. However, by age 12 they are carrying toasted tortillas to the men out working in the fields and returning with loads of corn.[6]

Similar situations are not unknown in industrial societies. In Naples, Italy, children play a significant role in the economy. At a very young age, girls begin to take on responsibilities for housework, leaving their mothers and older sisters free to earn money for the household. Nor is it long before little girls are apprenticed out to neighbors and kin, from whom they learn the skills that enable them, by age 14, to enter a small factory or workshop. Typically, girls turn over earned wages to their mothers. Boys, too, are apprenticed out at an early age, but

[5]Hawkes, K., O'Connell, J. F., & Blurton Jones, N. G. (1997). Hadza women's time allocation, offspring, provisioning, and the evolution of long postmenopausal life spans. *Current Anthropology 38*, 551–577.

[6]Vogt, E. Z. (1990). *The Zinacantecos of Mexico, a modern Maya way of life* (2nd ed., pp. 83–87). Fort Worth: Holt, Rinehart & Winston.

they may achieve more freedom from adult control by becoming involved in various street activities not available to girls.[7]

The use of child labor has become a matter of increasing concern as large capitalist corporations rely more and more on the low-cost manufacture of goods in the world's poorer countries. Although reliable figures are hard to come by, it is estimated that there are some 15 million bonded child laborers in South Asia alone, including some as young as 4 years old. Although the United States long ago passed laws prohibiting institutionalized child labor, the country imports at least $100 million worth of products manufactured by poorly paid children, ranging from rugs and carpets to clothing and soccer balls.[8]

Cooperative Labor

Cooperative work groups can be found everywhere—in foraging as well as food-producing and in nonindustrial as well as industrial societies. Often, if the effort involves the whole community, a festive spirit permeates the work. Jomo Kenyatta (see Anthropologist of Note), who became president of the East African country of Kenya after it won independence from British colonial rule in 1963, describes a happy moment in a communal work day of a Kikuyu farming village such as his own:

> If a stranger happens to pass by, he will have
> no idea that these people who are singing and
> dancing have completed their day's work. This is
> why most Europeans have erred by not realizing
> that the African in his own environment does
> not count hours or work by the movement of the
> clock, but works with good spirit and enthusiasm
> to complete the tasks before him.[9]

In some parts of East Africa, work parties begin with the display of a pot of millet beer to be consumed after the tasks have been finished. Home-brewed from millet, their major cereal crop, the beer is not really payment for the work; indeed, the labor involved is worth far more than the beer consumed. Rather, drinking the low-alcohol but highly nutritious beverage together is more of a symbolic activity to celebrate the spirit of friendship and mutual support, whereas recompense comes as individuals sooner or later participate in work parties for others.

In most human societies, the basic unit within which cooperation takes place is the household. It is both a unit of production and consumption; only in industrial societies have these two things been separated. The Maya farmer in Guatemala, for example, unlike his North American counterpart (but like peasant and subsistence farmers everywhere), is not so much running a commercial enterprise as he is a household. He is motivated by a desire to provide for the welfare of his own family; each family, as an economic unit, works as a group for its own good. Cooperative work may be undertaken outside the household, however, for other reasons, though not always voluntarily. It may be part of fulfilling duties to in-laws, or it may be performed for political officials or priests by command. Thus, institutions of family, kinship, religion, and the state all may act as organizing elements that define the nature and condition of each worker's cooperative obligations.

Craft Specialization

In contemporary industrial and postindustrial societies, there is a great diversity of specialized tasks to be performed, and no individual can even begin to know all of those customarily seen as fitting for his or her age and gender. However, although specialization has increased in these societies, modern technologies are making labor divisions based on gender less relevant. By contrast, in small-scale foraging and traditional crop-cultivating societies, where division of labor typically occurs along lines of age and gender, each person has knowledge and competence in all aspects of work appropriate to his or her age and gender. Yet, even in these nonindustrial societies there is a measure of specialization.

One example of specialization in a traditional society is afforded by the Afar people of the desolate Danakil Depression of northeastern Ethiopia, one of the lowest and hottest places on earth. Afar men are miners of salt, which since ancient times has been traded widely in East Africa. It is mined from the crust of an extensive salt plain, and to get to it is a risky and difficult business. L. M. Nesbitt, the first European to successfully cross this desert, called it "the hell-hole of creation."[10] The heat is extreme during the day, with shade temperatures of 140 to 156 degrees Fahrenheit not unusual. Shade is not found on the salt plain unless a shelter of salt blocks is built. Nor is there food or water for man or beast. To add to the difficulty, until recently the Muslim Afars and the Christian Tigrians, who also mine salt, were sworn enemies.

Successful mining, then, requires specialized skill at planning and organization, as well as physical strength

[7]Goddard, V. (1993). Child labor in Naples. In W. A. Haviland & R. J. Gordon (Eds.), *Talking about people* (pp. 105–109). Mountain View, CA: Mayfield.

[8]It's the law: Child labor protection. (1997, November/December). *Peace and Justice News*, 11.

[9]Herskovits, M. (1952). *Economic anthropology: A study in comparative economics* (2nd ed., p. 103). New York: Knopf.

[10]Nesbitt, L. M. (1935). *Hell-hole of creation*. New York: Knopf.

Anthropologists of Note
Jomo Kenyatta (1889–1978)

Jomo Kenyatta, Kenya's first president, was academically trained in anthropology and took the concept of cooperation from the local level and applied it to the state. His national slogan was *Harambee* ("Pull Together"), and with that sentiment he led his country to freedom from British colonial rule.

Born a Kikuyu, Kenya's largest ethnic group, he was originally named Kamau Ngengi. Later in life he adopted the name Jomo Kenyatta—Jomo meaning "burning spear" in his own language and Kenyatta referring to the beaded belt (*kinyata*) that he always wore. After his father died in 1896, he went to live with his grandfather, a medicine man. As a teenager, he attended primary school at a Scottish mission, followed by work as an apprentice carpenter. In 1915, he found work on a sisal farm, and in 1917 he moved to Narok where he lived with Maasai relatives while employed by an Asian contractor. A year later he found a job as a storekeeper in the capital city of Nairobi and took evening classes at another mission school. In 1919 he and his new wife turned part of their home into a little shop, which became a gathering place for friends from different ethnic groups who, like Kenyatta, were hungry for independence. Living outside of Nairobi, he also kept a small farm.

In the late 1920s, while working for the Nairobi City Council water department, Kenyatta became actively involved in the politics of land control and edited a newspaper on Kikuyu culture and new farming methods. As president of the Kikuyu Central Association, he traveled to London in 1929 and again in 1931 to argue for his people's right to the land on which British colonials had settled. Staying on in England, he completed studies at a Quaker college. In the mid-1930s he studied anthropology at the London School of Economics under the famous Bronislaw Malinowski. During this time he also penned various anticolonialism articles, taught at

© Bruce Dale/National Geographic Image Collection

University College in London, and wrote anthropological studies about his people. Most significantly he published an autobiography titled *Facing Mount Kenya*, sometimes referred to as the bible of Kenya's independence movement.

After serving as a key organizer of the 1945 Pan African Congress held in Manchester, England, Kenyatta went home to Kenya. In 1946 he became president of the Kenya African Union, which pressed for voting rights, an end to racial discrimination, and the return of indigenous lands. Dissatisfied with what appeared to be dead-end diplomacy, radical natives launched the "Mau Mau" uprising against British colonial rule. Responding with brutal force to guerrilla attacks that claimed about 100 British lives, British forces killed many thousands of native people and arrested those they suspected as instigators—including Kenyatta. During his seven years of imprisonment, Kenyatta gained all the more influence, and in 1960—just before his release—fellow natives in the colony elected him president of the newly founded Kenya African National Union. After his country finally won independence in 1963, he was elected as the republic's first president, holding that office until his death in 1978.

and the will to work under the most trying conditions.[11] Pack animals to carry the salt have to be fed in advance, for carrying sufficient fodder for them interferes with their ability to carry out salt. Food and water must be carried for the miners, who usually number thirty to forty per group. Travel is planned to take place at night to avoid the intense heat of day. In the past, measures to protect against attack had to be taken. Finally, timing is critical; a party has to return to sources of food and wa-

ter before their own supplies are too long exhausted and before their animals are unable to continue.

DISTRIBUTION AND EXCHANGE

In societies without a money economy, the rewards for labor are usually direct. The workers in a family group consume what they harvest, eat what the hunter or gatherer brings home, and use the tools they themselves make. But even where no formal medium of exchange such as money exists, some distribution of goods takes place. Anthropologists often classify the cultural sys-

[11]Mesghinua, H. M. (1966). Salt mining in Enderta. *Journal of Ethiopian Studies 4* (2); O'Mahoney, K. (1970). The salt trade. *Journal of Ethiopian Studies 8* (2).

These Ju/'hoansi are cutting up meat that will be shared by others in the camp. Food distribution practices of such food foragers are an example of generalized reciprocity.

tems of distributing material goods into three modes: reciprocity, redistribution, and market exchange.[12]

Reciprocity

Reciprocity refers to a transaction between two parties whereby goods and services of roughly equivalent value are exchanged. This may involve gift giving. Notably, individuals or groups in most cultures like to think that the main point of the transaction is the gift itself, yet what actually matters are the social ties that are created or reinforced between givers and receivers. Because reciprocity is about a relationship between the self and others, gift giving is seldom really selfless. The overriding (if unconscious) motive is to fulfill social obligations and perhaps to gain a bit of prestige in the process. Cultural traditions dictate the manner and occasion of exchange.

For example, when an animal is killed by a group of indigenous hunters in Australia, the meat is divided among the hunters' families and other relatives. Each person in the camp gets a share, the size depending on

the nature of the person's kinship tie to the hunters. Typically, if the animal is a kangaroo, the left hind leg goes to the brother of the hunter, the tail to his father's brother's son, the loins and the fat to his father-in-law, the ribs to his mother-in-law, the forelegs to his father's younger sister, the head to his wife, and the entrails and the blood to the hunter. If arguments were to arise over the apportionment, it would be because the principles of distribution were not followed properly. The hunter and his family seem to fare badly in this arrangement, but they have their turn when another man makes a kill. The giving and receiving is obligatory, as is the particularity of the distribution. Such sharing of food reinforces community bonds and ensures that everyone eats. By giving away part of a kill, the hunters get social credit for a similar amount of food in the future.

Reciprocity falls into several categories. The Australian food distribution example just noted constitutes an example of **generalized reciprocity**—exchange in which the value of what is given is not calculated, nor is the time of repayment specified. Gift giving, in the unselfish sense, also falls in this category. So, too, does the act of a kindhearted soul who stops to help a stranded motorist or someone else in distress and refuses payment with the admonition: "Pass it on to the next person in need."

Most generalized reciprocity, however, occurs among close kin or people who otherwise have very close ties with one another. Within such circles of intimacy, people give to others when they have the means and can count on receiving from others in time of need. Typically, participants will not consider such exchanges in economic terms but will couch them explicitly in terms of family and friendship social relations.

[12]Polanyi, K. (1968). The economy as instituted process. In E. E. LeClair, Jr., & H. K. Schneider (Eds.), *Economic anthropology: Readings in theory and analysis* (pp. 127–138). New York: Holt, Rinehart & Winston.

reciprocity The exchange of goods and services, of approximately equal value, between two parties.
generalized reciprocity A mode of exchange in which the value of what is given is not calculated, nor is the time of repayment specified.

© Stan Washburn/Anthro-Photo

Balanced reciprocity differs in that it is not part of a long-term process. The giving and receiving, as well as the time involved, are more specific. One has a direct obligation to reciprocate promptly in equal value in order for the social relationship to continue. Examples of balanced reciprocity in contemporary North American society include such customary practices as hosting a baby shower for young friends expecting their first baby; giving presents at birthdays, Christmas, and various other culturally prescribed "special" occasions; or buying drinks when one's turn comes at a gathering of friends or associates.

Examples from a traditional foraging society include those related by German American anthropologist Robert Lowie in his ethnography of the Crow (or Absaroke) Indians in Montana.[13] A woman skilled in the tanning of buffalo hides might offer her services to a neighbor who needed a new cover for her tepee. It took an expert to design and oversee the making of a tepee cover, which required from fourteen to twenty skins. The designer might need as many as twenty collaborators, whom she instructed in the sewing together of the skins and whom the tepee owner might thank by inviting them to be his guests at a feast. The designer herself would be given some special present of value by the tepee owner.

Giving, receiving, and sharing as so far described constitute a form of social security or insurance. A family contributes to others when they have the means and can count on receiving from others in time of need—promoting an egalitarian distribution of wealth over the long run.

Negative reciprocity is a third form of exchange, in which the aim is to get something for as little as possible. The parties involved have opposing interests and are not usually closely related; they may be strangers or even enemies. They are people with whom exchanges are often neither fair nor balanced and are usually not expected to be such. It may involve hard bargaining, manipulation, or outright cheating. An extreme form of negative reciprocity is to take something by force, while realizing that one's victim may seek compensation or retribution for losses.

Barter and Trade

Exchanges that occur within a group of relatives or between friends generally take the form of generalized or balanced reciprocity. However, when two or more partners from different groups negotiate a direct exchange of one trade good for another, we speak of *barter*. However, their arguing about the price and terms of the deal may well be in the form of negative reciprocity. This means

Scott Olson/Getty Images

Political fundraising in the United States involves elements of both balanced and negative reciprocity. Big contributors expect their generosity will buy influence with a candidate, resulting in benefits of equal value. The politician may seek to do as little as possible in return, but not so little as to jeopardize future donations. Those who accept too much and/or give too much in return risk legal repercussions. In 2006, a jury found former Illinois Governor George Ryan guilty of taking gifts and payoffs in return for government contracts, resulting in a prison sentence for this man who had been one of the most successful politicians in his state's history. Here we see Ryan speaking with the press outside the courtroom just after the guilty verdict was announced.

that there is the potential for suspicion and even the risk of hostility between both parties.

Although in barter each party seeks to get the best possible deal, both may negotiate until a relative balance has been found, and each feels satisfied at having achieved the better of the deal. Relative value is calculated, and despite an outward show of indifference, sharp trading is generally the rule, when compared to the more balanced nature of exchanges within a group.

An arrangement that combined elements of balanced reciprocity as well as barter existed in India between the Kota and three neighboring peoples. The Kota, the musicians and blacksmiths for the region, were able to provide their neighbors with tools and with music considered essential for ceremonial occasions. In exchange, the Toda, with whom they had an amicable relationship, offered *ghee* (a kind of butter used for certain ceremonies) and buffalo used for funerals. For grain, the Kota traded with the Badaga farmers, with whom they had a competitive relationship that sometimes led to one-sided trading practices (in which the Kota usually came out ahead). The forest-dwelling Kurumba, who were renowned as

balanced reciprocity A mode of exchange in which the giving and the receiving are specific as to the value of the goods and the time of their delivery.
negative reciprocity A form of exchange in which the aim is to get something for as little as possible. Neither fair nor balanced, it may involve hard bargaining, manipulation, and outright cheating.

[13]Lowie, R. (1956). *Crow Indians* (p. 75). New York: Holt, Rinehart & Winston. (orig. 1935)

sorcerers, had honey, canes, and occasionally fruits to offer, but their main contribution was protection against the supernatural. The Kota feared the Kurumba, and the Kurumba took advantage of this in their trade dealings, so that they always got more than they gave. Thus, great latent hostility existed between these two peoples.

Silent trade is a specialized form of barter in which no verbal communication takes place. In fact, it may involve no actual face-to-face contact at all. Such cases have often characterized the dealings between food-foraging peoples and their food-producing neighbors, as over the past 2,000 or so years, foragers have supplied various commodities in demand in a wider economy. A classic description of such trade follows:

> The forest people creep through the lianas to the trading place, and leave a neat pile of jungle products, such as wax, camphor, monkeys' gall bladders, birds' nests for Chinese soup. They creep back a certain distance, and wait in a safe place. The partners to the exchange, who are usually agriculturalists with a more elaborate and extensive set of material possessions but who cannot be bothered stumbling through the jungle after wax when they have someone else to do it for them, discover the little pile, and lay down beside it what they consider its equivalent in metal cutting tools, cheap cloth, bananas, and the like. They too discreetly retire. The shy folk then reappear, inspect the two piles, and if they are satisfied, take the second one away. Then the opposite group comes back and takes pile number one, and the exchange is completed. If the forest people are dissatisfied, they can retire once more, and if the other people want to increase their offering they may, time and again, until everyone is happy.[14]

To speculate about the reasons for silent trade, in some situations it may be silent for lack of a common language. More often silent trade may serve to control situations of distrust so as to keep relations peaceful. Good relations are maintained by preventing direct contact. Another possibility that does not exclude the others is that it makes exchange possible where problems of sta-

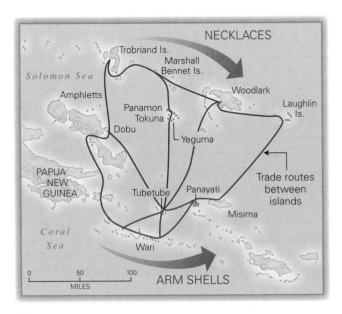

Figure 19.1

The ceremonial trading of shell necklaces and armbands in the Kula ring encourages trade throughout Melanesia.

tus might make verbal communication unthinkable. In any event, it provides for the exchange of goods between groups despite potential barriers.

The Kula Ring: Gift Giving and Trading in the South Pacific

Balanced reciprocity can take more complicated forms, whereby mutual gift giving serves to facilitate social interaction, "smoothing" social relations between traders wanting to do business and make profits or between politicians seeking favorable deals for themselves, their parties, or their countries. One classic ethnographic example of balanced reciprocity between trading partners seeking to be friends and do business at the same time is the **Kula ring** in the southwestern Pacific Ocean, as first described by Bronislaw Malinowski. Involving thousands of seafarers going to great lengths to establish and maintain good trade relations, this centuries-old ceremonial exchange system continues to this day.[15]

Kula participants are men of influence who travel to islands within the Trobriand ring to exchange prestige items—red shell necklaces (*soulava*), which are circulated around the ring of islands in a clockwise direction, and white shell armbands (*mwali*), which are carried in the opposite direction (Figure 19.1). Each man in the Kula is linked to partners on the islands that neighbor his own. To a partner residing on an island in the clockwise direc-

---

[14]Coon, C. S. (Ed.) (1948). *A reader in general anthropology* (p. 594). New York: Holt, Rinehart & Winston.

silent trade A form of barter in which no verbal communication takes place.
Kula ring A form of balanced reciprocity that reinforces trade relations among the seafaring Trobriand people, who inhabit a large ring of islands in the southwestern Pacific Ocean off the eastern coast of Papua New Guinea, and other Melanesians.

---

[15]Malinowski, B. (1922). *Argonauts of the western Pacific* (p. 94). London: Routledge & Kegan Paul; Weiner, A. B. (1988). *The Trobrianders of Papua New Guinea* (pp. 139–157). New York: Holt, Rinehart & Winston.

In Melanesia, men of influence paddle and sail within a large ring of islands in the southwestern Pacific off the eastern coast of Papua New Guinea to participate in the ceremonial trading of Kula shells, which smoothes trade relations and builds personal prestige.

tion, he offers a *soulava* and receives in return a *mwali*. He makes the reverse exchange of a *mwali* for a *soulava* to a partner living in the counterclockwise direction. Each of these trade partners eventually passes the object on to a Kula partner further along the chain of islands. *Soulava* and *mwali* are ranked according to their size, their color, how finely they are polished, and their particular histories. Such is the fame of some that, when they appear in a village, they create a sensation.

Traditionally, men make their Kula journeys in elaborately carved dugout canoes, sailing and paddling these 20- to 25-feet long boats across open waters to shores some 60 miles or more away. The adventure is often dangerous and may take men away from their homes for several weeks, sometimes even months. Although men on Kula voyages may use the opportunity to trade for practical goods, acquiring such goods is not always the reason for these voyages—nor is Kula exchange a necessary part of regular trade expeditions.

Perhaps the best way to view the Kula is as an indigenous insurance policy in an economic order fraught with danger and uncertainty. It establishes and reinforces social partnerships between traders doing business on distant shores, ensuring a welcome reception from people who have similar vested interests. That said, this ceremonial exchange network does more than simply smooth or enhance the trade of foods and other goods essential for survival. Melanesians participating in the

Kula ring have no doubt that their social position has to do with the company they keep, the circles in which they move. They derive their social prestige from the reputations of their partners and the valuables that they circulate. By giving and receiving armbands and necklaces that accumulate the histories of their travels and names of those who have possessed them, men proclaim their individual fame and talent, gaining considerable influence for themselves in the process.

Like other forms of currency, *soulava* and *mwali* must flow from hand to hand; once they stop flowing, they may lose their value. A man who takes these valuables out of their inter-island circuit invites criticism. He may lose not only prestige or social capital as a man of influence, but may become a target of sorcery for unraveling the cultural fabric that holds the islands together as a functioning social and economic order.

As this example from the South Pacific illustrates, the potential tension between trading partners may be resolved or lessened when they engage in a ritual of balanced reciprocity. As an elaborate complex of ceremony, political relationships, economic exchange, travel, magic, and social integration, the Kula ring illustrates how inseparable economic matters are from the rest of culture. Although perhaps difficult to recognize, this is just as true in modern industrial societies as it is in traditional Trobriand society—as evident when heads of state engage in ceremonial gift exchanges at official visits.

Redistribution

Redistribution is a form of exchange in which goods flow into a central place where they are sorted, counted, and reallocated. Commonly, it involves an element of power. In societies with a sufficient surplus to support some sort of government, goods in the form of gifts, tribute, taxes, and the spoils of war are gathered into storehouses controlled by a chief or some other type of leader. From there they are handed out again. The leadership has three motives in redistributing this income: The first is to gain or maintain a position of power through a display of wealth and generosity; the second is to assure those who support the leadership an adequate standard of living by providing them with desired goods; and the third is to establish alliances with leaders of other groups by hosting them at lavish parties and giving them valuable goods.

The redistribution system of the ancient Inca empire in the Andean highlands of South America was one of the most efficient the world has ever known, both in the collection of tribute (obligatory contributions or gifts in the form of crops, goods, and services) and in its methods of administrative control.[16] Administrators kept inventories of resources and a census of the population, which at its peak reached 6 million. Each craft specialist had to produce a specific quota of goods from materials supplied by overseers. Required labor was used for some agricultural and mining work. Unpaid labor was also used in a program of public works that included a remarkable system of roads and bridges throughout the mountainous terrain, aqueducts that guaranteed a supply of water, temples for worship, and storehouses that held surplus food for times of famine.

Careful accounts were kept of income and expenditures. A central administration, regulated by the Inca emperor and his relatives, had the responsibility for ensuring that production was maintained and that commodities were distributed. Holding power over this command economy, the ruling elite lived in great luxury, but sufficient goods were redistributed to the common people to ensure that no one would be left in dire need or face the indignity of pauperism.

---

[16]Mason, J. A. (1957). *The ancient civilizations of Peru.* Baltimore: Penguin.

redistribution A form of exchange in which goods flow into a central place, where they are sorted, counted, and reallocated.
conspicuous consumption A showy display of wealth for social prestige.
potlatch On the northwest coast of North America, a ceremonial event in which a village chief publicly gives away stockpiled food and other goods that signify wealth.

Taxes imposed by central governments of countries all around the world today are one form of redistribution—required payments typically based on a percentage of one's income and property value. Typically, a portion of the taxes goes toward supporting the government itself while the rest are redistributed either in cash (such as welfare payments and government loans or subsidies to businesses) or in the form of services (such as military defense, law enforcement, food and drug inspection, schools, highway construction, and the like). Tax codes vary greatly among countries. In many European countries, wealthy citizens pay considerably higher percentages of their incomes than those in the United States.

Spending Wealth to Gain Prestige

In societies where people devote most of their time to subsistence activities, gradations of wealth are small, kept that way through various cultural mechanisms and systems of reciprocity that serve to spread quite fairly what little wealth exists. It is a different situation in ranked societies where substantial surpluses are produced, and the gap between the have-nots and the have-lots can be considerable. In these societies, showy display for social prestige—known as **conspicuous consumption**—is a strong motivator for the distribution of wealth.

Obviously, excessive efforts to impress others with one's wealth or status also play a prominent role in industrial and postindustrial societies, as individuals compete for prestige. Indeed, many North Americans and Europeans spend much of their lives trying to impress others. This requires the display of symbolic prestige items—designer clothes, substantial jewelry, mansions, big cars, private planes—and fits neatly into an economy based on consumer wants.

A form of conspicuous consumption also occurs in some crop-cultivating and foraging societies—as illustrated by potlatches hosted by the chiefs of various American Indian groups living along the Pacific northwest coast, including the Tlingit, Haida, and Kwakwaka'wakw (Kwakiutl) peoples. A **potlatch** is a ceremonial event in which a village chief publicly gives away stockpiled food and other goods that signify wealth. (The term comes from the Chinook Indian word *patshatl,* which means "gift.")

Traditionally, a chief whose village had built up enough surplus to host such a feast for other villages in the region would give away large piles of sea otter furs, dried salmon, blankets, and other valuables while making boastful speeches about his generosity, greatness, and glorious ancestors. While other chiefs became indebted to him, he reaped the glory of successful and generous leadership and saw his prestige rise. In the future, his own village might face shortages, and he would find

Among Native Americans living along the northwest coast of North America, one gains prestige by giving away valuables at the potlatch feast. Here we see Tlingit clan members dressed in traditional Chilkat and Raven's Tail robes during a recent potlatch in Sitka, Alaska.

himself on the receiving end of a potlatch. Should that happen, he would have to listen to the self-serving and pompous speeches of rival chiefs. Obliged to receive, he would temporarily lose prestige and status.

In extreme displays of wealth, chiefs even destroyed some of their precious possessions. This occurred with some frequency in the second half of the 19th century, after European contact triggered a process of culture change that included new trade wealth. Outsiders might view such grandiose displays as wasteful in the extreme. However, these extravagant giveaway ceremonies have played an ecologically adaptive role in a coastal region where villages alternately faced periods of scarcity and abundance and relied upon alliances and trade relations with one another for long-term survival. The potlatch provided a ceremonial opportunity to strategically redistribute surplus food and goods among allied villages in response to periodic fluctuations in fortune.

A strategy that features this sort of accumulation of surplus goods for the express purpose of displaying wealth and giving it away to raise one's status is known as a **prestige economy.** In contrast to conspicuous consumption in industrial and postindustrial societies, the emphasis is not on amassing goods that then become unavailable to others. Instead, it is on gaining wealth in order to give it away for the sake of prestige and status.

Leveling Mechanisms

The potlatch is an example of a **leveling mechanism**—a cultural obligation compelling prosperous members of a community to give away goods, host public feasts, provide free service, or otherwise demonstrate generosity so that no one permanently accumulates significantly more wealth than anyone else. With leveling mechanisms at work, greater wealth brings greater social pres-

prestige economy Creation of a surplus for the express purpose of gaining prestige through a public display of wealth that is given away as gifts.

leveling mechanism A cultural obligation compelling prosperous members of a community to give away goods, host public feasts, provide free service, or otherwise demonstrate generosity so that no one permanently accumulates significantly more wealth than anyone else.

sure to spend and give generously. In exchange for such demonstrated altruism, a person not only increases his or her social standing in the community, but may also keep disruptive envy at bay.

Underscoring the value of collective well-being over individual self-interest, leveling mechanisms are important in the long-term survival of traditional communities. The potlatch is just one of many cultural varieties of leveling mechanisms. Another example can be found in Maya Indian towns in the highlands of Guatemala and southern Mexico. In these traditional communities, the higher public offices are those of councilmen, judges, and mayors, in addition to various ceremonial leadership positions. Because the people who are called upon to fill these roles are not paid, the positions are known as *cargos* (Spanish for "burdens"). In fact, Maya Indian officeholders are expected to personally pay for the food, liquor, music, fireworks, or whatever is required for community festivals or for feast meals associated with their particular post. For some cargos, the cost can be as much as a man can earn in four years!

After holding a cargo position, a man usually returns to his normal life for a period, during which he may accumulate sufficient resources to campaign for a higher office. Each successful male citizen of the community is socially obliged to serve in the community's cargo system at least once, and the social pressure to do so drives individuals who have once again accumulated surplus wealth to apply for higher offices in order to raise their social status. Ideally, while some individuals gain appreciably more prestige than others in their community, no one has significantly more wealth in the long run than anyone else.

By pressuring members into sharing their wealth in their own community rather than keeping it to themselves or privately investing it elsewhere, leveling mechanisms do more than keep resources in circulation. They also reduce social tensions among relatives, neighbors, and fellow town folk, promoting a collective sense of togetherness. An added practical benefit is that they ensure that necessary services within the community are performed.

Market Exchange

To an economist, **market exchange** has to do with the buying and selling of goods and services, with prices set by rules of supply and demand. Personal loyalties and moral values are not supposed to play a role, but they often do. Since the actual location of the transaction is not

market exchange The buying and selling of goods and services, with prices set by rules of supply and demand.

always relevant in today's world, we must distinguish between the "marketplace" and "market exchange."

Typically, until well into the 20th century, market exchange was carried out in specific localities or *marketplaces*. This is still the case in much of the nonindustrial world and even in numerous centuries-old European and Asian towns and cities. In food-producing societies, marketplaces overseen by a centralized political authority provide the opportunity for farmers or peasants in the surrounding rural territories to exchange some of their livestock and produce for needed items manufactured in factories or in the workshops of craft specialists living (usually) in towns and cities. Thus, some sort of complex division of labor as well as centralized political organization is necessary for the appearance of markets.

The traditional market is local, specific, and contained. Prices are typically set on the basis of face-to-face bargaining rather than by unseen market forces wholly removed from the transaction itself. Notably, sales do not necessarily involve money; instead, goods may be directly exchanged through some form of barter among the specific individuals involved.

In industrializing and industrial societies, many market transactions still take place in a specific identifiable location—including international trade fairs such as the semi-annual Canton Trade Fair in Guangzhou, China, which in spring 2005 featured some 10,000 Chinese enterprises and drew buyers from over 200 countries. However, it is possible and increasingly common for people living in technologically wired parts of the world to buy and sell everything from cattle to cars without ever being in the same city, let alone the same space. For example, think of Internet companies such as eBay where all buying and selling occurs electronically and irrespective of geographic distance. Thus, when people talk about a market in today's industrial or postindustrial world, the particular geographic location where something is bought or sold is often not important at all.

The faceless market exchanges that take place in industrial and postindustrial societies stand in stark contrast to experiences in the marketplaces of nonindustrial societies, which have much of the excitement of a fair. Traditional exchange centers are colorful places where a host of sights, sounds, and smells awaken the senses. Typically, vendors and/or their family members produced the goods they are selling, thereby personalizing the transactions. Dancers and musicians may perform, and feasting and fighting may mark the end of the day. In these markets social relationships and personal interactions are key elements, and noneconomic activities may even overshadow the economic. In short, such markets are gathering places where people renew friendships, see relatives, gossip, and keep up with the world,

VISUAL COUNTERPOINT

In many societies, particularly in developing countries, the market is an important focus of social as well as economic activity, as shown in the photo of a crowded outdoor marketplace in Aswan, Egypt. In contrast, the packer pictured on the left works at an Amazon.com distribution center in Fernley, Nevada, preparing orders purchased on the Internet. With the advent of online shopping, people can buy and sell with no social interaction whatsoever.

while procuring needed goods they cannot produce for themselves.[17]

Money: Invention and Spread of Coins as Means of Exchange

Although there have been marketplaces without money of any sort, money does facilitate trade. **Money** may be defined as something used to make payments for other goods and services as well as to measure their value. Its critical attributes are durability, transportability, divisibility, recognizability, and interchangeability. Items that have been used as money in various societies include salt, shells, precious stones, cacao beans, special beads, livestock, and of course valuable metals such as iron, copper, silver, and gold. Until recently, Indian Ocean cowry shells, for example, were widely used as a means of exchange in parts of Asia, Africa, and the Pacific Ocean. Indicative of its ancient use is the character for "money" in the Chinese writing system, which symbolically represents a cowry shell.

About 5,000 years ago, merchants and others in Mesopotamia (now part of Iraq) went beyond bartering in their trading activities and began using pieces of precious metal such as silver in their transactions. Once they agreed on the value of these pieces as a means of exchange, or money, at least within the boundaries of the political state, more complex commercial developments soon followed. As the means of exchange were standardized in terms of their value, it became easier to accumulate, lend, or borrow money for specified amounts and periods against payment of interest. In due time, some merchants began to do business with money itself and became bankers.

When the use of money began to spread far into neighboring territories and beyond, the metal units were adapted to long-term use, easy storage, and long-distance transportation. In many cultures, such pieces of iron, copper, or silver were cast as miniature models of especially valuable implements like sword blades, axes, or spades. In the ancient Mediterranean kingdom of

---

[17]Plattner, S. (1989). Markets and marketplaces. In S. Plattner (Ed.), *Economic anthropology* (p. 171). Stanford, CA: Stanford University Press.

money Something used to make payments for other goods and services as well as to measure their value.

Lydia (southwestern Turkey), however, these metal units took the shape of small metal disks, distinctively coined according to different size and weight, over 2,600 years ago.[18] Over the next few centuries, metal coins were also standardized in terms of the metal's purity and value, such as 100 units of copper equals 10 units of silver or 1 of gold.

By about 2,000 years ago, the commercial use of such coins was spreading throughout much of Europe and becoming increasingly common in parts of Asia and Africa, especially along trade routes and in urban centers. Meanwhile, new mines were opened to meet the growing demand for precious metals to produce more money. These mining operations, in turn, created growing demands for cheap human labor—demands that were often met by capturing people and forcing them to work as slaves.

About 500 years ago, Spanish explorers in search of wealth and glory discovered the great American civilizations of the Maya, the Aztecs, and the Incas, famous for their great cities, temples, and palaces. Impressed by the vast array of beautiful silver and gold objects, they not only looted Indian temples and palaces, but also lost no time locating the native gold and silver mines. During the first 150 years of Spanish colonial rule in the Americas, more than 7 million pounds of pure silver, much of it cast into heavy bars, was shipped to Spain's seaport city of Seville and later minted into Spanish or other coins. Having moved from hand to hand, pocket to pocket, and generation to generation, many of these coins have circulated around the globe more than once. In using them, merchants and bankers helped set into motion radical economic changes in many traditional societies and introduced what has been called merchant capitalism in many parts of the world.[19]

As revealed in this chapter's Biocultural Connection, there is much more to the story of some traditional non-Western forms of money than their economic exchange value.

LOCAL CULTURES AND ECONOMIC GLOBALIZATION

Failing to overcome cultural biases can have serious economic consequences, especially in this era of globalization. For example, it has led prosperous countries to impose inappropriate development schemes in parts of the world that they regard as economically underdeveloped. Typically, these schemes focus on increasing the target country's gross national product through large-scale pro-

A crowd of protesters demonstrating against World Trade Organization (WTO) policies that favor rich countries over poor ones during the organization's December 2005 meeting in Hong Kong. Established in 1995 and headquartered in Geneva, the WTO is the only global international organization with rules of trade among its 150 member countries.

duction that all too often boosts the well-being of a few but results in poverty, poor health, discontent, and a host of other ills for many.

In order to grow sisal for export to the United States, large-scale plantations were established in Brazil, taking over numerous small farms where peasants grew food to feed themselves. With this change, peasants were forced into the ranks of the unemployed or poorly paid wage laborers. Because they no longer had land for growing their own crops and did not earn enough to buy basic foodstuffs, they faced a dramatic increase in the incidence of malnutrition. Similarly, development projects in Africa, designed to bring about changes in local hydrology, vegetation, and settlement patterns—and even programs aimed at reducing certain diseases—have frequently led directly to *increased* disease rates.[20]

Such failures are tied to the fact that every culture is an integrated system (as illustrated by the barrel model)

---

[18]Davies, G. (2005). *A history of money from the earliest times to present day* (3rd ed.). Cardiff: University of Wales Press.

[19]See also Wolf, E. R. (1982). *Europe and the people without history* (pp. 135–141). Berkeley: University of California Press.

[20]Bodley, J. H. (1990). *Victims of progress* (3rd ed., p. 141). Mountain View, CA: Mayfield.

Biocultural Connection

Cacao: The Love Bean in the Money Tree

Several thousand years ago Indians in the tropical lowlands of southern Mexico discovered how to produce a hot brew from ground, roasted beans. They collected these beans from melon-shaped fruit pods growing in trees identified by today's scientists as *Theobroma cacao*. By adding honey, vanilla, and some flowers for flavoring, they produced a beverage that made them feel good and believed that these beans were gifts from their gods.

Soon, cacao beans became part of long-distance trade networks and appeared in the Mexican highlands, where the Aztec elite adopted this drink brewed from *cacahuatl*, calling it *chocolatl*. In fact, these beans were so highly valued that Aztecs also used them as money. When Spanish invaders conquered Guatemala and Mexico in the 1520s, they adopted the region's practice of using cacao beans as currency inside their new colony. They also embraced the custom of drinking chocolate, which they introduced to Europe, where it became a luxury drink as well as a medicine.[a]

In the next 500 years, chocolate developed into a $14 billion dollar global business, with the United States as top importer of cacao beans or cacao products. Women buy 75 percent of the chocolate products, and on Valentine's Day more than $1 billion worth of chocolate is sold.

What is it about chocolate that makes it a natural love drug? Other than carbohydrates, minerals, and vitamins, it contains about 300 chemicals, including some with mood-altering effects. For instance, cacao beans contain several chemical components that trigger feelings of pleasure in the human brain. In addition to tryptophan, which increases serotonin levels, chocolate also contains phenylethylamine, an amphetaminelike substance that stimulates the body's own dopamine and has slight antidepressant effects. Chocolate contains anandamide (*anan* means "bliss" in Sanskrit), a messenger molecule that triggers the brain's pleasure center. Also naturally pro-

duced in the brain, anandamide's mood-enhancing effect is the same as that obtained from marijuana leaves.[b] Finally, it also contains a mild stimulant called theobromine ("food of god"), which stimulates the human brain's production of natural opiates, reducing pain and increasing feelings of satisfaction and even euphoria.

These chemicals help explain why the last Aztec ruler Montezuma drank so much chocolate. A Spanish eyewitness, who visited his royal palace in the Aztec capital in 1519, later reported that Montezuma's servants sometimes brought their powerful lord "in cups of pure gold a drink made from the cocoa-plant, which they said he took before visiting his wives. . . . I saw them bring in a good fifty large jugs of this chocolate, all frothed up, of which he would drink a little. They always served it with great reverence."[c]

[a] For an excellent cultural history of chocolate, see Coe, S. D., & Coe, M. D. (1996). *The true history of chocolate*. New York: Thames and Hudson; Grivetti, L. E. (2005). From aphrodisiac to health food: A cultural history of chocolate. *Karger Gazette* (68).

[b] Personal communication, Lawrence C. Davis, Kansas State U.

[c] del Castillo, B. D. (1963). *The conquest of New Spain* (pp. 226–227) (translation and introduction by J. M. Cohen). New York: Penguin.

and that a shift in the infrastructure, or economic base, impacts interlinked elements of the society's social structure and superstructure. As the ethnographic examples of the potlatch and the Kula ring show, economic activities in traditional cultures are intricately intertwined with social and political relations and even involve spiritual elements. Development programs that do not take such complexities into consideration may have unintended negative consequences on a society. Fortunately, there is now a growing awareness on the part of development officials that future projects are unlikely to succeed without the expertise that anthropologically trained people can bring to bear.

Achieving a cross-cultural understanding of the economic organizations of other peoples that is not distorted or limited by the logic, hopes, and expectations of one's own society has also become important for corporate executives in today's world.

Recognizing how the economic structures are intertwined with other aspects of a culture could help business corporations avoid problems of the sort experienced by Gerber, when it began selling baby food in Africa. As in the United States, Gerber's labels featured a picture of a smiling baby. Only later did company officials learn that, in Africa, businesses routinely put pictures of the products themselves on the outside label, since many people cannot read. In a similar vein, Frank Perdue's line in ads for Perdue chickens, "It takes a strong man to make a tender chicken," was literally [mis]translated into Spanish as, "It takes an aroused man to make a chicken affectionate."[21]

As globalization increases so does corporate awareness of the cost of such cross-cultural miscues. So it is not surprising that business recruiters on college campuses in North America and elsewhere are now on the lookout for job candidates with the kind of cross-cultural understanding of the world anthropology provides. It is also of note that the business world has discovered that anthropological research methods are

[21] Madison Avenue relevance. (1999). *Anthropology Newsletter* 40 (4), 32.

Anthropology Applied

Anthropology in the Corporate Jungle ▪ By Karen Stephenson

For the first fifteen years of my career as an anthropologist, I did what most people in the discipline had done for more than a century: I focused my research on the cultures of "exotic" peoples living in remote, nonindustrial corners of the world. For me it was the rainforests of Central America and the deserts of the Sahara. Then I decided to turn the lens on my own culture and use anthropology's methods to study businesses, non-profit organizations, and governmental and educational institutions. I became part of a growing wave of corporate anthropologists, so-called because we study corporate groups.

What makes corporate anthropology an interesting addition to our discipline's repertoire is that fieldwork takes place in a contemporary organization rather than in the jungles of Guatemala, New Guinea, or Samoa. And when you think about it, you don't have to go far away to find the exotic. Many of us live in jungles, whether concrete or green and leafy. The challenge for all of us, not just anthropologists, is to critically see the most familiar and mundane cultural practice as a view from afar, and in that shift of perspective to gain new insight about how we live. Looking through an anthropological lens, some of those practices can at times seem quite bizarre!

Imagine, for example, observing a typical office meeting from an anthropological perspective. There are the tribal elders milling around a huge polished wooden slab, shaking hands and pounding each other on the back. The men are all dressed in the same costumes, their "loin cloths" held up by suspenders or a belt, their feet encased in black polished footwear. On occasion a female voice is heard, only to be drowned out by the bleating of the males. And then there's the question of what to do when you are the anthropologist and all of your informants are too busy to talk with you? I resorted to stocking my office

with exotic chocolates from all around the world and sprinkling Hershey's Kisses, like breadcrumbs, down the hallways so that people could find me easily. I was never lonely after that.

There are moments when this work is entertaining. That said, my research is serious business. It has a practical side, a purpose. It provides corporations with insights about their operations that can lead to problem-solving solutions that increase productivity and profitability. Let me offer a specific example.

I served as visiting anthropologist with IBM for ten years from 1990–2000. During that time IBM was struggling to respond to new market demands as the computer industry morphed from mainframes to personal computers in the late 1980s. Their slow reaction prompted their executives to seek help, and I was called in. I was placed in charge of developing a methodology for changing their culture, and, if successful, IBM would apply the same methodology on its many customers and vendors around the world (the inception of the IBM Consulting Group, now a part of Global Services). I explained how I had developed rapid analysis software that could "x-ray" the company's culture—the human

Courtesy of Karen Stephenson

networks of its current work processes. This was possible thanks to a database I'd created of more than 200 examples of corporate networks from all around the world. Using my database, I could quickly diagnose and benchmark IBM's culture to determine the nature of any pathology.

For the next several years, several divisions were analyzed, including their executive leadership. After a statistical analysis was performed, I developed a measure for cultural inertia (a resistance to change) and determined the sunk costs of operational inefficiencies. Fixing the problem was twofold:

1. Reorganizing the company by outsourcing divisions as independent companies partnering with IBM, reducing the overall employee population from 400,000 to 250,000.
2. Restructuring the pay and performance systems for the top executives so that they were rewarded for cooperating as a team rather than competing against neighboring divisions, perversely thwarting the overall organizational goals.

Both solutions were cultural in nature and difficult for those within the culture to detect. But with the help of my x-rays, IBMers saw for themselves how sometimes their best efforts were often misguided, hindering rather than helping. Accepting the findings and recommendations as objective and sound, they were willing to change their behaviors to improve productivity.

I also introduced another change at IBM: I was the first female executive to wear pants. When confronted with the news that I'd breached the fashion code, I just told them that females wearing pants was a more modest and conservative approach, totally in keeping with their cultural values. One vice president threw back his head and laughed: "I never thought of it that way!"

highly effective when it comes to identifying and analyzing what is and is not functioning within a particular corporate way of life. This has given rise to a career specialization known as business or corporate anthropology, as discussed in this chapter's Anthropology Applied.

That said, it is important to note that powerful corporations headquartered in the so-called developed world, often with subsidiaries overseas, are in business to make a profit, not to protect the weak, benefit the poor, support the sick, favor small producers, or save the environment. Their agenda is universally promoted through slogans such as "free trade," "free markets," and "free enterprise." The commercial success of such multinationals does not come without a price, and all too often that price is paid by still surviving indigenous foragers, small farmers, herders, fishermen, local artisans such as weavers and carpenters, and so on. From the viewpoint of these structurally disadvantaged groups of people, such slogans of freedom have the ring of "savage capitalism," a term now often used in Latin America for a new world order in which the powerless feel condemned to dependency and poverty.

Although political authorities in state-organized societies seek to govern and control economic activities for regulation and taxation purposes, they don't always succeed. Either because of insufficient government resources, bureaucratic mismanagement, and official corruption, or because of people seeking to escape from government regulations and tax-collectors, state-organized societies also possess a largely undocumented **informal economy**—a network of producing and circulating marketable commodities, labor, and services that for various reasons escape government control (enumeration, regulation, or other types of public monitoring or auditing). Such enterprises may encompass a range of activities: house cleaning, child care, gardening, repair or construction work, making and selling alcoholic beverages, street peddling, money lending, begging, prostitution,

gambling, drug dealing, pick-pocketing, and labor by illegal foreign workers, to mention just a few.

These off-the-books or black market activities have been known for a long time but generally have long been dismissed by economists as of marginal importance. Yet, in many countries of the world, the informal economy is, in fact, more important than the formal economy. In many places, large numbers of under- and unemployed people who have only limited access to the formal economic sector in effect improvise, "getting by" on scant resources. Meanwhile, more affluent members of society may dodge various regulations in order to maximize returns and/or to vent their frustrations at their perceived loss of self-determination in the face of increasing government regulation.

And now that globalization is connecting national, regional, and local markets in which natural resources, commodities, and human labor are bought and sold, people everywhere in the world face new economic opportunities and confront new challenges. Not only are natural environments more quickly and radically transformed by means of new powerful technologies, but long-established subsistence practices, economic arrangements, social organizations, and associated ideas, beliefs, and values are also under enormous pressure.

What is the future for the world's last remaining food-foraging societies? What about the hundreds of millions of independent herders, farmers, and peasants trying to make a living off the land like their ancestors? How will communities traditionally dependent on manufacturing handmade crafts—like basketry, pottery, weaving, blacksmithing, saddle or furniture making, and so on—fare now that mass-produced machine-made commodities are sold cheaper in nearby stores and markets?

informal economy A network of producing and circulating marketable commodities, labor, and services that for various reasons escape government control.

Questions for Reflection

1. Imagine that you have gone to live with a group of nomadic foragers who meet the challenges of survival by hunting, fishing, and gathering, rather than by shopping. How would that way of life challenge your current attitude on social relations, possessions, and the natural environment?

2. Consider the differences between reciprocity and market exchange. What role does each play in your own society?

3. As the potlatch ceremony shows, prestige may be gained by giving away wealth. Does such a prestige-building mechanism exist in your own society? If so, how does it work?

4. In the Kula ring, men of influence participate in a wide social network based on balanced reciprocity. Why would such a system not survive if individuals in this ring begin to operate on the basis of negative reciprocity?

5. As discussed in this chapter, economic relations in traditional cultures are usually wrapped up in social, political, and even spiritual issues. Can you think of any examples in your own society in which the economic sphere is inextricably intertwined with other structures in the cultural system? Would tinkering with the economic sphere affect these other aspects of your culture?

Suggested Readings

Blumberg, R. L. (1991). *Gender, family, and the economy: The triple overlap*. Newbury Park, CA: Sage.

A look at the interrelationship of gender, domestic life, and the economy.

Dalton, G. (1971). *Traditional tribal and peasant economies: An introductory survey of economic anthropology*. Reading, MA: Addison-Wesley.

This is just what the title says it is, by a major specialist in economic anthropology.

Halperin, R. H. (1994). *Cultural economies: Past and present*. Austin: University of Texas Press.

A cross-cultural approach to analyzing economic processes in cultural systems.

Plattner, S. (Ed.). (1989). *Economic anthropology*. Stanford, CA: Stanford University Press.

A collection of essays from twelve scholars in the field concerning a variety of issues ranging from economic behavior in foraging, horticultural, and "preindustrial" state, peasant, and industrial societies; to gender roles, common property resources, informal economics in industrial societies; and mass marketing in urban areas.

Wilk, R. R. (1996). *Economics and cultures: An introduction to economic anthropology*. Boulder, CO: Westview Press.

This lively primer traces the history of the dialogue between anthropology and economics and identifies the subdiscipline's basic practical and theoretical problems.

Thomson Audio Study Products

Enjoy the MP3-ready Audio Lecture Overviews for each chapter and a comprehensive audio glossary of key terms for quick study and review. Whether walking to class, doing laundry, or studying at your desk, you now have the freedom to choose when, where, and how you interact with your audio-based educational media. See the preface for information on how to access this on-the-go study and review tool.

The Anthropology Resource Center

www.thomsonedu.com/anthropology

The Anthropology Resource Center provides extended learning materials to reinforce your understanding of key concepts in the four fields of anthropology. For each of the four fields, the Resource Center includes dynamic exercises including video exercises, map exercises, simulations, and "Meet the Scientists" interviews, as well as critical thinking questions that can be assigned and e-mailed to instructors. The Resource Center also provides breaking news in anthropology and interesting material on applied anthropology to help you link what you are learning to the world around you.

20 Sex, Marriage, and Family

© Chao-Yang Chan/Alamy

CHALLENGE ISSUE

All around the world humans face the challenge of managing sexual relations and establishing social alliances essential to the survival of individuals and their offspring. Marriage and family, in various forms, provide cultural structures for meeting this challenge. Because each new generation becomes responsible for maintaining a group's overall well-being and advancing its collective interests, essential cultural know-how must be passed on to children to ensure the group's long-term survival. Adjusting to distinct environments and facing specific challenges, each group establishes its own arrangements in terms of child-rearing tasks, gender relations, household and family structures, and residence patterns. Because marriage, in all its varied forms, has played a fundamental role in determining these arrangements, wedding rituals are usually public—and often elaborate—events. In China they often include a procession, as pictured here.

What Is Marriage?

A nonethnocentric definition of marriage is a culturally sanctioned union between two or more people that establishes certain rights and obligations between the people, between them and their children, and between them and their in-laws. Although most marriages around the world involve unions between one woman and one man, numerous other arrangements exist. For example, many cultures not only permit but encourage marriage of one man to multiple wives. The specific form marriage takes is related to who has rights and obligations to offspring that may result from the marital union, as well as how property is distributed. In contrast to mating—the sexual bonding that all animal species do—marriage is a cultural institution, backed by economic, social, legal, and ideological forces.

What Is the Family?

Although the idea of family means different things to different people, in anthropological terms it is a group of two or more people related by blood, marriage, or adoption. The family may take many forms, ranging from a single parent with one or more children, to a married couple or polygamous spouses with offspring, to several generations of parents and their children. The particular form family takes within a society is related to distinct social, historical, and ecological circumstances.

What Is the Difference Between Family and Household?

Households are task-oriented residential units within which economic production, consumption, inheritance, child rearing, and shelter are organized and accomplished. In the vast majority of human societies, a household consists of a family or part of a family or their core members, even though some household members may not be relatives of the family around which it is built. In some societies, families may be less important in people's thinking than the households in which they live.

455

Among Trobriand Islanders in the southwestern Pacific, whose Kula voyages we examined in the previous chapter, children who have reached the age of 7 or 8 years begin playing erotic games and imitating adult seductive attitudes. Within another four or five years they begin to pursue sexual partners in earnest—experimenting sexually with a variety of individuals. By the time they are in their mid-teens, meetings between lovers may take up most of the night, and affairs are apt to last for several months. Ultimately, lovers begin to meet the same partner again and again, rejecting the advances of others. When the couple is ready, they appear together one morning outside the young man's house as a way of announcing their intention to be married.

For young Trobrianders, attracting sexual partners is an important matter, and they spend a great deal of time making themselves look attractive and seductive. Youthful conversations during the day are loaded with sexual innuendo, and magical spells as well as small gifts are employed to entice a prospective sex partner to the beach at night or to the house in which boys sleep apart from their parents. Because girls, too, sleep apart from their parents, youths and adolescents have considerable freedom in arranging their love affairs. Boys and girls play this game as equals, with neither having an advantage over the other.

Until the latter part of the 20th century, the Trobriand attitude toward adolescent sexuality was in marked contrast to that of most Western cultures in Europe and North America where individuals were not supposed to have sexual relations before or outside of marriage. Since

© Hideo Haga/HAGA/The Image Works

To attract lovers, young Trobriand men and woman must look as attractive and seductive as possible. This woman's beauty has been enhanced by face painting and adornments given by her father.

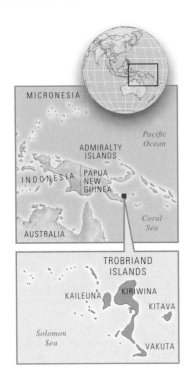

then, practices in much of Europe and North America have converged toward those of the Trobrianders, even though the traditional ideal of premarital abstinence has not been abandoned entirely.

As noted by anthropologist Annette Weiner who did ethnographic research among Trobrianders, all of this sexual activity is not a frivolous, adolescent pastime. Instead, she proposes that attracting lovers is:

> the first step toward entering the adult world of strategies, where the line between influencing others while not allowing others to gain control of oneself must be carefully learned. . . . Sexual liaisons give adolescents the time and occasion to experiment with all the possibilities and problems that adults face in creating relationships with those who are not relatives. Individual wills may clash, and the achievement of one's desire takes patience, hard work, and determination. The adolescent world of lovemaking has its own dangers and disillusionments. Young people, to

the degree they are capable, must learn to be both careful and fearless.[1]

CONTROL OF SEXUAL RELATIONS

One important human characteristic is the ability for the human female, like the human male, to engage in sexual relations at any time she wants or whenever her culture deems it appropriate. Although this ability to perform at any time when provided with the appropriate cue is not unusual for male mammals in general, it is unusual for females. Among most primate species, females whose offspring are weaned but who have not yet become pregnant again are likely to engage in sexual activity around the time of ovulation (approximately once a month), at which time they advertise their availability through highly visible physical signs. Otherwise, they are little interested in such activity. Bonobos, one of the species most closely related to us, are an exception. Whereas among chimpanzees, female genital swelling indicates ovulation and signals readiness for sexual activity, female bonobos are in a constant state of genital swelling, so that sexual activity may occur before, during, and after ovulation. Moreover, it may take place between individuals in virtually all combinations of ages and sex.

Among humans, female fertility is not signaled by any visible display, and couples are likely to engage in sex at any time, even when the female is pregnant. In some human societies, intercourse during pregnancy is thought to promote the growth of the fetus. Among Trobriand Islanders, for example, a child's identity is thought to come from its mother, but it is the father's job to build up and nurture the child, which he begins to do before birth through frequent intercourse with its mother.

As for the homosexual behavior seen among bonobos, that, too, is not uncommon among humans. While such behavior is absolutely condemned in some societies, many others are indifferent about such personal practices and openly tolerate individuals who engage in homosexual activities. Most languages do not even have a special term to distinguish such behavior as significant in its own right. In fact, in some cultures certain prescribed male-to-male sexual acts are part of male initiation rituals required of all boys to become respected adult men.[2] Certain New Guinea societies, for example, see the transmission of semen from older to younger boys, through oral sex, as vital for building up the strength needed to

protect against the supposedly debilitating effects of adult heterosexual intercourse.[3]

Even in the United States, with its long-standing obsession about and hostility toward homosexuality, the phenomenon is far from uncommon. Homosexuality is found in diverse contexts: from lifelong loving relationships to casual sexual encounters to supposedly celibate clergy to inmate populations in both men's and women's prisons. During the past few decades, public denigration or condemnation of homosexuality has diminished in general, and same-sex relationships have become an openly accepted part of the cosmopolitan lifestyle in urban cultural centers such as Amsterdam, London, and San Francisco. That said, the social rules and cultural meanings of *all* sexual behavior are subject to great variability from one society to another.

The ability of females as well as males to engage in sex at any time would have been advantageous to early humans and their ancestors to the extent that it acted, not alone but with other factors, to tie members of both sexes more firmly to the social groups so crucial to their survival. However, although sexual activity can reinforce group ties, it can also disrupt harmonious social relationships. The solution to this problem is to bring sexual activity under cultural control. Thus, just as a culture tells people what, when, and how they should eat, so does it tell them when, where, how, and with whom they should have sex.

Marriage and the Regulation of Sexual Relations

Given the potential for violent conflict resulting from unregulated sexual competition and the challenges of rearing and socializing the children that result from sexual contact, it is not surprising that all societies have cultural rules that seek to regulate those relations.

In much of North America and Europe, the traditional ideal was that all sexual activity outside of marriage was taboo. Individuals were expected to establish a family through marriage, by which one gained an exclusive right of sexual access to another person. According to strict Judeo-Christian law, as prescribed in the Book of Leviticus (20:10), adultery was punishable by death: "And the man that committeth adultery with another man's wife . . . , the adulterer and the adulteress shall surely be put to death." Deuteronomy (22:24) adds: "Then ye shall bring them both out unto the gate of that city, and ye shall stone them with stones that they die."

[1]Weiner, A. B. (1988). *The Trobrianders of Papua New Guinea* (p. 17). New York: Holt, Rinehart & Winston.

[2]Kirkpatrick, R. C. (2000). The evolution of human homosexual behavior. *Current Anthropology 41*, 385.

[3]Herdt, G. H. (1993). Semen transactions in Sambia culture. In D. N. Suggs & A. W. Mirade (Eds.), *Culture and human sexuality* (pp. 298–327). Pacific Grove, CA: Brooks/Cole.

VISUAL COUNTERPOINT

Although homosexuality is a widespread human phenomenon, in some societies it faces repression or ridicule. In parts of the United States, for example, public displays of same-sex affection between men in particular are often looked upon as distasteful or even disgusting. One nationwide exception is the football field, where an extreme measure of rough-and-tumble masculine behavior makes it possible for players to pat each other on the behind, exchange celebratory hugs, and even leap into each other's arms without bringing their sexual orientation into question.

Many centuries later, among Christian colonists in 17th- and 18th-century New England, adultery by women remained a serious crime. While it did not lead to stoning, women so accused were shunned by the community and could even be imprisoned. As recounted in *The Scarlet Letter* by Nathaniel Hawthorne, the adulteress was forced to have the letter "A" stitched on her dress, publicly signifying her transgression.

Such restrictions exist today in many traditional Muslim societies in northern Africa and western Asia, where age-old Shariah law continues or has been reinstated to regulate social behavior in strict accordance with religious standards of morality. Under this law,

THOMSON AUDIO STUDY PRODUCTS Take advantage of the MP3-ready Audio Lecture Overviews and comprehensive audio glossary of key terms for each chapter. See the preface for information on how to access this on-the-go study and review tool.

marriage A culturally sanctioned union between two or more people that establishes certain rights and obligations between the people, between them and their children, and between them and their in-laws. Such marriage rights and obligations most often include, but are not limited to, sex, labor, property, child rearing, exchange, and status.

women found guilty of having sexual relations outside marriage can be sentenced to death by stoning. In northern Nigeria, for example, a Muslim woman who committed adultery and had a child outside marriage was sentenced to death in 2002. Her sentence was ultimately overturned by an Islamic appeals court, but it nonetheless drove home the rule of Shariah law. Turning legal transgressions into a public spectacle, authorities reinforce public awareness of the rules of social conduct.

One positive side effect of such restrictive rules of sexual behavior is that they may limit the spread of sexually transmitted diseases. For instance, the global epidemic of HIV/AIDS has had relatively little impact in sexually restrictive societies. Such societies, however, are a minority. In fact, most cultures in the world are much more relaxed about sexuality and do not sharply regulate personal practices. Indeed, a majority of all cultures are considered sexually permissive or semi-permissive (the former having few or no restrictions on sexual experimentation before marriage, the latter allowing some experimentation but less openly). A minority of known societies—about 15 percent—have rules requiring that sexual involvement take place only within marriage.

This brings us to an anthropological definition of **marriage**—a culturally sanctioned union between two or more people that establishes certain rights and obligations between the people, between them and their children, and between them and their in-laws. Such marriage rights and obligations most often include, but are not limited to, sex, labor, property, child rearing, exchange, and status. Thus defined, marriage is universal. Notably, our definition of marriage refers to "people" rather than "a man and a woman" because in some countries same-sex marriages are considered socially acceptable and allowed by law, even though opposite-sex marriages are far more common. We will return to this point later in the chapter.

Sexual and Marriage Practices among the Nayar

In many cultures, marriage is considered the central and most important social institution. In such cultures, people will spend considerable time and energy on maintaining this institution. They may do so in various ways, including highlighting the ritual moment when the wedding takes place, festively memorializing the event at designated times such as anniversaries, and making it difficult to divorce.

In some societies, however, marriage is a relatively marginal institution and is not considered central to the establishing and maintenance of family life and society. For instance, marriage has lost much of its traditional significance in the Scandinavian societies of Iceland, Norway, Sweden, and Denmark, in part due to changes in the political economy, more balanced gender relations, and, last but not least, the shared public benefits of these capitalist welfare states.

But the relative insignificance of marriage is not unique to these wealthy European nations. For instance, this institution is also of marginal significance in the family life of the Nayar of Southwest India. Like the Scandinavians and Trobriand Islanders noted above, the Nayar are one of many examples of sexually permissive cultures.[4] A landowning warrior caste, their estates are held by corporations of sorts made up of kinsmen related in the female line. These blood relatives live together in a large household, with the eldest male serving as manager. Traditionally, Nayar boys began military training around the age of 7, and from this time through much of their young adulthood, they were away from home for significant stretches of time for military purposes.

Three traditional Nayar transactions are of interest in our discussion of sexual and marriage practices. The first occurred shortly before a girl experienced her first menstruation. It involved a ceremony that joined her with a "ritual husband" in a temporary union. This union, which did not necessarily involve sexual relations, lasted for a few days and then broke up. (Neither indi-

[4]Our interpretation of the Nayar follows Goodenough, W. H. (1970). *Description and comparison in cultural anthropology* (pp. 6–11). Chicago: Aldine.

vidual had any further obligation, although later, when the girl became a woman, she and her children typically participated in ritual mourning for the man when he died.) This temporary union established the girl as an adult ready for motherhood and eligible for sexual activity with men approved by her household.

The second transaction took place when a young Nayar woman entered into a continuing sexual liaison with a man approved by her family. This was a formal relationship that required the man to present her with gifts three times each year until the relationship was terminated. In return, the man could spend the nights with her. In spite of continuing sexual privileges, however, this "visiting husband" had no obligation to support his sex partner economically, nor was her home regarded as his home. In fact, she may have had such an arrangement with more than one man at the same time. Regardless of the number of men with whom she was involved, this second Nayar transaction, their version of marriage, clearly specified who had sexual rights to whom and included rules that deterred conflicts between the men.

In the absence of effective birth control devices, the usual outcome of sexual activity between individuals of opposite sex is that, sooner or later, the woman becomes pregnant. When this happens among the Nayar, one of the men with whom she has a relationship (who may or may not be the biological father) must formally acknowledge paternity. He does this by making gifts to the woman and the midwife. This third transaction establishes the child's birth rights. In this sense, it is the counterpart of the registration of birth in Western societies, which clearly establishes motherhood and fatherhood. However, once a man has formally acknowledged fatherhood by gift giving, he may continue to take interest in the child, but he has no further obligations. Support and education for the child are the responsibility of the mother and her brothers with whom she and her offspring live.

Indeed, unlike most other cultural groups in the world, the Nayar household includes only the mother, her children, and her other blood relatives, technically known as **consanguineal kin.** It does not include any of the "husbands." Nor does it include any other people related through marriage, technically known as **affinal kin.** In other words, sisters and their offspring all live together with their brothers and their mother and her brothers. This arrangement answers the need for security in a cultural group where, traditionally, warfare repeatedly pulled young men away from their homes. Among the Nayar, sexual relations are forbidden between consanguineal relatives and thus are permitted only with individuals who live in other households. This brings us to another human universal: the incest taboo.

The Incest Taboo

Just as marriage in its various forms is found in all cultures, so is the **incest taboo**—the prohibition of sexual contact between certain close relatives. But, what is defined as "close" is not the same in all cultures. Moreover, such definitions may be subject to change over time. The scope and details of the taboo vary across cultures and time, but almost all societies past and present strongly forbid sexual relations at least between parents and children and nearly always between siblings. In some societies the taboo extends to other close relatives, such as cousins, and even some relatives linked through marriage.

Anthropologists have long been fascinated by the incest taboo and have proposed many explanations for its cross-cultural existence and variation. The simplest explanation, based on the idea of "human nature," is that our species has an "instinctive" repulsion for incest. It has been documented that human beings raised together have less sexual attraction for one another. However, by itself this "familiarity breeds contempt" argument may simply substitute the result for the cause. The incest taboo ensures that children and their parents, who are constantly in close contact, avoid regarding one another as sexual objects. Besides this, if an instinctive horror of incest exists, how do we account for the far from rare violations of the incest taboo? (In the United States, for

instance, an estimated 10 to 14 percent of children under 18 years of age have been involved in incestuous relations.[5])

Moreover, so-called instinctive repulsion doesn't explain institutionalized incest, such as that requiring the divine ruler of the Inca empire in ancient Peru be married to his own (half) sister. Sharing the same father, both siblings belonged to the political dynasty that derived its sacred right to rule the empire from Inti, its ancestral Sun God. And by virtue of this royal lineage's godly origin, their children could claim the same sacred political status as their human god father and mother. Ancient emperors in Egypt also practiced such religiously prescribed incest based on a similar claim to godly status.

Early students of genetics argued that the incest taboo prevents the harmful effects of inbreeding. While this is so, it is also true that, as with domestic animals, inbreeding can increase desired characteristics as well as detrimental ones. Furthermore, undesirable effects will show up sooner than without inbreeding, so whatever genes are responsible for them are quickly eliminated from the population. That said, a preference for a genetically different mate does tend to maintain a higher level of genetic diversity within a population, and in evolution this variation works to a species' advantage. Without genetic diversity a species cannot adapt biologically to environmental change.

The inbreeding- or biological-avoidance theory can be challenged on several fronts. Detailed census records made in Roman Egypt about 2,000 years ago show that brother–sister marriages were not uncommon among ordinary members of the farming class.[6] Moreover, in a sample of 129 societies, anthropologist Nancy Thornhill found that only fifty-seven had specific rules against parent–child or sibling incest. Twice that number (114) had explicit rules to control activity with cousins, in-laws, or both.[7]

Some anthropologists have argued that the incest taboo exists as a cultural means to preserve the stability and integrity of the family, which is essential to maintaining social order. Sexual relations between members other than the husband and wife would introduce competition, destroying the harmony of a social unit fundamental to social order. A truly convincing explanation of the incest taboo has yet to be advanced.

---

consanguineal kin Biologically related relatives, commonly referred to as blood relatives.
affinal kin People related through marriage.
incest taboo The prohibition of sexual contact between certain close relatives, usually parent and child and sibling relations at a minimum.

[5]Whelehan, P. (1985). Review of incest, a biosocial view. *American Anthropologist 87*, 678. See also Langan, P., & Harlow, C. (1994). *Child rape victims, 1992.* Washington, D.C.: Bureau of Justice Statistics, U.S. Department of Justice.

[6]Leavitt, G. C. (1990). Sociobiological explanations of incest avoidance: A critical review of evidential claims. *American Anthropologist 92*, 982.

[7]Thornhill, N. (1993). Quoted in W. A. Haviland & R. J. Gordon (Eds.), *Talking about people* (p. 127). Mountain View, CA: Mayfield.

Biocultural Connection

Marriage Prohibitions in the United States
By Martin Ottenheimer

In the United States, every state has laws prohibiting some type of relatives from marrying each other. There is complete agreement when it comes to prohibiting parent–child marriage and preventing full siblings from marrying, but the laws vary when it comes to more distant relatives. Thirty-one states prohibit first cousins from marrying while nineteen do not. Furthermore, the prohibitions are not limited to people related by birth. A dozen states also forbid certain step-relatives and in-laws from intermarrying.

Although the marriage prohibitions apply to people not related by birth, North Americans commonly believe that these prohibitions are based on biological factors. It is assumed that the prohibitions protect families from potential genetic defects in children of parents who are biologically "too close." The

first-cousin prohibitions, in particular, are often defended for this reason.

There are two major problems with this idea. First, the cousin prohibitions began to be enacted in the United States around the middle of the 19th century, long before the emergence of modern genetics. Second, modern genetic research has shown that first-cousin marriage does not present any significantly greater risk to offspring than that from parents who are not related. Why, then, do some North Americans maintain this myth?

In the 19th-century United States, an evolutionary model of humans that included a notion about human progress dependent upon outbreeding became widely accepted. Cousin marriage was thought to be characteristic of savagery, considered a form of degeneration based on inbreeding, believed to inhibit the

intellectual development of humans, and feared as a threat to civilized life. With the development of modern genetics, it was wrongly assumed that genetic data supported this now-discredited evolutionary dogma.

Human reproduction is a biological process situated in a cultural context. Each culture develops a particular understanding about the nature of reproduction. This can change over time. At present, the Western model of reproduction is undergoing a transformation stimulated by the recent discovery of mitochondrial DNA and the introduction of new reproductive technologies.

The process well illustrates that biological processes and culture are intimately intertwined, each affecting and being affected by the other.

Endogamy and Exogamy

Whatever its cause, the utility of the incest taboo can be seen by examining its effects on social structure. Closely related to prohibitions against incest are cultural rules against **endogamy** (from Greek *endon,* "within," and *-gamos,* "marriage"), or marriage within a particular group of individuals (cousins and in-laws, for example). If the group is defined as one's immediate family alone, then societies generally prohibit or at least discourage endogamy, thereby promoting **exogamy** (from Greek *exo,* "outside," and *-gamos,* "marriage"), or marriage outside the group. Yet, a society that practices exogamy at one level may practice endogamy at another. Among the Trobriand Islanders, for example, each individual has to marry outside of his or her own clan and lineage (exogamy). However, since eligible sex partners are to be found within one's own community, village endogamy is commonly practiced.

Interestingly, societies vary widely concerning which relatives are or are not covered by rules of exogamy. For example, first cousins are prohibited from marrying each other in many countries where the Roman Catholic Church has long been a dominant institution. Such marriages are also illegal in thirty-one of the United States. Yet, in numerous other societies, first cousins are pre-

ferred spouses.[8] (See a discussion of U. S. marriage prohibitions in the Biocultural Connection.)

Early anthropologists suggested that our ancestors discovered the advantage of intermarriage as a means of creating bonds of friendship. French anthropologist Claude Lévi-Strauss elaborated on this idea. He saw exogamy as a form of inter-group social exchange in which "wife-giving" and "wife-taking" created social networks and alliances between distinct communities. By widening the human network, a larger number of people could pool natural resources and cultural information, including technology and other useful knowledge. (For more on this, see Anthropologist of Note.)

Building on Lévi-Strauss' theory, other anthropologists have proposed that exogamy is an important means of building and maintaining political alliances and promoting trade between groups, thereby ensuring mutual

---

[8]Ottenheimer, M. (1996). *Forbidden relatives: The American myth of cousin marriage* (pp. 116–133). Champaign: University of Illinois Press.

endogamy Marriage within a particular group or category of individuals.
exogamy Marriage outside the group.

Anthropologists of Note

Claude Lévi-Strauss (b. 1908)

Claude Lévi-Strauss is the leading exponent of French structuralism, which posits that the human mind imposes order by separating the perceived world into elementary bits of basic information. From this theoretical perspective, culture is viewed as the product of an underlying universal pattern of thought. Each culture is shaped and influenced by its unique physical and social environment as well as its history. Thus, cultures may vary considerably, even though the basic structure of the human thought processes responsible for them is the same for all people everywhere. The task of the anthropologist is to explain the fundamental principles by which humans accomplish this process and to uncover these underlying patterns.

According to Lévi-Strauss, human thought processes are structured into contrastive pairs of polar opposites, such as light versus dark, good versus evil, nature versus culture, dry versus wet, raw versus cooked, and male versus female. The ultimate contrastive pair is that of "self" versus "others," which is necessary for true symbolic communication to occur and upon which culture depends. Communication is a reciprocal exchange, which is extended to include goods and marital partners. Hence, the incest taboo stems from this fundamental contrastive pair of "self" versus "others." From this universal taboo are built the many and varied marriage rules ethnographers have described.

© Brissard Figaro/Getty Images

protection and access to needed goods and resources not otherwise available. Forging wider kinship networks, exogamy also functions to integrate distinctive groups and thus potentially reduces violent conflict.

Distinction Between Marriage and Mating

Having defined marriage, in part, in terms of sexual access, we must make clear the distinction between marriage and mating. All animals, including humans, mate—some for life and some not, some with a single individual and some with several. Mates are secured and held solely through personal effort and mutual consent. (Rape occurs when someone is pressured by one or more other individuals to submit to sexual acts, in particular sexual intercourse, by force. There exist a variety of cross-cultural differences in whether and how rapes are condoned or condemned.)

In contrast to mating, which is a personal affair, marriage is a culturally recognized right. Only marriage is backed by social, political, and ideological factors that regulate sexual relations as well as reproductive rights and obligations. Even among the Nayar, discussed above,

monogamy Marriage in which both partners have just one spouse.

where marriage seems to involve little other than a sexual relationship, a woman's husband is legally obligated to provide her with gifts at specified intervals. Nor may a Nayar woman legally have sex with a man to whom she is not married. Thus, while mating is biological, marriage is cultural. This is evident when we consider the various forms that marriage takes cross-culturally.

FORMS OF MARRIAGE

Within societies, and all the more so across cultures, we see contrasts in the constructs and contracts of marriage. Indeed, as evident in the definition of marriage given above, this institution comes in various forms—and these forms are distinct in terms of the number and gender of spouses involved.

Monogamy

Monogamy—marriage in which both partners have just one spouse—is the most common form of marriage worldwide. In North America and most of Europe, it is the only legally recognized form of marriage. Not only are other forms prohibited there, but also systems of inheritance, whereby property and wealth are transferred from one generation to the next, are based on the institution of monogamous marriage. In some parts of the world, such as North America and Europe where divorce rates are high and divorcees typically remarry, an increasingly common form of marriage is **serial monogamy,** whereby an individual marries a series of partners in succession.

Polygamy

While monogamy is the most common marriage form worldwide, it is not the most preferred. That distinction goes to **polygamy** (one individual having multiple spouses)—specifically to **polygyny,** in which a man is married to more than one woman. Favored in about 80 to 85 percent of the world's cultures, polygyny is commonly practiced in parts of Asia and much of sub-Saharan Africa.[9]

Although polygyny is the favored marriage form in these places, monogamy exceeds it, and the reason for this is economic rather than moral. In many polygynous societies, where a groom is usually expected to compensate a bride's family in cash or kind, a man must be fairly wealthy to be able to afford more than one wife. Recent multiple surveys of twenty-five sub-Saharan African countries where polygyny is common show that it declined by about half between the 1970s and 2001 but nonetheless remains highly significant with an overall average of 25 percent of married women in polygynous unions.[10]

Polygyny is particularly common in traditional food-producing societies that support themselves by herding grazing animals or growing crops and where women do the bulk of cultivation. Under these conditions, women are valued both as workers and as child bearers. Because the labor of wives in polygynous households generates wealth, and little support is required from husbands, the wives have a strong bargaining position within the household. Often, they have considerable freedom of movement and some economic independence from the sale of crafts or crops. Wealth-generating polygyny is found in its fullest elaboration in parts of sub-Saharan Africa and southwestern Asia, though it is known elsewhere as well.[11]

In societies practicing wealth-generating polygyny, most men and women do enter into polygynous marriages, although some are able to do so earlier in life than others. This is made possible by a female-biased sex ratio and/or a mean age at marriage for females that is significantly below that for males. In fact, this marriage pattern is frequently found in societies where violence, including war, is common and where many young males lose their lives in fighting. Their high combat mortality results in a population where women outnumber men.

By contrast, in societies where men are more heavily involved in productive work, generally only a small minority of marriages are polygynous. Under these circumstances, women are more dependent on men for support, so they are valued as child bearers more than for the work they do. This is commonly the case in pastoral nomadic societies where men are the primary owners and tenders of livestock. This makes women especially vulnerable if they prove incapable of bearing children, which is one reason a man may seek another wife.

Another reason for a man to take on secondary wives is to demonstrate his high position in society. But where men do most of the productive work, they must work extremely hard to support more than one wife, and few actually do so. Usually, it is the exceptional hunter or male shaman ("medicine man") in a food-foraging society or a particularly wealthy man in a horticultural, agricultural, or pastoral society who is most apt to practice polygyny. When he does, it is usually of the *sororal* type, with the co-wives being sisters. Having lived their lives together before marriage, the sisters continue to do so with their husband, instead of occupying separate dwellings of their own.

Polygyny also occurs in a few places in Europe. In 1972, for example, English laws concerning marriage changed to accommodate immigrants who traditionally practiced polygyny. Since that time polygamous marriages have been legal in England for some specific religious minorities, including Muslims and Sephardic Jews. According to one family law specialist, the real impetus behind this law change was a growing concern that "destitute immigrant wives, abandoned by their husbands, [were] overburdening the welfare state."[12]

[9]Lloyd, C. B. (Ed.). (2005). *Growing up global: The changing transitions to adulthood in developing countries* (pp. 450–453). Washington, D.C.: National Academies Press, Committee on Population, National Research Council, and Institute of Medicine of the National Academies.

[10]Lloyd, C. B. (Ed.). (2005). *Growing up global: The changing transitions to adulthood in developing countries* (pp. 450–453). Washington, D.C.: National Academies Press, Committee on Population, National Research Council, and Institute of Medicine of the National Academies.

[11]White, D. R. (1988). Rethinking polygyny: Co-wives, codes, and cultural systems. *Current Anthropology 29,* 529–572.

[12]Cretney, S. (2003). *Family law in the twentieth century: A history* (pp. 72–73). New York: Oxford University Press.

serial monogamy A marriage form in which an individual marries or lives with a series of partners in succession.
polygamy One individual having multiple spouses at the same time; from the Greek words *poly* ("many") and *gamous* ("marriage").
polygyny Marriage of a man to two or more women at the same time; a form of polygamy.

VISUAL **COUNTER**POINT

A Christian polygamist with his three wives and children in front of their dormitory-style home in Utah, and a Baranarna man of Upper Guinea with his two wives and children.

Even in the United States where it is illegal, somewhere between 20,000 and 60,000 people in the Rocky Mountain states live in households made up of a man with two or more wives.[13] Most consider themselves Mormons, even though the official Mormon Church does not approve of the practice. A growing minority, however, call themselves "Christian polygamists," citing the Bible as justification.[14] Despite its illegality, regional law enforcement officials have adopted a "live and let live" attitude toward polygyny in their region. One woman—a lawyer and one of nine co-wives—expresses her attitude toward polygyny as follows:

> I see it as the ideal way for a woman to have a career and children. In our family, the women can help each other care for the children. Women in monogamous relationships don't have that luxury. As I see it, if this lifestyle didn't already exist, it would have to be invented to accommodate career women.[15]

[13]Egan, T. (1999, February 28). The persistence of polygamy. *New York Times Magazine,* 52.

[14]Wolfson, H. (2000, January 22). Polygamists make the Christian connection. *Burlington Free Press,* 2c.

[15]Johnson, D. (1996). Polygamists emerge from secrecy, seeking not just peace but respect. In W. A. Haviland & R. J. Gordon (Eds.),

polyandry   Marriage of a woman to two or more men at one time; a form of polygamy.

In some societies, if a husband dies leaving a wife and children, it is customary that the wife marry the dead man's brother—but this does not preclude the brother having another wife then or in the future. This custom, called the *levirate,* not only provides social security for the widow and her children but also is a way for the husband's family to maintain the established relationship with her family and their rights over her sexuality and her future children: It acts to preserve relationships previously established. When a man marries the sister of his dead wife, it is called the *sororate;* in essence, a family of "wife givers" supplies one of "wife takers" with another spouse to take the dead one's place. In societies that have the levirate and sororate, the established in-law relationship between the two families is maintained even after the spouse's death.

Although monogamy and polygyny are the most common forms of marriage in the world today, other forms do occur. **Polyandry,** the marriage of one woman to two or more men simultaneously, is known in only a few societies, perhaps in part because a woman's life expectancy is usually longer than a man's, and female infant mortality is somewhat lower, so a surplus of women in a society is likely.

Fewer than a dozen societies are known to have favored this form of marriage, but they involve people as widely separated from one another as the eastern Inuit (Eskimos), Marquesan Islanders of Polynesia, and Tibet-

Talking about people (2nd ed., pp. 129–131). Mountain View, CA: Mayfield.

ans. In Tibet, where inheritance is in the male line and arable land is limited, the marriage of brothers to a single woman (*fraternal polyandry*) keeps the land together by preventing it from being repeatedly subdivided among sons from one generation to the next. Unlike monogamy, it also holds down population growth, thereby avoiding increased pressures on resources. Finally, among Tibetans who practice a mixed economy of farming, herding, and trading, fraternal polyandry provides the household with an adequate pool of male labor for all three subsistence activities.[16]

Other Forms of Marriage

There are several other marriage forms, each with its own particular cultural expressions and reasons for being. For instance, in a few societies the social practice of **group marriage** exists. Also known as *co-marriage,* this is a rare arrangement in which several men and women have sexual access to one another. Among Eskimos in northern Alaska, for instance, sexual relations between unrelated individuals implied ties of mutual aid and support. In order to create or strengthen such ties, a man could share his wife with another man for temporary sexual relationships:

> Thus, in attracting and holding members of a hunting crew, an *umialik* [whaleboat headman] could lend his wife to a crew member and borrow that man's wife in turn. These men thereafter entered into a partnership relationship, one virtually as strong as kinship. The children of such men, in fact, retained a recognized relationship to each other by virtue of the wife exchange of their parents.[17]

In contrast to group marriage, there are also arrangements anthropologists categorize as **fictive marriage**—marriage by proxy to the symbols of someone not physically present in order to establish a social status for a spouse and heirs. One major reason for such a marriage is to control rights to property in the next generation. One type of fictive marriage occurs in several traditional African societies, most famously among Nuer cattle herders of southern Sudan, where a woman can marry a man who has died without heirs. In such situations the deceased man's brother may become his stand-in, or proxy, and marry a woman on his behalf. The biological offspring will be considered as having been fathered by the dead man's spirit. Recognized as his

legitimate children, they are his rightful heirs. Because such spouses are absent in the flesh but believed to exist in spirit form, anthropologists refer to these fictive unions as *ghost marriages.*[18]

Fictive marriage variations also exist outside Africa. For instance, a form of ghost marriage can be found in traditional Christianity, in particular Roman Catholic monasteries, where women who remain virgins devote their lives to religious service. When a young woman decides to become a nun, she may enter a religious order as a novice. Being promised in spiritual marriage to Jesus Christ, deemed to be the divine bridegroom, she makes vows of celibacy and chastity, abstaining from regular marriage and renouncing all sexual pleasures. In a special marriage by proxy ceremony, such women are "wedded" as spouses of Christ, who they believe died as a human but lives on as divine spirit in heaven. Veiled and clothed as divine spouses, these nuns also receive a new name, thus completely shedding their old social identities.[19]

Other cultural forms of wedding by proxy can be found throughout the world. In the Netherlands, for example, a legal custom exists known as "marriage with the glove" (*huwelijk met de handschoen*). In this official ceremony, just one of the marriage partners appears before the civil authorities—the other is represented symbolically by an imaginary glove and physically by someone formally authorized as a legal proxy. Traditionally, such proxy marriage ceremonies accommodated physically separated partners such as Dutch seafarers or nationals residing in remote territories.

In several states in the United States, including Colorado and Texas, we find yet another example of marriage by proxy. It involves citizens who are incarcerated, deployed in the military, residing in a foreign country, or otherwise prevented from being physically present at the formal ceremony. In California, this legal wedding option is restricted to members of the U.S. armed forces in war or deployed in combat operations abroad.

Since the 1860s, a *double-proxy marriage* has been possible in Montana, where partners may become legally married in a civil wedding ceremony with neither party appearing before the official authorities. Because

---

[16]Levine, N. E., & Silk, J. B. (1997). Why polyandry fails. *Current Anthropology 38,* 375–398.

[17]Spencer, R. F. (1984). North Alaska Coast Eskimo. In D. Damas (Ed.), *Arctic: Handbook of North American Indians* (Vol. 5, pp. 320–337). Washington, D.C.: Smithsonian Institution.

[18]Evans-Pritchard, E. E. (1951). *Kinship and marriage among the Nuer.* New York: Oxford University Press.

[19]See also Pope Pius XII. (1954). *Sacra Virginitas. Encyclical on consecrated virginity.* The Catholic Encyclopedia Online: www.newadvent.org.

---

group marriage Marriage in which several men and women have sexual access to one another. Also called co-marriage.
fictive marriage Marriage by proxy to the symbols of someone not physically present to establish the social status of a spouse and heirs.

proxy marriages that take place in states where they are legal are officially recognized by the U.S. federal government and in all member states, these options are gaining acceptance in the military, especially among troops deployed in dangerous overseas combat operations. In cases of injury or death, a military person married in a proxy wedding ceremony may leave a partner (with or without children) with full military benefits. Those who survive and return home may opt to celebrate their already legal marriage in a religious or otherwise meaningful ceremony with family and friends.[20]

CHOICE OF SPOUSE

The Western egalitarian ideal that an individual should be free to marry whomever he or she chooses is a distinct arrangement, certainly not universally embraced.

---

[20]Shane III, L. (2005). Happy couple both no-show wedding: Deployed troops make use of double-proxy ceremony. *Stars & Stripes 3* (17), 6; see also www.MarriageByProxy.com.

In many societies, marriage and the establishment of a family are considered far too important to be left to the whims of young people. The individual relationship of two people who are expected to spend their lives together and raise their children together is viewed as incidental to the more serious matter of making allies of two families through the marriage bond. Marriage involves a transfer of rights between families, including rights to property and rights over children, as well as sexual rights. Thus, marriages tend to be arranged for the economic and political advantage of the family unit.

Although arranged marriages are rare in North American society, they do occur. Among ethnic minorities, they may serve to preserve traditional values that people fear might otherwise be lost. Among families of wealth and power, marriages may be arranged by segregating their children in private schools and carefully steering them toward "proper" marriages. The following Original Study illustrates how marriages may be arranged in societies where such practices are commonplace.

Original Study ▪ By Serena Nanda

Arranging Marriage in India

Six years [after my first field trip to India] I returned to do fieldwork among the middle class in Bombay, a modern, sophisticated city. From the experience of my earlier visit, I decided to include a study of arranged marriages in my project. By this time I had met many Indian couples whose marriages had been arranged and who seemed very happy. Particularly in contrast to the fate of many of my married friends in the United States who were already in the process of divorce, the positive aspects of arranged marriages appeared to me to outweigh the negatives. In fact, I thought I might even participate in arranging a marriage myself. I had been fairly successful in the United States in "fixing up" many of my friends, and I was confident that my matchmaking skills could be easily applied to this new situation, once I learned the basic rules. "After all," I thought, "how complicated can it be?"

An opportunity presented itself almost immediately. A friend from my previous Indian trip was in the process of arranging for the marriage of her eldest son. Since my friend's family was eminently respectable and the boy him-

self personable, well educated, and nice looking, I was sure that by the end of my year's fieldwork, we would have found a match.

The basic rule seems to be that a family's reputation is most important. It is understood that matches would be arranged only within the same caste and general social class, although some crossing of subcastes is permissible if the class positions of the bride's and groom's families are similar. Although dowry is now prohibited by law in India, extensive gift exchanges took place with every marriage. Even when the boy's family does not "make demands," every girl's family nevertheless feels the obligation to give the traditional gifts, to the girl, to the boy, and to the boy's family. Particularly when the couple would be living in the joint family—that is, with the boy's parents and his married brothers and their families, as well as with unmarried siblings, which is still very common even among the urban, upper-middle class in India—the girl's parents are anxious to establish smooth relations between their family and that of the boy. Offering the proper gifts, even when not called "dowry," is often an important factor in

influencing the relationship between the bride's and groom's families and perhaps, also, the treatment of the bride in her new home.

In a society where divorce is still a scandal and where, in fact, the divorce rate is exceedingly low, an arranged marriage is the beginning of a lifetime relationship not just between the bride and groom but between their families as well. Thus, while a girl's looks are important, her character is even more so, for she is being judged as a prospective daughter-in-law as much as a prospective bride. . . .

My friend is a highly esteemed wife, mother, and daughter-in-law. She is religious, soft-spoken, modest, and deferential. She rarely gossips and never quarrels, two qualities highly desirable in a woman. A family that has the reputation for gossip and conflict among its womenfolk will not find it easy to get good wives for their sons. Parents will not want to send their daughter to a house in which there is conflict.

Originally from North India, my friend's family had lived for forty years in Bombay, where her husband owned a business. The family had delayed in seeking a match for their eldest son because he had been an air force pilot for several years, stationed in such remote places that it had seemed fruitless to try to find a girl who would be willing to accompany him. In their social class, a military career, despite its economic security, has little prestige and is considered a drawback in finding a suitable bride. Many families would not allow their daughters to marry a man in an occupation so potentially dangerous and that requires so much moving around.

The son had recently left the military and joined his father's business. Since he was a college graduate, modern, and well traveled, from such a good family, and, I thought, quite handsome, it seemed to me that he, or rather his family, was in a position to pick and choose. I said as much to my friend. While she agreed that there were many advantages on their side, she also said, "We must keep in mind that my son is both short and dark; these are drawbacks in finding the right match." While the boy's height had not escaped my notice, "dark" seemed to me inaccurate; I would have called him "wheat" colored perhaps, and in any case, I did not realize that color would be a consideration. I discovered, however, that while a boy's skin color is a less important consideration than a girl's, it is still a factor.

An important source of contacts in trying to arrange her son's marriage was my friend's social club in Bombay. Many of the women had daughters of the right age, and some had already expressed an interest in my friend's son. I was most enthusiastic about the possibilities of one particular family who had five daughters, all of whom were pretty, demure, and well educated. Their mother had told my friend, "You can have your pick for your son, whichever one of my daughters appeals to you most." I saw a match in sight. "Surely," I said to my friend, "we will find one there. Let's go visit and make our choice." But my friend held back; she did not seem to share my enthusiasm, for reasons I could not then fathom.

When I kept pressing for an explanation of her reluctance, she admitted, "See, Serena, here is the problem. The

© Earl & Nazima Kowall/Corbis

family has so many daughters, how will they be able to provide nicely for any of them? We are not making any demands, but still, with so many daughters to marry off, one wonders whether she will even be able to make a proper wedding. Since this is our eldest son, it's best if we marry him to a girl who is the only daughter, then the wedding will truly be a gala affair." I argued that surely the quality of the girls themselves made up for any deficiency in the elaborateness of the wedding. My friend admitted this point but still seemed reluctant to proceed.

Is there something else," I asked her, "some factor I have missed?" "Well," she finally said, "there is one other thing. They have one daughter already married and living in Bombay. The mother is always complaining to me that the girl's in-laws don't let her visit her own family often enough. So it makes me wonder, will she be that kind of mother who always wants her daughter at her own home? This will prevent the girl from adjusting to our house. It is not a good thing." And so, this family of five daughters was dropped as a possibility.

Somewhat disappointed, I nevertheless respected my friend's reasoning and geared up for the next prospect. This was also the daughter of a woman in my friend's social club. There was clear interest in this family and I could see why. The family's reputation was excellent; in fact, they came from a subcaste slightly higher than my friend's own. The girl, who was an only daughter, was pretty and well educated and had a brother studying in the United States. Yet, after expressing an interest to me in this family, all talk of them suddenly died down and the search began elsewhere.

What happened to that girl as a prospect?" I asked one day. "You never mention her anymore. She is so pretty and so educated, what did you find wrong?"

"She is too educated. We've decided against it. My husband's father saw the girl on the bus the other day and thought her forward. A girl who 'roams about' the city by herself is not the girl for our family." My disappointment this time was even greater, as I thought the son would have liked the girl very much. . . . I learned that if the family of the girl has even a slightly higher social status than the family of the boy, the bride may think herself too good for them, and this too will cause problems. Later my friend admitted to me that this had been an important factor in her decision not to pursue the match. . . .

After one more candidate, who my friend decided was not attractive enough for her son, almost six months had passed and I had become anxious. My friend laughed at my impatience: "Don't be so much in a hurry," she said.

CONTINUED

CONTINUED

"You Americans want everything done so quickly. You get married quickly and then just as quickly get divorced. Here we take marriage more seriously. We must take all the factors into account. It is not enough for us to learn by our mistakes. This is too serious a business. If a mistake is made we have not only ruined the life of our son or daughter, but we have spoiled the reputation of our family as well. And that will make it much harder for their brothers and sisters to get married. So we must be very careful."

What she said was true and I promised myself to be more patient. I had really hoped and expected that the match would be made before my year in India was up. But it was not to be. When I left India my friend seemed no further along in finding a suitable match for her son than when I had arrived.

Two years later, I returned to India and still my friend had not found a girl for her son. By this time, he was close to 30, and I think she was a little worried. Since she knew I had friends all over India, and I was going to be there for a year, she asked me to "help her in this work" and keep an eye out for someone suitable. I was flattered that my judgment was respected, but I had lost my earlier confidence as a matchmaker. Nevertheless, I promised that I would try.

It was almost at the end of my year's stay in India that I met a family with a marriageable daughter whom I felt might be a good possibility for my friend's son. . . . This new family had a successful business in a medium-sized city in central India and were from the same subcaste as my friend. The daughter was pretty and chic; in fact, she had studied fashion design in college. Her parents would not allow her to go off by herself to any of the major cities in India where she could make a career, but they had compromised with her wish to work by allowing her to run a small dress-making boutique from their home. In spite of her desire to have a career, the daughter was both modest and home-loving and had had a traditional, sheltered upbringing.

I mentioned the possibility of a match with my friend's son. The girl's parents were most interested. Although their daughter was not eager to marry just yet, the idea of living in Bombay—a sophisticated, extremely fashion-conscious city where she could continue her education in clothing design—was a great inducement. I gave the girl's father my friend's address and suggested that when they went to Bombay on some business or whatever, they look up the boy's family.

Returning to Bombay on my way to New York, I told my friend of this newly discovered possibility. She seemed to feel there was potential but, in spite of my urging, would not make any moves herself. She rather preferred to wait for the girl's family to call upon them.

A year later I received a letter from my friend. The family had indeed come to visit Bombay, and their daughter and my friend's daughter, who were near in age, had become very good friends. During that year, the two girls had frequently visited each other. I thought things looked promising.

Last week I received an invitation to a wedding: My friend's son and the girl were getting married. Since I had found the match, my presence was particularly requested at the wedding. I was thrilled. Success at last! As I prepared to leave for India, I began thinking, "Now, my friend's younger son, who do I know who has a nice girl for him . . . ?"

(Excerpted from S. Nanda (1992). Arranging a marriage in India. In P. R. De Vita (Ed.). The naked anthropologist (pp. 139–143). Belmont, CA: Wadsworth.) ■

Cousin Marriage

While cousin marriage is prohibited in some societies, certain cousins are the preferred marriage partners in others. A **parallel cousin** is the child of a father's brother or a mother's sister (Figure 20.1). In some societies, the preferred spouse for a man is his father's brother's daughter (or, from the woman's point of view, her father's brother's son). This is known as *patrilateral parallel-cousin marriage*. Although not obligatory, such marriages have been favored historically among Arabs, the ancient Israelites, and the ancient Greeks. All of these societies are (or were) hierarchical in nature—that is, some people are ranked higher than others because they have more power and property—and although male dominance and descent are emphasized, property of value to men is inherited by daughters as well as sons. Thus, when a

parallel cousin Child of a father's brother or a mother's sister.
cross cousin Child of a mother's brother or a father's sister.

man marries his father's brother's daughter (or a woman marries her father's brother's son), property is retained within the single male line of descent. In these societies, generally speaking, the greater the property, the more this form of parallel-cousin marriage is apt to occur.

A **cross cousin** is the child of a mother's brother or a father's sister (Figure 20.1). Some societies favor *matrilateral cross-cousin marriage*—marriage of a man to his mother's brother's daughter, or a woman to her father's sister's son. This preference exists among food foragers (such as the Aborigines of Australia) and some farming cultures (including various peoples of South India). Among food foragers, who inherit relatively little in the way of property, such marriages help establish and maintain ties of solidarity between social groups. In agricultural societies, however, the transmission of property is an important determinant. In societies that trace descent exclusively in the female line, for instance, property and other important rights usually pass from a man to his sister's son; under cross-cousin marriage, the sister's son is also the man's daughter's husband.

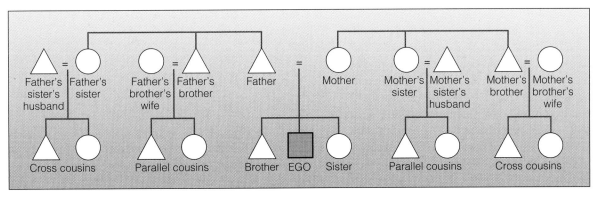

Figure 20.1
Anthropologists use diagrams of this sort to illustrate kinship relationships. Shown in this one is the distinction between cross cousins and parallel cousins. In such diagrams, males are always shown as triangles, females as circles, marital ties by an equal sign (=), sibling relationships as a horizontal line, and parent–child relationships as a vertical line. Terms are given from the perspective of the individual labeled EGO, who can be female or male.

Same-Sex Marriage

As noted earlier in this chapter, our definition of marriage refers to a union between "people" rather than "a man and a woman" because in some societies same-sex marriages are socially acceptable and officially allowed by law. Marriages between individuals of the same sex may provide a way of dealing with problems for which opposite-sex marriage offers no satisfactory solution. This is the case with woman–woman marriage, a practice permitted in many societies of sub-Saharan Africa, although in none does it involve more than a small minority of all women.

Details differ from one society to another, but woman–woman marriages among the Nandi of western Kenya may be taken as representative of such practices in Africa.[21] The Nandi are a pastoral people who also do considerable farming. Control of most significant property and the primary means of production—livestock and land—is exclusively in the hands of men and may only be transmitted to their male heirs, usually their sons. Since polygyny is the preferred form of marriage, a man's property is normally divided equally among his wives for their sons to inherit. Within the household, each wife has her own home in which she lives with her children, but all are under the authority of the woman's husband, who is a remote and aloof figure within the household. In such situations, the position of a woman who bears no sons is difficult; not only does she not help perpetuate her husband's male line—a major concern among the Nandi—but also she has no one to inherit the proper share of her husband's property.

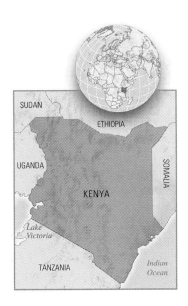

To get around these problems, a woman of advanced age who bore no sons may become a female husband by marrying a young woman. The purpose of this arrangement is for the young wife to provide the male heirs her female husband could not. To accomplish this, the woman's wife enters into a sexual relationship with a man other than her female husband's male husband; usually it is one of his male relatives. No other obligations exist between this woman and her male sex partner, and her female husband is recognized as the social and legal father of any children born under these conditions.

In keeping with her role as female husband, this woman is expected to abandon her female gender identity and, ideally, dress and behave as a man. In practice, the ideal is not completely achieved, for the habits of a lifetime are difficult to reverse. Generally, it is in the context of domestic activities, which are most highly symbolic of female identity, that female husbands most completely assume a male identity.

[21]The following is based on Obler, R. S. (1982). Is the female husband a man? Woman/woman marriage among the Nandi of Kenya. *Ethnology 19*, 69–88.

The individuals who are parties to woman–woman marriages enjoy several advantages. By assuming male identity, a barren or sonless woman raises her status considerably and even achieves near equality with men, who otherwise occupy a far more favored position in Nandi society than women. A woman who marries a female husband is usually one who is unable to make a good marriage, often because she (the female husband's wife) has lost face as a consequence of premarital pregnancy. By marrying a female husband, she too raises her status and also secures legitimacy for her children. Moreover, a female husband is usually less harsh and demanding, spends more time with her, and allows her a greater say in decision making than a male husband does. The one thing she may not do is engage in sexual activity with her marriage partner. In fact, female husbands are expected to abandon sexual activity altogether, including with their male husbands to whom they remain married even though the women now have their own wives.

In contrast to woman–woman marriages among the Nandi are same-sex marriages that include sexual activity between partners. Over the past decade, the legal recognition of such unions has become a matter of vigorous debate in some parts of the world. Several countries, including Spain, Belgium, Canada, and the Netherlands, have passed laws legalizing gay marriages. Meanwhile numerous U.S. states have adopted constitutional amendments barring same-sex marriage.

The arguments most commonly marshaled by opponents of same-sex unions are, first, that marriage has always been between males and females—but as we have just seen, this is not true. Same-sex marriages have been documented not only for a number of societies in Africa but in other parts of the world as well. As among the Nandi, they provide acceptable positions in society for individuals who might otherwise be marginalized.

A second argument against same-sex unions is that they legitimize gays and lesbians, whose sexual orientations have been widely regarded as unnatural. But again, as discussed in earlier chapters, neither cross-cultural studies nor studies of other animal species suggest that homosexual behavior is unnatural.

A third argument, that the function of marriage is to produce children, is at best a partial truth, as marriage involves economic, political, and legal considerations as well. Moreover, it is increasingly common for same-sex partners to have children through adoption or by turning to modern reproductive technologies. There is also the fact that in many societies, such as the Nandi, there is a separation between the sexual and reproductive attributes of women.

MARRIAGE AND ECONOMIC EXCHANGE

In the Trobriand Islands, when a young couple decides to get married, they sit in public on the veranda of the young man's adolescent retreat, where all may see them. Here they remain until the bride's mother brings the couple cooked yams, which they then eat together, making their marriage official. A day later the bride is presented with three long skirts by the husband's sister, a symbol of the fact that the sexual freedom of adolescence is now over for the newlywed woman. This is followed by a large presentation of uncooked yams by the bride's father and her mother's brother, who represent both her father's and her own lineages.

Meanwhile, the groom's father and mother's brother collect such valuables as stone axe blades, clay pots, money, and the occasional Kula shell (see Chapter 19) to present to the young wife's maternal kin and father. After the first year of the marriage, during which the bride's mother continues to provide the couple's meals of cooked yams, each of the young husband's relatives who provided valuables for his father and mother's brother to present to the bride's relatives will receive yams from her maternal relatives and father. All of this gift giving back and forth between the husband's and wife's lineages, as well as those of their fathers, serves to bind the four parties together in a way that makes people respect and honor the marriage and that creates obligations on the part of the woman's kin to take care of her husband in the future.

As among the Trobriand Islanders, marriages in many human societies are formalized by some sort of economic exchange. Among the Trobrianders, this takes the form of a gift exchange, as just described. Far more common is **bride-price**, sometimes called *bride wealth*, which involves payments of money or valuable goods to a bride's parents or other close kin. This usually happens in patrilineal societies where the bride will become a member of the household where her husband grew up; this household will benefit from her labor as well as from the offspring she produces. Thus, her family must be compensated for their loss.

Not only is bride-price *not* a simple "buying and selling" of women, but the bride's parents may use the money to purchase jewelry or household furnishings for her or to finance an elaborate and costly wedding celebration. It also contributes to the stability of the marriage, because it usually must be refunded if the couple separates. Other forms of compensation are an exchange of women between families—"My son will marry your

bride-price Money or valuable goods paid by the groom or his family to the bride's family upon marriage. Also called bride wealth.

In some societies when a woman marries, she receives her share of the family inheritance (her dowry), which she brings to her new family (unlike bride-price, which passes from the groom's family to the bride's family). Shown here are Slovakian women carrying the objects of a woman's dowry.

daughter if your son will marry my daughter." Yet another is **bride service,** a period of time during which the groom works for the bride's family.

In a number of societies more or less restricted to the western, southern, and eastern margins of Eurasia, where the economy is based on agriculture, women often bring a dowry with them at marriage. A form of dowry in the United States is the custom of the bride's family paying the wedding expenses. Another example is that a Roman Catholic woman joining a religious order as a consecrated nun, and thus entering into a spiritual marriage, as discussed earlier, also traditionally brings a dowry (*dos religiosa*) to that institution. In effect, a **dowry** is a woman's share of parental property that, instead of passing to her upon her parents' death, is distributed to her at the time of her marriage. This does not mean that she retains control of this property after marriage. In some European countries, for example, a woman's property traditionally falls exclusively under her husband's control. Having benefited by what she has brought to the marriage, however, he is obligated to look out for her future well-being, including her security after his death.

Thus, one of the functions of dowry is to ensure a woman's support in widowhood (or after divorce), an important consideration in a society where men carry out the bulk of productive work, and women are valued for their reproductive potential rather than for the work they do. In such societies, women incapable of bearing children are especially vulnerable, but the dowry they bring with them at marriage helps protect them against desertion. Another function of dowry is to reflect the economic status of the woman in societies where differ-

ences in wealth are important. It also permits women, with the aid of their parents and kin, to compete through dowry for desirable (that is, wealthy) husbands.

DIVORCE

Like marriage, divorce in most societies is a matter of great concern to the couple's families. Since marriage is less often a religious matter than it is an economic one, divorce arrangements can be made for a variety of reasons and with varying degrees of difficulty. Among the Gusii farmers of western Kenya, for instance, sterility and impotence are grounds for a divorce. Among certain aboriginal peoples in northern Canada and Chenchu foragers inhabiting the thickly forested hills in central India, divorce was discouraged after children were born; couples usually were urged by their families to adjust their differences. By contrast, in the southwestern United States, a Hopi Indian woman in Arizona could divorce her husband at any time merely by placing his belongings outside the door to indicate he was no longer welcome.

An adult unmarried woman is very rare in most non-Western societies where a divorced woman usually soon remarries. In many societies, economic considerations are often the strongest motivation to wed. On the island

bride service A designated period of time after marriage when the groom works for the bride's family.
dowry Payment of a woman's inheritance at the time of her marriage, either to her or to her husband.

of New Guinea, a man does not marry because of sexual needs, which he can readily satisfy out of wedlock, but because he needs a woman to make pots and cook his meals, to fabricate nets and weed his plantings. Likewise, women in communities that depend for security upon males capable of fighting need husbands who are raised to be able warriors as well as good hunters.

Although divorce rates may be high in various corners of the world, they have become so high in Western industrial and postindustrial societies that many worry about the future of what they view as traditional and familiar forms of marriage and the family. It is interesting to note that although divorce was next to impossible in Western societies between 1000 and 1800, few marriages lasted more than about ten or twenty years, due to high mortality rates caused in part by inadequate health care and medical expertise.[22] With increased longevity, separation by death has diminished, and separation by legal action has grown. In the United States today, some 50 percent of first marriages end in divorce—twice the 1960 divorce rate but slightly less than the high point in the early 1980s.[23]

---

[22]Stone, L. (1998). *Kinship and gender: An introduction* (p. 235). Boulder, CO: Westview Press.

[23]Whitehead, B. D. & Popenoe, D. (2004). *The state of our unions: The social health of marriage in America 2004.* Rutgers, NJ: Rutgers University National Marriage Project.

family Two or more people related by blood, marriage, or adoption. The family may take many forms, ranging from a single parent with one or more children, to a married couple or polygamous spouses with offspring, to several generations of parents and their children.

FAMILY AND HOUSEHOLD

Dependence on group living for survival is a basic human characteristic. We have inherited this from primate ancestors, although we have developed it in our own distinctly human way—through culture. However each culture may define what constitutes a family, this social unit forms the basic cooperative structure that ensures an individual's primary needs and provides the necessary care for children to develop as healthy and productive members of the group and thereby help ensure its future.

Comparative historical and cross-cultural studies reveal a wide variety of family patterns, and these patterns may change over time. Thus, the definition of **family** is necessarily broad: two or more people related by blood, marriage, or adoption. The family may take many forms, ranging from a single parent with one or more children, to a married couple or polygamous spouses with offspring, to several generations of parents and their children.

In all known cultures, past and present, gender plays at least some role in determining the division of labor. An effective way to facilitate economic cooperation between men and women and simultaneously provide for a close bond between mother and child is through the establishment of residential groups that include adults of both sexes. The differing nature of male and female roles, as defined by different cultures, makes it advantageous for a child to have an adult of the same sex available to serve as a proper model for the appropriate adult role. The presence of adult men and women in the same residential group provides for this. The men, however, need not be the women's husbands. In some societies

A celebration at the palace in the Yoruba city of Oyo, Nigeria. As is usual in societies where royal households are found, that of the Yoruba includes many individuals not related to the ruler, as well as the royal family.

they are the women's brothers—as in the case of the Nayar, discussed earlier in this chapter, where sisters and their children live together with their brothers and their mother and her brothers.

For purposes of cross-cultural comparison, anthropologists define the **household** as the basic residential unit where economic production, consumption, inheritance, child rearing, and shelter are organized and carried out. In the vast majority of human societies, most households are made up of families, but there are many other arrangements. For instance, among the Mundurucu Indians, a horticultural people living in the center of Brazil's Amazon rainforest, married men and women are members of separate households, meeting periodically for sexual activity. At age 13 boys join their fathers in the men's house. Meanwhile, their sisters continue to live with their mothers and the younger boys in two or three houses grouped around the men's house. Thus, the men's house constitutes one household inhabited by adult males and their sexually mature sons, and the women's houses, inhabited by adult women and prepubescent boys and girls, constitute others.

An array of other domestic arrangements can be found in other parts of the world, including situations in which co-residents of a household are not related biologically or by marriage—such as the service personnel in an elaborate royal household, apprentices in the household of craft specialists, low-status clients in the household of rich and powerful patrons, or groups of children being raised by paired teams of adult male and female community members in an Israeli kibbutz (a collectively owned and operated agricultural settlement). So it is that *family* and *household* are not always synonymous.

Forms of the Family

To discuss the various forms families take in response to particular social, historical, and ecological circumstances, we must, at the outset, make a distinction between a **conjugal family** (in Latin *conjugere* means "to join together"), which is formed on the basis of marital ties, and a **consanguineal family** (based on the Latin word *consanguineus,* literally meaning "of the same blood"), which consists of related women, their brothers, and the women's offspring.

Consanguineal families are not common, but there are more examples than the classic case of the Nayar described at the beginning of the chapter. Among these are the Musuo of southwestern China and the Tory Islanders, a Roman Catholic, Gaelic-speaking fisherfolk living off the coast of Ireland. The Tory Islanders, who do not marry until they are in their late 20s or early 30s, look at it this way: "Oh well, you get married at that age, it's too late to break up arrangements that you have already known for a long time. . . . You know, I have my sisters

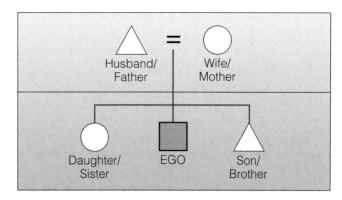

Figure 20.2
This diagram shows the relationships in a traditional nuclear family, a form that is common but declining in North America and much of Europe.

and brothers to look after, why should I leave home to go live with a husband? After all, he's got his sisters and his brothers looking after him."[24] Because the community numbers but a few hundred people, husbands and wives are within easy commuting distance of each other.

According to a cross-cultural survey of family types in 192 cultures around the world, the extended family is most common, present in about 48 percent of those cultures, compared to the nuclear family at 25 percent, and polygamous at 22 percent.[25] Each of these is discussed below.

The Nuclear Family

The smallest family unit is known as the **nuclear family,** a group consisting of one or two parents and dependent offspring, which may include a stepparent, stepsiblings, and adopted children (Figure 20.2). Until recently, the term *nuclear family* referred solely to the mother, father, and child(ren) unit—the family form that most Americans, Europeans, and many others now regard as the normal or natural nucleus of larger family units. In the United States father–mother–child(ren) nuclear fam-

---

[24]Fox, R. (1981, December 3). [Interview]. Coast Telecourses, Inc., Los Angeles.

[25]Winick, C. (Ed.). (1970). *Dictionary of anthropology* (p. 202). Totowa, NJ: Littlefield, Adams.

household The basic residential unit where economic production, consumption, inheritance, child rearing, and shelter are organized and carried out.
conjugal family A family established through marriage.
consanguineal family A family of "blood relatives" consisting of related women, their brothers, and the women's offspring.
nuclear family A group consisting of one or two parents and dependent offspring, which may include a stepparent, stepsiblings, and adopted children. (Until recently this term referred only to the father–mother–child(ren) unit.)

ily households reached their highest frequency around 1950, when 60 percent of all households conformed to this model.[26] Today such families comprise only 24 percent of U.S. households,[27] and the term *nuclear family* is used to cover the social reality of several types of small parent–child units, including single parents with children and same-sex couples with children.

Industrialization and market capitalism have played a historical role in shaping the nuclear family most of us are familiar with today. One reason for this is that factories, mining and transportation companies, warehouses, shops, and other businesses generally only pay individual wage earners for the jobs they are hired to do. Whether these workers are single, married, divorced, have siblings or children is really not a concern to the profit-seeking companies. Because jobs may come and go, individual wage earners must remain mobile to adapt to the labor markets. And since few wage earners have the financial resources to support large numbers of relatives without incomes of their own, industrial or postindustrial societies do not favor the continuance of larger extended families (discussed below), which are standard in most societies traditionally dependent on pastoral nomadism, agriculture, or horticulture.

Interestingly, the nuclear family is also likely to be prominent in traditional foraging societies such as that of the Eskimo people who live in the barren Arctic environments of eastern Siberia, Alaska, Greenland, and Canada (where Eskimos are now known as Inuit). In the winter the traditional Inuit husband and wife, with their children, roam the vast Arctic Canadian snowscape in their quest for food. The husband hunts and makes shelters. The wife cooks, is responsible for the children, and

---

[26]Stacey, J. (1990). *Brave new families* (pp. 5, 10). New York: Basic Books

[27]Irvine, M. (1999, November 24). Mom-and-pop houses grow rare. *Burlington Free Press; Current population survey.* (2002). U.S. Census Bureau.

makes the clothing and keeps it in good repair. One of her chores is to chew her husband's boots to soften the leather for the next day so that he can resume his quest for game. The wife and her children could not survive without the husband, and life for a man is unimaginable without a wife.

Similar to nuclear families in industrial societies, those living under especially harsh environmental conditions must be prepared to fend for themselves. Such isolation comes with its own set of challenges, including the difficulties of rearing children without multigenerational support and a lack of familial care for the elderly. Nonetheless, this form of family is well adapted to a mode of subsistence that requires a high degree of geographic mobility. For the Inuit in Canada, this mobility permits the hunt for food; for other North Americans, the hunt for jobs and improved social status requires a mobile form of family unit.

Not even among the Inuit, however, is the nuclear family as independent from other kin as it has become among most non-native North Americans. When Inuit families are off by themselves, it is regarded as a mat-

Among Inuit people in Canada who still hunt for much of their food, nuclear families such as the one shown here are typical. Their isolation from other relatives is usually temporary. Much of the time they are found in groups of at least a few related families.

John Eastcott/Eva Momatiuki/The Image Works

Extended family households exist in many parts of the world, including among the Maya people of Central America and Mexico.[30] In many of their communities, sons bring their wives to live in houses built on the edges of a small open plaza, on one edge of which their father's house already stands. Numerous household activities are carried out on this plaza—children play, while adults weave, do some other productive work, or socialize with guests. The head of the family is the sons' father, who makes most of the important decisions. All members of the family work together for the common good and deal with outsiders as a single unit.

ter of temporary expediency; most of the time, they are found in groups of at least a few families together, with members of one family having relatives in all of the others.[28] Thus families cooperate with one another on a daily basis, sharing food and other resources, looking out for one another's children, and sometimes even eating together.

The sense of shared responsibility for one another's children and for the general welfare in Inuit multifamily groups contrasts with families in the United States, which are basically "on their own." Here the states assign an individual sole responsibility to family for child care and the welfare of family members, with relatively little assistance from outside.[29] To be sure, families can and often do help one another out, but they are under no obligation to do so, and even if they wish to may find it impossible due to geographic separation born of high mobility. In fact, once children reach the age of majority (18), parents have no further legal obligation to them, nor do the children to their parents. When families do have difficulty fulfilling their assigned functions—as is increasingly the case even though it be through no fault of their own—less support is available to them from the community at large than in most of the world's "stateless" societies, including that of the Inuit.

The Extended Family

When two or more closely related nuclear families cluster together into a large domestic group, they form a unit known as the **extended family.** This larger family unit,

common in traditional horticultural, agricultural, and pastoral societies around the world, typically consists of siblings with their spouses and offspring, and often their parents. All of these kin, some related by blood and some by marriage, live and work together for the common good and deal with outsiders as a single unit.

Because members of the younger generation bring their husbands or wives to live in the family, extended families have continuity through time. As older members die off, new members are born into the family. Extended families have built into them particular challenges. Among these are difficulties that the in-marrying spouse is likely to have in adjusting to his or her spouse's family.

In North America, extended families can still be found on many American Indian reservations. They also exist in some non-Indian communities, for example along the Maine coast,[31] where they developed in response to a unique economy featuring a mix of farming and seafaring, coupled with an ideal of self-sufficiency. Because family farms were incapable of providing self-sufficiency, seafaring was taken up as an economic alternative. Sea-going commerce, however, was periodically afflicted by depression, so family farming remained important as a cushion against economic hard times. The need for a sufficient labor pool to tend the farm, while at the same time furnish officers, crew, or (frequently) both for locally owned vessels, was satisfied by the practice of

[28]Graburn, N. H. H. (1969). *Eskimos without igloos: Social and economic development in Sugluk* (pp. 56–58). Boston: Little Brown.

[29]Collier, J., Rosaldo, M. Z., & Yanagisako, S. (1982). Is there a family? New anthropological views. In B. Thorne & M. Yalom (Eds.), *Rethinking the family: Some feminist questions* (pp. 34–35). New York: Longman.

[30]Vogt, E. Z. (1990). *The Zinacantecos of Mexico, A modern Maya way of life* (2nd ed., pp. 30–34). Fort Worth: Holt, Rinehart & Winston.

[31]Haviland, W. A. (1973). Farming, seafaring and bilocal residence on the coast of Maine. *Man in the Northeast 6*, 31–44.

extended family Two or more closely related nuclear families clustered together into a large domestic group.

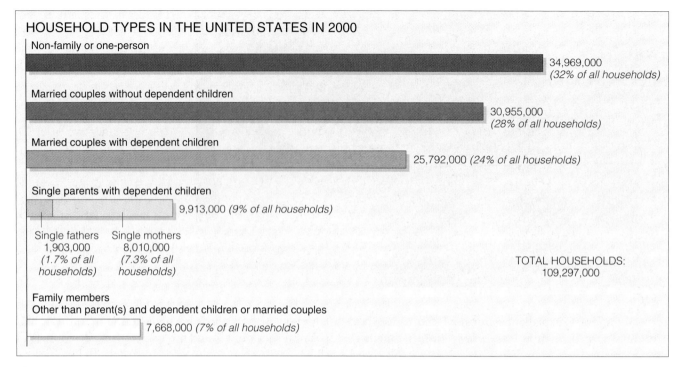

HOUSEHOLD TYPES IN THE UNITED STATES IN 2000

Non-family or one-person
34,969,000 (32% of all households)

Married couples without dependent children
30,955,000 (28% of all households)

Married couples with dependent children
25,792,000 (24% of all households)

Single parents with dependent children
9,913,000 (9% of all households)

Single fathers 1,903,000 (1.7% of all households)
Single mothers 8,010,000 (7.3% of all households)

TOTAL HOUSEHOLDS: 109,297,000

Family members
Other than parent(s) and dependent children or married couples
7,668,000 (7% of all households)

Figure 20.3
Household types in the United States, based on U.S. Census Bureau figures for 2000.

a newly married couple settling on the farm of either the bride's or the groom's parents. Thus, most people spent their lives cooperating on a day-to-day basis in economic activities with close relatives, all of whom lived together (even if in separate houses) on the same farm.

Nontraditional Families and Nonfamily Households

In North America and parts of Europe, increasing numbers of people live in nonfamily households, either alone or with nonrelatives. In fact, some 32 percent of households in the United States fall into this category (Figure 20.3). Many others live as members of what are often called *nontraditional families*. These include single-parent households. Such households are often the result of divorce or a marriage partner's death. They also stem from increased sexual activity outside of wedlock, combined with declining marriage rates among women of childbearing age, as well as a rise in the number of women actively choosing single motherhood. About a third of all births in the United States occur outside of marriage, and in several northwestern European countries, the nonmarital birthrate is close to 50 percent.[32]

The percentage of single-parent households in the United States has grown to 9 percent, while the number

comprised of married couples with children has dropped to 24 percent. Although single-parent households account for just 9 percent of all households in the United States, they are home to 28 percent of all children (under 18 years of age) in the country.[33] In the vast majority of cases, a child living in a single-parent household is with his or her mother. Fathers are usually required to pay child support but are not always able or willing to do so. And when they do pay, the amount is often insufficient for essential food, clothing, and medical care, let alone the cost of child care so that the woman can seek or continue income-producing work to support herself. Notably, single fathers in the United States are three times more likely to have a cohabiting partner in the home than are single mothers.

Not surprisingly, as the number of female-headed households has increased, so has the number of women (and, of course, their children) living below the poverty line. More than one-third of all female-headed households in the United States now fall into this category, and one-quarter of all children are poor.

Single-parent households headed by women are neither new nor restricted to industrial or postindustrial societies. They have been known and studied for a long time in the countries of the Caribbean Sea, where men historically have been exploited as a cheap source of la-

[32]*Recent demographic developments in Europe—2000.* Council of Europe.

[33]*Current population survey.* (2002). U.S. Census Bureau.

bor on sugar, coffee, or banana plantations. In more recent decades, many of these men are now also working as temporary migrant laborers in foreign countries, primarily in the United States. Under such seasonal or temporary work conditions, men are absent from their families for many months each year, have no social or political power and few economic rewards. Hence they are tenuously attached at best to any particular household. These are held together by women, who as producers of subsistence foods provide the means of economic survival for households. Similar female-headed households are becoming increasingly common in other "underdeveloped" countries, too, as development projects restrict the ability of women to earn a living wage (reasons for this are discussed in later chapters).

Residence Patterns

Where some form of conjugal or extended family is the norm, family exogamy requires that either the husband or wife, if not both, must move to a new household upon marriage. There are five common patterns of residence that a newly married couple may adopt—the prime determinant being ecological circumstances, although other factors enter in as well. Thus, postmarital residence arrangements, far from being arbitrary, are adaptive in character. Here we will mention only the four most common arrangements.

Patrilocal residence is when a married couple lives in the husband's father's place of residence. This arrangement is favorable in situations where men play a predominant role in subsistence, particularly if they own property that can be accumulated, if polygyny is customary, if warfare is prominent enough to make cooperation among men especially important, and if an elaborate political organization exists in which men wield authority. These conditions are most often found together in societies that rely on animal husbandry and/or intensive agriculture for their subsistence. Where patrilocal residence is customary, the bride often must move to a different band or community. In such cases, her parents' family is not only losing the services of a useful family member, but they are losing her potential offspring as well. Hence, some kind of compensation to her family, most commonly bride-price, is usual.

Matrilocal residence, in which a married couple lives in the wife's mother's place of residence, is a likely result if ecological circumstances make the role of the woman predominate for subsistence. It is found most often in horticultural societies, where political organization is relatively uncentralized and where cooperation among women is important. The Hopi Indians provide one example. Although it is the Hopi men who do the farming, the women control access to land and "own" the harvest. Indeed, men are not even allowed in the gra-

naries. Under matrilocal residence, men usually do not move very far from the family in which they were raised so they are available to help out there from time to time. Therefore, marriage usually does not involve compensation to the groom's family.

Ambilocal residence (*ambi* in Latin means "both"), a pattern in which a married couple may choose either matrilocal or patrilocal residence, is adaptive in situations where economic cooperation of more people than are available in the nuclear family is needed but where resources are limited in some way. Because the couple can join either the bride's or the groom's family, family membership is flexible, and the two can live where the resources look best or where their labor is most needed. This was once the situation on the peninsulas and islands along the coast of Maine, where, as already noted, extended family households were based upon ambilocal residence.

The same residential pattern is particularly common among food-foraging peoples, as among the Mbuti pygmies of Africa's Ituri forest. Typically, a Mbuti marries someone from another band, so that one spouse always has in-laws who live elsewhere. Thus, if foraging is bad in their part of the tropical rainforest, the couple has somewhere else to go where food may be more readily available. Ambilocality greatly enhances the Mbutis' opportunity to find food. It also provides a place to go if a dispute breaks out with someone in the band where the couple is currently living. Consequently, Mbuti camps are constantly changing their composition as people split off to go live with their in-laws, while others are joining from other groups. For a people like food foragers, who find their food in nature and who maintain an egalitarian social order, ambilocal residence can be a crucial factor in both survival and conflict resolution.

Under **neolocal residence,** a married couple forms a household in a separate location. This occurs where the independence of the nuclear family is emphasized. In industrial societies such as the United States, where most economic activity occurs outside rather than inside the family and where it is important for individuals to be able to move where jobs can be found, neolocal residence is better suited than any of the other patterns.

patrilocal residence A residence pattern in which a married couple lives in the husband's father's place of residence.
matrilocal residence A residence pattern in which a married couple lives in the wife's mother's place of residence.
ambilocal residence A residence pattern in which a married couple may choose either matrilocal or patrilocal residence.
neolocal residence A pattern in which a married couple establish their household in a location apart from either the husband's or the wife's relatives.

Many of China's 114 million migrant laborers work in factories and live in factory dormitories such as this.

MARRIAGE, FAMILY, AND HOUSEHOLD IN OUR GLOBALIZED AND TECHNOLOGIZED WORLD

In many countries the mosaic of marriage, family, and household forms has become more varied in recent decades. Many factors contribute to this, including global capitalism and large-scale emigration of peoples moving across cultural boundaries. Also significant are high rates of divorce and remarriage, resulting in *blended families* comprised of a married couple together raising children from previous unions. And although it has not been uncommon for childless couples in many cultures throughout human history to adopt children, including orphans and even captives, today it is a transnational practice for adults from industrial and postindustrial countries to travel across the world in search of infants to adopt, regardless of their ethnic heritage. Other contributing factors include *new reproductive technologies* (NRTs), such as in vitro fertilization, as well as open adoption, which make it possible for a child to have a relationship with both the biological and adoptive parents.

Also of note, worldwide, is the ever-growing number of households comprised of temporary and migrant workers. Today, China alone has 114 million of them, mostly young people who have quit the peasant villages of their childhood and traveled to fast-growing cities to work in factories, shops, restaurants, and other such places. Some pile into apartments with friends or co-workers, others live in factory dormitories—new, single-generation households that stand in stark contrast to the multigeneration extended family households in which they were raised. Similar scenes are repeated all around the world as individuals in this transient workforce set up house together far away from home in order to make a living. Although many countries have passed legislation intended to provide migrants with protections concerning housing, as well as work conditions and pay (such as the 1983 Migrant and Seasonal Agricultural Worker Protection Act in the United States), living conditions for these workers are often miserable.[34]

As the various ethnographic examples in this chapter illustrate, our species has invented a wide variety of marriage, family, and household forms, each in correspondence with related features in the social structure and conforming to the larger cultural system. In the face of new challenges, we explore and tinker in search of solutions, sometimes resulting in finding completely new forms, and other times returning to time-tested formulas of more traditional varieties.

---

[34]Chang, L. (2005, June 9). A Migrant worker sees rural home in new light. *Wall Street Journal.*

Questions for Reflection

1. Members of traditional communities in countries where the state is either weak or absent depend on relatives to help meet the basic challenges of survival. In such traditional societies, why would it be risky to choose marriage partners exclusively on the basis of romantic love? Can you imagine other factors playing a role if the long-term survival of your community is at stake?

2. Although most women in Europe and North America probably view polygyny as a marriage practice exclusively benefiting men, women in cultures where such marriages are traditional may stress more positive sides of sharing a husband with several co-wives. Under which conditions do you think polygyny could be considered as relatively beneficial for women?

3. Many people in North America and Europe choose to have children outside marriage. Considering some of the major functions of marriage, do you think there is a relationship

between the type of society an individual belongs to and the choice to forgo the traditional benefits of marriage? Under what cultural conditions might the choice to remain unmarried present serious challenges?

4. Raising children is a challenge not only for parents but also for the larger community. Why do you think your own culture has developed the kind of family and household organization most familiar to you? Why do you think those particular organizational forms came into being? Can you imagine under which circumstances these arrangements may become inadequate?

5. Single motherhood in North America has typically been seen as something tied to low income, yet it is becoming increasingly common among women across the economic spectrum. What do you consider to be the reasons for this, based on the barrel model of culture with its three tiers of infrastructure, social structure, and superstructure?

Suggested Readings

Coontz, S. (2005). *Marriage, a history: From obedience to intimacy, or how love conquered marriage.* New York: Viking Adult.

Challenging the idea that marriage is in crisis due to rising divorce rates, out-of-wedlock births, and same-sex unions, Coontz argues that marriage has always been in a state of flux and that "almost every marital and sexual arrangement we have seen in recent years . . . has been tried somewhere before." Placing current concepts of marriage in broad historical context, Coontz explains marriage as a political tool, a means of ensuring a domestic labor force, and a flexible reflection of changing social standards.

Holy, L. (1996). *Anthropological perspectives on kinship.* London: Pluto Press.

Holy investigates changes in the conceptualization of kinship brought about by new reproductive technologies and the growing interest in culturally specific notions of personhood and gender. Considering the extent to which Western assumptions have guided anthropological studies of kinship, the author offers critical reflection on cultural bias in approaches to the subject.

Hutter, M. (Ed.) (2003). *The family experience: A reader in cultural diversity* (4th ed.). Boston: Allyn & Bacon.

This readable anthology examines the cultural diversity of the American family by providing relevant articles integrating race, class, gender, and ethnicity. Taken as a whole, these readings reveal both historical trends and unique variations that widen our understanding of the diversity, patterns, and dynamics of the American family.

Modell, J. (1994). *Kinship with strangers: Adoption and interpretations of kinship in American culture.* Berkeley: University of California Press.

The author, an adopter and an anthropologist, analyzes the "core symbols" of kinship in American culture—birth, biology, and blood—and examines their impact on people who experience the "fictive" kinship of adoption.

Stockard, J. E. (2002). *Marriage in culture: Practice and meaning across diverse societies.* Ft. Worth: Harcourt College Publishers.

This innovative, accessible text explores the meaning of marriage in different cultures, using compelling ethnographic accounts of the !Kung San (Bushman), Chinese, Iroquois, and Tibetan societies to familiarize students with anthropologists' unique perspective on marriage in culture. Each chapter explores the ways in which different economic, political, family, and gender systems shape the practice and meaning of marriage.

Stone, L. (2005). *Kinship and gender: An introduction* (3rd ed.). Boulder, CO: Westview Press.

Focusing on gender, Stone considers the cross-cultural variations in marriage practices in the broader context of kinship studies. A particular strength is the inclusion of specific case studies to illustrate general principles. The book ends with a thought-provoking discussion of new reproductive technologies and their repercussions for both kinship and gender. This revised and updated edition features new case studies on primate kinship, American kinship, and new reproductive technologies.

Thomson Audio Study Products

 Enjoy the MP3-ready Audio Lecture Overviews for each chapter and a comprehensive audio glossary of key terms for quick study and review. Whether walking to class, doing laundry, or studying at your desk, you now have the freedom to choose when, where, and how you interact with your audio-based educational media. See the preface for information on how to access this on-the-go study and review tool.

The Anthropology Resource Center

www.thomsonedu.com/anthropology
The Anthropology Resource Center provides extended learning materials to reinforce your understanding of key concepts in the four fields of anthropology. For each of the four fields, the Resource Center includes dynamic exercises including video exercises, map exercises, simulations, and "Meet the Scientists" interviews, as well as critical thinking questions that can be assigned and e-mailed to instructors. The Resource Center also provides breaking news in anthropology and interesting material on applied anthropology to help you link what you are learning to the world around you.

21 Kinship and Descent

© Graeme Matthews/Photo New Zealand

CHALLENGE ISSUE All humans face the challenge of creating and maintaining a social network that reaches beyond the capabilities of immediate family or household to provide support and security. On a very basic level that network is arranged by kinship. We see such a kin-ordered arrangement with the Maori of New Zealand today. About seven centuries ago, their Polynesian ancestors arrived on the shores of this island country in a small fleet of large sailing canoes called *waka*. The chiefs and crewmembers of these canoes had children. Their offspring, in the course of generations, formed large descent groups known as *iwi* ("tribe"). Each Maori today belongs to such an *iwi* and can trace his or her family's genealogy back about twenty-five generations to a founding ancestor in one of these legendary canoes. For this reason, Maori refer to groups of related *iwi* sharing a territorial district as *waka,* and membership in one of these "canoes" gives them certain rights to cultural and natural resources as the indigenous heirs of New Zealand's first human settlers.

What Is Kinship?

Kinship is a social network of relatives within which individuals possess certain mutual rights and obligations. One's place in this network, or kinship status, determines what these rights and obligations are. Providing groups of relatives with a social structure, kinship helps shield them from the dangers of disorganization and fracture. Kinship is especially important in societies where other institutions such as a centralized government, a professional military, or financial banks are absent or do not function effectively. In such societies, individuals must depend on a wide network of relatives for support and protection.

What Are Descent Groups?

A descent group is a kind of kinship group in which being in the direct line of descent from a particular real or mythical ancestor is a criterion of membership. Descent may be traced exclusively through men or women, or through either at the discretion of the individual. Two different means of tracing descent may be used at the same time to assign individuals to different groups for different purposes. In societies without descent groups, such as many food-foraging as well as industrial and postindustrial societies, people rely instead on the kindred: an individual's close blood relatives on the maternal and paternal sides of his or her family. Because each kindred is an ego-centered family group, it is a less stable social unit than the descent group.

What Functions Do Kin-Ordered Groups Serve?

Kin-ordered groups of various kinds are social organizational devices for solving a number of specific challenges that commonly confront human societies: maintaining the integrity of resources that cannot be divided without being destroyed; providing work forces for tasks that require a labor pool larger than households can provide; and rallying support for purposes of self-defense or offensive attack. Kin-ordered organizations such as descent groups arise from extended family organization. Kinship terminology is affected by and adjusts to the kinds of descent or other kinship groups that are important in a society.

All societies rely on some form of family and/or household organization to effectively deal with basic human challenges: regulating sexual activities, coordinating work, and organizing child rearing. As efficient and flexible as family and household organization may be for meeting such challenges, many societies confront problems that are beyond the coping ability of family and household organization.

For example, members of one independent local group often need some means of interacting with neighboring groups, of claiming support and protection from individuals in another group. This can be important for defense against natural or human-made disasters. Also, a group frequently needs to share rights to a natural resource that is difficult to divide or exclusively control, such as a large tract of land, stretch of water, or a wild herd of migratory animals. Further, people often need some means of providing cooperative work forces for tasks that require more participants than households alone can provide. Finally, larger social units may be essential for pulling together support for self-defense against outside aggressors or offensive attacks against neighboring groups in order to gain control over scarce or choice resources.

THOMSON AUDIO STUDY PRODUCTS Take advantage of the MP3-ready Audio Lecture Overviews and comprehensive audio glossary of key terms for each chapter. See the preface for information on how to access this on-the-go study and review tool.

Humans have come up with many ways to widen their circles of support to meet such challenges. One is through a formal political system, with personnel to make and enforce laws, keep the peace, allocate resources, and perform other regulatory and societal functions. But the predominant way in societies not (or not effectively) organized as political states—especially foraging, crop-cultivating, and pastoral societies—is by means of **kinship**, a network of relatives within which individuals possess certain mutual rights and obligations.

kinship A network of relatives within which individuals possess certain mutual rights and obligations.

descent group Any kin-ordered social group with a membership in the direct line of descent from a real (historical) or fictional common ancestor.

unilineal descent Descent that establishes group membership exclusively through either the male or female line.

matrilineal descent Descent traced exclusively through the female line to establish group membership.

patrilineal descent Descent traced exclusively through the male line to establish group membership.

DESCENT GROUPS

A common way of organizing a society along kinship lines is by creating what anthropologists call descent groups. Found in many societies, a **descent group** is any kin-ordered social group with a membership in the direct line of descent from a real (historical) or fictional common ancestor. Members of a descent group trace their shared connections back to such an ancestor through a chain of parent–child links. The addition of a few culturally meaningful obligations and taboos acts as a kind of glue to help hold the structured social group together.

Membership in a descent group provides individuals with a wider social network of relatives without whom it is difficult or even impossible to effectively deal with the multiple challenges of survival hurled at them, including securing vitally important natural resources for food, fuel, shelter, and other necessities. Although many important functions of the descent group are taken over by other institutions when a society becomes politically organized as a state, elements of such kin-ordered groups may continue.

We see this with many traditional indigenous societies that have become part of larger state societies yet endure as distinctive kin-ordered communities. So it is with the Maori of New Zealand, featured in this chapter's Challenge Issue and the Biocultural Connection. Retaining key elements of their traditional social structure, they are still organized in about thirty large descent groups known as *iwi* ("tribes"), which form part of larger social and territorial units known as *waka* ("canoes").

Descent group membership must be sharply defined in order to operate effectively in a kin-ordered society. If membership is allowed to overlap, it is unclear where someone's primary loyalty belongs, especially when different descent groups have conflicting interests. Membership can be restricted in a number of ways. The most common way is what anthropologists refer to as *unilineal descent,* in which membership is determined by a direct line of descent from a common ancestor exclusively through one's male or female ancestors, but not both. In this way, each individual is automatically assigned from the moment of birth to his or her mother's or father's group and to that group only.

Unilineal Descent

Unilineal descent (sometimes called *unilateral descent*) establishes descent group membership exclusively through the male or the female line. In non-Western societies, unilineal descent groups are quite common. The individual is assigned at birth to membership in a specific descent group, which may be traced either by **matrilineal descent,** through the female line, or by **patrilineal descent,** through the male line, depending on the culture.

Maori Origins: Ancestral Genes and Mythical Canoes

Anthropologists have been fascinated to find that the oral traditions of Maori people in New Zealand fit quite well with scientific findings. New Zealand, an island country whose dramatic geography served as the setting for the *Lord of the Rings* film trilogy, lies in a remote corner of the Pacific Ocean some 1,200 miles southeast of Australia. Named by Dutch seafarers who landed on its shores in 1642, it was claimed by the British as a colony about 150 years later. Maoris, the country's indigenous people, fought back but were outgunned, outnumbered, and forced to lay down their arms in the early 1870s. Today, nearly 600,000 of New Zealand's 4.1 million citizens claim some Maori ancestry.

Maori have an age-old legend about how they came to Aotearoa ("Land of the Long White Cloud"), their name for New Zealand: More than twenty-five generations ago, their Polynesian ancestors arrived in a great fleet of sailing canoes from Hawaiki, their mythical homeland sometimes identified with Tahiti where the native language closely resembles their own. According to chants and genealogies passed down through the ages, this fleet consisted of at least seven (perhaps up to thirteen) seafaring canoes. Estimated to weigh about 5 tons, each of these large dugouts had a single claw-shaped sail and may have carried fifty to 120 people, plus food supplies, plants, and animals.

As described by Maori anthropologist Te Rangi Hiroa (Peter Buck), the seafaring skills of these voyagers enabled them to navigate by currents, winds, and stars across vast ocean expanses.[a] Perhaps escaping warfare and tribute payments in Hawaiki, they probably made the five-week long voyage around 1350 AD, although there were earlier and later canoes as well.

Traditional Maori society is organized into about thirty different *iwi* ("tribe"),

grouped in thirteen *waka* ("canoe"), each with its own traditional territory. Today, prior to giving a formal talk, Maoris still introduce themselves by identifying their *iwi*, their *waka*, and the major sacred places of their ancestral territory. Their genealogy connects them to their tribe's founding ancestor who was a crew member or perhaps even a chief in one of the giant canoes mentioned in the legend of the Great Fleet.[b]

Maori oral traditions about their origins fit quite well with scientific data based on anthropological and more recent genetic research. Study by outsiders can be controversial because Maori equate an individual's genes to his or her genealogy, which belongs to one's *iwi* or ancestral community. Considered sacred and entrusted to the tribal elders, genealogy is traditionally surrounded by *tapu* ("sacred prohibitions").[c] The Maori term for genealogy is *whakapapa* ("to set layer upon layer"), which is also a word for "gene." This Maori term captures something of the original *genous*, the Greek word for "begetting offspring"). Another Maori word for gene is *ira tangata* ("life spirit of mortals"), and for them, a gene has *mauri* (a "life force"). Given these spiritual associations, genetic investigations of Maori human DNA could not proceed until the Maori themselves became actively involved in the research.

Together with other researchers, Maori geneticist Adele Whyte has examined sex-linked genetic markers, namely mitochondrial DNA in women and Y chromosomes in men.[d] She recently calculated that the number of Polynesian females required to found New Zealand's

Maori population probably ranged between 170 to 230 women. If the original fleet sailing to Aotearoa consisted of seven large canoes, it may have carried a total of about 600 people (men, women, and children).

A comparison of the DNA of Maori with that of Polynesians across the Pacific Ocean and peoples from Southeast Asia reveals a genetic map of very ancient Maori migration routes. Mitochondrial DNA, which is passed along virtually unchanged from mothers to their children, provides a genetic clock linking today's Polynesians to southern Taiwan's indigenous coastal peoples, showing that female ancestors originally set out from that island off the southeast coast of China about 6,000 years ago.[e] In the next few thousand years, they migrated by way of the Philippines and then hopped south and east from island to island.

Adding to their gene pool in the course of later generations, Melanesian males from New Guinea and elsewhere joined the migrating bands before arriving in Aotearoa. In short, Maori cultural traditions in New Zealand are generally substantiated by anthropological as well as molecular biological data.

[a]Buck, P. H. (1938). *Vikings of the Pacific.* Chicago: University Press of Chicago.

[b]Hanson, A. (1989). The making of the Maori: Culture invention and its logic. *American Anthropologist 91* (4), 890–902.
[c]Mead, A. T. P. (1996). Genealogy, sacredness, and the commodities market. *Cultural Survival Quarterly 20* (2).
[d]Whyte, A. L. H. (2005). Human evolution in Polynesia. *Human Biology 77*(2), 157–177.

[e]Gene study suggests Polynesians came from Taiwan. (2005 , July 4). Reuters.

Gai Ming-sheng/HK China Tourism Press

Unlike the Han, the dominant ethnic majority in China who are patrilineal, several ethnic minorities in southwestern China are matrilineal, including the Mosuo. The women in the Mosuo family shown here are blood relatives of one another, and the men are their brothers. As among the Nayar, discussed in the previous chapter, Mosuo husbands live apart from their wives, in the households of their sisters.

In matrilineal societies females are culturally recognized as socially significant, for they are considered responsible for the group's continued existence. In patrilineal societies, this responsibility falls on the male members of the group, thereby enhancing their social importance.

The two major forms of a unilineal descent group, be it patrilineal or matrilineal, are the lineage and the clan. A **lineage** is a unilineal kinship group descended from a common ancestor or founder who lived four to six generations ago and in which relationships among members can be exactly stated in genealogical terms. A **clan** is an extended unilineal kinship group, often consisting of several lineages, whose members claim common descent from a remote ancestor, usually legendary or mythological.[1]

There is a close relationship between the descent system and a cultural system's infrastructure. Generally, patrilineal descent predominates where male labor is considered of prime importance, as among pastoralists and agriculturalists. Matrilineal descent predominates mainly among horticulturists in societies where female

work in subsistence is especially important. Numerous matrilineal societies are found in southern Asia, one of the earliest cradles of food production in the world. They are also prominent in parts of indigenous North America, South America's tropical lowlands, and parts of Africa.

Patrilineal Descent and Organization: A Chinese Example

Patrilineal descent (sometimes called *agnatic* or *male descent*) is the more widespread of the two unilineal descent systems. The male members of a patrilineal descent group trace through forefathers their descent from a common ancestor (Figure 21.1). Brothers and sisters belong to the descent group of their father's father, their father, their father's siblings, and their father's brother's children. A man's son and daughter also trace their descent back through the male line to their common ancestor. In the typical patrilineal group, authority over the children rests with the father or his elder brother. A woman belongs to the same descent group as her father and his brothers, but her children cannot trace their descent through them.

Patrilineal kinship organization is traditionally embedded in many cultures throughout the world and often endures despite radical political and economic changes. Such is also the case among the Han, the dominant ethnic majority in modern China. Until the communist takeover in 1949, most of rural Chinese society was strongly patrilineal, with a few exceptions such as the Mosuo in the southwestern part of the country. Since then, considerable changes have occurred, although vestiges of the old system persist in different regions. Traditionally, the basic unit for economic cooperation among the Han Chinese was the large extended family, typically including aged parents and their sons, their sons' wives, and their sons' children.[2]

Residence, therefore, was patrilocal, as defined in the previous chapter, so Han Chinese children grew up in a household dominated by their father and his male relatives. The father was a source of discipline from whom a child would maintain a respectful social distance. Often, the father's brother and his sons were members of the same household. Thus, one's paternal uncle was like a second father and deserving of obedience and respect, while his sons were like one's brothers. Accordingly, the Han Chinese kinship term applied to one's own father was extended to the father's brother, and the term for a brother was extended to the father's brother's sons. When families became too large and unwieldy, as frequently happened, one or more sons would move elsewhere to establish separate households. When a son did

[1]See Hoebel, E. A. (1949). *Man in the primitive world: An introduction to anthropology* (pp. 646, 652). New York: McGraw-Hill.

lineage A unilineal kinship group descended from a common ancestor or founder who lived four to six generations ago, and in which relationships among members can be exactly stated in genealogical terms.
clan An extended unilineal kinship group, often consisting of several lineages, whose members claim common descent from a remote ancestor, usually legendary or mythological.

[2]Most of the following is from Hsiaotung, F. (1939). *Peasant life in China*. London: Kegan, Paul, Trench & Truber.

so, however, the tie to the household in which he was born remained strong.

While family membership was important for each individual, the primary social unit was the lineage, or the *tsu,* as it is known among the Han in China. Each *tsu* consisted of men who traced their ancestry back through the male line to a common ancestor, usually within about five generations. Although a woman belonged to her father's *tsu,* for all practical purposes she was absorbed by the *tsu* of her husband, with whom she lived after marriage. Nonetheless, members of her natal (birth) *tsu* retained some interest in her after her departure. Her mother, for example, would assist her in the birth of her children, and her brother or some other male relative would look after her interests, perhaps even intervening if her husband or other members of his family treated her badly.

The function of the *tsu* was to help its members economically and to gather on ceremonial occasions such as weddings and funerals or to make offerings to the ancestors. Recently deceased ancestors, up to about three

generations back, were given offerings of food and paper money on the anniversaries of their births and deaths, while more distant ancestors were collectively worshiped five times a year. Each *tsu* maintained its own shrine for storage of ancestral tablets on which the names of all members were recorded. In addition to its economic and ritual functions, the *tsu* also functioned as a legal body, passing judgment on misbehaving members.

Just as families periodically split up into new ones, so would the larger descent groups periodically splinter along the lines of their main family branches. Causes included disputes among brothers over management of landholdings and suspicion of unfair division of profits. When such fissions occurred, a representative of the new *tsu* would return periodically to the ancestral temple in order to pay respect to the ancestors and record recent births and deaths in the official genealogy.

Ultimately, though the lineage tie to the old *tsu* still would be recognized, a copy of the old genealogy would be made and brought home to the younger *tsu,* and then only its births and deaths would be recorded. In this way, over many centuries, a whole hierarchy of descent groups developed, with all persons having the same surname considering themselves to be members of a great patrilineal clan. With this went surname exogamy, meaning that none of the many bearing the same clan name could marry anyone else within that large group. This marriage rule is still widely practiced today even though clan members no longer carry on ceremonial activities together.

The patrilineal system permeated all of rural Han Chinese social relations. Children owed obedience and respect to their fathers and older patrilineal relatives in life and had to marry whomever their parents chose for them. It was the duty of sons to care for their parents when they became old and helpless, and even after death

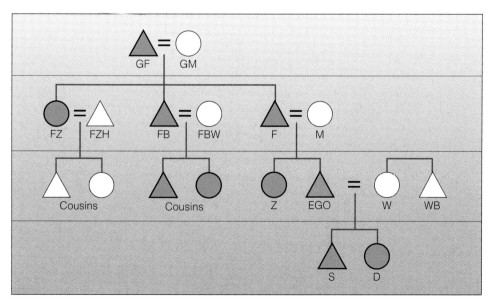

Figure 21.1

How patrilineal descent is traced. Only the individuals symbolized by a filled-in circle or triangle are in the same descent group as EGO (the central person from whom the degree of each kinship relationship is traced). The abbreviation F stands for father, B for brother, H for husband, S for son, M for mother, Z for sister, W for wife, and D for daughter, and G for grand.

In traditional Han Chinese society, offerings were made to the ancestors in special ancestral halls or temples such as the one pictured here, located in a family home in Taishun, Zhejiang Province. Among the Han, the dominant ethnic majority in China, almost all ancestral temples, or clan houses, are dedicated to male forebears, reflecting the country's long-established patrilineal rules of descent and cultural values.

sons had ceremonial obligations to them. Inheritance passed from fathers to sons, with an extra share going to the eldest, since he ordinarily made the greatest contribution to the household and had the greatest responsibility toward his parents after their death. Han Chinese women, by contrast, had no claims on their families' heritable property. Once married, a woman was in effect cast off by her own patrilineal kin (even though they might continue to take an interest in her) in order to produce children for her husband's family and *tsu*.

As the preceding suggests, a patrilineal society is very much a man's world. No matter how valued women may be, they inevitably find themselves in a difficult position. Far from resigning themselves to a subordinate position, however, they actively manipulate the system to their own advantage as best they can.

Matrilineal Descent and Organization: An American Indian Example

As the term implies, matrilineal descent is traced exclusively through the female line (Figure 21.2), just as patrilineal descent is through the male line. However, the matrilineal pattern differs from the patrilineal in that it does not automatically confer gender authority.

Although descent passes through the female line and women may have considerable power, they do not hold exclusive authority in the descent group. They share it with men. Usually, these are the brothers, rather than the husbands, of the women through whom descent is traced. Apparently, the adaptive purpose of matrilineal systems is to provide continuous female solidarity within the female work group. Matrilineal systems are usually found in horticultural societies in which women perform much of the work in the house and nearby gardens. In part because women's labor as crop cultivators is regarded as so important to the society, matrilineal descent prevails.

In a matrilineal system, brothers and sisters belong to the descent group of the mother, the mother's mother, the mother's siblings, and the mother's sisters' children. Thus, every male belongs to the same descent group as his mother, and a man's own children belong to his wife's descent group, not his.

Although not true of all matrilineal systems, a common feature is the relative weakness of the social tie between wife and husband. A woman's husband lacks au-

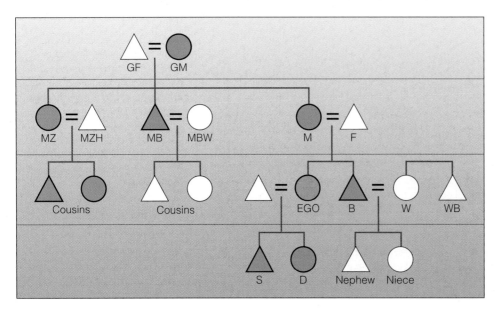

Figure 21.2

This diagram, which traces descent matrilineally, can be compared with that in Figure 21.1, showing patrilineal descent. The two patterns are virtually mirror images. Note that a man cannot transmit descent to his own children.

thority in the household they share. Her brother, and not the husband-father, distributes goods, organizes work, settles disputes, supervises rituals, and administers inheritance and succession rules. Meanwhile, her husband fulfills the same role in his own sister's household. Furthermore, his property and status are inherited by his sister's son rather than his son. Thus, brothers and sisters maintain lifelong ties with one another, whereas marital ties are easily severed. In matrilineal societies, unsatisfactory marriages are more easily ended than in patrilineal societies.

Among Hopi Indians, a farming people whose ancestors have lived in *pueblos* (villages) in northeastern Arizona for many centuries, society is divided into a number of clans based strictly on matrilineal descent.[3] (This is also true of many other Native American groups, such as the White Mountain Apache of Arizona.) At birth, every Hopi is assigned to his or her mother's clan. This affiliation is so important that, in a very real sense, a person has no social identity in the community apart from it. Two or more clans together constitute larger supra-clan units, which anthropologists refer to as *phratries* (discussed later in this chapter). There are nine phratries in Hopi society, and within each phratry member clans are expected to support one another and observe strict exogamy. Because people from all nine phratries can be found living in any given Hopi village, marriage partners usually can be found in one's home community. This same dispersal of membership provides individuals with rights of entry into villages other than their own.

Although phratries and clans are the major kinship units in Hopi culture, the actual functional social units consist of lineages, and there are several in each village. Each Hopi lineage is headed by a senior woman (usually the eldest), although it is her brother or mother's brother who keeps the sacred "medicine bundle" (objects of spiritual power considered essential for peoples' well-being) and plays an active role in running lineage affairs. However, the senior woman is no mere figurehead. She may act as mediator to help resolve disputes among group members. Also, although her brother or mother's brother have the right to offer her advice and criticism, they are equally obligated to listen to what she has to say, and she does not yield her authority to them.

Most female authority, however, is exerted within the household, which is the smallest distinct unit of Hopi society, and here men clearly take second place. These households consist of the women of the lineage with their husbands and unmarried sons, all of whom used to live in sets of adjacent rooms in single large buildings.

Nowadays, nuclear families often live (frequently with a maternal relative or two) in separate houses, but motorized vehicles enable related households to maintain close contact and cooperation as before.

Hopi lineages function as landholding corporations, allocating land for the support of member households. These lands are farmed by "outsiders," the husbands of the women whose lineage owns the land, and the harvest belongs to these women. Thus, Hopi men spend their lives laboring for their wives' lineages, and in return they are given food and shelter. Although sons learn from their fathers how to farm, a man has no real authority over his son. This is because a man's own children belong to his wife's lineage while his sister's children form part of his. Thus, when parents have difficulty with an unruly child, the mother's brother is called upon to mete out discipline. A man's loyalties are therefore divided between his wife's household on the one hand and his sisters' on the other. According to tradition, if a man is perceived as being an unsatisfactory husband, his wife merely has to place his personal belongings outside the door, and the marriage is over.

In addition to their economic and legal functions, lineages play a role in Hopi ceremonial activities. Although membership in the associations that actually perform ceremonies is open to all who have the proper qualifications, clans own and manage all the associations, and in each village, a leading lineage acts as its clan's representative. This lineage owns a special house where the clan's religious paraphernalia are stored and cared for by the "clan mother." Together with her brother, the clan's "big uncle," she helps manage ceremonial activity. Although men control most of the associations that do the actual performing, women still have vital roles to play. For example, they provide the cornmeal, symbolic of natural and spiritual life that is a necessary ingredient in virtually all ceremonies.

Traditionally, each Hopi village was politically autonomous, with its own chief and village council. Here again, however, descent group organization made itself

[3]Most of the following is from Connelly, J. C. (1979). Hopi social organization. In A. Ortiz (Ed.), *Handbook of North American Indians, Vol. 9, Southwest* (pp. 539–553). Washington, D.C.: Smithsonian Institution.

White Mountain Apaches in Arizona are organized in dozens of matrilineal clans. Closely related through the maternal line, small groups of these American Indian women lived and worked together, farming on the banks of streams in the mountains and gathering wild foods in ancestral territories. They trace their ancestry to *Is dzán naadleeshe'* (Changing Woman), a mythological founding mother. This photo shows three generations in prayer during a traditional puberty ceremony known as *na'ii'ees* ("getting her ready"), also called a Sunrise Dance. During this event, marking a girl's transition into womanhood, the sacred power of her clan's founding mother ritually passes to her.

© Lawrence Migdale/PIX

felt, for the council was made up of men who inherited their positions through their clans. Moreover, the powers of the chief and his council were limited; the chief's major job was to maintain harmony between his village and the spiritual world, and whatever authority he and his council wielded was directed at coordination of community effort, not enforcement of official decrees. Decisions were made on a consensual basis, and women's views had to be considered, as well as those of men.

Once again, although men held positions of authority, women had considerable control over their decisions in a behind-the-scenes way. These men, after all, lived in households women controlled, and their position within them depended largely on how well they got along with the senior women. Outside the household, women's refusal to play their part in the performance of ceremonies gave them veto power. Small wonder, then, that Hopi men readily admit that "women usually get their way."[4]

Other Forms of Descent

Among Samoan Islanders (and many other cultures in the Pacific as well as in Southeast Asia) a person has the option of affiliating with either the mother's or the father's descent group. Known as *ambilineal descent,* such a kin-ordered system provides a measure of flexibility. However, this flexibility also introduces a possibility of dispute and conflict as unilineal groups compete for members.

This problem does not arise under *double descent,* or double unilineal descent, a very rare system whereby descent is reckoned both patrilineally and matrilineally at the same time. Here descent is matrilineal for some purposes and patrilineal for others.

Generally, where double descent is traced, the matrilineal and patrilineal groups take action in different spheres of society. For example, among the Yakö of eastern Nigeria, property is divided into both patrilineal possessions and matrilineal possessions.[5] The patrilineage owns perpetual productive resources, such as land, whereas the matrilineage owns consumable property, such as livestock. The legally weaker matriline is somewhat more important in religious matters than the patriline. Through double descent, a Yakö might inherit grazing lands from the father's patrilineal group and certain ritual privileges from the mother's matrilineal group.

Finally, when descent derives from both the mother's and father's families equally, anthropologists use the term *bilateral descent.* In such a system people trace their descent from all ancestors, regardless of their gender or side of the family. We may recognize bilateral descent when individuals apply the same genealogical terms to identify similarly related individuals on both sides of the family—when they speak of a "grandmother" or "grandfather," for instance, no indication is given whether these relatives are on the paternal or maternal side of the family.

Bilateral descent exists in various foraging cultures and is also quite common in many contemporary state societies with agricultural, industrial, or postindustrial economies. For example, although most people in Eu-

[4]Schlegel, A. (1977). Male and female in Hopi thought and action. In A. Schlegel (Ed.), *Sexual stratification* (p. 254). New York: Columbia University Press.

[5]Forde, C. D. (1968). Double descent among the Yakö. In P. Bohannan & J. Middleton (Eds.), *Kinship and social organization* (pp. 179–191). Garden City, NY: Natural History Press.

rope, Australia, and North America typically inherit their father's family name (indicative of a culture's history in which patrilineal descent was the norm), they usually consider themselves as much a member of their mother's as their father's family.

DESCENT INTEGRATED IN THE CULTURAL SYSTEM

Regardless of how descent is traced, descent groups are usually more than mere sets of relatives providing emotional support and a sense of belonging. In nonindustrial societies they are tightly organized working units providing security and services in what can be a difficult, uncertain life. The tasks descent groups perform are manifold. Besides acting as economic units providing mutual aid to their members, they may act to support the aged and infirm and help with marriages and deaths. Often, they play a role in determining who an individual may or may not marry. The descent group also may act as a repository of religious traditions. Ancestor worship, for example, is often a powerful force acting to reinforce group solidarity.

In many societies an individual has no legal or political status except as a lineage member. Since "citizenship" is derived from lineage membership and legal status depends on it, political powers are derived from it as well. Because a lineage endures after the deaths of members with new members continually born into it, it has a con-

tinuing existence that enables it to act like a corporation, as in owning property, organizing productive activities, distributing goods and labor power, assigning status, and regulating relations with other groups. Thus it is a strong, effective base of social organization.

Beyond providing an important structure for social organization in kin-ordered societies, the descent group is also culturally represented in a society's worldview (superstructure), which provides relevant explanation and direction to its members. That is to say, there are certain important cultural ideas and values that members collectively subscribe to and reinforce by means of culturally appropriate rituals, ceremonies, and a range of social practices. As a traditional institution in a kin-ordered society, the descent group often endures in state-organized societies where political institutions are ineffective or weakly developed. Such is the case in many countries of the world today, especially in remote mountain or desert villages difficult to reach by state authorities.

Because the cultural ideas, values, and practices associated with traditional descent groups may be deeply embedded, such patterns of culture often endure in *diasporic communities* (among immigrants who have relocated from their ancestral homelands and retain their distinct cultural identities as ethnic minority groups in their new host countries). In such situations, it is not uncommon to find people seeking familiar kin-ordered cultural solutions to challenges faced in unfamiliar state-organized settings. We see an example of this in the following Original Study.

Original Study ■ By Clementine van Eck

Honor Killings in The Netherlands

When I first told my anthropology professors I wanted to write my dissertation on honor killing among Turkish immigrants in the Netherlands, they told me no way. It was the mid-1990s, and everyone seemed to feel that writing negative things about struggling immigrants was discriminatory. Better to choose a subject that would help them deal with the challenges of settling in Dutch society, such as the problems they experienced as foreigners in school or at work. But I was quite determined to investigate this issue and finally found a professor who shared my interest—Dr. Anton Blok. He himself was specialized in Italian mafia,[a]

[a]Blok, A. (1974). *The mafia of a Sicilian village 1860–1960.* New York: Harper & Row.

so quite used to violence of the cultural sort.

Before getting into some of the details of my research, I need to set the stage. Until the 1960s, the Netherlands was a relatively homogenous society (despite its colonial past). The major differences among its people were not ethnic but religious, namely their distinct ties to Catholicism or Protestantism (of various kinds). The country's population makeup began to change dramatically after the economic boom of the 1960s created a need for cheap labor and led to an influx of migrants from poor areas in Mediterranean countries seeking wage-earning opportunities.

These newcomers came not as immigrants but as "guest laborers"

(*gastarbeiders*) expected to return to their countries of origin, including Italy, Yugoslavia, Turkey, and Morocco. While many did go back home, numerous others did not. In contrast to most of the guest workers from southern European nations, those from Turkey and Morocco are mainly Muslim. And unlike southern European workers who stayed on as immigrants and successfully assimilated into Dutch society, many of the Muslim newcomers formed isolated, diasporic communities.

During the past three decades, these communities have expanded in size and are concentrated in certain areas of various cities. Today, the Turkish population in the Netherlands is about

CONTINUED

350,000. Most of them have become Dutch citizens, but they maintain some key cultural features of their historical "honor-and-shame" traditions. And this is what is at stake when we are dealing with the problem of honor killing.

Anthropologists have identified honor-and-shame traditions in many parts of the world, especially in remote traditional herding and farming societies where the power of the political state is either absent or ineffective. People in such areas, my professor, Dr. Blok, explained,

> cannot depend on stable centers of political control for the protection of life and patrimony. In the absence of effective state control, they have to rely on their own forces—on various forms of self-help. These conditions . . . put a premium on self-assertive qualities in men, involving the readiness and capacity to use physical force in order to guarantee the immunity of life and property, including women as the most precious and vulnerable part of the patrimony of men. The extremes of this sense of honour are reached when even merely glancing at a woman is felt as an affront, an incursion into a male domain, touching off a violent response.[b]

Beyond serving as a means of social control in isolated areas, honor-and-shame traditions may be used in situations where state mechanisms are alien to a certain group of people, as among some Turkish and Moroccan migrants in the Netherlands. Focusing on the latter, I tried to make sense of certain cultural practices that often baffle indigenous Dutch citizens accustomed to a highly organized bureaucratic state where our personal security and justice are effectively managed by social workers, police, courts, and so on. Most of all, I wanted to understand honor killings.

Honor killings are murders in the form of a ritual and they are carried out to purify tarnished honor—specifically honor having to do with something Turks refer to as *namus*. Both men and women pos-

[b]Blok, A. (1981). Rams and billy-goats: A key to the Mediterranean code of honour. *Man, New Series 16* (3), 427–440. See also Van Eck, C. (2003). *Purified by blood: honour killings amongst Turks in the Netherlands.* Amsterdam University Press.

sess *namus*. For women and girls *namus* means chastity, while for men it means having chaste family members. A man is therefore dependent for his *namus* on the conduct of the womenfolk in his family. This means in effect that women and girls must not have illicit contact with a member of the opposite sex and must avoid becoming the subject of gossip, since gossip alone can impugn *namus*. The victim of an honor killing can be the girl or woman who tarnished her honor, or the man who did this to her (usually her boyfriend). The girl or woman is killed by her family members, the man is killed by the family of the girl/woman whose honor he has violated.

As I was wrapping up my Ph.D. in 2000, Dutch society still didn't seem quite ready to acknowledge the phenomenon of honor killing. That year a Kurdish boy whose parents were born in Turkey tried to shoot the boyfriend of his sister. Because the attempt took place in a high school and resulted in injury to several students and a teacher, authorities focused on the issue of school safety rather than on the cultural reasons behind the murder attempt.

A shift in government and public awareness of honor killing took place in 2004. That year three Muslim Turkish women were killed by their former husbands on the street. Coming in quick succession, one after the other, these murders did not escape the attention of government officials or the media. Finally, honor killing was on the national agenda. In November of that year I was appointed as cultural anthropologist at the Dutch police force in The Hague district and began working with law enforcers on honor killing cases there (and soon in other areas of the country).

On 2 November 2004, the day I gave an opening speech about honor killings to colleagues at my new job, a radical Muslim migrant from Morocco shot the famous Dutch author and film director Theo van Gogh, well known for his critical, often mocking, views on Islam. Although his murder was not an honor killing, it had key elements of that cleansing ritual: It occurred in a public place (on the street) in front of many people, the victim had to die (injury would not suffice), the killer used many shots (or knife thrusts), the killing was planned (it was not the product of a sudden outburst), and the killer had no remorse.

Let me tell you about a recent and quite typical case. On a Friday evening the local police in an eastern Dutch community called in the help of our police team. A 17-year-old Turkish girl had run away to the family home of her Dutch boyfriend, also 17. Her father, who had discovered that this boy had a police record, telephoned his parents and asked them to send the daughter home. The parents tried to calm him down and told him his daughter was safe at their house. But as he saw it, she was in the most unsafe place in the world, for she was with the boy she loved. This could only mean that her virginity was in jeopardy and therefore the *namus* of the whole family.

My colleagues and I concluded that the girl had to be taken out of her boyfriend's home that same night: the father knew the place, he didn't want the boy as a son-in-law, and he believed his daughter not mature enough to make a decision about something as important as marriage. ("Just having a boyfriend" was not allowed. You either marry or you don't have a boyfriend, at least not an obvious one.) Because of my honor killing research, I was well aware of similar situations that ended in honor killings. To leave the girl where she was would invite disaster.

After we persuaded the prosecutor that intervention was necessary, the girl was taken from her boyfriend's house and brought to a guarded shelter to prevent her from fleeing back to him the next day. This is anthropology-in-action. You cannot always just wait and see what will happen (although I admit that as a scholar this is very tempting); you have to take responsibility and take action if you're convinced that a human life is at stake.

When I took up the study of cultural anthropology, I did so just because it intrigued me. I never imagined that what I learned might become really useful. So, what I would like to say to anthropology students is: Never give up on an interesting subject. One day it might just matter that you have become an expert in that area. At this moment I am analyzing all kinds of threatening cases and drawing up genealogies of the families involved—all in the effort to deepen our understanding of and help prevent honor killings. ∎

Clearly, descent carries codes of conduct. And, whatever form of descent predominates, the kin of both mother and father are important components of the social structure in all societies. Just because descent may be traced patrilineally, for example, does not mean that matrilineal relatives are necessarily unimportant. It simply means that, for purposes of group membership, the mother's relatives are excluded. Similarly, under matrilineal descent, the father's relatives are excluded for purposes of group membership.

By way of example, we have seen in preceding chapters how important paternal relatives are among the matrilineal Trobriand Islanders of the southern Pacific. Although children belong to their mother's descent groups, fathers play an important role in nurturing and educating them. Upon marriage, the bride's and groom's paternal relatives contribute to the exchange of gifts, and, throughout life, a man may expect his paternal kin to help him improve his economic and political position in society. Eventually, sons may expect to inherit personal property from their fathers.

In some cultures, lineages facing exceptional challenges to their survival may choose to ritually adopt individuals not related by birth. Such was the case among Iroquois Indians in Northeast America, for instance. In the 17th and 18th centuries, they often incorporated specially selected war captives and other valued strangers, including some Dutch, French, English, and other non-Indians, into their lineages in order to make up for population losses due to warfare and diseases. As soon as these newcomers were ceremonially naturalized, they acquired essentially the same birthright status as those actually born into the lineage.

Lineage Exogamy

A common characteristic of lineages is *exogamy.* As defined in the previous chapter, this means that lineage members must find their marriage partners in other lineages. One advantage of exogamy is that competition for desirable spouses within the group is curbed, promoting the group's solidarity. Lineage exogamy also means that each marriage is more than a union between two individuals; it is as well a new alliance between lineages. This helps to maintain them as components of larger social systems. Finally, lineage exogamy maintains open communication within a society, promoting the diffusion of knowledge from one lineage to another.

In contemporary North American Indian communities, kinship and descent play an essential role in tribal membership—as illustrated in this chapter's Anthropology Applied.

From Lineage to Clan

In the course of time, as generation succeeds generation and new members are born into the lineage, the kinship group's membership may become too large to be manageable or too much for the lineage's resources to support. When this happens, as we have seen with the Chinese *tsu,* **fission** occurs; that is, the original lineage splits into new, smaller lineages. Usually the members of the new lineages continue to recognize their original relationship to one another. The result of this process is the appearance of a larger kind of descent group: the clan.

As already noted, a clan—typically consisting of several lineages—is an extended unilineal descent group whose members claim common descent from a distant ancestor (usually legendary or mythological) but are unable to trace the precise genealogical links back to that ancestor. This stems from the great genealogical depth of the clan, whose founding ancestor lived so far in the past that the links must be assumed rather than known in detail. A clan differs from a lineage in another respect: It lacks the residential unity generally—although not invariably—characteristic of a lineage's core members. As with the lineage, descent may be patrilineal, matrilineal, or ambilineal.

Because clan membership is dispersed rather than localized, it usually does not involve a shared holding of tangible property. Instead, it involves shared participation in ceremonial and political matters. Only on special occasions will the membership gather together for specific purposes. Clans, however, may handle important integrative functions. Like lineages, they may regulate marriage through exogamy. Because of their dispersed membership, they give individuals the right of entry into local groups other than their own. Members usually are expected to give protection and hospitality to others in the clan. Hence, these can be expected in any local group that includes people who belong to a single clan.

Clans, lacking the residential unity of lineages, frequently depend on symbols—of animals, plants, natural forces, colors, and special objects—to provide members with solidarity and a ready means of identification. These symbols, called *totems,* often are associated with the clan's mythical origin and reinforce for clan members an awareness of their common descent.

The word *totem* comes from the Ojibwa American Indian word *ototeman,* meaning "he is a relative of mine." **Totemism** was defined by the British anthropologist A. R. Radcliffe-Brown as a set of customary beliefs

fission The splitting of a descent group into two or more new descent groups.
totemism The belief that people are related to particular animals, plants, or natural objects by virtue of descent from common ancestral spirits.

Anthropology Applied

Resolving a Native American Tribal Membership Dispute ▪ By Harald E. L. Prins

In autumn 1998, I received a call from the tribal chief of the Aroostook band of Micmacs in Northern Maine asking for help in resolving a bitter tribal membership dispute. The conflict centered on the fact that several hundred individuals had become tribal members without proper certification of their Micmac kinship status. Traditionalists in the community argued that their tribe's organization was being taken over by "non-Indians." With the formal status of so many members in question, the tribal administration could not properly determine who was entitled to benefit from the available health, housing, and education programs. After some hostile confrontations between the factions, tribal elders requested a formal inquiry into the membership controversy, and I was called in as a neutral party with a long history of working with the band.

My involvement as an advocacy anthropologist began in 1981, when these Micmacs (also spelled Mi'kmaq) first employed me (with Bunny McBride) as Co-Director of Research and Development. At the time, they formed a poor and landless community not yet officially recognized as a tribe. During that decade, we helped the band define its political strategies, which focused on petitioning for federal recognition of their Indian status, claiming traditional rights to hunt, trap, and fish, and even demanding return of lost ancestral lands.

To generate popular support for the effort, I co-produced a film about the community (*Our Lives in Our Hands*, 1986). Most important, we gathered oral histories and detailed archival documentation to address kinship issues and other government criteria for tribal recognition. The latter included important

genealogical records showing that most Micmac adults in the region were at least "half-blood" (having two of their grandparents officially recorded as Indians).

Based on this evidence, we effectively argued that Aroostook Micmacs could claim aboriginal title to lands in the region and convinced politicians in Washington, D.C., to introduce a special bill to acknowledge their tribal status and settle their land claims. When formal hearings were held in 1990, I testified in the U.S. Senate as expert witness for the Micmacs. The following year, the Aroostook band of Micmacs Settlement Act became federal law. This made the band eligible for the financial assistance (health, housing, education and child welfare) and economic development loans available to all federally recognized tribes in the United States. Moreover, it provided the band with funding to buy a 5,000-acre territorial base in Maine.

Flush with federal funding and rapidly expanding its activities, the 500-member band became overwhelmed by complex

© David Sanipass

The Sanipass-Lafford family cluster in Chapman, Maine, represents a traditional Micmac residential kin group. Such extended families typically include grandchildren and bilaterally related family members such as in-laws, uncles, and aunts. Taken from the Sanipass family album, this picture shows a handful of members in the mid-1980s: Marline Sanipass Morey with two of her nephews and uncles.

bureaucratic regulations now governing their existence. Without formally established ground rules determining who could apply for tribal membership, and overlooking federally imposed regulations, hundreds of new names were rather casually added to its tribal rolls.

By 1997, the Aroostook band population had ballooned to almost 1,200 members, and Micmac traditionalists were questioning the legitimacy of many whose names had been added to the band roll. With mounting tension threatening to destroy the band, the tribal chief invited me to evaluate critically the membership claims of more than half the tribe. In early 1999, I reviewed kinship records submitted by hundreds of individuals whose membership on the tribal rolls was in question. Several months later, I offered my final report to the Micmac community.

After traditional prayers, sweetgrass burning, drumming, and a traditional meal of salmon and moose, I formally presented my findings: Based on the official criteria, about 100 lineal descendants of the original members and just over 150 newcomers met the minimum required qualifications for membership; several hundred would have to be stripped from the tribal rolls. After singing, drumming, and closing prayers, the Micmac gathering dispersed.

Today, the band numbers about 850 members and is doing well. It has purchased several tracts of land (collectively over 600 acres), including a small residential reservation near Presque Isle, now home to about 200 Micmacs. Also located here are new tribal administration offices, a health clinic, and a cultural center.

Tsimshian people of Metlakatla, Alaska, raise a memorial totem pole gifted to the community by noted carver David Boxley, a member of the Eagle clan. The tradition of erecting totem poles to commemorate special events endures in several Native American communities in the Pacific Northwest. Carved from tall cedar trees, these spectacular monuments display a clan or lineage's ceremonial property and are prominently positioned as frontal house posts, as markers at grave sites, or at some other place of significance. Often depicting legendary ancestors and mythological animals, the painted carvings symbolically represent a descent group's cultural status and associated privileges in the community.

and practices "by which there is set up a special system of relations between the society and the plants, animals, and other natural objects that are important in the social life."[6] For example, Hopi Indian matrilineal clans in Arizona bear such totemic names as Bear, Bluebird, Butterfly, Lizard, Spider, and Snake.

Totemism varies among cultures. A reductive variation of totemism may be found in contemporary industrial and postindustrial societies, where sports teams are often given the names of such powerful wild animals as bears, lions, and wildcats. In the United States, this extends to the Democratic Party's donkey and the Republican Party's elephant, to the Elks, the Lions, and other fraternal and social organizations. These animal emblems, or mascots, however, do not involve the notion of biological descent and the strong sense of kinship that they have for clans, nor are they linked with the various ritual observances associated with clan totems.

In addition to the above-mentioned matrilineal clans (or matriclans), there are also patrilineal clans (or patriclans) tracing descent exclusively through men from a founding ancestor. Historically, a few dozen of such clans existed in the Scottish highlands, often identified with the prefix "Mac" or "Mc" (from an old Celtic word meaning "son of"). During the past few hundred years, large Scottish clans such as McGregor and Mackenzie broke apart as many members moved away in search of economic opportunity. Today, their descendants are dispersed all across the globe, especially in countries such as Australia, Canada, England, New Zealand, and the United States. During the past few decades, widely scat-

tered descendants have sought to re-establish their kinship ties to ancestral clans, and many travel from afar to attend the annual gathering of their clan, preferably in their traditional ancient homeland in the highlands of Scotland. These clan members express their kinship with one another by wearing woolen shawls, kilts, or other pieces of clothing made of their clan tartan—a distinct plaid pattern and color identifying their particular clan membership.

In the highlands of Scotland, as among many traditional peoples around the world, large kinship groups known as clans have been important units of social organization. Now dispersed all over the world, clan members gather and express their sense of kinship with one another by wearing a tartan skirt, or kilt, with a distinct plaid pattern and color identifying clan membership. Shown here is a Turnbull clan gathering in Stone Mountain, Georgia.

---

[6]Radcliffe-Brown, A. R. (1931) Social organization of Australian tribes. *Oceana Monographs 1*, 29.

Phratries and Moieties

Larger kinds of descent groups are phratries and moieties (Figure 21.3). A **phratry** (after the Greek word for "brotherhood") is a unilineal descent group composed of at least two clans that supposedly share a common ancestry, whether or not they really do. Like individuals in the clan, phratry members cannot trace precisely their descent links to a common ancestor, although they firmly believe such an ancestor existed.

If the entire society is divided into only two major descent groups, whether they are equivalent to clans or phratries, each group is called a **moiety** (after the French word *moitié,* for "half"). Members of the moiety believe themselves to share a common ancestor but cannot prove it through definite genealogical links. As a rule, the feelings of kinship among members of lineages and clans are stronger than those of members of phratries and moieties. This may be due to the much larger size and more diffuse nature of the latter groups.

Since feelings of kinship are often weaker between people from different clans, the moiety system is a cultural invention that keeps clan-based communities together by binding the clans into a social network of obligatory giving and receiving. That is to say, by institutionalizing reciprocity between groups of clans, the moiety system binds together families who otherwise would not be sufficiently invested in maintaining the commonwealth.

Like lineages and clans, phratries and moieties are often exogamous and so are bound together by marriages between their members. And like clans, they provide members rights of access to other communities as among the Hopi. In a community that does not include one's clan members, one's phratry members are still there to turn to for hospitality. Finally, moieties may perform reciprocal services for one another. Among them, individuals turn to members of the opposite "half" in their community for the necessary mourning rituals when a member of their own moiety dies. Such interdependence between moieties, again, serves to maintain the cohesion of the entire society.

The kin-ordered social structure of the Winnebago Indian nation (since 1993, known as the Ho-Chunk Nation—"People of the Sacred Language") offers an interesting ethnographic example of the moiety system. Organized in twelve patrilineal clans, these North American

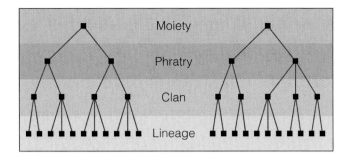

Figure 21.3

This diagram shows how lineages, clans, phratries, and moieties form an organizational hierarchy. Each moiety is subdivided into phratries, each phratry is subdivided into clans, and each clan is subdivided into lineages.

Indians, traditionally ranging the woodlands and prairies of southern Wisconsin, were divided between "those who are above" (Sky) and "those who are below" (Earth). The Sky moiety included the Eagle, Hawk, Pigeon, and Thunder clans, whereas those belonging to the Earth "half" consisted of the Bear, Buffalo, Deer, Elk, Fish, Snake, Water Spirit, and Wolf clans. These exogamous moieties not only regulated marriage and leadership positions among the Ho-Chunk, but even structured their traditional settlement patterns, with Sky clans inhabiting the southwest half of each village and those of the Earth moiety the northeast.[7] For archaeologists excavating ancient Ho-Chunk village sites, of course, the physical reflection in a traditional village layout of such clearly demarcated kinship patterns has considerable interpretive potential.

The principle of institutionalized reciprocity between groups of matrilineal clans organized into two equal halves, or moieties, is beautifully illustrated in the circular settlement pattern of many traditional Indian villages in the tropical forest of South America's Amazon region. Dwellings located in one-half of the village are those of clans belonging to one exogamous moiety, and those on the opposite side are the dwellings of clans belonging to the other. Since their clans are often matrilineal, the institutionalized rules of reciprocity in this kin-ordered community traditionally require that a woman marry a man from a clan house on the opposite side of the village, who then moves into her ancestral clan house. Their son, however, will one day have to find a wife from his father's original moiety and will have to move to his father's mother's side of the village. That is to say, the moiety system of institutionalized reciprocity functions like a social "zipper" between otherwise unconnected clans.

---

phratry A unilineal descent group composed of at least two clans that supposedly share a common ancestry, whether or not they really do.

moiety Each group that results from a division of a society into two halves on the basis of descent.

[7]Radin, P. (1923). The Winnebago tribe. In *37th annual report of the Bureau of American Ethnology, 1915–1916* (pp. 33–550). Washington, D.C.: Government Printing Office.

Many Amazonian Indians in South America's tropical woodlands traditionally live in circular villages socially divided into moieties. Here we see the Canela Indians' Escalvado village as it was in 1970. (Behind it is a smaller abandoned village where part of the tribe lived before uniting under one chief.) The village is 300 meters (nearly 1,000 feet) in diameter with a central plaza about 50 meters (165 feet) wide. The community's "upper" moiety meets in the eastern part (right) of the village, and the "lower" moiety meets in the western part. Nearly all 1,800 members of the Canela tribe reside in the village during festival seasons, but otherwise they are largely dispersed to their smaller, farm-centered circular villages. (Missionaries built the landing strip.)

BILATERAL KINSHIP AND THE KINDRED

Important though descent groups are in many societies, they are not found in all societies, nor are they the only kinds of extended kinship groups to be found. *Bilateral kinship,* a characteristic of most contemporary European and American societies as well as a number of food-foraging cultures, affiliates a person with genetically close relatives (but not in-laws) through both sexes. In other words, the individual traces descent through both parents, all four grandparents, and so forth, recognizing multiple ancestors. Theoretically, one is associated equally with all "blood" relatives on both the mother's and father's sides of the family. Thus, this principle relates an individual lineally to all eight great-grandparents and laterally to all third and fourth cousins.

Since such a huge group is too big to be socially practical, it is usually reduced to a smaller circle of paternal and maternal relatives, called the kindred. The **kindred** may be defined as an individual's close blood relatives on the maternal and paternal side of his or her family. Since the kindred is laterally rather than lineally organized—that is, **EGO,** or the central person from whom the degree of each relationship is traced, is the center of the group—it is not a true descent group (Figure 21.4).

Most North Americans are familiar with the kindred; those who belong are simply referred to as relatives. It includes those blood relatives on both sides of the family who are seen on important occasions, such as family weddings, reunions, and funerals. They can iden-

tify the members of their kindred up to grandparents and first, if not always second, cousins.

The limits of the kindred, however, are variable and indefinite. No one ever can be absolutely certain which relatives to invite to every important function and which to exclude. Inevitably, situations arise that require some debate about whether or not to invite particular, usually distant, relatives. Kindreds are thus not clearly bounded and lack the distinctiveness of the lineage. (They are also temporary, lasting only as long as the functions for which they are assembled.)

Unlike a descent group, the kindred is not self-perpetuating—it ceases with EGO's death. It has no constant leader, nor can it easily hold, administer, or pass on property. Because of its vagueness, temporary nature, and changing affiliation, the kindred cannot function as a group except in relation to EGO. In most cases, it cannot organize work, nor can it easily administer justice or assign status.

It can, however, be turned to for aid. In non-Western societies, for example, raiding or trading parties may be composed of kindreds. The group comes together to perform some particular function, shares the results, and then disbands. It also can act as a ceremonial group for rites of passage: initiation ceremonies and the like. In traditional European societies, kindreds acted

kindred An individual's close blood relatives on the maternal and paternal sides of his or her family.
EGO The central person from whom the degree of each relationship is traced.

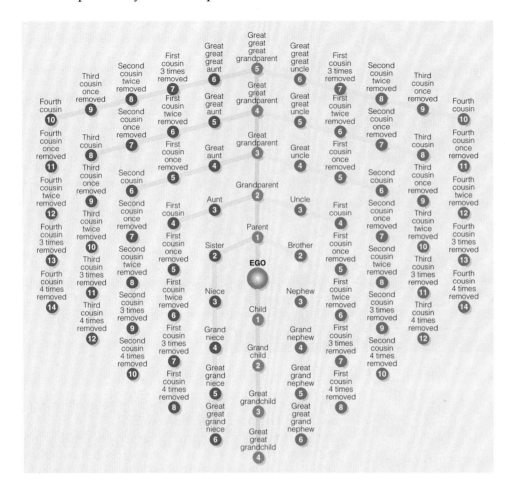

Figure 21.4
The kindred is traditionally of importance in many European cultures. It designates a person's exact degree of being related by blood to other relatives in the family. This degree of blood relatedness determines not only one's social obligations toward relatives but also one's rights. For instance, when a wealthy widowed great-aunt has died without children and without a will, specific surviving members of her kindred will be legally entitled to inherit from her.

to raise bail, compensate a victim's family, or take revenge for the murder or injury of someone in one's own kindred. Finally, kindreds also can regulate marriage through exogamy.

Kindreds are frequently found in industrial and postindustrial state societies where capitalist wage labor conditions bring on mobility and promote individualism, thereby weakening the importance of a strong kinship organization.

CULTURAL EVOLUTION OF THE DESCENT GROUP

Just as different types of families occur in different societies, so do different kinds of non-family kin groups. Descent groups, for example, are not a common feature of food-foraging societies, which are usually small. In many crop-cultivating or herding societies, however, the descent group usually provides the basic structural framework of the social system.

It is generally agreed that lineages arise from extended family organization, so long as organizational challenges exist that such structures help solve. All that is required, really, is that as members of existing ex-

tended families find it necessary to split off and establish new households elsewhere, they not move too far away; that the core members of such related families explicitly acknowledge their descent from a common ancestor; and that they continue to participate in common activities in an organized way. As this process proceeds, lineages will develop, and these may with time give rise to clans and ultimately moieties.

Another way that clans may arise is as fictive kin groups to politically integrate otherwise autonomous ethnic groups. The six Iroquois Indian nations of what now is New York State, for example, developed clans by simply behaving as if lineages of the same name in different villages were related. Thus, their members became fictitious "brothers" and "sisters." By this device, members of, say, a Bear clan in a Mohawk village could travel to a nearby Oneida village, or more distant Onondaga, Cayuga, Tuscarora, or even Seneca villages some 200 miles west of their homeland, and be welcomed in and hosted in any of these Iroquois settlements by members of local Bear clans. In this way, the six neighboring Iroquois nations achieved a wider cultural unity than had previously existed.

As larger, dispersed descent groups develop, the conditions that gave rise to extended families and lineages

KINSHIP TERMINOLOGY AND KINSHIP GROUPS

Any system of organizing people who are relatives into different kinds of groups—whether kindreds, lineages, or clans—influences how relatives are labeled in any given society. Kinship terminology systems vary considerably across cultures, reflecting the positions individuals occupy within their respective societies and helping to differentiate one relative from another. Distinguishing factors include gender, generational differences, or genealogical differences. In the various systems of kinship terminology, any one of these factors may be emphasized at the expense of others.

By looking at the terms people in a particular society use for their relatives, an anthropologist can tell how kinship groups are structured, what relationships are considered especially important, and sometimes what the prevailing attitudes are concerning various relationships. For instance, a number of languages use the same term to identify a brother and a cousin, and others have a single word for cousin, niece, and nephew. Some cultures find it useful to distinguish an oldest brother from his younger brothers and have different words for these brothers. And unlike English, many languages distinguish between an aunt who is mother's sister and one who is father's sister.

Regardless of the factors emphasized, all kinship terminologies accomplish two important tasks. First, they classify similar kinds of individuals into single specific categories; second, they separate different kinds of individuals into distinct categories. Generally, two or more kin are merged under the same term when the individuals have more or less the same rights and obligations with respect to the person referring to them as such. Such is the case among most English-speaking North Americans, for instance, when someone refers to a mother's sister and father's sister both as an "aunt." As far as the speaker is concerned, both relatives possess a similar status.

Several different systems of kinship terminology result from the application of the above principles just mentioned, including the Eskimo, Hawaiian, Iroquois, Crow, Omaha, Sudanese, Kariera, and Aranda systems, each named after the ethnographic example first or best described by anthropologists. The last five of these systems are fascinating in their complexity and are found among only a few of the world's societies. However, to illustrate some of the basic principles involved, we will focus our attention on the first three systems.

Eskimo System

The Eskimo system, comparatively rare among all the world's systems, is the one used by Euramericans, as well as by a number of food-foraging peoples (including

Clans among the Six Nations of the Iroquois confederacy in New York State are a kinship construct that allowed people to freely travel among multiple member villages. This portrait, done in 1710, shows Sa Ga Yeath Qua Pieth Tow, a chief of the Mohawk Nation. Behind him stands a bear, which represents his clan.

may change. For example, lineages may lose their economic bases if developing political institutions take control of resources. In such circumstances, lineages would be expected to disappear as important organizational units. Clans, however, might survive, if they continue to provide an important integrative function. Such is the case with the Scottish clans discussed earlier. This helps explain their continued strength and vitality even far outside Scotland today. They perform an integrative function among kin who are geographically dispersed as well as socially diverse—and they do this in a way that does not conflict with the mobility characteristic of industrial or postindustrial societies.

In societies where small domestic units—nuclear families or single-parent households—are of primary importance, bilateral kinship and kindred organization are likely to result. This can be seen in modern industrial and postindustrial societies, in newly emerging societies in the "underdeveloped" world, and in still-existing food-foraging societies throughout the world.

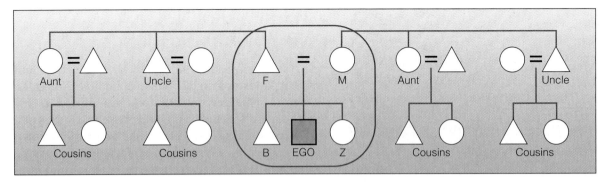

Figure 21.5

The Eskimo system of kinship terminology emphasizes the nuclear family (circled). EGO's father and mother are distinguished from EGO's aunts and uncles, and siblings from cousins.

the Inuit and other Eskimos; hence the name). Sometimes referred to as the *lineal system,* the **Eskimo system** emphasizes the nuclear family by specifically identifying mother, father, brother, and sister while lumping together all other relatives into a few large categories (Figure 21.5). For example, the father is distinguished from the father's brother (uncle); but the father's brother is not distinguished from the mother's brother (both are called "uncle"). The mother's sister and father's sister are treated similarly, both called "aunt." In addition, all the sons and daughters of aunts and uncles are called "cousin," thereby making a generational distinction but without indicating the side of the family to which they belong or even their gender.

Unlike other terminologies, the Eskimo system pro-

Eskimo system Kinship reckoning in which the nuclear family is emphasized by specifically identifying the mother, father, brother, and sister, while lumping together all other relatives into broad categories such as uncle, aunt, and cousin. Also referred to as lineal system.

Hawaiian system Kinship reckoning in which all relatives of the same sex and generation are referred to by the same term.

vides separate and distinct terms for the nuclear family members. This is probably because the Eskimo system is generally found in bilateral societies where the dominant kin group is the kindred, in which only immediate family members are important in day-to-day affairs. This is especially true of modern North American societies, where many families are independent, living apart from, and not directly involved with, other relatives except on special occasions. Thus, most North Americans (and others) generally distinguish between their closest kin (parents and siblings) but lump together (as aunts, uncles, cousins) other kin on both sides of the family.

Hawaiian System

The **Hawaiian system** of kinship terminology, common (as its name implies) in Hawaii and other islands in the southern central Pacific Ocean but found elsewhere as well, is the least complex system, in that it uses the fewest terms. The Hawaiian system is also called the *generational system,* since all relatives of the same generation and sex are referred to by the same term (Figure 21.6). For example, in one's parents' generation, the

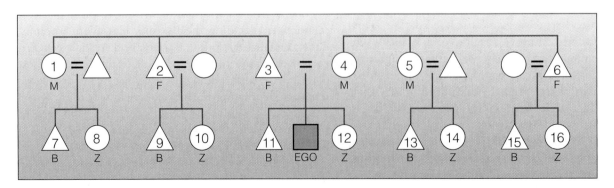

Figure 21.6

In the Hawaiian kinship system the men numbered 2 and 6 are called by the same term as father (3) by EGO; the women numbered 1 and 5 are called by the same term as mother (4). All cousins of EGO's own generation (7–16) are considered brothers (B) and sisters (Z).

Polynesian societies throughout the Pacific Ocean are traditionally structured conforming to the Hawaiian system of kinship terminology. With so many relatives identified as their fathers and mothers, children growing up in hamlets on islands such as Hawaii, as well as Tahiti, Samoa, Tonga, or Fiji are welcome in many homes where they share in meals and find a place to sleep like other brothers and sisters.

term used to refer to one's father is used as well for the father's brother and mother's brother. Similarly, one's mother, mother's sister, and father's sister are all lumped together under a single term. In EGO's generation, male and female cousins are distinguished by gender and are equated with brothers and sisters.

The Hawaiian system reflects the absence of strong unilineal descent, and members on both the father's and the mother's side are viewed as more or less equal. Thus, someone's father's and mother's siblings are all recognized as being similar relations and are merged under a single term appropriate for their gender. In like manner, the children of the mother's and father's siblings are related to EGO in the same way brother and sister are. Falling under the incest taboo, they are ruled out as potential marriage partners.

Iroquois System

In the **Iroquois system** of kinship terminology, the father and father's brother are referred to by a single term, as are the mother and mother's sister; however, the father's sister and mother's brother are given separate terms (Figure 21.7). In one's own generation, brothers, sisters, and parallel cousins (offspring of parental siblings of the same sex, that is, the children of the mother's sis-

Iroquois system Kinship reckoning in which a father and father's brother are referred to by a single term, as are a mother and mother's sister, but a father's sister and mother's brother are given separate terms. Parallel cousins are classified with brothers and sisters, while cross cousins are classified separately but not equated with relatives of some other generation.

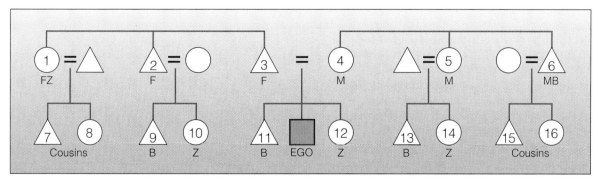

Figure 21.7

According to the Iroquois system of kinship terminology, EGO's father's brother (2) is called by the same term as the father (3); the mother's sister (5) is called by the same term as the mother (4); but the people numbered 1 and 6 are each referred to by a distinct term. Those people numbered 9 to 14 are all considered siblings, but 7, 8, 15, and 16 are considered cousins.

ter or father's brother) of the same sex are referred to by the same terms, which is logical enough considering that they are the offspring of people who are classified in the same category as EGO's actual mother and father. Cross cousins (offspring of parental siblings of opposite sex; that is, the children of the mother's brother or father's sister) are distinguished by terms that set them apart from all other kin. In fact, cross cousins are often preferred as spouses, for marriage to them reaffirms alliances between related lineages or clans.

Iroquois terminology, named for the Iroquoian Indians of northeastern North America's woodlands, is in fact very widespread and is usually found with unilineal descent groups. It was, for example, the terminology in use until recently in rural Chinese society.

Kinship Terms and New Reproductive Technologies

If systems of kinship reckoning other than one's own seem strange and complex, consider the implications of an event that took place in 1978: the production of the

new reproductive technologies (NRTs) Alternative means of reproduction such as surrogate motherhood and in vitro fertilization.

world's first test-tube baby, outside the womb, without sexual intercourse. Since then, thousands of babies have been created in this way, and all sorts of new technologies have become part of the reproductive repertoire. **New reproductive technologies** (**NRTs**) are alternative means of reproduction such as surrogate motherhood and in vitro fertilization.

These technologies have opened up a large—and sometimes mind-boggling—array of reproductive possibilities. For example, if a child is conceived from a donor egg, implanted in another woman's womb to be raised by yet another woman, who is its mother? To complicate matters even further, the egg may have been fertilized by sperm from a donor not married to, or in a sexual relationship with, any of these women. Indeed, it has been suggested that we need nearly a dozen different terms to cover the concepts of mother and father in today's changing societies.[8]

Clearly, the new reproductive technologies are impacting traditional notions of kinship. Beyond transforming our sense of being human, they force us to redefine established ideas about the status of relatives—challenging us to rethink what being "related" to others is about and, specifically, what our rights and obligations are toward such unfamiliar categories of kin.

---

[8]Stone, L. (1998) *Kinship and gender* (p. 272). Boulder, CO: Westview Press.

Questions for Reflection

1. Suppose that for reasons of support and security, you were forced to create and maintain a social network of relatives beyond your immediate family or household. How would you meet that challenge?

2. People growing up in modern industrial and postindustrial societies generally treasure ideas of personal freedom, individuality, and privacy as essential in their pursuit of happiness. Considering the social functions of kinship relations in traditional non-state societies, why do you think that such ideas may be considered unsociable and even dangerously selfish?

3. Why do you think that one of the simplest kinship terminology systems imaginable, namely the Eskimo system, is functionally adequate for most Europeans, North Americans, and others living in complex modern societies?

4. One major reason anthropologists are so interested in getting a handle on a culture's kinship terminology system is that it offers them a quick but crucially important insight into a group's social structure. Why do you think this is especially true for traditional communities of foragers, herders, and farmers but is less so for urban neighborhoods in industrial and postindustrial societies?

5. In some North American Indian languages, the English word for "loneliness" is translated as "I have no relatives." What does that tell you about the importance of kinship in these Native cultures?

Suggested Readings

Carsten, J. (Ed.). (2000). *Cultures of relatedness: New approaches to the study of kinship*. Cambridge, England: Cambridge University Press.

A cross-cultural examination of what it means to be a "relative" at a time when established ideas about kinship are being transformed by radical changes in marriage arrangements and gender relations, as well as new reproductive technologies.

Finkler, K. (2000). *Experiencing the new genetics: Family and kinship on the medical frontier*. Philadelphia: University of Pennsylvania Press.

An exploration of medical and genetic aspects of kinship and debates concerning the social impact of modern medical/genetic knowledge and practices.

Fox, R. (1968). *Kinship and marriage in an anthropological perspective*. Baltimore: Penguin.

This excellent book outlines some of the methods of analysis used in the anthropological treatment of kinship and marriage. It updates Radcliffe-Brown's *African Systems of Kinship and Marriage* and features a perspective focused on kinship groups and social organization.

Parkin, R. (1997). *Kinship: An introduction to basic concepts*. Cambridge, MA: Blackwell.

A solid, useful, readable text on the basics of kinship study.

Schusky, E. L. (1983). *Manual for kinship analysis* (2nd ed.). Lanham, MD: University Press of America.

This useful book discusses the elements of kinship, diagramming, systems classification, and descent with specific examples.

Thomson Audio Study Products

 Enjoy the MP3-ready Audio Lecture Overviews for each chapter and a comprehensive audio glossary of key terms for quick study and review. Whether walking to class, doing laundry, or studying at your desk, you now have the freedom to choose when, where, and how you interact with your audio-based educational media. See the preface for information on how to access this on-the-go study and review tool.

The Anthropology Resource Center

www.thomsonedu.com/anthropology
The Anthropology Resource Center provides extended learning materials to reinforce your understanding of key concepts in the four fields of anthropology. For each of the four fields, the Resource Center includes dynamic exercises including video exercises, map exercises, simulations, and "Meet the Scientists" interviews, as well as critical thinking questions that can be assigned and e-mailed to instructors. The Resource Center also provides breaking news in anthropology and interesting material on applied anthropology to help you link what you are learning to the world around you.

22 Grouping by Gender, Age, Common Interest, and Class

© Jeffrey David Ehrenreich

CHALLENGE ISSUE

Because ties of kinship and household are not always sufficient to handle all the challenges of human survival, people also establish other kinds of social groups. Such groups can be based on gender, age, common interest, and class or social rank. The latter—tied to differences in wealth, prestige, and power—may take the social form of class, caste, or "race" groups. Some groups embody more than one of these, as illustrated by this photo of "Black Indians" marching in the famous New Orleans' Mardi Gras parade. Usually Americans of African descent and belonging to the poor working class, these "Indians" are members of neighborhood social clubs or "tribes" that are, in part, spiritual and secret. During carnival week, when the normal social order is suspended, they publicly express ethnic pride in spectacular fashion.

What Principles Do People Use to Organize Societies?

Besides kinship and marriage, people group themselves by gender, age, common interest, and class or social rank within a society to deal with problems not conveniently handled by marriage, the family and/or household, descent group, or kindred.

What Is Age Grading?

Age grading—the formation of groups on an age basis—is a widely used means of organizing people in societies, including those of Europe and North America. In addition to age grades, some societies feature age sets—formally established groups of people born during a certain time span who move through the series of age-grade categories together.

What Are Common-Interest Associations?

Common-interest associations are formed to deal with specific challenges or opportunities. Membership may be voluntary to compulsory. Common-interest associations have been a feature of human societies since the appearance of the first farming villages several thousand years ago. They have become especially prominent in contemporary postindustrial, industrial, or industrializing societies. Assisted by electronic media, associations are also increasingly transnational in our globalizing world.

What Is Social Stratification?

Stratification is the division of society into two or more social classes of people who do not share equally in basic resources, power, or prestige. Such a hierarchical social structure is characteristic of all of the world's societies having large and heterogeneous populations with centralized political control. Among others, these include ancient kingdoms and empires, but also modern republics. Social classes can be relatively open, as in North America where membership is based primarily on personal achievement or wealth. They can also be closed, as in India where membership in hierarchically ranked groups known as castes is determined by birth and remains fixed for life.

Social organization based on kinship and marriage has received considerable attention from anthropologists. There are several reasons for this: In one way or another, kinship and marriage operate as organizing principles in all societies, and in the small stateless societies so often studied by anthropologists they are usually the most important organizational principles. There is, too, a certain fascination in the almost mathematical way kinship systems at least appear to work.

To the unwary, all this attention to kinship and marriage may give the impression that these are the only principles of social organization that really matter. Yet it is obvious from analyzing modern industrial societies that other principles of social organization not only exist but also may be quite important. These include grouping by gender, age, common interest, and class or social rank—each of which we will examine in this chapter.

GROUPING BY GENDER

As shown in preceding chapters, division of labor along gender lines occurs in all human societies. In some cultures—the previously discussed Ju/'hoansi in southern Africa for example—many tasks that men and women undertake may be shared. People may perform work normally assigned to the opposite sex without loss of face. In others, however, men and women are rigidly segregated in what they do. Such is the case in many maritime cultures, where seafarers aboard fishing, whaling, and trading ships are usually men. For instance, we find temporary all-male communities aboard ships of coastal Basque fishermen in northwest Spain, Yupik Eskimo whalers in Alaska, and Swahili merchants sailing along the East African coast. These seafarers commonly leave their wives, mothers, and daughters behind in their home ports, sometimes for months at a time.

Clearly demarcated grouping by gender also occurs in many traditional horticultural societies. For instance, among the Mohawk, Oneida, Onondaga, Cayuga, Seneca, and Tuscarora Indians of New York—the famous Six Nations of the Iroquois—society was divided into two parts consisting of sedentary women on the one hand and highly mobile men on the other. Women who were blood relatives to one another lived in the same village and shared the job of growing the corn, beans, and squash that all Iroquois relied upon for subsistence. Although men built the houses and the wooden palisades that protected villages and also helped women clear fields for cultivation, they did their most important work some distance away from the villages. This consisted of hunting, fishing, trading, warring, and diplomacy. As a consequence, men were mostly transients in the villages, being present for only brief periods.

Traditionally, the Iroquois viewed women's activities as less prestigious than those of men, but they explicitly acknowledged women as the sustainers of life. Moreover, women headed the longhouses (dwellings occupied by matrilocal extended families), descent and inheritance passed through women, and ceremonial life centered on women's activities. Although men held all leadership positions outside households—sitting on the councils of the villages, tribes, and the league of Six Nations—the women of their clans were the ones who nominated them for these positions and held veto power over them. Thus, Iroquois male leadership was balanced by female authority.

Overall, the phrase "separate but equal" accurately describes relations between the sexes in Six Nations Iroquois society, with members of neither sex being dominant nor submissive to the other. Related to this seems to have been a low incidence of rape, for outside observers in the 19th century widely commented upon its apparent absence within Iroquois communities. Even in warfare, sexual violation of female captives was virtually unheard of—as noted in this back-handed compliment made by U.S. Brigadier General James Clinton in 1779: "Bad as the savages are, they never violate the chastity of any women of their prisoners."[1]

Although Iroquoian men were often absent from the village, when present they ate and slept with women. This contrasts the habits of Mundurucu Indians of Brazil's Amazon rainforest. Mundurucu men and women work, eat, and sleep separately. From age 13 onward males live together in one large house, while women, girls, and preteen boys occupy two or three houses grouped around the men's house. For all intents and purposes, men associate with men, and women with women.

Among the Mundurucu, relations between the sexes is not harmonious but rather one of opposition. According to their belief, sex roles were once reversed: Women ruled over men and controlled the sacred trumpets that are the symbols of power and represent the reproductive capacities of women. But because women could not hunt, they could not supply the meat demanded by the ancient spirits that abided in the trumpets. This enabled the men to take the trumpets from the women, establishing their dominance in the process. Ever since, the trumpets have been carefully guarded and hidden in the men's house, and traditionally women were prohibited from even seeing them.

Thus, Mundurucu men express fear and envy toward women and seek to control them by force. For their part, the women neither like nor accept a submissive status,

---

[1]Littlewood, R. (1997). Military rape. *Anthropology Today 13* (2), 14.

Gender-based groups are common among the Mundurucu as well as numerous other Amazonian Indian nations such as the Yawalapiti pictured here, who live on the Tuatuari River in Brazil's upper Xingu region. Gender issues are symbolically worked out in their mythologies and ceremonial dances. One common theme concerns ownership of the sacred trumpets, which represents spiritual power. These trumpets are zealously guarded by the tribesmen, and traditionally women were forbidden to see them.

© Reuters/Corbis

and even though men occupy all formal positions of political and religious leadership, women are autonomous in the economic realm.

Alongside notable differences, there are also interesting similarities between the Mundurucu beliefs and those of traditional European and Euramerican cultures. For example, many 19th-century European and Euramerican intellectuals held to the idea that patriarchy (rule by men) had replaced an earlier state of matriarchy (rule by women). Moreover, the idea that men may use force to control women is deeply embedded in both Judaic, Christian, and Muslim traditions (and even today, despite changing attitudes, one out of three women in the United States is sexually assaulted at some time in her life). A major difference between Mundurucu and traditional European societies is that, in the latter, women often have not had control over their own economic activities. This has changed significantly over the past few decades, but women in North America and other Western countries still have some distance to go before they achieve economic parity with men.

GROUPING BY AGE

Age grouping is so familiar and so important that it and sex have been called the only universal factors that determine a person's positions in society. In North America today, for instance, a child's first friends are usually children of his or her own age. They begin preschool or kindergarten with age mates and typically move through a dozen or more years in the educational system together. At specified ages they are allowed to see certain movies, drive a car, and do things reserved for adults, such as voting, drinking alcoholic beverages, and serving in the military. Ultimately, North Americans retire from their jobs at a specified age and, increasingly, spend the final years of their lives in retirement communities, segregated from the rest of society. As North Americans age, they are labeled "teenagers," "middle-aged," and "senior citizens," whether they like it or not and for no other reason than the number of years they have lived.

Age classification also plays a significant role in non-Western societies, which, at a minimum, make a distinction between immature, mature, and older people whose physical powers are waning. In these societies old age often has profound significance, bringing with it the period of greatest respect (for women it may mean the first social equality with men). Rarely are the elderly shunted aside or abandoned. Even the Inuit of the Canadian Arctic, who are often cited as a people who literally abandon their aged relatives, do so only in truly desperate circumstances, when the group's physical survival is at stake. In all oral tradition societies, elders are the repositories of accumulated wisdom for their people. Recognized as such and no longer expected to carry out many subsistence activities, they play a major role in passing on cultural knowledge to their grandchildren.

In North America, however, elder status is becoming problematic because senior citizens 65 years and older now constitute 12 percent of the overall population, and experts predict their numbers will swell to about 70 million (20 percent of the overall population) by 2030.[2] With more and more people living longer, achieving old age seems less of an accomplishment than it once did and so commands less respect. An increasingly common view of the elderly is that they are unproductive and, even worse, a serious economic burden. The ultimate irony is that in the United States all of the ingenuity of modern science is used to keep alive the bodies of individuals who, in virtually every other way, society pushes aside.

All human societies recognize a number of life stages. The demarcation and duration of these stages vary across cultures. Each successive life stage provides distinctive social roles and comes with certain cultural features such as specific patterns of activity, attitudes, prohibitions, and obligations. In many cultures, the social position of an individual in a specific life stage is also marked by a distinctive outward appearance in terms of dress, hairstyle, body paint, tattoos, insignia, or some other symbolic distinction. Typically, these stages are designed to help the transition from one age to another, to teach needed skills, or to lend economic assistance. Often they are taken as the basis for the formation of organized groups.

THOMSON AUDIO STUDY PRODUCTS Take advantage of the MP3-ready Audio Lecture Overviews and comprehensive audio glossary of key terms for each chapter. See the preface for information on how to access this on-the-go study and review tool.

Institutions of Age Grouping

An organized category of people with membership on the basis of age is known as an **age grade.** Theoretically speaking, membership in an age grade ought to be automatic: One reaches the appropriate age and so is included, without question, in the particular age grade. Just such situations exist, for example, among the East African Tiriki, whose system we will examine shortly. Sometimes, though, individuals must buy their way into the age grade for which they are eligible. This was the case among some of the Indians of North America's plains, who required boys to purchase the appropriate

costumes, dances, and songs for age-grade membership. In societies where entrance fees are expensive, not all people eligible for membership in a particular age grade may actually be able to join.

Entry into and transfer out of age grades may be accomplished individually, either by a biological distinction, such as puberty, or by a socially recognized status, such as marriage or childbirth. Whereas age-grade members may have much in common, may engage in similar activities, may cooperate with one another, and may share the same orientation and aspirations, their membership may not be entirely parallel with physiological age. A specific time is often ritually established for moving from a younger to an older grade. An example of this is the traditional Jewish ceremony of the bar mitzvah (a Hebrew term meaning "son of the commandment"), marking that a 13-year-old boy has reached the age of religious duty and responsibility. (*Bat mitzvah,* meaning "daughter of the commandment," is the term for the equivalent ritual for a girl.)

Although members of senior groups commonly expect deference from and acknowledge certain responsibilities to their juniors, this does not necessarily mean that one grade is seen as better, or worse, or even more important than another. There can be standardized competition (opposition) between age grades, such as that traditionally between first-year students and sophomores on U.S. college campuses.

In addition to age grades, some societies feature age sets (sometimes referred to as *age classes*). An **age set** is a formally established group of people born during a certain time span who move through the series of age-grade categories together. Age sets, unlike age grades, end after a specified number of years; age set members usually remain closely associated throughout their lives. This is akin to but distinct from the broad and informal North American practice of identifying generation clusters comprised of all individuals born within a particular time frame—such as baby boomers (1946–1964), Gen-Xers (1961–1981), and the Internet generation (1986–1999) (year spans approximate).

The age-set notion implies strong feelings of loyalty and mutual support. Because such groups may possess property, songs, shield designs, and rituals and are internally organized for collective decision making and leadership, age sets are distinct from simple age grades. One also may distinguish between transitory age grades—and the comprehensive systems that affect people through the whole of their lives.

Age Grouping in African Societies

Although age is a criterion for group membership in many parts of the world, its most varied and elaborate use is found in Africa, south of the Sahara. An example may be seen among the Tiriki, one of several pastoral

---

[2]U.S. Census Bureau News. (2004, March 18).

age grade An organized category of people based on age; every individual passes through a series of such categories over his or her lifetime.

age set A formally established group of people born during a certain time span who move through the series of age-grade categories together.

© Louise Gubb/Corbis

Maasai subclans of western Kenya at the opening parade of the elaborate *eunoto* ceremony, marking the coming of age of *morans* (warriors). At the end of the ceremony, these men will be in the next age grade—junior adults—ready to marry and start families. Members of the same age set, they were initiated together into the warrior age grade as teenagers. They spent their warrior years raiding cattle (an old tradition that is now illegal, but nonetheless still practiced) and protecting their community homes and animal enclosures (from wild animals and other cattle raiders). The *eunoto* ceremony includes the ritual shaving of a warrior's hair by his mother, symbolizing the end of many freedoms and the passage to manhood.

nomadic groups living in Kenya.[3] In this culture of herders, each boy born within a 15-year period becomes a member of a particular age set then open for membership. Seven such named age sets exist, only one of which is open for membership at a time; when membership in one is closed, the next one is open for a 15-year period, and so on until the passage of 105 years (7 times 15), when the first set's membership is gone due to death, and it opens once again to take in new "recruits."

Members of Tiriki age sets remain together for life as they move through four successive age grades: Advancement in age grades occurs at fifteen-year intervals, coinciding with the closing of the oldest age set and the opening of a new one. Each age group has its own particular duties and responsibilities. Traditionally, the first, or Warrior age grade, served as guardians of the country, and members gained renown through fighting. Under British colonial rule, however, this traditional function fell by the wayside with the cessation of warfare, and members of this age grade now find excitement and adventure by leaving their community for extended employment or study elsewhere.

The next age grade, the Elder Warriors, had few specialized tasks in earlier days beyond learning skills they would need later on by assuming an increasing share of administrative activities. For example, they would chair the postfuneral gatherings held to settle property claims after someone's death. Traditionally, Elder Warriors also served as envoys between elders of different communities. Nowadays, they hold nearly all of the administrative and executive roles opened up by the creation and growth of a centralized Tiriki administrative bureaucracy.

Judicial Elders, the third age grade, traditionally handled most tasks connected with the administration and settlement of local disputes. Today, they still serve as the local judiciary body. Members of the "Ritual Elders,

[3]Sangree, W. H. (1965). The Bantu Tiriki of western Kenya. In J. L. Gibbs, Jr. (Ed.), *Peoples of Africa* (pp. 69–72). New York: Holt, Rinehart & Winston.

VISUAL COUNTERPOINT

The range of common-interest associations is astounding, as suggested by these photos of Shriners and Crips. The Shriners are a secret fraternal order of middle-class males in the United States committed to "fun, fellowship, and service" and named after the "Ancient Arabic Order of Nobles of the Mystic Shrine." The Crips are a violent urban gang, originating in poor Los Angeles neighborhoods, whose trademark is a blue bandana—in contrast to the red bandana of their rival gang, the Bloods. The notoriety of the Crips spread as a result of sensational stories in the media, spawning a network of independent satellite Crip gangs in other U.S. cities as well as in Europe and Central America.

the senior age grade, used to preside over the priestly functions of ancestral shrine observances on the household level, at subclan meetings, at semiannual community appeals, and at rites of initiation into the various age grades. They also were credited with access to special magical powers. With the decline of ancestor worship

common-interest associations Associations that result from an act of joining based on sharing particular activities, objectives, values, or beliefs.

over the past several decades, many of these traditional functions have been lost, and no new ones have arisen to take their places. Nonetheless, Ritual Elders continue to hold the most important positions in the initiation ceremonies, and their power as sorcerers and expungers of witchcraft are still recognized.

GROUPING BY COMMON INTEREST

The rise of urban, industrialized societies in which individuals are often separated from their kin has led to a proliferation of **common-interest associations**—associations that result from an act of joining and are based on sharing particular activities, objectives, values, or beliefs. As U.S. anthropologist Meredith Small observes,

> We often imprint lines of kinship on friends and colleagues, transferring familial expectations onto those with whom we share time but not blood or genes or vows, so that we can have the experience of an extended family. Young people join gangs, older people join clubs, and even babies are put into play groups. Pushed by a culture that favors independence and self-reliance, the social animal in us nonetheless seeks connections, even if they are bloodless and fragile.[4]

---

[4]Small, M. F. (2000). Kinship envy. *Natural History 109* (2), 88.

Moreover, common-interest associations help people meet a range of needs from companionship to safe work conditions to learning a new language and customs upon moving from one country to another.

Because common-interest associations are by nature flexible, they have often been turned to, both in cities and in traditional villages, as a way of meeting these needs. Common-interest associations are not, however, restricted to modernizing societies alone. They also are found in many traditional societies, and there is reason to believe they arose with the emergence of the first horticultural villages. Furthermore, associations in traditional societies may be just as complex and highly organized as those of countries such as the United States and Canada.

Common-interest associations have often been referred to in the anthropological literature as *voluntary associations,* but this term is misleading. The act of joining may range from fully voluntary to one required by law. For example, in the United States, under previous draft laws individuals often became members of the armed forces without choosing to join. It is not really compulsory to join a labor union, but unless one does, one cannot work in a union shop. What the term *voluntary association* really refers to are those associations not based on

sex, age, kinship, marriage, or territory that result from an act of joining. The act often may be voluntary, but it does not have to be.

Kinds of Common-Interest Associations

The variety of common-interest associations is astonishing. In the United States, they include such diverse entities as street gangs, private militias, sport and service clubs, churches and other religious organizations, political parties, labor unions, environmental organizations, women's and men's clubs of all sorts—the list could go on and on. Their goals may include the pursuit of friendship, recreation, and the promotion of certain values, as well as governing, seeking peace on a local or global scale, and the pursuit or defense of economic interests.

Associations also have served to preserve traditional songs, history, language, moral beliefs, and other customs among members of various ethnic minorities. A unique example can be found in the following Original Study, which illustrates how one ethnic minority group establishes a sense of traditional community within modern cities by means of symbolic geographic boundary markers.

Original Study ▪ By Susan Lees

The Jewish *Eruv:* Symbolic Place in Public Space

Cultural anthropologists are interested in how a geographic *space* becomes a culturally meaningful *place*—an area that we may think of as "our territory" or that we designate for one particular purpose or another, such as pasturing animals, playing football, gardening, or worshiping. As in a tennis court or baseball diamond, there are certain boundaries to such places. We may mark them off with symbols not readily comprehensible to outsiders, who may not understand why a ball has been hit "out of bounds" or is a "foul ball" until we explain the rules and the symbols.

At times, two different cultural groups may occupy the same geographic space, but each will see and divide it differently in terms that are meaningful only within their group. We see this on maps where the borders of many modern nation-states often cut through the traditional tribal or ethnic group territories. And we see it in various urban communities

that may divide up their spaces in ways perceptible only to themselves.

An intriguing example can be found among Orthodox Jews who practice an ancient tradition by ritually defining the boundaries of their communities for the purpose of Sabbath observance: On the Sabbath, the area enclosed by the boundaries becomes, by definition, a single shared symbolic domain. This symbolically enclosed space is called an *eruv,* which means "combination" or "amalgamation" of public and private space—that is, the private spaces of the household and the public areas of the sidewalks, streets, and perhaps parks are combined on the Sabbath as one big communal household.

The purpose of the *eruv* for Orthodox communities is to accommodate one of the many Sabbath prohibitions on religiously defined "work": the work of "carrying" objects from a private domain to a public one, or vice versa, or carrying objects for any distance in

a public domain. On the Sabbath, if there is an *eruv,* observant Orthodox Jews are permitted to treat carrying within the entire *eruv* enclosure as if they were in their own homes. Having an *eruv* means that strictly Orthodox Jews may push a baby stroller or a wheelchair within the ritually enclosed neighborhood—activities otherwise restricted by the "carrying" prohibition. This makes it possible for whole families—including small children and disabled individuals—to attend religious services in the synagogue or to socialize with one another and still be faithful to traditional law.

In ancient times, the boundaries of the *eruv* were in fact the walls of houses and courtyards and city walls within which communities were enclosed. But today, where there are no walls, communities sometimes erect thin strings or wires, or sometimes just use wires already there on utility poles (such as

CONTINUED

CONTINUED

phone or electricity wires) to demarcate the boundaries. These are known to members of the community but usually invisible to outsiders because they are part of the urban landscape anyway.

I was first drawn to the subject of the *eruv* nearly three decades ago, when I leafed through my mother's copy of the Code of Jewish Law still found in many Jewish households. Much of this text concerns rules about observing the Sabbath (the seventh day, the Lord's day reserved for worship and obligatory rest). Many of these seemed exotic and mysterious to me and hard to reconcile with life in the modern world.

As an anthropologist, I was intrigued by explanations given for certain practices because they heightened awareness of the special character of the Sabbath itself and *also* of the uniqueness of Jewish identity in a world where temptations to assimilate with the larger, dominant culture were strong. Most of all, the *eruv* captured my interest because it seemed to create, not just prohibit something. It transformed a group of diverse urban households into one common household, not just a community but a real "private" home. The symbolic "walls" around this collective domain were erected not to keep others out but to enclose its members and thus erase the actual walls of each individual household.

The ritual that creates an *eruv* requires that one member take a loaf of bread and make other members co-owners of that loaf; the symbolism of a household is shared ownership (not consumption) of this most symbolically meaningful food. The boundaries of the *eruv* "household" they co-inhabit must be contiguous, broken only by symbolic doorways through which they can pass as if through doorways of their individual homes. As long as the contiguity is maintained, they can extend the *eruv* to incorporate hundreds or even thousands of other houses. It occurred to me then that in a highly urbanized mass society of mostly strangers, this symbolic unification of sometimes widely separated

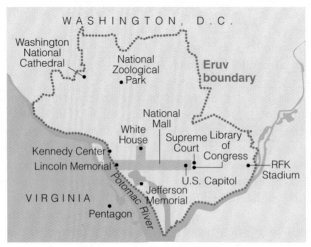

Boundaries of *eruv* in Washington, D.C.

Jewish households was an extraordinary thing.

The majority of North American Jews who are members of religious congregations belong to Reform synagogues (the other major groups are Conservative and Orthodox), and American Reform Judaism officially abandoned the *eruv* as a Sabbath practice in 1846. When I first became interested in the subject, there were rather few *eruvin* anywhere. Most Orthodox Jewish communities were still concentrated in a few large cities, particularly on the East Coast. After WWII, many Jews were able to move to the suburbs, where they integrated for the first time into the mainstream as "white folks."

But it was in the early 1970s that a shift in Jewish identity issues occurred, and some younger generation Jews began to turn purposefully to traditional practices that distinguished them from mainstream society and more assimilated Jews. Coming on the heels of the 1960s civil rights movement, this shift echoed the "Black Pride" movement of African Americans affirming their African roots. Other ethnic minorities developed their own distinct cultural expressions as the wider society seemed first to tolerate and then to respect such expressions. In this changing social climate young Orthodox Jews began to assert themselves as their forebears had not dared to. It was in this context that a proliferation of new *eruvin* occurred both in urban and suburban contexts. Meanwhile, some Jews resisted this expression of difference,

and within the wider Jewish community there was considerable strife over the question of the "authenticity" of the beliefs and practices of more assimilated Jews.

Most *eruvin* have been established without conflict, but a handful have been highly controversial, including one effort in North London, England, which faced a dozen years of legal struggles. The question of why a virtually invisible boundary that enables believers to exercise their religious obligations would be of such great significance to nonbelievers has generated considerable debate and touches on issues that are especially important in a globalized world of pluralistic societies that include many diasporic groups (people dispersed from their ancestral homeland). In these societies, diasporic cultures are created and developed through interaction with their surrounding communities, reacting in part to discrimination against them and in part to their own desire for continuity and connection with others sharing their origins and beliefs.

In my research, I was interested to find that Jews are among the principal parties on *both* sides of *eruv* conflicts. Opponents of the *eruv* appear to fear the creation, or re-creation, of ghettos of inassimilable Jews who neither conform to nor respect the ideals of the dominant or mainstream culture—who appear "foreign" in appearance and practices. Thus the *eruv* conflict appears on one level to be an argument among Jews adhering to different beliefs about how they should live in modern society with other groups and among themselves. (Interestingly, when Jewish religious leaders were first developing the laws of the *eruv* more than 2,000 years ago, this problem of how Jews could maintain a communal identity while living among others was among their primary concerns.)

Jews are not alone among diasporic groups in having this argument about assimilation and distinctiveness in the modern world, though the specifics of their conflict are their own. Like many others, they wish to live comfortably and without fear in a plural society with full rights of membership, yet also in communities of others like themselves, in which they can socialize and build institutions that tie them together.

The *eruv* is one symbolic device to reinforce community as neighborhood—to establish a meaningful *place* for a distinct group in a diverse society. Ethnic church parishes often have done the same for other urban groups. Neigh-

borhood identities like these can be the basis for disputes about exclusivity, but they can also ease the maintenance of cultural traditions and humanize life in the city.

Sometimes operating secretly, common-interest associations have helped maintain traditions. So it is among North American Indians, who since the late 1960s have been experiencing a resurgence of ethnic pride after generations of forced assimilation and schooling designed to stamp out their cultural identity. A very satisfying way of publicly expressing pride in their ethnic identity and cultural heritage is by way of ceremonial gatherings known as *powwows,* which take place not only on reservations but also in cities where most American Indians now live. Usually "pan-tribal," these festive gatherings feature American Indians from dozens of different nations or "tribes" dancing together in traditional regalia as the sounds of traditional songs and drumming fill the air. Gift offerings are part of the event, along with traditional Native foods such as frybread and the selling of Native crafts.[5]

Men's and Women's Associations

In some societies women have not established formal common-interest associations to the extent men have because they live in male-dominated cultures that re-

strict them or because women are absorbed on the domestic front with the constant and often unpredictable demands of rearing children. Moreover, some functions of men's associations—such as military duties—often are culturally defined as purely for men or repugnant to women.

Still, as cross-cultural research makes clear, women often play important roles in associations of their own as well as in those in which men predominate. Among the Crow (Apsaroke) Indians, women participated in the secret Tobacco Society, in addition to their own exclusive groups. Throughout Africa women's social clubs complement the men's and are concerned with educating women and with crafts, charitable, and wealth-generating activities—and increasingly with politics. In Sierra Leone, once-simple dancing societies have developed under urban conditions into complex organizations with a set of new objectives. The resulting dancing *compin* is made up of young women as well as men who together perform plays based on traditional music and dancing and raise money for various mutual benefit causes.[6]

[5]Ellis, C. (2006). *A dancing people: Powwow culture on the southern plains.* Lawrence: University Press of Kansas

[6]See Steady, F. C. (2001). *Women and the Amistad connection, Sierra Leone Krio Society* (pp. 71–80). Rochester, VT: Schenkman Books.

Courtesy of Women's Promotion and Assistance Association of Cameroon. Photo by Mousa.

Since the United Nations Decade for Women (1976–1985), the number of women's associations all around the world has grown significantly, from the local to the global. These associations often function as support systems for women while focusing on a range of issues and activities, including economic opportunities. For example, here we see members of a women's craft association in Bakingili, Cameroon (Africa), tie-dying fabric together.

Women's rights organizations, consciousness-raising groups, and professional organizations for women are examples of some of the associations arising directly or indirectly out of an ever-expanding feminist movement. These groups cover the entire range of association formation, from simple friendship and support groups to associations centered on politics, sports, the arts, spirituality, charity, and economic endeavors—on a national and even international scale. If an unresolved point does exist in the matter of women's participation, it is in determining why women are excluded from certain associations in some societies, while in others their participation is essentially equal to that of men.

Associations in the Postindustrial World

In spite of the diversity and vitality of common-interest associations, some have noted a recent decline in participation in all sorts of these groups, at least in North America. Those who have observed this trend see it as part of a more general drop in civic participation. People are spending less time socializing with others in bars, at dinner parties, having friends over, and so on.

One can only speculate on the causes, but they likely include further isolation of individuals as they spend more and more of their free time with an ever-growing array of electronic home entertainment options. For example, in the United States, adults spend an average of 4 hours each day watching television. Then, too, the frequency with which people move interferes with their ability to establish more than superficial friendships with others. Add to this the fact that North Americans work longer hours on average than people in almost all industrialized countries, leaving less time for socialization. In this connection, some have noted a 10 percent drop in civic participation for every 10 minutes of commuting time.

Finally, there is the rise of the Internet; as people spend more and more time online, they can stay in touch without having to leave home. The cyberworld has seen an explosion of what are, in effect, virtual common-interest associations, many of which are transnational, with members in far-flung corners of the world. In short, common-interest associations may not be showing a decline so much as a transformation.

stratified societies Societies in which people are hierarchically divided and ranked into social strata, or layers, and do not share equally in basic resources that support survival, influence, and prestige.
egalitarian societies Societies in which everyone has about equal rank, access to, and power over basic resources.
social class A category of individuals in a stratified society who enjoy equal or nearly equal prestige according to the system of evaluation.

With computer technology has come the rise of online common-interest associations, involving everything from ethnicity to hobbies to special education needs. Here, Inuit students in Canada use a computer to learn the Inuktitut syllabary—a phonetic writing system consisting of symbols representing syllables.

GROUPING BY CLASS OR SOCIAL RANK IN STRATIFIED SOCIETIES

Social stratification is a common and powerful structuring force in many of the world's societies. Basically, **stratified societies** are those in which people are hierarchically divided and ranked into social strata, or layers, and do not share equally in basic resources that support survival, influence, and prestige. Members of low-ranked strata typically have fewer privileges and less power than those in higher ranked strata. In addition, the restrictions and obligations they face are usually more oppressive, and they must work harder for less reward.

In short, social stratification amounts to institutionalized inequality. Without ranking—high versus low—no stratification exists; social differences without this do not constitute stratification. In the United States, Hispanic, African American, and American Indian groups are among those who have struggled with their positions in the low-ranked strata. As profiled in this chapter's Anthropology Applied, their needs are often ignored in development efforts.

Stratified societies stand in sharp contrast to **egalitarian societies,** in which everyone has about equal rank, access to, and power over basic resources. As we saw in earlier chapters, foraging societies are characteristically egalitarian, although there are some exceptions.

Social Class and Caste

A **social class** may be defined as a category of individuals in a stratified society who enjoy equal or nearly equal prestige according to the system of evaluation. The quali-

Anthropologists frequently do a type of policy research called a social impact assessment, which entails collecting data about a community or neighborhood for planners of development projects. Such an assessment seeks to determine a project's effect by determining how and upon whom its impact will fall and whether the impact is likely to be positive or negative.

In the United States, any project requiring a federal permit or license, or using federal funds, by law must be preceded by a social impact assessment as part of the environmental review process. Examples of such projects include highway construction, urban renewal, water diversion schemes, and land reclamation. Often, such projects are sited so that their impact falls most heavily on neighborhoods or communities inhabited by people in low socioeconomic strata—sometimes because the projects are seen as a way of improving the lives of poor people and sometimes because the poor people are seen as having less political power to block proposals that others conceive as in "the public interest."

As an illustration of this kind of work, anthropologist Sue Ellen Jacobs was hired to do a social impact assessment of a water diversion project in New Mexico planned by the Bureau of Land Recla-

mation in cooperation with the Bureau of Indian Affairs. This project proposed construction of a diversion dam and an extensive canal system for irrigation on the Rio Grande. Affected by this would be twenty-two communities inhabited primarily by Hispanic Americans, as well as two Indian pueblos. Unemployment was high in the region, and the project was seen as a way to promote a perceived trend to urbanism (which theoretically would be associated with industrial development), while bringing new land into production for intensive agriculture.

What the planners failed to take into account was that both the Hispanic and Indian populations were heavily committed to farming for household consumption (with some surpluses raised for the market), using a system of irrigation canals established as long as 300 years ago. These canals are maintained by elected supervisors familiar with the communities and knowledgeable about water laws, ditch management, and sustainable crop production. Such individuals can resolve conflicts concerning water allocation and land use—and often other issues as well. Under the proposed project, this system was to be given up in favor of one in which fewer people would control larger tracts of land, and water allocation would be in the hands of a government tech-

nocrat. One of the strongest measures of local government would be lost.

Not surprisingly, Jacobs discovered widespread community opposition to this project, and her report helped convince Congress that any positive impact was far outweighed by negative effects. One of the major objections to the construction of the project was that it would result in the obliteration of the centuries-old irrigation system structures. Project planners did not seem to recognize the antiquity and cultural significance of these traditional irrigation structures, referring to them as "temporary diversion structures." The fact that the old dams associated with the ditches were attached to local descent groups was simply not recognized by the official documents.

Beyond infringing on local control, the project threatened the community with a range of negative side effects: problems linked to population growth and relocation, a loss of fishing and other river-related resources, and new health hazards, including increased threat of drowning, insect breeding, and airborne dust.

(Adapted from J. van Willigen (1986). Applied anthropology (p. 169). South Hadley, MA: Bergin & Garvey.)

fication "nearly equal" is important, for a certain amount of inequality may occur even within a given class. Class distinctions are not always clear-cut and obvious in societies that have a wide and continuous range of differential privileges.

A **caste** is a closed social class in a stratified society in which membership is determined by birth and fixed for life. The opposite of the principle that all humans are born equal, the caste system is based on the principle that humans neither are nor can be equal. Castes are strongly endogamous, and offspring are automatically members of their parents' caste.

The classic ethnographic example is the traditional Hindu caste system of India. Perhaps the world's longest surviving social hierarchy, it encompasses a complex ranking of social groups on the basis of "ritual purity." Each of some 2,000 different castes considers itself as a distinct community higher or lower than other castes,

although their particular ranking varies among geographic regions and over time. The different castes are associated with specific occupations and customs, such as food habits and styles of dress, along with rituals involving notions of purity and pollution. Differences in status are traditionally justified by the religious doctrine of karma, a belief that one's place in life is determined by one's deeds in previous lifetimes.

All of these castes, or *jatis*, are organized into four basic orders or *varnas* (literally meaning "colors"), distinguished partly by occupation and ranked in order of descending religious status of purity. The religious foundation for this social hierarchy is found in a sacred text known as the Laws of Manu, an ancient work about

caste A closed social class in a stratified society in which membership is determined by birth and fixed for life.

2,000 years old and considered by traditional Hindus as the highest authority on their cultural institutions. It defines the Brahmans as the purest and therefore highest *varna*. As priests and lawgivers, Brahmans represent the world of religion and learning. Next comes the order of fighters and rulers, known as the Kshatriyas. Below them are the Vaisyas (merchants and traders), who are engaged in commercial, agricultural, and pastoral pursuits. At the bottom are the Shudras (artisans and laborers), an order required to serve the other three *varnas* and who also make a living by handicrafts.

Falling outside the *varna* system is a fifth category of degraded individuals known as "untouchables" or Dalits. Considered the most impure of all people, these outcasts can own neither land nor the tools of their trade. Untouchables constitute a large pool of cheap labor at the beck and call of those controlling economic and politi-

cal affairs. In an effort to bestow some dignity on these poverty-stricken victims of the caste system, Hindu nationalist leader Mahatma Gandhi renamed them *harijan* or "children of God."

Although India's national constitution of 1950 sought to abolish caste discrimination and the practice of untouchability, the caste system remains deeply entrenched in Hindu culture and is still widespread throughout southern Asia, especially in rural India. In what has been called India's "hidden apartheid," entire villages in many Indian states remain completely segregated by caste. Representing about 15 percent of India's population—or some 160 million people—the widely scattered Dalits endure near complete social isolation, humiliation, and discrimination based exclusively on their birth status. Even a Dalit's shadow is believed to pollute the upper castes. They may not cross the line dividing their part of the village from that occupied by higher castes, drink water from public wells, or visit the same temples as the higher castes. Dalit children are still often made to sit at the back of classrooms.

Castelike situations are known elsewhere in the world. In Bolivia, Ecuador, and several other South and Central American countries, for example, the wealthy upper class is almost exclusively white and rarely intermarries with people of non-European descent. In contrast, the lower class of working poor in those countries is primarily made up of American Indian laborers and peasants. Racial segregation also existed in the United States, where the nation's upper class was made up exclusively of individuals of European descent.

After the American Revolution, several states in New England joined Virginia and other southern states and made it illegal for whites to marry blacks or Ameri-

Dalits, known as "untouchables" in India's traditional caste system, light 100 "candles of freedom" at the 2004 World Social Forum held in Mumbai. Tens of thousands of activists from 130 countries attended the forum, debating and demonstrating against social, economic, and political inequality around the world.

© AFP/Getty Images

can Indians. After the U.S. federal government officially abolished slavery in 1863, these anti-miscegenation laws remained in force in many states from Maine to Florida for several decades.

In 1924, Virginia's General Assembly passed the Racial Integrity Act to prevent light-skinned individuals with some African ancestry from "passing" as whites. Known as the "one drop" rule, it codified the idea of white racial purity by classifying individuals as black if just one of their multiple ancestors was of African origin ("one drop of Negro blood"). However light-skinned, they were subject to a wide range of discriminatory practices not applicable to whites. Such institutionalized racial discrimination continued for a century after slavery was abolished, and today self-segregation exists in many parts of the United States.

Despite U.S. civil rights laws passed in the 1960s (prohibiting discrimination in accommodations, schools, employment, and voting for reasons of color, race, religion, or national origin), ethnic inequality persists in which the typical African American household has 54 cents of income and 12 cents of wealth for every corresponding dollar in the typical white American household[7] (Figure 22.1).[8]

Another castelike social system based on skin color and wealth officially existed in South Africa where until recently a minority of European origin imposed a political regime known as apartheid (an Afrikaans-Dutch term meaning "segregation" or "separation"). Based on a racist white superiority ideology, it relegated indigenous dark-skinned Africans to a low-ranking stratum in a racially divided society. Although the foundations for the policy of strict racial segregation were laid earlier, apartheid became national law in 1948.

During the next few decades, the European minority in control of the South African government enacted a series of racist laws and regulations creating a social order privileging themselves and discriminating against the indigenous African peoples. From then on, the government policy of segregation based on differences in skin color affected every level of social existence. In addition to prohibiting "racially mixed" marriages, apartheid laws also stipulated where "blacks" and "coloreds" were allowed to live, work, and play. Invading private lives, these laws even made "interracial" sexual relations a crime.

In the early 1960s, South Africa's apartheid regime declared that territories historically inhabited by South Africa's indigenous nations such as the Swazi, Xhosa, and Zulu were to become semi-independent countries

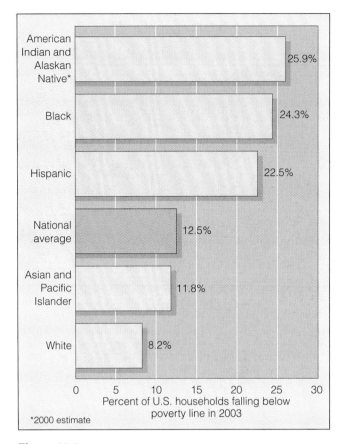

Figure 22.1

In the United States 70 percent of all wealth is in the hands of 10 percent of the population. The country's official poverty rate has increased for four consecutive years, from a 26-year low of 11.3 percent in 2000 to 12.7 percent in 2004. In real numbers 37 million people were below the official poverty thresholds in 2004—5.4 million more than in 2000. As this chart shows, poverty rates are much higher for minorities.

known as homelands. According to the apartheid regime, dark-skinned Africans were allowed to own property in these black homelands but could not own land in vast areas exclusively reserved for white settlement.

Internationally isolated and facing growing problems within the country, the South African government finally agreed to abolish the apartheid system in 1993. A year later, following the deeply divided country's first all-race multiparty elections, anti-apartheid activist Nelson Mandela, a lawyer born into the Xhosa-speaking Thembu nation, became the Republic of South Africa's first indigenous president. Today, more than a decade after the abolition of apartheid, the white minority no longer controls the government, and racial policies are no longer in effect. In daily practice, however, segregation still exists; few people of European descent can be found in South Africa's vast underclass of have-nots, who are almost all people of color.

All of this brings to mind the concepts of ritual purity and pollution so basic to the Indian caste system. In South Africa, whites feared pollution of their purity

---

[7]Boshara, R. (2003, January/February). Wealth inequality: The $6,000 solution. *Atlantic Monthly.*

[8]Kennickell, A. B. (2003, November). *A rolling tide: Changes in the distribution of wealth in the U.S. 1989–2001.* Levy Economics Institute.

VISUAL COUNTERPOINT

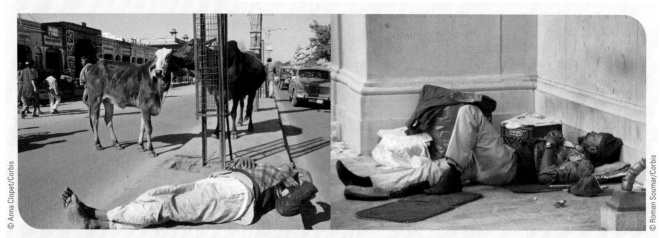

Homeless men sleeping on sidewalks—one in India, one in the United States. Outcast groups such as India's untouchables are a common feature of stratified societies. In the United States, nearly 13 percent of the population is trapped in poverty—according to the 2004 U.S. Census, which defined poverty as having an income under $19,300 for a four-person household, under $15,000 for three persons. Many sociologists and government officials argue that U.S. poverty is understated and that as much as 30 percent of Americans have trouble making ends meet. A disproportionate number in this underclass are African Americans, many still victimized by discrimination that is a remnant of slavery.

through improper contact with blacks. In India and South Africa, untouchables and blacks comprised categories of landless or near-landless people who served as a body of mobile laborers, always available for exploitation by those in political control. A similar mobile labor force of landless men at the state's disposal emerged in China as many as 2,200 years ago.

The basis of social class structure is role differentiation. Since great role diversity is most characteristic of civilizations—centrally organized state societies in which large numbers of people live in cities—it is not surprising they provide the greatest opportunities for stratification. Furthermore, the large size and heterogeneity of populations in civilizations create a need for classifying people into a manageable number of social categories. Small wonder, then, that social stratification is one of the defining characteristics of an urban civilization.

Social classes are manifest several ways. One is through *verbal evaluation*—what people say about others in their own society. For this, anything can be singled out for attention and spoken of favorably or unfavorably: political, military, religious, economic, or professional roles; wealth and property; kinship; physical qualities (skin color, for example); community activity; linguistic dialect; and a host of other traits. Cultures do this differently, and what may be spoken of favorably in one may be spoken of unfavorably in another and ignored in a third.

Furthermore, cultural values may change, so that something regarded favorably at one time may not be

at another. This is one reason why a researcher may be misled by verbal evaluation, for what people say may not correspond completely with social reality. As an example, the official language of Egypt is Classical Arabic, the language of the Koran (the holiest of Islamic texts). Though it is highly valued, no one in Egypt uses this language in daily interaction; rather, it is used for official documents or on formal occasions. Those most proficient in it are not of the upper class but, rather, of the lower middle classes. These are the people educated in the public schools (where Classical Arabic is the language of schooling) and who hold jobs in the government bureaucracy (which requires the most use of Classical Arabic). Upper-class Egyptians, by contrast, go to private schools, where they learn the foreign languages essential for success in diplomacy and in the global economy of business and industry.[9]

Social classes also are manifest through *patterns of association*—not just who interacts with whom but how and in what context. In Western society, informal, friendly relations take place mostly within one's own class. Relations with members of other classes tend to be more formal and occur in the context of specific situations. For example, a corporate executive and a janitor normally are members of different social classes. They may have frequent contact with each other, but it occurs in the setting of the corporate of-

---

[9]Haeri, N. (1997). The reproduction of symbolic capital: Language, state, and class in Egypt. *Current Anthropology 38*, 795–816.

Biocultural Connection

African Burial Ground Project ▪ By Michael Blakey

In 1991, construction workers in lower Manhattan unearthed what turned out to be an African burial ground, the final resting place of some 10,000 enslaved African captives brought to New York in the 17th and 18th centuries to build the city and provide the labor for its thriving economy. The discovery sparked controversy as the African American public held protests and prayer vigils to stop the part of a federal building project that nearly destroyed the site.

As a biological anthropologist and African American, I had a unique opportunity to work together with the descendant African American community to develop a plan that included both extensive biocultural research and the humane retention of the sacred nature of the site, ultimately through reburial and the creation of a fitting memorial. The research also involved archaeological and historical studies that used a broad African diasporic context for understanding the lifetime experiences of these people who were enslaved and buried in New York.

Studying a sample population of 419 individuals from the burial ground, our team used an exhaustive range of skeletal biological methods, producing a database

containing more than 200,000 observations of genetics, morphology, age, sex, growth and development, muscle development, trauma, nutrition, and disease. The bones revealed an unmistakable biocultural connection: physical wear and tear of an entire community brought on by the social institution of slavery.

We now know, based on this study, that life for Africans in colonial New York was characterized by poor nutrition, grueling physical labor that enlarged and often tore muscles, and death rates that were unusually high for 15- to 25-year-olds. Many of these young adults died soon after arriving on slaving ships. Few Africans lived past 40 years of age, and less than 2 percent lived beyond 55. Church records show strikingly different mortality trends

© A. J. Giordano/Corbis SABA

for the Europeans of New York: About eight times as many English as Africans lived past 55 years of age, and mortality in adolescence and the early 20s was relatively low.

Skeletal research also showed that those Africans who died as children and were most likely to have been born in New York exhibited stunted and disrupted growth and exposure to high levels of lead pollution—unlike those who had been born in Africa (and were distinguishable because they had filed teeth). Fertility was very low among enslaved women in New York, and infant mortality was high. In these respects, this northern colonial city was very similar to South Carolina and the Caribbean to which its economy was tied—regions where conditions for African captives were among the harshest.

Individuals in this deeply troubling burial ground came from warring African states including Calibar, Asante, Benin, Dahomey, Congo, Madagascar, and many others—states that wrestled with the European demand for human chattel. They resisted their enslavement through rebellion, and they resisted their dehumanization by carefully burying their dead and preserving what they could of their cultures.

fices and usually requires certain stereotyped behavior patterns.

A third way social classes are manifest is through *symbolic indicators.* For example, in the United States certain activities and possessions are indicative of class: occupation (a garbage collector has different class status than a medical specialist); wealth (rich people are generally in a higher social class than poor people); dress ("white collar" versus "blue collar"); form of recreation (upper-class people are expected to play golf rather than shoot pool down at the pool hall—but they can shoot pool at home or in a club); residential location (upper-class people do not ordinarily live in slums); kind of car; and so on. All sorts of status symbols are indicative of class position, including measures such as the number of

bathrooms in a person's house. That said, class rankings do not fully correlate with economic status or pay scales. The local garbage collector or unionized car-factory laborer typically makes more money than an average college professor with a doctorate.

Symbolic indicators involve factors of lifestyle, but differences in life chances may also signal differences in class standing. Life is apt to be less hard for members of an upper class as opposed to a lower class. This shows up in a tendency for lower infant mortality and longer life expectancy for the upper class. There is also a tendency for greater physical stature and robustness among upper-class people, the result of better diet and protection from serious illness in their juvenile years (see Biocultural Connection).

Social Mobility

Most stratified societies offer at least some **social mobility**—upward or downward change in one's social class position in a stratified society. For those who move upward in social ranking, this helps to ease the strains inherent in any system of inequality. Even the Indian caste system, with its guiding ideology that all hierarchical social arrangements within it are fixed, has a degree of flexibility and mobility, not all of it associated with the recent changes modernization has brought to India. Although individuals cannot move up or down the caste hierarchy, whole groups can do so depending on claims they can make for higher status and on how well they can manipulate others into acknowledging their claims.

Nonetheless, caste-structured societies exemplify *closed-class societies,* because of the limits on social mobility. Those that permit a great deal of mobility are referred to as *open-class societies.* Yet even in these, mobility is apt to be more limited than one might suppose. In the United States, despite its rags-to-riches ideology, most mobility involves a move up or down only a notch, although if this continues in a family over several generations, it may add up to a major change. Nonetheless, U.S. society makes much of relatively rare examples of great upward mobility consistent with its cultural values and does its best to overlook the numerous cases of little or no upward, not to mention downward, mobility.

The degree of mobility in a stratified society is related to the prevailing kind of family organization. Social mobility is most common in societies made up of independent nuclear families where the individual is closely tied to fewer people—especially when neolocal residence is the norm, and it is assumed that individuals will leave their family of birth when they become adults. In such social settings, through careful marriage, occupational success, and disassociation from the lower-class family in which they grew up, individuals can more easily move up in society.

In societies where the extended family is the usual form, mobility tends to be more difficult, because each individual is strongly tied to many relatives. Typically, if a person in such a society moves up to a higher social class, it is expected that he or she will help the rest of the family move up as well. In all likelihood, the extended families of the highly successful Ivory Coast soccer players described in this chapter's Globalscape have experienced upward social mobility through their ties to these athletes.

social mobility Upward or downward change in one's social class position in a stratified society.

Maintaining Stratification

Because social stratification of any kind generally makes life more difficult for large segments of a population, the lower classes are usually kept quiet through the cultural system's superstructure or worldview. This superstructure may be governed and directed by ruling elites, who impose their own ideas and values on a society by controlling information, staging public ceremonies, and other forms of ideological expression.

In India, for example, belief in reincarnation and the existence of an incorruptible supernatural power that assigns people to a particular caste position as a reward or punishment for the deeds and misdeeds of past lives justifies one's position in this life. If, however, individuals faithfully perform the duties appropriate to their caste in this lifetime, then they can expect to be reborn into a higher caste in a future existence. Truly exemplary performance of their duties may even release them from the cycle of rebirth, to be reunited with the divinity from which all existence springs.

In the minds of orthodox Hindus, then, one's caste position is something earned rather than the accident of birth as it appears to outside observers. Thus, although the caste system explicitly recognizes (and accepts as legitimate) inequality among people, an implicit assumption of ultimate equality underlies it. This contrasts with the situation in the United States, where the equality of all people is proclaimed even while various groups are repressed or otherwise discriminated against.

Although the cost is great—social classes do, after all, make life oppressive for large numbers of people—classes may nevertheless perform an integrative function in society. By cutting across some or all lines of kinship, residence, occupation, and age group, depending on the particular society, they counteract potential tendencies for society to fragment into separate entities. For instance, in India a succession of conquerors succeeded in moving into the caste hierarchy near its top as warriors. Coming from diverse ethnic and religious groups, they were incorporated into the larger state society by certification of their leaders as warriors and by marriage of their women to upper-caste Brahmans.

Nonetheless, stratification, by its very nature, provides a means by which one, usually small, group of people may dominate and make life miserable for large numbers of others. It provided 4.5 million people of European descent with justification to dominate 25 million indigenous people in South Africa and sanctioned the horrors of slavery in the United States and other parts of the world. Even without conquest or slavery, ethnic differences often are a factor in the definition of social classes, as not only African Americans but also members of other North American minorities have experienced

GLOBALSCAPE

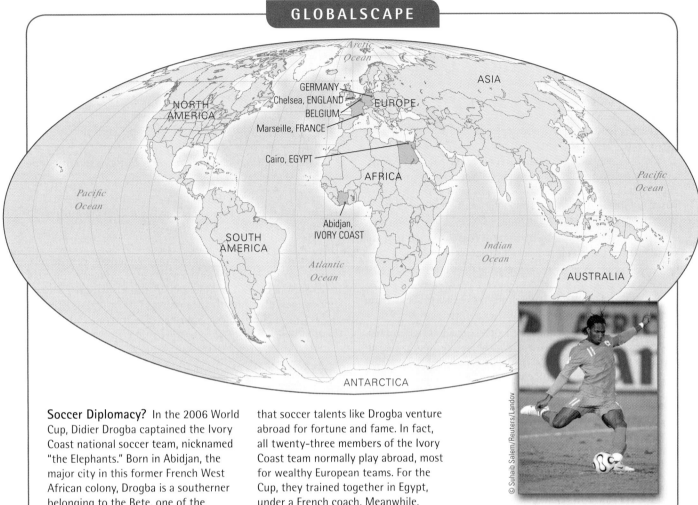

Soccer Diplomacy? In the 2006 World Cup, Didier Drogba captained the Ivory Coast national soccer team, nicknamed "the Elephants." Born in Abidjan, the major city in this former French West African colony, Drogba is a southerner belonging to the Bete, one of the country's sixty-five ethnic groups. He was recruited at an early age to play for a Belgian club. Emerging as a powerful striker, he was drafted by a French club for $8 million and moved to Marseille. Chosen French Player of the Year in 2004, after just one season he signed with England's champion team, Chelsea Football Club, for a record $42 million multi-year contract. In England, his annual salary (not counting endorsements) is more than $6 million.

Given that the average Ivorian earns just $1,600 per year, it is not surprising that soccer talents like Drogba venture abroad for fortune and fame. In fact, all twenty-three members of the Ivory Coast team normally play abroad, most for wealthy European teams. For the Cup, they trained together in Egypt, under a French coach. Meanwhile, their home country has been wracked by a brutal civil war in which southern ethnic groups are pitted against northern ones.

Ninety percent of the Ivory Coast's foreign exchange earnings come from cocoa beans. An international sports star, Drogba appears in ads promoting the sale of Ivorian chocolate in France and Germany. He also promotes peace: During the 2006 World Cup games in Germany, enthusiastically watched on television by millions of fellow Ivorians back home, he and his national soccer team (representing both southern and northern Ivory Coast) pleaded that the unity of the Elephants in the stadium would inspire fellow Ivorians to settle their conflict and reunite as a country.

Global Twister Why does the captain of Ivory Coast's national soccer team competing for the World Cup think that the Elephants can help bring together fellow Ivorians from rival factions?

through the racist stereotyping that leads to social and economic disadvantages.

In any system of stratification, those who dominate proclaim their supposedly superior status, commonly asserting it through intimidation or propaganda (in the form of gossip, media, religious doctrine, and so forth) that presents their position as normal, natural, divinely guided, or at least well-deserved. As U.S. anthropologist Laura Nader of the University of California, Berkeley, points out, "Systems of thought develop over time and reflect the interests of certain classes or groups in the society who manage to universalize their beliefs and values."[10]

_____

[10]Nader, L. (1997). Controlling processes: Tracing the dynamic components of power. *Current Anthropology 38,* 271.

So it is with certain religious ideologies that effectively assert that the social order is divinely fixed and therefore not to be questioned. With the aid of institutionalized thought structures, religious and otherwise, those in power hope that members of the lower classes will thereby "know their place" and not contest their domination by the "chosen elite." If, however, this domination is contested, the elite usually control the power of the state and use its institutions to protect their privileged position.

Questions for Reflection

1. When teenagers leave their parental home to go to college or find employment in a distant part of the country, they face the challenge of establishing social relationships that are not based on kinship but on common interest. To which common-interest associations do you belong and why?

2. At what point do you think kinship ceases to be the major organizational principle in a social structure?

3. Do you think that members of an upper class or caste in a socially stratified system have a greater vested interest in the idea of law and order than those forced to exist on the bottom of such societies? Why or why not?

4. Slavery in the United States was officially abolished in 1863, caste-based discrimination of untouchables became constitutionally outlawed in India in 1950, and race-based segregation in South Africa officially ended with the abolition of apartheid in 1993. Considering these important political changes, do you think that social repression against these groups has now ended for good?

5. In your own life, have you personally seen and experienced grouping by gender, age, and class? What do you see as the positive and negative aspects of these groupings?

Suggested Readings

Bernardi, B. (1985). *Age class systems: Social institutions and policies based on age.* New York: Cambridge University Press.

This is a cross-cultural analysis of age as a device for organizing society and seeing to the distribution and rotation of power.

Bradfield, R. M. (1998). *A natural history of associations.* New York: International Universities Press.

First published in 1973, this major anthropological study of common-interest associations attempts to provide a comprehensive theory of the origin of associations and their role in kin-based societies.

De Mott, B. (1990). *The imperial middle: Why Americans can't think straight about class.* New York: Morrow.

This critical commentary on the myth that the United States is a classless society demonstrates the great social and political costs of buying into that idea.

Lenski, G. E. (1984). *Power and privilege: A theory of social stratification.* New York: McGraw-Hill.

In this classic text, the author uses a historical and broadly comparative approach to analyze how stratification develops in societies.

Price, T. D., & Feinman, G. M. (Eds.). (1995). *Foundations of social inequality.* New York: Plenum.

A collection of essays by various contributors examining the emergence of social inequality.

Sanday, P. R. (1981). *Female power and male dominance: On the origins of sexual inequality.* Cambridge, England: Cambridge University Press.

A cross-cultural study of various ways that male–female relations are organized in human societies. Demonstrating that male dominance is not inherent in those relations, the author suggests that dominance emerges in situations of stress as a result of chronic food shortages, migration, and colonial domination.

Steady, F. C. (2005). *Women and collective action in Africa.* New York: Palgrave Macmillan.

This examination of women's movements and collective action in Africa begins in pre-colonial times and moves through to the present. It identifies and discusses the various arenas in which collective action has and can influence, including women's traditional, mutual-aid, and religious associations.

Thomson Audio Study Products

 Enjoy the MP3-ready Audio Lecture Overviews for each chapter and a comprehensive audio glossary of key terms for quick study and review. Whether walking to class, doing laundry, or studying at your desk, you now have the freedom to choose when, where, and how you interact with your audio-based educational media. See the preface for information on how to access this on-the-go study and review tool.

The Anthropology Resource Center

www.thomsonedu.com/anthropology
The Anthropology Resource Center provides extended learning materials to reinforce your understanding of key concepts in the four fields of anthropology. For each of the four fields, the Resource Center includes dynamic exercises including video exercises, map exercises, simulations, and "Meet the Scientists" interviews, as well as critical thinking questions that can be assigned and e-mailed to instructors. The Resource Center also provides breaking news in anthropology and interesting material on applied anthropology to help you link what you are learning to the world around you.

23 Politics, Power, and Violence

© Reuters/Corbis

CHALLENGE ISSUE

In all societies, from the largest to the smallest, people must decide who gets what, when, where, and how. This is the basic challenge of politics. Political organization takes many forms, of which the state is just one. Often, states are controlled by wealthy elites who use their positional power to defend their vested interests. They do so by means of government institutions, administrative bureaucracies, and armed forces equipped with the means of violence to impose or maintain law and order. Citizens seeking political change by staging public demonstrations, as in this photo of protestors in Japan, may be stopped by state security forces authorized to use violence, if necessary, to prohibit, control or even eliminate such opposition.

How Are Power and Political Organization Different?

All social relations involve power, which essentially refers to the ability of individuals or groups to impose their will upon others and make them do things even against their own wants or wishes. Power also operates on the level of entire societies. The ability to impose or maintain order and to resolve conflicts requires political organization, which refers to the means by which a society maintains order internally and manages its affairs with other societies externally. It may be relatively uncentralized and informal, as in bands and tribes, or more centralized and formal, as in chiefdoms and states.

How Are Social and Political Order Formed and Maintained?

Social controls may be internalized—in cultural values that are "built into" individuals—or externalized, in the form of sanctions. Positive sanctions encourage approved behavior, while negative sanctions discourage unacceptable behavior. Negative sanctions are called laws if they are formalized and enforced by an authorized political agency. Force may be employed to impose or maintain order within a society or between groups. Although states and chiefdoms frequently practice warfare as a means of achieving political objectives, some groups avoid such organized violence.

How Do Political Systems Obtain Popular Support?

In uncentralized systems people give loyalty and cooperation freely because everyone participates in making most decisions. Centralized systems, by contrast, rely more heavily on power, even coercion, although in the long run these may lessen the system's effectiveness. To a greater or lesser extent, political organizations all over the world seek to legitimize their power through recourse to supernatural ideas.

An irony of human life is that something as fundamental to our existence as cooperation should contain within it the seeds of its own destruction. It is nonetheless true that the groups people form to fulfill important organizational needs do not just facilitate cooperation among the members of those groups; they also create conditions that may lead to the disruption of society. We see this in a wide range of situations: in riots among fans rooting for different soccer teams, in the gang violence that takes place in many North American cities, and all the more seriously in bloody conflicts between neighboring ethnic groups such as Serbs and Albanians in southern Europe and Tutsi and Hutu in East Africa.

The attitude that "my group is better than your group" is not confined to any one of the world's cultures, and it commonly takes the form of rivalry between groups: descent group against descent group, men against women, age grade against age grade, social class against social class, and so forth. This does not mean that such rivalry has to be disruptive; indeed, it may function to ensure that the members of groups perform their jobs well so as not to lose face or be subject to ridicule. Rivalry, however, can become a serious problem if it erupts into violence.

The fact is, social living inevitably entails a certain amount of friction—not just between groups but between individual members of groups as well. Thus, any society can count on a degree of disruptive behavior by some of its members at one time or another. Yet, no one can know precisely when such outbursts will occur or what form they will take. Not only does this uncertainty go against the predictability social life demands, but it also goes against the deep-seated psychological need each individual has for structure and certainty. Therefore, every society must have means by which conflicts can be resolved and breakdown of the social order prevented. Today, throughout the world, state governments play a central role in maintaining social order.

 THOMSON AUDIO STUDY PRODUCTS Take advantage of the MP3-ready Audio Lecture Overviews and comprehensive audio glossary of key terms for each chapter. See the preface for information on how to access this on-the-go study and review tool.

power The ability of individuals or groups to impose their will upon others and make them do things even against their own wants or wishes.
political organization The way power is distributed and embedded in society; the means through which a society creates and maintains social order.

Complex political structures known as states first began to emerge over 5,000 years ago. Commonly unstable, many have disappeared in the course of history, some temporarily and others forever. Some were annexed by other states, and others collapsed or fragmented into smaller political units. Although some present-day states are very old—such as Japan, which has endured as a state for almost 1,500 years—few are older than the United States, an independent country since 1783.

Despite the predominance of state societies today, there are still groups where political organization consists of flexible and informal kinship systems whose leaders lack real **power**—the ability of individuals or groups to impose their will upon others and make them do things even against their own wants or wishes. Between these two polarities of kin-ordered and state-organized political systems lies a world of variety.

KINDS OF POLITICAL SYSTEMS

The term **political organization** refers to the way power is distributed and embedded in society, whether in organizing a giraffe hunt, managing irrigated farmlands, or raising an army. In short, it is the means through which a society creates and maintains social order. It assumes a variety of forms among the peoples of the world, but anthropologists have simplified this complex subject by identifying four basic kinds of political systems: bands, tribes, chiefdoms, and states (Figure 23.1). The first two are uncentralized systems; the latter two are centralized.

Uncentralized Political Systems

Until recently, many non-Western peoples have had neither chiefs with established rights and duties nor any fixed form of government, as those who live in modern states understand the term. Instead, marriage and kinship have formed their principal means of social organization. The economies of these societies are primarily of a subsistence type, and populations are typically small.

Leaders do not have real power to force compliance with the society's customs or rules, but if individuals do not conform, they may become targets of scorn and gossip or even be banished. Important decisions are usually made in a collective manner by agreement among adults. Dissenting members may decide to act with the majority, or they may choose to adopt some other course of action, including leaving the group. This egalitarian form of political organization provides great flexibility, which in many situations offers an adaptive advantage. Since power in these kin-ordered communities is shared, with nobody exercising exclusive control over collective

TYPES OF POLITICAL ORGANIZATION
The symbol → indicates that the attribute varies between less and more complex societies of that type.

	BAND	TRIBE	CHIEFDOM	STATE
MEMBERSHIP				
Number of people	Dozens and up	Hundreds and up	Thousands and up	Tens of thousands and up
Settlement pattern	Mobile	Mobile or fixed: 1 or more villages	Fixed: 2 or more villages	Fixed: Many villages and cities
Basis of relationships	Kin	Kin, descent groups	Kin, rank, and residence	Class and residence
Ethnicities and languages	1	1	1	1 or more
GOVERNMENT				
Decision making, leadership	"Egalitarian"	"Egalitarian" or Big Man	Centralized, hereditary	Centralized
Bureaucracy	None	None	None, or 1 or 2 levels	Many levels
Monopoly of force and information	No	No	No → Yes	Yes
Conflict resolution	Informal	Informal	Centralized	Laws, judges
Hierarchy of settlement	No	No	No → Paramount village or head town	Capital
ECONOMY				
Food production	No	No → Yes	Yes → Intensive	Intensive
Labor specialization	No	No	No → Yes	Yes
Exchanges	Reciprocal	Reciprocal	Redistributive ("tribute")	Redistributive ("taxes")
Control of land	Band	Descent group	Chief	Various
SOCIETY				
Stratified	No	No	Yes, ranked by kin	Yes, by class or caste
Slavery	No	No	Some, small-scale	Some, large-scale
Luxury goods for elite	No	No	Yes	Yes
Public architecture	No	No	No → Yes	Yes
Indigenous literacy	No	No	No → Some	Often

Figure 23.1
Four Kinds of Political Systems

resources or public affairs, individuals typically enjoy much more freedom than those who form part of larger and more complex political systems.

Band Organization
The **band** is a relatively small and loosely organized kin-ordered group that inhabits a specific territory and that may split periodically into smaller extended family groups that are politically independent. Typically, bands are found among food foragers and other nomadic societies where people organize into politically autonomous extended-family groups that usually camp together, although the members of such families may periodically break up into smaller groups to forage for food or visit other relatives. Thus, bands are kin groups, composed of men and/or women who are related (or are assumed to be) with their spouses and unmarried children.

Bands may be characterized as associations of related families who occupy a common (often loosely de-fined) territory and who live there together as long as environmental and subsistence circumstances are favorable. The band is probably the oldest form of political organization, since all humans were once food foragers and remained so until the development of farming and pastoralism over the past 10,000 years.

Since bands are egalitarian and small, numbering at most a few hundred people, no real need exists for formal, centralized political systems. Because everyone is related to—and knows on a personal basis—everyone else with whom dealings are required, there is high value placed on "getting along." Conflicts that do arise are usually settled informally through gossip, ridicule, direct negotiation, or mediation. When negotiation or

band A relatively small and loosely organized kin-ordered group that inhabits a specific territory and that may split periodically into smaller extended family groups that are politically independent.

mediation are used, the focus is on reaching a solution considered fair by all concerned parties, rather than on conforming to some abstract law or rule. Where all else fails, disgruntled individuals have the option of leaving to go live in another band where they may have relatives or trying to establish a new community of their own.

Decisions affecting a band are made with the participation of all its adult members, with an emphasis on achieving consensus—a collective agreement—rather than a simple majority. Individuals become leaders by virtue of their abilities and serve in that capacity only as long as they retain the confidence of the community. They have no real power to force people to abide by their decisions. A leader who exceeds what people are willing to accept quickly loses followers.

An example of the informal nature of band leadership is found among the Ju/'hoansi Bushmen of the Kalahari Desert mentioned in earlier chapters. Each Ju/'hoansi band is composed of a group of families that live together, linked through kinship to one another and to the headman (or, less often, headwoman). Although each band has rights to the territory it occupies and the resources within it, two or more bands may range over the same land. The head, called the *kxau,* or "owner," is the focal point for the band's claims on the territory. He or she does not personally own the land or resources but symbolically represents the rights of band members to them. If the head leaves the area to live elsewhere, people turn to someone else to lead them.

The head coordinates band migration when resources are no longer adequate for subsistence in a particular habitat. This leader's major duty is to plan when and where the group will move, and when the move

begins his or her position is at the head of the line. The leader selects the site for the new settlement and has the first choice of a spot for his or her own fire.

There are few other material rewards or duties. For example, a Ju/'hoansi head is not a judge and does not punish other band members. Wrongdoers are judged and held accountable by public opinion, usually expressed by gossip—which can play an important role in curbing socially unacceptable behavior. In small-scale communities where everyone is interdependent, public scolding or open expression of irritation may escalate into serious anger and lead to splits that jeopardize everyone's security.

Through gossip—talking behind someone's back and spreading rumors about behavior considered disruptive, shameful, or ridiculous—people accomplish several objectives while avoiding the potential disruption of open confrontation: They underscore and reinforce the cultural standards of "normal" people who abide by the unwritten rules of proper conduct; they punish those who violate standards of socially acceptable behavior; moreover, since gossip can damage a person's reputation and is often fueled by hidden jealousy or a secret desire to retaliate against someone considered too accomplished or successful, it may function like a leveling mechanism.

Another prime technique in small-scale societies for resolving disputes, or even avoiding them in the first place, is mobility. Those unable to get along with others of their group may choose or feel pressured to move to another group where existing kinship ties may give them rights of entry.

Tribal Organization

The second type of uncentralized authority system is the tribe. This term is problematic because it has many meanings. The English term is derived from the Latin word *tribus,* which referred to each of the three original divisions of the Roman people more than 2,500 years ago. Even after the number of Roman tribes increased to thirty-five, this term stuck, still referring to a major subdivision of a nation. When the biblical texts were translated from Hebrew into Latin, and much later into English, the term *tribe* was also applied to the twelve subdivisions of Israel. Over time, it came to be widely used as a label for any people not organized into states.

In the past few centuries, when the English and other Europeans expanded their powerful reach across the globe, the term gained popularity as a way to contrast people whom they regarded as inferior to their own supposedly superior civilization. The term was even applied to non-Western peoples who in fact had strongly centralized states (the Aztecs, for example).

The word is still often used in a negative or degrading way. For instance, political unrest in many parts of

Toma, a Ju/'hoansi headman, is known to many people worldwide through the ethnographic film *The Hunters.*

Documentary Educational Resources

Shown here is a meeting of the Navajo Tribal Council, a nontraditional governing body created in response to requirements set by the U.S. government in order for the Navajo to exercise national sovereignty.

the world is often blamed on "tribalism," when in fact the strife is usually the direct consequence of the creation of states that make it possible for the governing elite of one ethnic group or nationality to exploit others for their own benefit.[1]

To complicate matters, the term *tribe* also has a distinct legal meaning in some countries, including the United States. For instance, lumping together for administrative purposes a variety of groups historically organized as bands, tribes, or chiefdoms, U.S. law defines *tribe* as "any Indian tribe, band, nation, or other organized group or community . . . recognized as eligible for the special programs and services provided by the United States to Indians because of their status as Indians."[2]

In anthropology, this problematic term **tribe** refers to a wide range of kin-ordered groups that are politically integrated by some unifying factor and whose members share a common ancestry, identity, culture, language, and territory. In these larger political entities, people sacrifice a degree of household autonomy in return for greater security against such perils as enemy attacks or starvation.

Typically, though not invariably, a tribe has an economy based on some form of crop cultivation or herding.

Since these subsistence methods usually yield more food than those of the food-foraging band, tribal membership is usually larger than band membership. While band population densities are usually less than one person per square mile, tribal population densities generally exceed that and may be as high as 250 per square mile. Greater population density brings a new set of problems to be solved as opportunities for bickering, begging, adultery, and theft increase markedly, especially among people living in permanent villages.

Each tribe consists of one or more self-supporting and self-governing local communities that may then form alliances with others for various purposes. As in the band, political organization in the tribe is informal and temporary. Whenever a situation requiring political integration of all or several groups within the tribe arises—perhaps for defense, to carry out a raid, to pool resources in times of scarcity, or to capitalize on a windfall that must be distributed quickly lest it spoil—groups join to deal with the situation in a cooperative manner. When the problem is satisfactorily solved, each group then resumes autonomy.

In many tribal societies the organizing unit and seat of political authority is the clan, comprised of people who consider themselves descended from a common an-

[1]Whitehead, N. L., & Ferguson, R. B. (1993, November 10). Deceptive stereotypes about tribal warfare (p. A48). *Chronicle of Higher Education;* Van Den Berghe, P. L. (1992). The modern state: Nation builder or nation killer? *International Journal of Group Tensions 92*(3), 199–200.

[2]25 U.S. Code, par.450–450n.

tribe In anthropology, refers to a range of kin-ordered groups that are politically integrated by some unifying factor and whose members share a common ancestry, identity, culture, language, and territory.

cestor. Within the clan, elders or headmen and/or head-women regulate members' affairs and represent their clan in interactions with other clans. As a group, the elders of all the clans may form a council that acts within the community or for the community in dealings with outsiders. Because clan members usually do not all live together in a single community, clan organization facilitates joint action with members of related communities when necessary.

Leadership among tribes is also relatively informal, as evident in a wide array of past and present examples. The Navajo Indians in the southwestern United States, for example, traditionally did not think of government as something fixed and all-powerful, and leadership was not vested in a central authority. A local leader was a man respected for his age, integrity, and wisdom. Therefore, people sought his advice frequently, but he had no formal means of control and could not force any decision on those who asked for his help. Group decisions were made by public consensus, although the most influential man usually played a key role in reaching a decision. Social mechanisms that induced members to abide by group decisions included gossip, criticism, withdrawal of cooperation, and the belief that antisocial actions caused sickness and other misfortune.

Another example of tribal leadership is the Big Man. Common in the southern Pacific, such men are leaders of localized descent groups or of a territorial group. The Big Man combines a small amount of interest in his tribe's welfare with a great deal of cunning and calculation for his own personal gain. His authority is personal; he does not come to office in any formal sense, nor is he elected. His status is the result of acts that raise him above most other tribe members and attract to him a number of loyal followers.

The Kapauku of Western New Guinea typify this form of political organization. Among them, the Big Man is called the *tonowi*, or "rich one." To achieve this status, one must be male, wealthy, generous, and eloquent. Physical bravery and an ability to deal with the supernatural are also common *tonowi* characteristics,

but they are not essential. The *tonowi* functions as the headman of the village unit in a wide variety of situations within and beyond the community. He represents his group in dealing with outsiders and other villages and acts as negotiator and/or judge when disputes break out among his followers.

Because Kapauku culture places a high value on wealth, a well-to-do man is considered successful and admirable—provided he is also generous when it comes to making loans. Those who refuse to lend money to other villagers may be ostracized, ridiculed, and, in extreme cases, actually executed by a group of warriors. Such responses to tightfistedness ensure that economic wealth is distributed throughout the group.

The *tonowi* acquires political power through his loans. Other villagers comply with his requests because they are in his debt (often interest-free), and they do not want to have to repay their loans. Those who have not yet borrowed from him may wish to do so in the future, so they, too, want to keep his goodwill.

The *tonowi* gains further support by taking into his household young male apprentices who receive business

This Big Man from New Guinea is wearing his official regalia.

training along with food and shelter. He also gives them a loan that enables them to marry when the apprenticeship ends. In return, they act as messengers and bodyguards. After leaving, they remain tied to the *tonowi* by bonds of affection and gratitude. Political support also comes from the *tonowi*'s kinsmen, whose relationship brings with it varying obligations.

The *tonowi* functions as a leader in a wide variety of situations. He represents his group in dealing with outsiders and other villages and acts as negotiator and/or judge when disputes break out among his followers. As discussed in an earlier chapter, the *tonowi*'s wealth comes from his success at breeding pigs—the focus of the entire Kapauku economy. It is not uncommon for a *tonowi* to lose his fortune rapidly due to bad management or bad luck with his pigs. Thus the Kapauku political structure shifts frequently; as one man loses wealth and consequently power, another gains it and becomes a *tonowi*. These changes confer a degree of flexibility on the political organization and prevent any one *tonowi* from holding political power for too long.

Although it is far more common for tribal chiefs to be men, in some cultures women serve in such leadership positions, as discussed later in this chapter.

Political Integration Beyond the Kin Group

Age sets, age grades, and common-interest groups discussed in the previous chapter are among the mechanisms used by tribal societies as means of political integration. Cutting across territorial and kin groupings, these organizations link members from different lineages and clans. For example, among the Tiriki of East Africa (mentioned in the previous chapter) the Warrior age grade guards the village and grazing lands, while Judicial Elders resolve disputes. The oldest age grade, the Ritual Elders, advise on matters involving the well-being of all the Tiriki people. With the tribe's political affairs in the hands of the various age grades and their officers, this type of organization enables the largely independent kin groups to solve conflicts and sometimes even avoid feuding between the lineages.

Another system of political integration found among tribes in many parts of the world is the common-interest association, also discussed in the previous chapter. For example, among many Indian nations inhabiting North America's Great Plains in the 19th century, the band comprised the basic territorial and political unit. In addition, however, there existed a number of military societies or warrior clubs.

Among the Cheyenne, for instance, there were seven of these groups. A boy might be invited to join one of these societies when he achieved warrior status, whereupon he became familiar with the society's particular insignia, songs, and rituals. Beyond military functions,

the warrior societies also had ceremonial and social functions.

The Cheyenne warriors' daily tasks consisted of overseeing activities in the village, protecting families on the move to the next camping site, and enforcing rules against individual hunting when the whole tribe was on a buffalo hunt. In addition, each warrior society had its own repertoire of dances, performed on special ceremonial occasions. Since each Cheyenne band had identical military societies bearing identical names, the societies served to integrate the entire tribe for military and political purposes.[3]

Centralized Political Systems

In bands and tribes, political authority is not centralized, and each group is economically and politically autonomous. Political organization is vested in kinship, age, and common-interest groups. Populations are small and relatively homogeneous, with people engaged for the most part in the same sorts of activities throughout their lives. However, as a society's social life becomes more complex—as population rises, technology becomes more intricate, and specialization of labor and trade networks produce surplus goods—the opportunity increases for some individuals or groups to exercise control at the expense of others. In such societies, political authority and power are concentrated in a single individual (the chief) or in a body of individuals (the state).

Chiefdoms

A **chiefdom** is a regional polity (a politically organized society) in which two or more local groups are organized under a single ruling individual—the chief—who is at the head of a ranked hierarchy of people. An individual's status in such a polity is determined by the closeness of his or her relationship to the chief. Those closest are officially superior and receive deferential treatment from those in lower ranks.

The office of the chief is usually for life and often hereditary. Typically, it passes from a man to his son or his sister's son, depending on whether descent is traced patrilineally or matrilineally. Unlike the headmen or headwomen in bands and tribes, the leader of a chiefdom is generally a true authority figure, whose authority serves to unite members in all affairs and at all times. For

---

[3]Hoebel, E. A. (1960). *The Cheyennes: Indians of the Great Plains*. New York: Holt, Rinehart & Winston.

chiefdom A regional polity in which two or more local groups are organized under a single chief, who is at the head of a ranked hierarchy of people.

A Kpelle town chief in Liberia, West Africa, listens to a dispute in his district. Settling disputes is one of several ongoing traditional tasks that fall to paramount chiefs among Kpelle people.

example, a chief can distribute land among community members and recruit people into military service. Chiefdoms have a recognized hierarchy consisting of major and minor authorities who control major and minor subdivisions. Such an arrangement is, in effect, a chain of command, linking leaders at every level. It serves to bind groups in the heartland to the chief's headquarters, be it a mud and dung hut or a marble palace.

Although leaders of chiefdoms are almost always men, in some cultures a politically astute wife, sister, or single daughter of a deceased male chief could inherit such a powerful position as well. One historical example is Aimata, who succeeded her deceased half-brother Pomare III as leader of the Polynesian chiefdom of Tahiti in 1827, ruling as Queen Pomare IV until her death fifty years later.

Chiefs usually control the economic activities of those who fall under their political rule. Typically, chiefdoms involve redistributive systems, and the chief has control over surplus goods and perhaps even over the community's labor force. Thus, he (and sometimes she) may demand a quota of rice from farmers, which will then be redistributed to the entire community. Similarly, laborers may be recruited to build irrigation works, a palace, or a temple.

The chief may also amass a great amount of personal wealth and pass it on to offspring. Land, cattle, and luxury goods produced by specialists can be collected by the chief and become part of the power base. Moreover, high-ranking families of the chiefdom may engage in the same practice and use their possessions as evidence of noble status. An example of this form of political organi-

zation may be seen among the Kpelle of Liberia in West Africa.[4] Among them is a class of paramount chiefs, each of whom presides over one of the Kpelle chiefdoms (each of which is now a district of the Liberian state). The paramount chiefs' traditional tasks are hearing disputes, preserving order, seeing to the upkeep of trails, and various other supervising functions. In addition, they are now salaried officials of the Liberian government, mediating between it and their own people. Also, a paramount chief receives government commissions on taxes and court fees collected within his chiefdom, plus a commission for furnishing the rubber plantations with laborers. Moreover, he gets a stipulated amount of rice from each household and gifts from people who come to request favors and intercessions. In keeping with his exalted station in life, a paramount chief has at his disposal uniformed messengers, a literate clerk, and the symbols of wealth: many wives, embroidered gowns, and freedom from manual labor.

In a ranked hierarchy beneath each Kpelle paramount chief are several lesser chiefs: one for each district within the chiefdom, one for each town within a district, and one for each quarter of all but the smallest towns. Each acts as a kind of lieutenant for his chief of the next higher rank and also serves as a liaison between him and those of lower rank. Unlike paramount or district chiefs, who are comparatively remote, town and quarter chiefs are readily accessible to people at the local level.

[4]Gibbs, J. L., Jr. (1965). The Kpelle of Liberia. In J. L. Gibbs, Jr. (Ed.), *Peoples of Africa* (pp. 216–218). New York: Holt, Rinehart & Winston.

Traditionally, chiefdoms in all parts of the world have been highly unstable, with lesser chiefs trying to take power from higher ranking chiefs or paramount chiefs vying with one another for supreme power. In precolonial Hawaii, for example, war was the way to gain territory and maintain power; great chiefs set out to conquer one another in an effort to become paramount chief of all the islands. When one chief conquered another, the loser and all his nobles were dispossessed of all property and were lucky if they escaped alive. The new chief then appointed his own supporters to positions of political power. As a consequence, there was very little continuity of governmental or religious administration.

State Systems

The **state** is a centralized polity involving large numbers of people within a defined territory who are divided in social classes and organized and directed by a formal government that has the capacity and authority to make laws and to use force to defend the social order. This is the most formal of political organizations and represents one of the hallmarks of what is commonly referred to as *civilization*. From the perspective of the political elite in control of the state, its formation and endurance are typically represented as something positive—as progress. This view is not necessarily shared by those who exist on the political underside and do not possess much personal freedom to say and do as they please.

A large population in a state-organized society requires increased food production and wider distribution networks. Together, these lead to a transformation of the landscape by way of irrigation and terracing, carefully managed crop rotation cycles, intensive competition for clearly demarcated lands, roads, and enough farmers and other rural workers to support market systems and a specialized urban sector. Under such conditions, cor-

porate groups that stress exclusive membership proliferate, ethnic differentiation and ethnocentrism become more pronounced, and the potential for social conflict increases dramatically. Given these circumstances, state institutions, which minimally involve a bureaucracy, a military, and (usually) an official religion, provide the means for numerous and diverse groups to function together as an integrated whole.

Although their guiding ideology is that they are permanent and stable, since their first appearance some 5,000 years ago, states have been anything but permanent. Whatever stability they have achieved has been short term at best; over the long term, they show a clear tendency toward instability and transience. Nowhere have states even begun to show the staying power exhibited by less centralized political systems, the longest lasting social forms invented by humans.

An important distinction to make at this point is between state and nation. As noted in Chapter 1, a **nation** is a people who share a collective identity based on a common culture, language, territorial base, and history.[5] Today, there are roughly 200 internationally recognized states in the world, most of which did not exist before the end of World War II (1945). By contrast, there are about 5,000 nations (including tribes), many of which have existed since "time immemorial." Rarely do state and nation coincide, as they do, for example, in Iceland, Japan, and Swaziland.

About 73 percent of the world's states are pluralistic societies, having within their boundaries peoples of more than one nation.[6] Often, smaller nations (including tribes) and other groups find themselves at the mercy of one or more dominant nations or ethnic groups controlling the state. Frequently facing discrimination, even repression, some minority nations seek to improve their political position by founding an independent state. In the process, they usually encounter stiff opposition, even violent confrontations.

So it is with the Kurdish people inhabiting the borderlands of Iran, Iraq, and Turkey (Figure 23.2), the Pal-

---

[5]Clay, J. W. (1996). What's a nation? In W. A. Haviland & R. J. Gordon (Eds.), *Talking about people* (2nd ed., p. 188). Mountain View, CA: Mayfield.

[6]Van Den Berghe, P. L. (1992). The modern state: Nation builder or nation killer? *International Journal of Group Tensions 92* (3), 193.

---

state In anthropology, a centralized polity involving large numbers of people within a defined territory who are divided into social classes and organized and directed by a formal government that has the capacity and authority to make laws, and use force to defend the social order.

nation A people who share a collective identity based on a common culture, language, territorial base, and history.

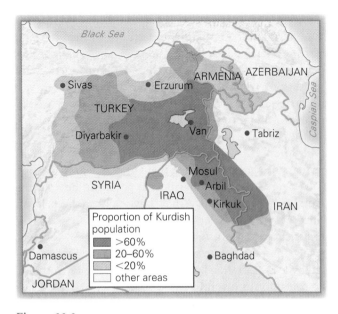

Figure 23.2

The Kurds, most of whom live in Iran, Iraq, and Turkey, are an example of a nation without a state.

estinians whose lands have been occupied by Israel for several decades, and the Chechens in the Russian federation, to cite but a few examples. While the outcome of armed struggle may be the formation of a new state (such as Bosnia's recent split from Serb-dominated Yugoslavia), some nations have forged their own states without open violence. Papua New Guinea in the southern Pacific, which became an independent state in 1975, is one example of this.

An important aspect of the state is its delegation of authority to maintain order within and outside its borders. Police, foreign ministries, war ministries, and other bureaucracies function to control and punish disruptive acts of crime, dissension, and rebellion. By such agencies the state asserts authority impersonally and in a consistent, predictable manner. Western forms of government, like that of the United States (in reality, a superstate), of course, are state governments, and their organization and workings are undoubtedly familiar to most everyone.

An example of a not-so-familiar state is Swaziland in southern Africa. One of the world's few true nation-states, it is home to the Swazi—a Bantu-speaking people.[7] Although the Swazi are primarily farmers, cattle raising is also practiced—and highly esteemed. In fact, the ritual, wealth, and power of their authority system are all intricately linked with cattle. In addition to farming and cattle raising, there is some specialization of

labor; certain people are specialists in ritual activities, metal smithing, wood carving, and pottery making. Their goods and services are traded, although the Swazi do not have elaborate markets.

The traditional Swazi authority system was characterized by a highly developed dual monarchy (now a thing of the past), a hereditary aristocracy, and elaborate kinship rituals, as well as by statewide age sets. The king and his mother were the central figures of all national activity, linking all the people of the Swazi state: They presided over higher courts, summoned national gatherings, controlled age classes, allocated land, disbursed national wealth, took precedence in ritual, and helped organize important social events.

Advising the king were the senior princes, who were usually his uncles and half-brothers. Between the king and the princes were two specially created *tinsila*, or "blood brothers," who were chosen from certain common clans. These men were his shields, protecting him from evildoers and serving him in intimate personal situations. In addition, the king was guided by two *tindvuna*, or counselors, one civil and one military. The people of the state made their opinions known through two councils: the *liqoqo*, or privy council (dissolved in 1986), composed of senior princes, and the *libanda*, or council of state, composed of chiefs and headmen and open to all adult males of the state. The *liqoqo* could advise the king, make decisions, and carry them out. For example, they could rule on questions about land, education, traditional ritual, court procedure, and transport.

Swazi government extended from the smallest local unit—the homestead—upward to the central administration. The head of a homestead had legal and administrative powers; he was responsible for the crimes of those under him, controlled their property, and spoke for them before his superiors. On the district level, political organization was similar to that of the central government. The relationship between a district chief, however, and his subjects was personal and familiar; he knew all the

---

[7]Kuper, H. (1965). The Swazi of Swaziland. In J. L. Gibbs, Jr. (Ed.), *Peoples of Africa* (pp. 475–512). New York: Holt, Rinehart & Winston.

Laura Nader has stood out among her peers from the start of her career in 1960, when she became the first woman faculty member in the anthropology department at the University of California, Berkeley.

Nader and her three siblings grew up in Winsted, Connecticut, children of immigrants from Lebanon. As she recalls, "My dad left Lebanon for political reasons, and when he came to the land of the free, he took it seriously. So we were raised to believe that you should be involved in public issues." They were also taught to question assumptions. Both Nader and her younger brother Ralph have made careers of doing this. She is an anthropologist noted for her cross-cultural research on law, justice, and social control and their connection to power structures. He is a consumer advocate and former U.S. presidential candidate who is a watchdog on issues of public health and the safety and quality of life.

Laura Nader's undergraduate studies included a study-abroad year in Mexico. Later, while earning her doctorate in anthropology at Radcliffe College, she returned to Mexico to do fieldwork in a Zapotec Indian peasant village in the Sierra Madre Mountains of Oaxaca. Re-

Courtesy of Laura Nader

flecting on this and subsequent research, she says, "In the 1950s, when I went to southern Mexico, I was studying how the Zapotec organize their lives, what they do with their problems, what they do when they go to court. And when I came back to this country, I started looking at American equivalents, at how Americans solve their consumer and service complaints."

Nader's first decade of teaching at Berkeley coincided with the Vietnam War, an era when the campus was in a perpetual state of turmoil with students demonstrating for peace and civil rights. Turning into a scholar-activist, she called upon colleagues to "study up" and do research on the world's power elite. "The

study of man," she wrote in 1972, "is confronted with an unprecedented situation: Never before have a few, by their actions and inactions, had the power of life and death over so many members of the species."

To date, the results of Nader's own research have appeared in over a hundred publications. Among these are her numerous books, including *Naked Science—Anthropological Inquiry into Boundaries, Power, and Knowledge* (1996), and *The Life of the Law: Anthropological Projects* (2002).

Playing a leading role in the development of the anthropology of law, Nader has taken on specialists in the fields of law, children's issues, nuclear energy, and science (including her own profession), critically questioning the basic assumptions ("central dogmas") under which these experts operate. She presses her students to do the same—to think critically, question authority, and break free from the "controlling processes" of the power elite. In 2000, Nader accepted one of the highest honors of the American Anthropological Association—an invitation to give the distinguished lecture at its annual gathering.

(Adapted from Interview with Laura Nader. California Monthly. *November 2000.)*

---

families in his district. The main check on any autocratic tendencies he might have exhibited rested in his subjects' ability to transfer their allegiance to a more responsive chief. Swazi officials held their positions for life and were dismissed only for treason or witchcraft. Incompetence, drunkenness, and stupidity were frowned upon, but they were not considered to be sufficient grounds for dismissal.

POLITICAL SYSTEMS AND THE QUESTION OF LEGITIMACY

Whatever form a society's political system may take, it must find some way to obtain and retain the people's allegiance. In uncentralized systems, where every adult participates in all decision making, loyalty and coopera-

tion are freely given, since each person is considered a part of the political system. As the group grows larger, however, and the organization becomes more formal, the problem of obtaining and keeping public support becomes greater.

Centralized political systems may rely upon coercion as a means of social control. This, however, carries a measure of risk since the personnel needed to apply force often must be numerous and may grow to be a political power. Also, the emphasis on force may create resentment and lessen cooperation. Thus, police states are generally short-lived; most societies choose less extreme forms of social coercion. In the United States, this is reflected in the increasing emphasis placed on cultural, as opposed to social, control. Laura Nader (see Anthropologist of Note) is well known for her anthropological research concerning issues of power, including social and cultural control.

VISUAL COUNTERPOINT

In contrast to countries such as the United States, where religion and state are constitutionally separated, countries such as Iran and Great Britain permit a much closer relationship between political and religious affairs. For instance, Shiite Muslim religious leader Ayatollah Khamenei is not only Iran's supreme spiritual leader but also his country's highest political authority. In England, Queen Elizabeth is not only her country's nominal head of state but also head of the Anglican Church.

Also basic to the political process is the concept of **legitimacy,** or the right of political leaders to govern—to hold, use, and allocate power. Like force, legitimacy is a form of support for a political system; unlike force, legitimacy is based on the values a particular society holds. For example, among the Kapauku of western New Guinea discussed above, the legitimacy of the *tonowi's* power comes from his wealth; the kings of Hawaii, and of England and France before their revolutions, were thought to have a divine right to rule; and the head of the traditional Dahomey state in what is now Benin, West Africa, acquired legitimacy through his age, as he was always the oldest living male.

While the basis for legitimacy varies across cultures, power based on legitimacy always results in authority. It is distinct from power based solely on force: Obedience to authority results from the belief that obedience is "right"; compliance to power based on force results from

legitimacy The right of political leaders to govern—to hold, use, and allocate power—based on the values of a particular society.

fear of being deprived of liberty, physical well-being, life, or material property. Thus, power based on legitimacy is symbolic and depends upon the positive expectations of those who recognize and accept it. If the expectations are not met regularly (if the head of state fails to deliver economic prosperity or the leader is continuously unsuccessful in preventing or dealing with calamities), the legitimacy of the recognized power figure erodes or may collapse altogether.

POLITICS AND RELIGION

Religion is often intricately connected with politics. Frequently it is religion that legitimizes the political order and leadership. Religious beliefs may influence or provide authoritative approval to customary rules and laws. For example, acts that people believe to be sinful, such as murder, are often illegal as well.

In both industrial and nonindustrial societies, belief in the supernatural is important and is reflected in people's political institutions. One place where the effect of religion on politics was well exemplified was in medieval Europe: Holy wars were fought over the smallest matter; labor was mobilized to build immense cathedrals in honor of the Virgin Mary and other saints; kings and queens ruled by "divine right" and (in the West) pledged allegiance to the pope and asked his blessing in all important ventures, were they marital or martial.

In Peru, the divine ruler of the Inca empire proclaimed absolute authority based on the proposition that he was descended from the Sun God. Mexico's ancient Aztec state was also a politico-religious one, having a divine ruler and engaging in nearly constant warfare to procure captives for human sacrifices thought necessary to assuage or please the gods. Modern Iran was proclaimed an "Islamic republic," and its first head of state was the most holy of all Shiite Muslim holy men.

The fact that the president of the United States takes the oath of office by swearing on the Bible is another instance of the use of religion to legitimize political power, as is the phrase "one nation, under God" in the Pledge of Allegiance. On U.S. coins is the phrase "In God We Trust," many meetings of government bodies begin with a prayer or invocation, and the phrase "so help me God" is routinely used in legal proceedings. In spite of an official separation of church and state, religious legitimization of government lingers.

POLITICAL LEADERSHIP AND GENDER

Irrespective of cultural configuration or type of political organization, women hold important positions of political leadership far less often than men. Furthermore, when they do occupy publicly recognized offices, their power and authority rarely exceed those of men. But significant exceptions occur. Historically, one might cite the female chiefs, or *sachems,* of Algonquian Indian communities in southern New England, as well as powerful queens in several Asian, African, and European monarchies.

Perhaps most notable is Queen Victoria, the long-reigning queen of England, Scotland, Wales, and Ireland. Also recognized as monarch in a host of colonies all over the world, Victoria even acquired the title Empress of India. Ruling the British empire from 1837 until 1901, she was perhaps the world's most powerful leader.

In addition to inheriting high positions of political leadership, growing numbers of women have also been elected as presidents or prime ministers. Countries with female heads of state now or in recent years include Indonesia, Pakistan, Ireland, Sri Lanka, Norway, India, Turkey, Liberia, Chile, Germany, and the Philippines, to

mention just a few. While such high-profile female leadership is still relatively rare, women regularly enjoy as much political power as men in a number of societies. In band societies, for example, it is common for females to have as much of a say in public affairs as males, even though more often than not the latter are the nominal leaders of their groups.

Among the Iroquois nations of New York State, all leadership positions above the household and clan level were, without exception, filled by men. Thus men held all positions on the village and tribal councils, as well as on the great council of the Iroquois Confederacy. However, they were completely beholden to women, for only women could nominate men to high office. Moreover, women actively lobbied the men on the councils and could have someone removed from office whenever it suited them.

Lower visibility in politics does not necessarily indicate that women lack power in political affairs. And just as there are various ways in which women play a role behind the scenes, so it is when they have more visible roles, as in the dual-sex system of the Igbo in Nigeria, West Africa. Among the Igbo, each political unit has separate political institutions for men and women, so that both have an autonomous sphere of authority, as well as an area of shared responsibility.[8] At the head of each political unit was a male *obi,* considered the head of government although in fact he presided over the male community, and a female *omu,* the acknowledged mother of the whole community but in practice concerned with the female section of the community. Unlike a queen (though both she and the *obi* were crowned), the *omu* was neither the *obi's* wife nor the previous *obi's* daughter.

---

[8]Okonjo, K. (1976). The dual-sex political system in operation: Igbo women and community politics in midwestern Nigeria. In N. Hafkin & E. Bay (Eds.), *Women in Africa.* Stanford, CA: Stanford University Press.

Liberian President Ellen Johnson Sirleaf inspects members of the Liberian police after taking the presidential oath in January 2006. Founded through the efforts of the American Colonization Society in 1821, this small West African country was settled mainly by freed slaves from the United States whose descendants became a powerful elite controlling Liberia's multi-ethnic population. After a military coup in 1980, the misgoverned state plunged into civil war. The first female president on the African continent, Sirleaf is a Harvard-educated economist who took the world by surprise when she won the elected head office in her war-torn and poverty-stricken country.

© AFP/Getty Images

Just as the *obi* had a council of dignitaries to advise him and act as a check against any arbitrary exercise of power, the *omu* was served by a council of women in equal number to the *obi*'s male councilors. The duties of the *omu* and her councilors involved such tasks as establishing rules and regulations for the community market (marketing was a woman's activity) and hearing cases involving women brought to her from throughout the town or village. If such cases also involved men, then she and her council would cooperate with the *obi* and his council. Widows also went to the *omu* for the final rites required to end their period of mourning for dead husbands. Since the *omu* represented all women, she had to be responsive to her constituency and would seek their approval and cooperation in all major decisions.

In addition to the *omu* and her council, the Igbo women's government included a representative body of women chosen from each quarter or section of the village or town. Moreover, political pressure groups of women acted at the village or lineage level to stop quarrels and prevent wars. These pressure groups included women born into a community (most of whom lived elsewhere since villages were exogamous and residence was patrilocal) and women who had married into the community. Their duties included helping companion wives in times of illness and stress and meting out discipline to lazy or recalcitrant husbands.

In the Igbo system, then, women managed their own affairs, and their interests were represented at all levels of government. Moreover, they had the right to enforce their decisions and rules with sanctions similar to those employed by men, including strikes, boycotts,

and "sitting on" someone. Political scientist Judith Van Allen, senior fellow at Cornell University's Institute for African Development, describes the latter:

> To "sit on" or "make war on" a man involved gathering at his compound, sometimes late at night, dancing, singing scurrilous songs which detailed the women's grievances against him and often called his manhood into question, banging on his hut with the pestles women used for pounding yams, and perhaps demolishing his hut or plastering it with mud and roughing him up a bit. A man might be sanctioned in this way for mistreating his wife, for violating the women's market rules, or for letting his cows eat the women's crops. The women would stay at his hut throughout the day, and late into the night if necessary, until he repented and promised to mend his ways.[9]

Given the high visibility of women in the Igbo political system, it may come as a surprise to learn that when the British imposed colonial rule on the Igbo in the late 1800s, they failed to recognize the autonomy and power of the women. One reason is that the British were blinded by their own cultural values, reflecting a male-dominated society in which the domestic sphere was seen as the ideal place for women. This is ironic because the long-reigning and powerful head of the British empire

[9]Van Allen, J. (1997). Sitting on a man: Colonialism and the lost political institutions of Igbo women. In R. Grinker & C. Steiner (Eds.), *Perspectives on Africa* (p. 450). Boston: Blackwell Press.

at the time was, as mentioned earlier, Queen Victoria. Nevertheless, unable to imagine that Igbo women might play important roles in politics, the British introduced "reforms" that destroyed traditional forms of female autonomy and power without providing alternative forms in exchange. As a result, Igbo women lost much of their traditional equality and became subordinate to men.

POLITICAL ORGANIZATION AND THE MAINTENANCE OF ORDER

Political organization always includes means of maintaining order that ensure people behave in acceptable ways and define what action will be taken when they do not. In chiefdoms and states, some sort of authority has the power to regulate the affairs of society. In bands and tribes, however, people behave generally as they are expected to, without the direct intervention of any centralized political authority. To a large degree, gossip, criticism, fear of supernatural forces, and the like serve as effective deterrents to antisocial behavior.

As an example of how such seemingly informal considerations serve to keep people in line, we may look at the Wape people of Papua New Guinea, who believe the spirits of deceased ancestors roam lineage lands, protecting them from trespassers and helping their hunting descendants by driving game their way.[10] These ancestral spirits also punish those who have wronged them or their descendants by preventing hunters from finding game or causing them to miss their shots, thereby depriving people of much needed meat.

Nowadays, the Wape hunt with shotguns, which the community purchases for the use of one man, whose job it is to hunt for all the others. The cartridges used in the hunt, however, are invariably supplied by individual community members. Thus, if the gunman shoots and misses, it is not viewed as his failing. Rather, it is because the owner of the fired shell, or some close relative, has quarreled or wronged another person whose deceased relative is securing revenge by causing the hunter to miss. Or, if the gunman cannot even find game, it is because vengeful ancestors have chased the animals away. As a proxy hunter for the villagers, the gunman is potentially subject to sanctions by ancestral spirits in response to collective wrongs by those for whom he hunts.

For the Wape, then, successful hunting depends upon avoiding quarrels and maintaining tranquility within the community so as not to antagonize anybody's deceased ancestor. Unfortunately, complete harmony is impossible to achieve in any human community, and the Wape are no exception. Thus, when hunting is poor, the gunman must discover what quarrels and wrongs have occurred within his village to identify the proper ancestral spirits to appeal to for renewed success. Usually, this is done in a special meeting where confessions of wrongdoing may be forthcoming. If not, questioning accusations are bandied about until resolution occurs, but even with no resolution, the meeting must end amicably to prevent new antagonisms. Thus, everyone's behavior comes under public scrutiny, reminding all of what is expected of them and encouraging all to avoid acts that will cast them in an unfavorable light.

Internalized Controls

The Wape concern about ancestral spirits is a good example of internalized, or cultural, controls—beliefs that are so thoroughly ingrained that each person becomes personally responsible for his or her own conduct. **Cultural control** may be thought of as control through beliefs and values deeply internalized in the minds of individuals, as opposed to **social control,** which involves external enforcement through open coercion.

Cultural controls are embedded in our consciousness and may rely on deterrents such as fear of supernatural punishment—ancestral spirits sabotaging the hunting, for example—and magical retaliation. Like the devout Christian who avoids sinning for fear of hell, the individual expects some sort of punishment, even though no one in the community may be aware of the wrongdoing.

Cultural controls can also be framed in positive terms, with customary ways and means that encourage individual sacrifice for the common good. For example, many cultures honor traditions of giving to, or volunteering for, charitable or humanitarian institutions. Performed out of a desire to help those in need, such personal sacrifices (Latin: *sacer,* "holy"; *facere,* "making") may be motivated by a spiritual or religious worldview. Often deeply rooted in basic ideas of a wider community and reciprocity, they are also cultural controls against self-seeking, self-serving, greedy opportunism that threaten the well-being of a larger community.

Externalized Controls

Because internalized controls are not wholly sufficient even in bands and tribes, every society develops externalized social controls known as **sanctions** designed to

---

[10]Mitchell, W. E. (1973, December). A new weapon stirs up old ghosts. *Natural History Magazine,* 77–84.

cultural control Control through beliefs and values deeply internalized in the minds of individuals.
social control External control through open coercion.
sanction An externalized social control designed to encourage conformity to social norms.

Formal sanctions may involve some form of regulated combat, seen here as armed dancers near Mount Hagen in New Guinea demand redress for murder.

encourage conformity to social norms. Operating within social groups of all sizes and involving a mix of cultural and social controls, sanctions may vary significantly within a given society, but they fall into one of two categories: positive or negative. Positive sanctions consist of incentives to conformity such as awards, titles, and recognition by one's neighbors. Negative sanctions consist of threats such as imprisonment, fines, corporal punishment, or ostracism from the community for violation of social norms.

For sanctions to be effective, they cannot be arbitrary. They must be applied consistently, and they must be generally known among members of the society. If some individuals are not convinced of the advantages of social conformity, they are still more likely to obey society's rules than to accept the consequences of not doing so.

Sanctions may also be categorized as either formal or informal, depending on whether or not a legal statute is involved. In the United States, the man who goes shirtless in shorts to a church service may be subject to a variety of informal sanctions, ranging from disapproving glances from the clergy to the chuckling of other parishioners. If, however, he were to show up without any clothing at all, he would be subject to the formal negative sanction of arrest for indecent exposure. Only in the second instance would he have been guilty of breaking the law.

Formal sanctions, such as laws, are always organized, because they attempt to precisely and explicitly regulate people's behavior, whether they are peacefully trading with each other or confronting each other on a battlefield. Other examples of organized sanctions include, on the positive side, military decorations and monetary rewards. On the negative side are loss of face, exclusion from social life and its privileges, seizure of property, imprisonment, and even bodily mutilation or death. Informal sanctions emphasize cultural control and are diffuse in nature, involving spontaneous expressions of approval or disapproval by members of the group or community. They are, nonetheless, very effective in enforcing a large number of seemingly unimportant customs. Because most people want to be accepted, they are willing to acquiesce to the rules that govern dress, eating, and conversation, even in the absence of actual laws.

Social Control through Witchcraft

In societies with or without centralized political systems, witchcraft sometimes functions as an agent of social control and involves both internal and external controls. An individual will think twice before offending a neighbor if convinced that the neighbor could retaliate by resorting to black magic. Similarly, individuals may not wish to be accused of practicing witchcraft, and so they behave with greater circumspection.

Among the Azande of the Sudan, people who think they have been bewitched may consult an oracle, who, after performing the appropriate mystical rites, then may establish or confirm the identity of the offending witch.[11] Confronted with this evidence, the "witch" will usually agree to cooperate in order to avoid any additional trouble. Should the victim die, the relatives of the deceased may choose to make magic against the witch, ultimately accepting the death of some villager both as evidence of guilt and of the efficacy of their magic.

For the Azande, witchcraft provides not only a sanction against antisocial behavior but also a means of dealing with natural hostilities and death. No one wishes to be thought of as a witch, and surely no one wishes to be victimized by one. By institutionalizing their emotional responses, the Azande successfully maintain social order.

SOCIAL CONTROL THROUGH LAW

Among the Inuit of northern Canada, all offenses are considered to involve disputes between individuals; thus, they must be settled between the disputants themselves. A traditional way of doing this is through a song duel, in which the individuals involved heap insults upon one another in songs specially composed for the occasion. Although society does not intervene, its interests are represented by spectators, whose applause determines the outcome. If, however, social harmony cannot be restored—and that is the goal, rather than assigning and punishing guilt—one or the other disputant may move to another band. Ultimately, there is no binding legal authority.

In Western society, by contrast, someone who commits an offense against another person may become subject to a series of complex legal proceedings. In criminal cases the primary concern is to assign and punish guilt rather than to help out the victim. The offender will be arrested by the police; tried before a judge and, perhaps, a jury; and, depending on the severity of the crime, may be fined, imprisoned, or even executed. Rarely does the victim receive restitution or compensation. Throughout this chain of events, the accused party is dealt with by police, judges, jurors, and jailers, who may have no personal acquaintance whatsoever with the plaintiff or the defendant. How strange this all seems from the standpoint of traditional Inuit culture! Clearly, the two systems operate under distinctly different assumptions.

Definition of Law

Once two Inuit settle a dispute by engaging in a song contest, the affair is considered closed; no further action is expected. Would we choose to describe the outcome

of such a contest as a legal decision? If every law is a sanction but not every sanction is a law, how are we to distinguish between social sanctions in general and those to which we apply the label "law"?

The definition of law has been a lively point of contention among anthropologists. In 1926, Bronislaw Malinowski argued that the rules of law are distinguished from the rules of custom in that "they are regarded as the obligation of one person and the rightful claim of another, sanctioned not by mere psychological motive, but by a definite social machinery of binding force based . . . upon mutual dependence."[12] In other words, laws exemplify social control because they employ overt coercion.

An example of one rule of custom in contemporary North American society might be the dictate that guests at a dinner party should repay the person who gave the party with entertainment in the future. A host or hostess who does not receive a return invitation may feel cheated out of something thought to be owed but has no legal claim against the ungrateful guest for the $30 spent on food and drinks. If, however, an individual was cheated out of the same sum by the grocer when shopping, the law could be invoked. Although Malinowski's definition introduced several important elements of law, his failure to distinguish adequately between legal and nonlegal sanctions left the problem of formulating a workable definition of law in the hands of later anthropologists.

According to E. Adamson Hoebel, an important pioneer in the anthropological study of law, "A social norm is legal if its neglect or infraction is regularly met, in threat or in fact, by the application of physical force by an individual or group possessing the socially recognized privilege of so acting."[13] In stressing the legitimate use of physical coercion, Hoebel de-emphasized the traditional association of law with a centralized court system. Although rules enacted by an authorized legislative body and enforced by the judicial mechanisms of the state are fundamental features of Western jurisprudence, they are not the universal backbone of human law. Can any concept of law be applied to societies for whom the notion of a centralized judiciary is virtually meaningless? How shall we categorize Inuit song duels and other socially condoned forms of self-help that seem to meet some but not all of the criteria of law?

Ultimately, it is always of greatest value to consider each case within its cultural context. After all, law reflects a society's basic postulates, so to understand any society's laws, one must understand the underlying values and assumptions. Nonetheless, a working definition of law is useful for purposes of discussion and cross-

[11]Evans-Pritchard, E. E. (1937). *Witchcraft, oracles and magic among the Azande*. London: Oxford University Press.

[12]Malinowski, B. (1951). *Crime and custom in savage society* (p. 55). London: Routledge.

[13]Hoebel, E. A. (1954). *The law of primitive man: A study in comparative legal dynamics* (p. 28). Cambridge, MA: Harvard University Press.

© Cunera Buijs

Having a song duel is the traditional approach to dispute resolution among the Inuit of northern Canada.

cultural comparison, and for this, **law** is adequately characterized as formal rules of conduct that, when violated, lead to negative sanctions.

Functions of Law

In Hoebel's 1954 book, *The Law of Primitive Man,* he described the generous sharing of private property as a fundamental principle in traditional Cheyenne Indian culture. However, he wrote, this principle shifted after some men assumed the privilege of borrowing other men's horses without bothering to obtain permission. When Wolf Lies Down complained of such unauthorized borrowing to the members of the Elk Soldier Society, the Elk Soldiers not only had his horse returned to him but also secured an award for damages from the offender. The Elk Soldiers then announced that, to avoid such difficulties in the future, horses no longer could be borrowed without permission. Furthermore, they declared their intention to retrieve any such property and whip anyone who resisted the return of improperly borrowed goods.

This case illustrates three basic functions of law. First, it defines relationships among society's members

law Formal rules of conduct that, when violated, effectuate negative sanctions.

and marks out proper behavior under specified circumstances. Knowledge of the law permits each person to know his or her rights and duties with respect to every other member of society. Second, law allocates the authority to employ coercion in the enforcement of sanctions. In societies with centralized political systems, such authority is generally vested in the government and its judiciary system. In societies that lack centralized political control, the authority to employ force may be allocated directly to the injured party. Third, law functions to redefine social relations and to ensure social flexibility. As new situations arise, law must determine whether old rules and assumptions retain their validity and to what extent they must be altered. Law, if it is to operate efficiently, must allow room for change.

In practice, law is never as neat as a written description about it. In any given society, people are usually members of various subgroups—and fall under the varied dictates of these diverse groups. For example, among the Kapauku of Papua New Guinea, discussed earlier in this chapter, each individual is simultaneously a member of a family, a household, a sublineage, and a confederacy—and is subject to all the (sometimes conflicting) rules and regulations of each. Furthermore, the power to employ sanctions may vary from level to level within a given society. Thus, the head of a Kapauku household in Papua New Guinea may punish a household member by slapping or beating, but the authority to confiscate property is vested exclusively in the headman of the lineage. Analogous distinctions exist in the United States among municipal, state, and federal jurisdictions. The complexity of legal jurisdiction within each society makes it difficult to generalize about law.

Crime

As we have observed, an important function of negative sanctions, legal or otherwise, is to discourage the breach of social norms. A person contemplating theft is aware of the possibility of being caught and punished. Yet, even in the face of severe sanctions, individuals in every society sometimes violate the norms and subject themselves to the consequences of their behavior.

In Western societies a clear distinction is made between offenses against the state and offenses against an individual. However, in non-state societies such as bands and tribes, all offenses are viewed as transgressions against individuals or kin-groups (families, lineages, clans, and so on).

Disputes between individuals or kin-groups may seriously disrupt the social order, especially in small groups where the number of disputants, though small in absolute numbers, may be a large percentage of the total population. For example, although the Inuit traditionally have no effective domestic or economic unit beyond the family, a dispute between two people will interfere with the ability of members of separate families to come to one another's aid when necessary and is consequently a matter of wider social concern. The goal of judicial proceedings in such instances is restoring social harmony rather than punishing an offender. When distinguishing between offenses of concern to the community as a whole and those of concern only to a few individuals, we may refer to them as *collective* or *personal*.

Basically, disputes are settled in one of two ways. First, disputing parties may, through argument and compromise, voluntarily arrive at a mutually satisfactory agreement. This form of settlement is referred to as **negotiation** or, if it involves the assistance of an unbiased third party, **mediation.** In bands and tribes a third party mediator has no coercive power and thus cannot force disputants to abide by such a decision, but as a person who commands great personal respect, the mediator frequently may help bring about a settlement.

Second, in chiefdoms and states, an authorized third party may issue a binding decision that the disputing parties will be compelled to respect. This process is referred to as **adjudication.** The difference between mediation and adjudication is basically a difference in authorization. In a dispute settled by adjudication, the disputing parties present their positions as compellingly as they can, but they do not participate in the ultimate decision making.

Although the adjudication process is not universally characteristic, every society employs some form of negotiation to settle disputes. Often negotiation acts as a prerequisite or an alternative to adjudication. For example, in the resolution of U.S. labor disputes, striking workers may first negotiate with management, often with the mediation of a third party. If the state decides the strike constitutes a threat to the public welfare, the disputing parties may be forced to submit to adjudication. In this case, the responsibility for resolving the dispute is transferred to a presumably impartial judge.

The judge's work is difficult and complex. In addition to sifting through evidence presented, he or she must consider a wide range of norms, values, and earlier rulings to arrive at a decision intended to be considered just not only by the disputing parties but by the public and other judges as well.

In many politically centralized societies, incorruptible supernatural, or at least nonhuman, powers are thought to make judgments through a "trial by ordeal." Among the Kpelle of Liberia, for example, when guilt is in doubt an "ordeal operator" licensed by the government may apply a hot knife to a suspect's leg. If the leg is burned, the suspect is guilty; if not, innocence is assumed. But the operator does not merely heat the knife and apply it. After massaging the suspect's legs and determining the knife is hot enough, the operator then strokes his own leg with it without being burned, demonstrating that the innocent will escape injury. The knife is then applied to the suspect.

Up to this point—consciously or unconsciously—the operator has read the suspect's nonverbal cues: gestures, the degree of muscular tension, amount of perspiration, and so forth. From this the operator can judge whether or not the accused is showing so much anxiety as to indicate probable guilt; in effect, a psychological stress evaluation has been made. As the knife is applied, it is manipulated to either burn or not burn the suspect, once this judgment has been made. The operator does this manipulation easily by controlling how long the knife is in the fire, as well as the pressure and angle at which it is pressed against the leg.[14]

Similar to this is the use of the lie detector (polygraph) in the United States, although the guiding ideol-

[14]Gibbs, J. L., Jr. (1983). [Interview]. *Faces of culture: Program 18.* Fountain Valley, CA: Coast Telecourses.

negotiation The use of direct argument and compromise by the parties to a dispute to arrive voluntarily at a mutually satisfactory agreement.
mediation Settlement of a dispute through negotiation assisted by an unbiased third party.
adjudication Mediation with an unbiased third party making the ultimate decision.

ogy is scientific rather than supernaturalistic. Nevertheless, an incorruptible nonhuman agency is thought to establish who is lying and who is not, whereas in reality the polygraph operator cannot just "read" the needles of the machine. He or she must judge whether or not they are registering a high level of anxiety brought on by the testing situation, as opposed to the stress of guilt. Thus, the polygraph operator has much in common with the Kpelle ordeal operator.

Restorative Justice and Conflict Resolution

Punitive justice, such as imprisonment, may be the most common approach to justice in North America, but it has not proven to be an effective way of changing criminal behavior. There are cultural alternatives.

For a number of years, Native American communities in Canada urged their federal government to reform justice services to make them more consistent with indigenous values and traditions. In 1999 Canada's Supreme Court amended sentencing law in the country's Criminal Code to include the following principle: "All available sanctions other than imprisonment that are reasonable in the circumstances should be considered for all offenders, with particular attention to the circumstances of aboriginal offenders."[15]

Native communities have pressed especially for restorative justice techniques such as the Talking Circle, traditionally used by Native American groups. For this, parties involved in a conflict come together in a circle with equal opportunity to express their views—one at a time, free of interruption. Usually, a "talking stick" (or eagle feather or some other symbolic tool) is held by whoever is speaking to signal that she or he has the right to talk at that moment and others have the responsibility to listen.

In the United States, over the past three decades there has been significant movement away from the courts in favor of outside negotiation and mediation to resolve a wide variety of disputes. Many jurists see this as a means to clear overloaded court dockets so as to concentrate on more important cases. A correlate of this move is a change in ideology, elevating order and harmony to positive values and replacing open coercion (seen as undemocratic) with control through persuasion.

In the abstract, this seems like a good idea and suggests a return to a system of cultural control characteristic of band and tribal societies. However, a crucial difference exists. In tribal and band societies, agreement is less likely to be coercive because all concerned individuals can negotiate and mediate on relatively equal terms. The

United States, by contrast, has great disparities in power, and evidence indicates that it is the stronger parties that prefer mediation and negotiation.

As anthropologist Laura Nader points out, there is now less emphasis on justice and concern with causes of disputes than on smoothing things over in ways that tend to be pacifying and restrictive—an emphasis that produces order of a repressive sort.[16] That said, leaders in the field of dispute resolution in the United States and other parts of the industrial and postindustrial world are finding effective ways to bring about balanced solutions to conflict. An example of this appears in the Anthropology Applied feature.

VIOLENT CONFLICT AND WARFARE

Although the regulation of internal affairs is an important function of any political system, it is by no means the sole function. Another is the management of external affairs—relations not just among different states but among different bands, lineages, clans, or whatever the largest autonomous political unit may be. And just as the threatened or actual use of force may be used to maintain order within a society, it also may be used in the conduct of external affairs.

Humans have a horrific track record when it comes to violence. Far more lethal than spontaneous and individual outbursts of aggression, organized violence in the form of war is responsible for enormous suffering and deliberate destruction of life and property. In the past 5,000 years or so, some 14,000 wars have been fought, resulting in many hundreds of millions of casualties.

Generally, we may distinguish among different motives, objectives, methods, and scales of warfare as organized violence. For instance, some societies engage in defensive wars only and avoid armed confrontations with others unless seriously threatened or actually attacked. Others initiate aggressive wars to pursue particular strategic objectives, including material benefits in the form of precious resources such as slaves, gold, or oil, as well as territorial expansion or control over trade routes. In some cultures, aggressive wars are waged for ideological reasons, such as spreading one's own worldview or religion and defeating "evil" ideas or heresies elsewhere.

The scope of violent conflict is wide, ranging from individual fights, local feuds, and raids to formally declared international wars fought by professional armed forces. In addition, we may distinguish among various civil wars (in which armies from different geographic

[15]Criminal Code of Canada, s.718.2(e).

[16]Nader, L. (1997). Controlling processes: Tracing the dynamic components of power. *Current Anthropology 38*, 714–715.

Anthropology Applied

Dispute Resolution and the Anthropologist ■ William Ury

In an era when the consequences of violent approaches to dispute resolution are more far-reaching than ever, conflict management is of growing importance. A world leader in this profession is anthropologist William L. Ury, an independent negotiations specialist.

In his first year at graduate school, Ury began looking for a way to apply anthropology to practical problems, including conflicts of all dimensions. He wrote a paper about the role of anthropology in peacemaking and on a whim sent it to Roger Fisher, a law professor noted for his work in negotiation and world affairs. Fisher, in turn, invited the young graduate student to co-author a kind of how-to book for international mediators. The book they researched and wrote together turned out to have a far wider audience, for it presented basic principles of negotiation that could be applied to household spats, management–employee conflicts, or international crises. Titled *Getting to Yes: Negotiating Agreement Without Giving In* (1981), it sold millions of copies, was translated into twenty-one languages, and earned the nickname "negotiator's bible."

While working on *Getting to Yes,* Ury and Fisher co-founded the Program on Negotiation (PON) at Harvard Law School, pulling together an interdisciplinary group of academics interested in new approaches to and applications of the negotiation process. Today this applied research center is a multiuniversity consortium that trains mediators, businesspeople, and government officials in negotiation skills. It has four key goals: (1) design, implement, and evaluate better dispute resolution practices; (2) promote collaboration among practitioners and

© Jay Dickman

scholars; (3) develop education programs and materials for instruction in negotiation and dispute resolution; (4) increase public awareness and understanding of successful conflict resolution efforts.

In 1982, Ury earned his doctorate in anthropology from Harvard with a dissertation titled *Talk Out or Walk Out: The Role and Control of Conflict in a Kentucky Coal Mine.* Afterward, he taught for several years while maintaining a leadership role at PON. In particular, he devoted himself to PON's Global Negotiation Project (initially known as the Project on Avoiding War). Today, having left his teaching post at Harvard, Ury continues to serve as director of the Global Negotiation Project, writing, consulting, and running regular workshops on dealing with difficult people and situations.

Utilizing a cross-cultural perspective sharpened through years of anthropo-

logical research, he specializes in ethnic and secessionist disputes, including those between white and black South Africans, Serbs and Croats, Turks and Kurds, Catholics and Protestants in Northern Ireland, and Russians and Chechens in the former Soviet Union.

Among the most effective tools in Ury's applied anthropology work are his books on dispute resolution. In 1993 he wrote *Getting Past No: Negotiating Your Way from Confrontation,* which explores ways to reach out to hostile parties who are not interested in negotiation. His 1999 book, *Getting to Peace: Transforming Conflict at Home, at Work, and in the World,* examines what he calls the "third side," which is the role that the surrounding community can play in preventing, resolving, and containing destructive conflict between two parties.[a]

His 2002 edited volume *Must We Fight?* challenges entrenched ideas that violence and war are inevitable and presents convincing evidence that human beings have as much inherent potential for cooperation and co-existence as they do for violent conflict. The key point in this book is that violence is a choice. In Ury's words, "Conflict is not going to end, but violence can."[b]

What Ury and others in this field are doing is helping create a culture of negotiation in a world where adversarial, win–lose attitudes are out of step with the increasingly interdependent relations between people.

---

[a]Pease, T. (2000, Spring). Taking the third side. *Andover Bulletin.*
[b]Ury, W. (2002, Winter). A global immune system. *Andover Bulletin;* see also www.PON .harvard.edu and www.thirdside.org.

sections, ethnic or religious groups, or political parties within the same state are pitted against each other) and low-intensity guerrilla warfare involving small-scale hit-and-run tactical operations instead of pitched battles.

Why do wars occur? Some argue that males of the human species are naturally aggressive (see this chapter's Biocultural Connection). As evidence, they point to aggressive group behavior exhibited by chimpanzees in Tanzania where researchers observed one group sys-

tematically destroy another and take over their territory. Also, they cite the behavior of people such as the Yanomami Indians who range on either side of the border between Brazil and Venezuela. These tropical horticulturalists and foragers have been described as living in a chronic state of war, and some scientists suggest this exemplifies the way all humans once behaved. However, as discussed in earlier chapters, warfare among humans, as well as aggressive group behavior among apes, may be

VISUAL **COUNTER**POINT

Public displays of human skulls may serve to commemorate victory over enemies slain in battle or sacri-ficed as war captives—as depicted on this stone wall in the ancient Maya city of Chichen Itza in south-eastern Mexico. Such displays may also serve as a gruesome monument of organized violence as in this Cambodian map made of skulls belonging to victims of the ruthless Khmer Rouge regime that claimed the lives of some 1.7 million innocent Cambodians in the 1970s.

situation specific rather than an unavoidable expression of biological predisposition.

This is not to say that violence was unknown among ancient humans. The occasional discovery of stone spear points embedded in human skeletons, such as that of a more than 9,000-year-old man found in Kennewick in the northwestern United States or even older ones from the Grimaldi caves in Italy prove otherwise. Nevertheless, it is clear that war is not a universal phenomenon, for in various parts of the world there are societies that do not practice warfare as we know it. Examples include people as diverse as the Ju/'hoansi Bushmen and pygmy peoples of southern Africa, the Arapesh of New Guinea, and the Jain of India, as well as the Amish of North America. Among societies that do practice warfare, levels of vio-lence may differ dramatically.

We have ample reason to suppose that war has be-come a problem only in the last 10,000 years, since the invention of food-production techniques and especially since the formation of centralized states 5,000 years ago. It has reached crisis proportions in the past 200 years, with the invention of modern weaponry and increased direction of violence against civilian populations. In con-temporary warfare, casualties not just of civilians but also of *children* far outnumber those of soldiers. Thus, war is not so much an age-old problem as it is a relatively recent one.

Among food foragers, with their uncentralized political systems, violence may erupt sporadically, but warfare was all but unknown until recent times. There are several reasons for this. First of all, since territorial boundaries and membership among food-foraging bands are usually fluid and loosely defined, a man who hunts with one band today may hunt with a neighboring band next month. This renders warfare impractical.

So, too, does the systematic exchange of marriage partners among food-foraging groups, which makes it likely that someone in each band will have a sister, a brother, or a cousin in a neighboring band. Moreover, the absence of a food surplus among foragers makes pro-longed combat difficult. Finally, a worldview in which people perceive themselves as part of the natural world rather than superior to it tends to work against exploita-tion of other people. In sum, where populations are small and see themselves as part of the natural world, where food surpluses are absent, property ownership minimal, and no state organization exists, the likelihood of orga-nized violence by one group against another is small.[17]

Despite the traditional view of the gardener or farmer as a gentle tiller of the soil, it is among such peo-ple, along with pastoralists, that warfare becomes prom-inent. One reason may be that food-producing peoples have a more exploitative worldview than do food forag-ers. Another is that they are far more prone to popula-tion growth than are food foragers, whose numbers are generally maintained well below carrying capacity. This population growth, if unchecked, can lead to resource depletion, one solution to which may be seizure of some other people's resources.

In addition, the commitment to a fixed piece of land inherent in farming makes such societies somewhat less

---

[17]Knauft, B. M. (1991). Violence and sociality in human evolution. *Current Anthropology 32*, 391–409.

Biocultural

Connection

Sex, Gender, and Human Violence

At the start of the 21st century, war and violence are no longer the strictly male domains that they were in many societies in the past. War has become embedded in civilian life in many parts of the world and impacts the daily lives of women and children. Moreover, women now serve in the military forces of several states, although their participation in combat is often limited. Some female soldiers in the United States argue that gender should not limit their participation in combat as they consider themselves as strong, capable, and well trained as their male counterparts. Others believe that biologically based sex differences make war a particularly male domain.

Scientists have long argued that males are more suited to combat because natural selection has made them on average larger and stronger than females. This idea, known as sexual selection, was first put forth by Darwin in the 19th century. At that time he proposed that the physical specializations of males in animal species—such as horns, vibrant plumage, and, in the case of humans, intelligence and tool use—demonstrate selection acting upon males to aid in the competition for mates. In these scenarios, male reproductive success is thought to be optimized through a strategy of "spreading seed"—in other words, by being sexually active with as many females as possible.

Females, on the other hand, are considered gatekeepers who optimize their reproductive success through car-ing for individual offspring. According to this theory of sexual selection, in species where male–male competition is high, males will be considerably larger than females, and aggression will serve males well. In monogamous species, males and females will be of similar sizes.

Primatologist Richard Wrangham has taken the idea of sexual selection even further. In his book *Demonic Males*, he explores the idea that both male aggression and patriarchy have an evolutionary basis. He states that humans, like our close cousins the chimpanzees, are "party gang" species characterized by strong bonds among groups of males who have dominion over an expandable territory. These features "suffice to account for natural selection's ugly legacy, the tendency to look for killing opportunities when hostile neighbors meet."[a] Violence in turn generates a male-dominated social order: "Patriarchy comes from biology in the sense that it emerges from men's temperaments out of their evolutionarily derived efforts to control women and at the same time have solidarity with fellow males in competition against outsiders."[b] While Wrangham allows that evolutionary forces have shaped women as well, he suggests that females' evolutionary interests cannot be met without cooperation with males.

Feminist scholars have pointed out that these scientific models are "gendered" in that they incorporate the gender norms derived from the scientists' culture. Darwin's original model of sexual selection incorporated the Victorian gender norms of the passive female and active male. U.S. primatologist Laura Fedigan suggests that in Darwinian models women evolved in positive directions only by a "coat tails" process whereby females were "pulled along" toward improved biological states by virtue of the progress of the genes they shared with males.[c] Wrangham's more recent *Demonic Males* theory is similarly shaped by culture. It incorporates the dominant world order (military states) and the gender norms (aggressive males) it values. In both cases, the putatively scientific theory has created a natural basis for a series of social conventions.

This does not mean that biological differences between the sexes cannot be studied in the natural world. Instead, scientists studying sex differences must be especially aware of how they may project cultural beliefs onto nature. Meanwhile, the attitudes of some women soldiers continue to challenge generalizations regarding "military specialization" by gender.

[a]Wrangham, R., & Peterson, D. (1996). *Demonic males* (p. 168). Boston: Houghton Mifflin.
[b]Wrangham, R., & Peterson, D. (1996). *Demonic males* (p. 125). Boston: Houghton Mifflin.

[c]Fedigan, L. M. (1986). The changing role of women in models of human evolution. *Annual Review of Anthropology 15*, 25–66.

---

fluid in their membership than those of food foragers. Instead of marrying distantly, farmers marry locally, depriving them of long-distance kin networks. In rigidly matrilocal or patrilocal societies, each new generation is bound to the same territory, no matter how small it may be or how large the group trying to live within it.

The availability of unoccupied lands may not serve as a sufficient detriment to the outbreak of war. Among swidden farmers, for example, competition for land cleared of old growth forest frequently leads to hostility and armed conflict. The centralization of political control and the possession of valuable property among farming people provide many more stimuli for warfare.

It is among such peoples, especially those organized into states, where the violence of warfare is most apt to result in indiscriminate killing. This development has reached its peak in modern states. Indeed, much (but not all) of the warfare that has been observed in recent stateless societies (so-called tribal warfare) has been induced by states as a reaction to colonial expansion.[18]

For example, although warfare was certainly present in northeastern America before the arrival of Europeans, intergroup conflicts began to increase and intensify in

---

[18]Whitehead, N. L., & Ferguson, R. B. (1993, November). Deceptive stereotypes about tribal warfare. *Chronicle of Higher Education*, A48.

Many armies around the world recruit children. Today, there are more than 250,000 child soldiers, many as young as 12 years old. Among them are these boys training to be guerrillas in Sahel, Eritrea.

© Dan Connell/The Image Works

the 16th century as a direct consequence of dispossession of Indian lands and the huge demand in Europe for precious furs, especially beaver ("soft gold"). Competition over game-rich territories, intensified by the availability of muskets and other deadly European weapons, led to violence. Alcohol introduced by Europeans as a trade commodity no doubt fueled the aggression, and each killing called for revenge. All of this triggered a cycle of bloody warfare commonly referred to as the Beaver Wars, involving virtually all native groups—food foragers and horticulturalists alike—from Cape Breton Island down to Chesapeake Bay and as far inland as the Great Lakes. These wars—periodic vicious outbursts—continued throughout much of the 17th century.[19]

Among the many American Indian groups involved in the Beaver Wars were the Iroquoian nations—Mohawk, Oneida, Onondaga, Cayuga, and Seneca. Before Europeans landed on their shores, these neighboring groups had resolved to end warfare among themselves by creating an alliance and directing their aggressive activities against outsiders. In this way the famous Iroquois Confederacy came into being.

Warring frequently against their immediate and more distant neighbors, members of the confederacy gained dominance and forced their victims to acknowledge Iroquoian superiority. The relation between victim and victor, however, was not outright subordination. Imposed payment of tribute purchased "protection" from the Iroquois. The price of protection went further than this, though; it included constant and public ceremonial

deference to the Iroquois, free passage for their war parties through the subordinate group's country, and the contribution of young men to Iroquoian war parties.

An instructive comparison can be made between the Iroquois nations and European Christians. In the year 1095 the Roman Catholic Pope Urban II launched the first crusade ("War of the Cross"), with a speech urging the Christian nobles of Europe to end their ceaseless wars against each other by directing their hostilities toward Muslim Turks and Arabs in the Middle East, who Europeans saw as infidels. In the same speech the pope also alluded to the economic benefits to be realized by seizing the resources of the "infidels." Although it is clear that the Crusades were motivated by more than religious ideology, they were justified as a holy war to liberate Jerusalem and the Holy Land from Muslims. Their success was limited, and twenty years after the ninth and final crusade of 1271 to 1272, the last Christian stronghold in Palestine surrendered to a Muslim army.

Within the next few centuries, however, Europe's Christian powers turned their attention to state building and colonial expansion in other parts of the world. Proceeding in concert with this growth and outward expansion was the development of the technology and organization of warfare. With the emergence of states (not just in Europe but in other parts of the world as well) has come a dramatic increase in the scale of warfare. Perhaps this is not surprising, given the state's acceptance of force as a legitimate tool for regulating human affairs and its ability to organize large numbers of people.

Consider, for example, the Aztec state in the central Mexican highlands, which engaged in continuous warfare from the mid-1400s until its demise in the early

---

[19]Prins, H. E. L. (1996). *The Mi'kmaq: Resistance, accommodation, and cultural survival* (p. 106). Orlando: Harcourt Brace.

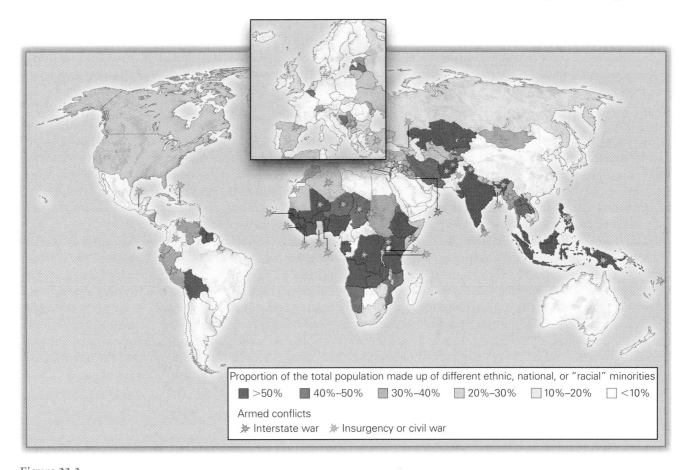

Figure 23.3

In multinational states, warfare is common as one nationality suppresses others within the country.

1520s. By way of battle, the state collected tribute and achieved regional dominance. Moreover, by waging war against their neighbors, Aztecs obtained prisoners to use as offerings for gods that they believed required human sacrifice to maintain the cosmic order: "The warrior slated for sacrifice was a *teomiqui,* 'he who dies in godlike fashion,' and would feed the sun so that it might shine upon the world and keep it in motion."[20]

Among Aztecs, this worldview justified, even sanctified, perpetual aggression. In fact, according to the noted anthropologist Eric Wolf, priests bearing the images of the Aztec war god Huitilopochtli and other deities walked ahead of the army and gave the signal to commence combat by lighting a fire and blowing on shell trumpets. The victory that followed, Wolf wrote, "always had the same results: long lines of captives, wooden collars about their necks, made the long journey to Tenochtitlán to be offered upon the altars of the gods."[21] Several thousand captives could be sacrificed after a

military campaign, and within a single year as many as 20,000 may have been offered to the gods in that capital city of the Aztec state.

This Aztec example, as well as that of the Christian Crusades, shows that ideological motivations and justifications for war are embedded in a society's worldview—the collective body of ideas that members of a culture generally share concerning the ultimate shape and substance of their reality. We will discuss other aspects of worldview in the following chapter, which focuses on religion and the supernatural.

Currently, there are several dozen wars going on in the world, often resulting in massive killing fields (Figure 23.3). And many contemporary wars are not between states but often occur within countries where the government is either corrupt, ineffective, or without popular support. Notably, many armies around the world recruit not only men, but also women and children. Today, more than 250,000 child soldiers, many as young as 12 years old, are participating in armed conflicts around the world.[22]

[20]Keen, B. (1971). *The Aztec image in Western thought* (p. 13). New Brunswick, NJ: Rutgers University Press.

[21]Wolf, E. R. (1999). *Envisioning power: Ideologies of dominance and crisis* (p. 263). Berkeley: University of California Press.

[22]Study estimates 250,000 active child soldiers. (2006, July 26). Associated Press.

The following examples offer some specific data. Between 1975 and 1979, Khmer Rouge soldiers in Cambodia murdered 1.7 million fellow citizens, or 20 percent of that country's population. In the 1990s, between 2 and 3 million died due to warfare in the southern Sudan. Another 5 million died in the recent war in Congo (1998–2003), which involved armies from a handful of neighboring states as well.

Moreover, the Middle East is in political turmoil, especially since the U.S. invasion of Iraq's oil-rich dictatorship in 2003, which has plunged that multi-ethnic country into violent chaos. In addition to many tens of thousands of fatalities, the vast majority of whom are Iraqi civilians, there is also massive destruction of the country's infrastructure. In the summer of 2006, Israel used its air force, army, and navy to fight an enemy Hezbollah (Shia Islamist) force on its northern border. Retaliating against a raid in which guerrillas kidnapped two Israeli soldiers, Israel staged a full-force invasion of the multi-ethnic country of Lebanon. Within a month of punishing warfare, much of which consisted of bombs, missiles, and small rockets, over a million people on both sides of the border were made refugees. The vast majority of fatalities in this war, which the state of Israel considers part of the global war against terror, were civilians; much of Lebanon's infrastructure—bridges, harbors, airports, roads, and other structures that make civilized life possible—was destroyed, along with countless homes.

Beyond these wars there are numerous so-called low-intensity wars involving guerrilla organizations, rebel armies, resistance movements, terrorist cells, and a host of other armed groups engaged in violent conflict with official state-controlled armed forces. Every year, confrontations result in hundreds of hot spots and violent flashpoints, most of which are never reported in Western news media.[23]

As the above examples show, the causes of warfare are complex, involving economic, political, and ideological factors. The challenge of eliminating human warfare has never been greater than it is in today's world—nor has the cost of *not* finding a way to do so. In the age of globalization, a new category—crimes against humanity—has been adopted by most countries in order to punish those responsible for mass murder; these crimes may be prosecuted in an international court of justice.

---

[23]icasualties.org.

Questions for Reflection

1. In many states, political power is concentrated in the hands of a wealthy elite—the have-lots. Imagine you belong to a group that is losing its traditional freedom or quality of life due to government policies but feel that your political representatives are unwilling or unable to defend your interests. Would you challenge the state authorities, as the Japanese demonstrators did in the chapter opening photo, or accept your degenerating condition without public protest?

2. Given the basic definition of politics presented in the beginning of this chapter, why do you think that power in egalitarian societies plays a relatively insignificant role?

3. If political organization functions to impose or maintain order and to resolve conflicts, why do you think that a government in a country such as yours is so interested in legitimizing its power? What happens when a government loses such legitimacy?

4. Which nationalities or ethnic groups do you know that are dominant, and which can you identify that are in a minority position or are repressed? What is the basis for this inequality?

5. When your own government declares war against another country, on which basis does it seek to justify its decision to send soldiers into battle? Do you know the death ratio of noncombatants to soldiers in your country's most recent war?

Suggested Readings

Cheater, A. (2005). *The anthropology of power*. London: Routledge.

Presents case studies from a wide range of societies to examine the issues surrounding power and empowerment and to question whether power is actually being transferred to the powerless. Explores how traditionally disempowered groups gain influence in postcolonial and multicultural settings. Surveys the relationships between empowerment and economic development, gender, and environmentalism.

Gledhill, J. (2000). *Power and its disguises: Anthropological perspectives on politics* (2nd ed.). Boulder, CO: Pluto Press.

Exploring the power relations that shape the global order, the author discusses the politics of agrarian civilizations and societies without indigenous states and then turns to the politics of domination and resistance within the colonial context, followed by an examination of contemporary politics of Africa, Asia, and Latin America.

Kertzer, D. I. (1989). *Ritual, politics, and power*. New Haven, CT: Yale University Press.

Using numerous examples from traditional and modern societies and writing in clear accessible prose, the author argues that political symbols manifested through rituals explain much of the political life of modern nations, contrary to the usual rational, utilitarian, and interest-group explanations. He discusses how elites use rituals to support the existing order, while revolutionaries use them to replace it.

Nader, L. (Ed.) (1997). *Law in culture and society.* Berkeley: University of California Press.

Classic anthology of studies on the process, structure, comparison, and perception of the law—reflecting the shift from what law is to what law does.

Ury, W. (Ed.). (2002). *Must we fight? From the battlefield to the schoolyard—A new perspective on violent conflict and its prevention.* Hoboken, NJ: Jossey-Bass.

This fresh exploration of the question of whether violence and war are inevitable presents evidence from leading anthropologists and others that human beings have as much inherent potential for cooperation and coexistence as they do for violent conflict.

Vincent, J. (2002). *The anthropology of politics: A reader in ethnography, theory, and critique.* Boston: Blackwell.

This sweeping historical and theoretical introduction to the field features readings from noted anthropologists past and present, enriched by Vincent's insightful headnotes.

Whitehead, N., & Ferguson, R. B. (Eds.) (1992). *War in the tribal zone.* Santa Fe: School of American Research Press.

The central point of this book is that the transformation and intensification of war, as well as the formation of tribes, result from complex interaction in the "tribal zone" that begins where centralized authority makes contact with stateless people it does not rule. In such zones, newly introduced plants, animals, diseases, and technologies often spread widely, even before colonizers appear. These and other changes disrupt existing social and political relationships, fostering new alliances and creating conflicts.

Thomson Audio Study Products

 Enjoy the MP3-ready Audio Lecture Overviews for each chapter and a comprehensive audio glossary of key terms for quick study and review. Whether walking to class, doing laundry, or studying at your desk, you now have the freedom to choose when, where, and how you interact with your audio-based educational media. See the preface for information on how to access this on-the-go study and review tool.

The Anthropology Resource Center

www.thomsonedu.com/anthropology

The Anthropology Resource Center provides extended learning materials to reinforce your understanding of key concepts in the four fields of anthropology. For each of the four fields, the Resource Center includes dynamic exercises including video exercises, map exercises, simulations, and "Meet the Scientists" interviews, as well as critical thinking questions that can be assigned and e-mailed to instructors. The Resource Center also provides breaking news in anthropology and interesting material on applied anthropology to help you link what you are learning to the world around you.

24 Spirituality, Religion, and the Supernatural

c-print, copyright Kuo-ming Sung

CHALLENGE ISSUE

As self-aware and self-reflecting beings, humans face challenges beyond biological survival. We face emotional and intellectual ones born of the need to make sense of our place in the universe. Among other fundamental concerns, each of us wrestles with basic existential questions about our own fate, life, and death. More broadly, we puzzle over human origin and destiny and truly big questions about time and space, the earth, and the universe. Throughout time and across the globe, humans have creatively addressed these ponderings and worked out answers articulated in sacred narratives and associated ceremonies, rituals, and other cultural forms of religious or spiritual expression. Here we see a Buddhist monk in crimson red robes walking alongside a row of prayer wheels in a temple gallery—spinning the wheels on the wall (and perhaps in his soul) as he goes.

What Are Religion and Spirituality?

Religion and spirituality form part of a cultural system's super-structure, which comprises a society's worldview. Religion is an organized system of ideas about spiritual reality, or the supernatural, along with associated beliefs and ceremonial practices. Spirituality, which also concerns the supernatural, involves less formalized spiritual beliefs and practices and is often individual rather than collective. Both guide humans in their attempts to give meaning to the world and their place in it and to deal with problems that defy ordinary explanation or solution through direct means. To overcome these challenges, people appeal to, or seek to influence and even manipulate, spiritual or supernatural beings and powers.

What Are the Identifying Features of Religion and Spirituality?

Religion (and spiritual practices in general) consists of various beliefs and rituals—prayers, songs, dances, offerings, and sacrifices—that people use to interpret, appeal to, and manipulate supernatural beings and powers to their advantage. These beings and powers may consist of gods and goddesses, ancestral and other spirits, or impersonal powers, either by themselves or in various combinations. In all societies certain individuals are especially skilled at dealing with these beings and powers and assist other members of society in their ritual activities. A body of myths rationalizes or explains the system in a manner consistent with people's experience in the world in which they live.

What Functions Do Religion and Spirituality Serve?

Whether or not a particular religion accomplishes what people believe it does, all religions serve a number of important emotional, psychological, and social functions. They reduce anxiety by explaining the unknown and offer comfort with the belief that supernatural aid is available in times of crisis. They provide notions of right and wrong, setting precedents for acceptable behavior and transferring the burden of decision making from individuals to supernatural powers. Through ritual, religion may be used to enhance the learning of oral traditions. Finally, religion plays an important role in maintaining social solidarity. Spirituality also serves emotional, psychological, and social functions, but it tends to be fitted to more personal preferences, and its form and expression are often uniquely creative.

From an anthropological point of view, spirituality and religion are part of a cultural system's superstructure, earlier defined as the collective body of ideas, beliefs, and values by which a group of people makes sense of the world and their place in it. In their studies of different religious and spiritual beliefs and practices, anthropologists seek to remain unbiased regarding any particular cultural tradition. Instead, they examine spirituality and religion in terms of a society's **worldview**— the collective body of ideas that members of a culture generally share concerning the ultimate shape and substance of their reality.

Among people in all cultures, particular spiritual or religious beliefs and practices fulfill numerous social and psychological needs, such as the need to confront and explain suffering and death. Religion gives meaning to individual and group life, drawing power from spiritual forces or beings and offering continuity of existence beyond death. It can provide the path by which people transcend their burdensome and mortal existence and attain, if only momentarily, spiritual hope and relief.

THOMSON AUDIO STUDY PRODUCTS Take advantage of the MP3-ready Audio Lecture Overviews and comprehensive audio glossary of key terms for each chapter. See the preface for information on how to access this on-the-go study and review tool.

Religion and spirituality also serve an array of social needs. A traditional religion reinforces group norms, provides moral sanctions for individual conduct, and furnishes the ideology of common purpose and values that support the well-being of the community. Also of note, people often turn to religion or spirituality in the hope of reaching a specific goal, such as the healing of physical, emotional, or social ills.

Perhaps it is because they fulfill these and numerous other social and psychological needs shared by humans across cultures that supernatural beliefs are universal. While recognizing that not all individuals believe in a supernatural force or entity, anthropologists know of no group of people anywhere on the face of the earth who, at any time over the past 100,000 years, has been without some manifestation of spirituality or religion. Not even in Russia and Albania, where atheism was the communist state dogma during much of the 20th century, did religion entirely disappear.

In the 19th century, the European intellectual tradition gave rise to the idea that modern science would ultimately replace religion by showing people the irrationality of their spiritual beliefs and practices. The expectation was that as valid scientific explanations became available, people would abandon their religious beliefs and rituals as superstitious myths and false worship. But to date, despite tremendous scientific advancements, that has not occurred. In fact, in many places, the opposite trend seems to prevail.

Far from causing religion's death, the growth of scientific knowledge in rapidly changing societies may have contributed to the continuing practice of religion in modern life by producing new anxieties and raising new questions about human existence. Although traditional, mainline Christian religions have shown some decline, nondenominational spirituality is on the rise. Also on the rise are fundamentalist religions, which often take a strong antiscience position. Examples include Islamic fundamentalism in countries such as Afghanistan, Algeria, and Iran; Jewish fundamentalism in Israel and the United States; and Hindu fundamentalism in India. Christian fundamentalism is represented in the dramatic growth of evangelical denominations in the United States, Central America, and sub-Saharan Africa.

Among the fastest-growing religious communities in the world are the indigenous churches of Africa. Over the last half century, the number of registered indigenous denominations in southern Africa alone has doubled from about 5,000 to about 10,000. There, it is estimated that more than half of Christian church members belong to indigenous churches, like the Amanazaretha Church founded by a Zulu prophet and popular among fellow Zulus in Natal.[1]

Within the United States, non-Christian religions are also growing. Islam (3 to 5 million followers—up from 527,000 in 1990), Buddhism (2 to 3 million—up from 401,000 in 1990), Hinduism (1.28 million—up from 227,000 in 1990), not to mention various new age options such as Wicca (a modern, nature-oriented religion that draws upon ancient western European and pre-Christian beliefs and now counting about 310,000 adherents).[2] Notably, just 16 percent of the adult population throughout the world claims to be nonreligious (Figure 24.1). This is not to say that those classified as nonreligious are all atheists, because this miscellaneous "negative" category actually includes many millions of individuals in dozens of countries who may reject or not fit under the label of any organized religion, but are metaphysically involved in creative arrangements of spiritual beliefs and practices of their own choosing.

worldview The collective body of ideas that members of a culture generally share concerning the ultimate shape and substance of their reality.

---

[1]Kunnie, J. (2003). Africa's fast growing indigenous churches. http://coh.arizona.edu/newandnotable/kunnie/kunnie.html

[2]U.S. Census 2000; www.adherents.com. See also *World Almanac.* (2004). New York: Press Publishing Co.; and pluralism.org (The Pluralism Project, Harvard University).

Members of the Church of Zion, an indigenous Christian church with a primarily Zulu congregation, perform a baptism in the Indian Ocean near Durban, South Africa. Over half of all Christian church members in South Africa belong to indigenous churches that combine some elements of their traditional African beliefs and rituals with those of Christianity.

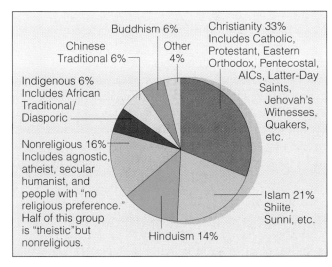

Figure 24.1

Major religions of the world and their percentage of all believers, 2005. (Note: Total adds up to more than 100 percent due to rounding and due to the upper-bound estimates used for each group.)

SOURCE: Adherents.com.

An inventory of the technological applications of modern science reveals the range of new anxieties facing our species. These include nuclear catastrophe, threats of chemical or biological terrorism, health hazards from pollution, and uneasiness about the consequences of developments in biotechnology such as cloning, production of new strains of genetically engineered organisms, ability to store human sperm and eggs for future fertilization, and manipulation of human DNA. On top of these, many people face emotional turmoil and psychological upheaval brought on by the breakup of traditional communities due to globalization, plus invasions of foreign ideas and values through mass media controlled by unfamiliar powers. In the face of these and other modern anxieties confronting the human species, religion offers social and psychological support.

The continuing strength of religion in the face of Western scientific rationalism clearly reveals that it remains a dominant and dynamic force in most contemporary societies. It is not the role of anthropologists to rank or pass judgment on the metaphysical truth of any particular religion or spiritual belief, but it is their task to show how each embodies a number of revealing facts about humans and the particular cultural system within which it is embedded.

THE ANTHROPOLOGICAL APPROACH TO RELIGION

Anthropologist Anthony F. C. Wallace defined religion as "a set of rituals, rationalized by myth, which mobilizes supernatural powers for the purpose of achieving or preventing transformations of state in man and nature."[3] Behind his definition lies a recognition that when people are unable to "fix" serious, anxiety-causing problems through technological or organizational means, they try to do so through manipulation of supernatural or spiritual beings and powers. This requires ritual, or "religion in action," which can be seen as a basic expression of religion. Its major functions are to reduce anxiety and boost confidence, thereby helping people cope with reality. It is this that gives religion survival value.

With these aspects in mind, we offer a somewhat simpler definition of **religion:** an organized system of ideas about the spiritual sphere or the supernatural, along with associated ceremonial practices by which people try to interpret and/or influence aspects of the universe otherwise beyond their control. Similar to religion, **spirituality** is also concerned with the sacred, as distinguished from material matters, but it is often individual rather than collective and does not require a distinctive format or traditional organization. Both are indicators that many aspects of the human experience are thought to be beyond scientific explanation.

Since no known culture, including those of modern industrial societies, has achieved complete certainty in controlling existing or future conditions and circumstances, spirituality and/or religion play a role in all known cultures. However, considerable variability exists here.

At one end of the spectrum are food-foraging peoples, whose technological ability to manipulate their en-

---

[3]Wallace, A. F. C. (1966). *Religion: An anthropological view.* New York: Random House.

religion An organized system of ideas about the spiritual sphere or the supernatural, along with associated ceremonial practices by which people try to interpret and/or influence aspects of the universe otherwise beyond their control.
spirituality Concern with the sacred, as distinguished from material matters. In contrast to religion, spirituality is often individual rather than collective and does not require a distinctive format or traditional organization.

vironment is limited and who tend to see themselves as part of, rather than masters of, nature. This may be referred to as a *naturalistic worldview.* Among food foragers religion is likely to be inseparable from the rest of daily life. It also mirrors and confirms the egalitarian nature of social relations in their societies, in that individuals do not plead with high-ranking deities for aid the way members of stratified societies do.

At the other end of the spectrum is Western civilization, with its ideological commitment to overcoming problems through technological and organizational skills. Here religion is less a part of daily activities and is restricted to more specific occasions. Moreover, with its hierarchy of supernatural beings—for instance, God, and (in some religions) the angels, saints, or holy people—it reflects and confirms the stratified nature of the society in which it is embedded.

Religious activity may be less prominent in the lives of social elites, who may see themselves as more in control of their own destinies, than it is in the lives of peasants or members of lower classes. Among the latter, religion may afford some compensation for a dependent position in society. Yet religion is still important to elite members of society, in that it rationalizes the system in such a way that less advantaged people are not as likely to question the existing social order as they might otherwise be. With hope for a better existence after death, one may be more willing to put up with a disadvantaged position in life. Thus, religious beliefs serve to influence and perpetuate certain ideas about the relationships, if not actual relations, between different classes of people.

THE PRACTICE OF RELIGION

Much of religion's value comes from the activities called for by its prescriptions and rules. Participation in religious ceremonies may bring a sense of personal lift—a wave of reassurance, a feeling of overwhelming joy, and even a sense of moving into a trancelike state—or a feeling of closeness to fellow participants. The beliefs and ceremonial practices of religions vary considerably. Yet, rituals that seem bizarre to an outsider can be shown to serve the same basic social and psychological functions as do his or her own distinct rituals.

Supernatural Beings and Powerss

A hallmark of religion is belief in supernatural beings and forces. In attempting to control by religious means what cannot be controlled in other ways, humans turn to prayer, sacrifice, and other religious or spiritual rituals. These presuppose the existence of spiritual forces that can be tapped into, or spiritual beings interested in human affairs and available for aid.

Beginning with spiritual beings, we may divide them into three categories: major deities (gods and goddesses), ancestral spirits, and other sorts of spirit beings. Although the variety of deities and spirits recognized by the world's cultures is tremendous, it is possible to make certain generalizations about them.

Gods and Goddesses

Gods and goddesses are the great and more remote beings. They are usually seen as controlling the universe. If more than one is recognized (known as **polytheism**), each has charge of a particular part of the universe. Such was the case with the gods and goddesses of ancient Greece: Zeus was lord of the sky, Poseidon was ruler of the sea, and Hades was lord of the underworld and ruler of the dead.

In addition to these three brothers, Greek mythology features a host of other deities, female as well as male, each similarly concerned with specific aspects of life and the universe. A **pantheon,** or the collection of gods and goddesses such as those of the Greeks, is common in non-Western states as well. Since states typically have grown through conquest, often their pantheons have expanded as local deities of conquered peoples were incorporated into the official state pantheon. Another frequent though not invariable feature of pantheons is the presence of a supreme deity, who may be all but totally ignored by humans. The Aztecs of the Mexican highlands, for instance, recognized a supreme pair to whom they paid little attention. After all, being so remote, this divine duo was unlikely to be interested in human affairs. The sensible practice, then, was to focus attention on less remote deities who were more directly concerned with human affairs.

Whether or not a people recognize gods, goddesses, or both has to do with how men and women relate to each other in everyday life. Generally speaking, societies that subordinate women to men define the supreme deity in masculine terms. For instance, in traditional Chris-tian religions believers speak of God as a "father" who had a divine "son" but do not entertain thoughts of God as a "mother" nor of a divine "daughter." Such male-privileging religions developed in traditional societies with economies based upon the herding of animals or intensive agriculture carried out or controlled by men, who are dominating figures to their children.

Goddesses, by contrast, are likely to be most prominent in societies where women play a significant role in the economy, where women enjoy relative equality with men, and where men are less controlling figures to their wives and children. Such societies are most often those that depend upon crop cultivation carried out solely or mostly by women.

As an illustration, the early Israelites, like other pastoral nomadic groups of the Middle East, described their god in masculine, authoritarian terms. By contrast, goddesses played central roles in religious ritual and in the popular imagination of the region's farming peoples. Associated with these goddesses were concepts of light, fertility, and procreation. About 3,200 years ago, the Israelite tribes crossed the Jordan River and entered the land of Canaan (Palestine) where they began to till the soil and grow crops, requiring them to establish a new kind of relationship with the land. As they settled down and became sedentary, dependent upon rainfall and concerned about seasonal cycles and soil fertility (as the region's Canaanites already were), they adopted many of the region's already established Canaanite goddess cults. Although diametrically opposed to the original Israelite supreme male deity cult, worship of these Canaanite female deities appealed to the farming people's desire for security by seeking to control the forces of fertility.

polytheism Belief in several gods and/or goddesses (as contrasted with monotheism—belief in one god or goddess).
pantheon The several gods and goddesses of a people.

The patriarchal nature of traditional Euramerican society is expressed in its Judeo-Christian theology, in which a supreme male deity gives life to the first man, as depicted here on the ceiling of the Sistine Chapel in Rome. Only later is the first woman created from the first man.

© Visual Arts Library (London)/Alamy

Later on, when the Israelite tribes sought national unity in the face of a military threat by neighboring nations and when they ethnocentrically strengthened their own identity as a supernaturally "chosen people," the goddess cults lost out to followers of the old masculine tribal god. This ancient masculine-authoritarian concept of god has been perpetuated down to the present, not just in the Judaic tradition but also by most Christians and Muslims, whose religions stem from the old Israelite religion. As a consequence, this masculine-authoritarian model has played an important role in perpetuating a relationship between men and women in which the latter traditionally have been expected to submit to the rule of men at every level of Jewish, Christian, and Islamic society.

Ancestral Spirits

A belief in ancestral spirits is consistent with the widespread notion that human beings are made up of two closely intertwined parts: a physical body and some mental component or spiritual self. For example, traditional belief of the Penobscot Indians in Maine holds that each person has a vital spirit capable of traveling apart from the body. Given such a concept, the idea of the spirit being freed from the body in trance and dreams or by death, and having an existence thereafter, seems quite reasonable. Frequently, where a belief in ancestral spirits exists, these beings are seen as retaining an active interest and even membership in society.

In the previous chapter, for instance, we discussed how the Wape Papuans in New Guinea believe that ancestral spirits act to provide or withhold meat from their living descendants. Like living persons, such spirit beings are viewed as benevolent or malevolent, but no one is ever quite sure what their behavior will be. The same feeling of uncertainty—How will they react to what I have done?—may be displayed toward ancestral spirits as it often is toward people of an older generation who hold authority over individuals. Beyond this, ancestral spirits closely resemble living humans in their appetites, feelings, emotions, and behavior. Thus, they reflect and reinforce social reality.

Belief in ancestral spirits of one sort or another is found in many parts of the world, especially among people having unilineal descent systems with their associated ancestor orientation. In several such African societies, the concept is highly elaborate. Here one frequently finds ancestral spirits behaving just like humans. They are able to feel hot, cold, and pain, and they may be capable of dying a second death by drowning or burning. They even may participate in family and lineage affairs, and seats will be provided for them, even though the spirits are invisible. If they are annoyed, they may send sickness or death. Eventually, they are reborn as new members of their lineage, and, in societies that hold such beliefs, adults need to observe infants closely to determine just who has been reborn. Such beliefs provide a strong sense of continuity that links the past, present, and future.

Ancestor spirits played an important role in the patrilineal society of traditional China. For the gift of life, a boy was forever indebted to his parents, owing them obedience, deference, and a comfortable old age. Even after their death, he had to provide for them in the spirit world, offering them food, money, and incense on the anniversaries of their births and deaths. In addition, people collectively worshiped all lineage ancestors periodically throughout the year. Giving birth to sons was regarded as an obligation to the ancestors, because boys inherited their father's ancestral duties.

To fulfill his ancestors' needs for descendants (and his own need to be respectable in a culture that demanded satisfying the needs of one's ancestors), a man would go so far as to marry a girl who had been adopted into his family as an infant so she could be raised as a dutiful wife for him, even when this arrangement went against the wishes of both parties. Furthermore, a father readily would force his daughter to marry a man against her will. In fact, a female child raised to be cast out by her natal family might not find acceptance in her husband's family for years. Not until after death, when her vital spirit was carried in a tablet and placed in the shrine of her husband's family, was she an official member of it. As a consequence, once a son was born to her, a woman worked long and hard to establish the strongest possible tie between herself and her son to ensure she would be looked after in life.

Strong beliefs in ancestral spirits are particularly appropriate in a society of descent-based groups with their associated ancestor orientation. But, more than this, as noted above, these beliefs provide a strong sense of continuity that links the past, present, and future.

Sacred Places

In addition to revering special supernatural figures such as deities, ancestral spirits, and other special beings, some religious traditions consider certain geographic places to be spiritually significant or even sacred. Typically, such sites are rivers, lakes, waterfalls, islands, forests, caves, and—especially—mountains. Often, their status is due to some unique shape or outstanding feature, such as a conical volcano capped with snow. Numerous mountains around the world fall into this category. Often they are associated with origin myths as splendid abodes of the gods. Or they are revered as dwelling places for the spirits of the dead, heights where prophets received their divine directions, or retreats for prayer, meditation, and vision quests.

Three sacred mountains are shared by the Jewish, Christian, and Muslim traditions: Mount Ararat in the Caucasus Mountain Range between Russia and Turkey where the ark of the ancient patriarch Noah is said to have landed after the Great Flood; Mount Horeb, the "mountain of God" in the Sinai Desert where the prophet Moses received the stone tablets with the ten sacred rules of behavior from his god; and Mount Zion at the old city of Jerusalem where Solomon, the Israelite king, is believed to have been divinely ordered to build the Great Temple and where an important Muslim mosque is also located. Another sacred mountain in that region is Mount Tabor in northern Israel where Christians believe the change in the appearance of Jesus as God's son took place.

© Images & Stories, Turkey

Pilgrims at Mount Kailash in Tibet. Rising 6,700 meters (about 22,000 feet), this mountain has been held sacred for thousands of years by Hindus, Buddhists, Jains, and followers of Bön (Tibet's indigenous religion). Year after year pilgrims follow the ancient tradition of circling the mountain on foot. The rugged, 52-kilometer (32-mile) trek, known as *parikarma*, is seen as a holy ritual that removes sins and brings good fortune. The most devout pilgrims make the journey lying down: Prostrating their bodies full-length, they extend their hands forward and make a mark on the ground with their fingers; then they rise, pray, crawl ahead on hands and knees to the mark, and then repeat the process again and again.

Similar traditions exist in many other cultures. For instance, the Japanese view the snow-capped perfect volcanic cone of Mount Fuji ("ever-lasting life") as a sacred place. Likewise, the Aztecs held several snow-capped volcanoes sacred, including Popocatepetl ("Smoking Mountain") just outside Mexico City. And the same can be said for Kirinyaga (Mount Kenya) in East Africa. Straddling the equator, it is seen as a holy place by the Kikuyu people who believe this "Mountain of Brightness" to be the earthly dwelling place of their creator god Ngai. Similarly, the ancient Greeks considered Mount Olympus to be the mythological abode of Zeus, the king of all their gods. In some religious traditions, such as among the Aymara of the Bolivian highlands, a volcanic mountain like Kaata is not only considered sacred, but is actually deified and worshiped as a living god.

Symbolic of the supreme being, or associated with various important deities or ancestral spirits, sacred mountains may feature in religious ceremonies or spiritual rituals. In some religious traditions, these towering geographic features are places of worship, like shrines, or are sacred destinies for spiritual journeys or pilgrimages. For example, every year thousands of Buddhist and Hindu worshipers make a long pilgrimage to the foot of Mount Kailash in Tibet. They do not deify this peak, but they believe it to be the sacred abode of Lord Shiva, a member of the supreme divine trinity—so sacred that they would not even dream of trying to climb it.

Among the many other mountains considered sacred is Bear Butte in the Paha Sapa, or Black Hills, of South Dakota. This mythological place is of great religious significance to dozens of American Indian nations in the Great Plains, especially the Lakota and Cheyenne who come to this domed mountain for meditation, prayers, and sacred vision quests. For outsiders unfamiliar with (or unsympathetic to) the indigenous religious traditions, these sacred mountains may be valued for commercial or recreational purposes, thus leading sometimes to bitter controversies and unfortunate consequences.

Animism

One of the most widespread concepts concerning supernatural beings is **animism,** a belief that nature is animated (enlivened or energized) by distinct personalized spirit beings separable from bodies. Spirits such as souls and ghosts are thought to dwell in humans and animals but also in human-made artifacts, plants, stones, mountains, wells, and other natural features. So too the woods may be full of a variety of unattached or free-ranging spirits.

animism A belief that nature is animated (enlivened or energized) by distinct personalized spirit beings separable from bodies.

The various spirits involved are a highly diverse lot. Generally speaking, though, they are less remote than gods and goddesses and are more involved in people's daily affairs. They may be benevolent, malevolent, or just plain neutral. They also may be awesome, terrifying, lovable, or mischievous. Since they may be pleased or irritated by human actions, people are obliged to be concerned about them.

Animism is typical of those who see themselves as being a part of nature rather than superior to it. This includes most food foragers, as well as those food-producing peoples who acknowledge little qualitative difference between a human life and any living entity from turtles to trees, or even rivers and mountains. In such societies, gods and goddesses are relatively unimportant, but the woods are full of spirits. Gods and goddesses, if they exist at all, may be seen as having created the world and perhaps making it fit to live in; but in animism, spirits are the ones to beseech when ill, the ones to help or hinder the shaman, and the ones who the ordinary hunter may meet when off in the woods.

Animatism

Although supernatural power is often thought of as being vested in supernatural beings, it does not have to be. Such is the case with **animatism**—the belief that nature is enlivened or energized by an impersonal spiritual power or supernatural potency.

The Melanesians, for example, think of *mana* as a force inherent in all objects—not unlike the idea of a cosmic energy passing into and through everything, affecting living and nonliving matter alike (similar to "the Force" in the *Star War* films). It is not in itself physical, but it can reveal itself physically. A warrior's success in fighting is not attributed to his own strength but to the *mana* contained in an amulet that hangs around his neck. Similarly, a farmer may know a great deal about horticulture, soil conditioning, and the correct time for sowing and harvesting, but nevertheless may depend upon *mana* for a successful crop, often building a simple altar to this power at one end of the field. If the crop is good, it is a sign that the farmer has in some way appropriated the necessary *mana*. Far from being a personalized force, *mana* is abstract in the extreme, a power or potency lying always just beyond reach of the senses.

This concept of impersonal potency or energy was widespread among North American Indians. The Algonquins called it *manitou;* to the Mohawk it was *orenda;* to the Lakota, *wakonda*. For instance, Bear Butte in the Black Hills, mentioned earlier, is a mountain where Lakota believers feel a strong presence of spirit power, or *wakonda,* which makes it a sacred site.

Nevertheless, though found on every continent, the concept of impersonal spirit power is not necessarily universal. In some cultures this energy is turned to for healing purposes. Notably, *animism* (as a belief in distinct spirit beings) and *animatism* (which lacks particular substance or individual form) are not mutually exclusive. They are often found in the same culture, as in Melanesian societies and also in the North American Indian societies just mentioned.

People trying to comprehend beliefs in the supernatural beings and powers that others recognize frequently ask how such beliefs are maintained. In part, the answer is through manifestations of power. Given a belief in animatism and/or the powers of supernatural beings, one is predisposed to see what appear to be results of the application of such powers. For example, if a Melanesian warrior is convinced of his power because he possesses the necessary *mana* and he is successful, he is likely to interpret this success as proof of the power of *mana:* "After all, I would have lost had I not possessed it, wouldn't I?" Beyond this, because of his confidence in his *mana,* he may be willing to take more chances in his fighting, and this indeed could mean the difference between success or failure.

Failures, of course, do occur, but they can be explained. Perhaps one's prayer was not answered because a deity or spirit was still angry about some past insult. Or perhaps the Melanesian warrior lost his battle because he was not as successful in bringing *mana* to bear or his opponent had more of it. In any case, humans generally emphasize successes over failures, and long after many of the latter have been forgotten, tales will still be told of striking cases of the workings of supernatural powers.

Beliefs are also maintained through myths—explanatory narratives that rationalize and reinforce religious beliefs and practices. We will discuss myths in more detail later in this chapter.

Religious Specialists

All human societies include individuals who guide and supplement the religious practices of others. Such individuals are seen to be highly skilled at contacting and influencing supernatural beings and manipulating supernatural forces. Often their qualification for this is that they have undergone special training. In addition, they may display certain distinctive personality traits that make them particularly well suited to perform these tasks.

animatism A belief that nature is enlivened or energized by an impersonal spiritual power or supernatural potency.

Priests and Priestesses

Within societies with the resources to support a full-time occupational specialist, a **priest** or **priestess** will have the role of guiding religious practices and influencing the supernatural. He or she is the socially initiated, ceremonially inducted member of a recognized religious organization, with a rank and function that belong to him or her as the holder of a position others have held before. The sources of power are the society and the institution within which the priest or priestess functions.

The priest, if not the priestess, is a familiar figure in Western societies; he is the priest, minister, imam, lama, rabbi, or whatever the official title may be in an organized religion. With their god defined historically in masculine, authoritarian terms, it is not surprising that, in the Judaic, Christian, and Islamic religions, the most important positions traditionally have been filled by men. Female religious specialists are likely to be found only in societies where women are acknowledged to contribute in a major way to the economy and where gods and goddesses are both recognized. In western Europe and North America, for instance, where women are now wage earners in almost every profession and occupy leadership positions in the workforce, they now have an increasing presence in the leadership of many Judeo-Christian religious groups.[4]

Although women still do not occupy the highest ranking religious leadership positions in the Roman Catholic Church (headed by a male pope and his all-male council, the College of Cardinals), this Christian religion does recognize important female saints. Most significant among these is the Virgin Mary, held to be the human mother of God's son. In many places where Roman Catholicism has spread, worshipers have created cults around this female saint. Moreover, all around the world women devoted to a religious life have formed their own places for religious exclusion as nuns jointly belonging to a cloister or convent, headed by an abbess. Such all-female religious institutions are not unique to Roman Catholicism. Convents of nuns are also part of Buddhist religious traditions and can be found in several Asian countries, including Thailand, as described by U.S. anthropologist Hillary Crane in this chapter's Biocultural Connection.

Shamans

Societies that lack full-time occupational specialization have existed far longer than those with such specialization, and they have always included individuals with special powers and skills that enable them to connect with and manipulate supernatural beings and forces. These powers have come to them through some personal experience, usually in solitude. In an altered state of consciousness, they receive a vision that empowers them to heal the sick, change the weather, control the movements of animals, and foretell the future. As they perfect these and related skills, they assume the role of shaman.

The word *shaman* originally referred to medical-religious specialists, or spiritual guides, among the Tungus and other Siberian pastoral nomads with animist beliefs. By means of various techniques such as fasting, drumming, chanting, or dancing, as well as hallucinogenic mushrooms, these Siberian shamans enter into a trance, or altered state of consciousness. While in this waking dream state, they experience visions of an alternate reality inhabited by spirit beings such as guardian animal spirits who may assist in the healing.

Cross-cultural research of shamanism shows that similar medical-religious healing practices also exist in traditional cultures outside Siberia. For that reason, the term *shaman* has also been applied to a variety of part-time spiritual leaders and traditional healers ("medicine men") active in North and South American indigenous communities and beyond.

As defined by U.S. anthropologist Michael Harner, famous for his participant observation among Shuar (or Jivaro) Indian shamans in the Amazon rainforest, a **shaman** is "a man or woman who enters an altered state of consciousness—at will—to contact and utilize an ordinarily hidden reality in order to acquire knowledge, power, and to help other persons. The shaman has at least one, and usually more, 'spirits' in his or her personal service."[5]

The term *shaman* has become so popular in recent decades that any non-Western local priest, healer, or diviner is often loosely referred to as one.[6] In the United States millions of people learned something about shamans through the popular autobiography of Black Elk, a traditional Lakota Indian Holy Man, and Carlos Castañeda's largely fictional accounts of his experiences with Don Juan, the Yaqui Indian shaman. Numerous books

[4]Lehman, E. C., Jr. (2002, Fall). Women's path into the ministry. *Pulpit & Pew Research Reports 1*, 4.

[5]Harner, M. (1980). *The way of the shaman: A guide to power and healing* (p. 20). San Francisco: Harper & Row.

[6]Kehoe, A. (2000). *Shamans and religion: An anthropological exploration in critical thinking*. Prospect Heights, IL: Waveland Press.

priest or **priestess** A full-time religious specialist formally recognized for his or her role in guiding the religious practices of others and for contacting and influencing supernatural powers.
shaman A person who enters an altered state of consciousness—at will—to contact and utilize an ordinarily hidden reality in order to acquire knowledge, power, and to help others.

Change Your Karma and Change Your Sex? ▪
By Hillary Crane

As Mahayana Buddhists, Taiwanese Chan (Zen) monastics believe that all humans are able to reach enlightenment and be released from reincarnation. But they believe it is easier for some because of the situation into which they are born—for example, if one is born in a country where Buddhism is practiced, in a family that teaches proper behavior, or with exceptional mental or physical gifts.

Chan monastics view contrasting human circumstances as the result of the karma accrued in previous lives. They believe certain behavior—such as diligently practicing Buddhism—improves karma and the chances of attaining spiritual goals in this lifetime or coming back in a better birth. Other behavior—such as killing a living being, eating meat, desiring or becoming attached to things or people—accrues bad karma.

One way karma manifests itself is in one's sex. Taiwanese Buddhists believe that being born female makes it harder to attain spiritual goals. This idea comes, in part, from the inferior status of women in Taiwan and the belief that their "complicated bodies" and monthly menstruation cycles can distract them. Moreover, they believe, women are more enmeshed in their families than men, and their emotional ties keep them focused on worldly rather than spiritual tasks.

Taiwanese Buddhists who decide to become monks and nuns must break from their families to enter a monastery. Since women are thought to be more attached to their families than are men, leaving home is seen as a particularly big step for nuns and a sign that they are more like men than most women. In fact, a nun's character is considered masculine, unlike the frightened, indecisive, and emotional traits usually associated with women in Taiwan. When they leave home nuns even stop referring to themselves as women and call one another *shixiong* ("dharma brother"). They use this linguistic change to signal that they identify themselves as men and to remind one another to behave like men, particularly like the monks at the temple.

Monastics also reduce their attachments to worldly things like music and food. Nuns usually emphasize forsaking food and eat as little as possible. Their appearance, already quite masculine because they shave their heads and wear loose, gray clothing, becomes even more so when they lose weight—particularly in their hips, breasts, and thighs. Also, after becoming monastics, they often experience a slowing or stopping of their menses. Although these physical changes can be attributed to change in diet and lifestyle, the nuns point to them as signs they are becoming men, making progress toward their spiritual goals, and improving their karma.

(For a more detailed treatment of this topic, see H. Crane (2001). Men in spirit: The masculinization of Taiwanese Buddhist nuns. Doctoral dissertation, Brown University.)

VISUAL COUNTERPOINT

Shamanism is by no means absent in modern industrial societies. Here we see a new age shaman in North America (left) and a traditional shaman in Mongolia. The Mongolian shaman's drum is crafted from the wood of a tree struck by lightning and covered with leather made from a female red deer. It is believed that when the shaman goes into trance, her drum transforms into a magic steed that carries her into the dark sky of her ancestors.

and other publications on shamanism have appeared over the past four decades, and some Euramericans have gone into practice as shamans, a development that has triggered considerable resentment among some Native Americans. ("They stole our land, now they are stealing our religion.") In addition to so-called new age enthusiasts, among whom shamanism is particularly popular, faith healers and other evangelists among fundamentalist Christians share many of the characteristics of shamanism.

Typically, one becomes a shaman by passing through stages of learning and practical experience, often involving psychological and emotional ordeals brought about by isolation, fasting, physical torture, sensory deprivation, and/or hallucinations. These hallucinations (derived from the Latin word for "mental wandering") occur when the shaman is in a trance, which may occur spontaneously but can also be induced by drumming or consuming mind-altering drugs such as psychoactive vines or mushrooms.

Among the Penobscot Indians in northern New England, for example, any person could become a shaman, since no formal institution provided rules and regulations to guide religious consciousness. The search for shamanic visions was pursued by most adult Penobscot males, who would go off alone and—through meditation, sensory deprivation, and hyperventilation—induce an altered state of consciousness in which they hoped to receive a vision. Not all were successful, but failure did not result in social disgrace. Those who did achieve success experienced a sense of being freed from their bodily existence in which they established a special relationship with a particular animal spirit that appeared in their trance state. This became the shaman's animal helper—a common element in shamanism—who thereafter would assist the individual in performing shamanic tasks.

Because shamanism is rooted in altered states of consciousness and the human nervous system that produces these trance states is universal, individuals involved in shamanism experience similarly structured visual, auditory, somatic (touch), olfactory (smell), and gustatory (taste) hallucinations. The widespread occurrence of shamanism and the remarkable similarities among shamanic traditions everywhere are consequences of this universal neurological inheritance. At the same time, the meanings ascribed to sensations experienced in altered states and made of their content are culturally determined; hence, despite their overall similarities, local traditions always vary in their details.

The shaman is essentially a religious go-between who acts on behalf of some human client, often to bring about healing or to foretell some future event. To do so, the shaman intervenes to influence or impose his or her will on supernatural powers. The shaman can be contrasted with the priest or priestess, whose "clients" are the deities. Priests and priestesses frequently tell people what to do; the shaman tells supernaturals what to do. In return for services rendered, the shaman may collect a fee—fresh meat, yams, or a favorite possession. In some cases, the added prestige, authority, and social power attached to the shaman's status are reward enough.

When a shaman acts on behalf of a client, he or she may put on something of a show—one that heightens the basic drama with a sense of danger. Typically, the shaman enters a trance state, in which he or she experiences the sensation of traveling to the alternate world and seeing and interacting with spirit beings. The shaman tries to impose his or her will upon these spirits, an inherently dangerous contest, considering the superhuman powers spirits usually are thought to possess.

An example of this can be seen in the trance dances of the Ju/'hoansi Bushmen of Africa's Kalahari Desert. Among the Ju/'hoansi, shamans constitute, on average, about half the men and a third of the older women in any group. Their most common reasons for going into trance are to bring rain, control animals, and to heal the sick. Healing is an important activity of shamans across cultures, and the following Original Study offers insight into shamanic healing as practiced among the Ju/'hoansi.

Original Study ▪ By Marjorie Shostak

Healing among the Ju/'hoansi of the Kalahari

One way the spirits affect humans is by shooting them with invisible arrows carrying disease, death, or misfortune. If the arrows can be warded off, illness will not take hold. If illness has already penetrated, the arrows must be removed to enable the sick person to recover. An ancestral spirit may exercise this power against the living if a person is not being treated well by others. If people argue with her frequently, if her husband shows how little he values her by carrying on blatant affairs, or if people refuse to cooperate or share with her, the spirit may conclude that no one cares whether or not she remains alive and may "take her into the sky."

CONTINUED

CONTINUED

Ju/'hoansi healers, when entering trance, are assisted by others among the trance dancers.

Interceding with the spirits and drawing out their invisible arrows is the task of [Ju/'hoansi] healers, men and women who possess the powerful healing force called *n/um* [the Ju/'hoansi equivalent of *mana*]. *N/um* generally remains dormant in a healer until an effort is made to activate it. Although an occasional healer can accomplish this through solo singing or instrumental playing, the usual way of activating *n/um* is through the medicinal curing ceremony or trance dance. To the sound of undulating melodies sung by women, healers dance around and around the fire, sometimes for hours. The music, the strenuous dancing, the smoke, the heat of the fire, and the healers' intense concentration cause their *n/um* to heat up. When it comes to a boil, trance is achieved.

At this moment the *n/um* becomes available as a powerful healing force, to serve the entire community. In trance, a healer lays hands on and ritually cures everyone sitting around the fire. His hands flutter lightly beside each person's head or chest or wherever illness is evident; his body trembles; his breathing becomes deep and coarse; and he becomes coated with a thick sweat—also considered to be imbued with power. Whatever "badness" is discovered in the person is drawn into the healer's own body and met by the *n/um* coursing up his spinal column. The healer gives a mounting cry that culminates in a soul-wrenching shriek as the illness is catapulted out of his body and into the air.

While in trance, many healers see various gods and spirits sitting just outside the circle of firelight, enjoying the spectacle of the dance. Sometimes the spirits are recognizable—departed relatives and friends—at other times they are "just people." Whoever these beings are, healers in trance usually blame them for whatever misfortune is being experienced by the community. They are barraged by hurled objects, shouted at, and aggressively warned not to take any of the living back with them to the village of the spirits.

To cure a very serious illness, the most experienced healers may be called upon, for only they have enough knowledge to undertake the dangerous spiritual exploration that may be necessary to effect a cure. When they are in a trance, their souls or vital spirits are said to leave their bodies and to travel to the spirit world to discover the cause of the illness or the problem. An ancestral spirit or a god is usually found responsible and asked to reconsider. If the healer is persuasive and the spirit agrees, the sick person recovers. If the spirit is elusive or unsympathetic, a cure is not achieved. The healer may go to the principal god, but even this does not always work. As one healer put it, "Sometimes, when you speak with God, he says, 'I want this person to die and won't help you make him better.' At other times, God helps; the next morning, someone who has been lying on the ground, seriously ill, gets up and walks again."

These journeys are considered dangerous because while the healer's soul is absent his body is in half-death. Akin to loss of consciousness, this state has been observed and verified by medical and scientific investigators. The power of other healers' *n/um* is all that is thought to protect the healer in this state from actual death. He receives lavish attention and care—his body is vigorously massaged, his skin is rubbed with sweat, and hands are laid on him. Only when consciousness returns—the signal that his soul has been reunited with his body—do the other healers cease their efforts.
(Excerpted from M. Shostak. (1983). Nisa: The life and words of a !Kung woman (pp. 291–293). New York: Vintage.)

In many human societies, sleight-of-hand tricks and ventriloquism occur at the same time as trancing. Among Arctic peoples, for example, a shaman may summon spirits in the dark and produce flapping noises and strange voices to impress the audience. Some Western observers regard this kind of trickery as evidence of the fraudulent nature of shamanism. However, those who have studied shamanic practices agree that even though shamans know perfectly well that they are manipulating people with their tricks, they really believe in their power to deal with supernatural forces and spirit beings. Their power, verified by the trance experience, gives them the right as well as the ability to manipulate people in minor technical matters. In short, the shaman regards his or her ability to perform extraordinary tricks as further proof of superior powers.

The importance of shamanism in a society should not be underestimated. It promotes, through the drama of performance, a trancelike feeling and a release of tension. And it provides psychological assurance that prevailing upon supernatural powers and spirits otherwise beyond human control can bring about invulnerability from attack, success at love, or the return of health. In fact, a frequent reason for a shamanic performance is poor health—a concept that is difficult to define effectively in cross-cultural terms. Not only do people in diverse cultures recognize and experience different types of illnesses, they may also view and explain them in different terms. The culturally defined diagnosis of an illness, in turn, determines how the patient will be treated according to the beliefs of the culture, in order to achieve healing.

Although the psychological effects of the shamanic treatment are not known, the connection between mind and body may contribute to the patient's recovery. From an anthropological perspective, shamanic healings can be understood by means of a three-cornered model we call the *shamanic complex* (Figure 24.2). This triangle is created by the relationships among the shaman and the patient and the community to which both belong.

For healing to take place, the shaman needs to be convinced of the effectiveness of his or her spiritual powers and techniques. Likewise, the patient must see the

shaman as a genuine healing master using appropriate techniques. Finally, to close the triangle's "magic field," the community within which the shaman operates on the patient must view the healing ceremony and its practitioner as potentially effective and beneficial.

Such dynamics are not unique to shamanic healing ceremonies, for similar social psychological processes are involved in Western medical treatments as well. Some people involved in modern medicine work collaboratively with practitioners of traditional belief systems toward the healing of various illnesses—as illustrated in this chapter's Anthropology Applied feature.

RITUALS AND CEREMONIES

Rituals, or ceremonial acts, are not all religious in nature (consider, for example, college graduation ceremonies in North America), but those that are play a crucial role in religious activity. Religious ritual is the means through which people relate to the supernatural; it is religion in action. Ritual serves to relieve social tensions and reinforce a group's collective bonds. More than this, it provides a means of marking many important events and lessening the social disruption and individual suffering of crises, such as death. Anthropologists have classified several different types of ritual. These include rites of passage and rites of intensification.

Rites of Passage

Rites of passage are rituals that mark important stages in an individual's life cycle. In one of anthropology's classic works, French social scientist Arnold van Gennep analyzed the rites of passage that help individuals through the crucial crises or major social transitions in their lives, such as birth, puberty, marriage, parenthood, advancement to a higher class, occupational specialization, and death.[7] He found it useful to divide ceremonies for all of these life crises into three stages: **separation, transition,** and **incorporation;** the first being ritual removal of the individual from everyday society, followed by a period

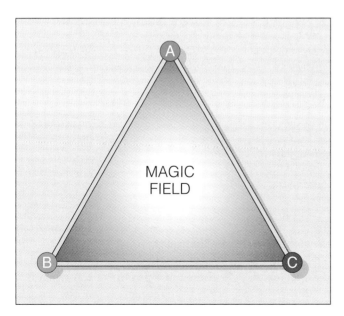

Figure 24.2
The shamanic complex. Shamanic healing takes place within a "magic field" created when the shaman (A) and patient (B), as well as their community (C), are all convinced that the shaman is a genuine healing master using appropriate techniques that are effective and beneficial. Similar psychological processes are involved in Western medical treatments.

---

[7]Van Gennep, A. (1960). *The rites of passage.* Chicago: University of Chicago Press.

---

rite of passage A ritual that marks an important stage in an individual's life cycle, such as birth, marriage, and death.
separation In a rite of passage, the ritual removal of the individual from society.
transition In a rite of passage, isolation of the individual following separation and prior to incorporation into society.
incorporation In a rite of passage, reincorporation of the individual into society in his or her new status.

Anthropology Applied

Reconciling Modern Medicine with Traditional Beliefs in Swaziland ▪ By Edward C. Green

Although the biomedical germ theory is generally known and accepted in Western societies today, this is not the case in many other societies around the world. In southern Africa's Swaziland, for example, many illnesses are generally thought to be caused by sorcery or by loss of ancestral protection. (Sexually transmitted diseases—STDs—and other contagious diseases are exceptions to these beliefs.)

Even where the effectiveness of Western medicine is recognized, the ultimate question remains: Why did a disease come to a particular person in the first place? Thus, for the treatment of disease, the Swazi have traditionally relied upon herbalists, diviner mediums through whom ancestor spirits are thought to work, and (more recently) Christian faith healers. Unfortunately, such individuals have usually been regarded as quacks and charlatans by the medical establishment. Yet, the herbal medicines used by traditional healers are effective in several ways, and the reassurance provided patient and family alike through rituals that reduce stress and anxiety plays an important role in the patient's recovery. In a country where there is one traditional healer for every 110 people, but only one physician for every 10,000, the potential benefit of cooperation between physicians and healers seems self-evident. Nevertheless, it was largely unrecognized until proposed by anthropologists D. M. Warren (in Ghana) and later, myself.

It was in 1981, when I was a Washington-based independent consultant, that I first went to Swaziland as a researcher for the Rural Water-Borne Disease Control Project, funded by the United States Agency for International Development. Assigned the task of finding out about knowledge, attitudes, and practices related to water and sanitation, and aware of the serious deficiencies of conventional surveys that rely on pre-coded questionnaires, I used instead the traditional anthropological techniques of open-ended interviews with key informants, along with participant observation. The key informants were traditional healers, their patients, and rural health motivators (women chosen by communities to receive eight weeks of training in preventive health care in regional clinics). Without such anthropological research, it would have been impossible to design and interpret a reliable survey instrument, but the added payoff was that I learned a great deal about Swazi theories of illness and its treatment.

Disposed at the outset to recognize the positive value of many traditional practices, I could also see how cooperation with physicians might be achieved. For example, traditional healers already recognized the utility of Western medicines for treatment of diseases considered not indigenous to Africa, and traditional preventive medicines were routinely given to children through inhalation, something like childhood vaccinations. Thus, nontraditional medicines and vaccinations might be accepted, if presented in ways that resembled traditional medicine.

Realizing the suspicion existing on both sides, I and my Swazi associate Lydia Makhubu (a chemist who had studied the properties of indigenous medicines) recommended to the minister of health a cooperative project focusing on a problem of concern to both health professionals and native healers: infant diarrheal diseases. These had recently become a health problem of high concern to the general public; healers wanted a means to prevent such diseases, and a means of treatment existed—oral rehydration therapy—that was compatible with traditional treatments for diarrhea (herbal preparations taken orally over a period of time). Packets of oral rehydration salts, along with instructions, were provided to healers in a pilot project, with positive results. This helped convince health professionals of the benefits of cooperation, while the healers saw the distribution of packets to them as a gesture of trust and cooperation on the part of their government.

Since then, further steps toward cooperation have been taken, such as work in prevention of AIDS, STDs, and TB. All of this demonstrates the importance of finding how to work in ways compatible with existing belief systems. Directly challenging traditional beliefs, as all too often happens, does little more than create stress, confusion, and resentment among people.

(See E. C. Green (1987). The planning of health education strategies in Swaziland, and the integration of modern and traditional health sectors in Swaziland. In R. M. Wulff & S. J. Fiske (Eds.), Anthropological praxis: Translating knowledge into action (pp. 15–25, 87–97). Boulder, CO: Westview Press.)

of isolation, and, finally, formal return and readmission back into society in his or her new status.

This sequence of stages is something that takes place in many forms in all cultures around the world, from military boot camps to college fraternity and sorority initiation ceremonies in the United States to a global array of puberty ceremonies that mark the transition from childhood to adulthood. For example, take the male initiation rites of the Aborigines of Australia. When the elders decide the time for initiation, the boys are taken from the village (separation), while the women cry and make a ritual show of resistance. At a place distant from the camp, groups of men from many villages gather. The elders sing and dance, while the initiates act as though they are dead. The climax of this part of the ritual is a bodily operation, such as circumcision or the knocking out of a tooth. Australian anthropologist A. P. Elkin comments:

This is partly a continuation of the drama of death. The tooth-knocking, circumcision or other symbolical act "killed" the novice; after this he does not return to the general camp and normally may not be seen by any woman. He is dead to the ordinary life of the tribe.[8]

In this transitional stage, the novice may be shown secret ceremonies and receive some instruction, but the most significant element is his complete removal from society. In the course of these Australian puberty rites, the initiate must learn the lore that all adult men are expected to know; he is given, in effect, a "cram course." The trauma of the occasion is a pedagogical technique that ensures he will learn and remember everything; in a nonliterate society the perpetuation of cultural traditions requires no less, and so effective teaching methods are necessary.

On his return to society (incorporation), the novice is welcomed with ceremonies, as though he had returned from the dead. This alerts the society at large to the individual's new status—that people can expect him to act in certain ways, and in return they must act in the appropriate ways toward him. The individual's new rights and duties are thus clearly defined. He is spared, for example, the problems of a teenager in North America, a time when an individual is neither adult nor child, a person whose status is ill defined.

In the Australian case just cited, boys are prepared not just for adulthood but also for *manhood*. In their society, for example, courage and endurance are considered important masculine virtues, and the pain of tooth-knocking and circumcision help instill these in initiates. In a similar way, female initiation rites help prepare Mende girls in West Africa for womanhood. After they have begun to menstruate, the girls are removed from society to spend weeks, or even months, in seclusion. There they discard the clothes of childhood, smear their bodies with white clay, and dress in short skirts and many strands of beads.

Shortly after entering this transitional stage, the girls undergo clitoridectomy, a form of female circumcision that they and Mende in general believe enhances their reproductive potential. Until their incorporation back into society, they are trained in the moral and practical responsibilities of potential child bearers by experienced women in the Sande association, an organization to which the initiates will belong once their training has ended. This training is not all harsh, however, for it is accompanied by a good deal of singing, dancing, and storytelling, and the initiates are very well fed. Thus, they acquire both a positive image of womanhood and a strong sense of sisterhood. Once their training is complete, a medicine made by brewing leaves in water is used for a ritual washing, removing the magical protection that has shielded them during the period of their confinement.

Mende women emerge from their initiation, then, as women in knowledgeable control of their sexuality, eligible for marriage and childbearing. The pain and danger of the surgery, endured in the context of intense social support from other women, serves as a metaphor for childbirth, which may well take place in the same place of seclusion, again with the support of women in the Sande association. It also has been suggested that, symbolically, the clitoridectomy (excision of the clitoris, the feminine version of the penis) removes sexual ambiguity.[9] Having gone through this ritual, a traditional Mende woman knows she is "all woman." Thus we have symbolic expression of gender as something important in people's cultural lives.

Anthropological commitment to cultural relativism permits an understanding of the practice of clitoridectomy in the Mende female initiation rites. However, as discussed early on in this book, cultural relativism does not preclude the anthropologist from criticizing a given practice. Apart from the pain and the effect of the operation on a woman's future sexual satisfaction, significant numbers of young women die from excessive bleeding, shock, various infections, or damage to the urethra or anus brought on by the procedure. Others face later risks when giving birth as scar tissue tears.

Not surprisingly, female circumcision—commonly referred to as female genital mutilation (FGM) and practiced in various forms in Asia and Africa especially—has been much condemned as a human rights violation in recent years. Committees to end the practice have been set up in twenty-two African countries.[10] (Notably, women's breast implant surgery has been compared to FGM as Western industrialized society's version of what it takes to be "all woman." The Original Study in the final chapter of this book addresses this issue in detail.)

Rites of Intensification

Rites of intensification are rituals that take place during a crisis in the life of the group and serve to bind individuals together. Whatever the precise nature of the crisis—a

---

[8]Elkin, A. P. (1964). *The Australian Aborigines*. Garden City, NY: Doubleday/Anchor Books.

[9]MacCormack, C. P. (1977). Biological events and cultural control. *Signs 3*, 98.

[10]Female genital mutilation. (2000). Fact sheet no. 241. World Health Organization; Dirie, W., & Miller, C. (1998). *Desert flower: The extraordinary journey of a desert nomad* (pp. 218, 219). New York: William Morrow.

rite of intensification A ritual that takes place during a crisis in the life of the group and serves to bind individuals together.

drought that threatens crops, the sudden appearance of an enemy war party, the onset of an epidemic—mass ceremonies are performed to ease the sense of danger. This unites people in a common effort so that fear and confusion yield to collective action and a degree of optimism. The balance in the relations of all concerned is restored to normal, and the community's values are celebrated and affirmed.

While an individual's death might be regarded as the ultimate crisis in that person's life, it is, as well, a crisis for the entire group, particularly if the group is small. A member of the community has been removed, so its composition has been seriously altered. The survivors, therefore, must readjust and restore balance. They also need to reconcile themselves to the loss of someone to whom they were emotionally tied.

Funerary ceremonies, then, can be regarded as rites of intensification that permit the living to express in nondisruptive ways their upset over the death while providing for social readjustment. Frequently such ceremonies feature ambivalence toward the dead person. For example, one part of the funerary rites of certain Melanesians was the eating of the dead person's flesh. This ritual can-

Ritual cannibalism appears in various societies in diverse forms. In Christianity, it is symbolic rather than actual, although millions of orthodox believers subscribe to the doctrine of transubstantiation, which holds that in Holy Communion the consecrated red wine and wafer or bread actually change into the divine blood and flesh of Christ, the Son of God.

nibalism, witnessed by anthropologist Malinowski, was performed with "extreme repugnance and dread and usually followed by a violent vomiting fit. At the same time it is felt to be a supreme act of reverence, love, and devotion."[11] This custom and the emotions accompanying it clearly reveal an ambiguous attitude toward death: On the one hand, there is the survivors' desire to maintain the tie to the dead person, and, on the other hand, they feel disgust and fear at the transformation wrought by death. According to Malinowski, funeral ceremonies provide an approved collective means for individuals to express these feelings while maintaining social cohesiveness and preventing disruption of society.

The performance of rites of intensification does not have to be limited to times of overt crisis. In regions where the seasons differ enough that human activities must change accordingly, they will take the form of annual ceremonies. These are particularly common among horticultural and agricultural people, with their planting and harvest ceremonies. These are critical times in the lives of people in such societies, and the ceremonies express a reverent attitude toward nature's forces of generation and fertility upon which people's very existence depends.

Participation in rituals of reverence and celebration during planting and harvest seasons reinforces group involvement. It also serves as a kind of dress rehearsal for crisis situations by promoting the habit of relying on supernatural forces—a habit that may make a crucial difference under stressful circumstances when it is important not to give way to fear and despair.

MAGIC

Among the most fascinating of ritual practices is application of the belief that supernatural powers can be compelled to act in certain ways for good or evil purposes by recourse to certain specified formulas. This is a classical anthropological notion of magic. Many societies have magical rituals to ensure good crops, the replenishment of game, the fertility of domestic animals, and the avoidance or healing of illness in humans.

Although many Western peoples today—seeking to objectify and demythologize their world—have tried to suppress magic mysteries in their own consciousness, they continue to be fascinated by them. Not only are books and films about demonic possession and witchcraft avidly devoured and discussed, but horoscope columns are a regular feature of daily newspapers in the United States. And magical rituals are still commonly practiced by many Westerners seeking some "luck"

[11]Malinowski, B. (1954). *Magic, science, and religion* (p. 50). Garden City, NY: Doubleday.

where the outcome is in doubt or beyond factual influence—from lighting a votive candle for someone going through a hard time, to wearing lucky boxers on a hot date, to the curious gesturing baseball pitchers do before each throw.

While it may raise few eyebrows that Abraham Lincoln's wife invited psychics to the White House, it caused a considerable stir when it was learned that President Reagan's wife regularly conferred with an astrologer. As for psychics or spirit mediums, they are consulted by growing numbers of people in the United States today. A 1996 Gallup poll found that 20 percent of the respondents believed the dead could contact the living, and another 22 percent thought it might be possible. Anthropologist Lauren Kendall notes,

> Many witches, wizards, druids, Cabalists, and shamans . . . practice modern magic in contemporary England and the United States, where their ranks are comfortably reckoned in the tens of thousands. . . . The usual magician is ordinary, generally middle class, and often highly intelligent—a noticeable number of them have something to do with computers.[12]

In the 19th century Scottish anthropologist Sir James George Frazer made a useful distinction between two fundamental principles of magic. The first principle, that "like produces like," he named **imitative magic** (sometimes called *sympathetic magic*). In Burma (Myanmar) in Southeast Asia, for example, a rejected lover might engage a sorcerer to make an image of his would-be love. If this image were tossed into water, to the accompaniment of certain charms, it was expected that the hapless girl would go mad. Thus, the girl would suffer a fate similar to that of her image.

Frazer called the second principle of thought on which magic is based **contagious magic**—the idea that things or persons once in contact can influence each other after the contact is broken. The most common example of contagious magic is the permanent relationship between an individual and any part of his or her body, such as hair, fingernails, or teeth. Frazer cited the Basutos of Lesotho in southern Africa, who were careful to conceal their extracted teeth, because these might fall into the hands of certain mythical beings who could harm the owners of the teeth by working magic on them. Related to this is the custom, in Western societies, of treasuring things that have been touched by special people. Such things range from a saint's relics to possessions of other admired or idolized individuals, such as the U.S. basketball star Michael Jordan or England's rock musician Mick Jagger of the Rolling Stones.

A hundred-year old carved wooden figure from the Congo believed to have magical powers. During a special ritual, based on the principle of imitative magic, iron nails were driven into this traditional African fetish with the motive of causing pain, disease, or even death to someone feared or detested.

WITCHCRAFT

In Salem, Massachusetts, 200 innocent citizens suspected of being witches were arrested in 1692; of these, thirteen women and six men were hanged, and one 80-year-old farmer was tortured to death. Despite awarding damages to descendants of some of the victims nineteen

---

imitative magic Magic based on the principle that like produces like; sometimes called sympathetic magic.
contagious magic Magic based on the principle that things or persons once in contact can influence each other after the contact is broken.

years later, it was not until 1957 that the last of the Salem witches were exonerated by the Massachusetts legislature. **Witchcraft** is an explanation of events based on the belief that certain individuals possess an innate psychic power capable of causing harm, including sickness and death.

Although many North Americans suppose it to be something that belongs to a less enlightened past, witchcraft is alive and well in the United States today. Indeed, starting in the 1960s, a "witch cult" known as Wicca began to undergo something of a boom in this country, including among highly educated segments of society. And, contrary to popular belief, the self-styled witches belonging to this neo-pagan religion are *not* concerned with "working evil."

Ibibio Witchcraft

North Americans are by no means alone in this. For example, as the Ibibio of Nigeria have become increasingly exposed to modern education and scientific training, their reliance on witchcraft as an explanation for misfortune has increased.[13] Furthermore, it is often the younger, more educated members of Ibibio society who accuse others of bewitching them. Frequently, the accused are older, more traditional members of society; thus, we have an expression of the intergenerational hostility that often exists in fast-changing traditional societies.

Ibibio witchcraft beliefs are highly developed and long-standing—as they are among most traditional peoples of sub-Saharan Africa. A rat that eats a person's crops is not really a rat but a witch that changed into one; if a young and enterprising man cannot get a job or fails an exam, he has been bewitched; if someone's money is wasted or if the person becomes sick, is bitten by a snake, or is struck by lightning, the reason is always the same—witchcraft.

Indeed, traditional Ibibio attribute virtually all misfortune, illness, or death to the malevolent activity of witches. The modern Ibibio's knowledge about the role microorganisms play in disease has little impact on this; after all, it says nothing about why these were sent to the afflicted individual. Although Ibibio religious beliefs provide alternative explanations for misfortune, those carry negative connotations and do not elicit nearly as

much sympathy from others. Thus, if evil befalls a person, witchcraft is a far more satisfying explanation than something such as offspring disobedience or violation of a taboo.

Ibibio witches are thought to be men or women who have within them a special substance acquired from another established witch. From swallowing this substance—made up of needles, colored threads, and other ingredients—one is believed to become endowed with a special power that causes injury, even death, to others regardless of whether its possessor intends harm or not. The power is purely psychic, and witches do not perform rites or make use of "bad medicine." It is believed to give them the ability to transform into animals and travel any distance at incredible speed to get at their unsuspecting victims, whom they may torture or kill by transferring the victim's soul or vital spirit into an animal, which is then eaten.

To identify a witch, an Ibibio looks for any person living in the region whose behavior is considered odd, out of the ordinary, immoral, or unsocial. Any combination of the following may cause someone to be labeled a witch: not being fond of greeting people; living alone in a place apart from others; charging too high a price for something; enjoying adultery or committing incest; walking about at night; not showing sufficient grief upon the death of a relative or other member of the community; taking improper care of one's parents, children, or wives; and hard-heartedness. Witches are apt to look and act mean and to be socially disruptive people in the sense that their behavior exceeds the range of variance considered acceptable.

The Ibibio make a distinction between *sorcerers*, whose acts are especially diabolical and destructive, and benign *witches*, whose witchcraft is relatively harmless, even though their powers are thought to be greater than those of their malevolent counterparts. Sorcerers are the very embodiment of a society's conception of evil—beings that flout the rules of sexual behavior and disregard

---

[13]Offiong, D. (1985). Witchcraft among the Ibibio of Nigeria. In A. C. Lehmann & J. E. Myers (Eds.), *Magic, witchcraft, and religion* (pp. 152–165). Palo Alto, CA: Mayfield.

witchcraft An explanation of events based on the belief that certain individuals possess an innate psychic power capable of causing harm, including sickness and death.

In North America, interest in and practice of witchcraft have grown significantly over the past thirty years, often among highly educated segments of society. Contrary to popular belief, witchcraft is *not* concerned exclusively, or even primarily, with working evil.

every other standard of decency. Benign witches are often the community's nonconformists. Typically, they are morose, arrogant, and unfriendly people who keep to themselves but otherwise cause little disturbance. Such witches are thought to be dangerous when offended— likely to retaliate by causing sickness, death, crop failure, cattle disease, or any number of lesser ills. Not surprisingly, people viewed as witches are usually treated with considerable caution, respect, and even fear.[14]

The Functions of Witchcraft

Why witchcraft? We might better ask, why not? In a world where there are few proven techniques for dealing with everyday crises, especially sickness, a belief in witches is not foolish; it is indispensable.[15] No one wants to resign oneself to illness, and if the malady is caused

by a witch's curse, then magical countermeasures should cure it.

Not only does the idea of personalized evil answer the problem of unmerited suffering, but it also provides an explanation for many happenings for which no cause can be discovered. Witchcraft, then, cannot be refuted. Even if we could convince a person that his or her illness was due to natural causes, the victim would still ask, as the Ibibio do, Why me? Why now? Such a view leaves no room for pure chance; everything must be assigned a cause or meaning. Witchcraft offers an explanation and, in so doing, also provides both the basis and the means for taking counteraction.

Nor is witchcraft always entirely harmful. Its positive functions are noted in many African societies where people traditionally believe sickness, death, or other harm may be caused by witches. If people in the community agree that evildoing magic is in play, the ensuing search for the perpetrator of the misfortune becomes, in effect, a communal probe into dysfunctional social behavior. A witch-hunt is, in fact, a systematic investigation, through a public hearing, into all social relationships involving the victim of the sickness or death. Was a husband or wife unfaithful or a son lacking in the performance of his duties? Were an individual's friends uncooperative, or was the victim guilty of any of these wrongs? Accusations are reciprocal, and before long just about every unsocial or hostile act that has occurred in that society since the last outbreak of witchcraft (as manifested in sickness, death, or some other misfortune) is brought into the open.[16]

Through such periodic public scrutiny of everyone's behavior, people are reminded of what their society regards as both strengths and weaknesses of character. This encourages individuals to suppress as best they can those personality traits that are looked upon with disapproval, for if they do not, they at some time may be accused of being a witch. A belief in witchcraft thus serves a function of social control.

Witchcraft among the Navajo

Widely known among American Indians are the Navajo of the southwestern United States, who possess a highly developed concept of witchcraft. Several types of witchcraft are distinguished. *Witchery* encompasses the practices of witches, who are said to meet at night to practice cannibalism and kill people at a distance. *Sorcery* is distinguished from witchery only by the methods used by the sorcerer, who casts spells on individuals using the victim's fingernails, hair, or discarded clothing. *Wizardry* is not distinguished so much by its effects as by its manner of working: Wizards kill by injecting a cursed

[14]See Mair, L. (1969). *Witchcraft* (p. 37). New York: McGraw-Hill.

[15]Mair, L. (1969). *Witchcraft*. New York: McGraw-Hill.

[16]Turnbull, C. M. (1983). *The human cycle* (p. 181). New York: Simon & Schuster.

substance, such as a tooth from a corpse, into the victim's body.

Whether or not a particular illness results from Navajo witchcraft is determined by **divination**—a magical procedure or spiritual ritual designed to find out about what is not knowable by ordinary means. Once a person is charged with witchcraft, he or she is publicly interrogated—in the past, possibly even tortured until there is a confession. It is believed the witch's own curse will turn against the witch once this happens, so it is expected that the witch will die within a year. Some confessed witches have been allowed to live in exile.

According to Clyde Kluckhohn, Navajo witchcraft serves to channel anxieties, tensions, and frustrations caused by the pressures from Euramericans.[17] The rigid rules of proper behavior among the Navajo allow little means for expression of hostility, except through accusations of witchcraft. Such accusations funnel pent-up negative emotions against individuals without upsetting the wider society. Another function of witchcraft accusations is that they permit direct expression of hostile feelings against people toward whom one ordinarily would be unable to express anger or enmity.

On a more positive note, individuals strive to behave in ways that will prevent them from being accused of witchcraft. Since excessive wealth is believed to result from witchcraft, individuals are encouraged to redistribute their assets among friends and relatives, thereby leveling economic differences. Similarly, because the Navajo believe elders, if neglected, will turn into witches, people are strongly motivated to take care of aged relatives. And because leaders are thought to be witches, people are understandably reluctant to go against their wishes, lest they suffer supernatural retribution.

The Consequences of Witchcraft

Anthropological research suggests that witchcraft, in spite of its often negative image, frequently functions in a very positive way to manage tensions within a society. Nonetheless, events may get out of hand, particularly in crisis situations, when widespread accusations may cause great suffering. This certainly was the case in the Salem witch trials, but even those pale in comparison to the half a million individuals executed as witches in Europe from the 15th through the 17th centuries. This was a time of profound change in European societies, marked

by a good deal of political and religious conflict. At such times, it is all too easy to search out scapegoats to blame for what people believe are undesirable changes.

THE FUNCTIONS OF RELIGION

Just as belief in witchcraft may serve a variety of psychological and social functions, so too do religious beliefs and practices in general. Here we may summarize these functions in a somewhat more systematic way.

One psychological function is to provide an orderly model of the universe, which plays a key role in establishing orderly human behavior. Through special stories, or myths, people find answers to important questions such as: What does the universe look like, how does it work, and what is my place in it? To many Euramericans, the word *myth* conjures up the idea of an invented story about imaginary events, something that did not factually happen. This is not true for those people for whom a particular myth comprises part of their worldview. To them myths are sacred and true stories, not unlike historical documents in contemporary European or North American culture. And even in these literate societies, myths exist, such as the accounts of creation in the Book of Genesis. Invariably, myths are full of accounts about the doings of various supernatural beings and thus serve to reinforce beliefs in them.

Beyond this, by explaining the unknown and making it understandable, religion reduces the fears and anxieties of individuals. As we have seen, these explanations typically assume the existence of supernatural beings and powers, which people may potentially appeal to or manipulate as a means for dealing with crises. Thus, at least theoretically, divine aid is available when all else fails.

A social function of religion is to prompt reflection concerning conduct. In this context, religion plays a role in social control, which, as we saw in the last chapter, does not rely on law alone. This is done through notions of right and wrong, good and evil. Right actions earn the approval of whatever supernatural powers are recognized by a particular culture. Wrong actions may cause revenge or punishment through supernatural agencies. In short, by deliberately *raising* people's feelings of guilt and anxiety about their actions, religion helps keep them in line.

Religion does more than this, though; it sets guidelines for acceptable behavior. We have noted already the connection between myths and religion. Usually, myths feature tales of extraordinary or supernatural beings that in various ways illustrate the society's ethical code in action. So it is that Gluskabe, the Penobscot Indian culture hero, is portrayed in that society's traditions as tricking and punishing those who lie, mock others, behave

---

[17]Kluckhohn, C. (1944). Navajo witchcraft. *Papers of the Peabody Museum of American Archaeology and Ethnology 22* (2).

divination   A magical procedure or spiritual ritual designed to find out about what is not knowable by ordinary means, such as foretelling the future by interpreting omens.

Buddhist monk prostrating in front of Jokhang temple in Lhasa, Tibet. Some religious devotees prostrate themselves for hours or days in an effort to demonstrate humility, transcend pain, and seek enlightenment. Some who make pilgrimages to sacred sites crawl the distance in a ritually prescribed ordeal for similar reasons.

greedily, overreact, or engage in other behaviors deemed inappropriate in Penobscot culture. Moreover, the specific situations relayed in myths serve as guidelines for human behavior in similar circumstances. The Old and New Testaments of the Bible are rich in the same sort of material, as is the Koran. Related to this, by the models religion presents and the morals it espouses, religion serves to justify and perpetuate a particular social order. Thus, in the Jewish, Christian, and Islamic traditions, a masculine-authoritarian godhead along with a creation story that portrays a woman as responsible for a fall from grace serve to justify a social order in which men exercise control over women.

A psychological function also is tied up in this. A society's moral code, since it is considered to be divinely ordained, lifts the burden of responsibility for conduct from the shoulders of the society's individual members, at least in important situations. It can be a tremendous relief to individuals to know that the responsibility for

the way things are rests with the gods or spirit forces rather than with themselves.

Another social function of religion is its role in the maintenance of social solidarity. In our discussion of shamans, we saw how such individuals provide focal points of interest, thus supplying one ingredient of assistance for maintaining group unity. In addition, common participation in rituals, coupled with a basic uniformity of beliefs, helps to bind people together and reinforce their identification with their group. Particularly effective may be their joint participation in rituals, when the atmosphere is charged with emotion. The ecstatic feelings people may experience in such circumstances serve as a positive reinforcement in that they feel good as a result. Here, once again, we find religion providing psychological assurance while fulfilling the needs of society.

One other area in which religion serves a social function is education. In our discussion of rites of passage, we noted that puberty rituals of Aborigines in Australia served as a kind of cram course in traditional lore. By providing a memorable occasion, initiation rites can enhance learning and so help ensure the perpetuation of a nonliterate culture. And as we saw in the female initiation rites among the Mende, they ensure that individuals have the knowledge they will need to fulfill their adult roles in society.

Education also may be served by rites of intensification. Frequently, such rites involve dramas that portray matters of cultural importance. For example, among a food-foraging people, dances may imitate the movement of game and techniques of hunting. Among farmers a fixed round of ceremonies may emphasize the steps necessary for good crops. All of this helps preserve knowledge important to a people's material well-being, gives expression to their worldview, and thereby reinforces their collective self-understanding.

In addition to all of the above, people often turn to religion in the hope of reaching a specific goal, such as the healing of physical, emotional, or social ills—as illustrated in this chapter's Original Study and the Anthropology Applied features.

RELIGION AND CULTURE CHANGE: REVITALIZATION MOVEMENTS

No anthropological consideration of religion is complete without some mention of **revitalization movements**—movements for radical culture reform in response to

revitalization movement A movement for radical cultural reform in response to widespread social disruption and collective feelings of great stress and despair.

A Sufi *sema* (prayer dance) in Istanbul, Turkey. Sufism, a mystical Muslim movement that emerged in the late 10th century, borrowing ideas from Buddhism, Christianity, and Neoplatonism, emphasizes the surrender of individual ego and attachment to worldly things in order to be receptive to God's grace. Known as "Whirling Dervishes," these Sufi dancers are part of the Mevlevi brotherhood founded by Mevlana Rumi in the 13th century. According to Mevlevi tradition, during the *sema* the soul is freed from earthly ties and able to jubilantly commune with the divine. (*Dervish* literally means "doorway" and is thought to be an entrance from the material world to the spiritual.) The felt hat represents personal ego's tombstone, and the wide skirt symbolizes its shroud.

widespread social disruption and collective feelings of great stress and despair. Many such movements developed in indigenous societies where European colonial exploitation caused enormous upheaval.

Among the various types of revitalization movements is the **cargo cult**—a spiritual movement (especially noted in Melanesia in the Southwest Pacific) in reaction to disruptive contact with Western capitalism, promising resurrection of deceased relatives, destruction or enslavement of white foreigners, and the magical arrival of utopian riches. Indigenous Melanesians referred to the white man's wealth as "cargo" (pidgin English for European trade goods). In times of great social stress, native prophets emerged, predicting that the time of suffering would come to an end, and a new paradise on earth would soon arrive. Their deceased ancestors would return to life, and the rich white man would magically disappear—swallowed by an earthquake or swept away by a huge wave. However, their cargo would be left for the

prophets and their cult followers who performed rituals to hasten this supernatural redistribution of wealth.[18]

One of many cargo cults took place in 1931 at Buka, in the Solomon Islands (in the Pacific Ocean). A native religious movement suddenly emerged there when prophets predicted that a deluge would soon engulf all whites, and a ship would then arrive filled with Western industrial commodities. The prophets told their followers to construct a storehouse for the goods and to prepare themselves to repulse the colonial police. They also spread word that the ship would come only after the natives had used up all their own supplies, and for this reason believers ceased working in the fields. Although the leaders of the movement were arrested, the cult continued for some years.

As deliberate efforts to construct a more satisfying culture, revitalization movements aim to reform not just the religious sphere of activity but an entire cultural system. Such drastic measures are taken when a group's anxiety and frustration have become so intense that the

---

cargo cult A spiritual movement (especially noted in Melanesia) in reaction to disruptive contact with Western capitalism, promising resurrection of deceased relatives, destruction or enslavement of white foreigners, and the magical arrival of utopian riches.

[18]For more on cargo cults, see Lindstrom, L. (1993). *Cargo cult: Strange stories of desire from Melanesia and beyond.* Honolulu: University of Hawaii Press; and Worsley, P. (1957). *The trumpet shall sound: A study of "cargo" cults in Melanesia.* London: Macgibbon & Kee.

only way to reduce the stress is to overturn the entire social system and replace it with a new one. From the cargo cults of Melanesia to the 1890 Ghost Dance of many North American Indians to the Mau Mau of the Kikuyu in Kenya in the 1950s, extreme and sometimes violent religious reactions to European domination are so common that anthropologists have sought to formulate their underlying causes and general characteristics.

Revitalization movements are by no means restricted to the colonial world, and in the United States alone hundreds of them have sprung up. These range from Mormonism, which began in the 19th century, to the more recent Unification Church led by Reverend Sun Myung Moon, the Branch Davidians led by Seventh-Day Adventist prophet David Koresh, and the Black Muslims led by Prophet Elijah Muhammad. Recent U.S. revitalization movements also include the American Indian revival of the spectacular Sun Dance ceremony, now held each summer at various reservations in the Great Plains.

Anthropologist Anthony Wallace outlined a sequence common to all expressions of the revitalization process.[19] First is the normal state of society, in which stress is not too great, and sufficient cultural means exist to satisfy needs. Under certain conditions, such as domination by a more powerful group or severe economic depression, stress and frustration are steadily amplified; this ushers in the second phase, or period of increased individual stress. If there are no significant adaptive changes, a period of cultural distortion follows in which stress becomes so chronic that socially approved methods of releasing tension begin to break down. This steady deterioration of the culture may be checked by a period of revitalization, during which a dynamic cult or religious movement grips a sizable portion of the population.

Sometimes the movement will be so out of touch with existing circumstances that it is doomed to failure from the beginning. This was the case with the Heaven's Gate cult, which mixed bits and pieces of apocalyptic Christian beliefs predicting destruction of the world at the end of the millennium with folk myths of contemporary North American culture, in particular those having to do with UFOs (alien spaceships). Its followers commit-

---

[19]Wallace, A. F. C. (1970). *Culture and personality* (2nd ed., pp. 191–196). New York: Random House.

ted mass suicide out of a conviction that their spiritual essences would reunite with higher extraterrestrial beings in a spaceship that awaited them behind the tail of the Hale-Bopp comet, ready to take them "home." A similar case of self-destruction took place among the Branch Davidians, whose hostility toward government authorities prompted an official assault on the cult's compound in Waco, Texas. In reaction, cult members set fire to their own headquarters, sending their movement and their lives up in flames.

More rarely, a movement may tap long-dormant adaptive forces underlying a culture, and an enduring religion may result. Such was the case with Mormonism. Though heavily persecuted at first and hounded from place to place, Mormons adapted to the point that their religion thrives in the United States today. Indeed, revitalization movements lie at the root of all known religions—Judaism, Christianity, and Islam included.

In Africa, during and following the period of foreign colonization and missionization, indigenous groups resisted or creatively revised Christian teachings and formed culturally appropriate religious movements. Since the 1970s, thousands of indigenous Christian churches have been founded, often born of alternative theological interpretations, new divinely inspired revelations, or cultural disagreements between African Christians and European or North American missionaries over the extent to which traditional African practices (such as animism, ancestor worship, and polygamy) were permissible. Today the African continent is as religiously diverse as ever. Although at least 40 percent of the population is Christian and more than another 40 percent is Muslim, African indigenous religious traditions persist and are often merged with Christianity and Islam.

Persistence of Religion

From the ongoing need to make sense of their existence, humans continue to explore metaphysically or spiritually as well as scientifically. All around the globe we see indications of the effort, not only in buildings and other structures created for religious purposes but in natural places that people have designated as sacred sites. The search for meaning is also evident in many works of art, as discussed in the next chapter.

Questions for Reflection

1. Beyond biological survival, humans face mental challenges born of the need to make meaningful sense of their existence. Do you ever ponder questions such as the meaning of your life and big issues such as the origin or destiny of the human species? How does your culture, including your religious or spiritual beliefs, offer you guidance in finding meaningful answers to such big questions?

2. You have read about female genital mutilation as a rite of passage in some cultures. Do you know of any genital mutilation practices in your society? Why are so many boys in the United States circumcised immediately after their birth?

3. Do the basic dynamics of the shamanic complex also apply to preachers or priests in modern churches and medical doctors working in modern hospitals? Can you think of some similarities among the shaman, preacher, and medical doctor in terms of their respective fields of operation?

4. Revitalization movements occur in reaction to the upheavals caused by rapid colonization and modernization. Do you think that the rise of Christian fundamentalism in the North American Bible Belt today is a response to such upheavals as well?

5. In postindustrial societies such as western Europe, the United States, and Canada, there is growing interest in shamanism and alternative healing techniques. Is there any relationship between globalization and this phenomenon?

Suggested Readings

Behrend, H., & Luig, U. (Eds.). (2000). *Spirit possession, modernity, and power in Africa.* Madison: University of Wisconsin Press.

This fascinating collection investigates how African spirit possession cults respond to local circumstances in a globalizing world. Contributors focus on power, histories, gender roles, and images of the Other in shaping these beliefs and practices, introducing pantheons of new holy spirits—such as spirits of airplanes and guitars in Central Africa or Christian spirits with names like "Hitler" fighting against the government of Uganda.

Bowen, J. R. (2004). *Religions in practice: An approach to the anthropology of religion* (3rd ed.). Boston: Allyn & Bacon.

Investigates how people from an array of spiritual traditions engage in special and everyday religious practices (prayer, sacrifice, pilgrimage, dress, rituals related to death) and discusses major issues of gender, states, and laws with respect to religion. Includes a review of religious studies theories from Hegel and Tylor to Geertz.

Bowie, F. (2006). *The anthropology of religion: An introduction* (2nd ed.). Malden, MA: Blackwell.

This readable introductory text presents the central theoretical ideas in the anthropology of religion, illustrating them with specific case studies. This edition features new chapters on mythology and pilgrimage, plus coverage of topics such as spirit possession and cargo cults.

Lambek, Michael (2002). *A reader in the anthropology of religion.* London: Blackwell.

This ambitious reader encompasses the breadth, depth, and complexity of anthropology's investigations into religion—

and aims to create a conversation between Western and non-Western cultures, as well as between anthropology and other disciplines in the social sciences and humanities. It features a general introduction, a comprehensive range of classical and recent readings, and an extensive bibliography that is indexed according to both ethnographic region and religious topics and practices.

Stein, R. L., & Stein, P. L. (2004). *Anthropology of religion, magic, and witchcraft.* Boston: Allyn & Bacon.

This concise introductory text emphasizes the major concepts of anthropology in general and the anthropology of religion in particular. Concepts are illustrated primarily with examples drawn from tribal or traditional societies, but the "world's great religions" are also included.

Tedlock, B. (2005). *The woman in the shaman's body: Reclaiming the feminine in religion and medicine.* New York: Random House.

Tracing the history of shamanism around the globe and illuminating the roles of women, the author integrates scholarship and her personal experience as a practicing shaman.

Thomson Audio Study Products

 Enjoy the MP3-ready Audio Lecture Overviews for each chapter and a comprehensive audio glossary of key terms for quick study and review. Whether walking to class, doing laundry, or studying at your desk, you now have the freedom to choose when, where, and how you interact with your audio-based educational media. See the preface for information on how to access this on-the-go study and review tool.

The Anthropology Resource Center

www.thomsonedu.com/anthropology
The Anthropology Resource Center provides extended learning materials to reinforce your understanding of key concepts in the four fields of anthropology. For each of the four fields, the Resource Center includes dynamic exercises including video exercises, map exercises, simulations, and "Meet the Scientists" interviews, as well as critical thinking questions that can be assigned and e-mailed to instructors. The Resource Center also provides breaking news in anthropology and interesting material on applied anthropology to help you link what you are learning to the world around you.

25 The Arts

© Vince Hemingson

CHALLENGE ISSUE

Humans in all cultures throughout time face the challenge of creatively articulating their feelings and ideas about themselves and the world around them. Although not all societies distinguish "art" as a special cultural domain, people everywhere have developed aesthetic forms—visual, verbal, musical, movement, and so on—to symbolically express, appreciate, and share experiences of beauty in all its variety. Several art forms are represented in this photo—dance, music, weaving, beadwork, and tattoos. Tattooing—puncturing and ingraining with indelible pigment the skin with special designs—is a widespread form of body art practiced by humans for thousands of years.

What Is Art?

Although difficult to define, art may be understood as the creative use of the human imagination to aesthetically interpret, express, and engage life, modifying experienced reality in the process. Many contemporary Western peoples consider art as exclusively aesthetic, serving no practical purpose, but most societies past and present have used art to give meaningful expression to almost every part of their culture, including ideas about religion, kinship, and ethnic identity. In fact, almost anything humans can lay their hands on can become an object of artistic creativity— skin, hair, dress, dwellings, vehicles, weapons, utensils, and so on.

Why Do Anthropologists Study Art?

Anthropologists have found that art often reflects a society's collective ideas, values, and concerns. From myths, songs, dances, paintings, carvings, and so on, anthropologists may learn how a people imagine their reality and understand themselves as well as other beings around them. Through the cross-cultural study of art and creativity, we discover much about different worldviews, religious beliefs, political ideas, social values, kinship structures, economic relations, and historical memory as well.

What Are the Functions of Art?

Aside from adding beauty and pleasure to everyday life, art serves a number of functions. Myths, for example, may offer basic explanations about the world and set cultural standards for right behavior. The verbal arts generally transmit and preserve a culture's customs and values. Songs, too, may do this within the structures imposed by musical form. And any art form, to the degree that it is characteristic of a particular society, may contribute to the cohesiveness or solidarity of that society. Yet, art may also express political themes and be used to influence events and create social change. Often it is created for religious purposes, to honor or beseech the aid of a divine power, a sacred being, an ancestral spirit, or an animal spirit.

Humans in all cultures throughout time have expressed feelings and ideas about themselves and the world around them through **art**—the creative use of the human imagination to aesthetically interpret, express, and engage life, modifying experienced reality in the process. It comes in many forms: visual, verbal, musical, dance, and so on. Most societies, past and present, have used art to symbolically express almost every part of their culture, including ideas about religion, kinship, and ethnic identity.

In North America, the arts often are seen as a luxury, an aesthetic pleasure that people engage in for personal or collective enjoyment quite apart from more useful or productive pursuits. This attitude becomes apparent whenever public funds are in short supply. On the local level, for example, in battles over school budgets, art programs are often the first to be cut. On the national level, fiscal conservatives repeatedly seek to curb funds for theater performances, museum exhibits, concerts, and other fine arts to be enjoyed by the general public on the premise that these lack the practical importance of roads, sewers, police, warplanes, office bureaucracies, and other governmental priorities.

THOMSON AUDIO STUDY PRODUCTS Take advantage of the MP3-ready Audio Lecture Overviews and comprehensive audio glossary of key terms for each chapter. See the preface for information on how to access this on-the-go study and review tool.

Indeed, a significant portion of the society views artists and their supporters as an elite group subsidized at the expense of "practical" tax-paying citizens. This is due in large part to the rather recent Western concept of *fine art* as a distinct cultural category of art for art's sake, unrelated to society at large but relished by specialists and wealthy collectors who chatter about, purchase, or even commission works of art for enjoyment in the privacy of their homes or showings in selective galleries and museums.

The idea of art serving purely aesthetic but non-practical purposes seems firmly entrenched in the thinking of many contemporary Western peoples. Today, for example, the objects from the ancient tomb of the young Egyptian king Tutankhamen are on display in a museum, where they may be seen and admired as the exquisite works of art that they are. They were made, however, not for human eyes but to guarantee the eternal life of the king and protect him from evil forces that might enter his body and gain control over it.

art The creative use of the human imagination to aesthetically interpret, express, and engage life, modifying experienced reality in the process.

Similarly, we may listen to the singing of a sea chantey purely for aesthetic pleasure, as a form of entertainment. But, in fact, in the days of sailing by wind power alone, sea chanteys served very useful and practical purposes. They set the appropriate rhythm for the performance of specific shipboard tasks such as hoisting or reefing sails, and the same qualities that make them pleasurable to listen to today served to coordinate joint tasks or relieve the boredom of those jobs.

Such links between art and other aspects of everyday life are common in human societies around the world. This can also be seen in the way that art has commonly been incorporated into everyday, functional objects—from pottery and baskets used to carry or store food to carpets and mats woven by herders to cover the ground inside their dwellings. Designs painted on or woven or carved into such objects typically express ideas, values, and things that have meaning to an entire community.

All of this goes to show that artistic expression is as basic to human beings as talking and is by no means limited to a special category of people called "artists." For example, all human beings adorn their bodies in certain ways and by doing so make a statement about who they are, both as individuals and as members of society. Similarly, people in all cultures tell stories in which they express their values, hopes, and concerns and in the process reveal much about themselves and the nature of the world as they see it. In short, all peoples engage in artistic expression. What's more, they have been doing this for at least 40,000 years. Far from being a luxury to be afforded or appreciated by a minority of sophisticated experts or frivolous lovers of art, creativity is a necessary activity in which everyone participates in one way or another.

Whether a particular work of art is intended to be appreciated purely for beauty or to serve some practical purpose, it will in every case require the same special combination of the symbolic representation of form and the expression of feeling that constitute the creative imagination. Since the creative use of the human ability to symbolize is universal, and both expresses and is shaped by cultural values and concerns, it is an important subject for anthropological study.

THE ANTHROPOLOGICAL STUDY OF ART

Anthropologists have found that art often reflects a society's collective ideas, values, and concerns. Indeed, through the cross-cultural study of art—myths, songs, dances, paintings, carvings, designs, and so on—we may discover much about different worldviews and religious beliefs, as well as political ideas, social values, kinship structures, economic relations, and historical memory.

VISUAL COUNTERPOINT

© Indiana University Art Museum, Bloomington

© Giraudon/Art Resource

On the left is a wooden spoon used by the Dan people of Ivory Coast, West Africa, carver unknown. On the right is a bronze sculpture, "Spoon Woman," created by Italian artist Alberto Giacometti in 1926. Both may be beautiful, but one is functional, the other purely aesthetic. Usually, traditional utilitarian objects, no matter how exquisite, are identified only in terms of the "primitive" or "tribal" cultures in which they were made. In contrast, "works of art" created for the sake of art itself are typically tied to the name of the person who made them. How curious it is that this great modern piece credited to the famous Giacometti was inspired by a now nameless West African person.

In approaching art as a cultural phenomenon, anthropologists have the pleasant task of cataloguing, photographing, recording, describing, and analyzing all possible forms of imaginative activity in any particular culture. An enormous variety of forms and modes of artistic expression exists in the world. Because people everywhere continue to create and develop in ever-new ways, there is no end in sight to the interesting process of collecting and describing the world's ornaments, ceremonial masks, body decorations, clothing variations, blanket and rug designs, pottery and basket styles, monuments, architectural embellishments, legends, work songs, dances, and other art forms—many of them rich with religious symbolism.

To study and analyze art, anthropologists employ a combination of aesthetic, narrative, and interpretive approaches. The distinction between these methods can be illustrated through a brief look at a famous work of West-

ern art, Leonardo da Vinci's painting *The Last Supper*.[1] A non-Christian viewing this late 15th-century mural in Italy will see thirteen people at a table, apparently enjoying a meal. Although one of the men clutches a bag of money and appears to have knocked over a dish of salt, nothing else in the scene seems out of the ordinary.

Aesthetically, our non-Christian observer may admire the way the composition fits the space available, the way the attitudes of the men are depicted, and the way the artist conveys a sense of movement. As *narrative,* the painting may be seen as a record of customs, table manners, dress, and architecture. But to *interpret* this picture—to perceive its real meaning—the viewer must be aware that in Western culture money symbol-

---

[1] This example is drawn from Lewis-Williams, J. D. (1990). *Discovering southern African rock art* (p. 9). Cape Town and Johannesburg: David Philip.

Leonardo da Vinci's *The Last Supper*. To really understand this painting, one must know something about Christianity and about the general cultural symbols and beliefs of the famous Italian artist (1452–1519) in his own place and time.

© Scala/Art Resource, NY

izes the root of all evil and spilling the salt symbolizes impending disaster. But even this is not enough; to fully understand this work of art, one must know something of the beliefs of Christianity. In other words, moving to the interpretive level of studying art requires knowledge of the symbols and beliefs of the people responsible for the art.

A good way to deepen our insight into the relationship between art and the rest of culture is to examine critically some of the generalizations that have already been made about specific art forms. Since it is impossible to cover all art forms in the space of a single chapter, we shall concentrate on just a few: visual, verbal, and musical—in that order.

VISUAL ART

For many people, the first thing that springs to mind in connection with the word *art* is some sort of visual image, be it a painting, drawing, sketch, or whatever. And indeed, in many parts of the world, people have been making pictures in one way or another for a very long time—etching in bone, engraving in rock, painting on cave walls and rock surfaces, carving and painting on wood, gourds, and clay pots, or painting on textiles, bark cloth, animal hide, or even their own bodies. Some form of visual art is a part of every historically known human culture.

As a type of symbolic expression, visual art may be representational (imitating closely the forms of nature)

or abstract (drawing from natural forms but representing only their basic patterns or arrangements). In some of the Indian art of North America's northwest coast, for example, animal figures may be so highly stylized as to be difficult for an outsider to identify. Although the art appears abstract, the artist has created it based on nature, even though he or she has exaggerated and deliberately transformed various shapes to express a particular feeling toward the animals. Because artists do these exaggerations and transformations according to the aesthetic principles of their Indian culture, their meanings are understood not just by the artist but by other members of the community as well.

This collective understanding of symbols is a hallmark in traditional art. Unlike modern Western art, which is judged in large part on its creative originality and the unique vision of an individual artist, traditional art is all about community and shared symbolism. As discussed in several earlier chapters, hunter–gatherers, nomadic herders, slash-and-burn horticulturists, and others living in small-scale traditional societies are profoundly interested in kinship relations—who is related to whom and how. In such societies, concerns about kinship may be symbolically expressed in stylized motifs and colorful designs. As described by North American art historian Carl Schuster and anthropologist Edmund Carpenter, cross-cultural and historical comparisons of certain widespread and recurrent geometric motifs—etched or painted on human skin, animal hides or bones, clay pottery, wood, rocks, or almost any other surface imaginable—indicate that many designs that we perceive as

© 1996 The Rock Foundation. Courtesy of Edmund Carpenter

Outstretched Limbs

Curved Limbs

Stepped Limbs

Hanging Limbs

Hourglass

Hocker

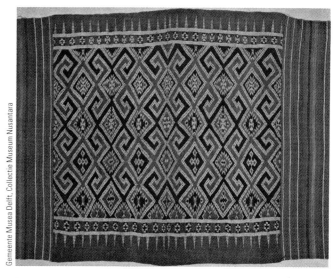

Gemeente Musea Delft, Collectie Museum Nusantara

In the figure at left, the two rows of diagrams at the top show the stylized human figures that are the basic "bricks" used in the construction of genealogical patterns. Each figure is designed to be joined limb-and-limb with adjacent figures to illustrate descent or other kin relationships. The diagrams in the two bottom rows show how these basic figures are linked arm-and-leg with diagonally adjacent figures to depict descent. For thousands of years people all over the world have linked such figures together, creating the familiar geometric patterns that we see in countless art forms, from pottery to sculpture to weaving—patterns that informed eyes recognize as genealogical.

purely decorative, ornamental, or abstract are actually symbolic. This symbolism, they show, can often be decoded in terms of a genealogical iconography primarily illustrating social relations of marriage and descent.[2]

Shared symbolism has also been fundamental to the traditional art of tattooing—although that is changing in some parts of the world, as discussed in the following Original Study.

---

[2]Schuster, C., & Carpenter, E. (1996). *Patterns that connect: Social symbolism in ancient and tribal art.* New York: Abrams; see also

Prins, H. E. L. (1998). Book review of Schuster, C., & Carpenter, E. *American Anthropologist* 100 (3), 841.

Original Study ▪ By Margo DeMello

The Modern Tattoo Community

As an anthropology graduate student in the early 1990s, I had no idea what (or, more accurately, whom) to study for my field research. Working as an animal advocate, I had a house full of creatures to care for, which left me in no position for long-term travel to a far-off field site.

Then one of my professors suggested a topic that was literally under

my nose—tattooing. I myself had several tattoos and spent quite a bit of time with other tattooed people, including my husband who had just become a professional tattooist. Yet, I had never thought about this as a research topic. Part of my everyday life, it didn't seem "exotic" enough. My professor assured me I was wrong, and I began my research assum-

ing that it would not be difficult since I was already accustomed to attending tattoo conventions, getting tattooed, and hanging around tattoo studios.

As it turned out I had unanticipated obstacles to overcome. Early on in my research, I, along with my husband, strove to find a way to "join" what is known as

CONTINUED

CONTINUED

the "tattoo community," finding that it was not as friendly and open as we had imagined it to be. As a tattooed person, married to a fledgling tattooist, I often felt excluded. But as an anthropologist I came to see that what I was experiencing was the lower rungs of a highly stratified social group, in which an artist's status is based on such features as class, geography, and professional and artistic credentials, and a "fan" might be judged on the type and extent of his or her tattoos, the artist(s) who created them, the level of media coverage achieved, and more. It was my personal experiences as both insider (tattooed person) and out-sider (anthropologist) with this community that in fact led to one of the major focuses of my work: how class and status increasingly came to define this once working-class art form.

Michael M. Phillips

For many U.S. Marines in Iraq, memorial tattoos are becoming a way to give ink-and-skin permanence to fallen friends. In memory of fellow Marine Lance Cpl. Michael Torres, Curt Stiver of Oshkosh, Wisconsin, had a tattoo artist copy onto his left chest a photograph taken of Torres in infantry school.

Ultimately, I spent almost five years studying and writing about tattoo-ing, finding my "community" wherever tattooed people talked about them-selves and each other—within the pages of tattoo magazines and mainstream newspapers, on Internet newsgroups, and at tattoo-oriented events across the country. I spent countless hours in tattoo shops watching the artists work; I collected what I call "tattoo narratives," which are often elaborate, sometimes spiritual, stories that people tell about their tattoos; and I followed the ca-reers of seminal artists. I even learned to tattoo a bit myself, placing a few particularly ugly images on my patient husband's body.

Tattoos are created by inserting ink or some other pigment through the epi-dermis (outer skin) into the dermis (the second layer of skin) through the use of needles. They may be beautiful as designs in and of themselves, but they can also express a multitude of meanings about the wearer and his or her place within the social group. Whether used in an overt punitive fashion (as in the tattooing of

slaves or prisoners) or to mark clan or cult membership, religious or tribal affiliation, social status, or marital position, tattoos have historically been a social sign. They have long been one of the simplest ways of establishing humans as social beings. In fact, tattooing is one of the most per-sistent and universal forms of body art and may date back as far as the Upper Paleolithic era (10,000–40,000 years ago).

Tattoos as signs derive their commu-nicative power from more than a simple sign-to-meaning correspondence: They also communicate through color, style, manner of execution, and location on the body. Traditionally inscribed on easily viewable parts of the body, tattoos were designed to be "read" by others and were part of a collectively understood system of inscription. However, for many middle-class North Americans today tattoos are more about private statement than public sign, and these individuals, especially women, tend to favor smaller tattoos in private spots.

The process by which tattooing has expanded in the United States from a working-class folk art into a more widespread and often refined aesthetic practice is related to a number of shifts in North American culture that occurred during the 1970s and 1980s. This time

period saw the introduction of finely trained artists into tattooing, bringing with them radically different backgrounds and artistic sensibilities to draw from. More and more middle-class men and women began getting tattooed, attracted by the expanded artistic choices and the new, more spiritual context of body decoration.

Tattoos have been partially transformed into fine art by a process of redefinition and framing based on formal quali-ties (that is, the skill of the artist, the iconic content of the tattoo, the style in which the tattoo is executed, and so on) and ideological qualities (the discourses that surround "artistic" tattoos, dis-courses that point to some higher reality on which the tattoo is based). When it is judged that a tattoo has certain formal artistic qualities as well as expresses a higher, often spiritual, reality, then it is seen as art.

While it may seem as though tattoos are not good candidates to be defined as art, due to their lack of permanence (the body, after all, ages and dies) and their seeming inability to be displayed within a gallery setting, modern tattoo art shows get around these problems by photographing tattoos and displaying them in a way that showcases the "art" and often minimizes the body. By both literally and figuratively "framing" tat-toos in a museum or gallery setting, or within an art book, the tattoo is removed from its social function and remade into art.

The basic working-class American tat-too designs (such as "Mother" or "Donna" inscribed alongside a heart) have been relegated to the bottom rung of today's tattoo hierarchy in the United States. Such tattoos are now seen by middle-class artists and fans as too literal, too transparently obvious, and too grounded in everyday experience and social life to qualify as art. The modern, artistic tat-toos that have increasingly gained favor are less "readable" and no longer have an easily recognizable function. Often derived from foreign (or "exotic") cultures (such as Polynesia) and custom-drawn for the wearer, they tend to eliminate the social aspect in favor of the highly individualistic. Some are purely decorative, and those that are intended to signify meaning often do so only for the individual or those in his or her intimate circle.

Tattoos in the United States have traveled a long way from the tattoo of old: brought to North America by way of Captain James Cook's 18th-century explorations of the Pacific, moving, over time, from a mark of affiliation to a highly individual statement of personal identity, losing and regaining function, meaning, and content along the way. In our increasingly global world, tattoo designs and motifs move swiftly and easily across cultural boundaries. As this happens, their original, communal meanings are often lost—but they are not meaningless. An animal crest tattoo traditionally worn by Indians on the Northwest Coast of North America to signify clan membership may now be worn by a non-Native in Boston as an artful, often private, sign of rebellion against Western "coat and tie" consumer culture. *(For a more detailed discussion of this topic, see DeMello, M. (2000).* Bodies of inscription: A cultural history of the modern tattoo community. *(2000). Durham: Duke University Press.)* ■

Southern Africa Rock Art

Rock art—paintings and engravings made on the faces of rock outcrops and on the interior walls of rock shelters—is one of the world's oldest art traditions. Bushmen in southern Africa practiced this art continually from at least 27,000 years ago until the beginning of the 20th century when European colonization led to the demise of their societies. Their art depicted humans and animals in highly sophisticated ways, sometimes in static poses but often in highly animated scenes. It also featured what appear to be abstract signs—dots, zigzags, nested curves, and the like. Until fairly recently, the significance of these abstract features puzzled non-Bushmen, as did the fact that new pictures were quite often created directly over existing images.

Because Bushman rock art, especially the paintings, are generally seen as beautiful and pleasurable to look at, it is not surprising that the specialists who first studied them took the aesthetic approach—analyzing *how* things were depicted. Investigating the various colored pigments, they found that the Bushmen had used charcoal and specularite for black; silica, china clay, and gypsum for white; and ferric oxide for red and reddish-brown hues—and that they had mixed the colors with fat, blood, and perhaps water. The paint had been applied to the rough rock with great skill. Indeed, the effectiveness of line and the way shading was used to suggest the contours of the animals' bodies elicits admiration, as does the realistic rendering of details such as the twist of an eland's horns or the black line running along its back.

In addition to the aesthetic approach of analyzing *how* Bushman rock paintings and engravings are created, specialists also study the art as "narrative," investigating *what* it depicts. Certainly, aspects of Bushman life are shown, as in several hunting scenes of men with bows, arrows, quivers, and hunting bags. Some depictions show hunting nets and also fish traps. Women are also portrayed—identifiable by their visible sexual characteristics and the stone-weighted digging sticks they carry.

Taking an interpretive approach to studying Bushman rock art—looking at it in light of contemporary ethnographic research among modern-day Bushman communities—we see that certain designs relate to the trance dance discussed in the previous chapter. This is symbolically indicated by several features: the numbers of people shown and the arrangement of hand-clapping women surrounding dancing men whose bodies are bent forward (in the distinctive posture caused by the cramping of abdominal muscles as they go into trance), whose noses are bleeding (common today when Bushmen trance), whose arms are stretched behind their backs (present-day Bushmen do this to gather more of the supernatural potency—*n/um*), and who are wearing dance rattles and carrying fly whisks (used to extract invisible arrows of sickness).

A fuller interpretation of this scene requires more than ethnographic knowledge about the Bushman trance dance. It calls for knowledge about the nature of trance gained through laboratory experiments in altered states of consciousness.

Laboratory research shows that humans typically move through three stages when entering a trance. In the first stage, the nervous system generates images of luminous, pulsating, revolving, and constantly shifting geometric patterns known as *entoptic phenomena*—similar to images seen during a migraine headache. Typically these include dots, zigzags, grids, filigrees, nested curves, and parallel lines, often in a spiral pattern.

In the second stage, the brain tries to make sense of these abstract forms (a process known as *construal*). Here, cultural influences come into play, so a trancing Bushman in southern Africa's Kalahari is likely to construe a grid pattern as markings on the skin of a giraffe, nested curves as a honeycomb (honey is a Bush delicacy), and so forth. A New York police officer or a Chinese priest would construe the patterns in very different ways.

During the third and deepest trance stage, people tend to feel as if they are at one with their visions, passing into a rotating tunnel or vortex. Typically, the tunnel

Bushmen in southern Africa created rock paintings and engravings depicting animals they believed possessed great supernatural powers. Shamans appear as well: In the painted example at the right, we see rain shamans with swallowtails acting in the spirit realm to protect people from the dangers of storms. Like contemporary Bushman shamans, several of these hold paired dance sticks. The idea of shamans transforming into birds, as well as being elongated and weightless as in flight or water, is based on altered states of consciousness experienced in trance.

has latticelike sides where **iconic images** of animals, humans, and monsters appear, merging with the entoptic forms of the early trance stages. Because these images are culture specific, individuals usually see things that have high significance within their culture. Thus, Bushmen often see the eland, a massive antelope they believe carries supernatural powers for rain-making. This given, one of the things shamans try to do in trance is to "capture" these envisioned elands ("rain animals") for purposes of making rain.

All of this helps us understand why elands are so prominent in the Bushman rock art. Moreover, it reveals the significance of the zigzags, dots, grids, and so forth that are so often a part of the compositions. It also leads to an understanding of other puzzling features of the art. For example, the third trance stage includes such sensations as being stretched out or elongated, weightlessness as in flight or in the water, and difficulty breathing as when under water. Hence we find depictions in the art of humans who appear to be abnormally long, as well as individuals who appear to be swimming or flying.

Another well-documented trance phenomenon is the sense of being transformed into some sort of animal. Such sensations are triggered in the deepest stage of trance if the individual sees or thinks of an animal, and the sensation accounts for the part human–part animal (therianthropes) in the art. Finally, the superpositioning of one work of art over another becomes comprehensible; not only are the visions seen in trance commonly superimposed on one another as they rotate and move,

but if the trancer stares at a painting or engraving of an earlier vision, the new one will appear as if projected on the old.

The interpretive approach makes clear, then, that the rock art of southern Africa—even in the case of compositions that otherwise might appear to be scenes of everyday life—is intimately connected with the practices and beliefs of shamanism. After shamans came out of trance and reflected on their visions, they proceeded to paint or engrave their recollections on the rock faces. But these were more than records of important visions; they had their own innate power, owing to their supposed supernatural origin. This being so, when the need arose for a new trance experience, it might be held where the old vision was recorded to draw power from it.

A similar interpretive analysis is needed to fully understand the art of Huichol Indians living in Mexico and profiled in this chapter's Biocultural Connection feature.

VERBAL ART

The verbal arts include narratives, dramas, poetry, incantations, proverbs, riddles, word games—as well as naming procedures, compliments, and insults, when these take structured and special forms. Narrative seems to be one of the easiest kinds of the verbal arts to record or collect. Perhaps because they also are the most reproducible of the arts and have considerable popular appeal, they have received considerable attention from linguists and anthropologists.

In the 19th century, when scholars began studying the unwritten stories (and other artistic traditions) of ru-

iconic images Culturally specific people, animals, and monsters seen in the deepest stage of trance.

Biocultural Connection

Peyote Art: Divine Visions among the Huichol

For generations, Huichol Indians living in Mexico's mountainous western Sierra Madre region have created art remarkable for its vibrant colors. They are especially noted for their spectacular beadwork and embroidery. Although many people far and wide appreciate the intricate beauty of Huichol art, most are probably unaware that the colorful designs express a religious worldview tied to the chemical substance of a sacred plant: a small cactus "button" known as peyote (*Lophophora williamsii*).[a]

Among the many Huichol gods and goddesses, all addressed in kinship terms, is Our Grandfather Fire. His principal spirit helper is Our Elder Brother Deer, a messenger between the gods and humans. Serving the Huichol as their spiritual guide, this divine deer is also the peyote cactus itself. Huichol Indians refer to peyote as *yawéi hikuri*, the "divine flesh of Elder Brother Deer." Guided by their shamans on a pilgrimage to harvest peyote, they "hunt" this "deer" in Wirikúta, the sacred desert highlands

where their ancestor deities dwell. Having found and "shot" the first cactus button with an arrow, they gather many more, later to be consumed in fresh, dried, or liquid form.

Participating in a holy communion with the creator god, Huichol shamans consume peyote (the divine flesh) as a

© Benjamin Chodroff

sacrament. Doing so, they enter into an ecstatic trance. With the help of peyote, their spiritual guide, they become hawks or eagles soaring high in the sky. Having visions extending far across the world, they interact directly with their gods and seek advice on behalf of those who need help in dealing with illness and other misfortunes.

From a purely chemical point of view, peyote contains a psychotropic substance identified by modern chemists as an alkaloid. By consuming some of this toxic organic substance, the Huichol move into an altered state of consciousness. In this dreamlike psychological state, which is also profoundly emotional, they experience religiously inspired, brilliantly colored visions from their spirit world.

These are reflected in Huichol art, such as the piece pictured here in which a stylized peyote button and deer have been rendered in rainbow-hued beading. The sacred cactus with its starlike shape is the most prominent symbolic design in Huichol art. Beaded onto fabric and objects of all kinds or embroidered on clothing, shoulder bags, and so forth, it can be found in almost all of their artwork—much of it now produced for sale abroad.

[a]Schaeffer, S. B., & Furst, P. T. (Eds.). (1996). *People of the peyote: Huichol Indian history, religion, and survival*. Albuquerque: University of New Mexico Press.

ral peoples, they coined the word **folklore** to distinguish between "folk art" and the "fine art" of the literate elite. Today, many linguists and anthropologists prefer to speak of a culture's oral traditions and verbal arts rather than its folklore and folktales, recognizing that the distinction between folk and fine art is a projection imposed by European and Euramerican elites. Generally, the narratives comprising the verbal arts have been divided into several basic and recurring categories, including myth, legend, and tale.

Myth

Derived from the Greek word *mythos*, meaning "speech" or "story," a **myth** is a sacred narrative that explains the fundamentals of human existence—where we and everything in our world came from, why we are here, and where we are going. Beyond this explanatory function, a myth provides a rationale for religious beliefs and

practices and sets cultural standards for "right" behavior. A typical creation or origin myth, traditional with the western Abenaki of northwestern New England and southern Quebec, goes as follows:

> In the beginning, *Tabaldak*, "The Owner," created all living things but one—the spirit being who was to accomplish the final transformation of the earth. Man and woman *Tabaldak* made out of a piece of stone, but he didn't like the result, their hearts being cold and hard. This being so,

folklore A term coined by 19th-century scholars studying the unwritten stories and other artistic traditions of rural peoples to distinguish between "folk art" and the "fine art" of the literate elite.

myth A sacred narrative that explains the fundamentals of human existence—where we and everything in our world came from, why we are here, and where we are going.

he broke them up, and their remains today can be seen in the many stones that litter the landscape of the Abenaki homeland. But *Tabaldak* tried again, this time using living wood, and from this came all later Abenakis. Like the trees from which the wood came, these people were rooted in the earth and (like trees when blown by the wind) could dance gracefully. The one living thing not created by *Tabaldak* was *Odzihózo*, "He Makes Himself from Something." This being seems to have created himself out of dust, but since he was a transformer, rather than creator, he wasn't able to accomplish it all at once. At first, he managed only his head, body, and arms; the legs came later, growing slowly as legs do on a tadpole. Not waiting until his legs were grown, he set out to transform the shape of the earth. He dragged his body about with his hands, gouging channels that became the rivers. To make the mountains, he piled dirt up with his hands. Once his legs grew, *Odzihózo's* task was made easier; by merely extending his legs, he made the tributaries of the main streams.

Odzihózo, then, was the Abenaki transformer who laid out the river channels and lake basins and shaped the hills and mountains. Just how long he took is a subject which Abenakis have discussed for as long as any can remember. Once he was finished, he surveyed his handiwork and found it was good. The last work he made was Lake Champlain and this he found especially good. He liked it so well that he climbed onto a rock in Burlington Bay and changed himself into stone so that he could sit there and enjoy his masterpiece through the ages. He still likes it, because he is still there and he is still given offerings of tobacco as Abenakis pass this way. The Abenaki call the rock *Odzihózo*, since it is the Transformer himself.[3]

Such a myth, insofar as it is believed, accepted, and perpetuated in a culture, may be said to express part of a people's traditional *worldview* (the collective body of ideas that members of a culture generally share concerning the ultimate shape and substance of their reality). Extrapolating from the details of this particular Abenaki myth, we might arrive at the conclusion that these people recognize a kinship among all living things; after all,

they were all part of the same creation, and humans even were made from living wood. Moreover, an attempt to make them of nonliving stone was not satisfactory.

This idea of closeness among all living things led the Abenaki to show special respect to the animals they hunted in order to sustain their own lives. For example, after killing a beaver, muskrat, or waterfowl, one could not unceremoniously toss its bones into the nearest garbage pit. Proper respect required that the bones be returned to the water, with a request to continue its kind. Similarly, before eating meat, the Abenaki placed an offering of grease on the fire to thank *Tabaldak*. More generally, waste was to be avoided so as not to offend the animals. Failure to respect their rights would result in an unwillingness to sacrifice their lives that people might live.

By transforming himself into stone in order to enjoy his work for all eternity, *Odzihózo* may be seen as setting an example for people; they should see the beauty in things as they are and not seek to alter what is already good. To question the goodness of existing reality would be to call into question the judgment of a powerful deity. A characteristic of explanatory myths, such as this one, is that the unknown is simplified and explained in terms of the known. This myth, in terms of human experience, accounts for the existence of rivers, mountains, lakes, and other features of the landscape, as well as of humans and all other living things. It also sanctions particular attitudes and behaviors. It is a product of creative imagination, and is a work of art, as well as a potentially religious statement.

The analysis of myths has been carried to great lengths, becoming a field of study almost unto itself. Myth making is an extremely significant kind of human creativity, and studying the myth-making process and its results can give valuable clues to the way people perceive and think about their world. The problems of interpretation, however, are great, as evidenced in these questions: Are myths literally believed or perhaps accepted symbolically or emotionally as a different kind of truth? To what extent do myths actually determine or reflect human behavior? Can an outsider discover the meaning that a myth has in its own culture? How do we account for contradictory myths in the same culture (such as the two distinct accounts of creation in the first and second chapters of the Bible's Book of Genesis)? New myths arise and old ones die. Is it then the myth's content or the structure that is important? All of these questions deserve, and are currently receiving, serious consideration.

[3]Haviland, W. A., & Power, M. W. (1994). *The original Vermonters: Native inhabitants, past and present* (2nd ed., p. 193). Hanover, NH: University Press of New England.

legend A story about a memorable event or figure handed down by tradition and told as true but without historical evidence.

Legend

A **legend** is a story about a memorable event or figure handed down by tradition and told as true but without historical evidence. An example of a modern urban legend in the United States is one that was often told by Ronald Reagan when he was president, about an African American woman on welfare in Chicago. Supposedly, her ability to collect something like 103 welfare checks under different names enabled her to live lavishly. Although proved to be false, the story was told as if true (by the president even after he was informed that it was not true) as legends are.

This particular legend illustrates a number of features all such narratives share: They cannot be attributed to any known author; they always exist in multiple versions, but, in spite of variation, they are told with sufficient detail to be plausible; and they tell us something about the cultures in which they are found. In this case, we learn something about popular anger against wasteful government spending of taxpayer dollars ("big government" policies to help the poor), mainstream society's views on self-reliant individualism and hard work (distrust, if not dislike of the poor), and last but not least, enduring racism in U.S. society (the story is told by whites, who identify the woman as African American).

As this illustration shows, legends (no more than myths) are not confined to nonliterate, nonindustrialized societies. Commonly, legends consist of pseudo-historical narratives that account for the deeds of heroes, the movements of peoples, and the establishment of local customs, typically with a mixture of realism and the supernatural or extraordinary. As stories, they are not necessarily believed or disbelieved, but they usually serve to entertain as well as to instruct and to inspire or bolster pride in family, community, or nation. Legends all around the world tell us something about the cultures in which they are found.

To a degree, in literate societies, the function of legends has been taken over by history. The trouble is that history does not always tell people what they want to hear about themselves, or, conversely, it tells them things that they would prefer not to hear. By projecting their culture's hopes and expectations onto the record of the past, they seize upon and even exaggerate some past events while ignoring or giving scant attention to others. Although this often takes place unconsciously, so strong is the motivation to transform history into legend that states often have gone as far as to deliberately rewrite it.

There are countless examples of the fact that different groups often recall and recount the same historical event in highly contrasting ways. For instance, white colonists and their descendants who settled in New England portrayed the region's 17th-century Indian rebellion led by Chief Metacomet (better known in American history books as "King Philip") as a treacherous uprising and described his defeat as a divinely guided military victory over heathen savages. In this violent conflict, thousands on both sides lost their lives. Although many Indian survivors found refuge among neighboring indigenous na-

tions, hundreds of Indian captives were sold as slaves and died in foreign lands. Unable to resist English colonial land grabs and repression, Indians who were allowed to remain in their homeland were confined to small reservations where they came under the administrative control of white agents.

In public commemorations and written historical accounts, the Indian side of this conflict remains largely unvoiced and unknown to the general public.[4] For this reason, American Indians sometimes joke bitterly about such one-sided versions of the past as "*his* story," and scholars attempting to separate historical fact from fiction frequently incur the wrath of people who refuse to abandon what they wish to believe is true, whether or not it really is.

A long dramatic narrative recounting the celebrated deeds of a historic or legendary hero—often sung or recited in poetic language—is known as an **epic.** In parts of western and central Africa, people hold remarkably elaborate and formalized recitations of extremely long legends, lasting several hours and even days. These long narratives have been described as veritable encyclopedias of a culture's most diverse aspects, with direct and indirect statements about history, institutions, relationships, values, and ideas. Epics are typically found in nonliterate societies with some form of state political organization; they serve to transmit and preserve a culture's legal and political precedents and practices.

Legends may incorporate mythological details, especially when they make an appeal to the supernatural, and are therefore not always clearly distinct from myth. Legends may also incorporate proverbs and incidental tales and thus be related to other forms of verbal art as well.

For the anthropologist, a major significance of the secular and apparently realistic portions of legends, whether long or short, is the clues they provide as to what constitutes a culture's approved or ideal ethical behavior. The subject matter of legends is essentially problem solving and mentoring, and the content is likely to include physical and psychological trials of many kinds. Certain questions may be answered explicitly or implicitly. In what circumstances, if any, does the culture permit homicide? What kinds of behavior are considered heroic or cowardly? Does the culture stress forgiveness over retaliation as an admirable trait?

[4]Calloway, C. (1997). Introduction: Surviving the dark ages. In C. G. Calloway (Ed.), *After King Philip's war: Presence and persistence in Indian New England* (pp. 1–28). Hanover, NH: University Press of New England.

epic A long dramatic narrative recounting the celebrated deeds of a historic or legendary hero—often sung or recited in poetic language

Here again, however, there are pitfalls in the process of interpreting art in relation to life. It is always possible that certain behaviors are acceptable or even admirable, with the distance or objectivity afforded by art, but are not at all so approved in daily life. In Euramerican culture, murderers, charlatans, and rascals sometimes have become popular heroes and the subjects of legends; North Americans would object, however, to an outsider's inference that they necessarily approved or wanted to emulate the morality of the notorious 19th-century Wild West outlaws Billy the Kid or Jesse James.

Tale

A third type of creative narrative, the **tale,** is recognized as fiction that is for entertainment but may also draw a moral or teach a practical lesson. Consider this brief summary of a tale from Ghana in West Africa, known as "Father, Son, and Donkey":

© Kevin Kelly

A scene such as this may bring to mind the internationally popular "Father, Son, and Donkey" tale. Told in different versions featuring localized draft animals, this tale conveys a basic motif or story situation—father and son trying in vain to please everyone.

> A father and his son farmed their corn, sold it, and spent part of the profit on a donkey. When the hot season came, they harvested their yams and prepared to take them to storage, using their donkey. The father mounted the donkey and they all three proceeded on their way until they met some people. "What? You lazy man!" the people said to the father. "You let your young son walk barefoot on this hot ground while you ride on a donkey? For shame!" The father yielded his place to the son, and they proceeded until they came to an old woman. "What? You useless boy!" said the old woman. "You ride on the donkey and let your poor father walk barefoot on this hot ground? For shame!" The son dismounted, and both father and son walked on the road, leading the donkey behind them until they came to an old man. "What? You foolish people!" said the old man. "You have a donkey and you walk barefoot on the hot ground instead of riding?" And so it goes. Listen: when you are doing something and other people come along, just keep on doing what you like.

This is precisely the kind of tale that is of special interest in traditional folklore studies. It is an internationally popular "numbskull" tale. Versions of it have been recorded in India, Southwest Asia, southern and western Europe, and North America, as well as in West Africa. It is classified or catalogued as exhibiting a basic **motif**

tale A creative narrative that is recognized as fiction for entertainment but may also draw a moral or teach a practical lesson.
motif A story situation in a tale.

or story situation—father and son trying to please everyone—one of the many thousands that have been found to recur in tales around the world. Despite variations in detail, every version follows the same basic structure in the sequence of events, sometimes called the *syntax* of the tale: A peasant father and son work together, a beast of burden is purchased, the three set out on a short excursion, the father rides and is criticized, the son rides and is criticized, both walk and are criticized, and a conclusion is drawn.

Tales of this sort (not to mention myths and legends) that are found to have wide geographic distribution raise the question: Where did they originate? Did the story arise only once and then pass from one culture to another (*diffusion*)? Or did the stories arise independently (*independent invention*) in response to like causes in similar settings, or perhaps as a consequence of inherited mental preferences and images deeply embedded in the evolutionary construction of the human brain? Or is it merely that there are logical limits to the structure of stories, so that, by coincidence, different cultures are bound to come up with similar motifs and syntax?[5]

A surprisingly large number of motifs in European and African tales are traceable to ancient sources in India, evidence of diffusion of tales. Of course, purely local tales also exist. Within any particular culture, anthropologists usually can categorize local types of tales: animal, human experience, trickster, dilemma, ghost, moral, scatological, nonsense tales, and so on. In West Africa, for example, there is a remarkable prevalence of stories with animal protagonists. Many were carried to the slaveholding areas of the Americas; the Uncle Remus stories about Brer Rabbit and Brer Fox may be part of this tradition.

The significance of tales for the anthropologist rests partly in this matter of their distribution. They provide evidence of either cultural contacts or cultural isolation and of limits of influence and cultural cohesion.

Anthropologists are interested, however, in more than these questions of distribution. Like legends, tales very often illustrate local solutions to universal human ethical problems, and in some sense they state a moral

---

[5]Gould, S. J. (2000). The narthex of San Marco and the pangenetic paradigm. *Natural History 109* (6), 29.

philosophy. Anthropologists see that whether the tale of the father, the son, and the donkey originated in West Africa or arrived there from Europe or the Middle East, the very fact it is told in West Africa suggests that it states something valid for that culture. The tale's lesson of a necessary degree of self-confidence in the face of arbitrary social criticism is therefore something that can be read into the culture's values and beliefs.

Other Verbal Art

Myths, legends, and tales, prominent as they are in anthropological studies, in many cultures turn out to be no more important than many other verbal arts. In the culture of the Awlad 'Ali Bedouins of Egypt's western desert, for example, poetry is a lively and active verbal art, especially as a vehicle for personal expression and private communication. These people use two forms of poetry. One is the elaborately structured and heroic poems men chant or recite only on ceremonial occasions and in specific public contexts. The other is the *ghinnáwas* or "little songs" that punctuate everyday conversations. Simple in structure, these deal with personal matters and feelings more appropriate to informal social situations, and

© Anthro-Photo

The *ghinnáwas* or "little songs" of the Awlad 'Ali Bedouins in Egypt punctuate conversations carried out while the people perform everyday chores, such as making bread, as these young women are doing. Through these "little songs," they can express what otherwise are taboo topics.

older men regard them as the unimportant productions of women and youths.

Despite this official devaluation in the male-dominated Bedouin society, however, "little songs" play a vital part in people's daily lives. In these poems individuals are shielded from the consequences of making statements and expressing sentiments that contravene the moral system. Paradoxically, by sharing these "immoral" sentiments only with intimates and veiling them in impersonal traditional formulas, those who recite them demonstrate that they have a certain control, which actually enhances their moral standing. As is often true of folklore in general, the "little songs" of the Awlad 'Ali provide a culturally appropriate outlet for otherwise taboo thoughts or opinions.[6] Disaster jokes are an example of this in contemporary North American society.

In all cultures the words of songs constitute a kind of poetry. Poetry and stories recited with gesture, movement, and props become drama. Drama combined with dance, music, and spectacle becomes a public celebration. The more we look at the individual arts, the clearer it becomes that they often are interrelated and interdependent. The verbal arts are, in fact, simply differing manifestations of the same creative imagination that produces music and the other arts.

MUSICAL ART

The study of music in specific cultural settings, beginning in the 19th century with the collection of folksongs, has developed into a specialized field of anthropological study called **ethnomusicology.** Like the study of folktales for their own sake, ethnomusicology is both related to and somewhat independent of anthropology. Nevertheless, it is possible to sort out several concerns that are of interest to the general discipline of anthropology.

To begin, we may ask, How does a culture conceive of music? What is considered of primary importance when distinguishing music from other modes of expression? Music to one person may be merely noise to another. Music is a form of communication that includes a nonverbal auditory component. The information it transmits is often abstract emotion rather than concrete ideas and is experienced in a variety of ways by different listeners. Such factors make music tough to define. In fact, no single definition of music can be agreed upon,

because different peoples may include or exclude different ideas within that category. Ethnomusicologists often distinguish between "music" and that which is "musical." The way to approach an unfamiliar kind of musical expression is to define it either in indigenous terms or in orthodox musicological terms such as melody, rhythm, and form.

Much of the historical development of ethnomusicology has been based upon musicology, which is primarily the study of European music. One problem has been the tendency to discuss music in terms of elements considered important in European music (tonality, rhythm, melody, and so on), when these may be of little importance to the practitioner. European music is defined, primarily, in terms of the presence of melody and rhythm. Melody is a function of tonality, and rhythm is an organizing concept involving tempo, stress, and measured repetition. Although these can be addressed in non-European music, they may not be the defining characteristics of a performance.

Early investigators of non-European song were struck by the apparent simplicity of *pentatonic* (five-tone) scales and a seemingly endless repetition of phrases. They often did not give sufficient credit to the formal function of repetition in such music, confusing repetition with lack of invention. A great deal of complex, sophisticated, non-European music was dismissed as primitive and formless and typically treated as trivial. Repetition, nevertheless, is a fact of music, including European music, and a basic formal principle.

In general, human music is said to differ from natural music—the songs of birds, wolves, and whales, for example—by being almost everywhere perceived in terms of a repertoire of tones at fixed or regular intervals: in other words, a scale. Scale systems and their modifications comprise what is known as **tonality** in music. These vary cross-culturally, so it is not surprising that something that sounds musical to one group of people may come across as noise to another.

Humans make closed systems out of a formless range of possible sounds by dividing the distance between a tone and its first *overtone* or sympathetic vibration (which always has exactly twice as many vibrations as the basic tone) into a series of measured steps. In the Western or European system, the distance between the basic tone and the first overtone is called the *octave;* it consists of seven steps—five *whole* tones and two *semitones.* The whole tones are further divided into semitones for a total working scale of twelve tones. Interestingly, some birds pitch their songs to the same scale as Western music,[7] perhaps influencing the way these people developed their scale.

---

[6]Abu-Lughod, L. (1986). *Veiled sentiments: Honor and poetry in a Bedouin society* (p. 252). Berkeley: University of California Press.

ethnomusicology The study of a society's music in terms of its cultural setting.
tonality In music, scale systems and their modifications.

---

[7]Gray, P. M., et al.. (2001). The music of nature and the nature of music. *Science 291,* 52.

Navajo Indian sand paintings, created for sacred healing rituals, are among countless examples of the interconnection of art, religion, and healing. A Navajo ceremonial "singer" directs the communal creation of these intricate works. Each painting features supernatural images "dry painted" with powders made from ground sandstone, ochre, lime, and charcoal on a surface of smooth clean sand. As shown in this photo, the patient sits at the painting's center, where a masked *yé'ii* (supernatural being) impersonator replaces illness with supernatural essences. Ritual acts include singing, anointing, and drinking medicine. When the ceremony is over, the supernatural presences depicted in the sand painting are brushed from the surface and sent home.

One of the most common alternatives to the semitonal system is the pentatonic system, which, as noted, divides the scale into five nearly equidistant tones. Such scales may be found all over the world, including in much European folk music. Arabic and Persian music have smaller units of a third of a tone with scales of seventeen and twenty-four steps in the octave. Even quarter-tone scales are used in India with subtleties of shading that are nearly indistinguishable to a Western ear. Small wonder, then, that even when Westerners can hear what sounds like melody and rhythm in these systems, the total result may sound peculiar to them, or "out of tune." Anthropologists need a practiced ear to learn to appreciate some of the music they hear, and only some of the most skilled folksong collectors have attempted to notate and analyze music that is not semitonal.

Another organizing factor in music, rhythm—whether regular or irregular—may be more important than tonality. One reason for this may be our constant exposure to natural pulses, such as our own heartbeat and rhythms of breathing and walking. Even before we are born, we are exposed to our mother's heartbeat and rhythms of her movements, and as infants we experience rhythmic touching, petting, stroking, and rocking.[8]

The rhythms of traditional European music are most often measured into recurrent patterns of two, three, and four beats, with combinations of weak and strong beats to mark the division and form patterns. Non-European music is likely to move in patterns of five, seven, or eleven beats, with complex arrangements of internal beats and sometimes *polyrhythms:* one instrument or singer using a pattern of three beats, for example, while another uses a pattern of five or seven. Polyrhythms are frequent in the drum music of West Africa, which shows remarkable precision in the overlapping of rhythmic lines. Non-European music also may contain shifting rhythms: a pattern of three beats, for example, followed by a pattern of two or five beats with little or no regular recurrence or repetition of any one pattern, although the patterns are fixed and identifiable as units.

Like other art forms, music is often created for religious purposes. Shamans drum to help create a trance state, Buddhist monks chant to focus their meditation, Christians sing hymns to praise God, and so on. Indeed, the division between art and religion is by no means sharply defined. However uniquely imagined or creatively expressed, art and religion are about feelings, values, and ideas people have about themselves and the world around them and as such form part of a culture's superstructure.

FUNCTIONS OF ART

Art in all its many forms has countless functions beyond providing aesthetic pleasure, some of which have been touched upon or hinted at in the preceding paragraphs. For anthropologists and others seeking to understand cultures beyond their own, art offers insights into a culture's worldview, giving clues about everything from gender and kinship relations to religious beliefs, political ideas, historical memory, and so on.

For those within a society, art may serve to display social status, spiritual identity, and political power. An

[8]Dissanayake, E. (2000). Birth of the arts. *Natural History 109* (10), 89.

example of this can be seen in the totem poles of Indians living along America's northwest coast. Erected in front of the homes of chiefs, these poles are inscribed with symbols that are visual reminders of the social hierarchy. Similarly, art is used to mark kinship ties, as seen in Scottish tartans designed to identify clan affiliation. It can also affirm group solidarity and identity beyond kinship lines, as evidenced in national emblems such as the dragon (Bhutan), bald eagle (United States), maple leaf (Canada), crescent moon (Turkey), or cedar tree (Lebanon) that typically appear on coins, government buildings, and so on. Sometimes art is employed to express political themes and influence events, as in the counterculture rock and folk music of the 1960s in the United States. Other times it is used to transmit traditional culture and ancestral ties, as in epic poems passed down from generation to generation.

As an activity or behavior that contributes to human well-being and that helps give shape and significance to life, art is related to, yet distinct from, religion. In an elaborate ceremony involving ornamentation, masks, costumes, songs, dances, and effigies, it is not easy to say precisely where art stops and religion begins. Furthermore music, dance, and other arts may be used, like magic, to "enchant"—to take advantage of the emotional or psychological predispositions of another person or group so as to cause them to perceive reality in a way favorable to the interests of the "enchanter." Often it is created to honor or beseech the aid of a deity, an ancestral spirit, or an animal spirit. Indeed, the arts may be used to manipulate a seemingly inexhaustible list of human passions, including desire, terror, wonder, love, fantasy, and vanity.[9] (Marketing specialists, of course, are well aware of this, which is why they routinely employ certain music and images in their advertising.)

Clearly, art in all its varied forms is used in a vast number of ways for a great array of purposes. To simplify our discussion of its numerous functions, we will consider a particular art form as embedded in a cultural system: music.

Functions of Music

Evidence of humans making music reaches far back in time. Bone flutes and whistles that date back some 40,000 years and resemble today's recorders have been found by archaeologists. And historically known food-foraging peoples were not without music. In the Kalahari Desert, for example, a Ju/'hoansi hunter off by himself would play a tune on his bow simply to help while

away the time (long before anyone thought of beating swords into plowshares, some genius discovered that bows could be used not just to kill but to make music as well). In northern New England, Abenaki shamans used cedar flutes to call game, lure enemies, and attract women. In addition, shamans would use a drum—over which two rawhide strings were stretched to produce a buzzing sound, representing singing—to allow communication with the spirit world.

Music is also a powerful identifier. Many marginalized groups have used it for purposes of self-identification—as a means of building group solidarity and distinguishing themselves from dominant culture and sometimes as a channel for direct social and political commentary. Examples of this range from ethnic groups sponsoring music festivals to rock bands such as Britain's Rolling Stones, Coldplay, and Radiohead to North American rap artists OutKast, Eminem, and Jay-Z. Music plays an important role in Native American potlatches and powwows where Native American groups gather to reaffirm and celebrate their ethnic identities. And Scottish gatherings would not be Scottish without the sound of the highland bagpipes and the fiddle.

This power of music to shape identity has had varying consequences. The English understood that the bagpipes created a strong sense of identity among the highland regiments of the British army and encouraged it within certain bounds, even as they suppressed piping in Scotland itself under the Disarming Act. Over time, the British military piping tradition was assimilated into the Scottish piping tradition and so was accepted and spread by Scottish pipers. As a result, much of the supposedly Scottish piping one hears today consists of marches written within the conventions of the musical tradition of England, though shaped to fit the physical constraints of the instrument. Less often heard is the "classical" music known in Scottish Gaelic as *Pibroch* ("pipering") or, as some prefer to call traditional pipe music, *Ceòl Mòr* ("great music"). This more traditional Scottish pipe music has been revived over the past century and is now often romantically associated with rising cultural pride and even nationalist sentiment.

The English adoption of the highland bagpipe into Scottish regiments is an instance of those in authority employing music to further a political agenda. So, too, in Spain, former dictator Francisco Franco (who came to power in the 1930s) established community choruses in even the smallest towns to promote the singing of patriotic songs. Similarly, in Ireland Comhaltas Ceoltoiri Eireann has promoted the collection and performance of traditional Irish music, and in Brittany and Galicia music is playing an important role in attempts to revive the spirits of the indigenous Celtic cultures in these regions of France and Spain.

---

[9]Gell, A. (1988). Technology and magic. *Anthropology Today 4* (2), 7; Lewis-Williams, J. D. (1997). Agency, art and altered consciousness: A motif in French (Quercy) upper Paleolithic parietal art. *Antiquity, 71*, 810–830.

R. Todd Hoffman

Laborers in Mali, West Africa, working to the beat of a drum, which serves to set the pace of work, unify the workforce, and relieve boredom.

The social function of music is perhaps most obvious in song, since these contain verbal text. Like other verbal forms, songs often express a group's values, beliefs, and concerns, but they do so with an increased formalism resulting from adherence to the restrictions of systematic rules or conventions of pitch, rhythm, timbre, and musical genre. For this reason, music plays an important part in the cultural preservation and revitalization efforts of indigenous peoples around the world whose traditions were repressed or nearly exterminated through colonialism.

Work songs have played an important part in manual labor, serving to coordinate efforts in heavy or dangerous labor (such as weighing anchor and furling sail on board ships), to synchronize axe or hammer strokes, and to pass time and relieve tedium as with oyster-shucking songs. Songs also have been used to soothe babies to sleep, to charm animals into giving more milk, to keep witchcraft at bay, and to advertise goods. Songs may also serve social and political purposes, spreading particular ideas swiftly and effectively by giving them a special form involving poetic language and rhythm and by attaching a pleasing and appropriate tune, be it solemn or light.

In the United States numerous examples exist of marginalized social and ethnic groups attempting to gain a larger audience and more compassion for their plight through song. Perhaps no better example exists than African Americans, whose ancestors were cap-

tured and carried across the Atlantic Ocean to be sold as slaves. Out of their experience emerged spirituals and, ultimately gospel, jazz, blues, rock and roll, and rap. These forms all found their way into the North American mainstream, and white performers such as Elvis Presley and Benny Goodman (the latter with integrated bands—unusual in the 1930s) presented their own versions of this music to white audiences. Even composers of so-called serious music ranging from Leonard Bernstein to George Gershwin to Antonin Dvořák to Francis Poulenc were influenced by the music of African Americans. In short, music of a marginalized group of former slaves eventually captivated the entire world, even while the descendants of those slaves have had to struggle continually to escape their subordinate status.

In the 1950s and 1960s performers such as Pete Seeger and Joan Baez gained great visibility when supporting civil and human rights causes in the United States. Indeed, both performers' celebrity status led to the broader dissemination of their social and political beliefs. Such celebrity status comes from skill in performing and communicating with the intended audience. So powerful a force was music in the civil rights and peace movements of the time that Seeger was targeted by right-wing Senator Joseph McCarthy's anti-Communist crusade, which aimed to discredit the political left as anti-American and unpatriotic. Seeger became one of many performers blacklisted by the entertainment industry due to this political witch-hunt.

GLOBALSCAPE

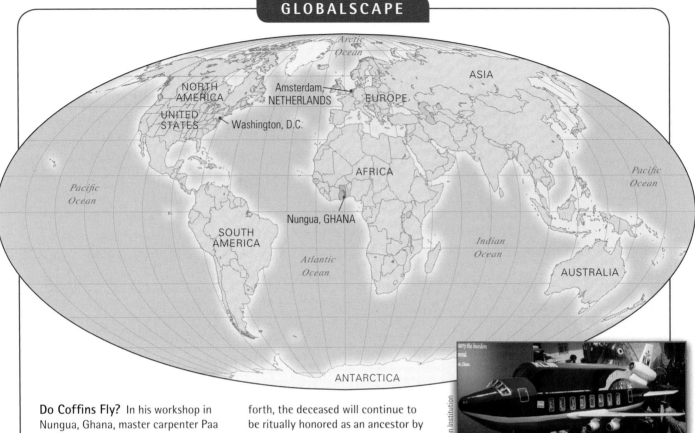

Smithsonian Institution

Do Coffins Fly? In his workshop in Nungua, Ghana, master carpenter Paa Joe makes unique painted wooden coffins for his clients in his Ga society and beyond. Some are spectacular, representing a richly colored tropical fish or even luxury cars, such as Mercedes-Benz. Celebrating the life accomplishments of the deceased, these designer coffins show off the family's prominent status and wealth.

As a collective expression of culturally shared ideas about the afterlife, a Ga funeral ceremony reminds the mourners of important values embodied in the departed individual. Seeing the deceased off on a journey to the afterlife, Ga mourners call out praises to this person, and some may even pour schnapps on the coffin. Hence-

forth, the deceased will continue to be ritually honored as an ancestor by descendants.

The 747 jumbo jet coffin pictured here confers upon the deceased the prestige and mystique of air travel. Its colors, blue and white, are those of the KLM Royal Dutch Airline, a long-time provider of air service between this West African country and the rest of the world. Its creator, Paa Joe, began working at age 15 for his cousin Kane Quaye, a carpenter known for designer coffins. Later, Joe started his own workshop, and before too long he began receiving orders from other parts of the world—not only from individuals but also from museums. Using wood, enamel paint, satin, and Christmas wrapping paper, Joe created this KLM airplane coffin in

1997 for the Smithsonian National Museum of Natural History in Washington, DC, where millions of visitors from all over the globe now admire this Ghanian funereal ritual object.

Global Twister When the Smithsonian museum purchased one of Paa Joe's remarkable coffins for public display, did this West African funereal ritual object transform into a work of art?
SOURCE: Based on script for African Voices *exhibition at NMNH, Smithsonian courtesy of Dr. Mari Jo Arnoldi.*

In Australia, certain ceremonial songs of the Aborigines have taken on a new legal function, as they are being introduced into court as evidence of early settlement patterns. These songs carry ancient stories recounting adventures of mythic ancestors who lived in "Dreamtime" and created waterholes, mountains, valleys, and other significant features in the landscape. The ancestors' tracks are known as *songlines,* and through ceremonial songs about them countless generations of Aborigines

have passed on sacred ecological knowledge. This oral tradition helps Aborigines to claim extensive indigenous land ownership, thus allowing them greater authority to use the land, as well as to negotiate and profit from the sale of natural resources. This had been impossible before. The British, upon their annexation of Australia, declared the land ownerless (*Terra Nullius*). Although the Aborigines had preserved their records of ownership in song and story, these were not admissible in the British

A concern with the arts of non-Western people has always been an important part of anthropology, as illustrated by the work of anthropologist Frederica de Laguna. Educated at Bryn Mawr College and Columbia University, where she earned her doctorate, she made her first trip into the field with a Danish expedition to Greenland in 1929. A year later, she began work in southeastern Alaska, a region to which she returned repeatedly until the end of the 20th century. Her first research there was archaeological, and she was a pioneer in southeastern Alaskan prehistory. But as her interest in native peoples grew, she became increasingly involved with ethnographic work as well. She found out that to understand the past, one had to know what it led to, just as to understand the present native people, one had to know their past.

In 1949, after many seasons of work in different localities, de Laguna began a project to trace the roots of the lifeways of the Tlingit Indians of Yakutat through combining archaeological and ethnographic research. This resulted in a monumental three-volume work published in

Laura Bliss Spaan

1972, *Under Mount St. Elias.* Considerable space in this trilogy is devoted to transcriptions of Tlingit songs and stories just as they were related and performed by elders now long dead. Beyond its

scientific anthropological value, this work has come to be of enormous importance to the Tlingit themselves.

When "Freddy" de Laguna began to work at Yakutat, Tlingit children were being sent to government boarding schools, where they were told nothing of their own culture and were harshly punished for even speaking their own language. The aim was to stamp out native culture to facilitate assimilation into mainstream American culture. Thus, as the elders died out, many traditions were being lost. But with the publication of de Laguna's trilogy, the community has been able to revitalize much that they were in danger of losing. As de Laguna said, songs and stories are for giving back, and so it was that in 1997 the Tlingit of Yakutat honored her with a potlatch ceremony in recognition of what she gave back to them.

Since her death at age 98 in 2004, generations of Tlingit with whom she worked readily acknowledge that much of their present-day cultural vigor and pride in who they are is due to "Grandmother Freddy's" work.

courts. In the early 1970s, however, the Aborigines exposed the injustice of the situation, and the Australian government began responding in a more favorable, if still limited, fashion, granting the claims of traditional ownership to groups in the Northern Territory. In 1992 the legitimacy of the concept of *Terra Nullius* was overturned, and native claims are now being presented in the other territories as well. These newer claimants are granted equal partnership with developers and others. Sacred sites are being recognized, and profits are being shared with the traditional owners. Proof of native ownership includes recordings of Aborigine songs indicative of traditional patterns of settlement, travel, and land use.[10]

Music gives basic human ideas a concrete form, made memorable and attractive with melody and rhythm, to basic human ideas. Whether a song's content is didactic,

satirical, inspirational, religious, political, or purely emotional, the formless has been given form, and feelings hard to express in words alone are communicated in a symbolic and memorable way that can be repeated and shared. The group is consequently united and has the sense that their shared experience, whatever it may be, has shape and meaning. This, in turn, shapes and gives meaning to the community.

ART, GLOBALIZATION, AND CULTURAL SURVIVAL

Clearly, there is more to art than meets the eye or ear (not to mention the nose and tongue—consider how burning incense or tobacco are part of the artfulness of sacred ceremonies, and imagine the cross-cultural array of smells and tastes in the cooking arts). In fact, art is such a significant part of any culture that many indigenous groups around the world whose lifeways have been threatened—first by colonialism and now by globaliza-

---

[10]Koch, G. (1997). Songs, land rights, and archives in Australia. *Cultural Survival Quarterly 20* (4). See also Berndt, R. M., & Berndt, C. H. (1989). *The Speaking Land: Myth and story in Aboriginal Australia.* New York: Penguin.

tion—are using aesthetic expressions as part of a cultural survival strategy. They are finding that a traditional art form—a dance, a song, a dress, a basket, a carving, or anything that is distinctly beautiful and well-made or performed—can serve as a powerful symbol that conveys the vital message, "We're still here, and we're still a culturally distinct people with our own particular beliefs and values." (See Anthropologist of Note box.)

There are many examples of art playing a role in indigenous rights efforts. Consider the native rights case of the Aroostook Band of Micmac Indians in northern Maine, described in the Anthropology Applied box in the Kinship and Descent chapter. Building support for this particular case involved making a documentary film to inform politicians and the general public about the band's cultural identity and tribulations.[11] At the time,

only a dozen or so families in this band still practiced traditional wood-splint basketry. However, it had been a common livelihood for many generations, and almost every band member had parents or grandparents who had made baskets.

Emblematic of Micmac identity, including their stubborn desire for self-determination, basketry became a focal point of the film, which ultimately played a key role in the success of the band's native rights case. More than this, the film helped create a wider market for Micmac baskets, and by conveying the diligence and real skill involved in making them, it justified raising the prices of the baskets to levels that make the craft a viable livelihood. This, in turn, has prompted young people to take up basketry and strengthened their relationships with Micmac elders who are now passing the age-old art on to a new generation.

A great array of similar examples of the link between art and cultural survival can be found all around the world.

---

[11]Prins, H. E. L., & Carter, K. (1986). *Our lives in our hands.* Video and 16mm. Color. 50 min. Distributed by Watertown, MA: Documentary Educational Resources and Bucksport, ME: Northeast Historic Film; see also Prins, H. E. L. (2002). Visual media and the primitivist perplex: Colonial fantasies, indigenous imagination, and advocacy in North America. In F. D. Ginsburg et al., *Media*

worlds: Anthropology on new terrain (pp. 58–74). Berkeley: University of California Press.

Questions for Reflection

1. Throughout history humans worldwide have creatively articulated their feelings and ideas about themselves and the world around them. Considering the range of possible art forms, how have people in your home community met this particular challenge? Can you identify specific examples in music, dance, imagery, or sculpture that are not only beautiful but also meaningful?

2. Among the Maori in New Zealand, tattooing is a traditional form of skin art, and their tattoo designs are typically based on cultural symbols understood by all members in the community. Are the tattoo designs in your culture based on traditional motifs that have a shared symbolic meaning?

3. Because kinship relations are important in small-scale traditional societies, these relationships are often symbolically represented in artistic designs and motifs. What are some of the major concerns in your society, and are these concerns reflected in any of your culture's art forms?

4. In some cultures art is produced not to be preserved and enjoyed by the living but to be buried along with the dead. In fact, in some cultures highly valued art objects may also be burned or otherwise destroyed. Can you think of any reason for such seemingly irrational cultural practices?

5. Many museums and private collectors in Europe and North America are interested in so-called tribal art, such as African statues or American Indian masks originally used in sacred rituals. Are there sacred objects such as paintings or carvings in your religion that might also be collected, bought, or sold as art?

Suggested Readings

Dundes, A. (1980). *Interpreting folklore.* Bloomington: Indiana University Press.

A collection of articles that assesses the materials folklorists have amassed and classified, this book seeks to broaden and refine traditional assumptions about the proper subject matter and methods of folklore.

Hannah, J. L. (1988). *Dance, sex, and gender.* Chicago: University of Chicago Press.

Like other art forms, dance is a social act that contributes to the continuation and emergence of culture. One of the oldest art forms, dance shares the same instrument, the human body, with sexuality. This book, written for a broad nonspecialist audience, explicitly examines sexuality and the construction of gender identities as they are played out in the production and visual imagery of dance.

Layton, R. (1991). *The anthropology of art* (2nd ed.). Cambridge, England: Cambridge University Press.

This readable introduction to the diversity of non-Western art deals with questions of aesthetic appreciation, the use of art, and the big question: What *is* art?

Morphy, H., & Perkins, M. (Eds.). (2006). *Anthropology of art: A reader.* Boston: Blackwell.

This illustrated anthology explores the art of different cultures at different times, covering the essential theoretical debates in the anthropology of art—including definitions of art and aesthetics, the nature of authenticity and representational processes, the Primitivism controversy, and the history of trade and commodification.

Seeger, A. (2004). *Why Suya sing: A musical anthropology.* Champaign: University of Illinois Press.

Examining the myth telling, speech making, and singing of Suyá Indians in Mato Grosso, Brazil, Seeger considers why music is important for them—and by extension for other groups. He reveals how Suyá singing creates euphoria out of silence, a village community out of a collection of houses, a socialized adult out of a boy, and contributes to the formation of ideas about time, space, and social identity.

Venbrux, E., Rosi, P. S., & Welsch, R. L. (Eds.) (2006). *Exploring world art.* Longrove, IL: Waveland Press.

Ethnographic case studies examine the contemporary art world from local and comparative global perspectives, spanning topics such as artistic agency, new art forms and media, arenas of cultural production, and the role of gender in these innovative traditions.

Thomson Audio Study Products

 Enjoy the MP3-ready Audio Lecture Overviews for each chapter and a comprehensive audio glossary of key terms for quick study and review. Whether walking to class, doing laundry, or studying at your desk, you now have the freedom to choose when, where, and how you interact with your audio-based educational media. See the preface for information on how to access this on-the-go study and review tool.

The Anthropology Resource Center

www.thomsonedu.com/anthropology
The Anthropology Resource Center provides extended learning materials to reinforce your understanding of key concepts in the four fields of anthropology. For each of the four fields, the Resource Center includes dynamic exercises including video exercises, map exercises, simulations, and "Meet the Scientists" interviews, as well as critical thinking questions that can be assigned and e-mailed to instructors. The Resource Center also provides breaking news in anthropology and interesting material on applied anthropology to help you link what you are learning to the world around you.

26 Processes of Change

CHALLENGE ISSUE

For long-term survival, human cultures have had to adapt to different environments and shifting circumstances. Today's technological and other major changes challenge us to adjust at an ever-faster pace. The challenge is all the more unsettling for traditional peoples around the world, for whom changes are often imposed by powerful outside forces undermining their customary ways of life. However, there are also many examples of traditional peoples confronting change on their own terms, welcoming certain new ideas, products, or practices into their lives as improvements. So it is with the means of transportation in developing countries such as Pakistan where the heavily-packed mules and camels that travel desert and mountain trails may also be found on city streets among cars, trucks, and buses. Since city traffic is often congested and slow-paced, it does not really matter whether one's transportation is a shrub-eating camel or a gas-fed vehicle.

Why Do Cultures Change?

All cultures change at one time or another for a variety of reasons. Although people may deliberately alter their ways in response to problems or challenges, much change is unforeseen, unplanned, and undirected. Changes in existing values and behavior may also come about due to contact with other peoples who introduce new ideas or tools. This may even involve the massive imposition of foreign ideas and practices through conquest of one group by another. Through cultural change, societies can adapt to altered conditions; however, not all change is positive or adaptive.

How Do Cultures Change?

The mechanisms of culture change include innovation, diffusion, cultural loss, and acculturation. Innovation is the discovery or creation of something that is then accepted by fellow members in a society. Diffusion is the borrowing of something from another group, and cultural loss is the abandonment of an existing practice or trait, with or without replacement. Acculturation is a massive change that comes about in a group due to intensive firsthand contact with another, usually more powerful, group. Typically, it occurs when dominant societies forcefully expand their activities beyond their borders, pressuring other societies to abandon their traditional cultures in favor of the foreign.

What Is Modernization?

Modernization is a problematic term referring to a process of change by which traditional, nonindustrial societies acquire characteristics of technologically complex societies. Accelerated modernization interconnecting all parts of the world is known as globalization. Although commonly assumed to be a good thing, modernization has also led to the destruction of treasured customs and values, leaving many people unsettled, disoriented, and demoralized.

Culture has become the primary medium through which the human species adapts to changes and solves the problems of existence. Various cultural institutions—such as religion, kinship and marriage, and political and economic organization—mesh to form an integrated cultural system. Because systems generally work to maintain stability, cultures are often fairly stable and remain so unless there is a critical change in one or more significant factors such as natural environment, technology, population density—or in human perceptions of the various conditions to which they are adapted.

Archaeological studies reveal how elements of a culture may persist for long periods. In northeastern North America, for example, the cultures of indigenous inhabitants remained relatively consistent over thousands of years because they successfully adapted to relatively minor fluctuations in their social conditions and natural environments, making changes from time to time in tools, utensils, and other material support.

Although stability may be a striking feature of many traditional cultures, all cultures are capable of adapting to changing conditions—climatic, economic, political, or ideological. Adaptation is a consequence of change that happens to work favorably for a population.

However, not all change is positive or adaptive, and not all cultures are equally well equipped for making the necessary adjustments in a timely fashion. In a stable society, change may occur gently and gradually, without altering in any fundamental way the culture's underlying structures, as was the case in much of North America before the European invasion several centuries ago. Sometimes, though, the pace of change may increase dramatically, to the point of destabilizing or even wrecking a cultural system. The modern world is full of examples of such radical changes, from the disintegration of the Soviet Union to the utter devastation of many indigenous communities in the Amazon caused by state efforts to develop Indian homelands and capitalize on the vast rainforest's natural resources.

The causes of change are many, including accidental discoveries, deliberate attempts to solve a perceived problem, and interaction with other people who introduce—or force—new ideas or tools or ways of life. Sometimes change is caused by the unexpected outcome of particular actions or events. Among countless examples is the establishment of European colonies in the homelands of Algonquian-speaking natives in northeastern America nearly 500 years ago. Many people today assume this came about because the culture of the newcomers was better or more advanced than that of the region's original inhabitants. However, one could just as well argue that it was the reverse, for at the time, these Indians had higher quality diets, enjoyed better health, and experienced less violence in their lives than did most Europeans.[1]

A deeper look at American history shows that the colonial settlements in New England were actually the outcome of a series of unrelated historical events that happened to coincide at a critical time. In the 1500s, economic and political developments in England drove large numbers of small farmers off the land during a period of population growth, thereby forcing an outward migration. By pure chance, this took place shortly after the European discovery of the Americas. Seeing the New World as an answer to its overpopulation, the English attempted to establish overseas colonies in lands they claimed and renamed New England. Early efforts failed, until an epidemic of unprecedented scope resulted in the sudden death of 75 to 90 percent of the indigenous inhabitants.

This devastating epidemic occurred because the region's native communities were exposed to a host of foreign diseases through contact with European fishermen and traders. It left the weakened remnants of indigenous survivors with few defenses against aggressive colonizers, many of whom possessed natural immunity to the diseases. (For centuries, Europeans had been living under conditions that were ideal for the incubation and spread of infectious diseases, which periodically killed off up to 80 percent of local populations. Since those who survived had a higher resistance to the diseases than those who succumbed, such resistance became more common in European populations over time. Indians at the time of the European invasion, by contrast, lacked all resistance to these diseases.)

Although the crucial issue of immunity played a huge role in England's North American colonization efforts, it is unlikely the English could have dispossessed the surviving indigenous peoples from their land were it not for one other important factor: They crossed the Atlantic Ocean equipped with the political and military techniques for dominating other peoples—tactics previously used to impose rule over the Scots, Irish, and Welsh. In addition, they came with the ideology of a "just war," which they believed justified dispossessing America's indigenous peoples who fought back in defense.

Change imposed upon one group by another continues in much of the world today as culture contact intensifies between societies unequal in power. Among those who have the power to drive and direct change in their favor, it is typically referred to as "progress." But progress is a relative term that implies improvement as de-

---

[1]Stannard, D. E. (1992). *American holocaust* (pp. 57–67). Oxford: Oxford University Press.

Like the millions of peasants about whom he wrote, Eric Wolf personally experienced radical upheaval in his life due to powerful outside political forces. A war refugee in his teens, he went on to survive the battlefields and mass murders of Nazi-occupied Europe. Driven by the inequities and atrocities he witnessed during World War II, he turned to anthropology to sort through issues of power. Viewing anthropology as the most scientific of the humanities and the most humane of the sciences, he became famous for his comparative historical studies on peasants, power, and the transforming impact of capitalism on traditional nations.

Eric Wolf's life began in Austria shortly after the First World War. During that terrible conflict, his Austrian father had been a prisoner of war in Siberia, where he met Wolf's mother, a Russian exile. When peace returned, the couple married and settled in Vienna, where Eric was born in 1923. Growing up in Austria's capital and then (because of his father's job) in Sudetenland in what is now the Czech Republic, young Eric enjoyed a life of relative ease. He relished summers spent in the Alps among local peasants in exotic costumes, and he drank in his mother's tales about her father's adventures with Siberian nomads.

Life changed for Eric in 1938 when Adolf Hitler grabbed power in Germany, annexed Austria and Sudetenland, and threatened Jews like the Wolfs. Seek-

© Sydel Silverman

ing security for their 15-year-old son, Eric's parents sent him to high school in England. In 1940, a year after World War II broke out, British authorities believed invasion was imminent and ordered aliens, including Eric, into an internment camp. There he met other refugees from Nazi-occupied Europe and had his first exposure to Marxist theories. Soon, he left England for New York City and enrolled at Queens College, where Professor Hortense Powdermaker, a former student of Malinowski, introduced him to anthropology.

In 1943, the 20-year-old refugee enlisted in the U.S. Army's 10th Mountain Division. Fighting in the mountains of Tuscany, Italy, he won a Silver Star for combat bravery. At the war's end, Wolf returned to the United States, completed his bachelor's degree, and went on to

graduate school at Columbia University, studying anthropology under Julian Steward and Ruth Benedict. After earning his doctorate in 1951, based on fieldwork in Puerto Rico, he did extensive research on Mexican peasants.

Following short stints at various U.S. universities, he became a professor at the University of Michigan in 1961. A prolific writer, Wolf gained tremendous recognition for his fourth book, *Peasant Wars of the Twentieth Century*, published in 1969 during the height of the Vietnam War. Against that war, he headed a newly founded ethics committee in the American Anthropological Association and helped expose counter-insurgency uses of anthropological research in Southeast Asia.

Wolf left Michigan in 1971, accepting a distinguished professorship at Lehman College in the Bronx, New York. There his classes were filled with working-class students of all ethnic backgrounds, including many who took the courses he taught in Spanish. In addition, he taught anthropology at the Graduate School of the City University of New York. After many more publications, Wolf wrote his award-winning book, *Europe and the People Without History* (1982). In 1990, he received a MacArthur "genius" prize. Shortly before his death of cancer in 1999, he published *Envisioning Power: Ideologies of Dominance and Crisis*, which explores how ideas and power are connected though the medium of culture.

---

fined by the people who profit or otherwise benefit from the changes set into motion. In other words, progress is in the eye of the beholder.

In recent decades, some anthropologists have focused on the historical impact European capitalist expansionism has had on indigenous cultures all around the world, radically changing or even destroying them. One of the first and most prominent among these anthropologists was Eric Wolf, who personally experienced the global havoc and upheaval of the 20th century (see Anthropologist of Note).

MECHANISMS OF CHANGE

Anthropologists are not only interested in the structures of cultures as systems of adaptation, which help us understand how a population maintains itself in a certain habitat, but also in explaining processes of culture change. Some of the major mechanisms involved in culture change are innovation, diffusion, and cultural loss. These types of change are typically voluntary and are not imposed on a population by outside forces.

A Hopi Indian woman firing pottery vessels. The earliest discovery that firing clay vessels makes them more durable took place in Asia, probably when clay-lined basins next to cooking fires were accidentally fired. Later, a similar innovation took place in the Americas.

© Stephen Trimble

Innovation

The ultimate source of all culture change is innovation: any new idea, method, or device that gains widespread acceptance in society. **Primary innovation** is the creation, invention, or chance discovery of a completely new idea, method, or device. A **secondary innovation** is a deliberate application or modification of an existing idea, method, or device.

An example of a primary innovation is the discovery that firing clay makes it permanently hard. Presumably, accidental firing of clay occurred frequently in ancient cooking fires—but a chance occurrence is of no account unless someone perceives an application of it. This perception took place about 25,000 years ago, when people began making figurines of fired clay. However, it was not until some time between 8,500 and 9,000 years ago that people recognized a highly practical application of fired clay and began using it to make pottery containers and cooking vessels—a secondary innovation.

THOMSON AUDIO STUDY PRODUCTS Take advantage of the MP3-ready Audio Lecture Overviews and comprehensive audio glossary of key terms for each chapter. See the preface for information on how to access this on-the-go study and review tool.

As nearly as we can reconstruct it, the development of the earliest known pottery vessels came about in the following way:[2] About 9,000 years ago, people in Southwest Asia still relied upon stone bowls, baskets, and animal-hide bags for containers. However, they were familiar with the working of clay, using it to build houses, line storage pits, and model figurines. In addition, their cooking areas included clay-lined basins built into the floor and clay ovens and hearths, making the accidental firing of clay inevitable. Once the significance of fired clay—the primary innovation—was understood, then the application of known techniques to it—secondary innovation—became possible. Clay could be modeled in the familiar way but now into the known shapes of existing containers. It could then be fired, either in an open fire or in the same facilities used for cooking food. The earliest known Southwest Asian pottery imitates leather and stone containers, but over time potters developed shapes and decorative techniques specifically suited to the new technology.

Archaeological research shows that the earliest known clay vessels produced were initially handmade, and the earliest furnaces or kilns were the same ovens used for cooking. As people became more adept at making pottery, they refined the technology. To aid in production, the clay could be modeled on a mat or other surface that could be turned as work progressed. Hence, the potter could sit in one place while working, without having to get up to move around the clay. A further re-

primary innovation The creation, invention, or chance discovery of a completely new idea, method, or device.
secondary innovation A new and deliberate application or modification of an existing idea, method, or device

_____

[2]Amiran, R. (1965). The beginnings of pottery-making in the Near East. In F. R. Matson (Ed.), *Ceramics and man* (pp. 240–247). Viking Fund Publications in Anthropology, 41.

Once one's reflexes become adjusted to doing something one way, it becomes difficult to do it differently. Thus, when a North American visits one of the world's many left-side drive countries (about sixty) such as Great Britain (or vice versa), learning to drive on the "wrong" side of the road is difficult.

finement was to mount the movable surface on a vertical rotating shaft—an application of a known principle used for drills—creating the potter's wheel and permitting mass production. Kilns, too, were modified for better heat circulation by separating the firing chamber from the fire itself. By chance, these improved kilns produced enough heat to smelt metal ores such as copper, tin, gold, silver, and lead. Presumably, this discovery was made by accident—another primary innovation—and set the stage for the eventual development of the forced-draft furnace out of the earlier pottery kiln.

The accidental discoveries responsible for primary innovations are not generated by environmental change or some other need, nor are they necessarily adaptive. They are, however, given structure by the cultural context. Thus, the outcome of the discovery of fired clay by migratory food foragers 25,000 years ago was very different from what it was when discovered later by more sedentary farmers in Southwest Asia, where it set off a cultural chain reaction as one invention led to another. Indeed, given particular sets of cultural goals, values, and knowledge, certain innovations are nearly inevitable.

Although a culture's internal dynamics may encourage certain innovative tendencies, they may discourage or remain neutral about others. Indeed, Polish astronomer Nicolaus Copernicus's discovery in the early 1500s of the rotation of the planets around the sun and the discovery of the basic laws of heredity in the early 1860s by botanist Gregor Mendel, a Roman Catholic monk in what is now the Czech Republic, are instances of genuine creative insights out of step with the established needs, values, and goals of their times and places. In fact, Mendel's work remained obscure until sixteen years

after his death, when three scientists working independently rediscovered, all in the same year (1900), the same laws of heredity. Thus, in the context of turn-of-the-century Western culture, Mendel's laws were bound to be discovered, even if Mendel's botanical experiments had not revealed them earlier.

Although an innovation must be reasonably consistent with a society's needs, values, and goals in order to gain acceptance, it takes more than this. Force of custom or habit tends to obstruct ready acceptance of the new or unfamiliar, for people typically stick with what they are used to rather than adopt something strange that requires adjustment on their part.

An example of this can be seen in the continued use of the QWERTY keyboard, named for the lineup of the top row of letters and familiar to all who use English language keyboards today. Devised in 1874, the QWERTY system was the first commercially successful typewriter. In 1932, after extensive study, U.S. education professor August Dvorak developed a more efficient system known as the Dvorak keyboard (Figure 26.1). Tests have shown that it can be learned in one-third the time it takes to master QWERTY. Moreover, once learned, the Dvorak system is less fatiguing and increases the average keyboard operator's accuracy by 68 percent and speed by 74 percent. So why has not Dvorak replaced QWERTY? The answer is commitment.

Because QWERTY had a head start, by the time Dvorak came along manufacturers, typists, teachers, salespeople, and office managers were committed to the old keyboard. It was what they were used to, and to this day it remains the standard on English language keyboards incorporated in a growing array of techno-

Figure 26.1

Dvorak and QWERTY keyboards, compared. Although superior to the latter in virtually every way, the Dvorak keyboard has not been adopted owing to the head start enjoyed by QWERTY.

Change, whether generated within a society or introduced from the outside, may encounter unexpected cultural obstacles. Such obstacles are often ideologically embedded in religious faith-based traditions, such as some conservative Mennonite sects in North America rejecting motorized vehicles in their rural communities. In several Asian and African countries primarily inhabited by Muslims, orthodox religious groups oppose modern development and the spread of what they consider immoral foreign influences. Instead, they seek to return to or maintain a society based on Muslim traditions. Here we see a class of traditional Muslim students in Lahore, Pakistan, studying the holy scriptures of the Koran at a *madrassah* (religious school).

logical innovations—from PCs and laptops to handheld computers.[3]

Obviously, an innovation is not assured of acceptance simply because it is notably better than the thing, method, or idea it might replace. Much depends on the prestige of the innovator and potential adopters. If the innovator's prestige is high, this will help gain more general acceptance for the innovation. If it is low, acceptance is less likely, unless the innovator can attract a sponsor who has high prestige.

Diffusion

The spread of certain ideas, customs, or practices from one culture to another is known as **diffusion.** So common is cross-cultural borrowing that North American anthropologist Ralph Linton suggested that it accounts

for as much as 90 percent of any culture's content. People are creative about their borrowing, however, picking and choosing from multiple possibilities and sources. Usually their selections are limited to those compatible with the existing culture. In Guatemala in the 1960s, for example, Maya Indians, who then (as now) made up more than half of that country's population, would adopt Western ways if the practical advantage of what they adopted was self-evident and did not conflict with deeply rooted traditional values and customs. The use of metal hoes, shovels, and machetes became standard early on, for they are superior to stone tools and yet compatible with the cultivation of corn in the traditional way by men using hand tools.

Yet, certain other modern practices that might seem advantageous to the Maya were resisted if they were perceived to be in conflict with Indian tradition. Pursuing these practices could make one a social outcast. This happened to a young farmer who tried using chemical fertilizers and pesticides to grow cash crops of vegetables not eaten by the Maya to sell in the city. He found he could not secure a "good" woman for a wife—a "good" woman (in his cultural context) being one who has never had sex with another man and is hard-working, skilled at

---

[3]Diamond, J. (1997). The curse of QWERTY. *Discover 18* (4), 34–42.

diffusion The spread of certain ideas, customs, or practices from one culture to another.

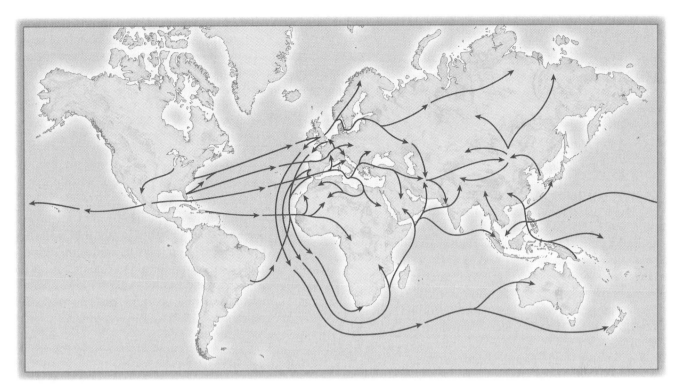

Figure 26.2
The diffusion of tobacco. Having spread from the tropics of the western hemisphere to much of the rest
of North and South America, it spread rapidly to the rest of the world after Italian explorer Christopher
Columbus first crossed the Atlantic in 1492.

domestic chores, and willing to attend to her husband's needs. However, after abandoning his unorthodox ways, he gained acceptance in his community as a "real" man—one who provides for his household by working steadily at farming and making charcoal in the traditional ways. No longer conspicuous as someone different from other local men, he married well within a short time.[4]

An awareness of the extent of cultural borrowing can be eye opening. Take, for example, the numerous things that people all around the globe have borrowed from American Indians. Domestic plants developed ("invented") by the Indians—potatoes, avocados, beans, squash, tomatoes, peanuts, manioc, chili peppers, chocolate, sweet potatoes, and corn or maize, to name a few—furnish a major portion of the world's food supply. In fact, American Indians are recognized as primary contributors to the world's varied cuisine and credited with developing the largest array of nutritious foods.[5]

As for drugs and stimulants introduced by Indians, tobacco is the best known (Figure 26.2), but others include the coca in cocaine, ephedra in ephedrine, datura

in pain relievers, and cascara in laxatives. Early on, Europeans discovered that Indians had a most sophisticated pharmacy. For instance, Spanish Jesuit missionaries in Peru and Ecuador in the 17th century learned from indigenous healers about the medicinal properties of the bitter tree bark of which quinine is extracted to treat malaria. All told, 200 plants and herbs used by Native Americans for medicinal purposes have at one time or another been included in official government-approved prescription and over the counter drugs.

On top of this, varieties of cotton developed by Indians supply much of the world's clothing needs, while the woolen poncho, the parka, and moccasins are universally familiar items. These borrowings are so thoroughly integrated into contemporary societies across the globe that few people are aware of their source.

Despite the obvious importance of diffusion, an innovation from another culture probably faces more obstacles when it comes to being accepted than does one that is "homegrown" simply because it is foreign. In the United States, for example, this is one reason why people have been so reluctant to abandon the cumbersome English system of weights and measures for the far more logical metric system. While all other countries in the world have essentially converted to metric, in the United States the switchover is still less than about 50 percent.

[4]Reina, R. E. (1966). *The law of the saints* (pp. 65–68). Indianapolis: Bobbs-Merrill.

[5]Weatherford, J. (1988). *Indian givers: How the Indians of the Americas transformed the New World* (p. 115). New York: Ballantine.

Hence, ethnocentrism may act as a barrier to cultural diffusion.

Cultural Loss

Most often people look at culture change as an accumulation of innovations. Frequently, however, the acceptance of a new innovation results in **cultural loss**—the abandonment of an existing practice or trait. For example, in ancient times chariots and carts were used widely in northern Africa and southwestern Asia, but wheeled vehicles virtually disappeared from Morocco to Afghanistan about 1,500 years ago. They were replaced by camels, not because of some reversion to the past but because camels used as pack animals worked better. The old Roman empire roads had deteriorated, and these sturdy animals traveled well with or without roads. Their endurance, longevity, and ability to ford rivers and traverse rough ground made pack camels admirably suited for the region. Plus, they were economical in terms of labor: A wagon required a man for every two draft animals, but a single person could manage up to six pack camels.

Reflecting on this, U.S. paleontologist Stephen Jay Gould commented that this surprises most Westerners because:

> Wheels have come to symbolize in our culture . . . intelligent exploitation and technological progress. . . . The success of camels reemphasizes a fundamental theme. . . . Adaptation, be it biological or cultural, represents a better fit to specific, local environments, not an inevitable stage in a ladder of progress. Wheels were a formidable invention, and their uses are manifold. . . . But camels may work better in some circumstances. Wheels, like wings, fins, and brains, are exquisite devices for certain purposes, not signs of intrinsic superiority.[6]

Often overlooked is another facet of losing apparently useful traits: loss without replacement. An example of this is the historical absence of boats among the indigenous inhabitants of the Canary Islands, a group of small islands isolated off North Africa's Atlantic coast. The ancestors of these people must have had boats, for without them they could never have transported themselves and their domestic livestock to the islands in the first place.

Later, without boats, they had no way to communicate between islands or with the mainland. This loss of something useful came about due to the islands' lack of stone suitable for making polished stone axes, which in turn limited the islanders' carpentry.[7]

REPRESSIVE CHANGE

Innovation, diffusion, and cultural loss all may take place among peoples who are free to decide for themselves what changes they will or will not accept. Not always, however, do people have the liberty to make their own choices. Frequently, changes they would not willingly make have been forced upon them by some other group, usually in the course of conquest and colonialism. A direct outcome in many cases is repressive culture change, which anthropologists call acculturation. The most radical form of repressive culture change is ethnocide.

Acculturation and Ethnocide

Acculturation is the massive culture change that occurs in a society when it experiences intensive firsthand contact with a more powerful society. It always involves an element of force, either directly, as in conquests, or indirectly, as in the implicit or explicit threat that force will be used if people refuse to make the demanded changes. Other variables include degree of cultural difference; circumstances, intensity, frequency, and hostility of contact; relative status of the agents of contact; who is dominant and who is submissive; and whether the nature of the flow is reciprocal or nonreciprocal. *Acculturation* and *diffusion* are not equivalent terms; one culture can borrow from another without being in the least acculturated.

In the course of cultural contact, any number of things may happen. Merger or fusion occurs when two cultures lose their separate identities and form a single culture, as historically expressed by the melting pot ideology of English-speaking, Protestant Euramerican culture in the United States. Sometimes, though, one of the cultures loses its autonomy but retains its identity as a subculture in the form of a caste, class, or ethnic group. This is typical of conquest or slavery situations, and the United States has examples of this in spite of its melting pot ideology—we need look no further than the nearest American Indian reservation.

In virtually all parts of the world today, people are faced with the tragedy of forced removal from their traditional homelands, as entire communities are uprooted to make way for hydroelectric projects, grazing lands for cattle, mining operations, or highway construction. In Brazil's rush to develop the vast Amazon rainforest,

---

[6]Gould, S. J. (1983). *Hens' teeth and horses' toes* (p. 159). New York: Norton.

cultural loss The abandonment of an existing practice or trait.
acculturation Massive culture change that occurs in a society when it experiences intensive firsthand contact with a more powerful society.

---

[7]Coon, C. S. (1954). *The story of man* (p. 174). New York: Knopf.

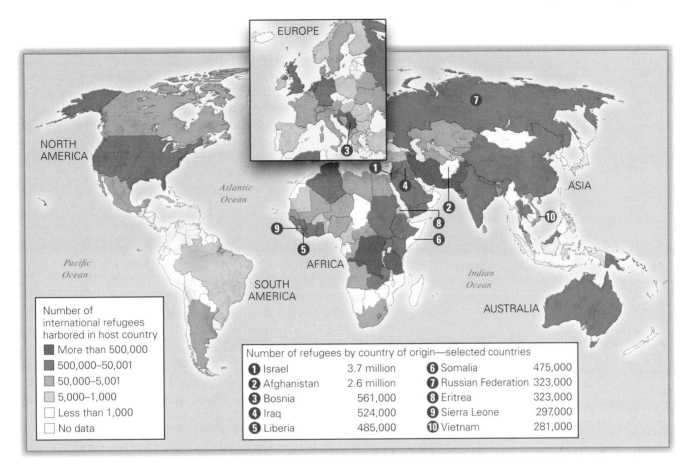

Figure 26.3
Increasing refugee populations, a consequence of conflict between nationalities living in multinational states, have become a burden and source of instability in the states to which they have fled.

for instance, entire indigenous communities have been relocated to "national parks," where resources are inadequate for the number of people and where former enemies are often forced to live in close proximity.

Ethnocide, the violent eradication of an ethnic group's collective cultural identity as a distinctive people, occurs when a dominant society deliberately sets out to destroy another society's cultural heritage. This may take place when a powerful nation aggressively expands its territorial control by annexing neighboring peoples and their territories, incorporating the conquered groups as subjects. A policy of ethnocide typically includes forbidding a subjugated nation's ancestral language, criminalizing their traditional customs, destroying their religion and demolishing sacred places and practices, breaking up their social organizations, and dispossessing or removing the survivors from their homelands—in essence, stopping short of physical extermination while removing all traces of their unique culture.

One tragic current example is Tibet, which could not defend itself against an invasion by the Chinese communist army in 1950. The Chinese government then initiated its ethnocidal policies by means of systematic attacks

against traditional Tibetan culture. Seeking to stamp out deeply rooted religious beliefs and practices, it ordered the demolition of most Buddhist temples and monasteries. Following a mass uprising, hundreds of thousands of Tibetans were killed or forced into exile abroad. Seeking to annihilate Tibetan identity, China sought to turn the surviving Tibetans into political subjects who would culturally identify themselves as Chinese nationals.[8]

Ethnocide may also take place when so many carriers of a culture die that those who manage to survive become refugees, living among peoples of different cultures. Examples of this may be seen in many parts of the world today (Figure 26.3). A particularly well-

_____

[8]http://www.savetibet.org/tibet/us/proceedings/senatefrmaur amoynihan.php. See also Avedon, John F. (1997). *In exile from the land of snows: The definitive account of the Dalai Lama and Tibet since the Chinese conquest.* New York: Harper.

ethnocide The violent eradication of an ethnic group's collective cultural identity as a distinctive people; occurs when a dominant society deliberately sets out to destroy another society's cultural heritage.

documented case occurred in Brazil's Amazon basin in 1968, when developers hired killers to wipe out several Indian groups, using arsenic, dynamite, and machine guns from light planes.

Violence continues to be used in Brazil as a means of dealing with indigenous peoples. For example, according to conservative estimates, at least 1,500 Yanomami Indians died in the 1980s, many the victims of deliberate massacres, as cattle ranchers and gold miners poured into northern Brazil. By 1990, 70 percent of Yanomami land in Brazil had been illegally expropriated; fish supplies were poisoned by mercury contamination of rivers; and malaria, venereal disease, and tuberculosis were running rampant. The Yanomami were dying at the rate of 10 percent a year, and their fertility had dropped to near zero. Many villages were left with no children or old people, and the survivors awaited their fate with a profound terror of extinction.[9]

The typical attitude of many Brazilians toward such situations is illustrated by their government's reaction to a diplomatic journey that two Kayapó Indian leaders and an anthropologist made to the United States. They ventured north to speak with World Bank authorities and various government officials in the U.S. Congress and State Department concerning the destruction of their land and way of life caused by internationally financed development projects. All three were charged with vio-

---

[9]Turner, T. (1991). Major shift in Brazilian Yanomami policy. *Anthropology Newsletter 32* (5), 1, 46.

genocide　The physical extermination of one people by another, either as a deliberate act or as the accidental outcome of activities carried out by one people with little regard for their impact on others.

lating Brazil's Foreign Sedition Act, which prohibits foreigners from secretly stirring up discontent, resistance, or revolt against the government in power. This charge and other relevant atrocities provoked international outrage, which in turn prompted Brazilian authorities to recommend policy changes that could favorably impact the country's indigenous peoples. However, whether their recommendations will be sufficient to effect positive change, or will even be acted upon fully, remains to be seen.

Genocide

The Brazilian Indian case just cited raises the issue of **genocide**—the physical extermination of one people by another, either as a deliberate act or as the accidental outcome of activities carried out by one people with little regard for their impact on others. Genocide, like ethnocide, is not new in the world. In North America in 1637, for example, a deliberate attempt was made to destroy the Pequot Indians by setting fire to their village at Mystic, Connecticut, and then shooting down all those—primarily unarmed elders, women, and children—who sought to escape the fire. To ensure that even their very memory would be stamped out, colonial authorities forbade the mention of the Pequot name. Numerous other massacres of Indian peoples occurred thereafter, up until the last one at Wounded Knee, South Dakota, in 1890.

Of course, such acts were by no means restricted to North America. One of the most famous 19th-century acts of genocide was the extermination of the indigenous inhabitants of Tasmania, a large island just south of Australia. In this case, the use of military force failed to achieve the complete elimination of the Tasmanians, but what the military could not achieve was done by George Augustus Robinson, a British Protestant missionary. He rounded up the surviving natives and brought them to his mission station, where they died from the combination of psychological depression and lack of resistance to European disease. Robinson retired to Britain to contemplate the horrible if unintended consequences of his actions, having brought about the demise of the last full-blooded Tasmanians.

The most widely known act of genocide in recent history was the attempt of the Nazis during World War II to wipe out European Jews and Roma (Gypsies) in the name of racial superiority and improvement of the human species. Unfortunately, the common practice of referring to this as *"the* Holocaust"—as if it were something unique, or at least exceptional—tends to blind us to the fact that this thoroughly monstrous act is but one example of an all-too-common phenomenon. Among many examples of mass murder in more recent years, Khmer Rouge soldiers in Cambodia killed 1.7 million fellow citi-

VISUAL COUNTERPOINT

© Bettmann/Corbis

© Scully/Getty Images

Two of many examples of attempted genocide in the 20th century: Hitler's Germany against Jews and Gypsies in the 1930s and the 1940s; and Hutus against Tutsis in Rwanda, as in this 1994 massacre.

zens in the 1970s. In the following decade, government-sponsored terrorism against indigenous communities in Guatemala reached its height, and Saddam Hussein's government used poison gas against the Kurdish ethnic minority in northern Iraq. In the 1990s, more than half a million Tutsi people were slaughtered by their Hutu neighbors in the African country of Rwanda, and today a genocidal campaign is waged against the non-Arab black peoples in the Darfur desert region of western Sudan. Estimates vary, but during the 20th century, as many as 83 million people died of genocide and tyranny.[10]

If such ugly practices are ever to end, we must gain a better understanding of what is behind them. Anthropologists are actively engaged in this, carrying out cross-cultural as well as specific case studies. One finding to

emerge is the regularity with which religious, economic, and political interests are allied in cases of genocide. In Tasmania, for example, British wool growers wanted the indigenous peoples off the island so that they could have it for their sheep. The government advanced their interests through its military campaigns against the natives, but it was the British missionary work that finally secured Tasmania for the commercial wool interests.

Directed Change

As we have seen, genocide is not about change but annihilation. The most extreme cases of forced cultural change, or acculturation, occur as a result of military conquest or massive invasion and breaking up of traditional political structures by dominant newcomers who know or care nothing about the culture they control. The indigenous people—unable to effectively resist imposed changes and obstructed in carrying out many of their own social, religious, and economic activities—may be

---

[10]White, M. (2001). *Historical atlas of the twentieth century.* http://users.erols.com/mwhite28/20centry.htm; see also Van Den Berghe, P. (1992). The modern state: Nation builder or nation killer? *International Journal of Group Tensions 22* (3), 198.

forced into new practices that tend to isolate individuals and destroy the integrity of their societies.

So it was with the Ju/'hoansi of Namibia in southern Africa. Rounded up in the early 1960s, these Bushmen were confined to a reservation in Tsumkwe where they could not possibly provide for their own needs. The government supplied them with rations, but these were insufficient to meet basic nutritional needs. In poor health and prevented from developing meaningful alternatives to traditional activities, the Ju/'hoansi became embittered and depressed, and their death rate came to exceed the birthrate. Within the next few years, however, surviving Ju/'hoansi began to take matters into their own hands. They returned to water holes in their traditional homeland, where, assisted by anthropologists and others concerned with their welfare, they are trying to sustain themselves by raising livestock. Whether this will succeed or not remains to be seen, as there are still many obstacles to success.

One by-product of colonial dealings with indigenous peoples has been the growth of *applied anthropology,* defined in Chapter 1 as the use of anthropological techniques and knowledge for the purpose of solving practical problems. For example, in the United States, the Bureau of American Ethnology was founded in 1876 to gather reliable data the government might use to formulate Indian policies. At the time, anthropologists were convinced of the practicality of their discipline, and many who did ethnographic work among Indians devoted a great deal of time, energy, and even money to assisting their informants, whose interests were frequently threatened from outside.

In the 20th century, the scope and intent of applied anthropology expanded. In the first part of that century, the applied work of Franz Boas—who almost single-handedly trained an entire generation of anthropologists in the United States—proved instrumental in reforming the country's immigration policies. With impressive statistical data based on comparative skull measurements and related physical anthropological studies, this German Jewish immigrant challenged popular race theories of the day. He demonstrated that theories privileging non-Jewish immigrants from western Europe and discriminating against Jews and others deemed undesirable as newcomers in the United States were based not on fact but on deeply rooted racial prejudice.

In the 1930s, anthropologists with clearly pragmatic objectives did a number of studies in industrial and other institutional settings in the United States. With World War II came increased involvement at colonial administration beyond U.S. borders, especially in the Pacific, by American officers trained in anthropology. The rapid postwar recovery of Japan was due in no small measure to the influence of anthropologists in structuring the U.S. occupation. Anthropologists continue to play an active role today in administering U.S. trust territories in the Pacific.

All too often, however, states and other powerful institutions directly intervening in the affairs of different ethnic groups or foreign societies fail to seek professional advice from anthropologists who possess relevant cross-cultural expertise and deeper insights. Such failures have contributed to a host of avoidable errors in planning and executing nation-building programs in ethnically divided countries such as Iraq and Afghanistan, both of which are now devastated by war and violence.

Today, applied anthropologists are in growing demand in the field of international development because of their specialized knowledge of social structure, value systems, and the functional interrelatedness of cultures targeted for development. Those working in this arena face a particular challenge: As anthropologists, they are bound to respect other peoples' dignity and cultural integrity, yet they are asked for advice on how to change certain aspects of those cultures. If the request comes from the people themselves, that is one thing, but more often than not, it comes from outsiders. Supposedly, the proposed change is for the good of the targeted population, yet members of that community do not always see it that way. Just how far applied anthropologists should go in advising outsiders how to manipulate people—especially those without the power to resist—to embrace changes proposed for them is a serious ethical question.

In direct response to such critical questions concerning the application and benefits of anthropological research, an alternative type of practical anthropology has emerged during the last half century. Known by a variety of names—including action anthropology and committed, engaged, involved, and advocacy anthropology—this involves community-based research and action in collaboration and solidarity with indigenous societies, ethnic minorities, and other besieged or repressed groups. In sum, the practical applications of anthropology are not only necessary, but there is a growing demand for anthropologically informed pragmatic solutions.

REACTIONS TO REPRESSIVE CHANGE

The reactions of indigenous peoples to the changes outsiders have thrust upon them have varied considerably. Some have responded by moving to the nearest available forest, desert, or other remote places in hopes of being left alone. In Brazil, a number of communities once located near the coast took this option a few hundred years ago and were successful until the great push to develop

© Jerry Leach

Indigenous peoples have reacted to colonialism in many different ways. When British missionaries pressed Trobriand Islanders of Melanesia to celebrate their regular yam harvests with a game of "civilized" cricket rather than traditional "wild" erotic dances, Trobrianders responded by transforming the staid British sport into an exuberant event that featured sexual chants and dances between innings. This is an example of syncretism—the creative blending of indigenous and foreign beliefs and practices into new cultural forms.

the Amazon forest began in the 1960s. Others, like many Indians of North America, took up arms to fight back but were ultimately forced to sign treaties and surrender much of their ancestral lands, after which they were reduced to an impoverished underclass in their own land. Today, they continue to fight through nonviolent means to retain their identities as distinct peoples and to regain control over natural resources on their lands.

In addition, ethnic groups may try to retain their distinctive identities by maintaining cultural boundaries such as holding on to traditional language, festive ceremonies, customary dress, ritual songs and dances, unique food, and so on. Indeed, in opposing modernization, people often seek cultural protection and emotional comfort from **tradition**—customary ideas and practices passed on from generation to generation, which in a modernizing society may form an obstacle to new ways of doing things.

When people are able to hold on to some of their traditions in the face of powerful outside domination, the result may be **syncretism**—the creative blending of indigenous and foreign beliefs and practices into new cultural forms. A fine illustration of this is the game of cricket as played by the Trobriand Islanders of Melanesia, some of whose practices we looked at in earlier chapters. When Trobrianders were under British rule, missionaries introduced them to this rather reserved British game to replace the erotic dancing and open sexuality that normally followed the yam harvests. Traditionally,

this was the season when chiefs sought to spread their fame by hosting nights of dancing, providing food for the hundreds of young married people who participated. For several months, there would be night after night of provocative dancing, accompanied by chanting and shouting full of sexual innuendo, each night ending as couples disappeared into the bush together.

Since no chief wished to be outdone by any other (being outdone brought into question the strength of one's magic), the dancing had a strong competitive element, and fighting sometimes erupted. To the British Protestant missionaries, cricket seemed a good way to end all of this in a way that would encourage conformity to "civilized" comportment in dress, religion, and sportsmanship. The Trobrianders, however, were determined to "rubbish" (throw out) the British rules of the game. They did this by turning it into the same kind of distinctly Trobriand event that their thrilling dance competitions had once been.

Making cricket their own, Trobrianders added battle dress and battle magic and incorporated erotic dancing into the game. Instead of inviting dancers each night,

tradition Customary ideas and practices passed on from generation to generation, which in a modernizing society may form an obstacle to new ways of doing things.
syncretism In acculturation, the creative blending of indigenous and foreign beliefs and practices into new cultural forms.

chiefs now arrange cricket matches. Pitching has been modified from the British style to one closer to their old way of throwing a spear. Following the game, they hold massive feasts, where wealth is displayed to enhance their prestige.

Cricket, in its altered form, has been made to serve traditional systems of prestige and exchange. Neither primitive nor passively accepted in its original form, Trobriand cricket was thoughtfully and creatively adapted into a sophisticated activity reflecting the importance of basic indigenous cultural premises. Exuberance and pride are displayed by everyone associated with the sport, and the players are as much concerned with conveying the full meaning of who they are as with scoring well. From the sensual dressing in preparation for the game to the team chanting songs full of sexual metaphors to the erotic chorus-line dancing between the innings, it is clear that each participant is playing for his own importance, for the fame of his team, and for the hundreds of attractive young women who watch the game.

Revitalization Movements

Another common reaction to repressive change is revitalization. As noted in an earlier chapter, revitalization movements are efforts for radical culture reform in response to widespread social disruption and collective feelings of anxiety and despair. When primary ties of culture, social relationships, and activities are broken and meaningless activity is imposed by outside forces, individuals and groups characteristically react by rejecting newly introduced cultural elements and reclaiming historical roots and traditional identity, as well as with spiritual imagination.

In the United States, revitalization movements have occurred often—whenever significant segments of the population have found their conditions in life to be at odds with the values of the American Dream. For example, the 1960s saw the emergence of revitalization movements among young people of middle-class and even upper-class families. In their case, the professed cultural values of peace, equality, and individual freedom were seen to be at odds with the realities of persistent war, poverty, and constraints on individual action imposed by a variety of impersonal institutions. Youths countered these realities by advocating free love, joining hippie communes, celebrating new forms of rock and folk music, using mind-altering drugs, challenging authority, growing their hair long, and wearing unconventional clothes.

By the 1980s revitalization movements were becoming prominent even among older, more affluent segments of U.S. society, as in the rise of the so-called religious right. In these cases, the reaction is not so much

Flanked by indigenous spiritual leaders, Bolivia's newly elected President Evo Morales was ceremonially inaugurated at the archaeological site of Tiwanaku, the ancient capital of a large indigenous empire in the Bolivian highlands surrounding Lake Titicaca. The first indigenous head of state elected since the Spanish conquest of Bolivia, Morales was dressed in traditional royal clothing. In their native tongue, he addressed a crowd that included thousands of Bolivian Indians, telling them, "Today begins a new era for the native peoples of the world." Morales chose this symbolic event to officially launch an indigenous cultural revitalization movement in a country where most citizens are members of Indian nations. Mostly poverty-stricken, these Bolivian Indians have seen their ancestral traditions repressed, marginalized, or ridiculed by Spanish-speaking European invaders and their descendants during the past five centuries.

against a perceived failure of the American Dream as it is against perceived threats to that dream by dissenters and activists within their society, by foreign governments, by new ideas that challenge other ideas they prefer to believe, and by the sheer complexity of modern life.

Clearly, when value systems are out of step with existing realities, a condition of cultural crisis is likely to build up that may breed reactive movements. Not all suppressed, conquered, or colonized people eventually rebel against established authority, although why they do not is debatable. When they do, however, cultural resistance may take one of several forms, all of which are varieties of revitalization movements. Some of these revitalization movements take on a revolutionary character, as did the Taliban in Afghanistan.

REBELLION AND REVOLUTION

When the scale of discontent within a society reaches a certain level, the possibilities are high for **rebellion**—organized armed resistance to an established government or authority in power. For instance, there have been many peasant rebellions around the world in the course of history. Often, such rebellions are triggered by repressive regimes imposing new taxes on the already struggling small farmers unable to feed their families under such unacceptable levels of exploitation.

One current example is the Zapatista Maya Indian uprising in southern Mexico, which began in the mid-1990s and has not yet been resolved. This rebellion involves thousands of poor Indian farmers whose livelihoods have been threatened by the disruptive outside changes imposed on them and whose human rights under the Mexican constitution have never been fully implemented.

In contrast to rebellions, which have rather limited objectives, a **revolution**—a radical change in a society or culture—involves a more radical transformation. Revolutions occur when the level of discontent in a society is very high. In the political arena, revolution involves the forced overthrow of an old government and the establishment of a completely new one.

Such was the case when Muslim fundamentalists in Iran toppled the imperial regime of the shah in 1979 and replaced him with Ayatollah Khomeini, a high-ranking Shiite Muslim religious leader. Returning to his homeland from exile and becoming Iran's new leader, he instituted a new social and political order.

The question of why revolutions erupt, as well as why they frequently fail to live up to the expectations of the people initiating them, is unsolved. It is clear, however, that the colonial policies of countries such as Britain, France, Spain, Portugal, and the United States during the 19th and early 20th centuries have created a worldwide situation in which revolution is nearly inevitable. Despite the political independence most colonies have gained since World War II, powerful countries continue to exploit many of these "underdeveloped" countries for their natural resources and cheap labor, causing a deep resentment of rulers beholden to foreign powers. Further discontent has been caused as governing elites in newly independent states try to assert their control over peoples living within their boundaries. By virtue of a common ancestry, possession of distinct cultures, persistent occupation of their own territories, and traditions of self-determination, the peoples they aim to control identify themselves as distinct nations and refuse to recognize the legitimacy of what they regard as a foreign government.

Thus, in many a former colony, large numbers of people have taken up arms to resist annexation and absorption by imposed state governments run by people of other nationalities. As they attempt to make their multiethnic states into unified countries, ruling elites of one nationality set about stripping the peoples of other nations within their states of their lands, resources, and particular cultural identities. The phenomenon is so common that it led Belgian sociologist Pierre van den Berghe to label what modern states refer to as "nation building" as, in fact, "nation killing."[11]

One of the most important facts of our time is that the vast majority of the distinct peoples of the world have never consented to rule by the governments of states within which they find themselves living.[12] In many newly emerging countries, such peoples feel they have no other option than to fight.

From an examination of various revolutions of the past, the following conditions have been offered as causes of rebellion and revolution:

1. Loss of prestige of established authority, often from the failure of foreign policy, financial difficulties, dismissals of popular ministers, or alteration of popular policies.
2. Threat to recent economic improvement. In France and Russia, sections of the population (professional classes and urban workers) whose economic fortunes previously had taken an upward swing were radicalized by unexpected setbacks, such as steeply rising food prices and unemployment.
3. Government indecisiveness, as exemplified by a lack of consistent policy. Such governments appear to be controlled by, rather than in control of, events.
4. Loss of support from the intellectual class. Such a loss deprived the prerevolutionary governments of France and Russia of philosophical support and popularity among the literate public.
5. A leader or group of leaders with enough charisma, or popular appeal, to mobilize a substantial part of the population against the establishment.

Apart from resistance to internal authority, such as in the Chinese, French, and Russian revolutions, many

---

[11]Van Den Berghe, P. (1992). The modern state: Nation builder or nation killer? *International Journal of Group Tensions* 22 (3), 191–207.

[12]Nietschmann, B. (1987). The third world war. *Cultural Survival Quarterly* 11 (3), 3.

---

rebellion Organized armed resistance to an established government or authority in power.
revolution Radical change in a society or culture. In the political arena, it involves the forced overthrow of an old government and establishment of a completely new one.

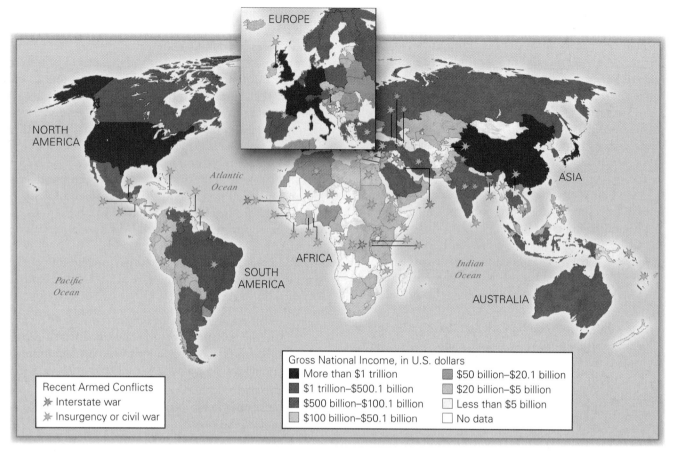

Figure 26.4

Today, the majority of armed conflicts are in the economically poor countries of Africa, Asia, Central and South America, many of which were at one time under European colonial domination. Most are between the state and one or more nations or ethnic groups within the state's borders who are seeking to maintain or regain control over their lives, lands, and resources.

revolutions in modern times have been struggles against an authority imposed by outsiders. Such resistance usually takes the form of independence movements that wage campaigns of armed defiance against colonial powers. The Algerian struggle for independence from France is a relevant example. Of the hundreds of armed conflicts in the world today, almost all are in the economically poor countries of Africa, Asia, Central and South America, many of which were at one time under European colonial domination (Figure 26.4). Of these wars, the majority are between the state and one or more nations or ethnic groups within the state's borders who are seeking to maintain or regain control of their personal lives, communities, lands, and resources in the face of what they regard as repression or subjugation by a foreign power.[13]

Revolutions do not always accomplish what they set out to do. One of the stated goals of the 1949 Chi-

nese communist revolution, for example, was to liberate women from the oppression of a strongly patriarchal society in which a woman owed lifelong obedience to some male relative—first her father, later her husband and, after his death, her oldest son. Although changes were (and continue to be) made, the transformation overall has been frustrated by the cultural lens through which the revolutionaries viewed their work. A tradition of deeply rooted patriarchy extending back at least 2,200 years is not easily overcome and has influenced many of the decisions made by communist China's leaders since the revolution.

In many parts of rural China today, as in the past, a woman's life is still largely determined by her relationship to a man, be it her father, husband, or son, rather than by her own efforts or failures. What's more, many rural women face official local policies that identify their primary roles as wives and mothers. When they do work outside the house, it is generally at jobs with low pay, low status, and no benefits. Indeed, the 1990s saw a major outbreak of the abduction and sale of women from ru-

---

[13] Nietschmann, B. (1987). The third world war. *Cultural Survival Quarterly* 11 (3), 7.

In China, women's labor has become critical to economic expansion. Much of this labor is controlled by male heads of families, who act as agents of the state in allocating labor.

ral areas as brides and workers. Women's no-wage home labor (and low-wage outside labor) for their husbands' households have been essential to China's economic expansion, which relies on the allocation of labor by the heads of patrilineal households.[14]

This situation shows that the undermining of revolutionary goals, if it occurs, is not necessarily by political opponents. Rather, it may be a consequence of the revolutionaries' own traditional cultural background. In rural China, as long as women marry out and their labor is controlled by male heads of families, women will be seen as a commodity.

It should be understood that revolution is a relatively recent phenomenon, occurring only during the past 5,000 years or so. The reason is that political rebellion requires a centralized political authority to rebel against, and states did not exist before 5,000 years ago. Obviously, then, in kin-ordered societies organized as tribes and bands, without a centralized government, there could be no rebellion or political revolution.

MODERNIZATION

One of the most frequently used terms to describe social and cultural changes as they are occurring today is **modernization.** This is most clearly defined as an all-encompassing and global process of political and socioeconomic change, whereby developing societies acquire some of the cultural characteristics common to Western industrial societies.

Derived from the Latin word *modo* ("just now"), modernization literally refers to something "in the pres-

ent time." The dominant idea behind this concept is that "becoming modern" is becoming like North American and other industrial societies, with the very clear implication that not to do so is to be stuck in the past—backward, inferior, and needing to be improved. It is unfortunate that the term *modernization* continues to be so widely used. Since we seem to be stuck with it, the best we can do at the moment is to recognize its problematic one-sidedness, even as we continue to use it.

The process of modernization may be best understood as consisting of four subprocesses, of which one is *technological development.* In the course of modernization, traditional knowledge and techniques give way to the application of scientific knowledge and techniques borrowed mainly from the industrialized West.

Another subprocess is *agricultural development,* represented by a shift in emphasis from subsistence farming to commercial farming. Instead of raising crops and livestock for their own use, people turn with growing frequency to the production of cash crops, with increased reliance on a cash economy and on global markets for selling farm products and purchasing goods.

A third subprocess is *industrialization,* with a greater emphasis placed on material forms of energy—especially fossil fuels—to drive machines. Human and animal power becomes less important, as do handicrafts in general. The fourth subprocess is *urbanization,* marked particularly by population movements from rural settlements into cities. Although all four subprocesses are interrelated, there is no fixed order of appearance.

[14]Gates, H. (1996). Buying brides in China—again. *Anthropology Today* 12 (4), 10.

modernization The process of political and socioeconomic change, whereby developing societies acquire some of the cultural characteristics of Western industrial societies.

In the 1960s, Saami reindeer herders in Scandinavia's Arctic tundra adopted newly invented snowmobiles, convinced that these modern machines would make traditional herding physically easier and economically more advantageous. Here, a young Saami man stands beside his tent and snowmobile, searching for his reindeer with binoculars.

As modernization proceeds, other changes are likely to follow. In the political realm, political parties and some sort of electoral apparatus frequently appear, along with the development of an administrative bureaucracy. In formal education, institutional learning opportunities expand, literacy increases, and an indigenous educated elite develops. Religion becomes less important in many areas of thought and behavior, as traditional beliefs and practices are undermined. Many traditional rights and duties connected with kinship are altered, if not eliminated, especially where distant relatives are concerned. Finally, where social stratification is a factor, social mobility increases as ascribed status becomes less important and personal achievement counts for more.

Self-Determination

A closer examination of traditional cultures that have felt the impact of modernization or other culture changes will help to pinpoint some of the problems such cultures have met. We will focus here on the Shuar Indians of Ecuador and the Skolt Lapps, one of several groups of Saami people living in the Arctic and sub-Arctic tundra of northwest Russia and Scandinavia.

Saami Herders: The Snowmobile Revolution and Its Unintended Consequences

In the 1960s Saami reindeer herders in Scandinavia eagerly adopted snowmobiles, expecting that the new technology would make herding physically easier and economically more advantageous. The choice to modernize was essentially theirs, but in Finland it backfired.

As snowmobile technology replaced traditional skills, the ability of the Saami (historically also known as Lapps) to creatively survive on their own diminished, and their dependency on the outside world grew. Given the high cost of buying, maintaining, and fueling the machines, they faced a sharp rise in their need for money. To obtain cash, men began going outside their communities for wage labor more than just occasionally, as had previously been the case.

One might argue that dependency on the larger economy and the need for cash are prices worth paying for an improved system of reindeer herding. However, snowmobiles contributed in a significant way to a disastrous decline in reindeer herding in some Saami communities, such as among the Skolt Lapps of northern Finland. Traditionally Skolt men tended the animals, moving about on wooden skis and associating closely with the herds—intensively from November to January and periodically from January to April. But once snowmobiles were introduced, the familiar, prolonged, and largely peaceful relationship between herder and beast changed into a noisy, traumatic one. The humans reindeer encountered came speeding out of the woods on noisy, smelly machines that invariably chased the animals, often for long distances. Instead of helping the reindeer in their winter food quest, aiding does with their calves, and protecting the herd from predators, men appeared periodically, either to slaughter or castrate the animals.

The reindeer became wary of people, resulting in de-domestication, with reindeer scattering and running off to less accessible areas. In addition, snowmobile harassment seemed to adversely affect birthing and the survival of calves. Within a decade the average size of the family herd among the Skolts had dropped from fifty to twelve—a number that is not economically viable.

This is a classic illustration that change, even when initiated by a community on its own volition, is not always advantageous. The financial cost of mechanized herding and the decline in domesticated herd size have led many to abandon herding altogether. Now, the majority of men are no longer herders at all. This constitutes a serious economic problem, since few local subsistence alternatives are available.[15]

Shuar Indians and Cattle in the Amazon: A Successful Experiment in Controlled Adaptation

In contrast to the Saami, the Shuar Indians of Ecuador's tropical forest deliberately avoided modernization until they felt that they had no other option if they were to

fend off the same outside forces that had destroyed whole societies elsewhere in the Amazon Basin. Traditionally organized in small autonomous groups that engaged in constant feuding, the Shuar (historically better known as Jivaro) survived on a mixed subsistence strategy of foraging and gardening. In 1964, threatened with the loss of their land base as more and more Ecuadoran colonists intruded into their territory, leaders from the many, widely scattered Shuar communities came together and founded a fully independent ethnic organization—the Shuar Federation—to take control over their own future.

Recognized by Ecuador's government, albeit reluctantly, the federation is officially dedicated to promotion of the social, economic, and moral advancement of the growing Shuar population and to coordinating development with official governmental agencies. Since its founding, the federation has secured title to more than 96,000 hectares of communal land; established a cattle herd of more than 15,000 head as the people's primary source of income; taken control of their own education, using their own language and mostly Shuar teachers; and established their own bilingual radio station and a bilingual newspaper.

Obviously, all of this has transformed daily life among the Shuar, but they have been able to maintain a variety of distinctive cultural markers, including their language, communal land tenure, cooperative production and distribution, a basically egalitarian economy, and kin-based communities that retain maximum autonomy. Thus, for all the changes, they feel they are still Shuar and distinct from other Ecuadorans.[16]

The Shuar case shows that indigenous peoples are capable of taking control of their own destinies even in the face of intense outside pressures, *if* allowed to do so. Unfortunately, until recently, few have had that op-

[15]Pelto, P. J. (1973). *The snowmobile revolution: Technology and social change in the Arctic.* Menlo Park, CA: Cummings.

[16]Bodley, J. H. (1990). *Victims of progress* (3rd ed., pp. 160–162). Mountain View, CA: Mayfield.

Anthropology Applied

Development Anthropology and Dams ▪ Michael M. Horowitz

Over a 35-year career in scholarly and applied work, Michael M. Horowitz, president and executive director of the Institute for Development Anthropology (IDA) and Distinguished Professor of Anthropology at the State University of New York at Binghamton, has made pioneering contributions to applied anthropology. His work has focused on achieving equitable economic growth, environmental sustainability, conflict resolution, and participatory government in the former colonial world.

Since co-founding IDA in 1976, Horowitz has been its principal leader. He has played a key role in bringing anthropology forward as an applied science in international development organizations such as the World Bank, the United Nations Fund for Women, and the US Agency for International Development (USAID), as well as nongovernmental organizations (NGOs) such as Oxfam and the International Union for the Conservation of Nature. He has mentored several generations of young scholars and professionals—paying particular attention to those from developing countries—encouraging the application of anthropology's comparative and holistic methodologies and theories to empower low-income majorities in the so-called underdeveloped world.

Horowitz's work with pastoralists and floodplain dwellers has had substantial positive impact on the well-being of small producers and small landholders in developing countries. A clear example of this is the impact of his work on the lives and livelihoods of people living downstream of a hydropower dam in West Africa. Beginning in the 1980s, he and his IDA team carried out rigorous anthropological research along the Senegal River, which flows through Mali, Senegal, and Mauritania. Their study showed that traditional, pre-dam, flood-recession

A local woman eats her breakfast overlooking the ship locks of China's Three Gorges hydroelectric dam on the Yangtze River. Under construction since 1992 and due for completion in 2009, the dam has been controversial since its inception, raising concerns among environmentalists around the world, not to mention among peasant farmers living downstream. If completed, the dam will result in the largest forced displacement of people in the world's history. Close to 2 million people are being relocated to make way for its 365-mile-long reservoir, and bitter complaints abound among those who have already been moved. *Unlike* the dam described in this Anthropology Applied box, not one social scientist was consulted in the planning and assessment phase of Three Gorges Dam.

farming yielded better results than irrigated agriculture and was better for the environment.

This finding influenced decisions made by these countries and affiliated NGOs to manage the system with a controlled release from the Manatali Dam in Mali in order to reproduce as nearly as possible the pre-dam flow system. Horowitz's long-term field research demonstrated that seasonal flooding would provide economic, environmental, and sociocultural benefits for nearly a million small producers.

Recognized by national governments, NGOs, and development funding agencies, the work of Horowitz and his IDA colleagues on the Senegal River Basin Monitoring Activity (SRBMA) was a breakthrough in the concepts of resettlement and river management, and it continues to influence development policy. Prior to IDA's work in West Africa, no hydropower dam had ever been managed with a controlled flood. Since then, IDA has been asked to help apply the SRMBA model to other parts of the world, including the lower Zambezi River in Mozambique and the Mekong River in Laos, Cambodia, and Vietnam.

(Adapted from W. Young (Ed.). (2000). Kimball Award winner. Anthropology News 41(8), 29, with update based on personal communication with IDA, November 2003.)

---

tion. Prior to European invasions of the Amazon rainforest, more than 700 distinct ethnic groups inhabited this vast region. By 1900 in Brazil, the number was down to 270, and today something like 180 remain.[17] Many of these survivors find themselves in situations not unlike that of the Yanomami, described earlier in this chapter. Nevertheless, some are showing resourcefulness in resisting the outside forces of destruction arrayed against

them. Some receive help from anthropologists, as discussed in this chapter's Anthropology Applied feature.

Globalization in the "Underdeveloped" World

Throughout the so-called underdeveloped world, in Africa, Asia, South and Central America, and elsewhere, whole countries are in the throes of radical political and

[17]*Cultural Survival Quarterly.* (1991). 15 (4), 38.

economic change and overall cultural transformation. In fact, inventions and major advances in industrial production, mass transportation, and communication and information technologies are transforming societies in Europe and North America as well. This worldwide process of accelerated modernization in which all parts of the earth are becoming interconnected in one vast interrelated and all-encompassing system is known as globalization—as defined in Chapter 1.

All around the globe we are witnessing the removal of economic activities—or at least their control—from the family and community setting. And we are seeing the altered structure of the family in the face of the changing labor market: young children relying increasingly on parents alone for affection, instead of on the extended family; parental authority generally declining; schools replacing the family as the primary educational unit; old people spending their last days in nursing homes rather than with family members; and many other changes.

In traditional societies, these changes are now happening very fast, without the time to adjust gradually. Changes that took generations to accomplish in Europe and North America are attempted within the span of a single generation in developing countries. In the process they frequently face the erosion of a number of dearly held values they had no intention of giving up. Anthropologists doing fieldwork in distant communities throughout the world have witnessed how these traditional cultures have been affected, and often destroyed, by powerful global forces.

Commonly, the burden of modernization falls most heavily on women. For example, the commercialization of agriculture often involves land reforms that overlook or ignore women's traditional land rights. This reduces their control of and access to resources at the same time that mechanization of food production and processing drastically reduces their opportunities for employment. As a consequence, women are confined more and more to traditional domestic tasks, which, as commercial production becomes peoples' dominant concern, are increasingly downgraded in value.

Moreover, the domestic workload tends to increase, because men are less available to help out, while tasks such as fuel gathering and water collection are made more difficult as common land and resources come to be privately owned and as woodlands are reserved for commercial exploitation. To top it all off, the growing of nonfood crops such as cotton and sisal or luxury crops such as tea, coffee, and cacao (source of chocolate) for the world market makes households vulnerable to wide price fluctuations. As a result, people cannot afford the high-quality diet subsistence farming provided and become malnourished. In short, with modernization, women frequently find themselves in an increasingly inferior position. As their workload increases, the value assigned to

the work they do declines, as does their relative educational status, not to mention their health and nutrition.

Globalization: Must It Be Painful?

Most anthropologists see the radical changes that affect traditional non-Western peoples caught up in the modern technological world as an ordeal. Yet, the more common attitude in the industrial West has been that modernization is both inevitable and good—that however disagreeable the "medicine" may be, it is worth it for the "backward" people to become just like people in the West. (For a serious look at the consequences of these changes, see the Biocultural Connection.)

This Western view has little to do with the cold political and economic realities of the contemporary world. It overlooks the stark fact that the standard of middle- and upper-class living in the Western world is based on a rate of consumption of nonrenewable resources whereby a small fraction of the world's population uses the vast majority of these precious resources. The imbalance continues, suggesting that it is impossible for most peoples of the world to achieve a material standard of living at all comparable to that of many people in Western countries in the near future. At the very least, the peoples of the industrial and postindustrial West would have to cut drastically their unrelenting and often wasteful consumption of resources. So far, few have shown a willingness to seriously adjust their standard of living in order to do this.

Countless people around the world today have been led to aspire to a material standard of living like that enjoyed by the middle class and well-to-do in many industrialized and postindustrialized countries, even as the gap between the rich and the poor continues to widen. Every year, many millions of people slide below the poverty level.[18] This has led to the development of what U.S. anthropologist Paul Magnarella called a new "culture of discontent" in which aspirations far exceed the bounds of local opportunities.

No longer satisfied with traditional values and often unable to sustain themselves in the rural backlands, people all over the world are moving to the large cities to find a better life. All too often they live out their days in poor, congested, and diseased slums while attempting to achieve what is usually beyond their reach. Unfortunately, despite rosy predictions about a better future, hundreds of millions of people in our world remain trapped in a wretched reality, struggling against poverty, hunger, poor health, and other dangers. In the next and final chapter of this book, we further explore the underlying structures and deeper causes of these problems, and look at the role anthropology can and does play in helping to meet these challenges.

---

[18]Kurth, P. (1998, October 14). Capitol crimes. *Seven Days,* 7.

Biocultural Connection

Studying the Emergence of New Diseases

Since the Neolithic, humans have had to cope with a host of new diseases that began as a consequence of changes in human behavior. Recently, this has become a renewed source of concern following the resurgence of infectious diseases and the spread of a host of new and lethal diseases.[a]

All told, more than thirty diseases new to medicine have emerged in the past twenty-five years. Perhaps the best known of these is AIDS, which has become a top killer among infectious diseases. Since 1981, more than 25 million people have died of AIDS, and today some 40 million people around the world are living with AIDS/HIV.[b] But there are others—like Ebola hemorrhagic fever, which causes victims to bleed to death; hemorrhagic fevers like dengue fever, Lassa fever, and hantavirus; invasive Streptococcus A, which consumes the victims' flesh; Legionnaire's disease; and Lyme disease.

What has sparked the appearance and spread of these new diseases remains a mystery, but one theory is that some are the result of human activities. In particular, the intrusion of people into new ecological settings, such as rainforests, along with construction of roads allows viruses and other infectious microbes to spread rapidly to large numbers of people. It is now generally accepted that the HIV virus responsible for AIDS transferred to humans from chimpanzees in the forests of the Democratic Republic of Congo as a consequence of hunting and butchering these animals for food. For the first thirty years, few people were affected; it was not until people began congregating in cities like Kinshasa that conditions were ripe for an epidemic.

To gain a better understanding of the interplay between ecological disturbance and the emergence of new diseases, U.S. medical anthropologist Carol Jenkins obtained a grant from the MacArthur Foundation in 1993. From her base at the Papua New Guinea Institute of Medical Research, she is tracking the health of local people in the wake of a massive logging operation. Her work should provide a better understanding of how disease organisms spread from animal hosts to humans.

Since most of the "new" viruses that have suddenly afflicted humans are in fact old ones that have been present in animals like monkeys (monkey pox), rodents (hantavirus), deer (Lyme disease), and insects (West Nile virus); it appears that something new has enabled them to jump from their animal hosts to humans.

A recent example comes from the Democratic Republic of Congo. Here civil war created a situation where villagers in the central part of the country were faced with starvation. Their response was to increase the hunting of animals, including monkeys, squirrels, and rats that carry a disease called monkey pox. Related to smallpox, the disease transfers easily to humans, resulting in the largest outbreak of this disease ever seen among humans. What makes this outbreak even more serious is an apparently new strain of the infection, enabling it to spread from person to person, instead of only from an animal host.[c]

Large-scale habitat disturbance is an obvious candidate for such disease transfers, but this needs to be confirmed and the process understood. So far, it is hard to make more than a circumstantial case, by looking back after a disease outbreak. The work of Jenkins and her team is unique in that she was able to get baseline health data on local people before their environment was disturbed. Thus, she is in a position to follow events as they unfold.

It will be some time before conclusions can be drawn from Jenkins's study. Its importance is obvious; in an era of globalization, as air travel allows diseases to spread worldwide, we need a fuller understanding of how viruses interact with their hosts if we are to devise effective preventive and therapeutic strategies to deal with them.

[a]Gibbons, A. (1993). Where are new diseases born? *Science 261*, 680–681.
[b]See www.avert.org/worldstats.htm.

[c]Cohen, J. (1997). Is an old virus up to new tricks? *Science 277*, 312–313.

Questions for Reflection

1. A people's ability to change their culture has always been a key requirement for long-term human survival. However, globalization radically challenges us to adjust at an ever-faster pace within increasingly complex transnational settings. Considering your own situation, can you identify any powerful outside force such as a government agency or large corporation that has had caused changes for your own family, community, or neighborhood? Do you feel that these changes are good for everyone?

2. What are some of the driving forces of culture change in the world today? Which groups are benefiting the most from free markets all across the globe?

3. On a regular basis, the news media are reporting about violent uprisings or rebellion and armed conflicts that result in death and destruction. Why do you think many people feel the need to fight?

4. When societies become involved in the modernizing process, all levels of their cultural systems are affected by these changes. Do you think that people are fully aware of the long-term consequences of the changes they themselves may have welcomed? Can you come up with any examples of unforeseen changes in your own community or neighborhood?

5. In many Muslim countries, orthodox religious groups may oppose modern developments that they associate with moral corruption and seek to maintain or return to a culture based on Muslim traditions. Do you know any religious groups that

identify themselves as fundamentalist, having similar tradition-based values and ideals? Would you feel comfortable if these groups controlled your country's government?

Suggested Readings

Bodley, J. H. (1999). *Victims of progress* (4th ed.). New York: McGraw-Hill.

Few North Americans are aware of the devastation unleashed upon indigenous peoples in the name of progress, nor are they aware that this continues on an unprecedented scale today and the extent of their own society's contributions to it. For most, this book will be a real eye-opener.

Spindler, G., & Stockard, J. E. (Eds.). (2006). *Globalization and change in fifteen cultures*. Belmont, CA: Wadsworth.

This collection of original articles reflects a world changed by globalization and an anthropology committed to documenting the effects of the vast cultural flows of people, information, goods, and technology, now in motion the world over. Spindler and Stockard's introduction frames the topic of cultural change, and the fifteen anthropologists in the anthology take readers on a return visit to their original field sites, asking questions for a new era and writing of peoples familiar to them yet transformed by global forces.

Inda, J. X., & Renato, R. (Eds.). (2001). *The anthropology of globalization: A reader*. Malden, MA, and Oxford: Blackwell.

This wide-ranging reader focuses simultaneously on the large-scale processes through which various cultures are becoming increasingly interconnected and on the ways that people around the world—from Africa and Asia to the Caribbean and North America—mediate these processes in culturally specific ways.

Maybury-Lewis, D. (2001). *Indigenous peoples, ethnic groups, and the state* (2nd ed.). Boston: Allyn & Bacon.

The author, who founded the organization Cultural Survival, summarizes modernization's effect on "tribalism and ethnic parochialism." Revealing the peculiar situation of indigenous peoples as ethnic minorities alien to the states in which they live, he describes the worldwide proliferation of ethnic conflicts and the growing demands for indigenous rights. The book stands on its own, while serving as introduction to a series of individual ethnographies on indigenous peoples and their struggles.

Prins, H. E. L. (1996). *The Mi'kmaq: Resistance, accommodation, and cultural survival*. Belmont, CA: Wadsworth.

This content-rich case study spans 500 years of history, chronicling the endurance of a tribal nation—its ordeals in the face of colonialism and its current struggle for self-determination and cultural revitalization. Rare for its multi-vocality.

Stannard, D. E. (1992). *American holocaust*. Oxford: Oxford University Press.

Stannard deals with 500 years of culture change in the Americas arising from contact between European and native cultures. In doing so, he focuses on genocide, relates it to the Holocaust of World War II, and demonstrates how deeply rooted the phenomenon is in Western culture and Christianity.

Thomson Audio Study Products

 Enjoy the MP3-ready Audio Lecture Overviews for each chapter and a comprehensive audio glossary of key terms for quick study and review. Whether walking to class, doing laundry, or studying at your desk, you now have the freedom to choose when, where, and how you interact with your audio-based educational media. See the preface for information on how to access this on-the-go study and review tool.

The Anthropology Resource Center

www.thomsonedu.com/anthropology
The Anthropology Resource Center provides extended learning materials to reinforce your understanding of key concepts in the four fields of anthropology. For each of the four fields, the Resource Center includes dynamic exercises including video exercises, map exercises, simulations, and "Meet the Scientists" interviews, as well as critical thinking questions that can be assigned and e-mailed to instructors. The Resource Center also provides breaking news in anthropology and interesting material on applied anthropology to help you link what you are learning to the world around you.

27 Global Challenges, Local Responses, and the Role of Anthropology

CHALLENGE ISSUE

For at least 10,000 years humans have met the challenges of survival not only by adapting to their natural environment but by transforming it to fit their needs. They have turned deserts, forests, swamps, and mountainsides into pastures and farmland, creating new survival opportunities for an ever-growing human population. During the past 200 years, global cultural development has relied on burning increasing quantities of fossil fuels such as coal, oil, and gas, which has had dire results: massive deforestation and desertification, along with severe air, water, and soil pollution threatening the health of all life. Fossil fuel use has dramatically increased carbon dioxide levels, trapping more heat in the earth's atmosphere. Rising temperatures are causing more and greater storms, droughts, and heat waves, devastating populations in vulnerable areas. And if the massive meltdown of Arctic ice now underway continues, rising sea levels will inundate low coastal areas worldwide. Entire islands may soon disappear, including thousands of villages and even large cities. Among those threatened is Malé, pictured here. It is the capital island of the Maldives, an Indian Ocean archipelago comprised of 1,200 low-lying islands (199 inhabited), home to 70,000 people.

What Can Anthropologists Tell Us of the Future?

Although anthropologists cannot accurately predict future cultural forms, they can identify certain patterns and trends and foresee some of the consequences these might have if they continue. Moreover, they can shed light on already identified problems by showing how they relate to each other and to cultural features and structures that are often below the radar of experts in other disciplines. This ability to systematically consider cultural facts and their underlying structures in a wider context and from a comparative perspective is a recognized anthropological specialty.

What Are the Cultural Trends in Our Globalizing World?

One major cultural trend is globalization, including worldwide adoption of the products, technologies, ideas, and cultural practices of powerful Western countries. This move toward a homogenized, global culture is countered by an opposite trend of ethnic and religious groups all over the world reasserting their distinctive cultural identities and emphasizing their unique historical traditions. A third trend is the growing concern that rising populations, spiraling energy use, and expanding consumption are devastating our natural resources, overwhelming us with waste, and poisoning our environment.

What Problems Must Be Solved for Humans to Have a Viable Future?

Creative, effective, and responsible solutions need to be found to deal with a host of serious problems posed by demographic shifts, unequal distribution of wealth, vanishing natural resources, environmental destruction, ever-more powerful technologies, and explosive population growth. One difficulty is that most people fail to recognize that many problems facing us are interconnected. Anthropology provides us with a critical and realistic understanding of the emergence of a global cultural system and its radical impact on local communities. Its cross-cultural and historically informed perspective is essential for solving problems and ensuring a future in which all peoples enjoy basic human rights.

623

Anthropology is superficially described by those who know little about it as an exotic discipline interested mainly in what happened long ago and far away. The most common popular stereotype is that anthropologists devote all of their attention to digging up the past and describing the last surviving tribal peoples with traditional ways of life. Yet, as noted earlier in this book, neither archaeologists nor paleoanthropologists (the anthropologists most devoted to looking into the past) limit their interests to ancient times, nor do ethnographers (who focus on contemporary cultures) overlook the ways and workings of industrial and postindustrial societies. Indeed, anthropologists are interested in the entire range of human cultures past and present—in their similarities and differences and in the multiple ways they influence one another.

Moreover, many anthropologists have a special concern with the future and the changes it may bring. They wonder what today's globalizing processes will create and what will be transformed, disrupted, or damaged beyond repair. As we saw in the preceding chapter, when traditional peoples are exposed to intense contact with technologically empowered Western peoples, their cultures typically change with unprecedented speed, often for the worse, becoming both less supportive and less adaptive. Since globalization seems unstoppable, we are compelled to ask: How can the thousands of different cultures, developed in the course of centuries if not millennia, deal successfully with the multiple challenges hurled at them?

THE CULTURAL FUTURE OF HUMANITY

To comprehend anthropology's role in understanding and solving problems in times to come, we must look at flaws frequently seen in publications and planning efforts focused on the future. First of all, rarely do futurists look more than about fifty years ahead, and more often than not the trends they project are those of recent history. This predisposes people to think that a trend that seems acceptable today will always be so. The danger of this assumption is neatly captured in anthropologist George Cowgill's comment: "It is worth recalling the story of the person who leaped from a very tall building and on being asked how things were going as he passed the 20th floor replied 'Fine, so far.'"[1]

A second flaw typical in futurist projections is a tendency to treat subjects in isolation, without reference to pertinent trends outside an expert's field of competence. For example, agricultural planning is often based on the

assumption that a certain amount of water is available for irrigation, whether or not urban planners or others have designs upon that same water. Thus, people may be counting on natural resources in the future that will not, in fact, be available.

This brings us to a third flaw common among futurists: The tendency to project the hopes and expectations of one's own social group or culture into the future interferes with the scientific objectivity necessary to see and address emerging problems. A recent example is the war in Iraq, where the hopes and expectations of the official U.S. and British planners blinded them to the complex problems that would emerge.

Against this background, anthropology's contribution to our understanding of the future is clear. With their holistic and integrative perspective, anthropologists are specialists at seeing how parts fit together into a larger whole. With their comparative and long-term historical perspective, they can place short-term trends in deeper and wider perspective. With more than a hundred years of cross-cultural research behind them—based on ancient archaeological finds, linguistic information, biological data, as well as participant observation within living cultures—anthropologists can recognize culture-bound assertions when they encounter them. Last but not least, they are familiar with alternative ways of dealing with a wide variety of problems.

Global Culture

Human populations have always been on the move. But today, more people travel faster and farther than ever before due to modern means of transportation (Figure 27.1). Moreover, revolutions in communication technology—from print media to telegraph and telephone to radio, television, satellites, and the Internet—make it possible to exchange more information with more people faster and over greater distances. Obviously, this global flow of humans, their products, and their ideas plays a major role in culture change.

A popular belief since the mid-1900s has been that the future world will see the development of a single homogeneous world culture. This idea is based largely on the observation that technological developments in communication, transportation, and trade are causing peoples of the world to increasingly watch the same television programs, read the same newspapers, eat the same foods, wear the same types of clothes, and communicate via satellites and the Internet.

Also of note, at least 175 million people (2.5 percent of the world's population) now live outside their countries of birth—not as refugees but as migrants who earn their living in one country while being citizens of another. The continuation of such trends, so this thinking goes, would mean that North Americans who travel in

[1]Cowgill, G. L. (1980). Letter, *Science 210*, 1,305.

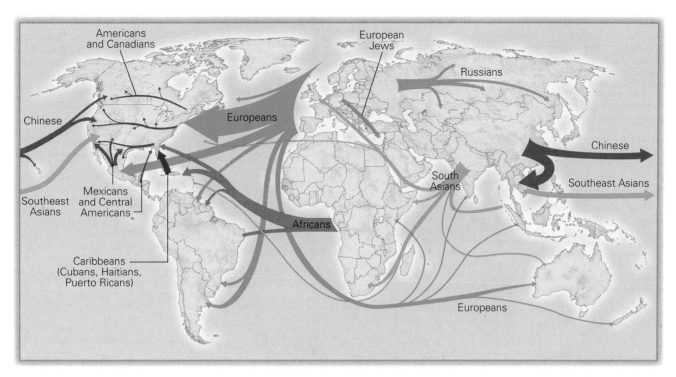

Figure 27.1

World Migrations Migration has had and continues to have a significant effect on world social geography, contributing to culture change and development, to the diffusion of ideas and innovations, and to the complex mixture of people and cultures found in the world today. Internal migration occurs within the boundaries of a country; external migration is movement from one country or region to another. Over the last fifty years, the most important migrations in the world have been internal, largely the rural-to-urban migration that has been responsible for the recent rise of global urbanization. Prior to the mid-20th century, three types of external migration were most important: voluntary, most often in search of better conditions and opportunities; involuntary or forced, involving people who have been driven from their homelands by war, political unrest, or environmental disasters, or transported as slaves or prisoners; and imposed, not entirely forced but made advisable by the circumstances.

SOURCE: From *Student Atlas of Anthropology* by John L. Allen and Audrey Shalinsky, p. 73. Copyright © 2003 McGraw-Hill/Dushkin Publishing.

the year 2100 to Afghanistan, Botswana, Colombia, or Denmark would find the local inhabitants living in a manner identical or similar to theirs. Yet, looking at ethnic conflicts around the world, we must ask if this prediction is likely to be accurate.

Is the World Coming Together or Coming Apart?

Certainly it is striking—the extent to which such items as Western-style clothing, bicycles, cars, cameras, computers, and soft drinks have spread to virtually all parts of the world. And many countries—Japan, for example—appear to have gone a long way toward becoming Westernized. Moreover, looking back over the past 5,000 years of human history, we see that political units have tended to become larger, more all-encompassing, and fewer in number. The logical outcome of this trend would be a

further reduction of autonomous political units into a single one taking in the entire globe.

Informed by comparative historical and cross-cultural research, anthropologists call attention to something that all large states throughout time have had in common: a tendency to come apart. Not only have the great empires of the past, without exception, broken up into numbers of smaller independent states, but states in virtually all parts of the world today show this same tendency to fragment, usually along major geographic and ethnic divisions.

The threat of political collapse is ever-present in multi-ethnic states, especially when these countries are large, difficult to travel in, and lack major unifying cultural forces such as a common national language. Such has been the case, for instance, with Afghanistan. This vast, mountainous country is inhabited by several major ethnic groups, including Pashtun who live mainly in the south, and Tajik, Uzbek, Hazara, and Turkmen who live

The worldwide spread of such products as Pepsi is taken by some as a sign that a homogeneous world is developing. Pepsi beverages include not only cola, but Mountain Dew, Lipton's Iced Tea, and Aquafina water—generating more than $26 billion in sales.

mainly in the north. Although the Pashtun are greatest in number and most dominant in the past 200 years, they were never able to successfully impose their political will on the other ethnic groups who maintain a great deal of independence; nor did they succeed in making their own native tongue, Pashto, the country's national language.

The tendency of multi-ethnic states to break apart has been especially noteworthy since the end of the Cold War between the United States and the former Soviet Union around 1990. For example, 1991 saw the dramatic breakup of the Soviet Union into about a dozen independent republics—Russia, Armenia, Kazakhstan, and Ukraine, among others. In 1992 Czechoslovakia split into the Czech and the Slovak republics. That same year the Republic of Yugoslavia began splintering into what are now six independent states in the Balkan Mountains.

The splintering tendency of multi-ethnic states can also be seen in separatist movements such as that of French-speaking peoples in Canada; Basques in Spain; Tibetans in China; the Karen in Burma (Myanmar); Tamils in Sri Lanka; Kurds in Turkey, Iran, and Iraq, and so on—this list is far from exhaustive. Nor is the United States immune, as can be seen in Native American nations seeking to secure greater political self-determination on their reservations.

All of these examples involve peoples who see themselves as members of distinct nations by virtue of their birth and their cultural and territorial heritage—nations over whom peoples of some other ethnic background have tried to assert political control. An estimated 5,000 such national groups exist in the world today, as opposed to a mere 192 states formally admitted as members of the United Nations (up from fewer than fifty in the 1940s).[2] Although some of these ethnic groups are small in population and area—100 or so people living on a few acres—many others are quite large. The Karen people inhabiting southern Burma (Myanmar), for example, number some 4.5 to 5 million, exceeding the population of nearly half of the countries in the world.

The reactions of such groups to forced annexation and domination by state regimes controlled by people of other nations range all the way from the nonviolence of Scottish and Welsh nationalism to bloody fights for national independence by the Irish, Algerians, Vietnamese, or Palestinians. Many struggles for independence have been going on for years. Today, about 35 million people in almost half of the world's countries are either internally displaced or have crossed international borders as refugees. Some 9 million of these unfortunates have been forced outside their countries, most of them suffering in makeshift camps where they cannot make a living.

In some cases, a large proportion of an ethnic group's entire population finds itself forced to abandon their homes and flee for their lives. For instance, some 18 million Africans are currently uprooted. In war-torn Sudan alone, more than 2.5 million people have been driven from their homes.

It is possible that we are reaching a point where the tendency for political units to increase in size while decreasing in number is being canceled out by the tendency for such units to fragment into a greater number of smaller ones. Despite these examples, there are also a

---

[2] *Cultural Survival Quarterly* (1991). *15* (4), 38.

Almost fifty years ago, when the Chinese communist government in Beijing annexed Tibet and imposed its rule over the Buddhist people in this Himalayan region, tens of thousands of Tibetans were forced to flee to neighboring Nepal and India, where they found safety in refugee camps. Among the many refugees is the Dalai Lama (left), Tibet's spiritual leader, who escaped his homeland across the freezing cold and snow-covered mountains in 1959 and still lives in exile.

few instances of reunification. Best known among these is the 1990 reunification of Germany, divided since the end of World War II as East and West Germany, into one large federal republic. Another notable exception is the recent integration of twenty-seven European countries into the European Union—however hindered by linguistic differences, distinctive cultural traditions, and bureaucratic red tape.

Global Culture: A Good Idea or Not?

The idea of a shared global culture may have a degree of popular appeal, in that it might diminish chances for the kinds of misunderstandings and conflicting viewpoints that so often in the past few hundred years have led to violent clashes and even full-scale wars. Anthropologists greet this prognosis with skepticism, though, suspecting that distinctive worldviews will persist as they have for hundreds of years, even in the face of massive changes. Indeed, one might argue that the chance for conflicting viewpoints actually increases, given the intensified interactions among people in the world today.

Some have argued that perhaps a generalized world culture would be desirable in the future, because some traditional cultures may be too specialized to adjust to a changed environment. For instance, when Amazonian Indians pursuing traditional ways of life that are well adapted to South America's tropical rainforest are confronted with sudden, radical changes brought on by

foreign invaders, their long-established cultures often collapse. The reason for this, it is argued, is that the forest dwellers' traditions and political and social organizations are not adapted to modern ways and that they are naturally destined to give way to the new.

A problem with this argument is that, far from being unable to adapt, such traditional peoples have been robbed repeatedly of the opportunity to work out their own adaptations based on their own agendas. Their demise is caused not by laws of nature but rather by the political and economic choices of the powerful, fueled by arrogance, intolerance, and greed, along with a willingness to invade and exploit lands already owned and long inhabited by indigenous people.

The possibility of Amazonian Indians adapting to the changing realities, if allowed to do so, without losing their distinctive ethnic and cultural identity, is demonstrated by the Shuar case in Ecuador, noted in the preceding chapter. However, the pressures to "develop" the Amazon rainforest in Brazil are so great that whole indigenous communities are dispossessed, swept aside, or even destroyed so that global timber, energy, and mining corporations and agribusinesses are free to pursue their unrestrained profit-making activities. People do not have much chance to work out their own adaptations to the globalizing world if they are driven from their homelands and abruptly deprived of their means of survival so that more acreage can be devoted to the raising of beef cattle. Much of this meat is refrigerated and shipped directly to Europe. And much of the profits also leave the country since the major ranches are owned and operated by foreign corporations. Although large tracts of land have been set aside as Indian reservations since the mid-1990s, the devastation process continues. In the globalization process, economically and technologically empowered people have defined others—indeed, whole societies—as inferior, subservient, irrelevant, and not entitled to human rights, including self-determination.

Ethnic Resurgence

Despite the worldwide adoption of such products as blue jeans, sunglasses, Coca-Cola, and the Big Mac, and despite ever-growing pressures on traditional cultures to disappear, it is clear that cultural differences are still with us in the world today. In fact, resistance to many aspects of globalization is growing in many parts of the world. We see evidence of this in examples already noted, as well as in repeated public protests around the globe against policies of the Geneva-based World Trade Organization. In addition, Greenpeace and a host of less radical environmental groups can be found demonstrating worldwide against such practices as French nuclear testing in the Pacific or Japanese commercial whaling. Other examples include symbolic attacks by small farmers in France against corporate control, genetically modified crops, industrial agriculture, and McDonald's fast-food outlets. Resistance to globalization is also evident in political movements in Bolivia and Venezuela, as well as Muslim fundamentalist movements from Algeria in northwest Africa to Indonesia in Southeast Asia. The remarkable recent revival of shamanism in former communist Mongolia is yet another example, as is the increasing political activism of many other indigenous peoples from every corner of the world.

During the 1970s the world's indigenous peoples (almost all of whom are minorities suffering repression or discrimination by more dominant nations or ethnic groups politically controlling the countries within which the indigenous groups have always lived) began to organize self-determination movements. Joining together across international borders, they established the World Council of Indigenous Peoples in 1975. This global organization now has official status as a nongovernmental organization of the United Nations, which allows it to present the plight of indigenous peoples before the world community. Movement leaders see their own traditional societies as community based, egalitarian, and close to the natural environment, and they are intent upon keeping them that way.

Representing 5 percent of the world's population, indigenous peoples gained important symbolic ground in 1992 when Rigoberta Menchú, a Maya Indian woman from Guatemala who won the Nobel Peace Prize in 1992 for her activism on behalf of indigenous rights. Receiving this honor in 1992 had particular political significance, because it was the year of the Columbian quincentennial in which people in Europe and the Americas commemorated the pioneering journey of Christopher Columbus across the Atlantic ocean—a journey that had devastating consequences for American Indians. The prize focused international attention on the ongoing repression of indigenous peoples in Guatemala and helped pave the way to peace accords in late December 1996.

In 1993, representatives of some 124 indigenous groups and organizations agreed to a draft Declaration of the Rights of Indigenous Peoples that had taken a decade to produce. Presented to the UN General Assembly, it contains some 150 articles urging respect for indigenous cultural heritages, calling for recognition of indigenous land titles and rights of self-determination, and demanding an end to all forms of oppression and discrimination as a principle of international law. So far, this drafted document is largely symbolic. It remains under consideration by the UN, which to date has agreed to only a handful of its articles. Whether it will be adopted remains to be seen.

The struggle by indigenous groups against domination and discrimination by more powerful peoples with different cultures is not only in defense of their human rights, but also resistance against imposed cultural values and foreign ethnocentrism—the belief that the ways of one's own culture are the only proper ones. North Americans, Europeans, and people in many other industrial or postindustrial societies often have difficulty adjusting to the fact that not everyone wants to be just like they are. In the United States, for example, children are taught to believe that the "American way of life" is one to which all other peoples aspire. Although it is true that many peoples from poor countries across the world seek to improve their living conditions and enjoy the fruits of freedom, such aspirations should not be confused with wanting to become "American." Moreover, in the globalizing world dominated by the United States, Japan, and a handful of European capitalist states today, whole countries that once valued Western ways are now drawing the line or even turning against many of these ideas, trends, and practices.

One striking case of such a cultural reaction was that of a group of Muslim religious fundamentalists in Afghanistan known as the Taliban (the Pashto word for "students," specifically of Islam). After helping to force the Russian army out of their country and ending the subsequent civil war, they rose to power in the 1990s and imposed a radical version of traditional Islamic law (Shariah) in an effort to create an Islamic republic based on strict religious values. A similar, though less radical, reaction against modernity is taking place in the United States, where "born again" and other fundamentalist politicians have been elected in recent years on a plat-

Often resistance to modernization takes the form of cultural tradition-alism and religious fundamentalism, as in Afghanistan during recent decades. This reactionary practice is evident in this family's clothing, the mother's veil, and the father's beard.

form of creating a national culture based on what they see as traditional Christian values.[3]

Cultural Pluralism and Multiculturalism

If a single homogenous global culture is not necessarily the wave of the future, what is? Some predict a world in which ethnic groups will become more nationalistic in response to globalization, each group stressing its unique cultural heritage and emphasizing differences with neighboring groups. But not all ethnic groups organize themselves politically as distinctive nations with their own state. In fact, it has been common for two or more neighboring ethnic groups or nations to draw together in a loose political union while maintaining their particular cultural identities. However, because such pluralistic societies lack a common cultural identity and

heritage, and often do not share the same language or religion, political relationships between them can be fraught with tension. When feelings of ethnonationalism are not far from the surface, political pressure may build up and result in separation and independence.

One way of curbing divisive pressures in pluralistic or multi-ethnic societies is the adoption of a public policy based on mutual respect and tolerance for cultural differences. Known as **multiculturalism,** such an official policy or doctrine asserts the value of different cultures co-existing within a country and stresses the reciprocal responsibility of all citizens to accept the rights of others to freely express their views and values. In contrast to state policies in which a dominant ethnic group uses its power to impose its own culture as the national standard, forcing other groups within the same state to assimilate, multiculturalism involves a public policy for managing a society's cultural diversity. Examples of long-established multiculturalism may be seen in states such as Switzerland (where German-, French-, Italian-, and Romansh-speaking peoples co-exist under the same government) and Canada (where French- and English-speaking Canadians, as well as dozens of indigenous nations live side by side).

THOMSON AUDIO STUDY PRODUCTS Take advantage of the MP3-ready Audio Lecture Overviews and comprehensive audio glossary of key terms for each chapter. See the preface for information on how to access this on-the-go study and review tool.

Although cultural pluralism is still more common than multiculturalism, several multi-ethnic countries have recently changed their official melting pot ideology and associated policies of assimilation. One example of a country that is moving toward multiculturalism is the United States, which now has over 120 different ethnic groups within its borders (in addition to hundreds of federally recognized American Indian groups). Another is Australia, now counting over a hundred ethnic groups and with eighty languages spoken within its territorial boundaries. Similar changes are also underway in many European countries where millions of foreign immigrants have settled during the past few decades. Such changes are not easy, and often engender protests along the way. In many pluralistic societies, however, governments lack the ideological commitment or political capacity to successfully structure a national cultural system.

We cannot ignore the fact that, historically, what has been called "nation building" in all parts of the world

[3]Marsella, J. (1982). Pulling it together: Discussion and comments. In S. Pastner & W. A. Haviland (Eds.), *Confronting the creationists* (pp. 79–80). *Northeastern Anthropological Association, Occasional Proceedings,* 1.

multiculturalism Public policy for managing cultural diversity in a multi-ethnic society, officially stressing mutual respect and tolerance for cultural differences within a country's borders.

In 1982 United Nations Sub-Commission on the Promotion and Protection of Human Rights established a Working Group on Indigenous Populations (WGIP). Eleven years later WGIP completed a draft Declaration of the Rights of Indigenous Peoples. The document has yet to be ratified, but indigenous peoples all around the world are increasingly organizing to defend their own interests against both developers and governments. Here we see delegates from Japan's ethnic Ainu community in the UN assembly hall at a recent WGIP gathering.

almost always involves attempts to destroy the cultures of peoples whose nationalities differ from those controlling the governments in those countries.[4] During the last two decades of the 20th century, states were borrowing more money to fight peoples within their own boundaries than for all other programs combined. Nearly all state debt in Africa and nearly half of all other debt in "underdeveloped" countries comes from the cost of weapons purchased by states to fight their own citizens.[5] The more divergent cultural traditions are, the more difficult it is to make pluralism work.

That said, states as political constructs are products of human imagination, and nothing prevents us from imagining in ways that are more tolerant of cultural pluralism or multiculturalism. For example, consider once again Switzerland, where multiculturalism has worked out to the satisfaction of all four ethnic groups. In this confederation of small states (cantons), a political tradition of direct democracy is combined with a political organization that does not interfere with the country's regional, linguistic, and religious differences.

Obviously, replicating such a success in other political arenas will take a good deal of work, but at least the international community recognizes the concept of *group* rights. Even though it often fails to act on it, the UN General Assembly's 1966 Covenant of Human Rights states unequivocally:

In those states in which ethnic, religious or linguistic minorities exist, persons belonging to such minorities shall not be denied the rights, in community with the other members of their group, to enjoy their own culture, to profess and practice their own religion or to use their own language.[6]

Ethnocentrism and Cultural Pluralism

The major problem associated with cultural pluralism has to do with ethnocentrism. To function effectively, we may expect a society to embrace at least a degree of ethnic pride and a loyalty to its unique cultural traditions, from which its people derive psychological support and a firm social bond to their group. In societies where one's self-identification derives from the group, belief that one's own distinct customs and cultural practices are ideal is essential to a sense of personal worth.

As illustrated again and again in this book, the problem with ethnocentrism is that it is all too easy to take it as a charter for condemning other cultures as inferior and to denigrate and exploit them for the benefit of one's own. Although this does have to be the result, when it is, unrest, hostility, and violence commonly result.

In the world today, powerful governments frequently operate on the basis of the political idea that no group has the right to stand in the way of "the greater good for the greater number." This concept is commonly used to justify the expropriation of natural resources in regions traditionally occupied by subsistence farmers, pastoral nomads, or food foragers—without any respect for the rights, concerns, or wishes of these peoples. But is it truly the greater good for the greater number? A look at the rise of global corporations helps to answer this question.

The Rise of Global Corporations

The resistance of the world to political integration might seem to be offset to some extent by the rise and ongoing growth of global corporations. Because these cut across the international boundaries between states, they are a force for worldwide integration despite the political, linguistic, religious, and other cultural differences that separate people.

Global corporations, rare before the latter half of the 20th century, now are a far-reaching economic and political force in the world. Modern-day business giants such as General Electric, Shell, and Toyota are actually clusters of several corporations joined by ties of com-

[4]Van Den Berghe, P. (1992). The modern state: Nation builder or nation killer? *International Journal of Group Tensions* 22 (3), 194–198.

[5]*Cultural Survival Quarterly* (1991). 15 (4), 38.

[6]Quoted in Bodley, J. H. (1990). *Victims of progress* (3rd ed., p. 99). Mountain View, CA: Mayfield.

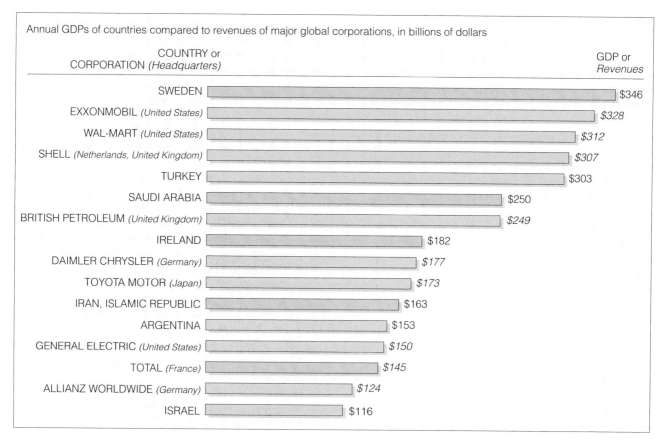

Annual GDPs of countries compared to revenues of major global corporations, in billions of dollars

COUNTRY or CORPORATION (Headquarters)	GDP or Revenues
SWEDEN	$346
EXXONMOBIL (United States)	$328
WAL-MART (United States)	$312
SHELL (Netherlands, United Kingdom)	$307
TURKEY	$303
SAUDI ARABIA	$250
BRITISH PETROLEUM (United Kingdom)	$249
IRELAND	$182
DAIMLER CHRYSLER (Germany)	$177
TOYOTA MOTOR (Japan)	$173
IRAN, ISLAMIC REPUBLIC	$163
ARGENTINA	$153
GENERAL ELECTRIC (United States)	$150
TOTAL (France)	$145
ALLIANZ WORLDWIDE (Germany)	$124
ISRAEL	$116

Figure 27.2

In today's consumer-driven world, it is not uncommon for the yearly revenues of large multinational corporations to equal and even exceed the total value of all goods and services produced within a country per year, known as a country's gross domestic product (GDP). This graph shows the annual GDPs of selected countries alongside the annual revenues of leading global corporations (Note: GDP says nothing about the unequal distribution of wealth within a country.)

SOURCE: Based on 2005 sales figures (www.forbes.com, May 2006) and GDP figures (www.worldbank.org, May 2006).

mon ownership and responsive to a common management strategy. Usually tightly controlled by a head office in one country, these enterprises organize and integrate production across the international boundaries of different countries for interests formulated in corporate boardrooms, irrespective of whether these are consistent with the interests of people in the countries where they operate. These megacorporations are the products of the technological revolution, for without sophisticated data-processing equipment and electronic communication, they could not keep adequate track of their worldwide operations.

Though typically thought of as responding impersonally to outside market forces, large corporations are in fact controlled by an increasingly smaller number of wealthy capitalists who benefit directly from their operations. Yet, unlike political leaders, the world's largest individual stockholders and most powerful directors are known to few people. For that matter, most people cannot even name the world's major global corporations,

which include Wal-Mart, British Petroleum, Shell, Exxon-Mobil, DaimlerChrysler, Toyota, and General Electric (Figure 27.2). Each of these business giants currently generates annual revenues above $150 billion, and three of them have passed the $300 billion mark.[7]

So great is the power of large businesses operating all across the globe that they increasingly thwart the wishes of national governments or international organizations such as the United Nations, Red Cross, International Court of Justice, or the World Council of Churches. Because the information these corporations process is kept from flowing in a meaningful way to the population at large, or even to lower levels within the organization, it becomes difficult for governments to get the information they need for informed policy decisions. It took years for the U.S. Congress to extract the information it needed from tobacco companies to decide what to do about tobacco legislation—and it is nearly as slow-going today

[7]Forbes International 500 List.

getting energy and media companies to provide data needed for regulatory purposes.

Beyond this, the global corporations have repeatedly shown they can overrule foreign policy decisions. While some might see this as a hopeful signal for getting beyond national vices and rivalries, it raises the unsettling issue of whether or not the global arena should be controlled by immensely large and powerful private corporations interested only in financial profits. According to one market research organization,

> Today, the top 100 companies control 33 percent of the world's assets, but employ only one percent of the world's workforce. General Motors is larger than Denmark, Wal-Mart bigger than South Africa. The mega-corporations roam freely around the globe, lobbying legislators, bankrolling elections and playing governments off against each other to get the best deals. Their private hands control the bulk of the world's news and information flows.[8]

If the ability of global corporations to ignore the wishes of sovereign governments is cause for concern, so is their ability to act in concert with such governments. Here, in fact, is where their worst excesses have occurred. One example took place in Brazil, where the situation is hardly unique but is especially well documented. After a 1964 military coup in that country, a partnership emerged between the new government, which was anxious to proceed as rapidly as possible with development of the Amazon rainforest, and a number of global corporations and international lending institutions. (The corporations included ALCOA, Borden, Union Carbide, Swift-Armour, and Volkswagen, among others, and the lending institutions included the Export-Import Bank, the Inter-American Development Bank, and the World Bank.[9])

To help bring about what they liked to call the Brazilian miracle, these allies initiated new road construction projects and introduced inappropriate technology and ecologically unsound practices into the region, converting vast woodlands into semi-desert. Far more shocking, however, has been the practice of uprooting whole human societies because they were seen as obstacles to economic growth.

Eager to alleviate acute land shortages in the country's impoverished northeastern region, but unwilling to break up the huge rural estates owned by a powerful elite and embark on much-needed land reform, govern-

© Harald E. L. Prins 1997

Maka Indian woman in Paraguay, South America. The poorest people in the world often wear clothing discarded by those who are better off—and people from all walks of life can be found wearing clothes with corporate logos. The power that big business (such as the Disney media corporation) has over individuals is illustrated by the ability of corporations to get consumers to pay for goods that advertise corporate products.

ment officials launched massive resettlement schemes. They lured millions of Brazilian peasants to the Amazon to clear the forest and settle as farmers in territories traditionally owned and long inhabited by many different indigenous nations. Soon, however, it became obvious that few of these newcomers could adequately support their families, so tens of thousands turned to gold mining. This, in turn, resulted in poisoning the rivers with mercury, creating serious health problems.

Bad as this was for these poor peasants, the disease, death, and human suffering that such schemes and policies unleashed upon the native Indians can only be described as massive. Entire indigenous groups have been (and are still being) destroyed with a thoroughness not achieved even by the communist dictator Stalin during his "Great Terror" in the Soviet Union of the 1930s or the Nazis in World War II. Were it not so well documented, it would be beyond belief.

[8]www.adbusters.org, accessed January 10, 2003. See also Hertz, N. (2001). *The silent takeover: Global capitalism and the death of democracy* (p. 43). New York: Arrow Books.

[9]Davis, S. H. (1982). *Victims of the miracle.* Cambridge, England: Cambridge University Press.

Megacorporations are changing the shape of the world and the lives of individuals from every walk of life, including those they employ. Anthropologist Jules Henry, in a classic 1965 study of life in the United States, observed that working for any large corporation—global or not—tends to generate "hostility, instability, and fear of being obsolete and unprotected. For most people their job was what they had to do rather than what they wanted to do, . . . taking a job, therefore, meant giving up part of their selves."[10]

Since Henry's day such feelings have grown in the ever more "sprawling, anonymous, networks" of global corporations.[11] Not only are business decisions typically made in corporate headquarters very far removed from where the actual business operations take place, but also, because corporations depend on sophisticated data-processing systems, many decisions can be and are being made by computers programmed for particular contingencies and strategies. In the face of such coldly calculating systems for making decisions exclusively in the corporate interest, workers become fearful that, if they ask too much of the company, it simply may shift its operations to another part of the world where it can find cheaper, more submissive personnel.

In the never-ending search for cheap labor, multinational corporations have returned to a practice once seen in the textile mills of 19th-century Britain and New England, but now on a much larger scale. More than ever before, they have come to favor women for low-skilled assembly jobs. In so-called underdeveloped countries, as subsistence farming gives way to mechanized agriculture for production of crops for export, women are less able to contribute to their families' survival. Together with the devaluation of domestic work, this places pressure on women to seek jobs outside the household to contribute to its support. Since most women in these countries do not have the time or resources to get an education or to develop special job skills, only low-paying jobs are open to them.

Corporate officials, for their part, assume female workers are strictly temporary, and high turnover means that wages can be kept low. Unmarried women are especially favored for employment, for it is assumed that they are free from family responsibilities until they marry, whereupon they will leave the labor force. Thus, the increasing importance of the multinationals in developing countries is contributing to the emergence of a marked gender-segregated division of labor. On top of their housework, women hold low-paying jobs that require little skill; altogether, they may work as many as 15 hours a day. Higher-paying jobs, or at least those

that require special skills, are generally held by men, whose workday may be shorter since they do not have additional domestic tasks to perform. Men who lack special skills—and many do—are often doomed to lives of unemployment.

Big business has created problems for consumers as well as workers. In a ten-year intensive study of relations between producers and consumers of products and services, anthropologist Laura Nader found repeated and documented offenses by North American businesses that could not be handled by existing complaint mechanisms, either in or out of court. Faceless relations between producers and consumers, among whom there is a grossly unequal distribution of power, have exacted a high cost: a terrible sense of apathy, even a loss of faith in the system itself.

In recent years, the power of corporations has become all the greater through media expansion. Over the past two decades, a global commercial media system has developed, dominated by a few megacorporations, most based in the United States. One such global media corporation is NBC, now owned by General Electric (GE), which is among the world's leading electronics and manufacturing firms with $150 billion in sales. In addition to NBC, GE owns various other broadcasting companies, including Paxson Communications and the Telemundo Communications Group. It also owns and operates a host of television stations in major urban markets such as New York, Los Angeles, Chicago, and Washington, D.C.—not to mention a digital media firm and three cable network companies, including CNBC and MSNBC. Moreover, GE owns companies such as GE Aircraft Engines, GE Commercial Finance, GE Consumer Products, GE Industrial Systems, GE Insurance, GE Medical Systems, GE Plastics, GE Power Systems, GE Specialty Materials, and GE Transportation Systems, and so on.

Having control of television and other media, as well as the advertising industry, gives global corporations such as GE and Disney enormous influence on the ideas and behavior of hundreds of millions of ordinary people across the world in ways most people little suspect and can hardly imagine.

Consider, for example, the powerful marketing messages that shape cultural standards concerning the ideal human body. The widespread nature of this concern is evident in highly popular reality TV programs like *Extreme Makeover,* which feature a few individuals chosen from many thousands of applicants to have their dream come true—to change their looks in an effort to lead better lives. They receive free plastic surgery and other radical cosmetic procedures in exchange for undergoing the knife on camera and allowing the details of their makeover to be broadcast on international television. The following Original Study offers details on what has become a lucrative cosmetic surgery industry.

---

[10]Henry, J. (1965). *Culture against man* (p. 127). New York: Vintage Books.

[11]Pitt, D. (1977). Comment. *Current Anthropology 18,* 628.

Original Study • By Laura Nader

Standardizing the Body: The Question of Choice

The question of choice is central to the story of how medicine and business generate controlling processes in the shaping of women's bodies. Images of the body appear natural within their specific cultural milieus. For example, breast implants are not seen as odd within the cultural milieu of the United States, and female circumcision and infibulation (also known as female genital mutilation or FGM) are not considered odd among people from the Sudan and several other African countries. However, many feminist writers differentiate FGM from breast implantation by arguing that North American women *choose* to have breast implants whereas in Africa women are presumably subject to indoctrination since they experience circumcision as young girls.

One of the most heated debates arising from the public health concern over breast implants is whether the recipients are freely situated—that is, whether their decision is voluntary or whether control is disguised as free will.

An informed response to the free choice argument requires knowing how the beauty-industrial complex works. Toward this end, corporate accountability researcher Linda Coco carried out fieldwork in multiple sites, gaining insights into the inner workings of a multibillion-dollar industry that segments the female body and manufactures commodities of and for the body.

Coco's research shows how some women get caught in the official beauty ideology, and in the case of silicone-gel breast implants some hundreds of thousands of women have been ensnared. But who gets caught and when are important to an understanding of the ecology of power. The average age of a woman having breast implantation is 36 years, and she has an average of two children. She is

the beauty industry's insecure consumer recast as a patient with an illness the industry defines as hypertrophy (small breasts).

Coco quotes a past president of the American Society of Plastic and Reconstructive Surgery (ASPRS): "There is substantial and enlarging medical knowledge to the effect that these deformities [small breasts] are really a disease which result in the patient's feelings of inadequacies, lack of self-confidence, distortion of body image, and a total lack of well-being due to a lack of self-perceived femininity. . . . Enlargement . . .

PROCEDURE	NUMBER DONE PER YEAR	PERCENT DONE FOR WOMEN
Chemical peel	1,033,581	89%
Eyelid surgery	230,697	86%
Nose reshaping	298,413	67%
Botox injection	3,839,387	92%
Face lift	150,401	90%
Breast enlargement	291,350	100%
Tummy tuck	134,746	96%
Liposuction	323,605	89%

Cosmetic surgical and nonsurgical procedures in the United States (2005) and the percentage carried out for women. In the United States in 2005 more than 2.1 million cosmetic surgeries were done and nearly 9.4 million nonsurgical procedures (chemical peels, Botox injections, and so on), at a total cost of about $12.4 billion. From 1997 to 2005, the number of cosmetic procedures performed increased 444 percent.

SOURCE: American Society for Aesthetic Plastic Surgery, 2006.

is therefore . . . necessary to ensure the quality of life for the patient." In other words, cosmetic surgery is necessary to the patient's psychological health.

The plastic surgeon regards the construction of the official breast as art, the aim being to reform the female body according to the ideals of classic Western art. One surgeon pioneering procedures for correcting deformity took as his ideal female figure that of ancient Greek statues, which he carefully measured, noticing the exact size and shape of the breasts, their vertical location between the third and seventh ribs, the horizontal between the line of the sternal (breast bone) border and the anterior axillary line, and so forth. In Coco's analysis the exercise of the plastic surgeon's technoart recreates a particular static, official breast shape and applies this creation ostensibly to relieve women's mental suffering. The surgeon becomes a psychological healer as well as an artist.

Along with art and psychology, there is, of course, the business of organized plastic surgery, which responds to the demands and opportunities of market economics (see figure). By the late 1970s and early 1980s there was a glut of plastic surgeons. The ASPRS began to operate like a commercial enterprise instead of a medical society, saturating the media with ads and even providing low-cost financing. The discourse became a sales pitch. Women "seek" breast implants to keep their husbands or their jobs, to attract men, or to become socially acceptable. Coco calls this "patriarchal capitalism" and questions whether this is free choice or "mind colonization."

Understanding "choice" led Coco to an examination of the power both in the doctor-patient relationship and in the control of information. She found that women "were told by the media, plastic surgeons, women's magazines, other women, and the business world that they could enhance their lives by enhancing their bust lines . . . the social imperative for appearance was personalized, psychologized, and normalized." Social surveys indicate that, to the extent that women internalize the social imperative, they feel they are making the decision on their own.

Not surprisingly, women whose surgery resulted in medical complications often came to recognize the external processes of coercive persuasion that had led them to seek implants. In some ways, they resembled former cult members who had been deprogrammed: Their disillusionment caused them to question the system that had encouraged them to make the decision in the first place. The result was a gradual building of protest against the industry, expressed in networks, newsletters, support groups, workshops, and seminars. As have some former cult members, women have brought suit, testified before lawmakers,

and challenged in other ways some of the largest corporations and insurance companies in the land.

The choice of implants, they learn, is part of a matrix of controlling processes in which women are subjects. Given the right circumstances it could happen to anyone. In the Sudan, the young girl is told that FGM procedures are done for her and not to her. In the United States the mutilation of natural breasts is also done for the recreation of femininity. Although power is exercised differently in these two cases, Coco notes the similarity: "The operation on the female breast in [North] America holds much of the same social symbolism and expression of cultural mandate as does FGM in Sudan. Thus, the question of why women choose breast augmentation becomes moot."

Breast implantation is now spreading elsewhere, most notably to China. Will it become a functional equivalent to footbinding in China as part of the competition between patriarchies East and West? Whatever the answer, many social think-

ers agree that people are always more vulnerable to intense persuasion during periods of historical dislocation—a break with structures and symbols familiar to the life cycle—in which the media can bring us images and ideas originating in past, contemporary, or even imaginary worlds.

Feminist researchers have sought to crack controlling paradigms such as those that define women's capacities and those that construct a standardized body shape and determine what is beautiful in women. Some of their writings are attempts to free the mind from the beauty constructions of cosmetic industries and fashion magazines. Others relay how the one model of Western beauty is affecting members of ethnic groups who aspire to look the way advertisements say they should. Choice is an illusion, since the restructuring of taste is inextricably linked to shifts in the organization of consumption.
(Adapted from L. Nader (1997). Controlling processes: Tracing the dynamics of power. Current Anthropology 38, 715–717.) ■

STRUCTURAL POWER IN THE AGE OF GLOBALIZATION

All of the above makes it clear that a new form of expansive international capitalism has emerged since the mid-1900s. Operating under the banner of globalization, it builds on earlier cultural structures of worldwide trade networks, and it is the successor to a system of colonialism in which a handful of powerful, mainly European, capitalist states ruled and exploited foreign nations inhabiting distant territories.

Enormously complex and turbulent, globalization is a dynamically structured process in which individuals, business corporations, and political institutions are actively rearranging and restructuring the social field of force to their own competitive advantage, vying for increasingly scarce natural resources, cheap labor, new commercial markets, and ever-larger profits in a huge political arena spanning the entire globe. Doing this, of course, requires a great deal of power.

As discussed previously, power refers to the ability of individuals or groups to impose their will upon others and make them do things even against their own wants or wishes. Power plays a major role in coordinating and regulating collective behavior toward imposing or main-

taining law and order within—and beyond—a particular community or society.

There are different levels of power within societies, as well as among societies. The recently deceased Austrian-American anthropologist Eric Wolf pointed out the importance of understanding a macro level of power that he referred to as **structural power**—power that organizes and orchestrates the systemic interaction within and among societies, directing economic and political forces on the one hand and ideological forces that shape public ideas, values, and beliefs on the other.[12]

The concept of structural power applies not only to regional political organizations such as chiefdoms or states but also captures the complex new cultural formations currently emerging in the globalization process. It focuses attention on the systemic interaction between the global forces directing the world's changing econo-

---

[12]Wolf, E. (1999). *Envisioning power: Ideologies of dominance and crisis* (p. 5). Berkeley: University of California Press.

structural power Power that organizes and orchestrates the systemic interaction within and among societies, directing economic and political forces on the one hand and ideological forces that shape public ideas, values, and beliefs on the other.

mies and political institutions on the one hand and those that shape public ideas, values, and beliefs on the other.

Joseph Nye, a political scientist, international security specialist, and former Assistant Secretary of Defense in the U.S. government, refers to these two major interacting forces in the worldwide arena as "hard power" and "soft power."[13] **Hard power** is the kind of coercive power that is backed up by economic and military force. **Soft power** is co-optive rather than coercive, pressing others through attraction and persuasion to change their ideas, beliefs, values, and behaviors. Although propaganda is a form of soft power, the exercise of ideological influence (the global struggle for hearts and minds) also operates through more subtle means, such as foreign aid, international diplomacy, news media, sports, entertainment, museum exhibits, and academic exchanges.

In today's globalization process, the United States has more hard power at its disposal than any of its allies or rivals worldwide. It is the global leader in military expenditure, spending more than $420 billion in 2005, followed by China ($62 billion), Russia ($62 billion), Britain ($51 billion), Japan ($45 billion—despite its pacifist constitution), France ($41 billion), and Germany ($30 billion). In fact, as the world's dominant superpower, the United States spends more on its armed forces than the next fourteen leading countries combined and is responsible for 43 percent of the $1 trillion spent on arms worldwide.[14]

Moreover, although there are seven other nuclear weapons states (Britain, France, and China, as well as Israel, India, Pakistan, and now also North Korea, collectively possessing nearly 900 active nuclear warheads), Russia and the United States have by far the largest nuclear arsenals at their disposal—minimally 5,830 and 5,735 operational warheads, respectively. (There are also nearly 16,000 intact but nonoperational warheads, almost all in the hands of the United States and Russia.)[15]

In addition to military might, hard power involves the use of economic strength as a political instrument of coercion or intimidation in the global structuring process. Among other things, this means that economic size and productivity, technological capability, and finance capital may be brought to bear on the global market, forcing weaker states to break down trade barriers protecting their workers, natural resources, and local markets.

As the world's largest economy and leading exporter, the United States has long pushed for free trade for its corporations doing business on a global scale. Sometimes it uses military power to impose changes on a foreign political landscape by means of armed interventions or full-scale invasions. For instance, when the United Fruit Company, owner of enormous banana plantations in Guatemala, saw its economic interests threatened by that country's democratically elected government, the U.S. government engineered a military coup in 1954 that resulted in a dictatorship favorable to U.S.-based corporations.

Through history, the United States (like several other powerful countries, including Russia, Britain, and France) has engaged in such military interventions around the world. Because of this, many see the United States as an ever-present threat, apt to use overwhelming military force in order to benefit its corporate interests from fruit to fuel, from microchips to automobiles. The corporations, in turn, wield enormous political and financial power over governments and international organizations, including the World Trade Organization, headquartered in Geneva, and global banking institutions such as the International Monetary Fund (IMF) and World Bank, both based in Washington, D.C.

Specializing in short-term loans to assist poor or developing countries, the IMF's financial resources weigh in at about $300 billion. The five wealthiest countries in the world (United States, Japan, Germany, France, and Britain) control 40 percent of this global fund and dominate its executive board. The IMF's structural power is evident not only in which development projects and policies it chooses to give financial support, but also in its surveillance practices, which involve monitoring a borrower's economic and financial developments.

The World Bank makes long-term loans ($20 billion annually) for economic development projects such as roads, schools, and health systems to reduce poverty in about a hundred developing countries. Like the IMF, it is largely controlled by a handful of powerful capitalist states. Operating under geopolitical constraints, these global banking institutions strategically direct capital flows to projects in certain parts of the world, financially supporting some governments and withholding capital from others.

Both the IMF and the World Bank have been accused of being insensitive to the political and cultural consequences of the projects they support. For example, in the 1990s the World Bank provided loans to a hydropower project in southern Chile to build dams in the upper Bio-Bio River without any serious consideration for

---

[13]Nye, J. (2002). *The paradox of American power: Why the world's only superpower can't go it alone.* New York: Oxford University Press.

[14]www.globalissue.org.

[15]Norris, R. S., & Kristensen, H. M. (2006, July/August). Global nuclear stockpiles, 1945–2006. *Bulletin of the Atomic Scientists 62* (4), 64–66.

hard power Coercive power that is backed up by economic and military force.
soft power Co-optive power that presses others through attraction and persuasion to change their ideas, beliefs, values, and behaviors.

Structural Power in the Age of Globalization 637

the human rights of local Pehuenche Indians. The dam flooded a large part of the Pehuenche's ancestral lands, forcing hundreds to be resettled against their own will. Likewise, the World Bank approved a $40 million loan to the Chinese government to relocate some of the country's poorest Han Chinese farmers to more fertile land in Qinghai, territory that Tibetans consider part of their homeland. Tibetans protested that the bank was supporting China's effort to dilute the Tibetan ethnic minority population in that region.

Globalization does more than create a worldwide field of force in which megacorporations reap megaprofits. It also wreaks havoc in many traditional cultures and disrupts long-established social organizations everywhere. By the early 21st century, the global trend of economic inequality is becoming clear: The poor are becoming poorer, and the rich are becoming richer. For the many thousands of big winners or have-lots, there are many millions of losers or have-nots.

As home base to more global corporations than any other country, the United States is endeavoring to protect its interests by investing in creating and controlling what it refers to as a *global security environment*. Numerous other countries, unable to afford expensive weapons systems (or blocked from developing or acquiring them), have invested in biological or chemical warfare technology. Still others, including relatively powerless political groups, have resorted to guerrilla tactics or terrorism as part of their local, regional, or even global warfare strategies.

In addition to reliance on military and economic hard power in the global quest for dominance and profit, competing states and corporations utilize the ideological persuasion of soft power as transmitted by means of electronic and digital media, communications satellites, and other forms of information and communication technology. One of the major tasks of soft power is to package and sell the general idea of globalization as something positive and progressive (as "freedom," "free" trade, "free" market) and to frame or brand anything that opposes capitalism in negative terms.

One outcome of this complex interaction between hard and soft power in structuring the global arena is the creation of a new collective awareness of worldwide connectivity, making peoples everywhere understand and possibly accept the new cultural order. Considering existing cultural differences, political divisions, and competing economic interests, combined with growing worldwide resistance against superpower domination, the emerging world system is inherently unstable, vulnerable, and unpredictable.

Structural power and its associated concepts of hard and soft power enable us to better understand the wider field of force in which local communities throughout the world are now compelled to operate. To comprehend it

Global mass media corporations like Cable News Network (CNN) possess enormous "soft power." This U.S.-based private company produces and distributes news and other information through transnational cable and satellite networks, as well as websites. With bureaus in over thirty countries, its 24-hour news coverage is available to 1.5 billion people all over the world. Like even larger media giants, such as the British Broadcasting Corporation (BBC), CNN not only reports news, but also selects the visual imagery and determines what to stress or repress. By means of their awesome soft power, these corporations influence public perception and action ("hearts and minds").

is to realize how unequal the distribution of power is in today's global arena.

That said, no matter how effectively a dominant state or corporation combines its hard and soft power, globalization does run into opposition. Pockets of resistance exist within the wealthy industrial and postindustrial states as well as elsewhere in the world. This resistance may manifest itself in the rise of traditionalisms and revitalization movements—efforts to return to life as it was (or how people think it was) before the familiar order became unhinged and people became unsettled. Some of these reactionary movements may take the form of resurgent ethnonationalism or religious fundamentalist movements. Others may find expression in alternative grassroots movements from radical environmental groups to peace groups.

Increasingly, such movements use the Internet to further their causes. While it is true that states and big corporations have expanded their power and influence through electronic communication technologies, it is also true that these same technologies present opportunities to individuals and groups that have traditionally been powerless. They provide a means of distributing information and promoting activities that are distinct from or in opposition to those of dominant society.

The far-reaching capabilities of modern electronic and digital technologies have led to the creation of a new global media environment that plays a major role in how individuals and even societies view themselves and their place in the world. Together with radio and

Anthropologists of Note

Arjun Appadurai (b. 1949)

Courtesy of Arjun Appadurai

Arjun Appadurai is one of millions of transnational migrants in the world. Growing up in India, he studied at the University of Bombay before heading to the United States, where he continued his education and chose a life in academia. Living abroad, he became interested in the dispersion of ethnic groups around the globe and in the question of how widely scattered members of these groups maintain their sense of cultural identity. His research—including fieldwork in India, South Africa, and the Philippines—shows that migrants form part of strong social networks, which, thanks to modern technology, reach far beyond traditional geographic boundaries.

Appadurai has developed theoretical concepts that help us understand the complex and largely unpredictable processes that are currently rearranging human relations and restructuring cultural systems worldwide. Although most people in today's world still function within geographically defined communities, Appadurai points out that territorial borders have become increasingly irrelevant given the "cultural flows"

in our emerging global environment. He marks out five global spaces or dimensions in which transnational cultural flows occur, identifying them as "scapes" (meaning something crafted, configured, or transformed by humans):

■ Ethnoscapes: the fluid and shifting landscape of migrants, refugees, exiles, tourists, and other moving groups and people
■ Technoscapes: the global configuration of technologies moving at high speeds across previously restrictive borders
■ Financescapes: the global crossroads of currency speculation and financial transfers
■ Mediascapes: the distribution of electronic media capabilities to produce and spread information, plus the large complex repertoire of narratives and visual images generated by these media
■ Ideoscapes: ideologies produced by the state and alternative ideologies developed by non-state and counter-hegemonic forces, around which societies organize their political cultures and collective cultural identities

Appadurai earned a doctorate from the University of Chicago in 1976 and has taught at the University of Pennsylvania, the University of Chicago, and Yale. Currently, he is provost at the New School University in New York City. Beyond university work, he has served as a consultant/advisor to a wide range of organizations, including the United Nations and the World Bank.

---

television, the Internet is now the dominant means of mass communication around the world. Today, the global flow of information made possible by fiber optic cables and communications satellites orbiting the earth is almost entirely digital-electronic and takes place in a new boundless cultural space that Indian anthropologist Arjun Appadurai refers to as a "global mediascape" (see Anthropologist of Note).

PROBLEMS OF STRUCTURAL VIOLENCE

Based on their capacity to harness, direct, and distribute global resources and energy flows, heavily armed states, megacorporations, and very wealthy elites are using their coercive and co-optive powers to structure or

structural violence Physical and/or psychological harm (including repression, environmental destruction, poverty, hunger, illness, and premature death) caused by impersonal, exploitative, and unjust social, political, and economic systems.

rearrange the emerging world system and direct global processes to their own competitive advantage. When such structural power undermines the well-being of others, we may speak of **structural violence**—physical and/or psychological harm (including repression, environmental destruction, poverty, hunger, illness, and premature death) caused by impersonal, exploitative, and unjust social, political, and economic systems.

Clearly, the current structures are positioned in a way that leads to more wealth, power, comfort, and glory for the happy few and little more than poverty, subservience, suffering, and death for multitudes. Every day millions of people around the world face famine, ecological disasters, health problems, political instability, and violence rooted in development programs or profit-making maneuvers directed by powerful states or global corporations.

A useful baseline for identifying structural violence is provided by the Universal Declaration of Human Rights, officially adopted by all members of the United Nations in 1948. Anthropologists played a key role in drafting this important document. The declaration's preamble begins with the statement that "recognition of the inherent dignity and of the equal and inalienable rights of all members of the human family is the foundation of freedom, justice, and peace in the world."[16] Generally speaking, structural violence concerns the impersonal systemic violation of the human rights of individuals and communities to a healthy, peaceful, and dignified life.

Although human rights abuses are nothing new, globalization has enormously expanded and intensified structural violence. For instance, it is leading to an ever-widening gap between the wealthiest and poorest peoples, the powerful and powerless. In 1960 the average income for the twenty wealthiest countries in the world was fifteen times that of the twenty poorest. Today it is thirty times higher.[17]

More remarkable is the fact that the world's 225 richest individuals have a combined wealth equal to the annual income of the poorest 47 percent of the entire world population. In fact, half of all people in the world get by on less than $2 per day, and more than 1.2 billion people live on just $1 a day. Measuring the gap in another way reveals that the poorest 80 percent of the human population make do with 14 percent of all goods and services in the world, the poorest 20 percent with a mere 1.3 percent. Meanwhile, the richest 20 percent enjoy 86 percent.[18]

Structural violence has countless manifestations in addition to widespread poverty. These range from the cultural destruction already indicated to hunger and obesity, environmental degradation, and emotional discontent, all discussed in the remaining pages of this chapter.

Overpopulation and Poverty

In 1750, 1 billion people lived on earth. Over the next two centuries our numbers climbed to nearly 2.5 billion. And between 1950 and 2000 the world population soared above 6 billion. Today, India and China alone have more than 1 billion inhabitants each. Such increases are highly significant because population growth increases the scale of hunger and pollution and the many problems tied to these two big issues. Although controlling population growth does not by itself make the other problems go away, it is unlikely those other problems can be solved unless population growth is stopped or even reversed.

For a population to hold steady, there must be a balance between birthrates and death rates. In other words, people must produce only enough offspring to replace themselves when they die. This is known as **replacement reproduction.** Prior to 1976, birthrates around the world generally exceeded death rates, with the exception of European and North American populations. Poor people, in particular, have tended to have large families because children have been their main resource. Children can provide a needed labor pool to work farms, and they are the only source of security for the elderly. Historically, people were apt to limit the size of their families only when they became wealthy enough that their money replaced children as their main resource; at that point, children actually *cost* them money. Given this, we can see why birthrates remained high for so long in the world's poorer countries. To those who live in poverty, children are seen as potentially valuable contributors to the household income.

Since the mid-1970s, birthrates have dropped below replacement level (which is about 2.1 children per woman) in virtually every industrialized country and also in nineteen developing countries—including China, the world's most populous country. Even in much of Africa, as well as South Asia and Central and South America (where most of the world's poorer nations are located), birthrates have also declined but far less dramatically.[19]

Despite progress in population control, the number of humans on earth continues to grow overall. Population projections are extremely tricky, given variables such as AIDS, but current projections suggest that global population will peak around 2050 at about 9.37 billion people.

The problem's severity becomes clear when it is realized that the present world population of more than 6 billion people can be sustained only by using up nonrenewable resources such as oil, which is like living off income-producing capital. It works for a time, but once the capital is gone, so is the possibility of even having an income to live on.

Hunger and Obesity

As frequently dramatized in media reports, hundreds of millions of people face hunger on a regular basis, leading to a variety of health problems, premature death, and other forms of suffering. Today, over a quarter of the world's countries do not produce enough food to feed their populations and cannot afford to import what

[16]www.ccnmtl.columbia.edu/projects/mmt/udhr.

[17]www.worldbank.org/poverty. (2003 statistics).

[18]Kurth, P. (1998, October 14). Capital crimes. *Seven Days*, 7; Swaminathan, M. S. (2000). Science in response to basic human needs. *Science 287*, 425. See also Human Development Report 2002, *Deepening democracy in a fragmented world*, United Nations Development Program.

[19]Bongaarts, J. (1998). Demographic consequences of declining fertility. *Science 282*, 419; Wattenberg, B. J. (1997, November 23). The population explosion is over. *New York Times Magazine*, 60.

replacement reproduction The point at which birthrates and death rates are in equilibrium; people producing only enough offspring to replace themselves when they die.

Hunger afflicts much of the world. It is caused not only by drought and pests, but also by violent ethnic, religious, or political conflicts that uproot families and by global food production and a distribution system geared to satisfy the needs and demands of the world's most powerful countries. Without adequate nutrition, humans lose their ability to resist diseases. And without access to adequate health care, many of the poverty-stricken sick have little chance to survive. For the poor, especially in refugee camps, slums, and other places with miserable living conditions, suffering is a normal condition of life, and death looms everywhere. Here, an African woman carries empty containers to be filled with water at Abu Shouk camp, home to some 100,000 refugees facing hunger and thirst in Sudan's ethnic war-torn Darfur region.

is needed. The majority of these countries are in sub-Saharan Africa.

All told, about 1 billion people in the world are undernourished. Some 6 million children aged 5 and under die every year due to hunger, and those who survive often suffer from physical and mental impairment.[20] For the victims of this situation, the effect is violent, even though it was not caused by the deliberate hostile act of a specific individual. The source of the violence may have been the unplanned yet devastatingly real impact of structural power—for instance, through the collapse of local markets due to subsidized foreign imports—and this is what structural violence is all about.

Ironically, while many millions of people in some parts of the world are starving, many millions of others are overeating—quite literally eating themselves to death. In fact, the number of overfed people now exceeds those who are underfed. According to the World Watch Institute in Washington, D.C., more than 1.1 billion people worldwide are now overweight. And 300 million of these are obese (but still often malnourished in that their diets lack certain nutrients).

Seriously concerned about the sharp rise in associated health problems (including stroke, diabetes, cancer, and heart disease), the World Health Organization classifies obesity as a global epidemic. Overeating is particularly unhealthy for individuals living in societies where machines have eased the physical burdens of work and other human activities, which helps explain why more than half of the people in some industrial and post-industrial countries are overweight.

However, the obesity epidemic is not due solely to excessive eating and lack of physical activity. A key ingredient is the high sugar and fat content of mass-marketed foods. The problem is spreading and has become a serious concern even in some developing countries. In fact, the highest rates of obesity in the world now exist among Pacific Islanders living in places such as Samoa and Fiji. On the island of Nauru, up to 65 percent of the men and 70 percent of the women are now classified as obese. (That said, not all people who are overweight or obese are so because they eat too much junk food and do too little exercise. In addition to cultural factors, being overweight or obese can also have genetic or other biological causes.)

As for hunger cases, about 10 percent of them can be traced to specific events—droughts or floods, as well as various social, economic, and political disruptions, including warfare. During the 20th century, 44 million people died due to human-made famine.[21] For example, in several sub-Saharan African countries plagued by chronic civil strife, it has been almost impossible to raise and harvest crops, for hordes of hungry refugees, roaming militias, and underpaid soldiers constantly raid fields. Another problem is that millions of acres in Africa, Asia, and Latin America once devoted to subsistence farming have been given over to the raising of cash crops for export. This has enriched members of elite social classes in these parts of the world, while satisfying the appetites of people in the developed countries for coffee, tea, chocolate, bananas, and beef. Those who used to farm the land for their own food needs have been relocated—either to urban areas, where all too often there is no employment for them, or to areas ecologically unsuited for farming.

In Africa, such lands are often occupied seasonally by pastoral nomads, and turning them over to cultiva-

[20]Hunger Project 2003; Swaminathan, M. S. (2000). Science in response to basic human needs. *Science 287*, 425.

[21]Hunger Project 2003; White, M. (2001). *Historical atlas of the twentieth century.* http://users.erols.com/mwhite28/20centry.htm.

tion has reduced pasture available for livestock and led to overgrazing. The increase in cleared land, coupled with overgrazing, has depleted both soil and water, with disastrous consequences to nomad and farmer alike. So it is that more than 250 million people can no longer grow crops on their farms, and 1 billion people in 100 countries are in danger of losing their ability to grow crops.[22]

One strategy urged upon so-called underdeveloped countries, especially by government officials and development advisors from Europe and the United States, has been to adopt practices that have made agriculture in industrialized societies incredibly productive. However, this strategy ignores the crucial fact that these large-scale, commercial farming practices require a financial investment that small farmers and poor countries cannot afford—a substantial outlay of cash for chemical fertilizers, pesticides, and herbicides, not to mention fossil fuels needed to run all the mechanized equipment.

U.S.-style farming has additional problems, including energy inefficiency. For every calorie produced, at least 8—some say as many as 20—calories go into its production and distribution.[23] By contrast, an Asian wet-rice farmer using traditional methods produces 300 calories for each 1 expended. North American agriculture is wasteful of other resources as well: About 30 pounds of fertile topsoil are ruined for every pound of food produced.[24] In the U.S. Midwest, about 50 percent of the topsoil has been lost over the past 100 years. Meanwhile, toxic substances from chemical nutrients and pesticides pile up in unexpected places, poisoning ground and surface waters; killing fish, birds, and other useful forms of life; upsetting natural ecological cycles; and causing major public health problems. Despite its spectacular short-term success, serious questions arise about whether such a profligate food production system can be sustained over the long run, even in North America.

Yet another problem with the idea of copying U.S. farming styles has to do with subsidies. Despite official rhetoric about free markets, governments of the wealthiest capitalist states in North America and western Europe spend between $100 billion and $300 billion annually on agriculture subsidies. In the United States, the world's largest agricultural exporter, 75 percent of these go to the wealthiest 10 percent of the farmers and large agricultural corporations.

Confronted with such economic forces in the global arena, small farmers in poor countries find themselves in

Spraying chemicals on crops, as here in California's Central Valley, trades short-term benefits for long-term pollution and health problems.

serious trouble when trying to sell their products on markets open to subsidized agricultural corporations dumping mass-produced and often genetically engineered crops and other farm products. Unable to compete under those structural conditions, many are forced to quit farming, leave their villages, and seek other livelihoods in cities or as migrant workers abroad. Such is the fate of many Maya Indians today. Since the early 1980s, when so many fled Guatemala's violence and poverty, thousands have made their way to places like southeastern Florida and taken low-paying jobs as illegal immigrants. Because of endemic poverty in their homeland where they would face starvation, these victims of structural violence have no choice but to remain where they are, condemned to an uncertain life in exile as cheap laborers without civil rights, Social Security, or health insurance.

Pollution

The effects of big agribusiness practices are part of larger problems of environmental degradation in which pollution is tolerated for the sake of higher profits that benefit select individuals and societies. Industrial activities are producing highly toxic waste at unprecedented rates, and factory emissions are poisoning the air. For example, smokestack gases are clearly implicated in acid rain, which is damaging lakes and forests all over northeastern North America. Air containing water vapor with a high acid content is, of course, harmful to the lungs, but the health hazard is greater than this. As ground and surface water becomes more acidic, the solubility of lead, cadmium, mercury, and aluminum, all of them toxic, rises sharply. For instance, aluminum contamination is high

[22]Godfrey, T. (2000, December 27). Biotech threatening biodiversity. *Burlington Free Press*, 10A.

[23]Bodley, J. H. (1985). *Anthropology and contemporary human problems* (2nd ed., p. 128). Palo Alto, CA: Mayfield.

[24]Chasin, B. H., & Franke, R. W. (1983). US farming: A world model? *Global Reporter* 1 (2), 10.

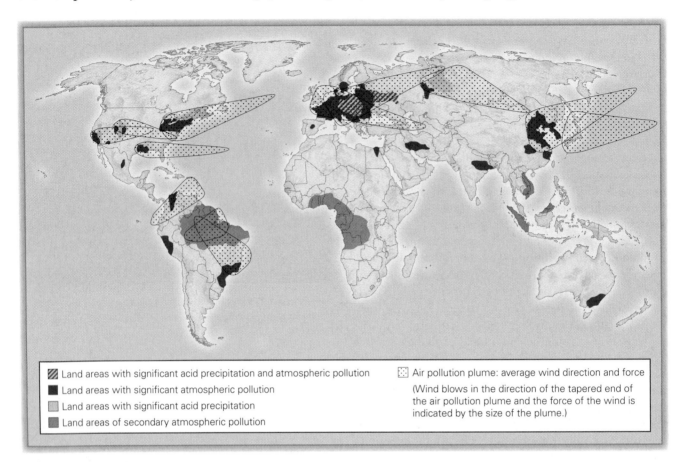

Figure 27.3

Global pollution. Almost all processes of physical geography begin and end with the flows of energy and matter among land, sea, and air. Because of the primacy of the atmosphere in this exchange system, air pollution is potentially one of the most dangerous human modifications in environmental systems. Pollutants such as various oxides of nitrogen or sulfur cause the development of acid precipitation, which damages soil, vegetation, and wildlife. Air pollution in the form of smog is often dangerous for human health. And most atmospheric scientists believe that the efficiency of the atmosphere in retaining heat— the so-called greenhouse effect—is being enhanced by increased carbon dioxide, methane, and other gases produced by industrial and agricultural activities. The result, a period of global warming, threatens to dramatically alter climates in all parts of the world.

SOURCE: From *Student Atlas of Anthropology,* by John Allen and Audrey Shalinksy, p. 132. Copyright © 2003 by the McGraw-Hill/Dushkin Publishing.

enough on 17 percent of the world's farmland to be toxic to plants—and has been linked to senile dementia, Alzheimer's, and Parkinson's diseases, three major health problems in industrial countries.

Finding their way into the world's oceans, toxic substances also create hazards for seafood consumers. For instance, Canadian Inuit face health problems related to eating fish and sea mammals that feed in waters contaminated by industrial chemical waste such as polychlorinated biphenyls (PCBs) (see Biocultural Connection).[25] Obviously, environmental poisoning affects peoples all across the globe (Figure 27.3).

Added to this is the problem of global warming— the greenhouse effect—caused primarily by the burning of fossil fuels (oil, gas, and coal). Although much is unknown about the extent of global warming, scientists now overwhelmingly agree it is real and poses a serious challenge. Experts predict that it will lead to an expansion of the geographic ranges of tropical diseases and increase the incidence of respiratory diseases due to additional smog caused by warmer temperatures. Also, they expect an increase in deaths due to heat waves, as witnessed in the 52,000 deaths attributed to the 2003 heat wave in Europe.[26]

[25]Inuit Tapiirit Kanatami. http://www.tapirisat.ca/english_text/ /departments/enviro/ncp.

[26]Larsen, J. (2006, July 28). Setting the record straight. Earth Policy Institute, Eco-economy updates.

Biocultural Connection

Toxic Breast Milk Threatens Arctic Culture

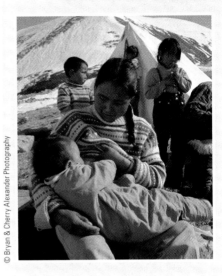

Asked to picture the Inuit people inhabiting the Arctic coasts of Canada, Greenland, and Labrador, you are likely to envision them dressed in fur parkas and moving across a pristine, snow-covered landscape on dogsleds—perhaps coming home from hunting seal, walrus, or whale.

Such imaginings are still true—except for the pristine part. Although Inuit live nearer to the North Pole than to any city, factory, or farm, they are not isolated from the pollutants of modern society. Chemicals originating in the cities and farms of North America, Europe, and Asia travel thousands of miles to Inuit territories via winds, rivers, and ocean currents. These toxins have a long life in the Arctic, breaking down very slowly due to icy temperatures and low sunlight. Ingested by zooplankton, the chemicals spread through the seafood chain as one species consumes another. The result is alarming levels of pesticides, mercury, and industrial chemicals in Arctic animals—and in

the Inuit people who rely on fishing and hunting for food.

Of particular note are toxic chemicals known as PCBs (polychlorinated biphenyls), used widely over several decades for numerous purposes, such as industrial lubricants, insulating materials, and paint stabilizers. Research shows a widespread presence of PCBs in the breast milk of women around the globe. But nowhere on earth is the concentration higher than among the Inuit—on average seven times that of nursing mothers in Canada's biggest cities![a]

PCBs have been linked to a wide range of health problems, from liver damage to weakened immune systems to cancer. Studies of children exposed to PCBs in the womb and through breast milk show impaired learning and memory functions. Beyond having a destructive impact on the health of humans (and other animal species), PCBs are impacting the economy, social organization, and psychological well-being of Arctic peoples. Nowhere is this more true than among the 450 Inuit living on Broughton Island, near Canada's Baffin Island. Here, word of skyrocketing PCB levels cost the community its valuable market for Arctic char fish. Other Inuits refer to them as "PCB people," and it is said that Inuit men now avoid marrying women from the island.[b]

The suggestion that the answer to these problems is a change of diet is soundly rejected by Inuit people, who have no real alternatives for afford-

able food. Abandoning the consumption of traditional seafood would destroy a 4,000-year-old culture based on hunting and fishing. Countless aspects of traditional Inuit culture—from worldview and social arrangements to vocabularies and myths—are linked to Arctic animals and the skills it takes to rely on them for food and so many other things. As one Inuit put it: "Our foods do more than nourish our bodies. They feed our souls. When I eat Inuit foods, I know who I am."[c]

The manufacture of PCBs is now banned in many western countries (including the United States), and PCB levels are gradually declining worldwide. However, because of their persistence (and widespread presence in remnant industrial goods such as fluorescent lighting fixtures and electrical appliances), they are still the highest-concentration toxins in breast milk, even among mothers born after the ban.

And even as PCBs decline, other commercial chemicals are finding their way northward. To date, about 200 hazardous compounds originating in industrialized regions have been detected in the bodies of Arctic peoples.[d] Global warming is fueling the problem, because as glaciers and snow melt, long-stored toxins are released.

[a]Colborn, T., et al. (1997). *Our stolen future* (pp. 107–108). New York: Plume (Penguin Books).
[b]AMAP. (2003). *AMAP assessment 2002: Human health in the Arctic* (pp. xii–xiii, 22–23). Oslo: Arctic Monitoring Assessment Project.

[c]Ingmar Egede, quoted in Cone, M. (2005) *Silent snow: The slow poisoning of the Arctic* (p. 1). New York: Grove Press.
[d]Additional sources: Johansen, B. E. (2002). The Inuit's struggle with dioxins and other organic pollutants. *The American Indian Quarterly 26* (3), 479–490; Natural Resources Defense Council. (2005, March 25). Healthy milk, healthy baby: Chemical pollution and mother's milk. www.NRDC.org; Williams, F. (2005, January 9). Toxic breast milk? *New York Times Magazine.*

Structural violence also manifests itself in the shifting of manufacturing and hazardous waste disposal from developed to developing countries. In the late 1980s, a tightening of environmental regulations in industrialized countries led to a dramatic rise in the cost of hazardous waste disposal. Seeking cheaper ways to get rid of the wastes, "toxic traders" began shipping hazard-

ous waste to Eastern Europe and especially to poor and underdeveloped countries in western Africa (see Globalscape). When news of this became public, international outrage led to the drafting and adoption of the Basel Convention to prohibit the export of hazardous wastes and minimize their generation. Today, the scope of the convention is severely limited by the fact that the United

GLOBALSCAPE

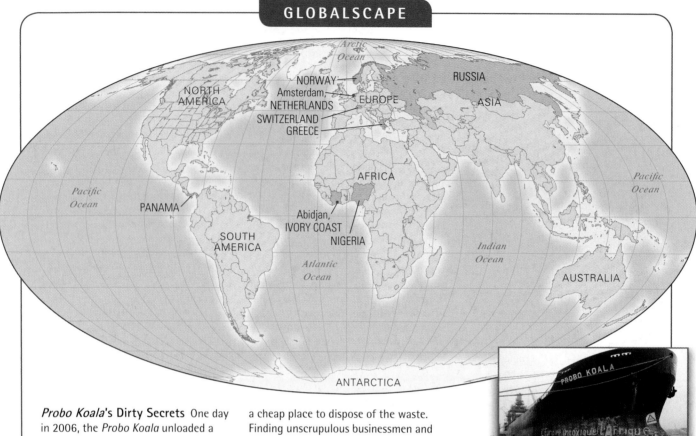

Probo Koala's Dirty Secrets One day in 2006, the *Probo Koala* unloaded a cargo of processed fuel in Nigeria, West Africa. Then the tanker sailed to Amsterdam where a Dutch treatment plant was to process its 400 tons of leftover toxic sludge. Navigating the oceans under the Panamanian flag, this ship's all-Russian crew serves under a Greek captain. Managed and operated by a Greek maritime company, the ship's registered owner is based in Norway. For this journey, it was chartered by a Dutch subsidiary of a multinational company headquartered in Switzerland and specialized in transporting oil and mineral products.

In Amsterdam, port authorities discovered that the *Probo Koala*'s captain had underreported the poison levels in his cargo, so the cost of treating the waste jumped to $600,000. Unwilling to pay the higher fee, the captain ordered his ship back to West Africa in search of

a cheap place to dispose of the waste. Finding unscrupulous businessmen and corrupt officials in Ivory Coast, he negotiated a dumping fee of about $18,000. The sludge was deposited in open-air waste pits on the edge of Abidjan, home to 5 million Africans. In the weeks that followed, some 40,000 locals were poisoned and fell ill; ten died almost immediately.

The *Probo Koala* forms part of a profitable global business network capitalizing on the more than 350 million tons of hazardous waste generated annually, primarily by industrial societies. Although most of this waste is now properly disposed, some companies avoid environmental regulations and high treatment costs within Europe and North America, seeking cheaper (possibly illegal) alternatives—including dumping at sea. Many millions of tons of hazardous waste are transported

across the oceans to underdeveloped countries. Remarkably, although over 150 states have signed treaties banning *import* of toxic and radioactive wastes (Ivory Coast is not among them), these agreements do not prohibit the *export* of waste.

Global Twister Although hazardous waste dumping by the *Probo Koala* resulted in the arrest of several African businessmen in Ivory Coast, should the other participants in this global crime be judged and punished? If so, under which laws?

States, the largest toxic residue producer in the world, has not ratified the agreement.[27] Moreover, the combination of unscrupulous entrepreneurs and corrupt government officials undermines people's health when it comes to circumventing international treaty obligations by

dumping hazardous wastes and poisoning soil, air, and drinking water.

Given a general awareness of the causes and dangers of pollution, why is it that the human species as a whole is not committed to controlling practices that foul its own nest? At least part of the answer lies in philosophical and theological traditions. As we saw in the chapter

[7]Hazardous waste trafficking. www.Choike.org.

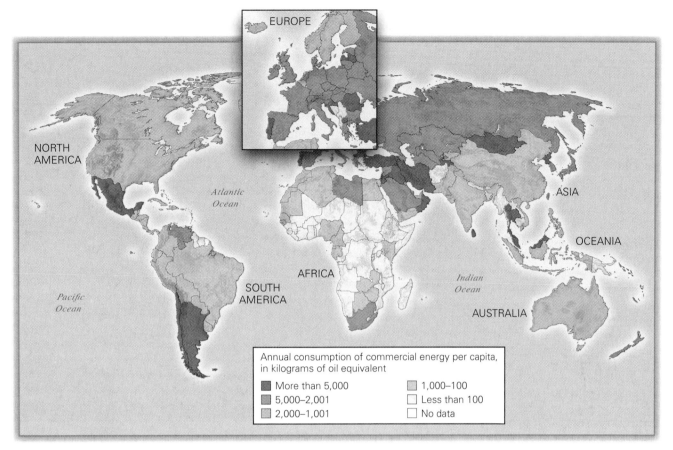

Figure 27.4

Global energy consumption. Most of the world's highest energy consumers are in North America and western Europe where at least 100 gigajoules of commercial energy per year are consumed by each person. (A gigajoule is the equivalent of about 3.5 metric tons of coal.) In some of these countries, such as the United States and Canada, the consumption rates are in the 300 gigajoule range (the equivalent of more than 10 metric tons of coal per person per year). At the other end of the scale are low-income countries, whose consumption rates are often less than 1 percent of those in the United States. (These figures do not include the consumption of noncommercial energy—the traditional fuels of firewood, animal dung, and other organic matter widely used in the less developed parts of the world.)

SOURCE: From *Student Atlas of Anthropology*, by Allen, J. L., & Shalinsky, A. C., p. 126. Copyright © 2004 McGraw-Hill/Dushkin Publishing.

on politics, Western industrialized societies accept the biblical assertion (found in the Koran as well) of human dominion over the earth, interpreting that it is their task to subdue and control the earth and all its inhabitants. These societies are the biggest contributors to global pollution. For example, on average, one North American consumes hundreds of times the resources of a single African, with all that implies with respect to waste disposal and environmental degradation (Figure 27.4). Moreover, each person in North America adds, on average, 20 tons of carbon dioxide (a greenhouse gas) a year to the atmosphere. In "underdeveloped" countries, less than 3 tons per person are emitted.[28] According to botanist Peter Ra-

ven, "if everyone lived like Americans, you'd need three planet earths . . . to sustain that level of consumption."[29]

The Culture of Discontent

For the past several decades, the world's poor countries have been sold on the idea they should and actually can enjoy a standard of living comparable to that of the rich countries. Yet, the resources necessary to maintain such a luxurious standard of living are not unlimited. This growing gap between expectations and realizations has led to the creation of a culture of discontent.

The problem involves not just population growth outstripping available natural resources, but also un-

[28]Broecker, W. S. (1992, April). Global warming on trial. *Natural History*, 14.

[29]Quoted in Becker, J. (2004, March). *National Geographic*, 90.

These Nambikwara children in southern Brazil are among the world's 300 million indigenous people to whom we have dedicated this book. With globalization now reaching even the most remote corners of the world, these Amazonian Indians are severely threatened, as are thousands of other small indigenous nations and ethnic minority groups that until now have survived the onslaught of colonialism, capitalist expansionism, and other forms of outside aggression. During the past five centuries, just a fraction of human existence, millions of indigenous peoples have perished due to foreign diseases, habitat destruction, warfare, and even genocide. Some 4,000 languages have disappeared due to acculturation, assimilation, or the physical extinction of their speakers. Yet, 6,000 languages remain, along with a still vast array of distinct peoples with unique cultures. Anthropologists study these different peoples for the sake of documenting their unique traditional cultures but also hope that information about their ways of life will lead to greater cross-cultural understanding, fostering tolerance and fundamental respect for human rights everywhere. Anthropologists have played and continue to play a valuable role in the long-term survival of indigenous groups—founding or helping to found organizations such as Cultural Survival, the Working Group on Indigenous Peoples, and Survival International.

equal access to decent jobs, housing, sanitation, health care, leisure, and adequate police and fire protection. It is one in which personal disappointments are echoed in a natural environment degraded by overcrowding, pollution, and soil erosion.

This culture of discontent is not limited to people living in poor and overpopulated countries. Because capitalism thrives on growing demands, powerful advertising strategies target people with financial means to purchase more and more luxury goods and services. In the process, even those whose needs are more than met will be made to feel the pinch of discontent and spend their money in pursuit of material dreams.

Some dramatic changes in cultural values and motivations, as well as in social institutions and the types of technologies we employ, are required if humans are going to realize a sustainable future for generations to come. The short-sighted emphasis on consumerism and individual self-interest so characteristic of the world's affluent countries needs to be abandoned in favor of a more balanced social and environmental ethic. This can be created from values still found in many of the world's non-Western cultures. Such values include a worldview that sees humanity as part of the natural world rather than superior to it. Included, too, is a sense of social responsibility that recognizes that no individual, people, or state has the right to expropriate resources at the expense of others. Finally, an awareness is needed of how important supportive ties are for individuals, such as seen in kinship or other associations in the world's traditional societies. Is humanity up to the challenge? And will anthropology play a role in meeting that challenge?

CONCLUDING REMARKS

As defined in this book's first chapter, anthropology is the comparative study of humankind everywhere and throughout time. It seeks to produce reliable knowledge about different peoples and cultures, their ideas and behaviors. Since the beginning of the discipline in the mid-1800s, generations of anthropologists have studied our species in all its cultural and biological varieties. In the process, they described in great detail an enormous number and range of different cultures and biological variations. They also collected a staggering volume of ethnographic artifacts and documented the sounds and sights of hundreds of different cultures with recording equipment and with still and motion cameras.

Today, many of the cultures studied by the earliest anthropologists more than a century ago have changed profoundly in response to powerful outside influences and internal dynamics. Others have disappeared as a result of deadly epidemics, violent conflicts, acculturation, ethnocide, or even genocide. All too often, the only detailed records we now possess of these altered and vanished cultures are those that some visiting anthropologist was able to document before it was too late.

But, anthropologists do much more than try to preserve precious information about distinctive peoples and cultures. As chronicled in the pages of this book, they also try to explain why cultures are similar or different, why and how they did or did not change. Moreover, they try to identify the particular knowledge and insights that each culture holds concerning the human condition—including contrasting views about humankind's place in the world, how natural resources are used and treated, and how one relates to fellow humans and other species.

Less apt than other scholarly specialists to see facts and activities as separate and unrelated, anthropologists are trained to understand and explain economic, social, political, ideological, and biological features and processes as parts of dynamic systems by means of theoretical concepts such as structural power and structural violence. Their cross-cultural and comparative historical perspective on local communities in the age of globalization enables them to make key contributions to our understanding of such troubling problems as overpopulation, food shortages, environmental destruction, and widespread strife and discontent in the world. This is evident, for instance, in hiring choices at the World Bank in the wake of a series of ill-conceived and mismanaged development projects that harmed more than helped local populations. Recognizing the value of anthropological knowledge and methods, the bank now employs and contracts dozens of professional anthropologists for projects all across the world. The same is true for other international organizations, as well as some global corporations and state government agencies.

Some anthropologists go beyond just studying different cultures and reach out to assist besieged groups that are struggling to survive in today's rapidly changing world. In so doing, they seek to put into practice their own knowledge about humankind—knowledge deepened through the comparative perspective of anthropology, which is cross-culturally, historically, and biologically informed.

The idea that anthropological research is fascinating in itself and also has the potential of helping solve practical problems on local and global levels has drawn and continues to draw a unique group of people into the discipline. Most of these individuals are inspired by the old but still valid idea that anthropology must aim to live up to its ideal as the most liberating of the sciences. As stated by noted anthropologist Margaret Mead, "Never doubt that a small group of committed people can change the world; indeed it is the only thing that ever has."

Questions for Reflection

1. No matter how divided peoples of the world are on economic, political, and ideological issues, all face the collective challenge of maintaining the long-term integrity of the planet we depend upon for survival. Do you think individuals like yourself can impact the current course toward environmental destruction that threatens all species, including our own? What steps do you think need to be taken individually and collectively to deal with this issue?

2. Most of the world's major global corporations are U.S. based, including Wal-Mart, which generates over $300 billion in annual revenues. Measured in economic terms, this business is bigger than Turkey, inhabited by nearly 75 million people. In what ways might such a megacorporation use its enormous economic power? Could it influence the U.S. government in terms of world trade policies? If so, would the company benefit more from free trade or protectionism?

3. Considering the relationship between structural power and structural violence, does your own lifestyle in terms of buying clothes and food, driving cars, and so on reflect or have an effect on the globalization process?

4. In the global mediascape, television viewers and Internet users are not only consumers of news and entertainment but

are also exposed to soft power. Can you think of an example of soft power in your daily life? And at which point does such influence turn into propaganda or manipulation?

5. The World Health Organization, UNESCO, Oxfam, and Amnesty International are global institutions concerned with structural violence and human rights violations. Confronted with genocidal conflicts, famines, epidemics, and torture of political prisoners, people active in these organizations try to improve the human condition. Why do you think that an anthropological perspective on such worldwide problems might be of practical use? Can you think of an example?

Suggested Readings

Appadurai, A. (1996). *Modernity at large: Cultural dimensions of globalization*. Minneapolis: University of Minnesota Press.

In this fundamental contribution to how globalization works, a leading anthropologist discusses how forces such as migration and electronic mediation acquire shaping roles in the production of contemporary culture.

Bodley, J. H. (2000). *Anthropology and contemporary human problems* (4th ed.). Palo Alto, CA: Mayfield.

Anthropologist Bodley examines some of the most serious problems in the world today: overconsumption, resource depletion, hunger and starvation, overpopulation, violence and war.

Friedman, J. (Ed.). (2003). *Globalization, the state, and violence*. Walnut Creek, CA: Altamira Press.

A vibrant, insightful analysis of globalization and the "lethal explosiveness" that characterizes the current world order. Friedman leads a group of distinguished contributors in examining the global processes and political forces that determine transnational networks of crime, commerce, and terror, leading to economic, social, and cultural fragmentation.

Ginsburg, F. D., Abu-Lughod, L., & Larkin, B. (Eds.). (2002). *Media worlds: Anthropology on new terrain*. Berkeley: University of California Press.

Groundbreaking essays by pioneers of media studies in anthropology, discussing the place and function of film, video, radio, television, and cinema in different cultures and showing that contemporary peoples and cultures cannot be understood without the mediascapes they inhabit.

Lewellen, T. C. (2002). *The anthropology of globalization: Cultural anthropology enters the 21st century*. Westport, CT: Greenwood Publishing Group/Bergin & Garvey.

Readable introduction, summary, and critique of globalization with telling and timely ethnographic examples.

Ong, A. (1999). *Flexible citizenship: The cultural logics of transnationality*. Durham, NC: Duke University Press.

Ong demonstrates how the Chinese transnational community confounds notions of peripheral non-Westerners and argues that the contemporary world is creating the context for the rise of China.

Trouillot, M. R. (2003). *Global transformations: Anthropology and the modern world*. New York: Palgrave Macmillan.

Examining anthropology's history and discussing future possibilities for the discipline, the author challenges colleagues to question dominant narratives of globalization and to radically rethink key concepts of the discipline.

Thomson Audio Study Products

 Enjoy the MP3-ready Audio Lecture Overviews for each chapter and a comprehensive audio glossary of key terms for quick study and review. Whether walking to class, doing laundry, or studying at your desk, you now have the freedom to choose when, where, and how you interact with your audio-based educational media. See the preface for information on how to access this on-the-go study and review tool.

The Anthropology Resource Center

www.thomsonedu.com/anthropology
The Anthropology Resource Center provides extended learning materials to reinforce your understanding of key concepts in the four fields of anthropology. For each of the four fields, the Resource Center includes dynamic exercises including video exercises, map exercises, simulations, and "Meet the Scientists" interviews, as well as critical thinking questions that can be assigned and e-mailed to instructors. The Resource Center also provides breaking news in anthropology and interesting material on applied anthropology to help you link what you are learning to the world around you.

Glossary

absolute or chronometric dating: In archaeology and paleoanthropology, dates for recovered archaeological material based on solar years, centuries, or other units of absolute time.

acclimatization: Long-term physiological adjustments made in order to attain an equilibrium with a specific environmental stimulus.

acculturation: Massive culture change that occurs in a society when it experiences intensive firsthand contact with a more powerful society.

Acheulean tradition: The tool-making tradition of *Homo erectus* in Africa, Europe, and Southwest Asia in which hand-axes were developed from the earlier Oldowan chopper.

action theory: The theory that self-serving actions by forceful leaders play a role in civilization's emergence.

adaptation: A series of beneficial adjustments to the environment.

adaptive radiation: Rapid diversification of an evolving population as it adapts to a variety of available niches.

adjudication: Mediation with an unbiased third party making the ultimate decision.

advocacy anthropology: Research that is community-based and politically involved.

affinal kin: People related through marriage.

age grade: An organized category of people based on age; every individual passes through a series of such categories over his or her lifetime.

age set: A formally established group of people born during a certain time span who move through the series of age-grade categories together.

agriculture: The cultivation of food plants in soil prepared and maintained for crop production. Involves using technologies other than hand tools, such as irrigation, fertilizers, and the wooden or metal plow pulled by harnessed draft animals.

allele: Alternate form of a single gene.

Allen's rule: The tendency of mammals living in cold climates to have shorter appendages (arms and legs) than members of the same species living in warm climates.

alphabet: A series of symbols representing the sounds of a language arranged in a traditional order.

altruism: Acts of selflessness or self-sacrificing behavior.

ambilocal residence: A residence pattern in which a married couple may choose either matrilocal or patrilocal residence.

anagenesis: A sustained directional shift in a population's average characteristics.

analogies: In biology, structures possessed by different organisms that are superficially similar due to similar function without sharing a common developmental pathway or structure.

ancestral: Characteristics possessed by an organism or group of organisms due to shared ancestry.

animatism: A belief that nature is enlivened or energized by an impersonal spiritual power or supernatural potency.

animism: A belief that nature is enlivened or energized by distinct personalized spirit beings separable from bodies.

Anthropoidea: A suborder of the primates that includes New World monkeys, Old World monkeys, and apes (including humans).

anthropology: The study of humankind in all times and places.

applied anthropology: The use of anthropological knowledge and methods to solve practical problems, often for a specific client.

arboreal: Living in the trees.

arboreal hypothesis: A theory for primate evolution that proposes that life in the trees was responsible for enhanced visual acuity and manual dexterity in primates.

archaeology: The study of human cultures through the recovery and analysis of material remains and environmental data.

Archaic cultures: Term used to refer to Mesolithic cultures in the Americas.

Ardipithecus ramidus: One of the earliest bipeds that lived in eastern Africa about 4.4 to 5.8 million years ago.

art: The creative use of the human imagination to aesthetically interpret, express, and engage life, modifying experienced reality in the process.

Aurignacian tradition: Tool-making tradition in Europe and western Asia at the beginning of the Upper Paleolithic.

Australopithecus: The genus including several species of early bipeds from southern, eastern, and central Africa living between about 1.1 and 4.3 million years ago, one of whom was directly ancestral to humans.

balanced reciprocity: A mode of exchange in which the giving and the receiving are specific as to the value of the goods and the time of their delivery.

band: A relatively small and loosely organized kin-ordered group that inhabits a specific territory and that may split periodically into smaller extended family groups that are politically independent.

Bergman's rule: The tendency for the bodies of mammals living in cold climates to be shorter and rounder than members of the same species living in warm climates.

binocular vision: Vision with increased depth perception from two eyes set next to each other allowing their visual fields to overlap.

bioarchaeology: The archaeological study of human remains emphasizing the preservation of cultural and social processes in the skeleton.

biocultural: Focusing on the interaction of biology and culture.

bipedalism: The mode of locomotion in which an organism walks upright on its two hind legs characteristic of humans and their ancestors.

blade technique: A technique of stone tool manufacture by which long, parallel-sided flakes are struck off the edges of a specially prepared core.

brachiation: Using the arms to swing from branch to branch, with the body hanging suspended beneath the arms.

bride-price: Money or valuable goods paid by the groom or his family to the bride's family upon marriage. Also called bride wealth.

burin: A stone tool with chisel-like edges used for working bone and antler.

cargo cult: A spiritual movement (especially noted in Melanesia) in reaction to disruptive contact with Western capitalism, promising resurrection of deceased relatives, destruction or enslavement of white foreigners, and the magical arrival of utopian riches.

carrying capacity: The number of individuals that the available resources can support at a given level of food-getting techniques.

caste: A closed social class in a stratified society in which membership is determined by birth and fixed for life.

Catarrhini: An anthropoid infraorder that includes Old World monkeys, apes, and humans.

chiefdom: A regional polity in which two or more local groups are organized under a single chief, who is at the head of a ranked hierarchy of people.

chromosome: In the cell nucleus, the structure visible during cellular division containing long strands of DNA combined with a protein.

civilization: In anthropology, a type of society marked by the presence of cities, social classes, and the state.

cladogenesis: Speciation through a branching mechanism whereby an ancestral population gives rise to two or more descendant populations.

clan: An extended unilineal kinship group, often consisting of several lineages, whose members claim common descent from a remote ancestor, usually legendary or mythological.

clavicle: The collarbone connecting the sternum (breastbone) with the scapula (shoulder blade).

cline: A gradual change in the frequency of an allele or trait over space.

code switching: Changing from one mode of language to another as the situation demands, whether from one language to another or from one dialect of a language to another.

codon: Three-base sequence of a gene that specifies a particular amino acid for inclusion in a protein.

cognitive capacity: A broad concept including intelligence, educability, concept formation, self-awareness, self-evaluation, attention span, sensitivity in discrimination, and creativity.

common-interest association: An association that results from the act of joining and is based on sharing particular activities, objectives, values, or beliefs.

community: A unit of primate social organization composed of fifty or more individuals who inhabit a large geographic area together.

conjugal family: A family established through marriage.

consanguineal family: A family of "blood relatives" consisting of related women, their brothers, and the women's offspring.

consanguineal kin: Biologically related relatives, commonly referred to as blood relatives.

conspicuous consumption: A showy display of wealth for social prestige.

contagious magic: Magic based on the principle that things once in contact can influence each other after the contact is broken.

continental drift: According to the theory of plate tectonics, the movement of continents embedded in underlying plates on the earth's surface in relation to one another over the history of life on earth.

convergent evolution: In biological evolution a process by which unrelated populations develop similarities to one another due to similar function rather than shared ancestry. In cultural evolution, the development of similar cultural adaptations to similar environmental conditions by different peoples with different ancestral cultures.

coprolites: Preserved fecal material providing evidence of the diet and health of past organisms.

core values: Those values especially promoted by a particular culture.

cranium: The braincase of the skull.

Cro-Magnon: A European of the Upper Paleolithic after about 36,000 years ago.

cross cousin: Child of a mother's brother or a father's sister.

cultural adaptation: A complex of ideas, activities, and technologies that enable people to survive and even thrive.

cultural anthropology: Also known as social or sociocultural anthropology. The study of customary patterns in human behavior, thought, and feelings. It focuses on humans as culture-producing and culture-reproducing creatures.

cultural control: Control through beliefs and values deeply internalized in the minds of individuals.

cultural evolution: Culture change over time (not to be confused with progress).

cultural loss: The abandonment of an existing practice or trait.

cultural relativism: The thesis that one must suspend judgment of other people's practices in order to understand them in their own cultural terms.

cultural resource management (CRM): A branch of archaeology tied to government policies for the protection of cultural resources and involving surveying and/or excavating archaeological and historical remains threatened by construction or development.

culture: A society's shared and socially transmitted ideas, values, and perceptions, which are used to make sense of experience and which generate behavior and are reflected in that behavior.

culture area: A geographic region in which a number of societies follow similar patterns of life.

culture core: Cultural features that are fundamental in the society's way of making its living—including food-producing techniques, knowledge of available resources, and the work arrangements involved in applying those techniques to the local environment.

datum point: The starting, or reference, point for a grid system.

dendrochronology: In archaeology, a method of chronometric dating based on the number of rings of growth found in a tree trunk.

density of social relations: The number and intensity of interactions among the members of a camp.

dental formula: The number of each tooth type (incisors, canines, premolars, and molars) on one half of each jaw. Unlike other mammals, primates possess equal numbers on their upper and lower jaws so the dental formula for the species is a single series of numbers.

dependence training: Child-rearing practices that foster compliance in the performance of assigned tasks and dependence on the domestic group, rather than reliance on oneself.

derived: Characteristics that define a group of organisms that did not exist in ancestral populations.

descent group: Any kinship group with a membership lineally descending from a real (historical) or fictional common ancestor.

developmental adaptation: A permanent phenotypic variation derived from interaction between genes and the environment during the period of growth and development.

dialects: Varying forms of a language that reflect particular regions, occupations, or social classes and that are similar enough to be mutually intelligible.

diastema: A space between the canines and other teeth allowing large projecting canines space within the jaw.

diffusion: The spread of certain ideas, customs, or practices from one culture to another.

digital ethnography: The use of digital technologies (audio and visual) for the collection, analysis, and representation of ethnographic data.

disease: Refers to a specific pathology; a physical or biological abnormality.

displacement: Referring to things and events removed in time and space.

divination: A magical procedure or spiritual ritual designed to find out about what is not knowable by ordinary means, such as foretelling the future by interpreting omens.

DNA: Deoxyribonucleic acid. The genetic material consisting of a complex molecule whose base structure directs the synthesis of proteins.

doctrine: An assertion of opinion or belief formally handed down by an authority as true and indisputable. Also known as dogma.

domestication: An evolutionary process whereby humans modify, either intentionally or unintentionally, the genetic makeup of a population of plants or animals, sometimes to the extent that members of the population are unable to survive and/or reproduce without human assistance.

dominance: In physical anthropology, the ability of one allele for a trait to mask the presence of another allele.

dominance hierarchies: An observed ranking system in primate societies ordering individuals from high (alpha) to low standing corresponding to predictable behavioral interactions including domination.

dowry: Payment of a woman's inheritance at the time of her marriage, either to her or to her husband.

ecological niche: A species' way of life considered in the full context of its environment, including factors such as diet, activity, terrain, vegetation, predators, prey, and climate.

ecosystem: A system, or a functioning whole, composed of both the natural environment and all the organisms living within it.

egalitarian societies: Societies in which everyone has about equal rank, access to, and power over basic resources.

EGO: The central person from whom the degree of each relationship is traced.

eliciting device: An activity or object used to draw out individuals and encourage them to recall and share information.

empirical: Based on observations of the world rather than on intuition or faith.

enculturation: The process by which a society's culture is transmitted from one generation to the next and individuals become members of their society.

endemic: The public health term for a disease that is widespread in a population.

endocast: A cast of the inside of a skull; helps determine the size and shape of the brain.

endogamy: Marriage within a particular group or category of individuals.

entoptic phenomena: Bright pulsating forms that are generated by the central nervous system and seen in states of trance.

enzyme: Protein that initiates and directs chemical reactions.

epic: A long dramatic narrative recounting the celebrated deeds of a historic or legendary hero—often sung or recited in poetic language

epicanthic eye fold: A fold of skin at the inner corner of the eye that covers the true corner of the eye; common in Asiatic populations.

Eskimo system: Kinship reckoning in which the nuclear family is emphasized by specifically identifying the mother, father, brother, and sister, while lumping together all other relatives into broad categories such as uncle, aunt, and cousin. Also referred to as lineal system.

estrus: In some primate females, the time of sexual receptivity during which ovulation is visibly displayed.

ethnic group: People who collectively and publicly identify themselves as a distinct group based on various cultural features such as shared ancestry and common origin, language, customs, and traditional beliefs.

ethnicity: This term, rooted in the Greek word *ethnikos* ("nation") and related to *ethnos* ("custom"), is the expression of the set of cultural ideas held by an ethnic group.

ethnic psychosis: A mental disorder specific to a particular ethnic group.

ethnocentrism: The belief that the ways of one's own culture are the only proper ones.

ethnocide: The violent eradication of an ethnic group's collective cultural identity as a distinctive people; occurs when a dominant society deliberately sets out to destroy another society's cultural heritage.

ethnographic fieldwork: Extended on-location research to gather detailed and in-depth information on a society's customary ideas, values, and practices through participation in its collective social life.

ethnography: A detailed description of a particular culture primarily based on fieldwork.

ethnohistory: A study of cultures of the recent past through oral histories, accounts of explorers, missionaries, and traders, and through analysis of records such as land titles, birth and death records, and other archival materials.

ethnolinguistics: A branch of linguistics that studies the relationships between language and culture and how they mutually influence and inform each other.

ethnology: The study and analysis of different cultures from a comparative or historical point of view, utilizing ethnographic accounts and developing anthropological theories that help explain why certain important differences or similarities occur among groups.

ethnomusicology: The study of a society's music in terms of its cultural setting.

evolution: Changes in allele frequencies in populations; also known as microevolution.

evolutionary medicine: An approach to human sickness and health combining principles of evolutionary theory and human evolutionary history.

exogamy: Marriage outside the group.

extended family: Two or more closely related nuclear families clustered together into a large domestic group.

fictive marriage: Marriage by proxy to the symbols of someone not physically present to establish the social status of a spouse and heirs.

fieldwork: The term anthropologists use for on-location research.

fission: The splitting of a descent group into two or more new descent groups.

flotation: An archaeological technique employed to recover very tiny objects by immersion of soil samples in water to separate heavy from light particles.

fluorine dating: In archaeology or paleoanthropology, a technique for relative dating based on the fact that the amount of fluorine in bones is proportional to their age.

folklore: A term coined by 19th-century scholars studying the unwritten stories and other artistic traditions of rural peoples to distinguish between "folk art" and the "fine art" of the literate elite.

food foraging: Hunting, fishing, and gathering wild plant foods.

foramen magnum: A large opening in the skull through which the spinal cord passes and connects to the brain.

forensic anthropology: Applied subfield of physical anthropology that specializes in the identification of human skeletal remains for legal purposes.

formal interview: A structured question/answer session carefully notated as it occurs and based on prepared questions.

fossil: Any mineralized trace or impression of an organism that has been preserved in the earth's crust from past geological time.

founder effect: A particular form of genetic drift deriving from a small founding population not possessing all the alleles present in the original population.

fovea centralis: A shallow pit in the retina of the eye that enables an animal to focus on an object while maintaining visual contact with its surroundings.

gender: The cultural elaborations and meanings assigned to the biological differentiation between the sexes.

gendered speech: Distinct male and female speech patterns, which vary across social and cultural settings.

gene: A portion of the DNA molecule containing a sequence of base pairs that is the fundamental physical and functional unit of heredity.

gene flow: The introduction of alleles from the gene pool of one population into that of another.

gene pool: All the genetic variants possessed by members of a population.

generalized reciprocity: A mode of exchange in which the value of what is given is not calculated, nor is the time of repayment specified.

genetic code: The sequence of three bases (a codon) that specifies the sequence of amino acids in protein synthesis.

genetic drift: Chance fluctuations of allele frequencies in the gene pool of a population.

genocide: The physical extermination of one people by another, either as a deliberate act or as the accidental outcome of activities carried out by one people with little regard for their impact on others.

genotype: The alleles possessed for a particular trait.

genus, genera (pl.): In the system of taxonomic classification, a group of like species.

gesture: Facial expressions and bodily postures and motions that convey intended as well as subconscious messages.

globalization: Worldwide interconnectedness, evidenced in global movements of natural resources, trade goods, human labor, finance capital, information, and infectious diseases.

glottochronology: In linguistics, a method for identifying the approximate time that languages branched off from a common ancestor. It is based on analyzing core vocabularies.

gracile australopithecines: Members of the genus *Australopithecus* possessing a more lightly built chewing apparatus; likely had a diet that included more meat than that of the robust australopithecines.

grade: A general level of biological organization seen among a group of species, useful for constructing evolutionary relationships.

grammar: The entire formal structure of a language, including morphology and syntax.

grave goods: Items such as utensils, figurines, and personal possessions, symbolically placed in the grave for the deceased person's use in the afterlife.

grid system: A system for recording data in three dimensions from an archaeological excavation.

grooming: The ritual cleaning of another animal's coat to remove parasites and other matter.

group marriage: Marriage in which several men and women have sexual access to one another. Also called co-marriage.

Haplorhini: In the alternate primate taxonomy, the suborder that includes tarsiers, monkeys, apes, and humans.

hard power: Coercive power that is backed up by economic and military force.

Hardy-Weinberg principle: Demonstrates algebraically that the percentage of individuals that are homozygous for the dominant allele, homozygous for the recessive allele, and heterozygous should remain constant from one generation to the next, provided that certain specified conditions are met.

Hawaiian system: Kinship reckoning in which all relatives of the same sex and generation are referred to by the same term.

health disparity: A difference in the health status between the wealthy elite and the poor in stratified societies.

hemoglobin: The protein that carries oxygen in the red blood cells.

heterochrony: Change in the timing of developmental events that is often responsible for changes in the shape or size of a body part.

heterozygous: Refers to a chromosome pair that bears different alleles for a single gene.

holistic perspective: A fundamental principle of anthropology: that the various parts of human culture and biology must be viewed in the broadest possible context in order to understand their interconnections and interdependence.

homeobox gene: A gene responsible for large-scale effects on growth and development that are frequently responsible for major reorganization of body plans in organisms.

homeotherm: An animal that maintains a relatively constant body temperature despite environmental fluctuations.

home range: The geographic area within which a group of primates usually moves.

hominid: African hominoid family that includes humans and their ancestors. Some scientists, recognizing the close relationship of humans, chimps, bonobos, and gorillas, use the term *hominid* to refer to all African hominoids. They then divide the hominid family into two subfamilies: the Paninae (chimps, bonobos, and gorillas) and the Homininae (humans and their ancestors).

hominin: The taxonomic subfamily or tribe within the primates that includes humans and our ancestors.

hominoid: The taxonomic division superfamily within the cattarrhine primates that includes gibbons, siamangs, orangutans, gorillas, chimpanzees, bonobos, and humans.

Homo erectus: "Upright man." A species within the genus *Homo* first appearing just after 2 million years ago in Africa and ultimately spreading throughout the Old World.

Homo habilis: "Handy man." The first fossil members of the genus *Homo* appearing 2.5 million years ago, with larger brains and smaller faces than australopithecines.

homologies: In biology, structures possessed by two different organisms that arise in similar fashion and pass through similar stages during embryonic development though they may possess different functions.

homozygous: Refers to a chromosome pair that bears identical alleles for a single gene.

horticulture: Cultivation of crops carried out with simple hand tools such as digging sticks or hoes.

household: The basic residential unit where economic production, consumption, inheritance, child rearing, and shelter are organized and carried out.

Human Relations Area Files (HRAF): A vast collection of cross-indexed ethnographic and archaeological data catalogued by cultural characteristics and geographic locations. Archived in about 300 libraries (on microfiche and/or online).

hunting response: A cyclic expansion and contraction of the blood vessels of the limbs that balances releasing enough heat to the limbs to prevent frostbite with maintaining heat in the body core.

hydraulic theory: The theory that explains civilization's emergence as the result of the construction of elaborate irrigation systems, the functioning of which required full-time managers whose control blossomed into the first governing body and elite social class.

hypoglossal canal: The opening in the skull that accommodates the tongue-controlling hypoglossal nerve.

iconic images: Culturally specific people, animals, and monsters seen in the deepest stage of trance.

idealist perspective: A theoretical approach stressing the primacy of superstructure in cultural research and analysis.

illness: Refers to the meanings and elaborations given to a particular physical state.

imitative magic: Magic based on the principle that like produces like; sometimes called sympathetic magic.

incest taboo: The prohibition of sexual relations between specified individuals, usually parent and child and sibling relations at a minimum.

incorporation: In rites of passage, reincorporation of the individual into society in his or her new status.

independence training: Child-rearing practices that promote independence, self-reliance, and personal achievement on the part of the child.

informal economy: Network of producing and circulating marketable commodities, labor, and services that for various reasons escape government control.

informal interview: An unstructured, open-ended conversation in everyday life.

informed consent: Formal, recorded agreement to participate in research.

infrastructure: The economic foundation of a society, including its subsistence practices and the tools and other material equipment used to make a living.

intersexual: A person born with reproductive organs, genitalia, and/or sex chromosomes that are not exclusively male or female.

Iroquois system: Kinship reckoning in which a father and father's brother are referred to by a single term, as are a mother and mother's sister, but a father's sister and mother's brother are given separate terms. Parallel cousins are classified with brothers and sisters, while cross cousins are classified separately but not equated with relatives of some other generation.

isolating mechanism: A factor that separates breeding populations, thereby preventing gene flow, creating divergent subspecies, and ultimately (if maintained) divergent species.

isotherm: An animal whose body temperature rises or falls according to the temperature of the surrounding environment.

Kenyanthropus platyops: A new proposed genus and species of bipeds contemporary with early australopithecines; may not be separate genus.

key consultant: A member of the society being studied, who provides information that helps researchers understand the meaning of what they observe; early anthropologists referred to such individuals as informants.

kindred: An individual's close blood relatives on the maternal and paternal sides of his or her family.

kinesics: A system of notating and analyzing postures, facial expressions, and bodily motions that convey messages.

kinship: A network of relatives within which individuals possess certain mutual rights and obligations.

k-selected: Reproduction involving the production of relatively few offspring with high parental investment in each.

Kula ring: A form of balanced reciprocity that reinforces trade relations among the seafaring Trobriand people, who inhabit a large ring of islands in the southwestern Pacific Ocean off the eastern coast of Papua New Guinea, and other Melanesians.

lactase: An enzyme in the small intestine that enables humans to assimilate lactose.

lactose: A sugar that is the primary constituent of fresh milk.

language: A system of communication using sounds or gestures that are put together in meaningful ways according to a set of rules.

language family: A group of languages descended from a single ancestral language.

law: Formal rules of conduct that, when violated, effectuate negative sanctions.

law of competitive exclusion: When two closely related species compete for the same niche, one will out-compete the other, bringing about the latter's extinction.

law of independent assortment: The Mendelian principle that genes controlling different traits are inherited independently of one another.

law of segregation: The Mendelian principle that variants of genes for a particular trait retain their separate identities through the generations.

legend: A story about a memorable event or figure handed down by tradition and told as true but without historical evidence.

legitimacy: The right of political leaders to govern—to hold, use, and allocate power—based on the values a particular society holds.

Levalloisian technique: Tool-making technique by which three or four long triangular flakes were detached from a specially prepared core. Developed by members of the genus *Homo* transitional from *H. erectus* to *H. sapiens*.

leveling mechanism: A cultural obligation compelling prosperous members of a community to give away goods, host public feasts, provide free service, or otherwise demonstrate generosity so that no one permanently accumulates significantly more wealth than anyone else.

lineage: A unilineal kinship group descended from a common ancestor or founder who lived four to six generations ago, and in which relationships among members can be exactly stated in genealogical terms.

linguistic anthropology: The study of human languages, looking at each language's structure, history, and/or its relation to social and cultural contexts.

linguistic determinism: The idea that language to some extent shapes the way in which we view and think about the world around us; sometimes called the Sapir-Whorf hypothesis after its originators Edward Sapir and his student Benjamin Lee Whorf.

linguistic divergence: The development of different languages from a single ancestral language.

linguistic nationalism: The attempt by ethnic minorities and even countries to proclaim independence by purging their language of foreign terms.

linguistic relativity: The idea that distinctions encoded in one language are unique to that language.

linguistics: The modern scientific study of all aspects of language.

Lower Paleolithic: The first part of the Old Stone Age beginning with the earliest Oldowan tools. It spanned from about 200,000 or 250,000 to 2.6 million years ago.

macroevolution: Evolution above the species level.

mammal: The class of vertebrate animals distinguished by bodies covered with fur, self-regulating temperature, and in females milk-producing mammary glands.

market exchange: The buying and selling of goods and services, with prices set by rules of supply and demand.

marriage: A culturally sanctioned union between two or more people that establishes certain rights and obligations between the people, between them and their children, and between them and their in-laws. Such marriage rights and obligations most often include, but are not limited to, sex, labor, property, child rearing, exchange, and status.

marrow: The tissue inside of long bones where blood cells are produced.

material culture: The durable aspects of culture such as tools, structures, and art.

materialist perspective: A theoretical approach stressing the primacy of infrastructure (material conditions) in cultural research and analysis.

matrilineal descent: Descent traced exclusively through the female line to establish group membership.

matrilocal residence: A residence pattern in which a married couple lives in the wife's mother's place of residence.

medical anthropology: A specialization in anthropology that brings theoretical and applied approaches from cultural and biological anthropology to the study of human health and disease.

medical pluralism: The presence of multiple medical systems, each with its own practices and beliefs in a society.

medical system: A patterned set of ideas and practices relating to illness.

meiosis: A kind of cell division that produces the sex cells, each of which has half the number of chromosomes found in other cells of the organism.

melanin: The chemical responsible for dark skin pigmentation that helps protect against damage from ultraviolet radiation.

Mesoamerica: The region encompassing southern Mexico and northern Central America.

Mesolithic: The Middle Stone Age period between the end of the Paleolithic and the start of the Neolithic; referred to as Archaic cultures in the Americas.

middens: A refuse or garbage disposal area in an archaeological site.

Middle Paleolithic: The middle part of the Old Stone Age characterized by the development of the Mousterian tradition of tool making and the earlier Levalloisian traditions.

mitosis: A kind of cell division that produces new cells having exactly the same number of chromosome pairs, and hence copies of genes, as the parent cell.

modal personality: The body of character traits that occur with the highest frequency in a culturally bounded population.

modernization: The process of political and socioeconomic change, whereby developing societies acquire some of the cultural characteristics of Western industrial societies.

moiety: Each group that results from a division of a society into two halves on the basis of descent.

molecular anthropology: A branch of biological anthropology that uses genetic and biochemical techniques to test hypotheses about human evolution, adaptation, and variation.

molecular clock: The hypothesis that dates of divergences among related species can be calculated through an examination of the genetic mutations that have accrued since the divergence.

money: Something used to make payments for other goods and services as well as to measure their value.

monogamous: In the animal kingdom, mating for life with a single individual of the opposite sex.

monogamy: Marriage in which both partners have just one spouse.

morpheme: The smallest unit of sound that carries a meaning in language. It is distinct from a phoneme, which can alter meaning but has no meaning by itself.

morphology: The study of the patterns or rules of word formation in a language (including such things as rules concerning verb tense, pluralization, and compound words). In biology, morphology refers to the shape or form of a structure.

motif: A story situation in a tale.

Mousterian tradition: The tool industry of the Neandertals and their contemporaries of Europe, Southwest Asia, and northern Africa from 40,000 to 125,000 years ago.

multiculturalism: Public policy for managing cultural diversity in a multi-ethnic society, officially stressing mutual respect and tolerance for cultural differences within a country's borders.

multiregional hypothesis: The hypothesis that modern humans originated through a process of simultaneous local transition from *Homo erectus* to *Homo sapiens* throughout the inhabited world.

multi-sited ethnography: The investigation and documentation of peoples and cultures embedded in the larger structures of a globalizing world, utilizing a range of methods in various locations of time and space.

mutation: Chance alteration of genetic material that produces new variation.

myth: A sacred narrative that explains the fundamentals of human existence—where we and everything in our world came from, why we are here, and where we are going.

naming ceremony: A special event or ritual to mark the naming of a child.

natal group: The group or the community an animal has inhabited since birth.

nation: A people who share a collective identity based on a common culture, language, territorial base, and history.

Natufian culture: A Mesolithic culture living in the lands that are now Israel, Lebanon, and western Syria, between about 12,500 and 10,200 years ago.

natural selection: The evolutionary process through which factors in the environment exert pressure, favoring some individuals over others to produce the next generation.

Neandertals: A distinct group within the genus *Homo* inhabiting Europe and Southwest Asia from approximately 30,000 to 125,000 years ago.

negative reciprocity: A form of exchange in which the aim is to get something for as little as possible. Neither fair nor balanced, it may involve hard bargaining, manipulation, and outright cheating.

Neolithic: The New Stone Age; prehistoric period beginning about 10,000 years ago in which peoples possessed stone-based technologies and depended on domesticated crops and/or animals.

Neolithic transition: Sometimes referred to as Neolithic revolution. The profound culture change beginning about 10,000 years ago and associated with the early domestication of plants and animals and settlement in villages.

neolocal residence: A pattern in which a married couple establish their household in a location apart from either the husband's or the wife's relatives.

new reproductive technologies (NRTs): Alternative means of reproduction such as surrogate motherhood and in vitro fertilization.

nocturnal: Active at night and at rest during the day.

notochord: A rodlike structure of cartilage that, in vertebrates, is replaced by the vertebral column.

nuclear family: A group consisting of one or more parents and dependent offspring, which may include a stepparent, stepsiblings, and adopted children. (Until recently this term referred only to the father–mother–child(ren) unit.)

Oldowan tool tradition: The first stone tool industry, beginning between 2.5 and 2.6 million years ago.

opposable: Able to bring the thumb or big toe in contact with the tips of the other digits on the same hand or foot in order to grasp objects.

ovulation: Moment when an egg released from the ovaries into the womb is receptive for fertilization.

paleoanthropology: The study of the origins and predecessors of the present human species.

Paleoindian: The earliest inhabitants of North America.

palynology: In archaeology and paleoanthropology, a method of relative dating based on changes in fossil pollen over time.

pantheon: The several gods and goddesses of a people.

paralanguage: Voice effects that accompany language and convey meaning. These include vocalizations such as giggling, groaning, or sighing, as well as voice qualities such as pitch and tempo.

parallel cousin: Child of a father's brother or a mother's sister.

parallel evolution: In cultural evolution, the development of similar cultural adaptations to similar environmental conditions by peoples whose ancestral cultures were already somewhat alike.

participant observation: In ethnography, the technique of learning a people's culture through social participation and personal observation within the community being studied, as well as interviews and discussion with individual members of the group over an extended period of time.

pastoralism: Breeding and managing migratory herds of domesticated grazing animals, such as goats, sheep, cattle, llamas, or camels.

patrilineal descent: Descent traced exclusively through the male line to establish group membership.

patrilocal residence: A residence pattern in which a married couple lives in the husband's father's place of residence.

peasant: A rural cultivator whose surpluses are transferred to a dominant group of rulers that uses the surpluses both to underwrite its own standard of living and to distribute the remainder to groups in society that do not farm but must be fed for their specific goods and services in turn.

percussion method: A technique of stone tool manufacture performed by striking the raw material with a hammerstone or by striking raw material against a stone anvil to remove flakes.

personality: The distinctive way a person thinks, feels, and behaves.

phenotype: The observable or testable appearance of an organism that may or may not reflect a particular genotype due to the variable expression of dominant and recessive alleles.

phoneme: The smallest unit of sound that makes a difference in meaning in a language.

phonetics: The systematic identification and description of distinctive speech sounds in a language.

phonology: The study of language sounds.

phratry: A unilineal descent group composed of at least two clans that supposedly share a common ancestry, whether or not they really do.

physical anthropology: Also known as biological anthropology. The systematic study of humans as biological organisms.

physiological adaptation: A short-term physiological change in response to a specific environmental stimulus. An immediate short-term response is not very efficient and is gradually replaced by a longer term response (see acclimatization).

Platyrrhini: An anthropoid infraorder that includes New World monkeys.

pluralistic society: A society in which two or more ethnic groups or nationalities are politically organized into one territorial state but maintain their cultural differences.

political organization: The way power is distributed and embedded in society; the means through which a society creates and maintains social order and reduces social disorder.

polyandry: Marriage of a woman to two or more men at one time; a form of polygamy.

polygamy: One individual having multiple spouses at the same time; from the Greek words *poly* ("many") and *gamous* ("marriage").

polygenetic inheritance: When two or more genes contribute to the phenotypic expression of single characteristic.

polygyny: Marriage of a man to two or more women at the same time; a form of polygamy.

polymerase chain reaction (PCR): A technique for amplifying or creating multiple copies of fragments of DNA so that it can be studied in the laboratory.

polymorphic: A term to describe species with alternative forms (alleles) of particular genes.

polytheism: Belief in several gods and/or goddesses (as contrasted with monotheism—belief in one god or goddess).

polytypic: The expression of genetic variants in different frequencies in different populations of a species.

population: In biology, a group of similar individuals that can and do interbreed.

potassium-argon dating: In archaeology and paleoanthropology, a technique for chronometric dating that measures the ratio of radioactive potassium to argon in volcanic debris associated with human remains.

potlatch: On the northwest coast of North America, a ceremonial event in which a village chief publicly gives away stockpiled food and other goods that signify wealth.

power: The ability of individuals or groups to impose their will upon others and make them do things even against their own wants or wishes.

preadapted: Possessing characteristics that, by chance, are advantageous in future environmental conditions.

prehensile: Having the ability to grasp.

prehistory: A conventional term used to refer to the period of time before the appearance of written records. Does not deny the existence of history in non-literate groups, merely of *written* history.

pressure flaking: A technique of stone tool manufacture in which a bone, antler, or wooden tool is used to press, rather than strike off, small flakes from a piece of flint or similar stone.

priest or priestess: A full-time religious specialist formally recognized for his or her role in guiding the religious practices of others and for contacting and influencing supernatural powers.

primary innovation: The creation, invention, or chance discovery of a completely new idea, method, or device.

primate: The group of mammals that includes lemurs, lorises, tarsiers, monkeys, apes, and humans.

primatology: The study of living and fossil primates.

prion: An infectious protein lacking any genetic material but capable of causing the reorganization and destruction of other proteins.

progress: The notion that humans are moving forward to a better, more advanced stage in their cultural development toward perfection.

Prosimii: A suborder of the primates that includes lemurs, lorises, and tarsiers.

proxemics: The cross-cultural study of humankind's perception and use of space.

punctuated equilibria: A model of macroevolutionary change that suggests evolution occurs via long periods of stability or stasis punctuated by periods of rapid change.

qualitative data: Nonstatistical information such as personal life stories and customary beliefs and practices.

quantitative data: Statistical or measurable information, such as demographic composition, the types and quantities of crops grown, or the ratio of spouses born and raised within or outside the community.

race: In biology, the taxonomic category of subspecies that is not applicable to humans because the division of humans into discrete types does not represent the true nature of human biological variation. In some societies race is an important social category.

racism: A doctrine of superiority by which one group justifies the dehumanization of others based on their distinctive physical characteristics.

radiocarbon dating: In archaeology and paleoanthropology, a technique for chronometric dating based on measuring the amount of radioactive carbon (^{14}C) left in organic materials found in archaeological sites.

rebellion: Organized armed resistance to an established government or authority in power.

recent African origins or "Eve" hypothesis: The hypothesis that all modern people are derived from one single population of archaic *H. sapiens* from Africa who migrated out of Africa after 100,000 years ago, replacing all other archaic forms due to their superior cultural capabilities. Also called the out of Africa hypothesis.

recessive: An allele for a trait whose expression is masked by the presence of a dominant allele.

reciprocity: The exchange of goods and services, of approximately equal value, between two parties.

redistribution: A form of exchange in which goods flow into a central place, where they are sorted, counted, and reallocated.

relative dating: In archaeology and paleoanthropology, designating an event, ob-

ject, or fossil as being older or younger than another.

religion: An organized system of ideas about the spiritual sphere or the supernatural, along with associated ceremonial practices by which people try to interpret and/or influence aspects of the universe otherwise beyond their control.

replacement reproduction: The point at which birthrates and death rates are in equilibrium; people producing only enough offspring to replace themselves when they die.

revitalization movement: A movement for radical cultural reform in response to widespread social disruption and collective feelings of great stress and despair.

revolution: Radical change in a society or culture. In the political arena, it involves the forced overthrow of an old government and establishment of a completely new one.

ribosomes: Structures in the cell where translation occurs.

rite of intensification: A ritual that takes place during a crisis in the life of the group and serves to bind individuals together.

rite of passage: A ritual that marks an important stage in an individual's life cycle, such as birth, marriage, and death.

RNA: Ribonucleic acid; similar to DNA but with uracil substituted for the base thymine. Transcribes and carries instructions from DNA from the nucleus to the ribosomes where it directs protein synthesis. Some simple life forms contain RNA only.

robust australopithecines: Several species within the genus *Australopithecus,* who lived from 2.5 and 1.1 million years ago in eastern and southern Africa; known for the rugged nature of their chewing apparatus (large back teeth, large chewing muscles, and a bony ridge on their skull tops for the insertion of these large muscles).

r-selected: Reproduction involving the production of large numbers of offspring with relatively low parental investment in each.

sagittal crest: A crest running from front to back on the top of the skull along the midline to provide a surface of bone for the attachment of the large temporal muscles for chewing.

Sahul: The greater Australian landmass including Australia, New Guinea, and Tasmania. At times of maximum glaciation and low sea levels, these areas were continuous.

sanction: An externalized social control designed to encourage conformity to social norms.

savannah: Semi-arid plains environment as in eastern Africa.

scapula: The shoulder blade.

secondary innovation: A new and deliberate application or modification of an existing idea, method, or device.

secular trend: A physical difference among related people from distinct generations that allows anthropologists to make inferences about environmental effects on growth and development.

self-awareness: The ability to identify oneself as an individual, to reflect on oneself, and to evaluate oneself.

separation: In rites of passage, the ritual removal of the individual from society.

serial monogamy: A marriage form in which a man or a woman marries or lives with a series of partners in succession.

seriation: A technique for relative dating by putting groups of objects into a sequence in relation to one another.

sexual dimorphism: Within a single species, differences in the shape or size of a feature for males and females in body features not directly related to reproduction such as body size or canine tooth shape and size.

shaman: A person who enters an altered state of consciousness—at will—to contact and utilize an ordinarily hidden reality in order to acquire knowledge, power, and to help others.

sickle-cell anemia: An inherited form of anemia caused by a mutation in the hemoglobin protein that causes the red blood cells to assume a sickle shape.

signal: An instinctive sound or gesture that has a natural or self-evident meaning.

silent trade: A form of barter in which no verbal communication takes place.

slash-and-burn cultivation: Also known as swidden farming. An extensive form of horticulture in which the natural vegetation is cut, the slash is subsequently burned, and crops are then planted among the ashes.

social class: A category of individuals in a stratified society who enjoy equal or nearly equal prestige according to the system of evaluation.

social control: External control through open coercion.

social mobility: Upward or downward change in one's social class position in a stratified society.

social structure: The rule-governed relationships—with all their rights and obligations—that hold members of a society together. This includes households, families, associations, and power relations, including politics.

society: An organized group or groups of interdependent people who generally share a common territory, language, and culture and who act together for collective survival and well-being.

sociolinguistics: The study of the relationship between language and society through examining how social categories (such as age, gender, ethnicity, religion, occupation, and class) influence the use and interpretation of distinctive styles of speech.

soft power: Co-optive power that presses others through attraction and persuasion to change their ideas, beliefs, values, and behaviors.

soil mark: A stain that shows up on the surface of recently plowed fields that reveals an archaeological site.

speciation: The process of forming new species.

species: The smallest working unit in the system of classification. Among living organisms, species are populations or groups of populations capable of interbreeding and producing fertile viable offspring.

spirituality: Concern with the sacred, as distinguished from material matters. In contrast to religion, spirituality is often individual rather than collective and does not require a distinctive format or traditional organization.

stabilizing selection: Natural selection acting to promote stability, rather than change, in a population's gene pool.

state: In anthropology, a centralized polity involving large numbers of people within a defined territory who are divided into social classes and organized and directed by a formal government that has the capacity and authority to make laws, and use force to defend the social order.

stratified: Layered; said of archaeological sites where the remains lie in layers, one upon another.

stratified societies: Societies in which people are hierarchically divided and ranked into social strata, or layers, and do not share equally in basic resources that support survival, influence, and prestige.

stratigraphy: In archaeology and paleoanthropology, the most reliable method of relative dating by means of strata.

Strepsirhini: In the alternate primate taxonomy, the suborder that includes the lemurs and lorises without the tarsiers.

structural power: Power that organizes and orchestrates the systemic interaction within and among societies, directing economic and political forces on the one hand and ideological forces that shape public ideas, values, and beliefs on the other.

structural violence: Physical and/or psychological harm (including repression, environmental destruction, poverty, hunger, illness, and premature death) caused by impersonal, exploitative, and unjust social, political, and economic systems.

subculture: A distinctive set of standards and behavior patterns by which a group within a larger society operates, while still sharing common standards with that larger society.

Sunda: The combined landmass of the contemporary islands of Java, Sumatra, Borneo, and Bali that was continuous with mainland Southeast Asia at times of low sea levels corresponding to maximum glaciation.

superstructure: A society's shared sense of identity and worldview. The collective body of ideas, beliefs, and values by which a group of people makes sense of the world—its shape, challenges, and opportunities—and their place in it. This includes religion and national ideology.

suspensory hanging apparatus: The broad powerful shoulder joints and muscles found in all the hominoids, allowing these large-bodied primates to hang suspended below the tree branches.

swidden farming: Also known as slash-and-burn. An extensive form of horticulture in which the natural vegetation is cut, the slash is subsequently burned, and crops are then planted among the ashes.

symbol: A sign, sound, emblem, or other thing that is arbitrarily linked to something else and represents it in a meaningful way.

syncretism: In acculturation, the creative blending of indigenous and foreign beliefs and practices into new cultural forms.

syntax: The patterns or rules by which morphemes are arranged into phrases and sentences.

taphonomy: The study of how bones and other materials come to be preserved in the earth as fossils.

tale: A creative narrative that is recognized as fiction for entertainment but may also draw a moral or teach a practical lesson.

taxonomy: The science of classification.

technology: Tools and other material equipment, together with the knowledge of how to make and use them.

tertiary scavenger: In a food chain, the third animal group (second to scavenge) to obtain meat from a kill made by a predator.

thrifty genotype: Human genotype that permits efficient storage of fat to draw on in times of food shortage and conservation of glucose and nitrogen.

tonality: In music, scale systems and their modifications.

tonal language: A language in which the sound pitch of a spoken word is an essential part of its pronunciation and meaning.

tool: An object used to facilitate some task or activity. Although tool making involves intentional modification of the material of which it is made, tool use may involve objects either modified for some particular purpose or completely unmodified.

totemism: The belief that people are related to particular animals, plants, or natural objects by virtue of descent from common ancestral spirits.

tradition: Customary ideas and practices passed on from generation to generation, which in a modernizing society may form an obstacle to new ways of doing things.

transcription: Process of conversion of instructions from DNA into RNA.

transgender: A person who crosses over or occupies a culturally accepted intermediate position in the binary male–female gender construction.

transition: In rites of passage, isolation of the individual following separation and prior to incorporation into society.

translation: Process of conversion of RNA instructions into proteins.

tribe: In anthropology, refers to a range of kin-ordered groups that are politically integrated by some unifying factor and whose members share a common ancestry, identity, culture, language, and territory.

unilineal descent: Descent that establishes group membership exclusively through either the male or female line.

Upper Paleolithic: The last part (10,000 to 40,000 years ago) of the Old Stone Age, featuring tool industries characterized by long slim blades and an explosion of creative symbolic forms.

urgent anthropology: Ethnographic research that documents endangered cultures; also known as salvage ethnography.

vertebrate: An animal with a backbone including fish, amphibians, reptiles, birds, and mammals.

visual predation: A hypothesis for primate evolution that proposes that hunting behavior in tree-dwelling primates was responsible for their enhanced visual acuity and manual dexterity.

witchcraft: An explanation of events based on the belief that certain individuals possess an innate psychic power capable of causing harm, including sickness and death.

worldview: The collective body of ideas that members of a culture generally share concerning the ultimate shape and substance of their reality.

writing system: A set of visible or tactile signs used to represent units of language in a systematic way.

Bibliography

Abbot, E. (2001). *A history of celibacy.* Cambridge, MA: Da Capo Press.

Aberle, D. F., Bronfenbrenner, U., Hess, E. H., Miller, D. R., Schneider, D. H., & Spuhler, J. N. (1963). The incest taboo and the mating patterns of animals. *American Anthropologist 65,* 253–265.

Abu-Lughod, L. (1986). *Veiled sentiments: Honor and poetry in a Bedouin society.* Berkeley: University of California Press.

Adams, R. E. W. (1977). *Prehistoric Mesoamerica.* Boston: Little, Brown.

Adams, R. M. (1966). *The evolution of urban society.* Chicago: Aldine.

Adams, R. M. (2001). Scale and complexity in archaic states. *Latin American Antiquity 11,* 188.

Adbusters. www.adbusters.org.

Alemseged, Z., et al. (2006, September 21). *Nature 443,* 296–301.

Alland, A., Jr. (1970). *Adaptation in cultural evolution: An approach to medical anthropology.* New York: Columbia University Press.

Alland, A., Jr. (1971). *Human diversity.* New York: Columbia University Press. Allen, J. L., & Shalinsky, A. C. (2004). *Student atlas of anthropology.* New York: McGraw-Hill.

Allen, J. S., & Cheer, S. M. (1996). The non-thrifty genotype. *Current Anthropology 37,* 831–842.

Alvard, M. S., & Kuznar, L. (2001). Deferred harvest: The transition from hunting to animal husbandry. *American Anthropologist 103* (2), 295–311.

Amábile-Cuevas, C. F., & Chicurel, M. E. (1993). Horizontal gene transfer. *American Scientist 81,* 332–341.

AMAP. (2003). *AMAP assessment 2002: Human health in the Arctic.* Oslo: Arctic Monitoring Assessment Project.

Ambrose, S. H. (2001). Paleolithic technology and human evolution. *Science 291,* 1,748–1,753.

American Anthropological Association. (1998). Statement on "race." www .ameranthassn.org.

Amiran, R. (1965). The beginnings of pottery-making in the Near East. In F. R. Matson (Ed.), *Ceramics and man* (pp. 240–247). Viking Fund Publications in Anthropology, 41.

Anderson, A. (2002). Faunal collapse, landscape change, and settlement history in Remote Oceania. *World Archaeology 33* (3), 375–390.

Andrews, L. B., & Nelkin, D. (1996). The Bell Curve: A statement. *Science 271,*13.

Angrosino, M. V. (2004). *Projects in ethnographic research.* Long Grove, IL: Waveland Press.

Ankel-Simons, F., Fleagle, J. G., & Chatrath, P. S. (1998). Femoral anatomy of *Aegyptopithecus zeuxis,* an early Oligocene anthropoid. *American Journal of Physical Anthropology 106,* 421–422.

Appadurai, A. (1996). *Modernity at large: Cultural dimensions of globalization.* Minneapolis: University of Minnesota Press.

Appenzeller, T. (1998). Art: Evolution or revolution? *Science 282,* 1,451–1,454.

Armstrong, D. F., Stokoe, W. C., & Wilcox, S. E. (1993). Signs of the origin of syntax. *Current Anthropology 34,* 349–368.

Ashmore, W. (Ed.). (1981). *Lowland Maya settlement patterns.* Albuquerque: University of New Mexico Press.

Aureli, F., & de Waal, F. B. M. (2000). *Natural conflict resolution.* Berkeley: University of California Press.

Avedon, J. F. (1997). *In exile from the land of snows: The definitive account of the Dalai Lama and Tibet since the Chinese conquest.* New York: Harper.

Babiker, M. A., Alumran, K., Alshahri, A., Almadan, M., & Islam, F. (1996). Unnecessary deprivation of common food items in glucose-6-phosphate dehydrogenase deficiency. *Annals of Saudi Arabia 16* (4), 462–463.

Bailey, R. C., & Aunger, R. (1989). Net hunters vs. archers: Variation in women's subsistence strategies in the Ituri Forest. *Human Ecology 17,* 273–297.

Baker, P. (Ed.) (1978). *The biology of high altitude peoples.* London: Cambridge University Press.

Balandier, G. (1971). *Political anthropology.* New York: Pantheon.

Balikci, A. (1970). *The Netsilik Eskimo.* Garden City, NY: Natural History Press.

Balter, M. (1998). On world AIDS day, a shadow looms over southern Africa. *Science 282,* 1,790.

Balter, M. (1998). Why settle down? The mystery of communities. *Science 282,* 1,442–1,444.

Balter, M. (1999). A long season puts Çatalhöyük in context. *Science 286,* 890– 891.

Balter, M. (2001). Did plaster hold Neolithic society together? *Science 294,* 2,278–2,281.

Balter, M. (2001). In search of the first Europeans. *Science 291,* 1,724.

Banton, M. (1968). Voluntary association: Anthropological aspects. In *International encyclopedia of the social sciences* (Vol. 16, pp. 357–362). New York: Macmillan.

Barber, B. (1957). *Social stratification.* New York: Harcourt.

Barham, L. S. (1998). Possible early pigment use in South-Central Africa. *Current Anthropology 39,* 703–710.

Barnard, A. (1995). Monboddo's *Orang Outang* and the definition of man. In R. Corbey & B. Theunissen (Eds.), *Ape, man, apeman: Changing views since 1600* (pp. 71–85). Leiden: Department of Prehistory, Leiden University.

Barnett, H. (1953). *Innovation: The basis of cultural change.* New York: McGraw- Hill.

Barnouw, V. (1985). *Culture and personality* (4th ed.). Homewood, IL: Dorsey Press.

Barr, R. G. (1997, October). The crying game. *Natural History, 47.*

Barth, F. (1961). *Nomads of South Persia: The Basseri tribe of the Khamseh confederacy.* Boston: Little, Brown (series in anthropology).

Barth, F. (1962). Nomadism in the mountain and plateau areas of Southwest Asia. *The problems of the arid zone* (pp. 341–355). Paris: UNESCO.

Bar-Yosef, O. (1986), The walls of Jericho: An alternative interpretation. *Current Anthropology 27,* 160.

Bar-Yosef, O., Vandermeesch, B., Arensburg, B., Belfer-Cohen, A., Goldberg, P., Laville, H., Meignen, L., Rak, Y., Speth, J. D., Tchernov, E., Tillier, A-M., & Weiner, S. (1992). The excavations in Kebara Cave, Mt. Carmel. *Current Anthropology 33,* 497–550.

Bascom, W. (1969). *The Yoruba of southwestern Nigeria.* New York: Holt, Rinehart & Winston.

Bates, D. G. (2001). *Human adaptive strategies: Ecology, culture, and politics* (2nd ed.). Boston: Allyn & Bacon.

Bates, D. G., & Plog, F. (1991). *Human adaptive strategies.* New York: McGraw-Hill.

Bednarik, R. G. (1995). Concept-mediated marking in the Lower Paleolithic. *Current Anthropology 36,* 606.

Beeman, W. O. (2000). Introduction: Margaret Mead, cultural studies, and international understanding. In M. Mead & R. Métraux (Eds.), *The study of culture at a distance* (pp. xiv–xxxi). New York and Oxford: Berghahn Books.

Behrend, H., & Luig, U. (Eds.) (2000). *Spirit possession, modernity, and power in Africa.* Madison: University of Wisconsin Press.

Behrensmeyer, A. K., Todd, N. E., Potts, R., & McBrinn, G. E. (1997). Late Pliocene faunal turnover in the Turkana basin, Kenya, and Ethiopia. *Science 278,* 1,589–1,594.

Belshaw, C. S. (1958). The significance of modern cults in Melanesian development. In W. Lessa & E. Z. Vogt (Eds.), *Reader in comparative religion: An anthropological approach.* New York: Harper & Row.

Benedict, R. (1959). *Patterns of culture.* New York: New American Library.

Bermúdez de Castro, J. M., Arsuaga, J. L., Cabonell, E., Rosas, A., Martinez, I., & Mosquera, M. (1997). A hominid from the lower Pleistocene of Atapuerca, Spain: Possible ancestor to Neandertals and modern humans. *Science 276,* 1,392–1,395.

Berndt, R. M., & Berndt, C. H. (1989). *The Speaking Land: Myth and story in Aboriginal Australia.* New York: Penguin. Berra, T. M. (1990). *Evolution and the myth of creationism.* Stanford, CA: Stanford University Press.

Bicchieri, M. G. (Ed.) (1972). *Hunters and gatherers today: A socioeconomic study of eleven such cultures in the twentieth century.* New York: Holt, Rinehart & Winston.

Binford, L. R. (1972). *An archaeological perspective.* New York: Seminar Press.

Binford, L. R., & Chuan, K. H. (1985). Taphonomy at a distance: Zhoukoudian, the cave home of Beijing man? *Current Anthropology 26,* 413–442.

Birdsell, J. H. (1977). The recalibration of a paradigm for the first peopling of Greater Australia. In J. Allen, J. Golson, & R. Jones (Eds.), *Sunda and Sahul: Prehistoric studies in Southeast Asia, Melanesia, and Australia* (pp. 113–167). New York: Academic Press.

Blackless, M., et al. (2000). How sexually dimorphic are we? Review and synthesis. *American Journal of Human Biology 12,* 151–166.

Blakey, M. (2003). *African Burial Ground Project.* Department of Anthropology, College of William & Mary.

Blok, A. (1974). *The mafia of a Sicilian village 1860–1960.* New York: Harper & Row.

Blok, A. (1981). Rams and billy-goats: A key to the Mediterranean code of honour. *Man, New Series 16* (3), 427–440.

Blom, A., et al. (2001). A survey of the apes in the Dzanga-Ndoki National Park, Central African Republic. *African Journal of Ecology 39,* 98–105.

Blumberg, R. L. (1991). *Gender, family, and the economy: The triple overlap.* Newbury Park, CA: Sage.

Blumer, M. A., & Byrne, R. (1991). The ecological genetics and domestication and the origins of agriculture. *Current Anthropology 32,* 30.

Boas, F. (1962). *Primitive art.* Gloucester, MA: Peter Smith.

Boas, F. (1966). *Race, language and culture.* New York: Free Press.

Bodley, J. H. (1985). *Anthropology and contemporary human problems* (2nd ed.). Palo Alto, CA: Mayfield.

Bodley, J. H. (1990). *Victims of progress* (3rd ed.). Mountain View, CA: Mayfield.

Boehm, C. (1984). *Blood revenge.* Lawrence: University of Kansas Press.

Boehm, C. (2000). The evolution of moral communities. *School of American Research, 2000 Annual Report,* 7.

Bogucki, P. (1999). *The origins of human society.* Oxford, England: Blackwell.

Bohannan, P. (Ed.) (1967). *Law and warfare: Studies in the anthropology of conflict.* Garden City, NY: Natural History Press.

Bohannan, P., & Middleton, J. (Eds.) (1968). *Kinship and social organization.* Garden City, NY: Natural History Press (American Museum Source Books in Anthropology).

Bohannan, P., & Middleton, J. (Eds.) (1968). *Marriage, family, and residence.* Garden City, NY: Natural History Press (American Museum Source Books in Anthropology).

Bolinger, D. (1968). *Aspects of language.* New York: Harcourt.

Bongaarts, J. (1998). Demographic consequences of declining fertility. *Science 182,* 419.

Bonvillain, N. (2000). *Language, culture, and communication: The meaning of messages* (3rd ed.). Upper Saddle River, NJ: Prentice-Hall.

Bordes, F. (1972). *A tale of two caves.* New York: Harper & Row.

Bornstein, M. H. (1975). The influence of visual perception on culture. *American Anthropologist 77* (4), 774–798.

Boshara, R. (2003, January/February). Wealth inequality: The $6,000 solution. *Atlantic Monthly.*

Bowen, J. R. (2004). *Religions in practice: An approach to the anthropology of religion* (3rd ed.). Boston: Allyn & Bacon.

Bowie, F. (2006). *The anthropology of religion: An introduction* (2nd ed.). Malden, MA: Blackwell.

Brace, C. L. (1981). Tales of the phylogenetic woods: The evolution and significance of phylogenetic trees. *American Journal of Physical Anthropology 56,* 411–429.

Brace, C. L. (1997). Cro-Magnons "R" us? *Anthropology Newsletter 38* (8), 1, 4.

Brace, C. L. (2000). *Evolution in an anthropological view.* Walnut Creek, CA: Altamira.

Brace, C. L., Nelson, H., & Korn, N. (1979). *Atlas of human evolution* (2nd ed.). New York: Holt, Rinehart & Winston.

Bradfield, R. M. (1998). *A natural history of associations* (2nd ed.). New York: International Universities Press.

Bradford, P. V., & Blume, H. (1992). *Ota Benga: The pygmy in the zoo.* New York: St. Martin's Press.

Braidwood, R. J. (1960). The agricultural revolution. *Scientific American 203,* 130–141.

Braidwood, R. J. (1975). *Prehistoric men* (8th ed.). Glenview, IL: Scott, Foresman.

Brain, C. K. (1968). Who killed the Swartkrans ape-men? *South African Museums Association Bulletin 9,* 127–139.

Brain, C. K. (1969). The contribution of Namib Desert Hottentots to an understanding of australopithecine bone accumulations. *Scientific Papers of the Namib Desert Research Station,* 13.

Branda, R. F., & Eatoil, J. W. (1978). Skin color and photolysis: An evolutionary hypothesis. *Science 201,* 625–626.

Brettell, C. B., & Sargent, C. F. (Eds.) (2000). *Gender in cross-cultural perspective* (3rd ed.). Upper Saddle River, NJ: Prentice-Hall.

Brew, J. O. (1968). *One hundred years of anthropology.* Cambridge, MA: Harvard University Press.

Brody, H. (1981). *Maps and dreams.* New York: Pantheon Books.

Broecker, W. S. (1992, April). Global warming on trial. *Natural History,* 14.

Brown, B., Walker, A., Ward, C. V., & Leakey, R. E. (1993). New *Australopithecus boisei* calvaria from East Lake Turkana, Kenya. *American Journal of Physical Anthropology 91,* 137–159.

Brown, D. E. (1991). *Human universals.* New York: McGraw-Hill.

Brown, P., et al. (2004). A new small-bodied hominin from the Late Pleistocene of Flores, Indonesia. *Nature 431,* 1,055–1,061.

Brues, A. M. (1977). *People and races.* New York: Macmillan.

Brunet, M., Beauvilain, A., Coppens, Y., Heintz, E., Moutaye, A. H., & Pilbeam, D. (1995). The first australopithecine 2,500 kilometers west of the Rift Valley (Chad). *Nature 16, 378* (6554), 273–275.

Brunet, M., et al. (2002). A new hominid from the Upper Miocene of Chad, Central Africa. *Nature 418,* 145–151.

Buck, P. H. (1938). *Vikings of the Pacific.* Chicago: University Press of Chicago.

Burling, R. (1969). Linguistics and ethnographic description. *American Anthropologist 71,* 817–827.

Burling, R. (1970). *Man's many voices: Language in its cultural context.* New York: Holt, Rinehart & Winston.

Burling, R. (1993). Primate calls, human language, and nonverbal communication. *Current Anthropology 34,* 25–53.

Burling, R. (2005). *The talking ape: How language evolved.* Oxford: Oxford University Press.

Butynski, T. M. (2001). Africa's great apes. In B. Beck et al. (Eds.), *Great apes and humans: The ethics of co-existence* (pp. 3–56). Washington, DC: Smithsonian Institution Press.

Butzer, K. (1971). *Environment and anthropology: An ecological approach to prehistory* (2nd ed.). Chicago: Aldine.

Byers, D. S. (Ed.) (1967). *The prehistory of the Tehuacan Valley: Vol. 1. Environment and subsistence.* Austin: University of Texas Press.

Cachel, S. (1997). Dietary shifts and the European Upper Paleolithic transition. *Current Anthropology 38,* 590.

Calloway, C. (1997). Introduction: Surviving the Dark Ages. In C. G. Calloway (Ed.), *After King Philip's war: Presence and persistence in Indian New England* (pp. 1–28). Hanover, NH: University Press of New England.

Carneiro, R. L. (1970). A theory of the origin of the state. *Science 169,* 733–738.

Carneiro, R. L. (2003). *Evolutionism in cultural anthropology: A critical history.* Boulder, CO: Westview Press.

Caroulis, J. (1996). Food for thought. *Pennsylvania Gazette 95* (3),16.

Carsten, J. (Ed.) (2000). *Cultures of relatedness: New approaches to the study of kinship.* Cambridge, England: Cambridge University Press.

Cartmill, M. (1998). The gift of gab. *Discover 19* (11), 64.

Cashdan, E. (1989). Hunters and gatherers: Economic behavior in bands. In S. Plattner (Ed.), *Economic anthropology* (pp. 21–48). Stanford, CA: Stanford University Press.

Catford, J. C. (1988). *A practical introduction to phonetics.* Oxford, England: Clarendon Press.

Caton, S. C. (1999). *Lawrence of Arabia: A film's anthropology.* Berkeley: University of California Press.

Cavalli-Sforza, L. L. (1977). *Elements of human genetics.* Menlo Park, CA: W. A. Benjamin.

Chagnon, N. A. (1988). Life histories, blood revenge, and warfare in a tribal population. *Science 239,* 935–992.

Chagnon, N. A. (1988). *Yanomamö: The fierce people* (3rd ed.). New York: Holt, Rinehart & Winston.

Chambers, R. (1983). *Rural development: Putting the last first.* New York: Longman.

Chang, K. C. (Ed.) (1968). *Settlement archaeology.* Palo Alto, CA: National Press.

Chang, L. (2005, June 9). A migrant worker sees rural home in new light. *Wall Street Journal.*

Chapple, E. D. (1970). *Cultural and biological man: Explorations in behavioral anthropology.* New York: Holt, Rinehart & Winston.

Chase, C. (1998). Hermaphrodites with attitude. *Gay and Lesbian Quarterly 4* (2), 189–211.

Chasin, B. H., & Franke, R. W. (1983). US farming: A world model? *Global Reporter 1* (2), 10.

Chatty, D. (1996). *Mobile pastoralists: Development planning and social change in Oman.* New York: Columbia University Press.

Cheater, A. (2005). *The anthropology of power.* London: Routledge.

Chicurel, M. (2001). Can organisms speed their own evolution? *Science 292,* 1,824–1,827.

Childe, V. G. (1951). *Man makes himself.* New York: New American Library. (orig. 1936)

Childe, V. G. (1954). *What happened in history.* Baltimore: Penguin.

Ciochon, R. L., & Fleagle, J. G. (Eds.) (1987). *Primate evolution and human origins.* Hawthorne, NY: Aldine.

Ciochon, R. L., & Fleagle, J. G. (1993). *The human evolution source book.* Englewood Cliffs, NJ: Prentice-Hall.

Clark, E. E. (1966). *Indian legends of the Pacific Northwest.* Berkeley: University of California Press.

Clark, G. (1967). *The Stone Age hunters.* New York: McGraw-Hill.

Clark, G. A. (1997). Neandertal genetics. *Science, 277,* 1,024.

Clark, G. A. (2002). Neandertal archaeology: Implications for our origins. *American Anthropologist 104* (1), 50–67.

Clark, W. E. L. (1960). *The antecedents of man.* Chicago: Quadrangle Books.

Clark, W. E. L. (1966). *History of the primates* (5th ed.). Chicago: University of Chicago Press.

Clark, W. E. L. (1967). *Man-apes or ape-men? The story of discoveries in Africa.* New York: Holt, Rinehart & Winston.

Clarke, R. J. (1998). First ever discovery of a well preserved skull and associated skeleton of *Australopithecus. South African Journal of Science 94,* 460–464.

Clarke, R. J., & Tobias, P. V. (1995). Sterkfontein member 2 foot bones of the oldest South African hominid. *Science 269,* 521–524.

Clottes, J., & Bennett, G. (2002). *World rock art* (conservation and cultural heritage series). San Francisco: Getty Trust Publication.

Coe, S. D., & Coe, M. D. (1996). *The true history of chocolate.* New York: Thames and Hudson.

Coe, W. R. (1967). *Tikal: A handbook of the ancient Maya ruins.* Philadelphia: University of Pennsylvania Museum.

Coe, W. R., & Haviland, W. A. (1982). *Introduction to the archaeology of Tikal.* Philadelphia: University Museum.

Cohen, J. (1997). Is an old virus up to new tricks? *Science 277,* 312–313.

Cohen, M. N. (1977). *The food crisis in prehistory.* New Haven, CT: Yale University Press.

Cohen, M. N. (1995). Anthropology and race: The Bell Curve phenomenon. *General Anthropology 2*(1), 1–4.

Cohen, M. N. (1998). *Culture of intolerance: Chauvinism, class, and racism in the United States.* New Haven, CT: Yale University Press.

Cohen, M. N., & Armelagos, G. J. (1984). *Paleopathology at the origins of agriculture.* Orlando: Academic Press.

Cohen, M. N., & Armelagos, G. J. (1984). Paleopathology at the origins of agriculture: Editors' summation. In *Paleopathology at the origins of agriculture* (p. 594). Orlando: Academic Press.

Colborn, T., et al. (1997). *Our stolen future.* New York: Plume/Penguin Books.

Colburn, T., Dumanoski, D., & Myers, J. P. (1996). Hormonal sabotage. *Natural History 3,* 45–46.

Cole, J. W., & Wolf, E. R. (1999). *The hidden frontier: Ecology and ethnicity in an alpine valley* (with a new introduction). Berkeley: University of California Press.

Cole, S. (1975). *Leakey's luck: The life of Louis Seymour Bazett Leakey. 1903–1972.* New York: Harcourt Brace Jovanovich.

Collier, J., & Collier, M. (1986). *Visual anthropology: Photography as a research method.* Albuquerque: University of New Mexico Press.

Collier, J., Rosaldo, M. Z., & Yanagisako, S. (1982). Is there a family? New anthropological views. In B. Thorne & M. Yalom (Eds.), *Rethinking the family: Some feminist questions* (pp. 25–39). New York: Longman.

Collier, J. F., & Yanagisako, S. J. (Eds.) (1987). *Gender and kinship: Essays toward a unified analysis.* Stanford, CA: Stanford University Press.

Cone, M. (2005) *Silent snow: The slow poisoning of the Arctic.* New York: Grove Press.

Connelly, J. C. (1979). Hopi social organization. In A. Ortiz (Ed.), *Handbook of North American Indians, Vol. 9, Southwest* (pp. 539–553). Washington, DC: Smithsonian Institution.

Conner, M. (1996). The archaeology of contemporary mass graves. *SAA Bulletin 14* (4), 6, 31.

Conroy, G. C. (1997). *Reconstructing human origins: A modern synthesis.* New York: Norton.

Coon, C. S. (Ed.) (1948). *A reader in general anthropology.* New York: Holt, Rinehart & Winston.

Coon, C. S. (1954). *The story of man.* New York: Knopf.

Coon, C. S. (1958). *Caravan: The story of the Middle East* (2nd ed.). New York: Holt, Rinehart & Winston.

Coontz, S. (2005). *Marriage, a history: From obedience to intimacy, or how love conquered marriage.* New York: Viking Adult.

Cooper, A., Poinar, H. N., Pääbo, S., Radovci, C. J., Debénath, A., Caparros, M., Barroso-Ruiz, C., Bertranpetit, J., Nielsen-March, C., Hedges, R. E. M., &

Sykes, B. (1997). Neanderthal genetics. *Science 277*, 1,021–1,024.

Coppa, A., et al. (2006). Early Neolithic tradition of dentistry. *Nature 440*, 755–756.

Coppens, Y., Howell, F. C., Isaac, G. L., & Leakey, R. E. F. (Eds.). (1976). *Earliest man and environments in the Lake Rudolf Basin: Stratigraphy, paleoecology, and evolution.* Chicago: University of Chicago Press.

Corballis, M. C. (2003). *From hand to mouth: The origins of human language.* Princeton, NJ: Princeton University Press.

Corbey, R. (1995). Introduction: Missing links, or the ape's place in nature. In R. Corbey & B. Theunissen (Eds.), *Ape, man, apeman: Changing views since 1600* (p.1). Leiden: Department of Prehistory, Leiden University.

Cornwell, T. (1995, November 10). Skeleton staff. *Times Higher Education*, 20.

Corruccini, R. S. (1992). Metrical reconsideration of the Skhul IV and IX and Border Cave I crania in the context of modern human origins. *American Journal of Physical Anthropology 87*, 433–445.

Courlander, H. (1971). *The fourth world of the Hopis.* New York: Crown.

Court says same-sex marriage is a right. (2004, February 5). *San Francisco Chronicle.*

Cowgill, G. L. (1980). Letter, *Science 210*, 1,305.

Cowgill, G. L. (1997). State and society at Teotihuacan, Mexico. *Annual Review of Anthropology 26*, 129–161.

Crane, H. (2001). *Men in spirit: The masculinization of Taiwanese Buddhist nuns.* Doctoral dissertation, Brown University.

Crane, L. B., Yeager, E., & Whitman, R. L. (1981). *An introduction to linguistics.* Boston: Little, Brown.

Cretney, S. (2003). *Family law in the twentieth century: A history.* New York: Oxford University Press.

Crocker, W. H., & Crocker, J. G. (1994). *The Canela, bonding through kinship, ritual, and sex.* Fort Worth: Harcourt Brace.

Crocker, W. H., & Crocker, J. G. (2004). *The Canela: Kinship, ritual, and sex in an Amazonian tribe.* Belmont, CA: Wadsworth.

Culbert, T. P. (Ed.) (1973). *The Classic Maya collapse.* Albuquerque: University of New Mexico Press.

Culotta, E. (1995). Asian hominids grow older. *Science 270*, 1,116–1,117.

Culotta, E. (1995). New finds rekindle debate over anthropoid origins. *Science 268*, 1,851.

Culotta, E., & Koshland, D. E., Jr. (1994). DNA repair works its way to the top. *Science 266*, 1,926.

Cultural Survival Quarterly. (1991). *15* (4), 5.

Cultural Survival Quarterly. (1991). *15* (4), 38.

Current population survey. (2002). U.S. Census Bureau.

Dalton, G. (Ed.) (1967). *Tribal and peasant economics: Readings in economic anthropology.* Garden City, NY: Natural History Press.

Dalton, G. (1971). *Traditional tribal and peasant economies: An introductory survey of economic anthropology.* Reading, MA: Addison-Wesley.

Daniel, G. (1970). *The first civilizations: The archaeology of their origins.* New York: Apollo Editions.

Dalton, G. (1971). *Traditional tribal and peasant economies: An introductory survey of economic anthropology.* Reading, MA: Addison-Wesley.

Daniel, G. (1975). *A hundred and fifty years of archaeology* (2nd ed.). London: Duckworth.

Darwin, C. (1936). *The descent of man and selection in relation to sex.* New York: Random House (Modern Library). (orig. 1871)

Darwin, C. (1967). *On the origin of species.* New York: Atheneum. (orig. 1859).

Davenport, W. (1959). Linear descent and descent groups. *American Anthropologist 61*, 557–573.

Davies, G. (2005). *A history of money from the earliest times to present day* (3rd ed.). Cardiff: University of Wales Press.

Davis, S. H. (1982). *Victims of the miracle.* Cambridge, England: Cambridge University Press.

Deevy, E. S., Jr. (1960). The human population. *Scientific American 203*, 194–204.

de Laguna, F. (1977). *Voyage to Greenland: A personal initiation into anthropology.* New York: Norton.

del Carmen Rodríguez Martínez, M., et al. (2006). Oldest writing in the New World. *Science 313* (5793), 1,610–1,614.

del Castillo, B. D. (1963). *The conquest of New Spain* (translation and introduction by J. M. Cohen). New York: Penguin.

Delson, E., Tattersal, I., Brooks, A., & Van Couvering, J. (1999). *Encyclopedia of human evolution and prehistory.* New York: Garland.

DeMello, M. (2000). *Bodies of inscription: A cultural history of the modern tattoo community.* Durham: Duke University Press.

d'Errico, F., Zilhão, J., Julien, M., Baffier, D., & Pelegrin, J. (1998). Neandertal acculturation in Western Europe? *Current Anthropology 39*, 521.

Desowitz, R. S. (1987). *New Guinea tapeworms and Jewish grandmothers.* New York: Norton.

Dettwyler, K. A. (1994). *Dancing skeletons: Life and death in West Africa.* Prospect Heights, IL: Waveland Press.

Dettwyler, K. A. (1997, October). When to wean. *Natural History*, 49.

DeVore, I. (Ed.). (1965). *Primate behavior: Field studies of monkeys and apes.* New York: Holt, Rinehart & Winston.

de Waal, F. B. M. (1998). Comment. *Current Anthropology 39*, 407.

de Waal, F. B. M. (2000). Primates—A natural heritage of conflict resolution. *Science 28*, 586–590.

de Waal, F. B. M. (2001). *The ape and the sushi master.* New York: Basic Books.

de Waal, F. B. M. (2001). Sing the song of evolution. *Natural History 110* (8), 77.

de Waal, F. B. M., & Johanowicz, D. L. (1993). Modification of reconciliation behavior through social experience: An experiment with two macaque species. *Child Development 64*, 897–908.

de Waal, F. B. M., Kano, T., & Parish, A. R. (1998). Comments. *Current Anthropology 39*, 408, 410, 413.

Diamond, J. (1996). Empire of uniformity. *Discover 17* (3), 83–84.

Diamond, J. (1997). The curse of QWERTY. *Discover 18* (4), 34–42.

Diamond, J. (1997). *Guns, germs, and steel.* New York: Norton.

Diamond, J. (1998). Ants, crops, and history. *Science 281*, 1,974–1,975.

Dicks, B., et al. (2005). *Qualitative research and hypermedia: Ethnography for the digital age (New technologies for social research).* Thousand Oaks, CA: Sage.

Dillehay, T. D. (2001). *The settlement of the Americas.* New York: Basic Books.

Dirie, W., & Miller, C. (1998). *Desert flower: The extraordinary journey of a desert nomad.* New York: William Morrow.

Dissanayake, E. (2000). Birth of the arts. *Natural History 109* (10), 89.

Dixon, J. E., Cann, J. R., & Renfrew, C. (1968). Obsidian and the origins of trade, *Scientific American 218*, 38–46.

Dobyns, H. F., Doughty, P. L., & Lasswell, H. D. (Eds.). (1971). *Peasants, power, and applied social change.* London: Sage.

Dobzhansky, T. (1962). *Mankind evolving.* New Haven, CT: Yale University Press.

Doist, R. (1997). Molecular evolution and scientific inquiry, misperceived. *American Scientist 85*, 475.

Dozier, E. (1970). *The Pueblo Indians of North America.* New York: Holt, Rinehart & Winston.

Draper, P. (1975). !Kung women: Contrasts in sexual egalitarianism in foraging and sedentary contexts. In R. Reiter (Ed.), *Toward an anthropology of women* (pp. 77–109). New York: Monthly Review Press.

Driver, H. (1964). *Indians of North America.* Chicago: University of Chicago Press.

Dubos, R. (1968). *So human an animal.* New York: Scribner.

Dumurat-Dreger, A. (1998, May/June). "Ambiguous sex" or ambivalent medicine? *The Hastings Center Report 28* (3), 2,435 (posted on the Intersex Society of North America website: www.isna.org).

Duncan, A. S., Kappelman, J., & Shapiro, L. J. (1994). Metasophalangeal joint function and positional behavior in *Australo-pithecus afarensis*. *American Journal of Physical Anthropology 93,* 67–81.

Dundes, A. (1980). *Interpreting folklore.* Bloomington: Indiana University Press.

Durant, J. C. (2000, April 23). Everybody into the gene pool. *New York Times Book Review,* 11.

Duranti, A. (2001). Linguistic anthropology: History, ideas, and issues. In A. Duranti (Ed.), *Linguistic anthropology: A reader* (pp. 1–38). Oxford: Blackwell.

Durkheim, E. (1964). *The division of labor in society.* New York: Free Press. (orig. 1893)

Durkheim, E. (1965). *The elementary forms of the religious life.* New York: Free Press. (orig. 1912)

duToit, B. M. (1991). *Human sexuality: Cross cultural readings.* New York: McGraw-Hill.

Eastman, C. M. (1990). *Aspects of language and culture* (2nd ed.). Novato, CA: Chandler & Sharp.

Edwards, J. (Ed.) (1999). *Technologies of procreation: Kinship in the age of assisted conception.* New York: Routledge (distributed by St. Martin's Press).

Edwards, S. W. (1978). Nonutilitarian activities on the Lower Paleolithic: A look at the two kinds of evidence. *Current Anthropology. 19* (l), 135–137.

Egan, T. (1999, February 28). The persistence of polygamy. *New York Times Magazine,* 52.

Eiseley, L. (1958). *Darwin's century: Evolution and the men who discovered it.* New York: Doubleday.

Eisenstadt, S. N. (1956). *From generation to generation: Age groups and social structure.* New York: Free Press.

El Guindi, F. (2004).*Visual anthropology: Essential method and theory.* Walnut Creek, CA: Altamira Press.

Elkin, A. P. (1964). *The Australian Aborigines.* Garden City, NY: Doubleday/Anchor Books.

Ellis, C. (2006). *A dancing people: Powwow culture on the southern plains.* Lawrence: University Press of Kansas.

Ellison, P. T. (1990). Human ovarian function and reproductive ecology: New hypotheses. *American Anthropologist 92,* 933–952.

Ember, C. R., & Ember, M. (1996). What have we learned from cross-cultural research? *General Anthropology 2* (2), 5.

Enard, W., et al. (2002). Molecular evolution of FOXP2, a gene involved in speech and language. *Nature 418,* 869–872.

Ervin-Tripp, S. (1973). *Language acquisition and communicative choice.* Stanford, CA: Stanford University Press.

Esber, G. S., Jr. (1987). Designing Apache houses with Apaches. In R. M. Wulff & S. J. Fiske (Eds.), *Anthropological praxis: Translating knowledge into action* (pp. 187–196). Boulder, CO: Westview Press.

Eugenides, J. (2002). *Middlesex: A novel.* New York: Farrar, Straus and Giroux.

Evans-Pritchard, E. E. (1951). *Kinship and marriage among the Nuer.* New York: Oxford University Press.

Evans-Pritchard, E. E. (1968). *The Nuer: A description of the modes of livelihood and political institutions of a Nilotic people.* London: Oxford University Press.

Fagan, B. M. (1995). *People of the earth* (8th ed.). New York: HarperCollins.

Fagan, B. M. (1999). *Archeology: A brief introduction* (7th ed.). New York: Longman.

Fagan, B. M. (2000). *Ancient lives: An introduction to archaeology.* Englewood Cliffs, NJ: Prentice-Hall.

Fagan, B. (2001). *The seventy great mysteries of the ancient world.* New York: Thames & Hudson.

Fagan, B. M., Beck, C., & Silberman, N. A. (1998). *The Oxford companion to archaeology.* New York: Oxford University Press.

Falk, D. (1975). Comparative anatomy of the larynx in man and the chimpanzee: Implications for language in Neanderthal. *American Journal of Physical Anthropology 43* (1), 123–132.

Falk, D. (1989). Apelike endocast of "apeman" Taung. *American Journal of Physical Anthropology 80,* 335–339.

Falk, D. (1992). *Braindance.* New York: Henry Holt & Company.

Falk, D. (1993). A good brain is hard to cool. *Natural History 102* (8), 65.

Falk, D. (1993). Hominid paleoneurology. In R. L. Ciochon & J. G. Fleagle (Eds.), *The human evolution source book.* Englewood Cliffs, NJ: Prentice-Hall.

Falk, D., et al. (2005). The brain of LB1, *Homo floresiensis. Science 308,* 242– 245.

Farmer, P. (1992). *AIDS and accusation: Haiti and the geography of blame.* Berkeley: University of California Press.

Farmer, P. (2001). *Infections and inequalities: The modern plagues* (updated edition with a new preface). Berkeley: University of California Press.

Farnell, B. (1995). *Do you see what I mean? Plains Indian sign talk and the embodiment of action.* Austin: University of Texas Press.

Fausto-Sterling, A. (1993, March/April). The five sexes: Why male and female are not enough. *The Sciences 33* (2), 20–24.

Fausto-Sterling, A. (2000, July/August). The five sexes revisited. *The Sciences 40* (4), 19–24.

Fausto-Sterling, A. (2003, August 2). Personal e-mail communication.

Feder, K. L. (1999). *Frauds, myths, and mysteries* (3rd ed.). Mountain View, CA: Mayfield.

Fedigan, L. M. (1986). The changing role of women in models of human evolution. *Annual Review of Anthropology 15,* 25–56.

Female genital mutilation. (2000). Fact sheet no. 241. World Health Organization.

Fernandez-Carriba, S., & Loeches, A. (2001). Fruit smearing by captive chimpanzees: A newly observed food-processing behavior. *Current Anthropology 42,* 143–147.

Ferrie, H. (1997). An interview with C. Loring Brace. *Current Anthropology 38,* 851–869.

Field, L. W. (2004). Beyond "applied" anthropology. In T. Biolsi (Ed.), *A companion to the anthropology of American Indians* (pp. 472–489). Oxford: Blackwell Publishing.

Finkler, K. (2000). *Experiencing the new genetics: Family and kinship on the medical frontier.* Philadelphia: University of Pennsylvania Press.

The first Americans, ca. 20,000 B.C. (1998). *Discover 19* (6), 24.

Firth, R. (1946). *Malay fishermen: Their peasant economy.* London: Kegan Paul, Trench, Trubner & Co., Ltd.

Firth, R. (1952). *Elements of social organization.* London: Watts.

Firth, R. (1957). *Man and culture: An evaluation of Bronislaw Malinowski.* London: Routledge.

Firth, R. (Ed.) (1967). *Themes in economic anthropology.* London: Tavistock.

Fisher, R., & Ury, W. L. (1991). *Getting to yes: Negotiating agreement without giving in* (2nd ed.). Boston: Houghton Mifflin.

Flannery, K. V. (1973). The origins of agriculture. In B. J. Siegel, A. R. Beals, & S. A. Tyler (Eds.), *Annual Review of Anthropology* (Vol. 2, pp. 271–310). Palo Alto, CA: Annual Reviews.

Flannery, K. V. (Ed.) (1976). *The Mesoamerican village.* New York: Seminar Press.

Fleagle, J. (1998). *Primate adaptation and evolution.* New York: Academic Press.

Folger, T. (1993). The naked and the bipedal. *Discover 14* (11), 34–35.

Forbes, J. D. (1964). *The Indian in America's past.* Englewood Cliffs, NJ: Prentice-Hall.

Forbes International 500 List. (2003).

Forde, C. D. (1955). The Nupe. In D. Forde (Ed.), *Peoples of the Niger-Benue confluence.* London: International African Institute (Ethnographic Survey of Africa. Western Africa, part 10).

Forde, C. D. (1968). Double descent among the Yakö. In P. Bohannan & J. Middleton (Eds.), *Kinship and social organization* (pp. 179–191). Garden City, NY: Natural History Press.

Fortes, M. (1950). Kinship and marriage among the Ashanti. In A. R. Radcliffe-Brown & C. D. Forde (Eds.), *African systems of kinship and marriage.* London: Oxford University Press.

Fortes, M. (1969). *Kinship and the social order: The legacy of Lewis Henry Morgan.* Chicago: Aldine.

Fortes, M., & Evans-Prichard, E. E. (Eds.) (1962). *African political systems.* London: Oxford University Press. (orig. 1940)

Fossey, D. (1983). *Gorillas in the mist.* Burlington, MA: Houghton Mifflin.

Foster, G. M. (1955). Peasant society and the image of the limited good. *American Anthropologist 67,* 293–315.

Fountain, H. (2000, January 30). Now the ancient ways are less mysterious. *New York Times,* News of the Week, 5.

Fox, R. (1968). *Kinship and marriage in an anthropological perspective.* Baltimore: Penguin.

Fox, R. (1981, December 3). [Interview]. Coast Telecourses, Inc., Los Angeles.

Frake, C. (1961). The diagnosis of disease among the Subinam of Mindinao. *American Anthropologist 63,*113–132.

Frake, C. O. (1992). Lessons of the Mayan sky. In A. F. Aveni (Ed.), *The sky in Mayan literature* (pp. 274–291). New York: Oxford University Press.

Frankfort, H. (1968). *The birth of civilization in the Near East.* New York: Barnes & Noble.

Fraser, D. (Ed.) (1966). *The many faces of primitive art: A critical anthology.* Englewood Cliffs, NJ: Prentice-Hall.

Frayer, D. W. (1981). Body size, weapon use, and natural selection in the European Upper Paleolithic and Mesolithic. *American Anthropologist 83,* 57–73.

Frazer, Sir J. G. (1961 reissue) *The new golden bough.* New York: Doubleday, Anchor Books.

Freeman, J. D. (1960). The Iban of western Borneo. In G. P. Murdock (Ed.), *Social structure in Southeast Asia.* Chicago: Quadrangle Books.

Freeman, L. G. (1992). *Ambrona and Torralba: New evidence and interpretation.* Paper presented at the 91st Annual Meeting, American Anthropological Association.

Fried, M. (1967). *The evolution of political society: An essay in political anthropology.* New York: Random House.

Fried, M., Harris, M., & Murphy, R. (1968). *War: The anthropology of armed conflict and aggression.* Garden City, NY: Natural History Press.

Friedl, E. (1975). *Women and men: An anthropologist's view.* New York: Holt, Rinehart & Winston.

Friedman, J. (Ed.) (2003). *Globalization, the state, and violence.* Walnut Creek, CA: Altamira Press.

Frisch, R. (2002). *Female fertility and the body fat connection.* Chicago: University of Chicago Press.

Fritz, G. J. (1994). Are the first American farmers getting younger? *Current Anthropology 35,* 305–309.

Frye, D. P. (2000). Conflict management in cross-cultural perspective. In F. Aureli & F. B. M. de Waal, *Natural conflict resolution* (pp. 334–351). Berkeley: University of California Press.

Furst, P. T. (1976). *Hallucinogens and culture* (p. 7). Novato, CA: Chandler & Sharp.

Galdikas, B. (1995). *Reflections on Eden: My years with the orangutans of Borneo.* New York: Little Brown.

Gamble, C. (1986). *The Paleolithic settlement of Europe.* Cambridge: Cambridge University Press.

Gardner, R. A., Gardner, B. T., & Van Cantfort, T. E. (Eds.) (1989). *Teaching sign language to chimpanzees.* Albany: State University of New York Press.

Gamst, F. C., & Norbeck, E. (1976). *Ideas of culture: Sources and uses.* New York: Holt, Rinehart & Winston.

Garn, S. M. (1970). *Human races* (3rd ed.). Springfield, IL: Charles C Thomas.

Gates, H. (1996). Buying brides in China—again. *Anthropology Today 12* (4), 10.

Gebo, D. L., Dagosto, D., Beard, K. C., & Tao, Q. (2001). Middle Eocene primate tarsals from China: Implications for haplorhine evolution. *American Journal of Physical Anthropology 116,* 83–107.

Geertz, C. (1965). The impact of the concept of culture on the concept of man. In J. R. Platt (Ed.), *New views of man.* Chicago: University of Chicago Press.

Geertz, C. (1973). *The interpretation of culture.* London: Hutchinson.

Geertz, C. (1984). Distinguished lecture: Antirelativism. *American Anthropologist 86,* 263–278.

Gell, A. (1988). Technology and magic. *Anthropology Today 4* (2), 6–9.

Gene study suggests Polynesians came from Taiwan. (2005, July 4). Reuters.

Gibbons, A. (1993). Where are new diseases born? *Science 261,* 680–681.

Gibbons, A. (1997). Ideas on human origins evolve at anthropology gathering. *Science 276,* 535–536.

Gibbons, A. (1998). Ancient island tools suggest *Homo erectus* was a seafarer. *Science 279,* 1,635.

Gibbons, A. (2001). The riddle of coexistence. *Science 291,* 1,726.

Gibbons, A. (2001). Studying humans—and their cousins and parasites. *Science 292,* 627.

Gibbs, J. L., Jr. (1965). The Kpelle of Liberia. In J. L. Gibbs, Jr. (Ed.), *Peoples of Africa* (pp. 216–218). New York: Holt, Rinehart & Winston.

Gibbs, J. L., Jr. (1983). [Interview]. *Faces of culture: Program 18.* Fountain Valley, CA: Coast Telecourses.

Giddens, A. (1990). *The consequences of modernity.* Stanford, CA: Stanford University Press.

Ginsburg, F. D., Abu-Lughod, L., & Larkin, B. (Eds.) (2002). *Media worlds: Anthropology on new terrain.* Berkeley: University of California Press.

Gladdol, D. (2006). *English next.* London: British Council.

Gledhill, J. (2000). *Power and its disguises: Anthropological perspectives on politics* (2nd ed.). Boulder, CO: Pluto Press.

Godfrey, T. (2000, December 27). Biotech threatening biodiversity. *Burlington Free Press,* 10A.

Godlier, M. (1971). Salt currency and the circulation of commodities among the Baruya of New Guinea. In G. Dalton (Ed.), *Studies in economic anthropology.* Washington, DC: American Anthropological Association (Anthropological Studies No. 7).

Goodall, J. (1986). *The chimpanzees of Gombe: Patterns of behavior.* Cambridge, MA: Belknap Press.

Goodall, J. (1990). *Through a window: My thirty years with the chimpanzees of Gombe.* Boston: Houghton Mifflin.

Goodall, J. (2000). *Reason for hope: A spiritual journey.* New York: Warner Books.

Goodenough, W. (Ed.). (1964). *Explorations in cultural anthropology: Essays in honor of George Murdock.* New York: McGraw–Hill.

Goodenough, W. (1965). Rethinking status and role: Toward a general model of the cultural organization of social relationships. In M. Benton (Ed.), *The relevance of models for social anthropology.* New York: Praeger (ASA Monographs l).

Goodenough, W. (1970). *Description and comparison in cultural anthropology.* Chicago: Aldine.

Goodenough, W. H. (1990). Evolution of the human capacity for beliefs. *American Anthropologist 92,* 601.

Goodman, A., & Armelagos, G. J. (1985). Death and disease at Dr. Dickson's mounds. *Natural History 94* (9), 12–18.

Goodman, M., Bailey, W. J., Hayasaka, K., Stanhope, M. J., Slightom J., & Czelusniak, J. (1994). Molecular evidence on primate phylogeny from DNA sequences. *American Journal of Physical Anthropology 94,* 7.

Goody, J. (1969). *Comparative studies in kinship.* Stanford, CA: Stanford University Press.

Goody, J. (1976). *Production and reproduction: A comparative study of the domestic domain.* Cambridge: Cambridge University Press.

Goody, J. (1983). *The development of the family and marriage in Europe.* Cambridge, MA: Cambridge University Press.

Gordon, R. J. (1992). *The Bushman myth: The making of a Namibian underclass.* Boulder, CO: Westview Press.

Gordon, R. J., & Megitt, M. J. (1985). *Law and order in the New Guinea highlands.* Hanover, NH: University Press of New England.

Gould, S. J. (1983). *Hen's teeth and horses' toes.* New York: Norton.

Gould, S. J. (1985). *The flamingo's smile: Reflections in natural history*. New York: Norton.

Gould, S. J. (1989). *Wonderful life*. New York: Norton.

Gould, S. J. (1991). *Bully for brontosaurus*. New York: Norton.

Gould, S. J. (1994). The geometer of race. *Discover 15* (11), 65–69.

Gould, S. J. (1996). *Full house: The spread of excellence from Plato to Darwin*. New York: Harmony Books.

Gould, S. J. (1996). *The mismeasure of man* (2nd ed.). New York: Norton.

Gould, S. J. (2000). The narthex of San Marco and the pangenetic paradigm. *Natural History 109* (6), 29.

Gould, S. J. (2000). What does the dreaded "E" word mean anyway? *Natural History 109* (1), 34–36.

Graburn, N. H. H. (1969). *Eskimos without igloos: Social and economic development in Sugluk*. Boston: Little, Brown.

Graburn, N. H. (1971). *Readings in kinship and social structure*. New York: Harper & Row.

Graves, J. L. (2001). *The emperor's new clothes: Biological theories of race at the millennium*. New Brunswick, NJ: Rutgers University Press.

Graves, P. (1991). New models and metaphors for the Neanderthal debate. *Current Anthropology, 32*(5), 513–543.

Gray, P. M., Krause, B., Atema, J., Payne, R., Krumhansl, C., & Baptista, L. (2001). The music of nature and the nature of music. *Science 291*, 52.

Greenberg, J. H. (1968). *Anthropological linguistics: An introduction*. New York: Random House.

Grine, F. E. (1993). Australopithecine taxonomy and phylogeny: Historical background and recent interpretation. In R. L. Ciochon & J. G. Fleagle (Eds.), *The human evolution source book*, Englewood Cliffs, NJ: Prentice-Hall.

Grivetti, L. E. (2005). From aphrodisiac to health food: A cultural history of chocolate. *Karger Gazette*, 68.

Grün, R., & Thorne, A. (1997). Dating the Ngandong humans, *Science 276*, 1,575.

Guillette, E. A., et al. (1998, June). An anthropological approach to the evaluation of preschool children exposed to pesticides in Mexico. *Environmental Health Perspectives 106*, 347.

Guthrie, S. (1993). *Faces in the clouds: A new theory of religions*. New York: Oxford University Press.

Gutin, J. A. (1995). Do Kenya tools root birth of modern thought in Africa? *Science 270*, 1,118–1,119.

Haeri, N. (1997). The reproduction of symbolic capital: Language, state and class in Egypt. *Current Anthropology 38*, 795–816.

Hafkin, N., & Bay, E. (Eds.) (1976). *Women in Africa*. Stanford, CA: Stanford University Press.

Hager, L. (1989). The evolution of sex differences in the hominid bony pelvis. Ph.D. dissertation, University of California, Berkeley.

Hall, E. T. (1959). *The silent language*. Garden City, NY: Anchor Press/Doubleday.

Hall, E. T., & Hall, M. R. (1986). The sounds of silence. In E. Angeloni (Ed.), *Anthropology 86/87* (pp. 65–70). Guilford, CT: Dushkin.

Hall, K. R. L., & DeVore, I. (1965). Baboon social behavior. In I. DeVore (Ed.), *Primate behavior*. New York: Holt, Rinehart & Winston.

Hallowell, A. I. (1955). *Culture and experience*. Philadelphia: University of Pennsylvania Press.

Halperin, R. H. (1994). *Cultural economies: Past and present*. Austin: University of Texas Press.

Halverson, J. (1989). Review of the book *Altimira Revisited and other essays on early art*. *American Antiquity 54*, 883.

Hannah, J. L. (1988). *Dance, sex and gender*. Chicago: University of Chicago Press.

Hanson, A. (1989). The making of the Maori: Culture invention and its logic. *American Anthropologist 91* (4), 890–902.

Harlow, H. F. (1962). Social deprivation in monkeys. *Scientific America, 206*, 1–10.

Harner, M. (1980). *The way of the shaman: A guide to power and healing*. San Francisco: Harper & Row.

Harpending, J. H., & Harpending, H. C. (1995). Ancient differences in population can mimic a recent African origin of modern humans. *Current Anthropology, 36*, 667–674.

Harris, M. (1965). The cultural ecology of India's sacred cattle. *Current Anthropology 7*, 51–66.

Harris, M. (1968). *The rise of anthropological theory: A history of theories of culture*. New York: Crowell.

Harris, M. (1979). *Cultural materialism: The struggle for a science of culture*. New York: Random House.

Harris, M. (1989). *Cows, pigs, wars, and witches: The riddles of culture*. New York: Vintage Books/Random House.

Harrison, G. G. (1975). Primary adult lactase deficiency: A problem in anthropological genetics. *American Anthropologist 77*, 815–819.

Hart, C. W., Pilling, A. R., & Goodale, J. (1988). *Tiwi of North Australia* (3rd ed.). New York: Holt, Rinehart & Winston.

Hart, D. (2006, April 21). Humans as prey. *Chronicle of Higher Education*.

Hart, D., & Sussman, R. W. (2005). *Man the hunted: Primates, predators, and human evolution*. Boulder, CO: Westview Press.

Hartwig, W. C. (2002). *The primate fossil record*. New York: Cambridge University Press.

Hartwig, W. C., & Doneski, K. (1998). Evolution of the hominid hand and toolmaking behavior. *American Journal of Physical Anthropology 106*, 401–402.

Hatch, E. (1983). *Culture and morality: The relativity of values in anthropology*. New York: Columbia University Press.

Hatcher, E. P. (1985). *Art as culture, an introduction to the anthropology of art*. New York: University Press of America.

Haviland, W. A. (1967). Stature at Tikal, Guatemala: Implications for ancient Maya, demography, and social organization. *American Antiquity 32*, 316–325.

Haviland, W. A. (1970). Tikal, Guatemala and Mesoamerican urbanism. *World Archaeology 2*, 186–198.

Haviland, W. A. (1972). A new look at Classic Maya social organization at Tikal. *Ceramica de Cultura Maya 8*, 1–16.

Haviland, W. A. (1974). Farming, seafaring and bilocal residence on the coast of Maine. *Man in the Northeast 6*, 31–44.

Haviland, W. A. (1997). Cleansing young minds, or what should we be doing in introductory anthropology? In C. P. Kottak, J. J. White, R. H. Furlow, & P. C. Rice (Eds.), *The teaching of anthropology: Problems, issues, and decisions* (p. 35). Mountain View, CA: Mayfield.

Haviland, W. A. (1997). The rise and fall of sexual inequality: Death and gender at Tikal, Guatemala. *Ancient Mesoamerica 8*, 1–12.

Haviland, W. A. (2002). Settlement, society and demography at Tikal. In J. Sabloff (Ed.), *Tikal*. Santa Fe: School of American Research.

Haviland, W. A. (2003). *Tikal, Guatemala: A Maya way to urbanism*. Paper prepared for 3rd INAH/Penn State Conference on Mesoamerican Urbanism.

Haviland, W. A., et al. (1985). *Excavations in small residential groups of Tikal: Groups 4F-1 and 4F-2*. Philadelphia: University Museum.

Haviland, W. A., & Moholy-Nagy, H. (1992). Distinguishing the high and mighty from the hoi polloi at Tikal, Guatemala. In A. F. Chase & D. Z. Chase (Eds.), *Mesoamerican elites: An archaeological assessment*. Norman: Oklahoma University Press.

Haviland, W. A., & Power, M. W. (1994). *The original Vermonters: Native inhabitants, past and present* (2nd ed.). Hanover, NH: University Press of New England.

Hawkes, K., O'Connell, J. F., & Blurton Jones, N. G. (1997). Hadza women's time allocation, offspring, provisioning, and the evolution of long postmenopausal life spans. *Current Anthropology 38*, 551–577.

Hawks, J. (2006, July 21). Neandertal Genome Project. http://johnhawks.net/weblog.

Hazardous waste trafficking. www.Choike.org.

Heita, K. (1999). Imanishi's world view. *Journal of Japanese Trade and Industry 18* (2), 15.

Heitzman, J., & R. L. Wordem, R. L. (Eds.). (2006). *India: A country study* (Sect. 2, 5th ed.). Washington, DC: Federal Research Division, Library of Congress.

Helm, J. (1962). The ecological approach in anthropology. *American Journal of Sociology 67,* 630–649.

Helman, C. B. (2003). *Culture, health, and illness: An introduction for health professionals.* New York: Butterworth Heinemann Medical.

Henry, D. O., et al. (2004). Human behavioral organization in the Middle Paleolithic: Were Neandertals different? *American Anthropologist 107* (1), 17–31.

Henry, J. (1965). *Culture against man.* New York: Vintage Books.

Henry, J. (1974). A theory for an anthropological analysis of American culture. In J. G. Jorgensen & M. Truzzi (Eds.), *Anthropology and American life.* Englewood Cliffs, NJ: Prentice-Hall.

Herdt, G. H. (1993). Semen transactions in Sambia culture. In D. N. Suggs & A. W. Mirade (Eds.), *Culture and human sexuality* (pp. 298–327). Pacific Grove, CA: Brooks/Cole.

Herskovits, M. J. (1952). *Economic anthropology: A study in comparative economics* (2nd ed.). New York: Knopf.

Hertz, N. (2001). *The silent takeover: Global capitalism and the death of democracy.* New York: Arrow Books.

Hewes, G. W. (1973). Primate communication and the gestural origin of language. *Current Anthropology 14,* 5–24.

Himmelfarb, E. J. (2000, January/February). First alphabet found in Egypt. Newsbrief. *Archaeology 53* (1).

Historical atlas of the twentieth century. http://users.erols.com/mwhite28/20centry.htm.

Hitchcock, R. K., & Enghoff, M. (2004). *Capacity-building of first people of the Kalahari, Botswana: An evaluation.* Copenhagen: International Work Group for Indigenous Affairs.

Hodgen, M. (1964). *Early anthropology in the sixteenth and seventeenth centuries.* Philadelphia: University of Pennsylvania Press.

Hoebel, E. A. (1949). *Man in the primitive world: An introduction to anthropology.* New York: McGraw-Hill.

Hoebel, E. A. (1954). *The law of primitive man: A study in comparative legal dynamics.* Cambridge, MA: Harvard University Press.

Hoebel, E. A. (1958). *Man in the primitive world: An introduction to anthropology.* New York: McGraw-Hill.

Hoebel, E. A. (1960). *The Cheyennes: Indians of the Great Plains.* New York: Holt, Rinehart & Winston.

Holden, C. (1996). Missing link for Miocene apes. *Science 271,* 151.

Holden, C. (1999). Ancient child burial uncovered in Portugal. *Science 283,* 169.

Hole, F. (1966). Investigating the origins of Mesopotamian civilization. *Science 153,* 605–611.

Hole, F., & Heizer, R. F. (1969). *An introduction to prehistoric archeology.* New York: Holt, Rinehart & Winston.

Holloway, R. L. (1980). The O. H. 7 (Olduvai Gorge, Tanzania) hominid partial brain endocast revisited. *American Journal of Physical Anthropology 53,* 267–274.

Holloway, R. L. (1981). The Indonesian *Homo erectus* brain endocast revisited. *American Journal of Physical Anthropology 55,* 503–521.

Holloway, R. L. (1981). Volumetric and asymmetry determinations on recent hominid endocasts: Spy I and II, Djebel Jhroud 1, and the Salb Homo erectus specimens, with some notes on Neanderthal brain size. *American Journal of Physical Anthropology 55,* 385–393.

Holloway, R. L., & de LaCoste-Lareymondie, M. C. (1982). Brain endocast asymmetry in pongids and hominids: Some preliminary findings on the paleontology of cerebral dominance. *American Journal of Physical Anthropology 58,* 101–110.

Holmes, L. D. (2000). Paradise bent (film review). *American Anthropologist 102* (3), 604–605.

Holy, L. (1996). *Anthropological perspectives on kinship.* London: Pluto Press.

Hostetler, J., & Huntington, G. (1971). *Children in Amish society.* New York: Holt, Rinehart &Winston.

Houle, A. (1999). The origin of platyrrhines: An evaluation of the Antarctic scenario and the floating island model. *American Journal of Physical Anthropology 109,* 554–556.

Howell, F. C. (1970). *Early man.* New York: Time-Life.

Hrdy, S. B. (1999). Body fat and birth control. *Natural History 108* (8), 88.

Hsiaotung, F. (1939). *Peasant life in China.* London: Kegan, Paul, Trench & Truber.

Hsu, F. L. (1961). *Psychological anthropology: Approaches to culture and personality.* Homewood, IL: Dorsey Press.

Hsu, F. L. K. (1979). The cultural problems of the cultural anthropologist. *American Anthropologist 81,* 517–532.

Hubert, H., & Mauss, M. (1964). *Sacrifice.* Chicago: University of Chicago Press.

Human development report. (2002). *Deepening democracy in a fragmented world.* United Nations Development Program.

Hunger Project. (2003). www.thp.org.

Hunt, R. C. (Ed.). (1967). *Personalities and cultures: Readings in psychological anthropology.* Garden City, NY: Natural History Press.

Hutter, M. (Ed.) (2003). *The family experience: A reader in cultural diversity* (4th ed.). Boston: Allyn & Bacon.

Hymes, D. (1964). *Language in culture and Society: A reader in linguistics and anthropology.* New York: Harper & Row.

Hymes, D. (Ed.) (1972). *Reinventing anthropology.* New York: Pantheon. icasualties.org.

Inda, J. X., & Rosaldo, R. (Eds.). (2001). *The anthropology of globalization: A reader.* Malden, MA, and Oxford: Blackwell.

Ingmanson, E. J. (1998). Comment. *Current Anthropology 39,* 409.

Inkeles, A., & Levinson, D. J. (1954). *National character: The study of modal personality and socio-cultural systems.* In G. Lindzey (Ed.), *Handbook of social psychology.* Reading, MA: Addison-Wesley.

International Union for Conservation of Nature and Natural Resources (IUCN). (2000).

Inuit Tapiirit Katami. http://www.taprisat.ca/english- text/itk/departments/enviro/ncp.

Irvine, M. (1999, November 24). Mom-and-pop houses grow rare. *Burlington Free Press.*

Italy-Germany verbal war hots up. (2003, July 9). *Deccan Herald.* (Bangalore, India).

It's the law: Child labor protection. (1997, November/December). *Peace and Justice News,* 11.

Jacobs, S. E. (1994). Native American two-spirits. *Anthropology Newsletter 35* (8), 7.

Jacoby, R., & Glauberman, N. (Eds.). (1995). *The Bell Curve debate.* New York: Random House.

Jennings, F. (1976). *The invasion of America.* New York: Norton.

Jennings, J. D. (1974). *Prehistory of North America* (2nd ed.). New York: McGraw-Hill.

Johansen, B. E. (2002). The Inuit's struggle with dioxins and other organic pollutants. *The American Indian Quarterly 26* (3), 479–490.

Johanson, D., & Shreeve, J. (1989). *Lucy's child: The discovery of a human ancestor.* New York: Avon.

Johanson, D. C., & Edey, M. (1981). *Lucy, the beginnings of humankind.* New York: Simon & Schuster.

Johanson, D. C, Edgar, B., & Brill, D. (1996). *From Lucy to language.* New York: Simon & Schuster.

Johanson, D. C., & White, T. D. (1979). A systematic assessment of early African hominids. *Science 203,* 321–330.

John, V. (1971). Whose is the failure? In C. L. Brace, G. R. Gamble, & J. T. Bond (Eds.), *Race and intelligence.* Washington, DC: American Anthropological Association (Anthropological Studies No. 8).

Johnson, A. (1989). Horticulturalists: Economic behavior in tribes. In S. Plattner (Ed.), *Economic anthropology* (pp. 49–77). Stanford, CA: Stanford University Press.

Johnson, A. W., & Earle, T. (1987). *The evolution of human societies, from forag-*

ing group to agrarian state. Stanford, CA: Stanford University Press.

Johnson, D. (1996). Polygamists emerge from secrecy, seeking not just peace but respect. In W. A. Haviland & R. J. Gordon (Eds.), *Talking about people* (2nd ed., pp. 129–131). Mountain View, CA: Mayfield.

Johnson, N. B. (1984). Sex, color, and rites of passage in ethnographic research. *Human Organization 43* (2), 108–120.

Jolly, A. (1985). *The evolution of primate behavior* (2nd ed.). New York: Macmillan.

Jolly, A. (1991). Thinking like a vervet. *Science 251*, 574.

Jolly, C. J. (1970). The seed eaters: A new model of hominid differentiation based on a baboon analogy. *Man 5*, 5–26.

Jones, S. (2005). Transhumance re-examined. *Journal of the Royal Anthropological Institute 11* (4), 841–842.

Jones, S., Martin, R., & Pilbeam, D. (1992). *Cambridge encyclopedia of human evolution.* New York: Cambridge University Press.

Jorgensen, J. (1972). *The sun dance religion.* Chicago: University of Chicago Press.

Joukowsky, M. A. (1980). *A complete field manual of archeology: Tools and techniques of field work for archaeologists.* Englewood Cliffs, NJ: Prentice-Hall.

Kaiser, J. (1994). A new theory of insect wing origins takes off. *Science 266*, 363.

Kalwet, H. (1988). *Dreamtime and inner space: The world of the shaman.* New York: Random House.

Kaplan, D. (1972). *Culture theory.* Englewood Cliffs, NJ: Prentice-Hall (Foundations of Modern Anthropology).

Kaplan, D. (2000). The darker side of the original affluent society. *Journal of Anthropological Research 53*(3), 301–324.

Karavani, I., & Smith, F. H. (2000). More on the Neanderthal problem: The Vindija case. *Current Anthropology 41*, 839.

Kay, R. F., Fleagle, J. G., & Simons, E. L. (1981). A revision of the Oligocene apes of the Fayum Province, Egypt. *American Journal of Physical Anthropology 55*, 293–322.

Kay, R. F., Ross, C., & Williams, B. A. (1997). Anthropoid origins. *Science 275*, 797–804.

Kay, R. F., Theweissen, J. G. M., & Yoder, A. D. (1992). Cranial anatomy of Ignacius graybullianus and the affinities of the plesiadapiformes. *American Journal of Physical Anthropology 89* (4), 477–498.

Kedia, S., &Van Willigen, J. (2005). *Applied anthropology: Domains of application.* New York: Praeger.

Keen, B. (1971). *The Aztec image in western thought.* New Brunswick, NJ: Rutgers University Press.

Kehoe, A. (1989). *The ghost dance: Ethnohistory and revitalization.* Fort Worth: Holt, Rinehart & Winston.

Kehoe, A. (2000). *Shamans and religion: An anthropological exploration in critical thinking.* Prospect Heights, IL: Waveland Press.

Keiser, L. (1991). *Friend by day, enemy by night: Organized vengeance in a Kohistani community.* Fort Worth: Holt, Rinehart & Winston.

Kelly, T. L. (2006). Sadhus, the great renouncers. Photography exhibit, Indigo Gallery, Naxal, Kathmandu, Nepal. www.asianart.com/exhibitions/sadhus/index.html.

Kendall, L. (1990, October). In the company of witches. *Natural History, 92.*

Kennickell, A. B. (2003, November). *A rolling tide: Changes in the distribution of wealth in the U.S. 1989–2001.* Levy Economics Institute.

Kertzer, D. I. (1989). *Ritual, politics, and power.* New Haven, CT: Yale University Press.

Key, M. R. (1975). *Paralanguage and kinesics: Nonverbal communication.* Metuchen, NJ: Scarecrow Press.

Kirkpatrick, R. C. (2000). The evolution of human homosexual behavior. *Current Anthropology 41*, 384.

Klass, M. (1995). *Ordered universes: Approaches to the anthropology of religion.* Boulder, CO: Westview Press.

Klass, M., & Weisgrau, M. (Eds.). (1999). *Across the boundaries of belief: Contemporary issues in the anthropology of religion.* Boulder, CO: Westview Press.

Klein, R. (2002). *The dawn of human culture.* New York: Wiley.

Klein, R. G., & Edgar, B. (2002). *The dawn of human culture.* New York: Wiley.

Kleinman, A. (1976). Concepts and a model for the comparison of medical systems as cultural systems. *Social Science and Medicine 12* (2B), 85–95.

Kluckhohn, C. (1970). *Mirror for man.* Greenwich, CT: Fawcett.

Kluckhohn, C. (1994). Navajo witchcraft. *Papers of the Peabody Museum of American Archaeology and Ethnology 22* (2).

Knauft, B. M. (1991). Violence and sociality in human evolution. *Current Anthropology 32*, 391–409.

Koch, G. (1997). Songs, land rights, and archives in Australia. *Cultural Survival Quarterly 20* (4).

Konner, M., & Worthman, C. (1980). Nursing frequency, gonadal function, and birth spacing among !Kung hunter-gatherers. *Science 207*, 788–791.

Koufos, G. (1993). Mandible of Ouranopithecus macedoniensis (hominidae: primates) from a new late Miocene locality in Macedonia (Greece). *American Journal of Physical Anthropology 91*, 225–234.

Krader, L. (1968). *Formation of the state.* Englewood Cliffs, NJ: Prentice-Hall (Foundation of Modern Anthropology).

Krajick, K. (1998). Greenfarming by the Incas? *Science 281*, 323.

Kramer, P. A. (1998). The costs of human locomotion: Maternal investment in child transport. *American Journal of Physical Anthropology 107*, 71–85.

Kraybill, D. B. (2001). *The riddle of Amish culture.* Baltimore: Johns Hopkins University Press.

Kroeber, A. (1958). Totem and taboo: An ethnologic psycho-analysis. In W. Lessa & E. Z. Vogt (Eds.), *Reader in comparative religion: An anthropological approach.* New York: Harper & Row.

Kroeber, A. L. (1939). Cultural and natural areas of native North America. *American Archaeology and Ethnology* (Vol. 38). Berkeley: University of California Press.

Kroeber, A. L. (1963). *Anthropology: Cultural processes and patterns.* New York: Harcourt.

Kroeber, A. L., & Kluckhohn, C. (1952). *Culture: A critical review of concepts and definitions.* Cambridge, MA: Harvard University Press (*Papers of the Peabody Museum of American Archaeology and Ethnology, 47*).

Kruger, J., et al. (2005, December). Egocentrism over e-mail: Can people communicate as well as they think? *Journal of Personality and Social Psychology 89* (6), 925–936.

Kummer, H. (1971). *Primate societies: Group techniques of ecological adaptation.* Chicago: Aldine.

Kunnie, J. (2003). Africa's fast growing indigenous churches. http://coh.arizona.edu/newandnotable/kunnie/kunnie.html. Kunzig, R. (1999). A tale of two obsessed archaeologists, one ancient city and nagging doubts about whether science can ever hope to reveal the past. *Discover 20* (5), 84–92.

Kuper, H. (1965). The Swazi of Swaziland. In J. L. Gibbs (Ed.), *Peoples of Africa* (pp. 479–511). New York: Holt, Rinehart & Winston.

Kurth, P. (1998, October 14). Capital crimes. *Seven Days, 7.*

Kurtz, D. V. (2001). *Political anthropology: Paradigms and power.* Boulder, CO: Westview Press.

Kushner, G. (1969). *Anthropology of complex societies.* Stanford, CA: Stanford University Press.

LaFont, S. (Ed.). (2003). *Constructing sexualities: Readings in sexuality, gender, and culture.* Upper Saddle River, NJ: Prentice-Hall.

Lai, C. S. L., et al. (2001). A forkhead-domain gene is mutated in severe speech and language disorder. *Nature 413*, 519–523.

Lakoff, R. T. (2004). *Language and woman's place.* M. Bucholtz (Ed.). New York: Oxford University Press.

Lambek, M. (2002). *A reader in the anthropology of religion.* London: Blackwell.

Lampl, M., Velhuis, J. D., & Johnson, M. L. (1992). Saltation and stasis: A model of human growth. *Science 258* (5083), 801–803.

Lancaster, J. B. (1975). *Primate behavior and the emergence of human culture.* New York: Holt, Rinehart & Winston.

Landau, M. (1991). *Narratives of human evolution.* New Haven, CT: Yale University Press.

Langan, P., & Harlow, C. (1994). *Child rape victims, 1992.* Washington, DC: Bureau of Justice Statistics, U.S. Department of Justice.

Lanning, E. P. (1967). *Peru before the Incas.* Englewood Cliffs, NJ: Prentice-Hall.

Larsen, C. S., Matter, R. M., & Gebo, D. L. (1998). *Human origins: The fossil record.* Long Grove, IL: Waveland Press.

Larsen, J. (2006, July 28). Setting the record straight. Earth Policy Institute, Ecoeconomy updates.

Lawler, A. (2001). Writing gets a rewrite. *Science 292,* 2,419.

Layton, R. (1991). *The anthropology of art* (2nd ed.). Cambridge: Cambridge University Press.

Leach, E. (1961). *Rethinking anthropology.* London: Athione Press.

Leach, E. (1962). The determinants of differential cross-cousin marriage. *Man 62,* 238.

Leach, E. (1962). On certain unconsidered aspects of double descent systems. *Man 214,* 13–34.

Leach, E. (1982). *Social anthropology.* Glasgow: Fontana Paperbacks.

Leacock, E. (1981). *Myths of male dominance: Collected articles on women cross culturally.* New York: Monthly Review Press.

Leacock, E. (1981). Women's status in egalitarian society: Implications for social evolution. In *Myths of male dominance: Collected articles on women cross culturally.* New York: Monthly Review Press.

Leakey, L. S. B. (1965). *Olduvai Gorge, 1951–1961* (Vol. 1). London: Cambridge University Press.

Leakey, L. S. B., Tobias, P. B., & Napier, J. R. (1964). A new species of the genus *Homo* from Olduvai Gorge. *Nature 202,* 7–9.

Leakey, M. G., Spoor, F., Brown, F. H., Gathogo, P. N., Kiare, C., Leakey, L. N., & McDougal, I. (2001). New hominin genus from eastern Africa shows diverse middle Pliocene lineages. *Nature 410,* 433–440.

Leakey, M. D. (1971). *Olduvai Gorge: Excavations in Beds I and II. 1960–1963.* London and New York: Cambridge University Press.

Leap, W. L. (1987). Tribally controlled culture change: The Northern Ute language revival project. In R. M. Wulff & S. J. Fiske (Eds.), *Anthropological praxis: Translating knowledge into action* (pp. 197–211). Boulder, CO: Westview Press.

Leavitt, G. C. (1990). Sociobiological explanations of incest avoidance: A critical review of evidential claims. *American Anthropologist 92,* 982.

Leclerc-Madlala, S. (2002). Bodies and politics: Healing rituals in the democratic South Africa. In V. Faure (Ed.), *Les cahiers de 'l'IFAS,* No. 2. Johannesburg: The French Institute.

Lee, R. B. (1993). *The Dobe Ju/'hoansi.* Ft. Worth: Harcourt Brace.

Lee, R. B., & Daly, R. H. (1999). *The Cambridge encyclopedia of hunters and gatherers.* New York: Cambridge University Press.

Lee, R. B., & DeVore, I. (Eds.) (1968). *Man the hunter.* Chicago: Aldine.

Lees, R. (1953). The basis of glottochronology. *Language 29,* 113–127.

Lehman, E. C., Jr. (2002, Fall). Women's path into the ministry. *Pulpit & Pew Research Reports 1,* 4.

Lehmann, A. C., & Myers, J. E. (Eds.) (2000). *Magic, witchcraft, and religion: An anthropological study of the supernatural* (5th ed.). Mountain View, CA: Mayfield.

Leigh, S. R., & Park, P. B. (1998). Evolution of human growth prolongation. *American Journal of Physical Anthropology 107,* 331–350.

Leinhardt, G. (1964). *Social anthropology.* London: Oxford University Press.

LeMay, M. (1975). The language capability of Neanderthal man. *American Journal of Physical Anthropology 43* (1), 9–14.

Lenski, G. (1966). *Power and privilege: A theory of social stratification.* New York: McGraw-Hill.

Leroi-Gourhan, A. (1968). The evolution of Paleolithic art. *Scientific American 218,* 58ff.

Lestel, D. (1998). How chimpanzees have domesticated humans. *Anthropology Today 12* (3).

Levine, N. E., & Silk, J. B. (1997). Why polyandry fails. *Current Anthropology 38,* 375–398.

Lévi-Strauss, C. (1963). The sorcerer and his magic. In *Structural anthropology.* New York: Basic Books.

Lewellen, T. C. (2002). *The anthropology of globalization: Cultural anthropology enters the 21st century.* Westport, CT: Greenwood Publishing Group/Bergin & Garvey.

Lewin, R. (1987). Four legs bad, two legs good. *Science 235,* 969.

Lewin, R. (1993). Paleolithic paint job. *Discover 14* (7), 64–70.

Lewis, I. M. (1976). *Social anthropology in perspective.* Harmondsworth, England: Penguin.

Lewis-Williams, J. D. (1990). *Discovering southern African rock art.* Cape Town and Johannesburg: David Philip.

Lewis-Williams, J. D. (1997). Agency, art, and altered consciousness: A motif in French (Quercy) Upper Paleolithic parietal art. *Antiquity 71,* 810–830.

Lewis-Williams, J. D., & Dowson, T. A. (1988). Signs of all times: Entoptic phenomena in Upper Paleolithic art. *Current Anthropology 29,* 201–245.

Lewis-Williams, J. D., & Dowson, T. A. (1993). On vision and power in the Neolithic: Evidence from the decorated monuments. *Current Anthropology 34,* 55–65.

Lewis-Williams, J. D., Dowson, T. A., & Deacon, J. (1993). Rock art and changing perceptions of Southern Africa's past: Ezeljagdspoort reviewed. *Antiquity 67,* 273–291.

Lewontin, R. C. (1972). The apportionment of human diversity. In T. Dobzhansky et al. (Eds.), *Evolutionary biology* (pp. 381–398). New York: Plenum Press.

Lewontin, R. C., Rose, S., & Kamin, L. J. (1984). *Not in our genes.* New York: Pantheon.

Li, X., Harbottle, G., Zhang, J., & Wang, C. (2003).The earliest writing? Sign use in the seventh millennium BC at Jiahu, Henan Province, China. *Antiquity 77,* 31–44.

Lieberman, P. (2006). *Toward an evolutionary biology of language.* Cambridge, MA : Belknap Press.

Lindenbaum, S. (1978). *Kuru sorcery: Disease and danger in the New Guinea highlands.* New York: McGraw-Hill.

Lindstrom, L. (1993). *Cargo cult: Strange stories of desire from Melanesia and beyond.* Honolulu: University of Hawaii Press.

Littlewood, R. (1997). Military rape. *Anthropology Today 13* (2), 14.

Livingstone, F. B. (1973). The distribution of abnormal hemoglobin genes and their significance for human evolution. In C. Loring Brace & J. Metress (Eds.), *Man in evolutionary perspective.* New York: Wiley.

Lloyd, C. B. (Ed.) (2005). *Growing up global: The changing transitions to adulthood in developing countries* (pp. 450–453). Washington, DC: National Academies Press, Committee on Population, National Research Council, and Institute of Medicine of the National Academies.

Lock, M. (2001). *Twice dead: Organ transplants and the reinvention of death.* Berkeley: University of California Press.

Louckey, J., & Carlsen, R. (1991). Massacre in Santiago Atitlán. *Cultural Survival Quarterly 15* (3), 70.

Louie, A. (2004). *Chineseness across borders: Renegotiating Chinese identities in China and the United States.* Durham and London: Duke University Press.

Lorenzo, C., Carretero, J. M., Arsuaga, J. L., Gracia, A., & Martinez, I. (1998). Intrapopulational body size variation and cranial capacity variation in middle Pleistocene humans: The Sima de los Huesos sample (Sierra de Atapuerca, Spain). *American Journal of Physical Anthropology 106,* 19– 33.

Lounsbury, F. (1964). The structural analysis of kinship semantics. In H. G.

Lunt (Ed.), *Proceedings of the Ninth International Congress of Linguists*. The Hague: Mouton.

Lovejoy, C. O. (1981). Origin of man. *Science 211* (4480), 341–350.

Lowie, R. H. (1948). *Social organization*. New York: Holt, Rinehart & Winston.

Lowie, R. H. (1956). *Crow Indians*. New York: Holt, Rinehart & Winston. (orig. 1935)

Lucy, J. A. (1997). Linguistic relativity. *Annual Review of Anthropology 26*, 291–312.

Lurie, N. O. (1973). Action anthropology and the American Indian. In *Anthropology and the American Indian: A symposium*. San Francisco: Indian Historical Press.

MacCormack, C. P. (1977). Biological events and cultural control. *Signs 3*, 93–100.

MacLarnon, A. M., & Hewitt, G. P. (1999). The evolution of human speech: The role of enhanced breathing control. *American Journal of Physical Anthropology 109*, 341–363.

MacNeish, R. S. (1992). *The origins of agriculture and settled life*. Norman: University of Oklahoma Press.

Madison Avenue relevance. (1999). *Anthropology Newsletter 40* (4), 32.

Mair, L. (1957). *An introduction to social anthropology*. London: Oxford University Press.

Mair, L. (1969). *Witchcraft*. New York: McGraw-Hill.

Mair, L. (1971). *Marriage*. Baltimore: Penguin.

Malefijt, A. de W. (1969). *Religion and culture: An introduction to anthropology of religion*. London: Macmillan.

Malinowski, B. (1922). *Argonauts of the western Pacific*. London: Routledge & Kegan Paul.

Malinowski, B. (1945). *The dynamics of culture change: An inquiry into race relations in Africa*. New Haven, CT: Yale University Press.

Malinowski, B. (1951). *Crime and custom in savage society*. London: Routledge.

Malinowski, B. (1954). *Magic, science, and religion*. Garden City, NY: Doubleday.

Mann, A., Lampl, M, & Monge, J. (1990). Patterns of ontogeny in human evolution: Evidence from dental development. *Yearbook of Physical Anthropology 33*, 111–150.

Mann, C. C. (2000). Misconduct alleged in Yanomamo studies. *Science 289*, 2, 253.

Mann, C. C. (2002).The real dirt on rainforest fertility. *Science 297*, 920–923.

Marcus, G. (1995). Ethnography in/of the world system: The emergence of multi-sited ethnography. *Annual Review of Anthropology 24*, 95–117.

Marcus, J., & Flannery, K. V. (1996). *Zapotec civilization: How urban society evolved in Mexico's Oaxaca Valley*. New York: Thames & Hudson.

Marks, J. (1995). *Human biodiversity: Genes, race and history*. Hawthorne, NY: Aldine.

Marks, J. (2000, May 12). 98% alike (what our similarity to apes tells us about our understanding of genetics). *Chronicle of Higher Education*, B7.

Marks, J. (2002). *What it means to be 98 percent chimpanzee: Apes, people, and their genes*. Berkeley: University of California Press.

Marsella, J. (1982). Pulling it together: Discussion and comments. In S. Pastner & W. A. Haviland (Eds.), *Confronting the creationists* (pp. 79–80). *Northeastern Anthropological Association, Occasional Proceedings, 1*.

Marshack, A. (1976). Some implications of the Paleolithic symbolic evidence for the origin of language. *Current Anthropology 17* (2), 274–282.

Marshack, A. (1989). Evolution of the human capacity: The symbolic evidence. *Yearbook of Physical Anthropology 32*, 1–34.

Marshall, E. (2001). Preclovis sites fight for acceptance. *Science 291*, 1,732.

Marshall, L. (1961). Sharing, talking and giving: Relief of social tensions among !Kung bushmen. *Africa 31*, 231–249.

Marshall, M. (1990). Two tales from the Trukese taproom. In P. R. DeVita (Ed.), *The humbled anthropologist* (pp. 12–17). Belmont, CA: Wadsworth.

Martin, E. (1994). *Flexible bodies: Tracking immunity in American culture—from the days of polio to the age of AIDS*. Boston: Beacon Press.

Martin, E. (1999). Flexible survivors. *Anthropology News 40* (6), 5–7.

Martorell, R. (1988). Body size, adaptation, and function. *GDP*, 335–347.

Mascia-Lees, F. E., & Black, N. J. (2000). *Gender and anthropology*. Prospect Heights, IL: Waveland Press.

Mason, J. A. (1957). *The ancient civilizations of Peru*. Baltimore: Penguin.

Maybury-Lewis, D. (1960). Parallel descent and the Apinaye anomaly. *Southwestern Journal of Anthropology 16*, 191–216.

Maybury-Lewis, D. (1984). The prospects for plural societies. *1982 Proceedings of the American Ethnological Society*.

Maybury-Lewis, D. (1993, fall). A new world dilemma: The Indian question in the Americas. *Symbols*, 17–23.

Maybury-Lewis, D. (2001). *Indigenous peoples, ethnic groups, and the state* (2nd ed.). Boston: Allyn & Bacon.

Maybury-Lewis, D. H. P. (1993). A special sort of pleading. In W. A. Haviland & R. J. Gordon (Eds.), *Talking about people* (2nd. ed., p. 17). Mountain View, CA: Mayfield.

Mayr, E., & Diamond, J. (2002). *What evolution is*. New York: Basic Books.

McCorriston, J., & Hole, F. (1991). The ecology of seasonal stress and the origins of agriculture in the Near East. *American Anthropologist 93*, 46–69.

McDermott, L. (1996). Self-representation in Upper Paleolithic female figurines. *Current Anthropology 37*, 227–276.

McElroy, A., & Townsend, P. K. (2003). *Medical anthropology in ecological perspective*. Boulder, CO: Westview Press.

McFee, M. (1972). *Modern Blackfeet: Montanans on a reservation*. New York: Holt, Rinehart & Winston.

McGrew, W. C. (2000). Dental care in chimps. *Science 288*, 1,747.

McHenry, H. (1975). Fossils and the mosaic nature of human evolution. *Science, 190*, 524–431.

McHenry, H. M. (1992). Body size and proportions in early hominids. *American Journal of Physical Anthropology 87*, 407–431.

McKenna, J. J. (1999). Co-sleeping and SIDS. In W. Trevathan, E. O. Smith, & J. J. McKenna (Eds.), *Evolutionary medicine*. London: Oxford University Press.

McKenna, J. J. (2002, September–October). Breastfeeding and bedsharing. *Mothering*, 28–37.

McKenna, J. J., & McDade, T. (2005, June). Why babies should never sleep alone: A review of the co-sleeping controversy in relation to SIDS, bedsharing, and breast feeding. *Pediatric Respiratory Reviews 6* (2), 134–152.

McNeill, W. (1992). *Plagues and people*. New York: Anchor Books.

Mead, A. T. P. (1996). Genealogy, sacredness, and the commodities market. *Cultural Survival Quarterly 20* (2).

Mead, M. (1928). *Coming of age in Samoa*. New York: Morrow.

Mead, M. (1960). Anthropology among the sciences. *American Anthropologist 63*, 475–482.

Mead, M. (1963). *Sex and temperament in three primitive societies* (3rd ed). New York: Morrow. (orig. 1935)

Mead, M., & Metraux, R. (Eds.) (1953). *The study of culture at a distance*. Chicago: University of Chicago Press.

Medicine, B. (1994). Gender. In M. B. Davis (Ed.), *Native America in the twentieth century*. New York: Garland.

Melaart, J. (1967). *Catal Hüyük: A Neolithic town in Anatolia*. London: Thames & Hudson.

Mellars, P. (1989). Major issues in the emergence of modern humans. *Current Anthropology 30*, 356–357.

Meltzer, D., Fowler, D., & Sabloff, J. (Eds.) (1986). *American archaeology: Past & future*. Washington, DC: Smithsonian Institution Press.

Merin, Y. (2002). *Equality for same-sex couples: The legal recognition of gay partnerships in Europe and the United States*. Chicago: University of Chicago Press.

Merriam, A. P. (1964). *The anthropology of music.* Chicago: Northwestern University Press.

Mesghinua, H. M. (1966). Salt mining in Enderta. *Journal of Ethiopian Studies 4* (2).

Miles, H. L. W. (1993). Language and the orangutan: The "old person" of the forest. In P. Cavalieri & P. Singer (Eds.), *The great ape project* (pp. 45–50). New York: St. Martin's Press.

Miller, J. M. A. (2000). Craniofacial variation in *Homo habilis:* An analysis of the evidence for multiple species. *American Journal of Physical Anthropology 112,* 122.

Millon, R. (1973). *Urbanization of Teotihuacán, Mexico: Vol. 1, Part 1. The Teotihuacán map.* Austin: University of Texas Press.

Mintz, S. (1996). A taste of history. In W. A. Haviland & R. J. Gordon (Eds.), *Talking about people* (2nd ed., pp. 81–82). Mountain View, CA: Mayfield.

Minugh-Purvis, N. (1992). The inhabitants of Ice Age Europe. *Expedition 34* (3), 23–36.

Mitchell, W. E. (1973, December). A new weapon stirs up old ghosts. *Natural History,* 77–84.

Mitchell, W. E. (1978). *Mishpokhe: A study of New York City Jewish family clubs.* The Hague: Mouton.

Modell, J. (1994). *Kinship with strangers: Adoption and interpretations of kinship in American culture.* Berkeley: University of California Press.

Molnar, S. (1992). *Human variation: Races, types and ethnic groups* (3rd ed.). Englewood Cliffs, NJ: Prentice-Hall.

Monaghan, L., Hinton, L., & Kephart, R. (1997). Can't teach a dog to be a cat? The dialogue on ebonics. *Anthropology Newsletter 38* (3), 1, 8, 9.

Montagu, A. (1964). *The concept of race.* London: Macmillan.

Montagu, A. (1964). *Man's most dangerous myth: The fallacy of race* (4th ed.) New York: World Publishing.

Montagu, A. (1975). *Race and IQ.* New York: Oxford University Press.

Moore, J. (1998). Comment. *Current Anthropology 39,* 412.

Morgan, L. H. (1877). *Ancient society.* New York: World Publishing.

Morphy, H., & Perkins, M. (Eds.). (2006). *Anthropology of art: A reader.* Boston: Blackwell.

Morse, D., et al. (1979). *Gestures: Their origins and distribution.* New York: Stein & Day.

Moscati, S. (1962). *The face of the ancient orient.* New York: Doubleday.

Murdock, G. P. (1960). Cognatic forms of social organization. In G. P. Murdock (Ed.), *Social structure in Southeast Asia* (pp. 1–14). Chicago: Quadrangle Books.

Murdock, G. P. (1965). *Social structure.* New York: Free Press.

Murphy, R. (1971). *The dialectics of social life: Alarms and excursions in anthropological theory.* New York: Basic Books.

Murphy, R., & Kasdan, L. (1959). The structure of parallel cousin marriage. *American Anthropologist 61,* 17–29.

Mydens, S. (2001, August 12). He's not hairy, he's my brother. *New York Times,* sec. 4, 5.

Myrdal, G. (1974). Challenge to affluence: The emergence of an "under-class." In J. G. Jorgensen & M. Truzzi (Eds.), *Anthropology and American life.* Englewood Cliffs, NJ: Prentice-Hall.

Nader, L. (Ed.) (1965). The ethnography of law, part II. *American Anthropologist 67* (6).

Nader, L. (Ed.) (1969). *Law in culture and society.* Chicago: Aldine.

Nader, L. (Ed.) (1996). *Naked science: Anthropological inquiry into boundaries, power, and knowledge.* New York: Routledge.

Nader, L. (1997). Controlling processes: Tracing the dynamics of power. *Current Anthropology 38,* 715–717.

Nader, L. (Ed.) (1997). *Law in culture and society.* Berkeley: University of California Press.

Nader, L. (2002). *The life of the law: Anthropological projects.* Berkeley: University of California Press.

Nader, L., & Todd, Jr., H. F. (1978). *The disputing process: Law in ten societies.* New York: Columbia University Press.

Nanda, S. (1990). *Neither man nor woman: The hijras of India.* Belmont, CA: Wadsworth.

Nanda, S. (1992). Arranging a marriage in India. In P. R. De Vita (Ed.), *The naked anthropologist* (pp. 139–143). Belmont, CA: Wadsworth.

Nash, J. (1976). Ethnology in a revolutionary setting. In M. A. Rynkiewich & J. P. Spradley (Eds.), *Ethics and anthropology: Dilemmas in fieldwork* (pp. 148–166). New York: Wiley.

Natural Resources Defense Council. (2005, March 25). Healthy milk, healthy baby: Chemical pollution and mother's milk. www.NRDC.org.

Needham, R. (Ed.) (1971). *Rethinking kinship and marriage.* London: Tavistock.

Needham, R. (1972). *Belief, language and experience.* Chicago: University of Chicago Press.

Neer, R. M. (1975). The evolutionary significance of vitamin D, skin pigment, and ultraviolet light. *American Journal of Physical Anthropology 43,* 409–416.

Nesbitt, L. M. (1935). *Hell-hole of creation.* New York: Knopf.

Nesse, R. M., & Williams, G. C. (1996). *Why we get sick.* New York: Vintage.

Netting, R. M., Wilk, R. R., & Arnould, E. J. (Eds.) (1984). *Households: Comparative and historical studies of the domestic group.* Berkeley: University of California Press.

Nietschmann, B. (1987). The third world war. *Cultural Survival Quarterly 11* (3), 1–16.

Norris, R. S., & Kristensen, H. M. (2006, July/August). Global nuclear stockpiles, 1945–2006. *Bulletin of the Atomic Scientists 62* (4), 64–66.

Nunney, L. (1998). Are we selfish, are we nice, or are we nice because we are selfish? *Science 281,* 1,619.

Nye, J. (2002). *The paradox of American power: Why the world's only superpower can't go it alone.* New York: Oxford University Press.

Oakley, K. P. (1964). *Man the tool-maker.* Chicago: University of Chicago Press.

O'Barr, W. M., & Conley, J. M. (1993). When a juror watches a lawyer. In W. A. Haviland & R. J. Gordon (Eds.), *Talking about people* (2nd. ed., pp. 42–45). Mountain View, CA: Mayfield.

Obler, R. S. (1982). Is the female husband a man? Woman/woman marriage among the Nandi of Kenya. *Ethnology 19,* 69–88.

Offiong, D. (1985). Witchcraft among the Ibibio of Nigeria. In A. C. Lehmann & J. E. Myers (Eds.), *Magic, witchcraft, and religion* (pp. 152–165). Palo Alto, CA: Mayfield.

Okonjo, K. (1976). The dual-sex political system in operation: Igbo women and community politics in midwestern Nigeria. In N. Hafkin & E. Bay (Eds.), *Women in Africa.* Stanford, CA: Stanford University Press.

Olszewski, D. I. (1991). Comment. *Current Anthropology 32,* 43.

O'Mahoney, K. (1970). The salt trade. *Journal of Ethiopian Studies 8* (2).

Ong, A. (1999). *Flexible citizenship: The cultural logics of transnationality.* Durham, NC: Duke University Press.

Orlando, L., et al. (6 June 2006). Correspondence: Revisiting Neandertal diversity with a 100,000 year old mtDNA sequence. *Current Biology 16,* 400–402.

Ortiz, A. (1969). *The Tewa world.* Chicago: The University of Chicago Press.

Oswalt, W. H. (1972). *Habitat and technology.* New York: Holt, Rinehart & Winston.

Otte, M. (2000). On the suggested bone flute from Slovenia. *Current Anthropology 41,* 271.

Otten, C. M. (1971). *Anthropology and art: Readings in cross-cultural aesthetics.* Garden City, NY: Natural History Press.

Ottenberg, P. (1965). The Afikpo Ibo of eastern Nigeria. In J. L. Gibbs (Ed.), *Peoples of Africa.* New York: Holt, Rinehart & Winston.

Ottenheimer, M. (1996). *Forbidden relatives: The American myth of cousin marriage.* Chicago: University of Illinois Press.

Otterbein, K. F. (1971). *The evolution of war.* New Haven, CT: HRAF Press.

Pandian, J. (1998). *Culture, religion, and the sacred self: A critical introduction to the anthropological study of religion.* Englewood Cliffs, NJ: Prentice-Hall.

Paredes, J. A., & Purdum, E. D. (1990). "Bye, bye Ted . . ." *Anthropology Today 6* (2), 9.

Parés, J. M., Perez-Gonzalez, A., Weil, A. B., & Arsuaga, J. L. (2000). On the age of hominid fossils at the Sima de los Huesos, Sierra de Atapuerca, Spain: Paleomagnetic evidence. *American Journal of Physical Anthropology 111,* 451–461.

Parish, A. R. (1998). Comment. *Current Anthropology 39,* 414.

Parker, R. G. (1991). *Bodies, pleasures, and passions: Sexual culture in contemporary Brazil.* Boston: Beacon Press.

Parkin, R. (1997). *Kinship: An introduction to basic concepts.* Cambridge, MA: Blackwell.

Parnell, R. (1999). Gorilla exposé. *Natural History 108* (8), 43

Partridge, W. (Ed.) (1984). *Training manual in development anthropology.* Washington, DC: American Anthropological Association.

Patterson, F., & Linden, E. (1981). *The education of Koko.* New York: Holt, Rinehart & Winston.

Peacock, J. L. (2002). *The anthropological lens: Harsh light, soft focus* (2nd ed.). New York: Cambridge University Press.

Pease, T. (2000, Spring). Taking the third side. *Andover Bulletin.*

Pelto, G. H., Goodman, A. H., & Dufour, D. L. (Eds.). (2000). *Nutritional anthropology: Biocultural perspectives on food and nutrition.* Mountain View, CA: Mayfield,

Pelto, P. J. (1973). *The snowmobile revolution: Technology and social change in the Arctic.* Menlo Park, CA: Cummings.

Pennisi, E. (1999). Genetic study shakes up out of Africa theory. *Science 283,* 1,828.

Peters, C. R. (1979). Toward an ecological model of African Plio-Pleistocene hominid adaptations. *American Anthropologist 81*(2), 261–278.

Petersen J. B., Neuves, E., & Heckenberger, M. J. (2001). Gift from the past: *Terra preta* and prehistoric American occupation in Amazonia. In C. McEwan and C. Barreo (Eds.) *Unknown Amazon* (pp. 86–105). London: British Museum Press.

Pfeiffer, J. E. (1978). *The emergence of man.* New York: Harper & Row.

Pfeiffer, J. E. (1985). *The creative explosion.* Ithaca, NY: Cornell University Press.

Piddocke, S. (1965). The potlatch system of the southern Kwakiutl: A new perspective. *Southwestern Journal of Anthropology 21,* 244–264.

Piggott, S. (1965). *Ancient Europe.* Chicago: Aldine.

Pilbeam, D. R. (1987). Rethinking human origins. In R. L. Ciochon & J. G. Fleagle (Eds.), *Primate evolution and human origins* (p. 217). Hawthorne, NY: Aldine de Gruyter.

Pimentel, D. (1991). Response. *Science 252,* 358.

Pimentel, D., Hurd, L. E., Bellotti, A. C., Forster, M. J., Oka, I. N., Sholes, O. D., & Whitman, R. J. (1973). Food Production and the Energy Crisis. *Science, 182.*

Pink, S. (2001). *Doing visual ethnography: Images, media and representation in research.* Thousand Oaks, CA: Sage.

Piperno, D. R., & Fritz, G. J. (1994). On the emergence of agriculture in the new world. *Current Anthropology 35,* 637–643.

Pitt, D. (1977). Comment. *Current Anthropology 18,* 628.

Pitts, V. (2003). *In the flesh: The cultural politics of body modification.* New York: Palgrave Macmillan.

Plane, A. M. (1996). Putting a face on colonization: Factionalism and gender politics in the life history of Awashunkes, the "Squaw Sachem" of Saconnet. In R. S. Grumet (Ed.), *Northeastern Indian Lives, 1632–1816* (pp.140–175). Amherst: University of Massachusetts Press.

Plattner, S. (Ed.) (1989). *Economic anthropology.* Stanford, CA: Stanford University Press.

Plattner, S. (1989). Markets and marketplaces. In S. Plattner (Ed.), *Economic anthropology.* Stanford, CA: Stanford University Press.

Pohl, M. E. D., Pope, K. O., & von Nagy, C. (2002). Olmec origins of Mesoamerican writing, *Science 298,* 1,984–1,987.

Polanyi, K. (1968). The economy as instituted process. In E. E. LeClair, Jr., & H. K. Schneider (Eds.), *Economic anthropology: Readings in theory and analysis* (pp. 127–138). New York: Holt, Rinehart & Winston.

Pollan, M. (2001). *The botany of desire: A plant's-eye view of the world.* New York: Random House.

Pope, G. (1989, October). Bamboo and human evolution. *Natural History 98,* 48–57.

Pope, G. G. (1992). Craniofacial evidence for the origin of modern humans in China. *Yearbook of Physical Anthropology 35,* 243–298.

Pope Pius XII. (1954). *Sacra Virginitas. encyclical on consecrated virginity.* The Catholic Encyclopedia Online: www.newadvent.org.

Pospisil, L. (1963). *The Kapauku Papuans of west New Guinea.* New York: Holt, Rinehart & Winston.

Pospisil, L. (1971). *Anthropology of law: A comparative theory.* New York: Harper & Row.

Potts, R. (1997). *Humanity's descent: The consequences of ecological instability.* New York: Avon.

Powdermaker, H. (1939). *After freedom: A cultural study in the Deep South.* New York: Viking.

Powdermaker, H. (1976). *Stranger and friend: The way of an anthropologist.* London: Secker and Warburg.

Power, M. G. (1995). Gombe revisited: Are chimpanzees violent and hierarchical in the free state? *General Anthropology 2* (1), 5–9.

Premack, A. J., & Premack, D. (1972). Teaching language to an ape. *Scientific American 277*(4), 92–99.

Price, T. D., & Feinman, G. M. (Eds.) (1995). *Foundations of social inequality.* New York: Plenum.

Pringle, H. (1997). Ice Age communities may be earliest known net hunters. *Science 277,* 1,203–1,204.

Pringle, H. (1998). The slow birth of agriculture. *Science 282,* 1,449.

Prins, A. H. J. (1953). *East African class systems.* Groningen, the Netherlands: J. B. Wolters.

Prins, H. E. L. (1996). *The Mi'kmaq: Resistance, accommodation, and cultural survival* (p. 106). Orlando: Harcourt Brace.

Prins, H. E. L. (1998). Book review of Schuster, C., & Carpenter, E. *American Anthropologist 100* (3), 841.

Prins, H. E. L. (2002). Visual media and the primitivist perplex: Colonial fantasies, indigenous imagination, and advocacy in North America. In F. D. Ginsburg et al., *Media worlds: Anthropology on new terrain* (pp. 58–74). Berkeley: University of California Press.

Prins, H. E. L., & Carter, K. (1986). *Our lives in our hands.* Video and 16mm. Color. 50 min. Distributed by Watertown, MA: Documentary Educational Resources and Bucksport, ME: Northeast Historic Film

Prins, H. E. L., & Krebs, E. (2006). Toward a land without evil: Alfred Métraux as UNESCO anthropologist 1948–1962. In *60 years of UNESCO history. Proceedings of the international symposium in Paris, 16–18 November 2005.* Paris: UNESCO.

Profet, M. (1991). The function of allergy: Immunological defense against toxins. *Quarterly Review of Biology 66* (1), 23–62.

Profet, M. (1995). *Protecting your baby to be.* New York: Addison Wesley.

Puleston, D. E. (1983). *The settlement survey of Tikal.* Philadelphia: University Museum.

Radcliffe-Brown, A. R. (1931). Social organization of Australian tribes. *Oceana Monographs 1,* 29.

Radcliffe-Brown, A. R., & Forde, C. D. (Eds.) (1950). *African systems of kinship and marriage.* London: Oxford University Press.

Radin, P. (1923). The Winnebago tribe. In *37th annual report of the Bureau of American Ethnology, 1915–1916* (pp. 33–550). Washington, DC: Government Printing Office.

Rapp, R. (1999). *Testing the woman, testing the fetus: The social impact of amniocentesis in America.* New York: Routledge.

Rappaport, R. A. (1969). Ritual regulation of environmental relations among a New Guinea people. In A. P. Vayda (Ed.), *Environment and cultural behavior* (pp. 181–201). Garden City, NY. Natural History Press.

Rappaport, R. A. (1984). *Pigs for the ancestors* (Enl. ed.). New Haven, CT: Yale University Press.

Rappaport, R. A. (1999). *Holiness and humanity: Ritual in the making of religious life.* New York: Cambridge University Press.

Rathke, L. (1989). To Maine for apples. *Salt Magazine 9* (4), 24–47.

Rathje, W. L. (1974). The garbage project: A new way of looking at the problems of archaeology. *Archaeology 27,* 236–241.

Rathje, W. L. (1993). Rubbish! In W. A. Haviland & R. J. Gordon (Eds.), *Talking about people: Readings in contemporary cultural anthropology.* Mountain View, CA: Mayfield.

Read-Martin, C. E., & Read, D. W. (1975). Australopithecine scavenging and human evolution: An approach from faunal analysis. *Current Anthropology 16*(3), 359–368.

Recent demographic developments in Europe—2000. Council of Europe.

Recer, P. (1998, February 16). Apes shown to communicate in the wild. *Burlington Free Press,* 12A.

Redfield, R. (1953). *The primitive world and its transformations.* Ithaca, NY: Cornell University Press.

Redman, C. L. (1978). *The rise of civilization: From early farmers to urban society in the ancient Near East.* San Francisco: Freeman.

Reid, J. J., Schiffer, M. B., & Rathje, W. L. (1975). Behavioral archaeology: Four strategies. *American Anthropologist 77,* 864–869.

Reina, R. E. (1966). *The law of the saints.* Indianapolis: Bobbs-Merrill.

Relethford, J. H. (2001). Absence of regional affinities of Neandertal DNA with living humans does not reject multiregional evolution. *American Journal of Physical Anthropology 115,* 95–98.

Relethford, J. H., & Harpending, H. C. (1994). Craniometric variation, genetic theory, and modern human origins. *American Journal of Physical Anthropology 95,* 249–270.

Renfrew, C. (1973). *Before civilization: The radiocarbon revolution and prehistoric Europe.* London: Jonathan Cape.

Reynolds, V. (1994). Primates in the field, primates in the lab. *Anthropology Today 10* (2), 4.

Rice, P. (2000). Paleoanthropology 2000—part 1. *General Anthropology 7* (1), 11.

Richmond, B. G., Fleagle, J. K., & Swisher III, C. C. (1998). First Hominoid elbow from the Miocene of Ethiopia and the evolution of the Catarrhine elbow. *American Journal of Physical Anthropology 105,* 257–277.

Ridley, M. (1999). *Genome: The autobiography of a species in 23 chapters.* New York: HarperCollins.

Rightmire, G. P. (1990). *The evolution of Homo erectus: Comparative anatomical studies of an extinct human species.* Cambridge: Cambridge University Press.

Rightmire, G. P. (1998). Evidence from facial morphology for similarity of Asian and African representatives of Homo erectus. *American Journal of Physical Anthropology 106,* 61–85.

Rindos, D. (1984). *The origins of agriculture: An evolutionary perspective.* Orlando: Academic Press.

Robben, A. C. G. M. (2007). Fieldwork identity: Introduction. In A. C. G. M. Robben & J. A. Sluka (Eds.), *Ethnographic fieldwork: An anthropological reader* (pp. 59–63). Malden, MA: Blackwell.

Robben, A. C. G. M. (2007). Reflexive ethnography: Introduction. In A. C. G. M. Robben & J. A. Sluka (Eds.), *Ethnographic fieldwork: An anthropological reader* (pp. 443–446). Malden, MA: Blackwell.

Robben, A. C. G. M., & Sluka, J. A. (Eds.) (2006). *Ethnographic fieldwork: An anthropological reader* (Part VII). Malden, MA: Blackwell.

Rogers, J. (1994). Levels of the genealogical hierarchy and the problem of hominid phylogeny. *American Journal of Physical Anthropology 94,* 81– 88.

Romer, A. S. (1945). *Vertebrate paleontology.* Chicago: University of Chicago Press.

Roosevelt, A. C. (1984). Population, health, and the evolution of subsistence: Conclusions from the conference. In M. N. Cohen & G. J. Armelagos (Eds.), *Paleopathology at the origins of agriculture* (pp. 572–574). Orlando: Academic Press.

Rosas, A., & Bermdez de Castro, J. M. (1998). On the taxonomic affinities of the Dmanisi mandible (Georgia). *American Journal of Physical Anthropology 107,* 145–162.

Roscoe, P. B. (1995). The perils of "positivism" in cultural anthropology. *American Anthropologist 97,* 497.

Roscoe, W. (1991). *Zuni man-woman.* Albuquerque: University of New Mexico Press.

Rowe, N., & Mittermeier, R. A. (1996). *The pictorial guide to the living primates.* East Hampton, NY: Pogonias Press.

Ruhlen, M. (1994). *The origin of language: Tracing the evolution of the mother tongue.* New York: Wiley.

Rupert, J. L., & Hochachka, P. W. (2001). The evidence for hereditary factors contributing to high altitude adaptation in Andean natives: A review. *High Altitude Medicine & Biology 2* (2), 235–256.

Ruvdo, M. (1994). Molecular evolutionary processes and conflicting gene trees: The hominoid case. *American Journal of Physical Anthropology 94,* 89– 113.

Sabloff, J. A. (1997). *The cities of ancient Mexico* (rev. ed.). New York: Thames & Hudson.

Sabloff, J. A., & Lambert-Karlovsky, C. C. (Eds.) (1974). *The rise and fall of civilizations, modern archaeological approaches to ancient cultures.* Menlo Park, CA: Cummings.

Sahlins, M. (1961). The segmentary lineage: An organization of predatory expansion. *American Anthropologist 63,* 322–343.

Sahlins, M. (1968). *Tribesmen.* Englewood Cliffs, NJ: Prentice-Hall (Foundations of Modern Anthropology).

Sahlins, M. (1972). *Stone age economics.* Chicago: Aldine.

Salzman, P. C. (1967). Political organization among nomadic peoples. *Proceedings of the American Philosophical Society 111,* 115–131.

Sanday, P. R. (1975). On the causes of IQ differences between groups and implications for social policy. In M. F. A. Montagu (Ed.), *Race and IQ* (pp. 232–238). New York: Oxford.

Sanday, P. R. (1981). *Female power and male dominance: On the origins of sexual inequality.* Cambridge, England: Cambridge University Press.

Sanday, P. R. (2002). *Women at the center: Life in a modern matriarchy.* Ithaca: Cornell University Press.

Sangree, W. H. (1965). The Bantu Tiriki of western Kenya. In J. L. Gibbs, Jr. (Ed.), *Peoples of Africa* (pp. 69–72). New York: Holt, Rinehart & Winston.

Sanjek, R. (1990). On ethnographic validity. In R. Sanjek (Ed.), *Field notes.* Ithaca, NY: Cornell University Press.

Sapir, E. (1921). *Language.* New York: Harcourt.

Savage-Rumbaugh, S., & Lewin, R. (1994). *Kanzi: The ape at the brink of the human mind.* New York: Wiley.

Scaglion, R. (1987). Contemporary law development in Papua New Guinea. In R. M. Wulff & S. J. Fiske (Eds.), *Anthropological praxis: Translating knowledge into action.* Boulder, CO: Westview Press.

Schaeffer, S. B., & Furst, P. T. (Eds.). (1996). *People of the peyote: Huichol Indian history, religion, and survival.* Albuquerque: University of New Mexico Press.

Scheflen, A. E. (1972). *Body language and the social order.* Englewood Cliffs, NJ: Prentice-Hall.

Schepartz, L.A. (1993). Language and human origins. *Yearbook of Physical Anthropology 36,* 91–126.

Scheper-Hughes, N., & Waquant, L. (2002). *Commodifying bodies.* London: Sage (Theory, Culture, and Society series).

Schlegel, A. (1977). Male and female in Hopi thought and action. In A. Schlegel (Ed.), *Sexual stratification* (pp. 245–269). New York: Columbia University Press.

Schoepfle, M. (2001). Ethnographic resource inventory and the National Park

Service. *Cultural Resource Management 5,* 1–7.

Schrire, C. (Ed.). (1984). *Past and present in hunter-gatherer studies.* Orlando: Academic Press.

Schusky, E. L. (1983). *Manual for kinship analysis* (2nd ed.). Lanham, MD: University Press of America.

Schuster, C., & Carpenter, E. (1996). *Patterns that connect: Social symbolism in ancient and tribal art.* New York: Abrams.

Schwartz, J. H. (1984). Hominoid evolution: A review and a reassessment. *Current Anthropology 25* (5), 655–672.

Schwartz, M. (1997). *A history of dogs in the early Americas.* New Haven: Yale University Press.

Scupin, R. (Ed.) (2000). *Religion and culture: An anthropological focus.* Upper Saddle River, NJ: Prentice-Hall.

Seeger, A. (2004). *Why Suya sing: A musical anthropology.* Champaign: University of Illinois Press.

Sellen, D. W., & Mace, R. (1997). Fertility and mode of subsistence: A phylogenetic analysis. *Current Anthropology 38,* 886.

Semenov, S. A. (1964). *Prehistoric technology.* New York: Barnes & Noble.

Senut, B., et al. (2001). First hominid from the Miocene (Lukeino formation, Kenya). *C. R. Academy of Science, Paris 332,*137–144.

Seyfarth, R. M., et al. (1980). Monkey responses to three different alarm calls: Evidence for predator classification and semantic communication. *Science 210,* 801–803.

Seymour, D. Z. (1986). Black children, black speech. In P. Escholz, A. Rosa, & V. Clark (Eds.), *Language awareness* (4th ed.). New York: St. Martin's Press.

Shane, L., III. (2005). Happy couple both no-show wedding: Deployed troops make use of double-proxy ceremony. *Stars & Stripes 3* (17), 6.

Shapiro, H. (Ed.) (1971). *Man, culture and society* (2nd ed.). New York: Oxford University Press.

Sharer, R. J., & Ashmore, W. (2002). *Archaeology: Discovering our past* (3rd ed.). New York: McGraw-Hill.

Shaw, D. G. (1984). A light at the end of the tunnel: Anthropological contributions toward global competence. *Anthropology Newsletter 25,* 16.

Shearer, R. R., & Gould, S. J. (1999). Of two minds and one nature. *Science 286,* 1093.

Sheets, P. (1993). Dawn of a new Stone Age in eye surgery. In R. J. Sharer & W. Ashmore, *Archaeology: Discovering our past* (2nd ed.). Palo Alto, CA: Mayfield.

Shipman, P. (1981). *Life history of a fossil: An introduction to taphonomy and paleoecology.* Cambridge, MA: Harvard University Press.

Shook, J. R., et al. (Eds.). (2004). *Dictionary of modern American philosophers, 1860–1960.* Bristol, England: Thoemmes Press.

Shore, B. (1996). *Culture in mind: Meaning, construction, and cultural cognition.* New York: Oxford University Press.

Shostak, M. (1983). *Nisa: The life and words of a !Kung woman.* New York: Vintage.

Shreeve, J. (1994). Terms of estrangement. *Discover 15* (11), 60.

Shreeve, J. (1995). *The Neandertal enigma: Solving the mystery of modern human origins.* New York: William Morrow.

Shuey, A. M. (1966). *The testing of Negro intelligence.* New York: Social Science Press.

Sillen, A., & Brain, C. K. (1990). Old flame. *Natural History 4,* 6–10.

Simons, E. L. (1972). *Primate evolution.* New York: Macmillan.

Simons, E. L. (1989) Human origins. *Science 245,* 1,349.

Simons, E. L. (1995). Skulls and anterior teeth of Catopithecus (primates: anthropoidea) from the Eocene and anthropoid origins. *Science 268,* 1,885–1,888.

Simons, E. L., Rasmussen, D. T., & Gebo, D. L. (1987). A new species of Propliopithecus from the Fayum, Egypt. *American Journal of Physical Anthropology 73,* 139–147.

Simpson, G. G. (1949). *The meaning of evolution.* New Haven, CT: Yale University Press.

Simpson, S. (1995, April). Whispers from the ice. *Alaska,* 23–28.

Sjoberg, G. (1960). *The preindustrial city.* New York: Free Press.

Sluka, J. A. (2007). Fieldwork relations and rapport: Introduction. In A. C. G. M. Robben & J. A. Sluka (Eds.), *Ethnographic fieldwork: An anthropological reader.* Malden, MA: Blackwell.

Small, M. F. (1997). Making connections. *American Scientist 85,* 503.

Small, M. F. (2000). Kinship envy. *Natural History 109* (2), 88.

Smedley, A. (1998). *Race in North America: Origin and evolution of a worldview.* Boulder, CO: Westview Press.

Smith, B. H. (1994). Patterns of dental development in *Homo, Australopithecus, Pan,* and gorilla. *American Journal of Physical Anthropology 94,* 307– 325.

Smith, F. H., & Raynard, G. C. (1980). Evolution of the supraorbital region in Upper Pleistocene fossil hominids from South-Central Europe. *American Journal of Physical Anthropology 53,* 589–610.

Smith, P. E. L. (1976). *Food production and its consequences* (2nd ed.). Menlo Park, CA: Cummings.

Snowden, C. T. (1990). Language capabilities of nonhuman animals. *Yearbook of Physical Anthropology 33,* 215–243.

Speck, F. G. (1920). Penobscot shamanism. *Memoirs of the American Anthropological Association 6,* 239–288.

Speck, F. G. (1970). *Penobscot man: The life history of a forest tribe in Maine.* New York: Octagon Books.

Spencer, F., & Smith, F. H. (1981). The significance of Ales Hrdlicka's "Neanderthal phase of man": A historical and current assessment. *American Journal of Physical Anthropology 56,* 435–459.

Spencer, H. (1896). *Principles of sociology.* New York: Appleton.

Spencer, R. F. (1984). North Alaska Coast Eskimo. In D. Damas (Ed.), *Arctic: Handbook of North American Indians* (Vol. 5, pp. 320–337). Washington, DC: Smithsonian Institution.

Spindler, G., & Stockard, J. E. (Eds.) (2006). *Globalization and change in fifteen cultures.* Belmont, CA: Wadsworth.

Spradley, J. P. (1979). *The ethnographic interview.* New York: Holt, Rinehart & Winston.

Spradley, J. P. (1980). *Participant observation.* New York: Holt, Rinehart & Winston.

Stacey, J. (1990). *Brave new families.* New York: Basic Books.

Stahl, A. B. (1984). Hominid dietary selection before fire. *Current Anthropology 25,* 151–168.

Stanford, C. B. (2001). *Chimpanzee and red colobus: The ecology of predator and prey.* Cambridge, MA: Harvard University Press.

Stanford, C. B. (2001). *The hunting apes: Meat eating and the origins of human behavior.* Princeton, NJ: Princeton University Press.

Stannard, D. E. (1992). *American holocaust.* Oxford: Oxford University Press.

Steady, F. C. (2001). *Women and the Amistad connection, Sierra Leone Krio Society.* Rochester, VT: Schenkman Books.

Steady, F. C. (2005). *Women and collective action in Africa.* New York: Palgrave Macmillan.

Stedman, H. H., et al. (2004). Myosin gene mutation correlates with anatomical changes in the human lineage. *Nature 428,* 415–418.

Stein, R. L., & Stein, P. L. (2004). *Anthropology of religion, magic, and witchcraft.* Boston: Allyn & Bacon.

Steward, J. H. (1972). *Theory of culture change: The methodology of multilinear evolution.* Urbana: University of Illinois Press.

Stiglitz, J.E. (2003). *Globalization and its discontents.* New York: Norton.

Stiles, D. (1979). Early Acheulean and developed Oldowan. *Current Anthropology 20* (l), 126–129.

Stockard, J. E. (2002). *Marriage in culture: Practice and meaning across diverse societies.* Ft. Worth: Harcourt College Publishers.

Stocking, G. W., Jr. (1968). *Race, culture and evolution: Essays in the history of anthropology.* New York: Free Press.

Stone, L. (1998). *Kinship and gender: An introduction.* Boulder, CO: Westview Press.

Stone, L. (2005). *Kinship and gender: An introduction* (3rd ed.). Boulder, CO: Westview Press.

Stone, R. (1995). If the mercury soars, so may health hazards. *Science 267, 958.*

Straus, W. L., & Cave, A. J. E. (1957). Pathology and the posture of Neanderthal man. *Quarterly Review of Biology, 32.*

Stringer, C. B., & McKie, R. (1996). *African exodus: The origins of modern humanity.* London: Jonathan Cape.

Stuart-MacAdam, P., & Dettwyler, K. A. (Eds.) (1995). *Breastfeeding: Biocultural perspectives.* New York: Aldine.

Study estimates 250,000 active child soldiers. (2006, July 26). Associated Press.

Suarez-Orozoco, M. M., Spindler, G., & Spindler, L. (1994). *The making of psychological anthropology, II.* Fort Worth: Harcourt Brace.

Susman, R. L. (1988). Hand of *Paranthropus robustus* from Member 1, Swartkrans: Fossil evidence for tool behavior. *Science 240,* 781–784.

Swadesh, M. (1959). Linguistics as an instrument of prehistory. *Southwestern Journal of Anthropology 15,* 20–35.

Swaminathan, M. S. (2000). Science in response to basic human needs. *Science 287, 425.*

Swartz, M. J., Turner, V. W., & Tuden, A. (1966). *Political anthropology.* Chicago: Aldine.

Swisher III, C. C., Curtis, G. H., Jacob, T., Getty, A. G., Suprijo, A., & Widiasmoro. (1994). Age of the earliest known hominids in Java, Indonesia. *Science 263,* 1,118–1,121.

Tannen, D. (1990). *You just don't understand: Women and men in conversation.* New York: Morrow.

Tapper, M. (1999). *In the blood: Sickle-cell anemia and the politics of race.* Philadelphia: University of Pennsylvania Press.

Tattersal, I. (1998). *Becoming human: Evolution and human uniqueness.* New York: Harcourt Brace.

Tattersall, I., & Schwartz, J. H. (1999). Hominids and hybrids: The place of Neanderthals in human evolution. *PNAS 96* (13), 7,117–7,119.

Tax, S. (1953). *Penny capitalism: A Guatemalan Indian economy.* Washington, DC: Smithsonian Institution, Institute of Social Anthropology, Pub. No. 16.

Taylor, G. (2000). *Castration: Abbreviated history of western manhood.* New York: Routledge.

Tedlock, B. (2005). *The woman in the shaman's body: Reclaiming the feminine in religion and medicine.* New York: Random House.

Templeton, A. R. (1994). Eve: Hypothesis compatibility versus hypothesis testing. *American Anthropologist 96* (1), 141–147.

Templeton, A. R. (1995). The "Eve" hypothesis: A genetic critique and reanalysis. *American Anthropologist 95* (1), 51–72.

Terashima, H. (1983). Mota and other hunting activities of the Mbuti archers: A socio-ecological study of subsistence technology. *African Studies Monograph* (Kyoto), 71–85.

Thomas, E. M. (1994). *The tribe of the tiger: Cats and their culture* (pp. 109–186). New York: Simon & Schuster.

Thomson, K. S. (1997). Natural selection and evolution's smoking gun. *American Scientist 85,* 516–518.

Thorne, A. G., & Wolpoff, M. D. H. (1981). Regional continuity in Australasian Pleistocene hominid evolution. *American Journal of Physical Anthropology 55,* 337–349.

Thornhill, N. (1993). Quoted in W. A. Haviland & R. J. Gordon (Eds.), *Talking about people* (p. 127). Mountain View, CA: Mayfield.

Tobias, P. V., & von Konigswald, G. H. R. (1964). A comparison between the Olduvai hominines and those of Java and some implications for hominid phylogeny. *Nature 204,* 515–518.

Trevathan, W., Smith, E. O., &.McKenna, J. J. (Eds.) (1999). *Evolutionary medicine.* London: Oxford University Press.

Trinkaus, E. (1986). The Neanderthals and modern human origins. *Annual Review of Anthropology 15,* 197.

Trinkaus, E., & Shipman, P. (1992). *The Neandertals: Changing the image of mankind.* New York: Knopf.

Trouillot, M. R. (1996). Culture, color, and politics in Haiti. In S. Gregory & R. Sanjek (Eds.), *Race.* New Brunswick, NJ: Rutgers University Press.

Trouillot, M. R. (2003). *Global transformations: Anthropology and the modern world.* New York: Palgrave Macmillan.

Tumin, M. M. (1967). *Social stratification: The forms and functions of inequality.* Englewood Cliffs, NJ: Prentice-Hall (Foundations of Modern Sociology).

Turnbull, C. M. (1983). *Mbuti Pygmies: Change and adaptation.* New York: Holt, Rinehart & Winston.

Turnbull, C. M. (1961). *The forest people.* New York: Simon & Schuster.

Turnbull, C. M. (1983). *The human cycle.* New York: Simon & Schuster.

Turner, T. (1991). Major shift in Brazilian Yanomami policy. *Anthropology Newsletter 32* (5), 1, 46.

Turner, V. W. (1957). *Schism and continuity in an African society.* Manchester, England: University Press.

Turner, V. W. (1969). *The ritual process.* Chicago: Aldine.

Tylor, E. B. (1871). *Primitive culture: Researches into the development of mythology, philosophy, religion, language, art and customs.* London: Murray.

Tylor, Sir E. B. (1931). Animism. In V. F. Calverton (Ed.), *The making of man: An outline of anthropology.* New York: Modern Library.

UNESCO. www.unesco.org/webworld/babel.

Urban, G. (2001). *Metaculture: How cultures move through the modern world.* Westport, CT: Greenwood Press.

Ury, W. L. (1993). *Getting past no: Negotiating your way from confrontation.* New York: Bantam Books.

Ury, W. L. (1999). *Getting to peace: Transforming conflict at home, at work, and in the world.* New York: Viking.

Ury, W. (2002, Winter). A global immune system. *Andover Bulletin.*

U.S. Census 2000. www.adherents.com.

U.S. Census Bureau News. (2004, March 18).

Van Allen, J. (1997). Sitting on a man: Colonialism and the lost political institutions of Igbo women. In R. Grinker & C. Steiner (Eds.), *Perspectives on Africa* (p. 450). Boston: Blackwell.

Van den Berghe, P. (1992). The modern state: Nation builder or nation killer? *International Journal of Group Tensions 22* (3), 191–207.

Van Eck, C. (2003). *Purified by blood: Honour killings amongst Turks in the Netherlands.* Amsterdam University Press.

Van Gennep, A. (1960). *The rites of passage.* Chicago: University of Chicago Press.

Van Tilburg, J. A. (1994). *Easter Island: Archaeology, ecology, and culture.* London: British Museum Press.

Van Willigen, J. (1986). *Applied anthropology.* South Hadley, MA: Bergin & Garvey.

Venbrux, E., Rosi, P. S., & Welsch, R. L. (Eds.) (2006). *Exploring world art.* Longrove, IL: Waveland Press.

Vincent, J. (2002). *The anthropology of politics: A reader in ethnography, theory, and critique.* Boston: Blackwell.

Vogt, E. Z. (1990). *The Zinacantecos of Mexico: A modern Maya way of life* (2nd ed.). Fort Worth: Holt, Rinehart & Winston.

Waldbaum, J. C. (2005, November/December). Tell it to the Marines: Teaching troops about cultural heritage. *Archaeology 58* (6).

Walker, A., & Shipman, P. (1997). *The wisdom of the bones: In search of human origins.* New York: Vintage Books.

Wallace, A. F. C. (1956). Revitalization movements. *American Anthropologist 58,* 264–281.

Wallace, A. F. C. (1966). *Religion: An anthropological view.* New York: Random House.

Wallace, A. F. C. (1970). *Culture and personality* (2nd ed.). New York: Random House.

Wallace, E., & Hoebel, E. A. (1952). *The Comanches.* Norman: University of Oklahoma Press.

Walrath, D. (2002). Decoding the discourses: Feminism and science, review essay. *American Anthropologist 104* (1), 327–330.

Walrath, D. (2003). Re-thinking pelvic typologies and the human birth mechanism. *Current Anthropology 44* (1), 5–31.

Walrath, D. (2006). Gender, genes, and the evolution of human birth. In P. L. Geller & M. K. Stockett (Eds.), *Feminist anthropology: Past, present, and future.* Philadelphia: University of Pennsylvania Press.

Ward, C. V., Walker, A., Teaford, M. F., & Odhiambo, I. (1993). Partial skeleton of Proconsul nyanzae from Mfangano Island, Kenya. *American Journal of Physical Anthropology 90,* 77–111.

Washburn, S. L., & Moore, R. (1980). *Ape into human: A study of human evolution* (2nd ed.). Boston: Little, Brown.

Wattenberg, B. J. (1997, November 23). The population explosion is over. *New York Times Magazine,* 60.

Weatherford, J. (1988). *Indian givers: How the Indians of the Americas transformed the world.* New York: Ballantine.

Weiner, A. B. (1977). Review of Trobriand cricket: An ingenious response to colonialism. *American Anthropologist 79,* 506.

Weiner, A. B. (1988). *The Trobrianders of Papua New Guinea.* New York: Holt, Rinehart & Winston.

Weiner, J. S. (1955). *The Piltdown forgery.* Oxford, England: Oxford University Press.

Weiss, M. L., & Mann, A. E. (1990). *Human biology and behavior* (5th ed.). Boston: Little, Brown.

Wells, S. (2002). *The journey of man: A genetic odyssey.* Princeton, NJ: Princeton University Press.

Werner, D. (1990). *Amazon journey.* Englewood Cliffs, NJ: Prentice-Hall.

Wheeler, P. (1993). Human ancestors walked tall, stayed cool. *Natural History 102* (8), 65–66.

Whelehan, P. (1985). Review of incest, a biosocial view. *American Anthropologist 87,* 678.

White, D. R. (1988). Rethinking polygyny: Co-wives, codes, and cultural systems. *Current Anthropology 29,* 529–572.

White, L. (1949). *The science of culture: A study of man and civilization.* New York: Farrar, Straus.

White, L. (1959). *The evolution of culture: The development of civilization to the fall of Rome.* New York: McGraw-Hill.

White, M. (2001). *Historical atlas of the twentieth century.* http://users.erols.com/ mwhite28/20centry.htm.

White, R. (2003). *Prehistoric art: The symbolic journey of humankind.* New York: Abrams.

White, T., Asfaw, B., Degusta, D., Gilbert, H., Richards, G., & Suwa, G., Howell, F. C. (2003). Pleistocene *Homo sapiens* from the Middle Awash, Ethiopia. *Nature 423,* 742–747.

White, T. D. (1979). Evolutionary implications of Pliocene hominid footprints. *Science 208,* 175–176.

White, T. D. (2003). Early hominids—diversity or distortion? *Science 299,* 1,994–1,997.

White, T. D., & Toth, N. (2000). Cutmarks on a Plio-Pleistocene hominid from Sterkfontein, South Africa. *American Journal of Physical Anthropology 111,* 579–584.

Whitehead, B. D. & Popenoe, D. (2004). *The state of our unions: The social health of marriage in America 2004.* Rutgers, NJ: Rutgers University National Marriage Project.

Whitehead, N. L., & Ferguson, R. B. (1993, November). Deceptive stereotypes about tribal warfare. *Chronicle of Higher Education,* A48.

Whiting, B. B. (Ed.) (1963). *Six cultures: Studies of child rearing.* New York: Wiley.

Whiting, J. W. M., & Child, I. L. (1953). *Child training and personality: A cross-cultural study.* New Haven, CT: Yale University Press.

Whiting, J. W. M., Sodergem, J. A., & Stigler, S. M. (1982). Winter temperature as a constraint to the migration of preindustrial peoples. *American Anthropologist 84,* 289.

Whyte, A. L. H. (2005). Human evolution in Polynesia. *Human Biology 77* (2), 157–177.

Wiley, A. S. (2004). An ecology of high-altitude infancy: A biocultural perspective series. *Cambridge Studies in Medical Anthropology 12.*

Wilk, R. R. (1996). *Economics and cultures: An introduction to economic anthropology.* Boulder, CO: Westview Press.

Willey, G. R. (1966). *An introduction to American archaeology: Vol. 1. North America.* Englewood Cliffs, NJ: Prentice-Hall.

Willey, G. R. (1971). *An introduction to American archaeology, Vol. 2: South America.* Englewood Cliffs, NJ: Prentice-Hall.

Williams, F. (2005, January 9). Toxic breast milk? *New York Times Magazine.*

Williamson, R. K. (1995). The blessed curse: Spirituality and sexual difference as viewed by Euramerican and Native American cultures. *The College News 18* (4).

Willigan, J. V. (1986). *Applied anthropology.* South Hadley, MA: Bergin and Garvey.

Wills, C. (1994). The skin we're in. *Discover 15* (11), 79.

Wilson, A. K., & Sarich, V. M. (1969). A molecular time scale for human evolution. *Proceedings of the National Academy of Science 63,* 1,089–1,093.

Wingert, P. (1965). *Primitive art: Its tradition and styles.* New York: World.

Winick, C. (Ed.). (1970). *Dictionary of anthropology.* Totowa, NJ: Littlefield, Adams.

Wirsing, R. L. (1985). The health of traditional societies and the effects of acculturation. *Current Anthropology 26* (3), 303–322.

Wittfogel, K. A. (1957). *Oriental despotism, a comparative study of total power.* New Haven, CT: Yale University Press.

Wolf, E. R. (1966). *Peasants.* Englewood Cliffs, NJ: Prentice-Hall.

Wolf, E. R. (1969). *Peasant wars of the twentieth century.* New York: Harper & Row.

Wolf, E. R. (1982). *Europe and the people without history.* Berkeley: University of California Press.

Wolf, E. R. (1999). *Envisioning power: Ideologies of dominance and crisis.* Berkeley: University of California Press.

Wolf, E. R., & Trager, G. L. (1971). Hortense Powdermaker 1900–1970. *American Anthropologist 73* (3), 784.

Wolf, M. (1985). *Revolution postponed: Women in contemporary China.* Stanford, CA: Stanford University Press.

Wolfson, H. (2000, January 22). Polygamists make the Christian connection. *Burlington Free Press,* 2c.

Wolpoff, M. H. (1993). Evolution in *Homo erectus:* The question of stasis. In R. L. Ciochon & J. G. Fleagle (Eds.), *The human evolution source book.* Englewood Cliffs, NJ: Prentice-Hall.

Wolpoff, M. H. (1993). Multiregional evolution: The fossil alternative to Eden. In R. L. Ciochon & J. G. Fleagle (Eds.), *The human evolution source book.* Englewood Cliffs, NJ: Prentice-Hall.

Wolpoff, M. (1996). *Australopithecus:* A new look at an old ancestor. *General Anthropology 3* (1), 2.

Wolpoff, M., & Caspari, R. (1997). *Race and human evolution: A fatal attraction.* New York: Simon & Schuster.

Wolpoff, M. H., Wu, X. Z., & Thorne, A. G. (1984). Modern *Homo sapiens* origins: A general theory of hominid evolution involving fossil evidence from east Asia. In F. H. Smith and F. Spencer (Eds.), *The origins of modern humans* (pp. 411–483). New York: Alan R. Liss.

Wood, B., & Aiello, L. C. (1998). Taxonomic and functional implications of mandibular scaling in early hominines. *American Journal of Physical Anthropology 105,* 523–538.

Wood, B., Wood, C., & Konigsberg, L. (1994). *Paranthropus boisei:* An example of evolutionary stasis? *American Journal of Physical Anthropology 95,* 117–136.

Woolfson, P. (1972). Language, thought, and culture. In V. P. Clark, P. A. Escholz, & A. F. Rosa (Eds.), *Language.* New York: St. Martin's Press.

World Almanac. (2004). New York: Press Publishing Co.

World Health Organization. http://www .who.int/about/definition/en.

World Meteorological Organization. (2003). Increasing heat waves and other health hazards. greenpeaceusa.org/climate/index.fpl/7096/article/907.html.

Worsley, P. (1957). *The trumpet shall sound: A study of "cargo" cults in Melanesia.* London: Macgibbon & Kee.

Worsley, P. (1959). Cargo cults. *Scientific American 200* (May), 117–128.

Wrangham, R., & Peterson, D. (1996). *Demonic males.* Boston: Houghton Mifflin.

Wulff, R. M., & Fiske, S. J. (1987). *Anthropological praxis: Translating knowledge into action.* Boulder, CO: Westview Press.

Yip, M. (2002). *Tone.* New York: Cambridge University Press.

Young, A. (1981). The creation of medical knowledge: Some problems in interpretation. *Social Science and Medicine 17,1,*205–1,211.

Young, W. (Ed.) (2000). Kimball award winner. *Anthropology News 41* (8), 29.

Zeder, M. A., & Hesse, B. (2000). The initial domestication of goats (*Capra hircus*) in the Zagros Mountains 10,000 years ago. *Science 287,* 2,254–2,257.

Zeresenay, A., Spoor, F., Kimbel, W. H., Bobe, R., Geraads, D., Reed, D., & Wynn, J. G. (2006). A juvenile early hominin skeleton from Dikika, Ethiopia. *Nature 443,* 296–301.

Zihlman, A. (2001). *The human evolution coloring book.* New York: Harper Resources.

Zilhão, J. (2000). Fate of the Neandertals. *Archaeology 53* (4), 30.

Zimmer, C. (1999). New date for the dawn of dream time. *Science 284,* 1,243.

Zimmer, C. (2001). *Evolution: The triumph of an idea.* New York: HarperCollins.

Zimmer, C. (2005) *Smithsonian intimate guide to human origins.* New York: HarperCollins.

Zohary, D., & Hopf, M. (1993). *Domestication of plants in the Old World* (2nd ed.). Oxford: Clarenden Press.

Index

Oligocene epoch, 116
Olmec Indians, 374
Olszewki, D. I., 227
Omaha Indians, 329
O'Mahoney, K., 439
"One drop" rule, 515
Oneida Indians, 546
On Man's Place in Nature (Huxley), 31
Onodaga Indians, 546
On the Natural Variety of Mankind (Blumenbach), 266
On the Origins of Species (Darwin), 31
Open adoption, 477
Open-class societies, 518
Open-ended questions, 338
Opposable toes, 61, 130
Oral histories, 329
Orangutans, 66
    body plan of, 118
    language and, 354–356
Orders, 28
Organ transplantation, 7
    sale of organs, 20
Origin of Species (Darwin), 106, 108, 183
Orrorin tugenensis, 122, 126, 134
Orthodox Jewish communities, 509–511
Ortiz, A., 487
Ostrich eggs, dating with, 100
Ota Benga, 266–267
Otte, Marcel, 190
Ottenheimer, Martin, 461
Ötzi, 83
Our Lives in Our Hands, 492
OutKast, 592
Out of Africa hypothesis, 192–193, 193, 195–198
Ovarian tissue, 394
Overgrazing, 641
Overpopulation, 639
Overtones, 590
Ovotestis, 394
Ovulation in primates, 72
Owsley, Doug, 96
Oxfam, 618
Ozone layer, 302

P

Pääbo, Svante, 191
Packard Humanities Institute, 258
Paha Sapa, 557, 558
Pair bonding of Australopithecus, 143
Paiute Indians, 411
    food production and, 418
Pakistan, 598
Paleoanthropology, 8, 82, 104
Paleocene epoch, 113–114
Paleoindians, 216
Paleolithic. *See also* Lower Paleolithic; Upper Paleolithic
    Middle Paleolithic, 186–193
    tattoos in, 582
Paleomagnetic reversals dating, 98, 101
Paleotourism, 155
Palestine, 555
    nationalism, 626
Palynology, 99
Pan genus, 56
Pantheon, 555
Pant-hoots, 74

Papua New Guinea, 532. *See also* Kapauku people
    Dani people, 229
    earliest sites in, 214
    Fore people, 299–300
    spread of people to, 213–214
    Wape people, 537, 556
Paralanguage, 371
Parallel cousins, 468
Parallel evolution, 409
Paredes, Anthony, 324
Parés, J. M., 180
Paris, Champs Elysées, 247
Parish, A. R., 69, 75
Park, P. B., 171
Parnell, R., 75
Participant observation, 9, 14, 336–337
Particulate, inheritance as, 32
Pashto language, 626
Pashtun peoples, 625–626
Passive bilingualism, 369
Pastner, S., 629
Pastoralism, 240, 424–428
    change and, 321
    Mesolithic roots of, 222–223
    nomadic pastoralism, 424–425
    warfare and, 544
Patacancha Valley, Peru, 422–423
Patriarchy
    capitalism, patriarchal, 634
    violence and, 545
Patrilateral parallel-cousin marriage, 468
Patrilineal clans, 493
Patrilineal descent, 482
    bilateral descent, 488–489
    cultural infrastructure and, 484
    Han Chinese example, 484–486
Patrilocal residence, 476–477
Patterns of association, 516–517
Patterns of Culture (Benedict), 389
Paxson Communications, 633
PCBs (polychlorinated biphenyls), 642
    in breast milk, 643
Peacock, Nadine, 338
Peasants, 426
    studies, 331–332
Peasant Wars of the Twentieth Century (Wolf), 601
Pease, T., 543
Pech Merle cave art, 211–212
Pei, W. C., 166
Peking Man, 166–167, 194
Pelto, G. H., 411
Pelto, P. J., 617
Pelvis of bipeds, 129
Penis fencing, 72
Pennsylvania Dutch, 313
Penobscot Indians
    myths of, 570–571
    shamans, 561
Pentatonic system, 591
Pepsi beverages, 626
Pequot Indians, 608
Percussion method, 154
Perdue, Frank, 449
Permian period, 112
Personality, 384–392
    combined dependence/independence training, 388

core values, 391–392
dependence training, 386–387
development of, 385–388
gender and, 385–386
group personality, 388, 390
independence training, 387–388
modal personality, 390
national character, 390–391
in social context, 397–402
Personal offenses, 541
Personal space, 370–371
Perspective, anthropological, 5–7
Pertussis
    animal domestication and, 239
    cities and, 259
Peru. *See also* Andean highlands; Incan culture
    Cusichaca Trust, 422–423
    Nazca Desert, 88
Pesticides, 303–304
Peterson, D., 545
Peterson, James B., 232
Petralona skull, 180
Peyote art, 585
Pharmaceutical drugs, 605
Pharynx, 359
Phenotypes, 34, 37
Phenylethylamine, 449
Philip, King, 587
Philippines, transgenders in, 397
Phoenician alphabet, 375
Phonemes, 358
Phonetics, 358
Phonology, 358
    differences, 361
Photography, 339, 340
Phratries, 494–495
Phyla, 28
Physical anthropology, 3, 8–9
Physical coercion, 540
Physiological adaptations, 8–9, 288–289
    to cold, 290
Physiological stress in Neolithic, 238–239
Pibloktoq, 401
Pibroch, 592
Pigments. *See also* Ochre
    Neandertal use of, 189
Pigs
    taboos, 349
    Tsembaga people and, 406–407
Pilbeam, David R., 118, 120
Piltdown specimens, 126–127
Pimentel, D., 303
Pine nuts, 413
Pipering, 592
Pitcairn Island, 41
Pithecanthropus erectus, 161
Pitt, D., 633
Pius XII, Pope, 465
Plains Apache Indians. *See* Apache Indians
Planning behavior, fire and, 171
Plant domestication, 418
Plastics, 304
Plattner, S., 447
Platyrrhini infraorder, 55–56, 62
Play in primates, 73–74
"Pledge of Allegiance," 535
Pleistocene epoch, 180